SHOWCASE PRESENTS

SHAZAM!

VOLUME ONE

Dan DiDio Senior VP-Executive Editor

Julius Schwartz, Joe Orlando, Jack C. Harris Editors-original series

Bob Joy Editor-collected edition

Robbin Brosterman Senior Art Director

Paul Levitz President & Publisher

Georg Brewer VP-Design & DC Direct Creative

Richard Bruning Senior VP-Creative Director

Patrick Caldon Executive VP-Finance & Operations

Chris Caramalis VP-Finance

John Cunningham VP-Marketing

Terri Cunningham VP-Managing Editor

Stephanie Fierman Senior VP-Sales & Marketing

Alison Gill VP-Manufacturing

Hank Kanalz VP-General Manager, WildStorm

Jim Lee Editorial Director-WildStorm

Paula Lowitt Senior VP-Business & Legal Affairs

MaryEllen McLaughlin VP-Advertising & Custom Publishing

John Nee VP-Business Development

Gregory Noveck Senior VP-Creative Affairs

Cheryl Rubin Senior VP-Brand Management

Jeff Trojan VP-Business Development, DC Direct

Bob Wayne VP-Sales

TABLE OF CONTENTS

SHAZAM! NO. 1
FEBRUARY 1973
COVER ARTIST: C. C. BECK
7

...IN THE BEGINNING...
WRITER: DENNY O'NEIL
ARTIST: C. C. BECK
8

THE WORLD'S WICKEDEST PLAN
WRITER: DENNY O'NEIL
ARTIST: C. C. BECK
14

SHAZAM & SON
WRITER: E. NELSON BRIDWELL
24

SHAZAM! NO. 2
APRIL 1973
COVER ARTIST: C. C. BECK
25

THE ASTONISHING ARCH ENEMY
WRITER: DENNY O'NEIL
ARTIST: C. C. BECK
26

THE NICEST GUY IN THE WORLD
WRITER: ELLIOT MAGGIN
ARTIST: C. C. BECK
36

SHAZAM! NO. 3
JUNE 1973
43

A SWITCH IN TIME
WRITER: DENNY O'NEIL
ARTIST: C. C. BECK
44

THE WIZARD OF PHONOGRAPH HILL
WRITER: ELLIOT MAGGIN
ARTIST: C. C. BECK
52

SHAZAM! NO. 4
JULY 1973
COVER ARTIST: C. C. BECK
60

¡BAC THE CURSED!
WRITER: DENNY O'NEIL
ARTIST: C. C. BECK
61

THE MIRRORS THAT PREDICTED THE FUTURE
WRITER: ELLIOT MAGGIN
ARTIST: C. C. BECK
69

SHAZAM! NO. 5
SEPTEMBER 1973
COVER ARTIST: C. C. BECK
77

THE MAN WHO WASN'T!
WRITER: ELLIOT MAGGIN
ARTIST: C. C. BECK
78

THE WORLD'S TOUGHEST GUY!
WRITER: ELLIOT MAGGIN
ARTIST: C. C. BECK
86

SHAZAM! NO. 6
OCTOBER 1973
COVER ARTIST: C. C. BECK
93

BETTER LATE THAN NEVER!
WRITER: DENNY O'NEIL
ARTIST: C. C. BECK
94

DEXTER KNOX AND HIS ELECTRIC GRANDMOTHER!
WRITER: ELLIOT MAGGIN
ARTIST: C. C. BECK
102

SHAZAM! NO. 7
NOVEMBER 1973
COVER ARTIST: C. C. BECK
109

THE TROUBLES OF THE TALKING TIGER!
WRITER : DENNY O'NEIL
ARTIST: C. C. BECK
110

WHAT'S IN A NAME? DOOMSDAY!
WRITER: E. NELSON BRIDWELL
COVER ARTIST: C. C. BECK
118

SHAZAM! NO. 8
DECEMBER 1973
COVER ARTIST: C. C. BECK
125

SHAZAM! NO. 9
JANUARY 1974
COVER ARTIST: C. C.BECK

126

WORMS OF THE WORLD, UNITE!
WRITER: DENNY O'NEIL
ARTIST: C. C. BECK

127

THE MYSTERY OF THE MISSING NEWSSTAND!
WRITER: ELLIOT MAGGIN
ARTIST: DAVE COCKRUM

135

THE DAY CAPTAIN MARVEL WENT APE!
WRITER: ELLIOT MAGGIN
ARTIST: C. C. BECK

140

SHAZAM! NO. 10
FEBRUARY 1974
COVER ARTIST: BOB OKSNER

147

INVASION OF THE SALAD MEN!
WRITER: ELLIOT MAGGIN
PENCILS: BOB OKSNER INKS: VINCE COLLETTA

148

THE THANKSGIVING THIEVES!
WRITER: E. NELSON BRIDWELL
ARTIST: BOB OKSNER

155

THE PRIZE CATCH OF THE YEAR
WRITER: E. NELSON BRIDWELL
ARTIST: C. C. BECK

161

SHAZAM! NO. 11
MARCH 1974
COVER ARTIST: BOB OKSNER

168

THE WORLD'S MIGHTIEST DESSERT!
WRITER: E. NELSON BRIDWELL
PENCILS: BOB OKSNER INKS: VINCE COLLETTA

169

THE INCREDIBLE CAPE-MAN
WRITER: ELLIOT MAGGIN
ARTIST: KURT SCHAFFENBERGER

176

THE YEAR WITHOUT A CHRISTMAS!
WRITER: ELLIOT MAGGIN
ARTIST: KURT SCHAFFENBERGER

182

SHAZAM! NO. 12
JUNE 1974
COVER ARTIST: BOB OKSNER

189

THE GOLDEN PLAGUE!
WRITER: E. NELSON BRIDWELL
ARTIST: BOB OKSNER

190

THE LONGEST BLOCK IN THE WORLD!
WRITER: ELLIOT MAGGIN
ARTIST: DICK GIORDANO

197

MIGHTY MASTER OF THE MARTIAL ARTS!
WRITER: ELLIOT MAGGIN
PENCILS: BOB OKSNER INKS: VINCE COLLETTA

203

SHAZAM! NO. 13
AUGUST 1974
COVER ARTIST: BOB OKSNER

210

THE CASE OF THE CHARMING CROOK!
WRITER: ELLIOT MAGGIN
ARTIST: BOB OKSNER

211

THE HAUNTED CLUBHOUSE!
WRITER: E. NELSON BRIDWELL
ARTIST: BOB OKSNER

223

SHAZAM! NO. 14
OCTOBER 1974
COVER ARTIST: BOB OKSNER

231

THE EVIL RETURN OF THE MONSTER SOCIETY!
WRITER: DENNY O'NEIL
ARTIST: KURT SCHAFFENBERGER

232

SHAZAM! NO. 15
DECEMBER 1974
COVER ARTIST: BOB OKSNER

252

CAPTAIN MARVEL MEETS LEX LUTHOR!?!
WRITER: DENNY O'NEIL
PENCILS: BOB OKSNER PENCILS: TEX BLAISDELL
253

THE MAN IN THE PAPER ARMOR!
WRITER: E. NELSON BRIDWELL
ARTIST: KURT SCHAFFENBERGER
265

SHAZAM! NO. 16
FEBRUARY 1975
COVER ARTIST: BOB OKSNER
273

THE MAN WHO STOLE JUSTICE!
WRITER: ELLIOT MAGGIN
ARTIST: KURT SCHAFFENBERGER
274

THE GREEN-EYED MONSTER!
WRITER: E. NELSON BRIDWELL
ARTIST: BOB OKSNER
286

SHAZAM! NO. 17
APRIL 1975
COVER ARTIST: BOB OKSNER
294

THE PIED UN-PIPER
WRITER: DENNY O'NEIL
ARTIST: KURT SCHAFFENBERGER
295

SHAZAM! NO. 18
JUNE 1975
COVER ARTIST: BOB OKSNER
315

**THE CELEBRATED TALKING FROG
OF BLACKSTONE FOREST**
WRITER: ELLIOT MAGGIN
ARTIST: BOB OKSNER
316

THE COIN-OPERATED CAPER!
WRITER: E. NELSON BRIDWELL
ARTIST: KURT SCHAFFENBERGER
327

SHAZAM! NO. 19
AUGUST 1975
COVER ARTIST: BOB OKSNER
334

WHO STOLE BILLY BATSON'S THUN
WRITER: ELLIOT MAGGIN
ARTIST: KURT SCHAFFENBERGER
335

**THE SECRET OF
SMILING SWORD**
WRITER: ELLIOT MAG
ARTIST: BOB OKSNE
346

SHAZAM! NO. 20
OCTOBER 1975
COVER ARTIST: KURT SCHAFFENBERGER
353

**THE STRANGE AND TERRIBLE
DISAPPEARANCE OF MAXWELL ZODIAC!**
WRITER: ELLIOT MAGGIN
ARTIST: KURT SCHAFFENBERGER
354

SHAZAM! NO. 21
DECEMBER 1975
COVER PENCILS: ERNIE CHUA
COVER INKS: BOB OKSNER
372

SHAZAM! NO. 22
FEBRUARY 1976
COVER ARTIST: KURT SCHAFFENBERGER
373

SHAZAM! NO. 23
WINTER 1976
COVER ARTIST: KURT SCHAFFENBERGER
374

SHAZAM! NO. 24
SPRING 1976
COVER PENCILS: ERNIE CHUA
COVER INKS: BOB OKSNER
375

SHAZAM! NO. 25
OCTOBER 1976
THE BICENTENNIAL VILLAIN
WRITER: E. NELSON BRIDWELL
ARTIST: KURT SCHAFFENBERGER
376

SHAZAM! NO. 26
DECEMBER 1976
COVER PENCILS: ERNIE CHUA
COVER INKS: KURT SCHAFFENBERGER

382

THE CASE OF THE KIDNAPPED CONGRESS
WRITER: E. NELSON BRIDWELL
ARTIST: KURT SCHAFFENBERGER

383

SHAZAM! NO. 27
FEBRUARY 1977
COVER ARTIST: KURT SCHAFFENBERGER

401

FEAR IN PHILADELPHIA!
WRITER: E. NELSON BRIDWELL
PENCILS: KURT SCHAFFENBERGER *INKS:* VINCE COLLETTA

402

SHAZAM! NO. 28
APRIL 1977
COVER ARTIST: KURT SCHAFFENBERGER

419

THE RETURN OF BLACK ADAM
WRITER: E. NELSON BRIDWELL *ARTIST:* KURT SCHAFFENBERGER

420

SHAZAM! NO. 29
JUNE 1977
COVER ARTIST: KURT SCHAFFENBERGER

437

IBAC MEETS AUNT MINERVA!
WRITER: E. NELSON BRIDWELL
PENCILS: KURT SCHAFFENBERGER *INKS:* VINCE COLLETTA

438

SHAZAM! NO. 30
AUGUST 1977
COVER ARTIST: KURT SCHAFFENBERGER

455

CAPTAIN MARVEL FIGHTS THE MAN OF STEEL
WRITER: E. NELSON BRIDWELL
PENCILS: KURT SCHAFFENBERGER *INKS:* VINCE COLLETTA

456

SHAZAM! NO. 31
OCTOBER 1977
COVER ARTIST: KURT SCHAFFENBERGER

473

THE RAINBOW SQUAD
WRITER: E. NELSON BRIDWELL
PENCILS: KURT SCHAFFENBERGER *INKS:* BOB WIACEK

474

SHAZAM! NO. 32
DECEMBER 1977
COVER ARTIST: KURT SCHAFFENBERGER

491

MR. TAWNY'S BIG GAME
WRITER: E. NELSON BRIDWELL
PENCILS: TENNY HENSON *INKS:* BOB SMITH

492

SHAZAM! NO. 33
FEBRUARY 1978
COVER ARTIST: KURT SCHAFFENBERGER

509

THE WORLD'S MIGHTIEST RACE
WRITER: E. NELSON BRIDWELL
PENCILS: TENNY HENSON
INKS: VINCE COLLETTA & KURT SCHAFFENBERGER

510

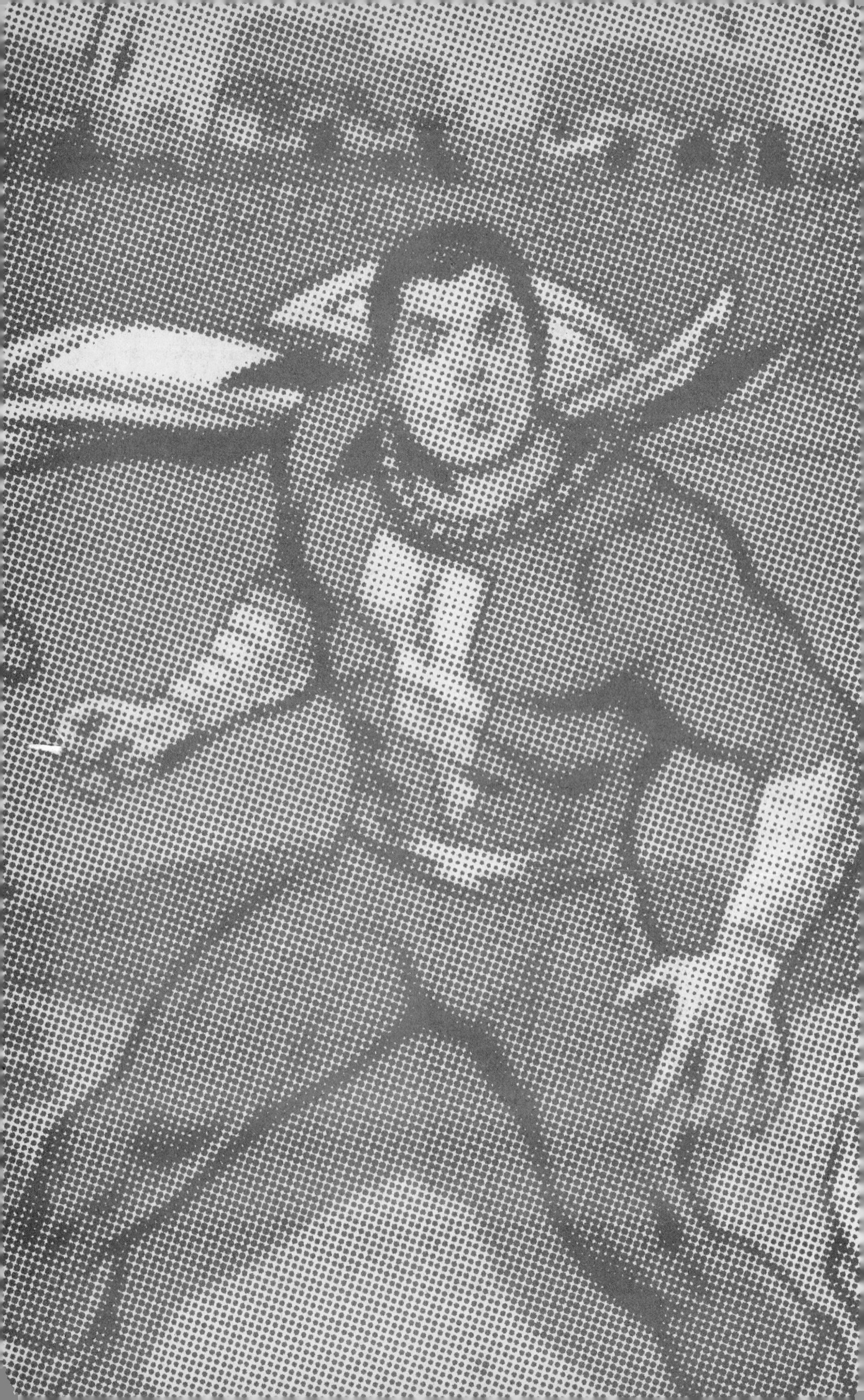

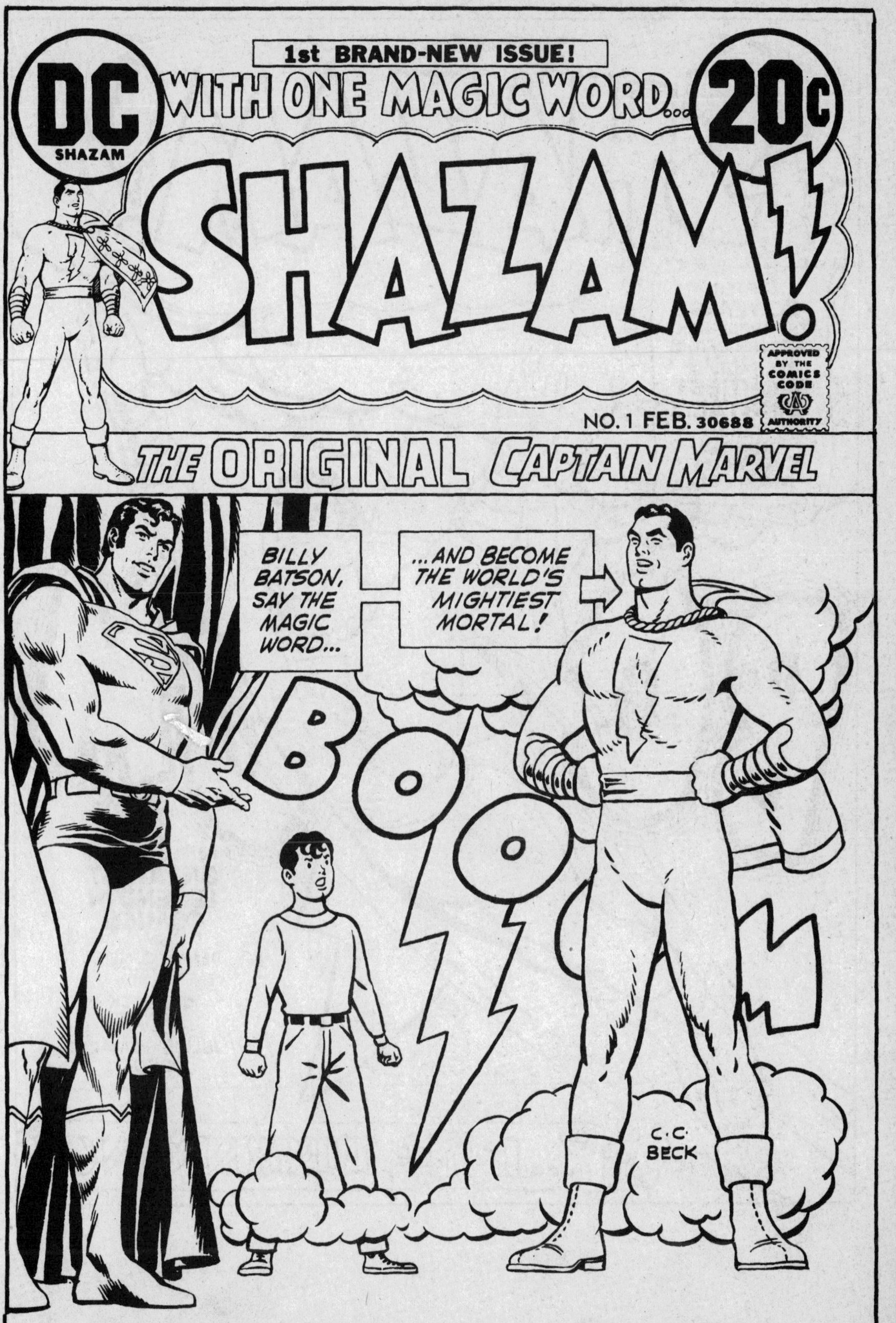
1st BRAND-NEW ISSUE!
DC SHAZAM
WITH ONE MAGIC WORD...
20¢
SHAZAM!
APPROVED BY THE COMICS CODE AUTHORITY
NO. 1 FEB. 30688
THE ORIGINAL CAPTAIN MARVEL
BILLY BATSON, SAY THE MAGIC WORD...
...AND BECOME THE WORLD'S MIGHTIEST MORTAL!
C.C. BECK

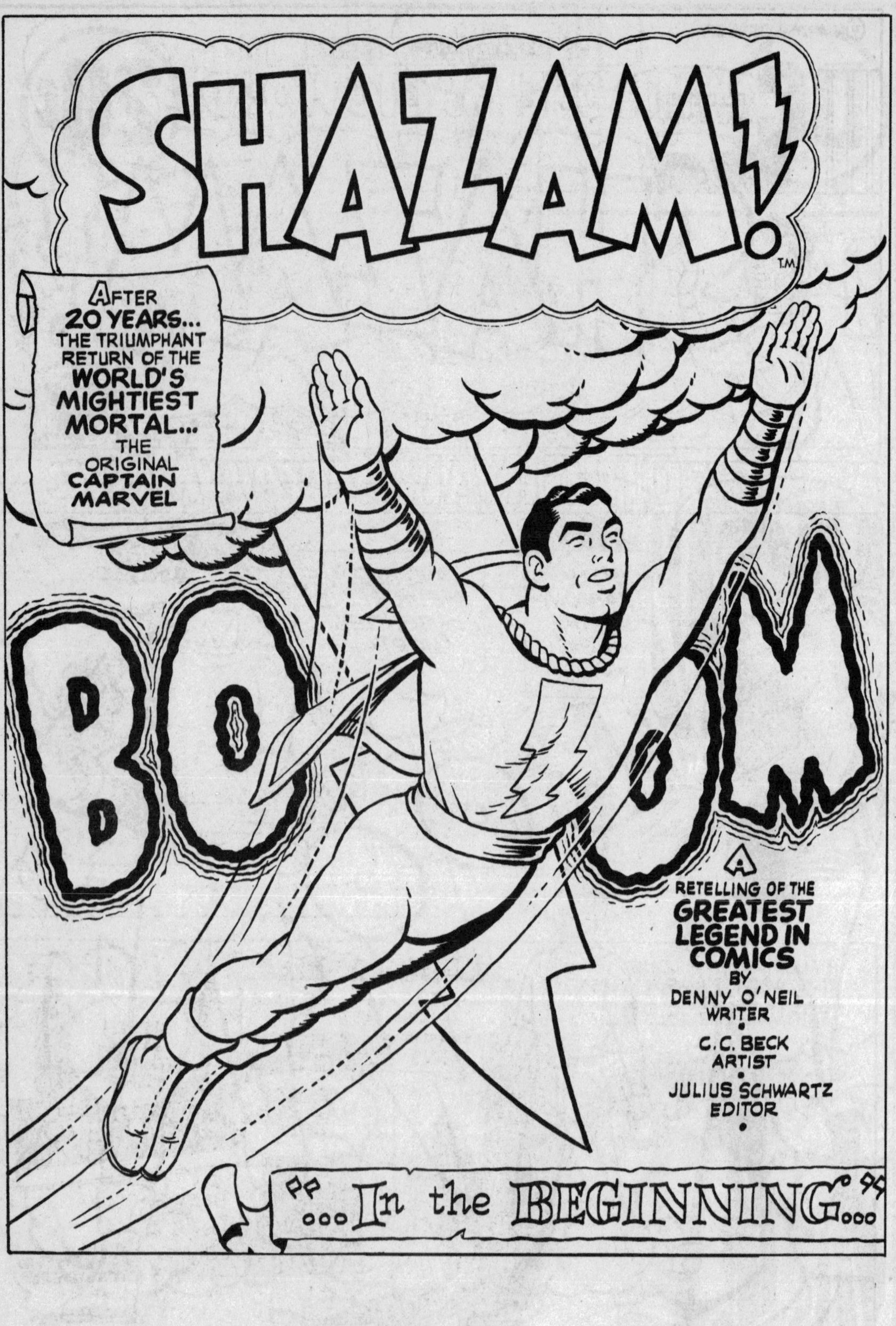
SHAZAM! T.M.
AFTER 20 YEARS... THE TRIUMPHANT RETURN OF THE WORLD'S MIGHTIEST MORTAL... THE ORIGINAL CAPTAIN MARVEL
BOOM
A RETELLING OF THE GREATEST LEGEND IN COMICS BY DENNY O'NEIL WRITER • C.C. BECK ARTIST • JULIUS SCHWARTZ EDITOR •
"...In the BEGINNING..."

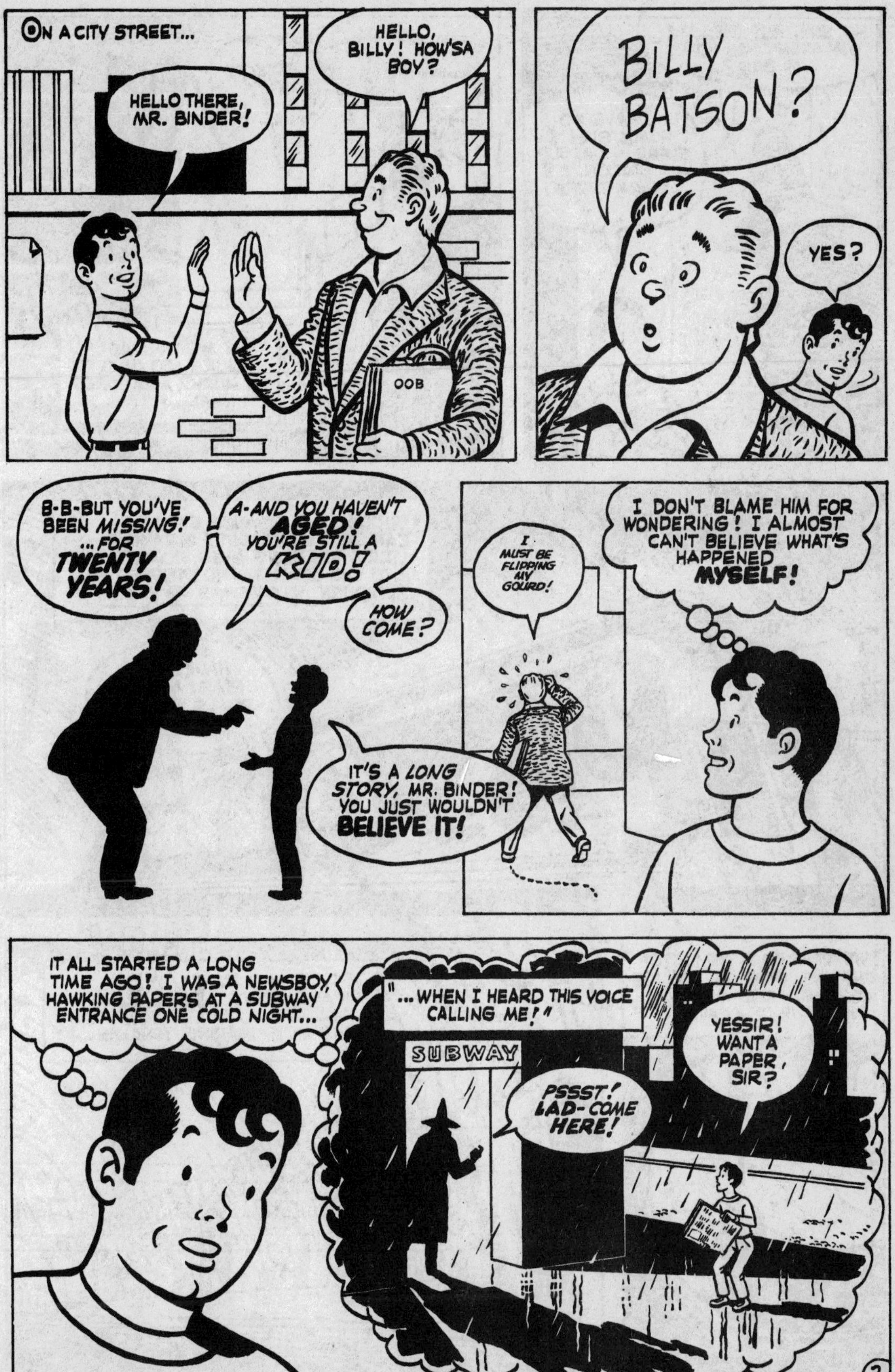
ON A CITY STREET...
HELLO THERE, MR. BINDER!
HELLO, BILLY! HOW'SA BOY?
OOB
BILLY BATSON?
YES?
B-B-BUT YOU'VE BEEN MISSING! ...FOR TWENTY YEARS!
A-AND YOU HAVEN'T AGED! YOU'RE STILL A KID!
HOW COME?
IT'S A LONG STORY, MR. BINDER! YOU JUST WOULDN'T BELIEVE IT!
I MUST BE FLIPPING MY GOURD!
I DON'T BLAME HIM FOR WONDERING! I ALMOST CAN'T BELIEVE WHAT'S HAPPENED MYSELF!
IT ALL STARTED A LONG TIME AGO! I WAS A NEWSBOY, HAWKING PAPERS AT A SUBWAY ENTRANCE ONE COLD NIGHT...
"...WHEN I HEARD THIS VOICE CALLING ME!"
SUBWAY
PSSST! LAD-COME HERE!
YESSIR! WANT A PAPER, SIR?
2

NO, SON, BUT IT'S LATE! WHY AREN'T YOU HOME IN BED?

I HAVE NO HOME, SIR! I SLEEP IN THE SUBWAY STATION. IT'S WARM THERE!

FOLLOW ME!

"THE MYSTERIOUS FIGURE LED ME INTO A MURKY, ABANDONED TUNNEL..."

"SUDDENLY, A STRANGE SUBWAY CAR, WITH HEADLIGHTS GLEAMING LIKE A DRAGON'S EYES, ROARED INTO THE STATION AND STOPPED --- ALTHOUGH *NO ONE WAS DRIVING IT!*"

HAVE NO FEAR! A MYSTIC POWER WILL GUIDE US SAFELY!

ENTER!

"WE TRAVELED TO THE END OF THE LINE, WHERE MY STRANGE COMPANION LED ME INTO THE MOUTH OF A CAVERN..."

"SUDDENLY I FOUND MYSELF IN AN ANCIENT UNDERGROUND HALL, CARVED OUT OF SOLID ROCK AND LIT BY FLARING TORCHES...!"

THE SEVEN DEADLY ENEMIES OF MAN

PRIDE   ENVY   GREED   HATRED   SELFISHNESS   LAZINESS   INJUSTICE

3

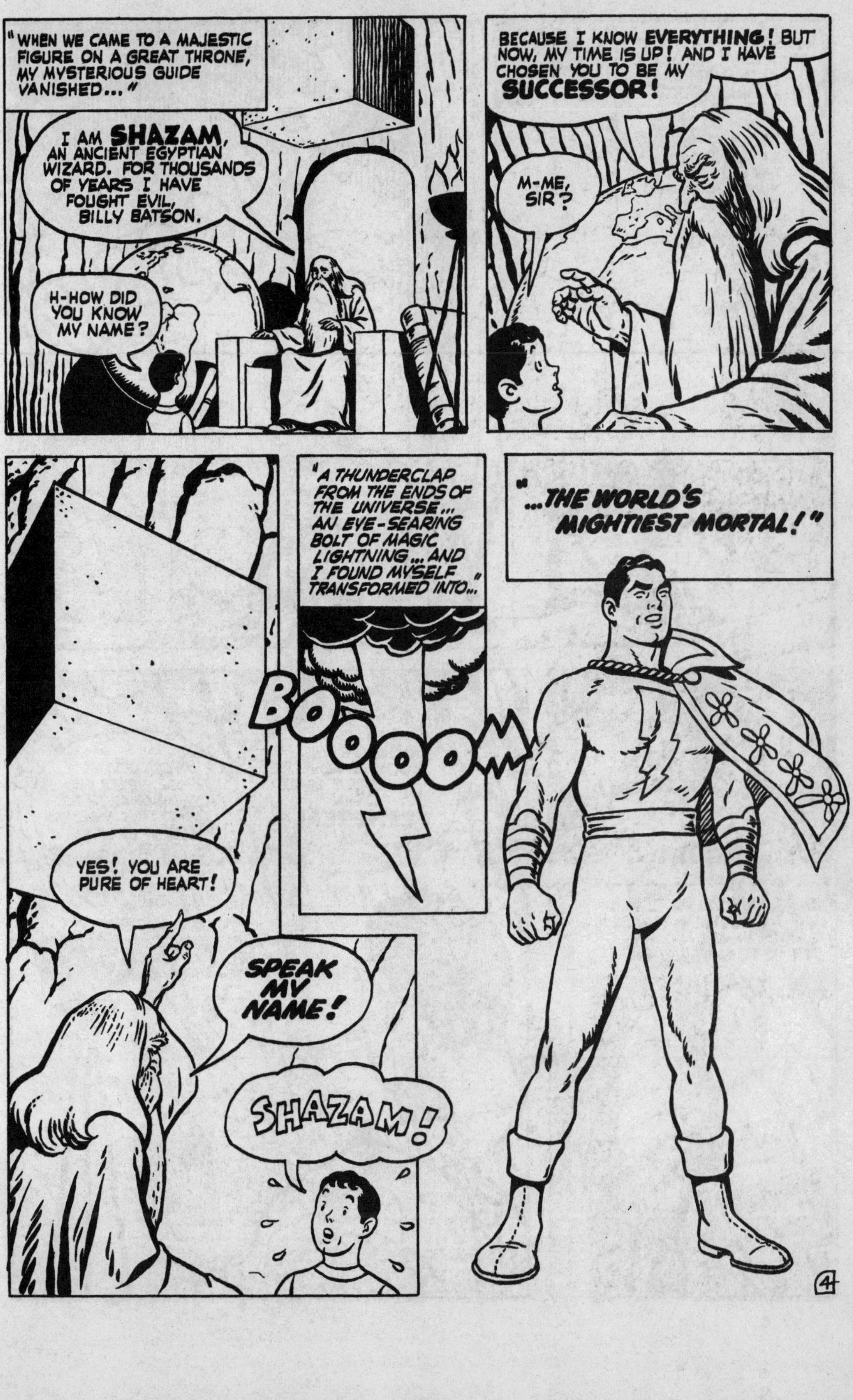
"WHEN WE CAME TO A MAJESTIC FIGURE ON A GREAT THRONE, MY MYSTERIOUS GUIDE VANISHED..."
I AM SHAZAM, AN ANCIENT EGYPTIAN WIZARD. FOR THOUSANDS OF YEARS I HAVE FOUGHT EVIL, BILLY BATSON.
H-HOW DID YOU KNOW MY NAME?
BECAUSE I KNOW EVERYTHING! BUT NOW, MY TIME IS UP! AND I HAVE CHOSEN YOU TO BE MY SUCCESSOR!
M-ME, SIR?
YES! YOU ARE PURE OF HEART!
SPEAK MY NAME!
SHAZAM!
"A THUNDERCLAP FROM THE ENDS OF THE UNIVERSE... AN EYE-SEARING BOLT OF MAGIC LIGHTNING... AND I FOUND MYSELF TRANSFORMED INTO..."
BOOOOOM
"...THE WORLD'S MIGHTIEST MORTAL!"
4

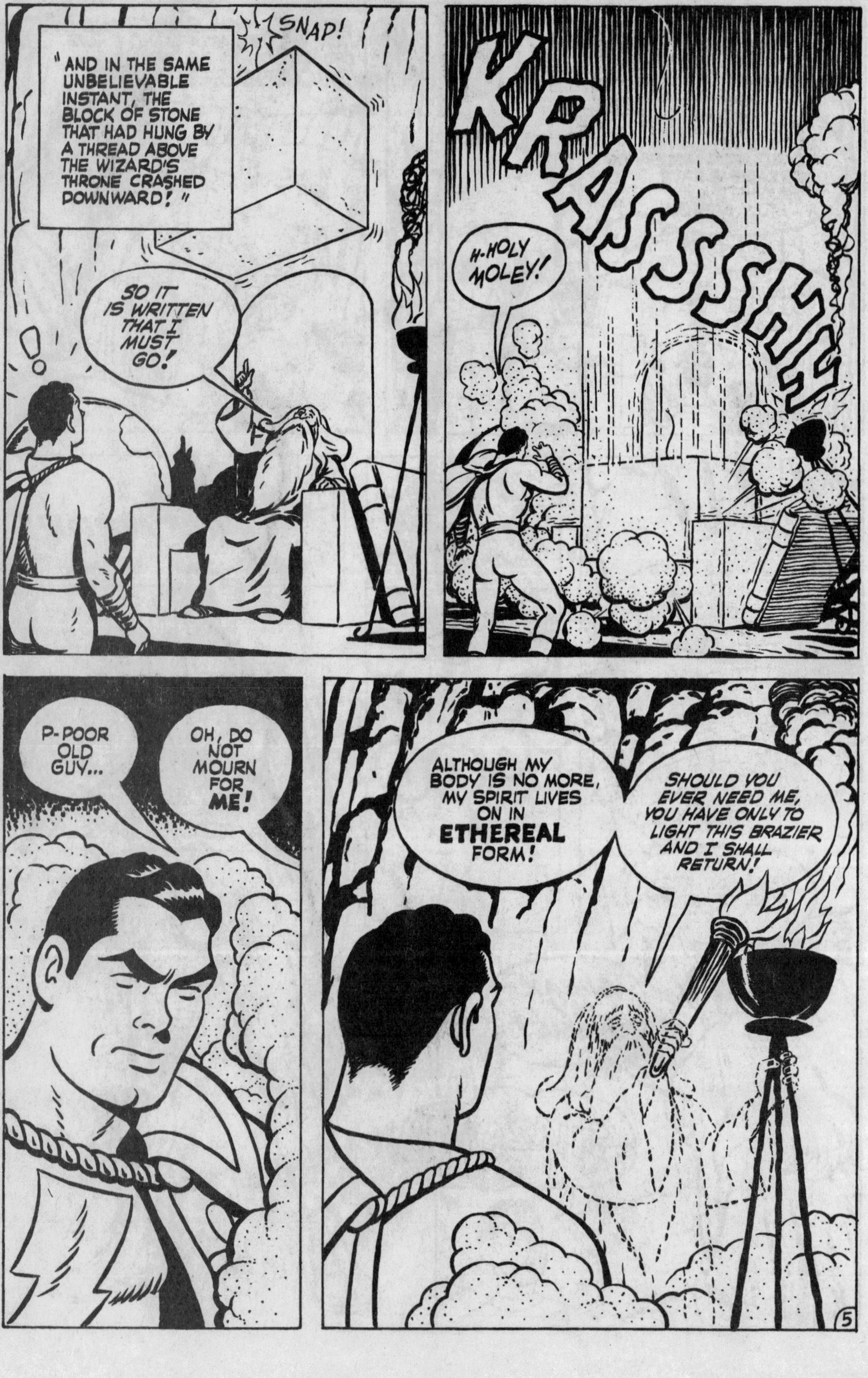
"AND IN THE SAME UNBELIEVABLE INSTANT, THE BLOCK OF STONE THAT HAD HUNG BY A THREAD ABOVE THE WIZARD'S THRONE CRASHED DOWNWARD!"
SNAP!
SO IT IS WRITTEN THAT I MUST GO!
KRASSSHH
H-HOLY MOLEY!
P-POOR OLD GUY...
OH, DO NOT MOURN FOR ME!
ALTHOUGH MY BODY IS NO MORE, MY SPIRIT LIVES ON IN ETHEREAL FORM!
SHOULD YOU EVER NEED ME, YOU HAVE ONLY TO LIGHT THIS BRAZIER AND I SHALL RETURN!
5

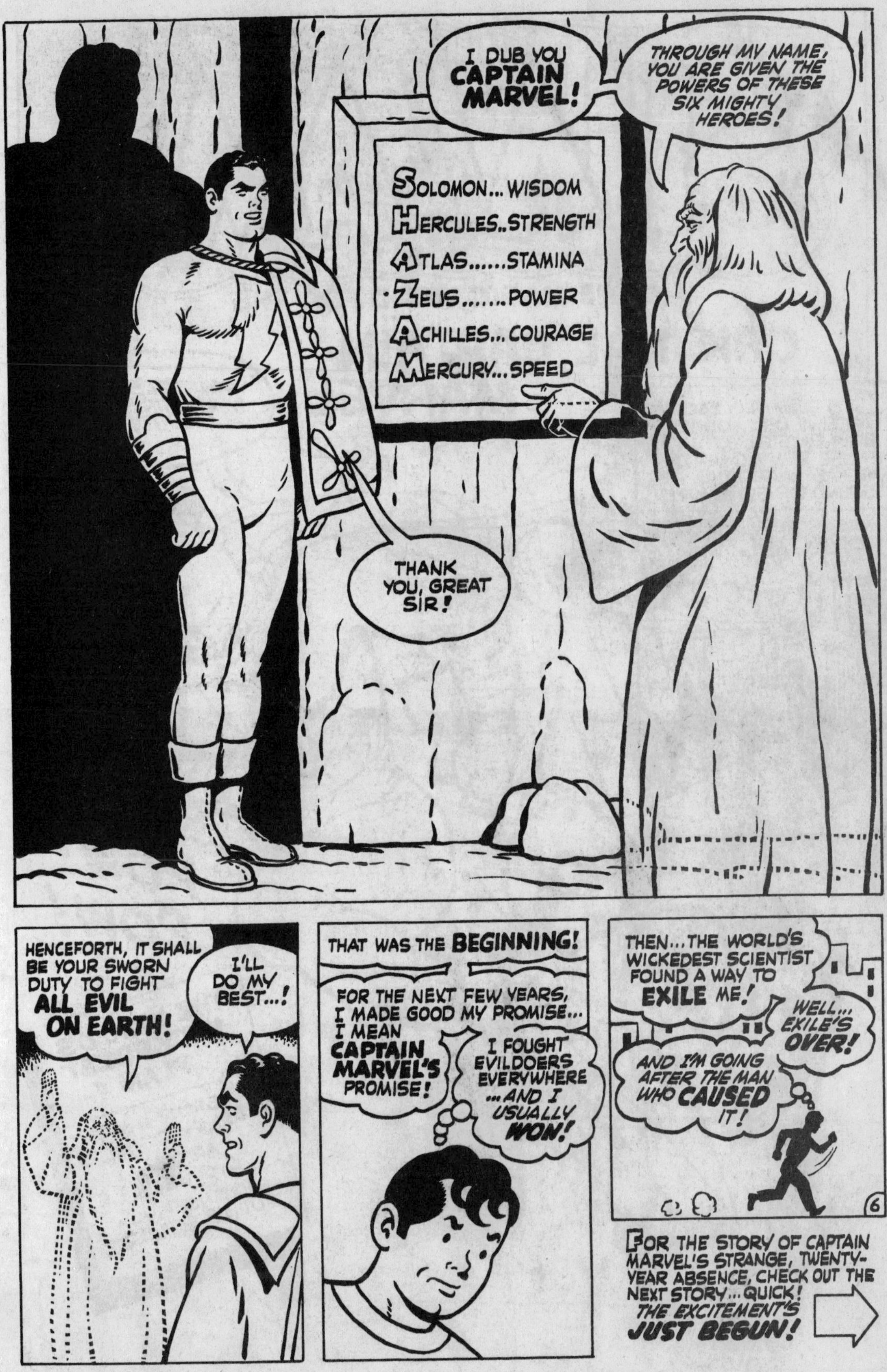
I DUB YOU CAPTAIN MARVEL!
THROUGH MY NAME, YOU ARE GIVEN THE POWERS OF THESE SIX MIGHTY HEROES!
SOLOMON... WISDOM
HERCULES.. STRENGTH
ATLAS...... STAMINA
ZEUS....... POWER
ACHILLES... COURAGE
MERCURY... SPEED
THANK YOU, GREAT SIR!
HENCEFORTH, IT SHALL BE YOUR SWORN DUTY TO FIGHT ALL EVIL ON EARTH!
I'LL DO MY BEST...!
THAT WAS THE BEGINNING!
FOR THE NEXT FEW YEARS, I MADE GOOD MY PROMISE... I MEAN CAPTAIN MARVEL'S PROMISE!
I FOUGHT EVILDOERS EVERYWHERE ...AND I USUALLY WON!
THEN... THE WORLD'S WICKEDEST SCIENTIST FOUND A WAY TO EXILE ME!
WELL... EXILE'S OVER!
AND I'M GOING AFTER THE MAN WHO CAUSED IT!
6
FOR THE STORY OF CAPTAIN MARVEL'S STRANGE, TWENTY-YEAR ABSENCE, CHECK OUT THE NEXT STORY... QUICK! THE EXCITEMENT'S JUST BEGUN!

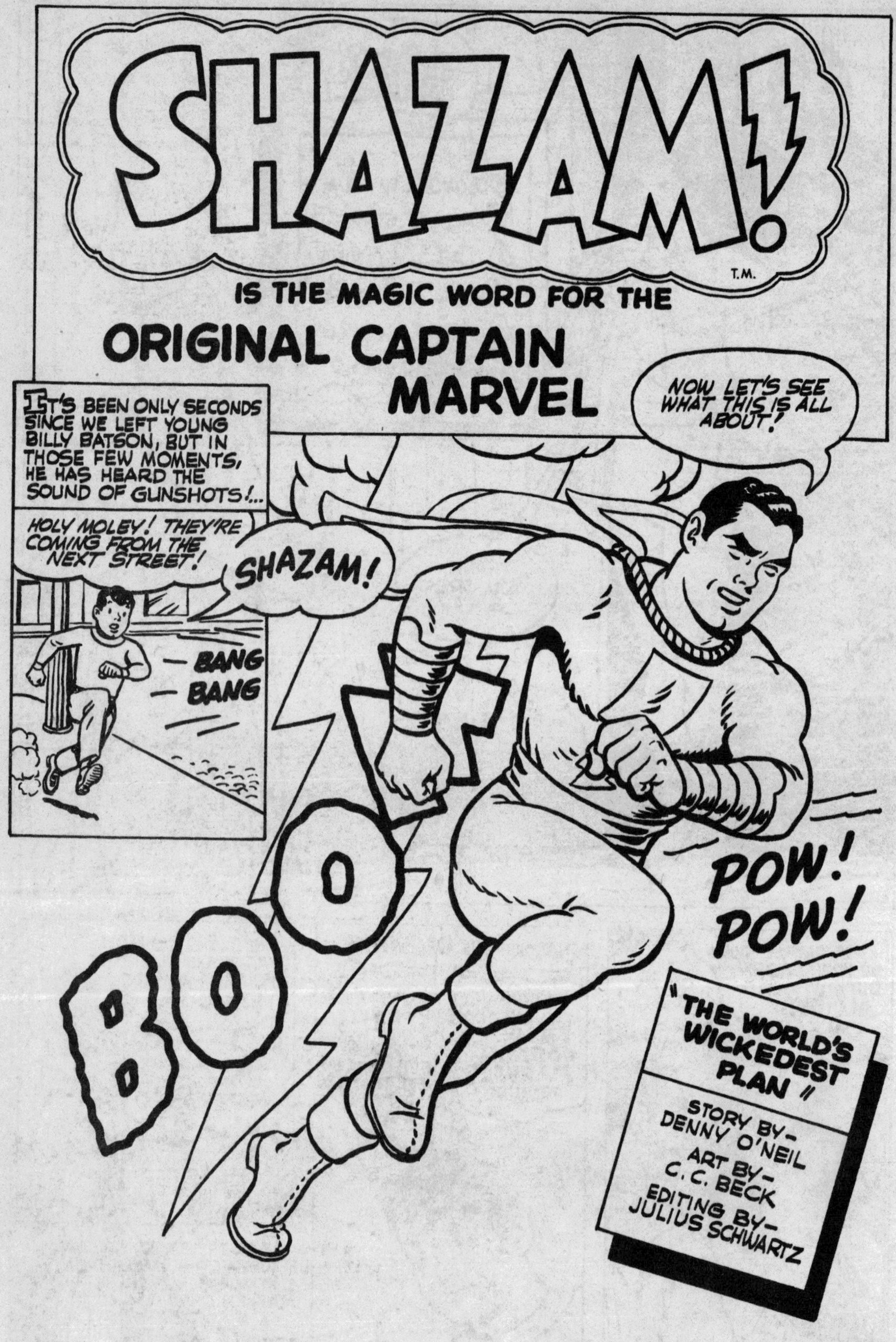
SHAZAM!
T.M.
IS THE MAGIC WORD FOR THE
ORIGINAL CAPTAIN MARVEL
IT'S BEEN ONLY SECONDS SINCE WE LEFT YOUNG BILLY BATSON, BUT IN THOSE FEW MOMENTS, HE HAS HEARD THE SOUND OF GUNSHOTS!...
HOLY MOLEY! THEY'RE COMING FROM THE NEXT STREET!
SHAZAM!
BANG
BANG
NOW LET'S SEE WHAT THIS IS ALL ABOUT!
BOOM
POW!
POW!
"THE WORLD'S WICKEDEST PLAN"
STORY BY- DENNY O'NEIL
ART BY- C.C. BECK
EDITING BY- JULIUS SCHWARTZ
1

CRIMINALS... RUNNING FROM THE POLICE! I SEE THINGS HAVEN'T CHANGED MUCH IN THE TWENTY YEARS I'VE BEEN AWAY!

KABANG KABANG

SCREECH

AROOOO

THERE ARE STILL *GOOD GUYS* AND *BAD GUYS*...

...AND I'M STILL ON THE SIDE OF THE *GOOD GUYS!*

KRASSH

Y'IPES! A HUMAN *ROADBLOCK!*

CH-CHARLIE... DO YOU SEE WHAT I SEE?

ZZZING

ZZZING

BAM

KAPOW

YEH, JULIE... EITHER THE BULLETS ARE BOUNCING OFF HIM... OR WE'RE USING *VERY INFERIOR BULLETS!*

YEP... THINGS HAVEN'T CHANGED MUCH AT *ALL!*

GOTCHA!

THANKS A LOT, MISTER.

NO THANKS ARE NECESSARY, OFFICER-- I WAS JUST DOING MY JOB!

2

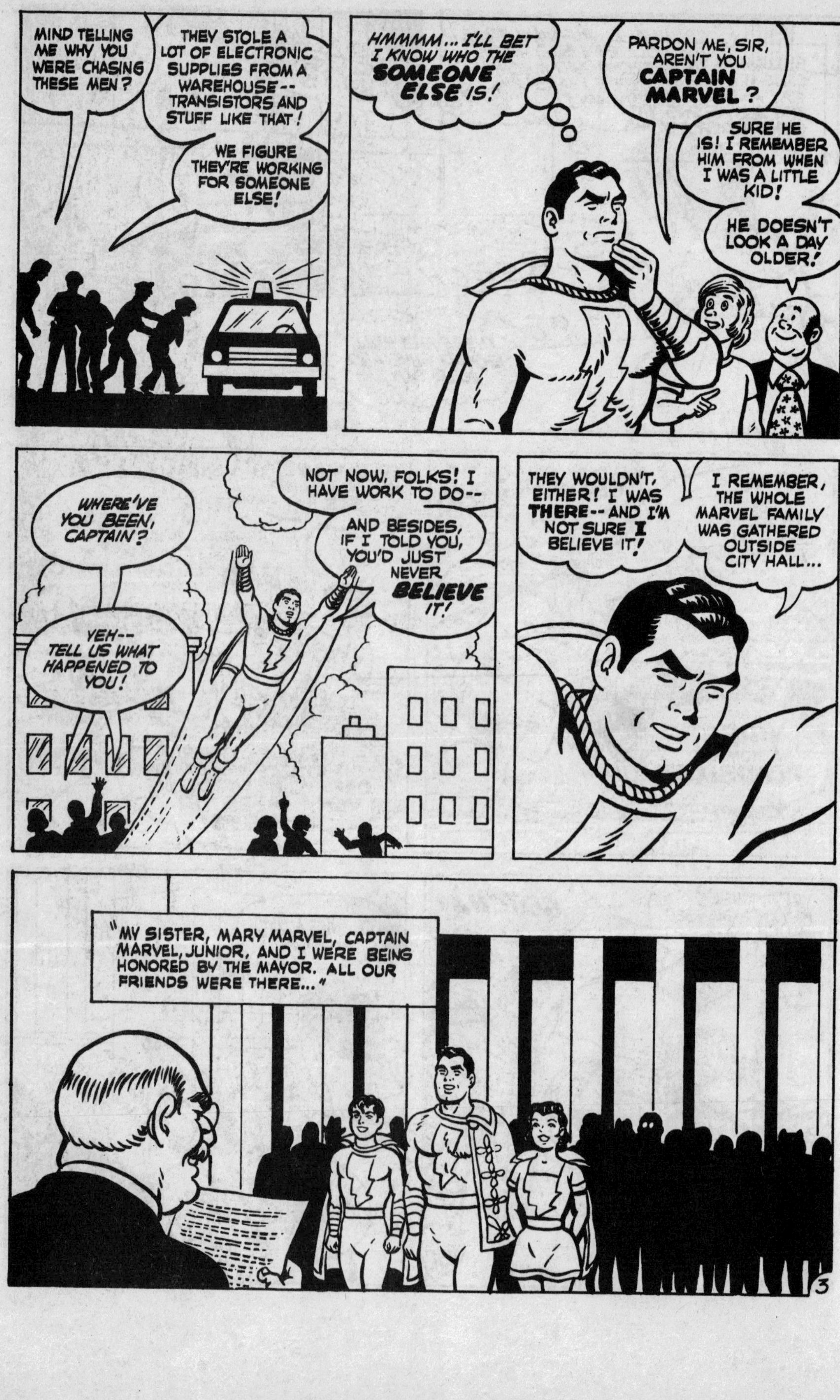
MIND TELLING ME WHY YOU WERE CHASING THESE MEN?
THEY STOLE A LOT OF ELECTRONIC SUPPLIES FROM A WAREHOUSE -- TRANSISTORS AND STUFF LIKE THAT!
WE FIGURE THEY'RE WORKING FOR SOMEONE ELSE!
HMMMM... I'LL BET I KNOW WHO THE SOMEONE ELSE IS!
PARDON ME, SIR, AREN'T YOU CAPTAIN MARVEL?
SURE HE IS! I REMEMBER HIM FROM WHEN I WAS A LITTLE KID!
HE DOESN'T LOOK A DAY OLDER!
WHERE'VE YOU BEEN, CAPTAIN?
YEH-- TELL US WHAT HAPPENED TO YOU!
NOT NOW, FOLKS! I HAVE WORK TO DO--
AND BESIDES, IF I TOLD YOU, YOU'D JUST NEVER BELIEVE IT!
THEY WOULDN'T, EITHER! I WAS THERE-- AND I'M NOT SURE I BELIEVE IT!
I REMEMBER, THE WHOLE MARVEL FAMILY WAS GATHERED OUTSIDE CITY HALL...
"MY SISTER, MARY MARVEL, CAPTAIN MARVEL, JUNIOR, AND I WERE BEING HONORED BY THE MAYOR. ALL OUR FRIENDS WERE THERE..."
3

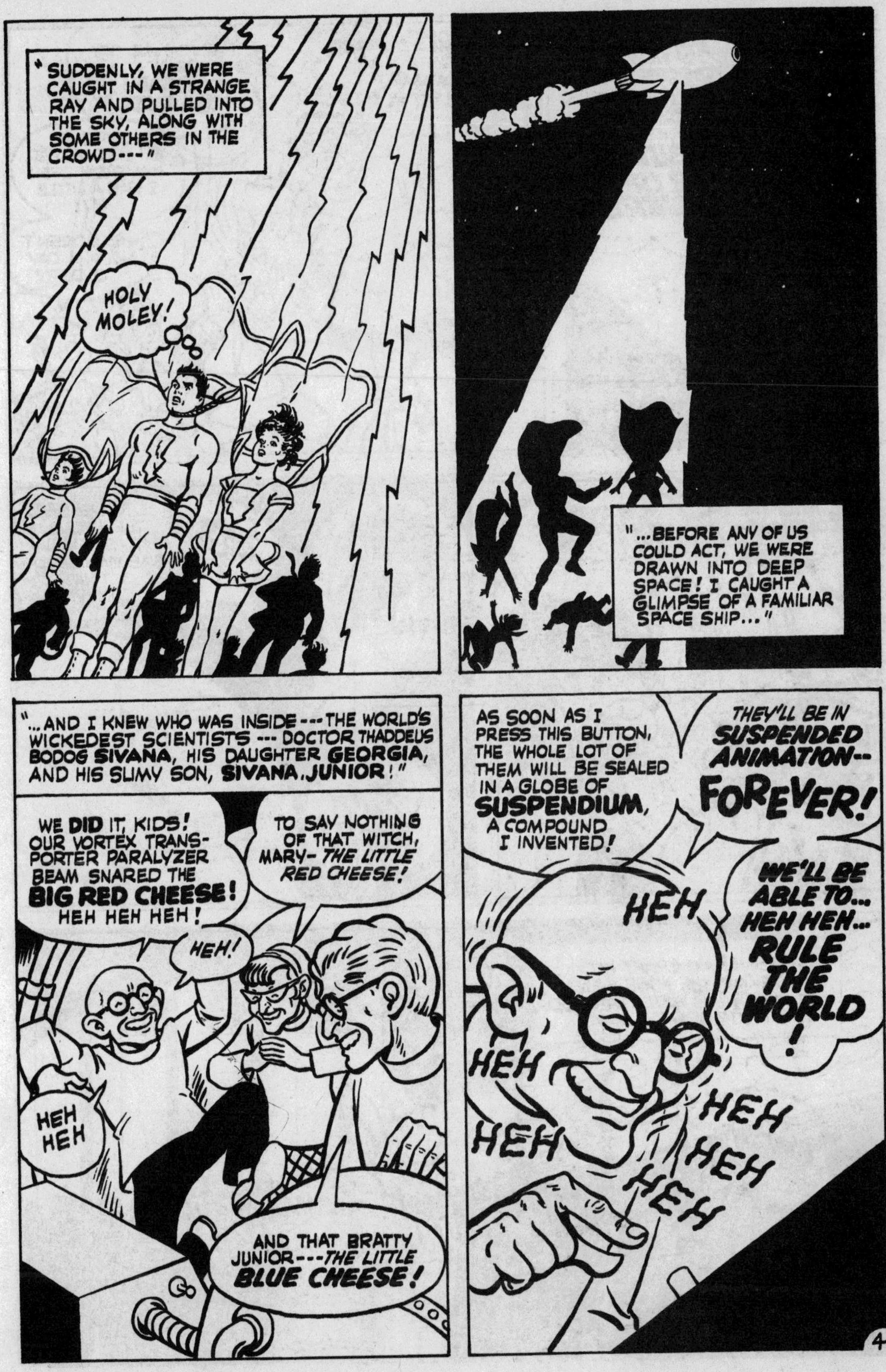
"SUDDENLY, WE WERE CAUGHT IN A STRANGE RAY AND PULLED INTO THE SKY, ALONG WITH SOME OTHERS IN THE CROWD---"
HOLY MOLEY!
"...BEFORE ANY OF US COULD ACT, WE WERE DRAWN INTO DEEP SPACE! I CAUGHT A GLIMPSE OF A FAMILIAR SPACE SHIP..."
"...AND I KNEW WHO WAS INSIDE---THE WORLD'S WICKEDEST SCIENTISTS --- DOCTOR THADDEUS BODOG SIVANA, HIS DAUGHTER GEORGIA, AND HIS SLIMY SON, SIVANA, JUNIOR!"
WE DID IT, KIDS! OUR VORTEX TRANSPORTER PARALYZER BEAM SNARED THE BIG RED CHEESE! HEH HEH HEH!
TO SAY NOTHING OF THAT WITCH, MARY- THE LITTLE RED CHEESE!
HEH!
HEH HEH
AND THAT BRATTY JUNIOR---THE LITTLE BLUE CHEESE!
AS SOON AS I PRESS THIS BUTTON, THE WHOLE LOT OF THEM WILL BE SEALED IN A GLOBE OF SUSPENDIUM, A COMPOUND I INVENTED!
THEY'LL BE IN SUSPENDED ANIMATION-- FOREVER!
WE'LL BE ABLE TO... HEH HEH... RULE THE WORLD!
HEH
HEH
HEH
HEH
HEH
HEH
4

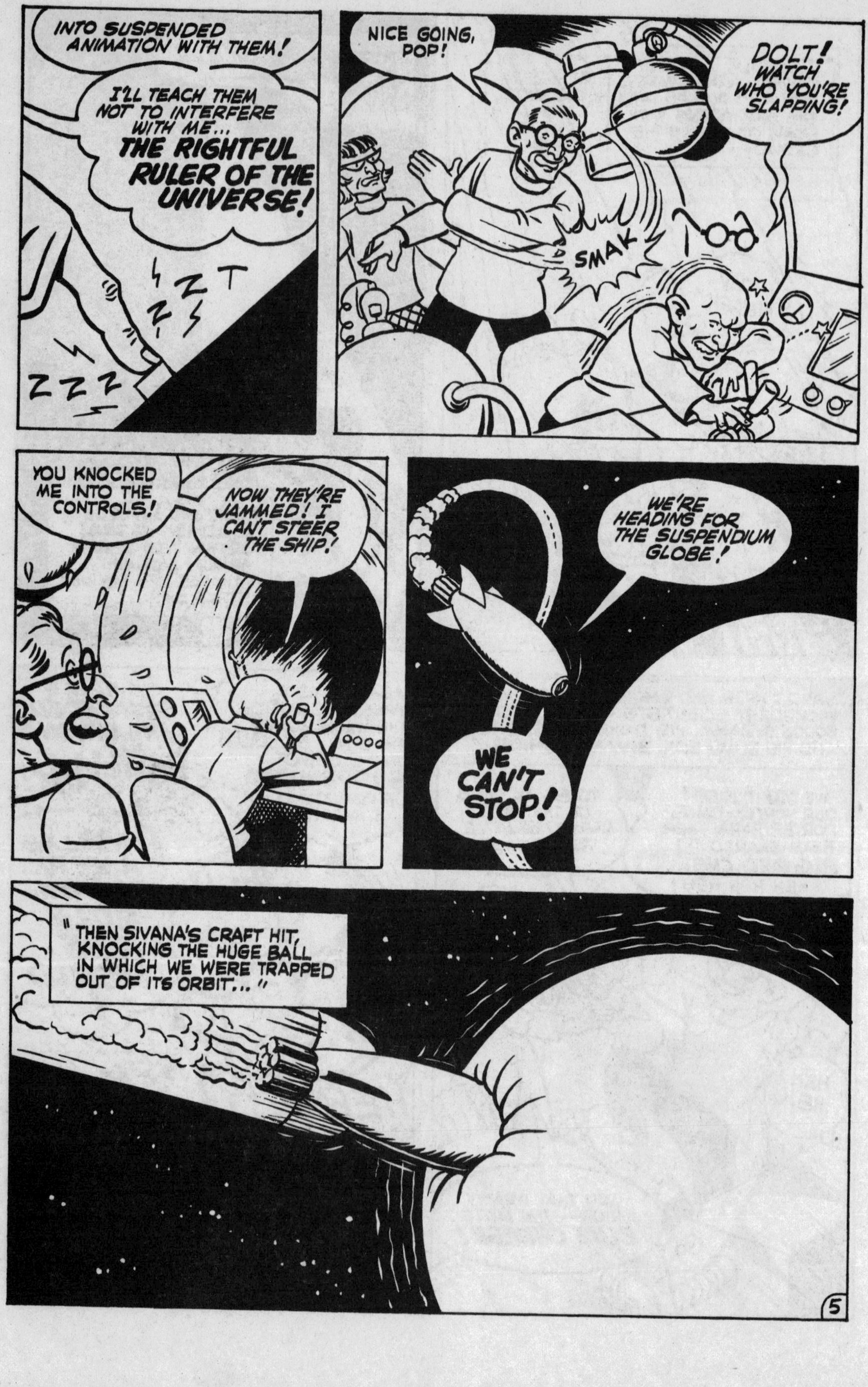
INTO SUSPENDED ANIMATION WITH THEM!
I'LL TEACH THEM NOT TO INTERFERE WITH ME... THE RIGHTFUL RULER OF THE UNIVERSE!
ZZZT
ZZZ
NICE GOING, POP!
DOLT! WATCH WHO YOU'RE SLAPPING!
SMAK
YOU KNOCKED ME INTO THE CONTROLS!
NOW THEY'RE JAMMED! I CAN'T STEER THE SHIP!
WE'RE HEADING FOR THE SUSPENDIUM GLOBE!
WE CAN'T STOP!
"THEN SIVANA'S CRAFT HIT, KNOCKING THE HUGE BALL IN WHICH WE WERE TRAPPED OUT OF ITS ORBIT..."
5

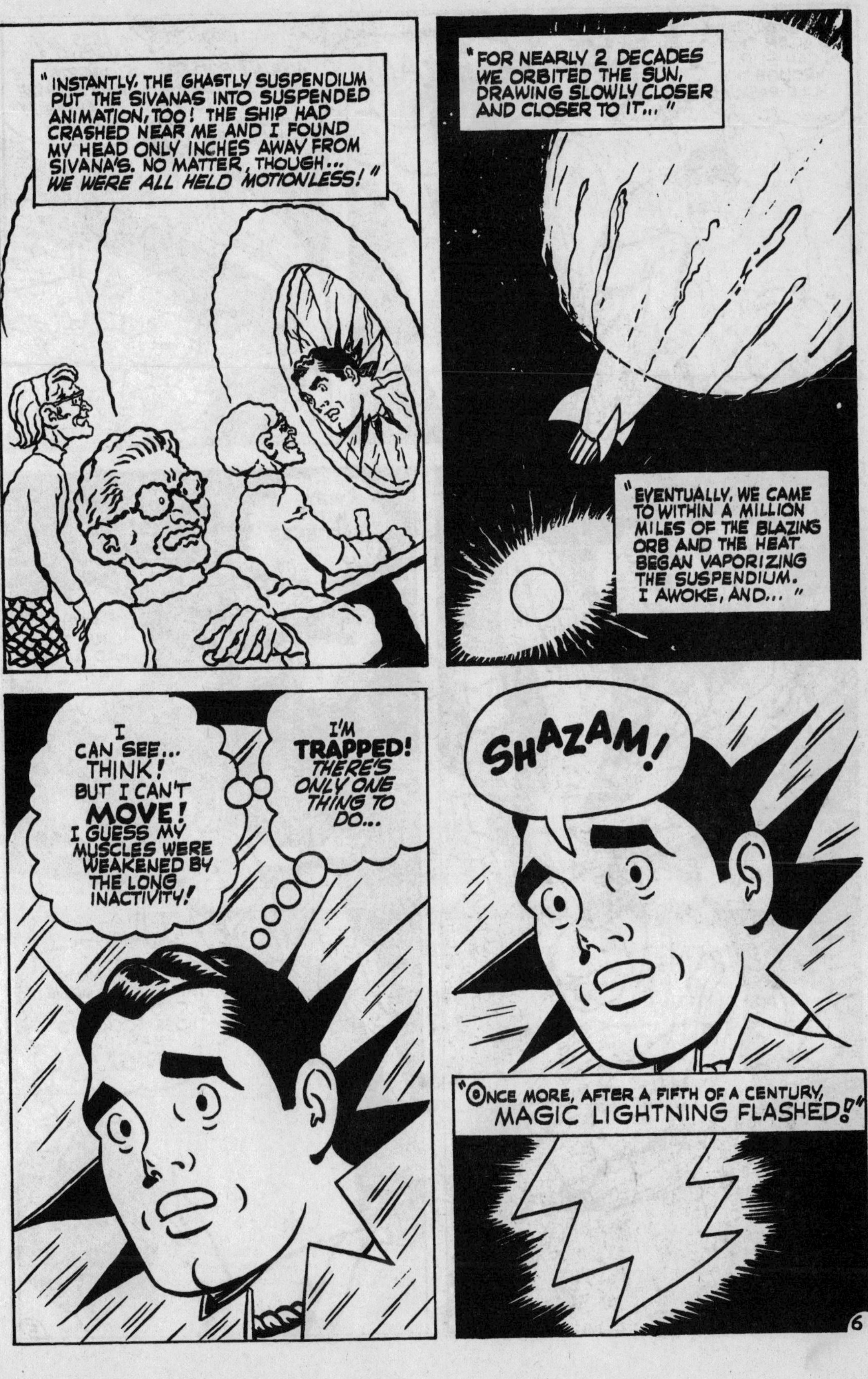
"INSTANTLY, THE GHASTLY SUSPENDIUM PUT THE SIVANAS INTO SUSPENDED ANIMATION, TOO! THE SHIP HAD CRASHED NEAR ME AND I FOUND MY HEAD ONLY INCHES AWAY FROM SIVANA'S. NO MATTER, THOUGH... WE WERE ALL HELD MOTIONLESS!"
"FOR NEARLY 2 DECADES WE ORBITED THE SUN, DRAWING SLOWLY CLOSER AND CLOSER TO IT..."
"EVENTUALLY, WE CAME TO WITHIN A MILLION MILES OF THE BLAZING ORB AND THE HEAT BEGAN VAPORIZING THE SUSPENDIUM. I AWOKE, AND..."
I CAN SEE... THINK! BUT I CAN'T MOVE! I GUESS MY MUSCLES WERE WEAKENED BY THE LONG INACTIVITY!
I'M TRAPPED! THERE'S ONLY ONE THING TO DO...
SHAZAM!
"ONCE MORE, AFTER A FIFTH OF A CENTURY, MAGIC LIGHTNING FLASHED!"
6

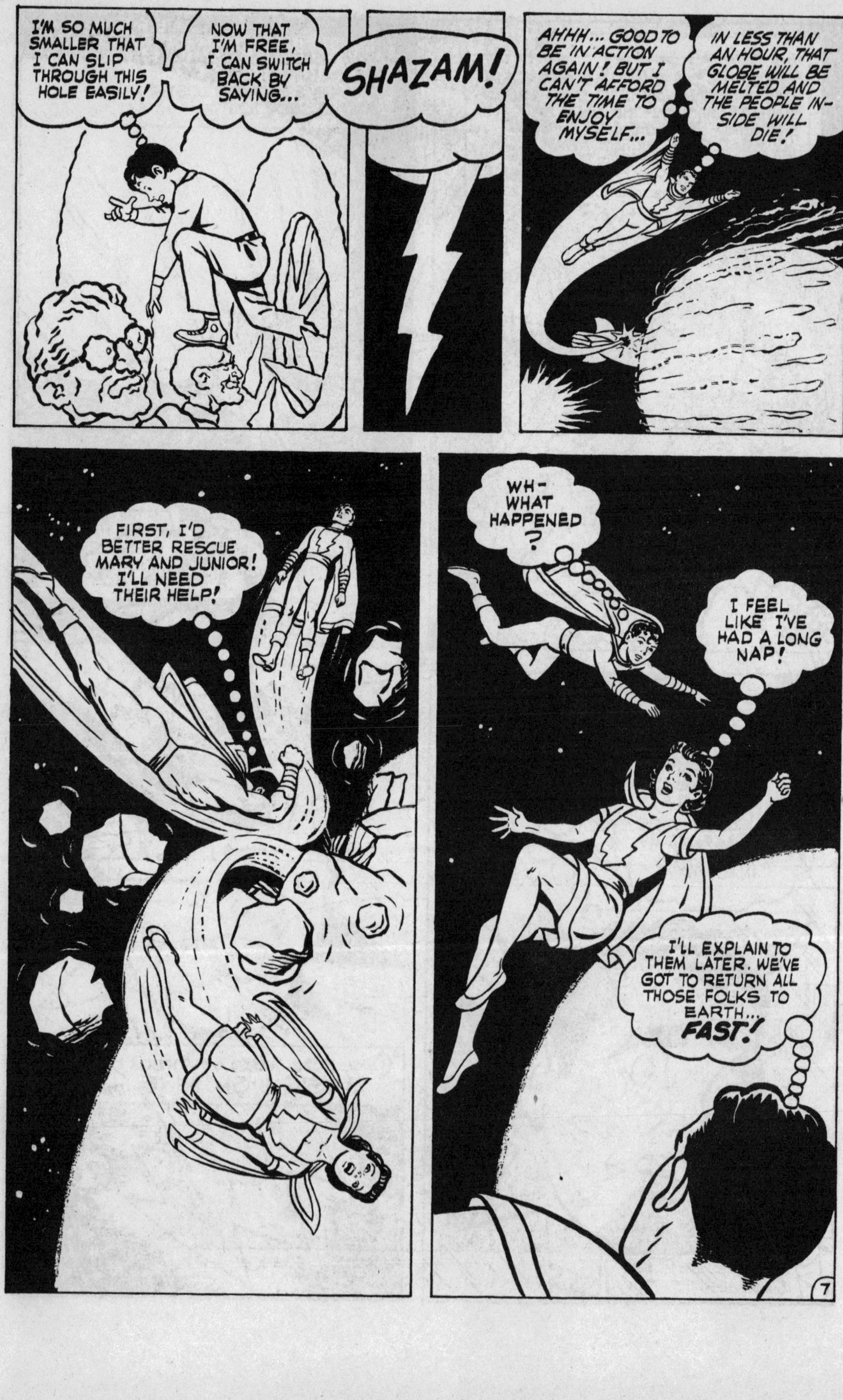
I'M SO MUCH SMALLER THAT I CAN SLIP THROUGH THIS HOLE EASILY!
NOW THAT I'M FREE, I CAN SWITCH BACK BY SAYING...
SHAZAM!
AHHH... GOOD TO BE IN ACTION AGAIN! BUT I CAN'T AFFORD THE TIME TO ENJOY MYSELF...
IN LESS THAN AN HOUR, THAT GLOBE WILL BE MELTED AND THE PEOPLE INSIDE WILL DIE!
FIRST, I'D BETTER RESCUE MARY AND JUNIOR! I'LL NEED THEIR HELP!
WH- WHAT HAPPENED ?
I FEEL LIKE I'VE HAD A LONG NAP!
I'LL EXPLAIN TO THEM LATER. WE'VE GOT TO RETURN ALL THOSE FOLKS TO EARTH... FAST!
7

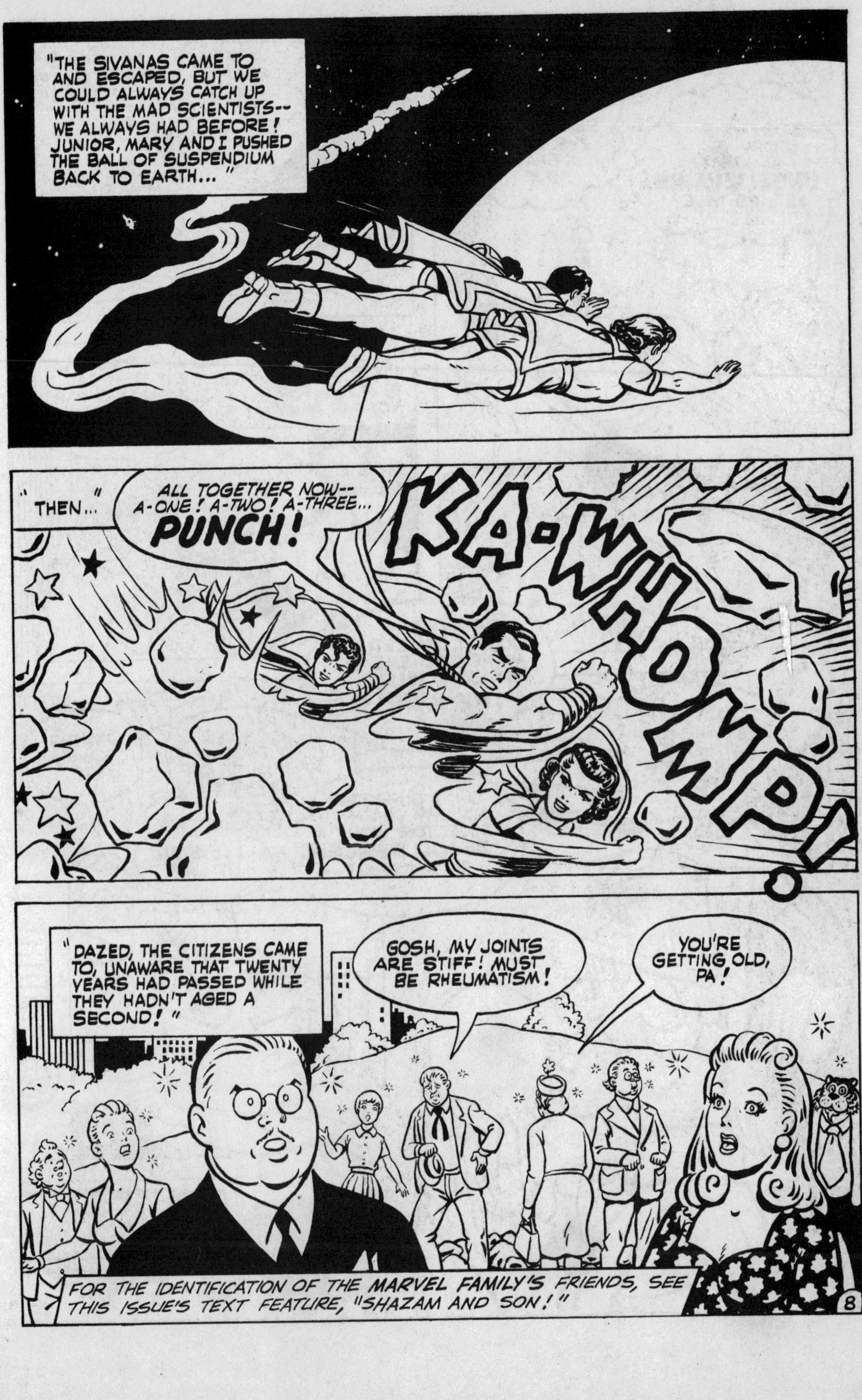

"THE SIVANAS CAME TO AND ESCAPED, BUT WE COULD ALWAYS CATCH UP WITH THE MAD SCIENTISTS-- WE ALWAYS HAD BEFORE! JUNIOR, MARY AND I PUSHED THE BALL OF SUSPENDIUM BACK TO EARTH..."
"THEN..."
ALL TOGETHER NOW-- A-ONE! A-TWO! A-THREE... PUNCH!
KA-WHOMP!
"DAZED, THE CITIZENS CAME TO, UNAWARE THAT TWENTY YEARS HAD PASSED WHILE THEY HADN'T AGED A SECOND!"
GOSH, MY JOINTS ARE STIFF! MUST BE RHEUMATISM!
YOU'RE GETTING OLD, PA!
FOR THE IDENTIFICATION OF THE MARVEL FAMILY'S FRIENDS, SEE THIS ISSUE'S TEXT FEATURE, "SHAZAM AND SON!"
8

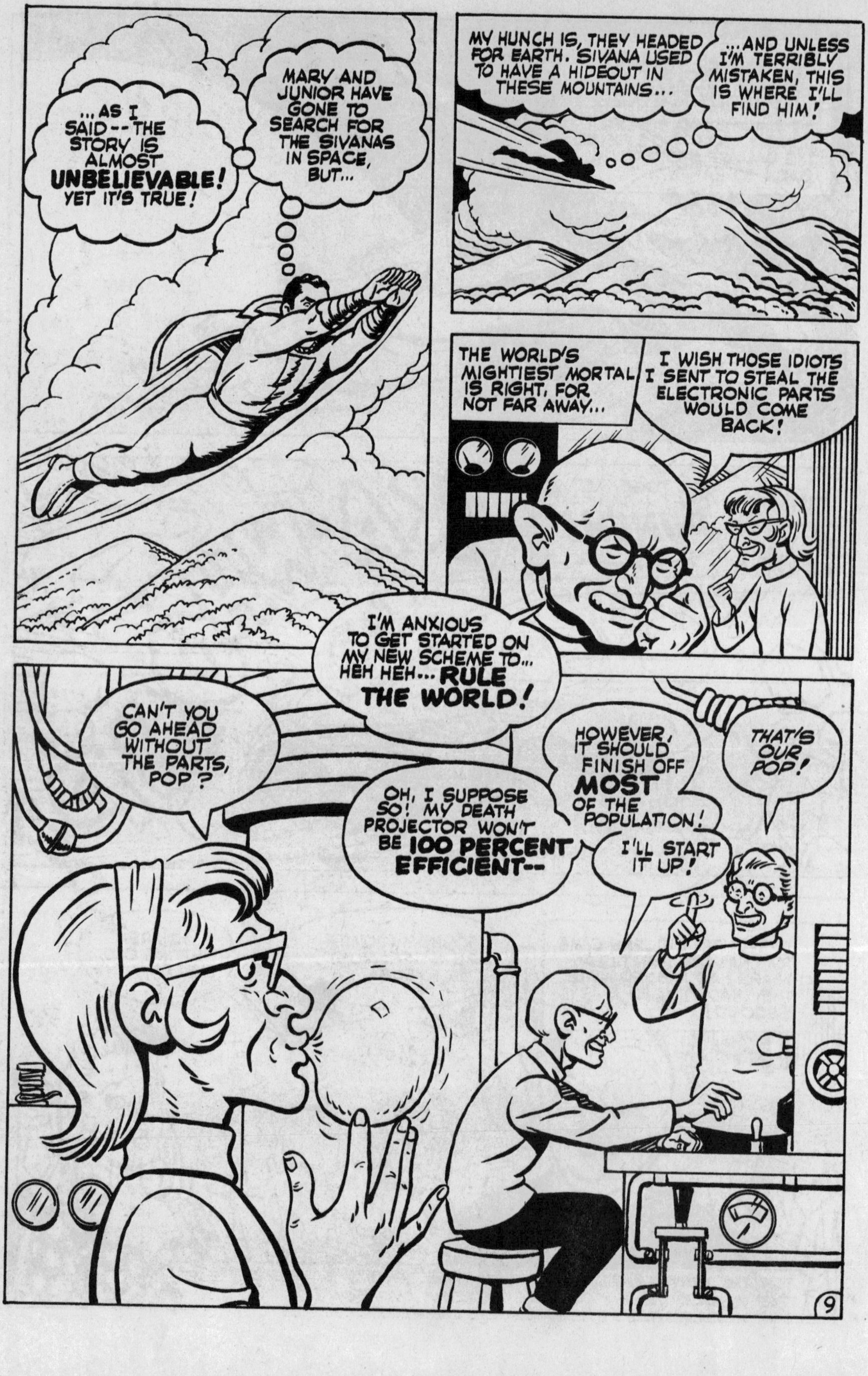
...AS I SAID--THE STORY IS ALMOST UNBELIEVABLE! YET IT'S TRUE!
MARY AND JUNIOR HAVE GONE TO SEARCH FOR THE SIVANAS IN SPACE, BUT...
MY HUNCH IS, THEY HEADED FOR EARTH. SIVANA USED TO HAVE A HIDEOUT IN THESE MOUNTAINS...
...AND UNLESS I'M TERRIBLY MISTAKEN, THIS IS WHERE I'LL FIND HIM!
THE WORLD'S MIGHTIEST MORTAL IS RIGHT, FOR NOT FAR AWAY...
I WISH THOSE IDIOTS I SENT TO STEAL THE ELECTRONIC PARTS WOULD COME BACK!
I'M ANXIOUS TO GET STARTED ON MY NEW SCHEME TO... HEH HEH... RULE THE WORLD!
CAN'T YOU GO AHEAD WITHOUT THE PARTS, POP?
OH, I SUPPOSE SO! MY DEATH PROJECTOR WON'T BE 100 PERCENT EFFICIENT--
HOWEVER, IT SHOULD FINISH OFF MOST OF THE POPULATION!
THAT'S OUR POP!
I'LL START IT UP!
9

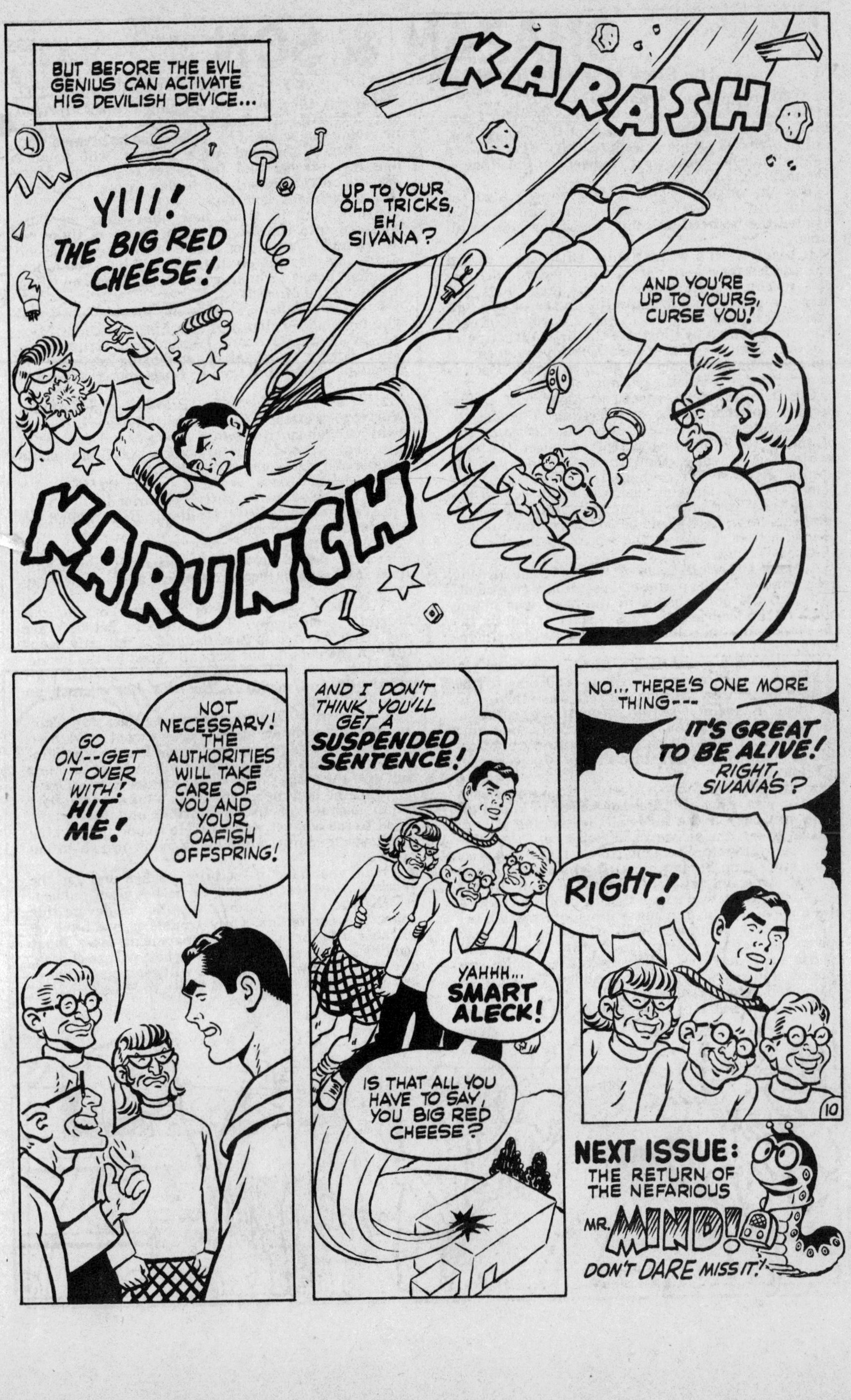
BUT BEFORE THE EVIL GENIUS CAN ACTIVATE HIS DEVILISH DEVICE...
KARASH
YIII! THE BIG RED CHEESE!
UP TO YOUR OLD TRICKS, EH, SIVANA?
AND YOU'RE UP TO YOURS, CURSE YOU!
KARUNCH
GO ON--GET IT OVER WITH! HIT ME!
NOT NECESSARY! THE AUTHORITIES WILL TAKE CARE OF YOU AND YOUR OAFISH OFFSPRING!
AND I DON'T THINK YOU'LL GET A SUSPENDED SENTENCE!
YAHHH... SMART ALECK!
IS THAT ALL YOU HAVE TO SAY, YOU BIG RED CHEESE?
NO... THERE'S ONE MORE THING---
IT'S GREAT TO BE ALIVE! RIGHT, SIVANAS?
RIGHT!
10
NEXT ISSUE: THE RETURN OF THE NEFARIOUS MR. MIND!
DON'T DARE MISS IT!

SHAZAM & SON

The Story of the World's Mightiest Mortal — By E. Nelson Bridwell

"You are my son, Captain Marvel!"

So old *Shazam* said once, in a story in *Whiz Comics*. And, in a way, it was true—for the ancient wizard had passed on his powers to *Billy Batson* when he died and his spirit went to dwell on the *Rock of Eternity.*

But the original *Captain Marvel* was also the brainchild of several other men, who together created the best-selling comic magazine hero of all time.

It began when a writer named Bill Parker turned out an idea for a hero named *Captain Thunder.* He was to combine the powers of six great gods and heroes, and he would debut in the first issue of a new magazine, *Whiz Comics.* Artist Charles Clarence Beck was chosen to illustrate the first adventure of *Captain Thunder,* and it was he who designed the red-and-gold costume of the hero. (Happily, Beck is back with this first issue of *Shazam!*)

But then, for some reason, accounts vary, it was decided to change the name from *Thunder* to —something else. I have heard Pete Costanza tell of the editorial meeting called to select the new name. For a while, they threw around various names. At last, Pete suggested "Captain Marvelous". Close—but someone wisely decided to lop off the "ous" and make it simply *Captain Marvel.* A few years later, Pete would be one of the top *Captain Marvel* artists; I suspect the reprint in this issue is Costanza's work.

A black-and-white issue of *Whiz #1* had already been printed, for the purpose of securing a copyright. Although the only change in the issue was in the name of the lead feature's hero, when it finally hit the newsstands, in color, it was *Whiz #2* (dated February, 1940).

Not since *Superman* had a hero so captured the imaginations of readers. Soon, in addition to the *Whiz* appearances, *Captain Marvel* was starring in his own magazine, *Captain Marvel Adventures,* which soon became the top-selling comix magazine in history! In time it went from quarterly publication to monthly, to every third Friday—to every other Friday.

In the very first *Captain Marvel* tale, a mysterious scientist was using a mysterious power to knock all radio stations off the air—and demanding a high ransom to free the air-waves. By chance, *Billy Batson* discovered the headquarters of the scientist (none other than *Sivana* himself), and told *Sterling Morris,* owner of radio station *WHIZ.* But *Morris* was so sure *Billy* was wrong that he promised to give him a job as a radio announcer if his information led to the villain's capture. Well, *Billy* used his new powers as *Captain Marvel* to capture *Sivana,* and *Morris* kept his word. *Billy* became a radio announcer and newscaster. *WHIZ* added TV early in 1946—well before NBC and CBS.

There were other members added to the *Marvel Family* as time went on, notably *Freddy Freeman,* crippled newsboy, whose life *Captain Marvel* saved by giving him some of his powers, so he became *Captain Marvel, Jr.;* and *Mary Batson,* who found a long-lost brother and the power to become *Mary Marvel* on the same historic day. More of them in this department next issue.

From time to time, new characters were introduced into the *Marvel* saga. Some of these are shown at the bottom of page 8 in this issue's second story. The diagram on this page will help you follow the list below, which gives a rundown on these friends of the *Marvels.*

1. *Uncle Dudley.* This is the lovable old fraud who pretends to change into a Marvel—Uncle Marvel—by saying "Shazam!" Actually, he strips off his outer clothes to reveal a home-made costume! As president of *Shazam, Inc.,* he raises money for charity.

2. *Miss Joan Jameson, Billy's* — and *Captain Marvel's*—secretary. She accidentally saw *Billy* slip away to change to *Captain Marvel,* and convinced him that a good secretary could save him some trouble and still conceal his identity.

3. *Sterling Morris,* owner of station *WHIZ.*

4. *Cissie Sommerly, Billy's* girl friend.

5. *Pa Potter, Billy's* landlord. *Billy* rented an apartment in his home.

6. *Ma Potter.*

7. *Prof. Edgewise,* eccentric scientific genius who lives in the same boarding house as *Freddy Freeman.*

8. *Beautia Sivana,* elder daughter of *Captain Marvel's* arch-enemy. The difference between her and sister *Georgia* is that *Beautia* is not only beautiful on the outside but basically good on the inside, as well . . . while *Georgia* resembles her father both physically and mentally. *Beautia* has a crush on *Captain Marvel.*

9. *Mr. Tawky Tawny,* the talking tiger. *Mr. Tawny* was an ordinary tiger once—except he'd been raised as a boy's pet. Later, an old hermit who'd invented a serum to raise the intelligence of animals and give them the power of speech tried it on *Tawny.* Once he became as smart as a human, the tiger began learning about civilization, and finally decided to see what it was like. He wound up working as a museum guide, while living in his own suburban home.

There you have it—a brief background on the *World's Mightiest Mortal,* as he has been dubbed. By the way, in the future, we plan to devote this space to your letters. Only trouble is, we have no suitable title for our letters department. How about sending in your suggestions? The best will be chosen, and the reader who submits it will get a special acknowledgement in *Shazam!* Write to SHAZAM*!*

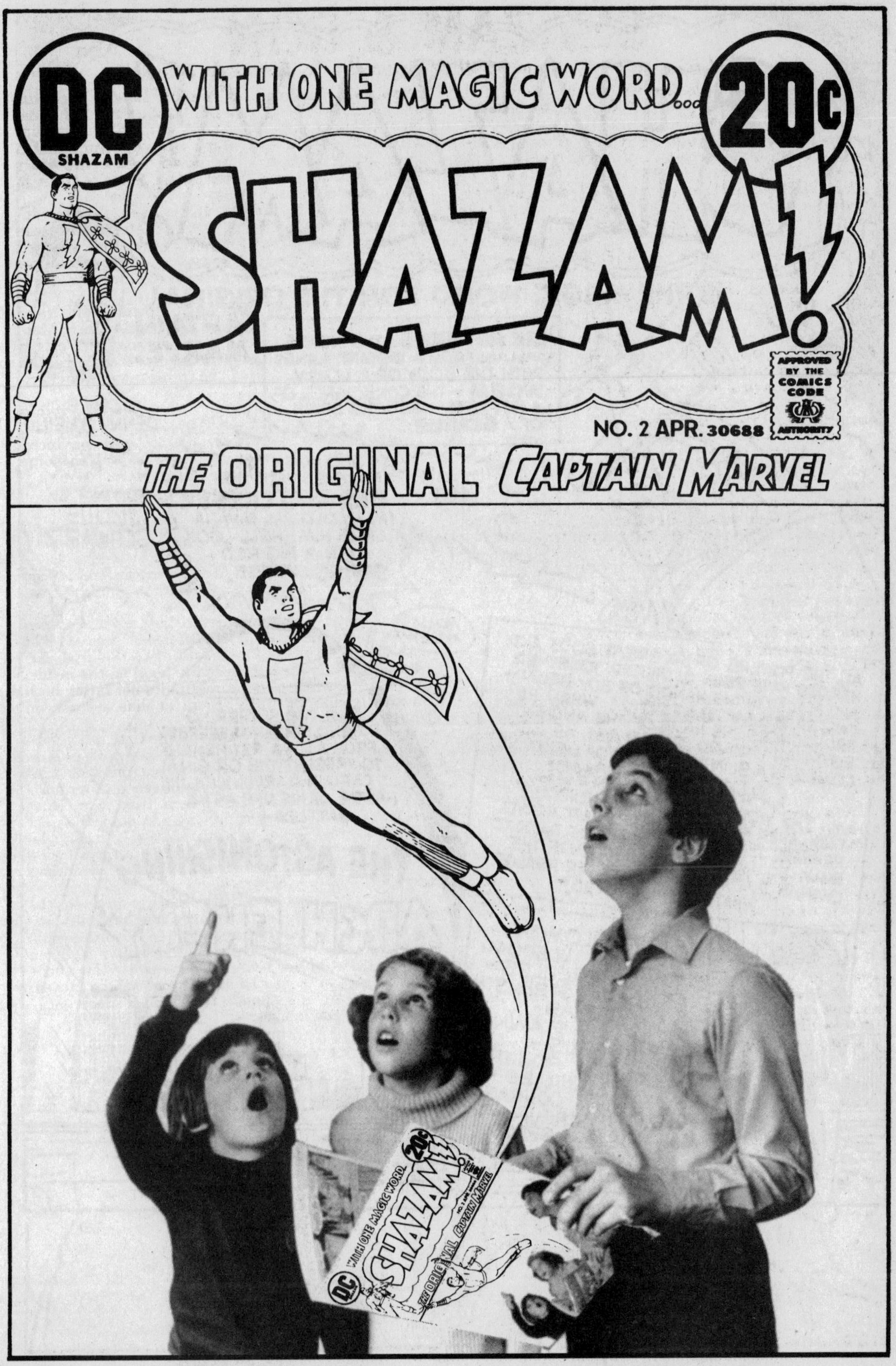
DC
SHAZAM
WITH ONE MAGIC WORD...
20¢
SHAZAM!
APPROVED BY THE COMICS CODE AUTHORITY
NO. 2 APR. 30688
THE ORIGINAL CAPTAIN MARVEL

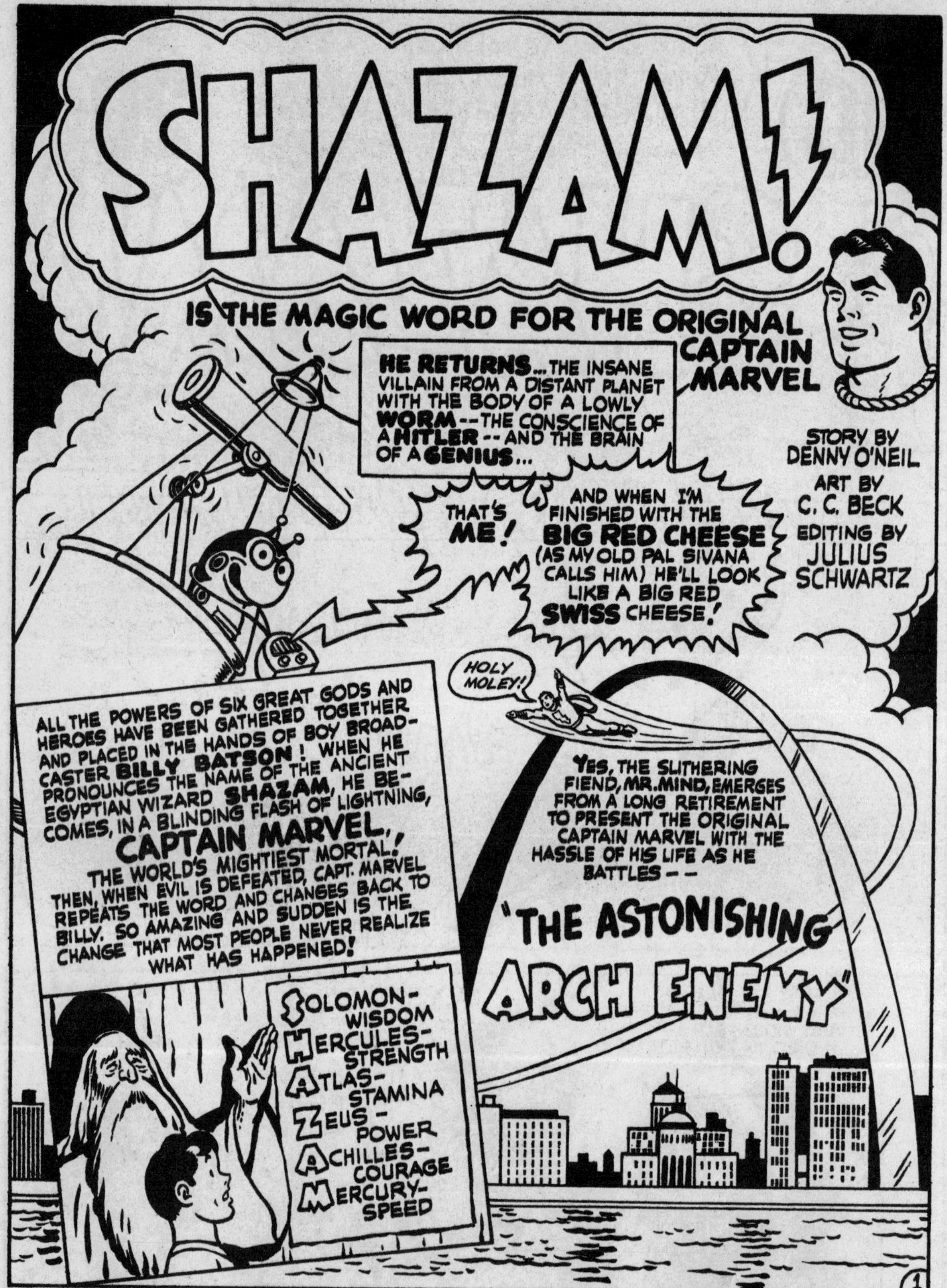
SHAZAM!
IS THE MAGIC WORD FOR THE ORIGINAL CAPTAIN MARVEL
HE RETURNS... THE INSANE VILLAIN FROM A DISTANT PLANET WITH THE BODY OF A LOWLY WORM -- THE CONSCIENCE OF A HITLER -- AND THE BRAIN OF A GENIUS...
STORY BY DENNY O'NEIL
ART BY C. C. BECK
EDITING BY JULIUS SCHWARTZ
THAT'S ME!
AND WHEN I'M FINISHED WITH THE BIG RED CHEESE (AS MY OLD PAL SIVANA CALLS HIM) HE'LL LOOK LIKE A BIG RED SWISS CHEESE!
HOLY MOLEY!
ALL THE POWERS OF SIX GREAT GODS AND HEROES HAVE BEEN GATHERED TOGETHER AND PLACED IN THE HANDS OF BOY BROAD-CASTER BILLY BATSON! WHEN HE PRONOUNCES THE NAME OF THE ANCIENT EGYPTIAN WIZARD SHAZAM, HE BE-COMES, IN A BLINDING FLASH OF LIGHTNING, CAPTAIN MARVEL, THE WORLD'S MIGHTIEST MORTAL! THEN, WHEN EVIL IS DEFEATED, CAPT. MARVEL REPEATS THE WORD AND CHANGES BACK TO BILLY. SO AMAZING AND SUDDEN IS THE CHANGE THAT MOST PEOPLE NEVER REALIZE WHAT HAS HAPPENED!
YES, THE SLITHERING FIEND, MR. MIND, EMERGES FROM A LONG RETIREMENT TO PRESENT THE ORIGINAL CAPTAIN MARVEL WITH THE HASSLE OF HIS LIFE AS HE BATTLES --
"THE ASTONISHING ARCH ENEMY"
SOLOMON-WISDOM
HERCULES-STRENGTH
ATLAS-STAMINA
ZEUS-POWER
ACHILLES-COURAGE
MERCURY-SPEED
1

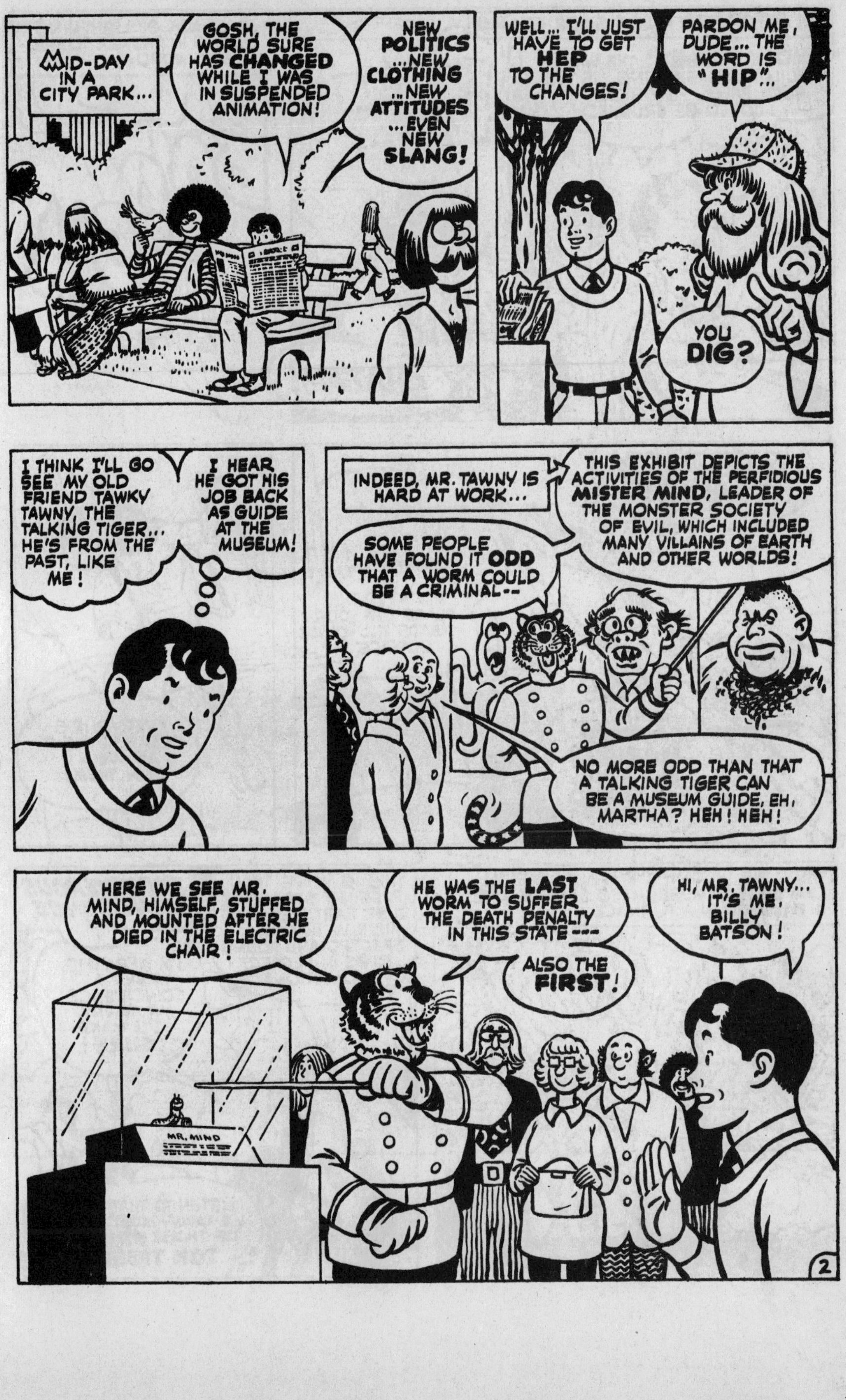
MID-DAY IN A CITY PARK...
GOSH, THE WORLD SURE HAS CHANGED WHILE I WAS IN SUSPENDED ANIMATION!
NEW POLITICS ...NEW CLOTHING ...NEW ATTITUDES ...EVEN NEW SLANG!
WELL... I'LL JUST HAVE TO GET HEP TO THE CHANGES!
PARDON ME, DUDE... THE WORD IS "HIP"...
YOU DIG?
I THINK I'LL GO SEE MY OLD FRIEND TAWKY TAWNY, THE TALKING TIGER... HE'S FROM THE PAST, LIKE ME!
I HEAR HE GOT HIS JOB BACK AS GUIDE AT THE MUSEUM!
INDEED, MR. TAWNY IS HARD AT WORK...
THIS EXHIBIT DEPICTS THE ACTIVITIES OF THE PERFIDIOUS MISTER MIND, LEADER OF THE MONSTER SOCIETY OF EVIL, WHICH INCLUDED MANY VILLAINS OF EARTH AND OTHER WORLDS!
SOME PEOPLE HAVE FOUND IT ODD THAT A WORM COULD BE A CRIMINAL--
NO MORE ODD THAN THAT A TALKING TIGER CAN BE A MUSEUM GUIDE, EH, MARTHA? HEH! HEH!
HERE WE SEE MR. MIND, HIMSELF, STUFFED AND MOUNTED AFTER HE DIED IN THE ELECTRIC CHAIR!
HE WAS THE LAST WORM TO SUFFER THE DEATH PENALTY IN THIS STATE---
ALSO THE FIRST!
HI, MR. TAWNY... IT'S ME, BILLY BATSON!
MR. MIND
2

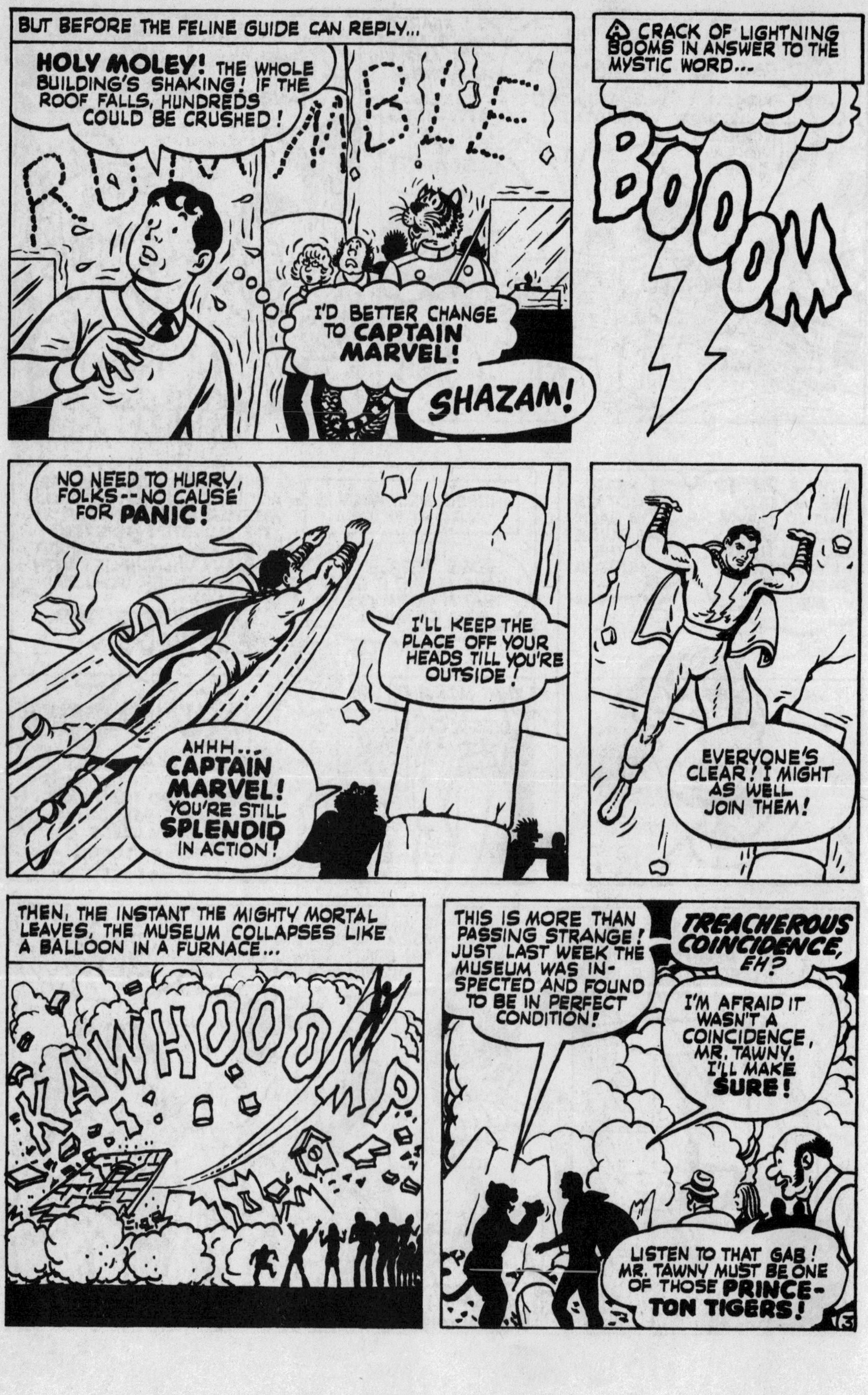
BUT BEFORE THE FELINE GUIDE CAN REPLY...
HOLY MOLEY! THE WHOLE BUILDING'S SHAKING! IF THE ROOF FALLS, HUNDREDS COULD BE CRUSHED!
RUMMBLE
I'D BETTER CHANGE TO CAPTAIN MARVEL!
SHAZAM!
A CRACK OF LIGHTNING BOOMS IN ANSWER TO THE MYSTIC WORD...
BOOOOM
NO NEED TO HURRY, FOLKS--NO CAUSE FOR PANIC!
I'LL KEEP THE PLACE OFF YOUR HEADS TILL YOU'RE OUTSIDE!
AHHH... CAPTAIN MARVEL! YOU'RE STILL SPLENDID IN ACTION!
EVERYONE'S CLEAR! I MIGHT AS WELL JOIN THEM!
THEN, THE INSTANT THE MIGHTY MORTAL LEAVES, THE MUSEUM COLLAPSES LIKE A BALLOON IN A FURNACE...
KAWHOOOMP
THIS IS MORE THAN PASSING STRANGE! JUST LAST WEEK THE MUSEUM WAS INSPECTED AND FOUND TO BE IN PERFECT CONDITION!
TREACHEROUS COINCIDENCE, EH?
I'M AFRAID IT WASN'T A COINCIDENCE, MR. TAWNY. I'LL MAKE SURE!
LISTEN TO THAT GAB! MR. TAWNY MUST BE ONE OF THOSE PRINCE-TON TIGERS!
13

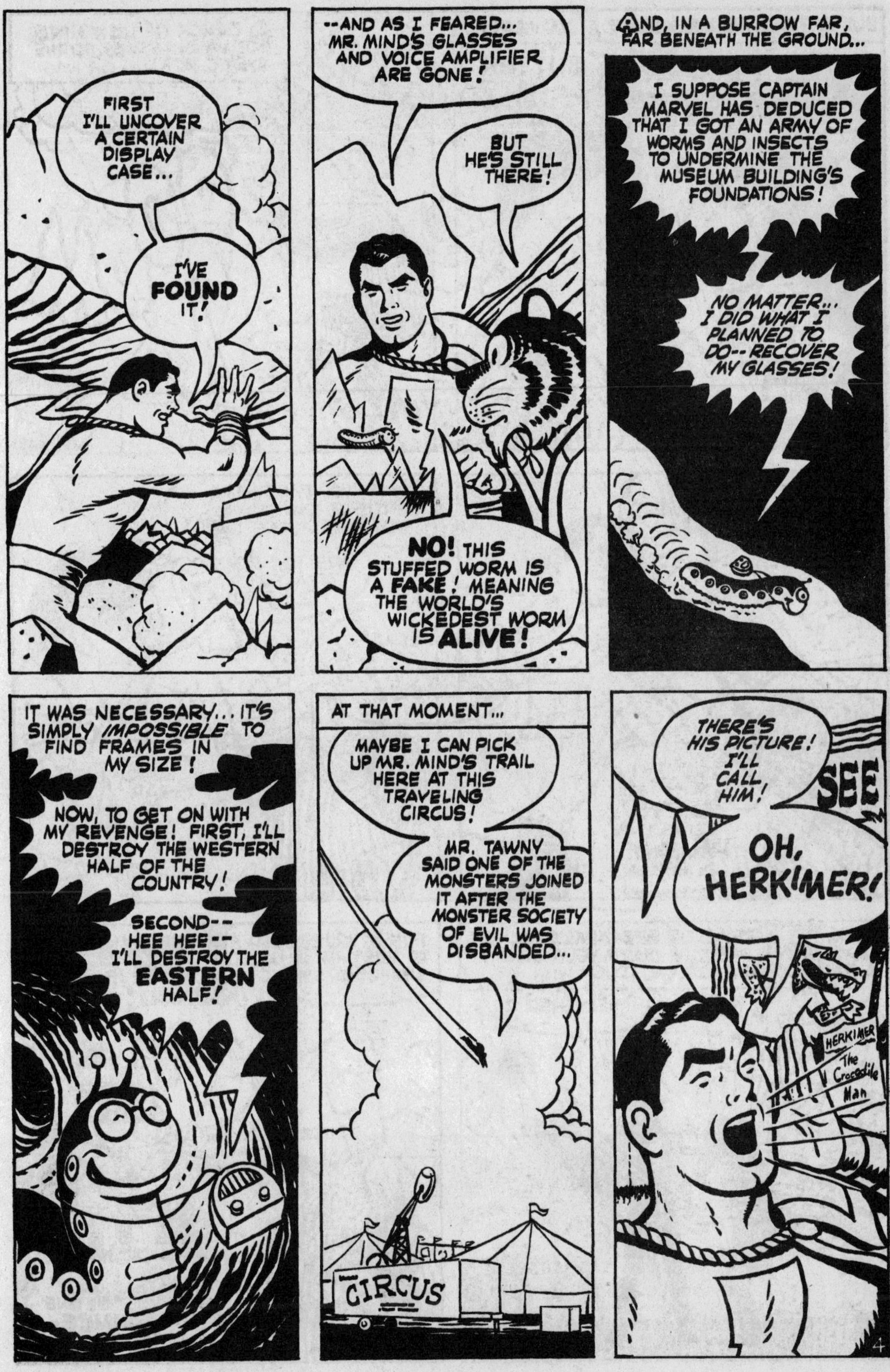
FIRST I'LL UNCOVER A CERTAIN DISPLAY CASE...
I'VE FOUND IT!
--AND AS I FEARED... MR. MIND'S GLASSES AND VOICE AMPLIFIER ARE GONE!
BUT HE'S STILL THERE!
NO! THIS STUFFED WORM IS A FAKE! MEANING THE WORLD'S WICKEDEST WORM IS ALIVE!
AND, IN A BURROW FAR, FAR BENEATH THE GROUND...
I SUPPOSE CAPTAIN MARVEL HAS DEDUCED THAT I GOT AN ARMY OF WORMS AND INSECTS TO UNDERMINE THE MUSEUM BUILDING'S FOUNDATIONS!
NO MATTER... I DID WHAT I PLANNED TO DO-- RECOVER MY GLASSES!
IT WAS NECESSARY... IT'S SIMPLY IMPOSSIBLE TO FIND FRAMES IN MY SIZE!
NOW, TO GET ON WITH MY REVENGE! FIRST, I'LL DESTROY THE WESTERN HALF OF THE COUNTRY!
SECOND-- HEE HEE-- I'LL DESTROY THE EASTERN HALF!
AT THAT MOMENT...
MAYBE I CAN PICK UP MR. MIND'S TRAIL HERE AT THIS TRAVELING CIRCUS!
MR. TAWNY SAID ONE OF THE MONSTERS JOINED IT AFTER THE MONSTER SOCIETY OF EVIL WAS DISBANDED...
CIRCUS
THERE'S HIS PICTURE! I'LL CALL HIM!
SEE
OH, HERKIMER!
HERKIMER
The Crocodile Man
4

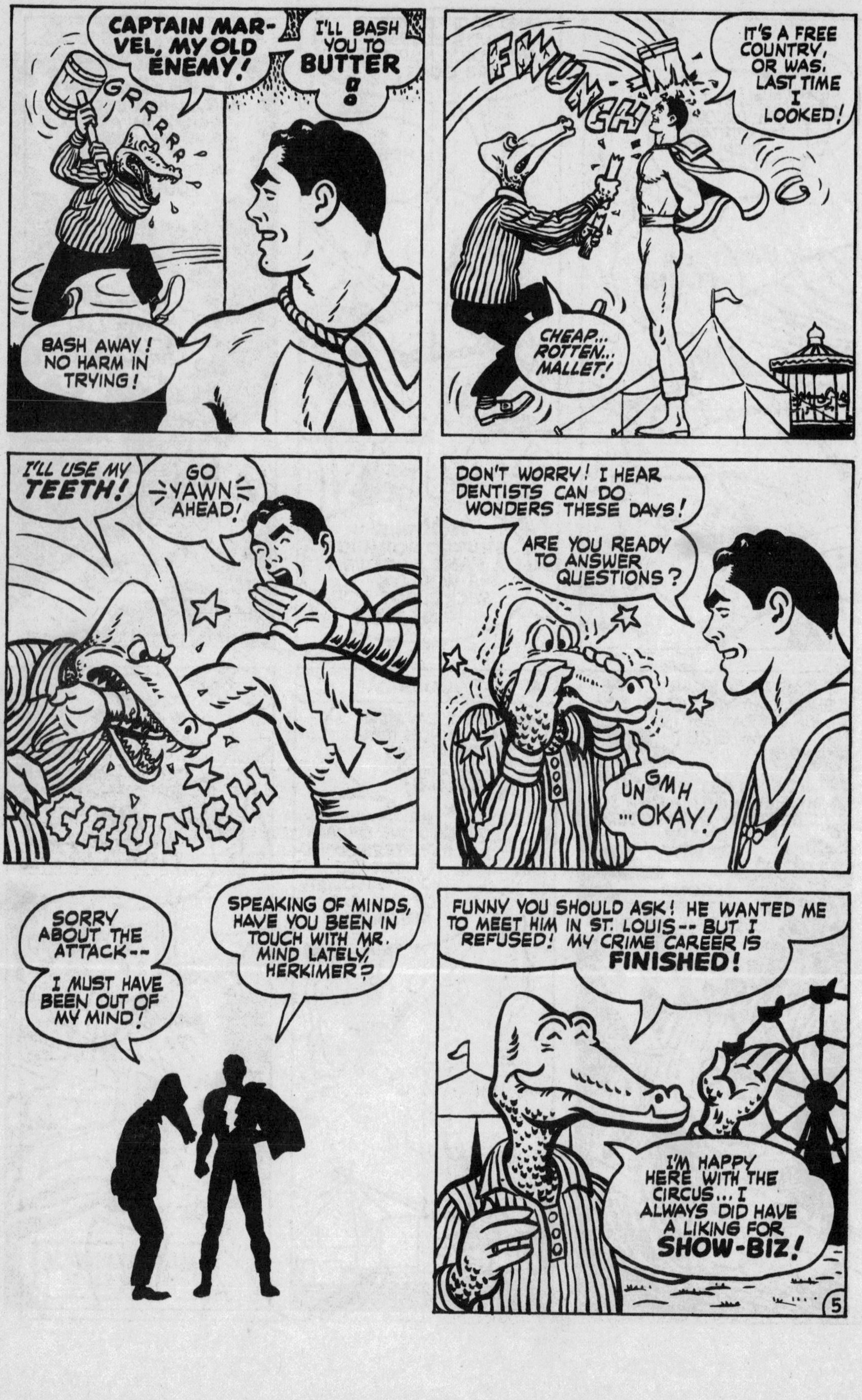
CAPTAIN MAR-VEL, MY OLD ENEMY!
I'LL BASH YOU TO BUTTER!
GRRRRRR
BASH AWAY! NO HARM IN TRYING!
FWUNCH
IT'S A FREE COUNTRY, OR WAS, LAST TIME I LOOKED!
CHEAP... ROTTEN... MALLET!
I'LL USE MY TEETH!
GO YAWN AHEAD!
CRUNCH
DON'T WORRY! I HEAR DENTISTS CAN DO WONDERS THESE DAYS!
ARE YOU READY TO ANSWER QUESTIONS?
UNGMH ...OKAY!
SORRY ABOUT THE ATTACK--
I MUST HAVE BEEN OUT OF MY MIND!
SPEAKING OF MINDS, HAVE YOU BEEN IN TOUCH WITH MR. MIND LATELY, HERKIMER?
FUNNY YOU SHOULD ASK! HE WANTED ME TO MEET HIM IN ST. LOUIS-- BUT I REFUSED! MY CRIME CAREER IS FINISHED!
I'M HAPPY HERE WITH THE CIRCUS... I ALWAYS DID HAVE A LIKING FOR SHOW-BIZ!
5

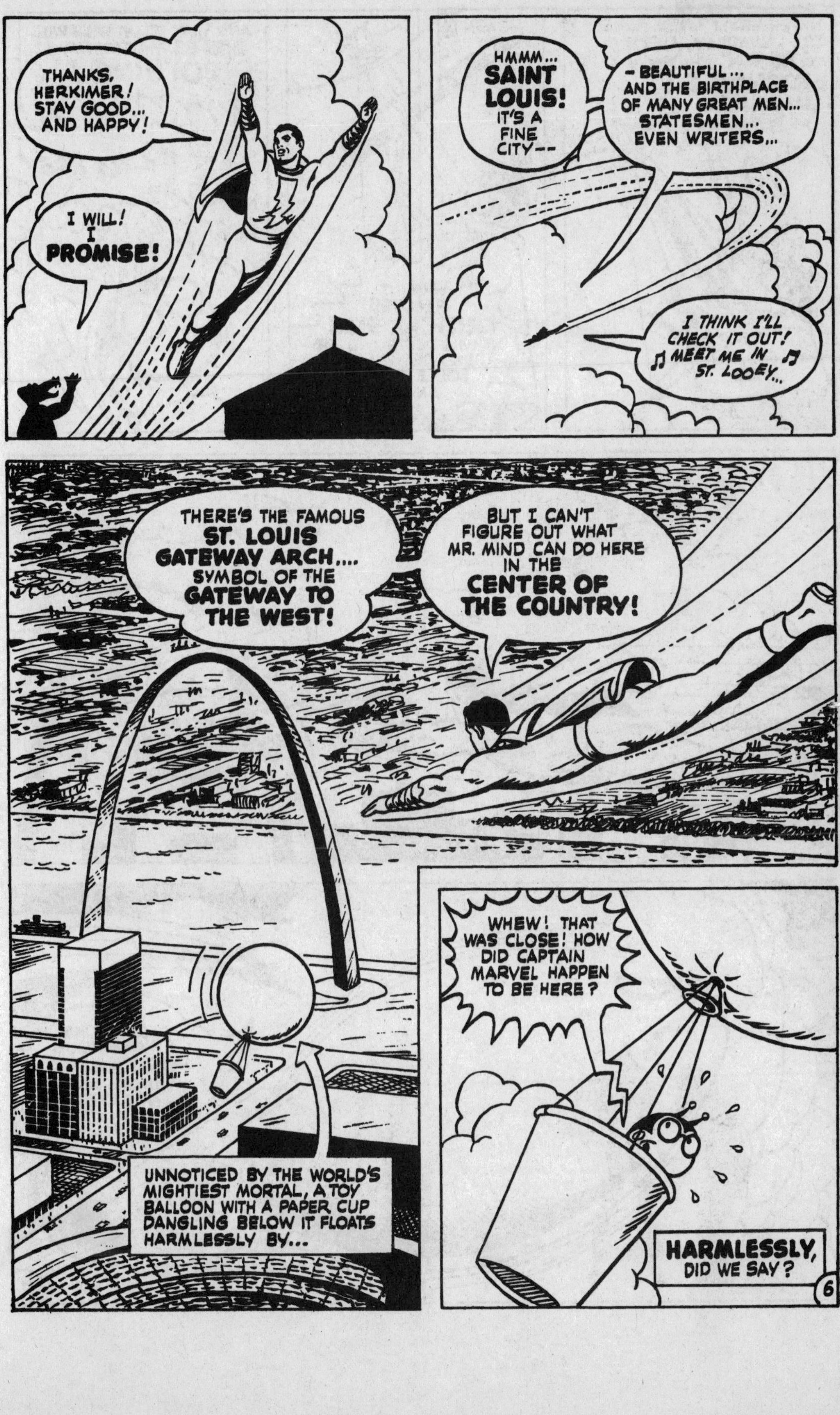
THANKS, HERKIMER! STAY GOOD... AND HAPPY!
I WILL! I PROMISE!
HMMM... SAINT LOUIS! IT'S A FINE CITY--
-BEAUTIFUL... AND THE BIRTHPLACE OF MANY GREAT MEN... STATESMEN... EVEN WRITERS...
I THINK I'LL CHECK IT OUT! ♫ MEET ME IN ST. LOOEY... ♫
THERE'S THE FAMOUS ST. LOUIS GATEWAY ARCH.... SYMBOL OF THE GATEWAY TO THE WEST!
BUT I CAN'T FIGURE OUT WHAT MR. MIND CAN DO HERE IN THE CENTER OF THE COUNTRY!
UNNOTICED BY THE WORLD'S MIGHTIEST MORTAL, A TOY BALLOON WITH A PAPER CUP DANGLING BELOW IT FLOATS HARMLESSLY BY...
WHEW! THAT WAS CLOSE! HOW DID CAPTAIN MARVEL HAPPEN TO BE HERE?
HARMLESSLY, DID WE SAY?
6

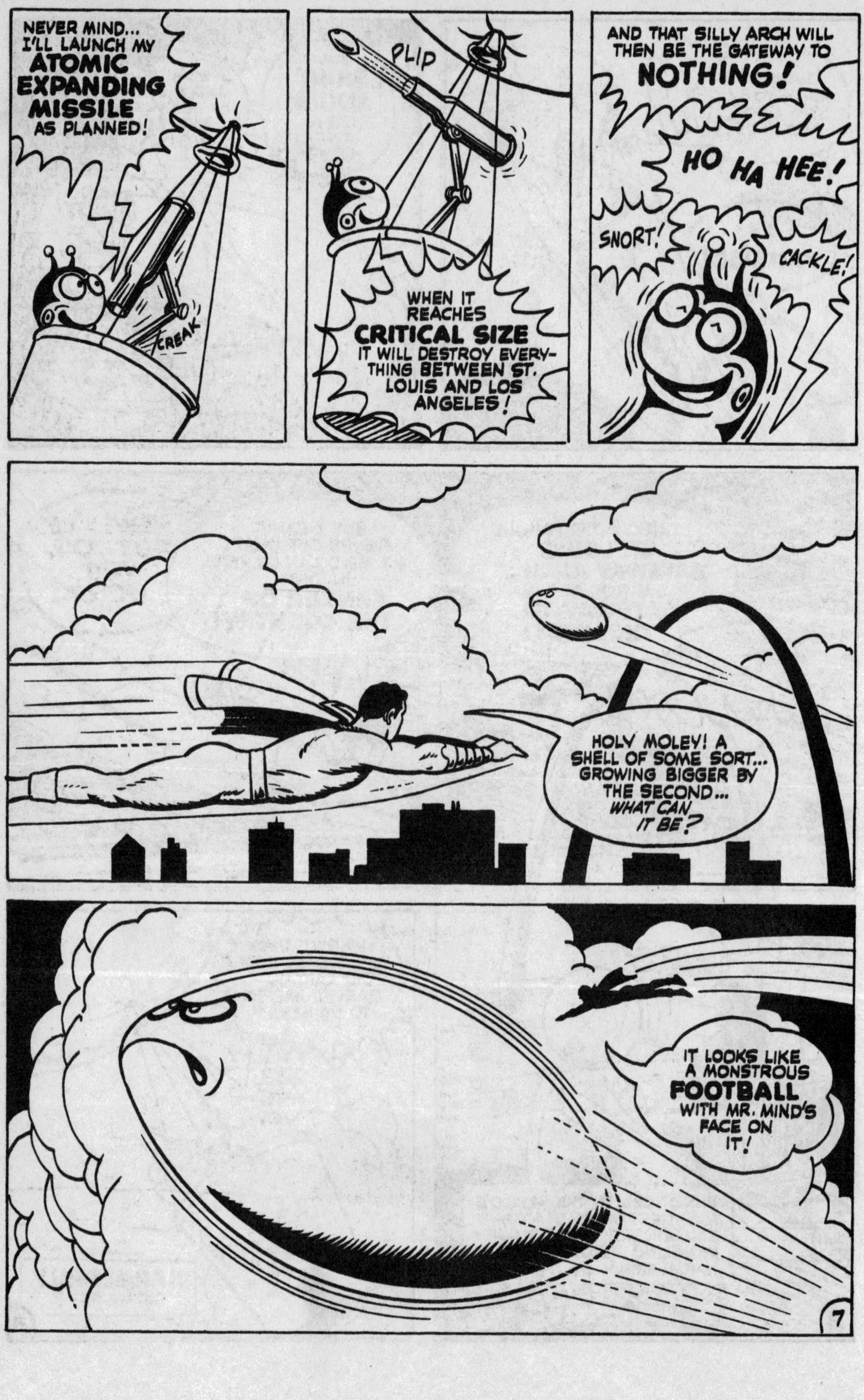
NEVER MIND... I'LL LAUNCH MY ATOMIC EXPANDING MISSILE AS PLANNED!
CREAK
PLIP
WHEN IT REACHES CRITICAL SIZE IT WILL DESTROY EVERY-THING BETWEEN ST. LOUIS AND LOS ANGELES!
AND THAT SILLY ARCH WILL THEN BE THE GATEWAY TO NOTHING!
HO HA HEE!
SNORT!
CACKLE!
HOLY MOLEY! A SHELL OF SOME SORT... GROWING BIGGER BY THE SECOND... WHAT CAN IT BE?
IT LOOKS LIKE A MONSTROUS FOOTBALL WITH MR. MIND'S FACE ON IT!
7

SO I'LL JUST MAKE LIKE A FOOTBALL PLAYER--
--AND BOOT IT INTO DEEP SPACE!
CURSES! THAT BIG RED MEDDLER HAS FOILED MY FOULEST SCHEME! I SPENT YEARS PERFECTING THAT WEAPON!
NEXT HE'LL FOUL ME... UNLESS I ESCAPE!
HAW! I'VE GOT YOU, YOU WORM!
PLOP!
EMPTY!
MR. MIND HAS GOTTEN AWAY!
BUT HE WON'T GET FAR!
HEE HEE HAW!
8

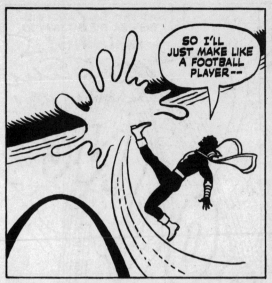

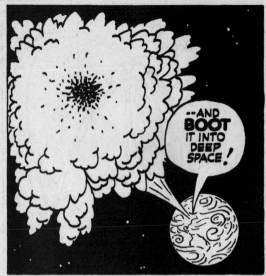

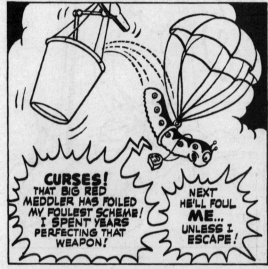

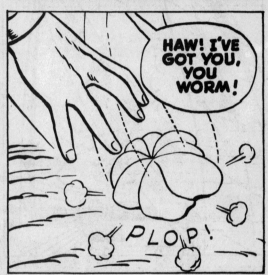

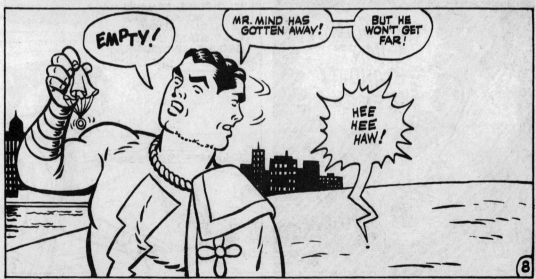

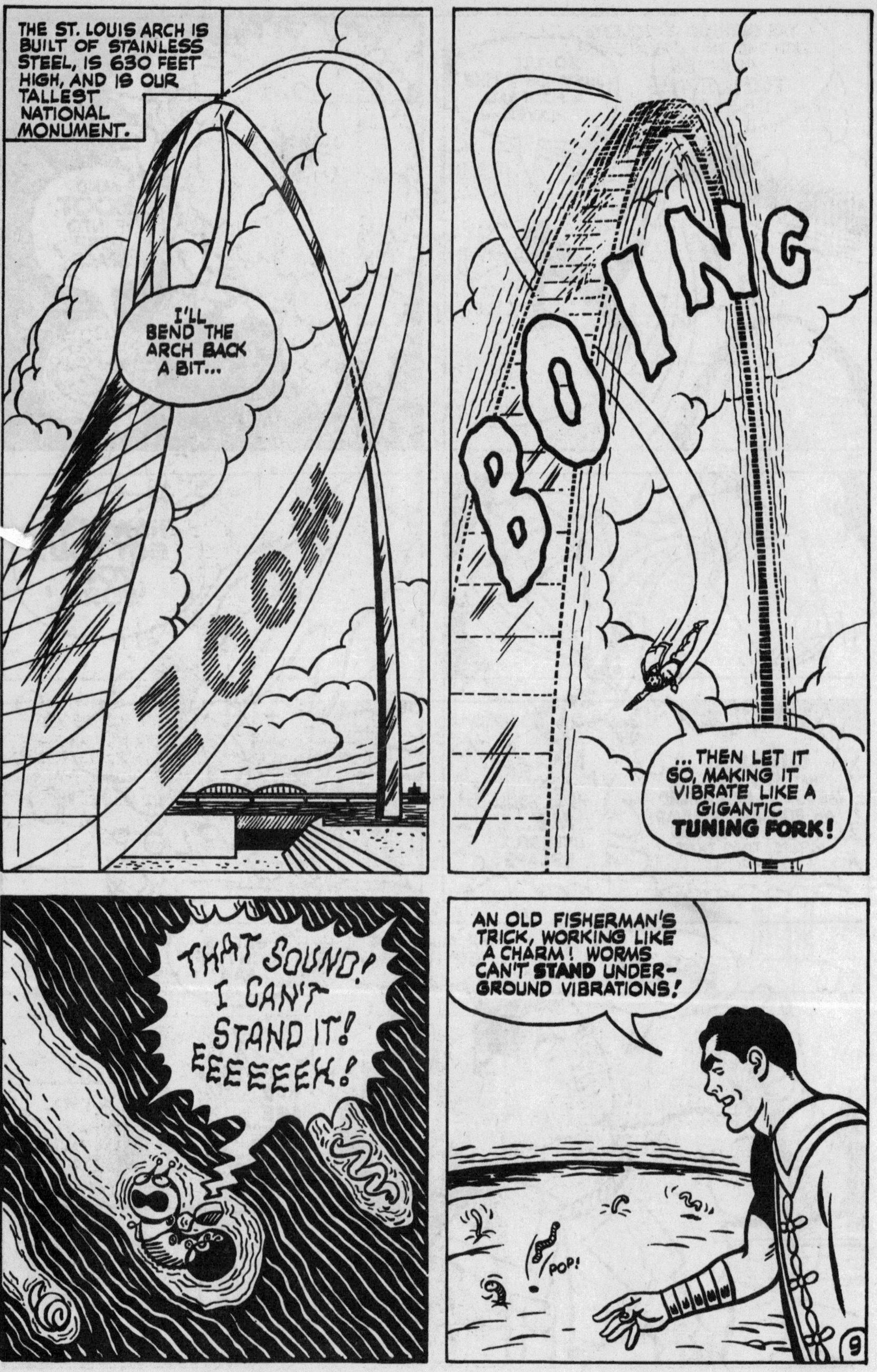
THE ST. LOUIS ARCH IS BUILT OF STAINLESS STEEL, IS 630 FEET HIGH, AND IS OUR TALLEST NATIONAL MONUMENT.
I'LL BEND THE ARCH BACK A BIT...
ZOOOM
BOING
...THEN LET IT GO, MAKING IT VIBRATE LIKE A GIGANTIC **TUNING FORK!**
THAT SOUND! I CAN'T STAND IT! EEEEEEK!
AN OLD FISHERMAN'S TRICK, WORKING LIKE A CHARM! WORMS CAN'T **STAND** UNDER-GROUND VIBRATIONS!
POP!
9

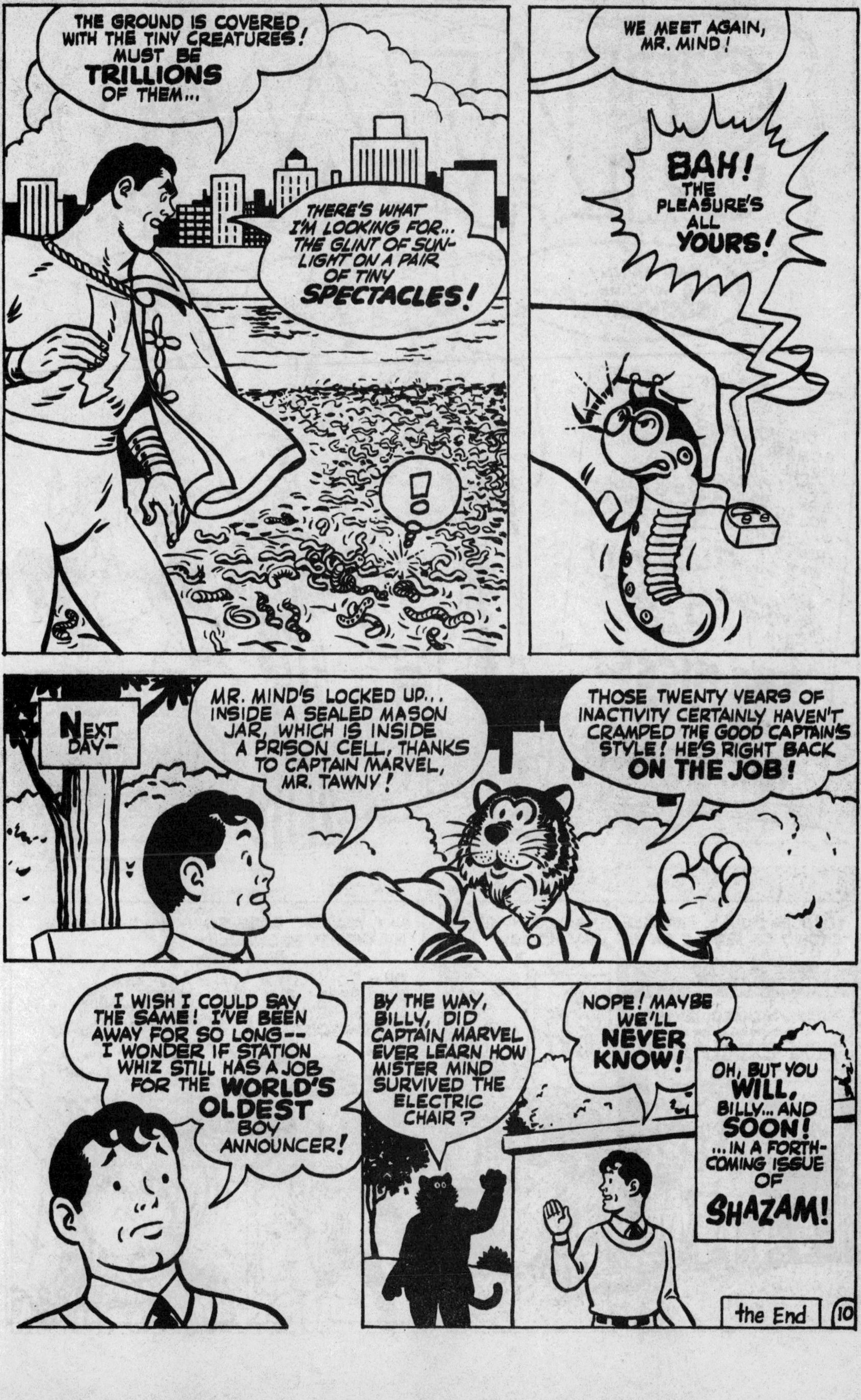
THE GROUND IS COVERED WITH THE TINY CREATURES! MUST BE TRILLIONS OF THEM...
THERE'S WHAT I'M LOOKING FOR... THE GLINT OF SUN-LIGHT ON A PAIR OF TINY SPECTACLES!
!
WE MEET AGAIN, MR. MIND!
BAH! THE PLEASURE'S ALL YOURS!
NEXT DAY--
MR. MIND'S LOCKED UP... INSIDE A SEALED MASON JAR, WHICH IS INSIDE A PRISON CELL, THANKS TO CAPTAIN MARVEL, MR. TAWNY!
THOSE TWENTY YEARS OF INACTIVITY CERTAINLY HAVEN'T CRAMPED THE GOOD CAPTAIN'S STYLE! HE'S RIGHT BACK ON THE JOB!
I WISH I COULD SAY THE SAME! I'VE BEEN AWAY FOR SO LONG-- I WONDER IF STATION WHIZ STILL HAS A JOB FOR THE WORLD'S OLDEST BOY ANNOUNCER!
BY THE WAY, BILLY, DID CAPTAIN MARVEL EVER LEARN HOW MISTER MIND SURVIVED THE ELECTRIC CHAIR?
NOPE! MAYBE WE'LL NEVER KNOW!
OH, BUT YOU WILL, BILLY... AND SOON! ...IN A FORTH-COMING ISSUE OF SHAZAM!
the End
10

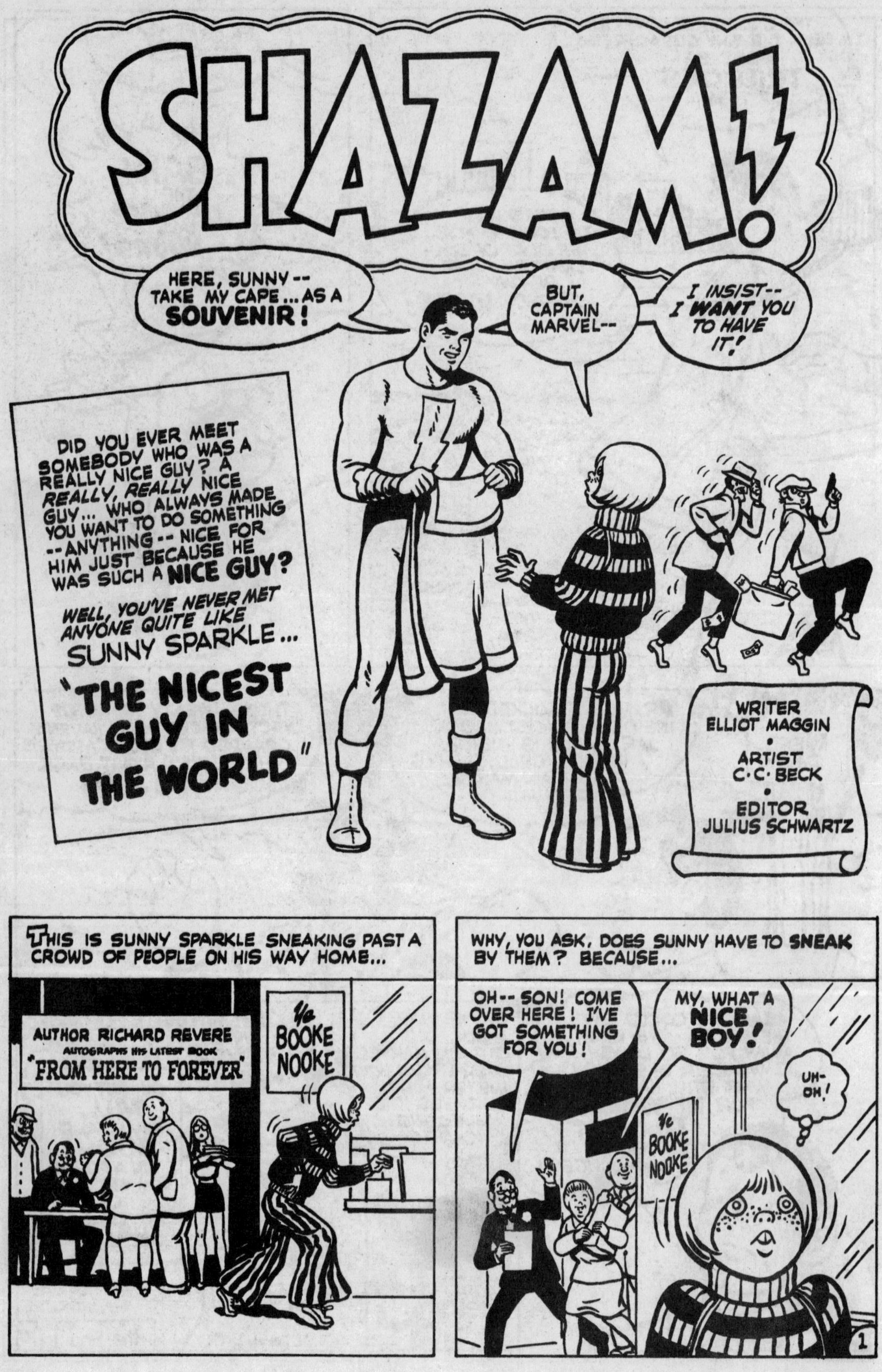
SHAZAM!
HERE, SUNNY -- TAKE MY CAPE ... AS A SOUVENIR!
BUT, CAPTAIN MARVEL--
I INSIST-- I WANT YOU TO HAVE IT!
DID YOU EVER MEET SOMEBODY WHO WAS A REALLY NICE GUY? A REALLY, REALLY NICE GUY... WHO ALWAYS MADE YOU WANT TO DO SOMETHING -- ANYTHING -- NICE FOR HIM JUST BECAUSE HE WAS SUCH A NICE GUY?
WELL, YOU'VE NEVER MET ANYONE QUITE LIKE SUNNY SPARKLE...
"THE NICEST GUY IN THE WORLD"
WRITER ELLIOT MAGGIN • ARTIST C·C· BECK • EDITOR JULIUS SCHWARTZ
THIS IS SUNNY SPARKLE SNEAKING PAST A CROWD OF PEOPLE ON HIS WAY HOME...
AUTHOR RICHARD REVERE AUTOGRAPHS HIS LATEST BOOK "FROM HERE TO FOREVER"
Ye BOOKE NOOKE
WHY, YOU ASK, DOES SUNNY HAVE TO SNEAK BY THEM? BECAUSE...
OH -- SON! COME OVER HERE! I'VE GOT SOMETHING FOR YOU!
MY, WHAT A NICE BOY!
UH-OH!
Ye BOOKE NOOKE
1

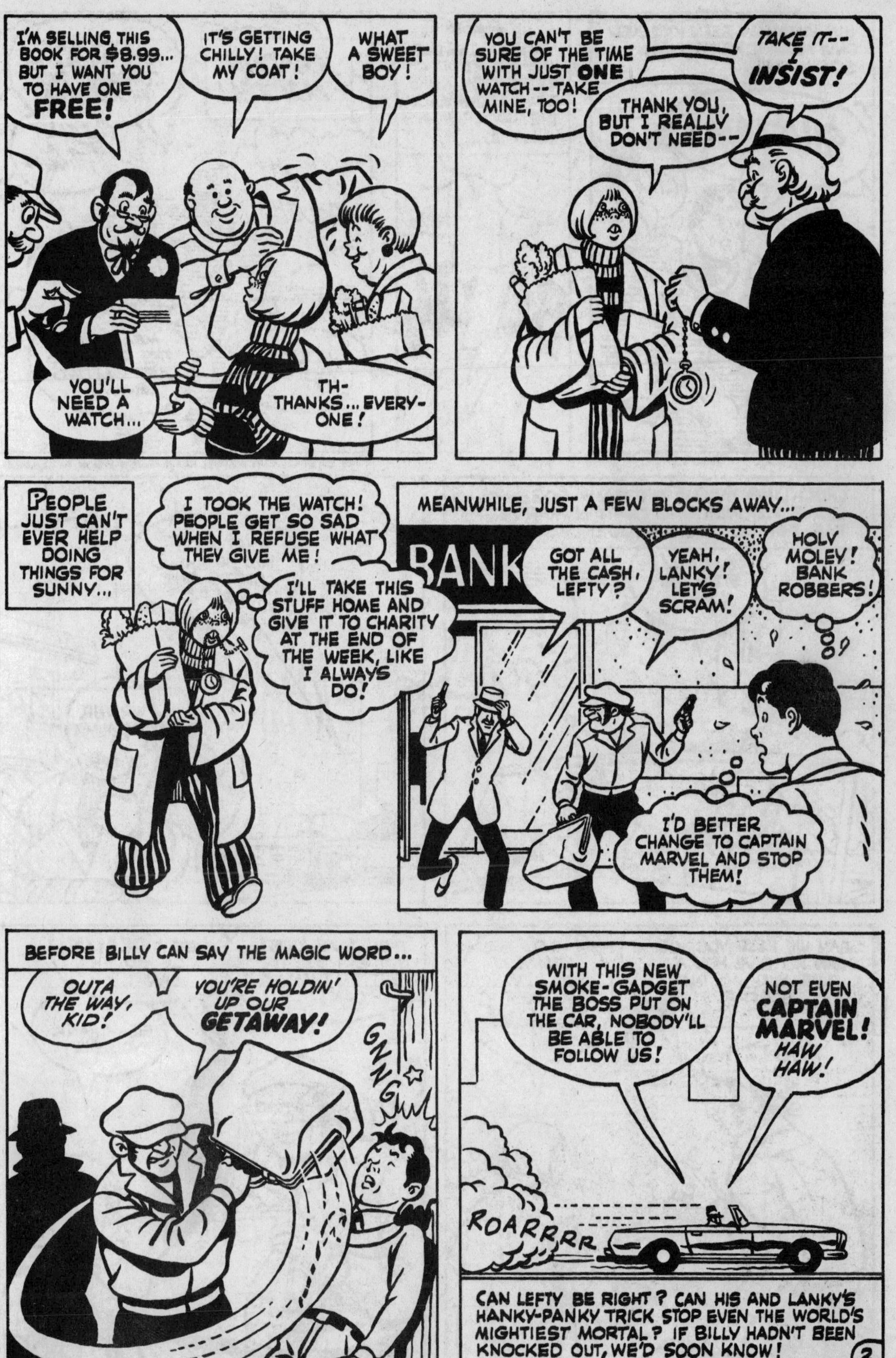
I'M SELLING THIS BOOK FOR $8.99... BUT I WANT YOU TO HAVE ONE FREE!
IT'S GETTING CHILLY! TAKE MY COAT!
WHAT A SWEET BOY!
YOU'LL NEED A WATCH...
TH- THANKS... EVERY-ONE!
YOU CAN'T BE SURE OF THE TIME WITH JUST ONE WATCH -- TAKE MINE, TOO!
TAKE IT-- I INSIST!
THANK YOU, BUT I REALLY DON'T NEED--
PEOPLE JUST CAN'T EVER HELP DOING THINGS FOR SUNNY...
I TOOK THE WATCH! PEOPLE GET SO SAD WHEN I REFUSE WHAT THEY GIVE ME!
I'LL TAKE THIS STUFF HOME AND GIVE IT TO CHARITY AT THE END OF THE WEEK, LIKE I ALWAYS DO!
MEANWHILE, JUST A FEW BLOCKS AWAY...
BANK
GOT ALL THE CASH, LEFTY?
YEAH, LANKY! LET'S SCRAM!
HOLY MOLEY! BANK ROBBERS!
I'D BETTER CHANGE TO CAPTAIN MARVEL AND STOP THEM!
BEFORE BILLY CAN SAY THE MAGIC WORD...
OUTA THE WAY, KID!
YOU'RE HOLDIN' UP OUR GETAWAY!
GNNG
WITH THIS NEW SMOKE-GADGET THE BOSS PUT ON THE CAR, NOBODY'LL BE ABLE TO FOLLOW US!
NOT EVEN CAPTAIN MARVEL! HAW HAW!
ROARRRRR
CAN LEFTY BE RIGHT? CAN HIS AND LANKY'S HANKY-PANKY TRICK STOP EVEN THE WORLD'S MIGHTIEST MORTAL? IF BILLY HADN'T BEEN KNOCKED OUT, WE'D SOON KNOW!
2

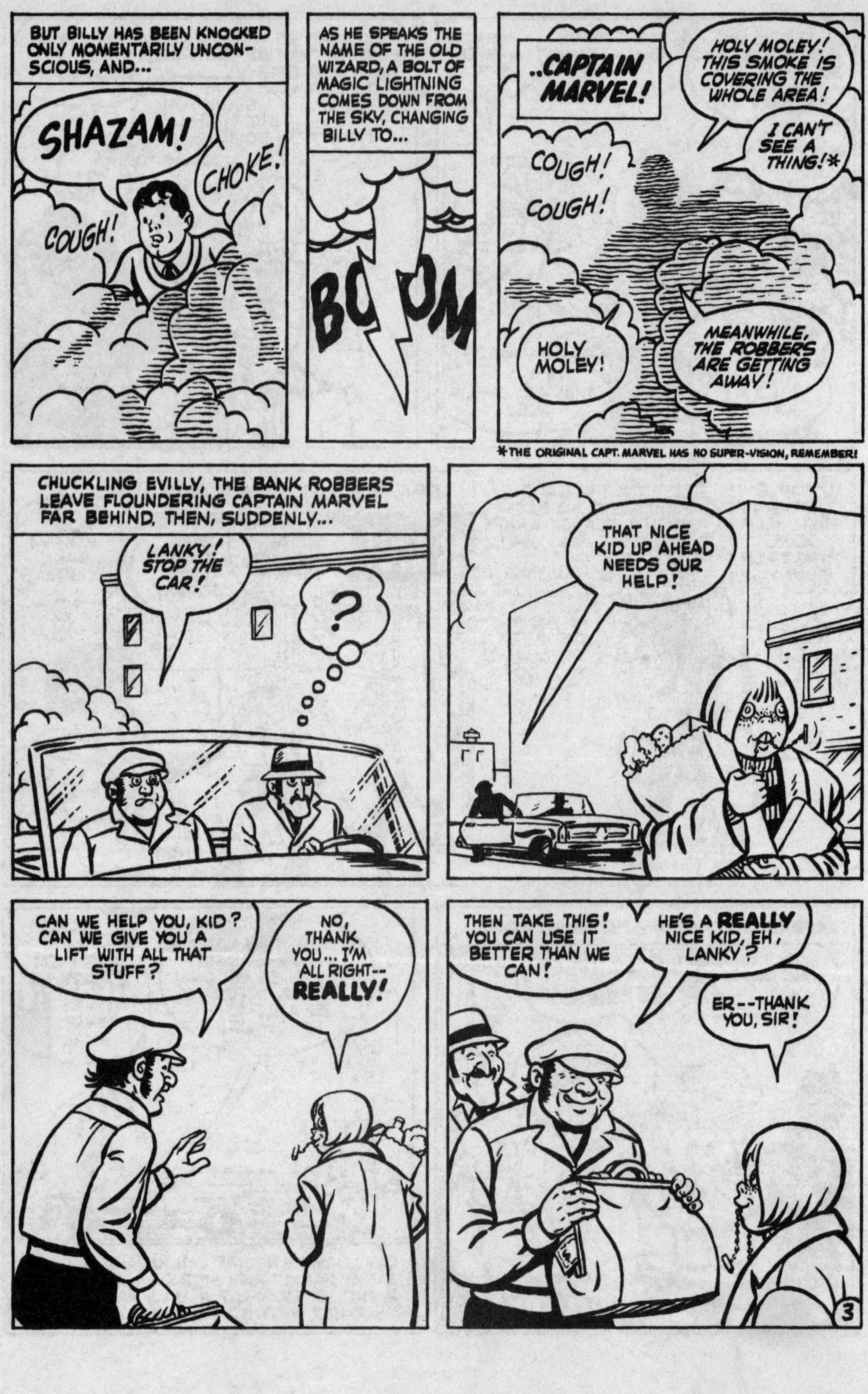

BUT BILLY HAS BEEN KNOCKED ONLY MOMENTARILY UNCONSCIOUS, AND...
SHAZAM!
CHOKE!
COUGH!
AS HE SPEAKS THE NAME OF THE OLD WIZARD, A BOLT OF MAGIC LIGHTNING COMES DOWN FROM THE SKY, CHANGING BILLY TO...
BOOM
..CAPTAIN MARVEL!
HOLY MOLEY! THIS SMOKE IS COVERING THE WHOLE AREA!
I CAN'T SEE A THING!*
COUGH!
COUGH!
HOLY MOLEY!
MEANWHILE, THE ROBBERS ARE GETTING AWAY!
*THE ORIGINAL CAPT. MARVEL HAS NO SUPER-VISION, REMEMBER!
CHUCKLING EVILLY, THE BANK ROBBERS LEAVE FLOUNDERING CAPTAIN MARVEL FAR BEHIND. THEN, SUDDENLY...
LANKY! STOP THE CAR!
?
THAT NICE KID UP AHEAD NEEDS OUR HELP!
CAN WE HELP YOU, KID? CAN WE GIVE YOU A LIFT WITH ALL THAT STUFF?
NO, THANK YOU... I'M ALL RIGHT-- REALLY!
THEN TAKE THIS! YOU CAN USE IT BETTER THAN WE CAN!
HE'S A REALLY NICE KID, EH, LANKY?
ER--THANK YOU, SIR!
3

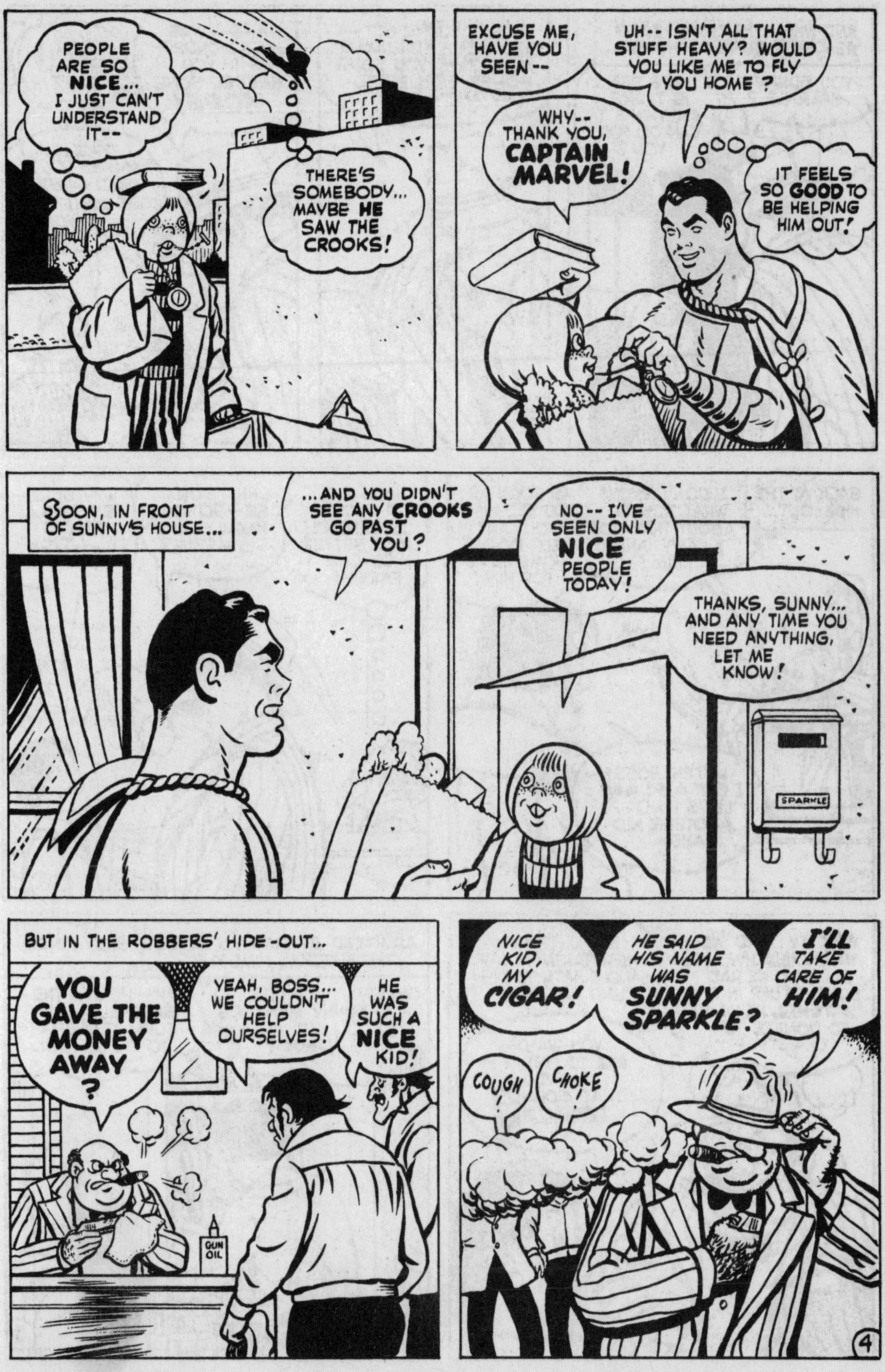
PEOPLE ARE SO NICE... I JUST CAN'T UNDERSTAND IT--
THERE'S SOMEBODY... MAYBE HE SAW THE CROOKS!
EXCUSE ME, HAVE YOU SEEN--
UH-- ISN'T ALL THAT STUFF HEAVY? WOULD YOU LIKE ME TO FLY YOU HOME ?
WHY-- THANK YOU, CAPTAIN MARVEL!
IT FEELS SO GOOD TO BE HELPING HIM OUT!
SOON, IN FRONT OF SUNNY'S HOUSE...
...AND YOU DIDN'T SEE ANY CROOKS GO PAST YOU?
NO-- I'VE SEEN ONLY NICE PEOPLE TODAY!
THANKS, SUNNY... AND ANY TIME YOU NEED ANYTHING, LET ME KNOW!
SPARKLE
BUT IN THE ROBBERS' HIDE-OUT...
YOU GAVE THE MONEY AWAY?
YEAH, BOSS... WE COULDN'T HELP OURSELVES!
HE WAS SUCH A NICE KID!
GUN OIL
NICE KID, MY CIGAR!
HE SAID HIS NAME WAS SUNNY SPARKLE?
I'LL TAKE CARE OF HIM!
COUGH!
CHOKE!
4

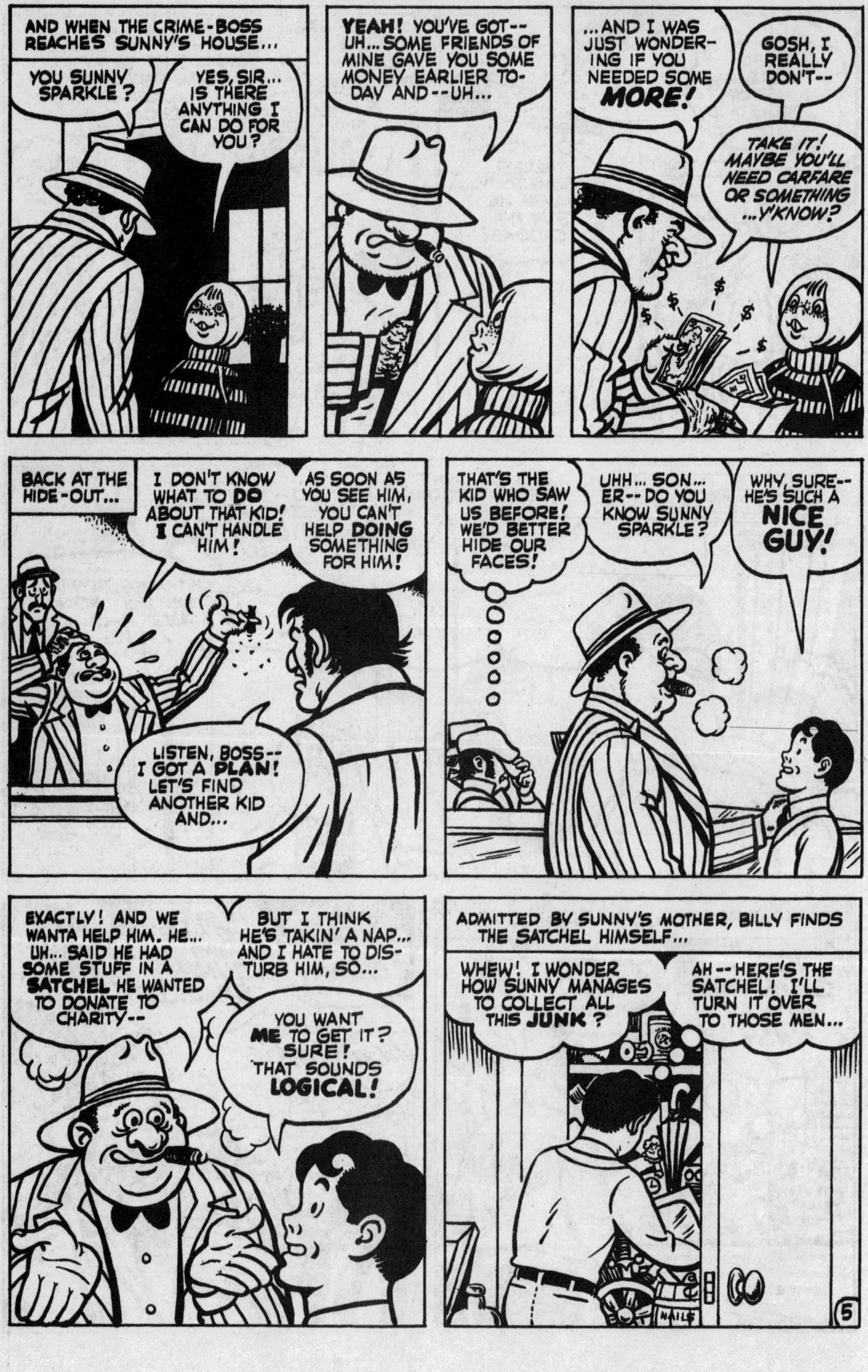
AND WHEN THE CRIME-BOSS REACHES SUNNY'S HOUSE...
YOU SUNNY SPARKLE?
YES, SIR... IS THERE ANYTHING I CAN DO FOR YOU?
YEAH! YOU'VE GOT-- UH... SOME FRIENDS OF MINE GAVE YOU SOME MONEY EARLIER TO-DAY AND--UH...
...AND I WAS JUST WONDER-ING IF YOU NEEDED SOME MORE!
GOSH, I REALLY DON'T--
TAKE IT! MAYBE YOU'LL NEED CARFARE OR SOMETHING ...Y'KNOW?
BACK AT THE HIDE-OUT...
I DON'T KNOW WHAT TO DO ABOUT THAT KID! I CAN'T HANDLE HIM!
AS SOON AS YOU SEE HIM, YOU CAN'T HELP DOING SOMETHING FOR HIM!
LISTEN, BOSS-- I GOT A PLAN! LET'S FIND ANOTHER KID AND...
THAT'S THE KID WHO SAW US BEFORE! WE'D BETTER HIDE OUR FACES!
UHH... SON... ER-- DO YOU KNOW SUNNY SPARKLE?
WHY, SURE-- HE'S SUCH A NICE GUY!
EXACTLY! AND WE WANTA HELP HIM. HE... UH... SAID HE HAD SOME STUFF IN A SATCHEL HE WANTED TO DONATE TO CHARITY--
BUT I THINK HE'S TAKIN' A NAP... AND I HATE TO DIS-TURB HIM, SO...
YOU WANT ME TO GET IT? SURE! THAT SOUNDS LOGICAL!
ADMITTED BY SUNNY'S MOTHER, BILLY FINDS THE SATCHEL HIMSELF...
WHEW! I WONDER HOW SUNNY MANAGES TO COLLECT ALL THIS JUNK?
AH--HERE'S THE SATCHEL! I'LL TURN IT OVER TO THOSE MEN...
NAILS
5

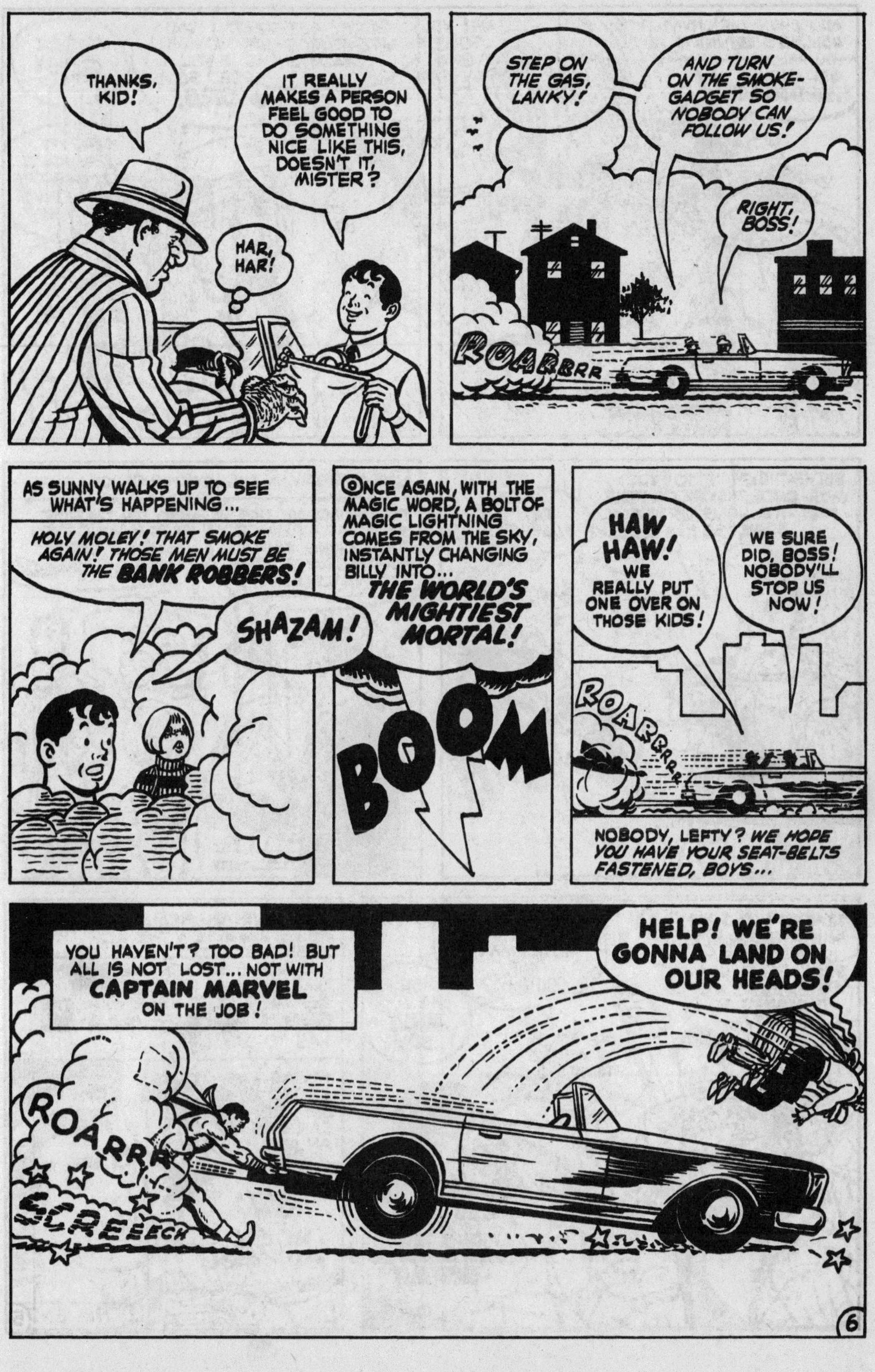
THANKS, KID!
IT REALLY MAKES A PERSON FEEL GOOD TO DO SOMETHING NICE LIKE THIS, DOESN'T IT, MISTER?
HAR, HAR!
STEP ON THE GAS, LANKY!
AND TURN ON THE SMOKE-GADGET SO NOBODY CAN FOLLOW US!
RIGHT, BOSS!
ROARRRRR
AS SUNNY WALKS UP TO SEE WHAT'S HAPPENING...
HOLY MOLEY! THAT SMOKE AGAIN! THOSE MEN MUST BE THE BANK ROBBERS!
SHAZAM!
ONCE AGAIN, WITH THE MAGIC WORD, A BOLT OF MAGIC LIGHTNING COMES FROM THE SKY, INSTANTLY CHANGING BILLY INTO... THE WORLD'S MIGHTIEST MORTAL!
BOOM
HAW HAW! WE REALLY PUT ONE OVER ON THOSE KIDS!
WE SURE DID, BOSS! NOBODY'LL STOP US NOW!
ROARRRRR
NOBODY, LEFTY? WE HOPE YOU HAVE YOUR SEAT-BELTS FASTENED, BOYS...
YOU HAVEN'T? TOO BAD! BUT ALL IS NOT LOST... NOT WITH CAPTAIN MARVEL ON THE JOB!
HELP! WE'RE GONNA LAND ON OUR HEADS!
ROARRR
SCREEECH
6

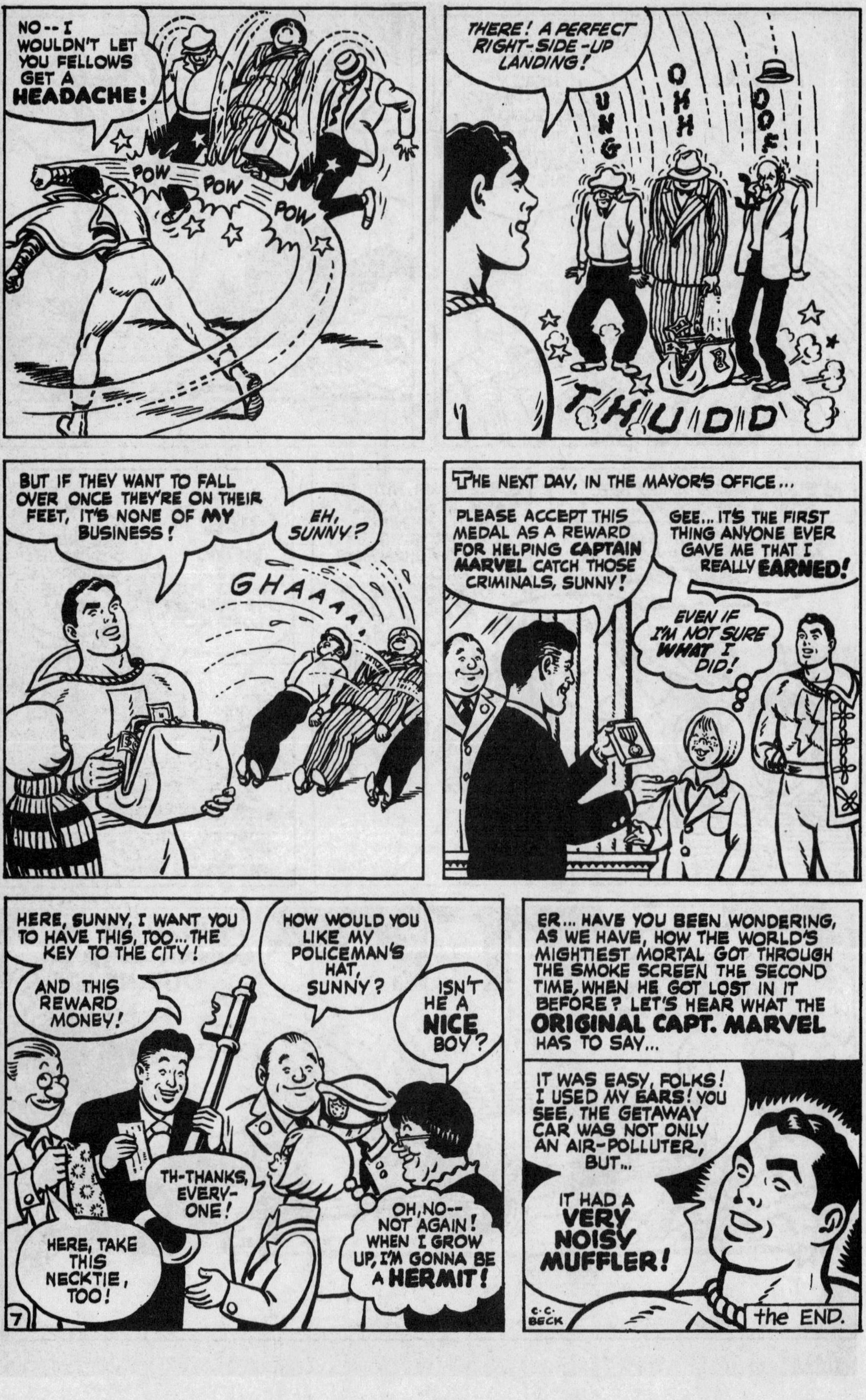
NO-- I WOULDN'T LET YOU FELLOWS GET A HEADACHE!
POW
POW
POW
THERE! A PERFECT RIGHT-SIDE-UP LANDING!
UNG
OHH
OOF
THUDD
BUT IF THEY WANT TO FALL OVER ONCE THEY'RE ON THEIR FEET, IT'S NONE OF MY BUSINESS!
EH, SUNNY?
GHAAAAA
THE NEXT DAY, IN THE MAYOR'S OFFICE...
PLEASE ACCEPT THIS MEDAL AS A REWARD FOR HELPING CAPTAIN MARVEL CATCH THOSE CRIMINALS, SUNNY!
GEE... IT'S THE FIRST THING ANYONE EVER GAVE ME THAT I REALLY EARNED!
EVEN IF I'M NOT SURE WHAT I DID!
HERE, SUNNY, I WANT YOU TO HAVE THIS, TOO... THE KEY TO THE CITY!
AND THIS REWARD MONEY!
HOW WOULD YOU LIKE MY POLICEMAN'S HAT, SUNNY?
ISN'T HE A NICE BOY?
TH-THANKS, EVERY-ONE!
HERE, TAKE THIS NECKTIE, TOO!
OH, NO-- NOT AGAIN! WHEN I GROW UP, I'M GONNA BE A HERMIT!
7
ER... HAVE YOU BEEN WONDERING, AS WE HAVE, HOW THE WORLD'S MIGHTIEST MORTAL GOT THROUGH THE SMOKE SCREEN THE SECOND TIME, WHEN HE GOT LOST IN IT BEFORE? LET'S HEAR WHAT THE ORIGINAL CAPT. MARVEL HAS TO SAY...
IT WAS EASY, FOLKS! I USED MY EARS! YOU SEE, THE GETAWAY CAR WAS NOT ONLY AN AIR-POLLUTER, BUT...
IT HAD A VERY NOISY MUFFLER!
C.C. BECK
the END.

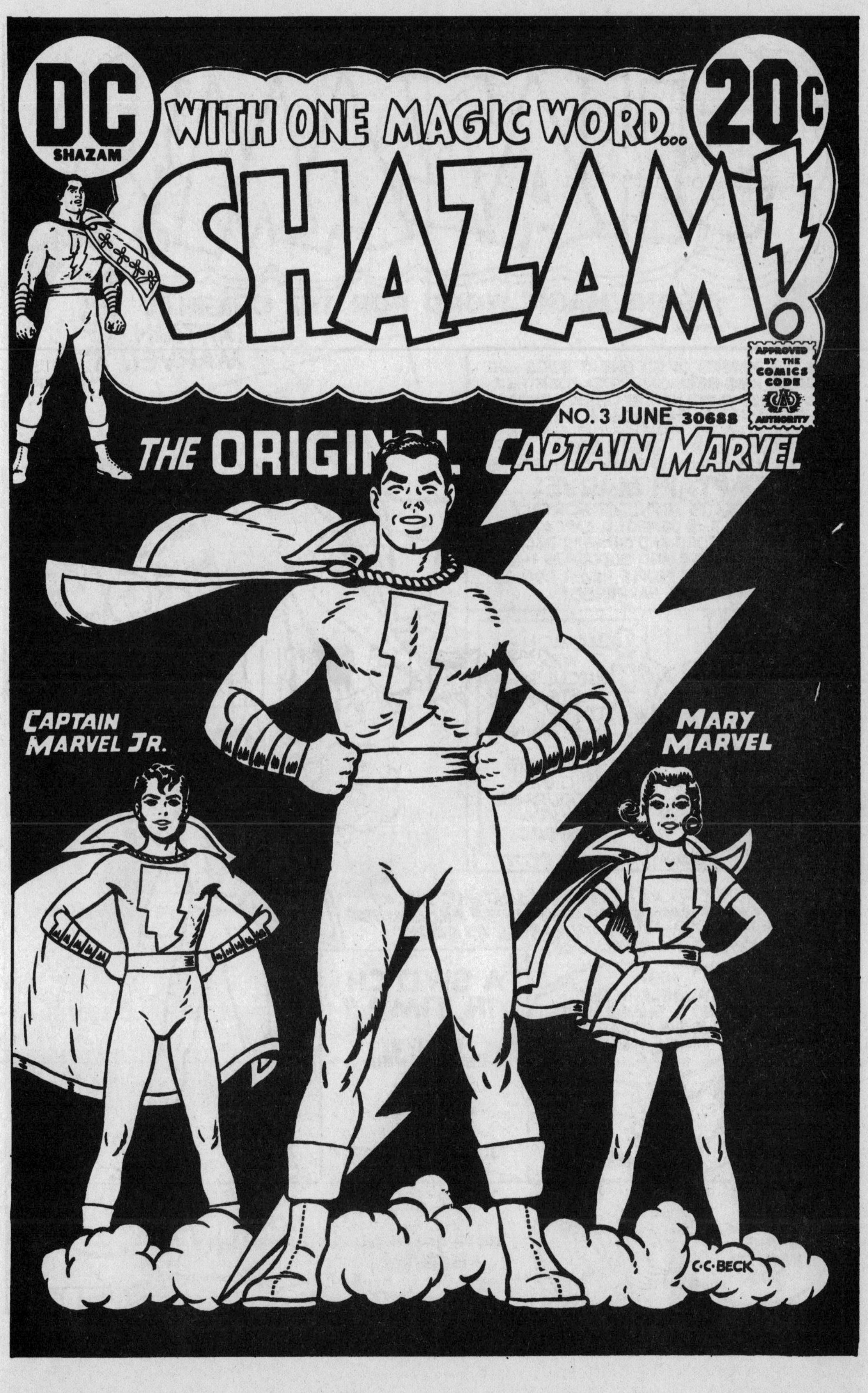
DC
SHAZAM
WITH ONE MAGIC WORD...
SHAZAM!
20¢
APPROVED BY THE COMICS CODE AUTHORITY
NO. 3 JUNE 30688
THE ORIGINAL CAPTAIN MARVEL
CAPTAIN MARVEL JR.
MARY MARVEL
C.C. BECK

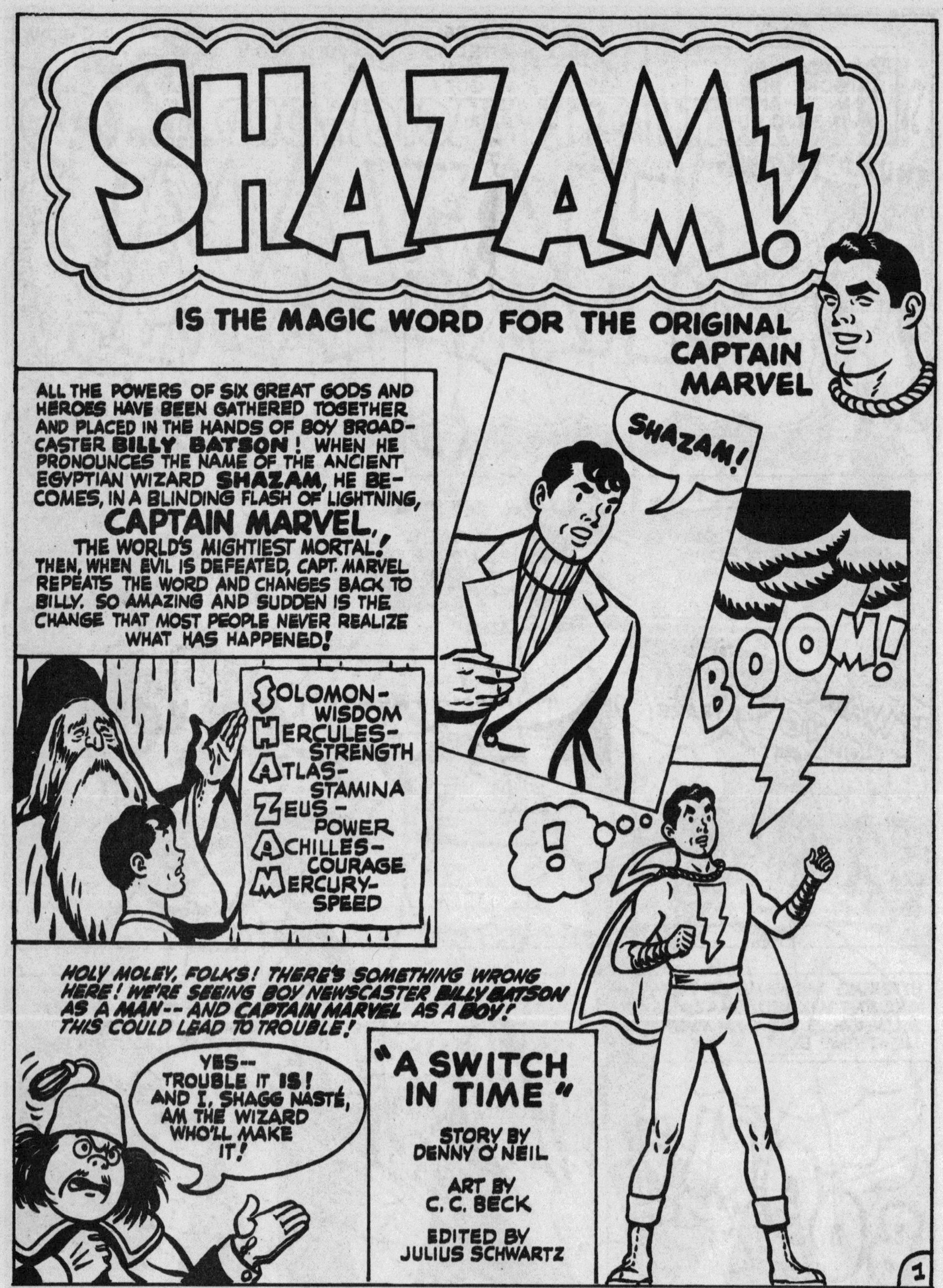
SHAZAM!
IS THE MAGIC WORD FOR THE ORIGINAL CAPTAIN MARVEL
ALL THE POWERS OF SIX GREAT GODS AND HEROES HAVE BEEN GATHERED TOGETHER AND PLACED IN THE HANDS OF BOY BROADCASTER BILLY BATSON! WHEN HE PRONOUNCES THE NAME OF THE ANCIENT EGYPTIAN WIZARD SHAZAM, HE BECOMES, IN A BLINDING FLASH OF LIGHTNING,
CAPTAIN MARVEL,
THE WORLD'S MIGHTIEST MORTAL! THEN, WHEN EVIL IS DEFEATED, CAPT. MARVEL REPEATS THE WORD AND CHANGES BACK TO BILLY. SO AMAZING AND SUDDEN IS THE CHANGE THAT MOST PEOPLE NEVER REALIZE WHAT HAS HAPPENED!
SHAZAM!
BOOM!
SOLOMON-WISDOM
HERCULES-STRENGTH
ATLAS-STAMINA
ZEUS-POWER
ACHILLES-COURAGE
MERCURY-SPEED
!
HOLY MOLEY, FOLKS! THERE'S SOMETHING WRONG HERE! WE'RE SEEING BOY NEWSCASTER BILLY BATSON AS A MAN-- AND CAPTAIN MARVEL AS A BOY! THIS COULD LEAD TO TROUBLE!
YES-- TROUBLE IT IS! AND I, SHAGG NASTÉ, AM THE WIZARD WHO'LL MAKE IT!
"A SWITCH IN TIME"
STORY BY DENNY O'NEIL
ART BY C. C. BECK
EDITED BY JULIUS SCHWARTZ
1

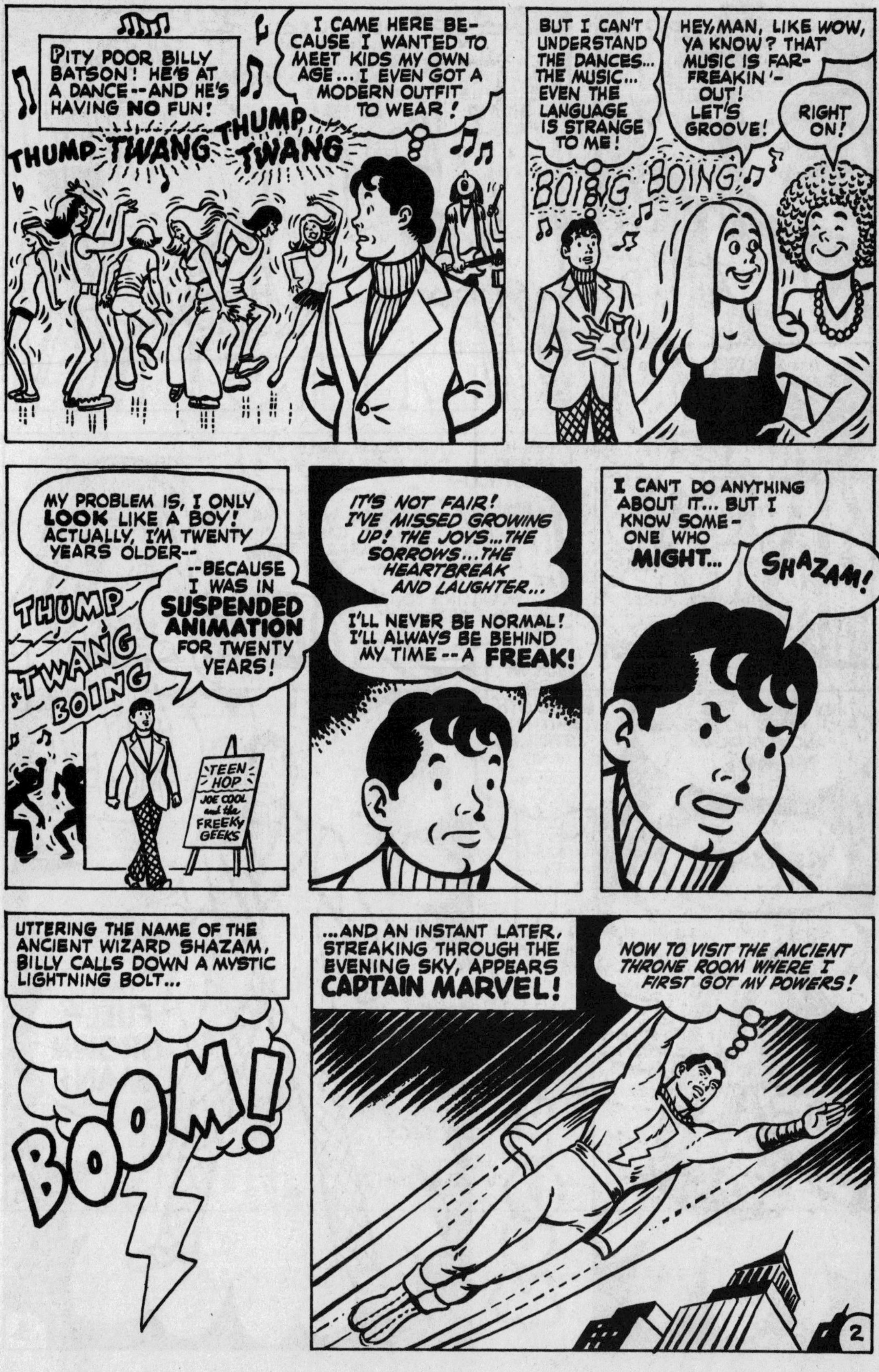
PITY POOR BILLY BATSON! HE'S AT A DANCE--AND HE'S HAVING NO FUN!
I CAME HERE BE-CAUSE I WANTED TO MEET KIDS MY OWN AGE... I EVEN GOT A MODERN OUTFIT TO WEAR!
THUMP TWANG THUMP TWANG
BUT I CAN'T UNDERSTAND THE DANCES... THE MUSIC... EVEN THE LANGUAGE IS STRANGE TO ME!
HEY, MAN, LIKE WOW, YA KNOW? THAT MUSIC IS FAR-FREAKIN'-OUT! LET'S GROOVE!
RIGHT ON!
BOING BOING
MY PROBLEM IS, I ONLY LOOK LIKE A BOY! ACTUALLY, I'M TWENTY YEARS OLDER--
--BECAUSE I WAS IN SUSPENDED ANIMATION FOR TWENTY YEARS!
THUMP TWANG BOING
TEEN HOP JOE COOL and the FREEKY GEEKS
IT'S NOT FAIR! I'VE MISSED GROWING UP! THE JOYS...THE SORROWS...THE HEARTBREAK AND LAUGHTER...
I'LL NEVER BE NORMAL! I'LL ALWAYS BE BEHIND MY TIME--A FREAK!
I CAN'T DO ANYTHING ABOUT IT... BUT I KNOW SOME-ONE WHO MIGHT...
SHAZAM!
UTTERING THE NAME OF THE ANCIENT WIZARD SHAZAM, BILLY CALLS DOWN A MYSTIC LIGHTNING BOLT...
BOOM!
...AND AN INSTANT LATER, STREAKING THROUGH THE EVENING SKY, APPEARS CAPTAIN MARVEL!
NOW TO VISIT THE ANCIENT THRONE ROOM WHERE I FIRST GOT MY POWERS!
2

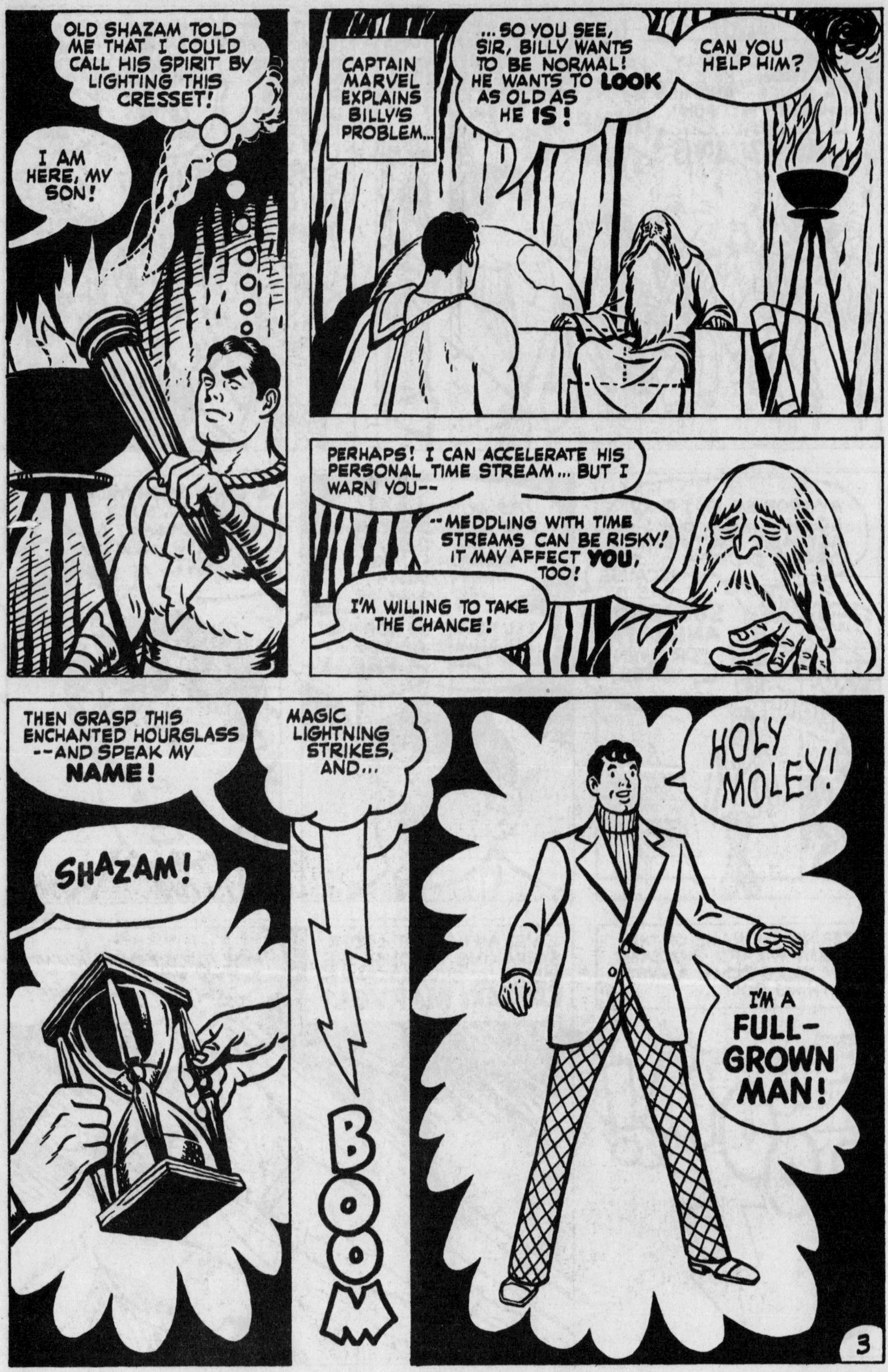

OLD SHAZAM TOLD ME THAT I COULD CALL HIS SPIRIT BY LIGHTING THIS CRESSET!
I AM HERE, MY SON!
CAPTAIN MARVEL EXPLAINS BILLY'S PROBLEM...
...SO YOU SEE, SIR, BILLY WANTS TO BE NORMAL! HE WANTS TO LOOK AS OLD AS HE IS!
CAN YOU HELP HIM?
PERHAPS! I CAN ACCELERATE HIS PERSONAL TIME STREAM... BUT I WARN YOU--
--MEDDLING WITH TIME STREAMS CAN BE RISKY! IT MAY AFFECT YOU, TOO!
I'M WILLING TO TAKE THE CHANCE!
THEN GRASP THIS ENCHANTED HOURGLASS --AND SPEAK MY NAME!
SHAZAM!
MAGIC LIGHTNING STRIKES, AND...
BOOM
HOLY MOLEY!
I'M A FULL-GROWN MAN!
3

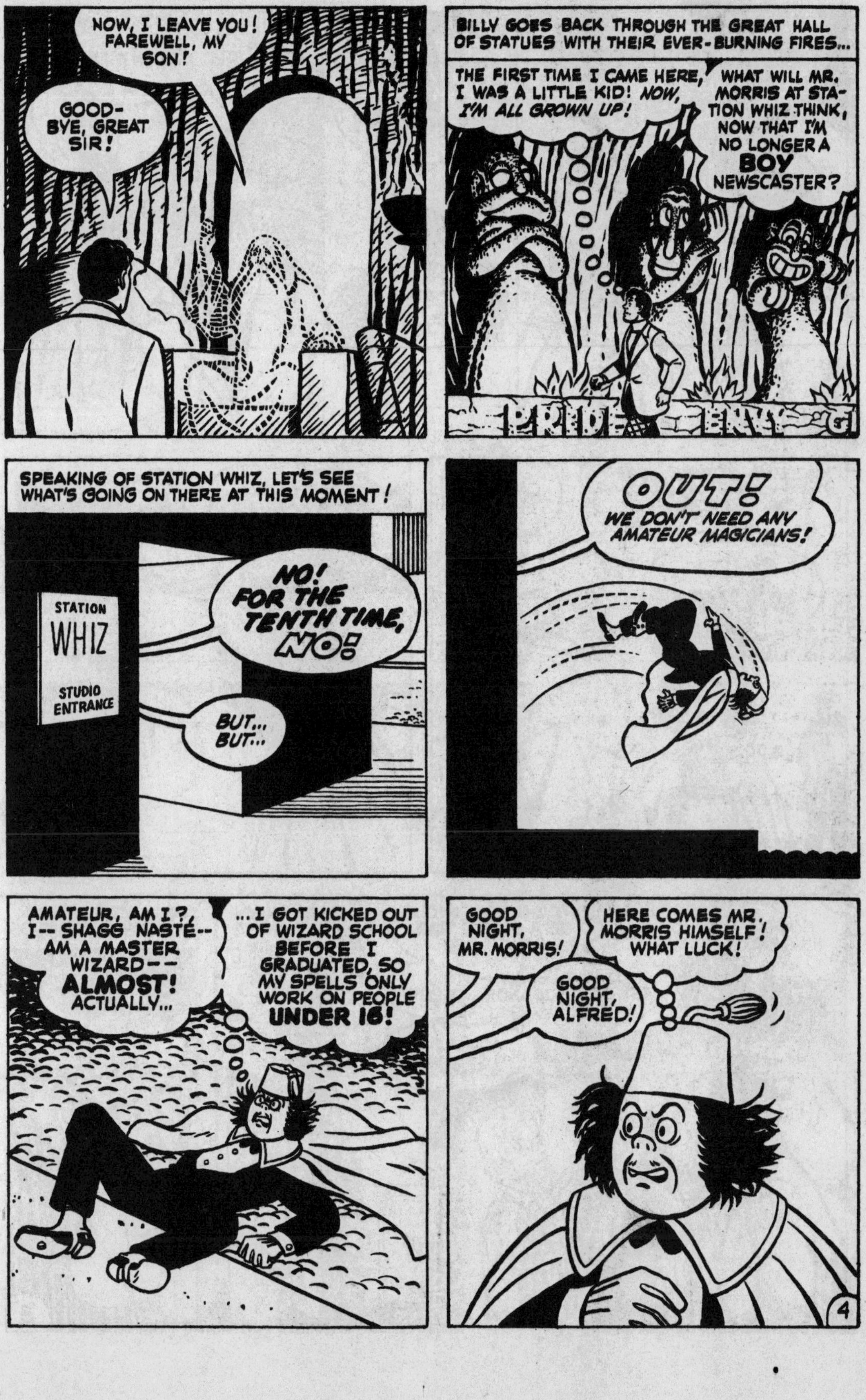
NOW, I LEAVE YOU! FAREWELL, MY SON!
GOOD-BYE, GREAT SIR!
BILLY GOES BACK THROUGH THE GREAT HALL OF STATUES WITH THEIR EVER-BURNING FIRES...
THE FIRST TIME I CAME HERE, I WAS A LITTLE KID! NOW, I'M ALL GROWN UP!
WHAT WILL MR. MORRIS AT STATION WHIZ THINK, NOW THAT I'M NO LONGER A BOY NEWSCASTER?
PRID
ENVY
SPEAKING OF STATION WHIZ, LET'S SEE WHAT'S GOING ON THERE AT THIS MOMENT!
STATION WHIZ STUDIO ENTRANCE
NO! FOR THE TENTH TIME, NO!
BUT... BUT...
OUT! WE DON'T NEED ANY AMATEUR MAGICIANS!
AMATEUR, AM I?, I-- SHAGG NASTÉ-- AM A MASTER WIZARD-- ALMOST! ACTUALLY...
...I GOT KICKED OUT OF WIZARD SCHOOL BEFORE I GRADUATED, SO MY SPELLS ONLY WORK ON PEOPLE UNDER 16!
GOOD NIGHT, MR. MORRIS!
HERE COMES MR. MORRIS HIMSELF! WHAT LUCK!
GOOD NIGHT, ALFRED!
4

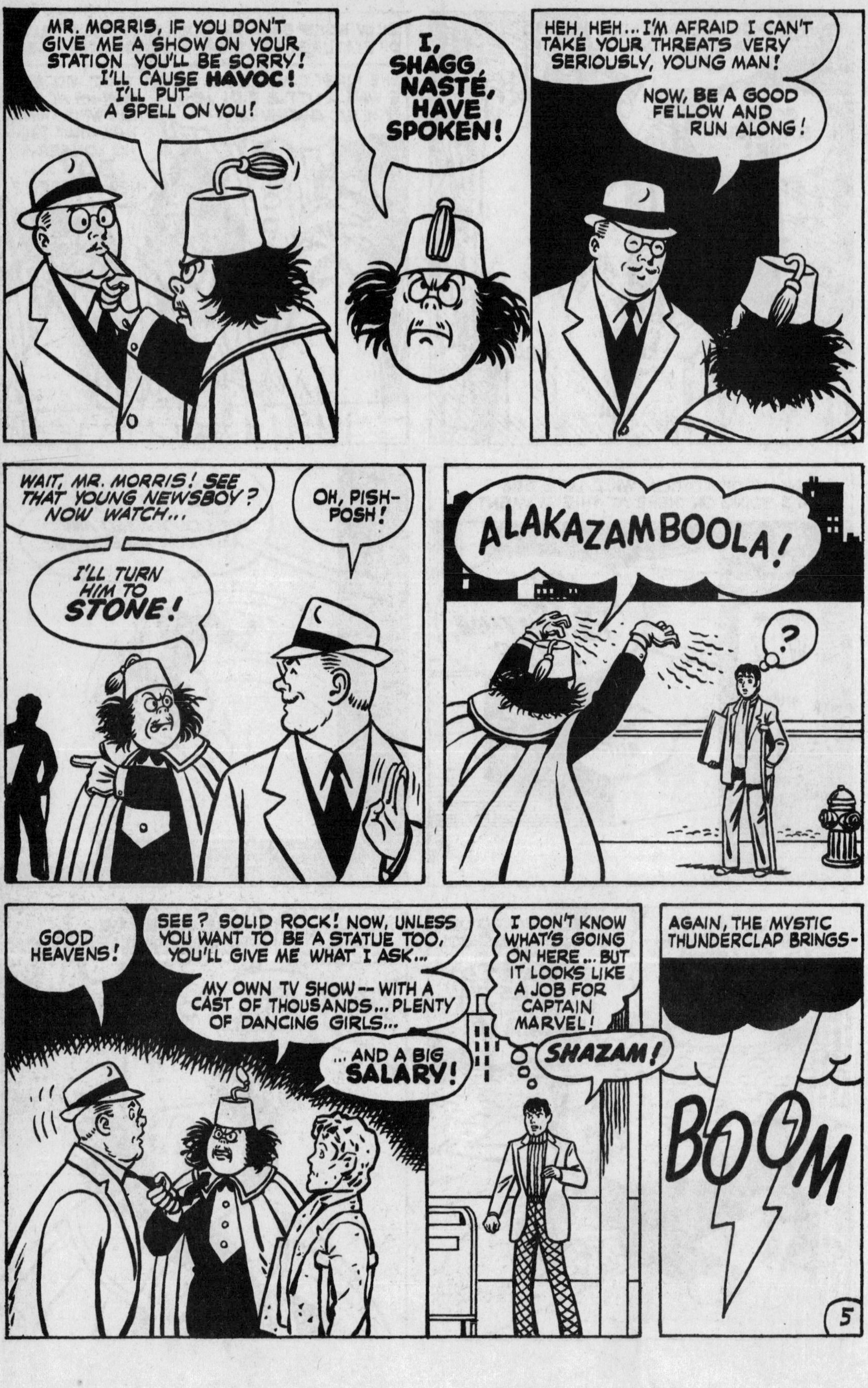
MR. MORRIS, IF YOU DON'T GIVE ME A SHOW ON YOUR STATION YOU'LL BE SORRY! I'LL CAUSE HAVOC! I'LL PUT A SPELL ON YOU!
I, SHAGG NASTÉ, HAVE SPOKEN!
HEH, HEH... I'M AFRAID I CAN'T TAKE YOUR THREATS VERY SERIOUSLY, YOUNG MAN!
NOW, BE A GOOD FELLOW AND RUN ALONG!
WAIT, MR. MORRIS! SEE THAT YOUNG NEWSBOY? NOW WATCH...
I'LL TURN HIM TO STONE!
OH, PISH-POSH!
ALAKAZAMBOOLA!
?
GOOD HEAVENS!
SEE? SOLID ROCK! NOW, UNLESS YOU WANT TO BE A STATUE TOO, YOU'LL GIVE ME WHAT I ASK...
MY OWN TV SHOW -- WITH A CAST OF THOUSANDS... PLENTY OF DANCING GIRLS...
...AND A BIG SALARY!
I DON'T KNOW WHAT'S GOING ON HERE... BUT IT LOOKS LIKE A JOB FOR CAPTAIN MARVEL!
SHAZAM!
AGAIN, THE MYSTIC THUNDERCLAP BRINGS-
BOOM
5

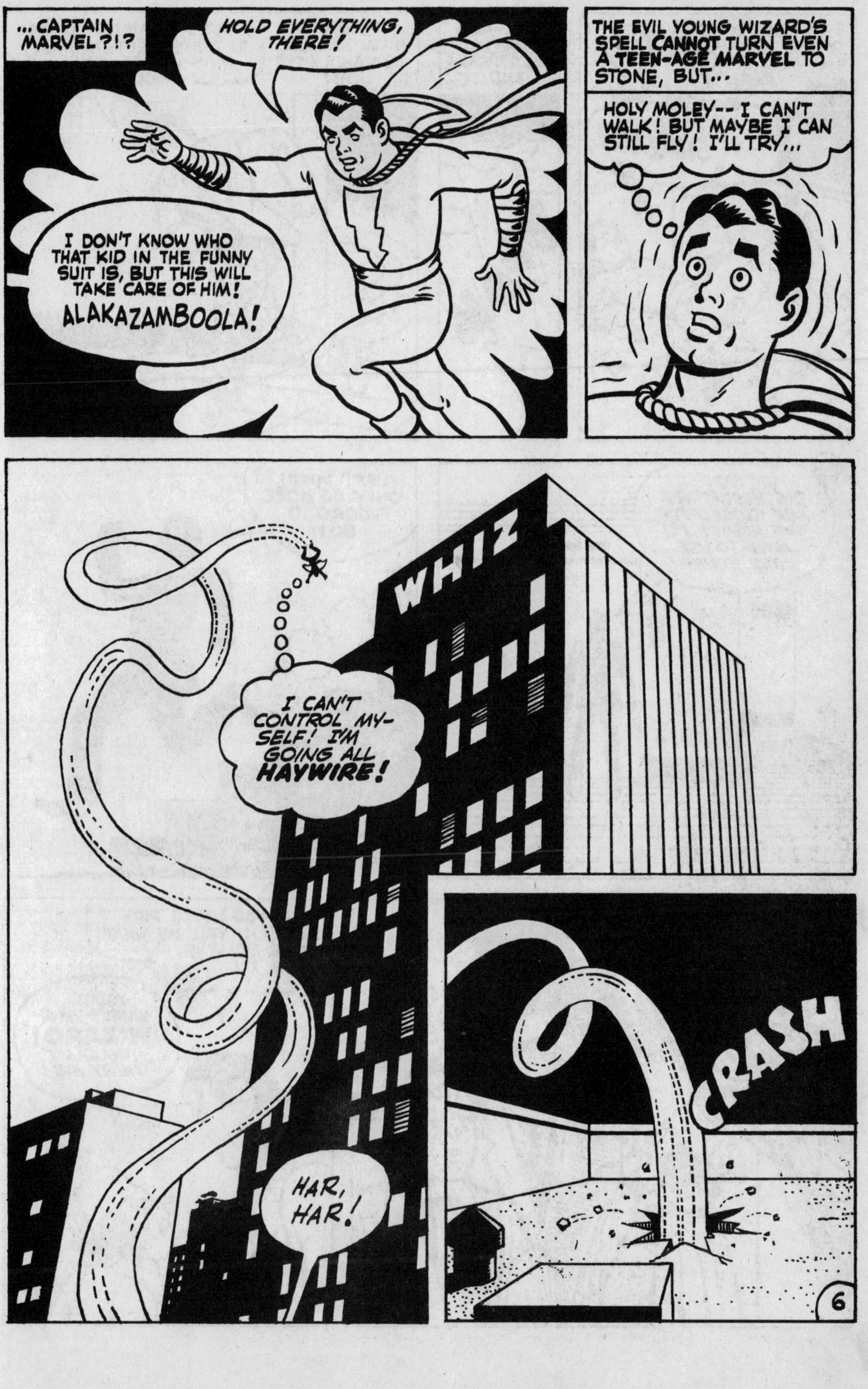
...CAPTAIN MARVEL?!?
HOLD EVERYTHING, THERE!
I DON'T KNOW WHO THAT KID IN THE FUNNY SUIT IS, BUT THIS WILL TAKE CARE OF HIM! ALAKAZAMBOOLA!
THE EVIL YOUNG WIZARD'S SPELL CANNOT TURN EVEN A TEEN-AGE MARVEL TO STONE, BUT...
HOLY MOLEY-- I CAN'T WALK! BUT MAYBE I CAN STILL FLY! I'LL TRY...
WHIZ
I CAN'T CONTROL MY-SELF! I'M GOING ALL HAYWIRE!
HAR, HAR!
CRASH
6

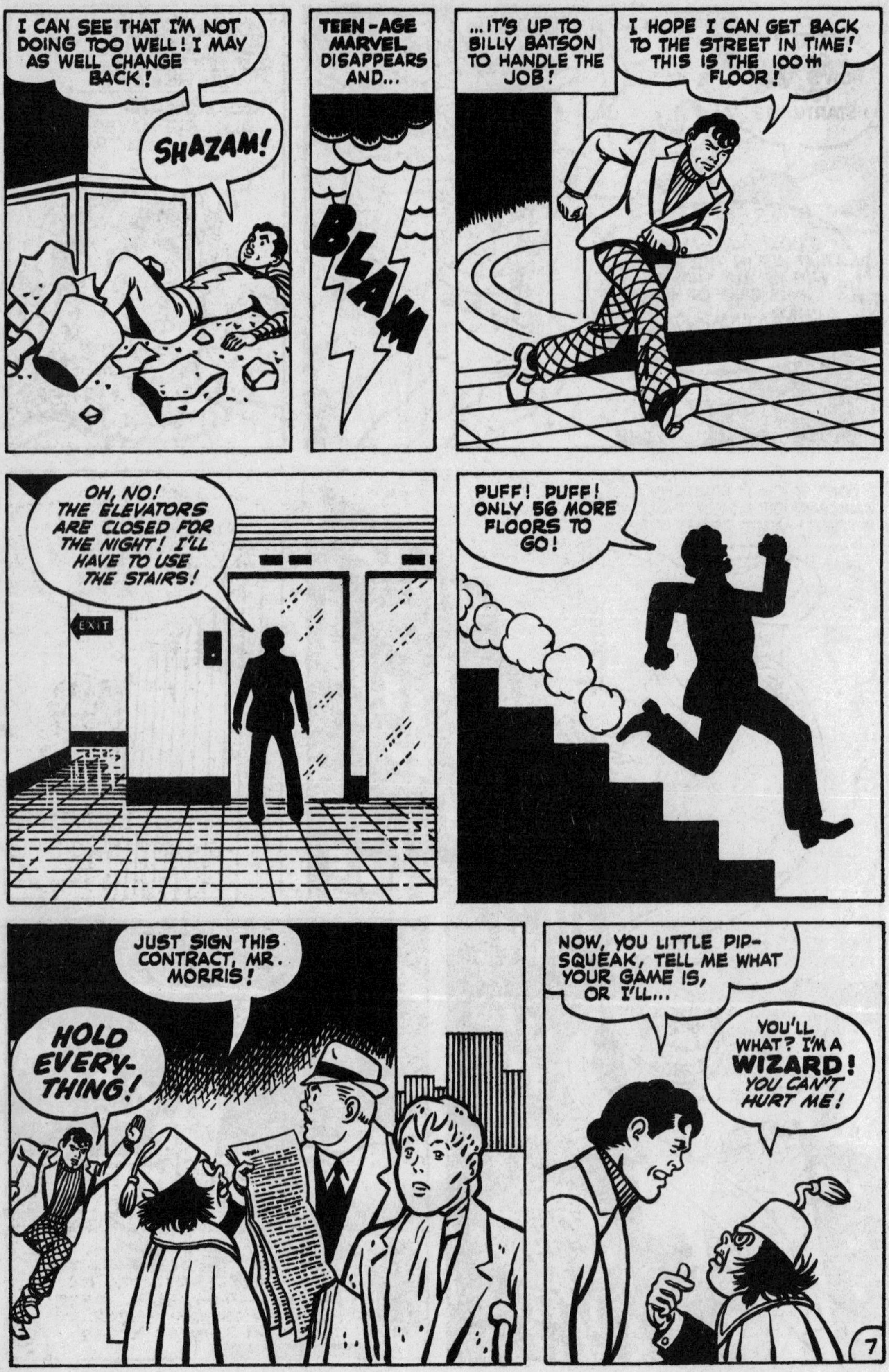
I CAN SEE THAT I'M NOT DOING TOO WELL! I MAY AS WELL CHANGE BACK!
SHAZAM!
TEEN-AGE MARVEL DISAPPEARS AND...
BLAM
...IT'S UP TO BILLY BATSON TO HANDLE THE JOB!
I HOPE I CAN GET BACK TO THE STREET IN TIME! THIS IS THE 100th FLOOR!
OH, NO! THE ELEVATORS ARE CLOSED FOR THE NIGHT! I'LL HAVE TO USE THE STAIRS!
EXIT
PUFF! PUFF! ONLY 56 MORE FLOORS TO GO!
JUST SIGN THIS CONTRACT, MR. MORRIS!
HOLD EVERY-THING!
NOW, YOU LITTLE PIP-SQUEAK, TELL ME WHAT YOUR GAME IS, OR I'LL...
YOU'LL WHAT? I'M A WIZARD! YOU CAN'T HURT ME!
7

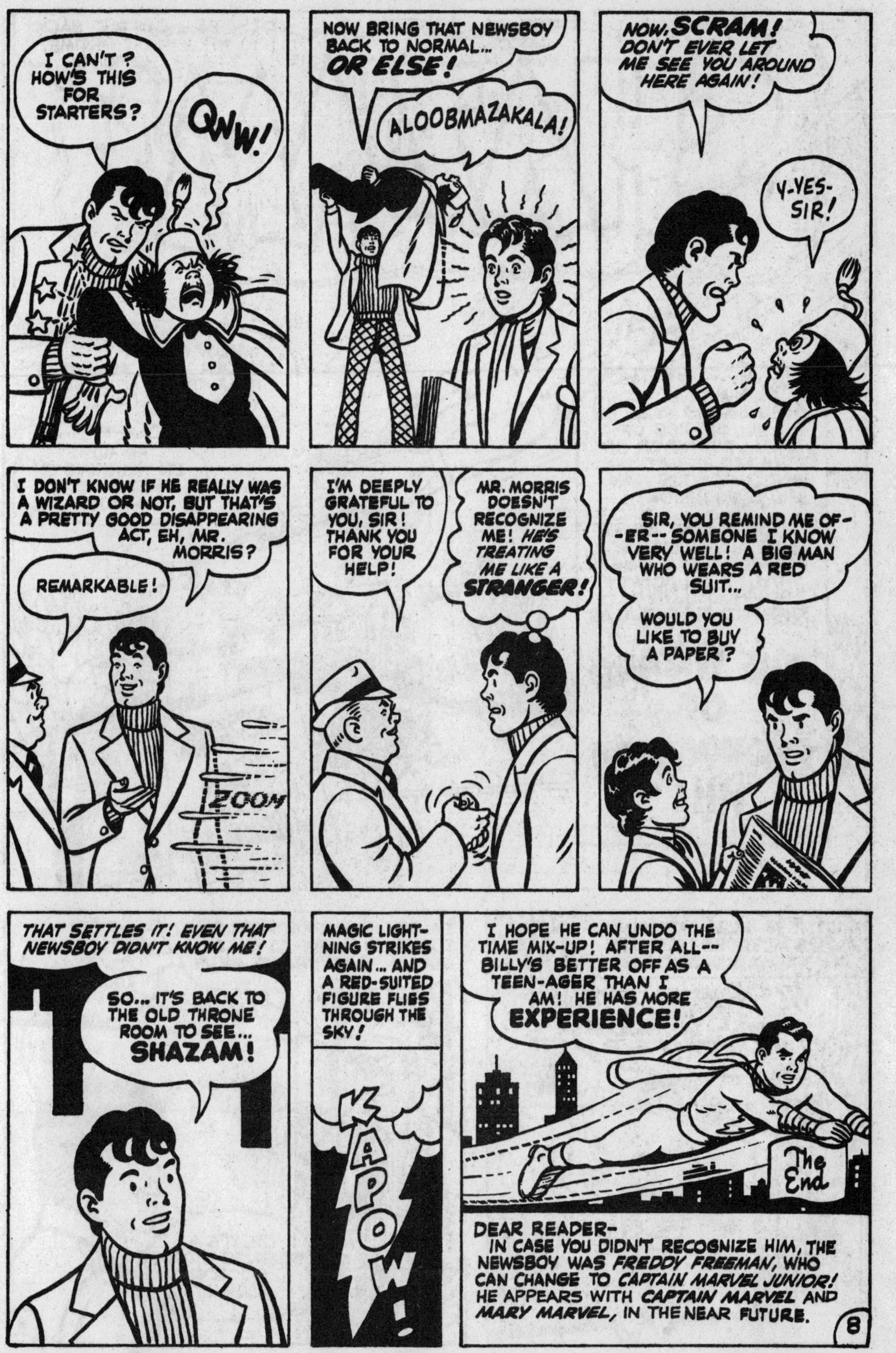
I CAN'T? HOW'S THIS FOR STARTERS?
QNW!
NOW BRING THAT NEWSBOY BACK TO NORMAL... OR ELSE!
ALOOBMAZAKALA!
NOW, SCRAM! DON'T EVER LET ME SEE YOU AROUND HERE AGAIN!
Y-YES-SIR!
I DON'T KNOW IF HE REALLY WAS A WIZARD OR NOT, BUT THAT'S A PRETTY GOOD DISAPPEARING ACT, EH, MR. MORRIS?
REMARKABLE!
ZOOM
I'M DEEPLY GRATEFUL TO YOU, SIR! THANK YOU FOR YOUR HELP!
MR. MORRIS DOESN'T RECOGNIZE ME! HE'S TREATING ME LIKE A STRANGER!
SIR, YOU REMIND ME OF--ER-- SOMEONE I KNOW VERY WELL! A BIG MAN WHO WEARS A RED SUIT...
WOULD YOU LIKE TO BUY A PAPER?
THAT SETTLES IT! EVEN THAT NEWSBOY DIDN'T KNOW ME!
SO... IT'S BACK TO THE OLD THRONE ROOM TO SEE... SHAZAM!
MAGIC LIGHTNING STRIKES AGAIN... AND A RED-SUITED FIGURE FLIES THROUGH THE SKY!
KAPOW!
I HOPE HE CAN UNDO THE TIME MIX-UP! AFTER ALL-- BILLY'S BETTER OFF AS A TEEN-AGER THAN I AM! HE HAS MORE EXPERIENCE!
The End
DEAR READER-
IN CASE YOU DIDN'T RECOGNIZE HIM, THE NEWSBOY WAS FREDDY FREEMAN, WHO CAN CHANGE TO CAPTAIN MARVEL JUNIOR! HE APPEARS WITH CAPTAIN MARVEL AND MARY MARVEL, IN THE NEAR FUTURE.
8

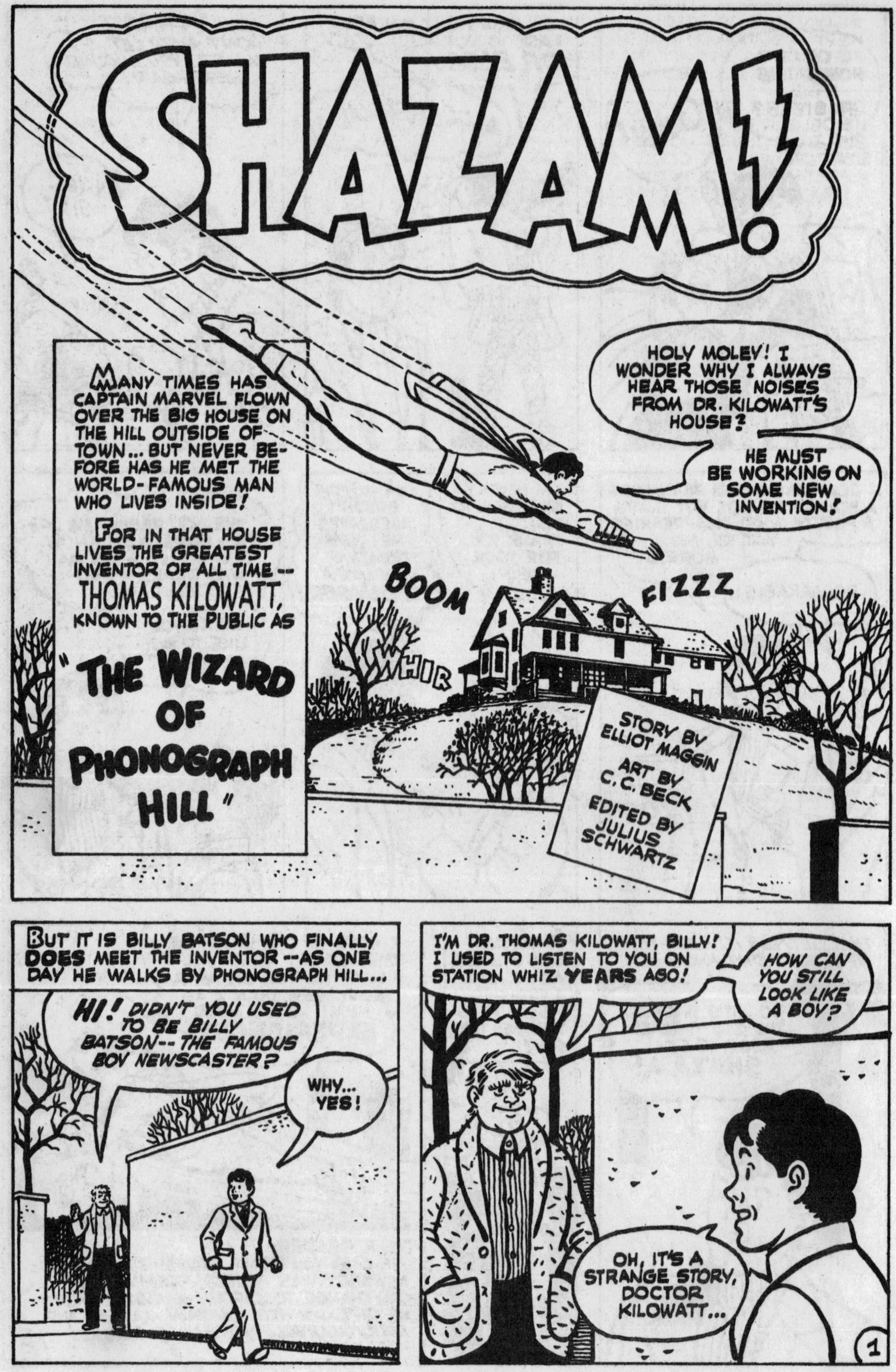
SHAZAM!
MANY TIMES HAS CAPTAIN MARVEL FLOWN OVER THE BIG HOUSE ON THE HILL OUTSIDE OF TOWN... BUT NEVER BEFORE HAS HE MET THE WORLD-FAMOUS MAN WHO LIVES INSIDE!
FOR IN THAT HOUSE LIVES THE GREATEST INVENTOR OF ALL TIME -- THOMAS KILOWATT, KNOWN TO THE PUBLIC AS
"THE WIZARD OF PHONOGRAPH HILL"
HOLY MOLEY! I WONDER WHY I ALWAYS HEAR THOSE NOISES FROM DR. KILOWATT'S HOUSE?
HE MUST BE WORKING ON SOME NEW INVENTION!
BOOM
WHIR
FIZZZ
STORY BY ELLIOT MAGGIN
ART BY C. C. BECK
EDITED BY JULIUS SCHWARTZ
BUT IT IS BILLY BATSON WHO FINALLY DOES MEET THE INVENTOR -- AS ONE DAY HE WALKS BY PHONOGRAPH HILL...
HI! DIDN'T YOU USED TO BE BILLY BATSON -- THE FAMOUS BOY NEWSCASTER?
WHY... YES!
I'M DR. THOMAS KILOWATT, BILLY! I USED TO LISTEN TO YOU ON STATION WHIZ YEARS AGO!
HOW CAN YOU STILL LOOK LIKE A BOY?
OH, IT'S A STRANGE STORY, DOCTOR KILOWATT...
1

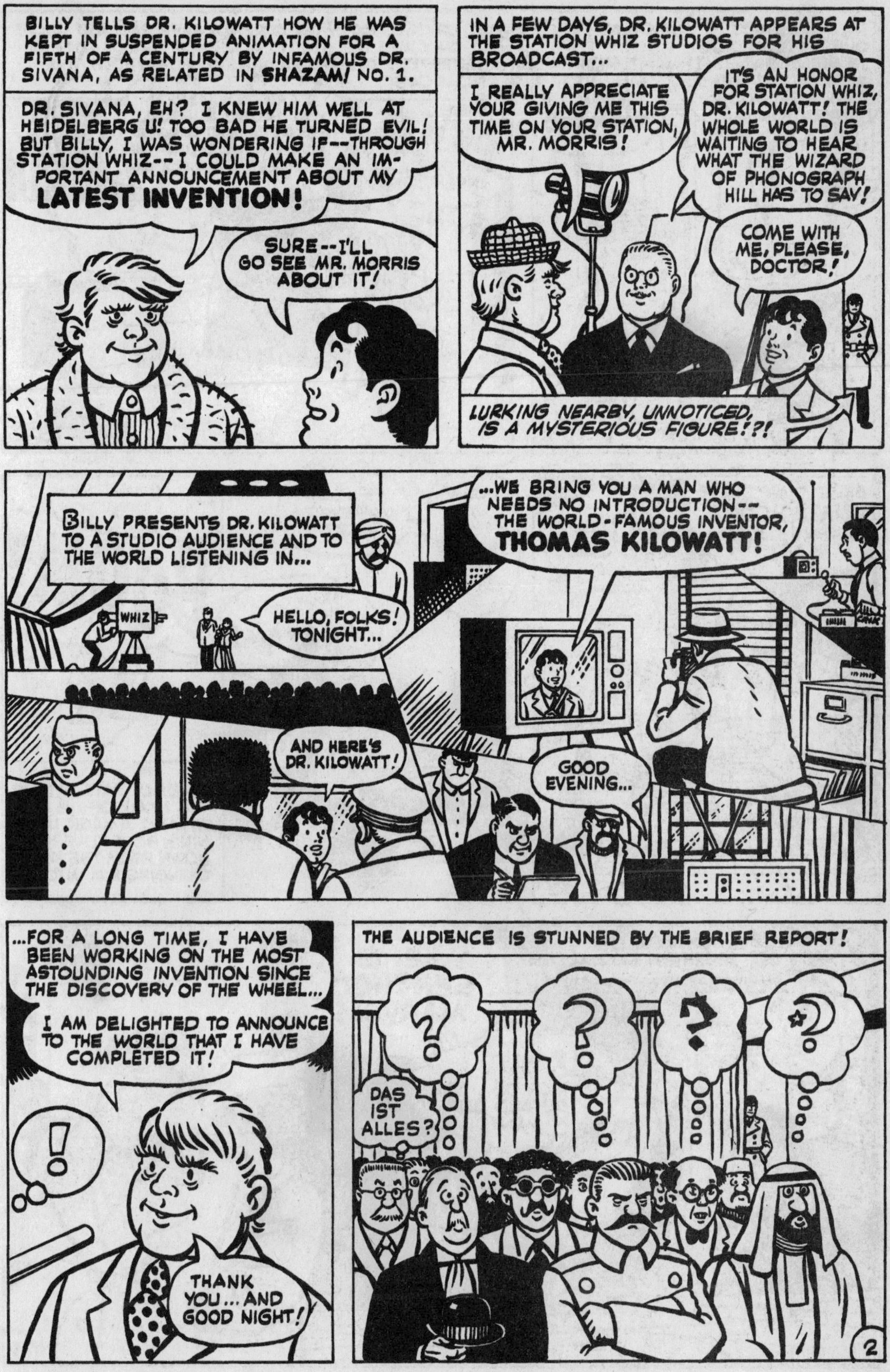
BILLY TELLS DR. KILOWATT HOW HE WAS KEPT IN SUSPENDED ANIMATION FOR A FIFTH OF A CENTURY BY INFAMOUS DR. SIVANA, AS RELATED IN SHAZAM! NO. 1.
DR. SIVANA, EH? I KNEW HIM WELL AT HEIDELBERG U! TOO BAD HE TURNED EVIL! BUT BILLY, I WAS WONDERING IF--THROUGH STATION WHIZ--I COULD MAKE AN IMPORTANT ANNOUNCEMENT ABOUT MY LATEST INVENTION!
SURE--I'LL GO SEE MR. MORRIS ABOUT IT!
IN A FEW DAYS, DR. KILOWATT APPEARS AT THE STATION WHIZ STUDIOS FOR HIS BROADCAST...
I REALLY APPRECIATE YOUR GIVING ME THIS TIME ON YOUR STATION, MR. MORRIS!
IT'S AN HONOR FOR STATION WHIZ, DR. KILOWATT! THE WHOLE WORLD IS WAITING TO HEAR WHAT THE WIZARD OF PHONOGRAPH HILL HAS TO SAY!
COME WITH ME, PLEASE, DOCTOR!
LURKING NEARBY, UNNOTICED, IS A MYSTERIOUS FIGURE!?!
BILLY PRESENTS DR. KILOWATT TO A STUDIO AUDIENCE AND TO THE WORLD LISTENING IN...
WHIZ
HELLO, FOLKS! TONIGHT...
...WE BRING YOU A MAN WHO NEEDS NO INTRODUCTION-- THE WORLD-FAMOUS INVENTOR, THOMAS KILOWATT!
AND HERE'S DR. KILOWATT!
GOOD EVENING...
...FOR A LONG TIME, I HAVE BEEN WORKING ON THE MOST ASTOUNDING INVENTION SINCE THE DISCOVERY OF THE WHEEL...
I AM DELIGHTED TO ANNOUNCE TO THE WORLD THAT I HAVE COMPLETED IT!
!
THANK YOU... AND GOOD NIGHT!
THE AUDIENCE IS STUNNED BY THE BRIEF REPORT!
DAS IST ALLES?
?
?
2

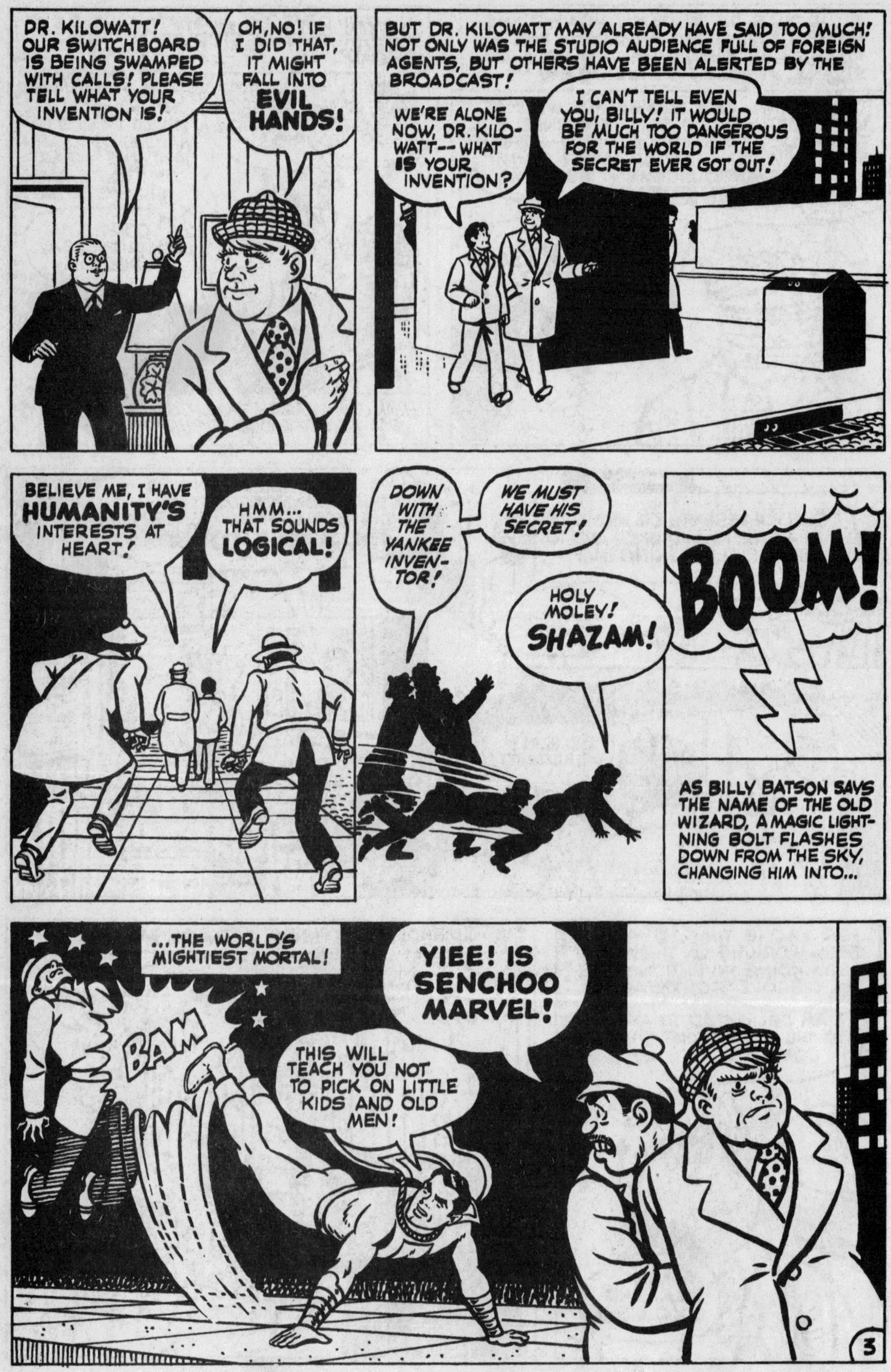
DR. KILOWATT! OUR SWITCHBOARD IS BEING SWAMPED WITH CALLS! PLEASE TELL WHAT YOUR INVENTION IS!
OH, NO! IF I DID THAT, IT MIGHT FALL INTO EVIL HANDS!
BUT DR. KILOWATT MAY ALREADY HAVE SAID TOO MUCH! NOT ONLY WAS THE STUDIO AUDIENCE FULL OF FOREIGN AGENTS, BUT OTHERS HAVE BEEN ALERTED BY THE BROADCAST!
WE'RE ALONE NOW, DR. KILO-WATT-- WHAT IS YOUR INVENTION?
I CAN'T TELL EVEN YOU, BILLY! IT WOULD BE MUCH TOO DANGEROUS FOR THE WORLD IF THE SECRET EVER GOT OUT!
BELIEVE ME, I HAVE HUMANITY'S INTERESTS AT HEART!
HMM... THAT SOUNDS LOGICAL!
DOWN WITH THE YANKEE INVEN-TOR!
WE MUST HAVE HIS SECRET!
HOLY MOLEY! SHAZAM!
BOOM!
AS BILLY BATSON SAYS THE NAME OF THE OLD WIZARD, A MAGIC LIGHT-NING BOLT FLASHES DOWN FROM THE SKY, CHANGING HIM INTO...
...THE WORLD'S MIGHTIEST MORTAL!
BAM
YIEE! IS SENCHOO MARVEL!
THIS WILL TEACH YOU NOT TO PICK ON LITTLE KIDS AND OLD MEN!
3

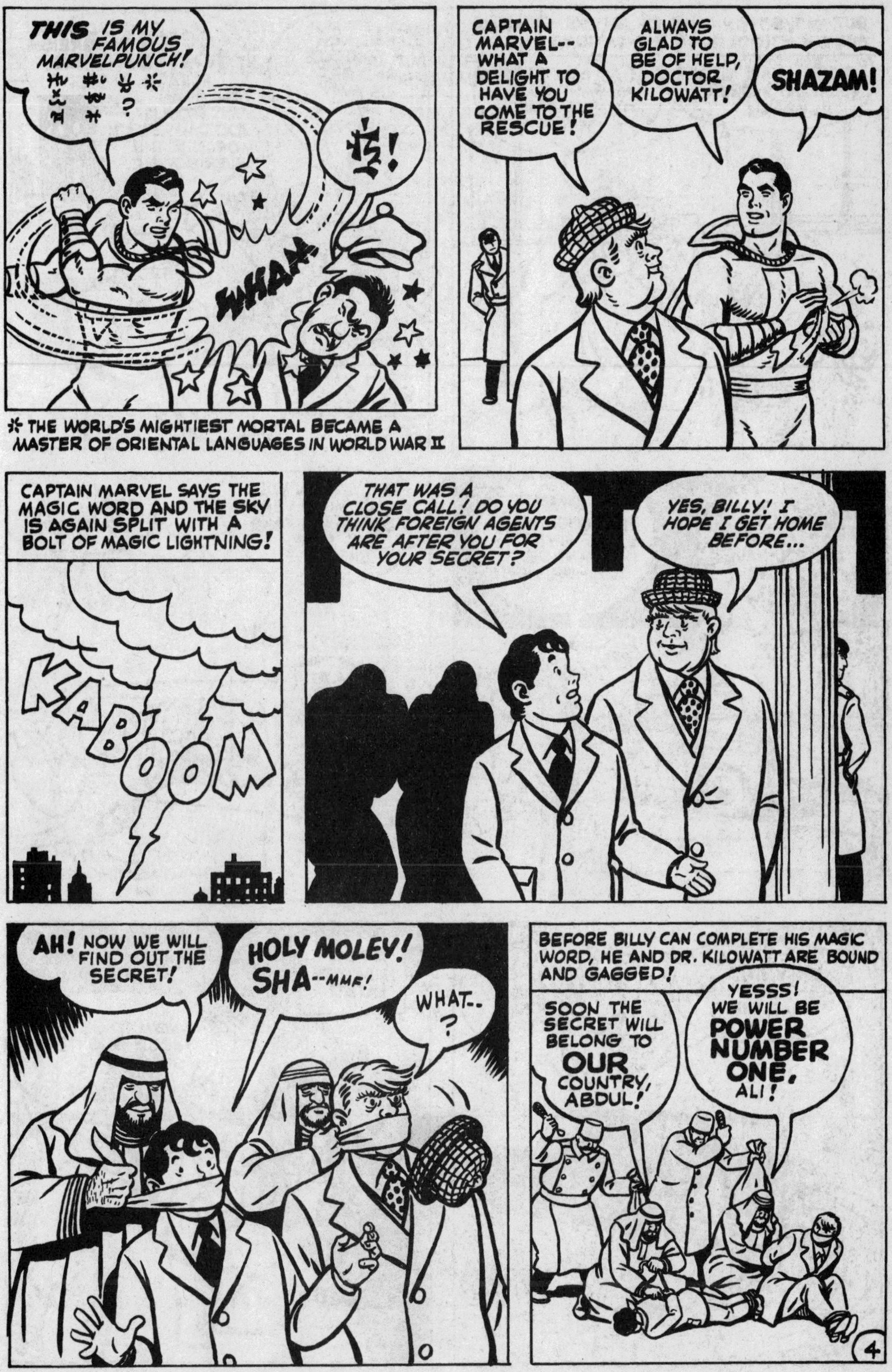
THIS IS MY FAMOUS MARVELPUNCH!
WHAM
* THE WORLD'S MIGHTIEST MORTAL BECAME A MASTER OF ORIENTAL LANGUAGES IN WORLD WAR II
CAPTAIN MARVEL-- WHAT A DELIGHT TO HAVE YOU COME TO THE RESCUE!
ALWAYS GLAD TO BE OF HELP, DOCTOR KILOWATT!
SHAZAM!
CAPTAIN MARVEL SAYS THE MAGIC WORD AND THE SKY IS AGAIN SPLIT WITH A BOLT OF MAGIC LIGHTNING!
KABOOM
THAT WAS A CLOSE CALL! DO YOU THINK FOREIGN AGENTS ARE AFTER YOU FOR YOUR SECRET?
YES, BILLY! I HOPE I GET HOME BEFORE...
AH! NOW WE WILL FIND OUT THE SECRET!
HOLY MOLEY! SHA--MMF!
WHAT..?
BEFORE BILLY CAN COMPLETE HIS MAGIC WORD, HE AND DR. KILOWATT ARE BOUND AND GAGGED!
SOON THE SECRET WILL BELONG TO OUR COUNTRY, ABDUL!
YESSS! WE WILL BE POWER NUMBER ONE, ALI!
4

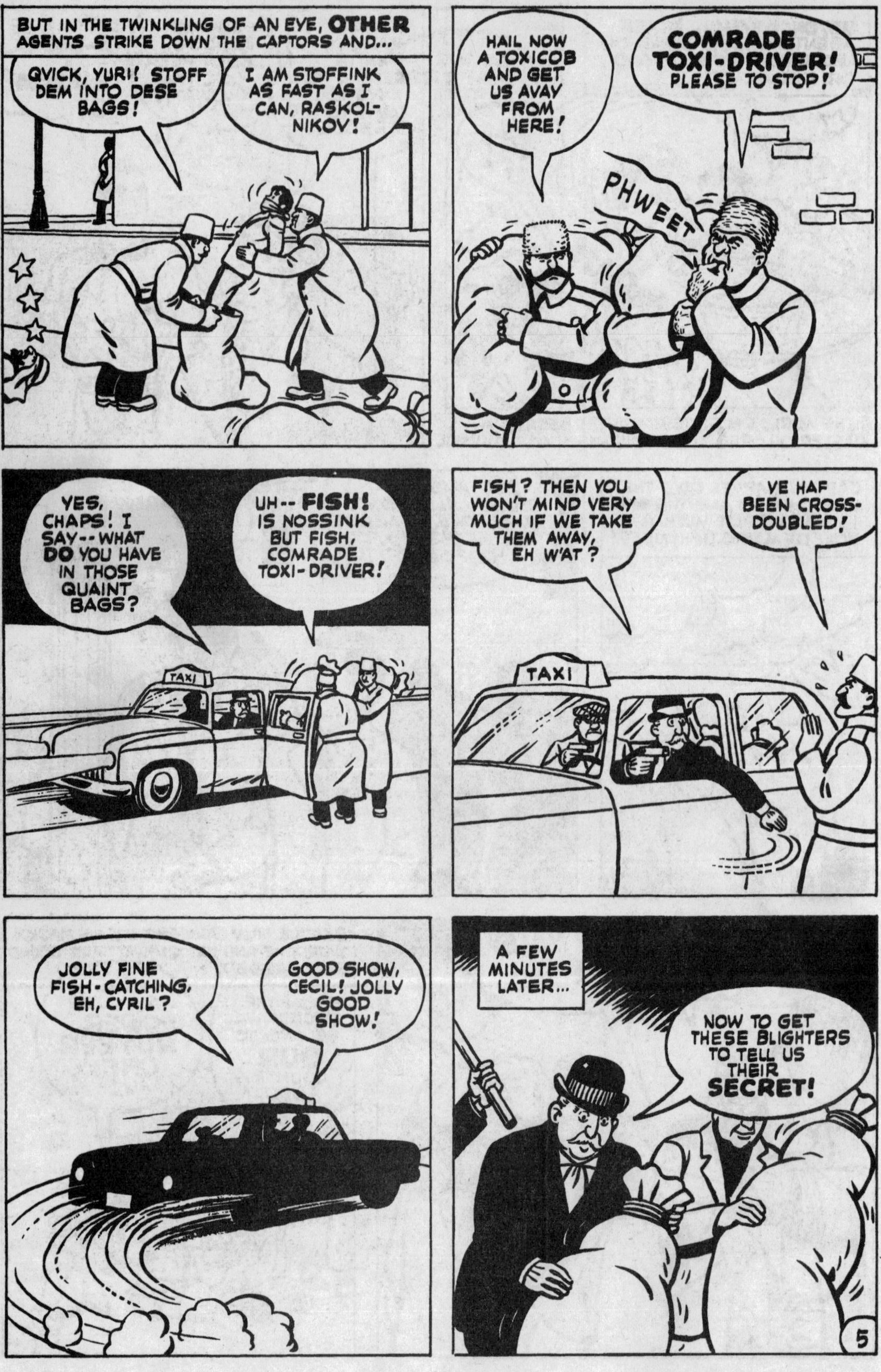
BUT IN THE TWINKLING OF AN EYE, OTHER AGENTS STRIKE DOWN THE CAPTORS AND...
QVICK, YURI! STOFF DEM INTO DESE BAGS!
I AM STOFFINK AS FAST AS I CAN, RASKOLNIKOV!
HAIL NOW A TOXICOB AND GET US AVAY FROM HERE!
COMRADE TOXI-DRIVER! PLEASE TO STOP!
PHWEET
YES, CHAPS! I SAY--WHAT DO YOU HAVE IN THOSE QUAINT BAGS?
UH--FISH! IS NOSSINK BUT FISH, COMRADE TOXI-DRIVER!
TAXI
FISH? THEN YOU WON'T MIND VERY MUCH IF WE TAKE THEM AWAY, EH W'AT?
VE HAF BEEN CROSS-DOUBLED!
TAXI
JOLLY FINE FISH-CATCHING, EH, CYRIL?
GOOD SHOW, CECIL! JOLLY GOOD SHOW!
A FEW MINUTES LATER...
NOW TO GET THESE BLIGHTERS TO TELL US THEIR SECRET!
5

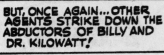

BUT, ONCE AGAIN...OTHER AGENTS STRIKE DOWN THE ABDUCTORS OF BILLY AND DR. KILOWATT!

CLONK! SOCK!

WE 'AVE ZEM! QUEEK, INTO ZE TRUCK!

NOW-- YOU WEEL TELL US ZE BEEG SECRET OR... ZUT! RIGHT ACROSS ZE THROATS!

NEVER! I'LL NOT SAV A WORD!

BUT I WILL...

SHAZAM!

KABOOOM!

AGAIN, THE BOLT OF MAGIC LIGHTNING CHANGES BILLY TO--

LE CAPITAINE MARVEL!

RIGHT! OTHERWISE KNOWN AS...

...THE WORLD'S MIGHTIEST MORTAL!

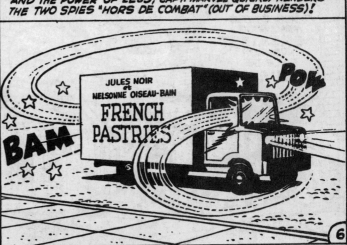

WITH THE SPEED OF MERCURY, THE STRENGTH OF HERCULES, AND THE POWER OF ZEUS, CAPT. MARVEL QUICKLY RENDERS THE TWO SPIES "HORS DE COMBAT" (OUT OF BUSINESS)!

JULES NOIR et NELSONNE OISEAU-BAIN FRENCH PASTRIES

POW

BAM

6

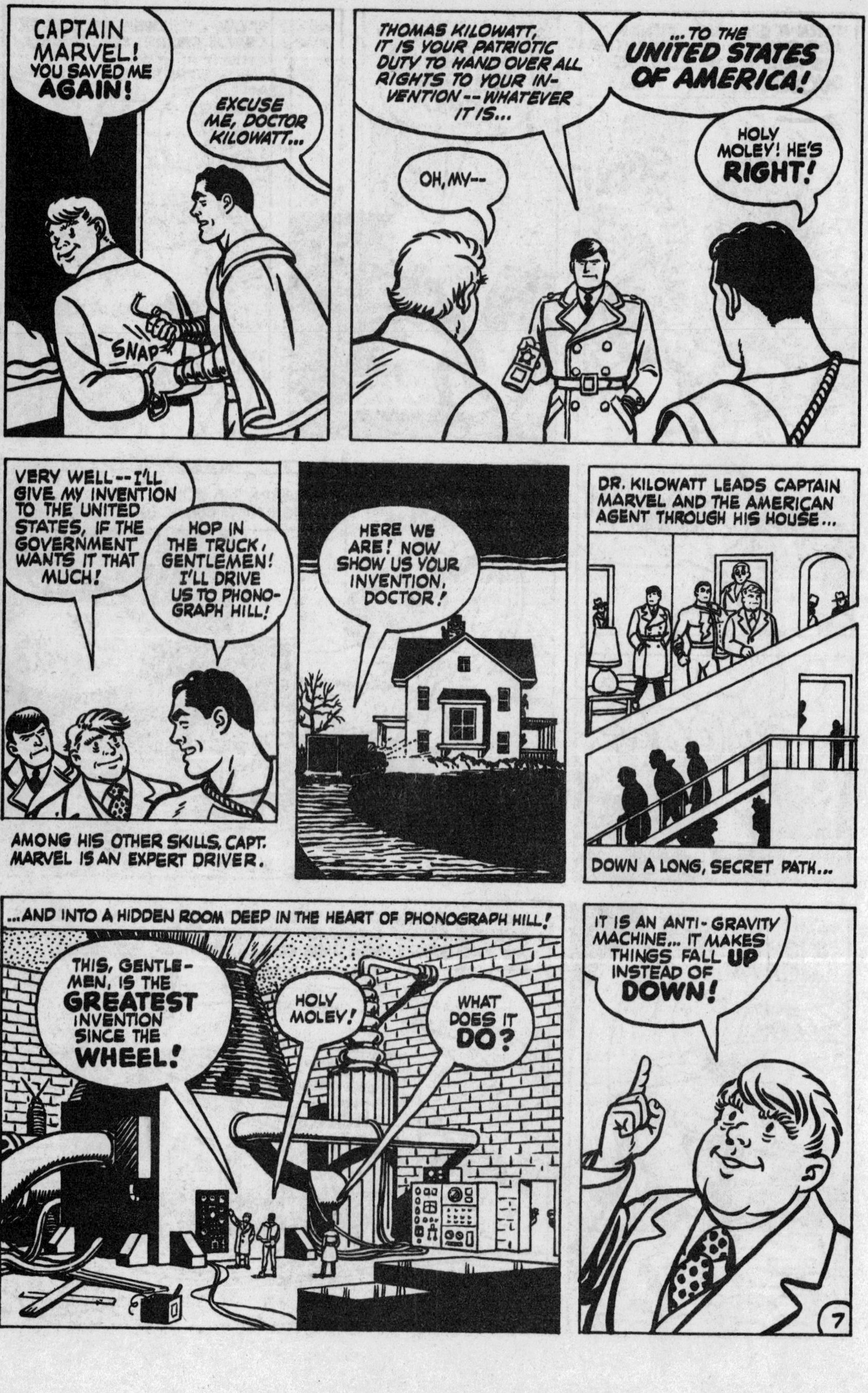
CAPTAIN MARVEL! YOU SAVED ME AGAIN!
EXCUSE ME, DOCTOR KILOWATT...
SNAP
THOMAS KILOWATT, IT IS YOUR PATRIOTIC DUTY TO HAND OVER ALL RIGHTS TO YOUR INVENTION -- WHATEVER IT IS...
...TO THE UNITED STATES OF AMERICA!
OH, MY--
HOLY MOLEY! HE'S RIGHT!
VERY WELL -- I'LL GIVE MY INVENTION TO THE UNITED STATES, IF THE GOVERNMENT WANTS IT THAT MUCH!
HOP IN THE TRUCK, GENTLEMEN! I'LL DRIVE US TO PHONOGRAPH HILL!
AMONG HIS OTHER SKILLS, CAPT. MARVEL IS AN EXPERT DRIVER.
HERE WE ARE! NOW SHOW US YOUR INVENTION, DOCTOR!
DR. KILOWATT LEADS CAPTAIN MARVEL AND THE AMERICAN AGENT THROUGH HIS HOUSE...
DOWN A LONG, SECRET PATH...
...AND INTO A HIDDEN ROOM DEEP IN THE HEART OF PHONOGRAPH HILL!
THIS, GENTLEMEN, IS THE GREATEST INVENTION SINCE THE WHEEL!
HOLY MOLEY!
WHAT DOES IT DO?
IT IS AN ANTI-GRAVITY MACHINE... IT MAKES THINGS FALL UP INSTEAD OF DOWN!
7

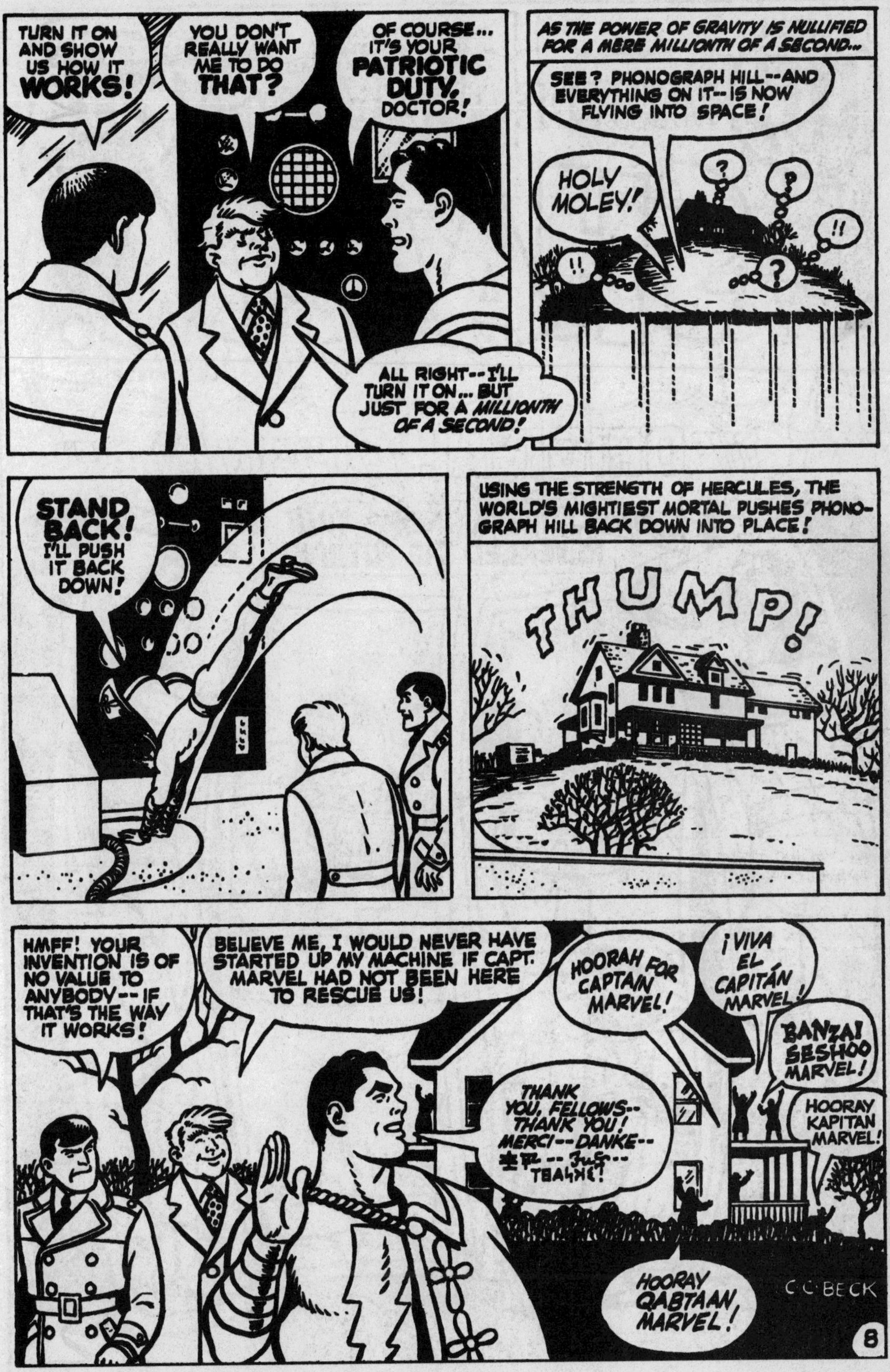
TURN IT ON AND SHOW US HOW IT WORKS!
YOU DON'T REALLY WANT ME TO DO THAT?
OF COURSE... IT'S YOUR PATRIOTIC DUTY, DOCTOR!
ALL RIGHT--I'LL TURN IT ON... BUT JUST FOR A MILLIONTH OF A SECOND!
AS THE POWER OF GRAVITY IS NULLIFIED FOR A MERE MILLIONTH OF A SECOND...
SEE? PHONOGRAPH HILL--AND EVERYTHING ON IT--IS NOW FLYING INTO SPACE!
HOLY MOLEY!
?
?
!!
!!
?
STAND BACK! I'LL PUSH IT BACK DOWN!
USING THE STRENGTH OF HERCULES, THE WORLD'S MIGHTIEST MORTAL PUSHES PHONOGRAPH HILL BACK DOWN INTO PLACE!
THUMP!
HMFF! YOUR INVENTION IS OF NO VALUE TO ANYBODY--IF THAT'S THE WAY IT WORKS!
BELIEVE ME, I WOULD NEVER HAVE STARTED UP MY MACHINE IF CAPT. MARVEL HAD NOT BEEN HERE TO RESCUE US!
HOORAH FOR CAPTAIN MARVEL!
¡VIVA EL CAPITÁN MARVEL!
BANZAI SESHOO MARVEL!
HOORAY KAPITAN MARVEL!
THANK YOU, FELLOWS--THANK YOU! MERCI--DANKE--
HOORAY QABTAAN MARVEL!
C.C. BECK
8

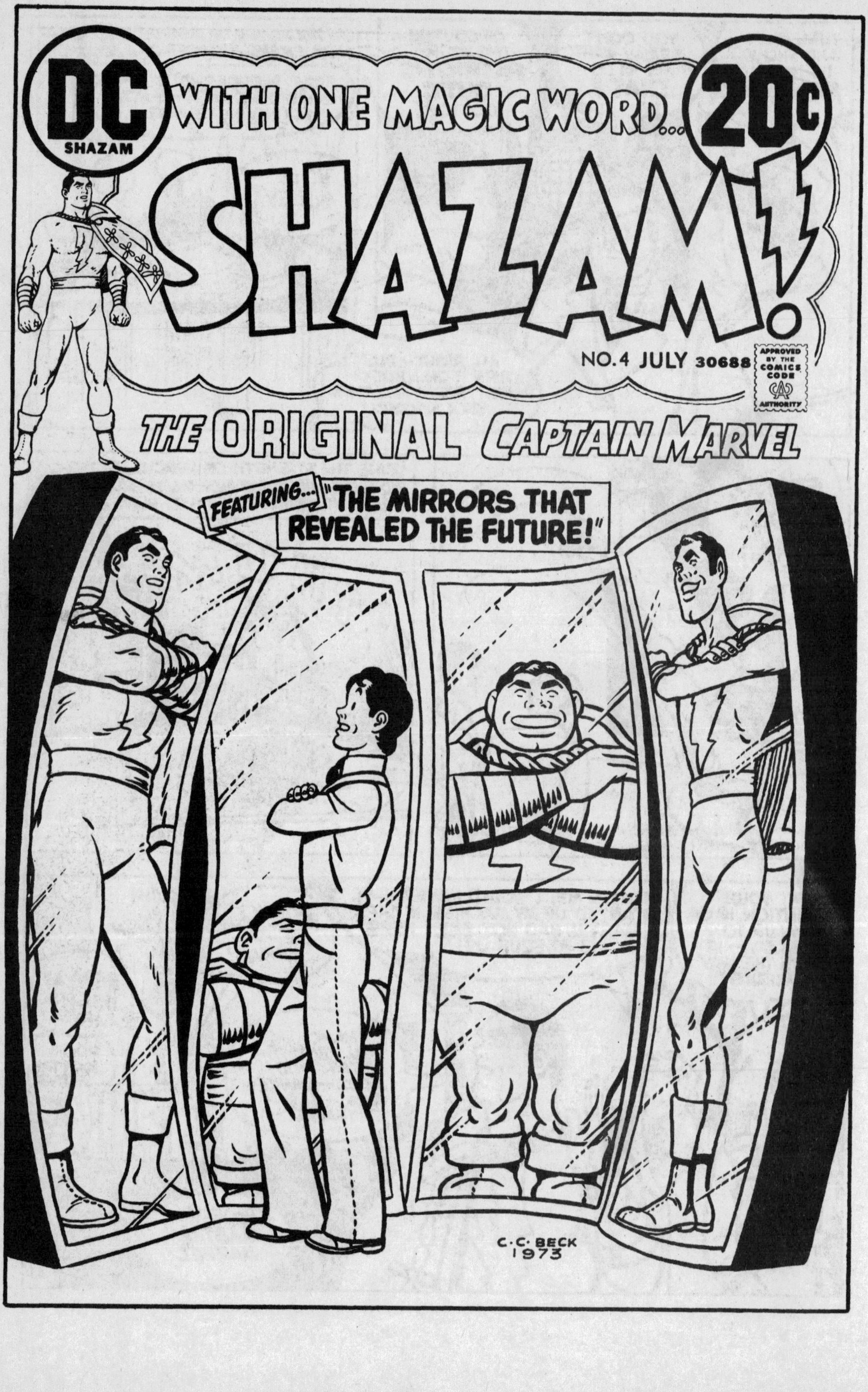
DC
SHAZAM
WITH ONE MAGIC WORD...
20¢
SHAZAM!
NO.4 JULY 30688
APPROVED BY THE COMICS CODE AUTHORITY
THE ORIGINAL CAPTAIN MARVEL
FEATURING... "THE MIRRORS THAT REVEALED THE FUTURE!"
C.C. BECK 1973

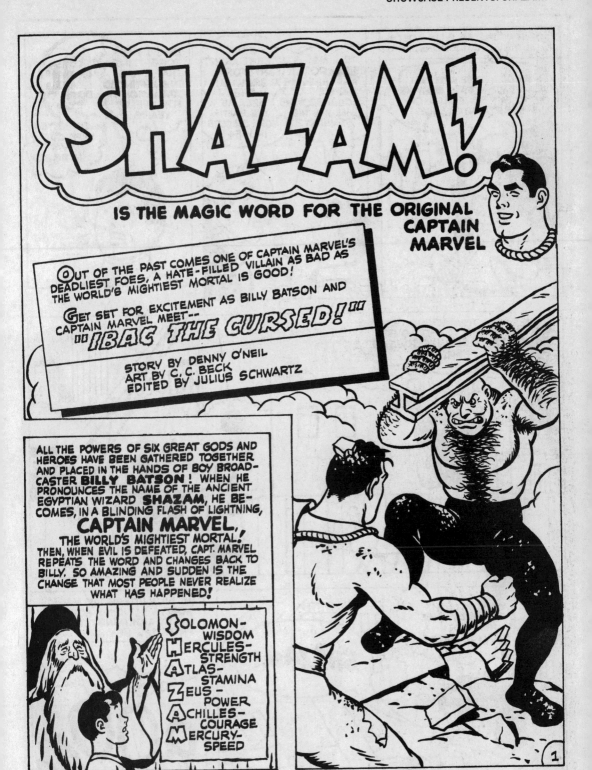

SHAZAM!

IS THE MAGIC WORD FOR THE ORIGINAL CAPTAIN MARVEL

Out of the past comes one of Captain Marvel's deadliest foes, a hate-filled villain as bad as the world's mightiest mortal is good!

Get set for excitement as Billy Batson and Captain Marvel meet--

"IBAC THE CURSED!"

STORY BY DENNY O'NEIL
ART BY C. C. BECK
EDITED BY JULIUS SCHWARTZ

ALL THE POWERS OF SIX GREAT GODS AND HEROES HAVE BEEN GATHERED TOGETHER AND PLACED IN THE HANDS OF BOY BROADCASTER **BILLY BATSON**! WHEN HE PRONOUNCES THE NAME OF THE ANCIENT EGYPTIAN WIZARD **SHAZAM**, HE BECOMES, IN A BLINDING FLASH OF LIGHTNING,
CAPTAIN MARVEL, THE WORLD'S MIGHTIEST MORTAL! THEN, WHEN EVIL IS DEFEATED, CAPT. MARVEL REPEATS THE WORD AND CHANGES BACK TO BILLY. SO AMAZING AND SUDDEN IS THE CHANGE THAT MOST PEOPLE NEVER REALIZE WHAT HAS HAPPENED!

SOLOMON- WISDOM
HERCULES- STRENGTH
ATLAS- STAMINA
ZEUS- POWER
ACHILLES- COURAGE
MERCURY- SPEED

1

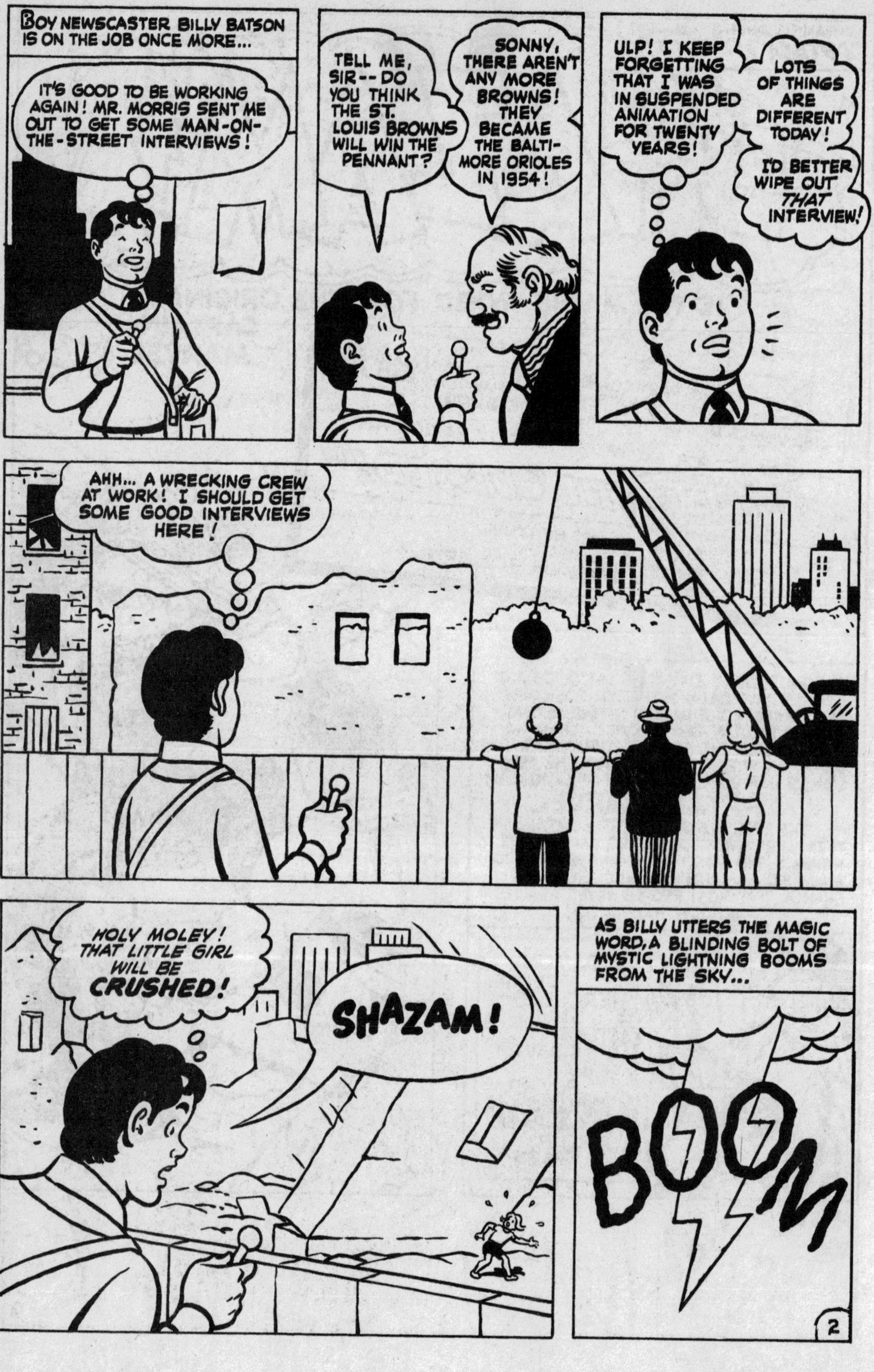
BOY NEWSCASTER BILLY BATSON IS ON THE JOB ONCE MORE...
IT'S GOOD TO BE WORKING AGAIN! MR. MORRIS SENT ME OUT TO GET SOME MAN-ON-THE-STREET INTERVIEWS!
TELL ME, SIR -- DO YOU THINK THE ST. LOUIS BROWNS WILL WIN THE PENNANT?
SONNY, THERE AREN'T ANY MORE BROWNS! THEY BECAME THE BALTI-MORE ORIOLES IN 1954!
ULP! I KEEP FORGETTING THAT I WAS IN SUSPENDED ANIMATION FOR TWENTY YEARS!
LOTS OF THINGS ARE DIFFERENT TODAY!
I'D BETTER WIPE OUT THAT INTERVIEW!
AHH... A WRECKING CREW AT WORK! I SHOULD GET SOME GOOD INTERVIEWS HERE!
HOLY MOLEY! THAT LITTLE GIRL WILL BE CRUSHED!
SHAZAM!
AS BILLY UTTERS THE MAGIC WORD, A BLINDING BOLT OF MYSTIC LIGHTNING BOOMS FROM THE SKY...
BOOM
2

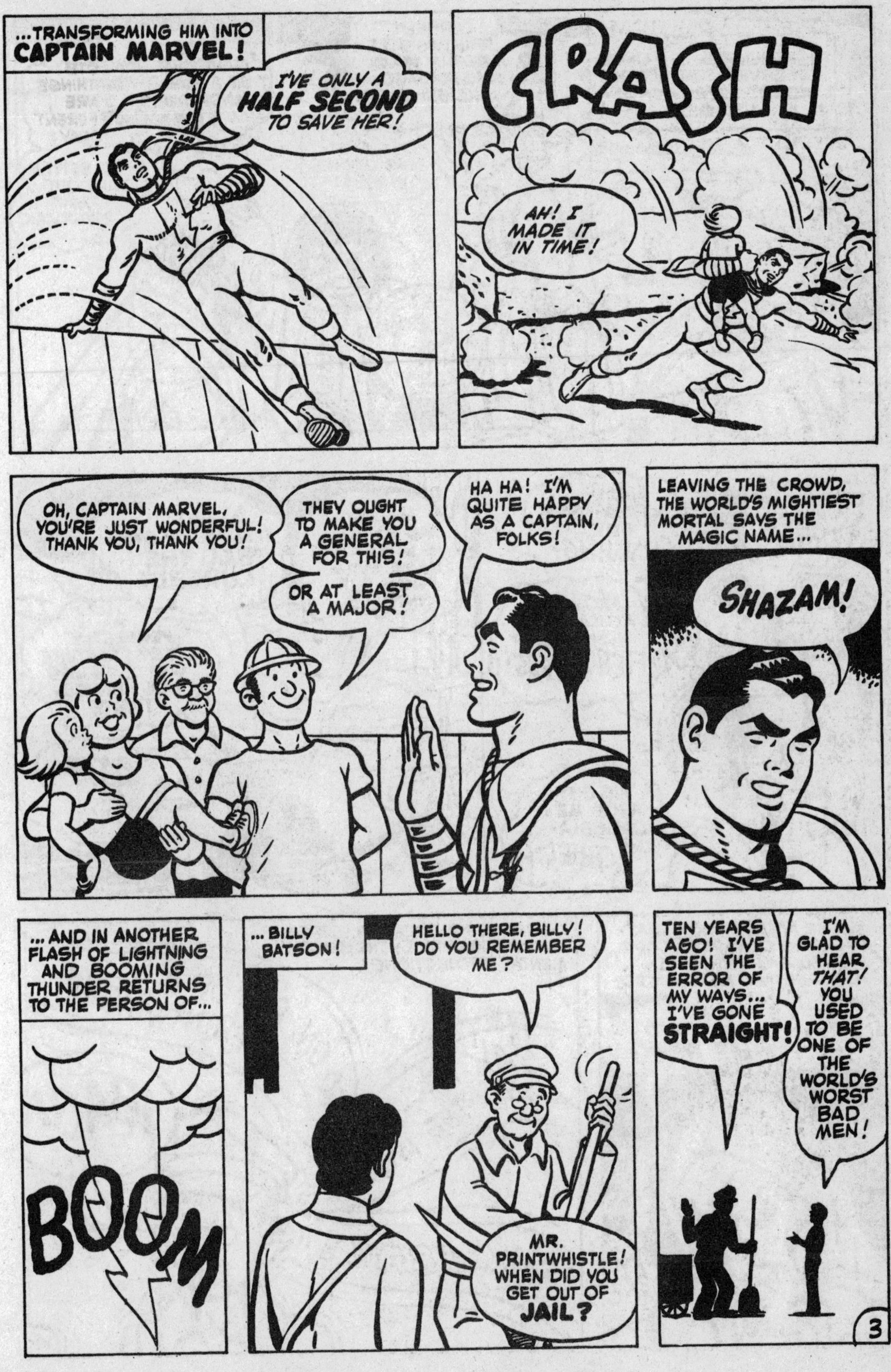
...TRANSFORMING HIM INTO CAPTAIN MARVEL!
I'VE ONLY A HALF SECOND TO SAVE HER!
CRASH
AH! I MADE IT IN TIME!
OH, CAPTAIN MARVEL, YOU'RE JUST WONDERFUL! THANK YOU, THANK YOU!
THEY OUGHT TO MAKE YOU A GENERAL FOR THIS!
OR AT LEAST A MAJOR!
HA HA! I'M QUITE HAPPY AS A CAPTAIN, FOLKS!
LEAVING THE CROWD, THE WORLD'S MIGHTIEST MORTAL SAYS THE MAGIC NAME...
SHAZAM!
... AND IN ANOTHER FLASH OF LIGHTNING AND BOOMING THUNDER RETURNS TO THE PERSON OF...
BOOM
... BILLY BATSON!
HELLO THERE, BILLY! DO YOU REMEMBER ME?
MR. PRINTWHISTLE! WHEN DID YOU GET OUT OF JAIL?
TEN YEARS AGO! I'VE SEEN THE ERROR OF MY WAYS... I'VE GONE STRAIGHT!
I'M GLAD TO HEAR THAT! YOU USED TO BE ONE OF THE WORLD'S WORST BAD MEN!
3

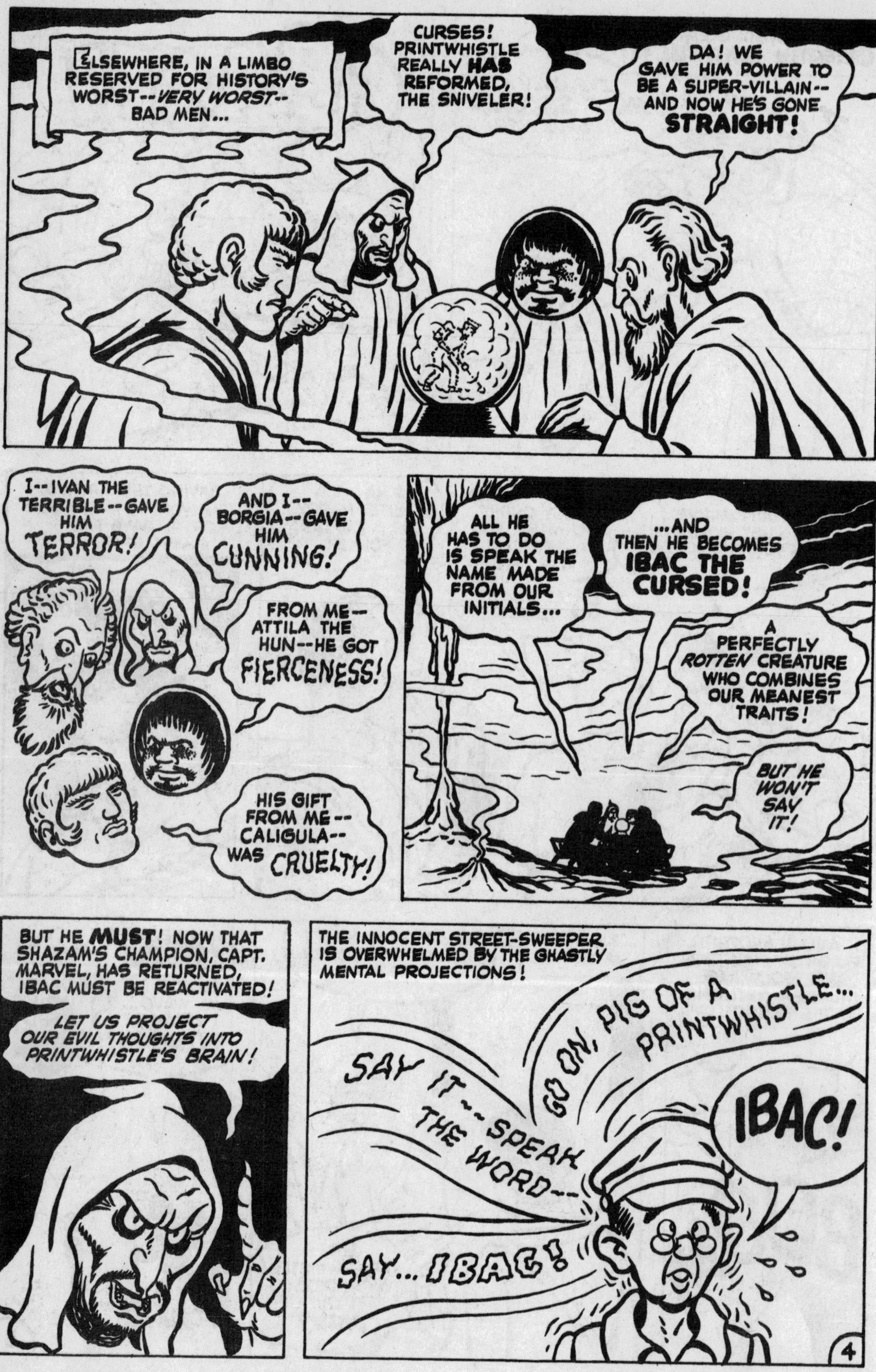
ELSEWHERE, IN A LIMBO RESERVED FOR HISTORY'S WORST--*VERY WORST*--BAD MEN...
CURSES! PRINTWHISTLE REALLY **HAS** REFORMED, THE SNIVELER!
DA! WE GAVE HIM POWER TO BE A SUPER-VILLAIN--AND NOW HE'S GONE **STRAIGHT!**
I--IVAN THE TERRIBLE--GAVE HIM TERROR!
AND I--BORGIA--GAVE HIM CUNNING!
FROM ME--ATTILA THE HUN--HE GOT FIERCENESS!
HIS GIFT FROM ME--CALIGULA--WAS CRUELTY!
ALL HE HAS TO DO IS SPEAK THE NAME MADE FROM OUR INITIALS...
...AND THEN HE BECOMES **IBAC THE CURSED!**
A PERFECTLY *ROTTEN* CREATURE WHO COMBINES OUR MEANEST TRAITS!
BUT HE WON'T SAY IT!
BUT HE **MUST**! NOW THAT SHAZAM'S CHAMPION, CAPT. MARVEL, HAS RETURNED, IBAC MUST BE REACTIVATED!
LET US PROJECT OUR EVIL THOUGHTS INTO PRINTWHISTLE'S BRAIN!
THE INNOCENT STREET-SWEEPER IS OVERWHELMED BY THE GHASTLY MENTAL PROJECTIONS!
GO ON, PIG OF A PRINTWHISTLE...
SAY IT--SPEAK THE WORD--
SAY... IBAC!
IBAC!
4

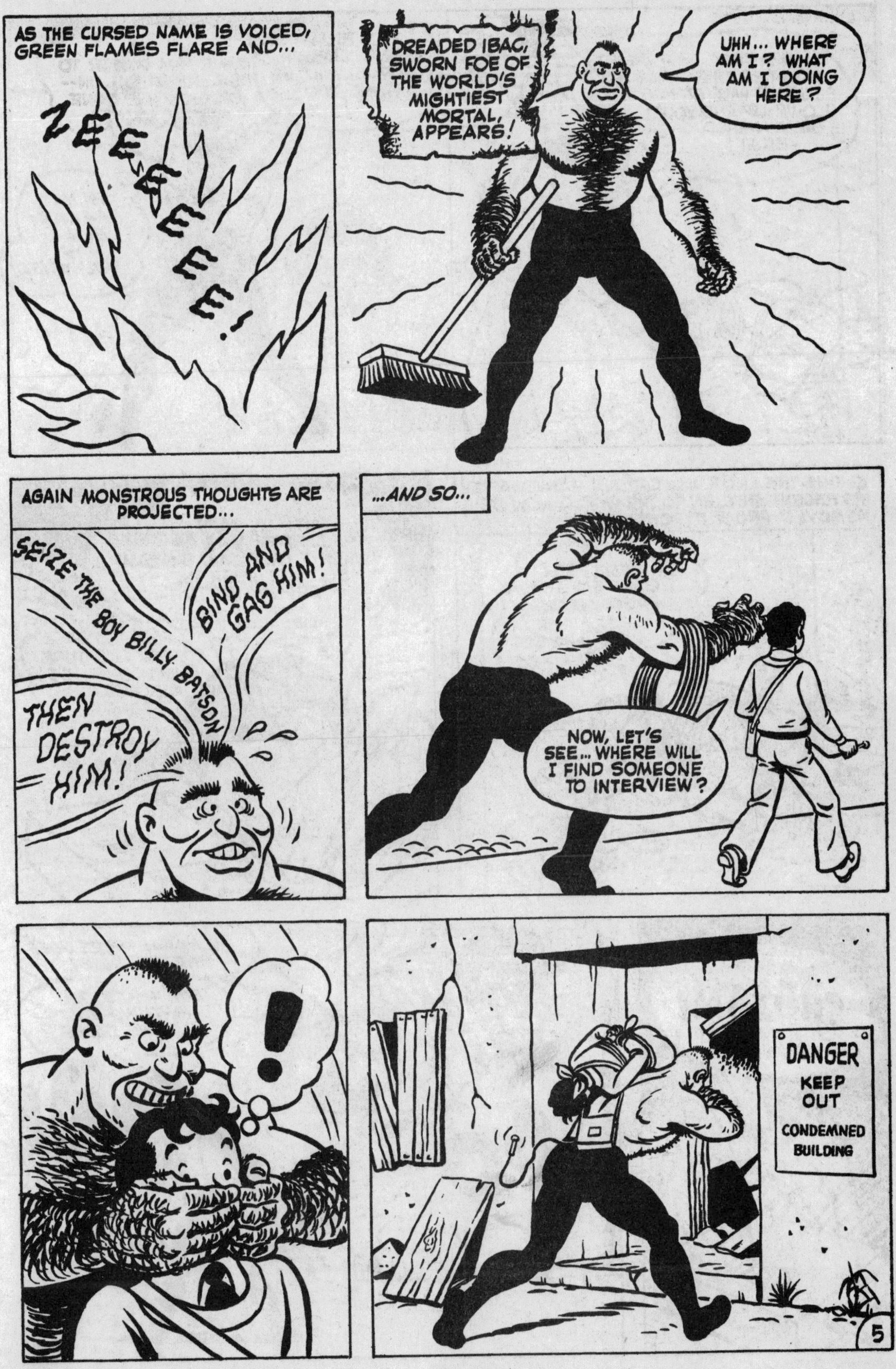
AS THE CURSED NAME IS VOICED, GREEN FLAMES FLARE AND...
ZEEEEEEE!
DREADED IBAC, SWORN FOE OF THE WORLD'S MIGHTIEST MORTAL, APPEARS!
UHH... WHERE AM I? WHAT AM I DOING HERE?
AGAIN MONSTROUS THOUGHTS ARE PROJECTED...
SEIZE THE BOY BILLY BATSON
BIND AND GAG HIM!
THEN DESTROY HIM!
...AND SO...
NOW, LET'S SEE... WHERE WILL I FIND SOMEONE TO INTERVIEW?
!
DANGER
KEEP OUT
CONDEMNED BUILDING
5

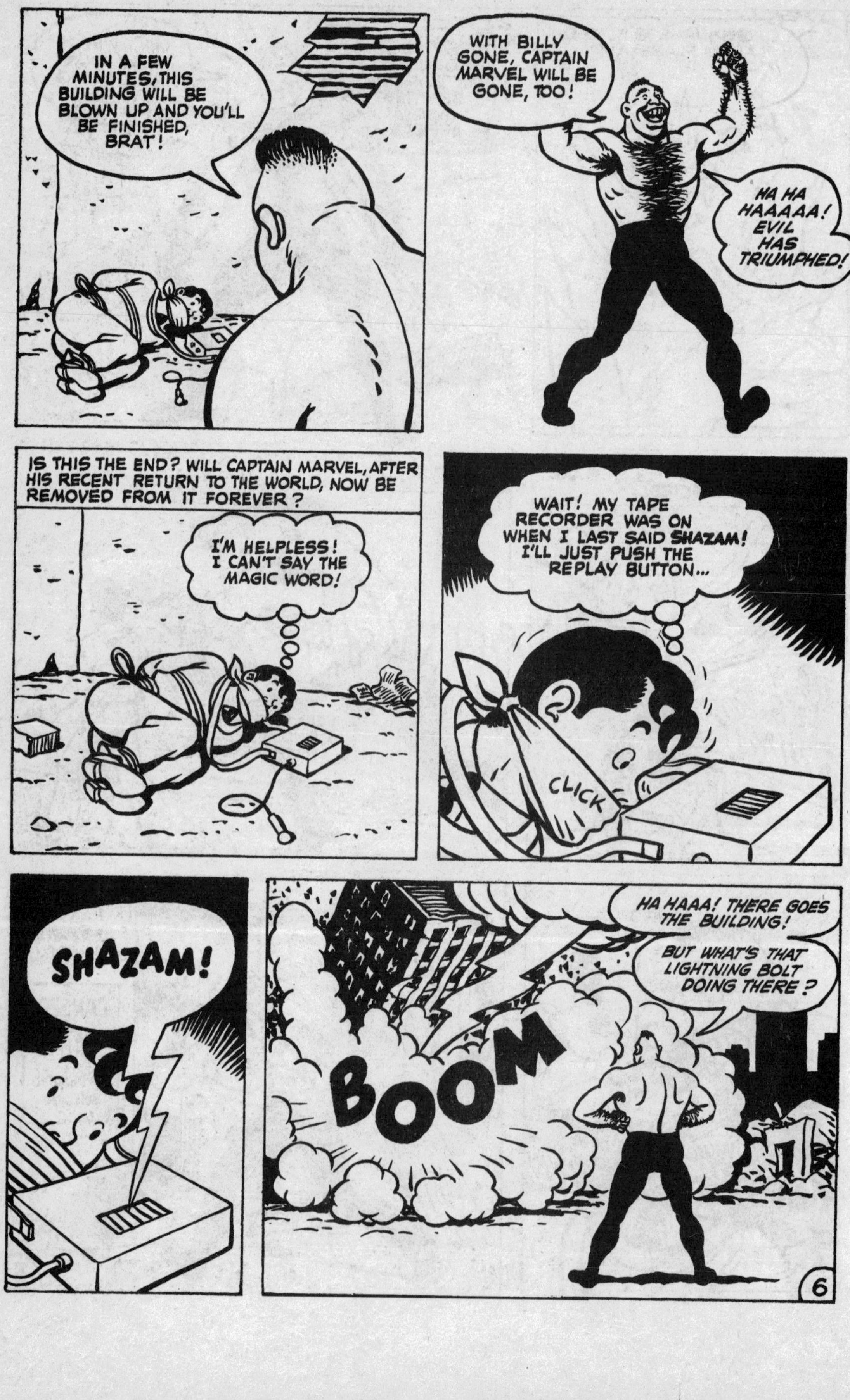
IN A FEW MINUTES, THIS BUILDING WILL BE BLOWN UP AND YOU'LL BE FINISHED, BRAT!
WITH BILLY GONE, CAPTAIN MARVEL WILL BE GONE, TOO!
HA HA HAAAAA! EVIL HAS TRIUMPHED!
IS THIS THE END? WILL CAPTAIN MARVEL, AFTER HIS RECENT RETURN TO THE WORLD, NOW BE REMOVED FROM IT FOREVER?
I'M HELPLESS! I CAN'T SAY THE MAGIC WORD!
WAIT! MY TAPE RECORDER WAS ON WHEN I LAST SAID SHAZAM! I'LL JUST PUSH THE REPLAY BUTTON...
CLICK
SHAZAM!
HA HAAA! THERE GOES THE BUILDING!
BUT WHAT'S THAT LIGHTNING BOLT DOING THERE?
BOOM
6

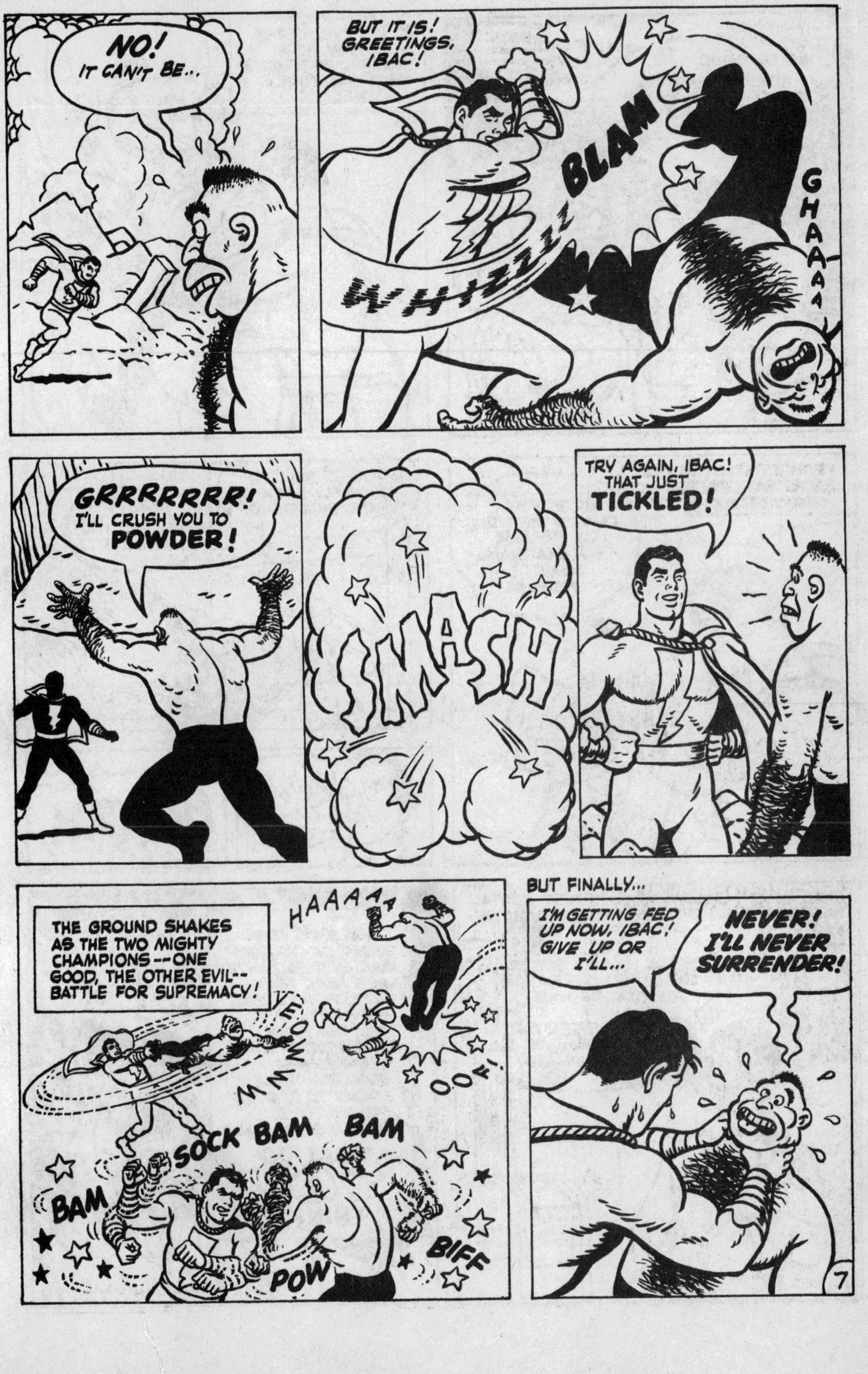
NO! IT CAN'T BE...
BUT IT IS! GREETINGS, IBAC!
BLAM
WHIZZZ
GHAAAAA
GRRRRRRR! I'LL CRUSH YOU TO POWDER!
SMASH
TRY AGAIN, IBAC! THAT JUST TICKLED!
THE GROUND SHAKES AS THE TWO MIGHTY CHAMPIONS--ONE GOOD, THE OTHER EVIL--BATTLE FOR SUPREMACY!
HAAAAA
EEOWWMMM
OOF!
SOCK BAM BAM
BAM
POW
BIFF
BUT FINALLY...
I'M GETTING FED UP NOW, IBAC! GIVE UP OR I'LL...
NEVER! I'LL NEVER SURRENDER!
7

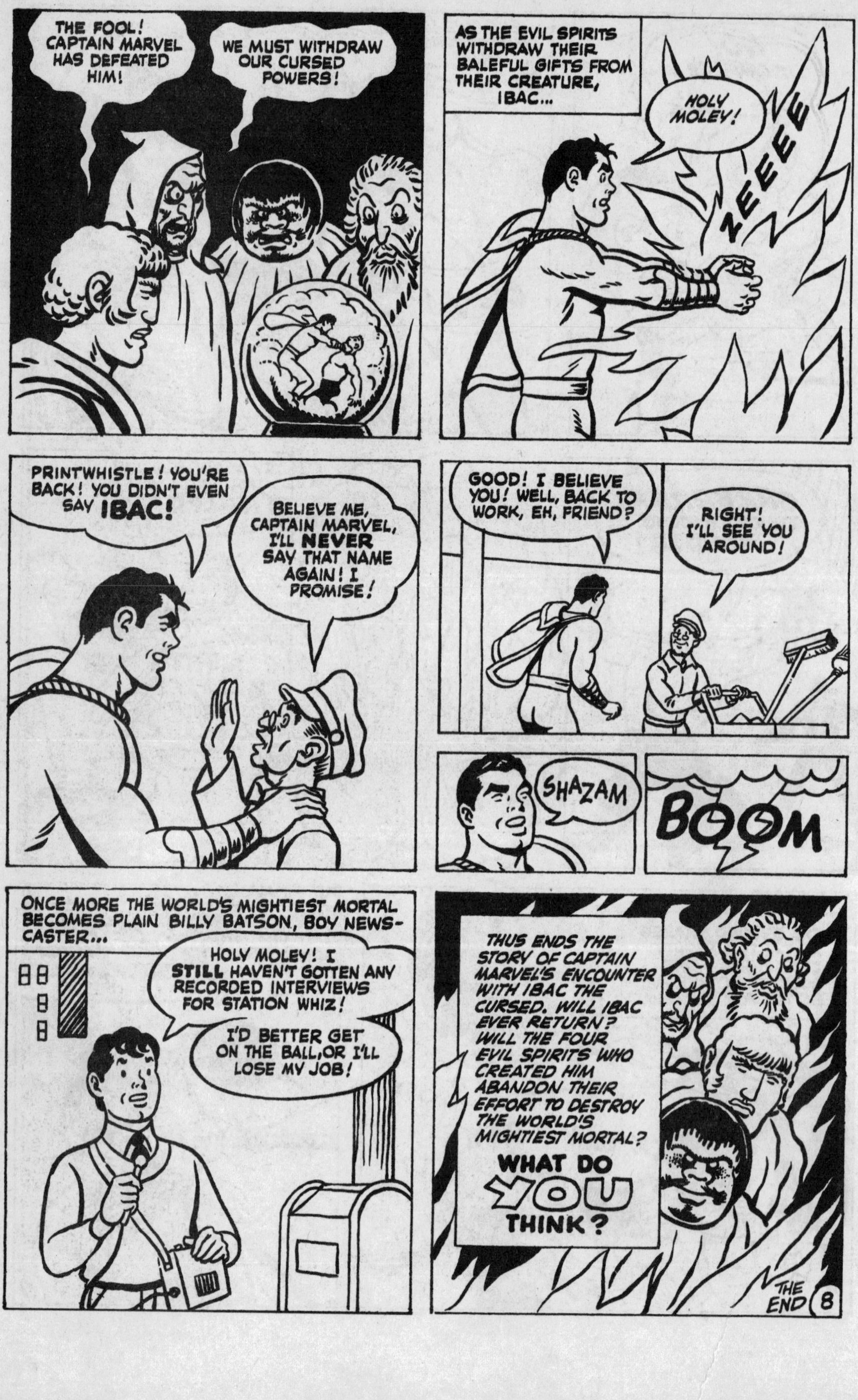
THE FOOL! CAPTAIN MARVEL HAS DEFEATED HIM!
WE MUST WITHDRAW OUR CURSED POWERS!
AS THE EVIL SPIRITS WITHDRAW THEIR BALEFUL GIFTS FROM THEIR CREATURE, IBAC...
HOLY MOLEY!
ZEEEE
PRINTWHISTLE! YOU'RE BACK! YOU DIDN'T EVEN SAY IBAC!
BELIEVE ME, CAPTAIN MARVEL, I'LL NEVER SAY THAT NAME AGAIN! I PROMISE!
GOOD! I BELIEVE YOU! WELL, BACK TO WORK, EH, FRIEND?
RIGHT! I'LL SEE YOU AROUND!
SHAZAM
BOOM
ONCE MORE THE WORLD'S MIGHTIEST MORTAL BECOMES PLAIN BILLY BATSON, BOY NEWS-CASTER...
HOLY MOLEY! I STILL HAVEN'T GOTTEN ANY RECORDED INTERVIEWS FOR STATION WHIZ!
I'D BETTER GET ON THE BALL, OR I'LL LOSE MY JOB!
THUS ENDS THE STORY OF CAPTAIN MARVEL'S ENCOUNTER WITH IBAC THE CURSED. WILL IBAC EVER RETURN? WILL THE FOUR EVIL SPIRITS WHO CREATED HIM ABANDON THEIR EFFORT TO DESTROY THE WORLD'S MIGHTIEST MORTAL?
WHAT DO YOU THINK?
THE END
8

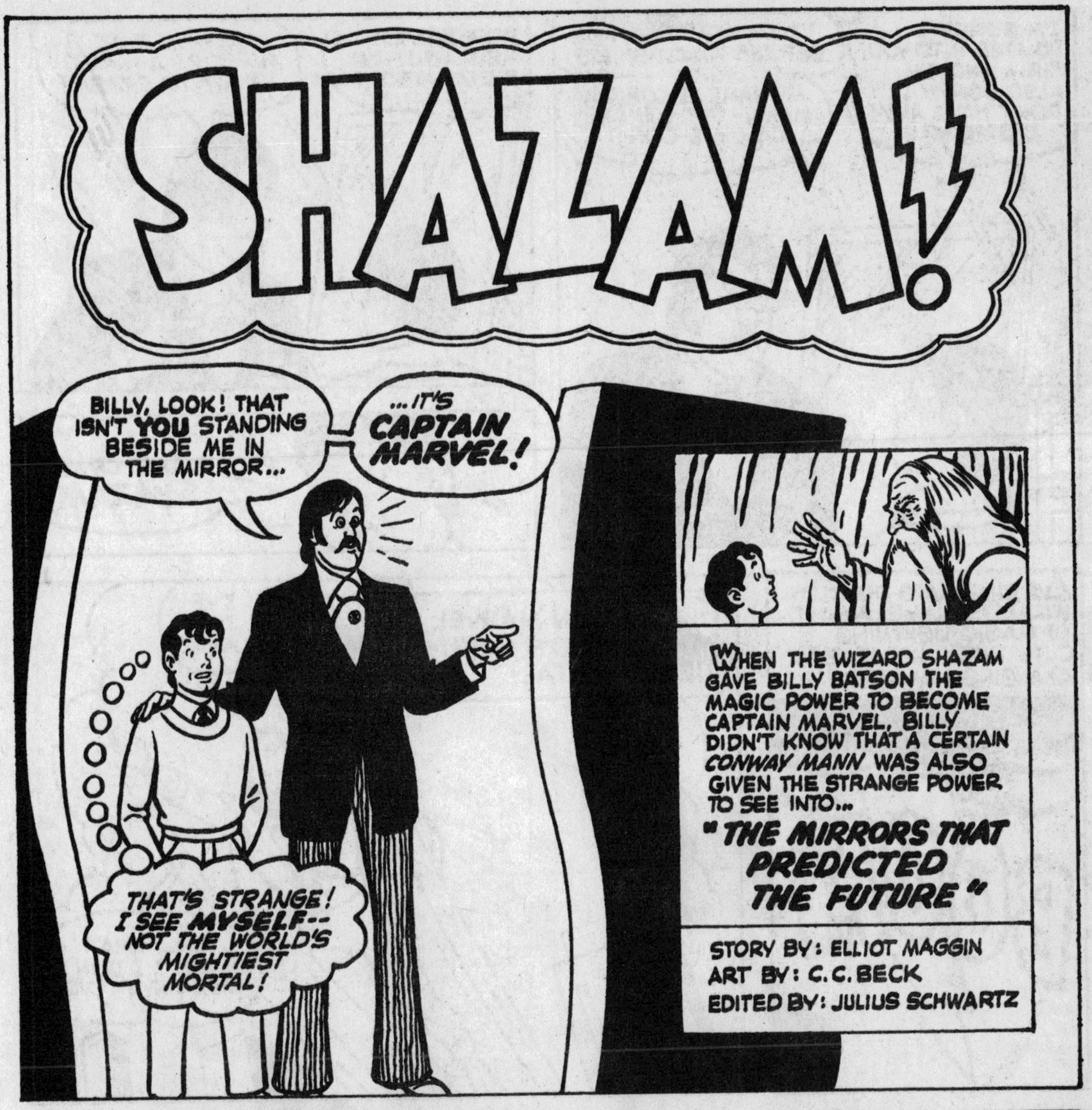
SHAZAM!
BILLY, LOOK! THAT ISN'T YOU STANDING BESIDE ME IN THE MIRROR...
...IT'S CAPTAIN MARVEL!
THAT'S STRANGE! I SEE MYSELF--NOT THE WORLD'S MIGHTIEST MORTAL!
WHEN THE WIZARD SHAZAM GAVE BILLY BATSON THE MAGIC POWER TO BECOME CAPTAIN MARVEL, BILLY DIDN'T KNOW THAT A CERTAIN CONWAY MANN WAS ALSO GIVEN THE STRANGE POWER TO SEE INTO...
"THE MIRRORS THAT PREDICTED THE FUTURE"
STORY BY: ELLIOT MAGGIN
ART BY: C.C. BECK
EDITED BY: JULIUS SCHWARTZ

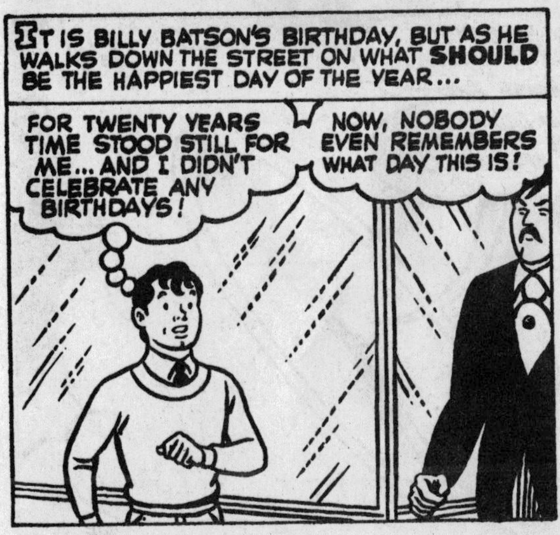
IT IS BILLY BATSON'S BIRTHDAY, BUT AS HE WALKS DOWN THE STREET ON WHAT SHOULD BE THE HAPPIEST DAY OF THE YEAR...
FOR TWENTY YEARS TIME STOOD STILL FOR ME... AND I DIDN'T CELEBRATE ANY BIRTHDAYS!
NOW, NOBODY EVEN REMEMBERS WHAT DAY THIS IS!

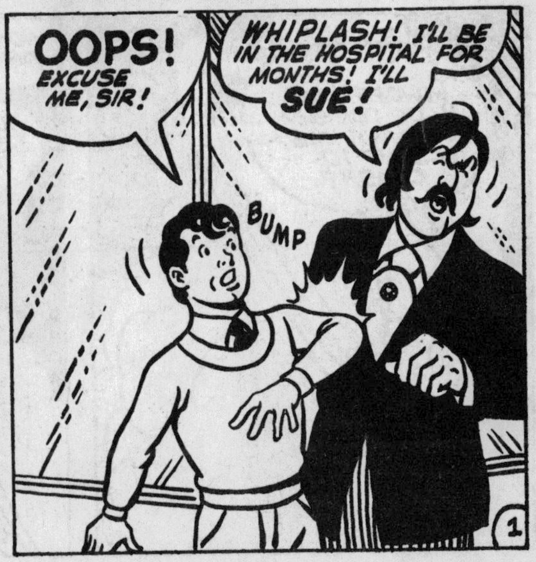
OOPS! EXCUSE ME, SIR!
WHIPLASH! I'LL BE IN THE HOSPITAL FOR MONTHS! I'LL SUE!
BUMP
1

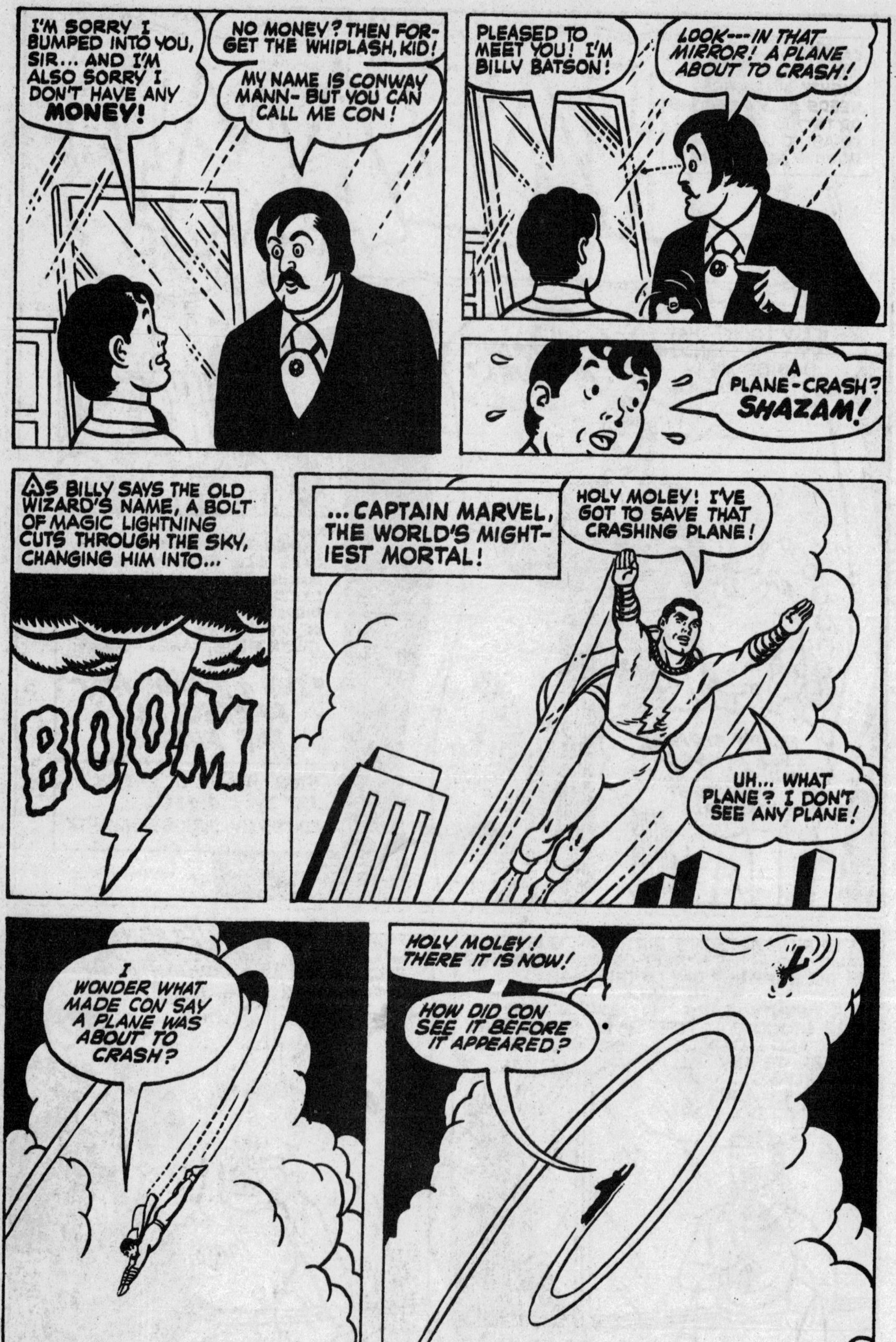
I'M SORRY I BUMPED INTO YOU, SIR... AND I'M ALSO SORRY I DON'T HAVE ANY MONEY!
NO MONEY? THEN FORGET THE WHIPLASH, KID!
MY NAME IS CONWAY MANN- BUT YOU CAN CALL ME CON!
PLEASED TO MEET YOU! I'M BILLY BATSON!
LOOK---IN THAT MIRROR! A PLANE ABOUT TO CRASH!
A PLANE-CRASH? SHAZAM!
AS BILLY SAYS THE OLD WIZARD'S NAME, A BOLT OF MAGIC LIGHTNING CUTS THROUGH THE SKY, CHANGING HIM INTO...
BOOM
...CAPTAIN MARVEL, THE WORLD'S MIGHTIEST MORTAL!
HOLY MOLEY! I'VE GOT TO SAVE THAT CRASHING PLANE!
UH... WHAT PLANE? I DON'T SEE ANY PLANE!
I WONDER WHAT MADE CON SAY A PLANE WAS ABOUT TO CRASH?
HOLY MOLEY! THERE IT IS NOW!
HOW DID CON SEE IT BEFORE IT APPEARED?
2

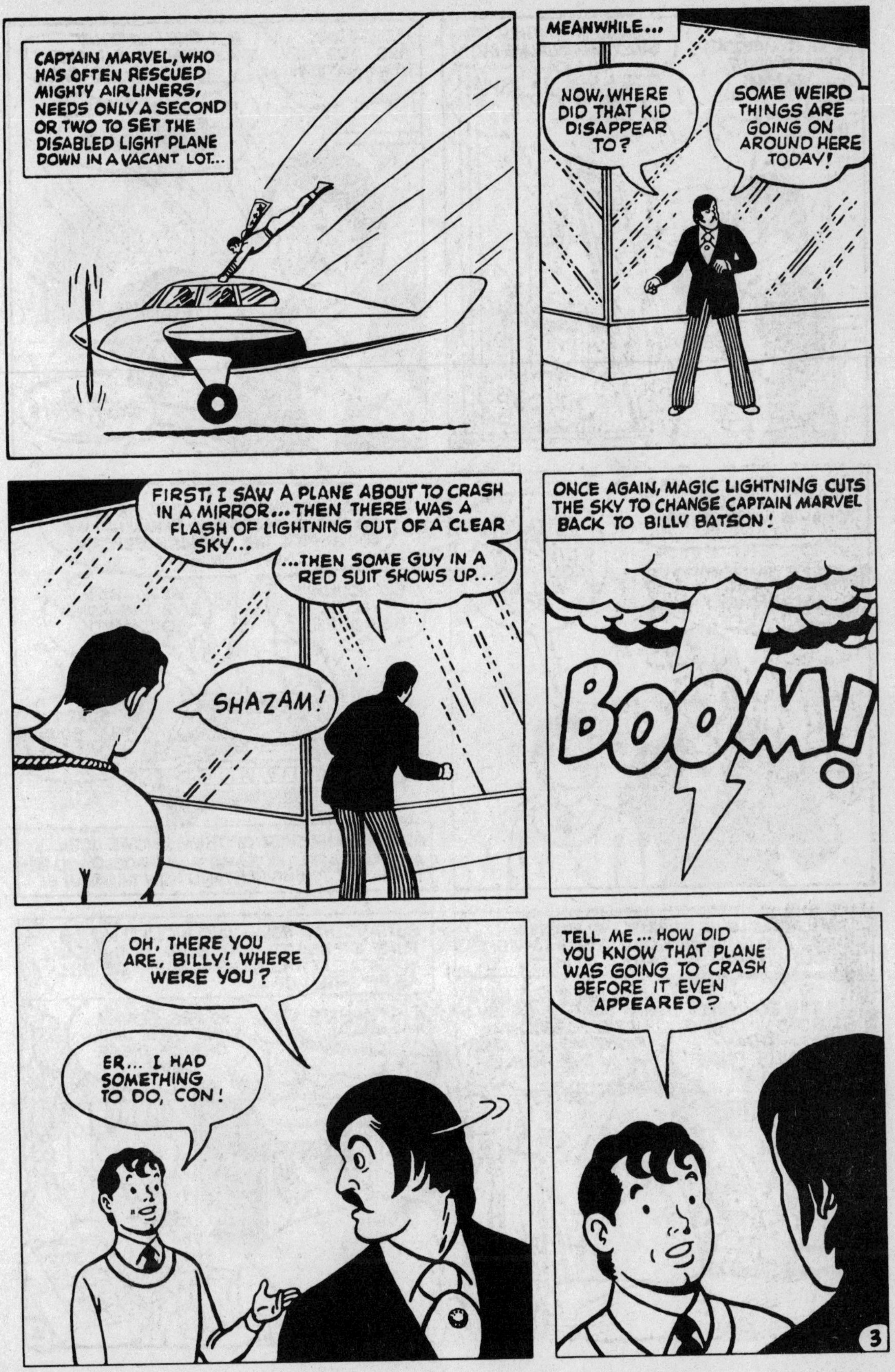
CAPTAIN MARVEL, WHO HAS OFTEN RESCUED MIGHTY AIRLINERS, NEEDS ONLY A SECOND OR TWO TO SET THE DISABLED LIGHT PLANE DOWN IN A VACANT LOT...
MEANWHILE...
NOW, WHERE DID THAT KID DISAPPEAR TO?
SOME WEIRD THINGS ARE GOING ON AROUND HERE TODAY!
FIRST, I SAW A PLANE ABOUT TO CRASH IN A MIRROR... THEN THERE WAS A FLASH OF LIGHTNING OUT OF A CLEAR SKY...
...THEN SOME GUY IN A RED SUIT SHOWS UP...
SHAZAM!
ONCE AGAIN, MAGIC LIGHTNING CUTS THE SKY TO CHANGE CAPTAIN MARVEL BACK TO BILLY BATSON!
BOOM!
OH, THERE YOU ARE, BILLY! WHERE WERE YOU?
ER... I HAD SOMETHING TO DO, CON!
TELL ME... HOW DID YOU KNOW THAT PLANE WAS GOING TO CRASH BEFORE IT EVEN APPEARED?
3

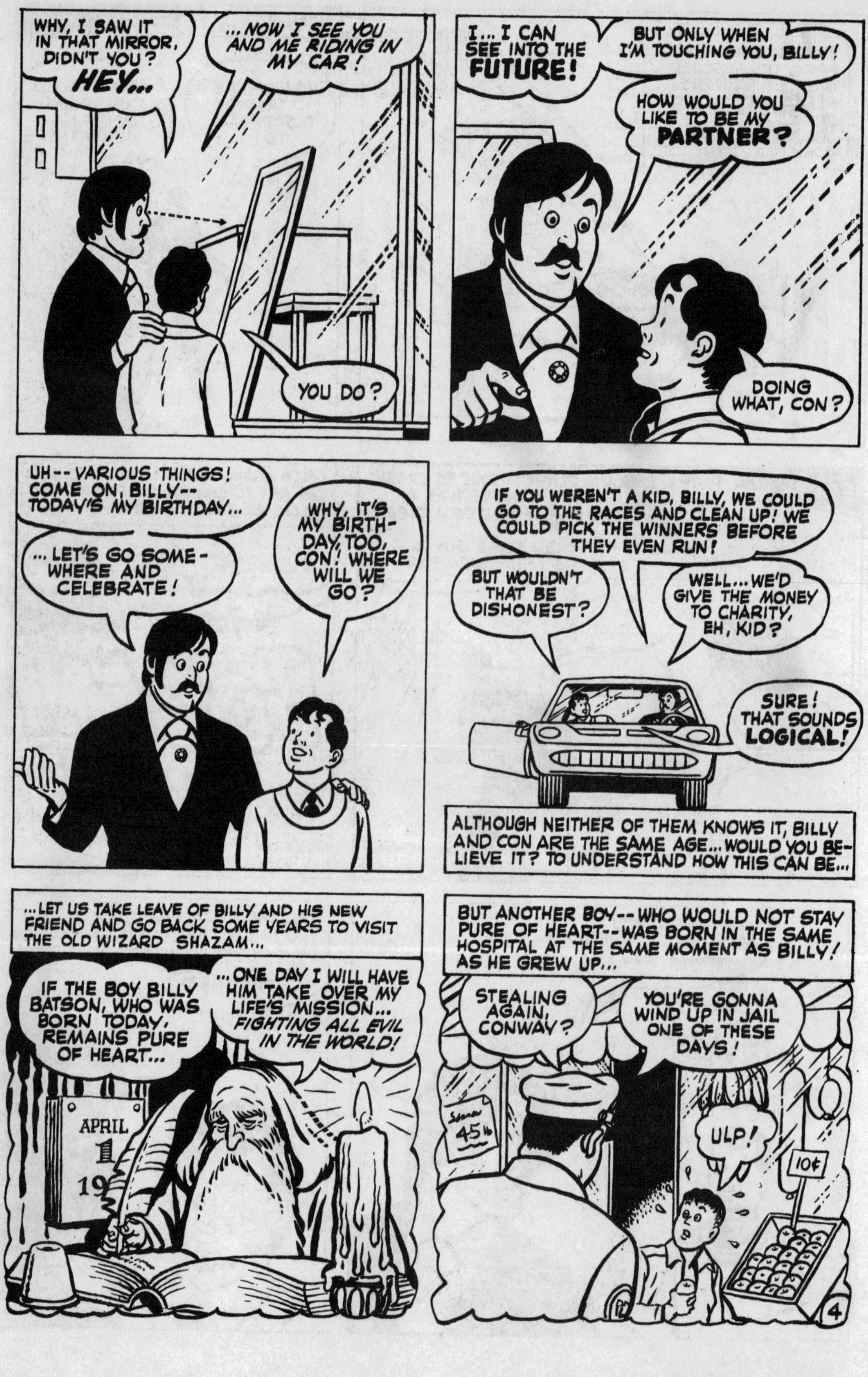
WHY, I SAW IT IN THAT MIRROR, DIDN'T YOU? HEY...
...NOW I SEE YOU AND ME RIDING IN MY CAR!
YOU DO?
I... I CAN SEE INTO THE FUTURE!
BUT ONLY WHEN I'M TOUCHING YOU, BILLY!
HOW WOULD YOU LIKE TO BE MY PARTNER?
DOING WHAT, CON?
UH-- VARIOUS THINGS! COME ON, BILLY-- TODAY'S MY BIRTHDAY...
... LET'S GO SOME-WHERE AND CELEBRATE!
WHY, IT'S MY BIRTH-DAY, TOO, CON! WHERE WILL WE GO?
IF YOU WEREN'T A KID, BILLY, WE COULD GO TO THE RACES AND CLEAN UP! WE COULD PICK THE WINNERS BEFORE THEY EVEN RUN!
BUT WOULDN'T THAT BE DISHONEST?
WELL... WE'D GIVE THE MONEY TO CHARITY, EH, KID?
SURE! THAT SOUNDS LOGICAL!
ALTHOUGH NEITHER OF THEM KNOWS IT, BILLY AND CON ARE THE SAME AGE... WOULD YOU BE-LIEVE IT? TO UNDERSTAND HOW THIS CAN BE...
...LET US TAKE LEAVE OF BILLY AND HIS NEW FRIEND AND GO BACK SOME YEARS TO VISIT THE OLD WIZARD SHAZAM...
IF THE BOY BILLY BATSON, WHO WAS BORN TODAY, REMAINS PURE OF HEART...
...ONE DAY I WILL HAVE HIM TAKE OVER MY LIFE'S MISSION... FIGHTING ALL EVIL IN THE WORLD!
APRIL 1 19
BUT ANOTHER BOY-- WHO WOULD NOT STAY PURE OF HEART-- WAS BORN IN THE SAME HOSPITAL AT THE SAME MOMENT AS BILLY! AS HE GREW UP...
STEALING AGAIN, CONWAY?
YOU'RE GONNA WIND UP IN JAIL ONE OF THESE DAYS!
ULP!
10¢
4

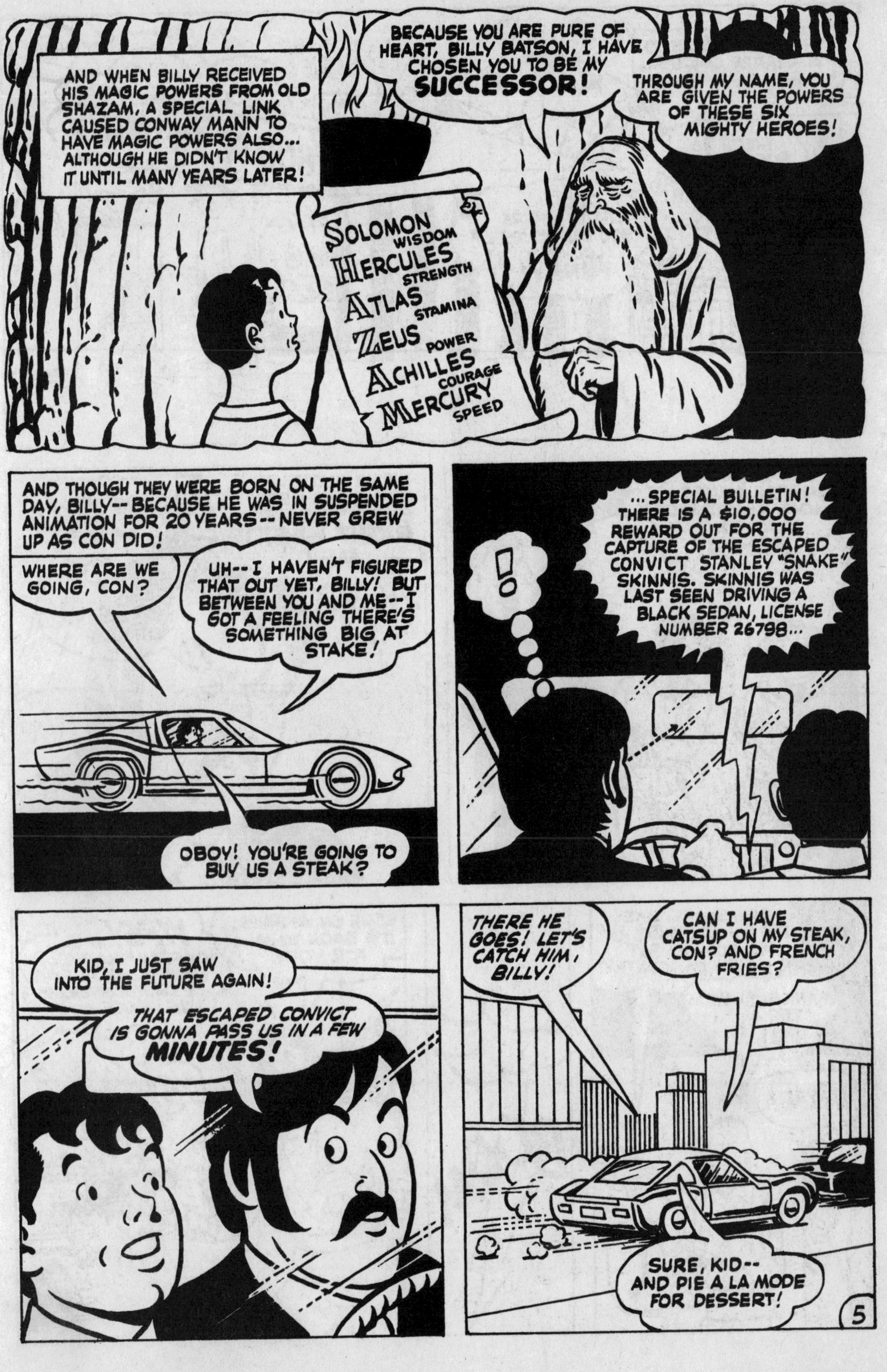
AND WHEN BILLY RECEIVED HIS MAGIC POWERS FROM OLD SHAZAM, A SPECIAL LINK CAUSED CONWAY MANN TO HAVE MAGIC POWERS ALSO... ALTHOUGH HE DIDN'T KNOW IT UNTIL MANY YEARS LATER!
BECAUSE YOU ARE PURE OF HEART, BILLY BATSON, I HAVE CHOSEN YOU TO BE MY SUCCESSOR!
THROUGH MY NAME, YOU ARE GIVEN THE POWERS OF THESE SIX MIGHTY HEROES!
SOLOMON WISDOM
HERCULES STRENGTH
ATLAS STAMINA
ZEUS POWER
ACHILLES COURAGE
MERCURY SPEED
AND THOUGH THEY WERE BORN ON THE SAME DAY, BILLY-- BECAUSE HE WAS IN SUSPENDED ANIMATION FOR 20 YEARS -- NEVER GREW UP AS CON DID!
WHERE ARE WE GOING, CON?
UH-- I HAVEN'T FIGURED THAT OUT YET, BILLY! BUT BETWEEN YOU AND ME-- I GOT A FEELING THERE'S SOMETHING BIG AT STAKE!
OBOY! YOU'RE GOING TO BUY US A STEAK?
...SPECIAL BULLETIN! THERE IS A $10,000 REWARD OUT FOR THE CAPTURE OF THE ESCAPED CONVICT STANLEY "SNAKE" SKINNIS. SKINNIS WAS LAST SEEN DRIVING A BLACK SEDAN, LICENSE NUMBER 26798...
!
KID, I JUST SAW INTO THE FUTURE AGAIN!
THAT ESCAPED CONVICT IS GONNA PASS US IN A FEW MINUTES!
THERE HE GOES! LET'S CATCH HIM, BILLY!
CAN I HAVE CATSUP ON MY STEAK, CON? AND FRENCH FRIES?
SURE, KID-- AND PIE A LA MODE FOR DESSERT!
5

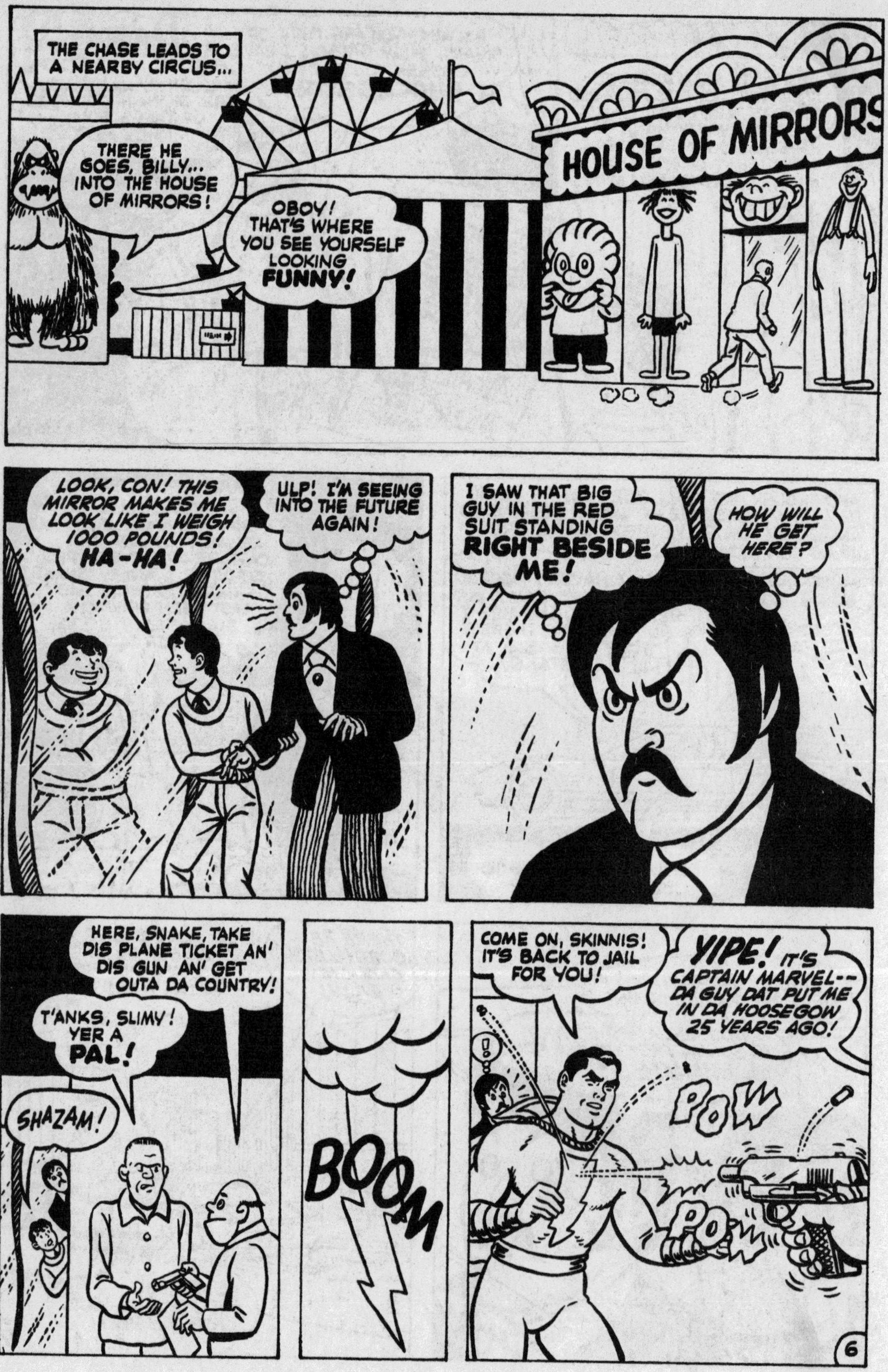
THE CHASE LEADS TO A NEARBY CIRCUS...
HOUSE OF MIRRORS
THERE HE GOES, BILLY... INTO THE HOUSE OF MIRRORS!
OBOY! THAT'S WHERE YOU SEE YOURSELF LOOKING FUNNY!
LOOK, CON! THIS MIRROR MAKES ME LOOK LIKE I WEIGH 1000 POUNDS! HA-HA!
ULP! I'M SEEING INTO THE FUTURE AGAIN!
I SAW THAT BIG GUY IN THE RED SUIT STANDING RIGHT BESIDE ME!
HOW WILL HE GET HERE?
HERE, SNAKE, TAKE DIS PLANE TICKET AN' DIS GUN AN' GET OUTA DA COUNTRY!
T'ANKS, SLIMY! YER A PAL!
SHAZAM!
BOOM
COME ON, SKINNIS! IT'S BACK TO JAIL FOR YOU!
YIPE! IT'S CAPTAIN MARVEL-- DA GUY DAT PUT ME IN DA HOOSEGOW 25 YEARS AGO!
!
POW
POW
6

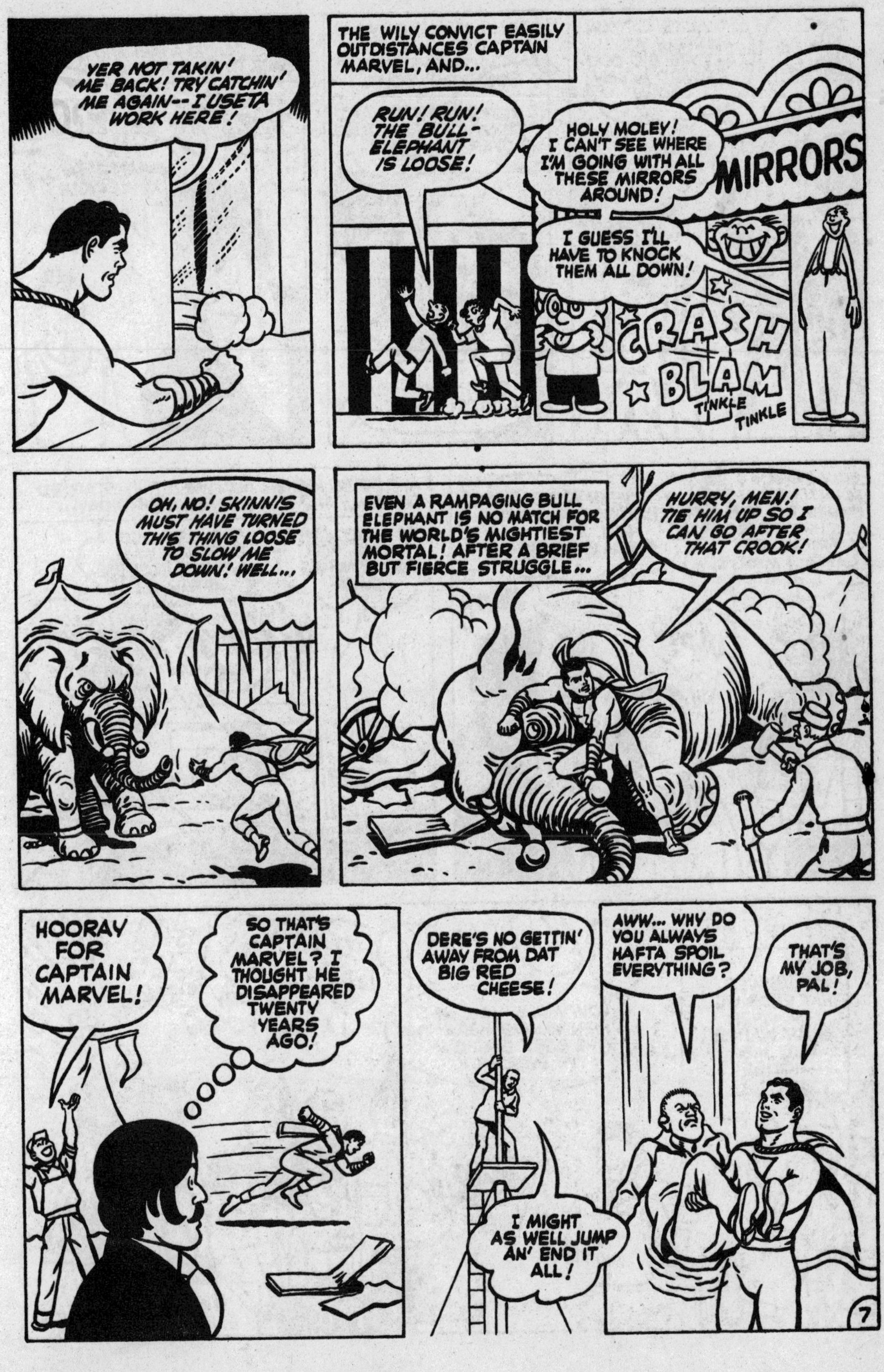
YER NOT TAKIN' ME BACK! TRY CATCHIN' ME AGAIN-- I USETA WORK HERE!
THE WILY CONVICT EASILY OUTDISTANCES CAPTAIN MARVEL, AND...
RUN! RUN! THE BULL-ELEPHANT IS LOOSE!
HOLY MOLEY! I CAN'T SEE WHERE I'M GOING WITH ALL THESE MIRRORS AROUND!
I GUESS I'LL HAVE TO KNOCK THEM ALL DOWN!
MIRRORS
CRASH
BLAM
TINKLE
TINKLE
OH, NO! SKINNIS MUST HAVE TURNED THIS THING LOOSE TO SLOW ME DOWN! WELL...
EVEN A RAMPAGING BULL ELEPHANT IS NO MATCH FOR THE WORLD'S MIGHTIEST MORTAL! AFTER A BRIEF BUT FIERCE STRUGGLE...
HURRY, MEN! TIE HIM UP SO I CAN GO AFTER THAT CROOK!
HOORAY FOR CAPTAIN MARVEL!
SO THAT'S CAPTAIN MARVEL? I THOUGHT HE DISAPPEARED TWENTY YEARS AGO!
DERE'S NO GETTIN' AWAY FROM DAT BIG RED CHEESE!
I MIGHT AS WELL JUMP AN' END IT ALL!
AWW... WHY DO YOU ALWAYS HAFTA SPOIL EVERYTHING?
THAT'S MY JOB, PAL!
7

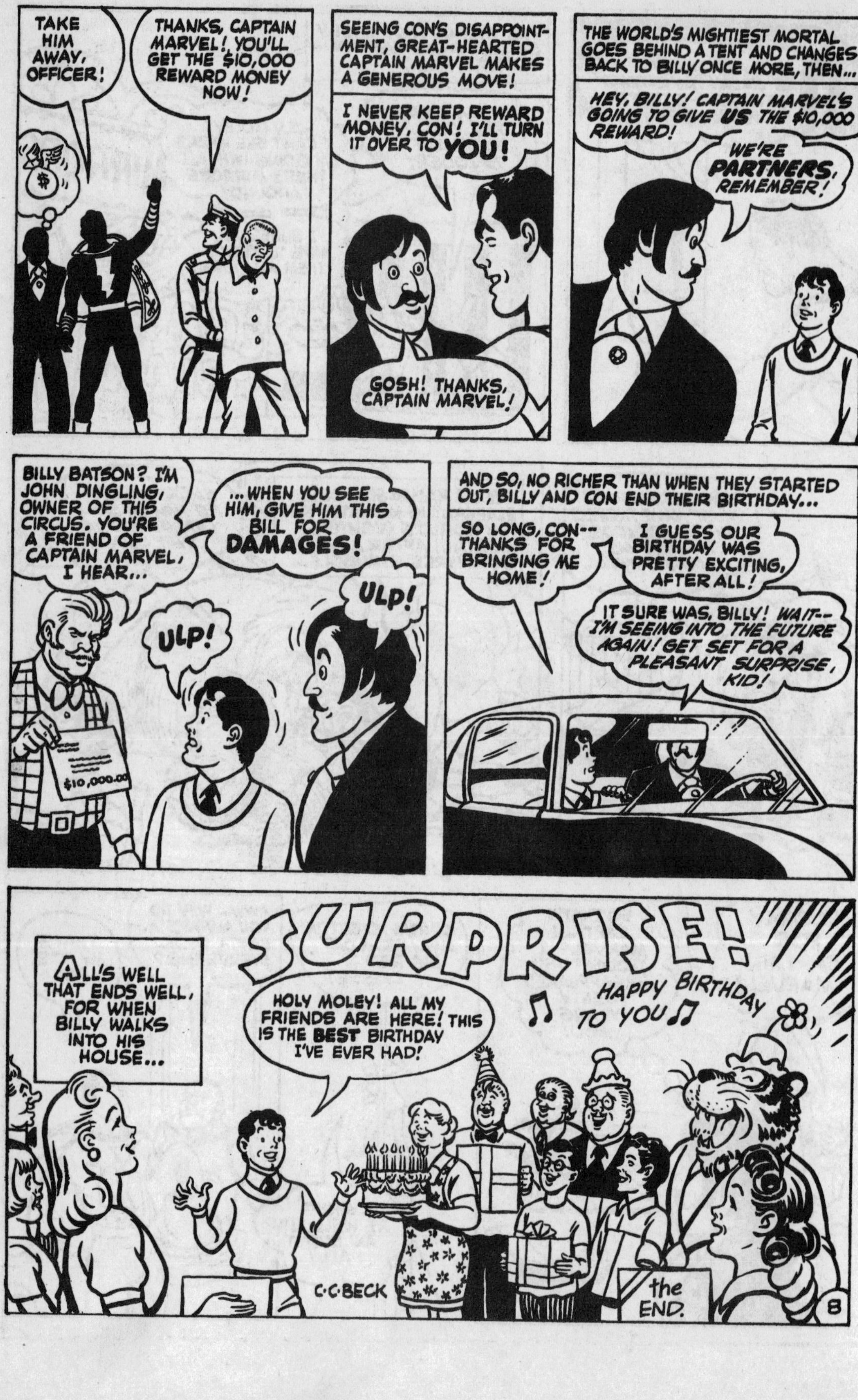
TAKE HIM AWAY, OFFICER!
THANKS, CAPTAIN MARVEL! YOU'LL GET THE $10,000 REWARD MONEY NOW!
$
SEEING CON'S DISAPPOINTMENT, GREAT-HEARTED CAPTAIN MARVEL MAKES A GENEROUS MOVE!
I NEVER KEEP REWARD MONEY, CON! I'LL TURN IT OVER TO YOU!
GOSH! THANKS, CAPTAIN MARVEL!
THE WORLD'S MIGHTIEST MORTAL GOES BEHIND A TENT AND CHANGES BACK TO BILLY ONCE MORE, THEN...
HEY, BILLY! CAPTAIN MARVEL'S GOING TO GIVE US THE $10,000 REWARD!
WE'RE PARTNERS, REMEMBER!
BILLY BATSON? I'M JOHN DINGLING, OWNER OF THIS CIRCUS. YOU'RE A FRIEND OF CAPTAIN MARVEL, I HEAR...
...WHEN YOU SEE HIM, GIVE HIM THIS BILL FOR DAMAGES!
ULP!
ULP!
$10,000.00
AND SO, NO RICHER THAN WHEN THEY STARTED OUT, BILLY AND CON END THEIR BIRTHDAY...
SO LONG, CON-- THANKS FOR BRINGING ME HOME!
I GUESS OUR BIRTHDAY WAS PRETTY EXCITING, AFTER ALL!
IT SURE WAS, BILLY! WAIT-- I'M SEEING INTO THE FUTURE AGAIN! GET SET FOR A PLEASANT SURPRISE, KID!
SURPRISE!
ALL'S WELL THAT ENDS WELL, FOR WHEN BILLY WALKS INTO HIS HOUSE...
HOLY MOLEY! ALL MY FRIENDS ARE HERE! THIS IS THE BEST BIRTHDAY I'VE EVER HAD!
HAPPY BIRTHDAY TO YOU
C·C·BECK
the END.
8

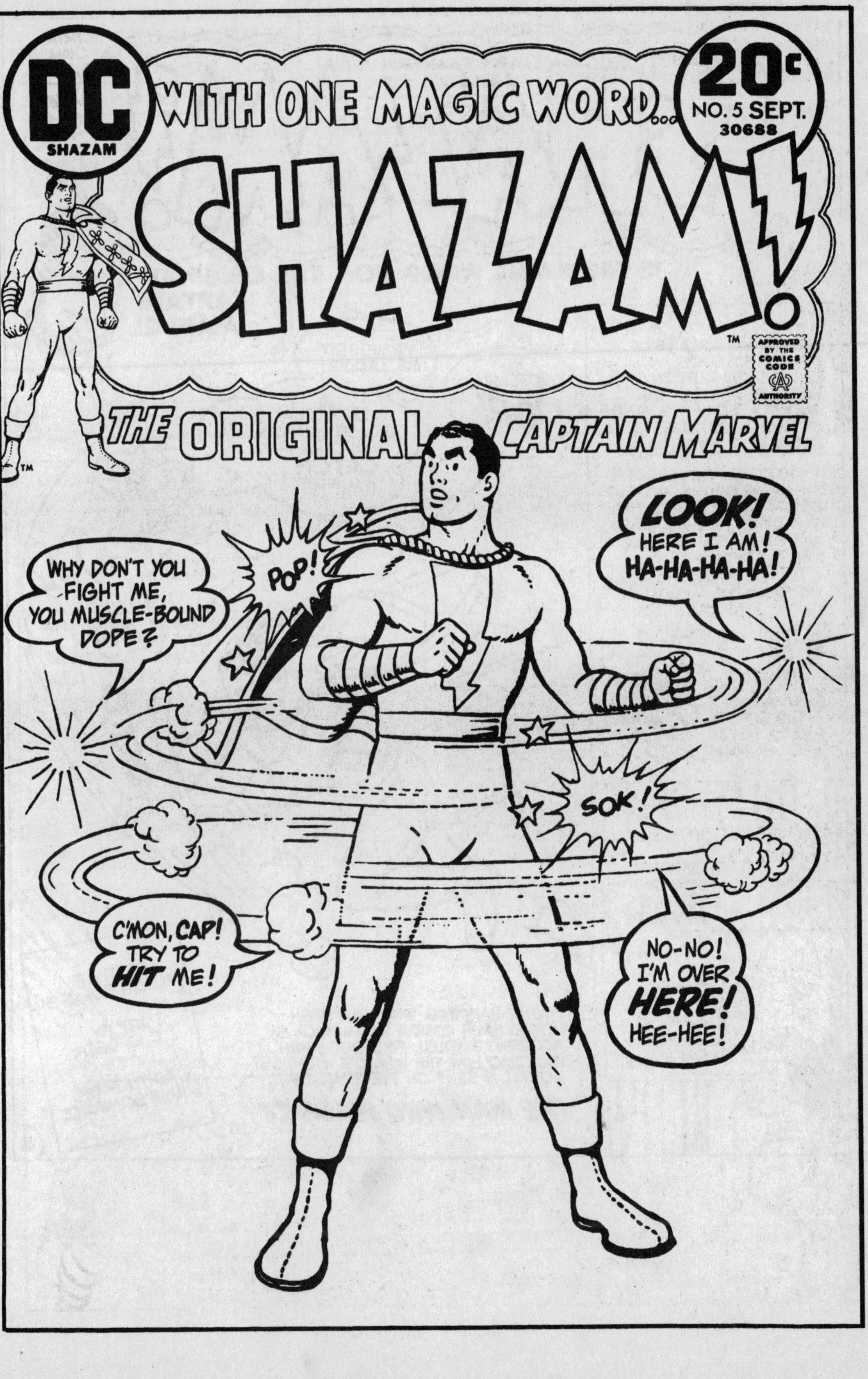
DC
SHAZAM
WITH ONE MAGIC WORD...
20¢
NO. 5 SEPT.
30688
SHAZAM!
TM
APPROVED BY THE COMICS CODE AUTHORITY
THE ORIGINAL CAPTAIN MARVEL
TM
LOOK! HERE I AM! HA-HA-HA-HA!
WHY DON'T YOU FIGHT ME, YOU MUSCLE-BOUND DOPE?
POP!
SOK!
C'MON, CAP! TRY TO HIT ME!
NO-NO! I'M OVER HERE! HEE-HEE!

SHAZAM!

IS THE MAGIC WORD FOR THE ORIGINAL CAPTAIN MARVEL

ALL THE POWERS OF SIX GREAT GODS AND HEROES HAVE BEEN GATHERED TOGETHER AND PLACED IN THE HANDS OF BOY BROADCASTER **BILLY BATSON!**

WHEN HE PRONOUNCES THE NAME OF THE ANCIENT EGYPTIAN WIZARD *SHAZAM*, HE BECOMES, IN A BLINDING FLASH OF LIGHTNING, **CAPTAIN MARVEL,** THE WORLD'S MIGHTIEST MORTAL!

THEN, WHEN EVIL IS DEFEATED, CAPTAIN MARVEL REPEATS THE WORD AND CHANGES BACK TO BILLY! SO AMAZING AND SUDDEN IS THE CHANGE THAT MOST PEOPLE NEVER REALIZE WHAT HAS HAPPENED!

SOLOMON— *WISDOM*
HERCULES— *STRENGTH*
ATLAS— *STAMINA*
ZEUS— *POWER*
ACHILLES— *COURAGE*
MERCURY— *SPEED*

GOTCHA-- OOP!

YE MISSED ME, LADDIE!

A LEPRECHAUN WILL BE GRANTIN' Y'R WISH ONLY IF YE **CATCH** HIM FIRST!

ZIP

WHAT HAPPENS WHEN AN IRISH LEPRECHAUN COMES TO AMERICA BY ACCIDENT? YOU'LL FIND OUT WHEN YOU READ HOW THE WORLD'S MIGHTIEST MORTAL IS SENT ON THE TRAIL OF... "*THE MAN WHO WASN'T!*"

STORY BY ELLIOT S. MAGGIN

ART BY C. C. BECK

EDITING BY JULIUS SCHWARTZ

1

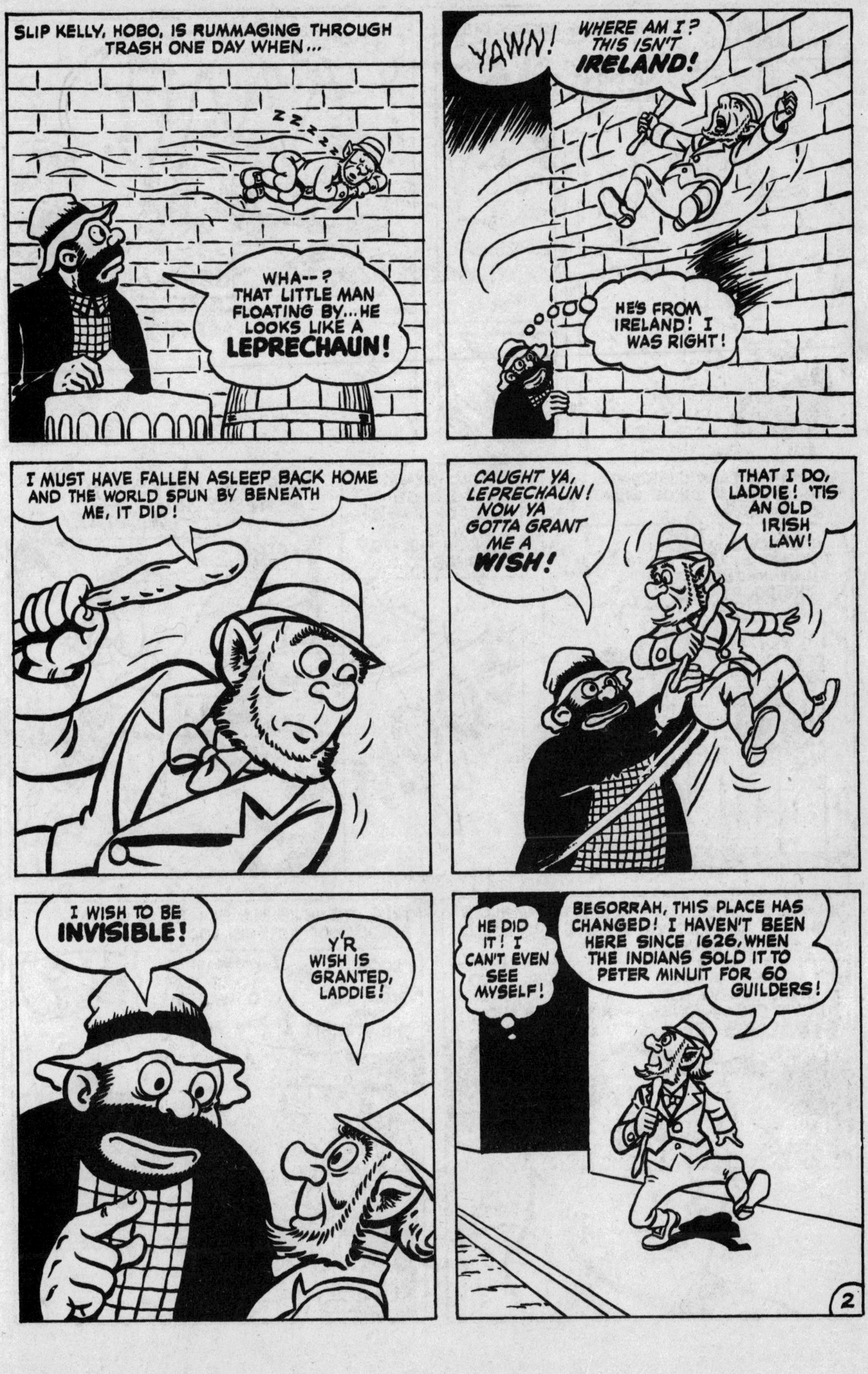
SLIP KELLY, HOBO, IS RUMMAGING THROUGH TRASH ONE DAY WHEN...
Z Z Z Z Z
WHA--? THAT LITTLE MAN FLOATING BY... HE LOOKS LIKE A LEPRECHAUN!
YAWN!
WHERE AM I? THIS ISN'T IRELAND!
HE'S FROM IRELAND! I WAS RIGHT!
I MUST HAVE FALLEN ASLEEP BACK HOME AND THE WORLD SPUN BY BENEATH ME, IT DID!
CAUGHT YA, LEPRECHAUN! NOW YA GOTTA GRANT ME A WISH!
THAT I DO, LADDIE! 'TIS AN OLD IRISH LAW!
I WISH TO BE INVISIBLE!
Y'R WISH IS GRANTED, LADDIE!
HE DID IT! I CAN'T EVEN SEE MYSELF!
BEGORRAH, THIS PLACE HAS CHANGED! I HAVEN'T BEEN HERE SINCE 1626, WHEN THE INDIANS SOLD IT TO PETER MINUIT FOR 60 GUILDERS!
2

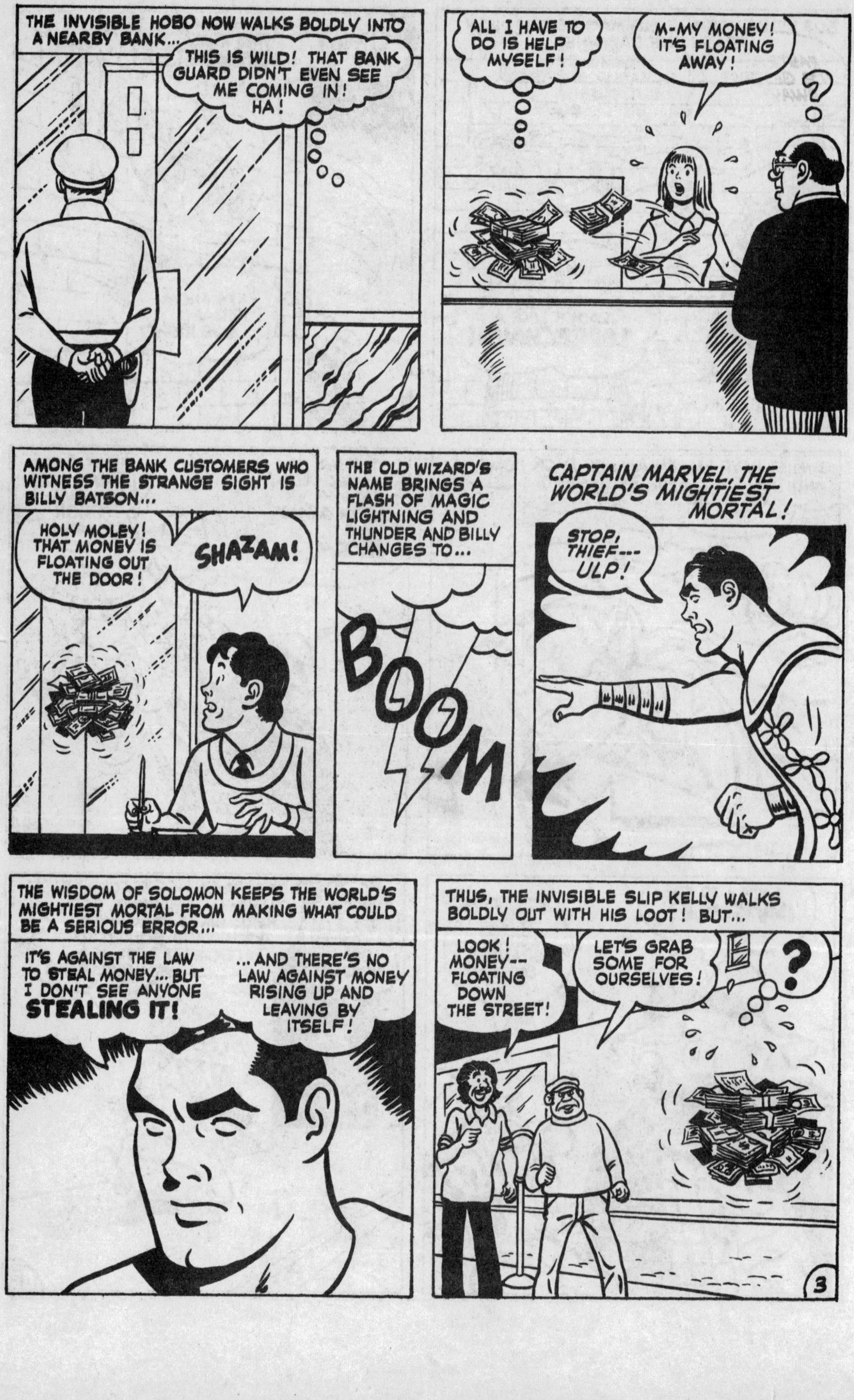
THE INVISIBLE HOBO NOW WALKS BOLDLY INTO A NEARBY BANK...
THIS IS WILD! THAT BANK GUARD DIDN'T EVEN SEE ME COMING IN! HA!
ALL I HAVE TO DO IS HELP MYSELF!
M-MY MONEY! IT'S FLOATING AWAY!
?
AMONG THE BANK CUSTOMERS WHO WITNESS THE STRANGE SIGHT IS BILLY BATSON...
HOLY MOLEY! THAT MONEY IS FLOATING OUT THE DOOR!
SHAZAM!
THE OLD WIZARD'S NAME BRINGS A FLASH OF MAGIC LIGHTNING AND THUNDER AND BILLY CHANGES TO...
BOOM
CAPTAIN MARVEL, THE WORLD'S MIGHTIEST MORTAL!
STOP, THIEF--- ULP!
THE WISDOM OF SOLOMON KEEPS THE WORLD'S MIGHTIEST MORTAL FROM MAKING WHAT COULD BE A SERIOUS ERROR...
IT'S AGAINST THE LAW TO STEAL MONEY... BUT I DON'T SEE ANYONE STEALING IT!
...AND THERE'S NO LAW AGAINST MONEY RISING UP AND LEAVING BY ITSELF!
THUS, THE INVISIBLE SLIP KELLY WALKS BOLDLY OUT WITH HIS LOOT! BUT...
LOOK! MONEY-- FLOATING DOWN THE STREET!
LET'S GRAB SOME FOR OURSELVES!
?
3

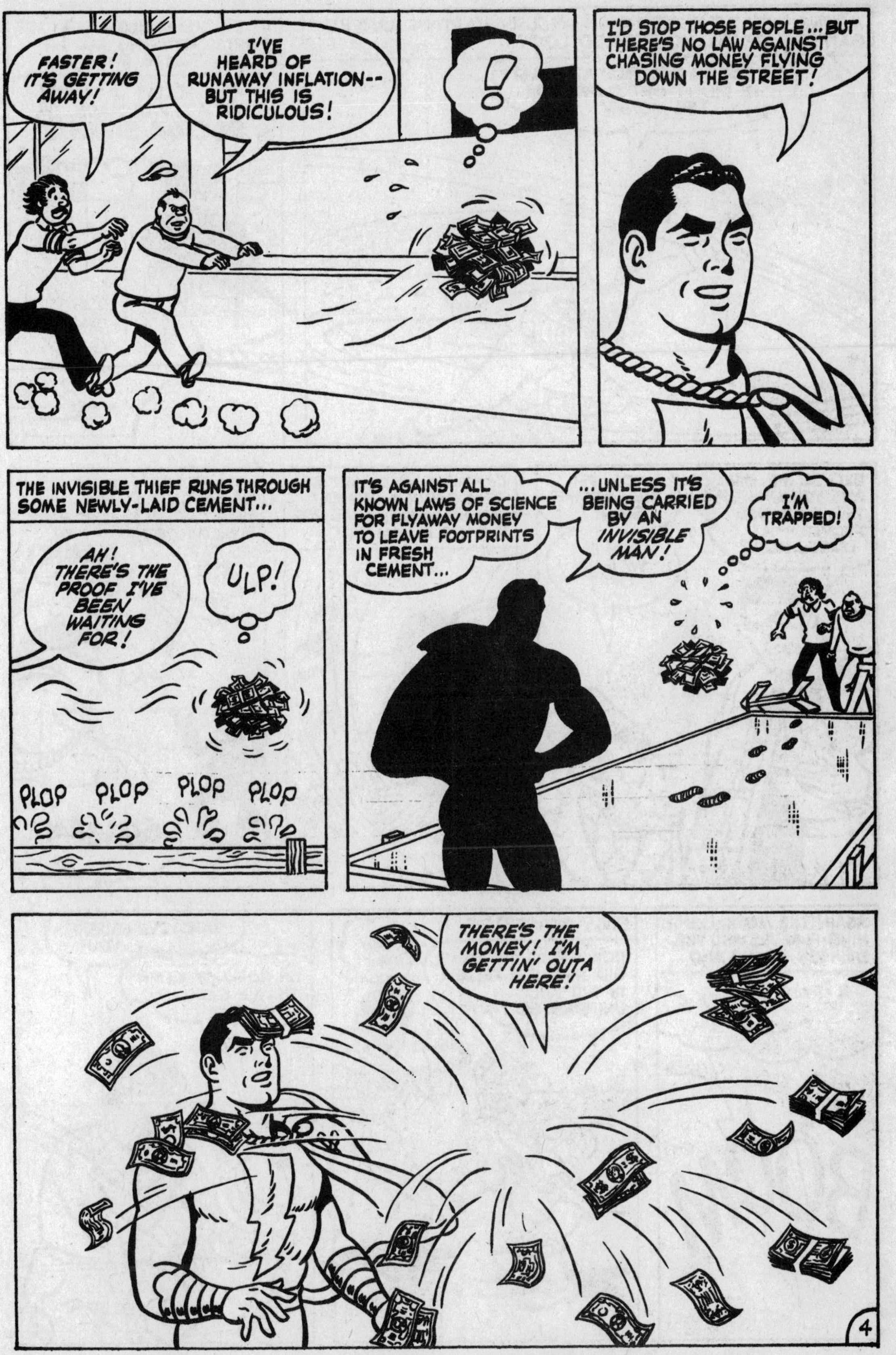
FASTER! IT'S GETTING AWAY!
I'VE HEARD OF RUNAWAY INFLATION-- BUT THIS IS RIDICULOUS!
!
I'D STOP THOSE PEOPLE ... BUT THERE'S NO LAW AGAINST CHASING MONEY FLYING DOWN THE STREET!
THE INVISIBLE THIEF RUNS THROUGH SOME NEWLY-LAID CEMENT...
AH! THERE'S THE PROOF I'VE BEEN WAITING FOR!
ULP!
PLOP PLOP PLOP PLOP
IT'S AGAINST ALL KNOWN LAWS OF SCIENCE FOR FLYAWAY MONEY TO LEAVE FOOTPRINTS IN FRESH CEMENT...
...UNLESS IT'S BEING CARRIED BY AN INVISIBLE MAN!
I'M TRAPPED!
THERE'S THE MONEY! I'M GETTIN' OUTA HERE!
4

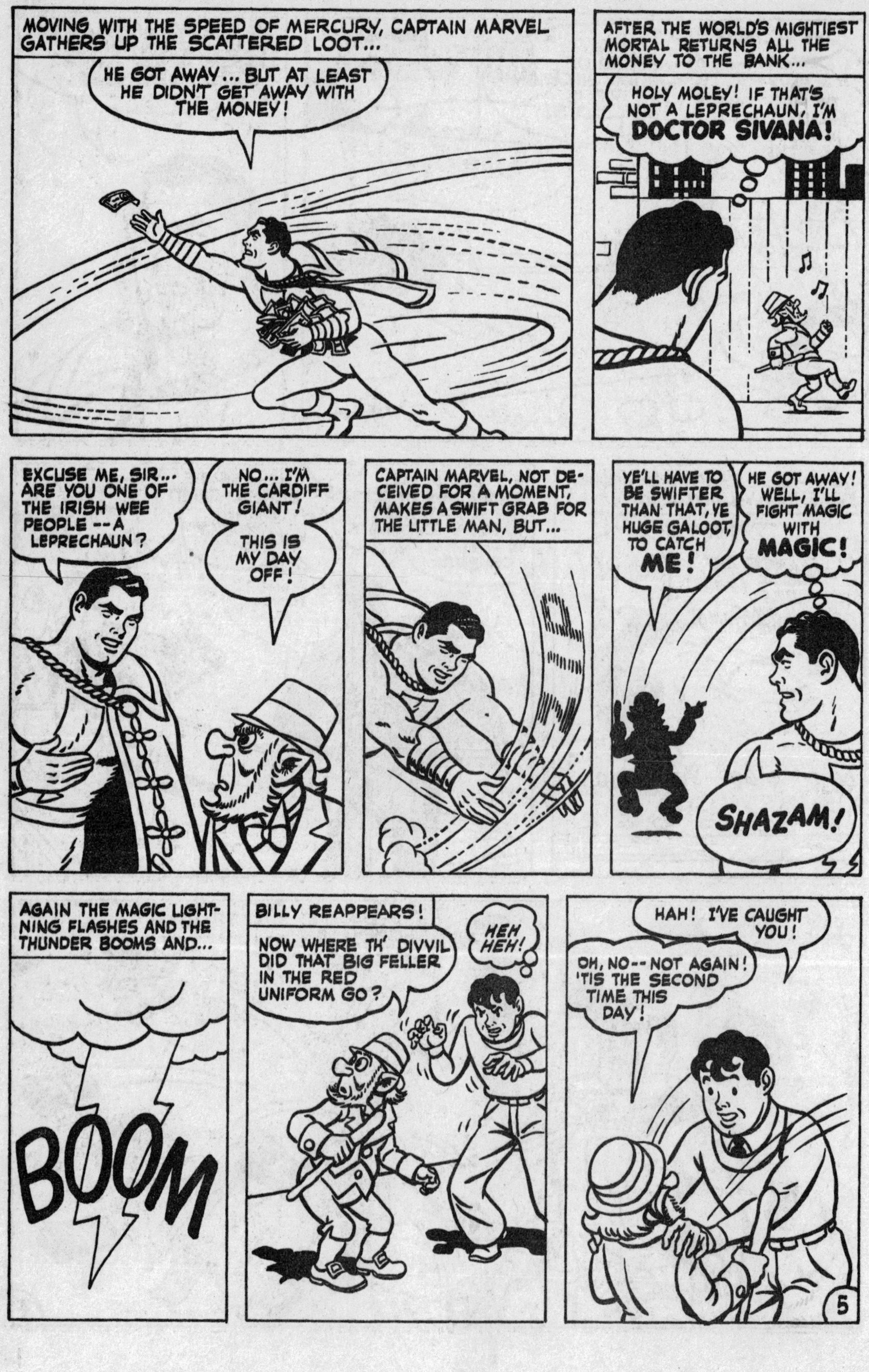
MOVING WITH THE SPEED OF MERCURY, CAPTAIN MARVEL GATHERS UP THE SCATTERED LOOT...
HE GOT AWAY... BUT AT LEAST HE DIDN'T GET AWAY WITH THE MONEY!
AFTER THE WORLD'S MIGHTIEST MORTAL RETURNS ALL THE MONEY TO THE BANK...
HOLY MOLEY! IF THAT'S NOT A LEPRECHAUN, I'M DOCTOR SIVANA!
EXCUSE ME, SIR... ARE YOU ONE OF THE IRISH WEE PEOPLE -- A LEPRECHAUN?
NO... I'M THE CARDIFF GIANT!
THIS IS MY DAY OFF!
CAPTAIN MARVEL, NOT DECEIVED FOR A MOMENT, MAKES A SWIFT GRAB FOR THE LITTLE MAN, BUT...
YE'LL HAVE TO BE SWIFTER THAN THAT, YE HUGE GALOOT, TO CATCH ME!
HE GOT AWAY! WELL, I'LL FIGHT MAGIC WITH MAGIC!
SHAZAM!
AGAIN THE MAGIC LIGHTNING FLASHES AND THE THUNDER BOOMS AND...
BOOM
BILLY REAPPEARS!
NOW WHERE TH' DIVVIL DID THAT BIG FELLER IN THE RED UNIFORM GO?
HEH HEH!
HAH! I'VE CAUGHT YOU!
OH, NO-- NOT AGAIN! 'TIS THE SECOND TIME THIS DAY!
5

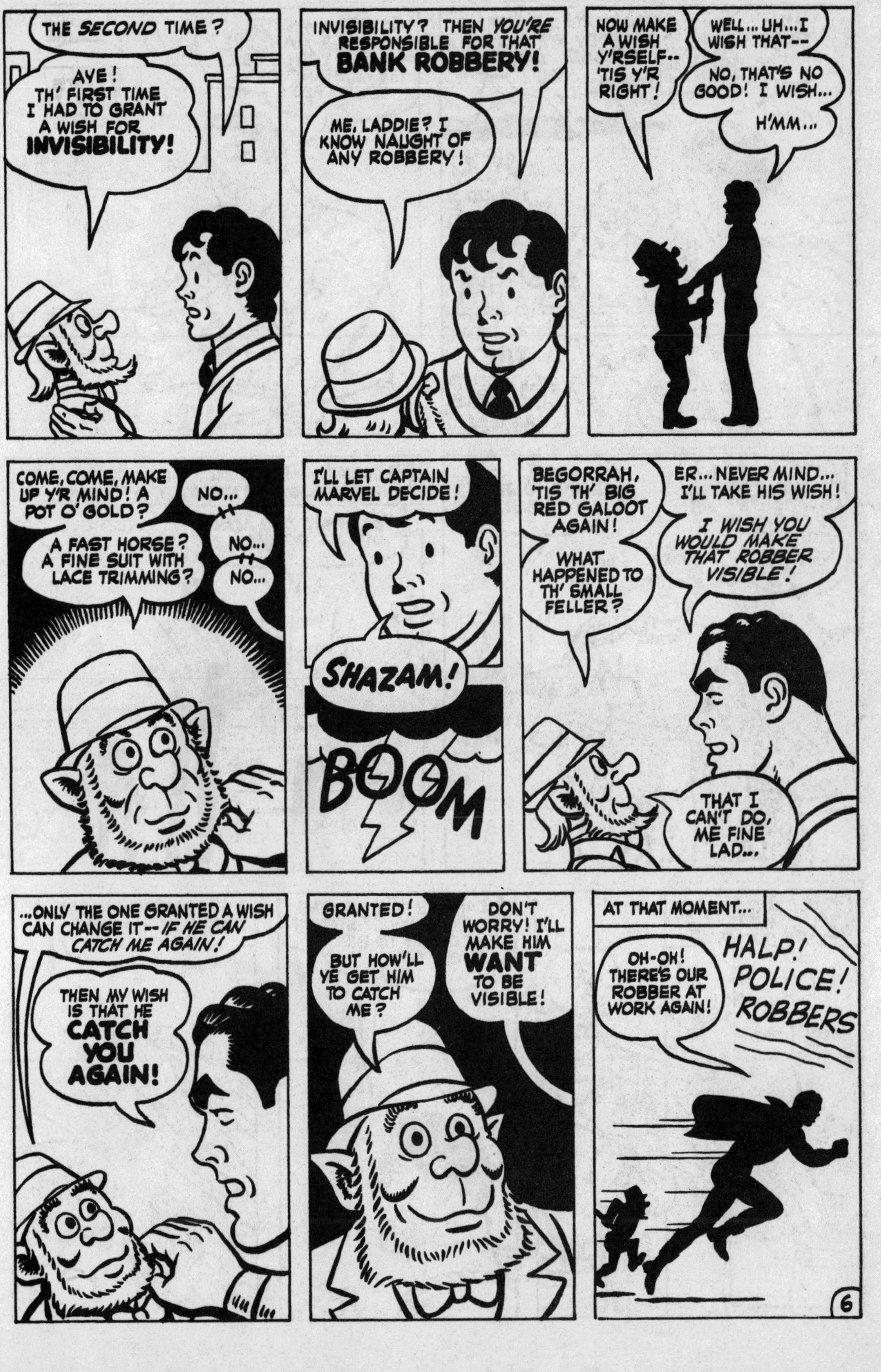
THE SECOND TIME?
AYE! TH' FIRST TIME I HAD TO GRANT A WISH FOR INVISIBILITY!
INVISIBILITY? THEN YOU'RE RESPONSIBLE FOR THAT BANK ROBBERY!
ME, LADDIE? I KNOW NAUGHT OF ANY ROBBERY!
NOW MAKE A WISH Y'RSELF-- 'TIS Y'R RIGHT!
WELL... UH... I WISH THAT--
NO, THAT'S NO GOOD! I WISH...
H'MM...
COME, COME, MAKE UP Y'R MIND! A POT O' GOLD?
NO...
A FAST HORSE? A FINE SUIT WITH LACE TRIMMING?
NO...
NO...
I'LL LET CAPTAIN MARVEL DECIDE!
SHAZAM!
BOOM
BEGORRAH, 'TIS TH' BIG RED GALOOT AGAIN!
WHAT HAPPENED TO TH' SMALL FELLER?
ER... NEVER MIND... I'LL TAKE HIS WISH!
I WISH YOU WOULD MAKE THAT ROBBER VISIBLE!
THAT I CAN'T DO, ME FINE LAD...
...ONLY THE ONE GRANTED A WISH CAN CHANGE IT -- IF HE CAN CATCH ME AGAIN!
THEN MY WISH IS THAT HE CATCH YOU AGAIN!
GRANTED!
BUT HOW'LL YE GET HIM TO CATCH ME?
DON'T WORRY! I'LL MAKE HIM WANT TO BE VISIBLE!
AT THAT MOMENT...
OH-OH! THERE'S OUR ROBBER AT WORK AGAIN!
HALP! POLICE! ROBBERS
6

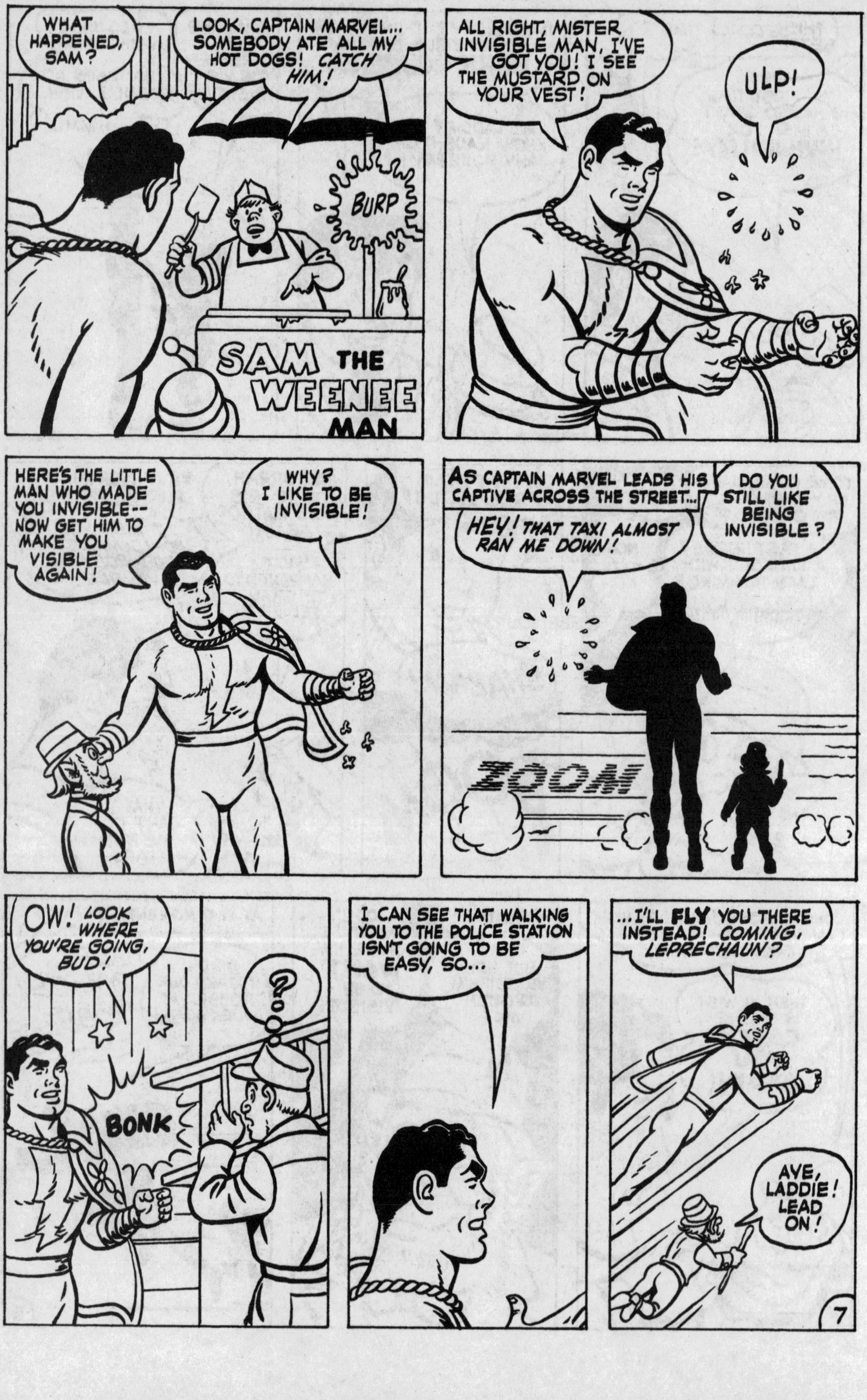

WHAT HAPPENED, SAM?
LOOK, CAPTAIN MARVEL... SOMEBODY ATE ALL MY HOT DOGS! CATCH HIM!
BURP
SAM THE WEENEE MAN
ALL RIGHT, MISTER INVISIBLE MAN, I'VE GOT YOU! I SEE THE MUSTARD ON YOUR VEST!
ULP!
HERE'S THE LITTLE MAN WHO MADE YOU INVISIBLE--NOW GET HIM TO MAKE YOU VISIBLE AGAIN!
WHY? I LIKE TO BE INVISIBLE!
AS CAPTAIN MARVEL LEADS HIS CAPTIVE ACROSS THE STREET...
HEY! THAT TAXI ALMOST RAN ME DOWN!
DO YOU STILL LIKE BEING INVISIBLE?
ZOOM
OW! LOOK WHERE YOU'RE GOING, BUD!
?
BONK
I CAN SEE THAT WALKING YOU TO THE POLICE STATION ISN'T GOING TO BE EASY, SO...
...I'LL FLY YOU THERE INSTEAD! COMING, LEPRECHAUN?
AYE, LADDIE! LEAD ON!
7

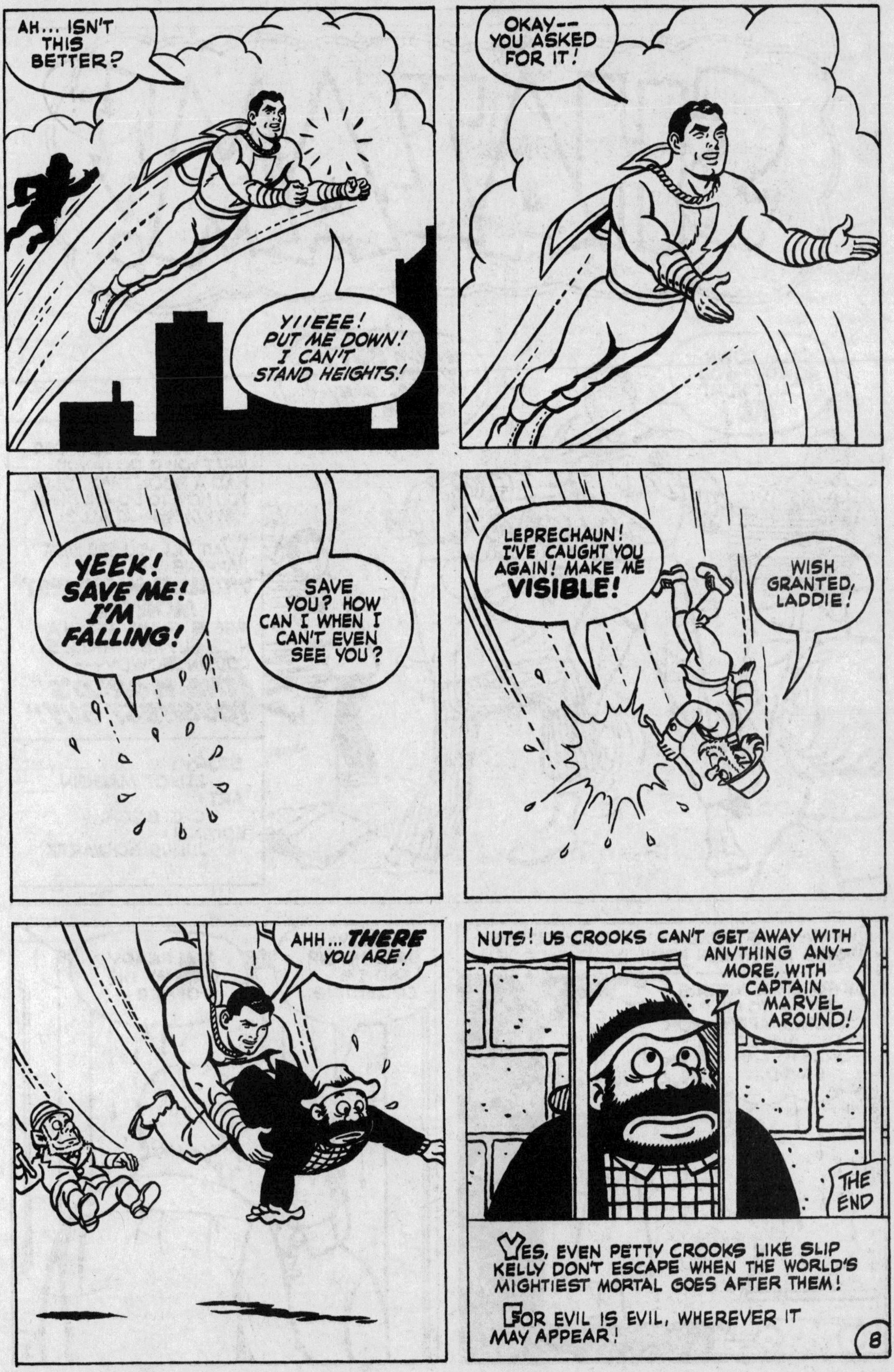
AH... ISN'T THIS BETTER?
YIIEEE! PUT ME DOWN! I CAN'T STAND HEIGHTS!
OKAY-- YOU ASKED FOR IT!
YEEK! SAVE ME! I'M FALLING!
SAVE YOU? HOW CAN I WHEN I CAN'T EVEN SEE YOU?
LEPRECHAUN! I'VE CAUGHT YOU AGAIN! MAKE ME VISIBLE!
WISH GRANTED, LADDIE!
AHH... THERE YOU ARE!
NUTS! US CROOKS CAN'T GET AWAY WITH ANYTHING ANY-MORE, WITH CAPTAIN MARVEL AROUND!
THE END
YES, EVEN PETTY CROOKS LIKE SLIP KELLY DON'T ESCAPE WHEN THE WORLD'S MIGHTIEST MORTAL GOES AFTER THEM!
FOR EVIL IS EVIL, WHEREVER IT MAY APPEAR!
8

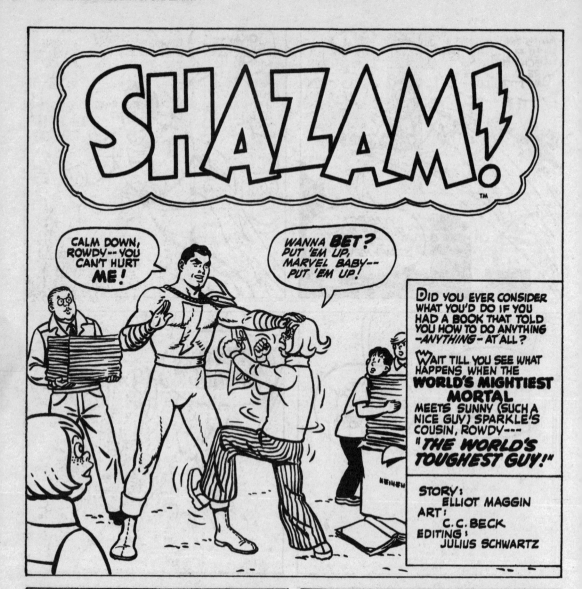

SHAZAM!

CALM DOWN, ROWDY-- YOU CAN'T HURT **ME!**

WANNA **BET?** PUT 'EM UP, MARVEL BABY-- PUT 'EM UP!

DID YOU EVER CONSIDER WHAT YOU'D DO IF YOU HAD A BOOK THAT TOLD YOU HOW TO DO ANYTHING --ANYTHING-- AT ALL?

WAIT TILL YOU SEE WHAT HAPPENS WHEN THE **WORLD'S MIGHTIEST MORTAL** MEETS SUNNY (SUCH A NICE GUY) SPARKLE'S COUSIN, ROWDY---

"*THE WORLD'S TOUGHEST GUY!*"

STORY:
    ELLIOT MAGGIN
ART:
    C.C. BECK
EDITING:
    JULIUS SCHWARTZ

ONE RAINY AFTERNOON, AS BILLY BATSON DRAGS HIS WAGON FROM DOOR TO DOOR...

MY BOSS, MR. MORRIS, ASKED ME TO HELP COLLECT OLD NEWSPAPERS FOR RECYCLING SO THE FORESTS CAN BE SAVED...

I'M BILLY BATSON, SIR, AND I'M COLLECTING...

I ALREADY GAVE AT THE OFFICE!

1

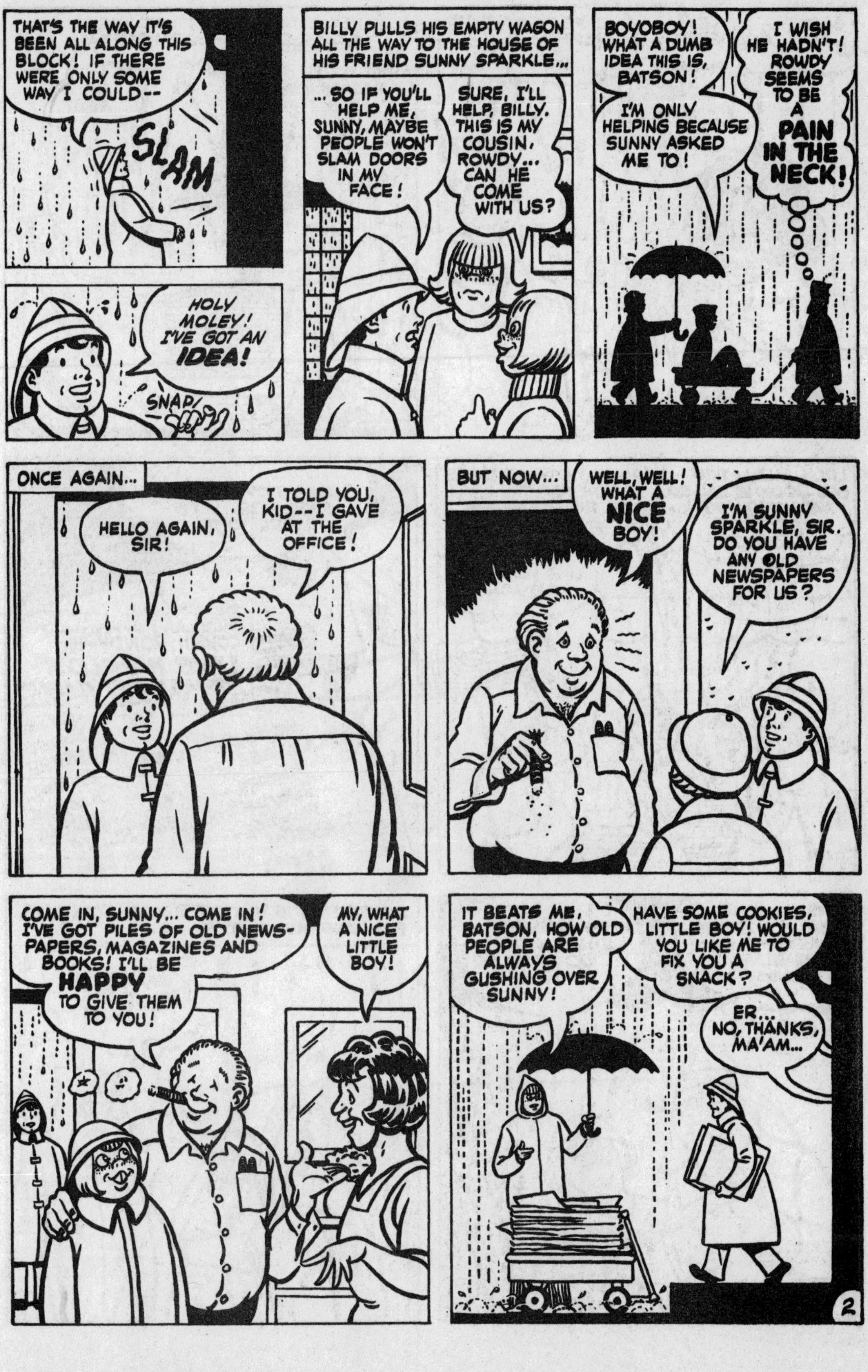
THAT'S THE WAY IT'S BEEN ALL ALONG THIS BLOCK! IF THERE WERE ONLY SOME WAY I COULD--
SLAM
HOLY MOLEY! I'VE GOT AN IDEA!
SNAP!
BILLY PULLS HIS EMPTY WAGON ALL THE WAY TO THE HOUSE OF HIS FRIEND SUNNY SPARKLE...
...SO IF YOU'LL HELP ME, SUNNY, MAYBE PEOPLE WON'T SLAM DOORS IN MY FACE!
SURE, I'LL HELP, BILLY. THIS IS MY COUSIN, ROWDY... CAN HE COME WITH US?
BOYOBOY! WHAT A DUMB IDEA THIS IS, BATSON!
I'M ONLY HELPING BECAUSE SUNNY ASKED ME TO!
I WISH HE HADN'T! ROWDY SEEMS TO BE A PAIN IN THE NECK!
ONCE AGAIN...
HELLO AGAIN, SIR!
I TOLD YOU, KID--I GAVE AT THE OFFICE!
BUT NOW...
WELL, WELL! WHAT A NICE BOY!
I'M SUNNY SPARKLE, SIR. DO YOU HAVE ANY OLD NEWSPAPERS FOR US?
COME IN, SUNNY... COME IN! I'VE GOT PILES OF OLD NEWSPAPERS, MAGAZINES AND BOOKS! I'LL BE HAPPY TO GIVE THEM TO YOU!
MY, WHAT A NICE LITTLE BOY!
IT BEATS ME, BATSON, HOW OLD PEOPLE ARE ALWAYS GUSHING OVER SUNNY!
HAVE SOME COOKIES, LITTLE BOY! WOULD YOU LIKE ME TO FIX YOU A SNACK?
ER... NO, THANKS, MA'AM...
2

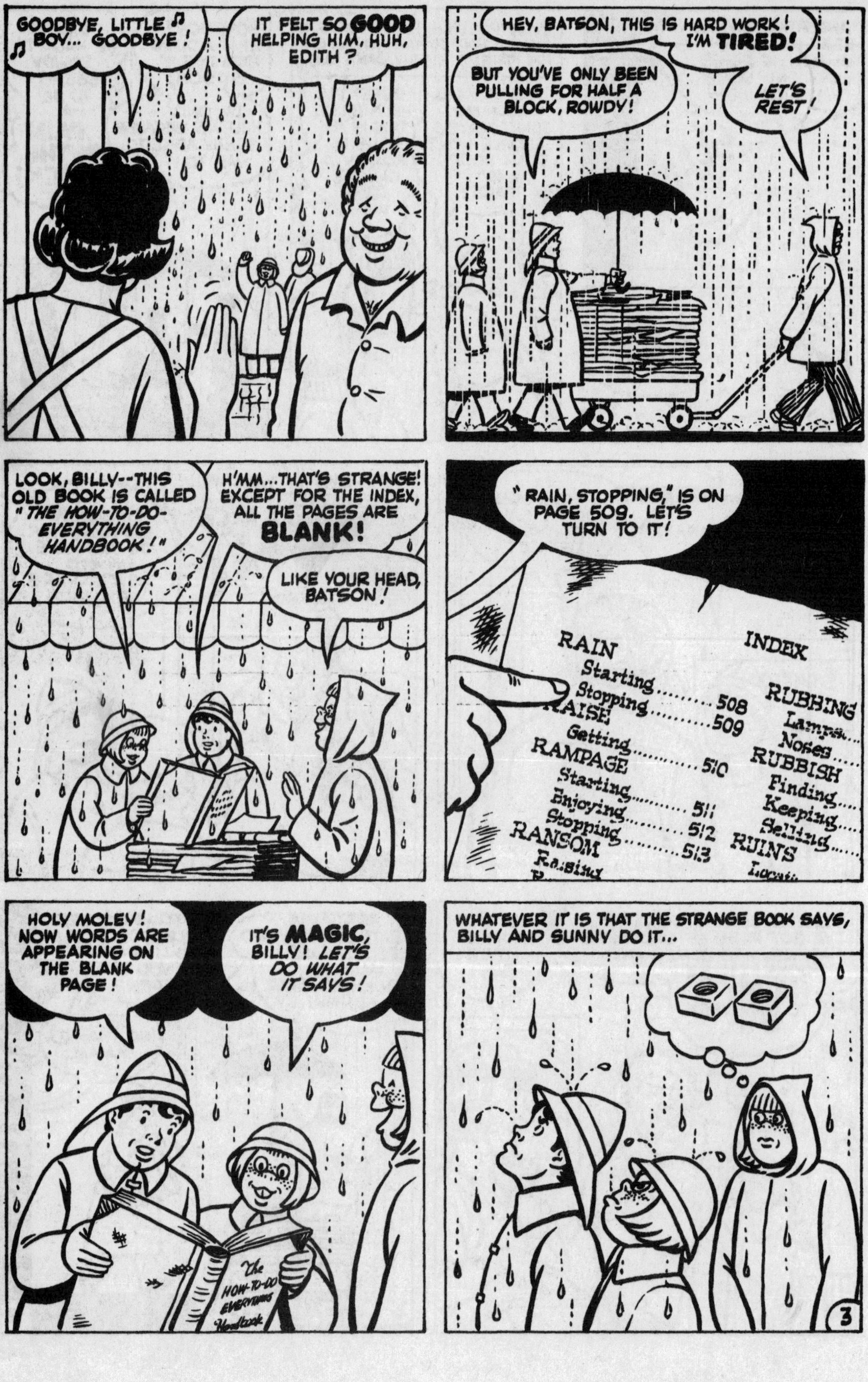
GOODBYE, LITTLE BOY... GOODBYE!
IT FELT SO GOOD HELPING HIM, HUH, EDITH?
HEY, BATSON, THIS IS HARD WORK! I'M TIRED!
BUT YOU'VE ONLY BEEN PULLING FOR HALF A BLOCK, ROWDY!
LET'S REST!
LOOK, BILLY--THIS OLD BOOK IS CALLED "THE HOW-TO-DO-EVERYTHING HANDBOOK!"
H'MM...THAT'S STRANGE! EXCEPT FOR THE INDEX, ALL THE PAGES ARE BLANK!
LIKE YOUR HEAD, BATSON!
"RAIN, STOPPING," IS ON PAGE 509. LET'S TURN TO IT!
RAIN
INDEX
Starting
Stopping.........508
RUBBING
RAISE..........509
Lamps
Getting
Noses
RAMPAGE..........510
RUBBISH
Starting
Finding
Enjoying..........511
Keeping
Stopping..........512
Selling
RANSOM..........513
RUINS
HOLY MOLEY! NOW WORDS ARE APPEARING ON THE BLANK PAGE!
IT'S MAGIC, BILLY! LET'S DO WHAT IT SAYS!
The HOW-TO-DO EVERYTHING Handbook
WHATEVER IT IS THAT THE STRANGE BOOK SAYS, BILLY AND SUNNY DO IT...
3

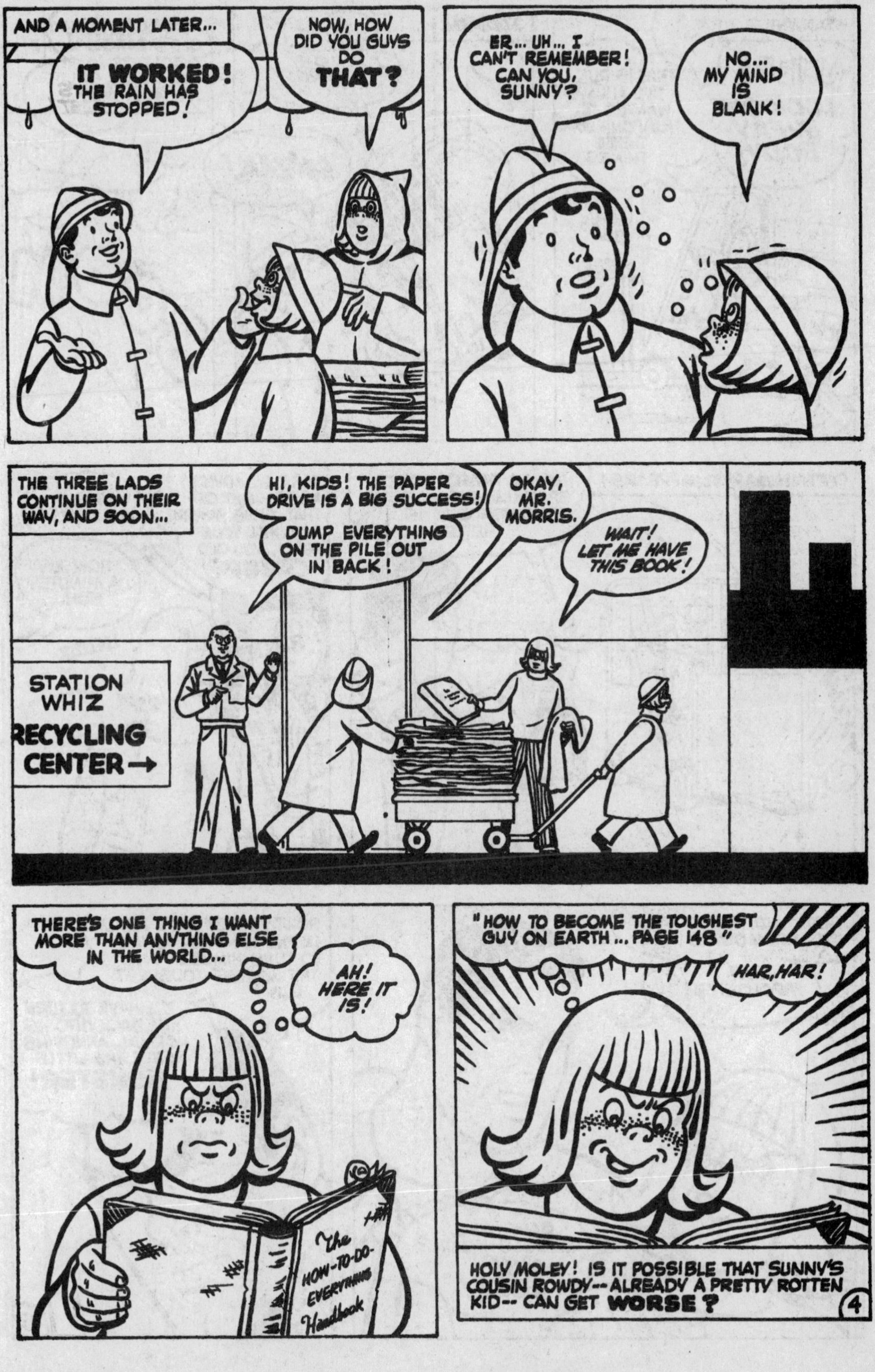

AND A MOMENT LATER...
IT WORKED! THE RAIN HAS STOPPED!
NOW, HOW DID YOU GUYS DO THAT?
ER... UH... I CAN'T REMEMBER! CAN YOU, SUNNY?
NO... MY MIND IS BLANK!
THE THREE LADS CONTINUE ON THEIR WAY, AND SOON...
HI, KIDS! THE PAPER DRIVE IS A BIG SUCCESS!
DUMP EVERYTHING ON THE PILE OUT IN BACK!
OKAY, MR. MORRIS.
WAIT! LET ME HAVE THIS BOOK!
STATION WHIZ
RECYCLING CENTER →
THERE'S ONE THING I WANT MORE THAN ANYTHING ELSE IN THE WORLD...
AH! HERE IT IS!
The HOW-TO-DO-EVERYTHING Handbook
"HOW TO BECOME THE TOUGHEST GUY ON EARTH ... PAGE 148"
HAR, HAR!
HOLY MOLEY! IS IT POSSIBLE THAT SUNNY'S COUSIN ROWDY-- ALREADY A PRETTY ROTTEN KID-- CAN GET WORSE?
4

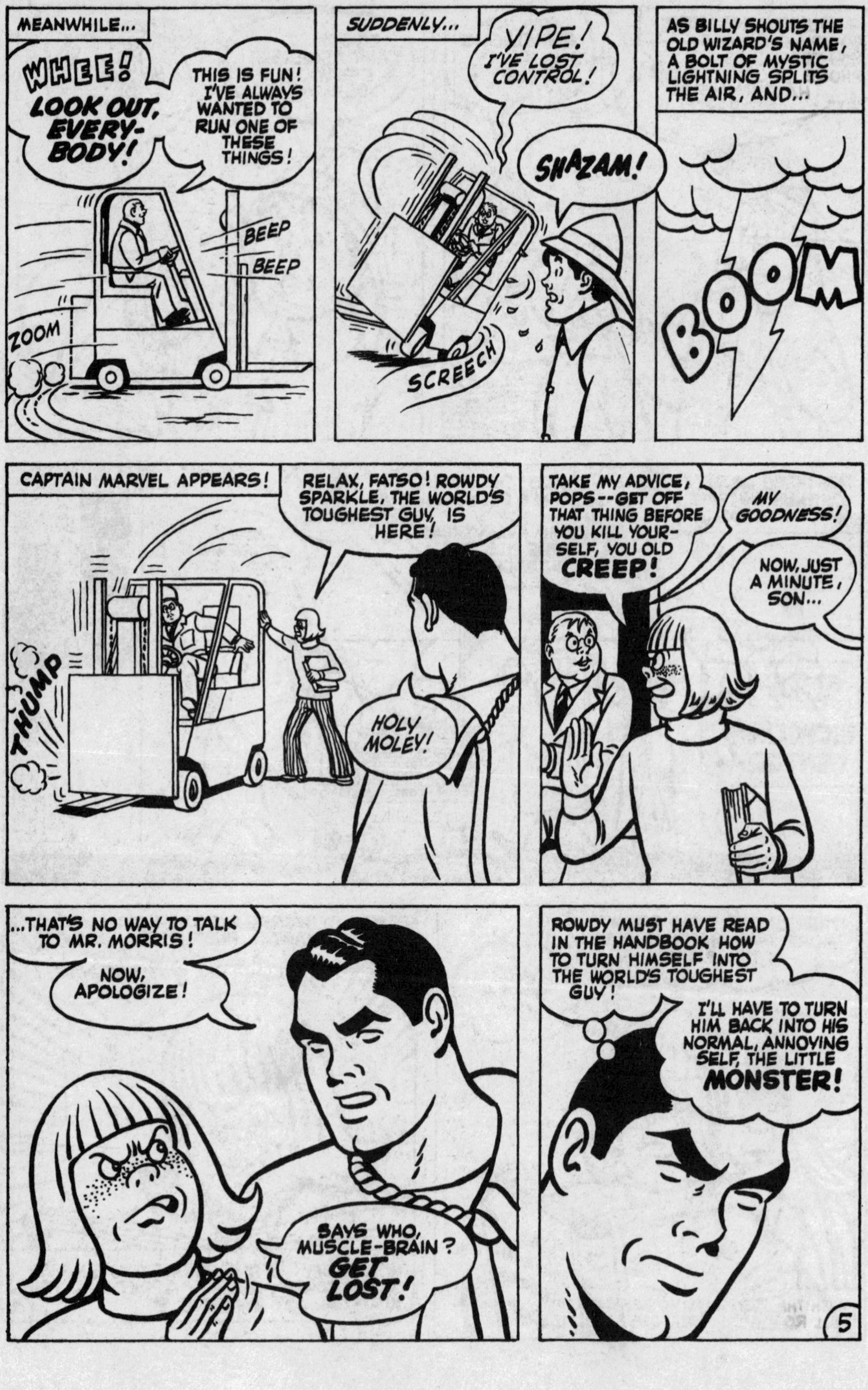
MEANWHILE...
WHEE! LOOK OUT, EVERY-BODY!
THIS IS FUN! I'VE ALWAYS WANTED TO RUN ONE OF THESE THINGS!
BEEP
BEEP
ZOOM
SUDDENLY...
YIPE! I'VE LOST CONTROL!
SHAZAM!
SCREECH
AS BILLY SHOUTS THE OLD WIZARD'S NAME, A BOLT OF MYSTIC LIGHTNING SPLITS THE AIR, AND...
BOOM
CAPTAIN MARVEL APPEARS!
RELAX, FATSO! ROWDY SPARKLE, THE WORLD'S TOUGHEST GUY, IS HERE!
THUMP
ZOOM
HOLY MOLEY!
TAKE MY ADVICE, POPS--GET OFF THAT THING BEFORE YOU KILL YOUR-SELF, YOU OLD CREEP!
MY GOODNESS!
NOW, JUST A MINUTE, SON...
...THAT'S NO WAY TO TALK TO MR. MORRIS!
NOW, APOLOGIZE!
SAYS WHO, MUSCLE-BRAIN? GET LOST!
ROWDY MUST HAVE READ IN THE HANDBOOK HOW TO TURN HIMSELF INTO THE WORLD'S TOUGHEST GUY!
I'LL HAVE TO TURN HIM BACK INTO HIS NORMAL, ANNOYING SELF, THE LITTLE MONSTER!
5

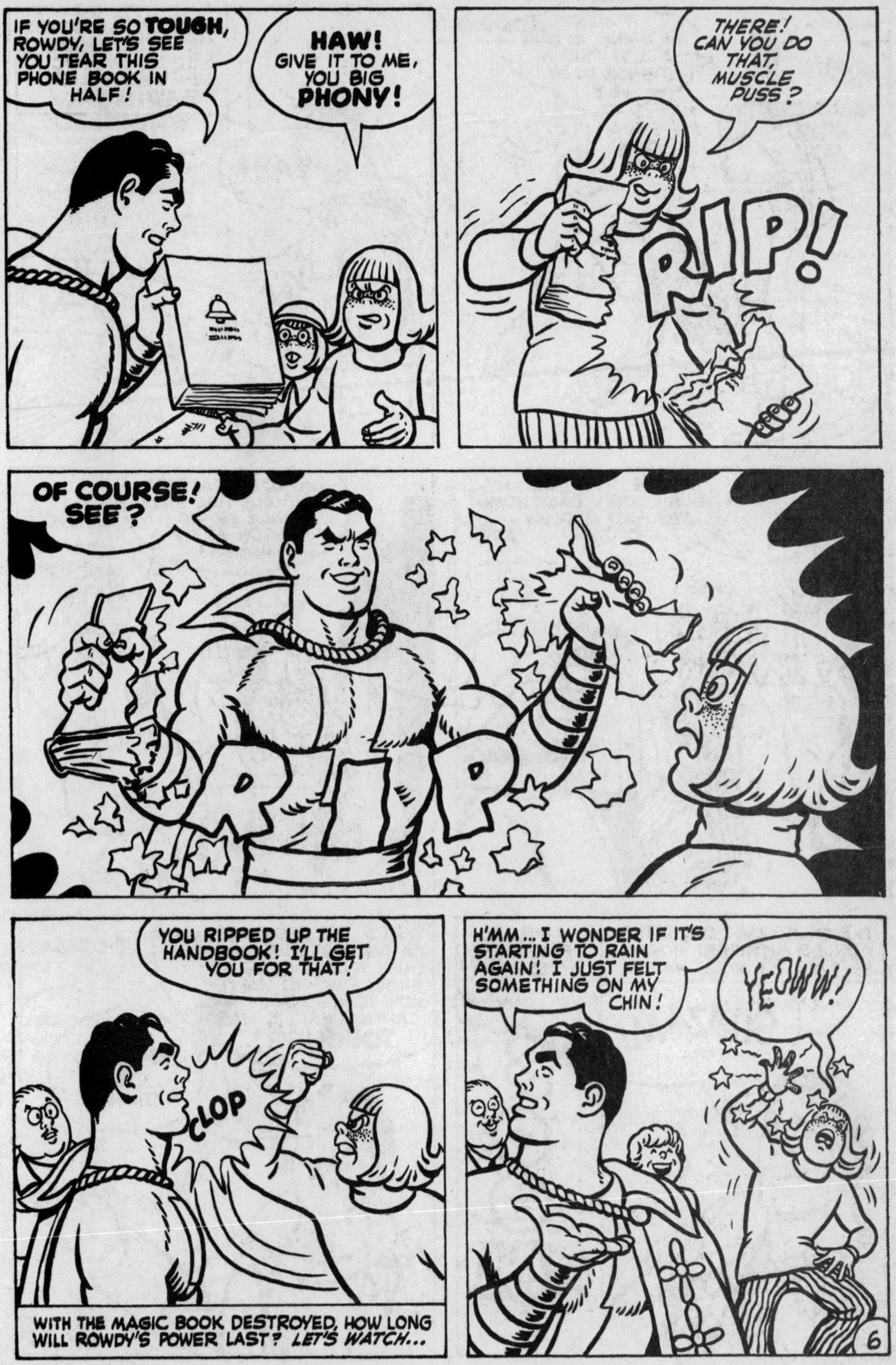
IF YOU'RE SO TOUGH, ROWDY, LET'S SEE YOU TEAR THIS PHONE BOOK IN HALF!
HAW! GIVE IT TO ME, YOU BIG PHONY!
THERE! CAN YOU DO THAT, MUSCLE PUSS?
RIP!
OF COURSE! SEE?
RIP
YOU RIPPED UP THE HANDBOOK! I'LL GET YOU FOR THAT!
CLOP
WITH THE MAGIC BOOK DESTROYED, HOW LONG WILL ROWDY'S POWER LAST? LET'S WATCH...
H'MM... I WONDER IF IT'S STARTING TO RAIN AGAIN! I JUST FELT SOMETHING ON MY CHIN!
YEOWW!
6

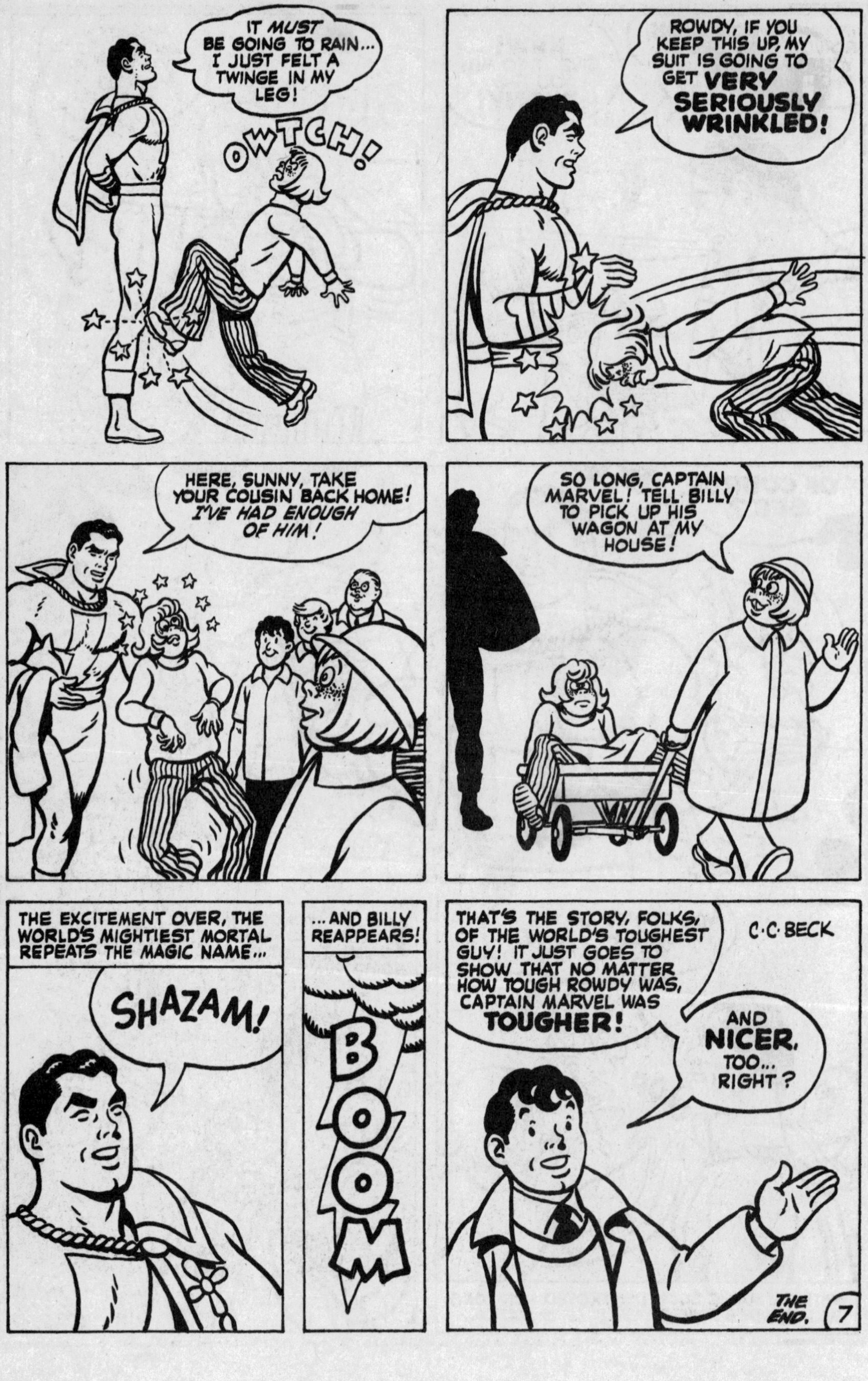
IT MUST BE GOING TO RAIN... I JUST FELT A TWINGE IN MY LEG!
OWTCH!
ROWDY, IF YOU KEEP THIS UP, MY SUIT IS GOING TO GET VERY SERIOUSLY WRINKLED!
HERE, SUNNY, TAKE YOUR COUSIN BACK HOME! I'VE HAD ENOUGH OF HIM!
SO LONG, CAPTAIN MARVEL! TELL BILLY TO PICK UP HIS WAGON AT MY HOUSE!
THE EXCITEMENT OVER, THE WORLD'S MIGHTIEST MORTAL REPEATS THE MAGIC NAME...
SHAZAM!
...AND BILLY REAPPEARS!
BOOM
THAT'S THE STORY, FOLKS, OF THE WORLD'S TOUGHEST GUY! IT JUST GOES TO SHOW THAT NO MATTER HOW TOUGH ROWDY WAS, CAPTAIN MARVEL WAS TOUGHER!
C·C·BECK
AND NICER, TOO... RIGHT?
THE END.
7

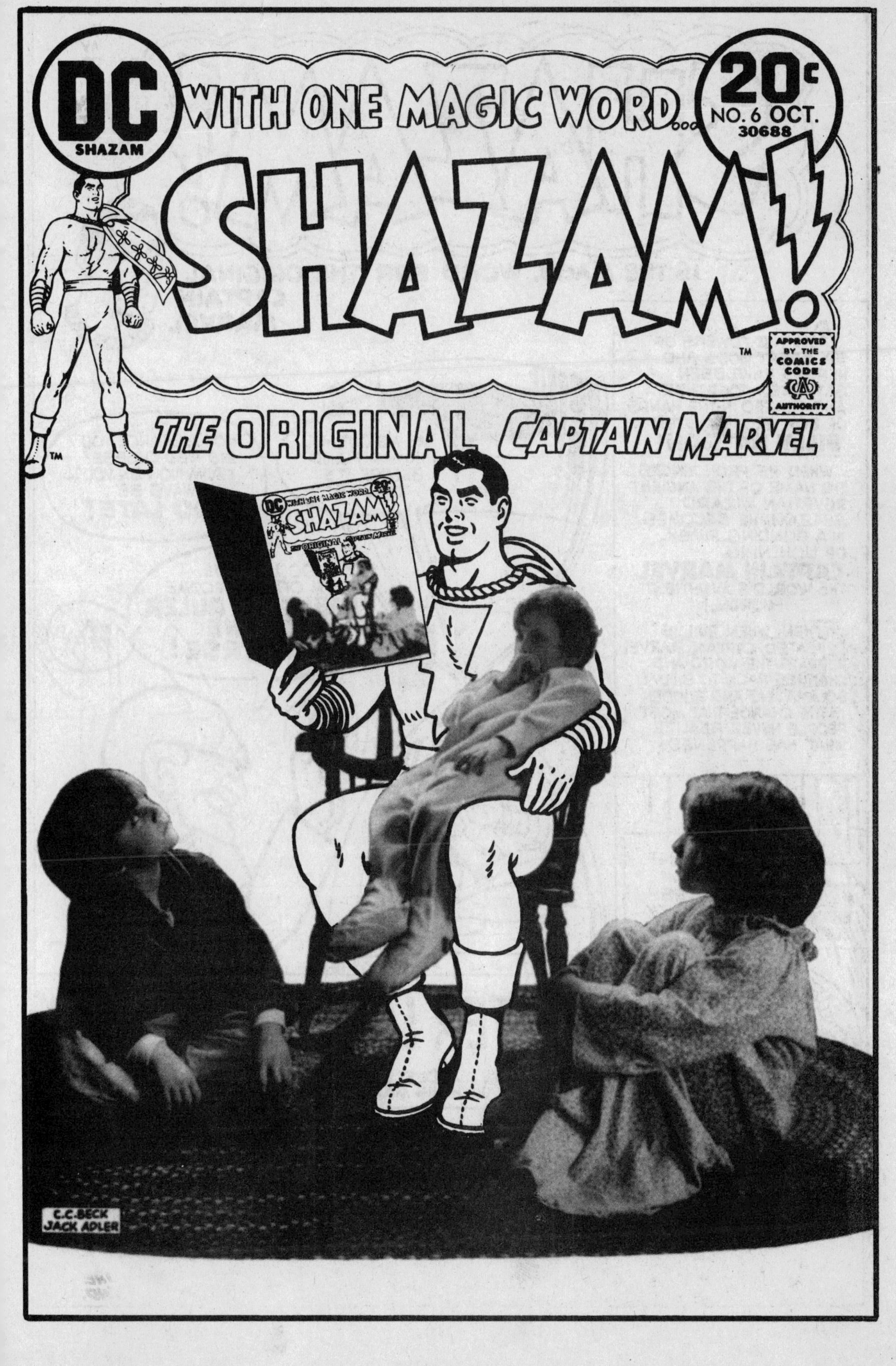
DC
SHAZAM
WITH ONE MAGIC WORD...
20¢
NO. 6 OCT.
30688
SHAZAM!
APPROVED BY THE COMICS CODE AUTHORITY
THE ORIGINAL CAPTAIN MARVEL
C.C. BECK
JACK ADLER

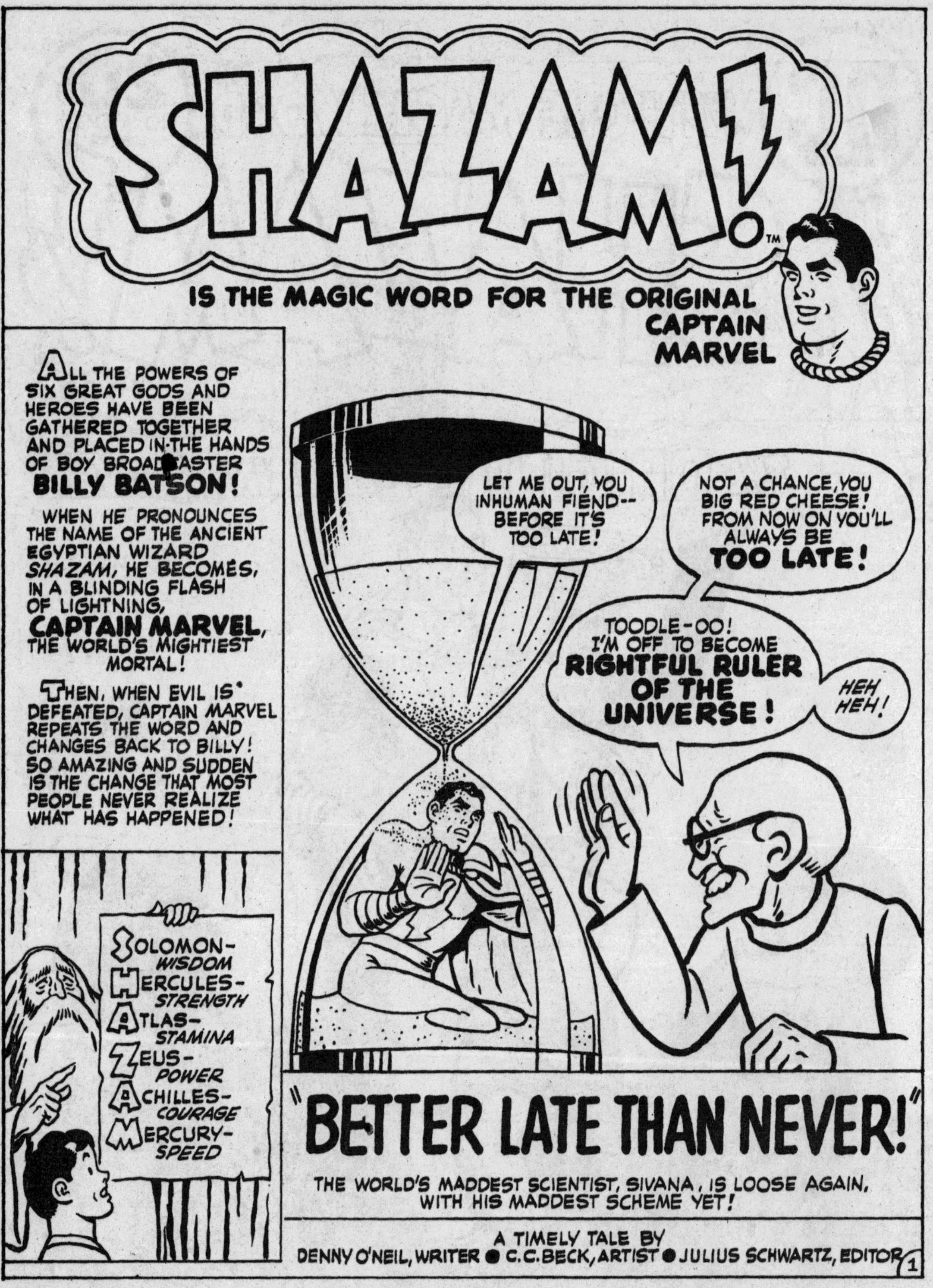
SHAZAM!™
IS THE MAGIC WORD FOR THE ORIGINAL CAPTAIN MARVEL
ALL THE POWERS OF SIX GREAT GODS AND HEROES HAVE BEEN GATHERED TOGETHER AND PLACED IN THE HANDS OF BOY BROADCASTER BILLY BATSON!
WHEN HE PRONOUNCES THE NAME OF THE ANCIENT EGYPTIAN WIZARD SHAZAM, HE BECOMES, IN A BLINDING FLASH OF LIGHTNING, CAPTAIN MARVEL, THE WORLD'S MIGHTIEST MORTAL!
THEN, WHEN EVIL IS DEFEATED, CAPTAIN MARVEL REPEATS THE WORD AND CHANGES BACK TO BILLY! SO AMAZING AND SUDDEN IS THE CHANGE THAT MOST PEOPLE NEVER REALIZE WHAT HAS HAPPENED!
SOLOMON- WISDOM
HERCULES- STRENGTH
ATLAS- STAMINA
ZEUS- POWER
ACHILLES- COURAGE
MERCURY- SPEED
LET ME OUT, YOU INHUMAN FIEND-- BEFORE IT'S TOO LATE!
NOT A CHANCE, YOU BIG RED CHEESE! FROM NOW ON YOU'LL ALWAYS BE TOO LATE!
TOODLE-OO! I'M OFF TO BECOME RIGHTFUL RULER OF THE UNIVERSE!
HEH HEH!
"BETTER LATE THAN NEVER!"
THE WORLD'S MADDEST SCIENTIST, SIVANA, IS LOOSE AGAIN, WITH HIS MADDEST SCHEME YET!
A TIMELY TALE BY
DENNY O'NEIL, WRITER ● C.C. BECK, ARTIST ● JULIUS SCHWARTZ, EDITOR
1

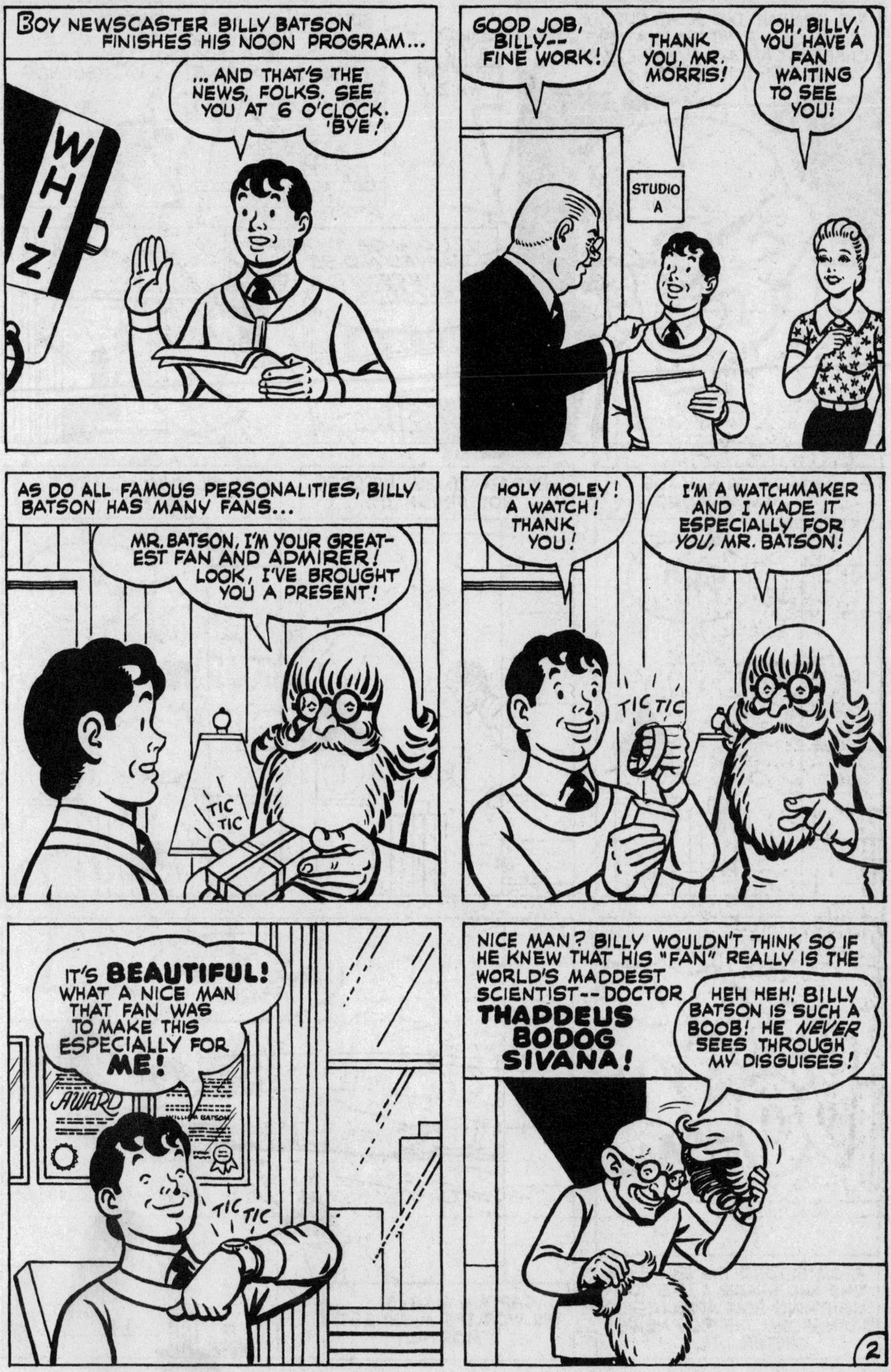
BOY NEWSCASTER BILLY BATSON FINISHES HIS NOON PROGRAM...
... AND THAT'S THE NEWS, FOLKS. SEE YOU AT 6 O'CLOCK. 'BYE!
WHIZ
GOOD JOB, BILLY-- FINE WORK!
THANK YOU, MR. MORRIS!
OH, BILLY, YOU HAVE A FAN WAITING TO SEE YOU!
STUDIO A
AS DO ALL FAMOUS PERSONALITIES, BILLY BATSON HAS MANY FANS...
MR. BATSON, I'M YOUR GREATEST FAN AND ADMIRER! LOOK, I'VE BROUGHT YOU A PRESENT!
TIC TIC
HOLY MOLEY! A WATCH! THANK YOU!
I'M A WATCHMAKER AND I MADE IT ESPECIALLY FOR YOU, MR. BATSON!
TIC TIC
IT'S BEAUTIFUL! WHAT A NICE MAN THAT FAN WAS TO MAKE THIS ESPECIALLY FOR ME!
AWARD
TIC TIC
NICE MAN? BILLY WOULDN'T THINK SO IF HE KNEW THAT HIS "FAN" REALLY IS THE WORLD'S MADDEST SCIENTIST-- DOCTOR THADDEUS BODOG SIVANA!
HEH HEH! BILLY BATSON IS SUCH A BOOB! HE NEVER SEES THROUGH MY DISGUISES!
2

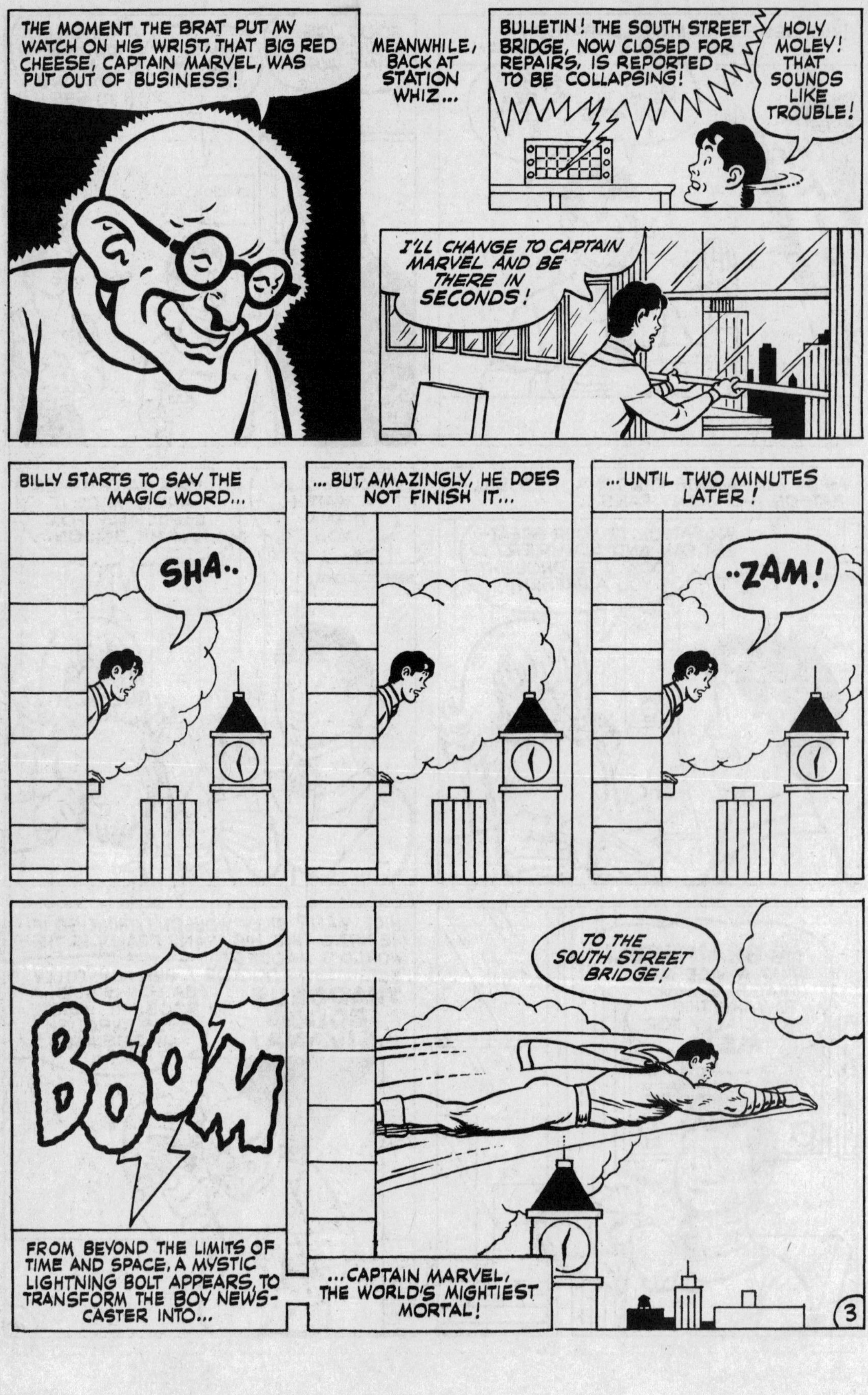
THE MOMENT THE BRAT PUT MY WATCH ON HIS WRIST, THAT BIG RED CHEESE, CAPTAIN MARVEL, WAS PUT OUT OF BUSINESS!
MEANWHILE, BACK AT STATION WHIZ...
BULLETIN! THE SOUTH STREET BRIDGE, NOW CLOSED FOR REPAIRS, IS REPORTED TO BE COLLAPSING!
HOLY MOLEY! THAT SOUNDS LIKE TROUBLE!
I'LL CHANGE TO CAPTAIN MARVEL AND BE THERE IN SECONDS!
BILLY STARTS TO SAY THE MAGIC WORD...
SHA..
...BUT, AMAZINGLY, HE DOES NOT FINISH IT...
...UNTIL TWO MINUTES LATER!
..ZAM!
BOOM
FROM BEYOND THE LIMITS OF TIME AND SPACE, A MYSTIC LIGHTNING BOLT APPEARS, TO TRANSFORM THE BOY NEWS-CASTER INTO...
...CAPTAIN MARVEL, THE WORLD'S MIGHTIEST MORTAL!
TO THE SOUTH STREET BRIDGE!
3

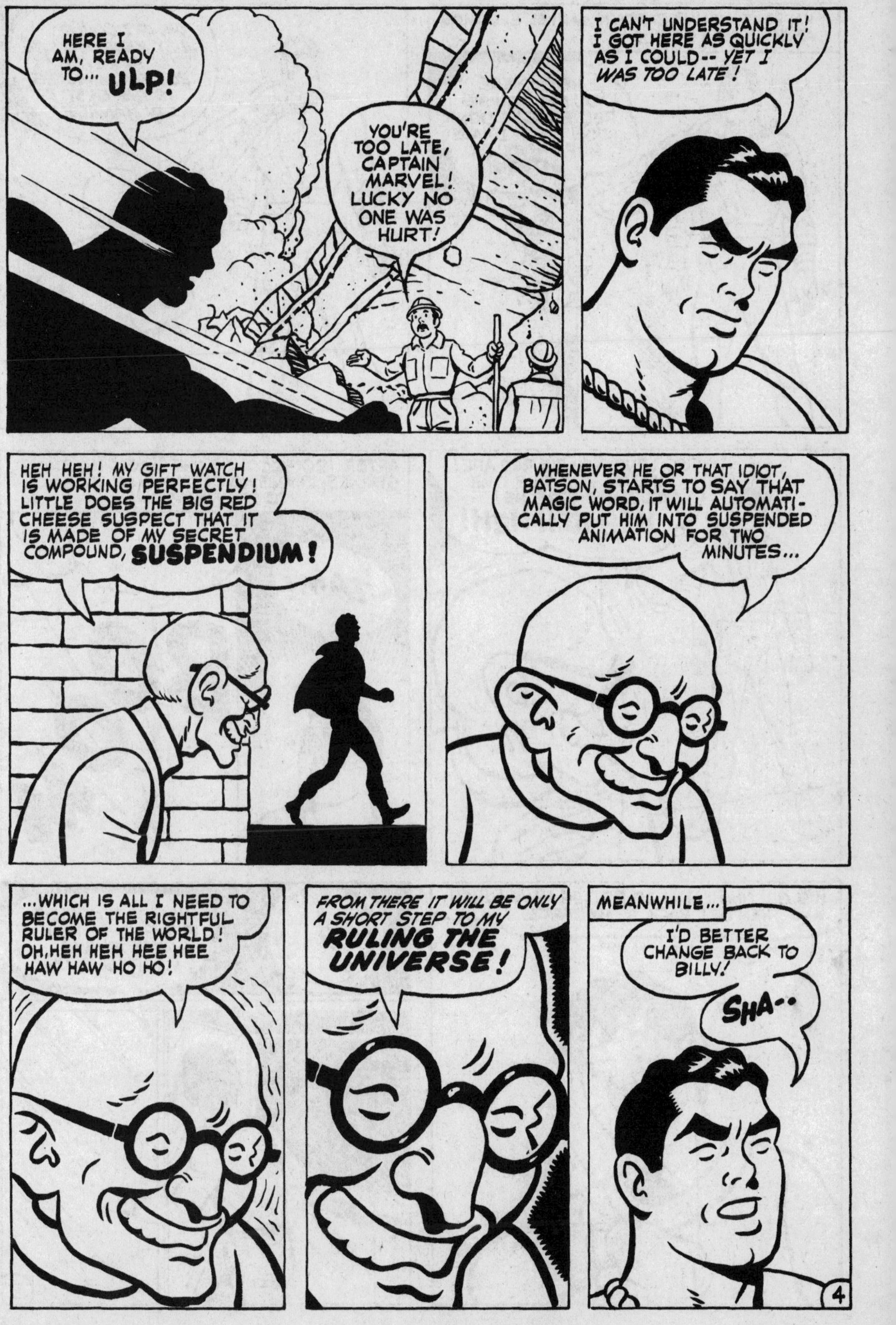
HERE I AM, READY TO... ULP!
YOU'RE TOO LATE, CAPTAIN MARVEL! LUCKY NO ONE WAS HURT!
I CAN'T UNDERSTAND IT! I GOT HERE AS QUICKLY AS I COULD-- YET I WAS TOO LATE!
HEH HEH! MY GIFT WATCH IS WORKING PERFECTLY! LITTLE DOES THE BIG RED CHEESE SUSPECT THAT IT IS MADE OF MY SECRET COMPOUND, SUSPENDIUM!
WHENEVER HE OR THAT IDIOT, BATSON, STARTS TO SAY THAT MAGIC WORD, IT WILL AUTOMATICALLY PUT HIM INTO SUSPENDED ANIMATION FOR TWO MINUTES...
...WHICH IS ALL I NEED TO BECOME THE RIGHTFUL RULER OF THE WORLD! OH, HEH HEH HEE HEE HAW HAW HO HO!
FROM THERE IT WILL BE ONLY A SHORT STEP TO MY RULING THE UNIVERSE!
MEANWHILE...
I'D BETTER CHANGE BACK TO BILLY!
SHA-..
4

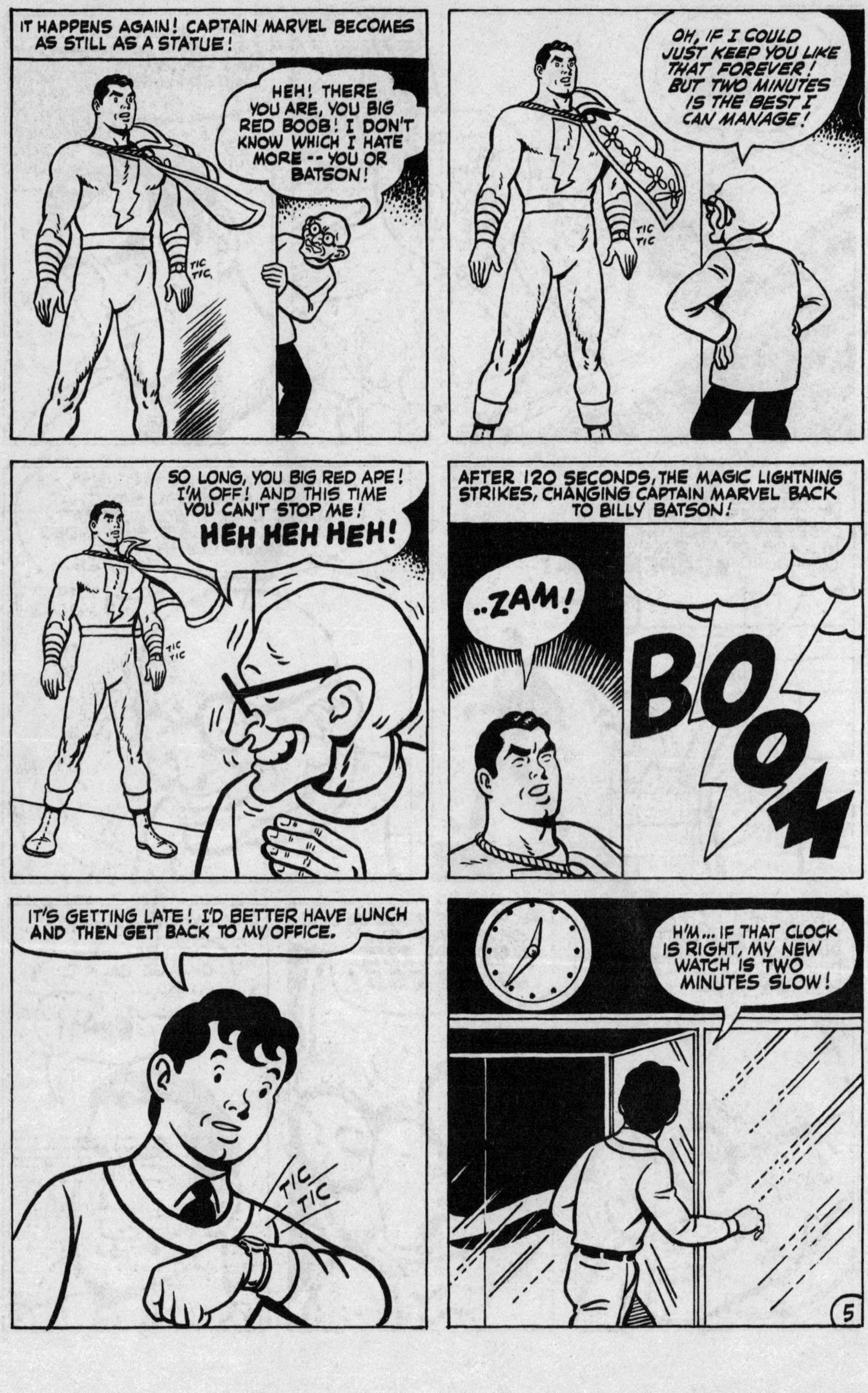
IT HAPPENS AGAIN! CAPTAIN MARVEL BECOMES AS STILL AS A STATUE!
HEH! THERE YOU ARE, YOU BIG RED BOOB! I DON'T KNOW WHICH I HATE MORE -- YOU OR BATSON!
TIC TIC
OH, IF I COULD JUST KEEP YOU LIKE THAT FOREVER! BUT TWO MINUTES IS THE BEST I CAN MANAGE!
TIC TIC
SO LONG, YOU BIG RED APE! I'M OFF! AND THIS TIME YOU CAN'T STOP ME! HEH HEH HEH!
TIC TIC
AFTER 120 SECONDS, THE MAGIC LIGHTNING STRIKES, CHANGING CAPTAIN MARVEL BACK TO BILLY BATSON!
..ZAM!
BOOM
IT'S GETTING LATE! I'D BETTER HAVE LUNCH AND THEN GET BACK TO MY OFFICE.
TIC TIC
H'M... IF THAT CLOCK IS RIGHT, MY NEW WATCH IS TWO MINUTES SLOW!
5

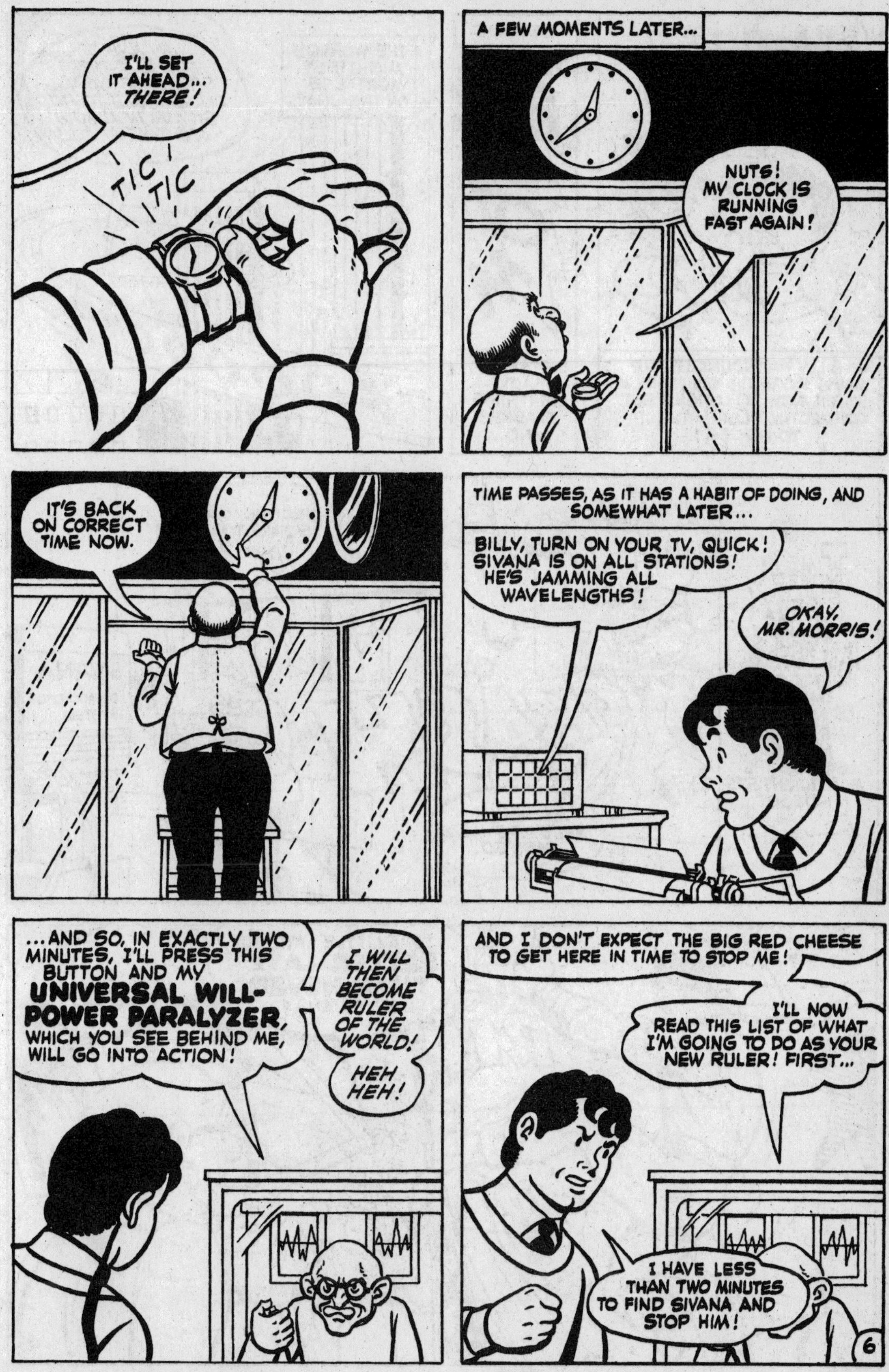
I'LL SET IT AHEAD... THERE!
TIC TIC
A FEW MOMENTS LATER...
NUTS! MY CLOCK IS RUNNING FAST AGAIN!
IT'S BACK ON CORRECT TIME NOW.
TIME PASSES, AS IT HAS A HABIT OF DOING, AND SOMEWHAT LATER...
BILLY, TURN ON YOUR TV, QUICK! SIVANA IS ON ALL STATIONS! HE'S JAMMING ALL WAVELENGTHS!
OKAY, MR. MORRIS!
...AND SO, IN EXACTLY TWO MINUTES, I'LL PRESS THIS BUTTON AND MY UNIVERSAL WILL-POWER PARALYZER, WHICH YOU SEE BEHIND ME, WILL GO INTO ACTION!
I WILL THEN BECOME RULER OF THE WORLD!
HEH HEH!
AND I DON'T EXPECT THE BIG RED CHEESE TO GET HERE IN TIME TO STOP ME!
I'LL NOW READ THIS LIST OF WHAT I'M GOING TO DO AS YOUR NEW RULER! FIRST...
I HAVE LESS THAN TWO MINUTES TO FIND SIVANA AND STOP HIM!
6

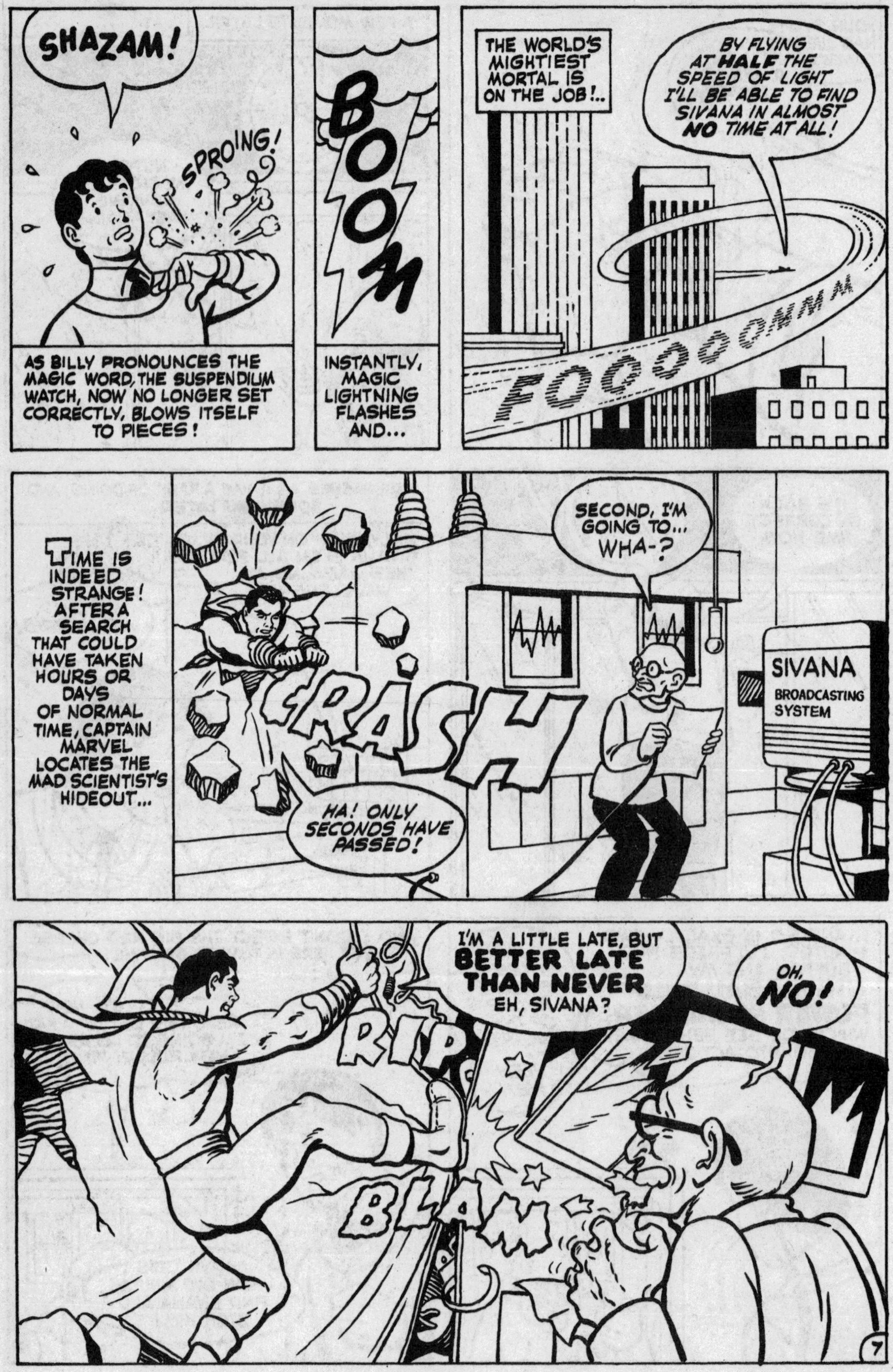
SHAZAM!
SPROING!
AS BILLY PRONOUNCES THE MAGIC WORD, THE SUSPENDIUM WATCH, NOW NO LONGER SET CORRECTLY, BLOWS ITSELF TO PIECES!
BOOM
INSTANTLY, MAGIC LIGHTNING FLASHES AND...
THE WORLD'S MIGHTIEST MORTAL IS ON THE JOB!..
BY FLYING AT HALF THE SPEED OF LIGHT I'LL BE ABLE TO FIND SIVANA IN ALMOST NO TIME AT ALL!
FOOOOOOOMMM
TIME IS INDEED STRANGE! AFTER A SEARCH THAT COULD HAVE TAKEN HOURS OR DAYS OF NORMAL TIME, CAPTAIN MARVEL LOCATES THE MAD SCIENTIST'S HIDEOUT...
CRASH
HA! ONLY SECONDS HAVE PASSED!
SECOND, I'M GOING TO... WHA-?
SIVANA
BROADCASTING SYSTEM
I'M A LITTLE LATE, BUT BETTER LATE THAN NEVER EH, SIVANA?
OH, NO!
RIP
BLAM
7

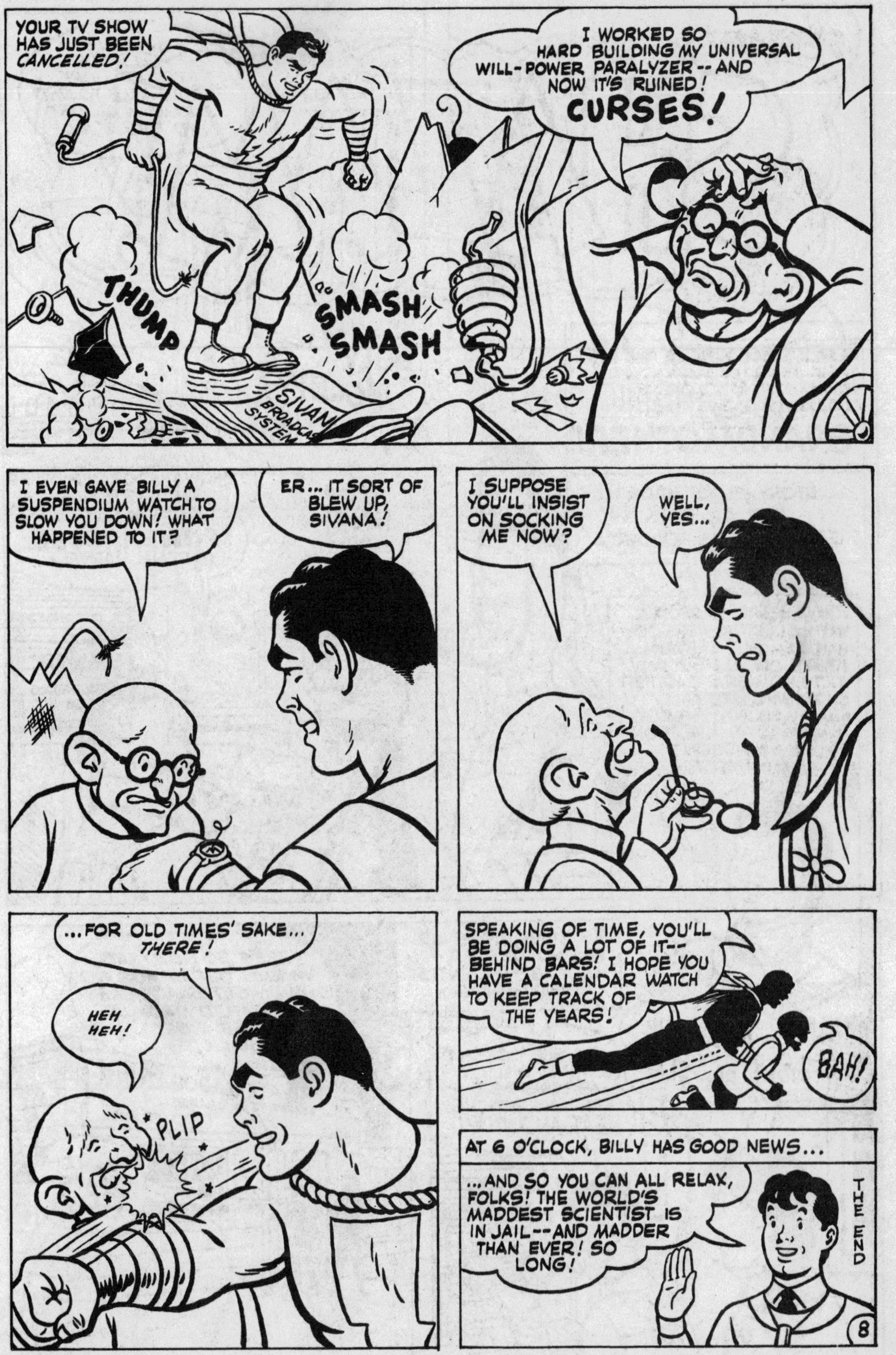
YOUR TV SHOW HAS JUST BEEN CANCELLED!
I WORKED SO HARD BUILDING MY UNIVERSAL WILL-POWER PARALYZER -- AND NOW IT'S RUINED! CURSES!
THUMP
SMASH SMASH
SIVAN BROADCAS SYSTEM
I EVEN GAVE BILLY A SUSPENDIUM WATCH TO SLOW YOU DOWN! WHAT HAPPENED TO IT?
ER... IT SORT OF BLEW UP, SIVANA!
I SUPPOSE YOU'LL INSIST ON SOCKING ME NOW?
WELL, YES...
...FOR OLD TIMES' SAKE... THERE!
HEH HEH!
PLIP
SPEAKING OF TIME, YOU'LL BE DOING A LOT OF IT-- BEHIND BARS! I HOPE YOU HAVE A CALENDAR WATCH TO KEEP TRACK OF THE YEARS!
BAH!
AT 6 O'CLOCK, BILLY HAS GOOD NEWS...
...AND SO YOU CAN ALL RELAX, FOLKS! THE WORLD'S MADDEST SCIENTIST IS IN JAIL--AND MADDER THAN EVER! SO LONG!
THE END
8

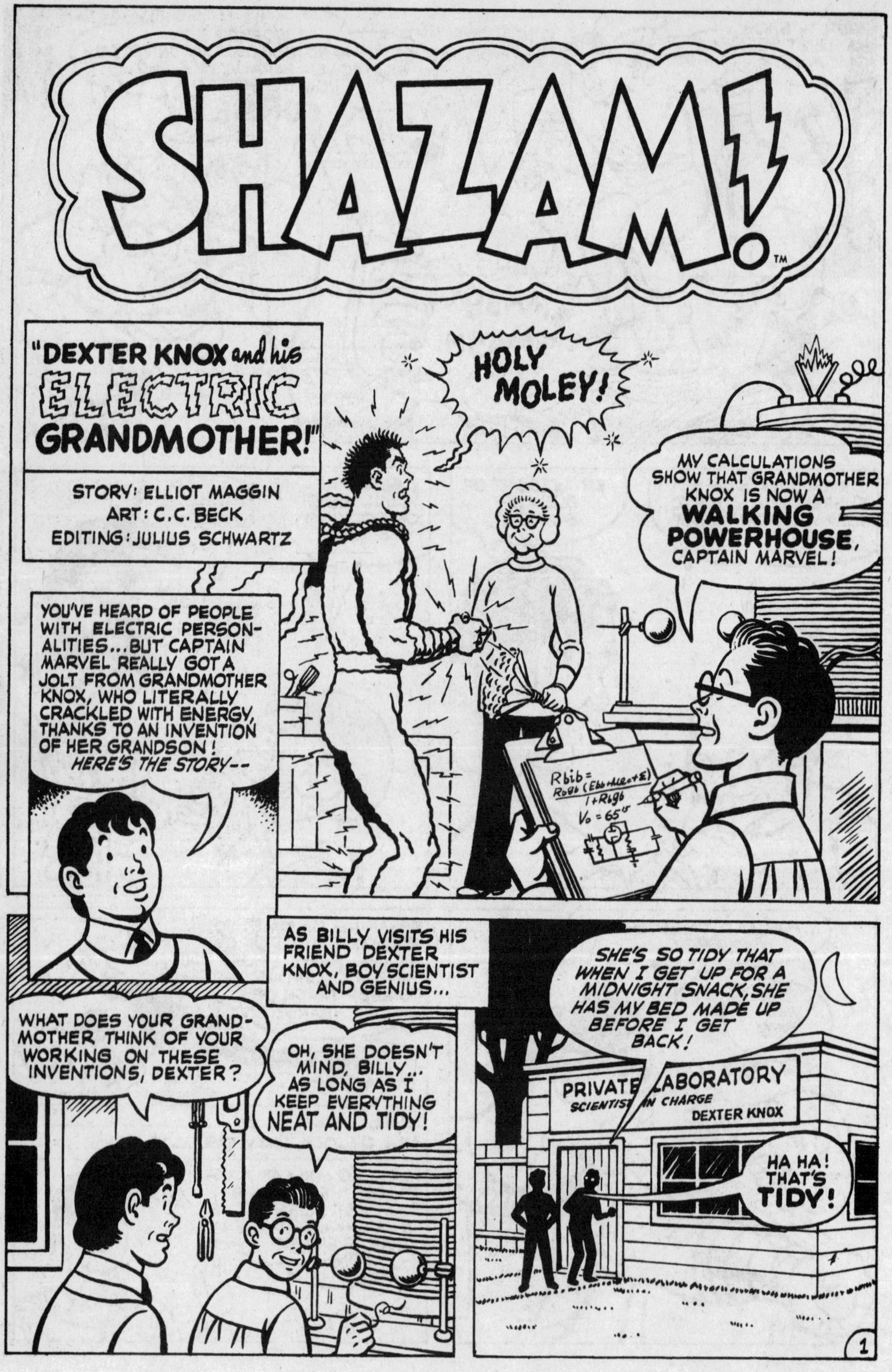
SHAZAM!
"DEXTER KNOX and his ELECTRIC GRANDMOTHER!"
STORY: ELLIOT MAGGIN
ART: C.C. BECK
EDITING: JULIUS SCHWARTZ
HOLY MOLEY!
MY CALCULATIONS SHOW THAT GRANDMOTHER KNOX IS NOW A WALKING POWERHOUSE, CAPTAIN MARVEL!
YOU'VE HEARD OF PEOPLE WITH ELECTRIC PERSONALITIES... BUT CAPTAIN MARVEL REALLY GOT A JOLT FROM GRANDMOTHER KNOX, WHO LITERALLY CRACKLED WITH ENERGY, THANKS TO AN INVENTION OF HER GRANDSON! HERE'S THE STORY--
AS BILLY VISITS HIS FRIEND DEXTER KNOX, BOY SCIENTIST AND GENIUS...
WHAT DOES YOUR GRANDMOTHER THINK OF YOUR WORKING ON THESE INVENTIONS, DEXTER?
OH, SHE DOESN'T MIND, BILLY... AS LONG AS I KEEP EVERYTHING NEAT AND TIDY!
SHE'S SO TIDY THAT WHEN I GET UP FOR A MIDNIGHT SNACK, SHE HAS MY BED MADE UP BEFORE I GET BACK!
PRIVATE LABORATORY
SCIENTIST IN CHARGE
DEXTER KNOX
HA HA! THAT'S TIDY!
1

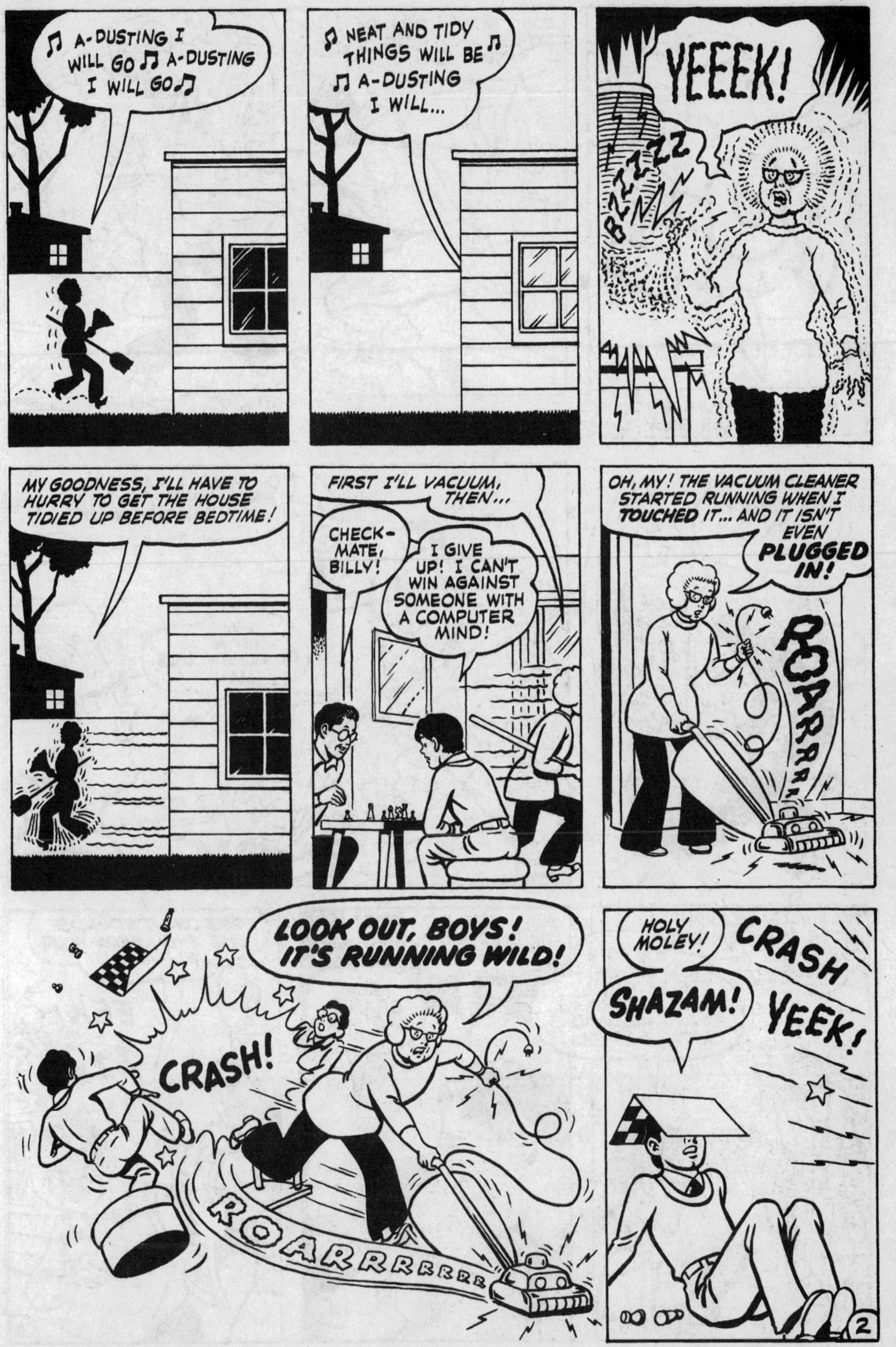
♫ A-DUSTING I WILL GO ♫ A-DUSTING I WILL GO ♫
♫ NEAT AND TIDY THINGS WILL BE ♫ ♫ A-DUSTING I WILL...
YEEEK!
BZZZZZZ
MY GOODNESS, I'LL HAVE TO HURRY TO GET THE HOUSE TIDIED UP BEFORE BEDTIME!
FIRST I'LL VACUUM, THEN...
CHECK-MATE, BILLY!
I GIVE UP! I CAN'T WIN AGAINST SOMEONE WITH A COMPUTER MIND!
OH, MY! THE VACUUM CLEANER STARTED RUNNING WHEN I TOUCHED IT... AND IT ISN'T EVEN PLUGGED IN!
ROARRRRR
LOOK OUT, BOYS! IT'S RUNNING WILD!
CRASH!
ROARRRRRRRR
HOLY MOLEY!
CRASH
SHAZAM!
YEEK!
2

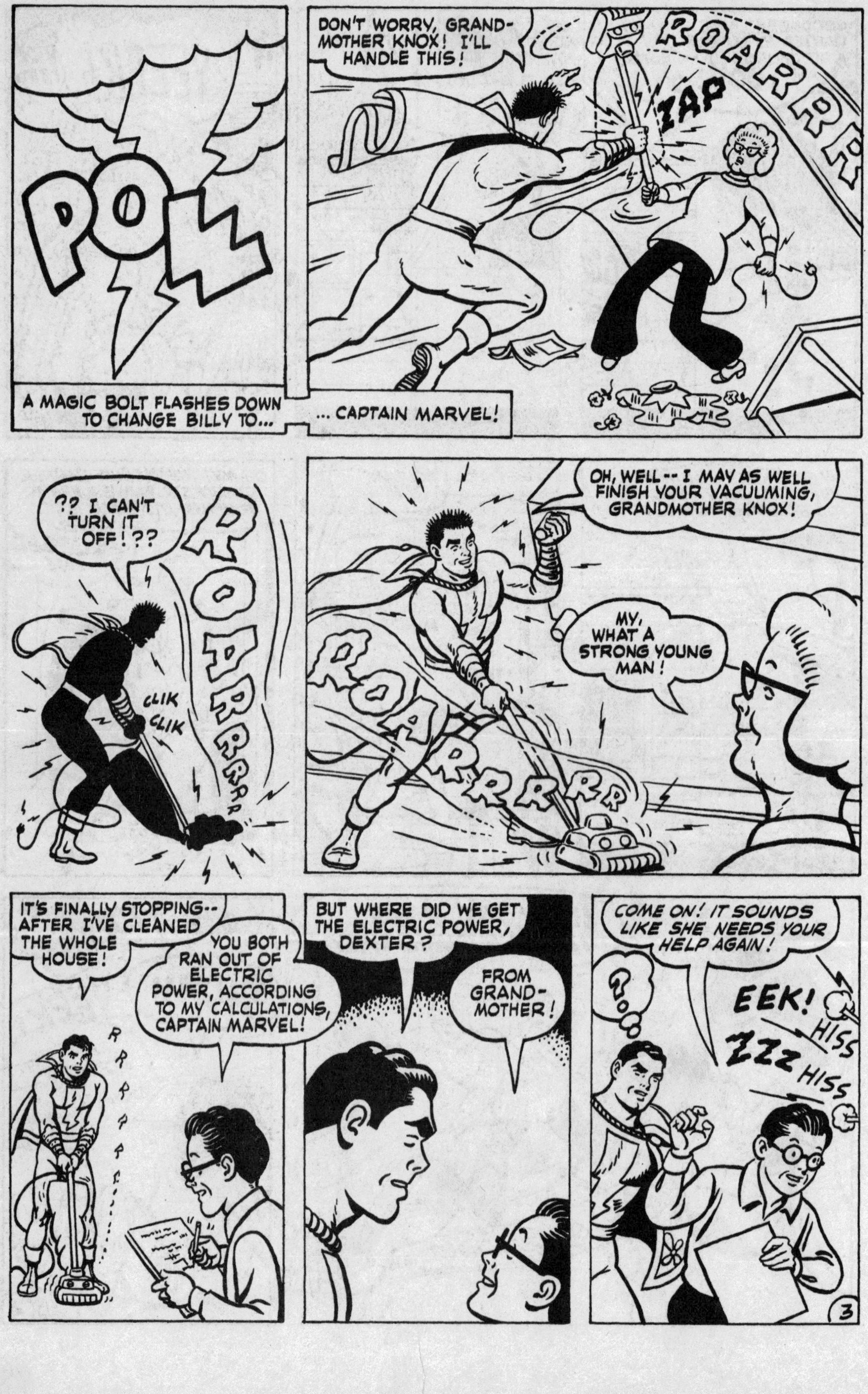
POW
A MAGIC BOLT FLASHES DOWN TO CHANGE BILLY TO...
... CAPTAIN MARVEL!
DON'T WORRY, GRANDMOTHER KNOX! I'LL HANDLE THIS!
ROARRRR
ZAP
?? I CAN'T TURN IT OFF! ??
ROARRRRR
CLIK CLIK
OH, WELL -- I MAY AS WELL FINISH YOUR VACUUMING, GRANDMOTHER KNOX!
MY, WHAT A STRONG YOUNG MAN!
ROARRRRRRR
IT'S FINALLY STOPPING-- AFTER I'VE CLEANED THE WHOLE HOUSE!
YOU BOTH RAN OUT OF ELECTRIC POWER, ACCORDING TO MY CALCULATIONS, CAPTAIN MARVEL!
RRRRR
BUT WHERE DID WE GET THE ELECTRIC POWER, DEXTER?
FROM GRANDMOTHER!
COME ON! IT SOUNDS LIKE SHE NEEDS YOUR HELP AGAIN!
?
EEK!
ZZZ
HISS
HISS
3

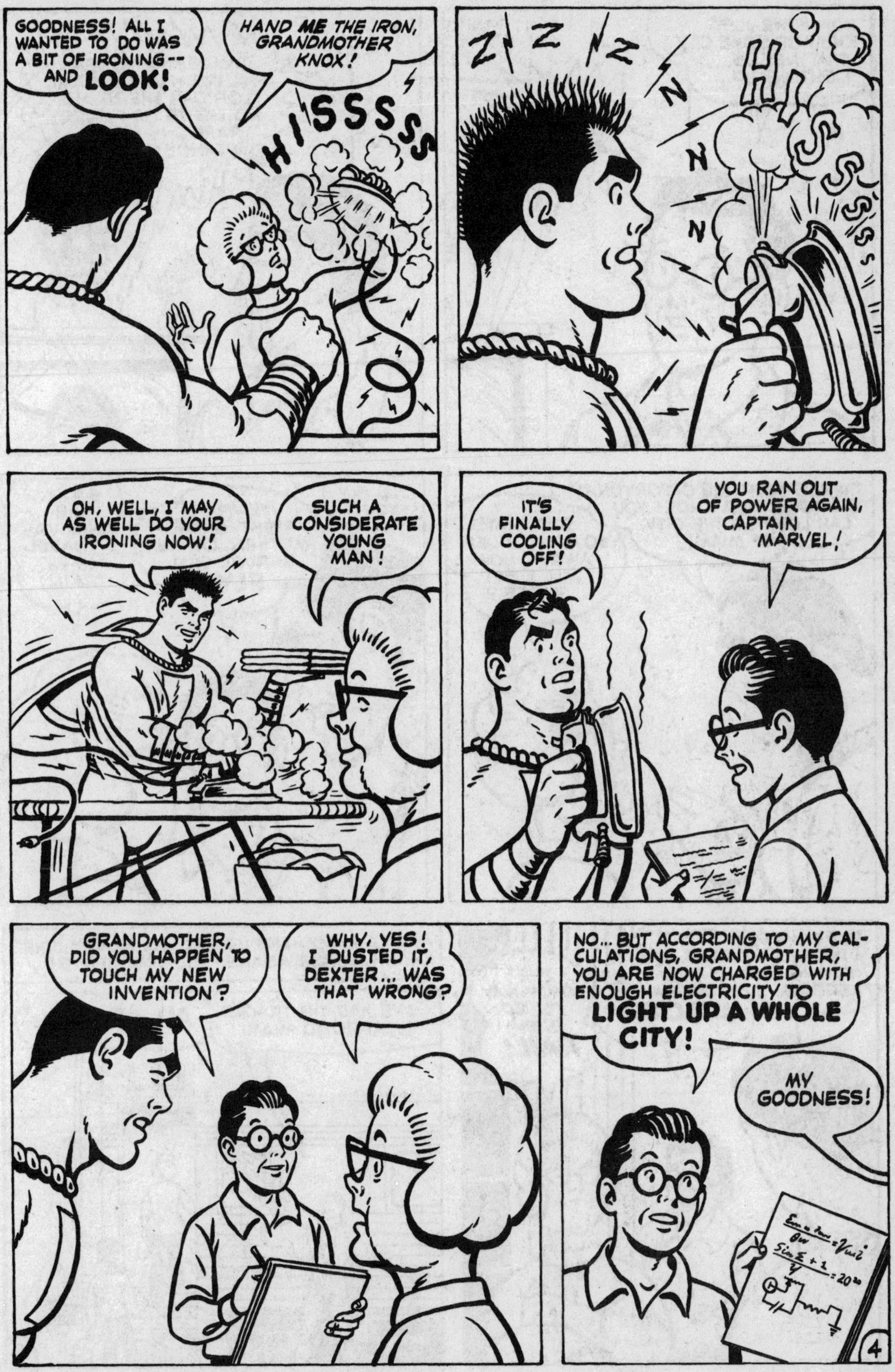
GOODNESS! ALL I WANTED TO DO WAS A BIT OF IRONING-- AND LOOK!
HAND ME THE IRON, GRANDMOTHER KNOX!
HISSSSSS
ZZZZZ
HISSSSSS
OH, WELL, I MAY AS WELL DO YOUR IRONING NOW!
SUCH A CONSIDERATE YOUNG MAN!
IT'S FINALLY COOLING OFF!
YOU RAN OUT OF POWER AGAIN, CAPTAIN MARVEL!
GRANDMOTHER, DID YOU HAPPEN TO TOUCH MY NEW INVENTION?
WHY, YES! I DUSTED IT, DEXTER... WAS THAT WRONG?
NO... BUT ACCORDING TO MY CALCULATIONS, GRANDMOTHER, YOU ARE NOW CHARGED WITH ENOUGH ELECTRICITY TO LIGHT UP A WHOLE CITY!
MY GOODNESS!
4

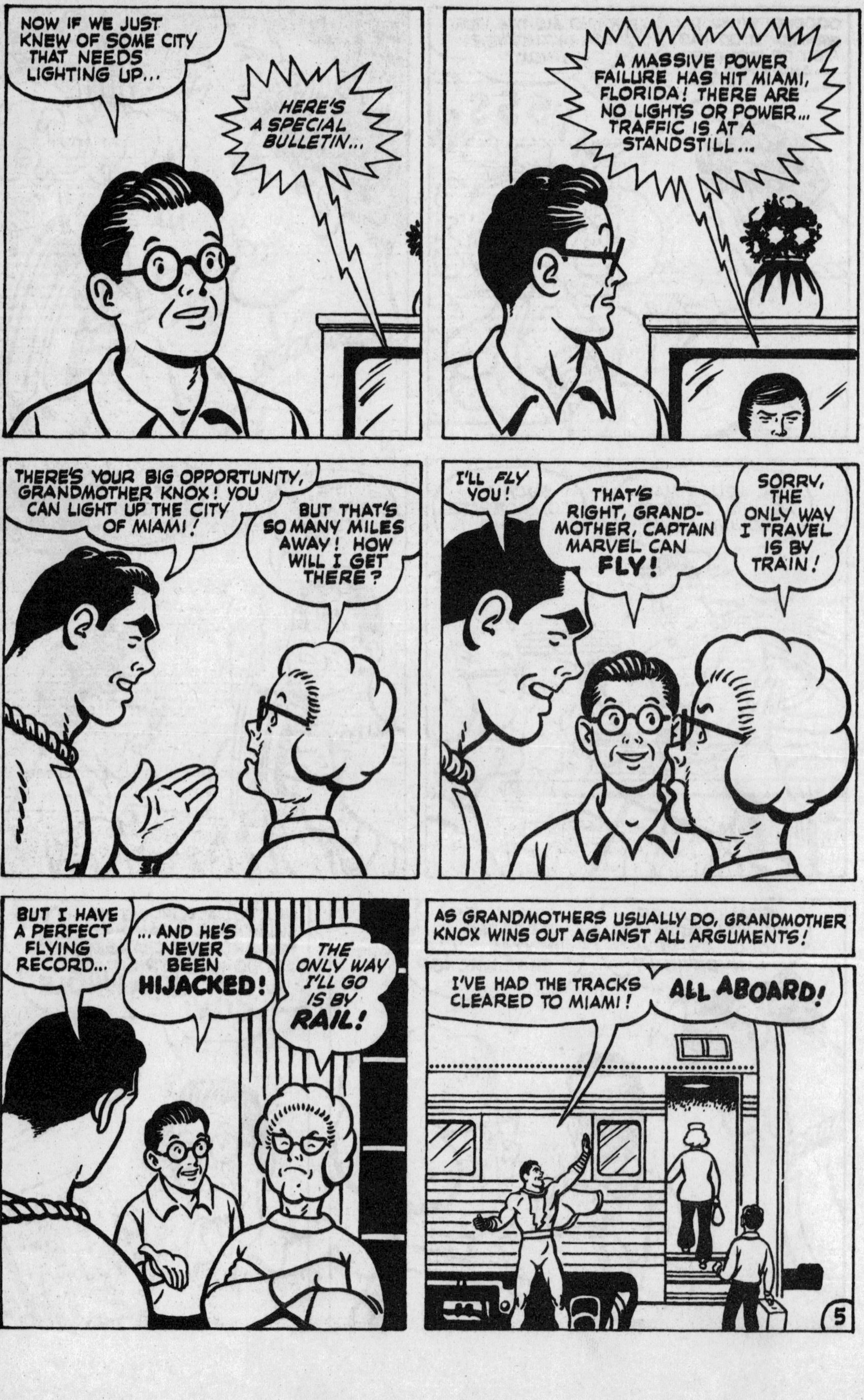
NOW IF WE JUST KNEW OF SOME CITY THAT NEEDS LIGHTING UP...
HERE'S A SPECIAL BULLETIN...
A MASSIVE POWER FAILURE HAS HIT MIAMI, FLORIDA! THERE ARE NO LIGHTS OR POWER... TRAFFIC IS AT A STANDSTILL...
THERE'S YOUR BIG OPPORTUNITY, GRANDMOTHER KNOX! YOU CAN LIGHT UP THE CITY OF MIAMI!
BUT THAT'S SO MANY MILES AWAY! HOW WILL I GET THERE?
I'LL FLY YOU!
THAT'S RIGHT, GRAND-MOTHER, CAPTAIN MARVEL CAN FLY!
SORRY, THE ONLY WAY I TRAVEL IS BY TRAIN!
BUT I HAVE A PERFECT FLYING RECORD...
...AND HE'S NEVER BEEN HIJACKED!
THE ONLY WAY I'LL GO IS BY RAIL!
AS GRANDMOTHERS USUALLY DO, GRANDMOTHER KNOX WINS OUT AGAINST ALL ARGUMENTS!
I'VE HAD THE TRACKS CLEARED TO MIAMI!
ALL ABOARD!
5

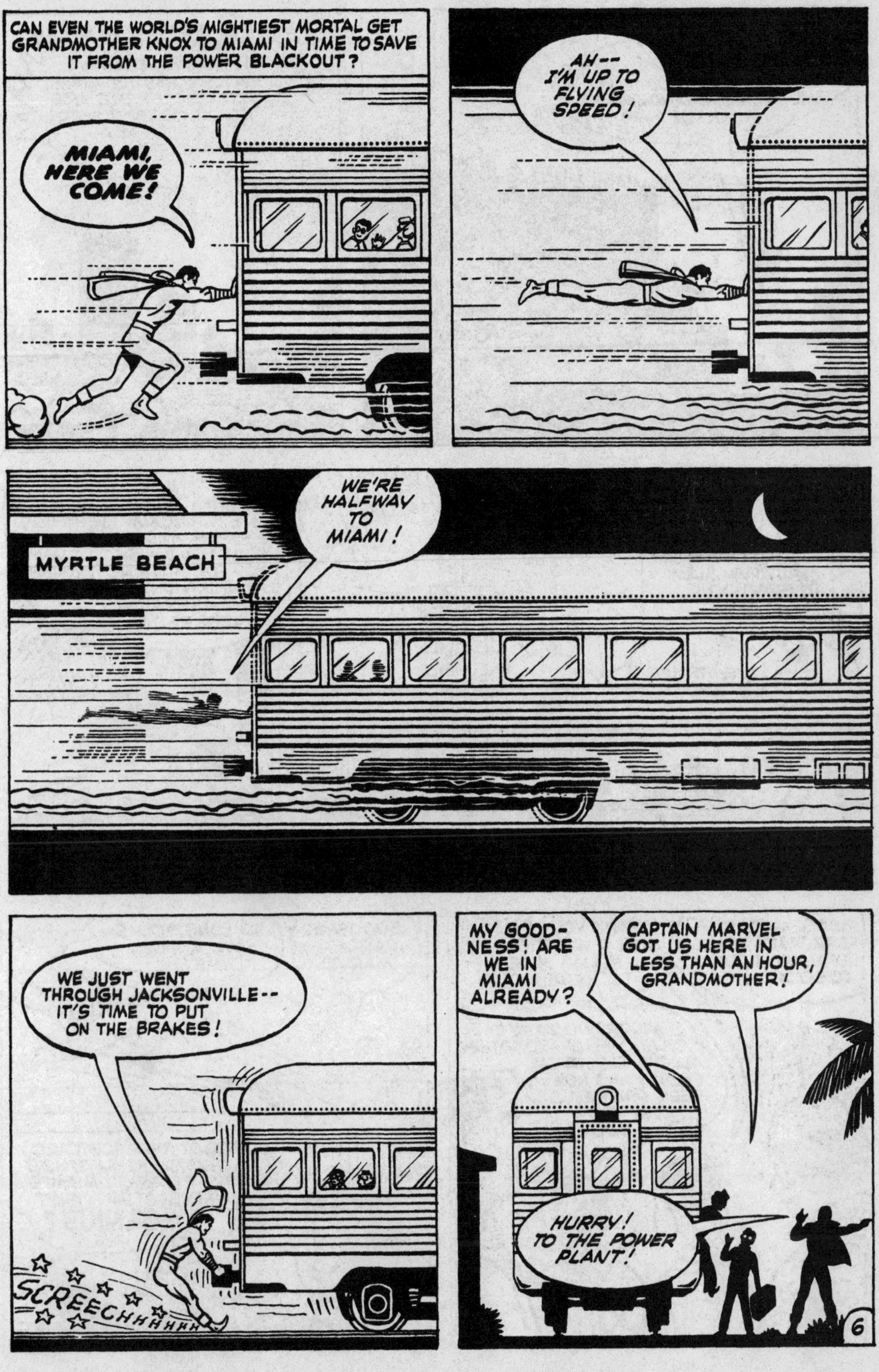
CAN EVEN THE WORLD'S MIGHTIEST MORTAL GET GRANDMOTHER KNOX TO MIAMI IN TIME TO SAVE IT FROM THE POWER BLACKOUT?
MIAMI, HERE WE COME!
AH-- I'M UP TO FLYING SPEED!
MYRTLE BEACH
WE'RE HALFWAY TO MIAMI!
WE JUST WENT THROUGH JACKSONVILLE-- IT'S TIME TO PUT ON THE BRAKES!
SCREECHHHHHH
MY GOODNESS! ARE WE IN MIAMI ALREADY?
CAPTAIN MARVEL GOT US HERE IN LESS THAN AN HOUR, GRANDMOTHER!
HURRY! TO THE POWER PLANT!
6

HERE'S WHERE YOU DO YOUR THING, GRANDMOTHER KNOX!

MIAMI LIGHT & POWER

AS GRANDMOTHER KNOX'S SUPER-CHARGED BODY CONNECTS WITH THE POWER CABLES...

...THOUSANDS OF KILOWATTS OF ELECTRICITY BRING BEAUTIFUL MIAMI TO SPARKLING LIFE!

THE LIGHTS ARE ON!

HOORAY!

NEXT MORN-ING...

MRS. KNOX, IN BEHALF OF THE MIAMI LIGHT AND POWER COMPANY, I WISH TO THANK YOU FOR KEEPING THINGS RUNNING UNTIL WE GOT THE GENERATORS REPAIRED!

PLEASE ACCEPT A FREE VACATION HERE, WITH OUR COMPLIMENTS!

THANK YOU! I CAN USE A VACATION... I FEEL A MITE TUCKERED-OUT!

ACCORDING TO MY CAL-CULATIONS, GRANDMOTHER, ALL THE ELECTRICAL ENERGY HAS NOW BEEN DRAINED FROM YOUR BODY!

C.C. BECK

GOODBYE, CAPTAIN MARVEL!

SO LONG, FOLKS-- HAVE A NICE TIME!

AWARD

I JUST GOT THIS POSTCARD FROM DEXTER! HE SAYS HE'S HELPING REDESIGN MIAMI'S POWER SYSTEM... ISN'T HE A **GENIUS?**

THE END 7

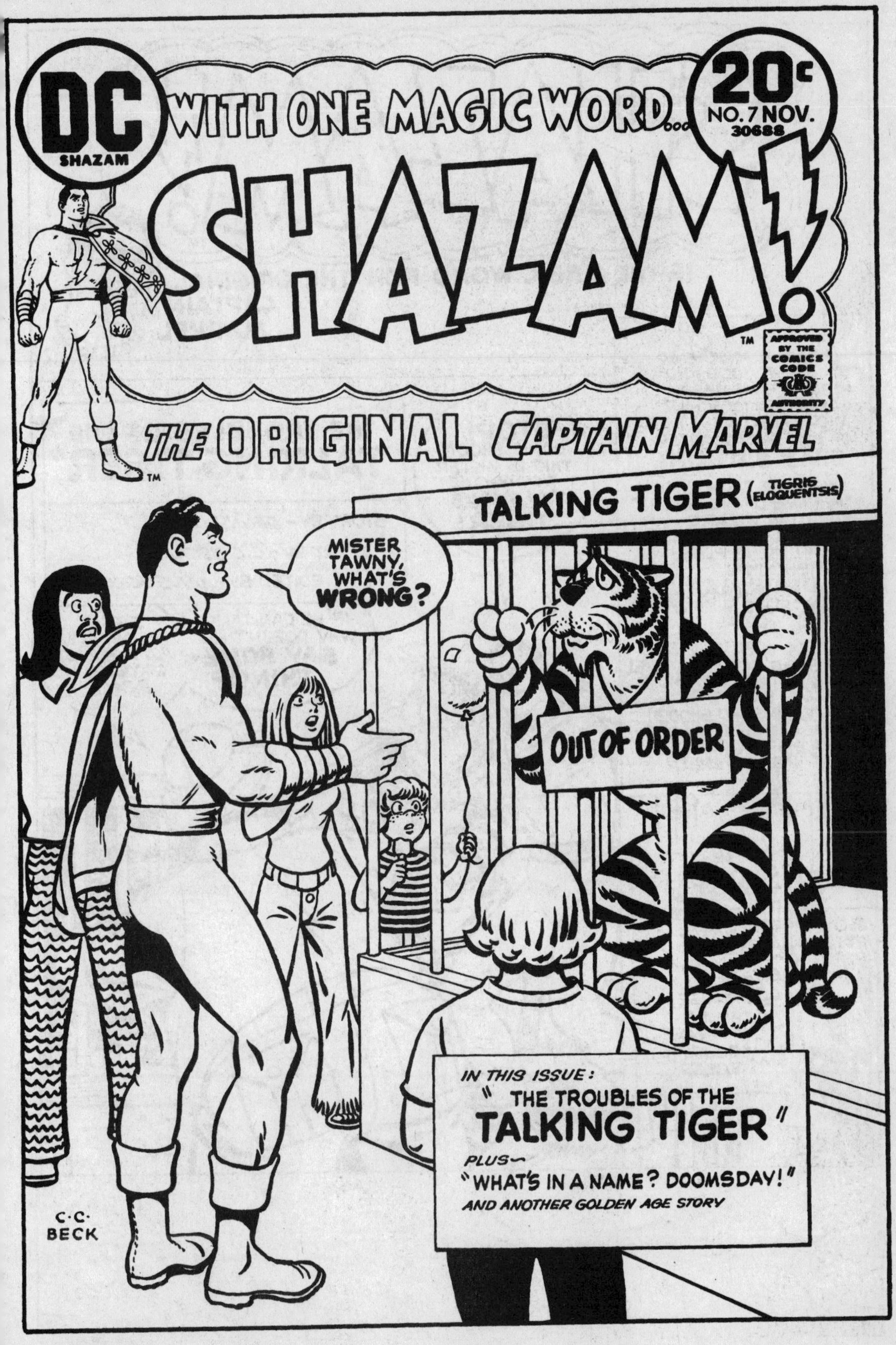
DC SHAZAM
WITH ONE MAGIC WORD...
20¢ NO. 7 NOV. 30688
SHAZAM!
APPROVED BY THE COMICS CODE AUTHORITY
THE ORIGINAL CAPTAIN MARVEL
TALKING TIGER (TIGRIS ELOQUENTSIS)
MISTER TAWNY, WHAT'S WRONG?
OUT OF ORDER
IN THIS ISSUE: "THE TROUBLES OF THE TALKING TIGER"
PLUS— "WHAT'S IN A NAME? DOOMSDAY!"
AND ANOTHER GOLDEN AGE STORY
C.C. BECK

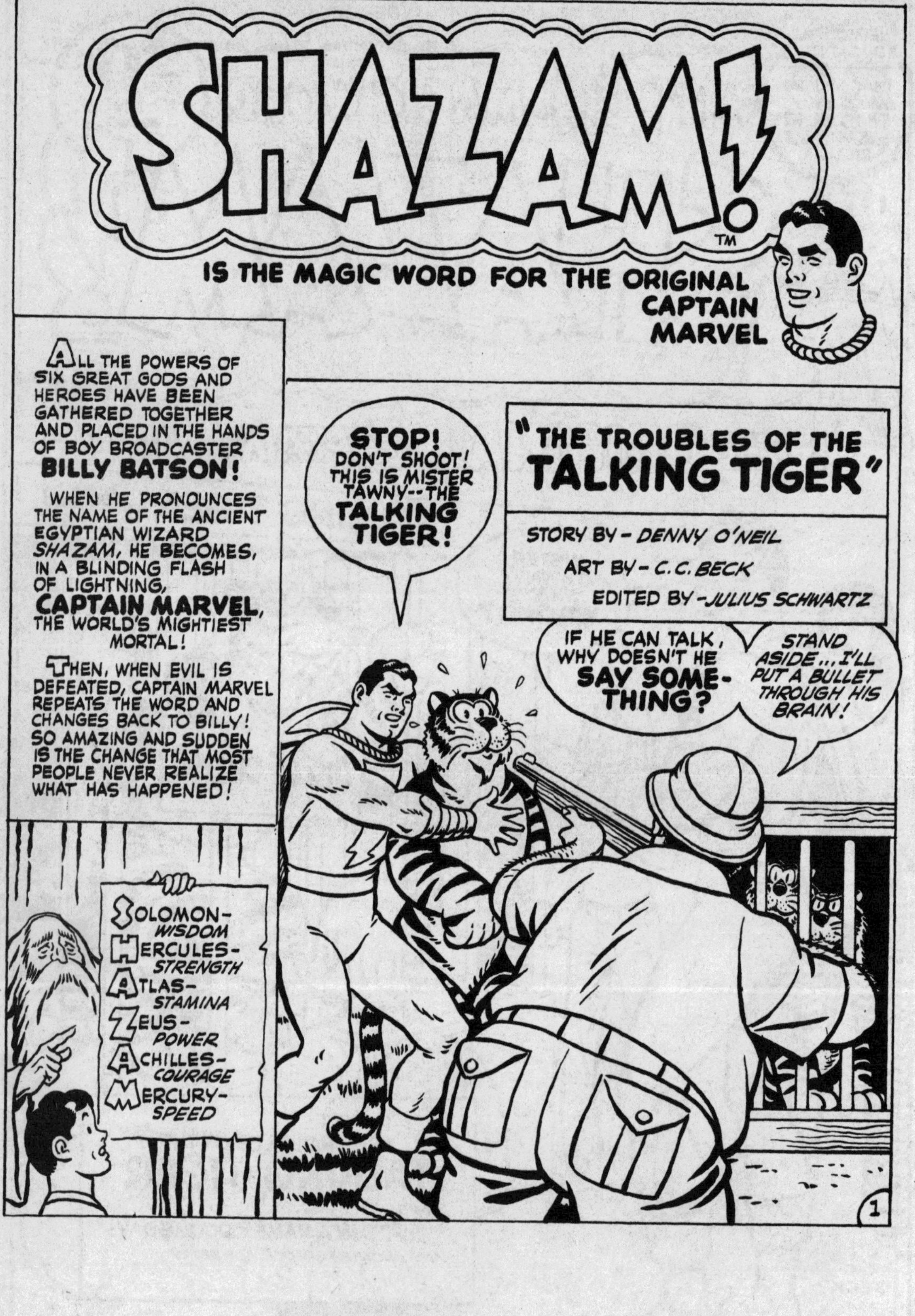
SHAZAM!
TM
IS THE MAGIC WORD FOR THE ORIGINAL CAPTAIN MARVEL
ALL THE POWERS OF SIX GREAT GODS AND HEROES HAVE BEEN GATHERED TOGETHER AND PLACED IN THE HANDS OF BOY BROADCASTER BILLY BATSON!
WHEN HE PRONOUNCES THE NAME OF THE ANCIENT EGYPTIAN WIZARD SHAZAM, HE BECOMES, IN A BLINDING FLASH OF LIGHTNING, CAPTAIN MARVEL, THE WORLD'S MIGHTIEST MORTAL!
THEN, WHEN EVIL IS DEFEATED, CAPTAIN MARVEL REPEATS THE WORD AND CHANGES BACK TO BILLY! SO AMAZING AND SUDDEN IS THE CHANGE THAT MOST PEOPLE NEVER REALIZE WHAT HAS HAPPENED!
SOLOMON- WISDOM
HERCULES- STRENGTH
ATLAS- STAMINA
ZEUS- POWER
ACHILLES- COURAGE
MERCURY- SPEED
STOP! DON'T SHOOT! THIS IS MISTER TAWNY--THE TALKING TIGER!
"THE TROUBLES OF THE TALKING TIGER"
STORY BY - DENNY O'NEIL
ART BY - C. C. BECK
EDITED BY - JULIUS SCHWARTZ
IF HE CAN TALK, WHY DOESN'T HE SAY SOMETHING?
STAND ASIDE...I'LL PUT A BULLET THROUGH HIS BRAIN!
1

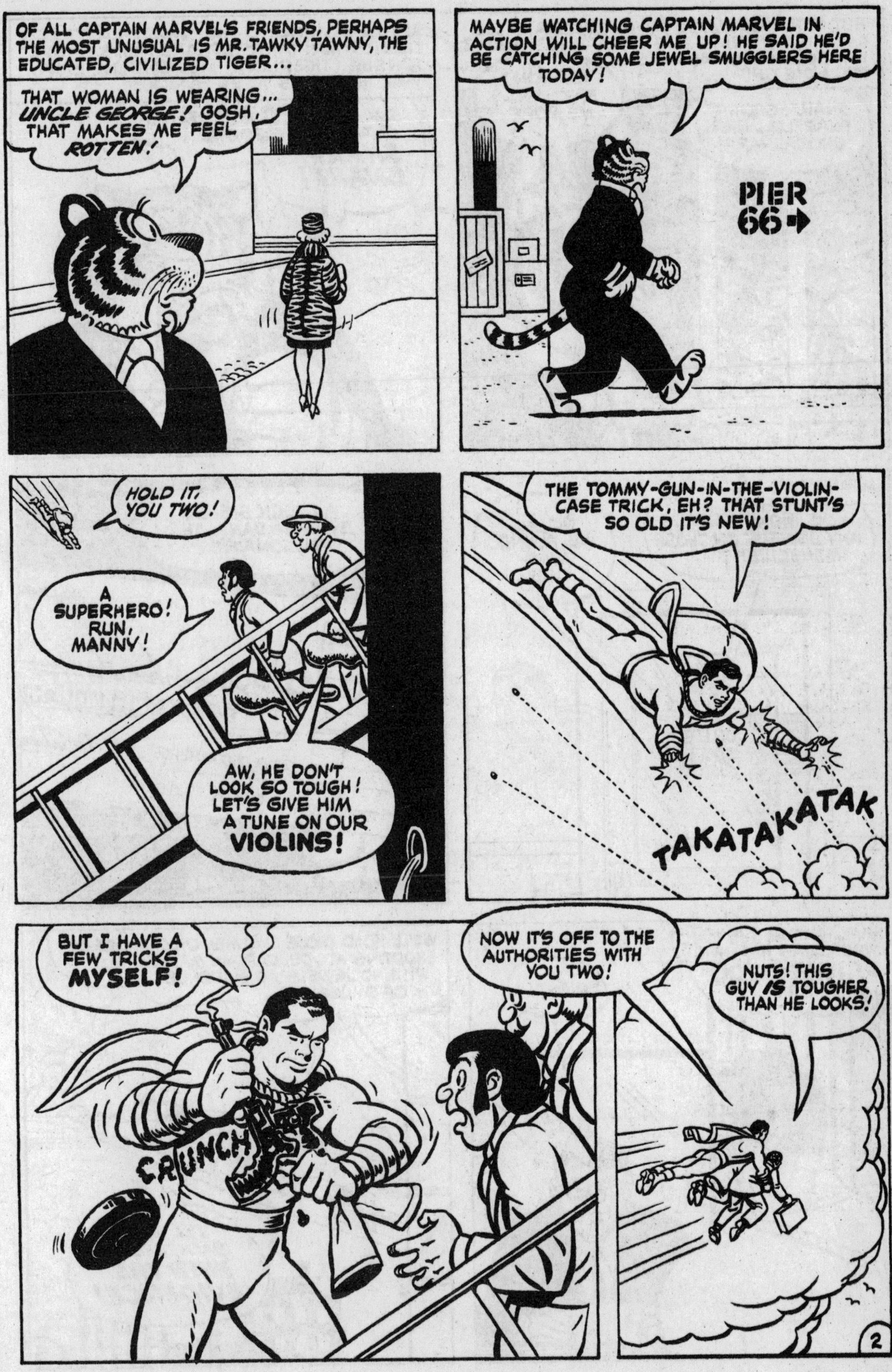
OF ALL CAPTAIN MARVEL'S FRIENDS, PERHAPS THE MOST UNUSUAL IS MR. TAWKY TAWNY, THE EDUCATED, CIVILIZED TIGER...
THAT WOMAN IS WEARING... UNCLE GEORGE! GOSH, THAT MAKES ME FEEL ROTTEN!
MAYBE WATCHING CAPTAIN MARVEL IN ACTION WILL CHEER ME UP! HE SAID HE'D BE CATCHING SOME JEWEL SMUGGLERS HERE TODAY!
PIER 66
HOLD IT, YOU TWO!
A SUPERHERO! RUN, MANNY!
AW, HE DON'T LOOK SO TOUGH! LET'S GIVE HIM A TUNE ON OUR VIOLINS!
THE TOMMY-GUN-IN-THE-VIOLIN-CASE TRICK, EH? THAT STUNT'S SO OLD IT'S NEW!
TAKATAKATAK
BUT I HAVE A FEW TRICKS MYSELF!
CRUNCH
NOW IT'S OFF TO THE AUTHORITIES WITH YOU TWO!
NUTS! THIS GUY IS TOUGHER THAN HE LOOKS!
2

BUT STRANGELY, MR. TAWNY ISN'T WATCHING CAPTAIN MARVEL AT ALL! INSTEAD, HE'S TALKING WITH SOME CAGED ANIMALS FROM THE SHIP!...

SNARF! GROWF SNARFLE... GRR GROWFSNARF!

YOU DON'T SAY! TELL ME MORE!

AFTER TALKING TO THE NEWLY-CAPTURED TIGERS, MR. TAWNY SPEAKS IN HIS NATIVE TONGUE (TIGERIAN)! WHATEVER HE IS SAYING, HE SEEMS TO BE SERIOUS!...

SNARL! GROWF! SNARF SNARFLE ... GROWFL SNARF SNARF!

MEANWHILE...

YOU DIDN'T FIND ANY JEWELS ON THOSE MEN, CHIEF?

NO, ALL WE FOUND WAS THIS...

UNITED STATES CUSTOMS

OFFICE OF CHIEF

... A CHECK SIGNED BY DANA DANA, THE MILLIONAIRE.

NO. 17654

PAY TO THE ORDER OF *Animal Importers Inc.*

EXACTLY $10,000 & 00

BANK OF COMMERCE

Dana Dana

HMM...ISN'T HE THE MAN WHO OWNS HIS OWN **PRIVATE ZOO**, CHIEF?

RIGHT!

WE'LL HOLD THOSE TWO MEN ON CHARGES OF SHOOTING AT YOU, CAPTAIN MARVEL, BUT WITH NO JEWELS AS EVIDENCE OF SMUGGLING...

I'LL BE BACK, CHIEF, **WITH THE EVIDENCE!**

3

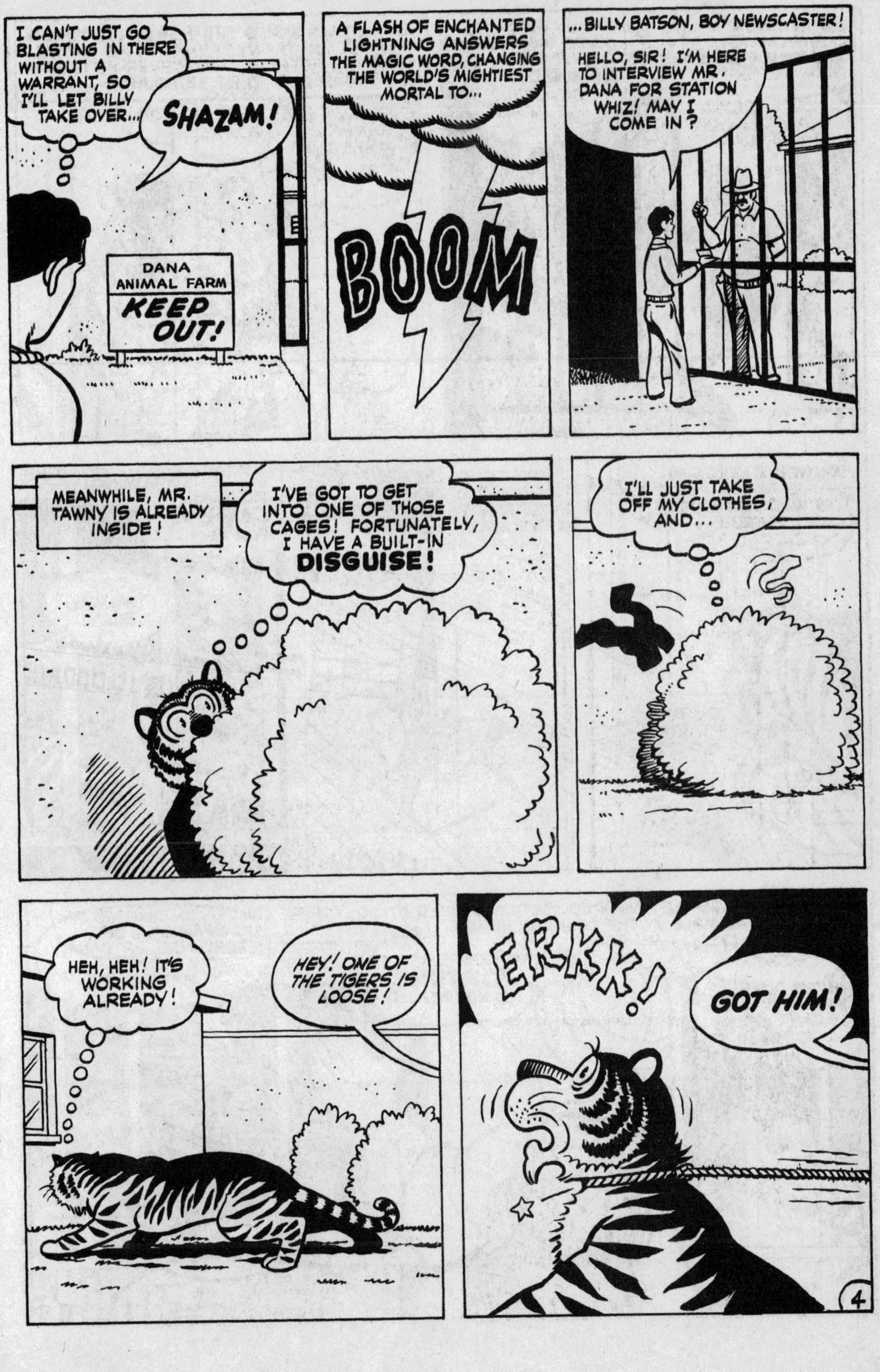
I CAN'T JUST GO BLASTING IN THERE WITHOUT A WARRANT, SO I'LL LET BILLY TAKE OVER...
SHAZAM!
DANA ANIMAL FARM
KEEP OUT!
A FLASH OF ENCHANTED LIGHTNING ANSWERS THE MAGIC WORD, CHANGING THE WORLD'S MIGHTIEST MORTAL TO...
BOOM
...BILLY BATSON, BOY NEWSCASTER!
HELLO, SIR! I'M HERE TO INTERVIEW MR. DANA FOR STATION WHIZ! MAY I COME IN?
MEANWHILE, MR. TAWNY IS ALREADY INSIDE!
I'VE GOT TO GET INTO ONE OF THOSE CAGES! FORTUNATELY, I HAVE A BUILT-IN DISGUISE!
I'LL JUST TAKE OFF MY CLOTHES, AND...
HEH, HEH! IT'S WORKING ALREADY!
HEY! ONE OF THE TIGERS IS LOOSE!
ERKK!
GOT HIM!
4

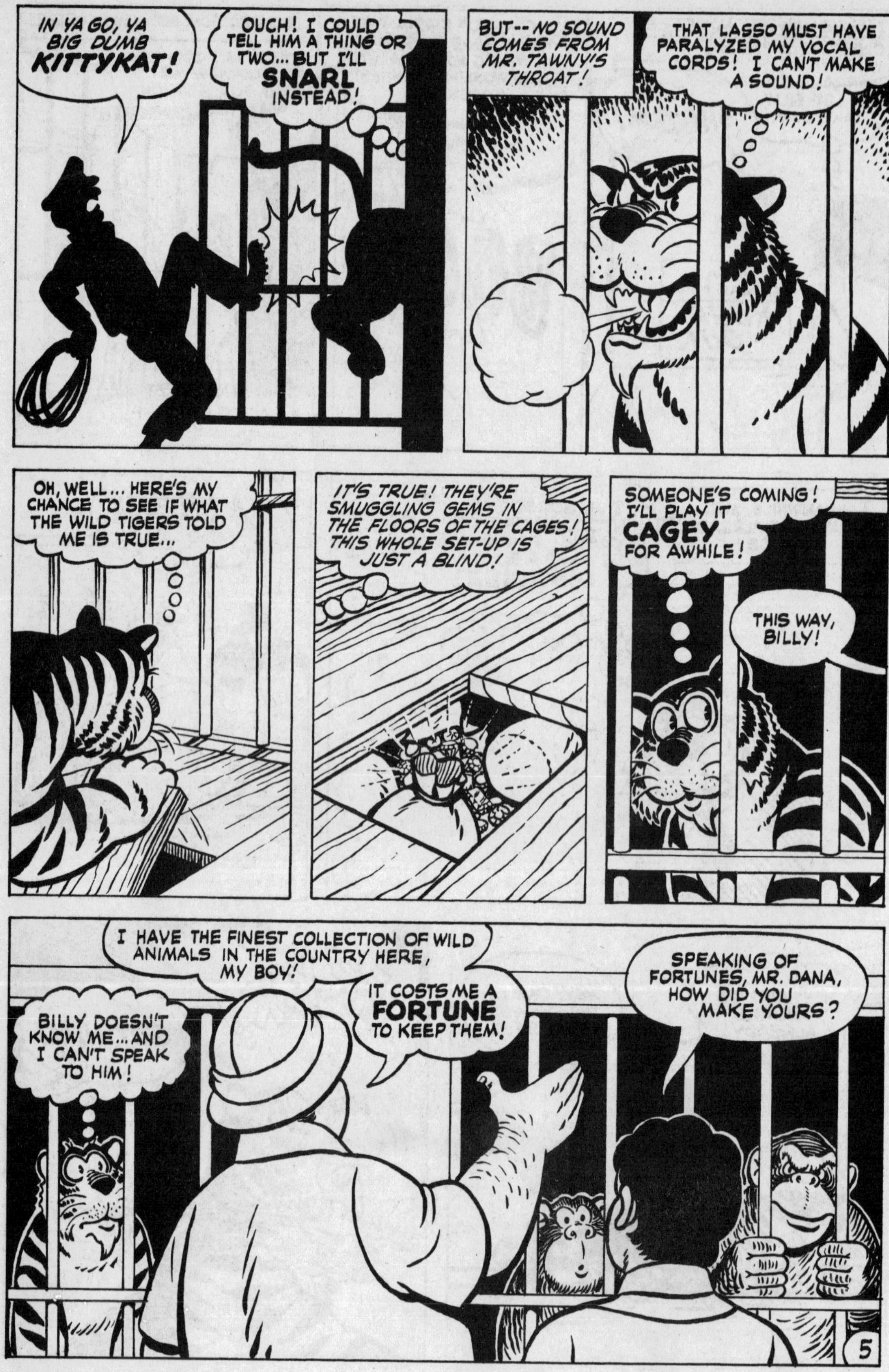
IN YA GO, YA BIG DUMB KITTYKAT!
OUCH! I COULD TELL HIM A THING OR TWO... BUT I'LL SNARL INSTEAD!
BUT-- NO SOUND COMES FROM MR. TAWNY'S THROAT!
THAT LASSO MUST HAVE PARALYZED MY VOCAL CORDS! I CAN'T MAKE A SOUND!
OH, WELL... HERE'S MY CHANCE TO SEE IF WHAT THE WILD TIGERS TOLD ME IS TRUE...
IT'S TRUE! THEY'RE SMUGGLING GEMS IN THE FLOORS OF THE CAGES! THIS WHOLE SET-UP IS JUST A BLIND!
SOMEONE'S COMING! I'LL PLAY IT CAGEY FOR AWHILE!
THIS WAY, BILLY!
I HAVE THE FINEST COLLECTION OF WILD ANIMALS IN THE COUNTRY HERE, MY BOY!
BILLY DOESN'T KNOW ME... AND I CAN'T SPEAK TO HIM!
IT COSTS ME A FORTUNE TO KEEP THEM!
SPEAKING OF FORTUNES, MR. DANA, HOW DID YOU MAKE YOURS?
5

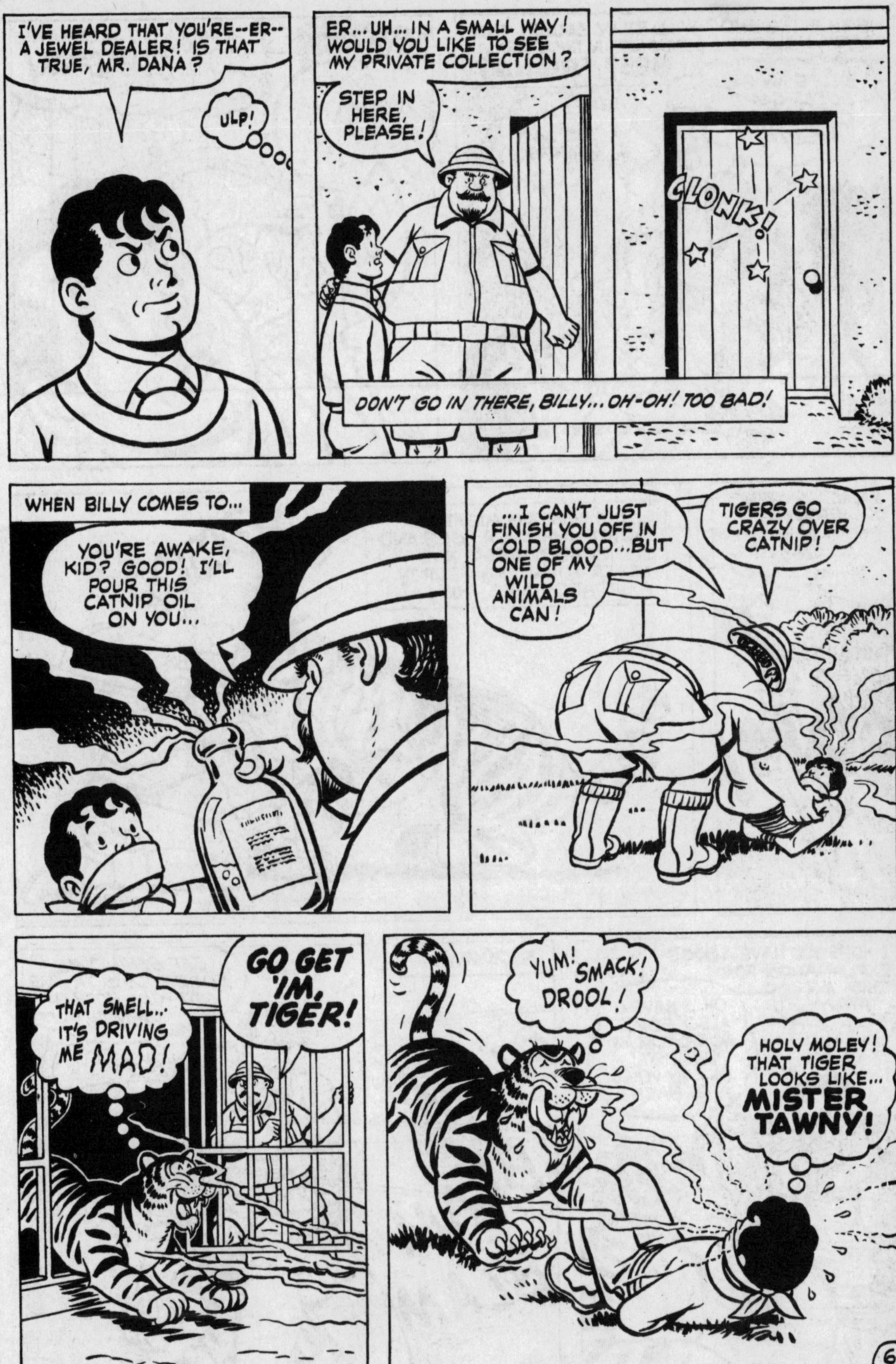
I'VE HEARD THAT YOU'RE--ER-- A JEWEL DEALER! IS THAT TRUE, MR. DANA?
ULP!
ER... UH... IN A SMALL WAY! WOULD YOU LIKE TO SEE MY PRIVATE COLLECTION?
STEP IN HERE, PLEASE!
CLONK!
DON'T GO IN THERE, BILLY... OH-OH! TOO BAD!
WHEN BILLY COMES TO...
YOU'RE AWAKE, KID? GOOD! I'LL POUR THIS CATNIP OIL ON YOU...
...I CAN'T JUST FINISH YOU OFF IN COLD BLOOD...BUT ONE OF MY WILD ANIMALS CAN!
TIGERS GO CRAZY OVER CATNIP!
THAT SMELL... IT'S DRIVING ME MAD!
GO GET 'IM, TIGER!
YUM! SMACK! DROOL!
HOLY MOLEY! THAT TIGER LOOKS LIKE... MISTER TAWNY!
6

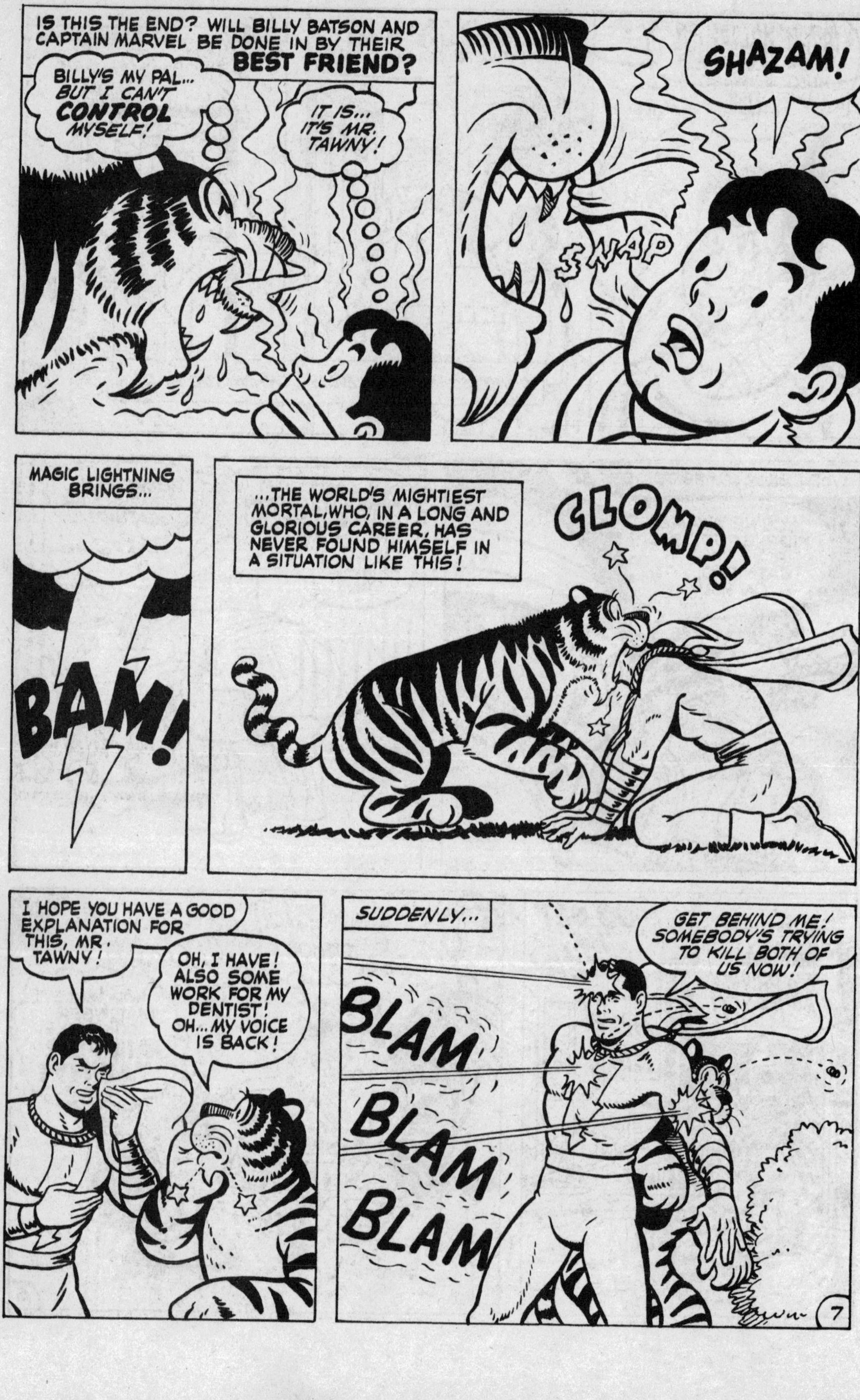
IS THIS THE END? WILL BILLY BATSON AND CAPTAIN MARVEL BE DONE IN BY THEIR BEST FRIEND?
BILLY'S MY PAL... BUT I CAN'T CONTROL MYSELF!
IT IS... IT'S MR. TAWNY!
SHAZAM!
SNAP
MAGIC LIGHTNING BRINGS...
BAM!
...THE WORLD'S MIGHTIEST MORTAL, WHO, IN A LONG AND GLORIOUS CAREER, HAS NEVER FOUND HIMSELF IN A SITUATION LIKE THIS!
CLOMP!
I HOPE YOU HAVE A GOOD EXPLANATION FOR THIS, MR. TAWNY!
OH, I HAVE! ALSO SOME WORK FOR MY DENTIST! OH... MY VOICE IS BACK!
SUDDENLY...
GET BEHIND ME! SOMEBODY'S TRYING TO KILL BOTH OF US NOW!
BLAM
BLAM
BLAM
7

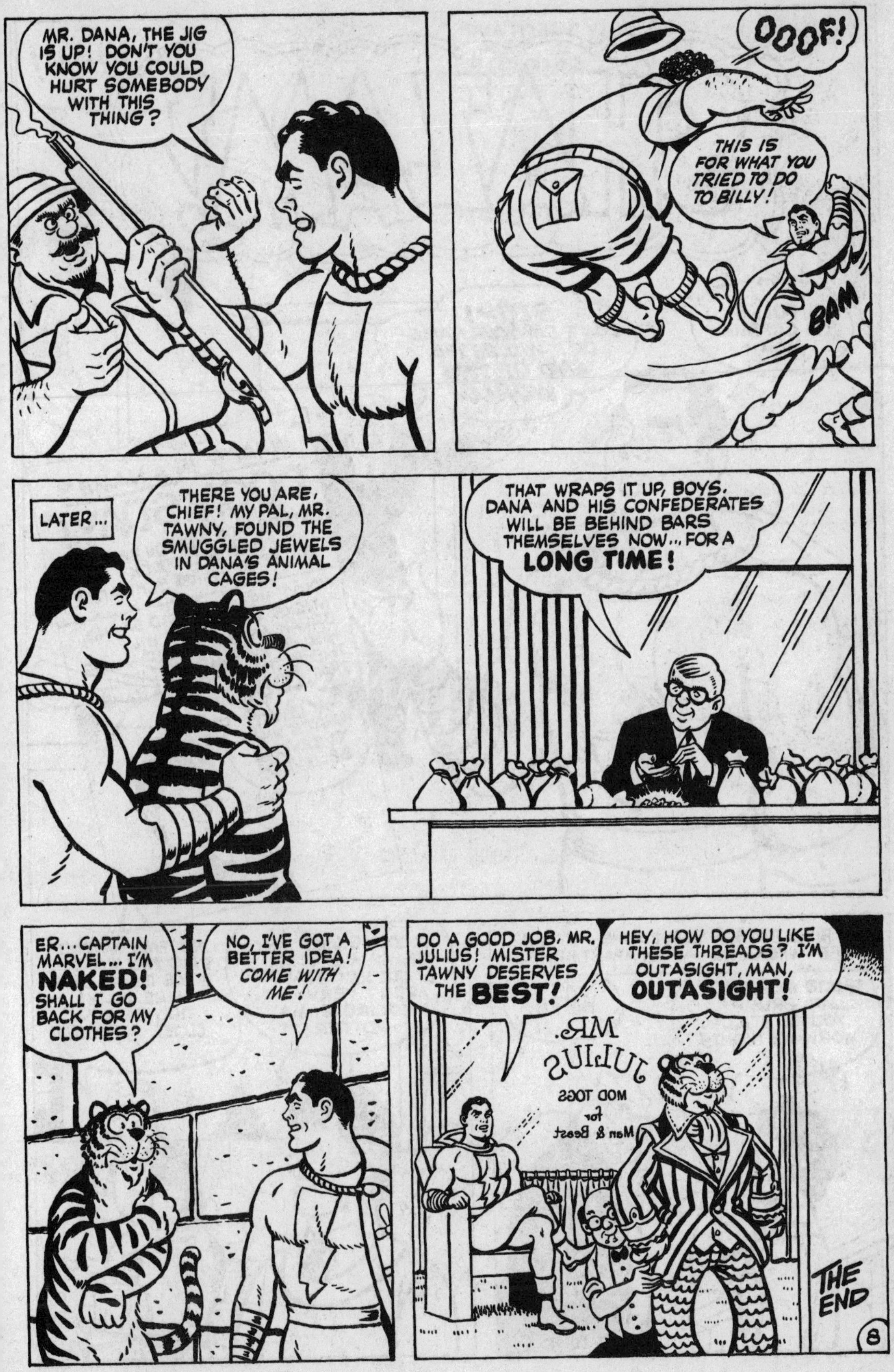
MR. DANA, THE JIG IS UP! DON'T YOU KNOW YOU COULD HURT SOMEBODY WITH THIS THING?
OOOF!
THIS IS FOR WHAT YOU TRIED TO DO TO BILLY!
BAM
LATER...
THERE YOU ARE, CHIEF! MY PAL, MR. TAWNY, FOUND THE SMUGGLED JEWELS IN DANA'S ANIMAL CAGES!
THAT WRAPS IT UP, BOYS. DANA AND HIS CONFEDERATES WILL BE BEHIND BARS THEMSELVES NOW... FOR A LONG TIME!
ER... CAPTAIN MARVEL... I'M NAKED! SHALL I GO BACK FOR MY CLOTHES?
NO, I'VE GOT A BETTER IDEA! COME WITH ME!
DO A GOOD JOB, MR. JULIUS! MISTER TAWNY DESERVES THE BEST!
HEY, HOW DO YOU LIKE THESE THREADS? I'M OUTASIGHT, MAN, OUTASIGHT!
MR. JULIUS MOD TOGS for Man & Beast
THE END
8

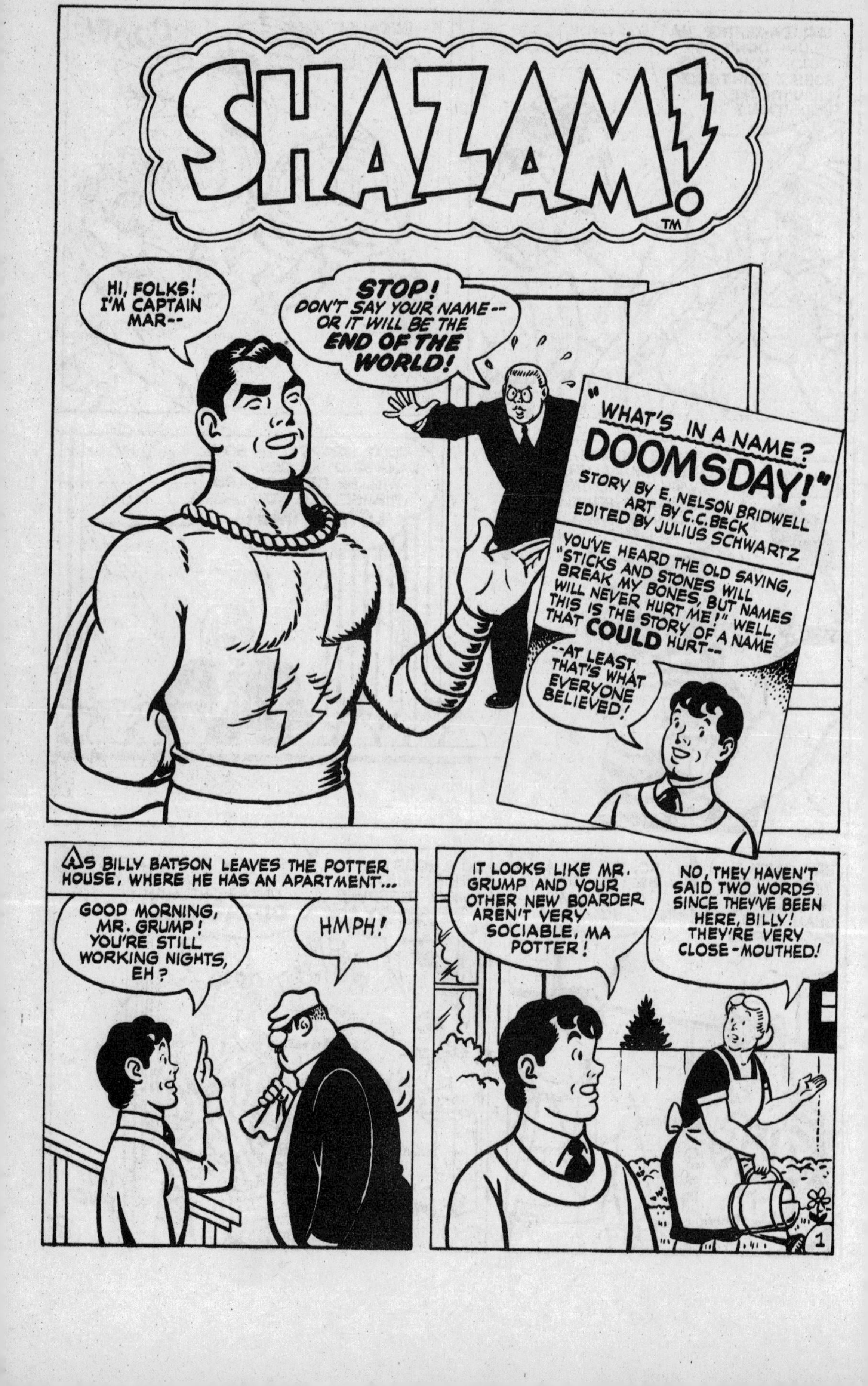
SHAZAM!
TM
HI, FOLKS! I'M CAPTAIN MAR--
STOP! DON'T SAY YOUR NAME-- OR IT WILL BE THE END OF THE WORLD!
"WHAT'S IN A NAME? DOOMSDAY!"
STORY BY E. NELSON BRIDWELL
ART BY C.C. BECK
EDITED BY JULIUS SCHWARTZ
YOU'VE HEARD THE OLD SAYING, "STICKS AND STONES WILL BREAK MY BONES, BUT NAMES WILL NEVER HURT ME!" WELL, THIS IS THE STORY OF A NAME THAT COULD HURT--
--AT LEAST, THAT'S WHAT EVERYONE BELIEVED!
AS BILLY BATSON LEAVES THE POTTER HOUSE, WHERE HE HAS AN APARTMENT...
GOOD MORNING, MR. GRUMP! YOU'RE STILL WORKING NIGHTS, EH?
HMPH!
IT LOOKS LIKE MR. GRUMP AND YOUR OTHER NEW BOARDER AREN'T VERY SOCIABLE, MA POTTER!
NO, THEY HAVEN'T SAID TWO WORDS SINCE THEY'VE BEEN HERE, BILLY! THEY'RE VERY CLOSE-MOUTHED!
1

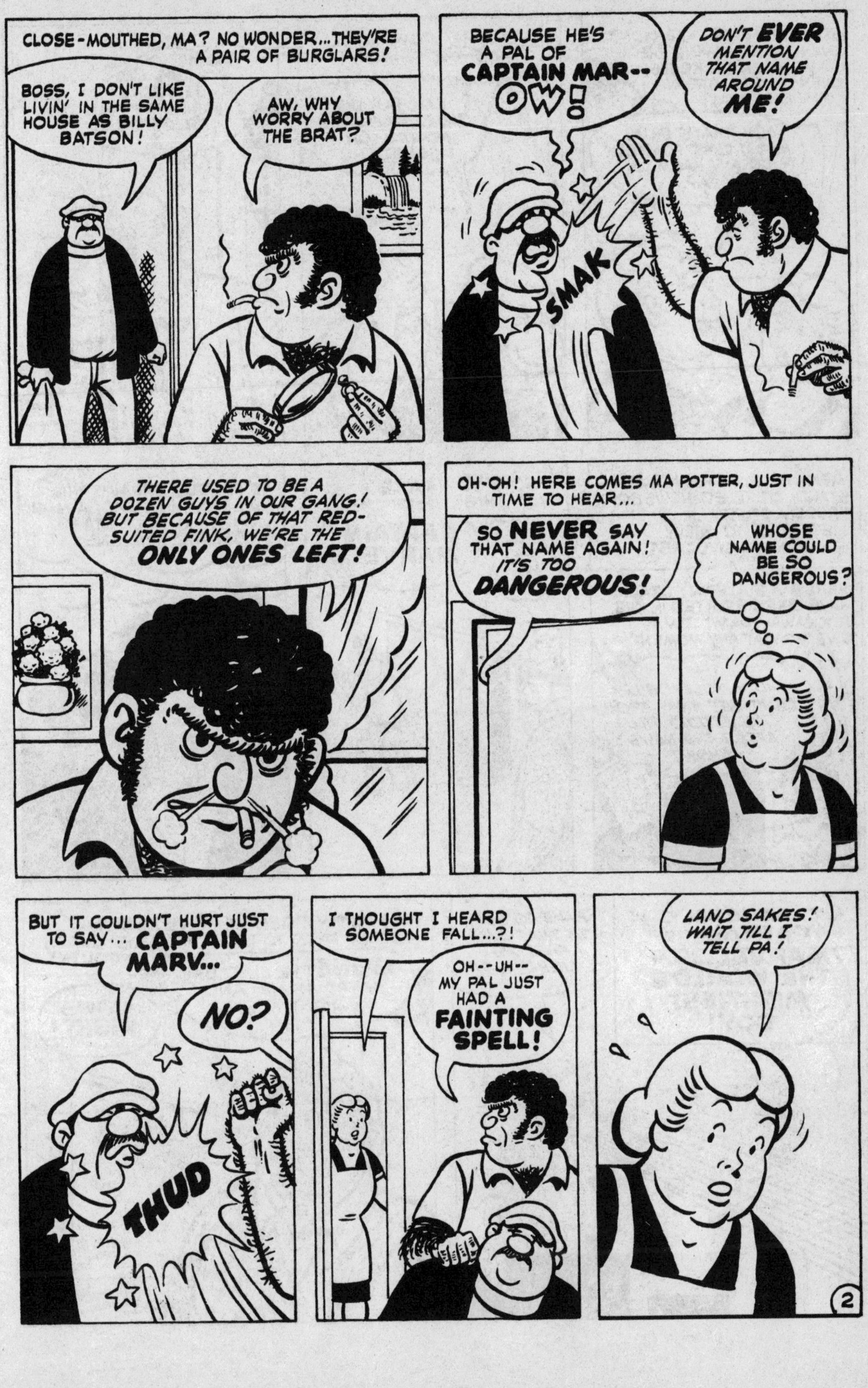
CLOSE-MOUTHED, MA? NO WONDER...THEY'RE A PAIR OF BURGLARS!
BOSS, I DON'T LIKE LIVIN' IN THE SAME HOUSE AS BILLY BATSON!
AW, WHY WORRY ABOUT THE BRAT?
BECAUSE HE'S A PAL OF CAPTAIN MAR-- OW!
DON'T EVER MENTION THAT NAME AROUND ME!
SMAK
THERE USED TO BE A DOZEN GUYS IN OUR GANG! BUT BECAUSE OF THAT RED-SUITED FINK, WE'RE THE ONLY ONES LEFT!
OH-OH! HERE COMES MA POTTER, JUST IN TIME TO HEAR...
SO NEVER SAY THAT NAME AGAIN! IT'S TOO DANGEROUS!
WHOSE NAME COULD BE SO DANGEROUS?
BUT IT COULDN'T HURT JUST TO SAY... CAPTAIN MARV...
NO?
THUD
I THOUGHT I HEARD SOMEONE FALL...?!
OH--UH-- MY PAL JUST HAD A FAINTING SPELL!
LAND SAKES! WAIT TILL I TELL PA!
2

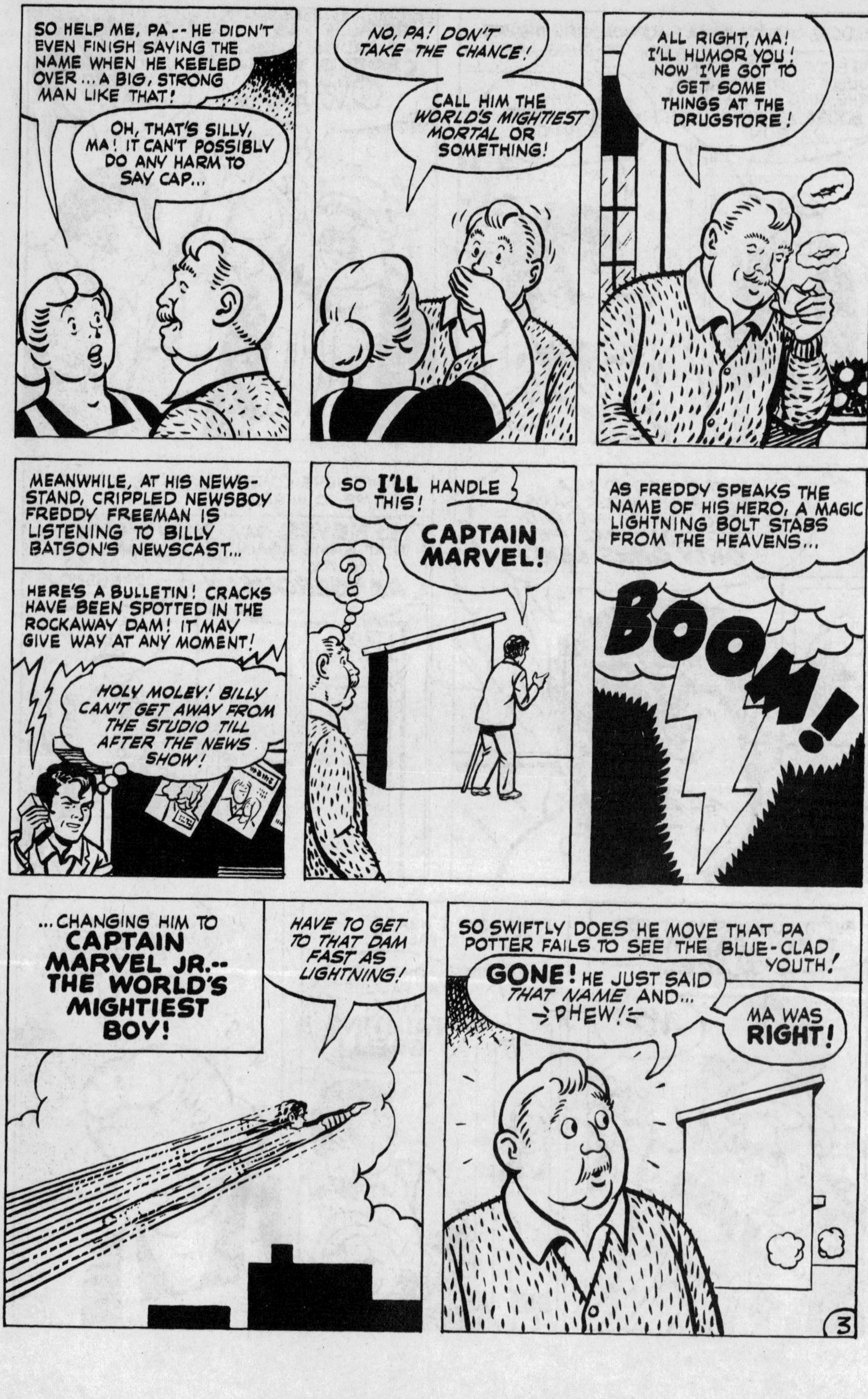
SO HELP ME, PA -- HE DIDN'T EVEN FINISH SAYING THE NAME WHEN HE KEELED OVER ... A BIG, STRONG MAN LIKE THAT!
OH, THAT'S SILLY, MA! IT CAN'T POSSIBLY DO ANY HARM TO SAY CAP...
NO, PA! DON'T TAKE THE CHANCE!
CALL HIM THE WORLD'S MIGHTIEST MORTAL OR SOMETHING!
ALL RIGHT, MA! I'LL HUMOR YOU! NOW I'VE GOT TO GET SOME THINGS AT THE DRUGSTORE!
MEANWHILE, AT HIS NEWS-STAND, CRIPPLED NEWSBOY FREDDY FREEMAN IS LISTENING TO BILLY BATSON'S NEWSCAST...
HERE'S A BULLETIN! CRACKS HAVE BEEN SPOTTED IN THE ROCKAWAY DAM! IT MAY GIVE WAY AT ANY MOMENT!
HOLY MOLEY! BILLY CAN'T GET AWAY FROM THE STUDIO TILL AFTER THE NEWS SHOW!
SO I'LL HANDLE THIS!
CAPTAIN MARVEL!
?
AS FREDDY SPEAKS THE NAME OF HIS HERO, A MAGIC LIGHTNING BOLT STABS FROM THE HEAVENS...
BOOM!
...CHANGING HIM TO CAPTAIN MARVEL JR.-- THE WORLD'S MIGHTIEST BOY!
HAVE TO GET TO THAT DAM FAST AS LIGHTNING!
SO SWIFTLY DOES HE MOVE THAT PA POTTER FAILS TO SEE THE BLUE-CLAD YOUTH!
GONE! HE JUST SAID THAT NAME AND... PHEW!
MA WAS RIGHT!
3

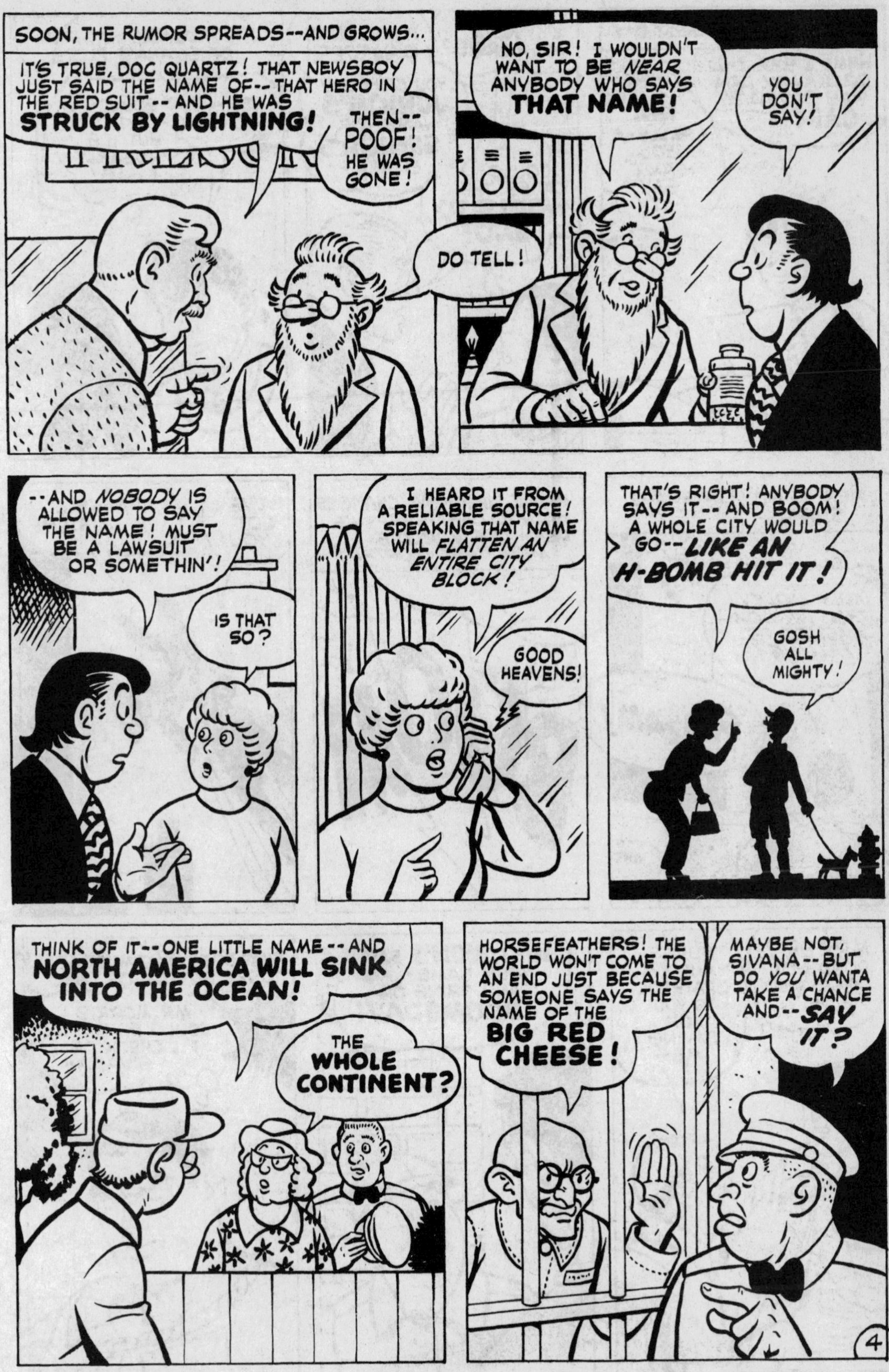
SOON, THE RUMOR SPREADS--AND GROWS...
IT'S TRUE, DOC QUARTZ! THAT NEWSBOY JUST SAID THE NAME OF--THAT HERO IN THE RED SUIT--AND HE WAS STRUCK BY LIGHTNING!
THEN--POOF! HE WAS GONE!
DO TELL!
NO, SIR! I WOULDN'T WANT TO BE NEAR ANYBODY WHO SAYS THAT NAME!
YOU DON'T SAY!
--AND NOBODY IS ALLOWED TO SAY THE NAME! MUST BE A LAWSUIT OR SOMETHIN'!
IS THAT SO?
I HEARD IT FROM A RELIABLE SOURCE! SPEAKING THAT NAME WILL FLATTEN AN ENTIRE CITY BLOCK!
GOOD HEAVENS!
THAT'S RIGHT! ANYBODY SAYS IT--AND BOOM! A WHOLE CITY WOULD GO--LIKE AN H-BOMB HIT IT!
GOSH ALL MIGHTY!
THINK OF IT--ONE LITTLE NAME--AND NORTH AMERICA WILL SINK INTO THE OCEAN!
THE WHOLE CONTINENT?
HORSEFEATHERS! THE WORLD WON'T COME TO AN END JUST BECAUSE SOMEONE SAYS THE NAME OF THE BIG RED CHEESE!
MAYBE NOT, SIVANA--BUT DO YOU WANTA TAKE A CHANCE AND--SAY IT?
4

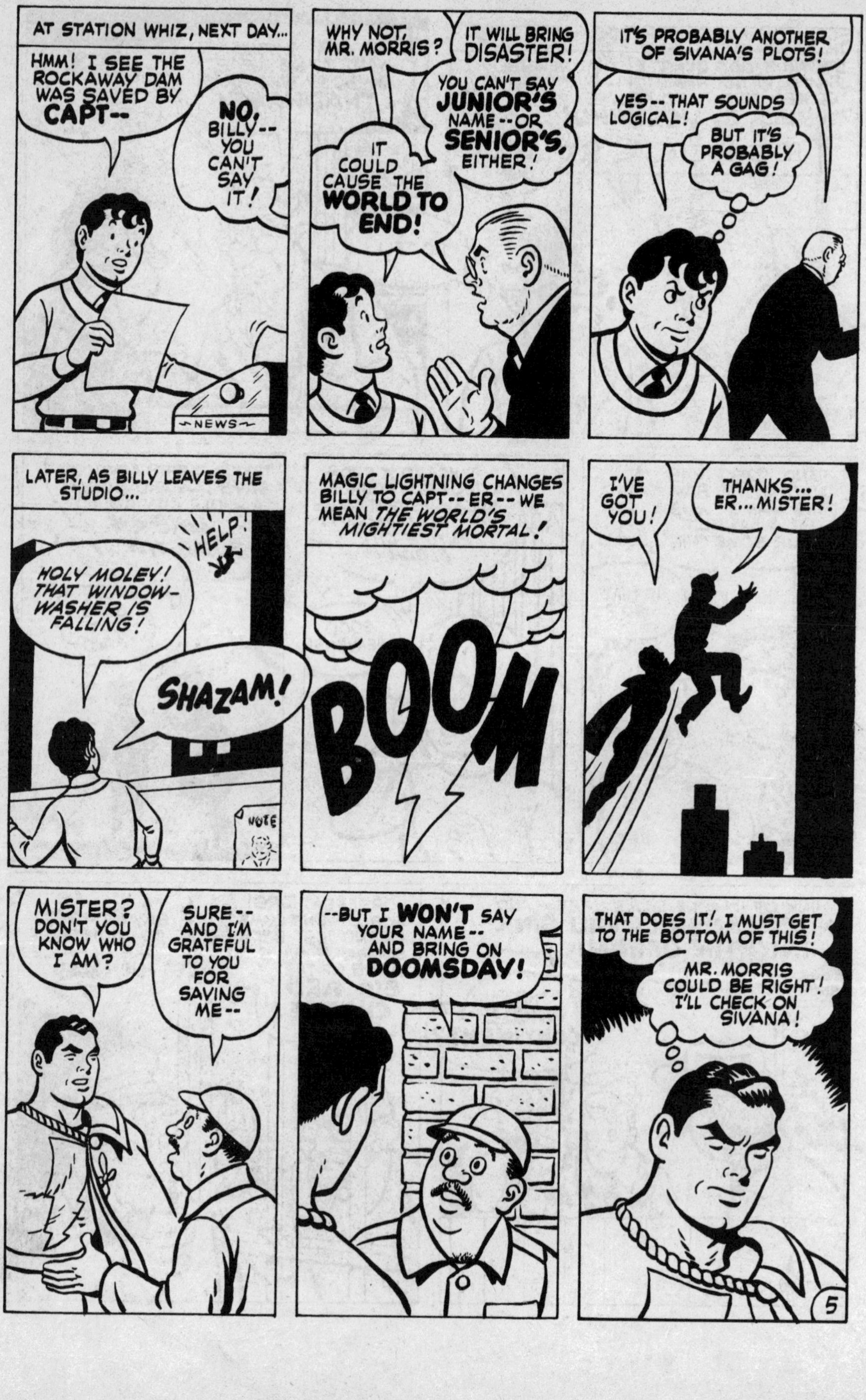
AT STATION WHIZ, NEXT DAY...
HMM! I SEE THE ROCKAWAY DAM WAS SAVED BY CAPT--
NO, BILLY-- YOU CAN'T SAY IT!
NEWS
WHY NOT, MR. MORRIS?
IT WILL BRING DISASTER!
YOU CAN'T SAY JUNIOR'S NAME--OR SENIOR'S, EITHER!
IT COULD CAUSE THE WORLD TO END!
IT'S PROBABLY ANOTHER OF SIVANA'S PLOTS!
YES-- THAT SOUNDS LOGICAL!
BUT IT'S PROBABLY A GAG!
LATER, AS BILLY LEAVES THE STUDIO...
HELP!
HOLY MOLEY! THAT WINDOW-WASHER IS FALLING!
SHAZAM!
NOTE
MAGIC LIGHTNING CHANGES BILLY TO CAPT-- ER-- WE MEAN THE WORLD'S MIGHTIEST MORTAL!
BOOM
I'VE GOT YOU!
THANKS... ER... MISTER!
MISTER? DON'T YOU KNOW WHO I AM?
SURE-- AND I'M GRATEFUL TO YOU FOR SAVING ME--
--BUT I WON'T SAY YOUR NAME-- AND BRING ON DOOMSDAY!
THAT DOES IT! I MUST GET TO THE BOTTOM OF THIS!
MR. MORRIS COULD BE RIGHT! I'LL CHECK ON SIVANA!
5

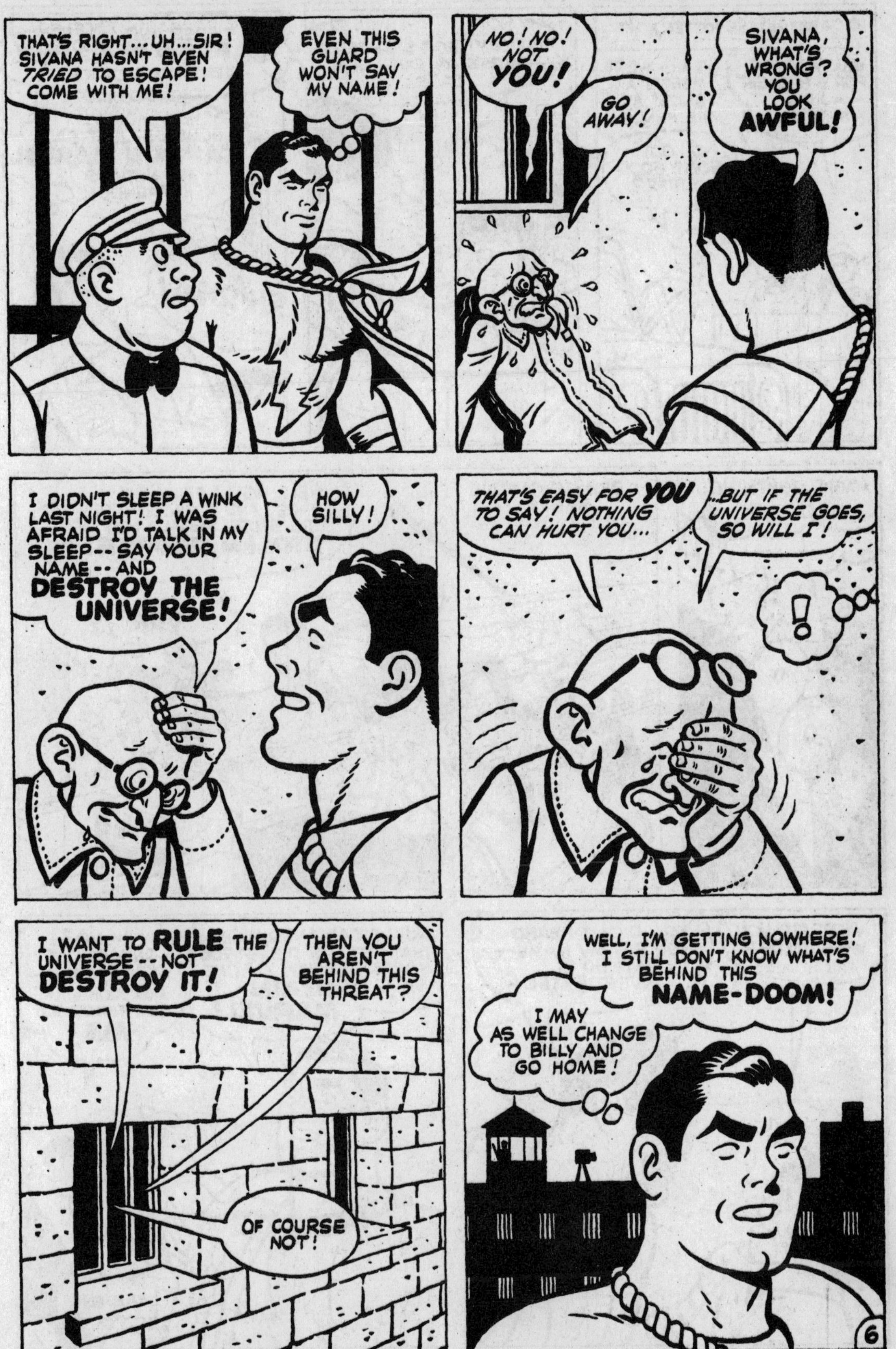
THAT'S RIGHT... UH... SIR! SIVANA HASN'T EVEN TRIED TO ESCAPE! COME WITH ME!
EVEN THIS GUARD WON'T SAY MY NAME!
NO! NO! NOT YOU!
GO AWAY!
SIVANA, WHAT'S WRONG? YOU LOOK AWFUL!
I DIDN'T SLEEP A WINK LAST NIGHT! I WAS AFRAID I'D TALK IN MY SLEEP-- SAY YOUR NAME-- AND DESTROY THE UNIVERSE!
HOW SILLY!
THAT'S EASY FOR YOU TO SAY! NOTHING CAN HURT YOU...
...BUT IF THE UNIVERSE GOES, SO WILL I!
!
I WANT TO RULE THE UNIVERSE-- NOT DESTROY IT!
THEN YOU AREN'T BEHIND THIS THREAT?
OF COURSE NOT!
WELL, I'M GETTING NOWHERE! I STILL DON'T KNOW WHAT'S BEHIND THIS NAME-DOOM!
I MAY AS WELL CHANGE TO BILLY AND GO HOME!
6

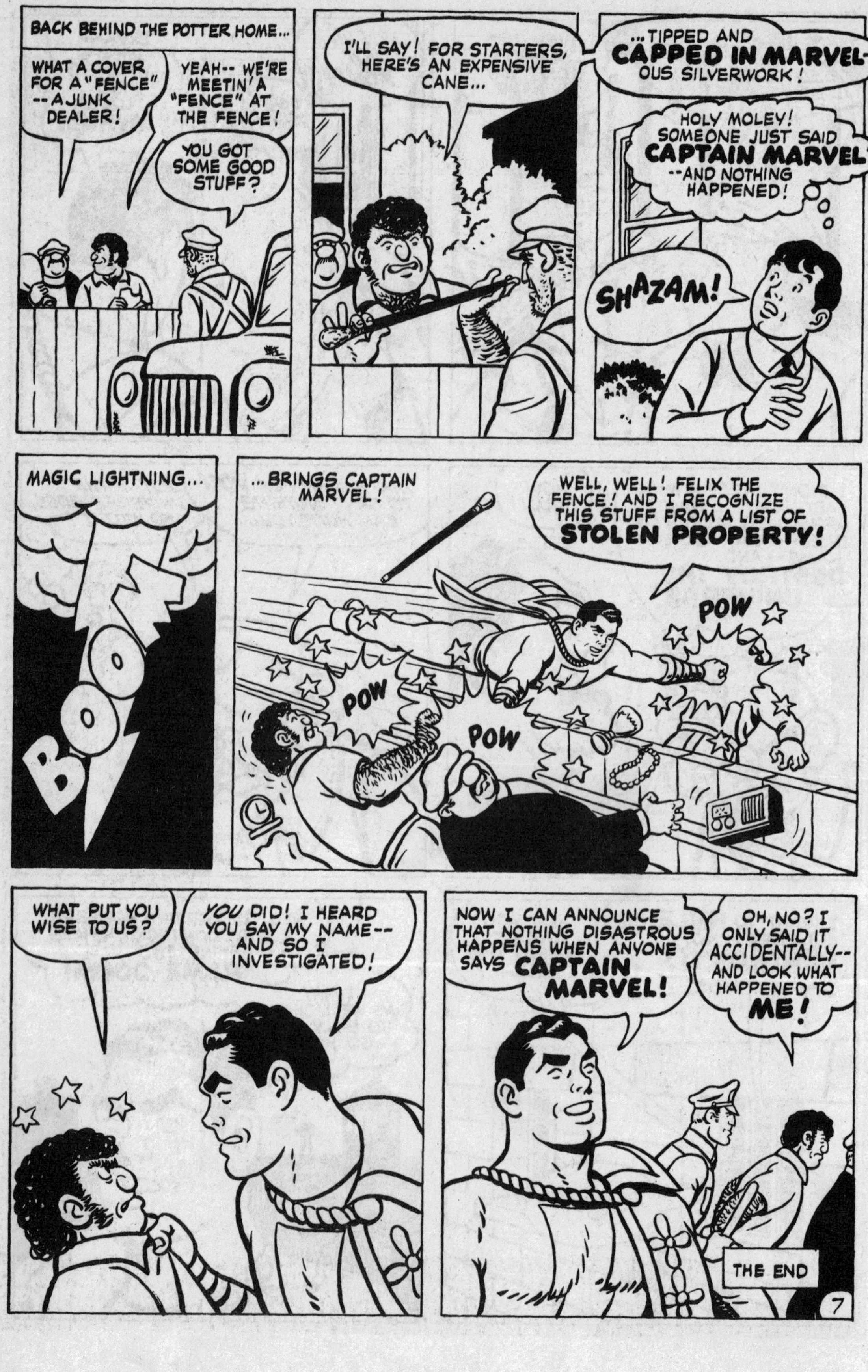
BACK BEHIND THE POTTER HOME...
WHAT A COVER FOR A "FENCE" --A JUNK DEALER!
YEAH-- WE'RE MEETIN' A "FENCE" AT THE FENCE!
YOU GOT SOME GOOD STUFF?
I'LL SAY! FOR STARTERS, HERE'S AN EXPENSIVE CANE...
...TIPPED AND CAPPED IN MARVEL-OUS SILVERWORK!
HOLY MOLEY! SOMEONE JUST SAID CAPTAIN MARVEL --AND NOTHING HAPPENED!
SHAZAM!
MAGIC LIGHTNING...
BOOM
...BRINGS CAPTAIN MARVEL!
WELL, WELL! FELIX THE FENCE! AND I RECOGNIZE THIS STUFF FROM A LIST OF STOLEN PROPERTY!
POW
POW
POW
WHAT PUT YOU WISE TO US?
YOU DID! I HEARD YOU SAY MY NAME-- AND SO I INVESTIGATED!
NOW I CAN ANNOUNCE THAT NOTHING DISASTROUS HAPPENS WHEN ANYONE SAYS CAPTAIN MARVEL!
OH, NO? I ONLY SAID IT ACCIDENTALLY-- AND LOOK WHAT HAPPENED TO ME!
THE END
7

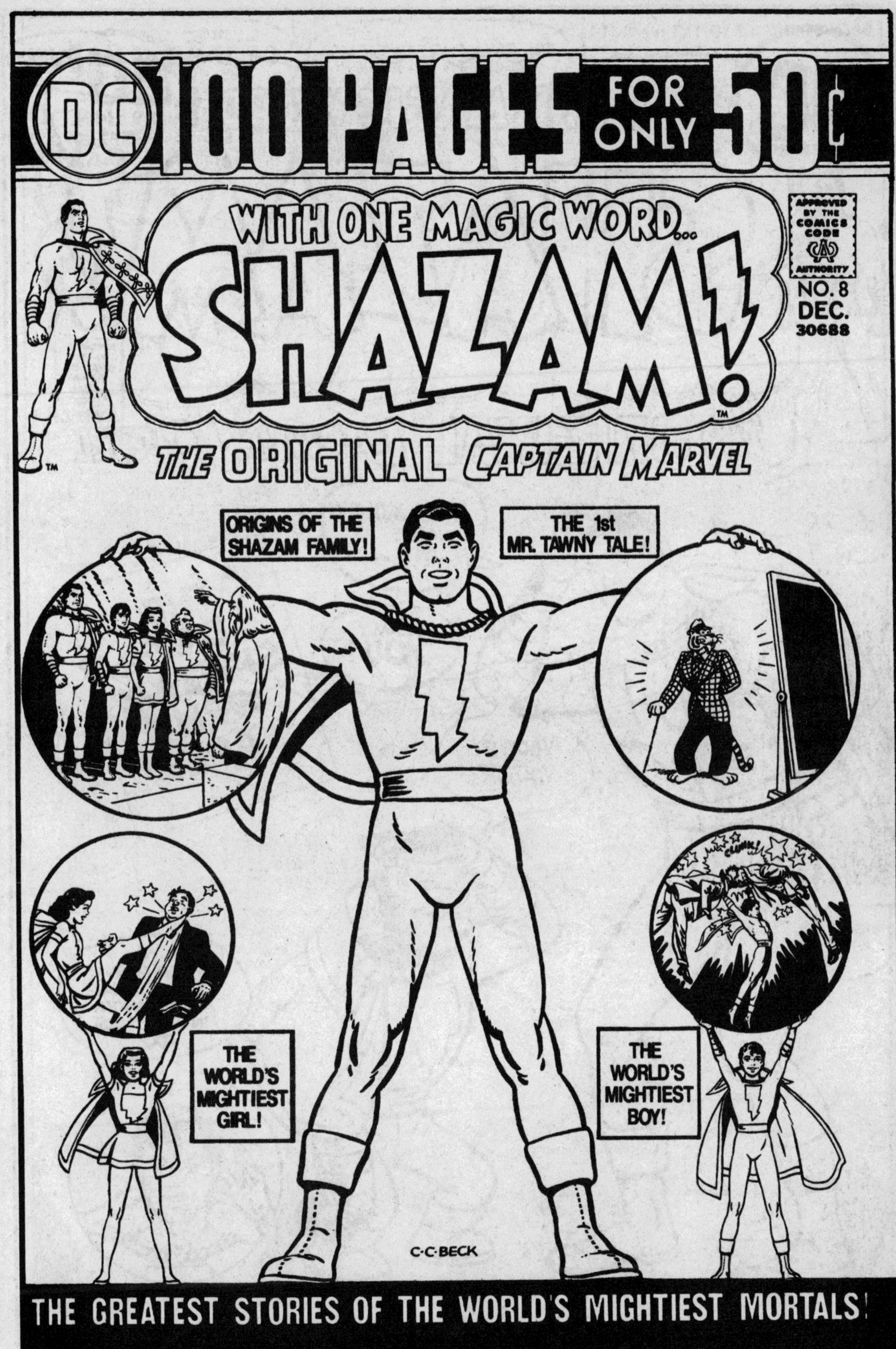
DC
100 PAGES FOR ONLY 50¢
WITH ONE MAGIC WORD...
SHAZAM!
APPROVED BY THE COMICS CODE AUTHORITY
NO. 8
DEC.
30688
THE ORIGINAL CAPTAIN MARVEL
ORIGINS OF THE SHAZAM FAMILY!
THE 1st MR. TAWNY TALE!
THE WORLD'S MIGHTIEST GIRL!
THE WORLD'S MIGHTIEST BOY!
C·C·BECK
THE GREATEST STORIES OF THE WORLD'S MIGHTIEST MORTALS!

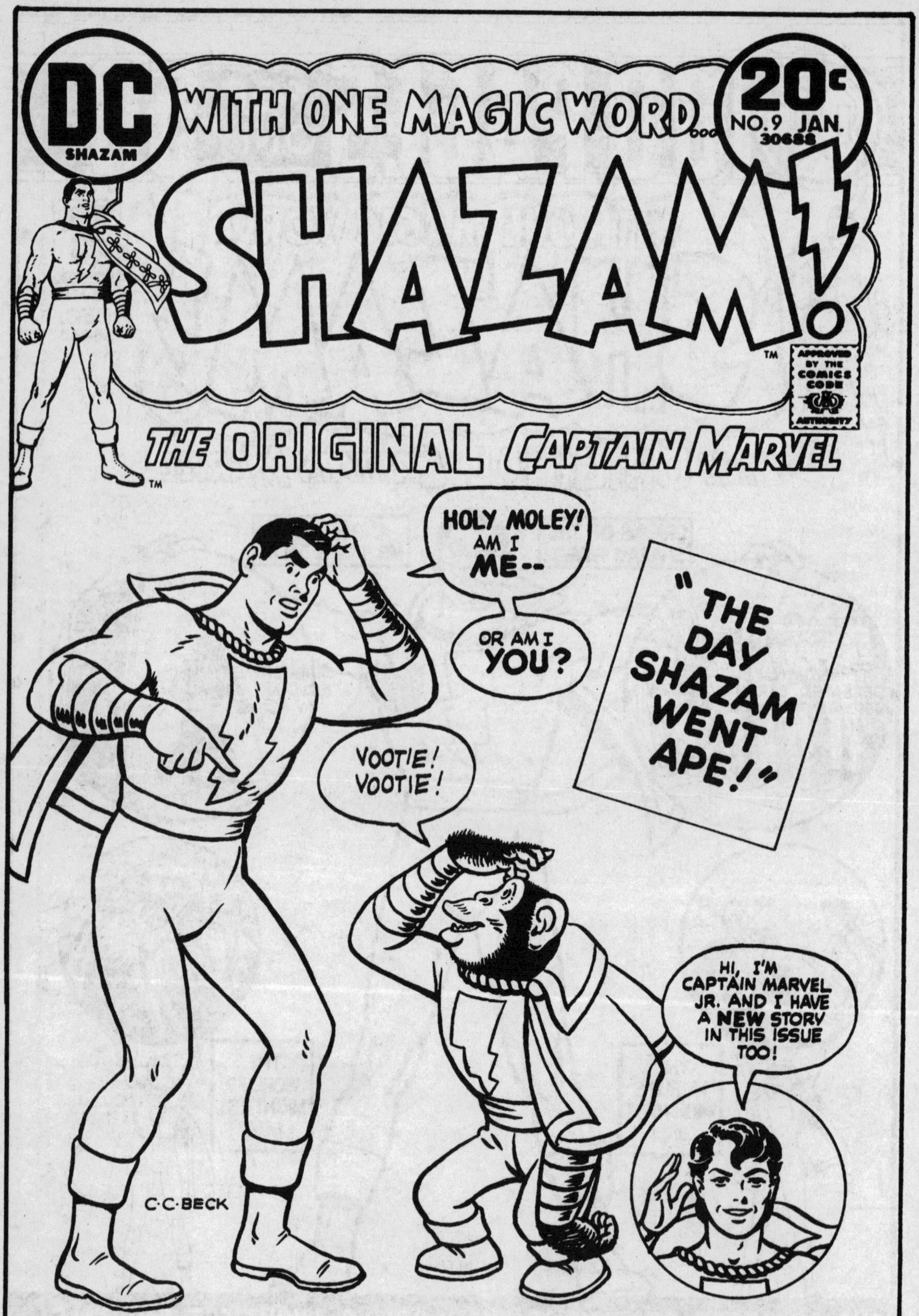
DC
SHAZAM
WITH ONE MAGIC WORD...
20¢
NO.9 JAN.
30688
SHAZAM!
TM
APPROVED BY THE COMICS CODE AUTHORITY
THE ORIGINAL CAPTAIN MARVEL
TM
HOLY MOLEY! AM I ME--
OR AM I YOU?
"THE DAY SHAZAM WENT APE!"
VOOTIE! VOOTIE!
HI, I'M CAPTAIN MARVEL JR. AND I HAVE A NEW STORY IN THIS ISSUE TOO!
C.C.BECK

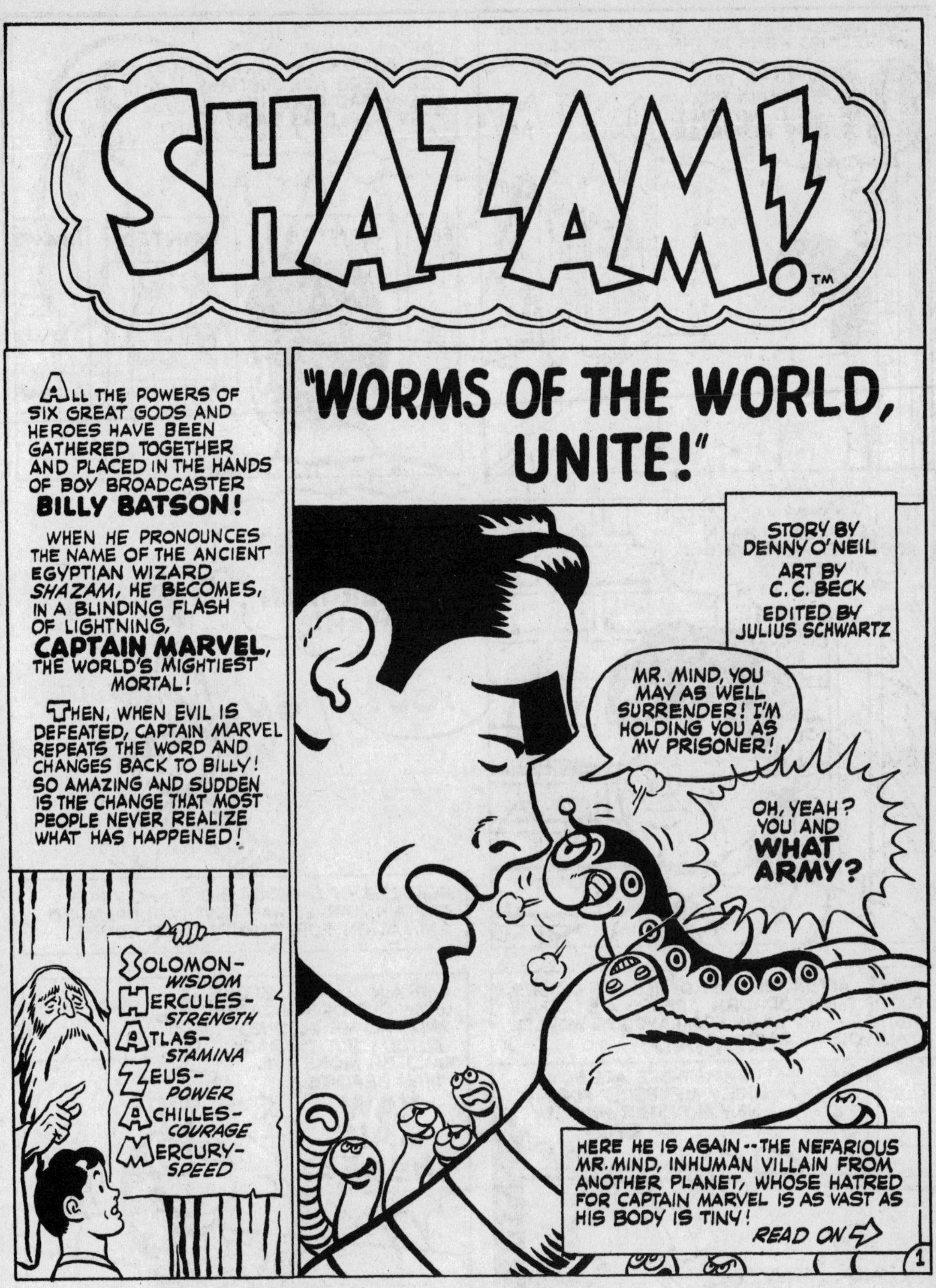
SHAZAM! TM
ALL THE POWERS OF SIX GREAT GODS AND HEROES HAVE BEEN GATHERED TOGETHER AND PLACED IN THE HANDS OF BOY BROADCASTER BILLY BATSON!
WHEN HE PRONOUNCES THE NAME OF THE ANCIENT EGYPTIAN WIZARD SHAZAM, HE BECOMES, IN A BLINDING FLASH OF LIGHTNING, CAPTAIN MARVEL, THE WORLD'S MIGHTIEST MORTAL!
THEN, WHEN EVIL IS DEFEATED, CAPTAIN MARVEL REPEATS THE WORD AND CHANGES BACK TO BILLY! SO AMAZING AND SUDDEN IS THE CHANGE THAT MOST PEOPLE NEVER REALIZE WHAT HAS HAPPENED!
SOLOMON-WISDOM
HERCULES-STRENGTH
ATLAS-STAMINA
ZEUS-POWER
ACHILLES-COURAGE
MERCURY-SPEED
"WORMS OF THE WORLD, UNITE!"
STORY BY DENNY O'NEIL
ART BY C.C. BECK
EDITED BY JULIUS SCHWARTZ
MR. MIND, YOU MAY AS WELL SURRENDER! I'M HOLDING YOU AS MY PRISONER!
OH, YEAH? YOU AND WHAT ARMY?
HERE HE IS AGAIN--THE NEFARIOUS MR. MIND, INHUMAN VILLAIN FROM ANOTHER PLANET, WHOSE HATRED FOR CAPTAIN MARVEL IS AS VAST AS HIS BODY IS TINY!
READ ON
1

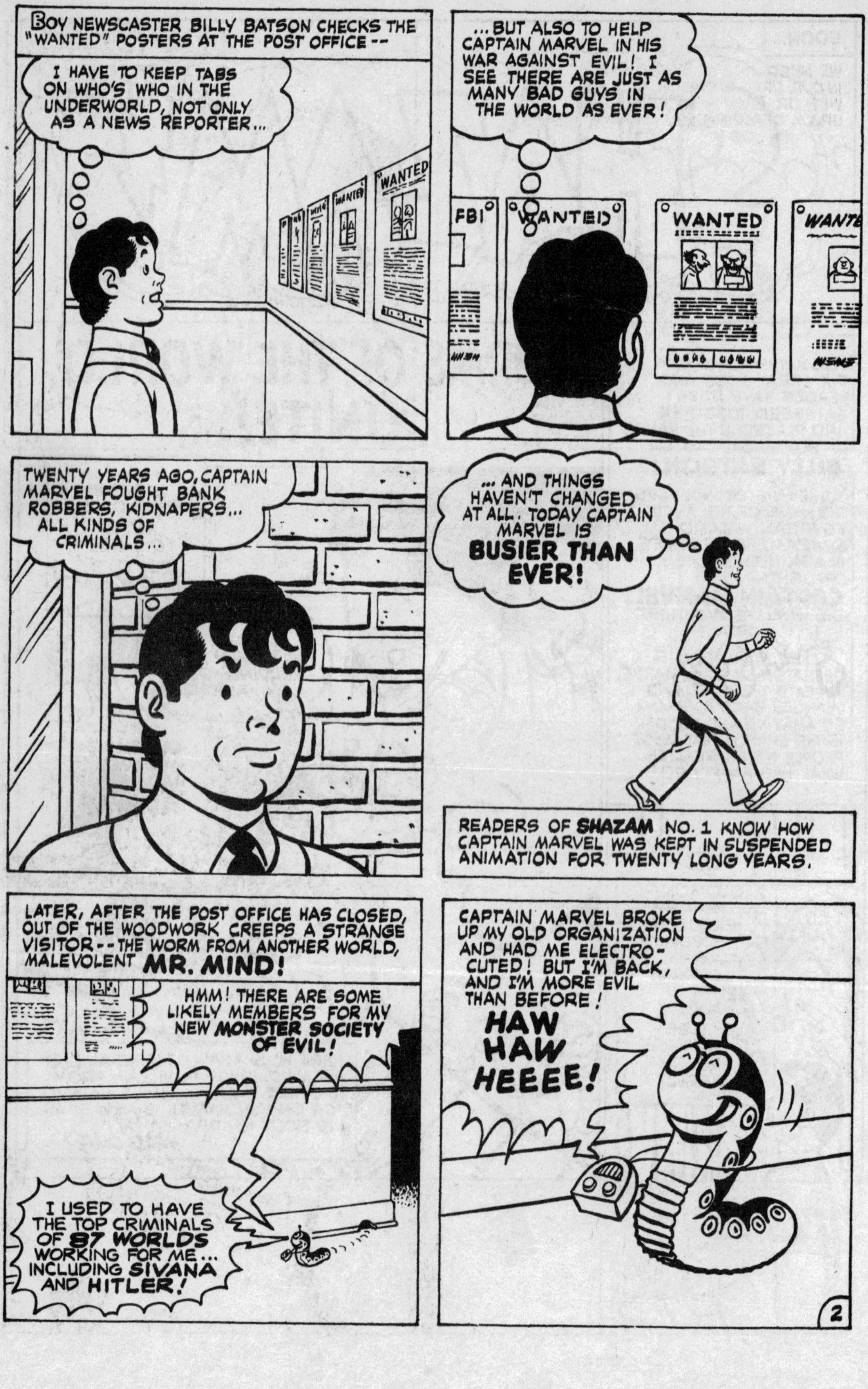
BOY NEWSCASTER BILLY BATSON CHECKS THE "WANTED" POSTERS AT THE POST OFFICE --
I HAVE TO KEEP TABS ON WHO'S WHO IN THE UNDERWORLD, NOT ONLY AS A NEWS REPORTER...
WANTED
...BUT ALSO TO HELP CAPTAIN MARVEL IN HIS WAR AGAINST EVIL! I SEE THERE ARE JUST AS MANY BAD GUYS IN THE WORLD AS EVER!
FBI
WANTED
WANTED
TWENTY YEARS AGO, CAPTAIN MARVEL FOUGHT BANK ROBBERS, KIDNAPERS... ALL KINDS OF CRIMINALS...
...AND THINGS HAVEN'T CHANGED AT ALL. TODAY CAPTAIN MARVEL IS BUSIER THAN EVER!
READERS OF SHAZAM NO. 1 KNOW HOW CAPTAIN MARVEL WAS KEPT IN SUSPENDED ANIMATION FOR TWENTY LONG YEARS.
LATER, AFTER THE POST OFFICE HAS CLOSED, OUT OF THE WOODWORK CREEPS A STRANGE VISITOR--THE WORM FROM ANOTHER WORLD, MALEVOLENT MR. MIND!
HMM! THERE ARE SOME LIKELY MEMBERS FOR MY NEW MONSTER SOCIETY OF EVIL!
I USED TO HAVE THE TOP CRIMINALS OF 87 WORLDS WORKING FOR ME... INCLUDING SIVANA AND HITLER!
CAPTAIN MARVEL BROKE UP MY OLD ORGANIZATION AND HAD ME ELECTRO-CUTED! BUT I'M BACK, AND I'M MORE EVIL THAN BEFORE!
HAW HAW HEEEE!
2

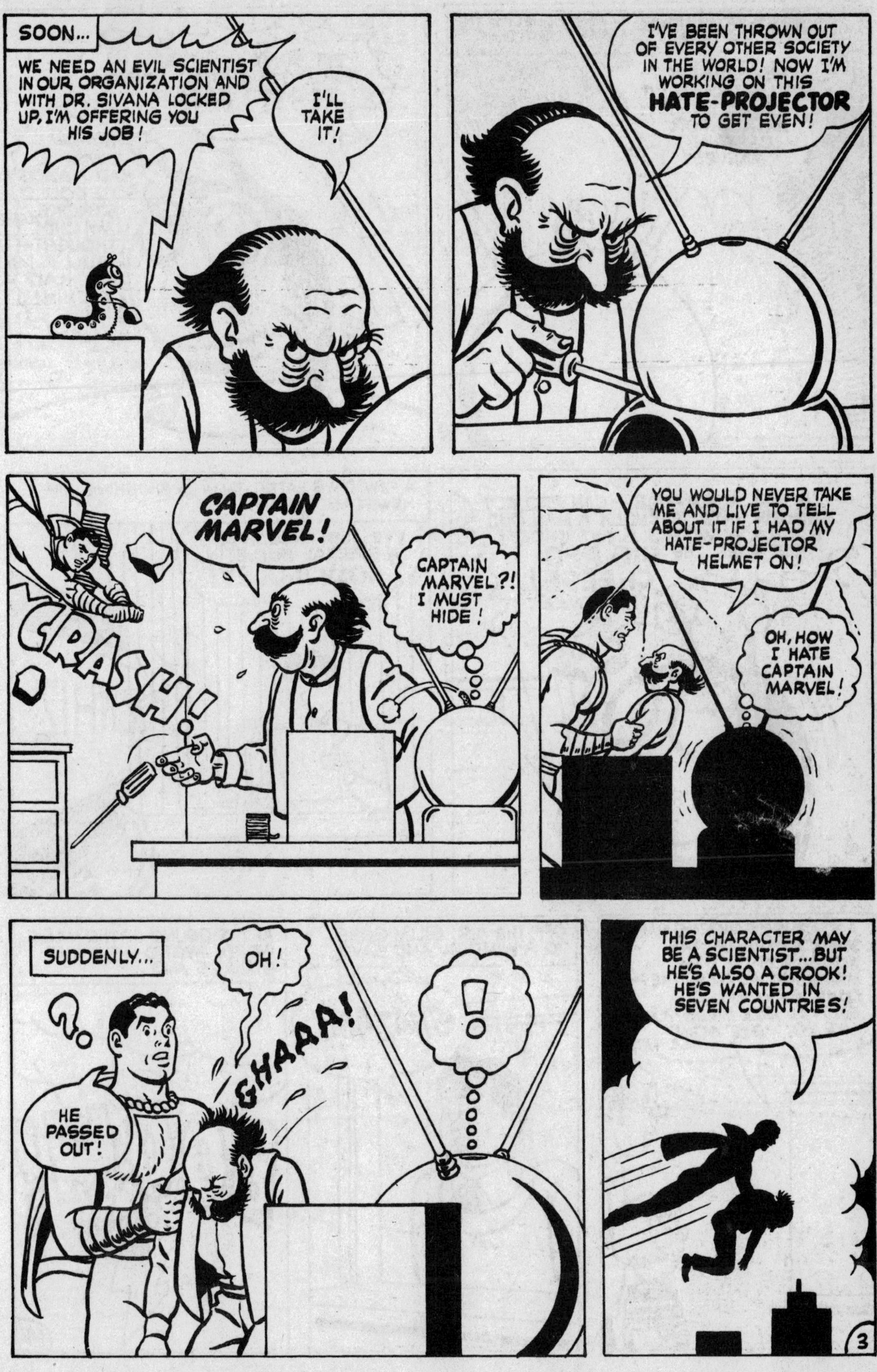
SOON...
WE NEED AN EVIL SCIENTIST IN OUR ORGANIZATION AND WITH DR. SIVANA LOCKED UP, I'M OFFERING YOU HIS JOB!
I'LL TAKE IT!
I'VE BEEN THROWN OUT OF EVERY OTHER SOCIETY IN THE WORLD! NOW I'M WORKING ON THIS HATE-PROJECTOR TO GET EVEN!
CAPTAIN MARVEL!
CRASH!
CAPTAIN MARVEL?! I MUST HIDE!
YOU WOULD NEVER TAKE ME AND LIVE TO TELL ABOUT IT IF I HAD MY HATE-PROJECTOR HELMET ON!
OH, HOW I HATE CAPTAIN MARVEL!
SUDDENLY...
OH!
GHAAA!
?
!
HE PASSED OUT!
THIS CHARACTER MAY BE A SCIENTIST...BUT HE'S ALSO A CROOK! HE'S WANTED IN SEVEN COUNTRIES!
3

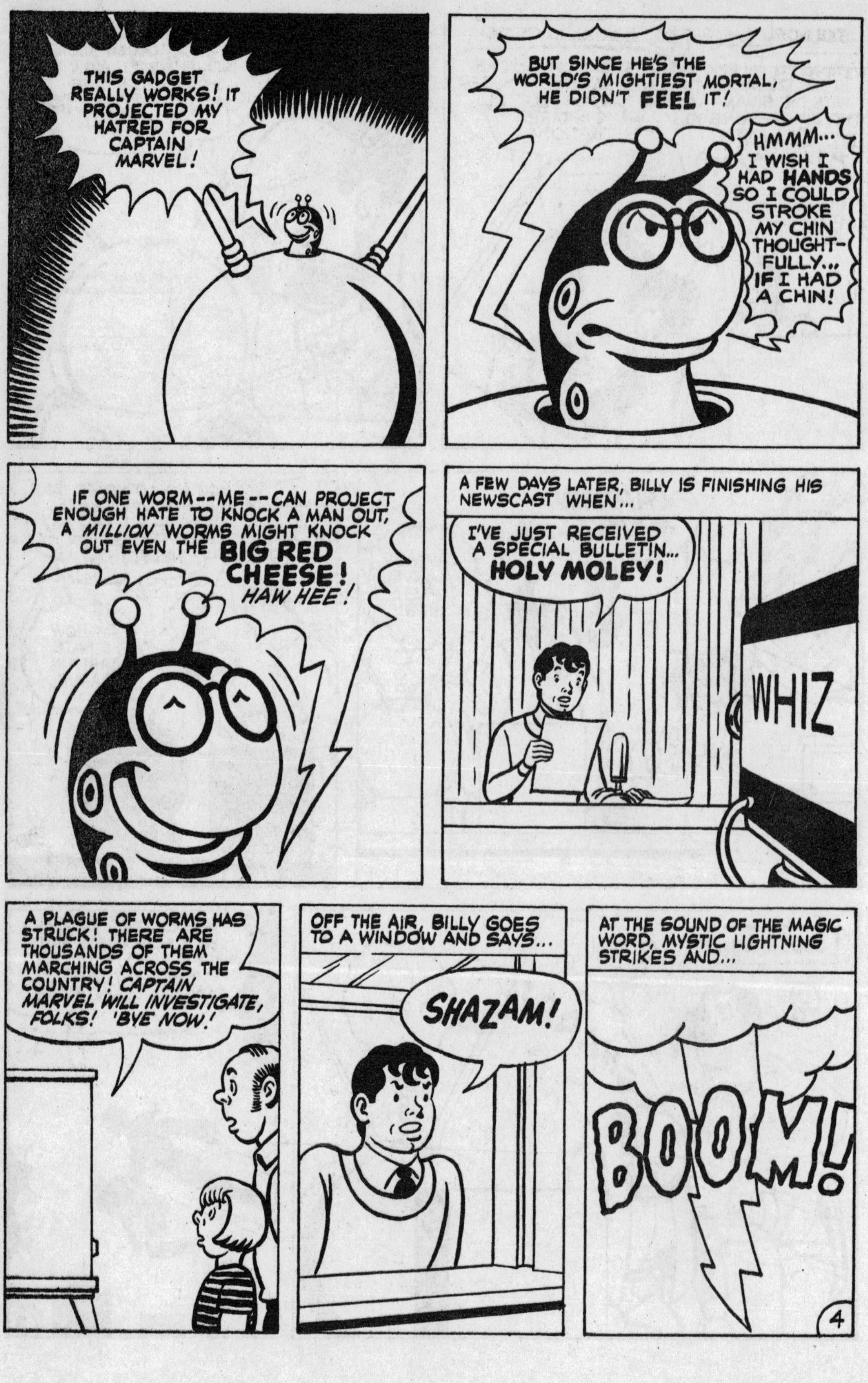
THIS GADGET REALLY WORKS! IT PROJECTED MY HATRED FOR CAPTAIN MARVEL!
BUT SINCE HE'S THE WORLD'S MIGHTIEST MORTAL, HE DIDN'T FEEL IT!
HMMM... I WISH I HAD HANDS SO I COULD STROKE MY CHIN THOUGHT-FULLY... IF I HAD A CHIN!
IF ONE WORM--ME--CAN PROJECT ENOUGH HATE TO KNOCK A MAN OUT, A MILLION WORMS MIGHT KNOCK OUT EVEN THE BIG RED CHEESE! HAW HEE!
A FEW DAYS LATER, BILLY IS FINISHING HIS NEWSCAST WHEN...
I'VE JUST RECEIVED A SPECIAL BULLETIN... HOLY MOLEY!
WHIZ
A PLAGUE OF WORMS HAS STRUCK! THERE ARE THOUSANDS OF THEM MARCHING ACROSS THE COUNTRY! CAPTAIN MARVEL WILL INVESTIGATE, FOLKS! 'BYE NOW!
OFF THE AIR, BILLY GOES TO A WINDOW AND SAYS...
SHAZAM!
AT THE SOUND OF THE MAGIC WORD, MYSTIC LIGHTNING STRIKES AND...
BOOM!
4

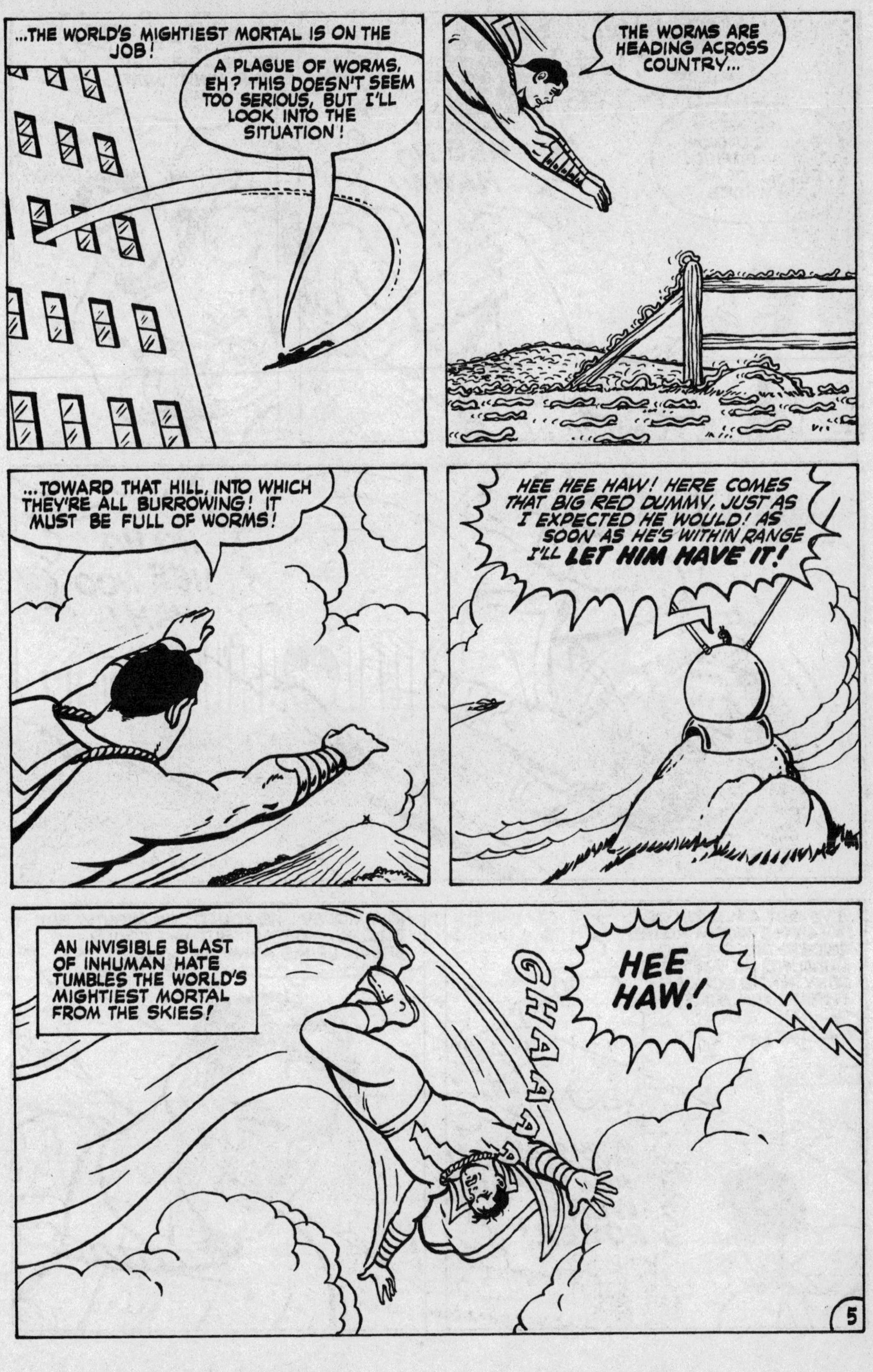
...THE WORLD'S MIGHTIEST MORTAL IS ON THE JOB!
A PLAGUE OF WORMS, EH? THIS DOESN'T SEEM TOO SERIOUS, BUT I'LL LOOK INTO THE SITUATION!
THE WORMS ARE HEADING ACROSS COUNTRY...
...TOWARD THAT HILL, INTO WHICH THEY'RE ALL BURROWING! IT MUST BE FULL OF WORMS!
HEE HEE HAW! HERE COMES THAT BIG RED DUMMY, JUST AS I EXPECTED HE WOULD! AS SOON AS HE'S WITHIN RANGE I'LL LET HIM HAVE IT!
AN INVISIBLE BLAST OF INHUMAN HATE TUMBLES THE WORLD'S MIGHTIEST MORTAL FROM THE SKIES!
GHAAAA
HEE HAW!
5

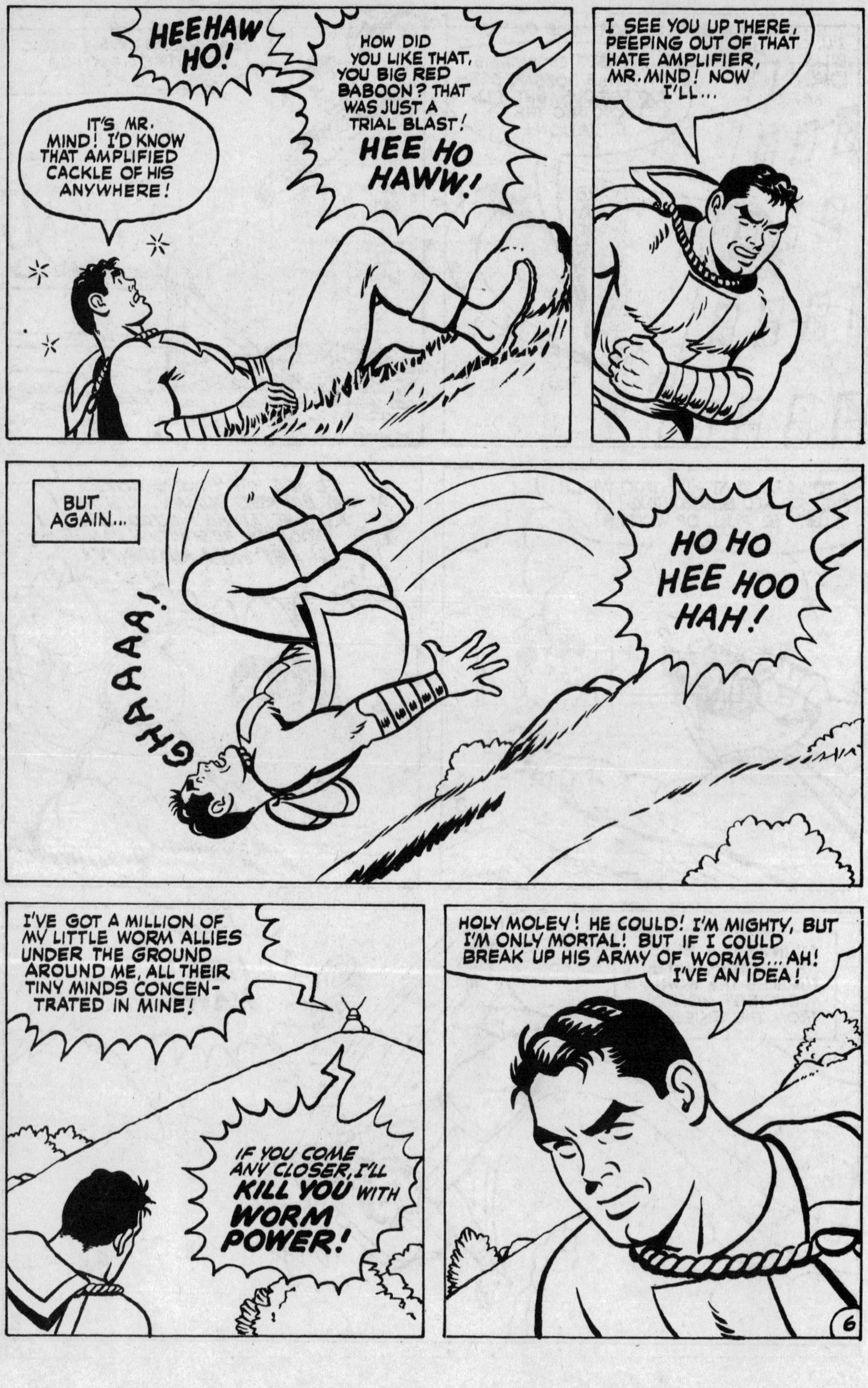
HEEHAW HO!
IT'S MR. MIND! I'D KNOW THAT AMPLIFIED CACKLE OF HIS ANYWHERE!
HOW DID YOU LIKE THAT, YOU BIG RED BABOON? THAT WAS JUST A TRIAL BLAST! HEE HO HAWW!
I SEE YOU UP THERE, PEEPING OUT OF THAT HATE AMPLIFIER, MR. MIND! NOW I'LL...
BUT AGAIN...
GHAAAA!
HO HO HEE HOO HAH!
I'VE GOT A MILLION OF MY LITTLE WORM ALLIES UNDER THE GROUND AROUND ME, ALL THEIR TINY MINDS CONCENTRATED IN MINE!
IF YOU COME ANY CLOSER, I'LL KILL YOU WITH WORM POWER!
HOLY MOLEY! HE COULD! I'M MIGHTY, BUT I'M ONLY MORTAL! BUT IF I COULD BREAK UP HIS ARMY OF WORMS...AH! I'VE AN IDEA!
6

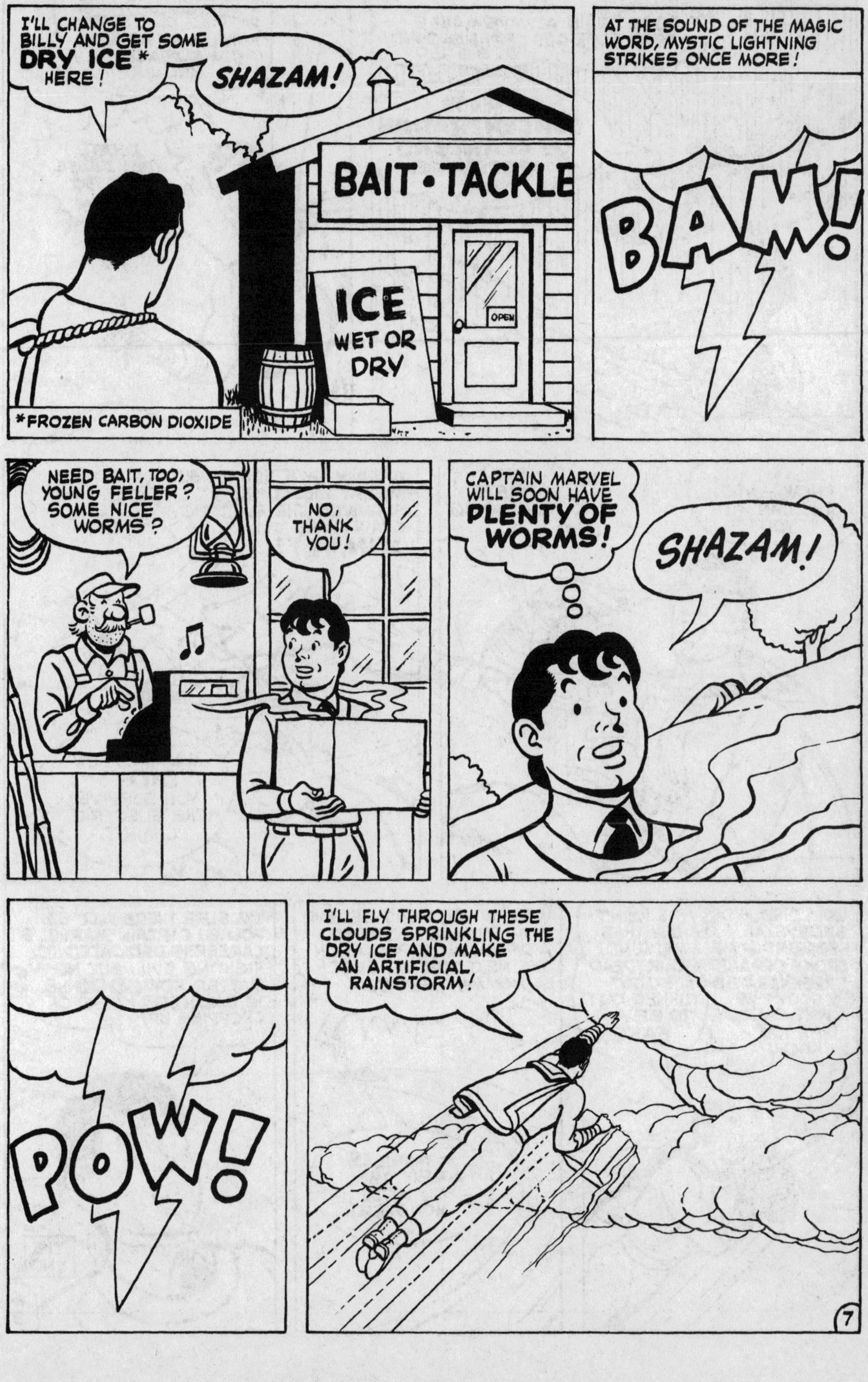
I'LL CHANGE TO BILLY AND GET SOME DRY ICE* HERE!
SHAZAM!
BAIT • TACKLE
ICE WET OR DRY
OPEN
*FROZEN CARBON DIOXIDE
AT THE SOUND OF THE MAGIC WORD, MYSTIC LIGHTNING STRIKES ONCE MORE!
BAM!
NEED BAIT, TOO, YOUNG FELLER? SOME NICE WORMS?
NO, THANK YOU!
CAPTAIN MARVEL WILL SOON HAVE PLENTY OF WORMS!
SHAZAM!
POW!
I'LL FLY THROUGH THESE CLOUDS SPRINKLING THE DRY ICE AND MAKE AN ARTIFICIAL RAINSTORM!
7

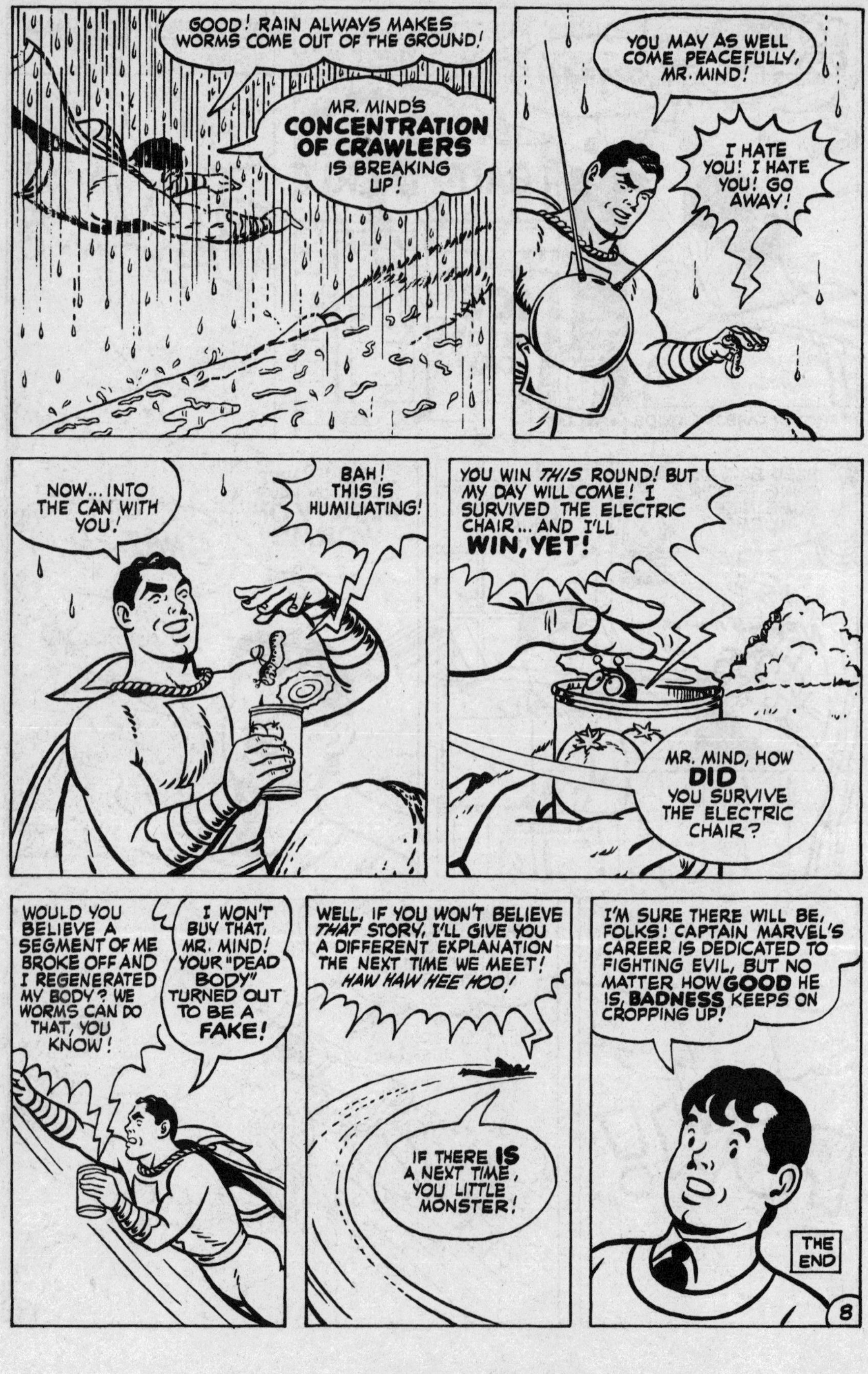
GOOD! RAIN ALWAYS MAKES WORMS COME OUT OF THE GROUND!
MR. MIND'S CONCENTRATION OF CRAWLERS IS BREAKING UP!
YOU MAY AS WELL COME PEACEFULLY, MR. MIND!
I HATE YOU! I HATE YOU! GO AWAY!
NOW... INTO THE CAN WITH YOU!
BAH! THIS IS HUMILIATING!
YOU WIN THIS ROUND! BUT MY DAY WILL COME! I SURVIVED THE ELECTRIC CHAIR... AND I'LL WIN, YET!
MR. MIND, HOW DID YOU SURVIVE THE ELECTRIC CHAIR?
WOULD YOU BELIEVE A SEGMENT OF ME BROKE OFF AND I REGENERATED MY BODY? WE WORMS CAN DO THAT, YOU KNOW!
I WON'T BUY THAT, MR. MIND! YOUR "DEAD BODY" TURNED OUT TO BE A FAKE!
WELL, IF YOU WON'T BELIEVE THAT STORY, I'LL GIVE YOU A DIFFERENT EXPLANATION THE NEXT TIME WE MEET! HAW HAW HEE HOO!
IF THERE IS A NEXT TIME, YOU LITTLE MONSTER!
I'M SURE THERE WILL BE, FOLKS! CAPTAIN MARVEL'S CAREER IS DEDICATED TO FIGHTING EVIL, BUT NO MATTER HOW GOOD HE IS, BADNESS KEEPS ON CROPPING UP!
THE END
8

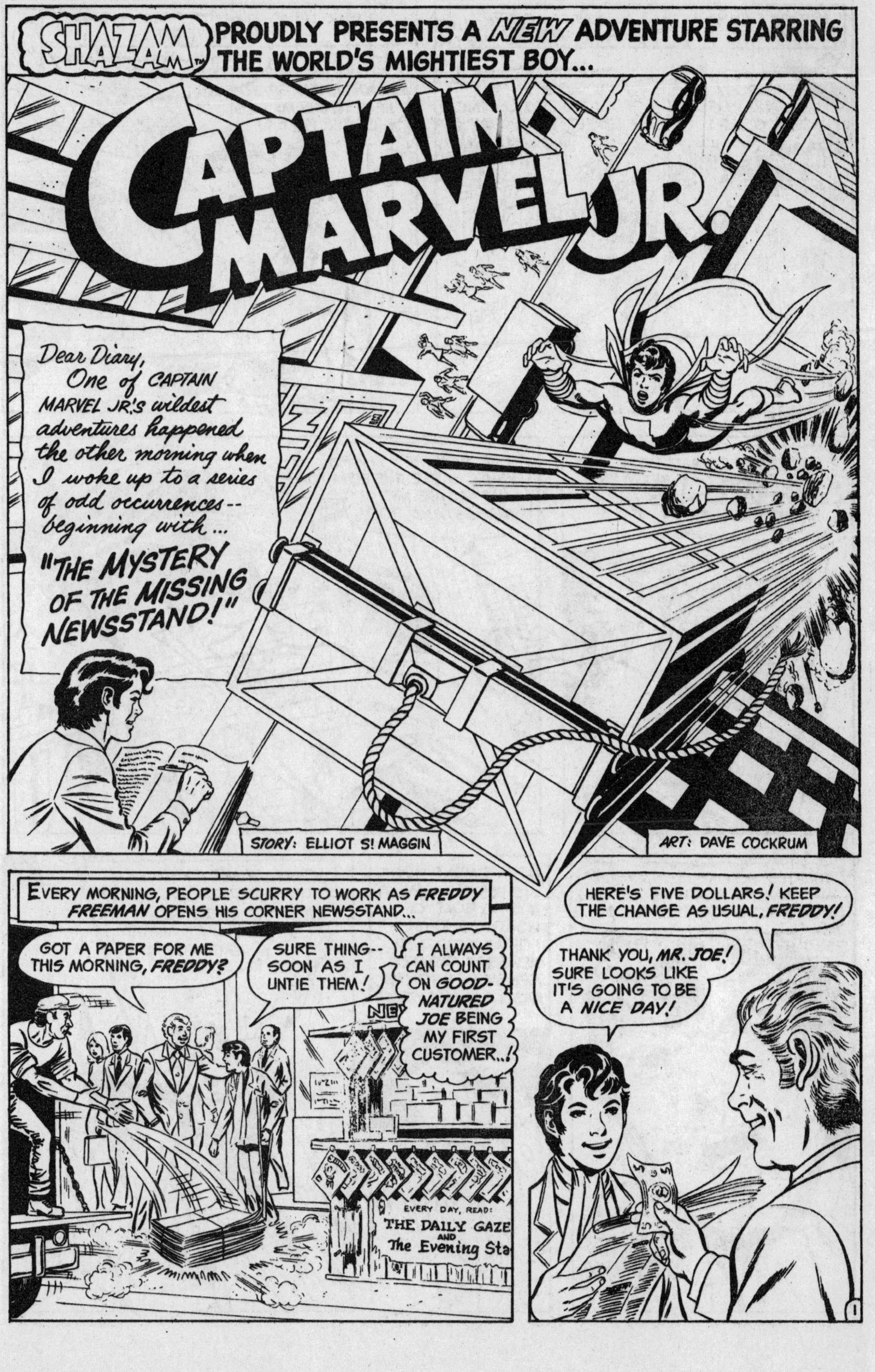
SHAZAM PROUDLY PRESENTS A NEW ADVENTURE STARRING THE WORLD'S MIGHTIEST BOY...
CAPTAIN MARVEL JR.
Dear Diary, One of CAPTAIN MARVEL JR.'s wildest adventures happened the other morning when I woke up to a series of odd occurrences -- beginning with ...
"THE MYSTERY OF THE MISSING NEWSSTAND!"
STORY: ELLIOT S! MAGGIN
ART: DAVE COCKRUM
EVERY MORNING, PEOPLE SCURRY TO WORK AS FREDDY FREEMAN OPENS HIS CORNER NEWSSTAND...
GOT A PAPER FOR ME THIS MORNING, FREDDY?
SURE THING-- SOON AS I UNTIE THEM!
I ALWAYS CAN COUNT ON GOOD-NATURED JOE BEING MY FIRST CUSTOMER..!
EVERY DAY, READ: THE DAILY GAZE AND The Evening Sta
HERE'S FIVE DOLLARS! KEEP THE CHANGE AS USUAL, FREDDY!
THANK YOU, MR. JOE! SURE LOOKS LIKE IT'S GOING TO BE A NICE DAY!
1

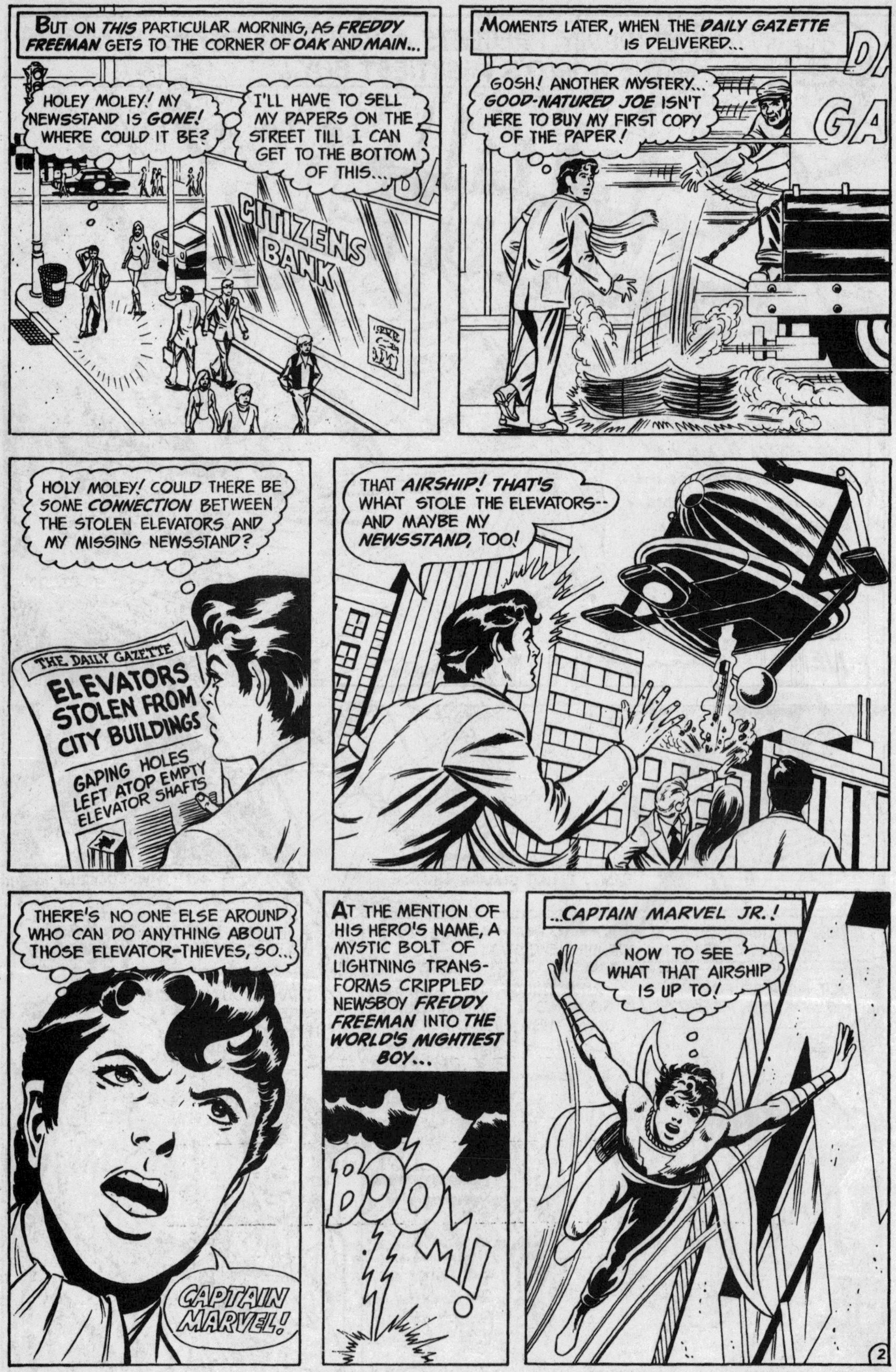
BUT ON THIS PARTICULAR MORNING, AS FREDDY FREEMAN GETS TO THE CORNER OF OAK AND MAIN...
HOLEY MOLEY! MY NEWSSTAND IS GONE! WHERE COULD IT BE?
I'LL HAVE TO SELL MY PAPERS ON THE STREET TILL I CAN GET TO THE BOTTOM OF THIS...
CITIZENS BANK
MOMENTS LATER, WHEN THE DAILY GAZETTE IS DELIVERED...
GOSH! ANOTHER MYSTERY... GOOD-NATURED JOE ISN'T HERE TO BUY MY FIRST COPY OF THE PAPER!
HOLY MOLEY! COULD THERE BE SOME CONNECTION BETWEEN THE STOLEN ELEVATORS AND MY MISSING NEWSSTAND?
THE DAILY GAZETTE
ELEVATORS STOLEN FROM CITY BUILDINGS
GAPING HOLES LEFT ATOP EMPTY ELEVATOR SHAFTS
THAT AIRSHIP! THAT'S WHAT STOLE THE ELEVATORS-- AND MAYBE MY NEWSSTAND, TOO!
THERE'S NO ONE ELSE AROUND WHO CAN DO ANYTHING ABOUT THOSE ELEVATOR-THIEVES, SO...
CAPTAIN MARVEL!
AT THE MENTION OF HIS HERO'S NAME, A MYSTIC BOLT OF LIGHTNING TRANSFORMS CRIPPLED NEWSBOY FREDDY FREEMAN INTO THE WORLD'S MIGHTIEST BOY...
BOOM!
...CAPTAIN MARVEL JR.!
NOW TO SEE WHAT THAT AIRSHIP IS UP TO!
2

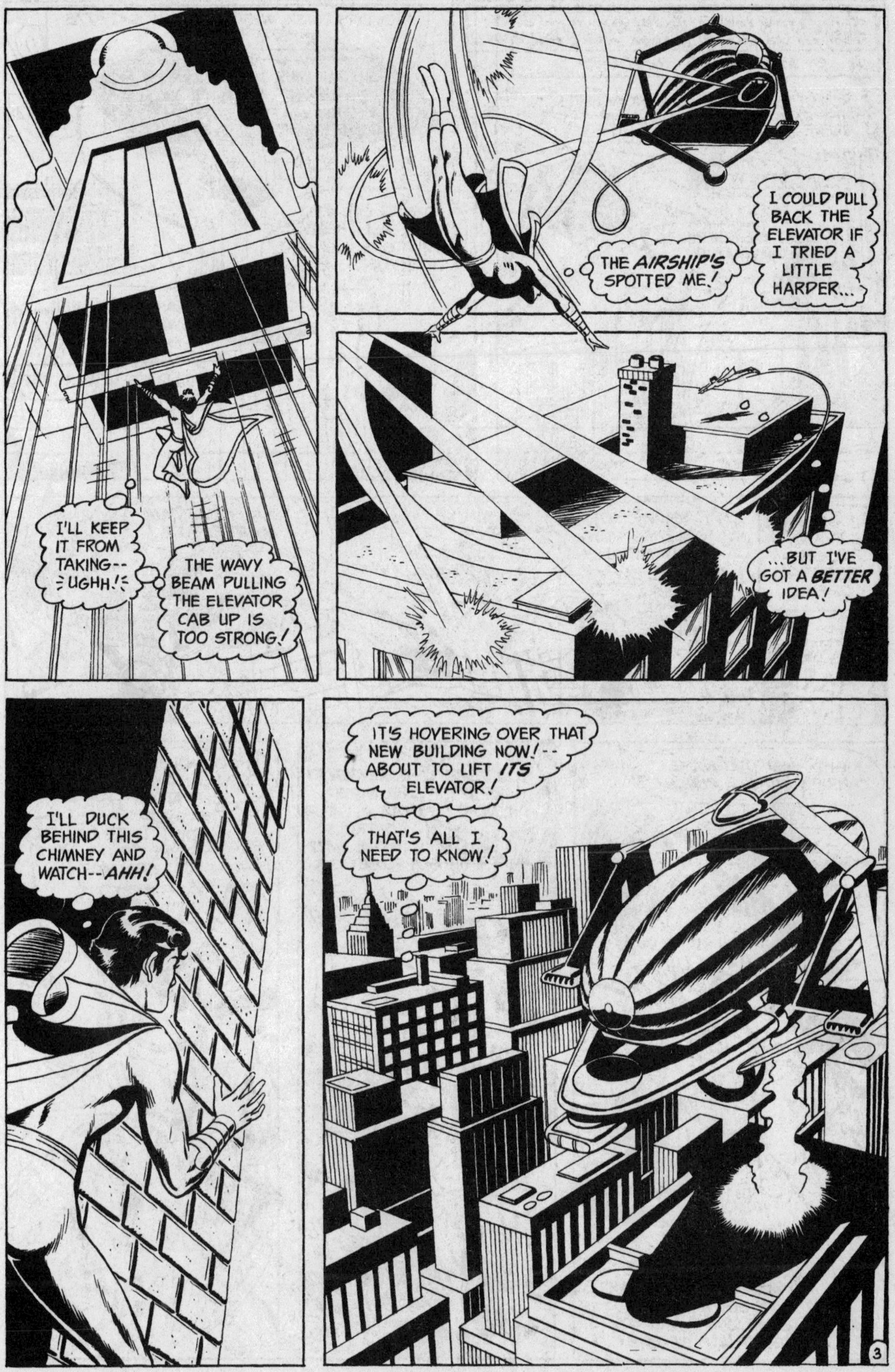
I'LL KEEP IT FROM TAKING-- UGHH!
THE WAVY BEAM PULLING THE ELEVATOR CAB UP IS TOO STRONG!
THE AIRSHIP'S SPOTTED ME!
I COULD PULL BACK THE ELEVATOR IF I TRIED A LITTLE HARDER...
...BUT I'VE GOT A BETTER IDEA!
I'LL DUCK BEHIND THIS CHIMNEY AND WATCH--AHH!
IT'S HOVERING OVER THAT NEW BUILDING NOW!-- ABOUT TO LIFT ITS ELEVATOR!
THAT'S ALL I NEED TO KNOW!
3

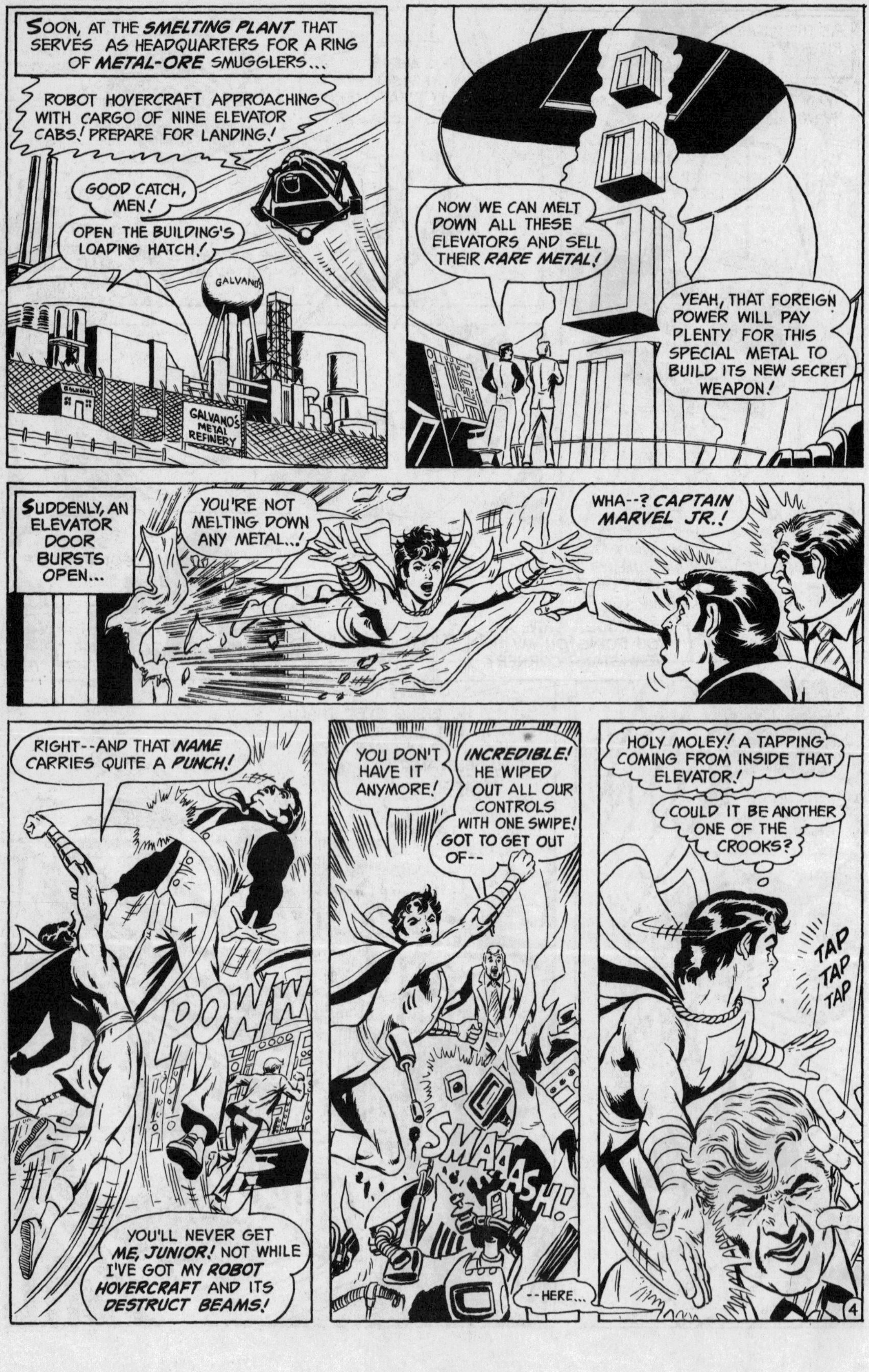
SOON, AT THE SMELTING PLANT THAT SERVES AS HEADQUARTERS FOR A RING OF METAL-ORE SMUGGLERS...
ROBOT HOVERCRAFT APPROACHING WITH CARGO OF NINE ELEVATOR CABS! PREPARE FOR LANDING!
GOOD CATCH, MEN!
OPEN THE BUILDING'S LOADING HATCH!
GALVANO'S
GALVANO'S METAL REFINERY
NOW WE CAN MELT DOWN ALL THESE ELEVATORS AND SELL THEIR RARE METAL!
YEAH, THAT FOREIGN POWER WILL PAY PLENTY FOR THIS SPECIAL METAL TO BUILD ITS NEW SECRET WEAPON!
SUDDENLY, AN ELEVATOR DOOR BURSTS OPEN...
YOU'RE NOT MELTING DOWN ANY METAL...!
WHA--? CAPTAIN MARVEL JR.!
RIGHT--AND THAT NAME CARRIES QUITE A PUNCH!
POWW
YOU'LL NEVER GET ME, JUNIOR! NOT WHILE I'VE GOT MY ROBOT HOVERCRAFT AND ITS DESTRUCT BEAMS!
YOU DON'T HAVE IT ANYMORE!
INCREDIBLE! HE WIPED OUT ALL OUR CONTROLS WITH ONE SWIPE! GOT TO GET OUT OF--
SMAAASH!
--HERE...
HOLY MOLEY! A TAPPING COMING FROM INSIDE THAT ELEVATOR!
COULD IT BE ANOTHER ONE OF THE CROOKS?
TAP TAP TAP
4

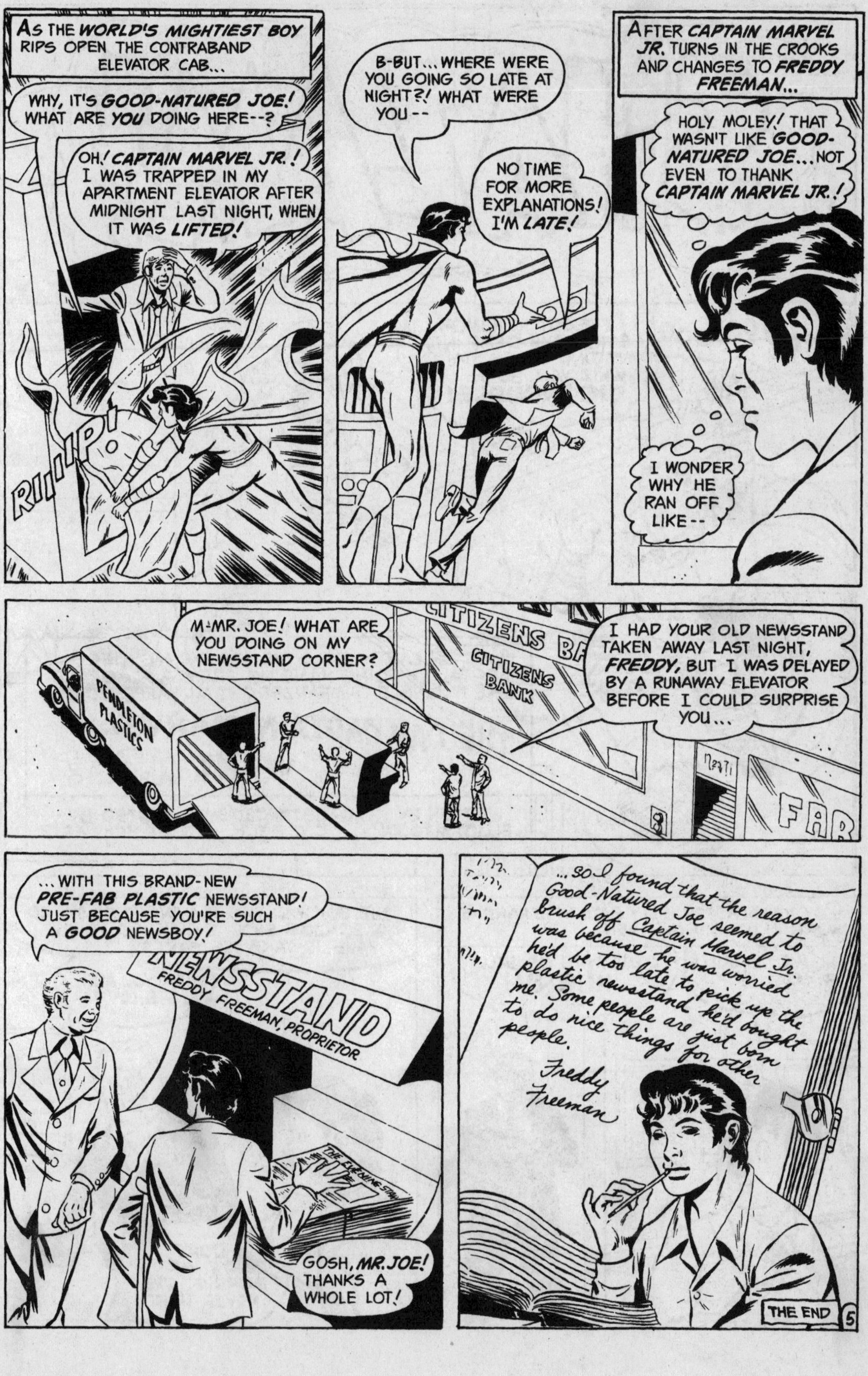
AS THE WORLD'S MIGHTIEST BOY RIPS OPEN THE CONTRABAND ELEVATOR CAB...
WHY, IT'S GOOD-NATURED JOE! WHAT ARE YOU DOING HERE--?
OH! CAPTAIN MARVEL JR.! I WAS TRAPPED IN MY APARTMENT ELEVATOR AFTER MIDNIGHT LAST NIGHT, WHEN IT WAS LIFTED!
RIIIIP!
B-BUT... WHERE WERE YOU GOING SO LATE AT NIGHT?! WHAT WERE YOU --
NO TIME FOR MORE EXPLANATIONS! I'M LATE!
AFTER CAPTAIN MARVEL JR. TURNS IN THE CROOKS AND CHANGES TO FREDDY FREEMAN...
HOLY MOLEY! THAT WASN'T LIKE GOOD-NATURED JOE... NOT EVEN TO THANK CAPTAIN MARVEL JR.!
I WONDER WHY HE RAN OFF LIKE --
M-MR. JOE! WHAT ARE YOU DOING ON MY NEWSSTAND CORNER?
CITIZENS BA
CITIZENS BANK
PENDLETON PLASTICS
I HAD YOUR OLD NEWSSTAND TAKEN AWAY LAST NIGHT, FREDDY, BUT I WAS DELAYED BY A RUNAWAY ELEVATOR BEFORE I COULD SURPRISE YOU...
...WITH THIS BRAND-NEW PRE-FAB PLASTIC NEWSSTAND! JUST BECAUSE YOU'RE SUCH A GOOD NEWSBOY!
NEWSSTAND
FREDDY FREEMAN, PROPRIETOR
GOSH, MR. JOE! THANKS A WHOLE LOT!
...so I found that the reason Good-Natured Joe seemed to brush off Captain Marvel Jr. was because he was worried he'd be too late to pick up the plastic newsstand he'd bought me. Some people are just born to do nice things for other people.
Freddy Freeman
THE END
5

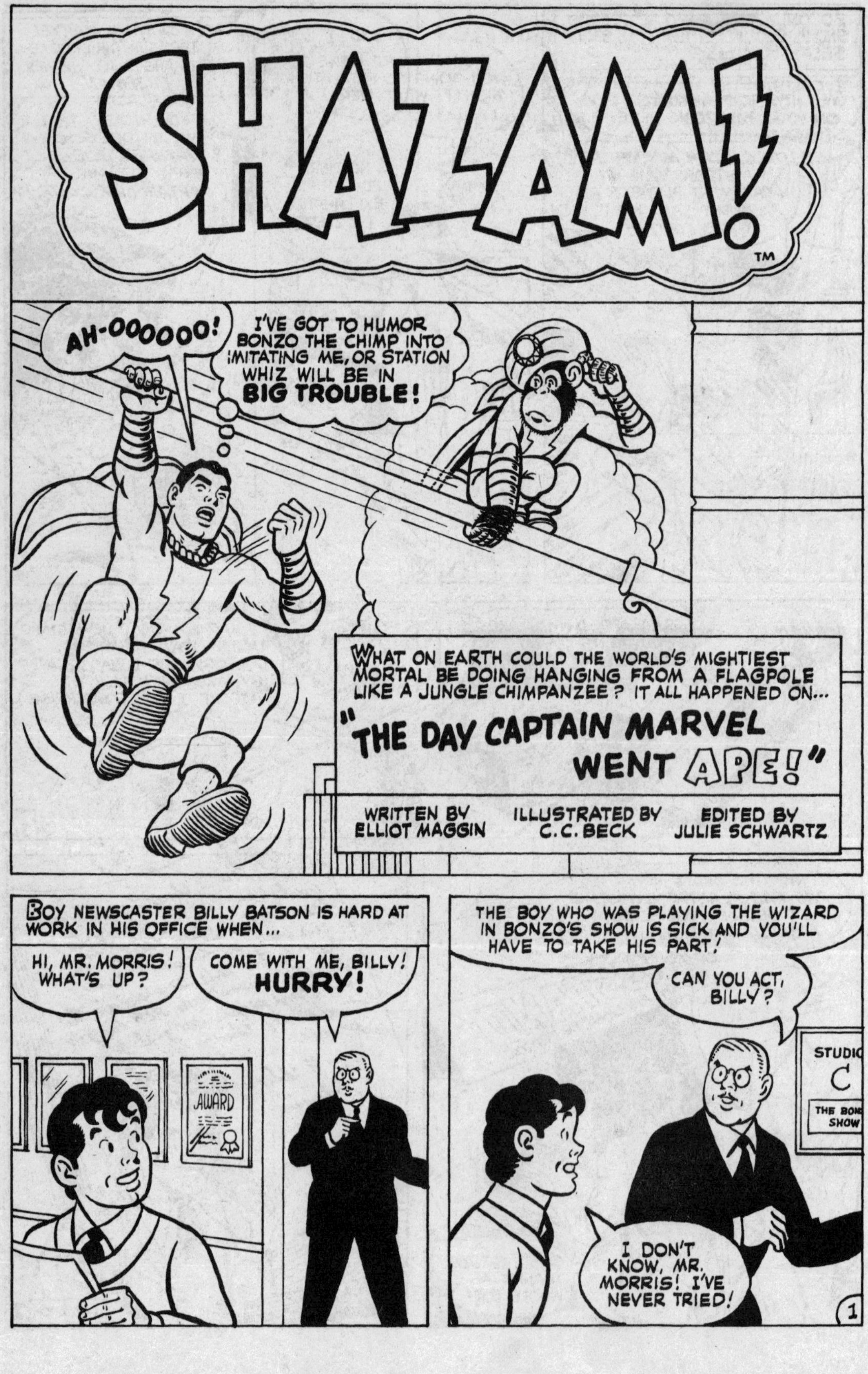

SHAZAM!™
AH-OOOOOO!
I'VE GOT TO HUMOR BONZO THE CHIMP INTO IMITATING ME, OR STATION WHIZ WILL BE IN BIG TROUBLE!
WHAT ON EARTH COULD THE WORLD'S MIGHTIEST MORTAL BE DOING HANGING FROM A FLAGPOLE LIKE A JUNGLE CHIMPANZEE? IT ALL HAPPENED ON...
"THE DAY CAPTAIN MARVEL WENT APE!"
WRITTEN BY ELLIOT MAGGIN
ILLUSTRATED BY C.C. BECK
EDITED BY JULIE SCHWARTZ
BOY NEWSCASTER BILLY BATSON IS HARD AT WORK IN HIS OFFICE WHEN...
HI, MR. MORRIS! WHAT'S UP?
COME WITH ME, BILLY! HURRY!
AWARD
THE BOY WHO WAS PLAYING THE WIZARD IN BONZO'S SHOW IS SICK AND YOU'LL HAVE TO TAKE HIS PART!
CAN YOU ACT, BILLY?
STUDIO C
THE BON SHOW
I DON'T KNOW, MR. MORRIS! I'VE NEVER TRIED!
1

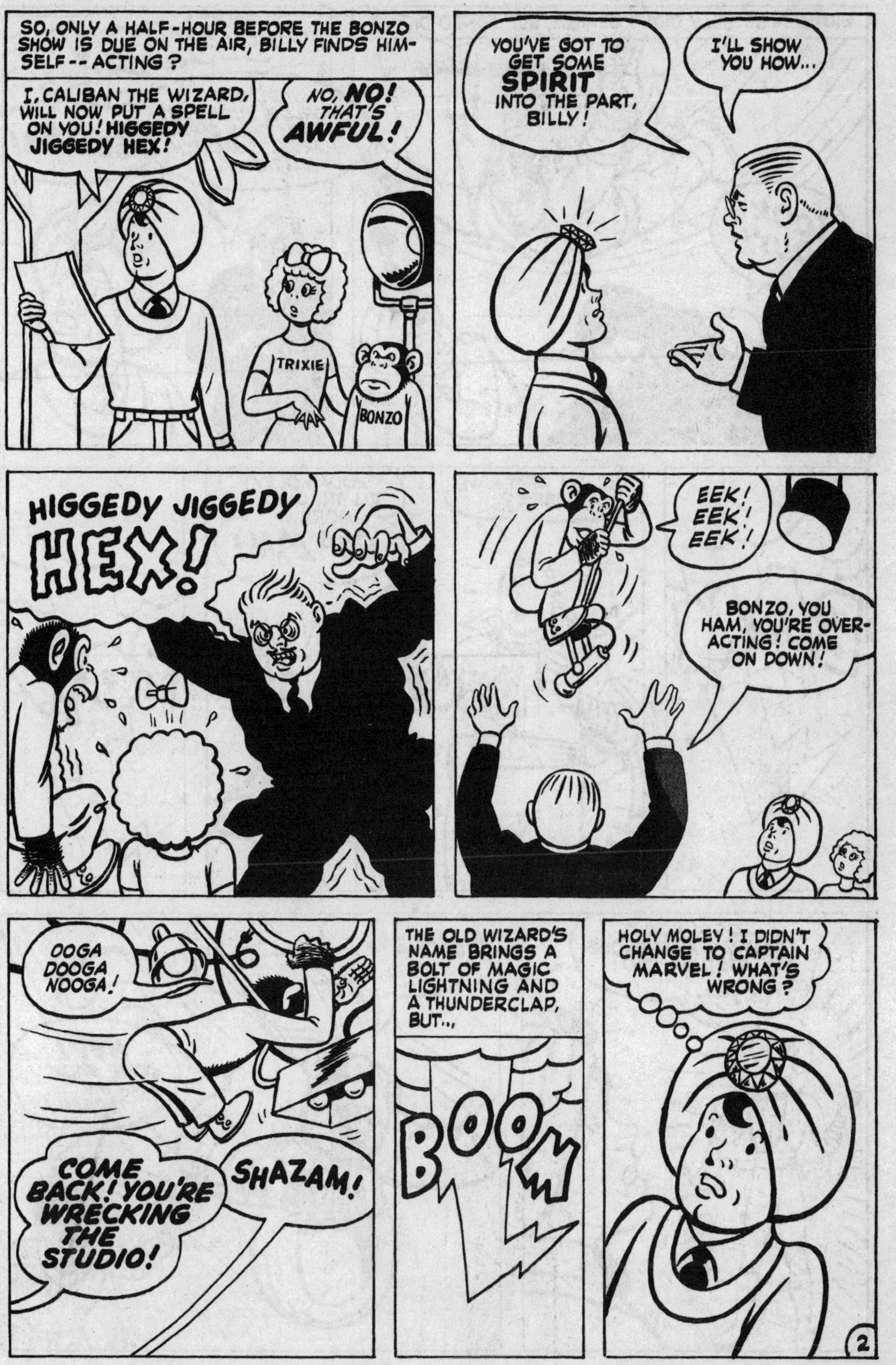
SO, ONLY A HALF-HOUR BEFORE THE BONZO SHOW IS DUE ON THE AIR, BILLY FINDS HIMSELF -- ACTING?
I, CALIBAN THE WIZARD, WILL NOW PUT A SPELL ON YOU! HIGGEDY JIGGEDY HEX!
NO, NO! THAT'S AWFUL!
TRIXIE
BONZO
YOU'VE GOT TO GET SOME SPIRIT INTO THE PART, BILLY!
I'LL SHOW YOU HOW...
HIGGEDY JIGGEDY HEX!
EEK! EEK! EEK!
BONZO, YOU HAM, YOU'RE OVERACTING! COME ON DOWN!
OOGA DOOGA NOOGA!
COME BACK! YOU'RE WRECKING THE STUDIO!
SHAZAM!
THE OLD WIZARD'S NAME BRINGS A BOLT OF MAGIC LIGHTNING AND A THUNDERCLAP, BUT...
BOOM
HOLY MOLEY! I DIDN'T CHANGE TO CAPTAIN MARVEL! WHAT'S WRONG?
2

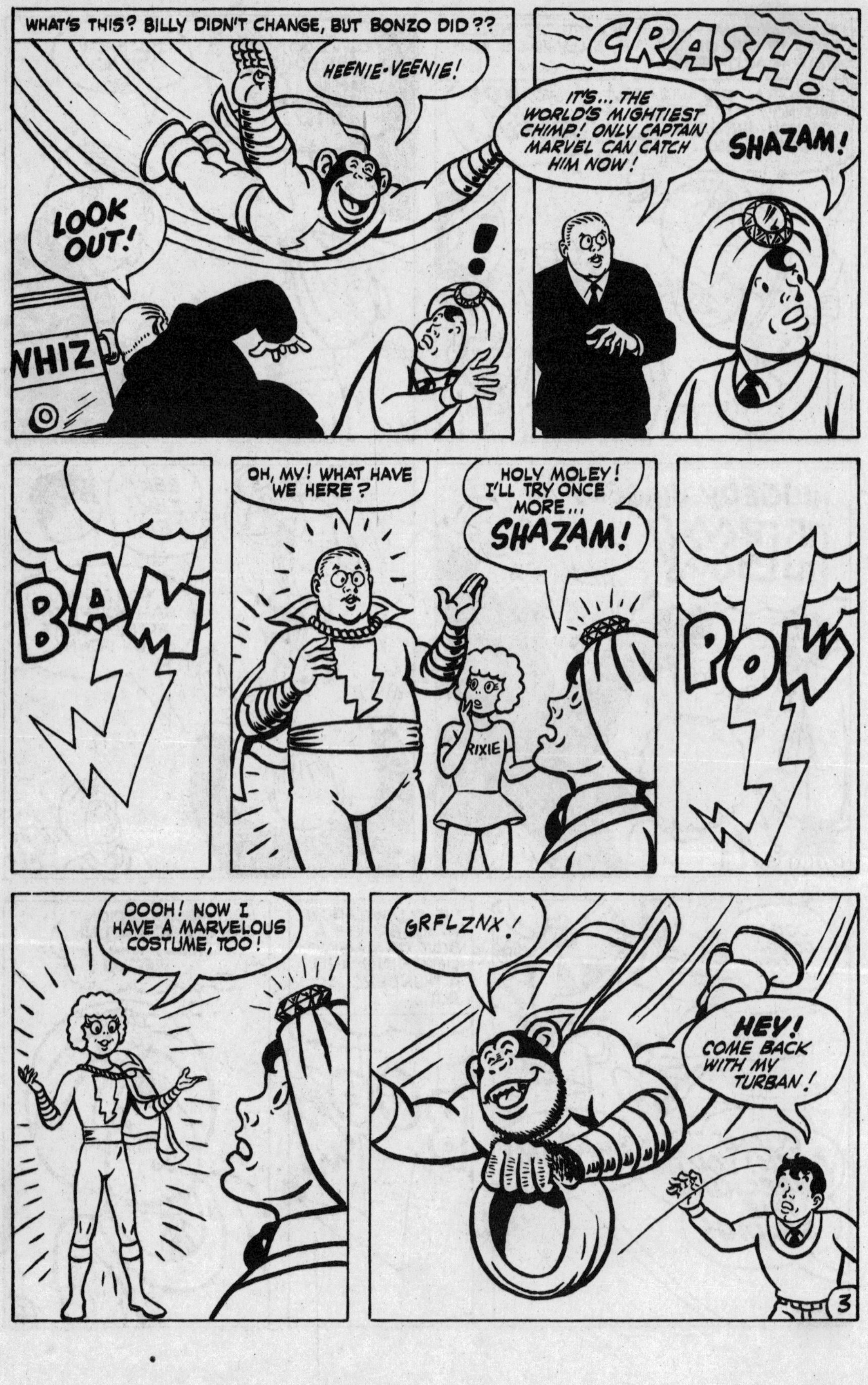
WHAT'S THIS? BILLY DIDN'T CHANGE, BUT BONZO DID??
HEENIE-VEENIE!
LOOK OUT!
WHIZ
CRASH!
IT'S... THE WORLD'S MIGHTIEST CHIMP! ONLY CAPTAIN MARVEL CAN CATCH HIM NOW!
SHAZAM!
BAM
OH, MY! WHAT HAVE WE HERE?
HOLY MOLEY! I'LL TRY ONCE MORE... SHAZAM!
RIXIE
POW
OOOH! NOW I HAVE A MARVELOUS COSTUME, TOO!
GRFLZNX!
HEY! COME BACK WITH MY TURBAN!
3

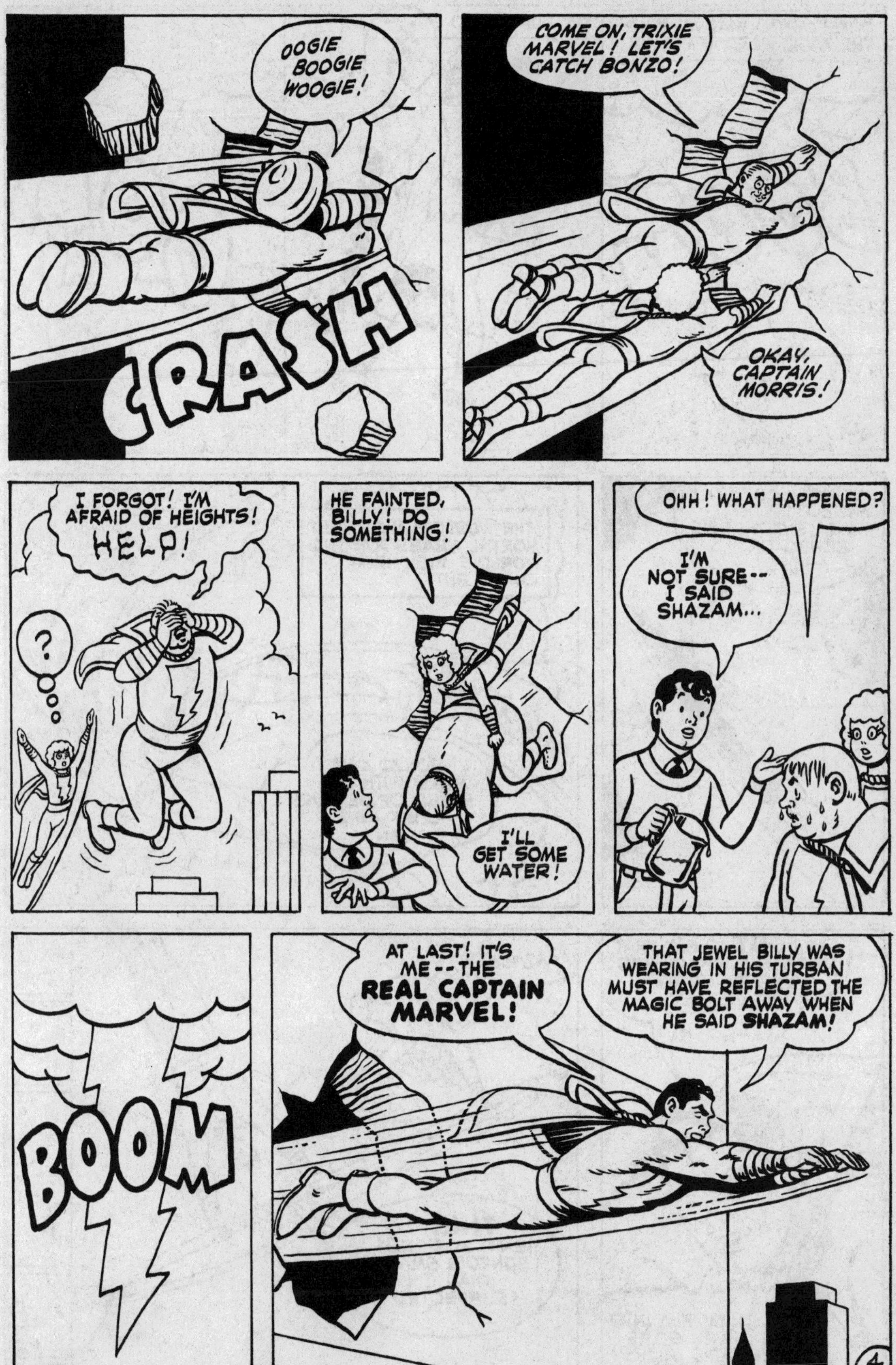
OOGIE BOOGIE WOOGIE!
CRASH
COME ON, TRIXIE MARVEL! LET'S CATCH BONZO!
OKAY, CAPTAIN MORRIS!
I FORGOT! I'M AFRAID OF HEIGHTS! HELP!
?
HE FAINTED, BILLY! DO SOMETHING!
I'LL GET SOME WATER!
OHH! WHAT HAPPENED?
I'M NOT SURE-- I SAID SHAZAM...
BOOM
AT LAST! IT'S ME--THE REAL CAPTAIN MARVEL!
THAT JEWEL BILLY WAS WEARING IN HIS TURBAN MUST HAVE REFLECTED THE MAGIC BOLT AWAY WHEN HE SAID SHAZAM!
4

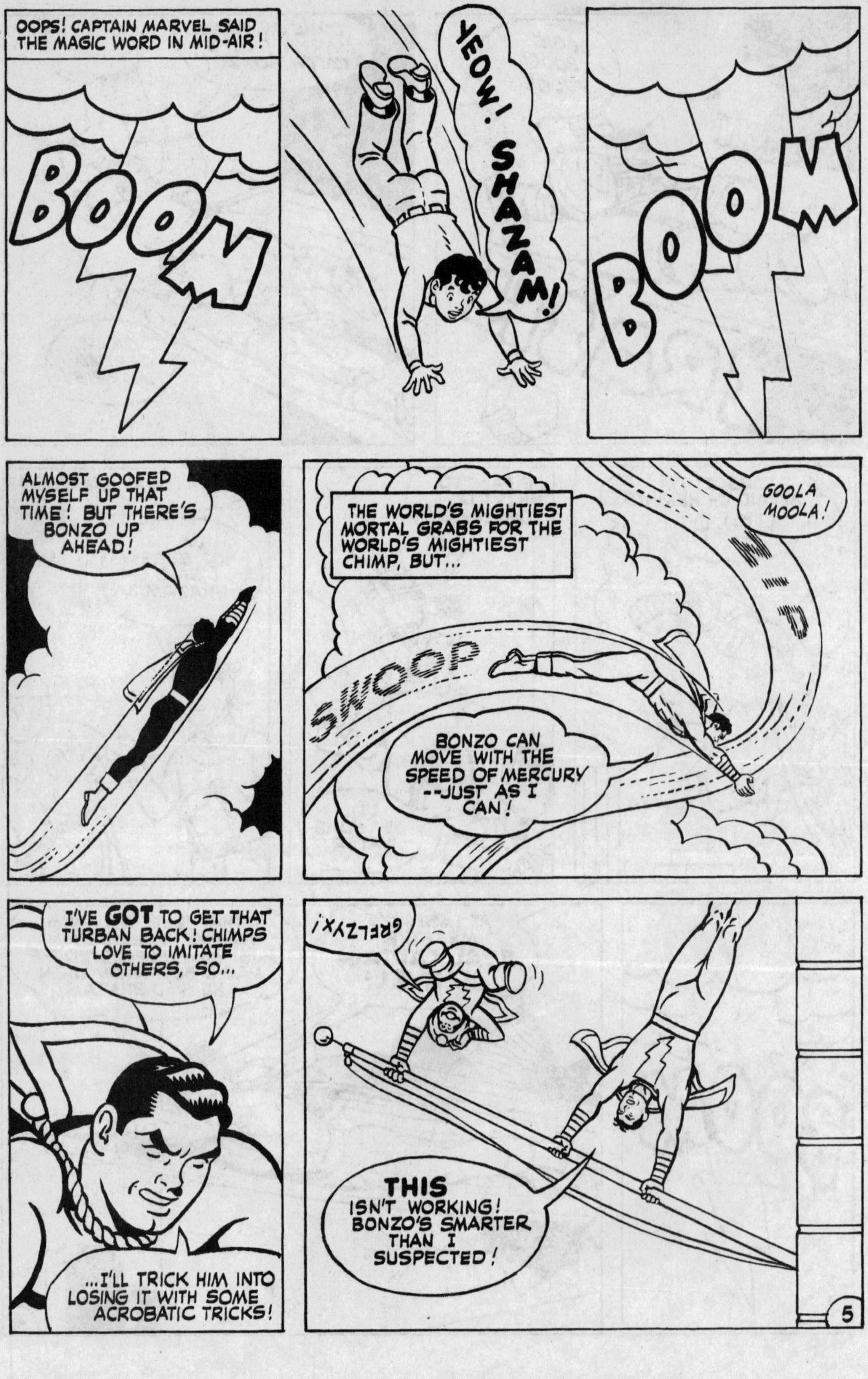
OOPS! CAPTAIN MARVEL SAID THE MAGIC WORD IN MID-AIR!
BOOM
YEOW! SHAZAM!
BOOM
ALMOST GOOFED MYSELF UP THAT TIME! BUT THERE'S BONZO UP AHEAD!
THE WORLD'S MIGHTIEST MORTAL GRABS FOR THE WORLD'S MIGHTIEST CHIMP, BUT...
GOOLA MOOLA!
SWOOP
BONZO CAN MOVE WITH THE SPEED OF MERCURY --JUST AS I CAN!
I'VE GOT TO GET THAT TURBAN BACK! CHIMPS LOVE TO IMITATE OTHERS, SO...
...I'LL TRICK HIM INTO LOSING IT WITH SOME ACROBATIC TRICKS!
GRFLZYX!
THIS ISN'T WORKING! BONZO'S SMARTER THAN I SUSPECTED!
5

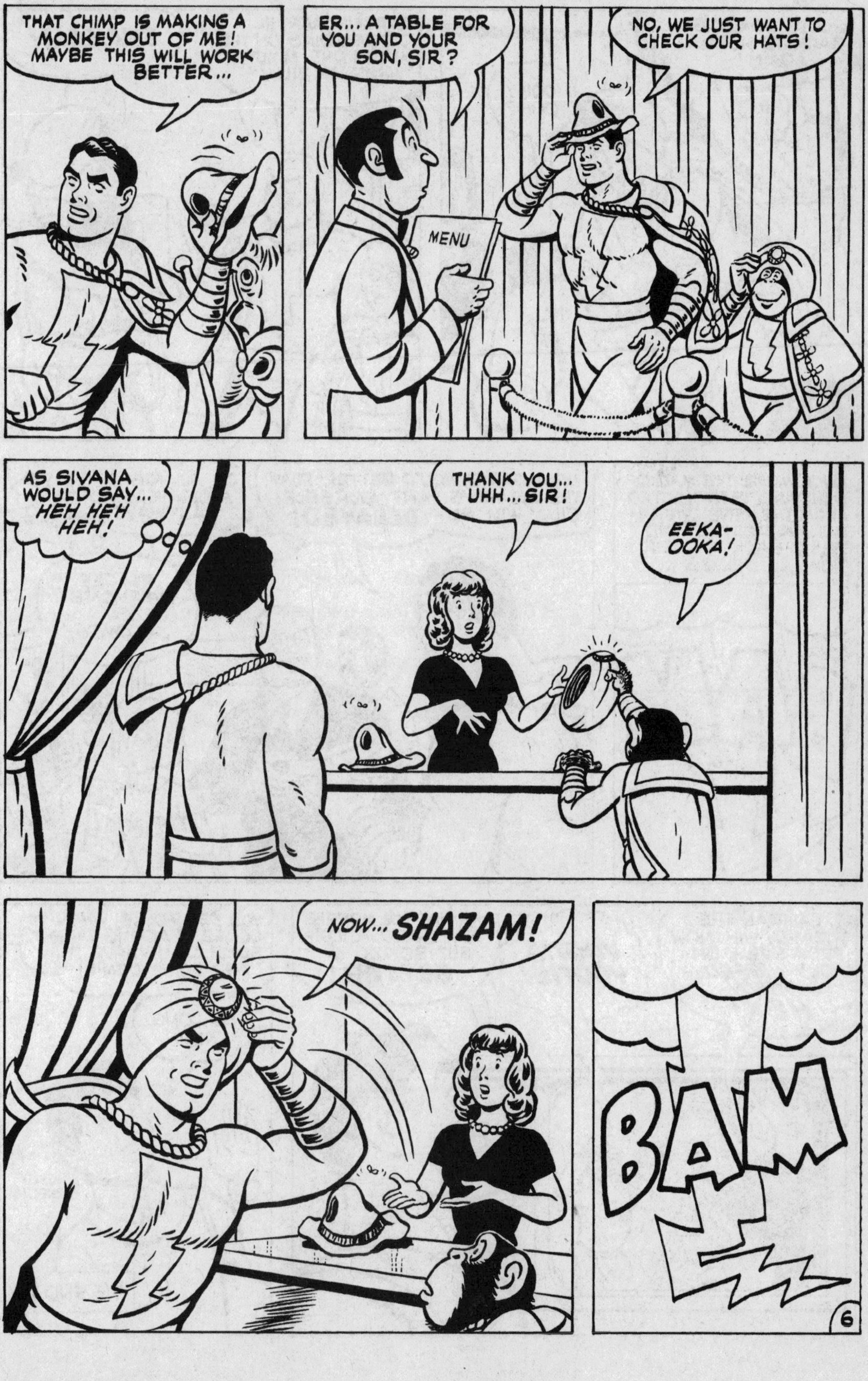
THAT CHIMP IS MAKING A MONKEY OUT OF ME! MAYBE THIS WILL WORK BETTER...
ER... A TABLE FOR YOU AND YOUR SON, SIR?
MENU
NO, WE JUST WANT TO CHECK OUR HATS!
AS SIVANA WOULD SAY... HEH HEH HEH!
THANK YOU... UHH... SIR!
EEKA-OOKA!
NOW... SHAZAM!
BAM
6

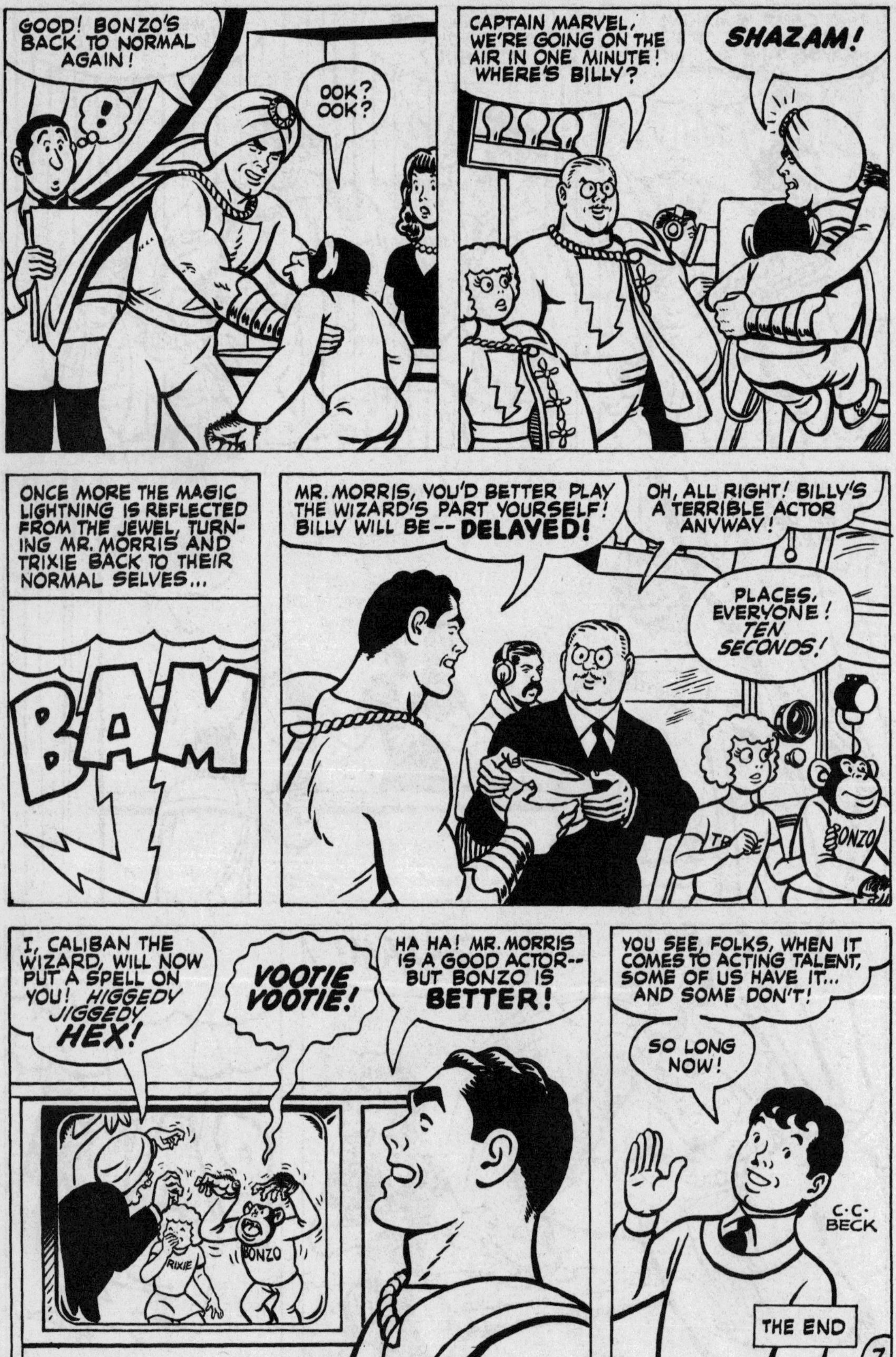
GOOD! BONZO'S BACK TO NORMAL AGAIN!
OOK? OOK?
CAPTAIN MARVEL, WE'RE GOING ON THE AIR IN ONE MINUTE! WHERE'S BILLY?
SHAZAM!
ONCE MORE THE MAGIC LIGHTNING IS REFLECTED FROM THE JEWEL, TURNING MR. MORRIS AND TRIXIE BACK TO THEIR NORMAL SELVES...
BAM
MR. MORRIS, YOU'D BETTER PLAY THE WIZARD'S PART YOURSELF! BILLY WILL BE -- DELAYED!
OH, ALL RIGHT! BILLY'S A TERRIBLE ACTOR ANYWAY!
PLACES, EVERYONE! TEN SECONDS!
BONZO
I, CALIBAN THE WIZARD, WILL NOW PUT A SPELL ON YOU! HIGGEDY JIGGEDY HEX!
VOOTIE VOOTIE!
TRIXIE
BONZO
HA HA! MR. MORRIS IS A GOOD ACTOR-- BUT BONZO IS BETTER!
YOU SEE, FOLKS, WHEN IT COMES TO ACTING TALENT, SOME OF US HAVE IT... AND SOME DON'T!
SO LONG NOW!
C.C. BECK
THE END
7

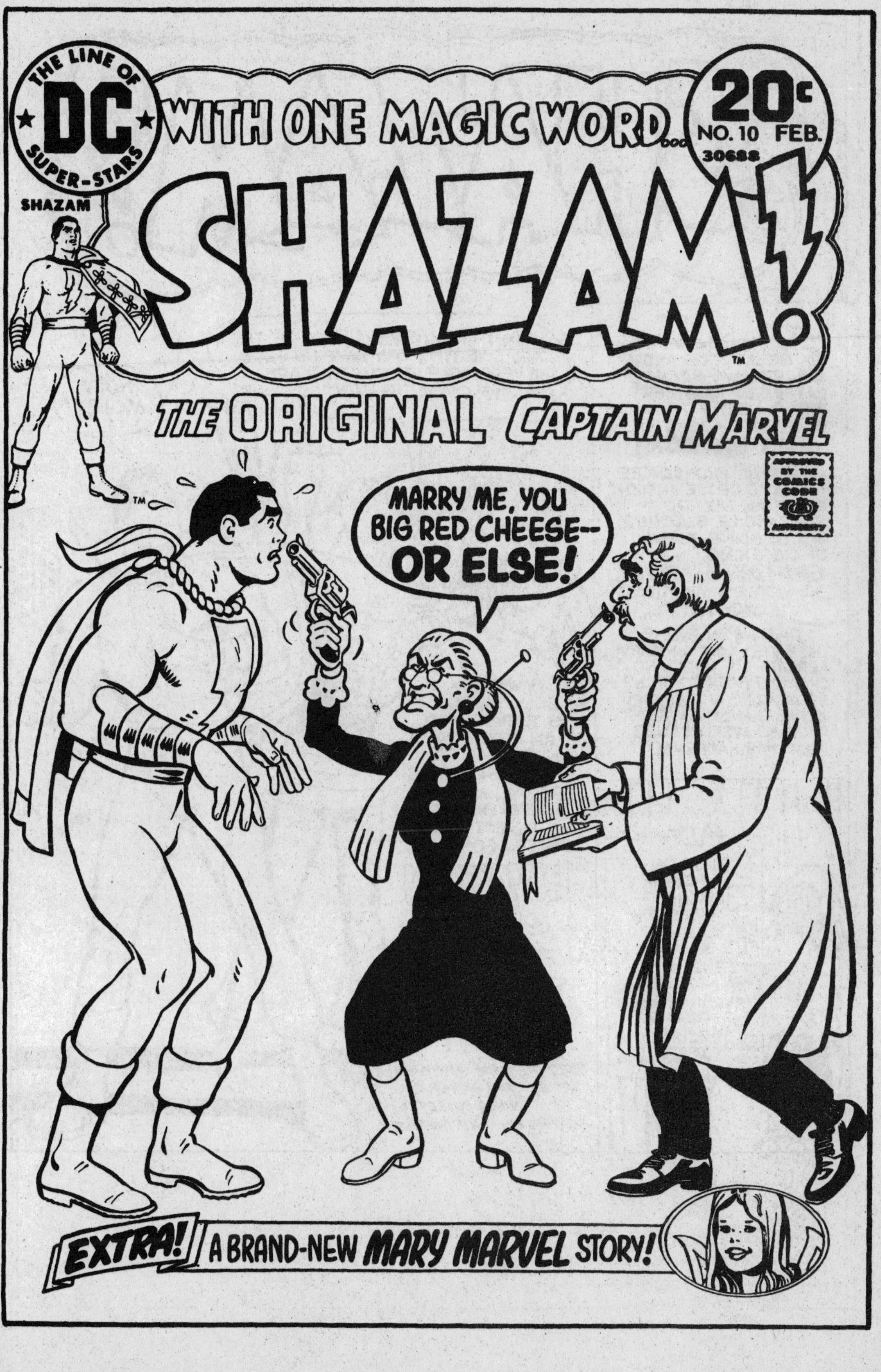
THE LINE OF DC SUPER-STARS
SHAZAM
WITH ONE MAGIC WORD...
20¢
NO. 10 FEB.
30688
SHAZAM!
THE ORIGINAL CAPTAIN MARVEL
APPROVED BY THE COMICS CODE AUTHORITY
MARRY ME, YOU BIG RED CHEESE-- OR ELSE!
EXTRA! A BRAND-NEW MARY MARVEL STORY!

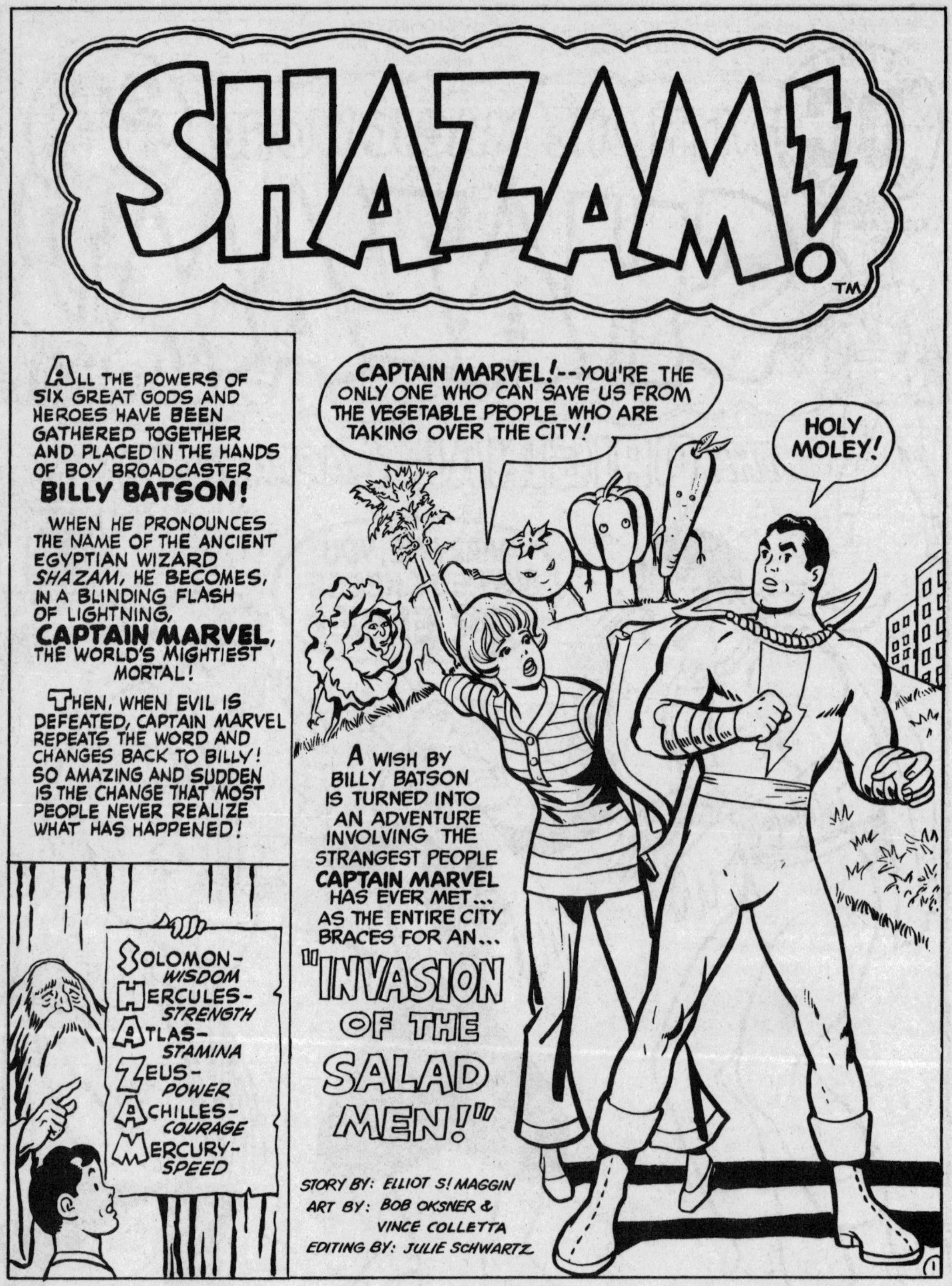
SHAZAM!
TM
ALL THE POWERS OF SIX GREAT GODS AND HEROES HAVE BEEN GATHERED TOGETHER AND PLACED IN THE HANDS OF BOY BROADCASTER BILLY BATSON!
WHEN HE PRONOUNCES THE NAME OF THE ANCIENT EGYPTIAN WIZARD SHAZAM, HE BECOMES, IN A BLINDING FLASH OF LIGHTNING, CAPTAIN MARVEL, THE WORLD'S MIGHTIEST MORTAL!
THEN, WHEN EVIL IS DEFEATED, CAPTAIN MARVEL REPEATS THE WORD AND CHANGES BACK TO BILLY! SO AMAZING AND SUDDEN IS THE CHANGE THAT MOST PEOPLE NEVER REALIZE WHAT HAS HAPPENED!
SOLOMON-WISDOM
HERCULES-STRENGTH
ATLAS-STAMINA
ZEUS-POWER
ACHILLES-COURAGE
MERCURY-SPEED
CAPTAIN MARVEL!--YOU'RE THE ONLY ONE WHO CAN SAVE US FROM THE VEGETABLE PEOPLE WHO ARE TAKING OVER THE CITY!
HOLY MOLEY!
A WISH BY BILLY BATSON IS TURNED INTO AN ADVENTURE INVOLVING THE STRANGEST PEOPLE CAPTAIN MARVEL HAS EVER MET... AS THE ENTIRE CITY BRACES FOR AN...
"INVASION OF THE SALAD MEN!"
STORY BY: ELLIOT S! MAGGIN
ART BY: BOB OKSNER & VINCE COLLETTA
EDITING BY: JULIE SCHWARTZ
1

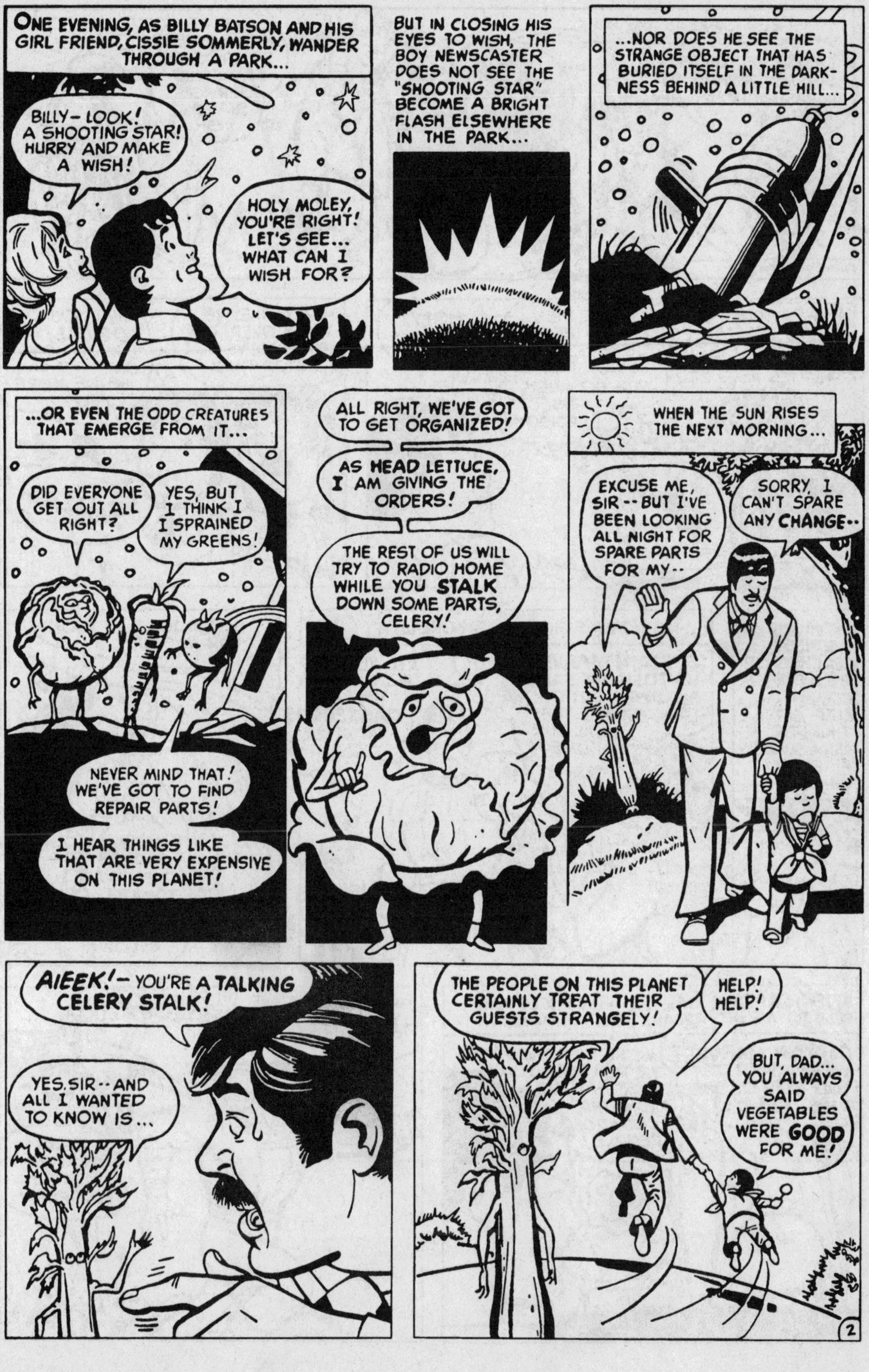
ONE EVENING, AS BILLY BATSON AND HIS GIRL FRIEND, CISSIE SOMMERLY, WANDER THROUGH A PARK...
BILLY-- LOOK! A SHOOTING STAR! HURRY AND MAKE A WISH!
HOLY MOLEY, YOU'RE RIGHT! LET'S SEE... WHAT CAN I WISH FOR?
BUT IN CLOSING HIS EYES TO WISH, THE BOY NEWSCASTER DOES NOT SEE THE "SHOOTING STAR" BECOME A BRIGHT FLASH ELSEWHERE IN THE PARK...
...NOR DOES HE SEE THE STRANGE OBJECT THAT HAS BURIED ITSELF IN THE DARKNESS BEHIND A LITTLE HILL...
...OR EVEN THE ODD CREATURES THAT EMERGE FROM IT...
DID EVERYONE GET OUT ALL RIGHT?
YES, BUT I THINK I SPRAINED MY GREENS!
NEVER MIND THAT! WE'VE GOT TO FIND REPAIR PARTS!
I HEAR THINGS LIKE THAT ARE VERY EXPENSIVE ON THIS PLANET!
ALL RIGHT, WE'VE GOT TO GET ORGANIZED!
AS HEAD LETTUCE, I AM GIVING THE ORDERS!
THE REST OF US WILL TRY TO RADIO HOME WHILE YOU STALK DOWN SOME PARTS, CELERY!
WHEN THE SUN RISES THE NEXT MORNING...
EXCUSE ME, SIR -- BUT I'VE BEEN LOOKING ALL NIGHT FOR SPARE PARTS FOR MY --
SORRY, I CAN'T SPARE ANY CHANGE --
AIEEK! -- YOU'RE A TALKING CELERY STALK!
YES, SIR -- AND ALL I WANTED TO KNOW IS...
THE PEOPLE ON THIS PLANET CERTAINLY TREAT THEIR GUESTS STRANGELY!
HELP! HELP!
BUT, DAD... YOU ALWAYS SAID VEGETABLES WERE GOOD FOR ME!
2

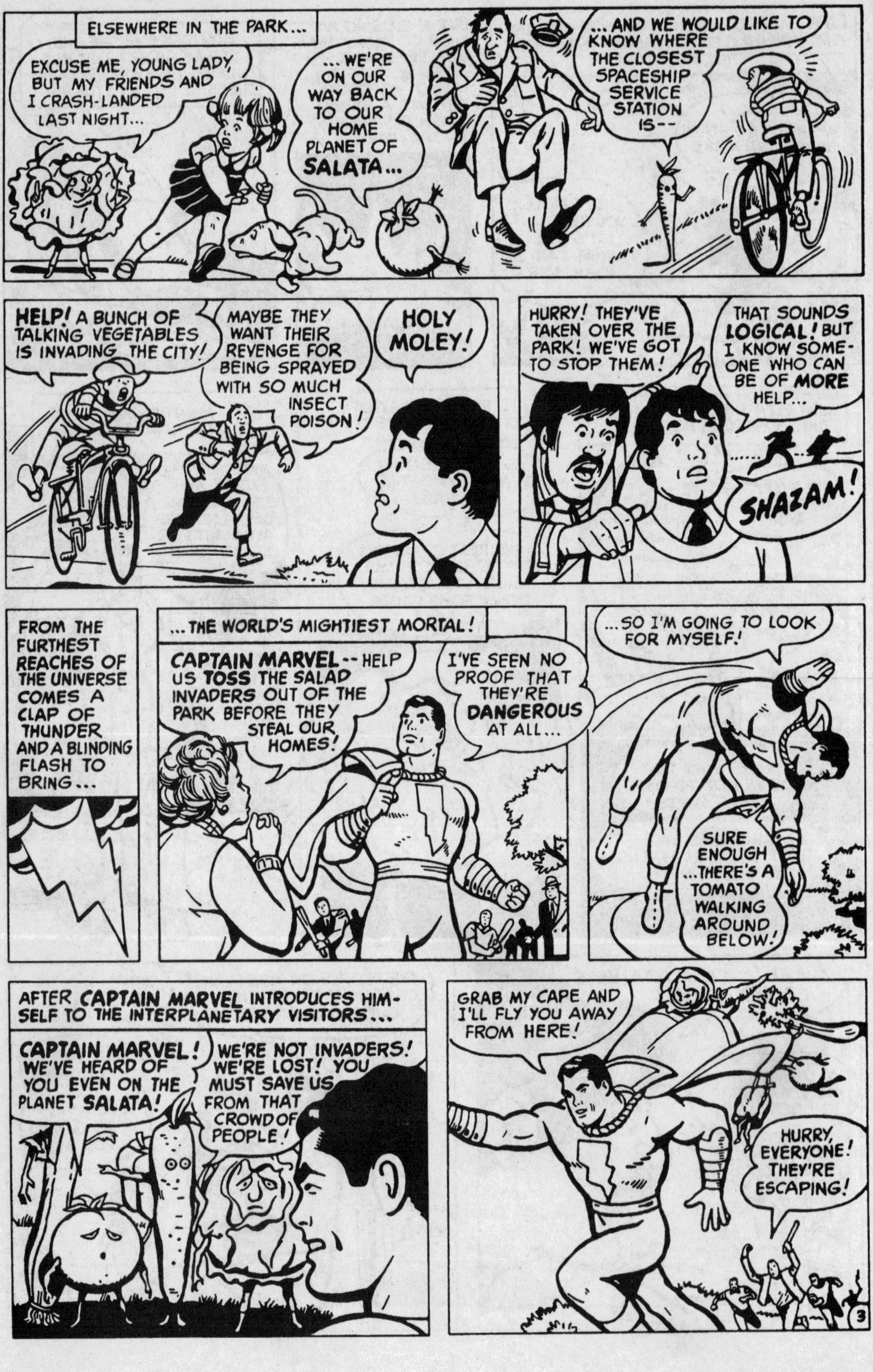
ELSEWHERE IN THE PARK...
EXCUSE ME, YOUNG LADY, BUT MY FRIENDS AND I CRASH-LANDED LAST NIGHT...
...WE'RE ON OUR WAY BACK TO OUR HOME PLANET OF SALATA...
...AND WE WOULD LIKE TO KNOW WHERE THE CLOSEST SPACESHIP SERVICE STATION IS--
HELP! A BUNCH OF TALKING VEGETABLES IS INVADING THE CITY!
MAYBE THEY WANT THEIR REVENGE FOR BEING SPRAYED WITH SO MUCH INSECT POISON!
HOLY MOLEY!
HURRY! THEY'VE TAKEN OVER THE PARK! WE'VE GOT TO STOP THEM!
THAT SOUNDS LOGICAL! BUT I KNOW SOME-ONE WHO CAN BE OF MORE HELP...
SHAZAM!
FROM THE FURTHEST REACHES OF THE UNIVERSE COMES A CLAP OF THUNDER AND A BLINDING FLASH TO BRING...
...THE WORLD'S MIGHTIEST MORTAL!
CAPTAIN MARVEL-- HELP US TOSS THE SALAD INVADERS OUT OF THE PARK BEFORE THEY STEAL OUR HOMES!
I'VE SEEN NO PROOF THAT THEY'RE DANGEROUS AT ALL...
...SO I'M GOING TO LOOK FOR MYSELF!
SURE ENOUGH ...THERE'S A TOMATO WALKING AROUND BELOW!
AFTER CAPTAIN MARVEL INTRODUCES HIM-SELF TO THE INTERPLANETARY VISITORS...
CAPTAIN MARVEL! WE'VE HEARD OF YOU EVEN ON THE PLANET SALATA!
WE'RE NOT INVADERS! WE'RE LOST! YOU MUST SAVE US FROM THAT CROWD OF PEOPLE!
GRAB MY CAPE AND I'LL FLY YOU AWAY FROM HERE!
HURRY, EVERYONE! THEY'RE ESCAPING!
3

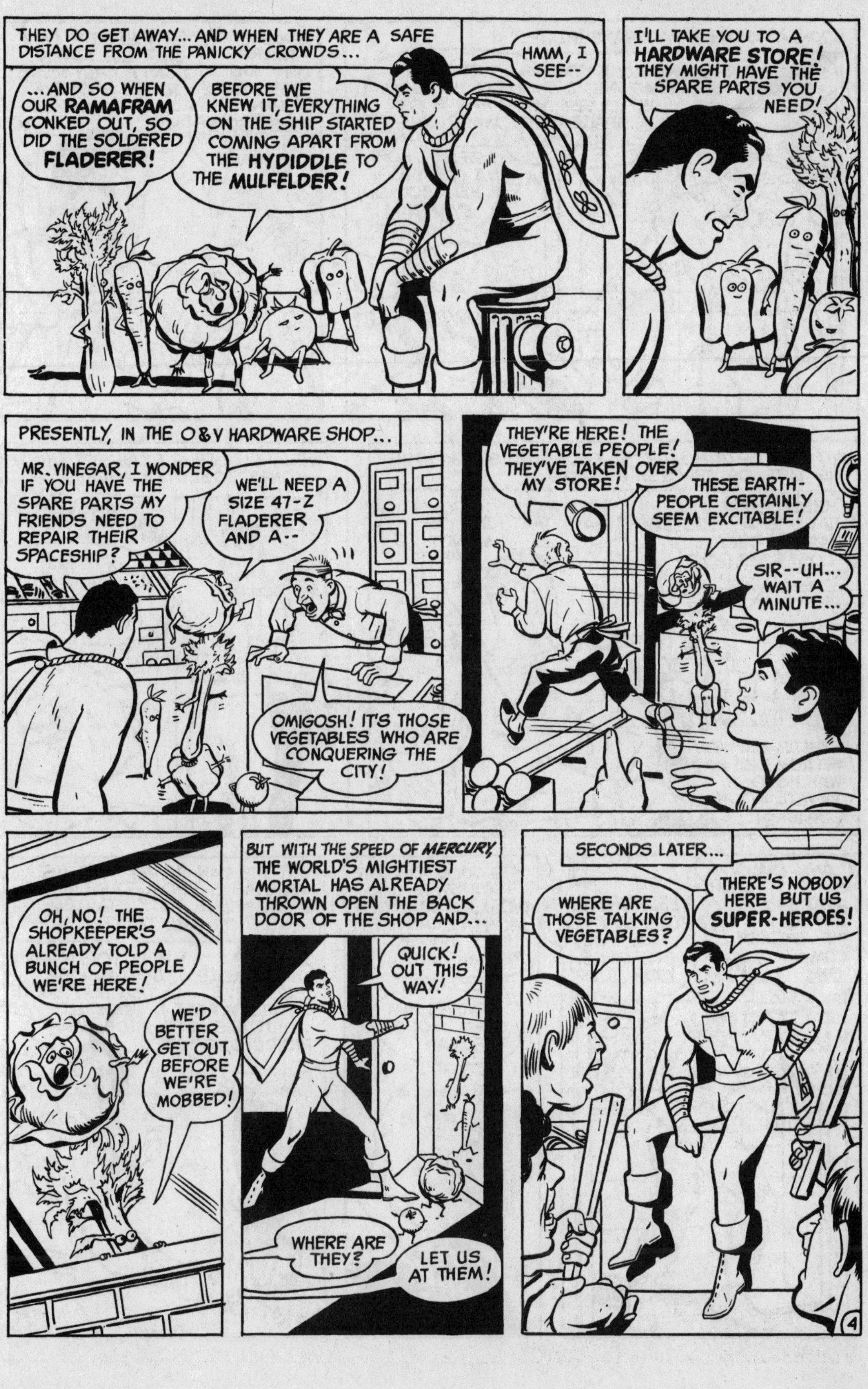
THEY DO GET AWAY... AND WHEN THEY ARE A SAFE DISTANCE FROM THE PANICKY CROWDS...
...AND SO WHEN OUR RAMAFRAM CONKED OUT, SO DID THE SOLDERED FLADERER!
BEFORE WE KNEW IT, EVERYTHING ON THE SHIP STARTED COMING APART FROM THE HYDIDDLE TO THE MULFELDER!
HMM, I SEE--
I'LL TAKE YOU TO A HARDWARE STORE! THEY MIGHT HAVE THE SPARE PARTS YOU NEED!
PRESENTLY, IN THE O&V HARDWARE SHOP...
MR. VINEGAR, I WONDER IF YOU HAVE THE SPARE PARTS MY FRIENDS NEED TO REPAIR THEIR SPACESHIP?
WE'LL NEED A SIZE 47-Z FLADERER AND A--
OMIGOSH! IT'S THOSE VEGETABLES WHO ARE CONQUERING THE CITY!
THEY'RE HERE! THE VEGETABLE PEOPLE! THEY'VE TAKEN OVER MY STORE!
THESE EARTH-PEOPLE CERTAINLY SEEM EXCITABLE!
SIR--UH... WAIT A MINUTE...
OH, NO! THE SHOPKEEPER'S ALREADY TOLD A BUNCH OF PEOPLE WE'RE HERE!
WE'D BETTER GET OUT BEFORE WE'RE MOBBED!
BUT WITH THE SPEED OF MERCURY, THE WORLD'S MIGHTIEST MORTAL HAS ALREADY THROWN OPEN THE BACK DOOR OF THE SHOP AND...
QUICK! OUT THIS WAY!
WHERE ARE THEY?
LET US AT THEM!
SECONDS LATER...
WHERE ARE THOSE TALKING VEGETABLES?
THERE'S NOBODY HERE BUT US SUPER-HEROES!
4

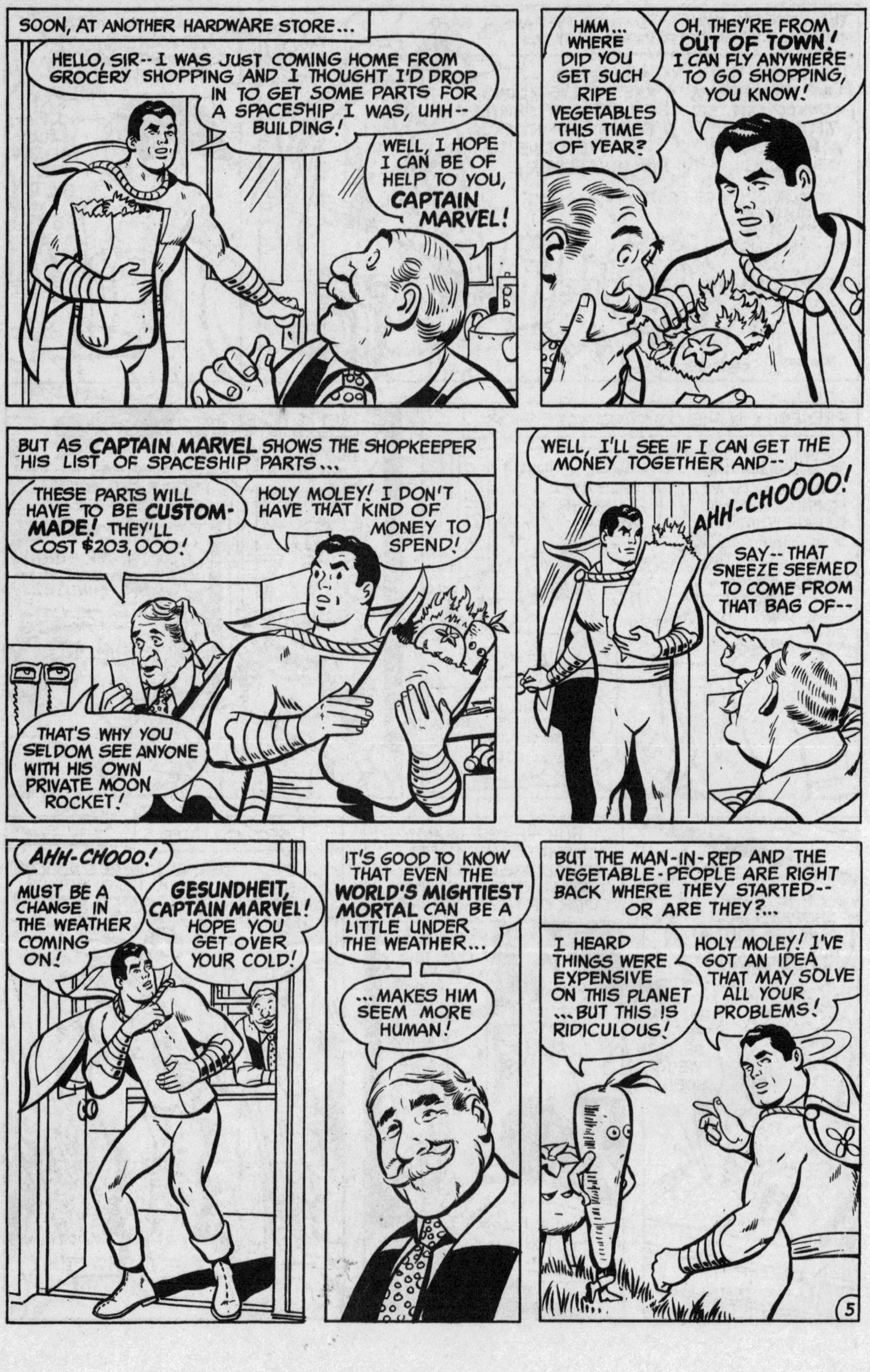
SOON, AT ANOTHER HARDWARE STORE...
HELLO, SIR-- I WAS JUST COMING HOME FROM GROCERY SHOPPING AND I THOUGHT I'D DROP IN TO GET SOME PARTS FOR A SPACESHIP I WAS, UHH-- BUILDING!
WELL, I HOPE I CAN BE OF HELP TO YOU, CAPTAIN MARVEL!
HMM... WHERE DID YOU GET SUCH RIPE VEGETABLES THIS TIME OF YEAR?
OH, THEY'RE FROM OUT OF TOWN! I CAN FLY ANYWHERE TO GO SHOPPING, YOU KNOW!
BUT AS CAPTAIN MARVEL SHOWS THE SHOPKEEPER HIS LIST OF SPACESHIP PARTS...
THESE PARTS WILL HAVE TO BE CUSTOM-MADE! THEY'LL COST $203,000!
HOLY MOLEY! I DON'T HAVE THAT KIND OF MONEY TO SPEND!
THAT'S WHY YOU SELDOM SEE ANYONE WITH HIS OWN PRIVATE MOON ROCKET!
WELL, I'LL SEE IF I CAN GET THE MONEY TOGETHER AND--
AHH-CHOOOO!
SAY-- THAT SNEEZE SEEMED TO COME FROM THAT BAG OF--
AHH-CHOOO!
MUST BE A CHANGE IN THE WEATHER COMING ON!
GESUNDHEIT, CAPTAIN MARVEL! HOPE YOU GET OVER YOUR COLD!
IT'S GOOD TO KNOW THAT EVEN THE WORLD'S MIGHTIEST MORTAL CAN BE A LITTLE UNDER THE WEATHER...
...MAKES HIM SEEM MORE HUMAN!
BUT THE MAN-IN-RED AND THE VEGETABLE-PEOPLE ARE RIGHT BACK WHERE THEY STARTED-- OR ARE THEY?...
I HEARD THINGS WERE EXPENSIVE ON THIS PLANET ...BUT THIS IS RIDICULOUS!
HOLY MOLEY! I'VE GOT AN IDEA THAT MAY SOLVE ALL YOUR PROBLEMS!
5

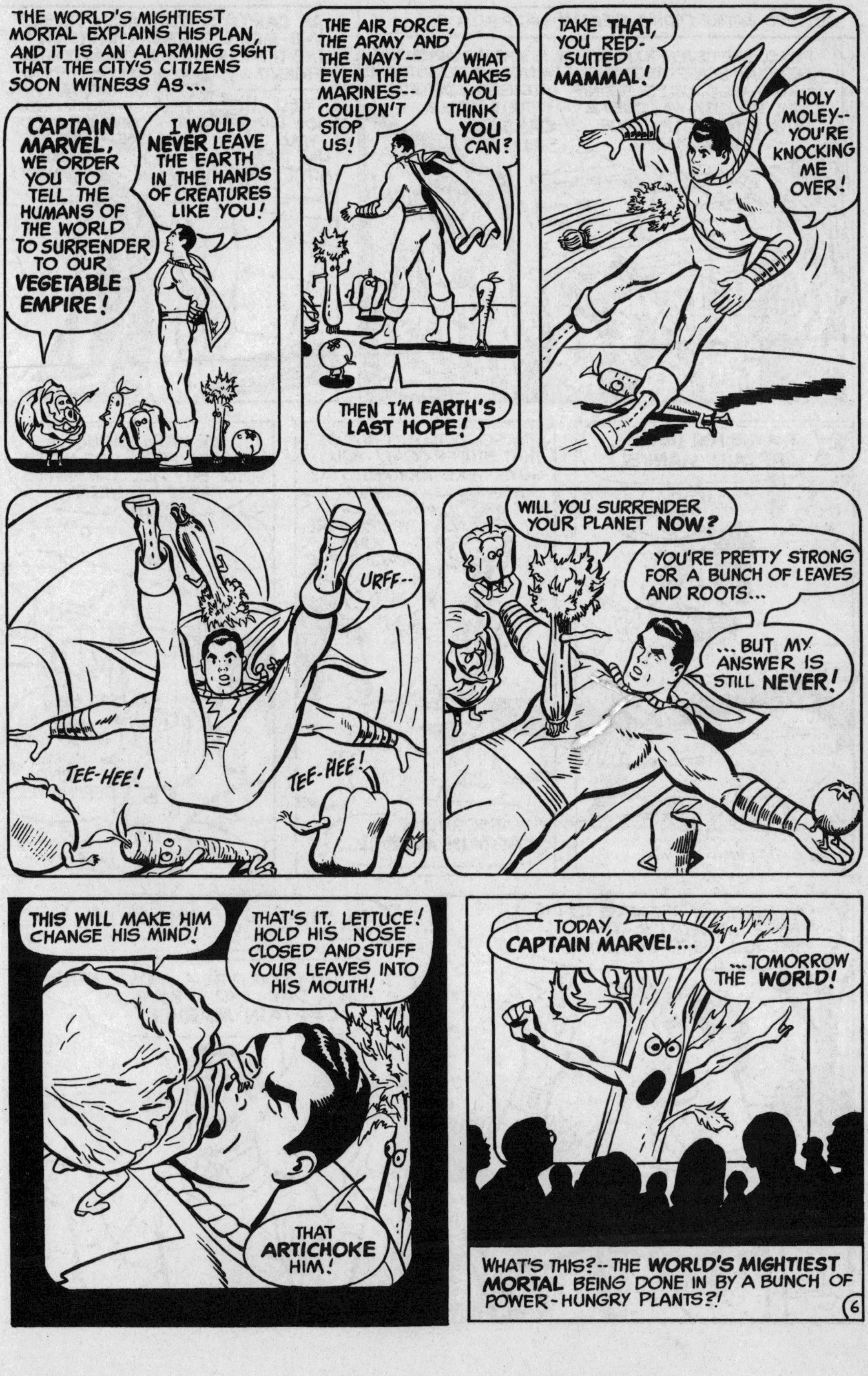
THE WORLD'S MIGHTIEST MORTAL EXPLAINS HIS PLAN, AND IT IS AN ALARMING SIGHT THAT THE CITY'S CITIZENS SOON WITNESS AS...
CAPTAIN MARVEL, WE ORDER YOU TO TELL THE HUMANS OF THE WORLD TO SURRENDER TO OUR VEGETABLE EMPIRE!
I WOULD NEVER LEAVE THE EARTH IN THE HANDS OF CREATURES LIKE YOU!
THE AIR FORCE, THE ARMY AND THE NAVY-- EVEN THE MARINES-- COULDN'T STOP US!
WHAT MAKES YOU THINK YOU CAN?
THEN I'M EARTH'S LAST HOPE!
TAKE THAT, YOU RED-SUITED MAMMAL!
HOLY MOLEY-- YOU'RE KNOCKING ME OVER!
URFF--
TEE-HEE!
TEE-HEE!
WILL YOU SURRENDER YOUR PLANET NOW?
YOU'RE PRETTY STRONG FOR A BUNCH OF LEAVES AND ROOTS...
...BUT MY ANSWER IS STILL NEVER!
THIS WILL MAKE HIM CHANGE HIS MIND!
THAT'S IT, LETTUCE! HOLD HIS NOSE CLOSED AND STUFF YOUR LEAVES INTO HIS MOUTH!
THAT ARTICHOKE HIM!
TODAY, CAPTAIN MARVEL...
...TOMORROW THE WORLD!
WHAT'S THIS?-- THE WORLD'S MIGHTIEST MORTAL BEING DONE IN BY A BUNCH OF POWER-HUNGRY PLANTS?!
6

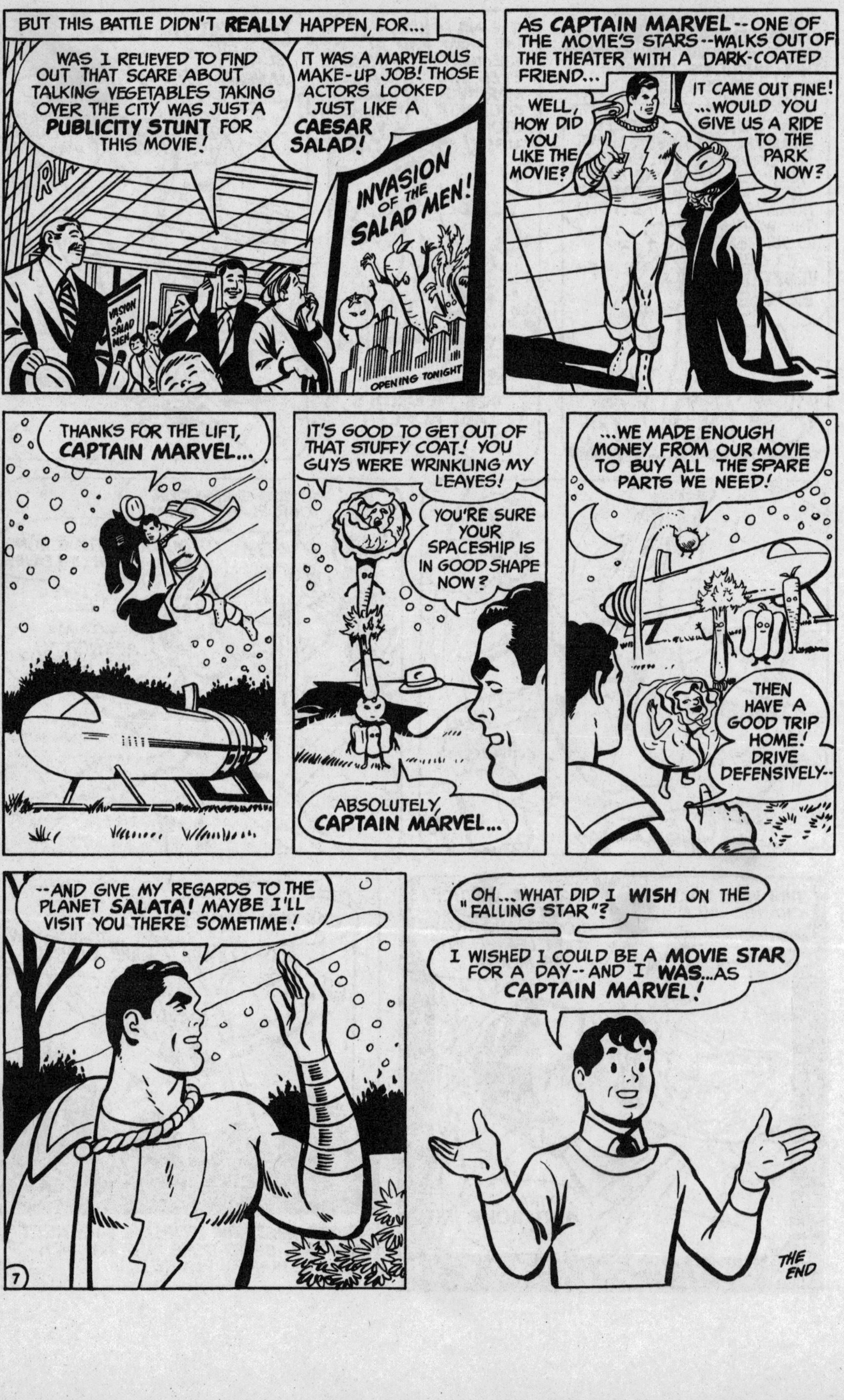
BUT THIS BATTLE DIDN'T REALLY HAPPEN, FOR...
WAS I RELIEVED TO FIND OUT THAT SCARE ABOUT TALKING VEGETABLES TAKING OVER THE CITY WAS JUST A PUBLICITY STUNT FOR THIS MOVIE!
IT WAS A MARVELOUS MAKE-UP JOB! THOSE ACTORS LOOKED JUST LIKE A CAESAR SALAD!
INVASION OF THE SALAD MEN!
OPENING TONIGHT
AS CAPTAIN MARVEL -- ONE OF THE MOVIE'S STARS -- WALKS OUT OF THE THEATER WITH A DARK-COATED FRIEND...
WELL, HOW DID YOU LIKE THE MOVIE?
IT CAME OUT FINE! ...WOULD YOU GIVE US A RIDE TO THE PARK NOW?
THANKS FOR THE LIFT, CAPTAIN MARVEL...
IT'S GOOD TO GET OUT OF THAT STUFFY COAT! YOU GUYS WERE WRINKLING MY LEAVES!
YOU'RE SURE YOUR SPACESHIP IS IN GOOD SHAPE NOW?
ABSOLUTELY, CAPTAIN MARVEL...
...WE MADE ENOUGH MONEY FROM OUR MOVIE TO BUY ALL THE SPARE PARTS WE NEED!
THEN HAVE A GOOD TRIP HOME! DRIVE DEFENSIVELY--
--AND GIVE MY REGARDS TO THE PLANET SALATA! MAYBE I'LL VISIT YOU THERE SOMETIME!
7
OH ... WHAT DID I WISH ON THE "FALLING STAR"?
I WISHED I COULD BE A MOVIE STAR FOR A DAY -- AND I WAS...AS CAPTAIN MARVEL!
THE END

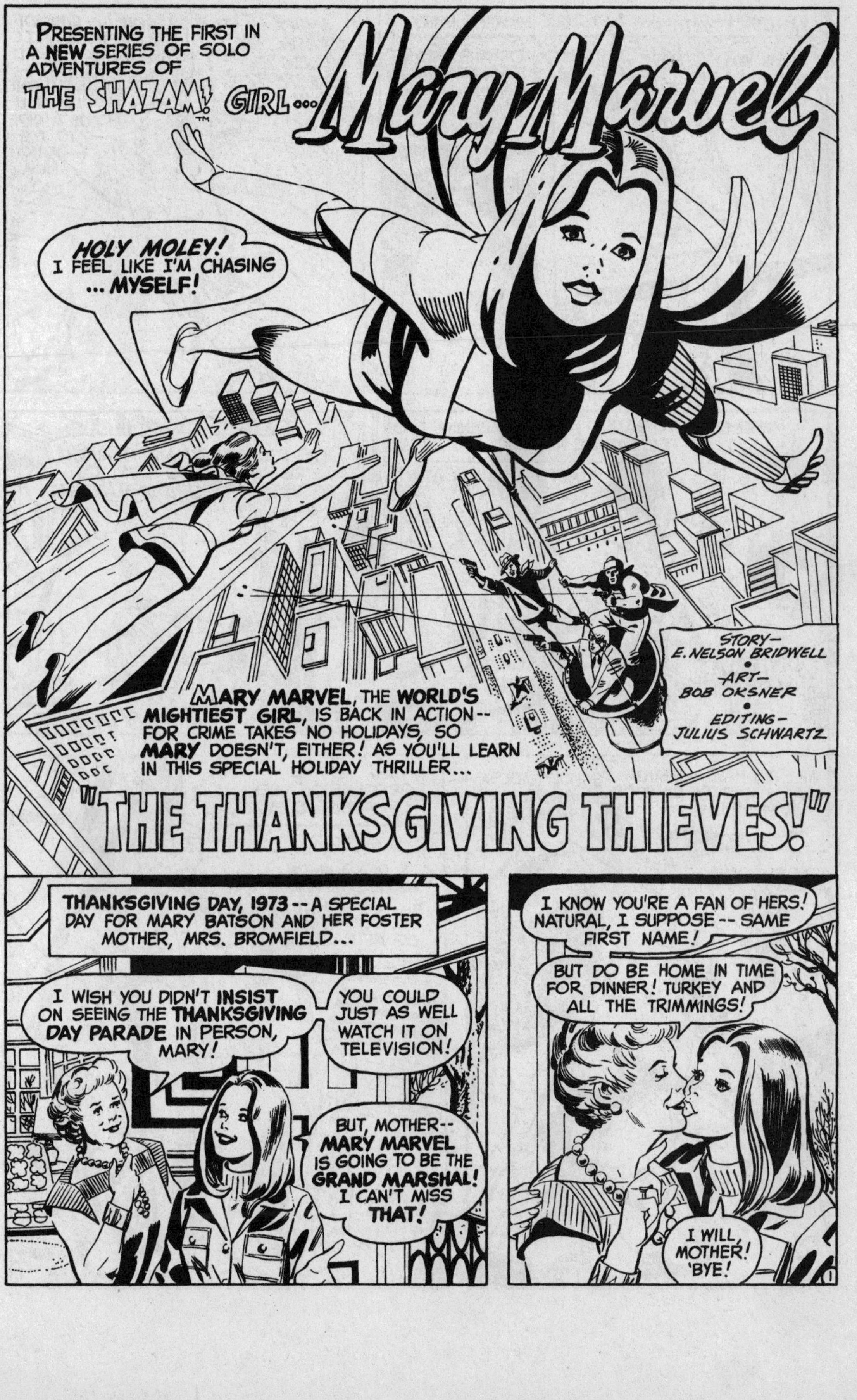
PRESENTING THE FIRST IN A NEW SERIES OF SOLO ADVENTURES OF THE SHAZAM! GIRL... Mary Marvel
HOLY MOLEY! I FEEL LIKE I'M CHASING ... MYSELF!
MARY MARVEL, THE WORLD'S MIGHTIEST GIRL, IS BACK IN ACTION-- FOR CRIME TAKES NO HOLIDAYS, SO MARY DOESN'T, EITHER! AS YOU'LL LEARN IN THIS SPECIAL HOLIDAY THRILLER...
STORY— E. NELSON BRIDWELL • ART— BOB OKSNER • EDITING— JULIUS SCHWARTZ
"THE THANKSGIVING THIEVES!"
THANKSGIVING DAY, 1973 -- A SPECIAL DAY FOR MARY BATSON AND HER FOSTER MOTHER, MRS. BROMFIELD...
I WISH YOU DIDN'T INSIST ON SEEING THE THANKSGIVING DAY PARADE IN PERSON, MARY!
YOU COULD JUST AS WELL WATCH IT ON TELEVISION!
BUT, MOTHER-- MARY MARVEL IS GOING TO BE THE GRAND MARSHAL! I CAN'T MISS THAT!
I KNOW YOU'RE A FAN OF HERS! NATURAL, I SUPPOSE -- SAME FIRST NAME!
BUT DO BE HOME IN TIME FOR DINNER! TURKEY AND ALL THE TRIMMINGS!
I WILL, MOTHER! 'BYE!
1

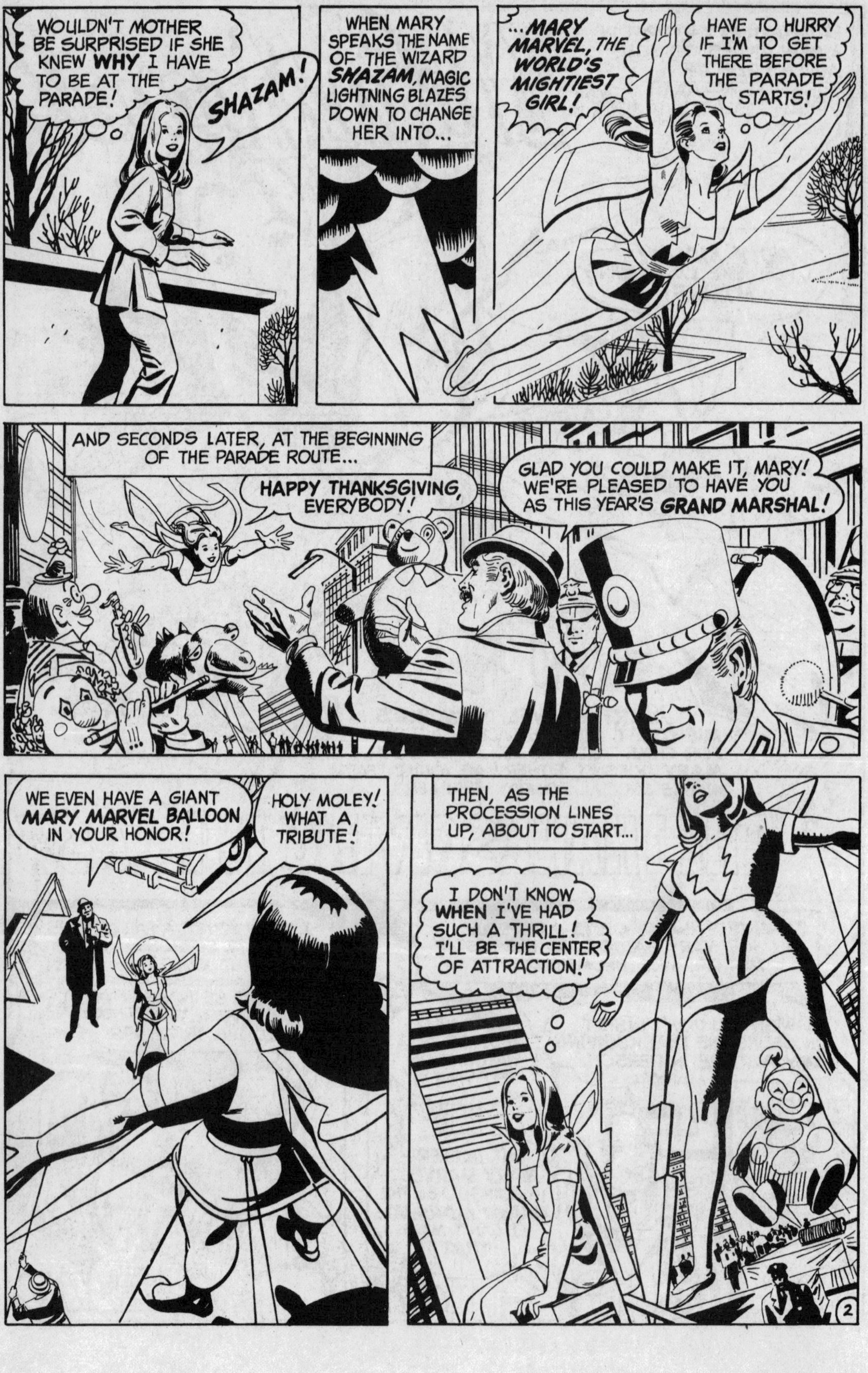
WOULDN'T MOTHER BE SURPRISED IF SHE KNEW **WHY** I HAVE TO BE AT THE PARADE!
SHAZAM!
WHEN MARY SPEAKS THE NAME OF THE WIZARD ***SHAZAM***, MAGIC LIGHTNING BLAZES DOWN TO CHANGE HER INTO...
...***MARY MARVEL***, THE ***WORLD'S MIGHTIEST GIRL***!
HAVE TO HURRY IF I'M TO GET THERE BEFORE THE PARADE STARTS!
AND SECONDS LATER, AT THE BEGINNING OF THE PARADE ROUTE...
HAPPY THANKSGIVING, EVERYBODY!
GLAD YOU COULD MAKE IT, MARY! WE'RE PLEASED TO HAVE YOU AS THIS YEAR'S **GRAND MARSHAL**!
WE EVEN HAVE A GIANT **MARY MARVEL BALLOON** IN YOUR HONOR!
HOLY MOLEY! WHAT A TRIBUTE!
THEN, AS THE PROCESSION LINES UP, ABOUT TO START...
I DON'T KNOW **WHEN** I'VE HAD SUCH A THRILL! I'LL BE THE CENTER OF ATTRACTION!
2

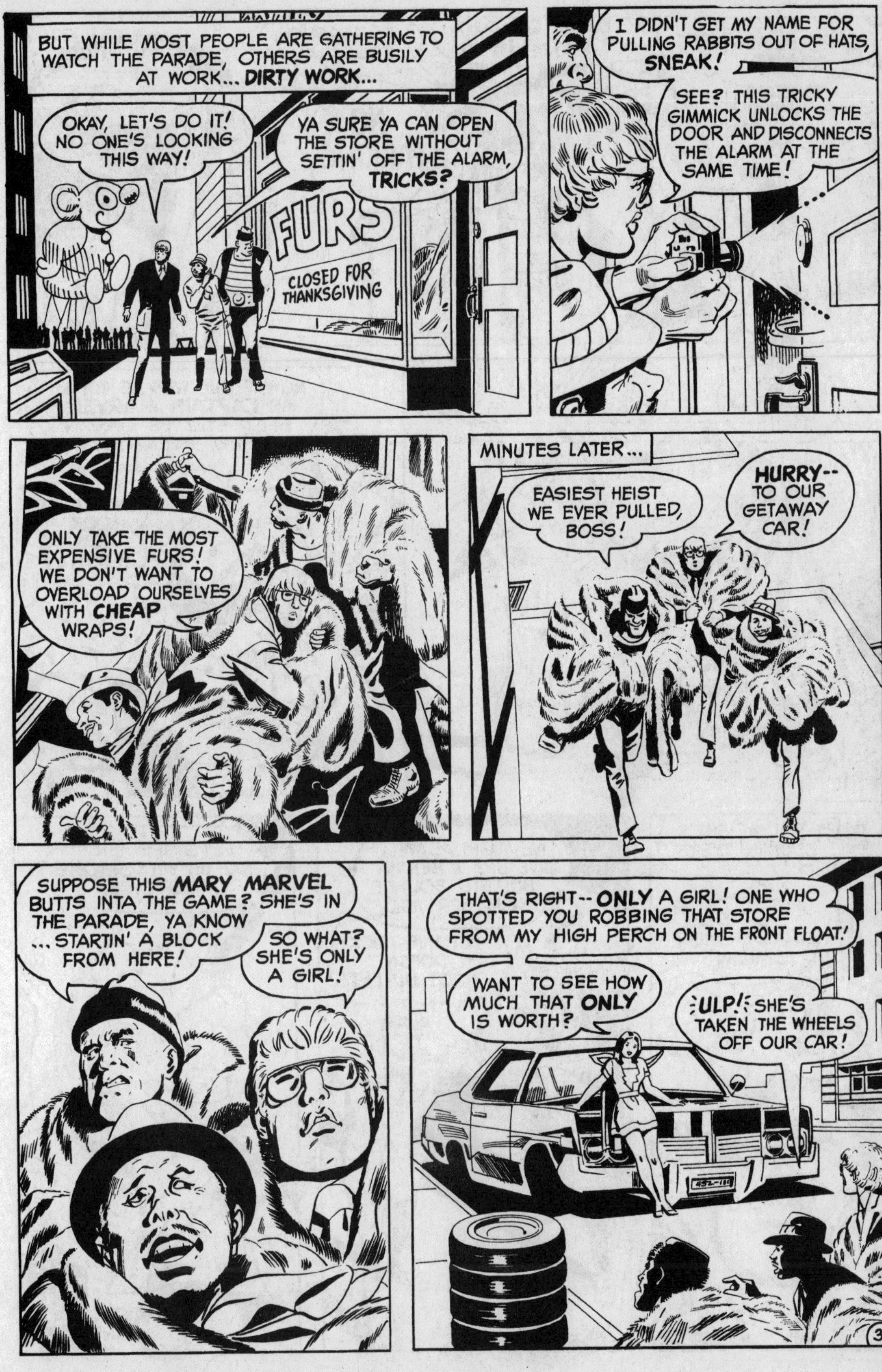
BUT WHILE MOST PEOPLE ARE GATHERING TO WATCH THE PARADE, OTHERS ARE BUSILY AT WORK... DIRTY WORK...
OKAY, LET'S DO IT! NO ONE'S LOOKING THIS WAY!
YA SURE YA CAN OPEN THE STORE WITHOUT SETTIN' OFF THE ALARM, TRICKS?
FURS
CLOSED FOR THANKSGIVING
I DIDN'T GET MY NAME FOR PULLING RABBITS OUT OF HATS, SNEAK!
SEE? THIS TRICKY GIMMICK UNLOCKS THE DOOR AND DISCONNECTS THE ALARM AT THE SAME TIME!
ONLY TAKE THE MOST EXPENSIVE FURS! WE DON'T WANT TO OVERLOAD OURSELVES WITH CHEAP WRAPS!
MINUTES LATER...
EASIEST HEIST WE EVER PULLED, BOSS!
HURRY-- TO OUR GETAWAY CAR!
SUPPOSE THIS MARY MARVEL BUTTS INTA THE GAME? SHE'S IN THE PARADE, YA KNOW ...STARTIN' A BLOCK FROM HERE!
SO WHAT? SHE'S ONLY A GIRL!
THAT'S RIGHT-- ONLY A GIRL! ONE WHO SPOTTED YOU ROBBING THAT STORE FROM MY HIGH PERCH ON THE FRONT FLOAT!
WANT TO SEE HOW MUCH THAT ONLY IS WORTH?
ULP! SHE'S TAKEN THE WHEELS OFF OUR CAR!
3

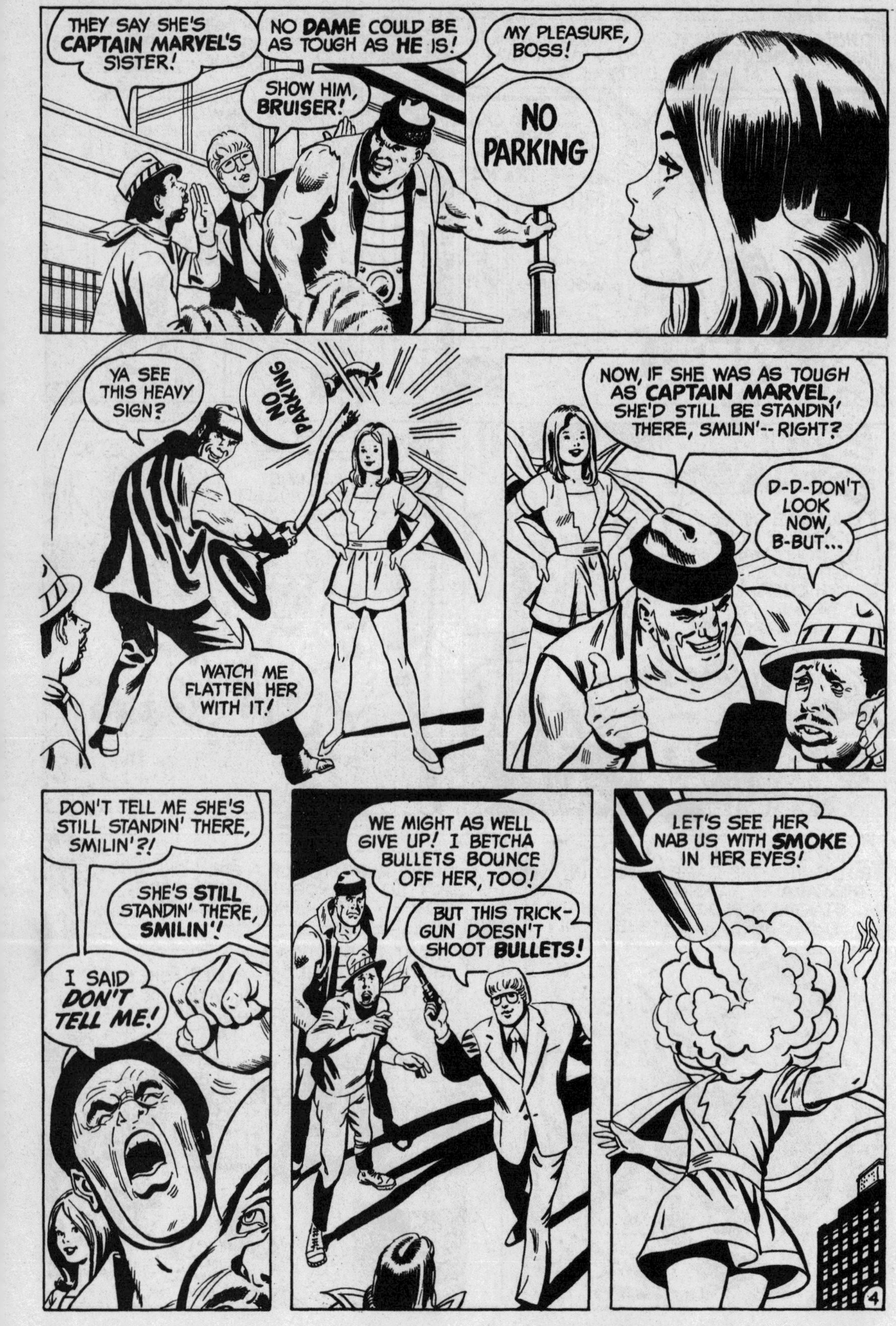
THEY SAY SHE'S CAPTAIN MARVEL'S SISTER!
NO DAME COULD BE AS TOUGH AS HE IS!
SHOW HIM, BRUISER!
MY PLEASURE, BOSS!
NO PARKING
YA SEE THIS HEAVY SIGN?
NO PARKING
WATCH ME FLATTEN HER WITH IT!
NOW, IF SHE WAS AS TOUGH AS CAPTAIN MARVEL, SHE'D STILL BE STANDIN' THERE, SMILIN'-- RIGHT?
D-D-DON'T LOOK NOW, B-BUT...
DON'T TELL ME SHE'S STILL STANDIN' THERE, SMILIN'?!
SHE'S STILL STANDIN' THERE, SMILIN'!
I SAID DON'T TELL ME!
WE MIGHT AS WELL GIVE UP! I BETCHA BULLETS BOUNCE OFF HER, TOO!
BUT THIS TRICK-GUN DOESN'T SHOOT BULLETS!
LET'S SEE HER NAB US WITH SMOKE IN HER EYES!
4

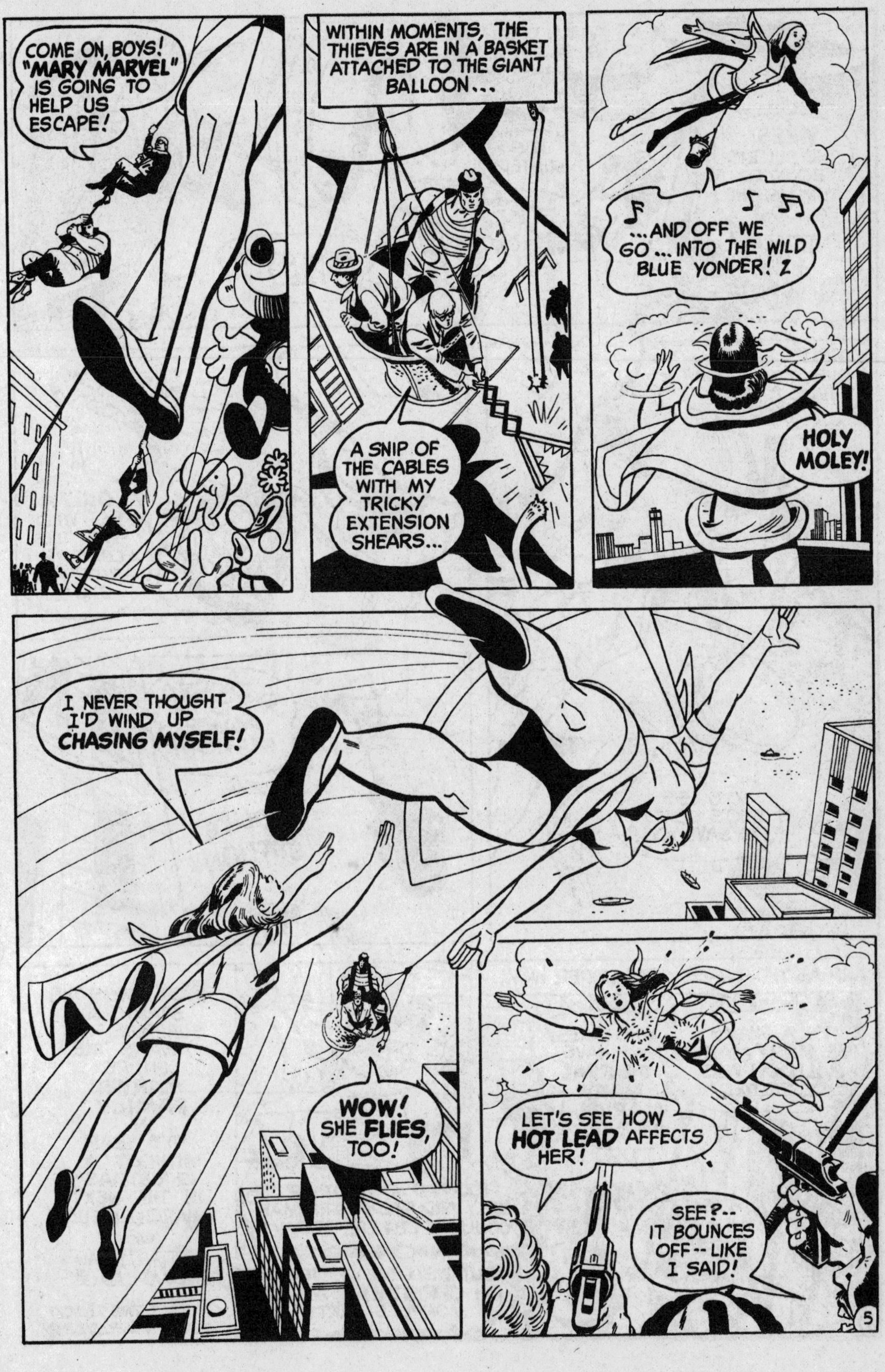
COME ON, BOYS! "MARY MARVEL" IS GOING TO HELP US ESCAPE!
WITHIN MOMENTS, THE THIEVES ARE IN A BASKET ATTACHED TO THE GIANT BALLOON...
A SNIP OF THE CABLES WITH MY TRICKY EXTENSION SHEARS...
...AND OFF WE GO... INTO THE WILD BLUE YONDER!
HOLY MOLEY!
I NEVER THOUGHT I'D WIND UP CHASING MYSELF!
WOW! SHE FLIES, TOO!
LET'S SEE HOW HOT LEAD AFFECTS HER!
SEE?-- IT BOUNCES OFF-- LIKE I SAID!
5

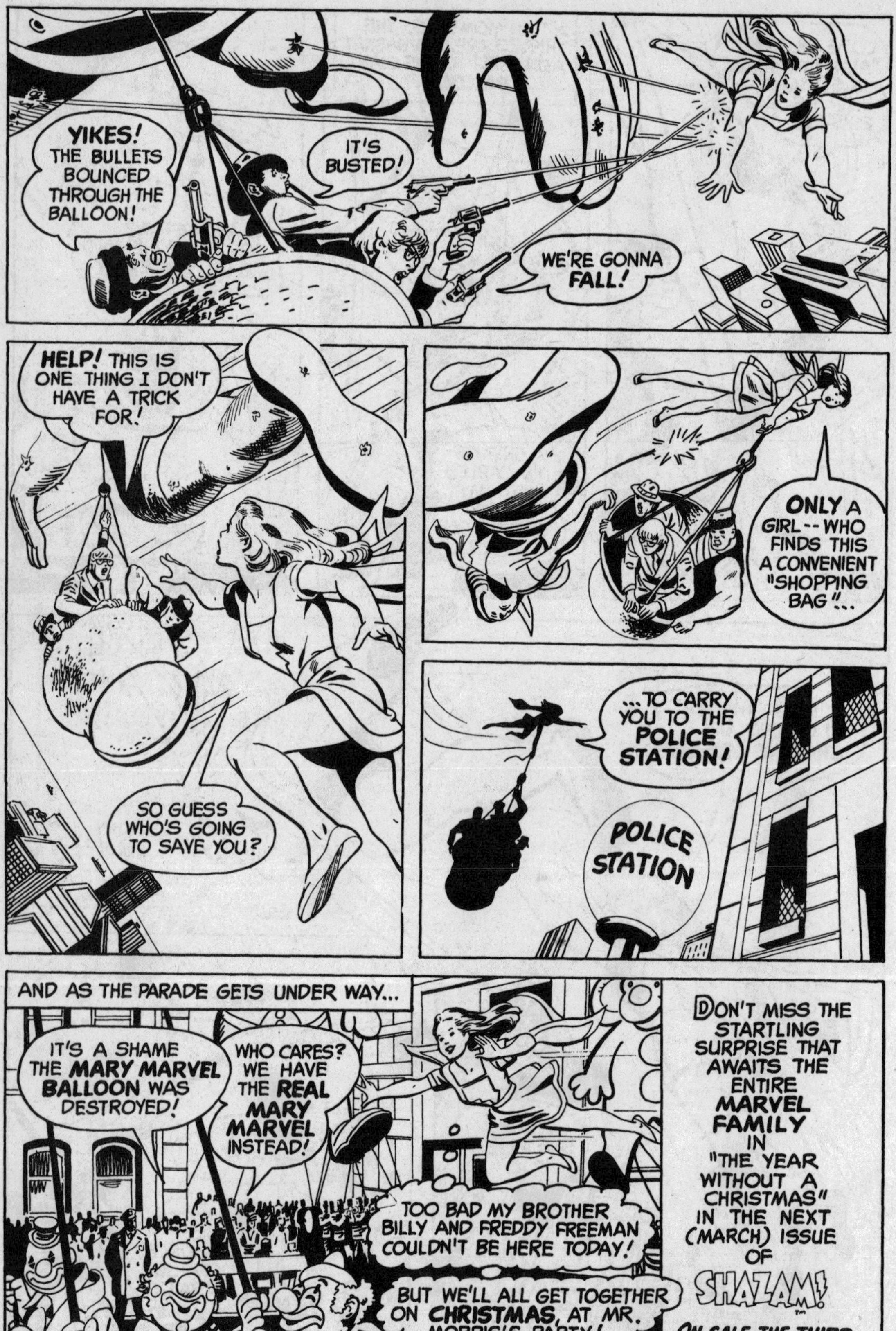
YIKES! THE BULLETS BOUNCED THROUGH THE BALLOON!
IT'S BUSTED!
WE'RE GONNA FALL!
HELP! THIS IS ONE THING I DON'T HAVE A TRICK FOR!
SO GUESS WHO'S GOING TO SAVE YOU?
ONLY A GIRL -- WHO FINDS THIS A CONVENIENT "SHOPPING BAG"...
...TO CARRY YOU TO THE POLICE STATION!
POLICE STATION
AND AS THE PARADE GETS UNDER WAY...
IT'S A SHAME THE MARY MARVEL BALLOON WAS DESTROYED!
WHO CARES? WE HAVE THE REAL MARY MARVEL INSTEAD!
TOO BAD MY BROTHER BILLY AND FREDDY FREEMAN COULDN'T BE HERE TODAY!
BUT WE'LL ALL GET TOGETHER ON CHRISTMAS, AT MR. MORRIS'S PARTY!
6
THE END.
DON'T MISS THE STARTLING SURPRISE THAT AWAITS THE ENTIRE MARVEL FAMILY IN "THE YEAR WITHOUT A CHRISTMAS" IN THE NEXT (MARCH) ISSUE OF
SHAZAM!
ON SALE THE THIRD WEEK IN DECEMBER.

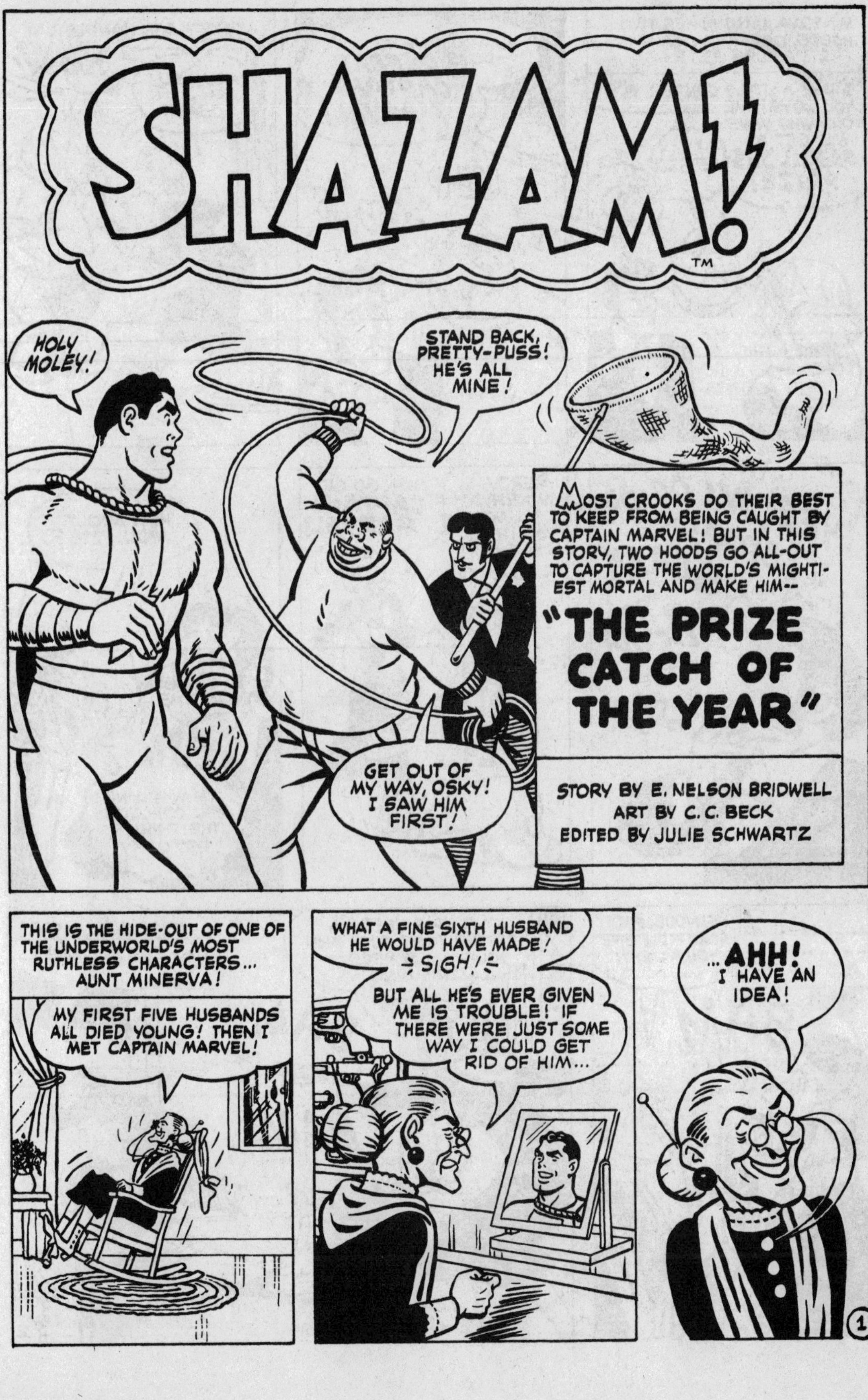
SHAZAM!
TM
HOLY MOLEY!
STAND BACK, PRETTY-PUSS! HE'S ALL MINE!
MOST CROOKS DO THEIR BEST TO KEEP FROM BEING CAUGHT BY CAPTAIN MARVEL! BUT IN THIS STORY, TWO HOODS GO ALL-OUT TO CAPTURE THE WORLD'S MIGHTIEST MORTAL AND MAKE HIM--
"THE PRIZE CATCH OF THE YEAR"
GET OUT OF MY WAY, OSKY! I SAW HIM FIRST!
STORY BY E. NELSON BRIDWELL
ART BY C. C. BECK
EDITED BY JULIE SCHWARTZ
THIS IS THE HIDE-OUT OF ONE OF THE UNDERWORLD'S MOST RUTHLESS CHARACTERS... AUNT MINERVA!
MY FIRST FIVE HUSBANDS ALL DIED YOUNG! THEN I MET CAPTAIN MARVEL!
WHAT A FINE SIXTH HUSBAND HE WOULD HAVE MADE!
SIGH!
BUT ALL HE'S EVER GIVEN ME IS TROUBLE! IF THERE WERE JUST SOME WAY I COULD GET RID OF HIM...
...AHH! I HAVE AN IDEA!
1

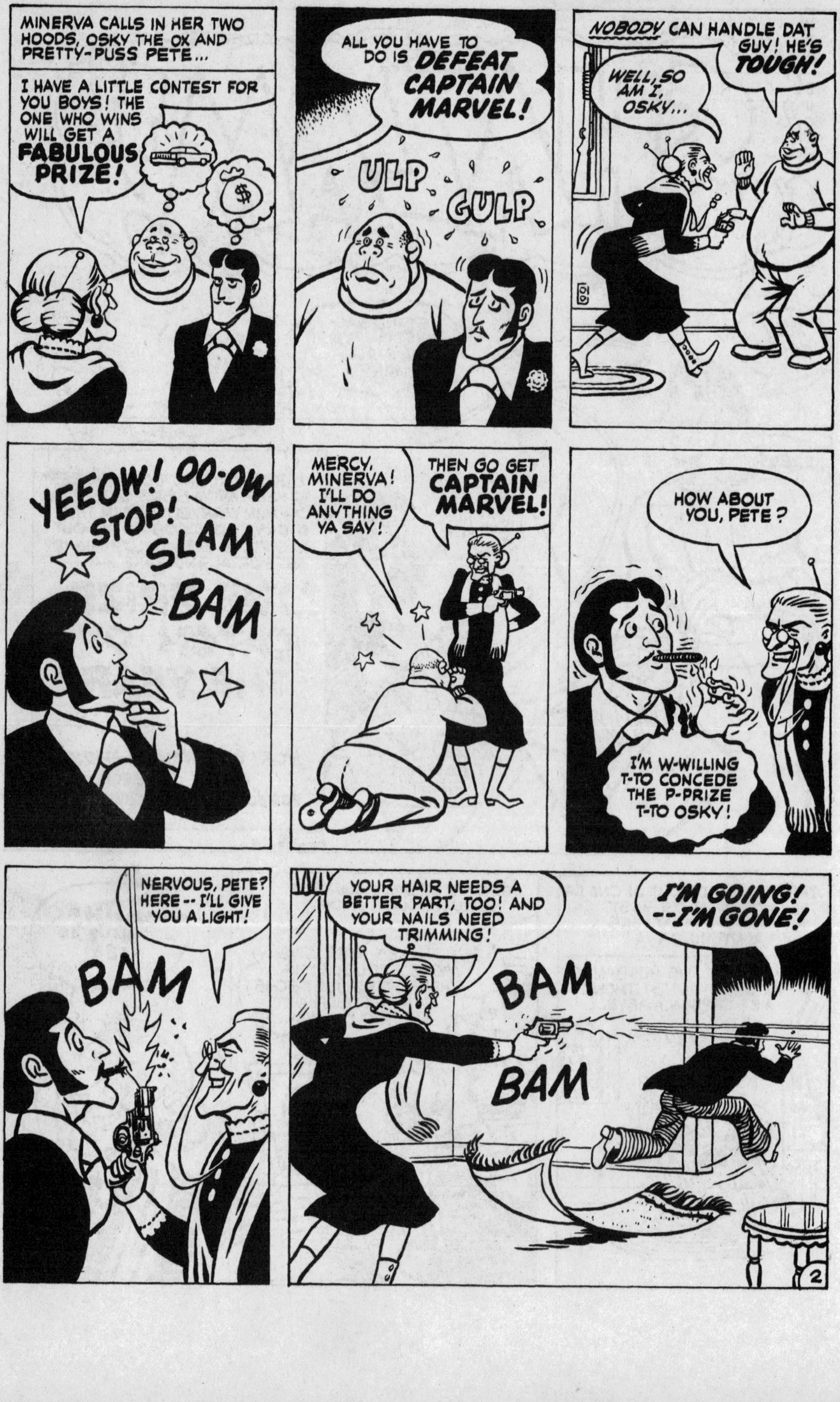
MINERVA CALLS IN HER TWO HOODS, OSKY THE OX AND PRETTY-PUSS PETE...
I HAVE A LITTLE CONTEST FOR YOU BOYS! THE ONE WHO WINS WILL GET A FABULOUS PRIZE!
$
ALL YOU HAVE TO DO IS DEFEAT CAPTAIN MARVEL!
ULP
GULP
NOBODY CAN HANDLE DAT GUY! HE'S TOUGH!
WELL, SO AM I, OSKY...
YEEOW! OO-OW STOP!
SLAM
BAM
MERCY, MINERVA! I'LL DO ANYTHING YA SAY!
THEN GO GET CAPTAIN MARVEL!
HOW ABOUT YOU, PETE?
I'M W-WILLING T-TO CONCEDE THE P-PRIZE T-TO OSKY!
NERVOUS, PETE? HERE -- I'LL GIVE YOU A LIGHT!
BAM
YOUR HAIR NEEDS A BETTER PART, TOO! AND YOUR NAILS NEED TRIMMING!
I'M GOING! --I'M GONE!
BAM
BAM
2

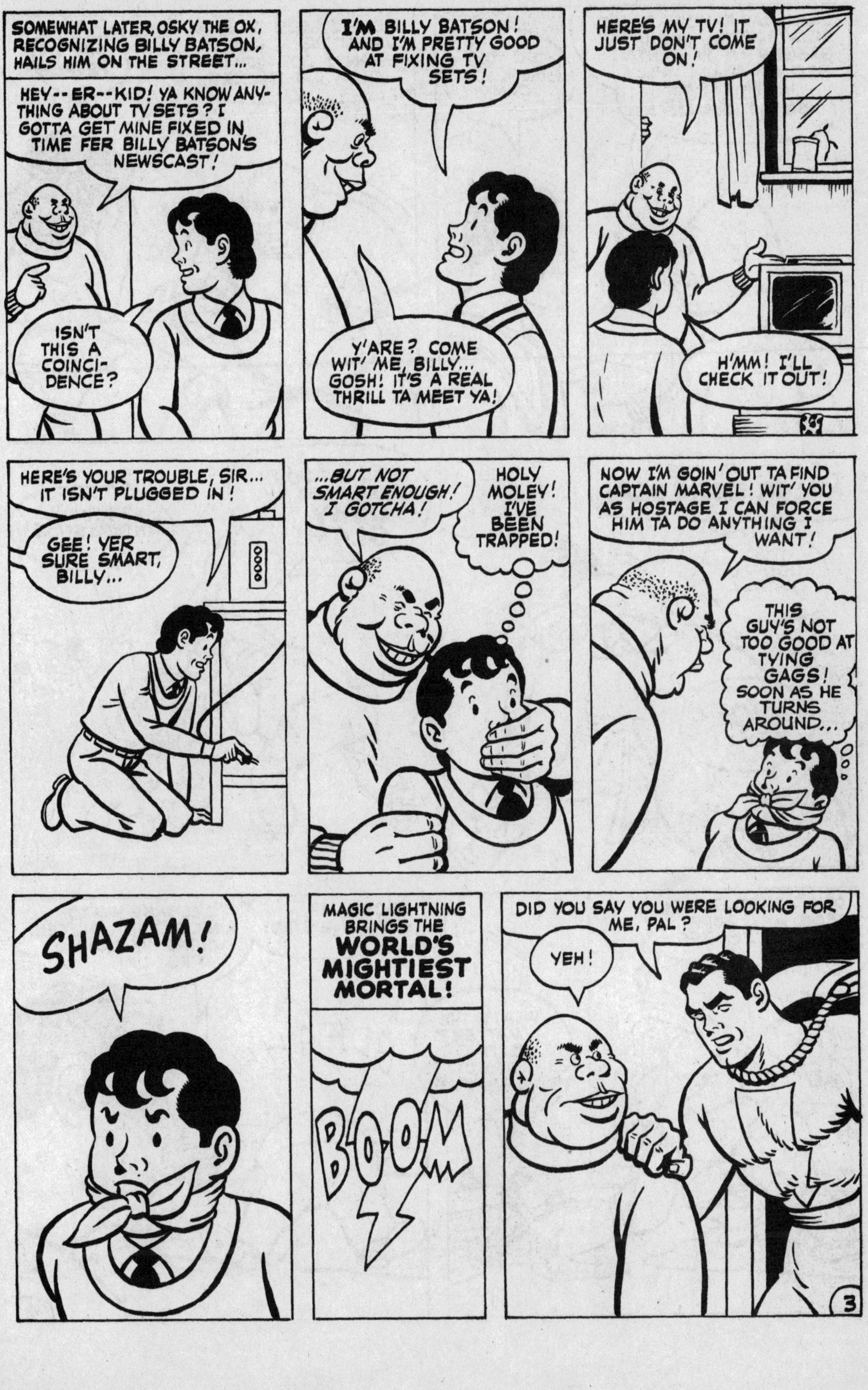

SOMEWHAT LATER, OSKY THE OX, RECOGNIZING BILLY BATSON, HAILS HIM ON THE STREET...
HEY--ER--KID! YA KNOW ANYTHING ABOUT TV SETS? I GOTTA GET MINE FIXED IN TIME FER BILLY BATSON'S NEWSCAST!
ISN'T THIS A COINCIDENCE?
I'M BILLY BATSON! AND I'M PRETTY GOOD AT FIXING TV SETS!
Y'ARE? COME WIT' ME, BILLY... GOSH! IT'S A REAL THRILL TA MEET YA!
HERE'S MY TV! IT JUST DON'T COME ON!
H'MM! I'LL CHECK IT OUT!
HERE'S YOUR TROUBLE, SIR... IT ISN'T PLUGGED IN!
GEE! YER SURE SMART, BILLY...
...BUT NOT SMART ENOUGH! I GOTCHA!
HOLY MOLEY! I'VE BEEN TRAPPED!
NOW I'M GOIN' OUT TA FIND CAPTAIN MARVEL! WIT' YOU AS HOSTAGE I CAN FORCE HIM TA DO ANYTHING I WANT!
THIS GUY'S NOT TOO GOOD AT TYING GAGS! SOON AS HE TURNS AROUND...
SHAZAM!
MAGIC LIGHTNING BRINGS THE WORLD'S MIGHTIEST MORTAL!
BOOM
DID YOU SAY YOU WERE LOOKING FOR ME, PAL?
YEH!
3

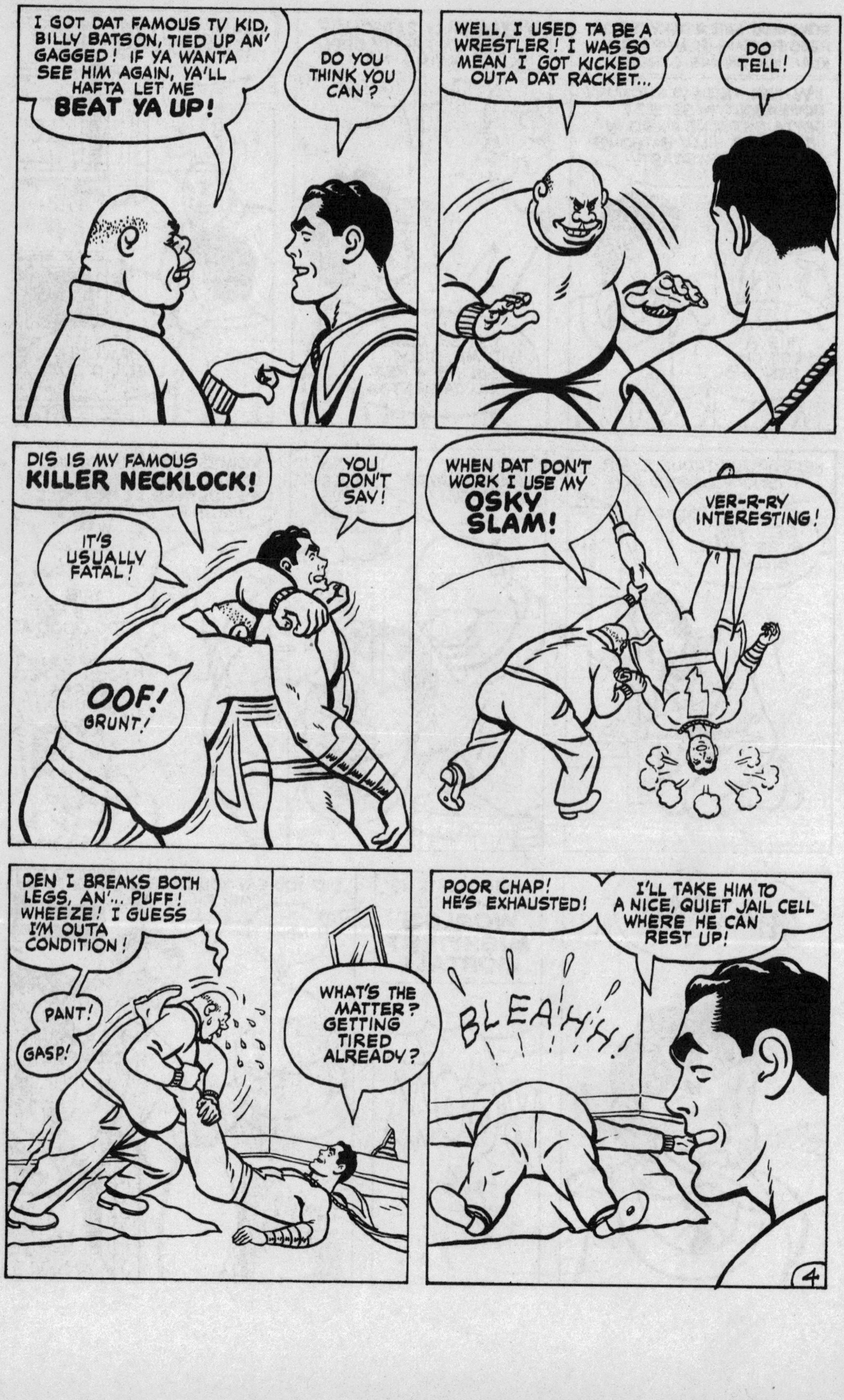
I GOT DAT FAMOUS TV KID, BILLY BATSON, TIED UP AN' GAGGED! IF YA WANTA SEE HIM AGAIN, YA'LL HAFTA LET ME BEAT YA UP!
DO YOU THINK YOU CAN?
WELL, I USED TA BE A WRESTLER! I WAS SO MEAN I GOT KICKED OUTA DAT RACKET...
DO TELL!
DIS IS MY FAMOUS KILLER NECKLOCK!
YOU DON'T SAY!
IT'S USUALLY FATAL!
OOF! GRUNT!
WHEN DAT DON'T WORK I USE MY OSKY SLAM!
VER-R-RY INTERESTING!
DEN I BREAKS BOTH LEGS, AN'... PUFF! WHEEZE! I GUESS I'M OUTA CONDITION!
PANT!
GASP!
WHAT'S THE MATTER? GETTING TIRED ALREADY?
POOR CHAP! HE'S EXHAUSTED!
I'LL TAKE HIM TO A NICE, QUIET JAIL CELL WHERE HE CAN REST UP!
BLEAHHH!
4

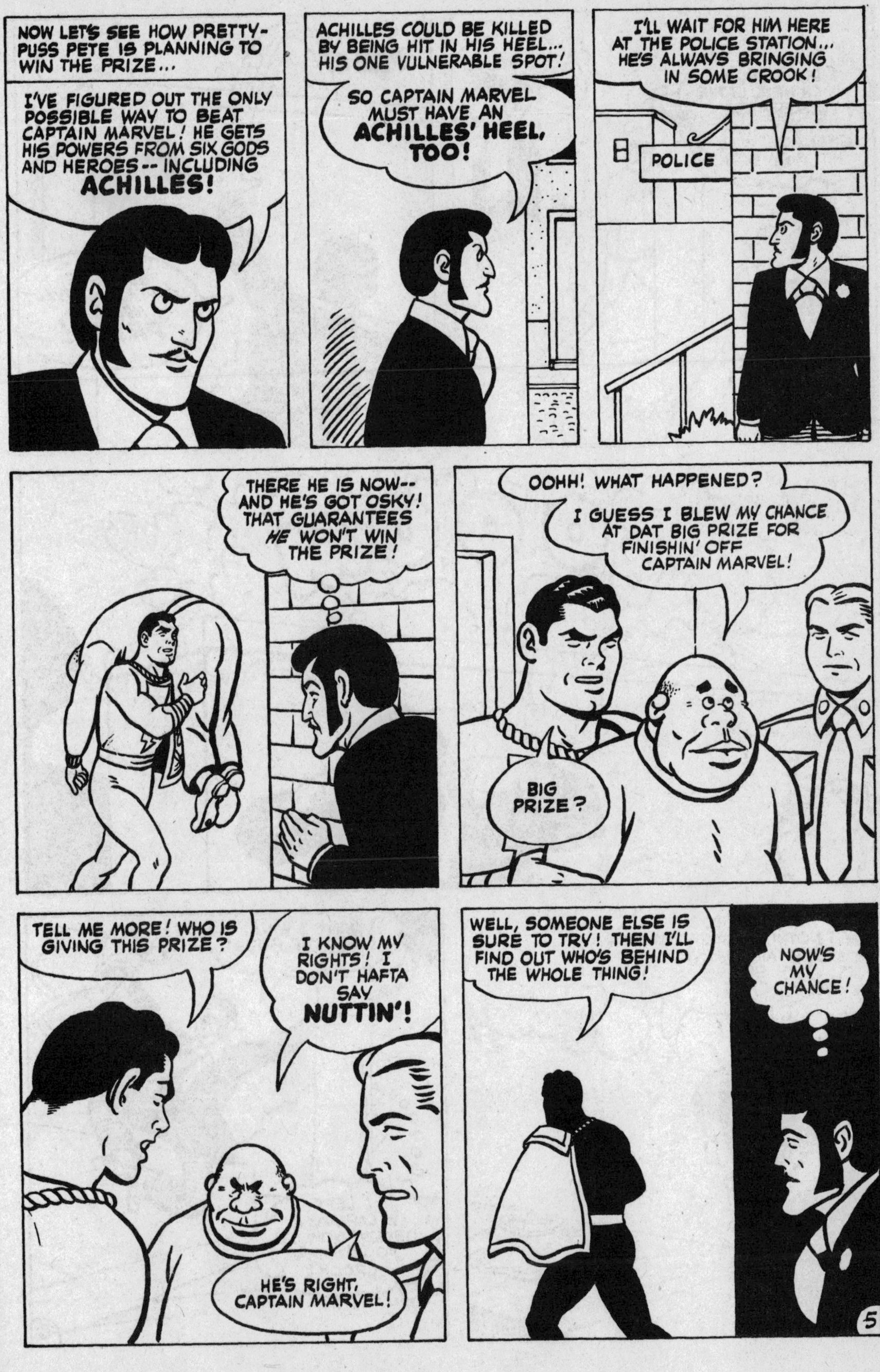
NOW LET'S SEE HOW PRETTY-PUSS PETE IS PLANNING TO WIN THE PRIZE...
I'VE FIGURED OUT THE ONLY POSSIBLE WAY TO BEAT CAPTAIN MARVEL! HE GETS HIS POWERS FROM SIX GODS AND HEROES -- INCLUDING ACHILLES!
ACHILLES COULD BE KILLED BY BEING HIT IN HIS HEEL... HIS ONE VULNERABLE SPOT!
SO CAPTAIN MARVEL MUST HAVE AN ACHILLES' HEEL, TOO!
I'LL WAIT FOR HIM HERE AT THE POLICE STATION... HE'S ALWAYS BRINGING IN SOME CROOK!
POLICE
THERE HE IS NOW-- AND HE'S GOT OSKY! THAT GUARANTEES HE WON'T WIN THE PRIZE!
OOHH! WHAT HAPPENED?
I GUESS I BLEW MY CHANCE AT DAT BIG PRIZE FOR FINISHIN' OFF CAPTAIN MARVEL!
BIG PRIZE?
TELL ME MORE! WHO IS GIVING THIS PRIZE?
I KNOW MY RIGHTS! I DON'T HAFTA SAY NUTTIN'!
HE'S RIGHT, CAPTAIN MARVEL!
WELL, SOMEONE ELSE IS SURE TO TRY! THEN I'LL FIND OUT WHO'S BEHIND THE WHOLE THING!
NOW'S MY CHANCE!
5

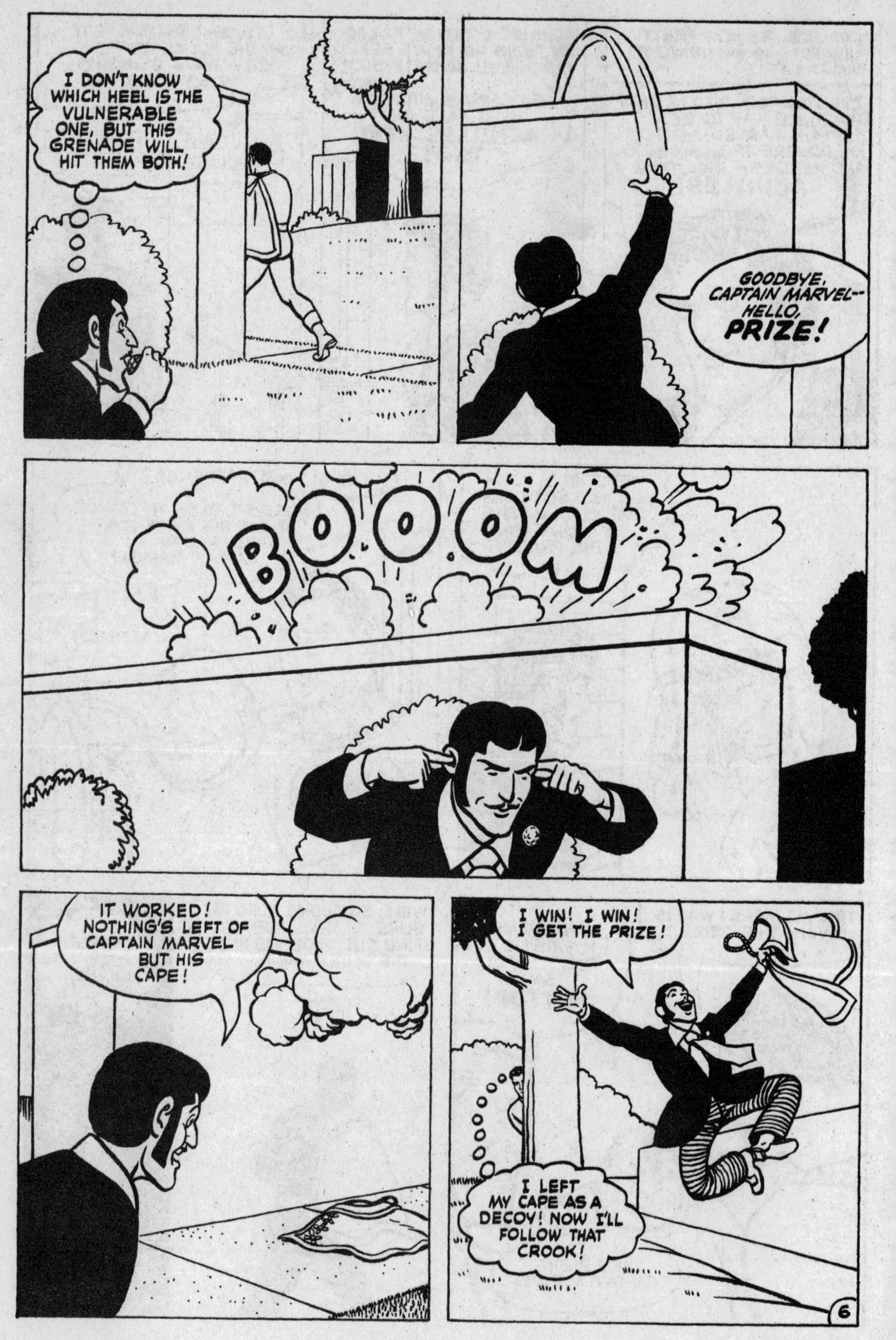
I DON'T KNOW WHICH HEEL IS THE VULNERABLE ONE, BUT THIS GRENADE WILL HIT THEM BOTH!
GOODBYE, CAPTAIN MARVEL-- HELLO, PRIZE!
BOOOM
IT WORKED! NOTHING'S LEFT OF CAPTAIN MARVEL BUT HIS CAPE!
I WIN! I WIN! I GET THE PRIZE!
I LEFT MY CAPE AS A DECOY! NOW I'LL FOLLOW THAT CROOK!
6

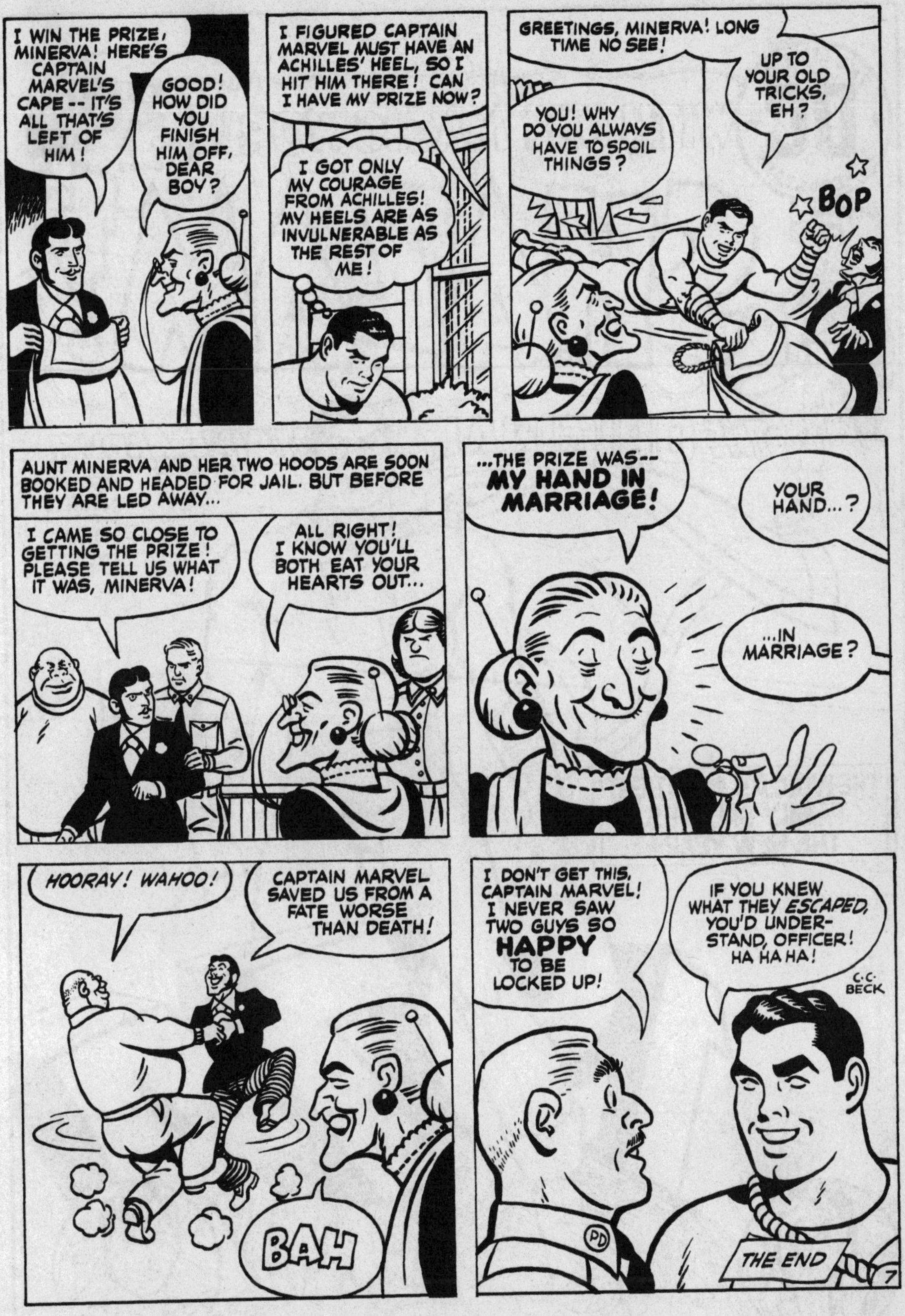
I WIN THE PRIZE, MINERVA! HERE'S CAPTAIN MARVEL'S CAPE -- IT'S ALL THAT'S LEFT OF HIM!
GOOD! HOW DID YOU FINISH HIM OFF, DEAR BOY?
I FIGURED CAPTAIN MARVEL MUST HAVE AN ACHILLES' HEEL, SO I HIT HIM THERE! CAN I HAVE MY PRIZE NOW?
I GOT ONLY MY COURAGE FROM ACHILLES! MY HEELS ARE AS INVULNERABLE AS THE REST OF ME!
GREETINGS, MINERVA! LONG TIME NO SEE!
YOU! WHY DO YOU ALWAYS HAVE TO SPOIL THINGS?
UP TO YOUR OLD TRICKS, EH?
BOP
AUNT MINERVA AND HER TWO HOODS ARE SOON BOOKED AND HEADED FOR JAIL. BUT BEFORE THEY ARE LED AWAY...
I CAME SO CLOSE TO GETTING THE PRIZE! PLEASE TELL US WHAT IT WAS, MINERVA!
ALL RIGHT! I KNOW YOU'LL BOTH EAT YOUR HEARTS OUT...
...THE PRIZE WAS-- MY HAND IN MARRIAGE!
YOUR HAND...?
...IN MARRIAGE?
HOORAY! WAHOO!
CAPTAIN MARVEL SAVED US FROM A FATE WORSE THAN DEATH!
BAH
I DON'T GET THIS, CAPTAIN MARVEL! I NEVER SAW TWO GUYS SO HAPPY TO BE LOCKED UP!
IF YOU KNEW WHAT THEY ESCAPED, YOU'D UNDERSTAND, OFFICER! HA HA HA!
C.C. BECK
PD
THE END
7

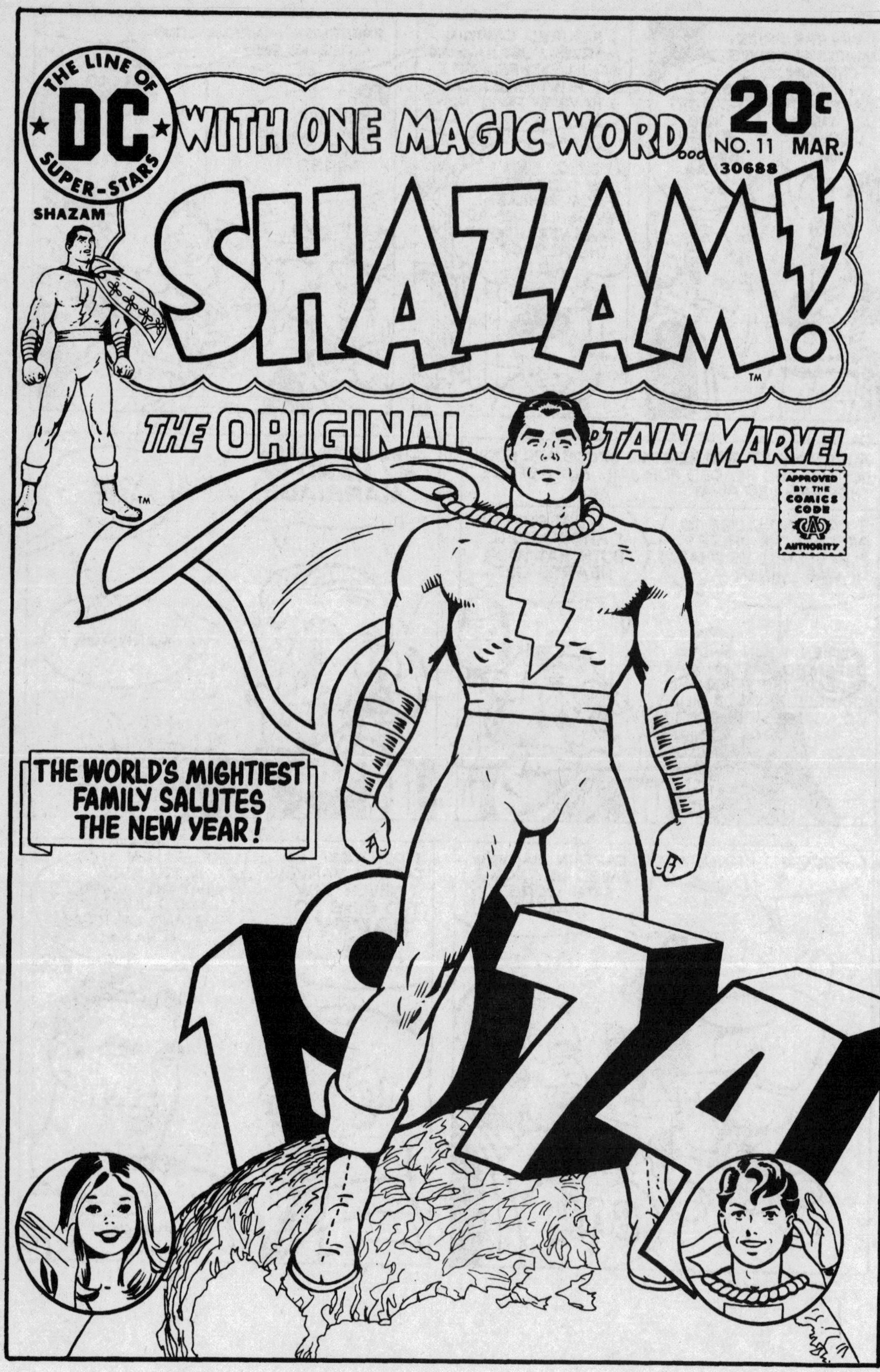

THE LINE OF DC SUPER-STARS
SHAZAM
WITH ONE MAGIC WORD...
20¢
NO. 11 MAR.
30688
SHAZAM!
TM
THE ORIGINAL CAPTAIN MARVEL
TM
APPROVED BY THE COMICS CODE AUTHORITY
THE WORLD'S MIGHTIEST FAMILY SALUTES THE NEW YEAR!
1974

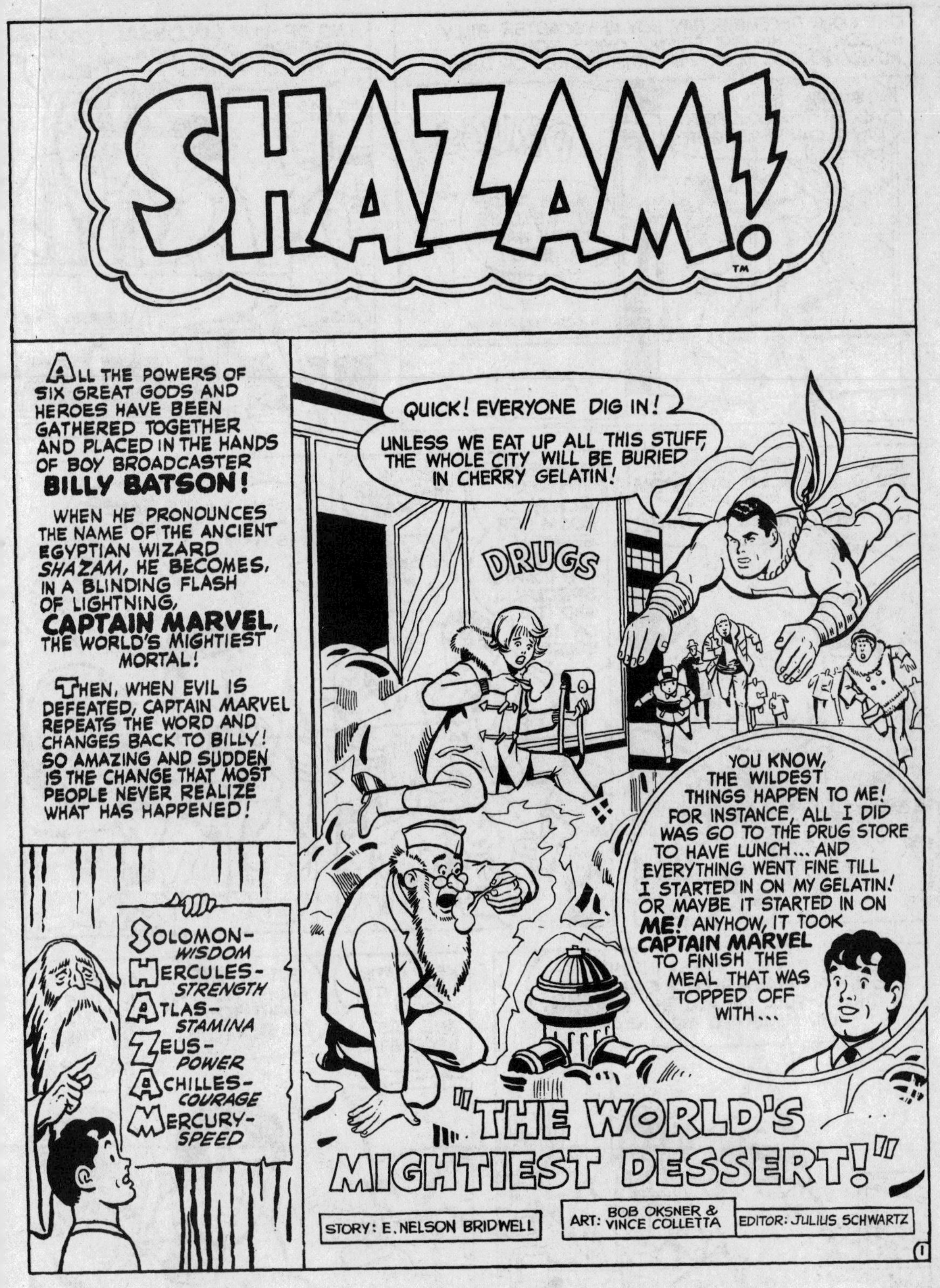
SHAZAM!™
ALL THE POWERS OF SIX GREAT GODS AND HEROES HAVE BEEN GATHERED TOGETHER AND PLACED IN THE HANDS OF BOY BROADCASTER BILLY BATSON!
WHEN HE PRONOUNCES THE NAME OF THE ANCIENT EGYPTIAN WIZARD SHAZAM, HE BECOMES, IN A BLINDING FLASH OF LIGHTNING, CAPTAIN MARVEL, THE WORLD'S MIGHTIEST MORTAL!
THEN, WHEN EVIL IS DEFEATED, CAPTAIN MARVEL REPEATS THE WORD AND CHANGES BACK TO BILLY! SO AMAZING AND SUDDEN IS THE CHANGE THAT MOST PEOPLE NEVER REALIZE WHAT HAS HAPPENED!
SOLOMON-WISDOM
HERCULES-STRENGTH
ATLAS-STAMINA
ZEUS-POWER
ACHILLES-COURAGE
MERCURY-SPEED
QUICK! EVERYONE DIG IN! UNLESS WE EAT UP ALL THIS STUFF, THE WHOLE CITY WILL BE BURIED IN CHERRY GELATIN!
DRUGS
YOU KNOW, THE WILDEST THINGS HAPPEN TO ME! FOR INSTANCE, ALL I DID WAS GO TO THE DRUG STORE TO HAVE LUNCH... AND EVERYTHING WENT FINE TILL I STARTED IN ON MY GELATIN! OR MAYBE IT STARTED IN ON ME! ANYHOW, IT TOOK CAPTAIN MARVEL TO FINISH THE MEAL THAT WAS TOPPED OFF WITH...
"THE WORLD'S MIGHTIEST DESSERT!"
STORY: E. NELSON BRIDWELL
ART: BOB OKSNER & VINCE COLLETTA
EDITOR: JULIUS SCHWARTZ
1

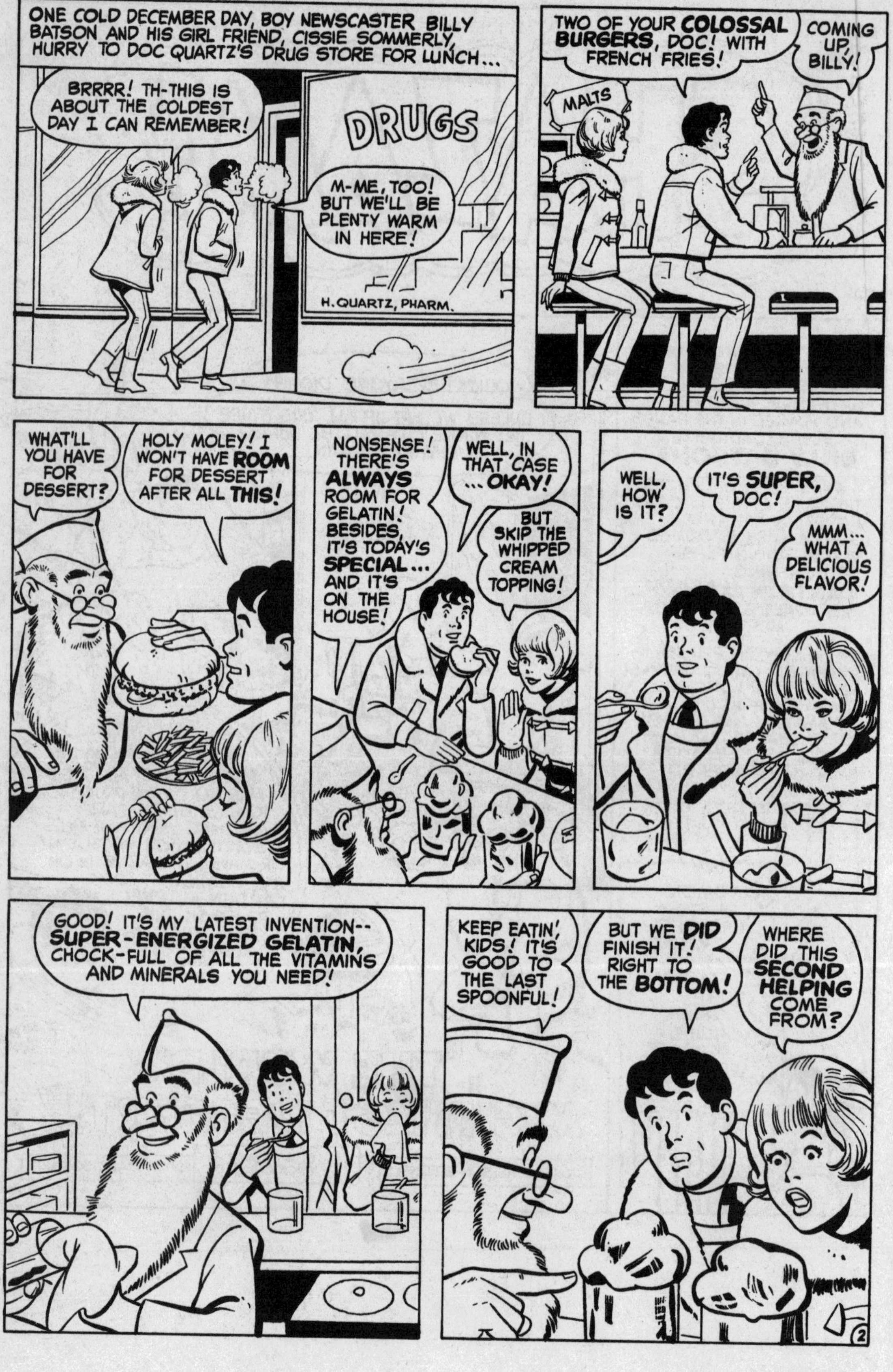
ONE COLD DECEMBER DAY, BOY NEWSCASTER BILLY BATSON AND HIS GIRL FRIEND, CISSIE SOMMERLY, HURRY TO DOC QUARTZ'S DRUG STORE FOR LUNCH...
BRRRR! TH-THIS IS ABOUT THE COLDEST DAY I CAN REMEMBER!
DRUGS
M-ME, TOO! BUT WE'LL BE PLENTY WARM IN HERE!
H. QUARTZ, PHARM.
TWO OF YOUR **COLOSSAL BURGERS**, DOC! WITH FRENCH FRIES!
COMING UP, BILLY!
MALTS
WHAT'LL YOU HAVE FOR DESSERT?
HOLY MOLEY! I WON'T HAVE **ROOM** FOR DESSERT AFTER ALL **THIS**!
NONSENSE! THERE'S **ALWAYS** ROOM FOR GELATIN! BESIDES, IT'S TODAY'S **SPECIAL**... AND IT'S ON THE HOUSE!
WELL, IN THAT CASE ...**OKAY**!
BUT SKIP THE WHIPPED CREAM TOPPING!
WELL, HOW IS IT?
IT'S **SUPER**, DOC!
MMM... WHAT A DELICIOUS FLAVOR!
GOOD! IT'S MY LATEST INVENTION-- **SUPER-ENERGIZED GELATIN**, CHOCK-FULL OF ALL THE VITAMINS AND MINERALS YOU NEED!
KEEP EATIN', KIDS! IT'S GOOD TO THE LAST SPOONFUL!
BUT WE **DID** FINISH IT! RIGHT TO THE **BOTTOM**!
WHERE DID THIS **SECOND HELPING** COME FROM?
2

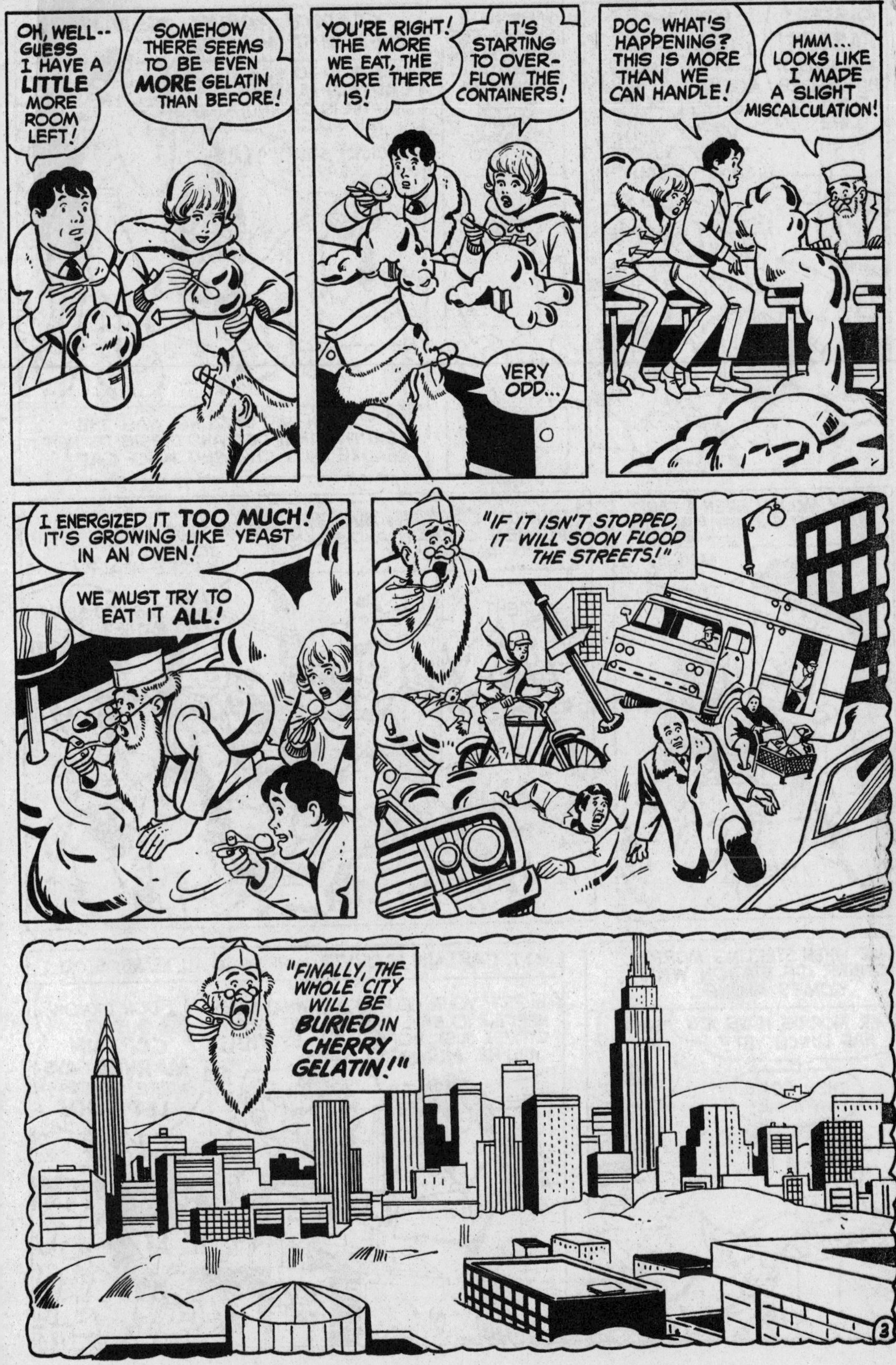
OH, WELL-- GUESS I HAVE A LITTLE MORE ROOM LEFT!
SOMEHOW THERE SEEMS TO BE EVEN MORE GELATIN THAN BEFORE!
YOU'RE RIGHT! THE MORE WE EAT, THE MORE THERE IS!
IT'S STARTING TO OVER-FLOW THE CONTAINERS!
VERY ODD...
DOC, WHAT'S HAPPENING? THIS IS MORE THAN WE CAN HANDLE!
HMM... LOOKS LIKE I MADE A SLIGHT MISCALCULATION!
I ENERGIZED IT TOO MUCH! IT'S GROWING LIKE YEAST IN AN OVEN!
WE MUST TRY TO EAT IT ALL!
"IF IT ISN'T STOPPED, IT WILL SOON FLOOD THE STREETS!"
"FINALLY, THE WHOLE CITY WILL BE BURIED IN CHERRY GELATIN!"
3

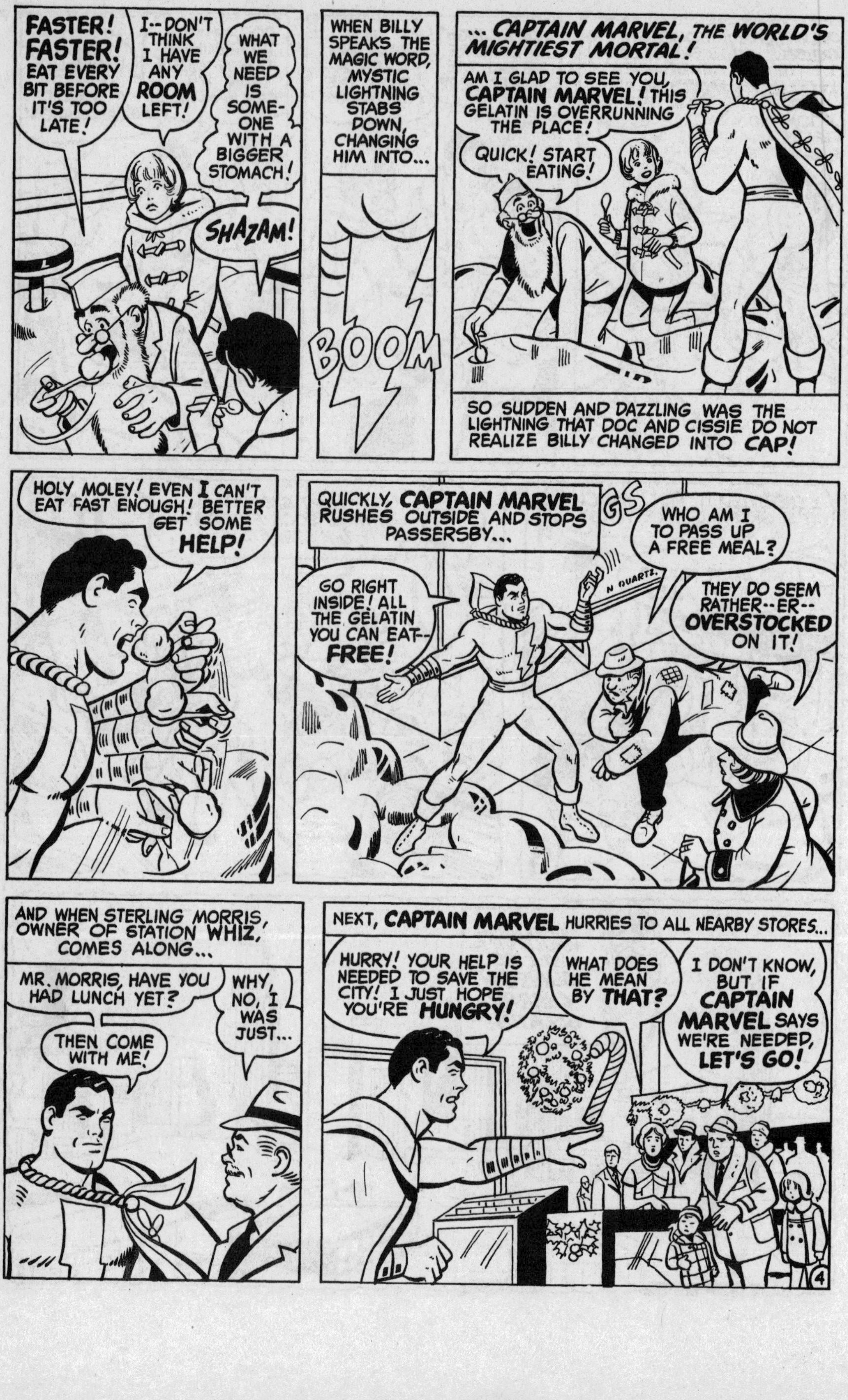
FASTER! FASTER! EAT EVERY BIT BEFORE IT'S TOO LATE!
I--DON'T THINK I HAVE ANY ROOM LEFT!
WHAT WE NEED IS SOME-ONE WITH A BIGGER STOMACH!
SHAZAM!
WHEN BILLY SPEAKS THE MAGIC WORD, MYSTIC LIGHTNING STABS DOWN, CHANGING HIM INTO...
BOOM
... CAPTAIN MARVEL, THE WORLD'S MIGHTIEST MORTAL!
AM I GLAD TO SEE YOU, CAPTAIN MARVEL! THIS GELATIN IS OVERRUNNING THE PLACE!
QUICK! START EATING!
SO SUDDEN AND DAZZLING WAS THE LIGHTNING THAT DOC AND CISSIE DO NOT REALIZE BILLY CHANGED INTO CAP!
HOLY MOLEY! EVEN I CAN'T EAT FAST ENOUGH! BETTER GET SOME HELP!
QUICKLY, CAPTAIN MARVEL RUSHES OUTSIDE AND STOPS PASSERSBY...
WHO AM I TO PASS UP A FREE MEAL?
GO RIGHT INSIDE! ALL THE GELATIN YOU CAN EAT--FREE!
THEY DO SEEM RATHER--ER--OVERSTOCKED ON IT!
AND WHEN STERLING MORRIS, OWNER OF STATION WHIZ, COMES ALONG...
MR. MORRIS, HAVE YOU HAD LUNCH YET?
WHY, NO, I WAS JUST...
THEN COME WITH ME!
NEXT, CAPTAIN MARVEL HURRIES TO ALL NEARBY STORES...
HURRY! YOUR HELP IS NEEDED TO SAVE THE CITY! I JUST HOPE YOU'RE HUNGRY!
WHAT DOES HE MEAN BY THAT?
I DON'T KNOW, BUT IF CAPTAIN MARVEL SAYS WE'RE NEEDED, LET'S GO!
4

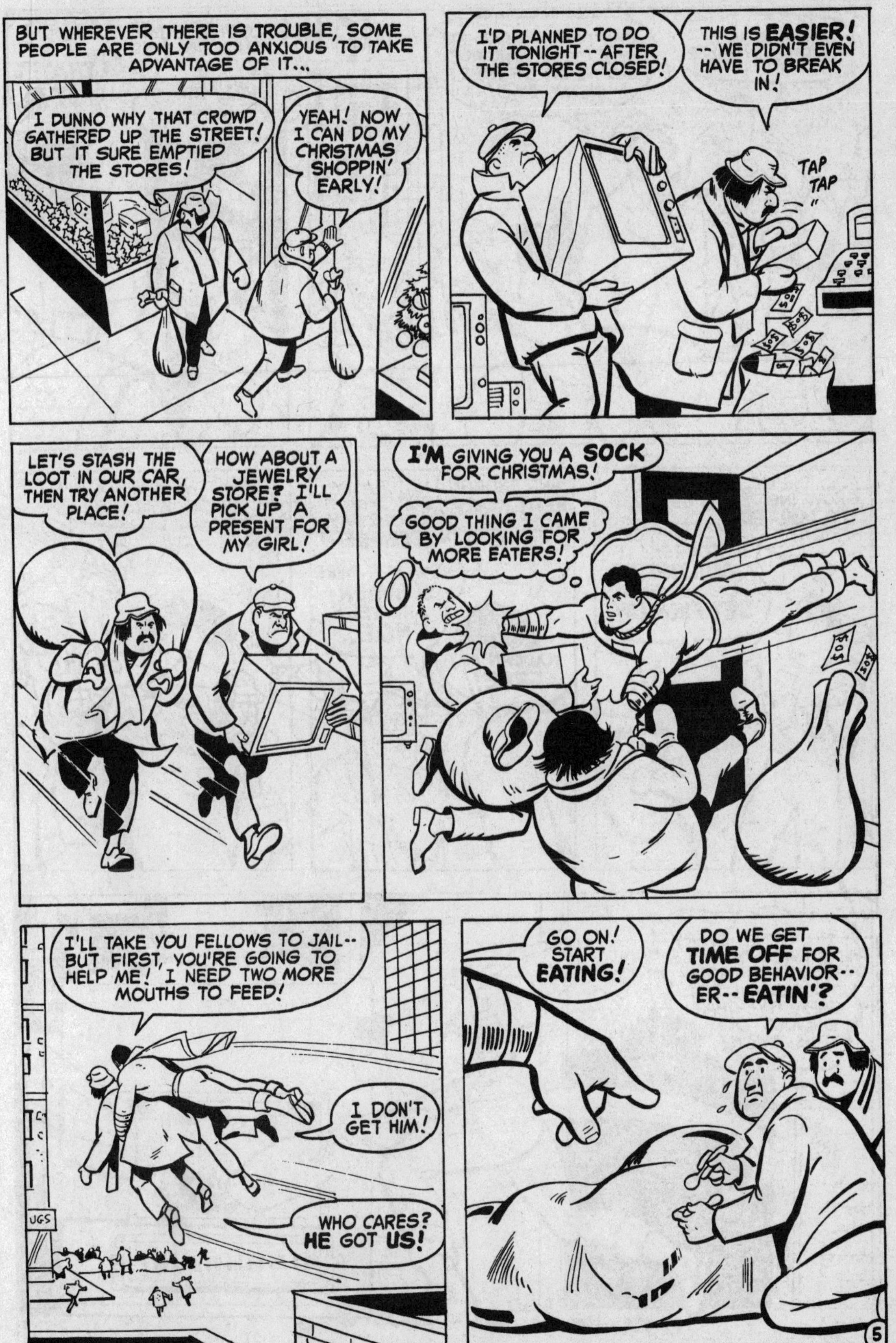
BUT WHEREVER THERE IS TROUBLE, SOME PEOPLE ARE ONLY TOO ANXIOUS TO TAKE ADVANTAGE OF IT...
I DUNNO WHY THAT CROWD GATHERED UP THE STREET! BUT IT SURE EMPTIED THE STORES!
YEAH! NOW I CAN DO MY CHRISTMAS SHOPPIN' EARLY!
I'D PLANNED TO DO IT TONIGHT -- AFTER THE STORES CLOSED!
THIS IS **EASIER!** -- WE DIDN'T EVEN HAVE TO BREAK IN!
TAP TAP
LET'S STASH THE LOOT IN OUR CAR, THEN TRY ANOTHER PLACE!
HOW ABOUT A JEWELRY STORE? I'LL PICK UP A PRESENT FOR MY GIRL!
I'M GIVING YOU A **SOCK** FOR CHRISTMAS!
GOOD THING I CAME BY LOOKING FOR MORE EATERS!
I'LL TAKE YOU FELLOWS TO JAIL-- BUT FIRST, YOU'RE GOING TO HELP ME! I NEED TWO MORE MOUTHS TO FEED!
I DON'T GET HIM!
WHO CARES? **HE** GOT **US!**
UGS
GO ON! START **EATING!**
DO WE GET **TIME OFF** FOR GOOD BEHAVIOR-- ER-- **EATIN'?**
5

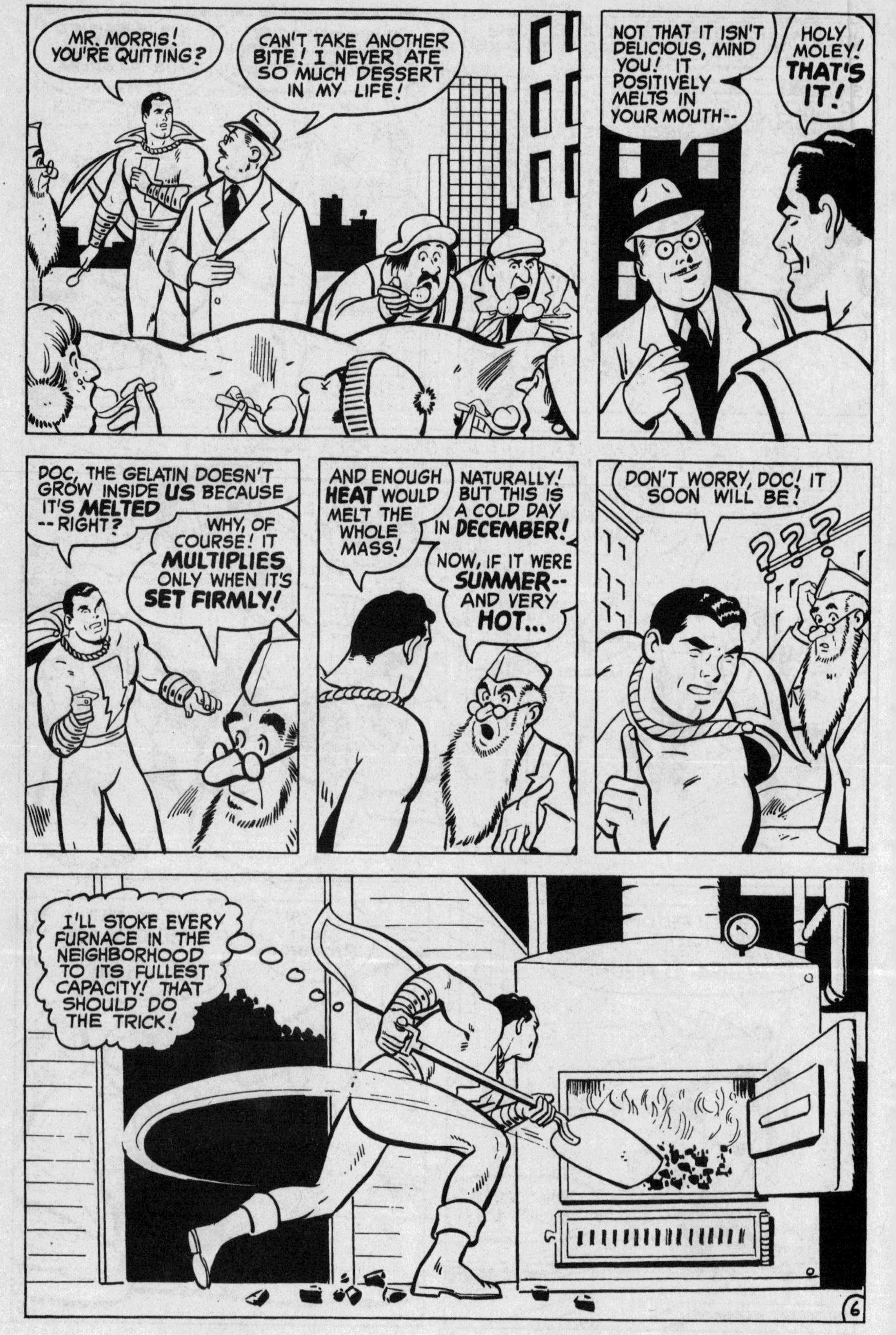
MR. MORRIS! YOU'RE QUITTING?
CAN'T TAKE ANOTHER BITE! I NEVER ATE SO MUCH DESSERT IN MY LIFE!
NOT THAT IT ISN'T DELICIOUS, MIND YOU! IT POSITIVELY MELTS IN YOUR MOUTH--
HOLY MOLEY! THAT'S IT!
DOC, THE GELATIN DOESN'T GROW INSIDE US BECAUSE IT'S MELTED --RIGHT?
WHY, OF COURSE! IT MULTIPLIES ONLY WHEN IT'S SET FIRMLY!
AND ENOUGH HEAT WOULD MELT THE WHOLE MASS!
NATURALLY! BUT THIS IS A COLD DAY IN DECEMBER!
NOW, IF IT WERE SUMMER-- AND VERY HOT...
DON'T WORRY, DOC! IT SOON WILL BE!
???
I'LL STOKE EVERY FURNACE IN THE NEIGHBORHOOD TO ITS FULLEST CAPACITY! THAT SHOULD DO THE TRICK!
6

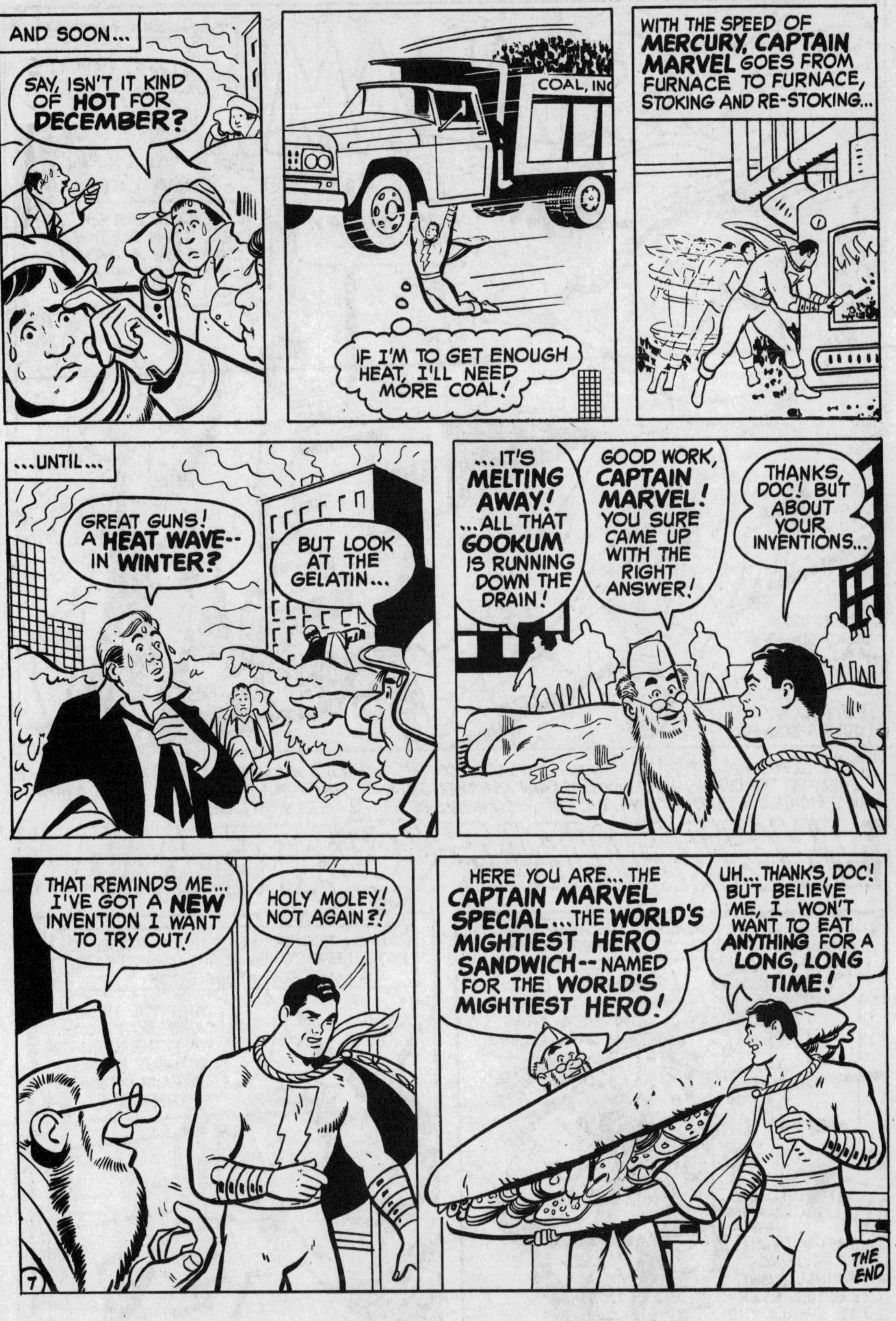
AND SOON...
SAY, ISN'T IT KIND OF HOT FOR DECEMBER?
COAL, INC
IF I'M TO GET ENOUGH HEAT, I'LL NEED MORE COAL!
WITH THE SPEED OF MERCURY, CAPTAIN MARVEL GOES FROM FURNACE TO FURNACE, STOKING AND RE-STOKING...
...UNTIL...
GREAT GUNS! A HEAT WAVE-- IN WINTER?
BUT LOOK AT THE GELATIN...
...IT'S MELTING AWAY! ...ALL THAT GOOKUM IS RUNNING DOWN THE DRAIN!
GOOD WORK, CAPTAIN MARVEL! YOU SURE CAME UP WITH THE RIGHT ANSWER!
THANKS, DOC! BUT ABOUT YOUR INVENTIONS...
THAT REMINDS ME... I'VE GOT A NEW INVENTION I WANT TO TRY OUT!
HOLY MOLEY! NOT AGAIN?!
7
HERE YOU ARE... THE CAPTAIN MARVEL SPECIAL...THE WORLD'S MIGHTIEST HERO SANDWICH-- NAMED FOR THE WORLD'S MIGHTIEST HERO!
UH...THANKS, DOC! BUT BELIEVE ME, I WON'T WANT TO EAT ANYTHING FOR A LONG, LONG TIME!
THE END

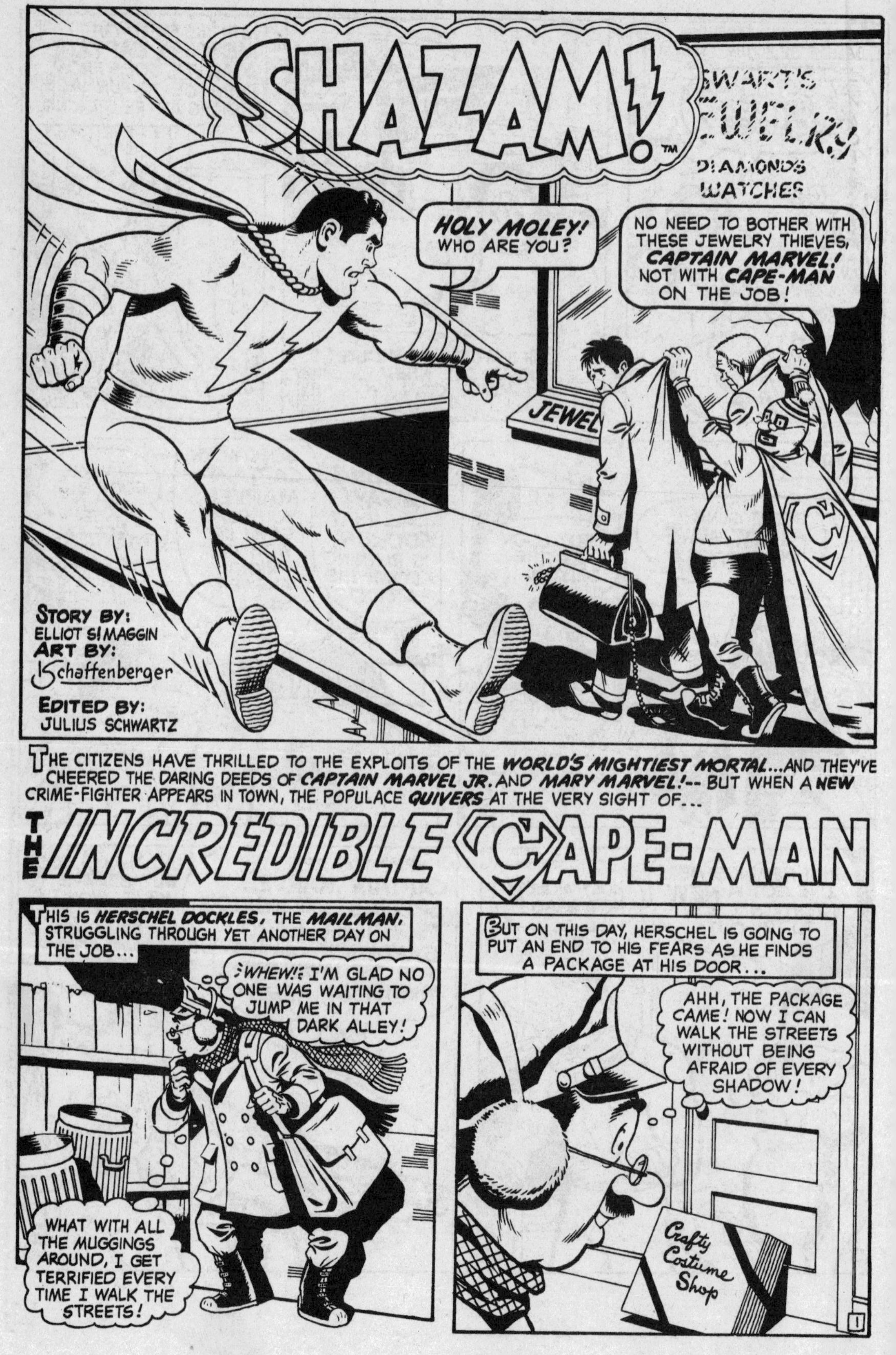
SHAZAM!™
DIAMONDS
WATCHES
HOLY MOLEY! WHO ARE YOU?
NO NEED TO BOTHER WITH THESE JEWELRY THIEVES, CAPTAIN MARVEL! NOT WITH CAPE-MAN ON THE JOB!
JEWEL
STORY BY: ELLIOT S! MAGGIN
ART BY: K. Schaffenberger
EDITED BY: JULIUS SCHWARTZ
THE CITIZENS HAVE THRILLED TO THE EXPLOITS OF THE WORLD'S MIGHTIEST MORTAL...AND THEY'VE CHEERED THE DARING DEEDS OF CAPTAIN MARVEL JR. AND MARY MARVEL!-- BUT WHEN A NEW CRIME-FIGHTER APPEARS IN TOWN, THE POPULACE QUIVERS AT THE VERY SIGHT OF...
THE INCREDIBLE CAPE-MAN
THIS IS HERSCHEL DOCKLES, THE MAILMAN, STRUGGLING THROUGH YET ANOTHER DAY ON THE JOB...
WHEW!! I'M GLAD NO ONE WAS WAITING TO JUMP ME IN THAT DARK ALLEY!
WHAT WITH ALL THE MUGGINGS AROUND, I GET TERRIFIED EVERY TIME I WALK THE STREETS!
BUT ON THIS DAY, HERSCHEL IS GOING TO PUT AN END TO HIS FEARS AS HE FINDS A PACKAGE AT HIS DOOR...
AHH, THE PACKAGE CAME! NOW I CAN WALK THE STREETS WITHOUT BEING AFRAID OF EVERY SHADOW!
Crafty Costume Shop
1

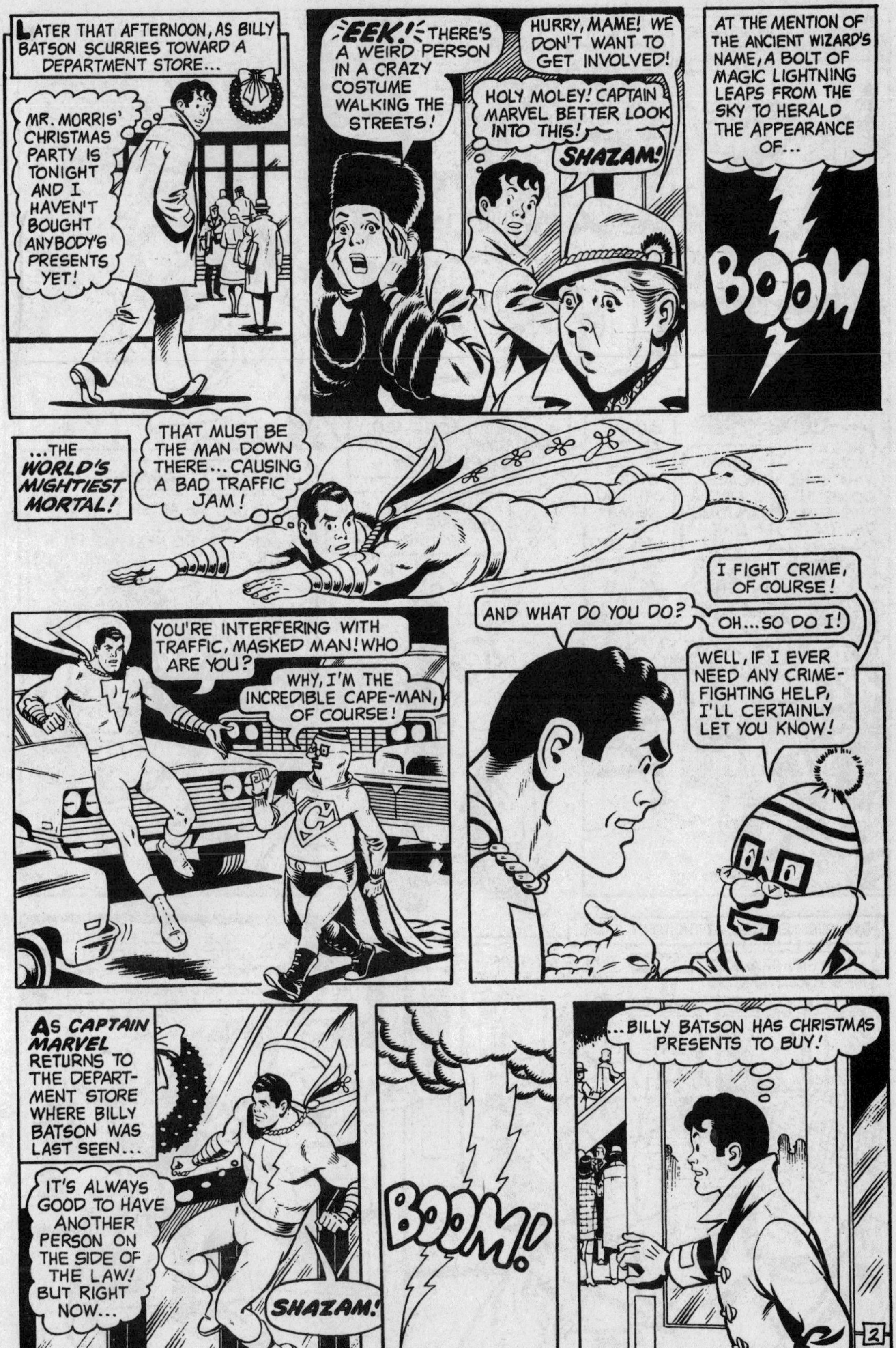
LATER THAT AFTERNOON, AS BILLY BATSON SCURRIES TOWARD A DEPARTMENT STORE...
MR. MORRIS' CHRISTMAS PARTY IS TONIGHT AND I HAVEN'T BOUGHT ANYBODY'S PRESENTS YET!
EEK! THERE'S A WEIRD PERSON IN A CRAZY COSTUME WALKING THE STREETS!
HURRY, MAME! WE DON'T WANT TO GET INVOLVED!
HOLY MOLEY! CAPTAIN MARVEL BETTER LOOK INTO THIS!
SHAZAM!
AT THE MENTION OF THE ANCIENT WIZARD'S NAME, A BOLT OF MAGIC LIGHTNING LEAPS FROM THE SKY TO HERALD THE APPEARANCE OF...
BOOM
...THE WORLD'S MIGHTIEST MORTAL!
THAT MUST BE THE MAN DOWN THERE... CAUSING A BAD TRAFFIC JAM!
YOU'RE INTERFERING WITH TRAFFIC, MASKED MAN! WHO ARE YOU?
WHY, I'M THE INCREDIBLE CAPE-MAN, OF COURSE!
AND WHAT DO YOU DO?
I FIGHT CRIME, OF COURSE!
OH... SO DO I!
WELL, IF I EVER NEED ANY CRIME-FIGHTING HELP, I'LL CERTAINLY LET YOU KNOW!
AS CAPTAIN MARVEL RETURNS TO THE DEPARTMENT STORE WHERE BILLY BATSON WAS LAST SEEN...
IT'S ALWAYS GOOD TO HAVE ANOTHER PERSON ON THE SIDE OF THE LAW! BUT RIGHT NOW...
SHAZAM!
BOOM!
...BILLY BATSON HAS CHRISTMAS PRESENTS TO BUY!
2

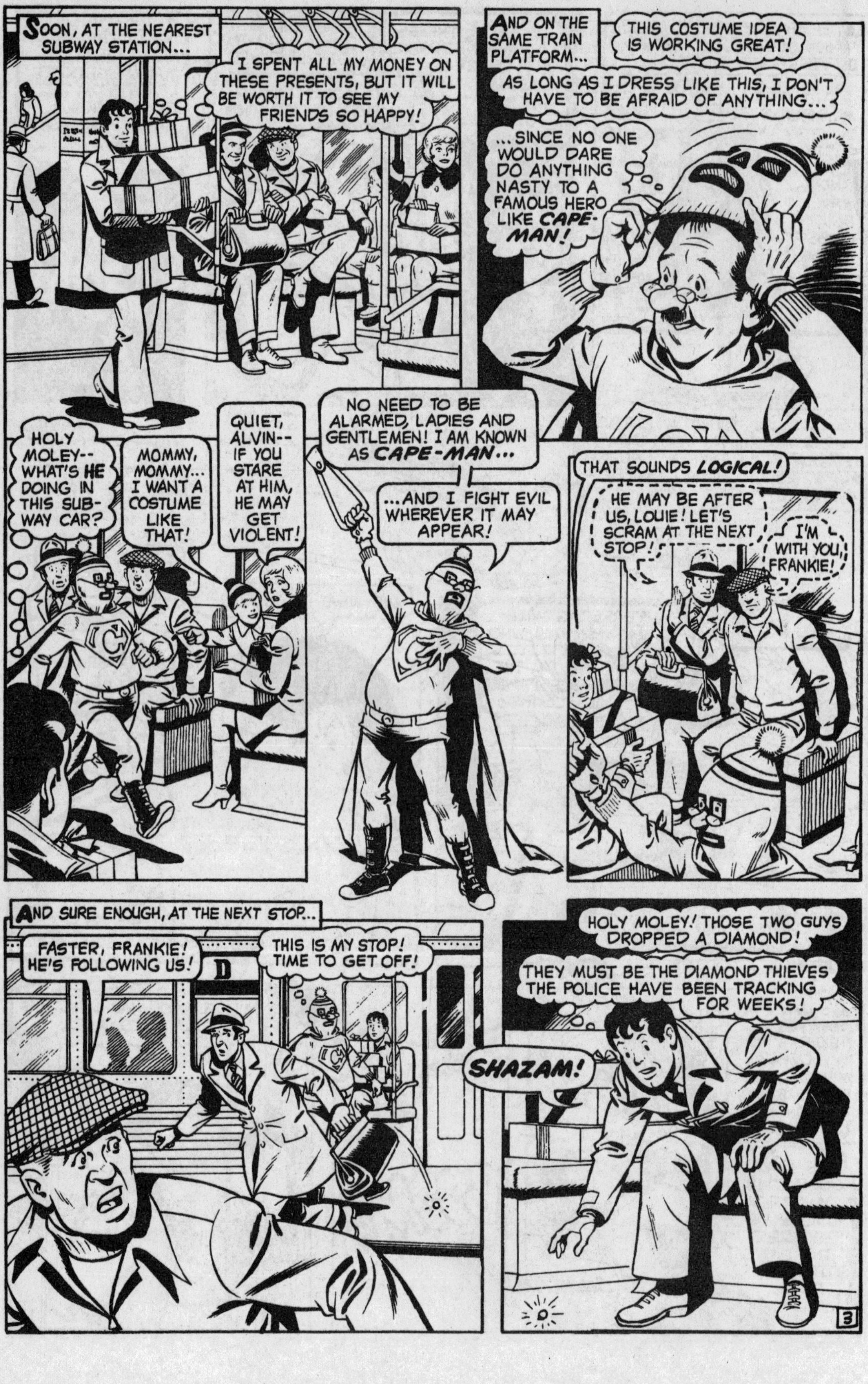
SOON, AT THE NEAREST SUBWAY STATION...
I SPENT ALL MY MONEY ON THESE PRESENTS, BUT IT WILL BE WORTH IT TO SEE MY FRIENDS SO HAPPY!
AND ON THE SAME TRAIN PLATFORM...
THIS COSTUME IDEA IS WORKING GREAT!
AS LONG AS I DRESS LIKE THIS, I DON'T HAVE TO BE AFRAID OF ANYTHING...
...SINCE NO ONE WOULD DARE DO ANYTHING NASTY TO A FAMOUS HERO LIKE CAPE-MAN!
HOLY MOLEY-- WHAT'S HE DOING IN THIS SUBWAY CAR?
MOMMY, MOMMY... I WANT A COSTUME LIKE THAT!
QUIET, ALVIN-- IF YOU STARE AT HIM, HE MAY GET VIOLENT!
NO NEED TO BE ALARMED, LADIES AND GENTLEMEN! I AM KNOWN AS CAPE-MAN...
...AND I FIGHT EVIL WHEREVER IT MAY APPEAR!
THAT SOUNDS LOGICAL!
HE MAY BE AFTER US, LOUIE! LET'S SCRAM AT THE NEXT STOP!
I'M WITH YOU, FRANKIE!
AND SURE ENOUGH, AT THE NEXT STOP...
FASTER, FRANKIE! HE'S FOLLOWING US!
THIS IS MY STOP! TIME TO GET OFF!
D
HOLY MOLEY! THOSE TWO GUYS DROPPED A DIAMOND!
THEY MUST BE THE DIAMOND THIEVES THE POLICE HAVE BEEN TRACKING FOR WEEKS!
SHAZAM!
3

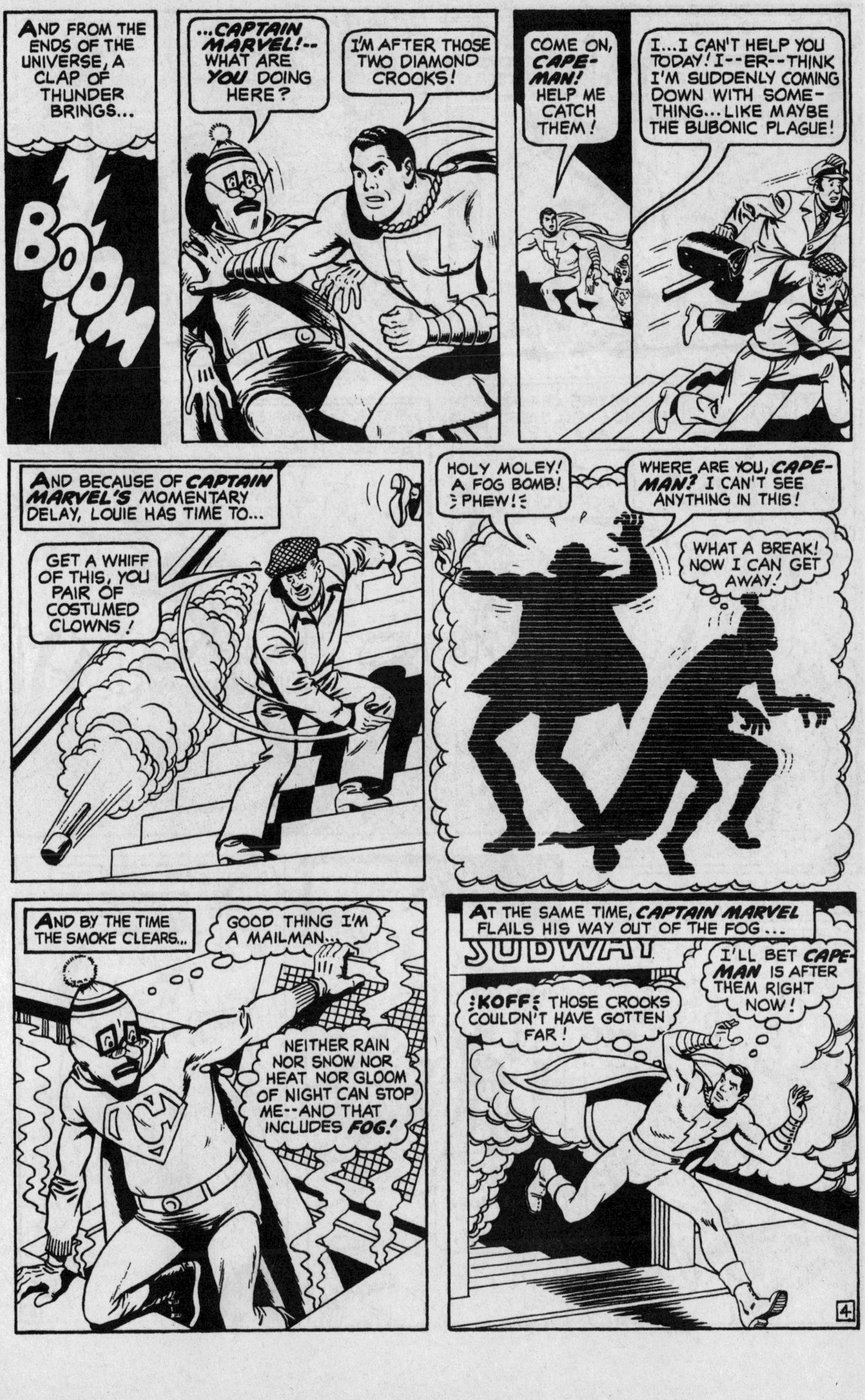

AND FROM THE ENDS OF THE UNIVERSE, A CLAP OF THUNDER BRINGS...
BOOM
...CAPTAIN MARVEL!-- WHAT ARE YOU DOING HERE?
I'M AFTER THOSE TWO DIAMOND CROOKS!
COME ON, CAPE-MAN! HELP ME CATCH THEM!
I...I CAN'T HELP YOU TODAY! I--ER--THINK I'M SUDDENLY COMING DOWN WITH SOME-THING...LIKE MAYBE THE BUBONIC PLAGUE!
AND BECAUSE OF CAPTAIN MARVEL'S MOMENTARY DELAY, LOUIE HAS TIME TO...
GET A WHIFF OF THIS, YOU PAIR OF COSTUMED CLOWNS!
HOLY MOLEY! A FOG BOMB! PHEW!
WHERE ARE YOU, CAPE-MAN? I CAN'T SEE ANYTHING IN THIS!
WHAT A BREAK! NOW I CAN GET AWAY!
AND BY THE TIME THE SMOKE CLEARS...
GOOD THING I'M A MAILMAN...
NEITHER RAIN NOR SNOW NOR HEAT NOR GLOOM OF NIGHT CAN STOP ME--AND THAT INCLUDES FOG!
AT THE SAME TIME, CAPTAIN MARVEL FLAILS HIS WAY OUT OF THE FOG...
SUBWAY
I'LL BET CAPE-MAN IS AFTER THEM RIGHT NOW!
KOFF THOSE CROOKS COULDN'T HAVE GOTTEN FAR!
4

AND SURE ENOUGH, LESS THAN A BLOCK AWAY...

LET'S GET OUTA HERE QUICK, LOUIE!

YEAH-- BEFORE THOSE TWO HERO GUYS FIND OUT WHAT HIT 'EM!

LOOKIT! -- IT'S *CAPE-MAN!* RUN 'IM DOWN!

OH, MY!

TH-THEY'RE CHASING ME! HOW WILL I GET AWAY?

AHH-- UP THIS LIGHT-POLE!

AFTER THE THIEVES CIRCLE THE POLE SEVERAL TIMES...

WE CAN'T GET HIM UP THERE!

LET'S SCRAM BEFORE THE OTHER ONE SEES US!

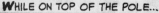

WHILE ON TOP OF THE POLE...

OH, MY! I FORGOT THAT I'M AFRAID OF HEIGHTS!

HELP ME! *HELP!*

THOSE CROOKS ARE RACING OFF... BUT *CAPE-MAN* IS IN TROUBLE!

I'LL SAVE YOU, PAL!

NO! LET *GO!* I'M EVEN *MORE* SCARED OF *FLYING!*

B-BUT, *CAPE-MAN!* I'VE GOT TO...

"...SAVE YOU?

5

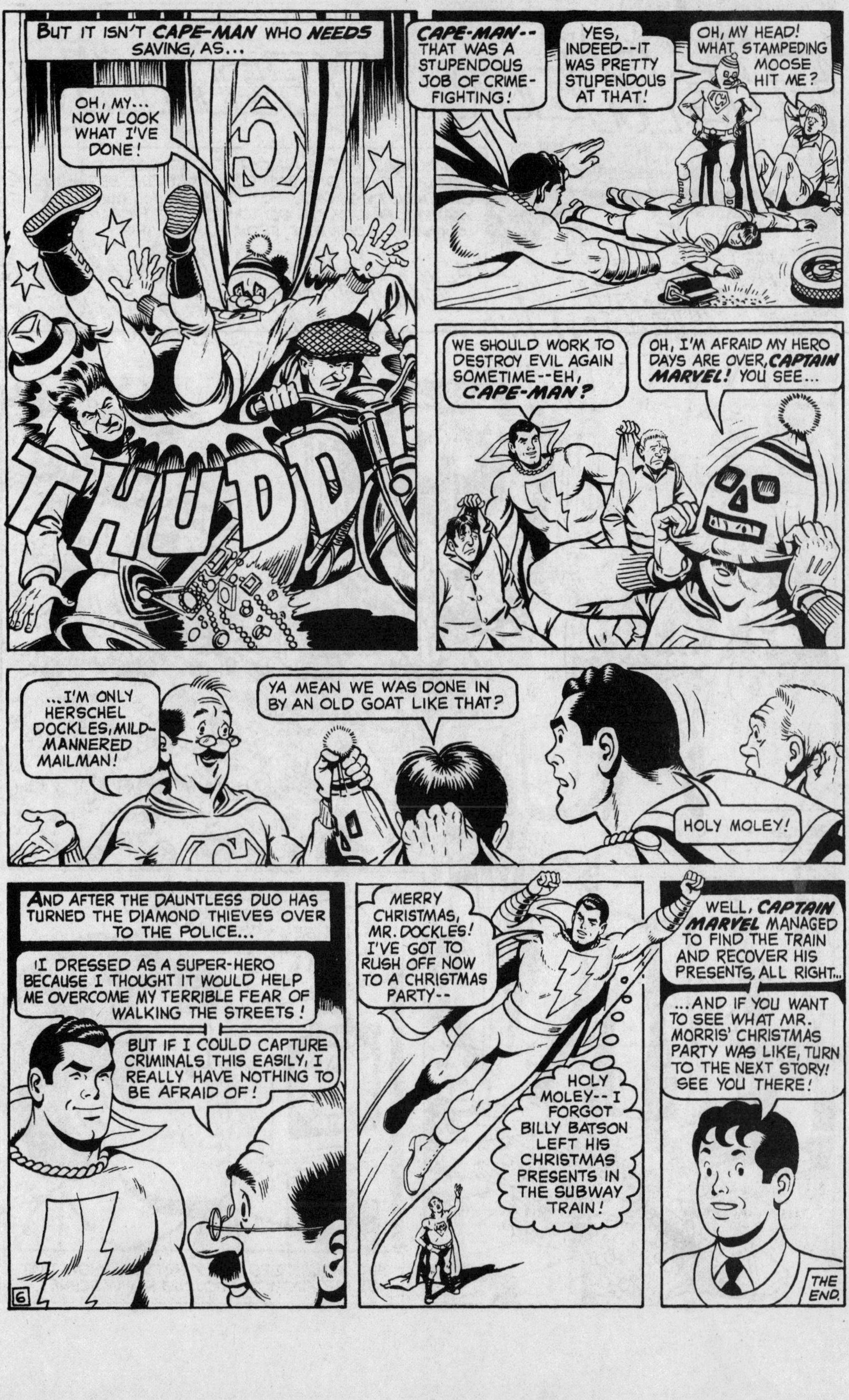
BUT IT ISN'T CAPE-MAN WHO NEEDS SAVING, AS...
OH, MY... NOW LOOK WHAT I'VE DONE!
THUDD!
CAPE-MAN-- THAT WAS A STUPENDOUS JOB OF CRIME-FIGHTING!
YES, INDEED--IT WAS PRETTY STUPENDOUS AT THAT!
OH, MY HEAD! WHAT STAMPEDING MOOSE HIT ME?
WE SHOULD WORK TO DESTROY EVIL AGAIN SOMETIME--EH, CAPE-MAN?
OH, I'M AFRAID MY HERO DAYS ARE OVER, CAPTAIN MARVEL! YOU SEE...
...I'M ONLY HERSCHEL DOCKLES, MILD-MANNERED MAILMAN!
YA MEAN WE WAS DONE IN BY AN OLD GOAT LIKE THAT?
HOLY MOLEY!
AND AFTER THE DAUNTLESS DUO HAS TURNED THE DIAMOND THIEVES OVER TO THE POLICE...
I DRESSED AS A SUPER-HERO BECAUSE I THOUGHT IT WOULD HELP ME OVERCOME MY TERRIBLE FEAR OF WALKING THE STREETS!
BUT IF I COULD CAPTURE CRIMINALS THIS EASILY, I REALLY HAVE NOTHING TO BE AFRAID OF!
6
MERRY CHRISTMAS, MR. DOCKLES! I'VE GOT TO RUSH OFF NOW TO A CHRISTMAS PARTY--
HOLY MOLEY-- I FORGOT BILLY BATSON LEFT HIS CHRISTMAS PRESENTS IN THE SUBWAY TRAIN!
WELL, CAPTAIN MARVEL MANAGED TO FIND THE TRAIN AND RECOVER HIS PRESENTS, ALL RIGHT...
...AND IF YOU WANT TO SEE WHAT MR. MORRIS' CHRISTMAS PARTY WAS LIKE, TURN TO THE NEXT STORY! SEE YOU THERE!
THE END.

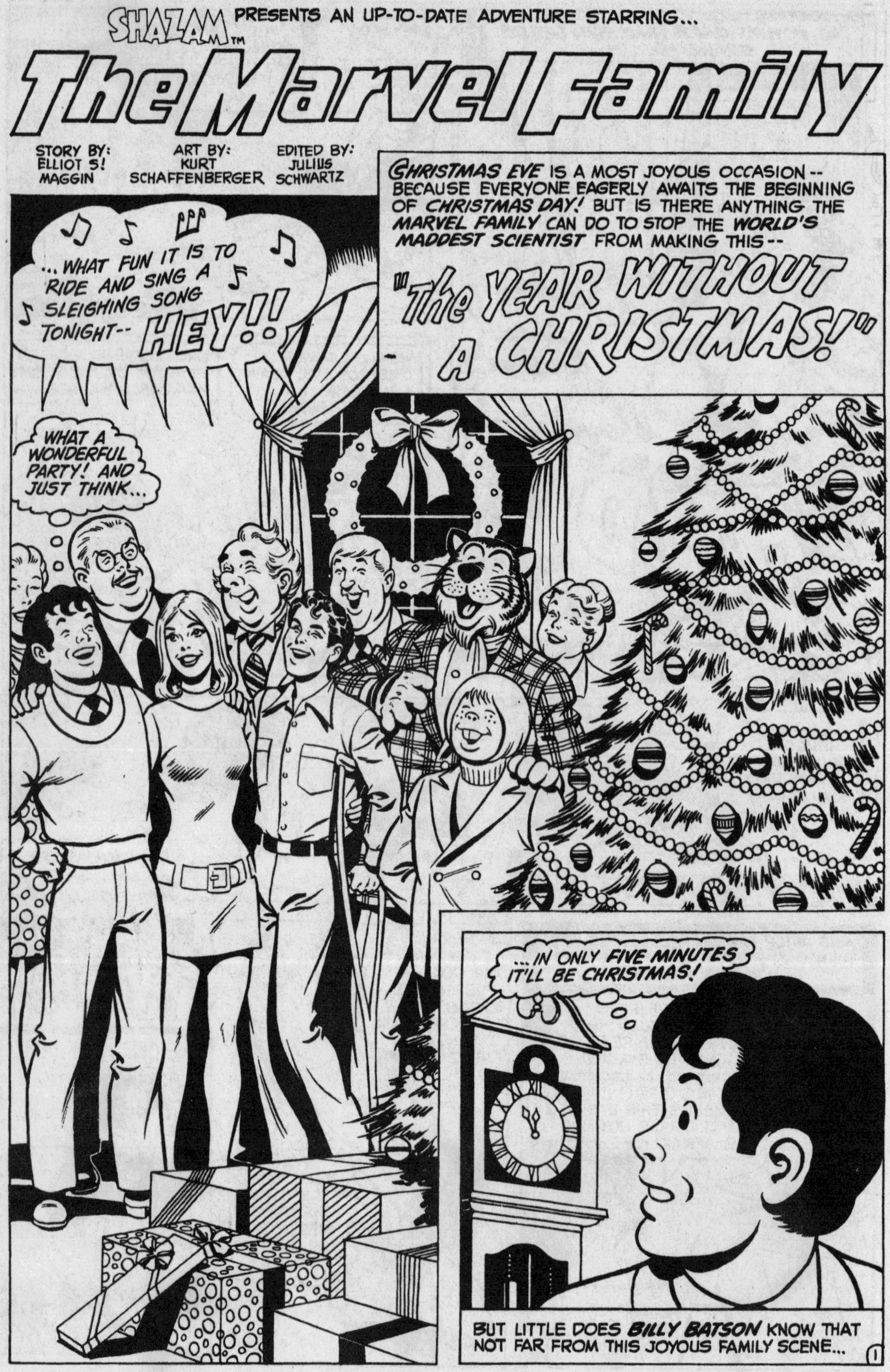
SHAZAM™ PRESENTS AN UP-TO-DATE ADVENTURE STARRING...
The Marvel Family
STORY BY: ELLIOT S! MAGGIN
ART BY: KURT SCHAFFENBERGER
EDITED BY: JULIUS SCHWARTZ
CHRISTMAS EVE IS A MOST JOYOUS OCCASION -- BECAUSE EVERYONE EAGERLY AWAITS THE BEGINNING OF CHRISTMAS DAY! BUT IS THERE ANYTHING THE MARVEL FAMILY CAN DO TO STOP THE WORLD'S MADDEST SCIENTIST FROM MAKING THIS --
"The YEAR WITHOUT A CHRISTMAS!"
...WHAT FUN IT IS TO RIDE AND SING A SLEIGHING SONG TONIGHT-- HEY!!
WHAT A WONDERFUL PARTY! AND JUST THINK...
...IN ONLY FIVE MINUTES IT'LL BE CHRISTMAS!
BUT LITTLE DOES BILLY BATSON KNOW THAT NOT FAR FROM THIS JOYOUS FAMILY SCENE...
1

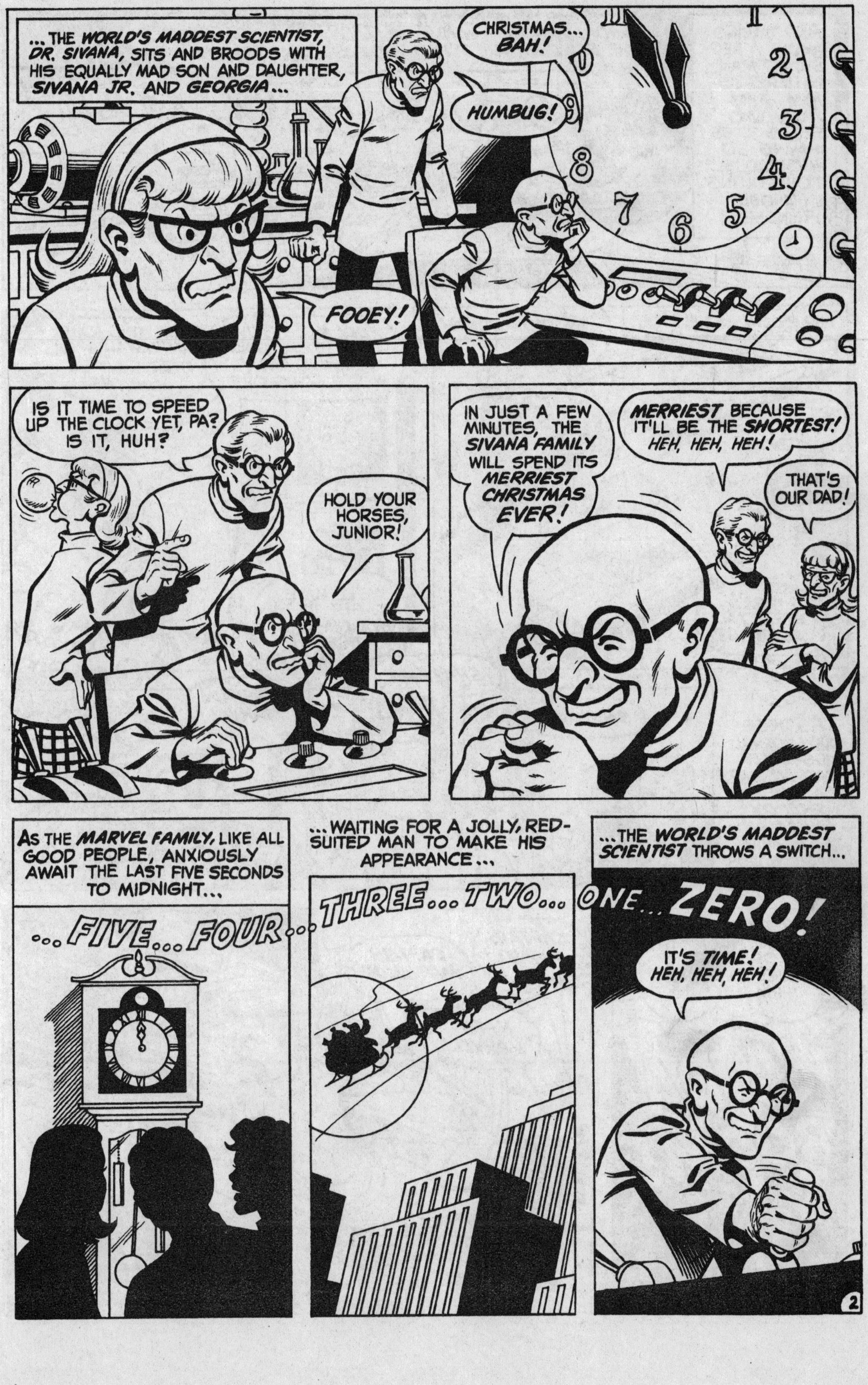
...THE WORLD'S MADDEST SCIENTIST, DR. SIVANA, SITS AND BROODS WITH HIS EQUALLY MAD SON AND DAUGHTER, SIVANA JR. AND GEORGIA...
CHRISTMAS... BAH!
HUMBUG!
FOOEY!
IS IT TIME TO SPEED UP THE CLOCK YET, PA? IS IT, HUH?
HOLD YOUR HORSES, JUNIOR!
IN JUST A FEW MINUTES, THE SIVANA FAMILY WILL SPEND ITS MERRIEST CHRISTMAS EVER!
MERRIEST BECAUSE IT'LL BE THE SHORTEST! HEH, HEH, HEH!
THAT'S OUR DAD!
AS THE MARVEL FAMILY, LIKE ALL GOOD PEOPLE, ANXIOUSLY AWAIT THE LAST FIVE SECONDS TO MIDNIGHT...
...WAITING FOR A JOLLY, RED-SUITED MAN TO MAKE HIS APPEARANCE...
...THE WORLD'S MADDEST SCIENTIST THROWS A SWITCH...
...FIVE... FOUR... THREE... TWO... ONE... ZERO!
IT'S TIME! HEH, HEH, HEH!
2

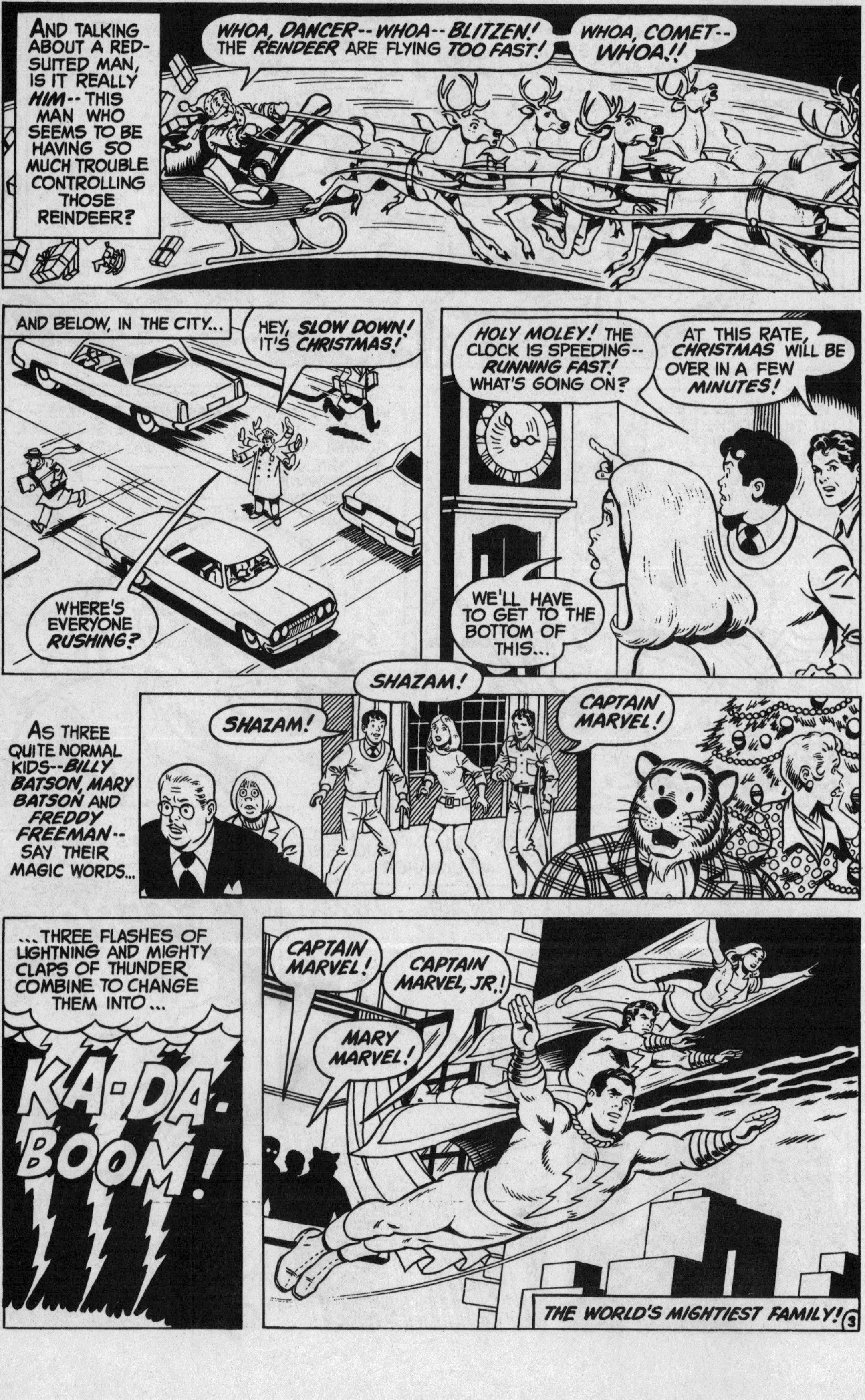
AND TALKING ABOUT A RED-SUITED MAN, IS IT REALLY *HIM*-- THIS MAN WHO SEEMS TO BE HAVING SO MUCH TROUBLE CONTROLLING THOSE REINDEER?
WHOA, DANCER-- *WHOA*-- *BLITZEN!* THE *REINDEER* ARE FLYING *TOO FAST!*
WHOA, COMET-- WHOA!!
AND BELOW, IN THE CITY...
HEY, *SLOW DOWN!* IT'S *CHRISTMAS!*
WHERE'S EVERYONE *RUSHING?*
HOLY MOLEY! THE CLOCK IS SPEEDING-- *RUNNING FAST!* WHAT'S GOING ON?
AT THIS RATE, *CHRISTMAS* WILL BE OVER IN A FEW *MINUTES!*
WE'LL HAVE TO GET TO THE BOTTOM OF THIS...
AS THREE QUITE NORMAL KIDS-- *BILLY BATSON, MARY BATSON* AND *FREDDY FREEMAN*-- SAY THEIR MAGIC WORDS...
SHAZAM!
SHAZAM!
CAPTAIN MARVEL!
...THREE FLASHES OF LIGHTNING AND MIGHTY CLAPS OF THUNDER COMBINE TO CHANGE THEM INTO...
KA-DA-BOOM!
CAPTAIN MARVEL!
CAPTAIN MARVEL, JR.!
MARY MARVEL!
THE WORLD'S MIGHTIEST FAMILY!
3

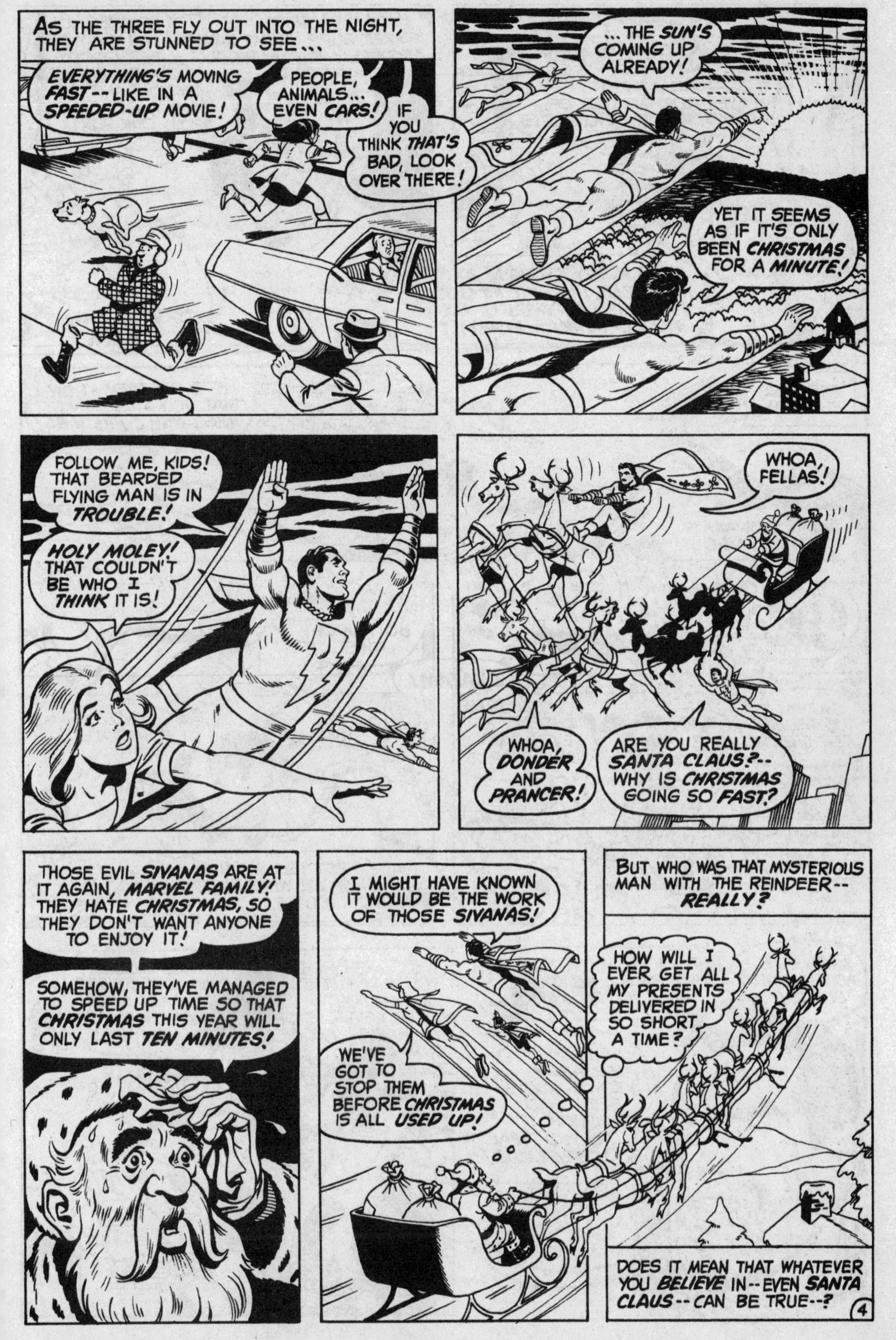
AS THE THREE FLY OUT INTO THE NIGHT, THEY ARE STUNNED TO SEE...
EVERYTHING'S MOVING FAST--LIKE IN A SPEEDED-UP MOVIE!
PEOPLE, ANIMALS... EVEN CARS!
IF YOU THINK THAT'S BAD, LOOK OVER THERE!
...THE SUN'S COMING UP ALREADY!
YET IT SEEMS AS IF IT'S ONLY BEEN CHRISTMAS FOR A MINUTE!
FOLLOW ME, KIDS! THAT BEARDED FLYING MAN IS IN TROUBLE!
HOLY MOLEY! THAT COULDN'T BE WHO I THINK IT IS!
WHOA, FELLAS!
WHOA, DONDER AND PRANCER!
ARE YOU REALLY SANTA CLAUS?--WHY IS CHRISTMAS GOING SO FAST?
THOSE EVIL SIVANAS ARE AT IT AGAIN, MARVEL FAMILY! THEY HATE CHRISTMAS, SO THEY DON'T WANT ANYONE TO ENJOY IT!
SOMEHOW, THEY'VE MANAGED TO SPEED UP TIME SO THAT CHRISTMAS THIS YEAR WILL ONLY LAST TEN MINUTES!
I MIGHT HAVE KNOWN IT WOULD BE THE WORK OF THOSE SIVANAS!
WE'VE GOT TO STOP THEM BEFORE CHRISTMAS IS ALL USED UP!
BUT WHO WAS THAT MYSTERIOUS MAN WITH THE REINDEER--REALLY?
HOW WILL I EVER GET ALL MY PRESENTS DELIVERED IN SO SHORT A TIME?
DOES IT MEAN THAT WHATEVER YOU BELIEVE IN--EVEN SANTA CLAUS--CAN BE TRUE--?
4

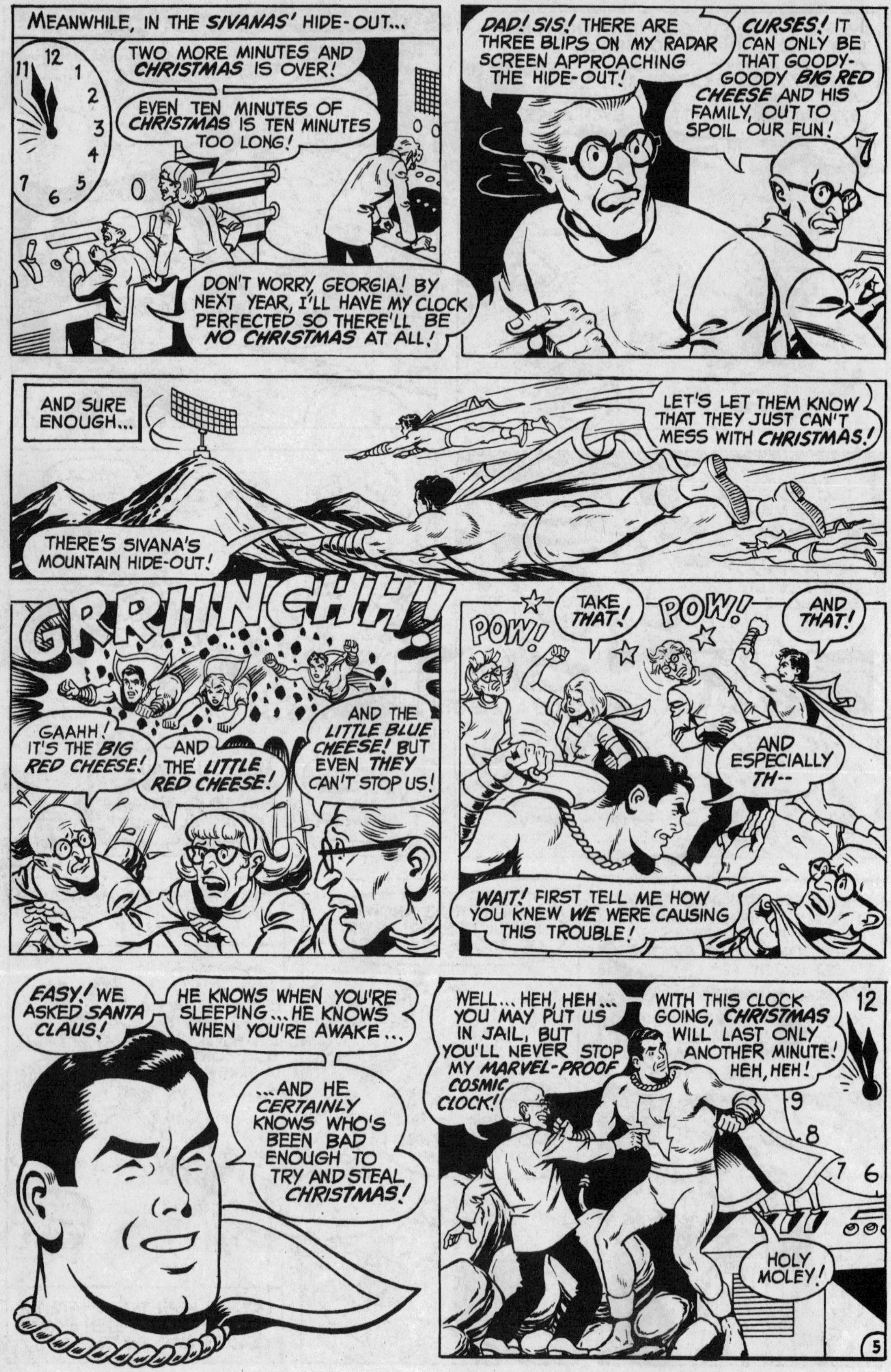
MEANWHILE, IN THE SIVANAS' HIDE-OUT...
TWO MORE MINUTES AND CHRISTMAS IS OVER!
EVEN TEN MINUTES OF CHRISTMAS IS TEN MINUTES TOO LONG!
DON'T WORRY, GEORGIA! BY NEXT YEAR, I'LL HAVE MY CLOCK PERFECTED SO THERE'LL BE NO CHRISTMAS AT ALL!
DAD! SIS! THERE ARE THREE BLIPS ON MY RADAR SCREEN APPROACHING THE HIDE-OUT!
CURSES! IT CAN ONLY BE THAT GOODY-GOODY BIG RED CHEESE AND HIS FAMILY, OUT TO SPOIL OUR FUN!
AND SURE ENOUGH...
LET'S LET THEM KNOW THAT THEY JUST CAN'T MESS WITH CHRISTMAS!
THERE'S SIVANA'S MOUNTAIN HIDE-OUT!
GRRIINCHH!
GAAHH! IT'S THE BIG RED CHEESE!
AND THE LITTLE RED CHEESE!
AND THE LITTLE BLUE CHEESE! BUT EVEN THEY CAN'T STOP US!
POW!
TAKE THAT!
POW!
AND THAT!
AND ESPECIALLY TH--
WAIT! FIRST TELL ME HOW YOU KNEW WE WERE CAUSING THIS TROUBLE!
EASY! WE ASKED SANTA CLAUS!
HE KNOWS WHEN YOU'RE SLEEPING... HE KNOWS WHEN YOU'RE AWAKE...
...AND HE CERTAINLY KNOWS WHO'S BEEN BAD ENOUGH TO TRY AND STEAL CHRISTMAS!
WELL... HEH, HEH... YOU MAY PUT US IN JAIL, BUT YOU'LL NEVER STOP MY MARVEL-PROOF COSMIC CLOCK!
WITH THIS CLOCK GOING, CHRISTMAS WILL LAST ONLY ANOTHER MINUTE! HEH, HEH!
HOLY MOLEY!
5

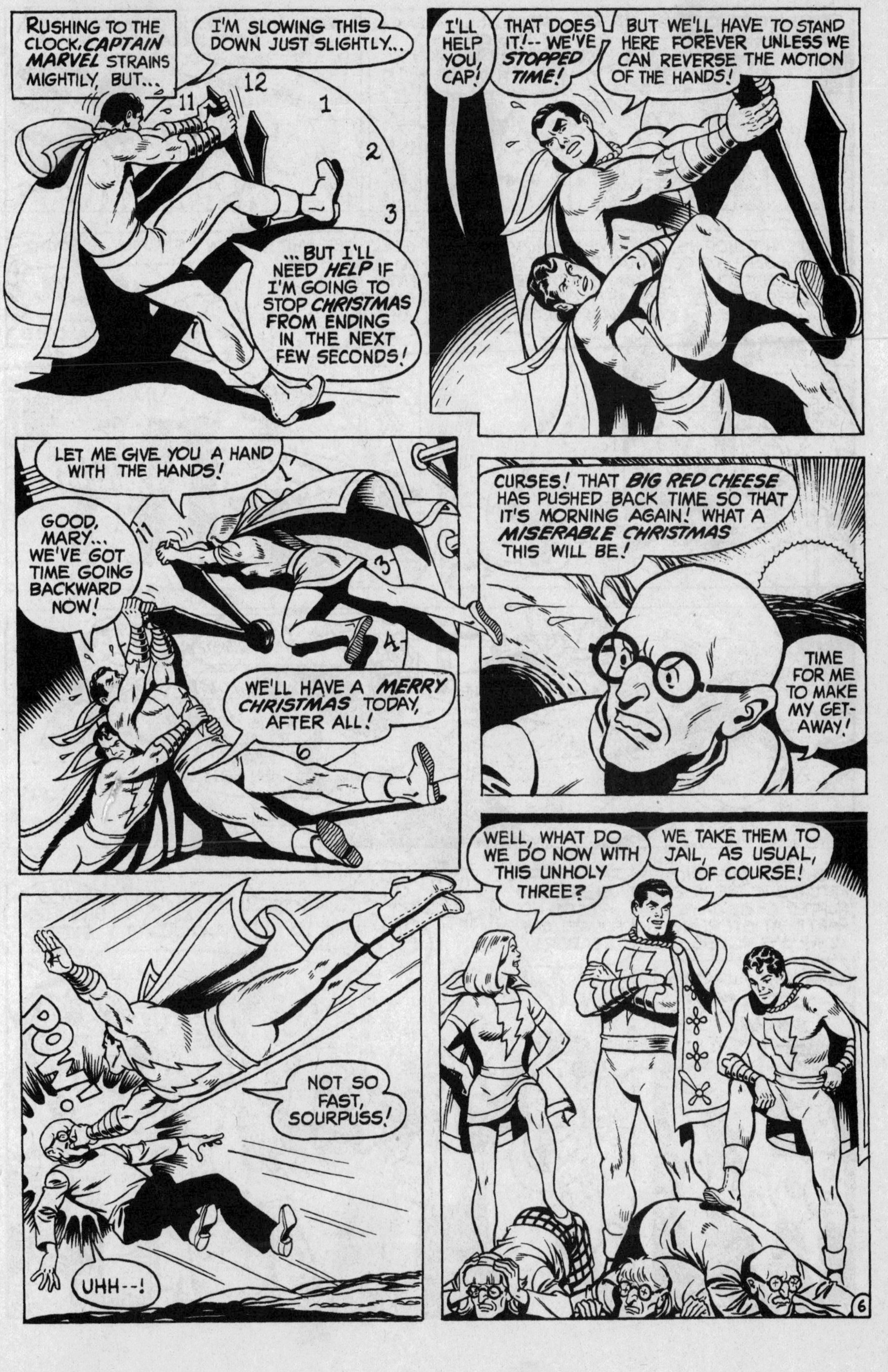
RUSHING TO THE CLOCK, CAPTAIN MARVEL STRAINS MIGHTILY, BUT...
I'M SLOWING THIS DOWN JUST SLIGHTLY...
12
11
1
2
3
... BUT I'LL NEED HELP IF I'M GOING TO STOP CHRISTMAS FROM ENDING IN THE NEXT FEW SECONDS!
I'LL HELP YOU, CAP!
THAT DOES IT!-- WE'VE STOPPED TIME!
BUT WE'LL HAVE TO STAND HERE FOREVER UNLESS WE CAN REVERSE THE MOTION OF THE HANDS!
LET ME GIVE YOU A HAND WITH THE HANDS!
GOOD, MARY... WE'VE GOT TIME GOING BACKWARD NOW!
WE'LL HAVE A MERRY CHRISTMAS TODAY, AFTER ALL!
CURSES! THAT BIG RED CHEESE HAS PUSHED BACK TIME SO THAT IT'S MORNING AGAIN! WHAT A MISERABLE CHRISTMAS THIS WILL BE!
TIME FOR ME TO MAKE MY GET-AWAY!
POW!
NOT SO FAST, SOURPUSS!
UHH--!
WELL, WHAT DO WE DO NOW WITH THIS UNHOLY THREE?
WE TAKE THEM TO JAIL, AS USUAL, OF COURSE!
6

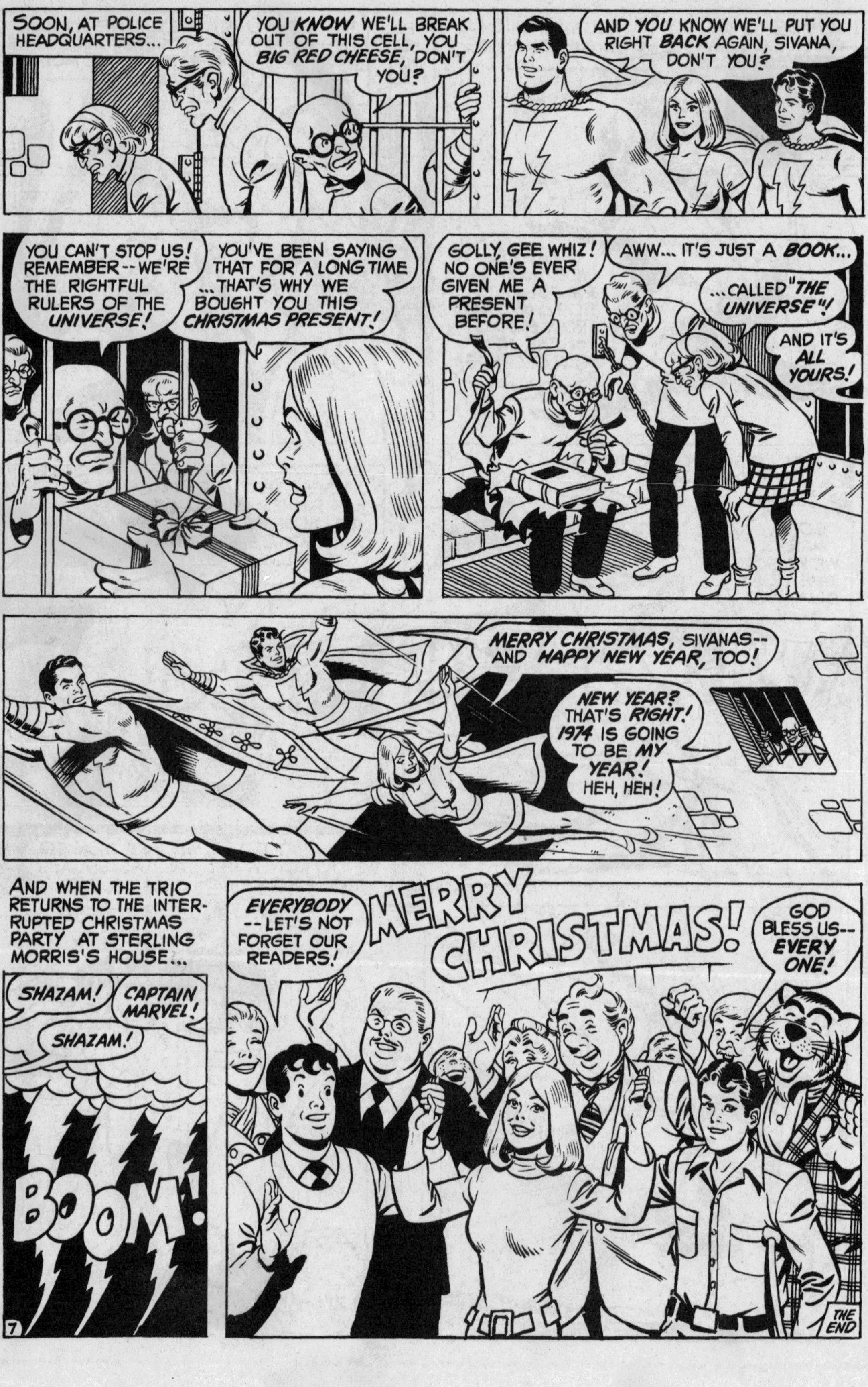
SOON, AT POLICE HEADQUARTERS...
YOU KNOW WE'LL BREAK OUT OF THIS CELL, YOU BIG RED CHEESE, DON'T YOU?
AND YOU KNOW WE'LL PUT YOU RIGHT BACK AGAIN, SIVANA, DON'T YOU?
YOU CAN'T STOP US! REMEMBER--WE'RE THE RIGHTFUL RULERS OF THE UNIVERSE!
YOU'VE BEEN SAYING THAT FOR A LONG TIME ...THAT'S WHY WE BOUGHT YOU THIS CHRISTMAS PRESENT!
GOLLY, GEE WHIZ! NO ONE'S EVER GIVEN ME A PRESENT BEFORE!
AWW... IT'S JUST A BOOK...
...CALLED "THE UNIVERSE"!
AND IT'S ALL YOURS!
MERRY CHRISTMAS, SIVANAS-- AND HAPPY NEW YEAR, TOO!
NEW YEAR? THAT'S RIGHT! 1974 IS GOING TO BE MY YEAR! HEH, HEH!
AND WHEN THE TRIO RETURNS TO THE INTERRUPTED CHRISTMAS PARTY AT STERLING MORRIS'S HOUSE...
SHAZAM!
CAPTAIN MARVEL!
SHAZAM!
BOOM!
7
EVERYBODY --LET'S NOT FORGET OUR READERS!
MERRY CHRISTMAS!
GOD BLESS US-- EVERY ONE!
THE END

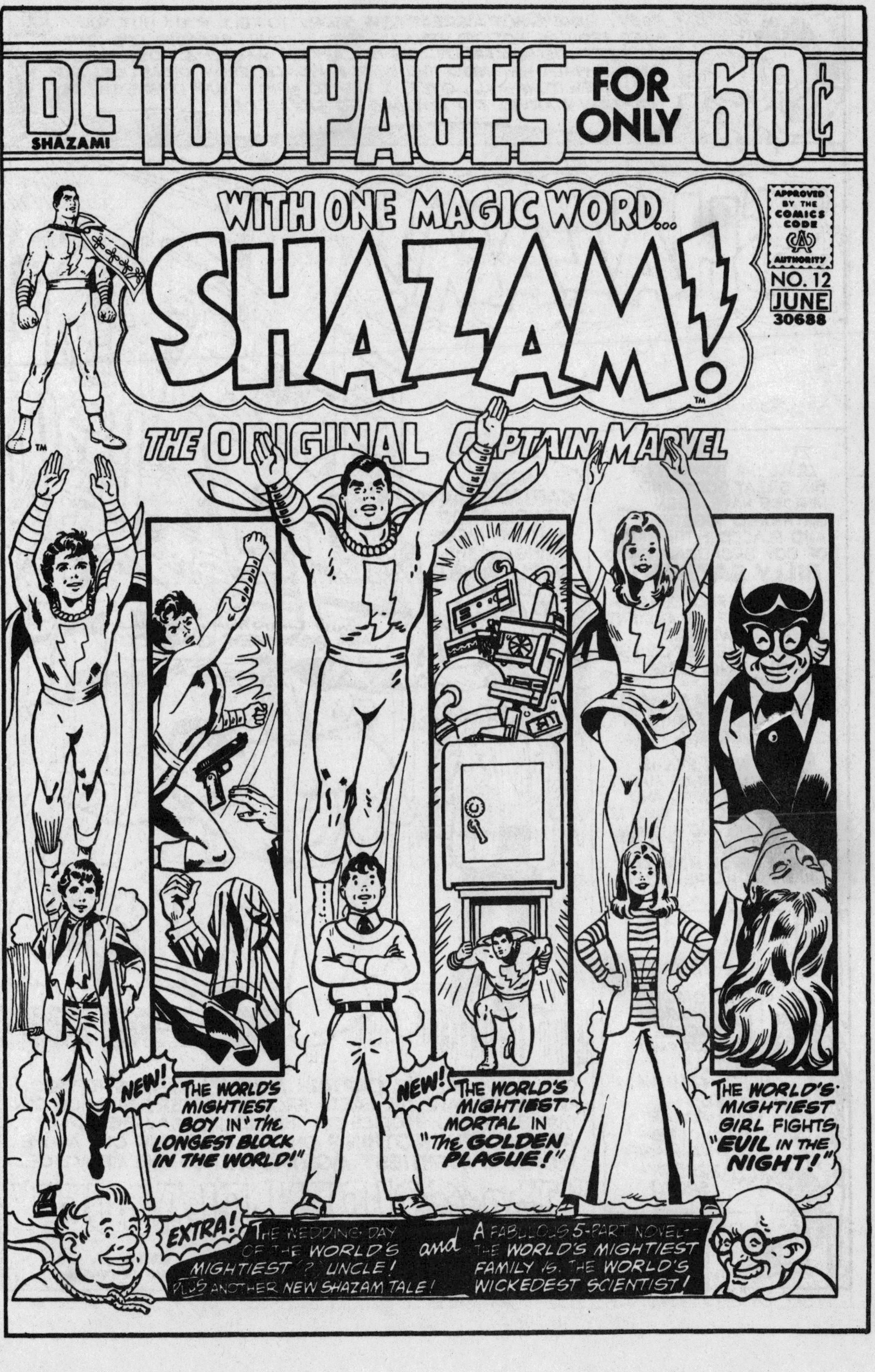
DC
SHAZAM!
100 PAGES FOR ONLY 60¢
WITH ONE MAGIC WORD...
SHAZAM!
APPROVED BY THE COMICS CODE AUTHORITY
NO. 12
JUNE
30688
THE ORIGINAL CAPTAIN MARVEL
NEW!
THE WORLD'S MIGHTIEST BOY IN "THE LONGEST BLOCK IN THE WORLD!"
NEW!
THE WORLD'S MIGHTIEST MORTAL IN "THE GOLDEN PLAGUE!"
THE WORLD'S MIGHTIEST GIRL FIGHTS "EVIL IN THE NIGHT!"
EXTRA!
THE WEDDING DAY OF THE WORLD'S MIGHTIEST (?) UNCLE! PLUS ANOTHER NEW SHAZAM TALE!
and
A FABULOUS 5-PART NOVEL -- THE WORLD'S MIGHTIEST FAMILY VS. THE WORLD'S WICKEDEST SCIENTIST!

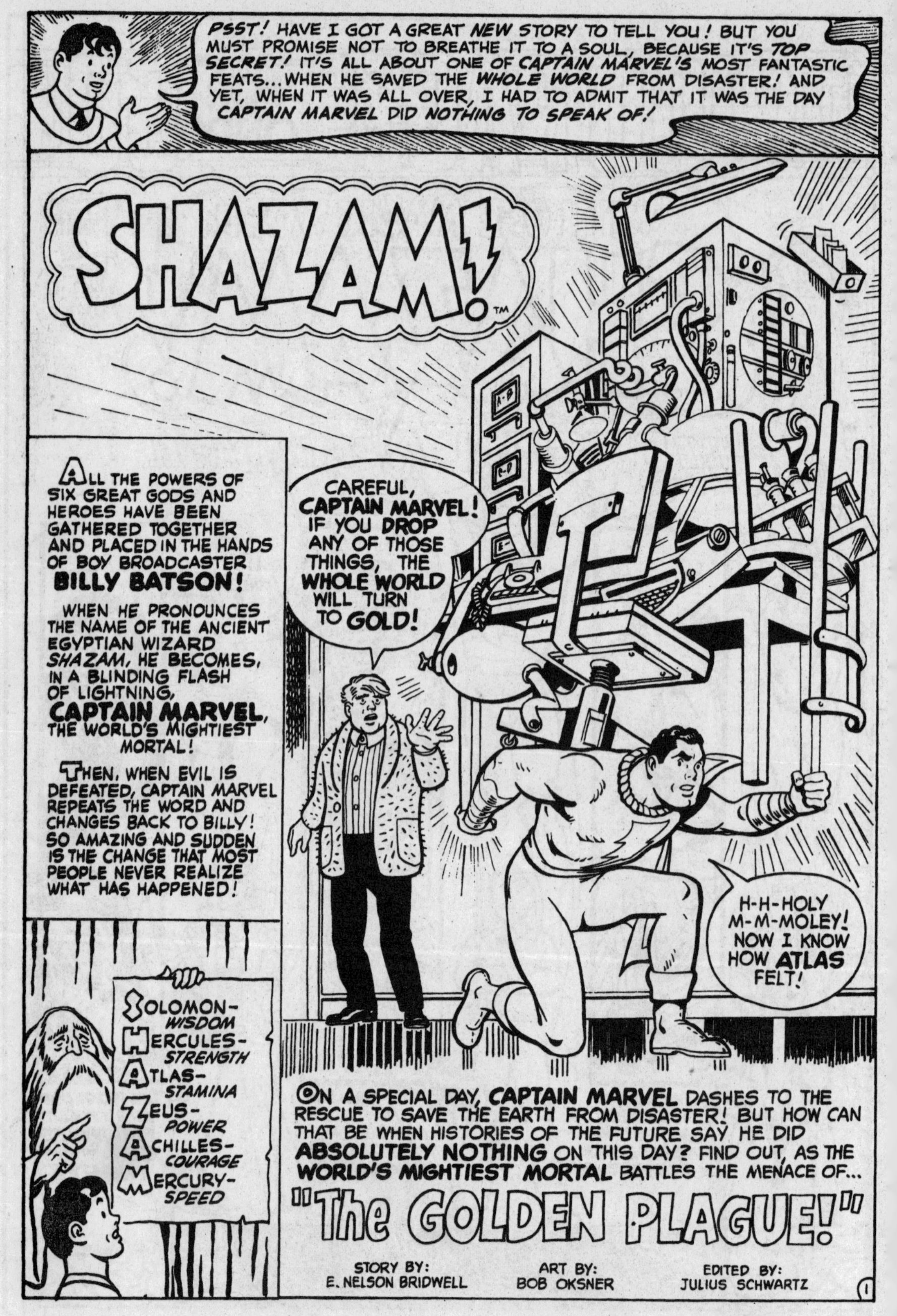

PSST! HAVE I GOT A GREAT NEW STORY TO TELL YOU! BUT YOU MUST PROMISE NOT TO BREATHE IT TO A SOUL, BECAUSE IT'S TOP SECRET! IT'S ALL ABOUT ONE OF CAPTAIN MARVEL'S MOST FANTASTIC FEATS...WHEN HE SAVED THE WHOLE WORLD FROM DISASTER! AND YET, WHEN IT WAS ALL OVER, I HAD TO ADMIT THAT IT WAS THE DAY CAPTAIN MARVEL DID NOTHING TO SPEAK OF!
SHAZAM!™
ALL THE POWERS OF SIX GREAT GODS AND HEROES HAVE BEEN GATHERED TOGETHER AND PLACED IN THE HANDS OF BOY BROADCASTER BILLY BATSON!
WHEN HE PRONOUNCES THE NAME OF THE ANCIENT EGYPTIAN WIZARD SHAZAM, HE BECOMES, IN A BLINDING FLASH OF LIGHTNING, CAPTAIN MARVEL, THE WORLD'S MIGHTIEST MORTAL!
THEN, WHEN EVIL IS DEFEATED, CAPTAIN MARVEL REPEATS THE WORD AND CHANGES BACK TO BILLY! SO AMAZING AND SUDDEN IS THE CHANGE THAT MOST PEOPLE NEVER REALIZE WHAT HAS HAPPENED!
SOLOMON- WISDOM
HERCULES- STRENGTH
ATLAS- STAMINA
ZEUS- POWER
ACHILLES- COURAGE
MERCURY- SPEED
CAREFUL, CAPTAIN MARVEL! IF YOU DROP ANY OF THOSE THINGS, THE WHOLE WORLD WILL TURN TO GOLD!
H-H-HOLY M-M-MOLEY! NOW I KNOW HOW ATLAS FELT!
ON A SPECIAL DAY, CAPTAIN MARVEL DASHES TO THE RESCUE TO SAVE THE EARTH FROM DISASTER! BUT HOW CAN THAT BE WHEN HISTORIES OF THE FUTURE SAY HE DID ABSOLUTELY NOTHING ON THIS DAY? FIND OUT, AS THE WORLD'S MIGHTIEST MORTAL BATTLES THE MENACE OF...
"The GOLDEN PLAGUE!"
STORY BY: E. NELSON BRIDWELL
ART BY: BOB OKSNER
EDITED BY: JULIUS SCHWARTZ
1

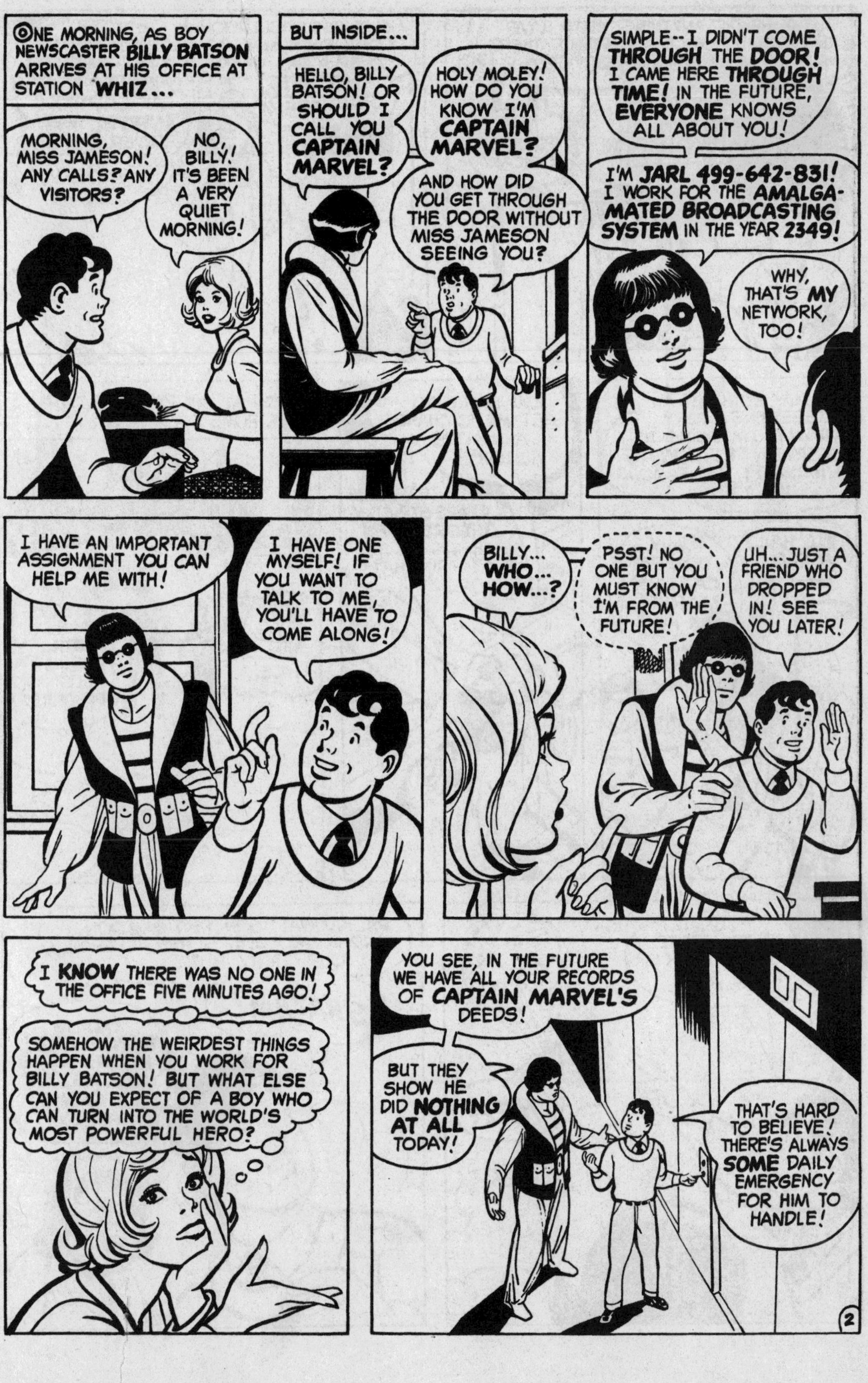

ONE MORNING, AS BOY NEWSCASTER BILLY BATSON ARRIVES AT HIS OFFICE AT STATION WHIZ...
MORNING, MISS JAMESON! ANY CALLS? ANY VISITORS?
NO, BILLY! IT'S BEEN A VERY QUIET MORNING!
BUT INSIDE...
HELLO, BILLY BATSON! OR SHOULD I CALL YOU CAPTAIN MARVEL?
HOLY MOLEY! HOW DO YOU KNOW I'M CAPTAIN MARVEL?
AND HOW DID YOU GET THROUGH THE DOOR WITHOUT MISS JAMESON SEEING YOU?
SIMPLE--I DIDN'T COME THROUGH THE DOOR! I CAME HERE THROUGH TIME! IN THE FUTURE, EVERYONE KNOWS ALL ABOUT YOU!
I'M JARL 499-642-831! I WORK FOR THE AMALGAMATED BROADCASTING SYSTEM IN THE YEAR 2349!
WHY, THAT'S MY NETWORK, TOO!
I HAVE AN IMPORTANT ASSIGNMENT YOU CAN HELP ME WITH!
I HAVE ONE MYSELF! IF YOU WANT TO TALK TO ME, YOU'LL HAVE TO COME ALONG!
BILLY... WHO... HOW...?
PSST! NO ONE BUT YOU MUST KNOW I'M FROM THE FUTURE!
UH... JUST A FRIEND WHO DROPPED IN! SEE YOU LATER!
I KNOW THERE WAS NO ONE IN THE OFFICE FIVE MINUTES AGO!
SOMEHOW THE WEIRDEST THINGS HAPPEN WHEN YOU WORK FOR BILLY BATSON! BUT WHAT ELSE CAN YOU EXPECT OF A BOY WHO CAN TURN INTO THE WORLD'S MOST POWERFUL HERO?
YOU SEE, IN THE FUTURE WE HAVE ALL YOUR RECORDS OF CAPTAIN MARVEL'S DEEDS!
BUT THEY SHOW HE DID NOTHING AT ALL TODAY!
THAT'S HARD TO BELIEVE! THERE'S ALWAYS SOME DAILY EMERGENCY FOR HIM TO HANDLE!
2

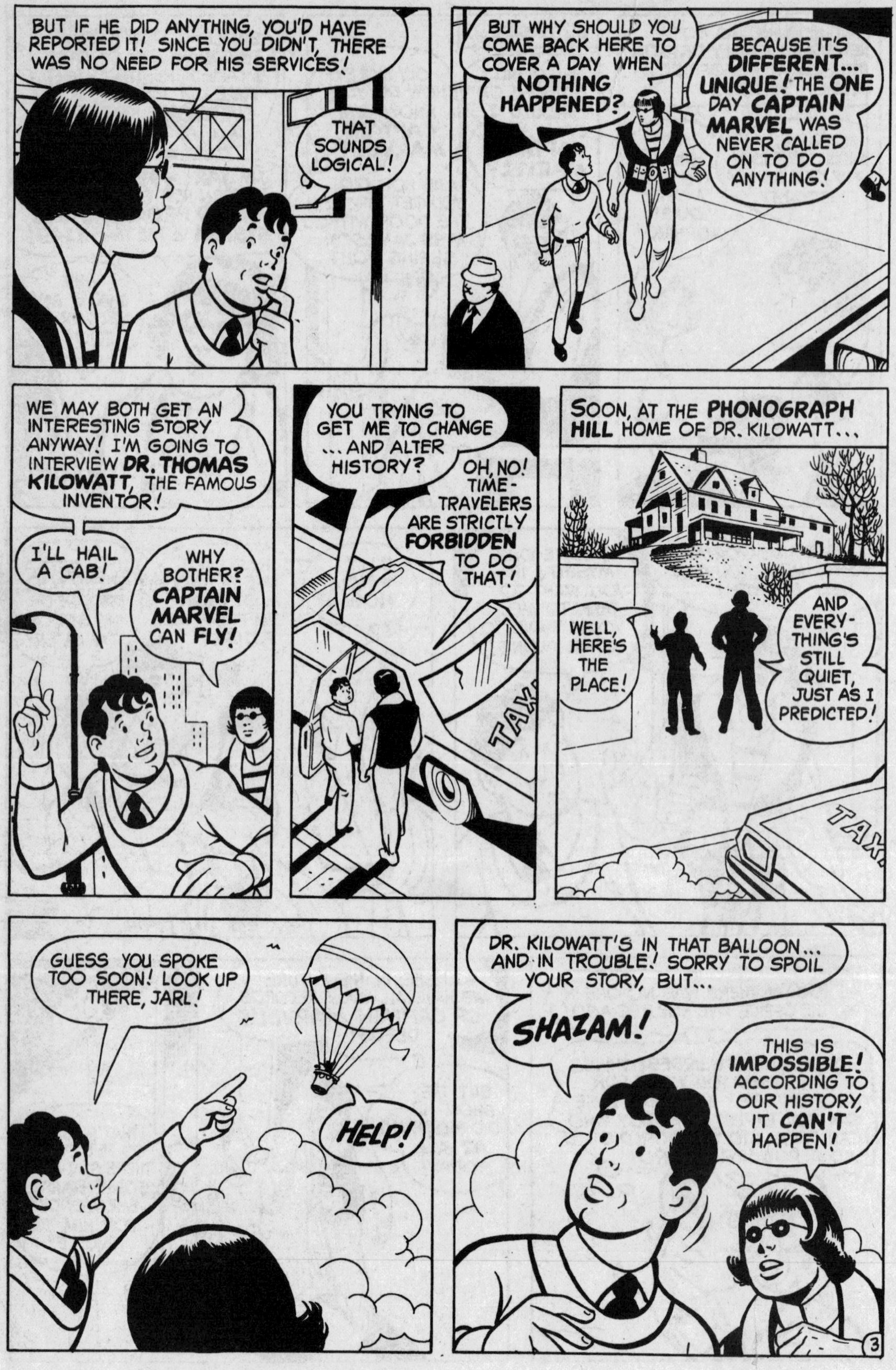
BUT IF HE DID ANYTHING, YOU'D HAVE REPORTED IT! SINCE YOU DIDN'T, THERE WAS NO NEED FOR HIS SERVICES!
THAT SOUNDS LOGICAL!
BUT WHY SHOULD YOU COME BACK HERE TO COVER A DAY WHEN NOTHING HAPPENED?
BECAUSE IT'S DIFFERENT... UNIQUE! THE ONE DAY CAPTAIN MARVEL WAS NEVER CALLED ON TO DO ANYTHING!
WE MAY BOTH GET AN INTERESTING STORY ANYWAY! I'M GOING TO INTERVIEW DR. THOMAS KILOWATT, THE FAMOUS INVENTOR!
I'LL HAIL A CAB!
WHY BOTHER? CAPTAIN MARVEL CAN FLY!
YOU TRYING TO GET ME TO CHANGE ... AND ALTER HISTORY?
OH, NO! TIME-TRAVELERS ARE STRICTLY FORBIDDEN TO DO THAT!
TAXI
SOON, AT THE PHONOGRAPH HILL HOME OF DR. KILOWATT...
WELL, HERE'S THE PLACE!
AND EVERYTHING'S STILL QUIET, JUST AS I PREDICTED!
TAXI
GUESS YOU SPOKE TOO SOON! LOOK UP THERE, JARL!
HELP!
DR. KILOWATT'S IN THAT BALLOON... AND IN TROUBLE! SORRY TO SPOIL YOUR STORY, BUT...
SHAZAM!
THIS IS IMPOSSIBLE! ACCORDING TO OUR HISTORY, IT CAN'T HAPPEN!
3

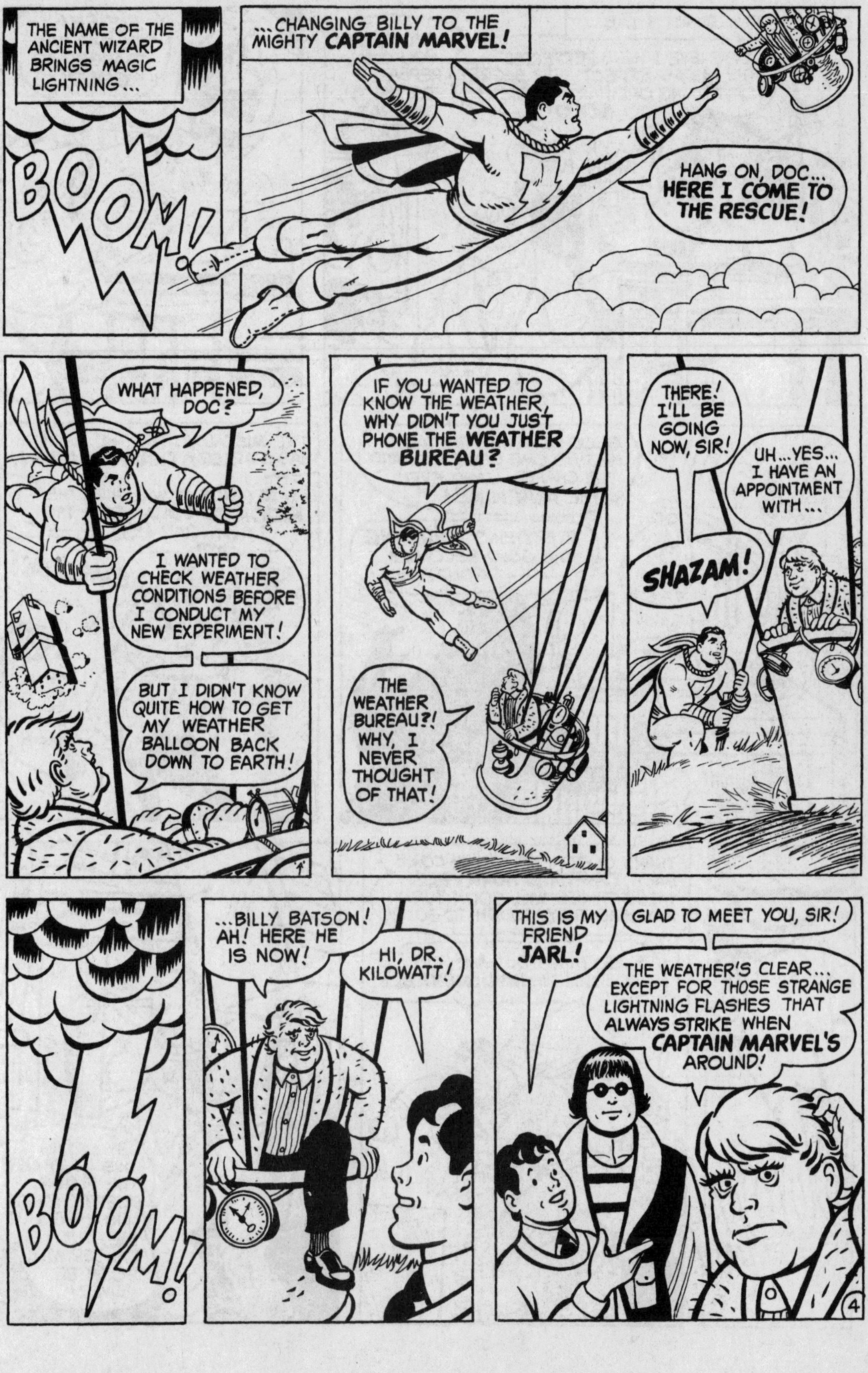
THE NAME OF THE ANCIENT WIZARD BRINGS MAGIC LIGHTNING...
BOOM!
...CHANGING BILLY TO THE MIGHTY **CAPTAIN MARVEL!**
HANG ON, DOC... **HERE I COME TO THE RESCUE!**
WHAT HAPPENED, DOC?
I WANTED TO CHECK WEATHER CONDITIONS BEFORE I CONDUCT MY NEW EXPERIMENT!
BUT I DIDN'T KNOW QUITE HOW TO GET MY WEATHER BALLOON BACK DOWN TO EARTH!
IF YOU WANTED TO KNOW THE WEATHER, WHY DIDN'T YOU JUST PHONE THE **WEATHER BUREAU?**
THE WEATHER BUREAU?! WHY, I NEVER THOUGHT OF THAT!
THERE! I'LL BE GOING NOW, SIR!
UH...YES... I HAVE AN APPOINTMENT WITH...
SHAZAM!
BOOM!
...BILLY BATSON! AH! HERE HE IS NOW!
HI, DR. KILOWATT!
THIS IS MY FRIEND **JARL!**
GLAD TO MEET YOU, SIR!
THE WEATHER'S CLEAR... EXCEPT FOR THOSE STRANGE LIGHTNING FLASHES THAT ALWAYS STRIKE WHEN **CAPTAIN MARVEL'S** AROUND!
4

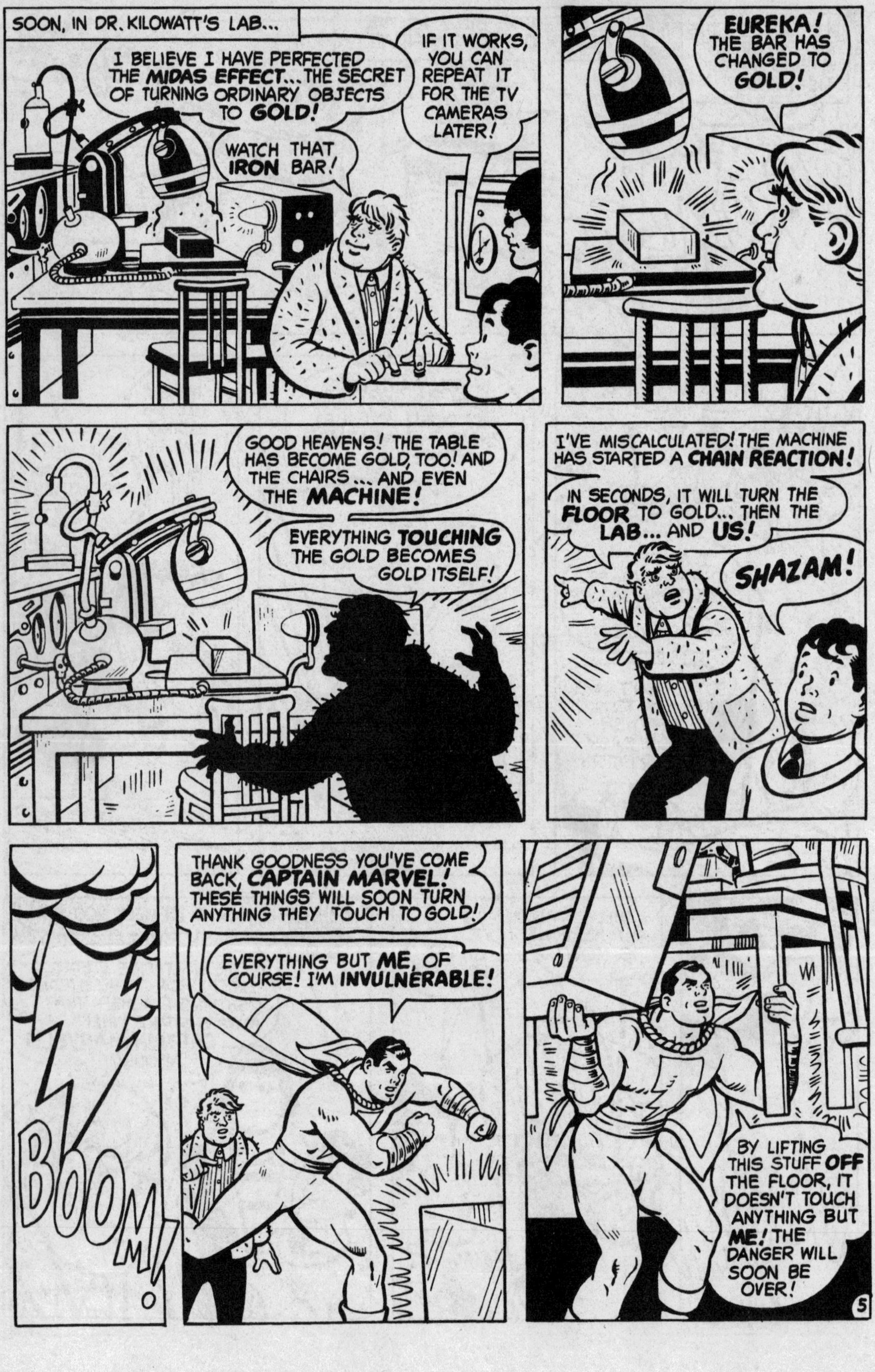

SOON, IN DR. KILOWATT'S LAB...
I BELIEVE I HAVE PERFECTED THE MIDAS EFFECT... THE SECRET OF TURNING ORDINARY OBJECTS TO GOLD!
IF IT WORKS, YOU CAN REPEAT IT FOR THE TV CAMERAS LATER!
WATCH THAT IRON BAR!
EUREKA! THE BAR HAS CHANGED TO GOLD!
GOOD HEAVENS! THE TABLE HAS BECOME GOLD, TOO! AND THE CHAIRS... AND EVEN THE MACHINE!
EVERYTHING TOUCHING THE GOLD BECOMES GOLD ITSELF!
I'VE MISCALCULATED! THE MACHINE HAS STARTED A CHAIN REACTION!
IN SECONDS, IT WILL TURN THE FLOOR TO GOLD... THEN THE LAB... AND US!
SHAZAM!
BOOM!
THANK GOODNESS YOU'VE COME BACK, CAPTAIN MARVEL! THESE THINGS WILL SOON TURN ANYTHING THEY TOUCH TO GOLD!
EVERYTHING BUT ME, OF COURSE! I'M INVULNERABLE!
BY LIFTING THIS STUFF OFF THE FLOOR, IT DOESN'T TOUCH ANYTHING BUT ME! THE DANGER WILL SOON BE OVER!
5

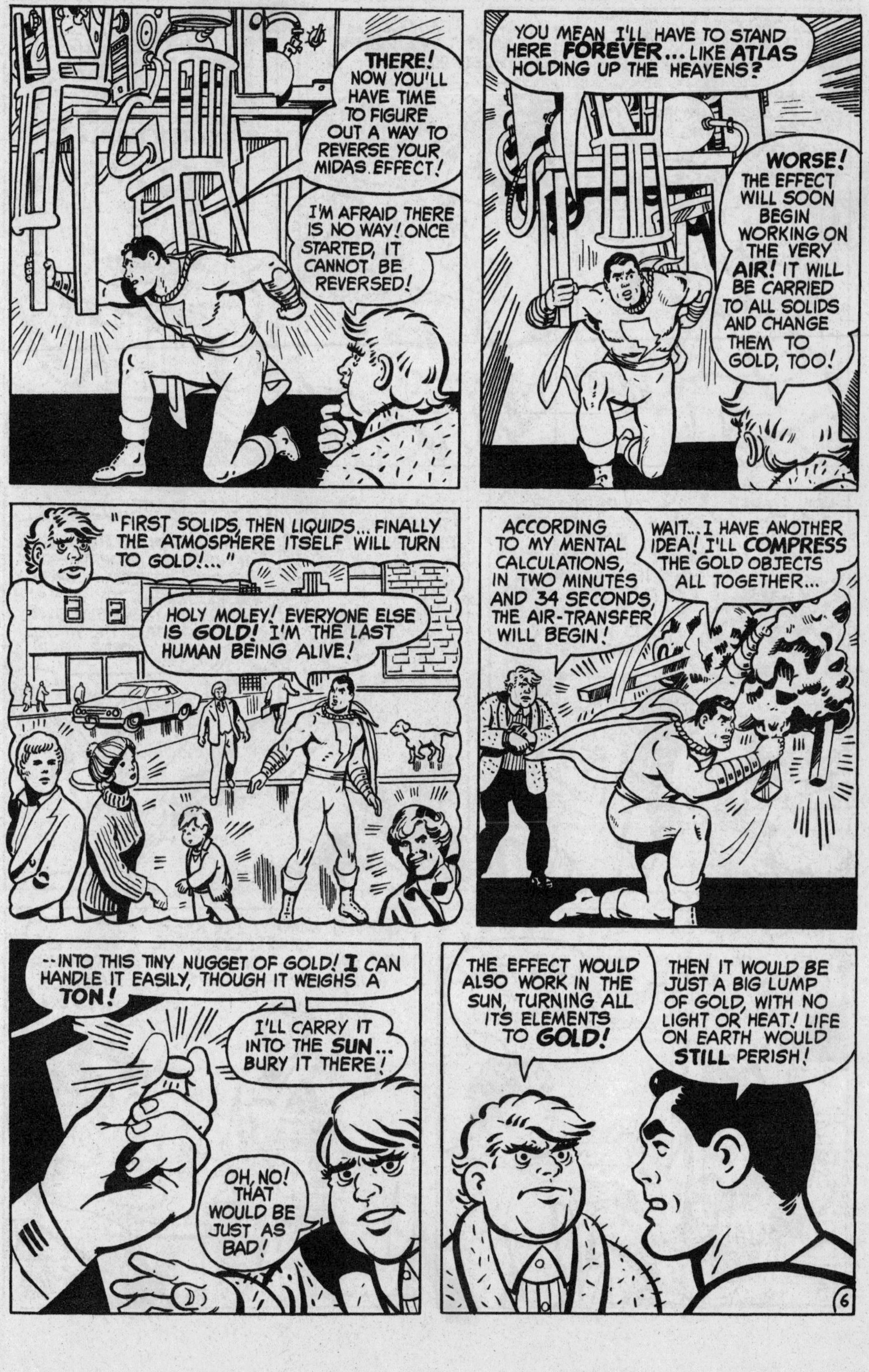
THERE! NOW YOU'LL HAVE TIME TO FIGURE OUT A WAY TO REVERSE YOUR MIDAS EFFECT!
I'M AFRAID THERE IS NO WAY! ONCE STARTED, IT CANNOT BE REVERSED!
YOU MEAN I'LL HAVE TO STAND HERE FOREVER... LIKE ATLAS HOLDING UP THE HEAVENS?
WORSE! THE EFFECT WILL SOON BEGIN WORKING ON THE VERY AIR! IT WILL BE CARRIED TO ALL SOLIDS AND CHANGE THEM TO GOLD, TOO!
"FIRST SOLIDS, THEN LIQUIDS... FINALLY THE ATMOSPHERE ITSELF WILL TURN TO GOLD!..."
HOLY MOLEY! EVERYONE ELSE IS GOLD! I'M THE LAST HUMAN BEING ALIVE!
ACCORDING TO MY MENTAL CALCULATIONS, IN TWO MINUTES AND 34 SECONDS, THE AIR-TRANSFER WILL BEGIN!
WAIT... I HAVE ANOTHER IDEA! I'LL COMPRESS THE GOLD OBJECTS ALL TOGETHER...
--INTO THIS TINY NUGGET OF GOLD! I CAN HANDLE IT EASILY, THOUGH IT WEIGHS A TON!
I'LL CARRY IT INTO THE SUN... BURY IT THERE!
OH, NO! THAT WOULD BE JUST AS BAD!
THE EFFECT WOULD ALSO WORK IN THE SUN, TURNING ALL ITS ELEMENTS TO GOLD!
THEN IT WOULD BE JUST A BIG LUMP OF GOLD, WITH NO LIGHT OR HEAT! LIFE ON EARTH WOULD STILL PERISH!
6

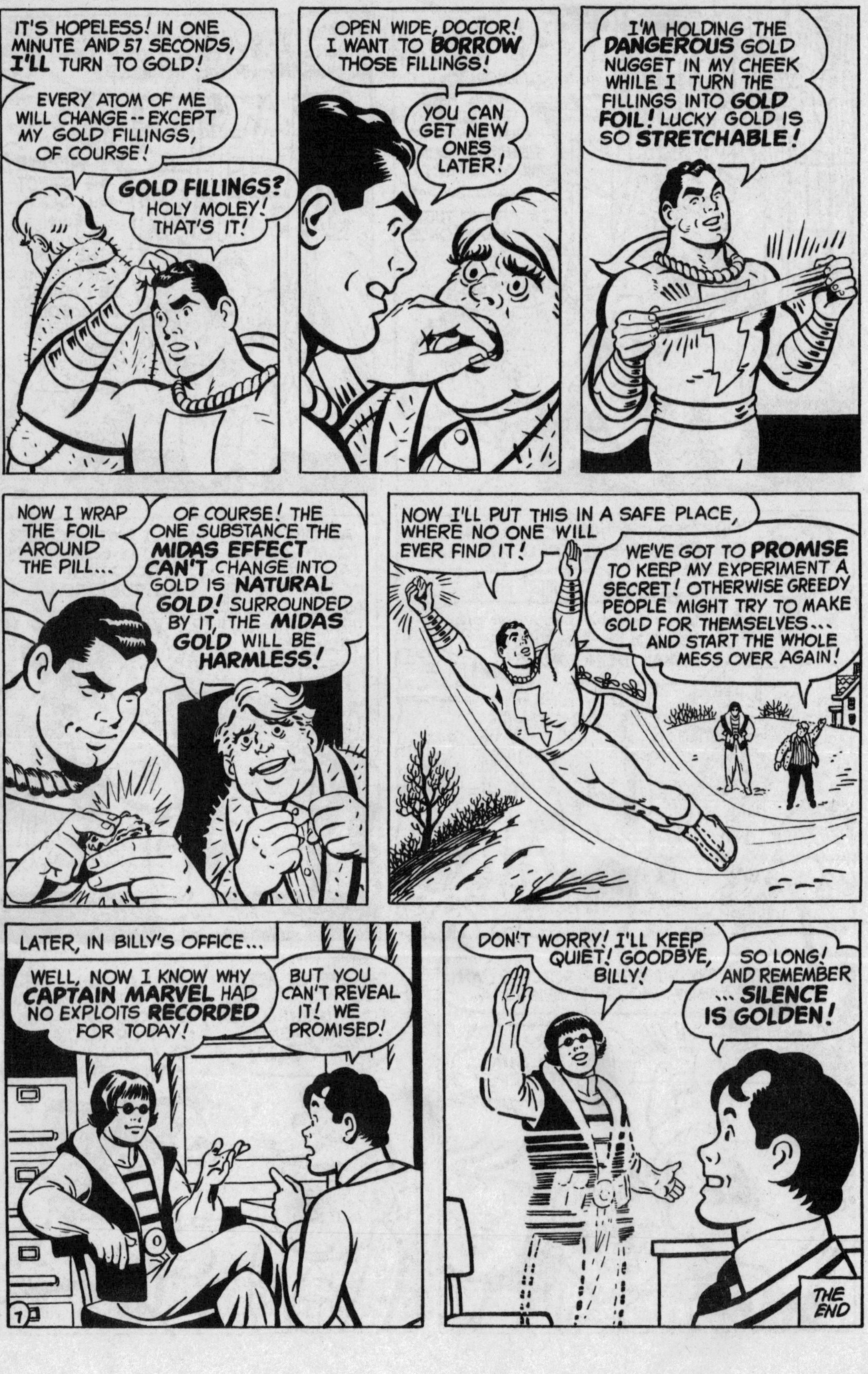
IT'S HOPELESS! IN ONE MINUTE AND 57 SECONDS, I'LL TURN TO GOLD!
EVERY ATOM OF ME WILL CHANGE -- EXCEPT MY GOLD FILLINGS, OF COURSE!
GOLD FILLINGS? HOLY MOLEY! THAT'S IT!
OPEN WIDE, DOCTOR! I WANT TO BORROW THOSE FILLINGS!
YOU CAN GET NEW ONES LATER!
I'M HOLDING THE DANGEROUS GOLD NUGGET IN MY CHEEK WHILE I TURN THE FILLINGS INTO GOLD FOIL! LUCKY GOLD IS SO STRETCHABLE!
NOW I WRAP THE FOIL AROUND THE PILL...
OF COURSE! THE ONE SUBSTANCE THE MIDAS EFFECT CAN'T CHANGE INTO GOLD IS NATURAL GOLD! SURROUNDED BY IT, THE MIDAS GOLD WILL BE HARMLESS!
NOW I'LL PUT THIS IN A SAFE PLACE, WHERE NO ONE WILL EVER FIND IT!
WE'VE GOT TO PROMISE TO KEEP MY EXPERIMENT A SECRET! OTHERWISE GREEDY PEOPLE MIGHT TRY TO MAKE GOLD FOR THEMSELVES... AND START THE WHOLE MESS OVER AGAIN!
LATER, IN BILLY'S OFFICE...
WELL, NOW I KNOW WHY CAPTAIN MARVEL HAD NO EXPLOITS RECORDED FOR TODAY!
BUT YOU CAN'T REVEAL IT! WE PROMISED!
7
DON'T WORRY! I'LL KEEP QUIET! GOODBYE, BILLY!
SO LONG! AND REMEMBER ... SILENCE IS GOLDEN!
THE END

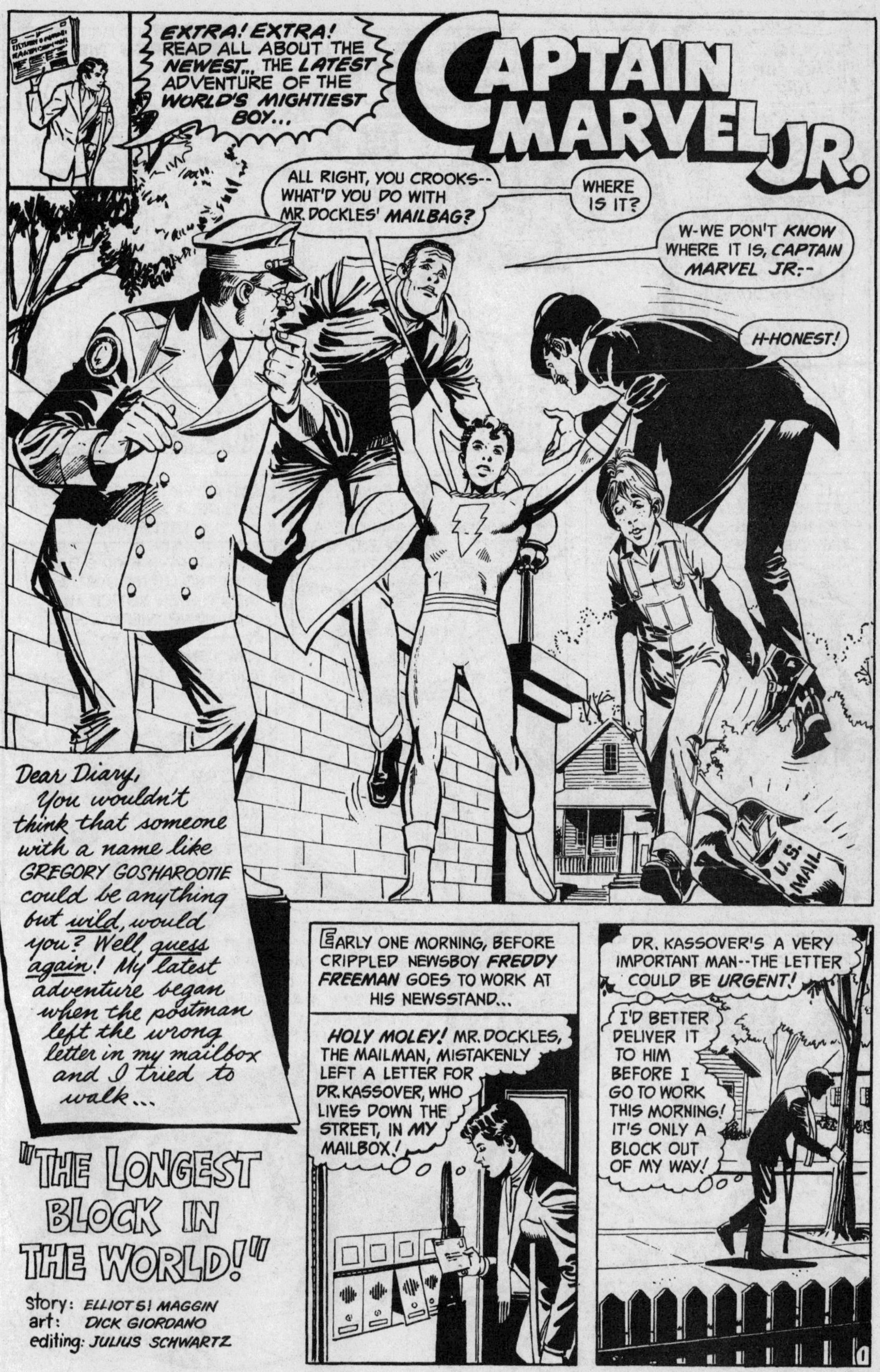
EXTRA! EXTRA! READ ALL ABOUT THE NEWEST... THE LATEST ADVENTURE OF THE WORLD'S MIGHTIEST BOY...
CAPTAIN MARVEL JR.
ALL RIGHT, YOU CROOKS-- WHAT'D YOU DO WITH MR. DOCKLES' MAILBAG?
WHERE IS IT?
W-WE DON'T KNOW WHERE IT IS, CAPTAIN MARVEL JR.--
H-HONEST!
U.S. MAIL
Dear Diary, You wouldn't think that someone with a name like GREGORY GOSHAROOTIE could be anything but wild, would you? Well, guess again! My latest adventure began when the postman left the wrong letter in my mailbox and I tried to walk...
"THE LONGEST BLOCK IN THE WORLD!"
story: ELLIOT S! MAGGIN
art: DICK GIORDANO
editing: JULIUS SCHWARTZ
EARLY ONE MORNING, BEFORE CRIPPLED NEWSBOY FREDDY FREEMAN GOES TO WORK AT HIS NEWSSTAND...
HOLY MOLEY! MR. DOCKLES, THE MAILMAN, MISTAKENLY LEFT A LETTER FOR DR. KASSOVER, WHO LIVES DOWN THE STREET, IN MY MAILBOX!
DR. KASSOVER'S A VERY IMPORTANT MAN--THE LETTER COULD BE URGENT!
I'D BETTER DELIVER IT TO HIM BEFORE I GO TO WORK THIS MORNING! IT'S ONLY A BLOCK OUT OF MY WAY!
1

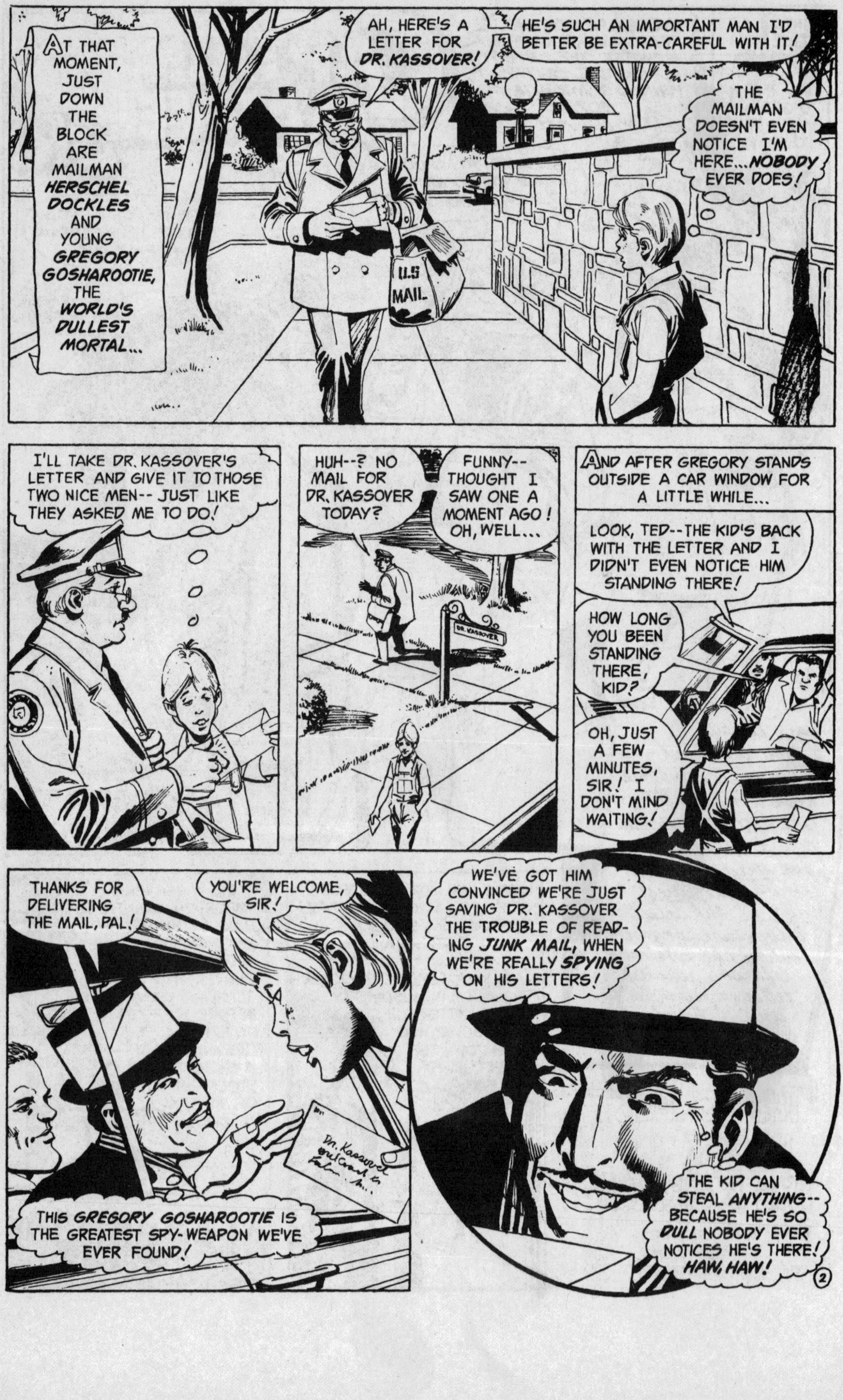
AT THAT MOMENT, JUST DOWN THE BLOCK ARE MAILMAN HERSCHEL DOCKLES AND YOUNG GREGORY GOSHAROOTIE, THE WORLD'S DULLEST MORTAL...
AH, HERE'S A LETTER FOR DR. KASSOVER!
HE'S SUCH AN IMPORTANT MAN I'D BETTER BE EXTRA-CAREFUL WITH IT!
THE MAILMAN DOESN'T EVEN NOTICE I'M HERE...NOBODY EVER DOES!
U.S MAIL
I'LL TAKE DR. KASSOVER'S LETTER AND GIVE IT TO THOSE TWO NICE MEN-- JUST LIKE THEY ASKED ME TO DO!
HUH--? NO MAIL FOR DR. KASSOVER TODAY?
FUNNY-- THOUGHT I SAW ONE A MOMENT AGO! OH, WELL...
DR. KASSOVER
AND AFTER GREGORY STANDS OUTSIDE A CAR WINDOW FOR A LITTLE WHILE...
LOOK, TED--THE KID'S BACK WITH THE LETTER AND I DIDN'T EVEN NOTICE HIM STANDING THERE!
HOW LONG YOU BEEN STANDING THERE, KID?
OH, JUST A FEW MINUTES, SIR! I DON'T MIND WAITING!
THANKS FOR DELIVERING THE MAIL, PAL!
YOU'RE WELCOME, SIR!
THIS GREGORY GOSHAROOTIE IS THE GREATEST SPY-WEAPON WE'VE EVER FOUND!
WE'VE GOT HIM CONVINCED WE'RE JUST SAVING DR. KASSOVER THE TROUBLE OF READING JUNK MAIL, WHEN WE'RE REALLY SPYING ON HIS LETTERS!
THE KID CAN STEAL ANYTHING-- BECAUSE HE'S SO DULL NOBODY EVER NOTICES HE'S THERE! HAW, HAW!
2

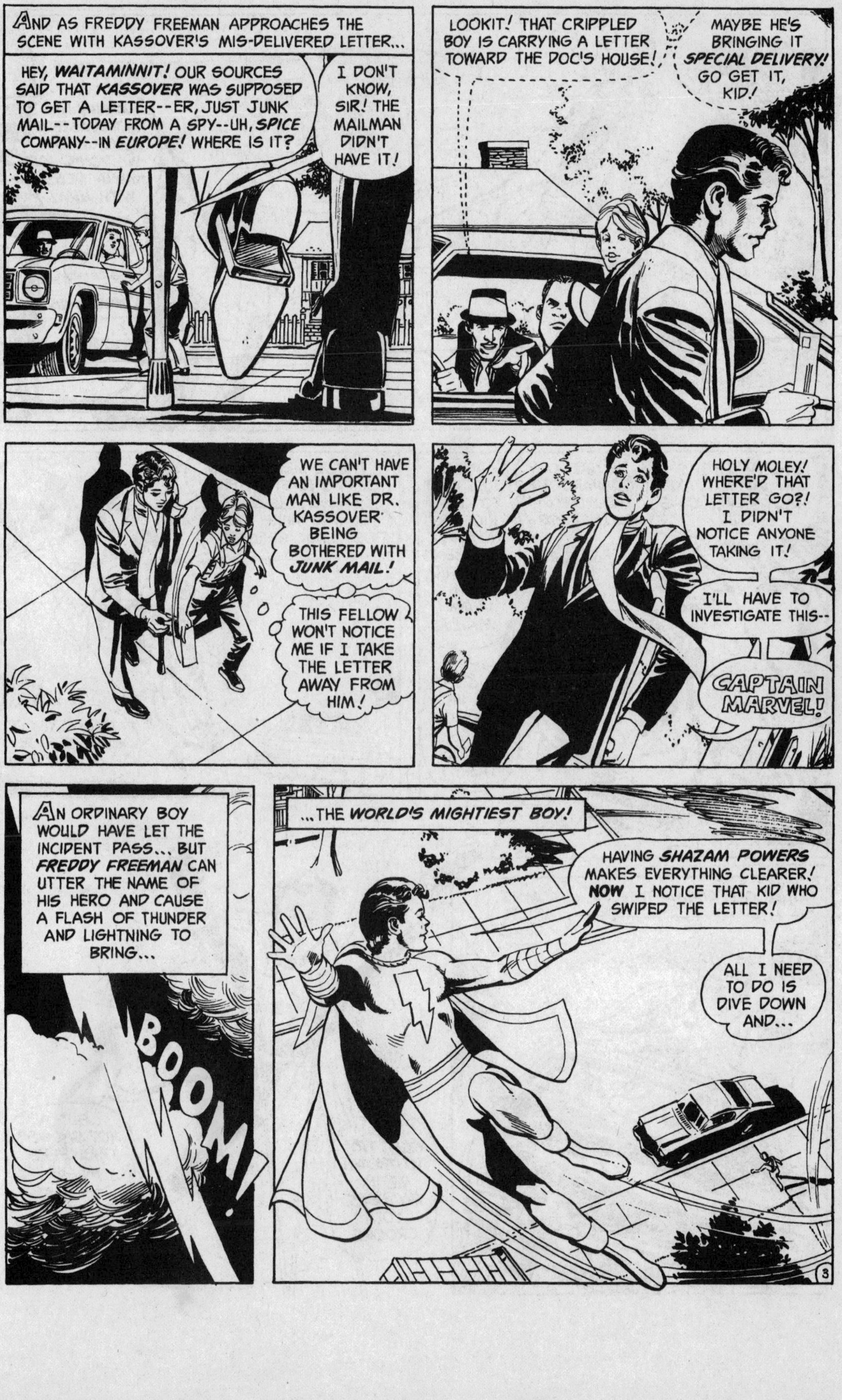
AND AS FREDDY FREEMAN APPROACHES THE SCENE WITH KASSOVER'S MIS-DELIVERED LETTER...
HEY, WAITAMINNIT! OUR SOURCES SAID THAT KASSOVER WAS SUPPOSED TO GET A LETTER--ER, JUST JUNK MAIL--TODAY FROM A SPY--UH, SPICE COMPANY--IN EUROPE! WHERE IS IT?
I DON'T KNOW, SIR! THE MAILMAN DIDN'T HAVE IT!
LOOKIT! THAT CRIPPLED BOY IS CARRYING A LETTER TOWARD THE DOC'S HOUSE!
MAYBE HE'S BRINGING IT SPECIAL DELIVERY! GO GET IT, KID!
WE CAN'T HAVE AN IMPORTANT MAN LIKE DR. KASSOVER BEING BOTHERED WITH JUNK MAIL!
THIS FELLOW WON'T NOTICE ME IF I TAKE THE LETTER AWAY FROM HIM!
HOLY MOLEY! WHERE'D THAT LETTER GO?! I DIDN'T NOTICE ANYONE TAKING IT!
I'LL HAVE TO INVESTIGATE THIS--
CAPTAIN MARVEL!
AN ORDINARY BOY WOULD HAVE LET THE INCIDENT PASS... BUT FREDDY FREEMAN CAN UTTER THE NAME OF HIS HERO AND CAUSE A FLASH OF THUNDER AND LIGHTNING TO BRING...
BOOM!
...THE WORLD'S MIGHTIEST BOY!
HAVING SHAZAM POWERS MAKES EVERYTHING CLEARER! NOW I NOTICE THAT KID WHO SWIPED THE LETTER!
ALL I NEED TO DO IS DIVE DOWN AND...
3

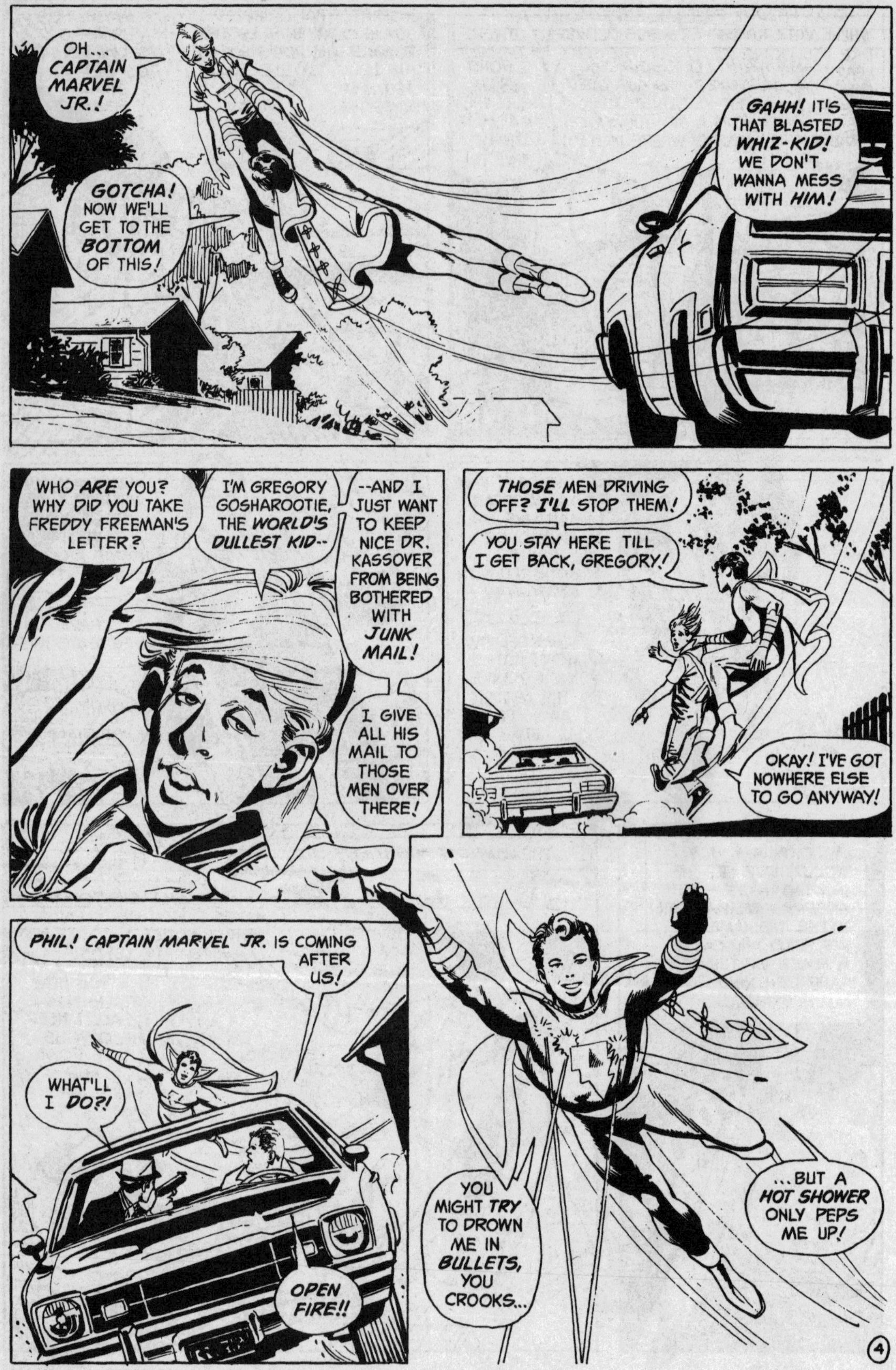
OH... CAPTAIN MARVEL JR.!
GOTCHA! NOW WE'LL GET TO THE BOTTOM OF THIS!
GAHH! IT'S THAT BLASTED WHIZ-KID! WE DON'T WANNA MESS WITH HIM!
WHO ARE YOU? WHY DID YOU TAKE FREDDY FREEMAN'S LETTER?
I'M GREGORY GOSHAROOTIE, THE WORLD'S DULLEST KID--
--AND I JUST WANT TO KEEP NICE DR. KASSOVER FROM BEING BOTHERED WITH JUNK MAIL!
I GIVE ALL HIS MAIL TO THOSE MEN OVER THERE!
THOSE MEN DRIVING OFF? I'LL STOP THEM!
YOU STAY HERE TILL I GET BACK, GREGORY!
OKAY! I'VE GOT NOWHERE ELSE TO GO ANYWAY!
PHIL! CAPTAIN MARVEL JR. IS COMING AFTER US!
WHAT'LL I DO?!
OPEN FIRE!!
YOU MIGHT TRY TO DROWN ME IN BULLETS, YOU CROOKS...
...BUT A HOT SHOWER ONLY PEPS ME UP!
4

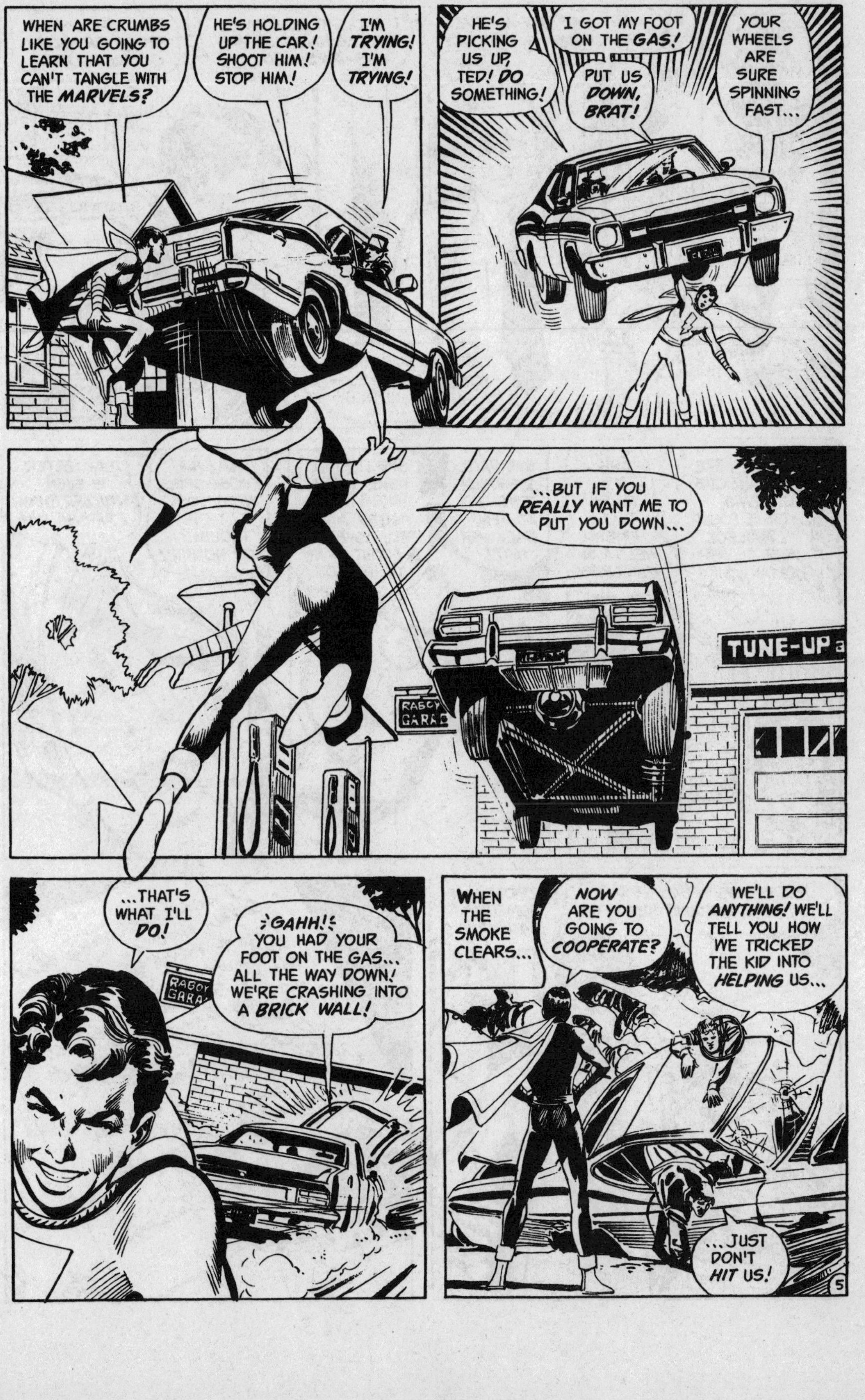
WHEN ARE CRUMBS LIKE YOU GOING TO LEARN THAT YOU CAN'T TANGLE WITH THE MARVELS?
HE'S HOLDING UP THE CAR! SHOOT HIM! STOP HIM!
I'M TRYING! I'M TRYING!
HE'S PICKING US UP, TED! DO SOMETHING!
I GOT MY FOOT ON THE GAS!
PUT US DOWN, BRAT!
YOUR WHEELS ARE SURE SPINNING FAST...
...BUT IF YOU REALLY WANT ME TO PUT YOU DOWN...
TUNE-UP
RABOY GARA
...THAT'S WHAT I'LL DO!
GAHH! YOU HAD YOUR FOOT ON THE GAS... ALL THE WAY DOWN! WE'RE CRASHING INTO A BRICK WALL!
RABOY GARA
WHEN THE SMOKE CLEARS...
NOW ARE YOU GOING TO COOPERATE?
WE'LL DO ANYTHING! WE'LL TELL YOU HOW WE TRICKED THE KID INTO HELPING US...
...JUST DON'T HIT US!
5

AND WHEN *GREGORY* AND *CAPTAIN MARVEL JR.* FINALLY REACH *DR. KASSOVER'S* HOUSE AT THE END OF THE BLOCK...

ACH! CAPTAIN MARVEL JR. ... COME IN, MEIN BOY!

I BROUGHT YOUR MAIL, DR. KASSOVER... IT WAS *MIS-DIRECTED!*

OHH... THIS IS MY FRIEND *GREGORY GOSHAROOTIE!*

THERE IS SOMEBODY MIT YOU?-- OHH, YES-- I DIDN'T NOTICE!

TWO SPIES WERE MIGHTY ANXIOUS TO GET *THIS* LETTER I FOUND IN MY MAILBOX! IT MUST BE VERY IMPORTANT, SIR!

AHH! IT'S FROM MY FRIEND *HELGA* IN *HEIDELBERG!*

SHE SAYS I SHOULD REMEMBER TO SEND BACK HER *HAT!*

SHE LEFT IT HERE WHEN SHE LAST VISITED AND FELL ASLEEP IN FRONT OF MY TELEVISION!

HA! HA! THOSE SPIES WENT TO A LOT OF TROUBLE FOR NOTHIN'!

THAT LETTER IS EVEN *DULLER* THAN I AM! HA, HA!

JUNIOR, MEIN BOY-- DID YOU HEAR A SOUND JUST DEN?

ALMOST LIKE SOMEBOY *LAUGHING!*

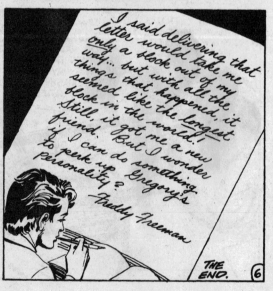

I said delivering that letter would take me only a block out of my way... but with all the things that happened, it seemed like the longest block in the world! Still, it got me a new friend. But I wonder if I can do something to perk up Gregory's personality?

Freddy Freeman

THE END. 6

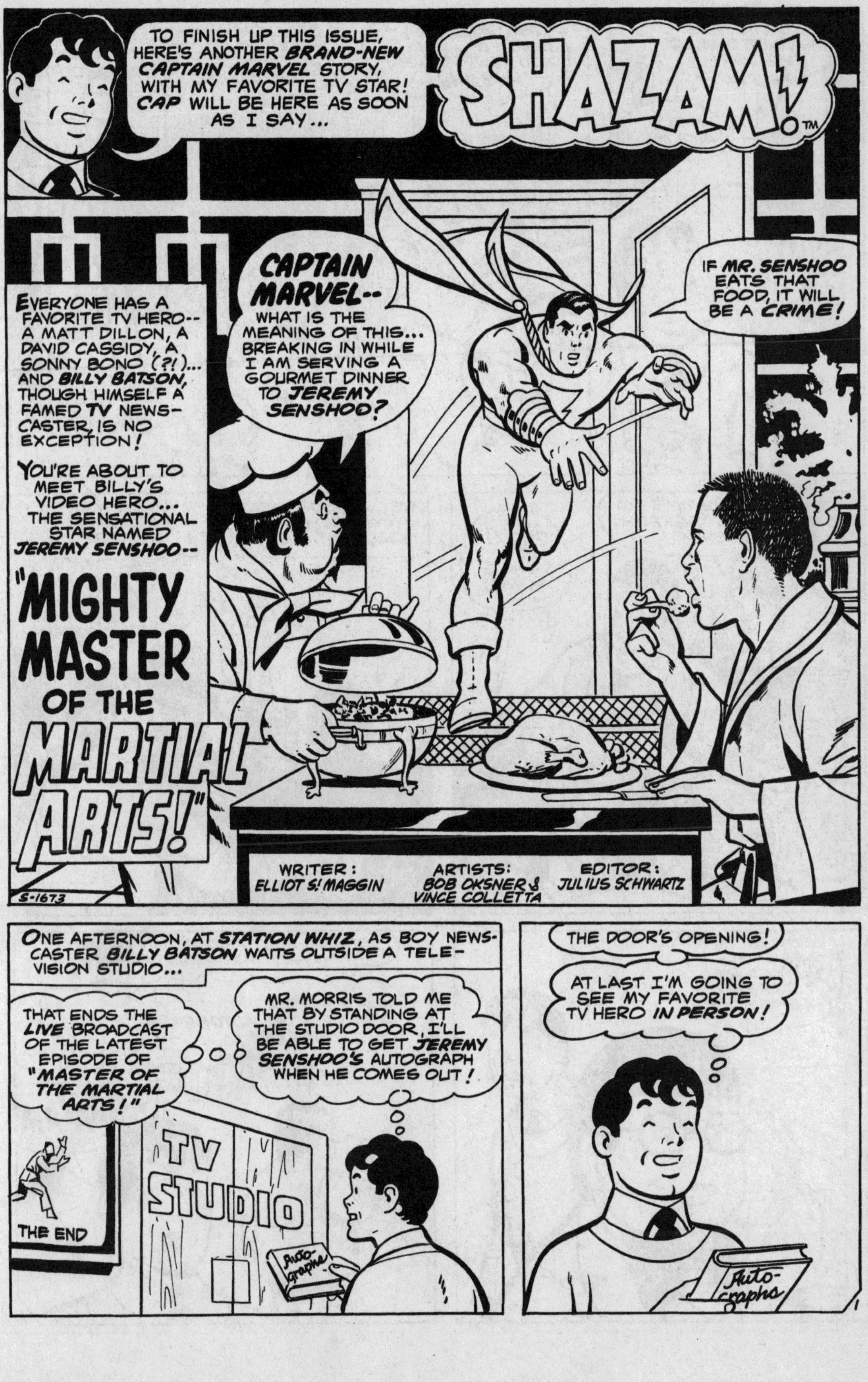
TO FINISH UP THIS ISSUE, HERE'S ANOTHER BRAND-NEW CAPTAIN MARVEL STORY, WITH MY FAVORITE TV STAR! CAP WILL BE HERE AS SOON AS I SAY...
SHAZAM!™
EVERYONE HAS A FAVORITE TV HERO-- A MATT DILLON, A DAVID CASSIDY, A SONNY BONO (?!)... AND BILLY BATSON, THOUGH HIMSELF A FAMED TV NEWS-CASTER, IS NO EXCEPTION!
YOU'RE ABOUT TO MEET BILLY'S VIDEO HERO... THE SENSATIONAL STAR NAMED JEREMY SENSHOO--
"MIGHTY MASTER OF THE MARTIAL ARTS!"
CAPTAIN MARVEL-- WHAT IS THE MEANING OF THIS... BREAKING IN WHILE I AM SERVING A GOURMET DINNER TO JEREMY SENSHOO?
IF MR. SENSHOO EATS THAT FOOD, IT WILL BE A CRIME!
WRITER: ELLIOT S! MAGGIN
ARTISTS: BOB OKSNER & VINCE COLLETTA
EDITOR: JULIUS SCHWARTZ
S-1673
ONE AFTERNOON, AT STATION WHIZ, AS BOY NEWS-CASTER BILLY BATSON WAITS OUTSIDE A TELE-VISION STUDIO...
THAT ENDS THE LIVE BROADCAST OF THE LATEST EPISODE OF "MASTER OF THE MARTIAL ARTS!"
THE END
MR. MORRIS TOLD ME THAT BY STANDING AT THE STUDIO DOOR, I'LL BE ABLE TO GET JEREMY SENSHOO'S AUTOGRAPH WHEN HE COMES OUT!
TV STUDIO
Auto-graphs
THE DOOR'S OPENING!
AT LAST I'M GOING TO SEE MY FAVORITE TV HERO IN PERSON!
Auto-graphs
1

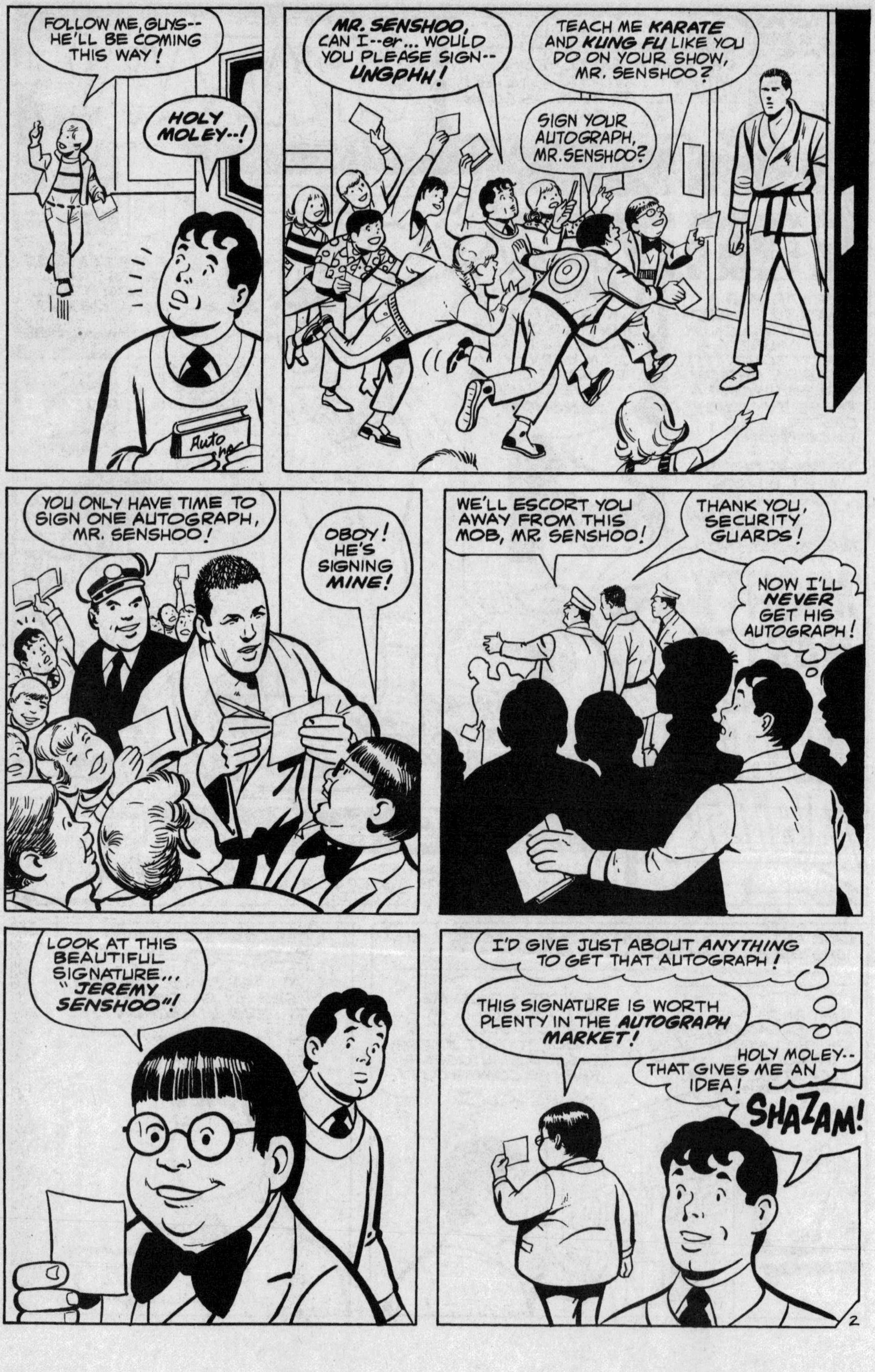
FOLLOW ME, GUYS-- HE'LL BE COMING THIS WAY!
HOLY MOLEY--!
Auto
MR. SENSHOO, CAN I--er... WOULD YOU PLEASE SIGN-- UNGPHH!
TEACH ME KARATE AND KUNG FU LIKE YOU DO ON YOUR SHOW, MR. SENSHOO?
SIGN YOUR AUTOGRAPH, MR. SENSHOO?
YOU ONLY HAVE TIME TO SIGN ONE AUTOGRAPH, MR. SENSHOO!
OBOY! HE'S SIGNING MINE!
WE'LL ESCORT YOU AWAY FROM THIS MOB, MR. SENSHOO!
THANK YOU, SECURITY GUARDS!
NOW I'LL NEVER GET HIS AUTOGRAPH!
LOOK AT THIS BEAUTIFUL SIGNATURE... "JEREMY SENSHOO"!
I'D GIVE JUST ABOUT ANYTHING TO GET THAT AUTOGRAPH!
THIS SIGNATURE IS WORTH PLENTY IN THE AUTOGRAPH MARKET!
HOLY MOLEY-- THAT GIVES ME AN IDEA!
SHAZAM!
2

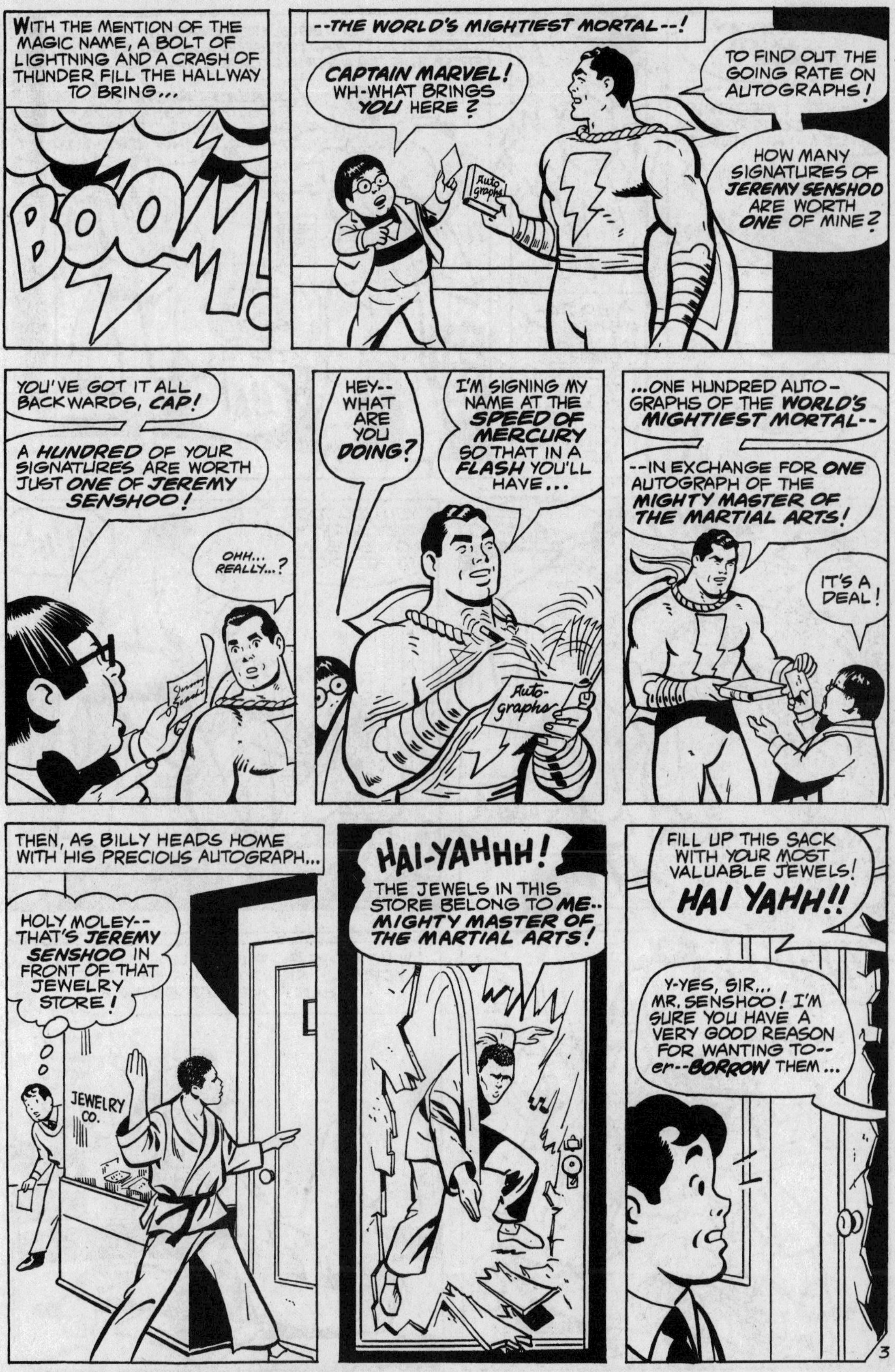
WITH THE MENTION OF THE MAGIC NAME, A BOLT OF LIGHTNING AND A CRASH OF THUNDER FILL THE HALLWAY TO BRING...
BOOM!
--THE WORLD'S MIGHTIEST MORTAL--!
CAPTAIN MARVEL! WH-WHAT BRINGS YOU HERE?
TO FIND OUT THE GOING RATE ON AUTOGRAPHS!
HOW MANY SIGNATURES OF JEREMY SENSHOO ARE WORTH ONE OF MINE?
Autographs
YOU'VE GOT IT ALL BACKWARDS, CAP!
A HUNDRED OF YOUR SIGNATURES ARE WORTH JUST ONE OF JEREMY SENSHOO!
OHH... REALLY...?
HEY-- WHAT ARE YOU DOING?
I'M SIGNING MY NAME AT THE SPEED OF MERCURY SO THAT IN A FLASH YOU'LL HAVE...
Auto-graphs
...ONE HUNDRED AUTOGRAPHS OF THE WORLD'S MIGHTIEST MORTAL--
--IN EXCHANGE FOR ONE AUTOGRAPH OF THE MIGHTY MASTER OF THE MARTIAL ARTS!
IT'S A DEAL!
THEN, AS BILLY HEADS HOME WITH HIS PRECIOUS AUTOGRAPH...
HOLY MOLEY-- THAT'S JEREMY SENSHOO IN FRONT OF THAT JEWELRY STORE!
JEWELRY CO.
HAI-YAHHH!
THE JEWELS IN THIS STORE BELONG TO ME.. MIGHTY MASTER OF THE MARTIAL ARTS!
FILL UP THIS SACK WITH YOUR MOST VALUABLE JEWELS! HAI YAHH!!
Y-YES, SIR... MR. SENSHOO! I'M SURE YOU HAVE A VERY GOOD REASON FOR WANTING TO-- er--BORROW THEM...
3

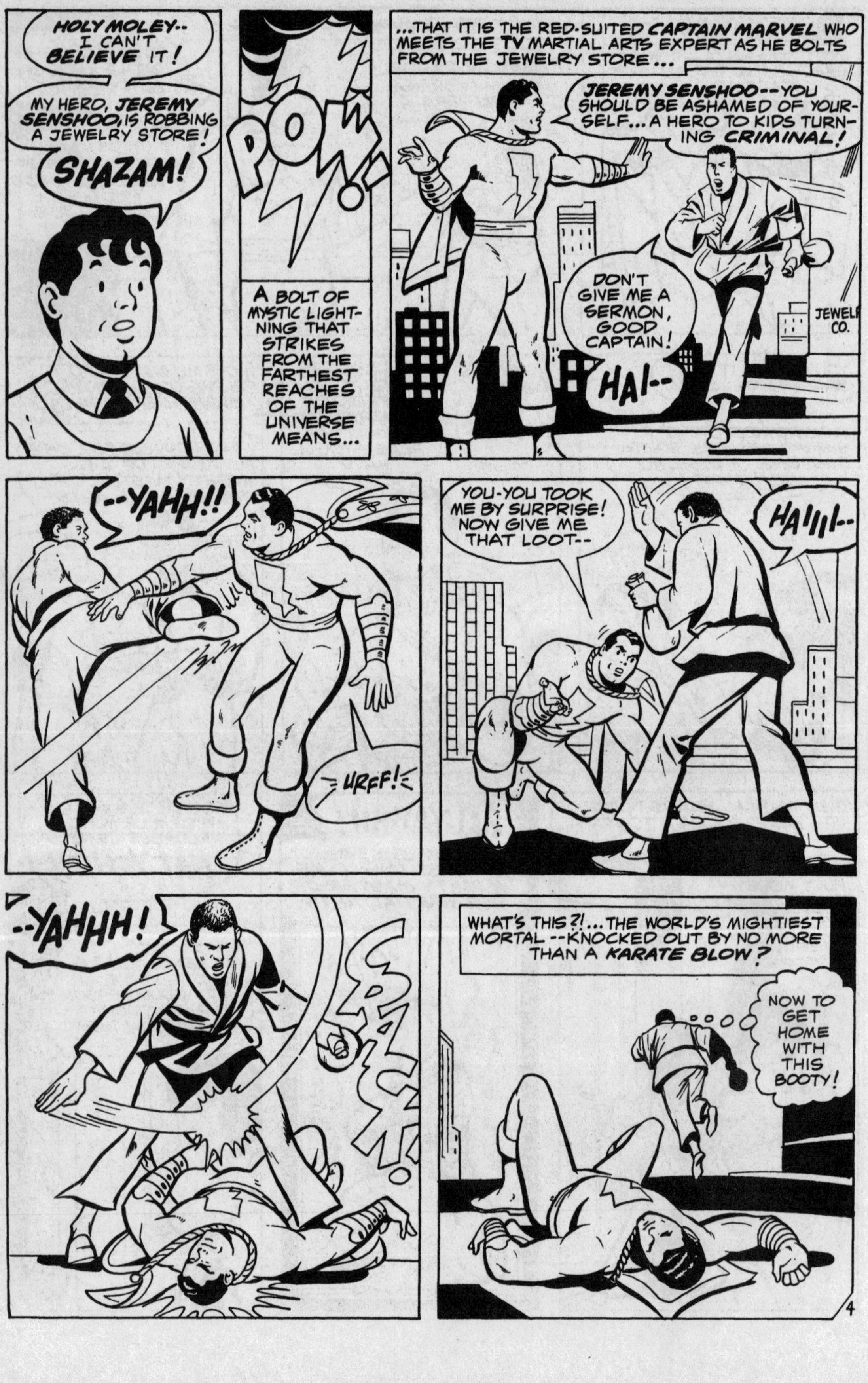
HOLY MOLEY-- I CAN'T BELIEVE IT!
MY HERO, JEREMY SENSHOO, IS ROBBING A JEWELRY STORE!
SHAZAM!
POW!
A BOLT OF MYSTIC LIGHTNING THAT STRIKES FROM THE FARTHEST REACHES OF THE UNIVERSE MEANS...
...THAT IT IS THE RED-SUITED CAPTAIN MARVEL WHO MEETS THE TV MARTIAL ARTS EXPERT AS HE BOLTS FROM THE JEWELRY STORE...
JEREMY SENSHOO--YOU SHOULD BE ASHAMED OF YOURSELF... A HERO TO KIDS TURNING CRIMINAL!
DON'T GIVE ME A SERMON, GOOD CAPTAIN!
HAI--
JEWEL CO.
--YAHH!!
URFF!
YOU-YOU TOOK ME BY SURPRISE! NOW GIVE ME THAT LOOT--
HAIIII--
--YAHHH!
CRACK!
WHAT'S THIS?!... THE WORLD'S MIGHTIEST MORTAL--KNOCKED OUT BY NO MORE THAN A KARATE BLOW?
NOW TO GET HOME WITH THIS BOOTY!
4

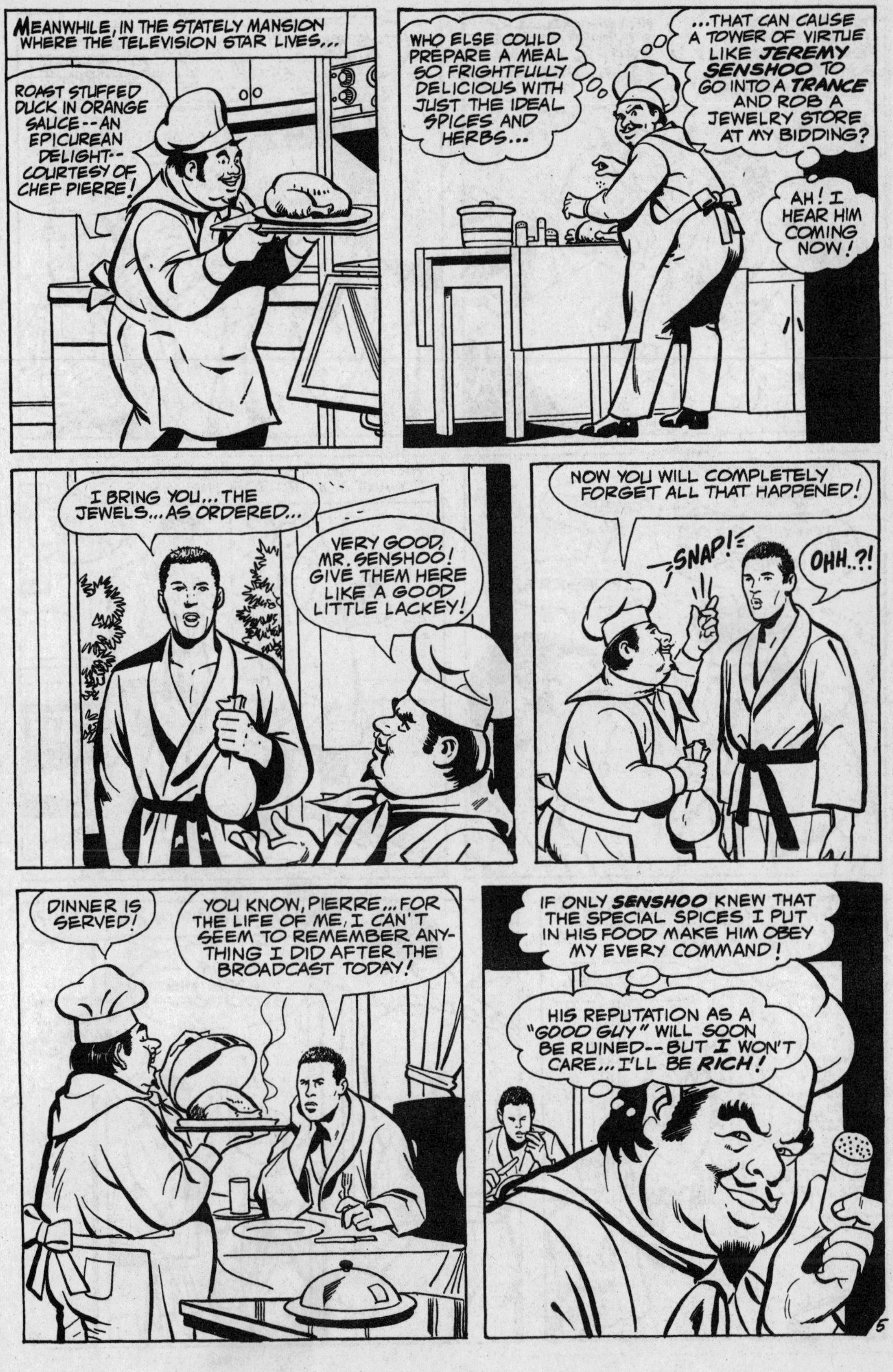
MEANWHILE, IN THE STATELY MANSION WHERE THE TELEVISION STAR LIVES,..
ROAST STUFFED DUCK IN ORANGE SAUCE--AN EPICUREAN DELIGHT--COURTESY OF CHEF PIERRE!
WHO ELSE COULD PREPARE A MEAL SO FRIGHTFULLY DELICIOUS WITH JUST THE IDEAL SPICES AND HERBS...
...THAT CAN CAUSE A TOWER OF VIRTUE LIKE JEREMY SENSHOO TO GO INTO A TRANCE AND ROB A JEWELRY STORE AT MY BIDDING?
AH! I HEAR HIM COMING NOW!
I BRING YOU... THE JEWELS... AS ORDERED...
VERY GOOD, MR. SENSHOO! GIVE THEM HERE LIKE A GOOD LITTLE LACKEY!
NOW YOU WILL COMPLETELY FORGET ALL THAT HAPPENED!
SNAP!
OHH..?!
DINNER IS SERVED!
YOU KNOW, PIERRE... FOR THE LIFE OF ME, I CAN'T SEEM TO REMEMBER ANYTHING I DID AFTER THE BROADCAST TODAY!
IF ONLY SENSHOO KNEW THAT THE SPECIAL SPICES I PUT IN HIS FOOD MAKE HIM OBEY MY EVERY COMMAND!
HIS REPUTATION AS A "GOOD GUY" WILL SOON BE RUINED--BUT I WON'T CARE... I'LL BE RICH!
5

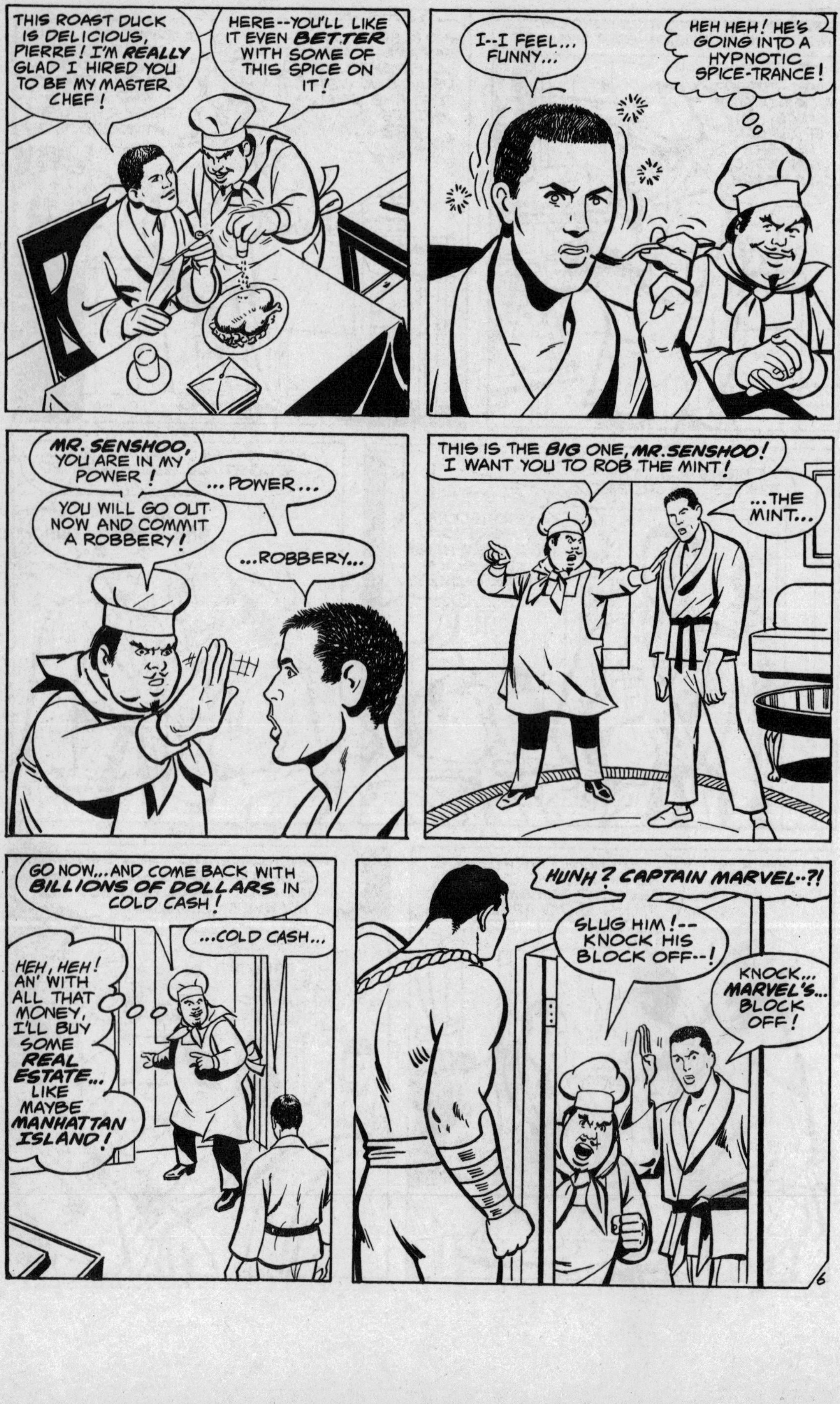
THIS ROAST DUCK IS DELICIOUS, PIERRE! I'M REALLY GLAD I HIRED YOU TO BE MY MASTER CHEF!
HERE--YOU'LL LIKE IT EVEN BETTER WITH SOME OF THIS SPICE ON IT!
I--I FEEL... FUNNY...
HEH HEH! HE'S GOING INTO A HYPNOTIC SPICE-TRANCE!
MR. SENSHOO, YOU ARE IN MY POWER!
...POWER...
YOU WILL GO OUT NOW AND COMMIT A ROBBERY!
...ROBBERY...
THIS IS THE BIG ONE, MR. SENSHOO! I WANT YOU TO ROB THE MINT!
...THE MINT...
GO NOW...AND COME BACK WITH BILLIONS OF DOLLARS IN COLD CASH!
...COLD CASH...
HEH, HEH! AN' WITH ALL THAT MONEY, I'LL BUY SOME REAL ESTATE... LIKE MAYBE MANHATTAN ISLAND!
HUNH? CAPTAIN MARVEL..?!
SLUG HIM!--KNOCK HIS BLOCK OFF--!
KNOCK... MARVEL'S... BLOCK OFF!
6

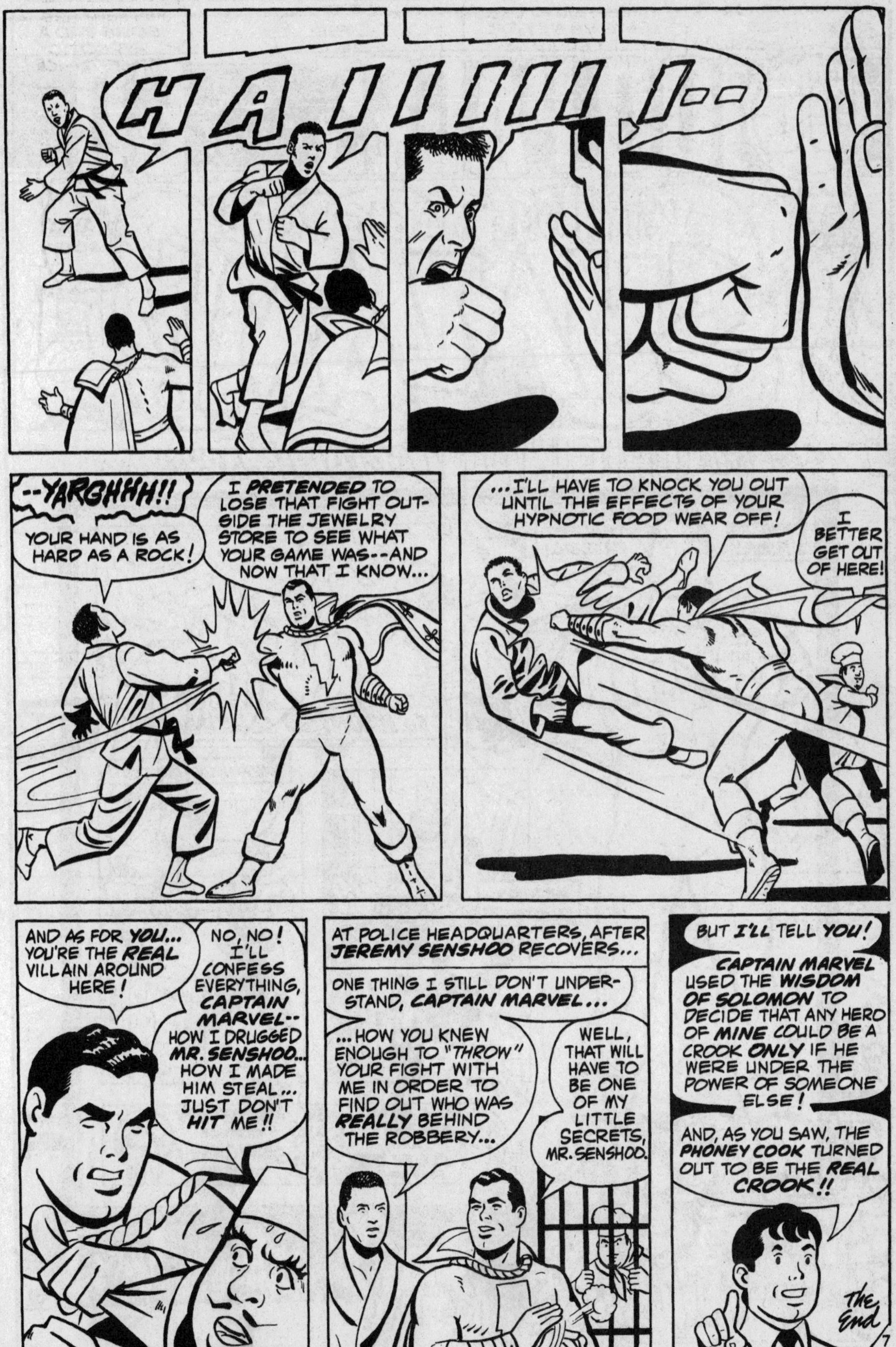
HAIIIII--
--YARGHHH!!
YOUR HAND IS AS HARD AS A ROCK!
I PRETENDED TO LOSE THAT FIGHT OUTSIDE THE JEWELRY STORE TO SEE WHAT YOUR GAME WAS--AND NOW THAT I KNOW...
...I'LL HAVE TO KNOCK YOU OUT UNTIL THE EFFECTS OF YOUR HYPNOTIC FOOD WEAR OFF!
I BETTER GET OUT OF HERE!
AND AS FOR YOU... YOU'RE THE REAL VILLAIN AROUND HERE!
NO, NO! I'LL CONFESS EVERYTHING, CAPTAIN MARVEL-- HOW I DRUGGED MR. SENSHOO... HOW I MADE HIM STEAL... JUST DON'T HIT ME!!
AT POLICE HEADQUARTERS, AFTER JEREMY SENSHOO RECOVERS...
ONE THING I STILL DON'T UNDERSTAND, CAPTAIN MARVEL...
...HOW YOU KNEW ENOUGH TO "THROW" YOUR FIGHT WITH ME IN ORDER TO FIND OUT WHO WAS REALLY BEHIND THE ROBBERY...
WELL, THAT WILL HAVE TO BE ONE OF MY LITTLE SECRETS, MR. SENSHOO.
BUT I'LL TELL YOU!
CAPTAIN MARVEL USED THE WISDOM OF SOLOMON TO DECIDE THAT ANY HERO OF MINE COULD BE A CROOK ONLY IF HE WERE UNDER THE POWER OF SOMEONE ELSE!
AND, AS YOU SAW, THE PHONEY COOK TURNED OUT TO BE THE REAL CROOK!!
THE END
7

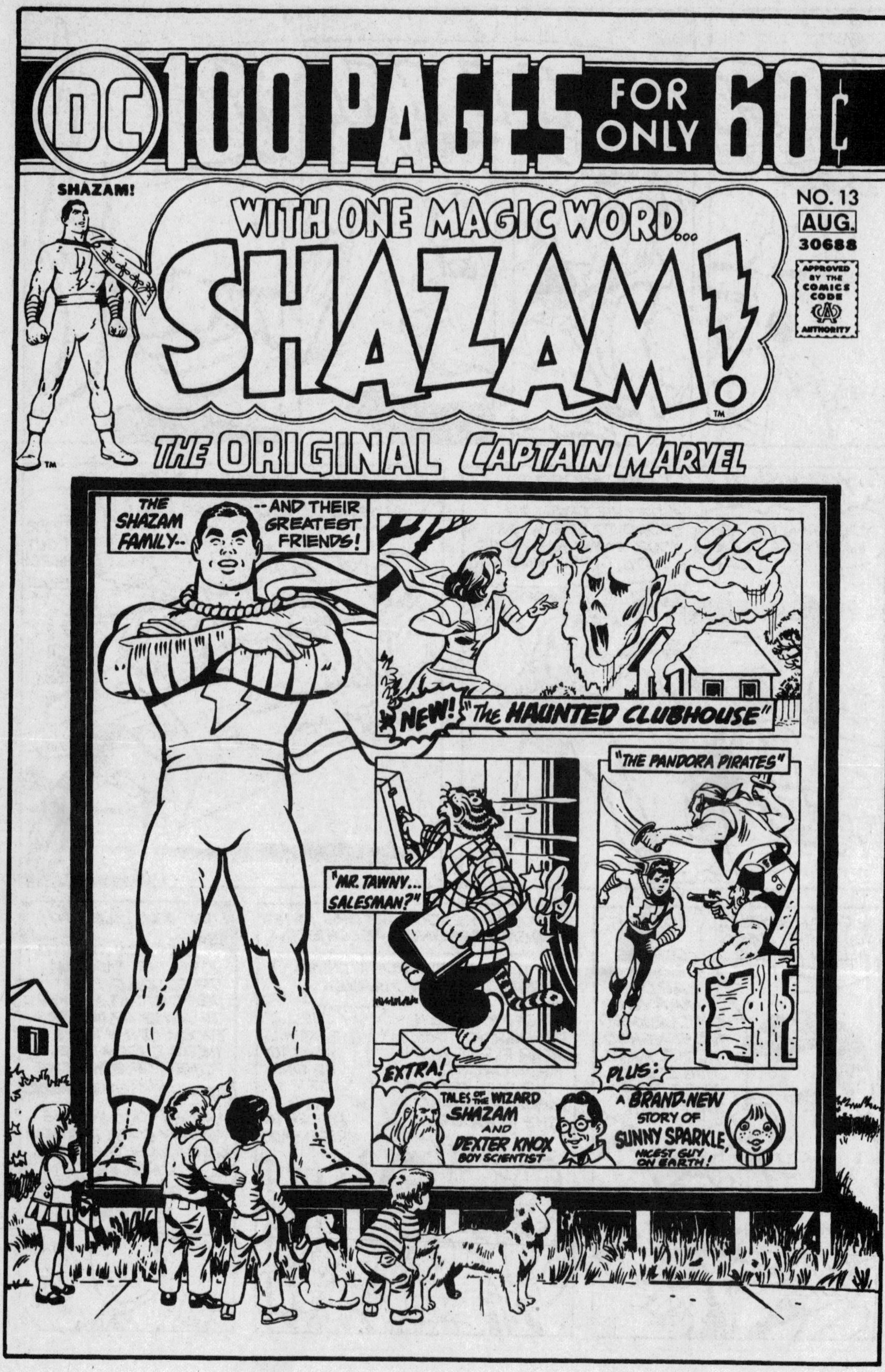
DC
100 PAGES FOR ONLY 60¢
SHAZAM!
WITH ONE MAGIC WORD...
SHAZAM!
NO. 13
AUG.
30688
APPROVED BY THE COMICS CODE AUTHORITY
THE ORIGINAL CAPTAIN MARVEL
THE SHAZAM FAMILY--
--AND THEIR GREATEST FRIENDS!
NEW! "The HAUNTED CLUBHOUSE"
"THE PANDORA PIRATES"
"MR. TAWNY... SALESMAN?"
EXTRA!
PLUS:
TALES OF THE WIZARD SHAZAM
AND
DEXTER KNOX BOY SCIENTIST
A BRAND-NEW STORY OF SUNNY SPARKLE, NICEST GUY ON EARTH!

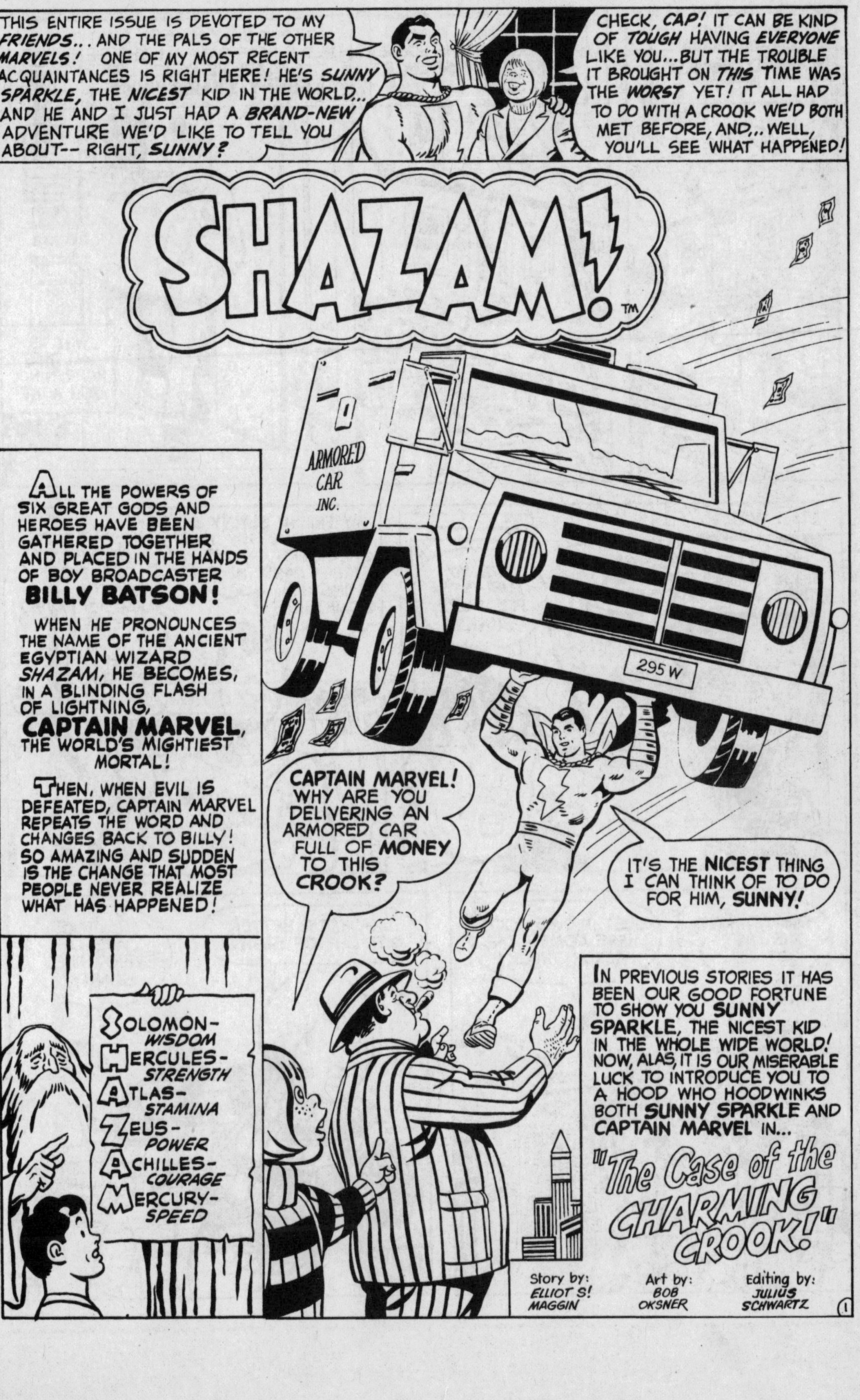
THIS ENTIRE ISSUE IS DEVOTED TO MY FRIENDS... AND THE PALS OF THE OTHER MARVELS! ONE OF MY MOST RECENT ACQUAINTANCES IS RIGHT HERE! HE'S SUNNY SPARKLE, THE NICEST KID IN THE WORLD... AND HE AND I JUST HAD A BRAND-NEW ADVENTURE WE'D LIKE TO TELL YOU ABOUT-- RIGHT, SUNNY?
CHECK, CAP! IT CAN BE KIND OF TOUGH HAVING EVERYONE LIKE YOU...BUT THE TROUBLE IT BROUGHT ON THIS TIME WAS THE WORST YET! IT ALL HAD TO DO WITH A CROOK WE'D BOTH MET BEFORE, AND... WELL, YOU'LL SEE WHAT HAPPENED!
SHAZAM! TM
ALL THE POWERS OF SIX GREAT GODS AND HEROES HAVE BEEN GATHERED TOGETHER AND PLACED IN THE HANDS OF BOY BROADCASTER BILLY BATSON!
WHEN HE PRONOUNCES THE NAME OF THE ANCIENT EGYPTIAN WIZARD SHAZAM, HE BECOMES, IN A BLINDING FLASH OF LIGHTNING, CAPTAIN MARVEL, THE WORLD'S MIGHTIEST MORTAL!
THEN, WHEN EVIL IS DEFEATED, CAPTAIN MARVEL REPEATS THE WORD AND CHANGES BACK TO BILLY! SO AMAZING AND SUDDEN IS THE CHANGE THAT MOST PEOPLE NEVER REALIZE WHAT HAS HAPPENED!
ARMORED CAR INC.
295 W
CAPTAIN MARVEL! WHY ARE YOU DELIVERING AN ARMORED CAR FULL OF MONEY TO THIS CROOK?
IT'S THE NICEST THING I CAN THINK OF TO DO FOR HIM, SUNNY!
SOLOMON- WISDOM
HERCULES- STRENGTH
ATLAS- STAMINA
ZEUS- POWER
ACHILLES- COURAGE
MERCURY- SPEED
IN PREVIOUS STORIES IT HAS BEEN OUR GOOD FORTUNE TO SHOW YOU SUNNY SPARKLE, THE NICEST KID IN THE WHOLE WIDE WORLD! NOW, ALAS, IT IS OUR MISERABLE LUCK TO INTRODUCE YOU TO A HOOD WHO HOODWINKS BOTH SUNNY SPARKLE AND CAPTAIN MARVEL IN...
"The Case of the CHARMING CROOK!"
Story by: ELLIOT S! MAGGIN
Art by: BOB OKSNER
Editing by: JULIUS SCHWARTZ
1

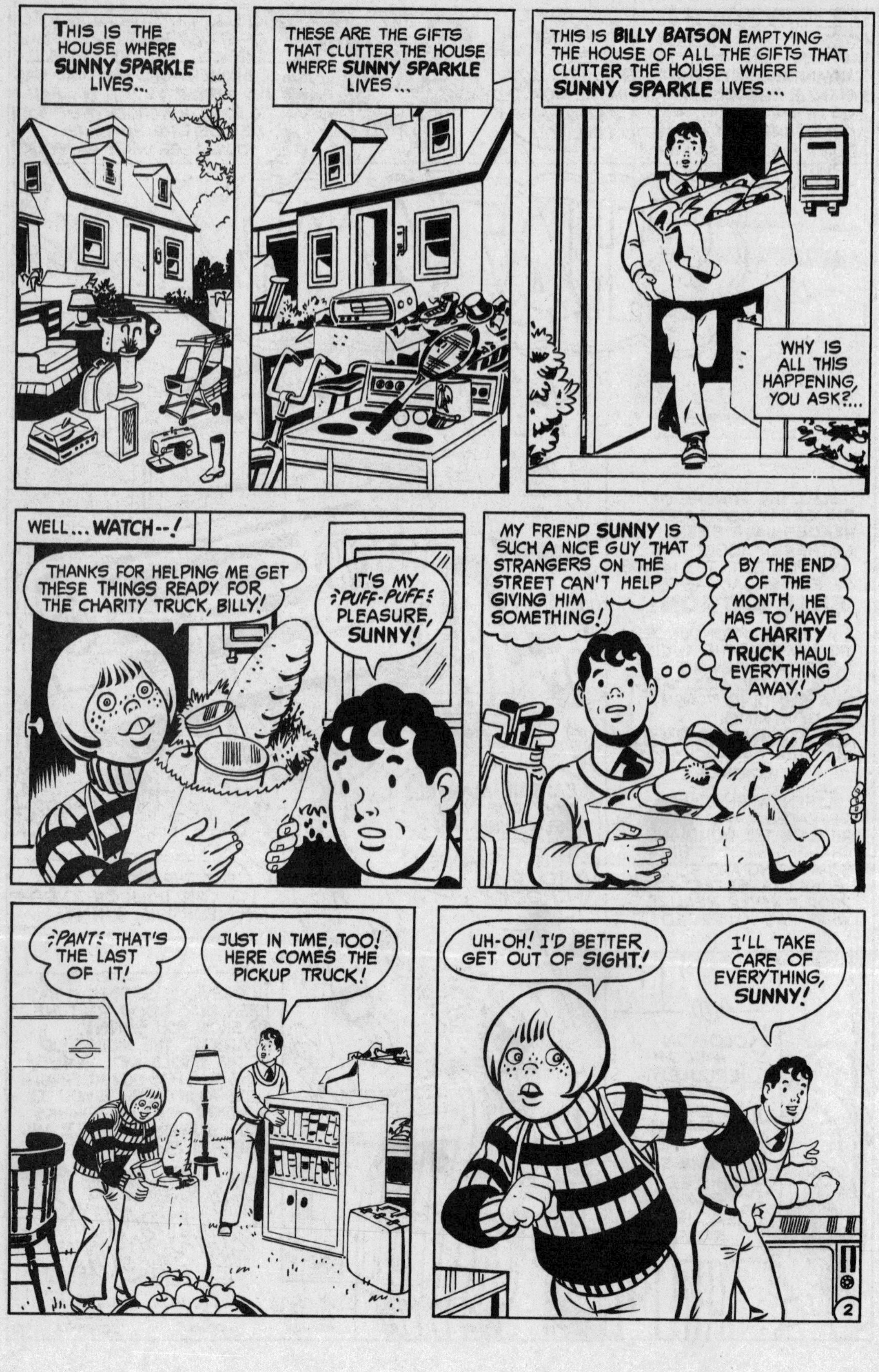
THIS IS THE HOUSE WHERE SUNNY SPARKLE LIVES...
THESE ARE THE GIFTS THAT CLUTTER THE HOUSE WHERE SUNNY SPARKLE LIVES...
THIS IS BILLY BATSON EMPTYING THE HOUSE OF ALL THE GIFTS THAT CLUTTER THE HOUSE WHERE SUNNY SPARKLE LIVES...
WHY IS ALL THIS HAPPENING, YOU ASK?...
WELL... WATCH--!
THANKS FOR HELPING ME GET THESE THINGS READY FOR THE CHARITY TRUCK, BILLY!
IT'S MY PUFF-PUFF PLEASURE, SUNNY!
MY FRIEND SUNNY IS SUCH A NICE GUY THAT STRANGERS ON THE STREET CAN'T HELP GIVING HIM SOMETHING!
BY THE END OF THE MONTH, HE HAS TO HAVE A CHARITY TRUCK HAUL EVERYTHING AWAY!
PANT THAT'S THE LAST OF IT!
JUST IN TIME, TOO! HERE COMES THE PICKUP TRUCK!
UH-OH! I'D BETTER GET OUT OF SIGHT!
I'LL TAKE CARE OF EVERYTHING, SUNNY!
2

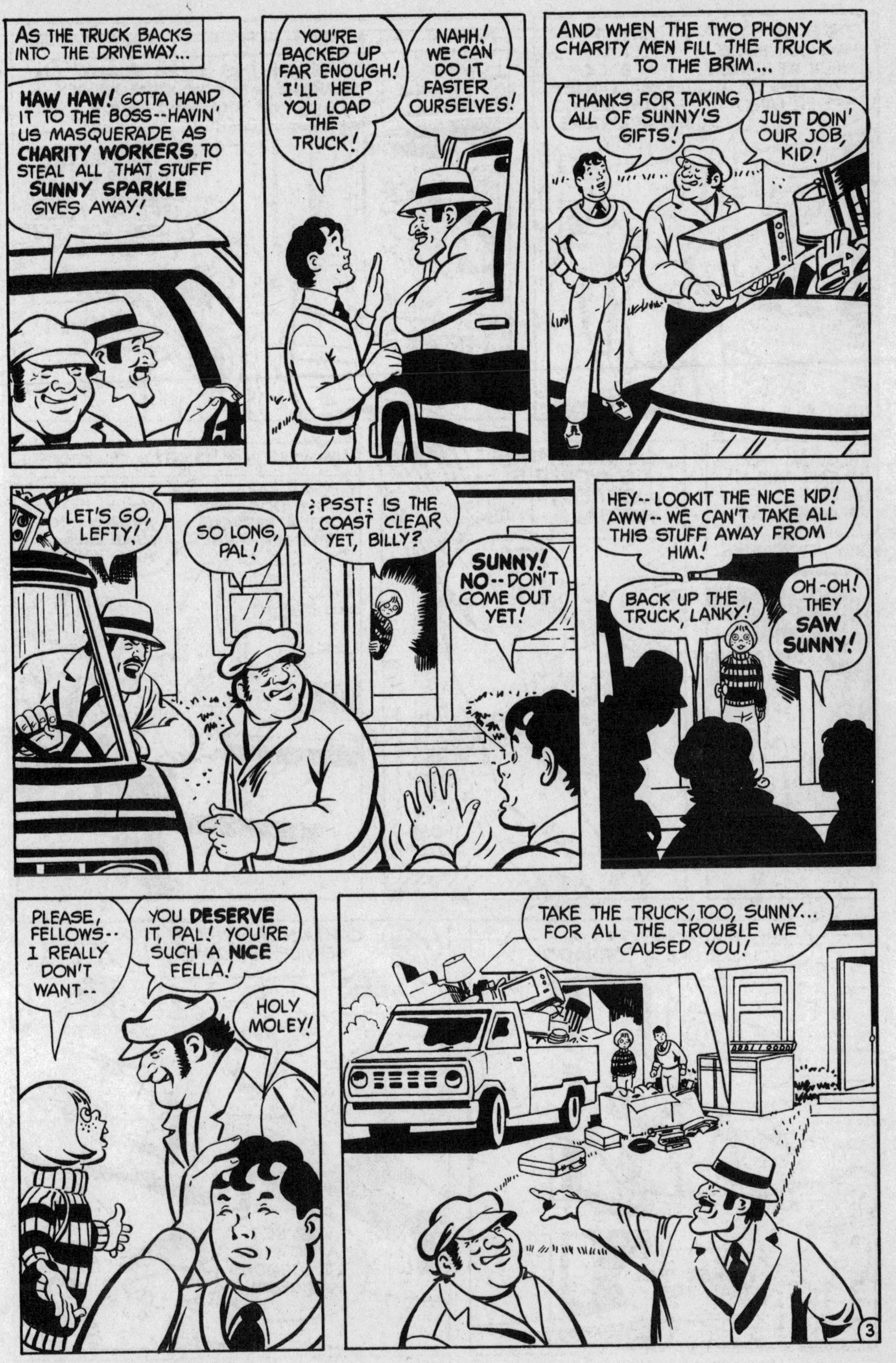
AS THE TRUCK BACKS INTO THE DRIVEWAY...
HAW HAW! GOTTA HAND IT TO THE BOSS--HAVIN' US MASQUERADE AS CHARITY WORKERS TO STEAL ALL THAT STUFF SUNNY SPARKLE GIVES AWAY!
YOU'RE BACKED UP FAR ENOUGH! I'LL HELP YOU LOAD THE TRUCK!
NAHH! WE CAN DO IT FASTER OURSELVES!
AND WHEN THE TWO PHONY CHARITY MEN FILL THE TRUCK TO THE BRIM...
THANKS FOR TAKING ALL OF SUNNY'S GIFTS!
JUST DOIN' OUR JOB, KID!
LET'S GO, LEFTY!
SO LONG, PAL!
PSST! IS THE COAST CLEAR YET, BILLY?
SUNNY! NO--DON'T COME OUT YET!
HEY--LOOKIT THE NICE KID! AWW--WE CAN'T TAKE ALL THIS STUFF AWAY FROM HIM!
BACK UP THE TRUCK, LANKY!
OH-OH! THEY SAW SUNNY!
PLEASE, FELLOWS--I REALLY DON'T WANT--
YOU DESERVE IT, PAL! YOU'RE SUCH A NICE FELLA!
HOLY MOLEY!
TAKE THE TRUCK, TOO, SUNNY... FOR ALL THE TROUBLE WE CAUSED YOU!
3

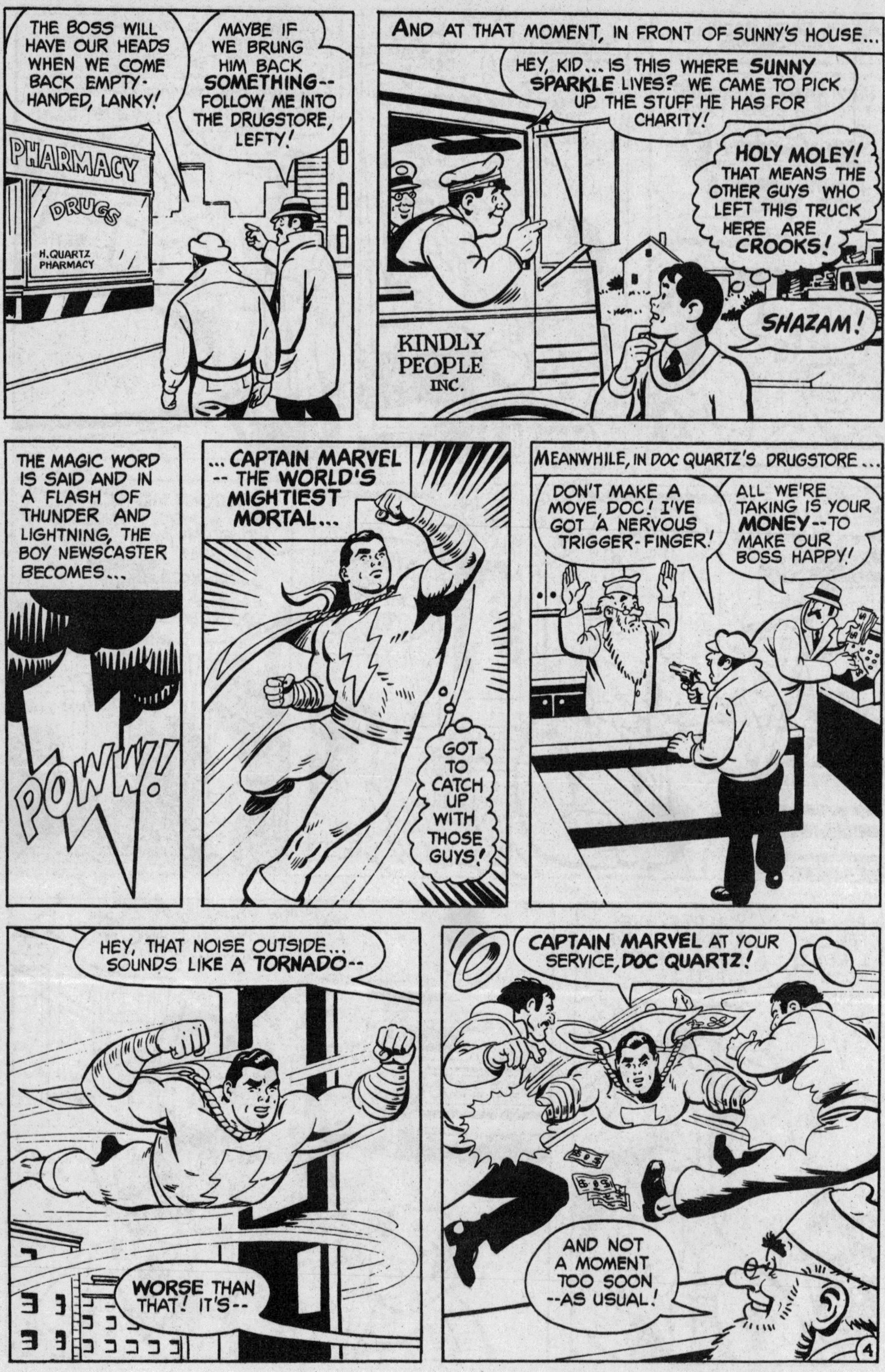
THE BOSS WILL HAVE OUR HEADS WHEN WE COME BACK EMPTY-HANDED, LANKY!
MAYBE IF WE BRUNG HIM BACK SOMETHING-- FOLLOW ME INTO THE DRUGSTORE, LEFTY!
PHARMACY
DRUGS
H. QUARTZ PHARMACY
AND AT THAT MOMENT, IN FRONT OF SUNNY'S HOUSE...
HEY, KID... IS THIS WHERE SUNNY SPARKLE LIVES? WE CAME TO PICK UP THE STUFF HE HAS FOR CHARITY!
HOLY MOLEY! THAT MEANS THE OTHER GUYS WHO LEFT THIS TRUCK HERE ARE CROOKS!
SHAZAM!
KINDLY PEOPLE INC.
THE MAGIC WORD IS SAID AND IN A FLASH OF THUNDER AND LIGHTNING, THE BOY NEWSCASTER BECOMES...
POWW!
... CAPTAIN MARVEL -- THE WORLD'S MIGHTIEST MORTAL...
GOT TO CATCH UP WITH THOSE GUYS!
MEANWHILE, IN DOC QUARTZ'S DRUGSTORE...
DON'T MAKE A MOVE, DOC! I'VE GOT A NERVOUS TRIGGER-FINGER!
ALL WE'RE TAKING IS YOUR MONEY--TO MAKE OUR BOSS HAPPY!
HEY, THAT NOISE OUTSIDE... SOUNDS LIKE A TORNADO--
WORSE THAN THAT! IT'S--
CAPTAIN MARVEL AT YOUR SERVICE, DOC QUARTZ!
AND NOT A MOMENT TOO SOON --AS USUAL!
4

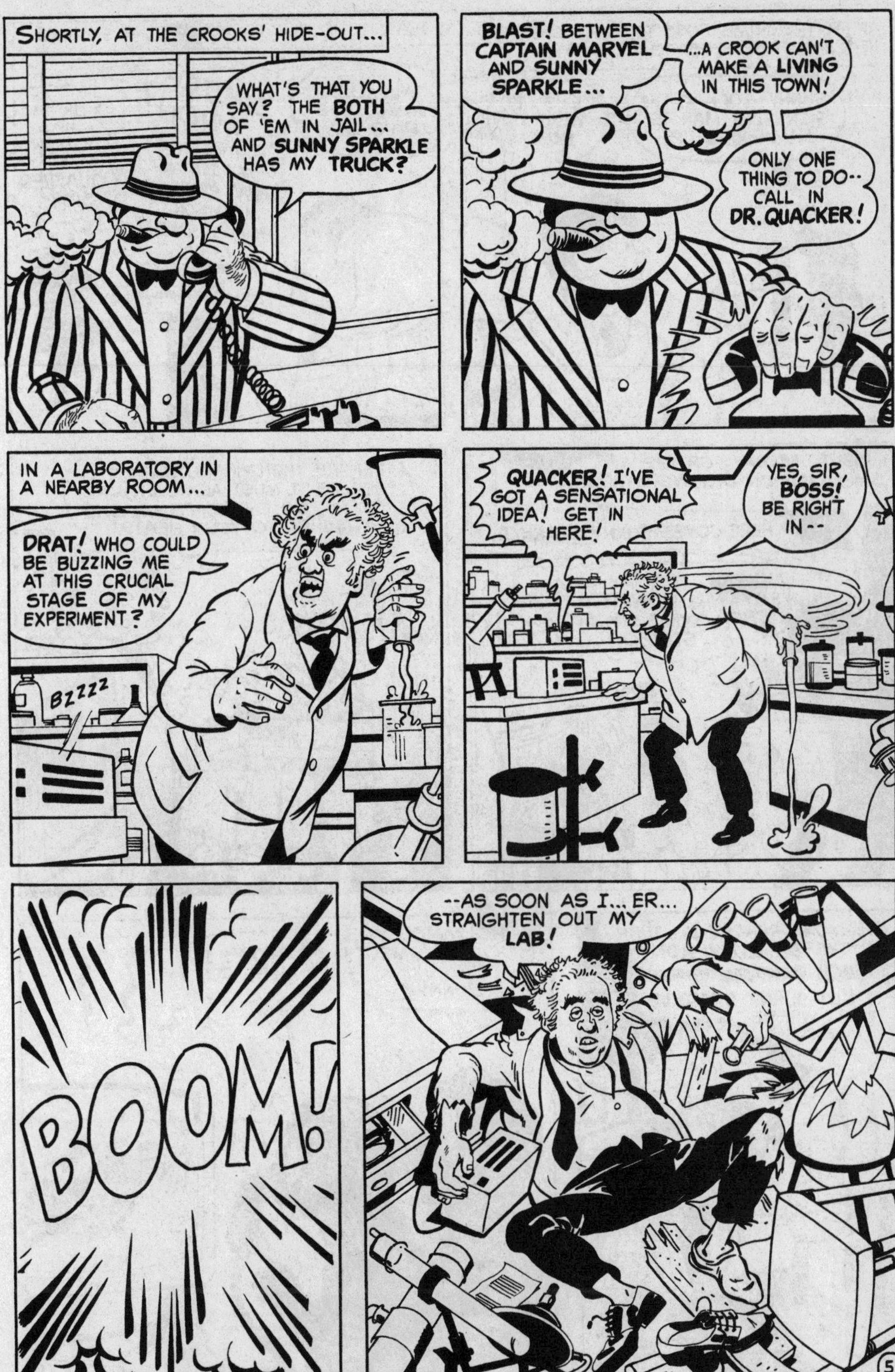
SHORTLY, AT THE CROOKS' HIDE-OUT...
WHAT'S THAT YOU SAY? THE BOTH OF 'EM IN JAIL... AND SUNNY SPARKLE HAS MY TRUCK?
BLAST! BETWEEN CAPTAIN MARVEL AND SUNNY SPARKLE...
...A CROOK CAN'T MAKE A LIVING IN THIS TOWN!
ONLY ONE THING TO DO-- CALL IN DR. QUACKER!
IN A LABORATORY IN A NEARBY ROOM...
DRAT! WHO COULD BE BUZZING ME AT THIS CRUCIAL STAGE OF MY EXPERIMENT?
BZZZZ
QUACKER! I'VE GOT A SENSATIONAL IDEA! GET IN HERE!
YES, SIR, BOSS! BE RIGHT IN--
BOOM!
--AS SOON AS I... ER... STRAIGHTEN OUT MY LAB!
5

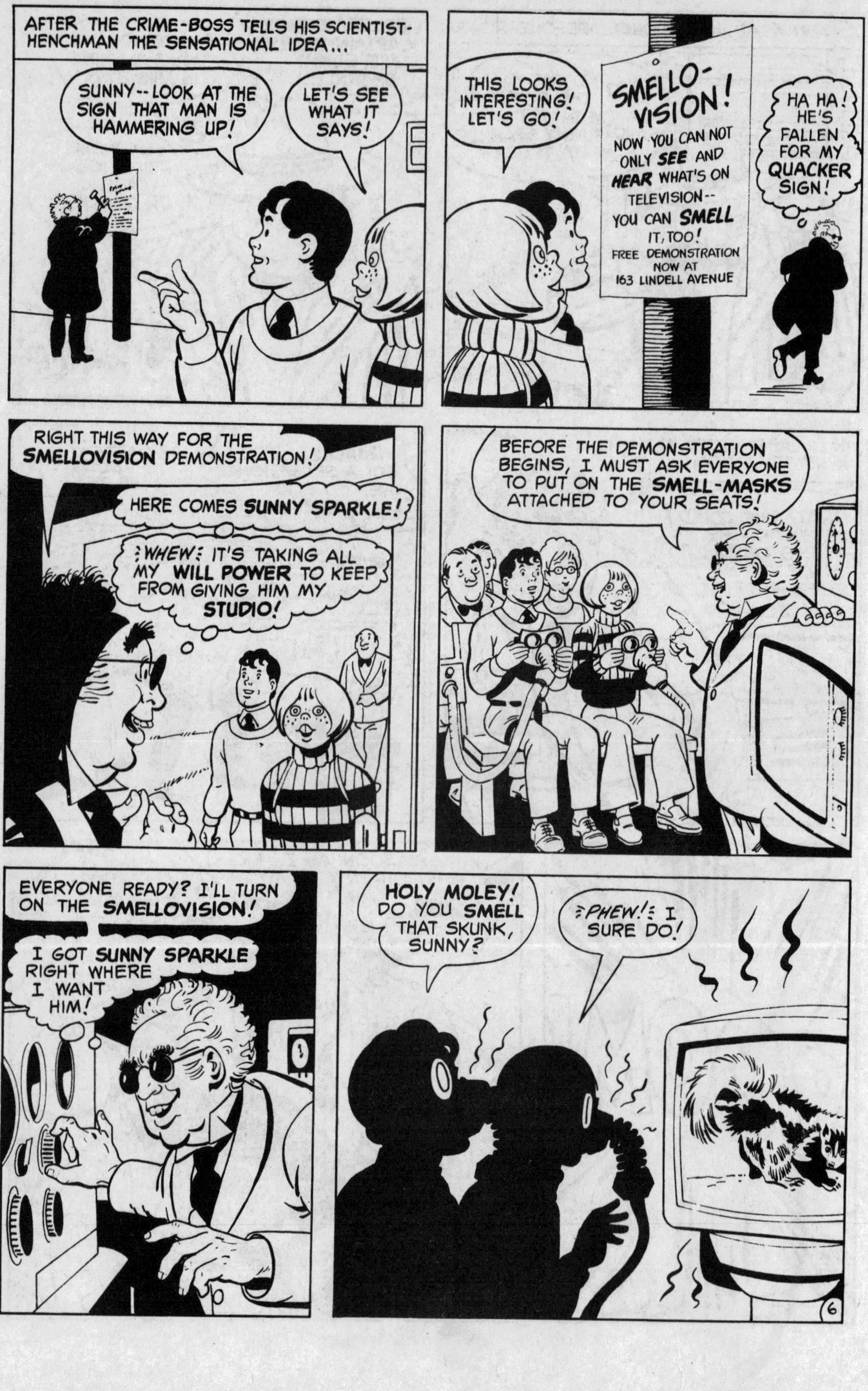
AFTER THE CRIME-BOSS TELLS HIS SCIENTIST-HENCHMAN THE SENSATIONAL IDEA...
SUNNY--LOOK AT THE SIGN THAT MAN IS HAMMERING UP!
LET'S SEE WHAT IT SAYS!
THIS LOOKS INTERESTING! LET'S GO!
SMELLO-VISION! NOW YOU CAN NOT ONLY SEE AND HEAR WHAT'S ON TELEVISION-- YOU CAN SMELL IT, TOO! FREE DEMONSTRATION NOW AT 163 LINDELL AVENUE
HA HA! HE'S FALLEN FOR MY QUACKER SIGN!
RIGHT THIS WAY FOR THE SMELLOVISION DEMONSTRATION!
HERE COMES SUNNY SPARKLE!
WHEW! IT'S TAKING ALL MY WILL POWER TO KEEP FROM GIVING HIM MY STUDIO!
BEFORE THE DEMONSTRATION BEGINS, I MUST ASK EVERYONE TO PUT ON THE SMELL-MASKS ATTACHED TO YOUR SEATS!
EVERYONE READY? I'LL TURN ON THE SMELLOVISION!
I GOT SUNNY SPARKLE RIGHT WHERE I WANT HIM!
HOLY MOLEY! DO YOU SMELL THAT SKUNK, SUNNY?
PHEW! I SURE DO!
6

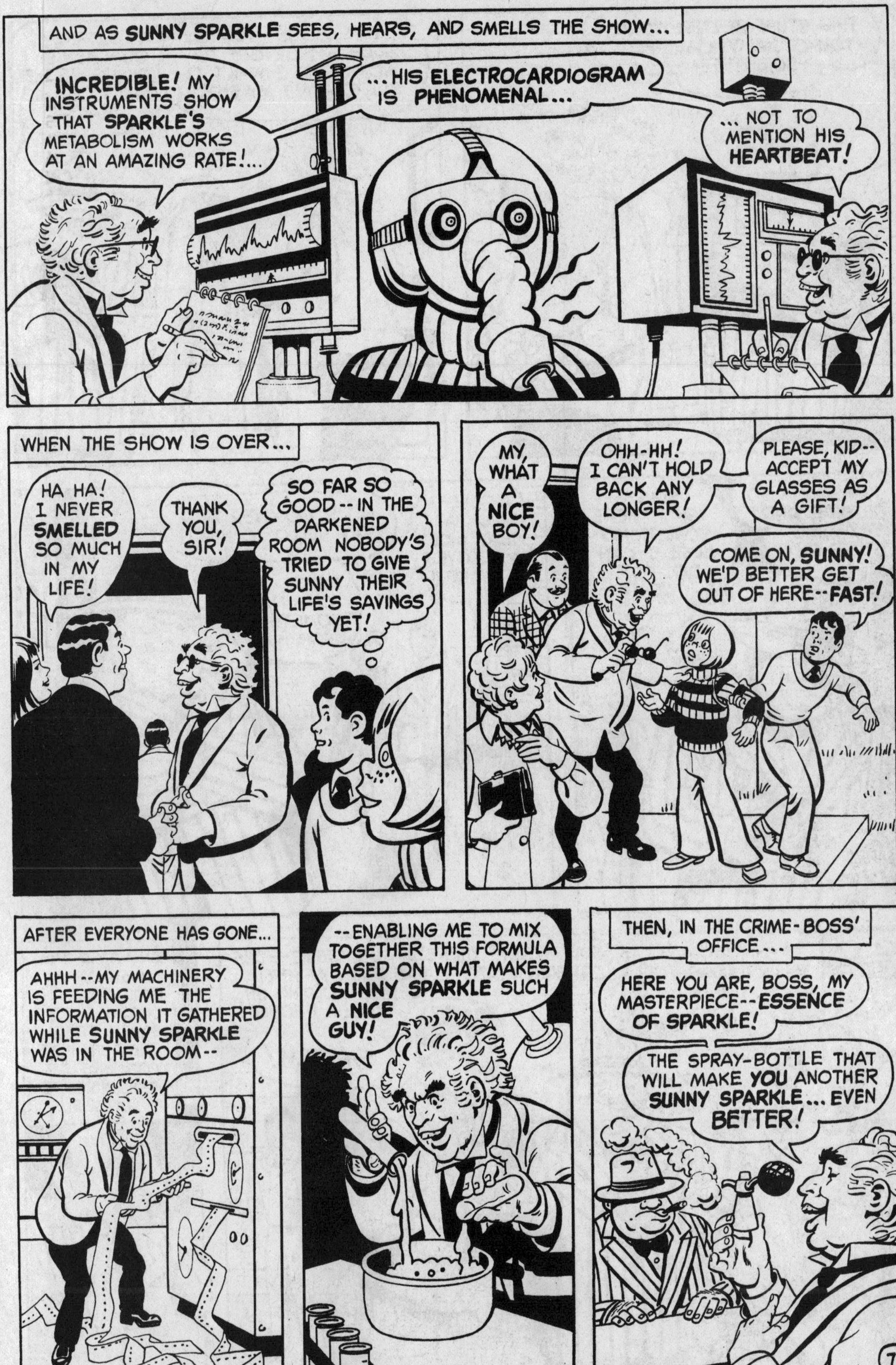
AND AS SUNNY SPARKLE SEES, HEARS, AND SMELLS THE SHOW...
INCREDIBLE! MY INSTRUMENTS SHOW THAT SPARKLE'S METABOLISM WORKS AT AN AMAZING RATE!...
...HIS ELECTROCARDIOGRAM IS PHENOMENAL...
...NOT TO MENTION HIS HEARTBEAT!
WHEN THE SHOW IS OVER...
HA HA! I NEVER SMELLED SO MUCH IN MY LIFE!
THANK YOU, SIR!
SO FAR SO GOOD -- IN THE DARKENED ROOM NOBODY'S TRIED TO GIVE SUNNY THEIR LIFE'S SAVINGS YET!
MY, WHAT A NICE BOY!
OHH-HH! I CAN'T HOLD BACK ANY LONGER!
PLEASE, KID-- ACCEPT MY GLASSES AS A GIFT!
COME ON, SUNNY! WE'D BETTER GET OUT OF HERE--FAST!
AFTER EVERYONE HAS GONE...
AHHH--MY MACHINERY IS FEEDING ME THE INFORMATION IT GATHERED WHILE SUNNY SPARKLE WAS IN THE ROOM--
--ENABLING ME TO MIX TOGETHER THIS FORMULA BASED ON WHAT MAKES SUNNY SPARKLE SUCH A NICE GUY!
THEN, IN THE CRIME-BOSS' OFFICE...
HERE YOU ARE, BOSS, MY MASTERPIECE--ESSENCE OF SPARKLE!
THE SPRAY-BOTTLE THAT WILL MAKE YOU ANOTHER SUNNY SPARKLE... EVEN BETTER!
7

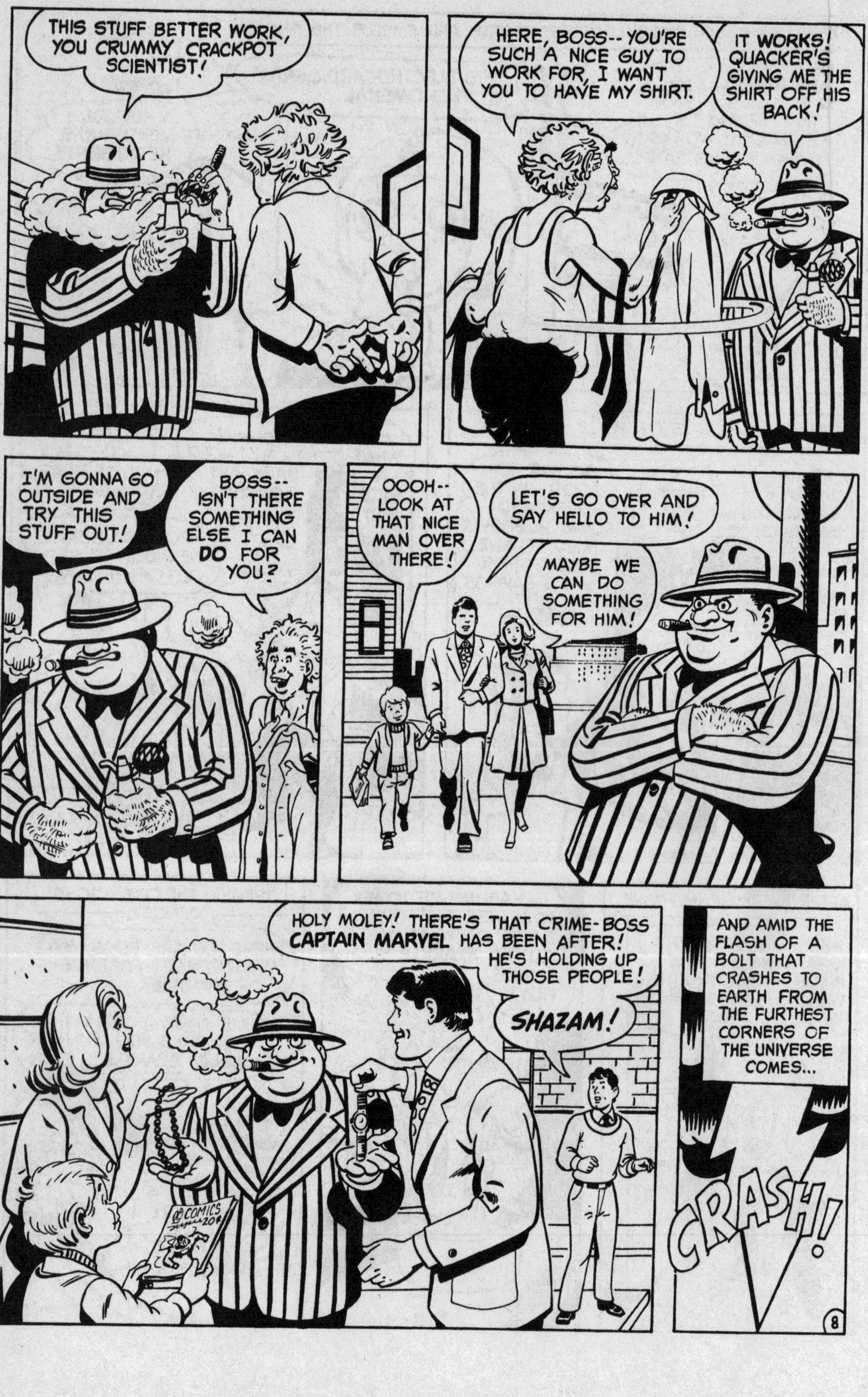
THIS STUFF BETTER WORK, YOU CRUMMY CRACKPOT SCIENTIST!
HERE, BOSS--YOU'RE SUCH A NICE GUY TO WORK FOR, I WANT YOU TO HAVE MY SHIRT.
IT WORKS! QUACKER'S GIVING ME THE SHIRT OFF HIS BACK!
I'M GONNA GO OUTSIDE AND TRY THIS STUFF OUT!
BOSS--ISN'T THERE SOMETHING ELSE I CAN DO FOR YOU?
OOOH--LOOK AT THAT NICE MAN OVER THERE!
LET'S GO OVER AND SAY HELLO TO HIM!
MAYBE WE CAN DO SOMETHING FOR HIM!
HOLY MOLEY! THERE'S THAT CRIME-BOSS CAPTAIN MARVEL HAS BEEN AFTER! HE'S HOLDING UP THOSE PEOPLE!
SHAZAM!
AND AMID THE FLASH OF A BOLT THAT CRASHES TO EARTH FROM THE FURTHEST CORNERS OF THE UNIVERSE COMES...
CRASH!
8

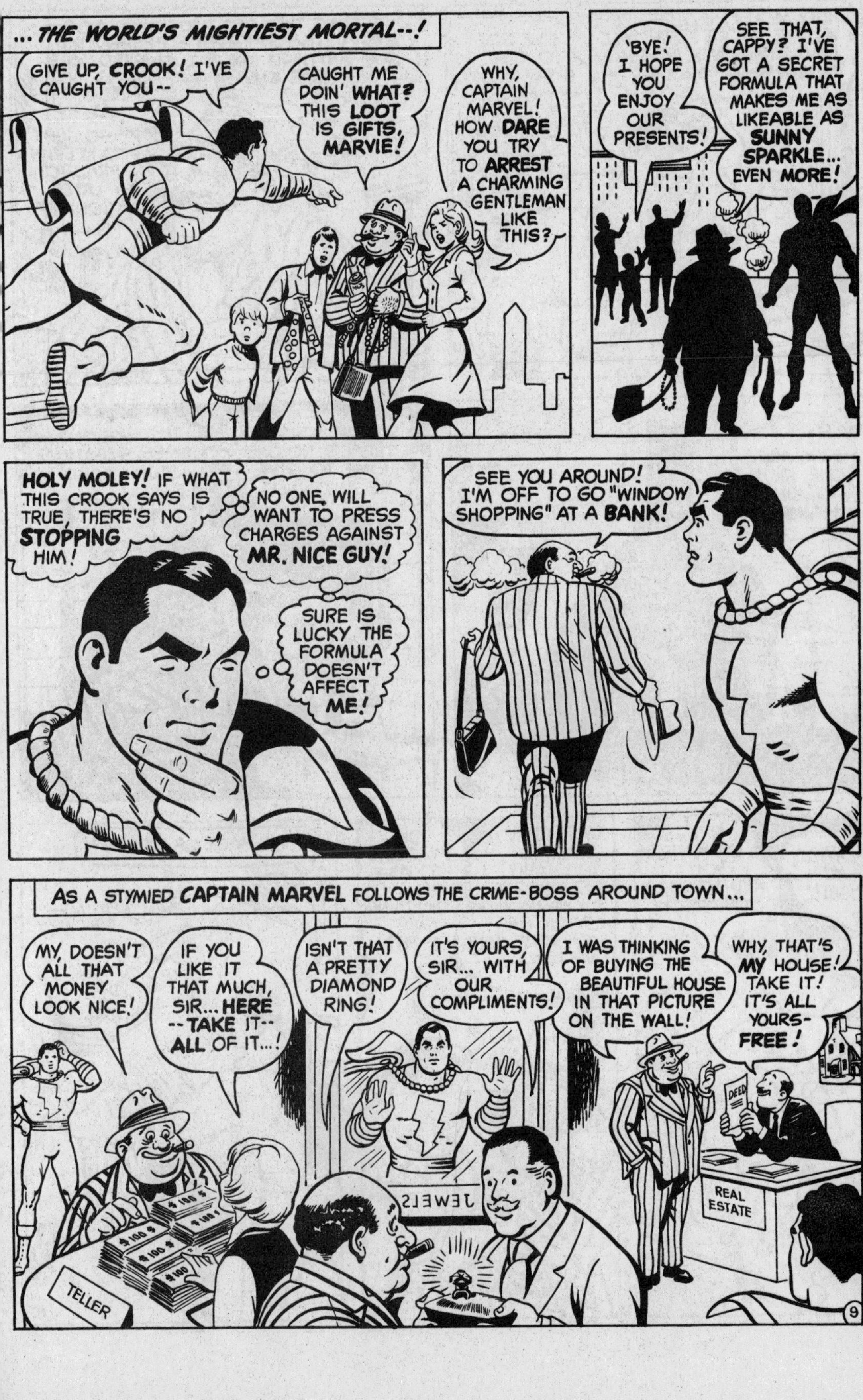
...THE WORLD'S MIGHTIEST MORTAL--!
GIVE UP, CROOK! I'VE CAUGHT YOU--
CAUGHT ME DOIN' WHAT? THIS LOOT IS GIFTS, MARVIE!
WHY, CAPTAIN MARVEL! HOW DARE YOU TRY TO ARREST A CHARMING GENTLEMAN LIKE THIS?
'BYE! I HOPE YOU ENJOY OUR PRESENTS!
SEE THAT, CAPPY? I'VE GOT A SECRET FORMULA THAT MAKES ME AS LIKEABLE AS SUNNY SPARKLE... EVEN MORE!
HOLY MOLEY! IF WHAT THIS CROOK SAYS IS TRUE, THERE'S NO STOPPING HIM!
NO ONE WILL WANT TO PRESS CHARGES AGAINST MR. NICE GUY!
SURE IS LUCKY THE FORMULA DOESN'T AFFECT ME!
SEE YOU AROUND! I'M OFF TO GO "WINDOW SHOPPING" AT A BANK!
AS A STYMIED CAPTAIN MARVEL FOLLOWS THE CRIME-BOSS AROUND TOWN...
MY, DOESN'T ALL THAT MONEY LOOK NICE!
IF YOU LIKE IT THAT MUCH, SIR... HERE --TAKE IT-- ALL OF IT...!
ISN'T THAT A PRETTY DIAMOND RING!
IT'S YOURS, SIR... WITH OUR COMPLIMENTS!
I WAS THINKING OF BUYING THE BEAUTIFUL HOUSE IN THAT PICTURE ON THE WALL!
WHY, THAT'S MY HOUSE! TAKE IT! IT'S ALL YOURS-FREE!
JEWELS
DEED
REAL ESTATE
TELLER
9

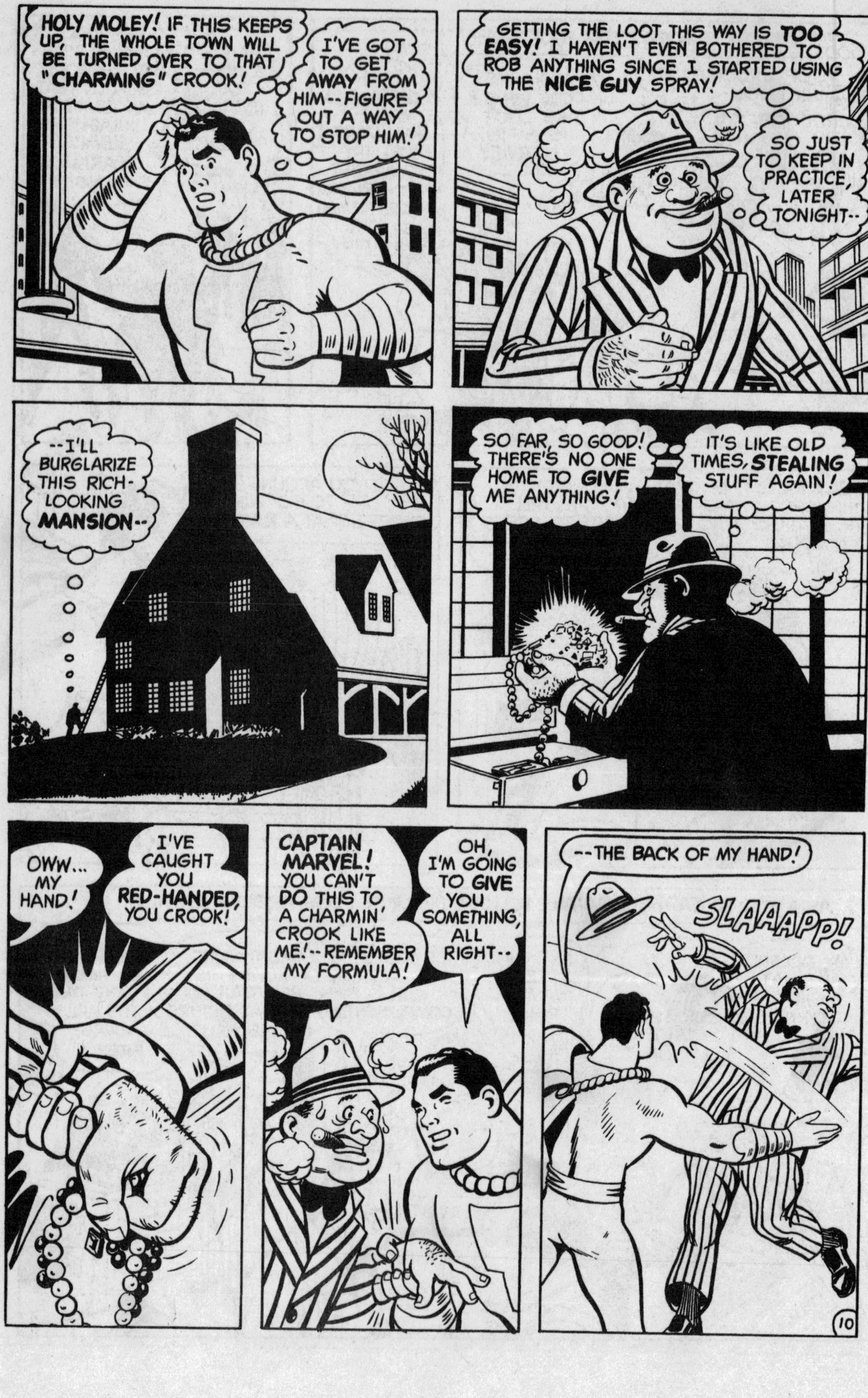
HOLY MOLEY! IF THIS KEEPS UP, THE WHOLE TOWN WILL BE TURNED OVER TO THAT "CHARMING" CROOK!
I'VE GOT TO GET AWAY FROM HIM--FIGURE OUT A WAY TO STOP HIM!
GETTING THE LOOT THIS WAY IS TOO EASY! I HAVEN'T EVEN BOTHERED TO ROB ANYTHING SINCE I STARTED USING THE NICE GUY SPRAY!
SO JUST TO KEEP IN PRACTICE, LATER TONIGHT--
--I'LL BURGLARIZE THIS RICH-LOOKING MANSION--
SO FAR, SO GOOD! THERE'S NO ONE HOME TO GIVE ME ANYTHING!
IT'S LIKE OLD TIMES, STEALING STUFF AGAIN!
OWW... MY HAND!
I'VE CAUGHT YOU RED-HANDED, YOU CROOK!
CAPTAIN MARVEL! YOU CAN'T DO THIS TO A CHARMIN' CROOK LIKE ME!--REMEMBER MY FORMULA!
OH, I'M GOING TO GIVE YOU SOMETHING, ALL RIGHT--
--THE BACK OF MY HAND!
SLAAAPP!
10

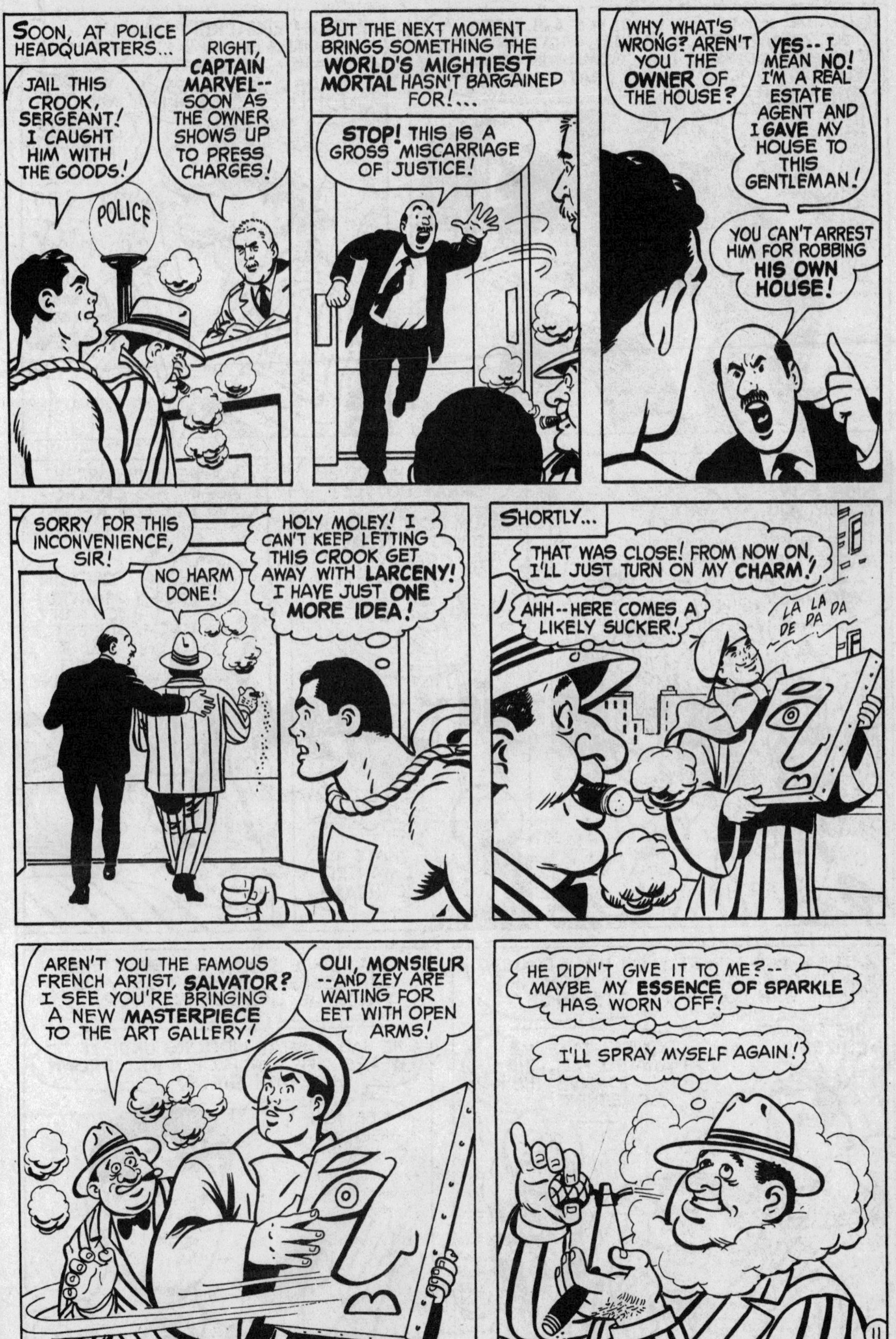
SOON, AT POLICE HEADQUARTERS...
JAIL THIS CROOK, SERGEANT! I CAUGHT HIM WITH THE GOODS!
RIGHT, CAPTAIN MARVEL-- SOON AS THE OWNER SHOWS UP TO PRESS CHARGES!
POLICE
BUT THE NEXT MOMENT BRINGS SOMETHING THE WORLD'S MIGHTIEST MORTAL HASN'T BARGAINED FOR!...
STOP! THIS IS A GROSS MISCARRIAGE OF JUSTICE!
WHY, WHAT'S WRONG? AREN'T YOU THE OWNER OF THE HOUSE?
YES-- I MEAN NO! I'M A REAL ESTATE AGENT AND I GAVE MY HOUSE TO THIS GENTLEMAN!
YOU CAN'T ARREST HIM FOR ROBBING HIS OWN HOUSE!
SORRY FOR THIS INCONVENIENCE, SIR!
NO HARM DONE!
HOLY MOLEY! I CAN'T KEEP LETTING THIS CROOK GET AWAY WITH LARCENY! I HAVE JUST ONE MORE IDEA!
SHORTLY...
THAT WAS CLOSE! FROM NOW ON, I'LL JUST TURN ON MY CHARM!
AHH--HERE COMES A LIKELY SUCKER!
LA LA DE DA DA
AREN'T YOU THE FAMOUS FRENCH ARTIST, SALVATOR? I SEE YOU'RE BRINGING A NEW MASTERPIECE TO THE ART GALLERY!
OUI, MONSIEUR --AND ZEY ARE WAITING FOR EET WITH OPEN ARMS!
HE DIDN'T GIVE IT TO ME?-- MAYBE MY ESSENCE OF SPARKLE HAS WORN OFF!
I'LL SPRAY MYSELF AGAIN!
11

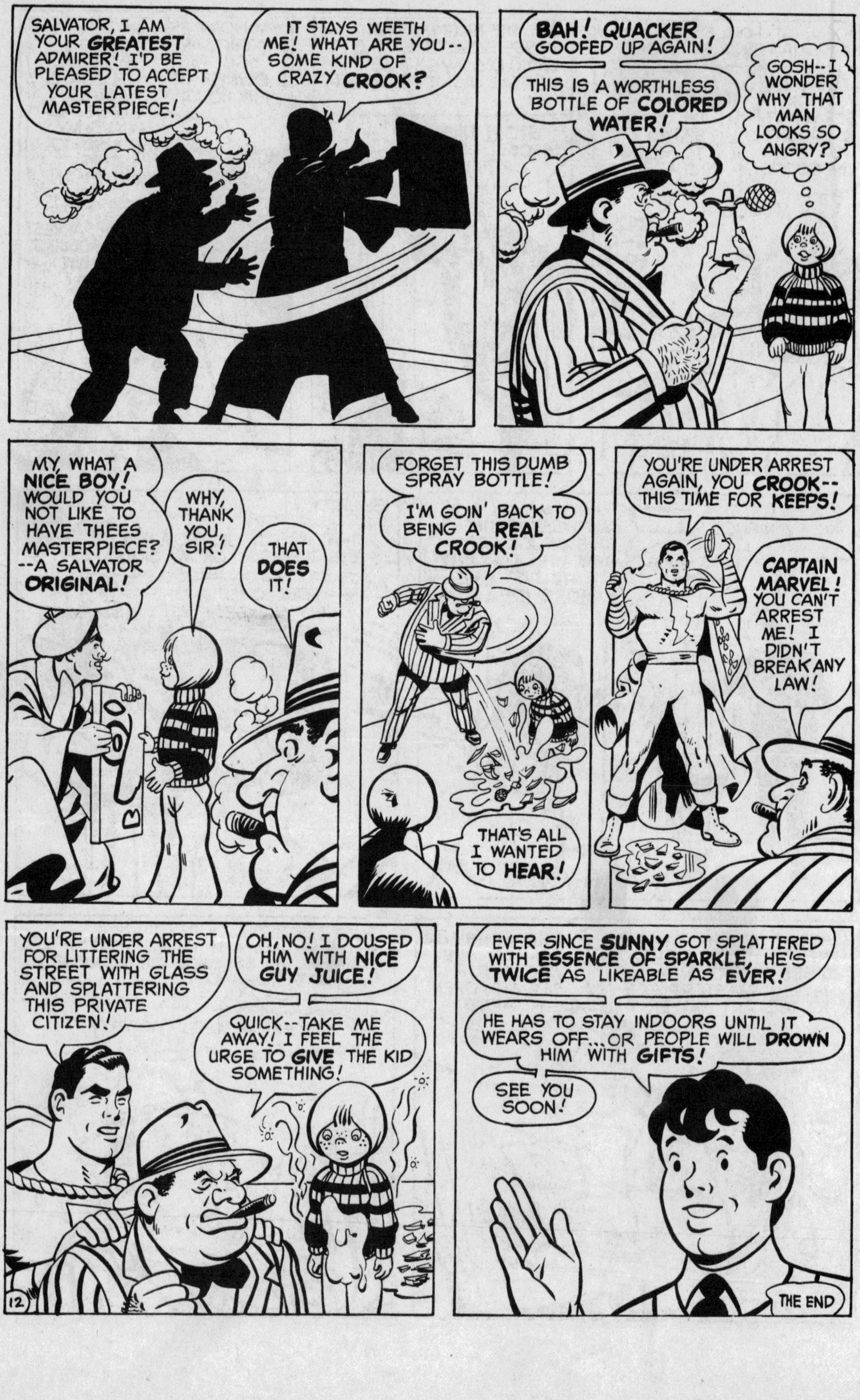
SALVATOR, I AM YOUR GREATEST ADMIRER! I'D BE PLEASED TO ACCEPT YOUR LATEST MASTERPIECE!
IT STAYS WEETH ME! WHAT ARE YOU--SOME KIND OF CRAZY CROOK?
BAH! QUACKER GOOFED UP AGAIN!
THIS IS A WORTHLESS BOTTLE OF COLORED WATER!
GOSH--I WONDER WHY THAT MAN LOOKS SO ANGRY?
MY, WHAT A NICE BOY! WOULD YOU NOT LIKE TO HAVE THEES MASTERPIECE? --A SALVATOR ORIGINAL!
WHY, THANK YOU, SIR!
THAT DOES IT!
FORGET THIS DUMB SPRAY BOTTLE!
I'M GOIN' BACK TO BEING A REAL CROOK!
THAT'S ALL I WANTED TO HEAR!
YOU'RE UNDER ARREST AGAIN, YOU CROOK--THIS TIME FOR KEEPS!
CAPTAIN MARVEL! YOU CAN'T ARREST ME! I DIDN'T BREAK ANY LAW!
YOU'RE UNDER ARREST FOR LITTERING THE STREET WITH GLASS AND SPLATTERING THIS PRIVATE CITIZEN!
OH, NO! I DOUSED HIM WITH NICE GUY JUICE!
QUICK--TAKE ME AWAY! I FEEL THE URGE TO GIVE THE KID SOMETHING!
12
EVER SINCE SUNNY GOT SPLATTERED WITH ESSENCE OF SPARKLE, HE'S TWICE AS LIKEABLE AS EVER!
HE HAS TO STAY INDOORS UNTIL IT WEARS OFF...OR PEOPLE WILL DROWN HIM WITH GIFTS!
SEE YOU SOON!
THE END

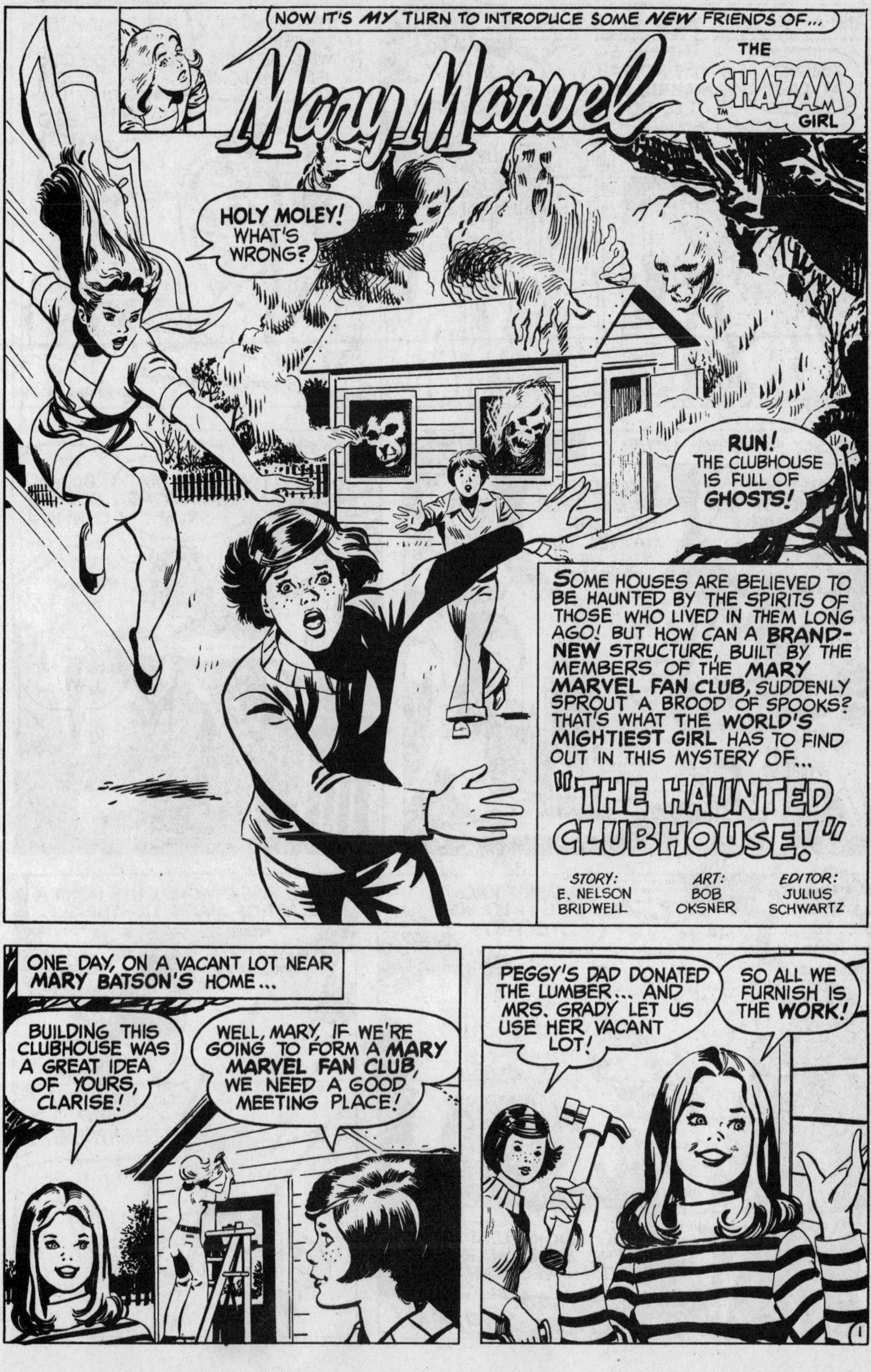
NOW IT'S MY TURN TO INTRODUCE SOME NEW FRIENDS OF...
Mary Marvel
THE SHAZAM GIRL
HOLY MOLEY! WHAT'S WRONG?
RUN! THE CLUBHOUSE IS FULL OF GHOSTS!
SOME HOUSES ARE BELIEVED TO BE HAUNTED BY THE SPIRITS OF THOSE WHO LIVED IN THEM LONG AGO! BUT HOW CAN A BRAND-NEW STRUCTURE, BUILT BY THE MEMBERS OF THE MARY MARVEL FAN CLUB, SUDDENLY SPROUT A BROOD OF SPOOKS? THAT'S WHAT THE WORLD'S MIGHTIEST GIRL HAS TO FIND OUT IN THIS MYSTERY OF...
"THE HAUNTED CLUBHOUSE!"
STORY: E. NELSON BRIDWELL
ART: BOB OKSNER
EDITOR: JULIUS SCHWARTZ
ONE DAY, ON A VACANT LOT NEAR MARY BATSON'S HOME...
BUILDING THIS CLUBHOUSE WAS A GREAT IDEA OF YOURS, CLARISE!
WELL, MARY, IF WE'RE GOING TO FORM A MARY MARVEL FAN CLUB, WE NEED A GOOD MEETING PLACE!
PEGGY'S DAD DONATED THE LUMBER... AND MRS. GRADY LET US USE HER VACANT LOT!
SO ALL WE FURNISH IS THE WORK!
1

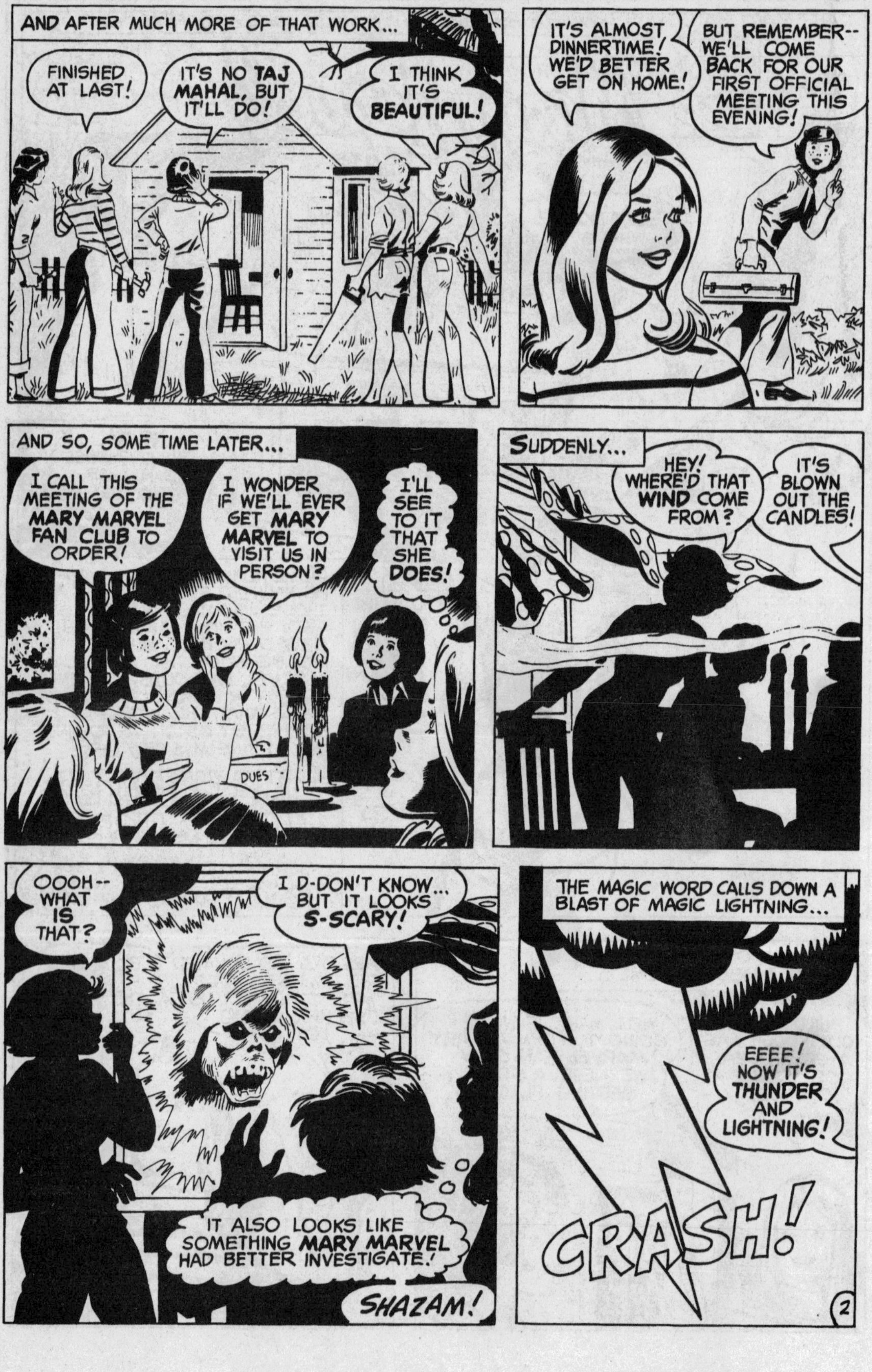
AND AFTER MUCH MORE OF THAT WORK...
FINISHED AT LAST!
IT'S NO TAJ MAHAL, BUT IT'LL DO!
I THINK IT'S BEAUTIFUL!
IT'S ALMOST DINNERTIME! WE'D BETTER GET ON HOME!
BUT REMEMBER-- WE'LL COME BACK FOR OUR FIRST OFFICIAL MEETING THIS EVENING!
AND SO, SOME TIME LATER...
I CALL THIS MEETING OF THE MARY MARVEL FAN CLUB TO ORDER!
I WONDER IF WE'LL EVER GET MARY MARVEL TO VISIT US IN PERSON?
I'LL SEE TO IT THAT SHE DOES!
DUES
SUDDENLY...
HEY! WHERE'D THAT WIND COME FROM?
IT'S BLOWN OUT THE CANDLES!
OOOH-- WHAT IS THAT?
I D-DON'T KNOW... BUT IT LOOKS S-SCARY!
IT ALSO LOOKS LIKE SOMETHING MARY MARVEL HAD BETTER INVESTIGATE!
SHAZAM!
THE MAGIC WORD CALLS DOWN A BLAST OF MAGIC LIGHTNING...
EEEE! NOW IT'S THUNDER AND LIGHTNING!
CRASH!
2

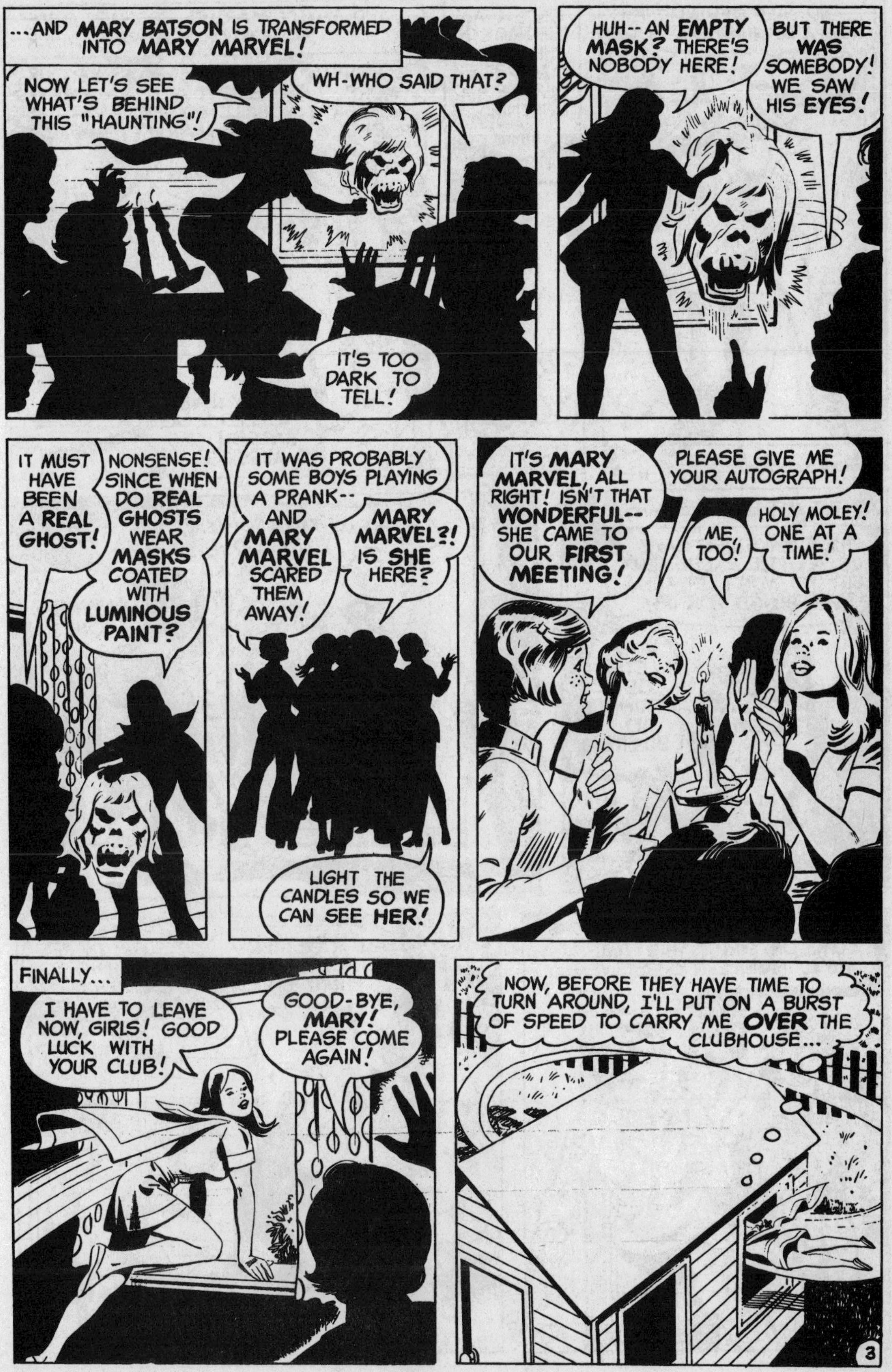

...AND MARY BATSON IS TRANSFORMED INTO MARY MARVEL!
NOW LET'S SEE WHAT'S BEHIND THIS "HAUNTING"!
WH-WHO SAID THAT?
IT'S TOO DARK TO TELL!
HUH--AN EMPTY MASK? THERE'S NOBODY HERE!
BUT THERE WAS SOMEBODY! WE SAW HIS EYES!
IT MUST HAVE BEEN A REAL GHOST!
NONSENSE! SINCE WHEN DO REAL GHOSTS WEAR MASKS COATED WITH LUMINOUS PAINT?
IT WAS PROBABLY SOME BOYS PLAYING A PRANK-- AND MARY MARVEL SCARED THEM AWAY!
MARY MARVEL?! IS SHE HERE?
LIGHT THE CANDLES SO WE CAN SEE HER!
IT'S MARY MARVEL, ALL RIGHT! ISN'T THAT WONDERFUL-- SHE CAME TO OUR FIRST MEETING!
PLEASE GIVE ME YOUR AUTOGRAPH!
ME, TOO!
HOLY MOLEY! ONE AT A TIME!
FINALLY...
I HAVE TO LEAVE NOW, GIRLS! GOOD LUCK WITH YOUR CLUB!
GOOD-BYE, MARY! PLEASE COME AGAIN!
NOW, BEFORE THEY HAVE TIME TO TURN AROUND, I'LL PUT ON A BURST OF SPEED TO CARRY ME OVER THE CLUBHOUSE...
3

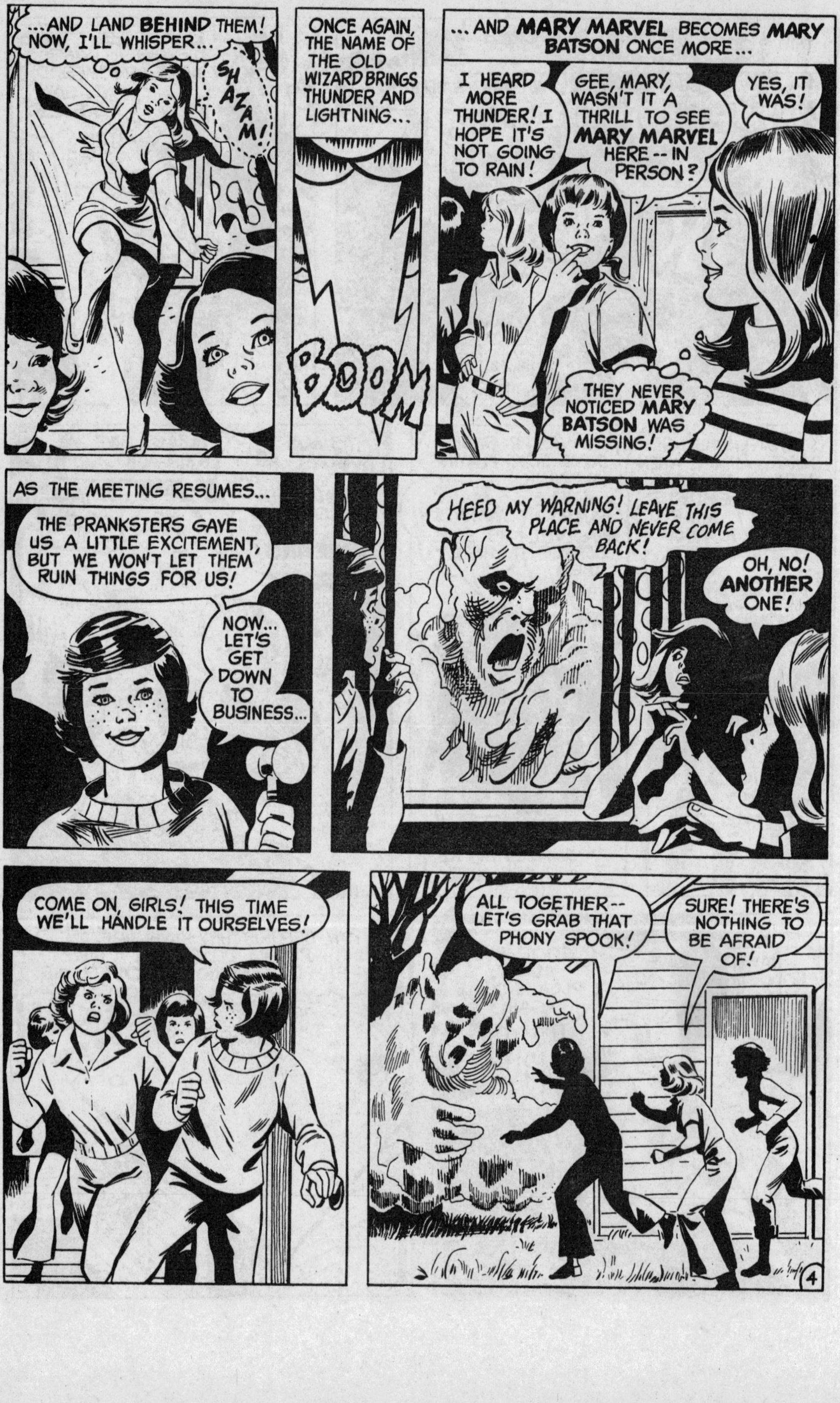
...AND LAND BEHIND THEM! NOW, I'LL WHISPER...
SHAZAM!
ONCE AGAIN, THE NAME OF THE OLD WIZARD BRINGS THUNDER AND LIGHTNING...
BOOM
...AND MARY MARVEL BECOMES MARY BATSON ONCE MORE...
I HEARD MORE THUNDER! I HOPE IT'S NOT GOING TO RAIN!
GEE, MARY, WASN'T IT A THRILL TO SEE MARY MARVEL HERE -- IN PERSON?
YES, IT WAS!
THEY NEVER NOTICED MARY BATSON WAS MISSING!
AS THE MEETING RESUMES...
THE PRANKSTERS GAVE US A LITTLE EXCITEMENT, BUT WE WON'T LET THEM RUIN THINGS FOR US!
NOW... LET'S GET DOWN TO BUSINESS...
HEED MY WARNING! LEAVE THIS PLACE AND NEVER COME BACK!
OH, NO! ANOTHER ONE!
COME ON, GIRLS! THIS TIME WE'LL HANDLE IT OURSELVES!
ALL TOGETHER-- LET'S GRAB THAT PHONY SPOOK!
SURE! THERE'S NOTHING TO BE AFRAID OF!
4

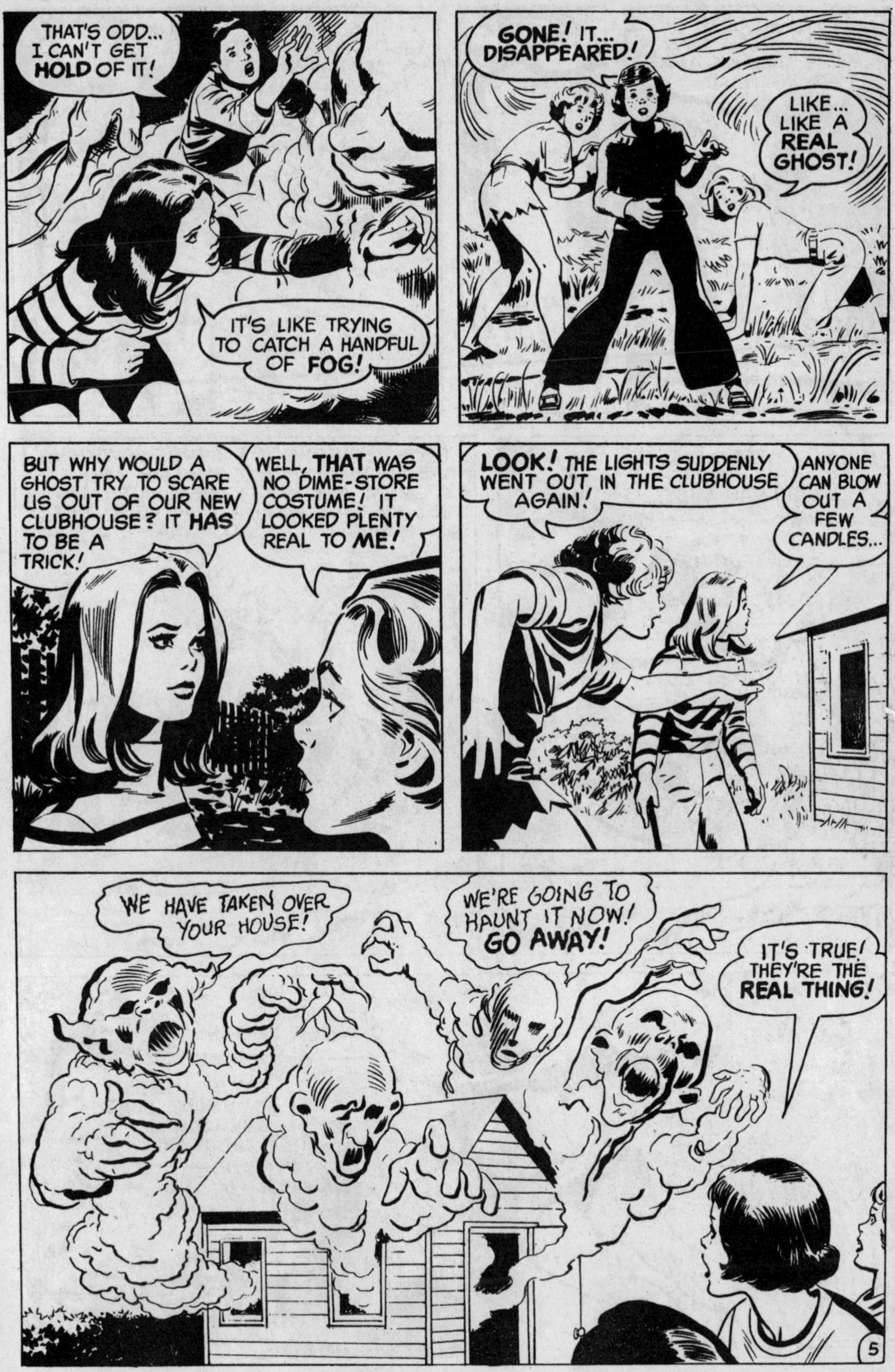
THAT'S ODD... I CAN'T GET HOLD OF IT!
IT'S LIKE TRYING TO CATCH A HANDFUL OF FOG!
GONE! IT... DISAPPEARED!
LIKE... LIKE A REAL GHOST!
BUT WHY WOULD A GHOST TRY TO SCARE US OUT OF OUR NEW CLUBHOUSE? IT HAS TO BE A TRICK!
WELL, THAT WAS NO DIME-STORE COSTUME! IT LOOKED PLENTY REAL TO ME!
LOOK! THE LIGHTS SUDDENLY WENT OUT IN THE CLUBHOUSE AGAIN!
ANYONE CAN BLOW OUT A FEW CANDLES...
WE HAVE TAKEN OVER YOUR HOUSE!
WE'RE GOING TO HAUNT IT NOW! GO AWAY!
IT'S TRUE! THEY'RE THE REAL THING!
5

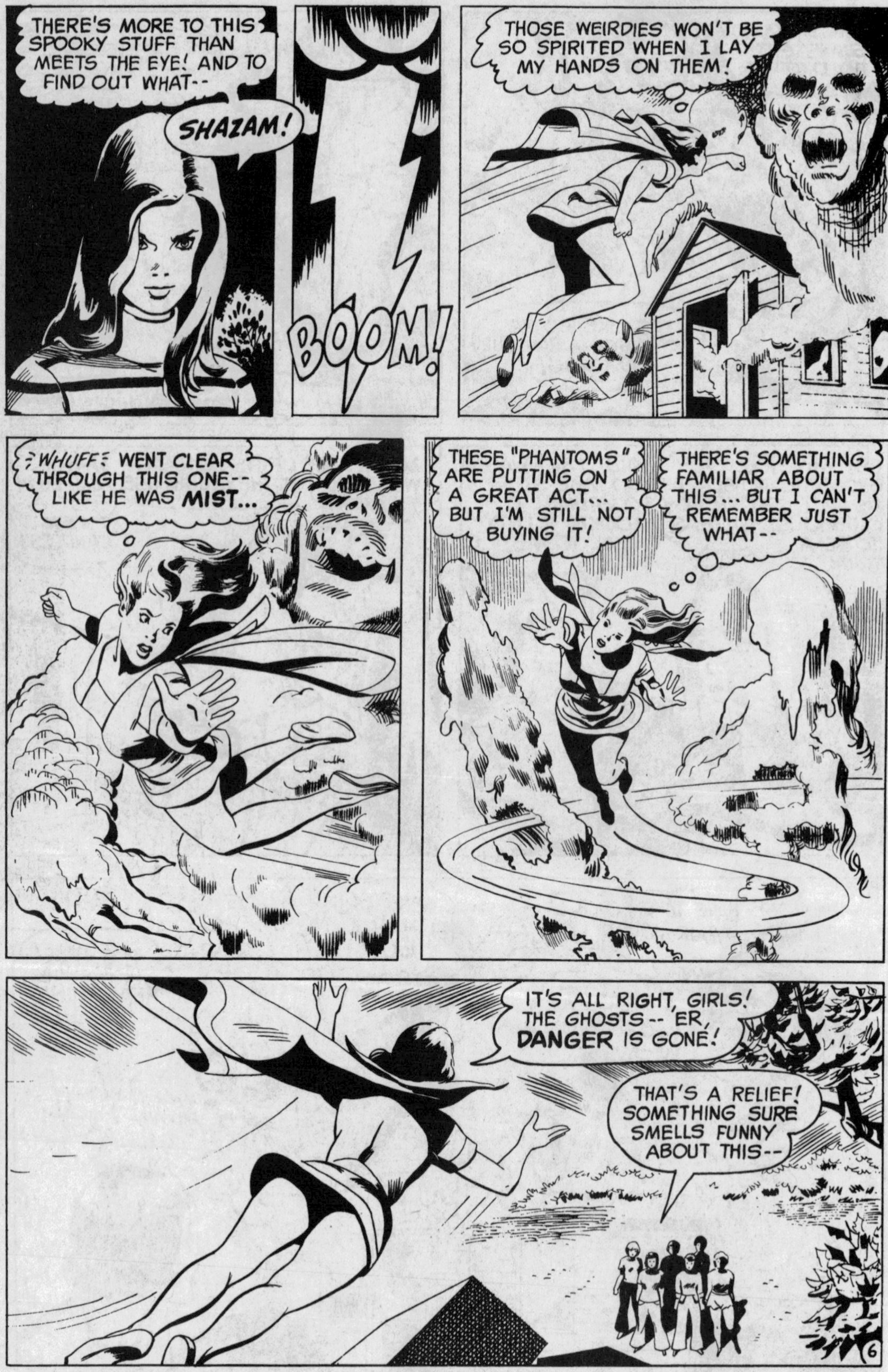
THERE'S MORE TO THIS SPOOKY STUFF THAN MEETS THE EYE! AND TO FIND OUT WHAT--
SHAZAM!
BOOM!
THOSE WEIRDIES WON'T BE SO SPIRITED WHEN I LAY MY HANDS ON THEM!
WHUFF! WENT CLEAR THROUGH THIS ONE-- LIKE HE WAS MIST...
THESE "PHANTOMS" ARE PUTTING ON A GREAT ACT... BUT I'M STILL NOT BUYING IT!
THERE'S SOMETHING FAMILIAR ABOUT THIS... BUT I CAN'T REMEMBER JUST WHAT--
IT'S ALL RIGHT, GIRLS! THE GHOSTS-- ER, DANGER IS GONE!
THAT'S A RELIEF! SOMETHING SURE SMELLS FUNNY ABOUT THIS--
6

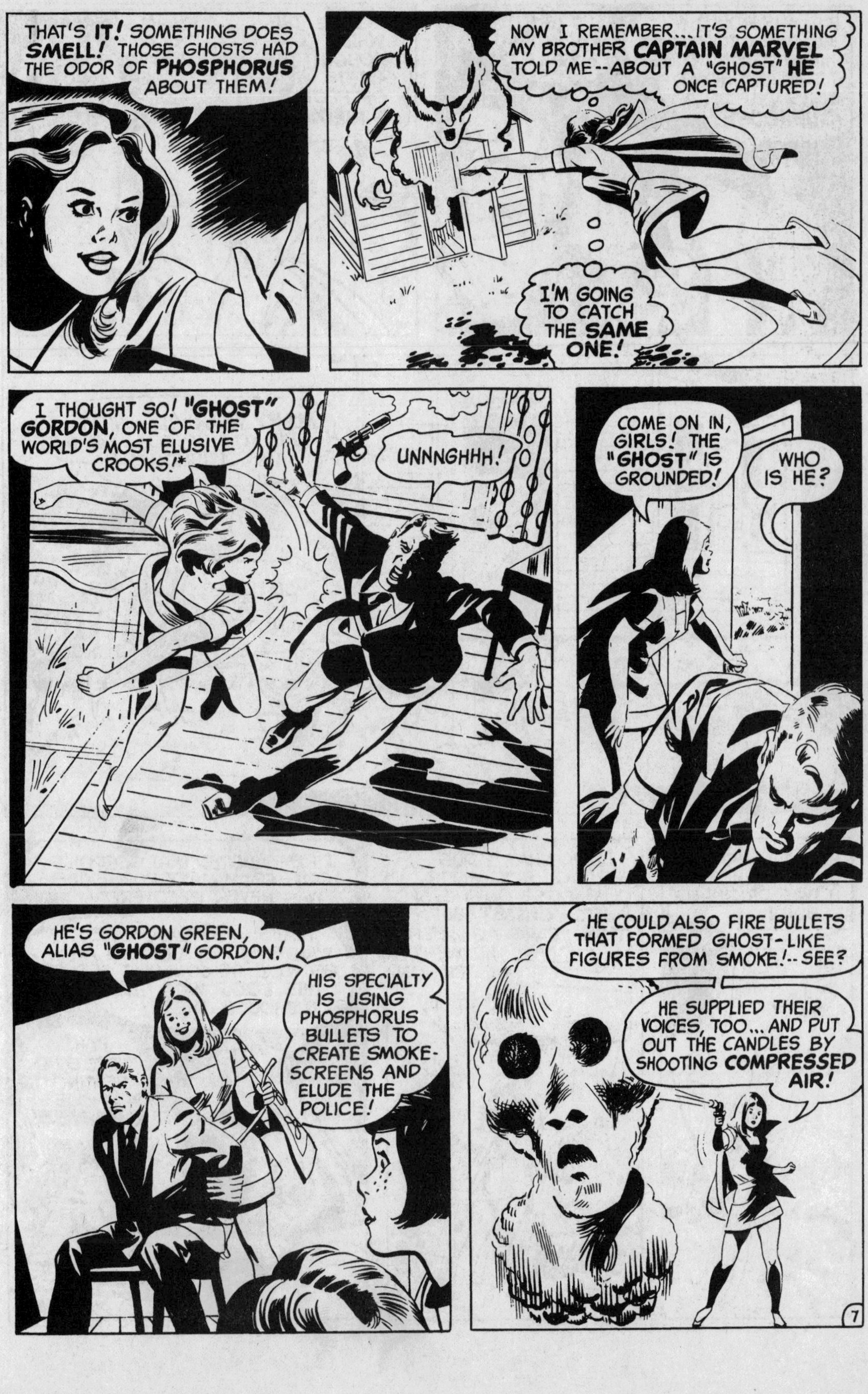
THAT'S IT! SOMETHING DOES SMELL! THOSE GHOSTS HAD THE ODOR OF PHOSPHORUS ABOUT THEM!
NOW I REMEMBER... IT'S SOMETHING MY BROTHER CAPTAIN MARVEL TOLD ME--ABOUT A "GHOST" HE ONCE CAPTURED!
I'M GOING TO CATCH THE SAME ONE!
I THOUGHT SO! "GHOST" GORDON, ONE OF THE WORLD'S MOST ELUSIVE CROOKS!*
UNNNGHHH!
COME ON IN, GIRLS! THE "GHOST" IS GROUNDED!
WHO IS HE?
HE'S GORDON GREEN, ALIAS "GHOST" GORDON!
HIS SPECIALTY IS USING PHOSPHORUS BULLETS TO CREATE SMOKE-SCREENS AND ELUDE THE POLICE!
HE COULD ALSO FIRE BULLETS THAT FORMED GHOST-LIKE FIGURES FROM SMOKE!--SEE?
HE SUPPLIED THEIR VOICES, TOO... AND PUT OUT THE CANDLES BY SHOOTING COMPRESSED AIR!
7

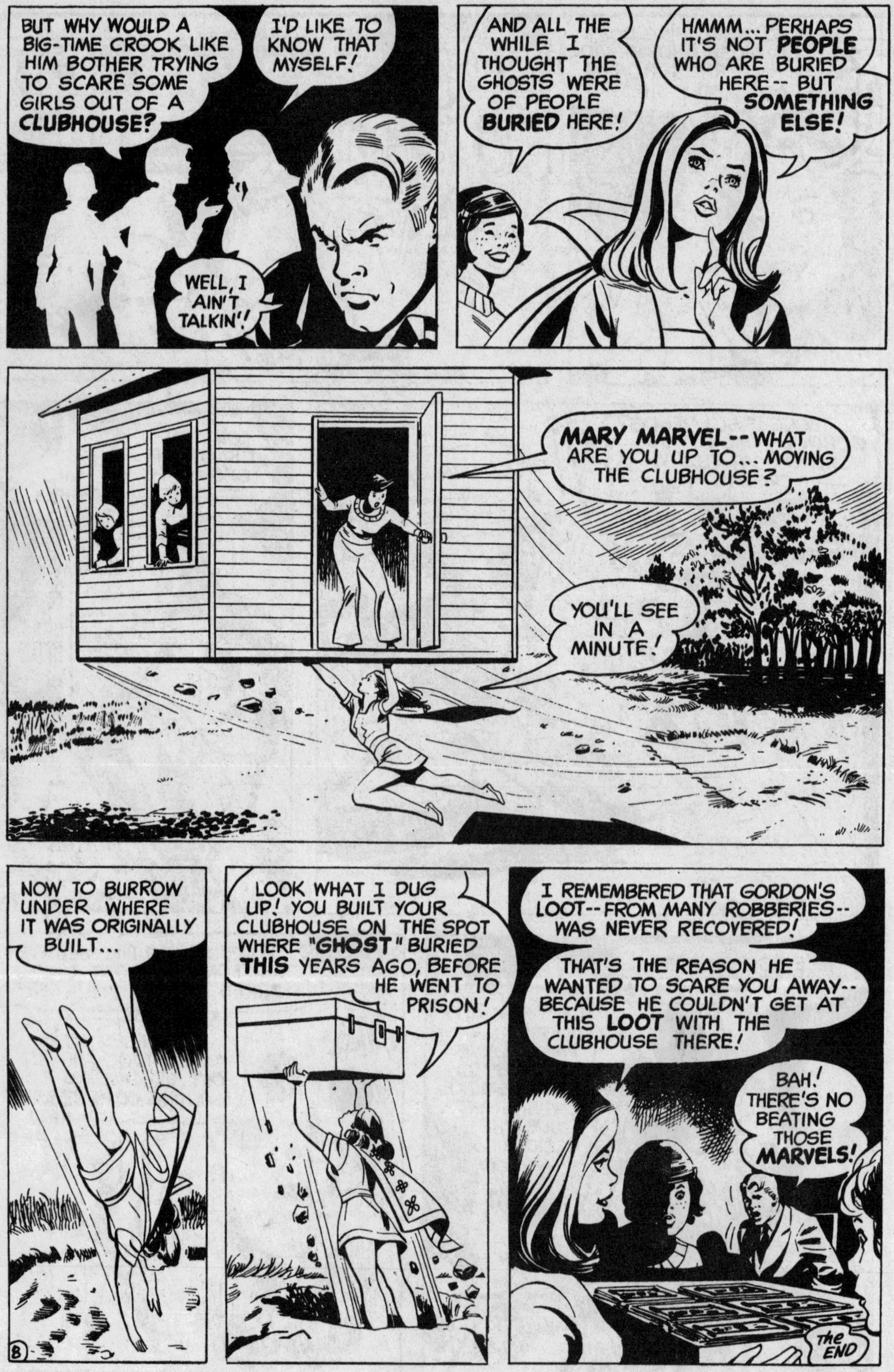
BUT WHY WOULD A BIG-TIME CROOK LIKE HIM BOTHER TRYING TO SCARE SOME GIRLS OUT OF A CLUBHOUSE?
I'D LIKE TO KNOW THAT MYSELF!
WELL, I AIN'T TALKIN'!
AND ALL THE WHILE I THOUGHT THE GHOSTS WERE OF PEOPLE BURIED HERE!
HMMM... PERHAPS IT'S NOT PEOPLE WHO ARE BURIED HERE-- BUT SOMETHING ELSE!
MARY MARVEL--WHAT ARE YOU UP TO... MOVING THE CLUBHOUSE?
YOU'LL SEE IN A MINUTE!
NOW TO BURROW UNDER WHERE IT WAS ORIGINALLY BUILT...
8
LOOK WHAT I DUG UP! YOU BUILT YOUR CLUBHOUSE ON THE SPOT WHERE "GHOST" BURIED THIS YEARS AGO, BEFORE HE WENT TO PRISON!
I REMEMBERED THAT GORDON'S LOOT--FROM MANY ROBBERIES--WAS NEVER RECOVERED!
THAT'S THE REASON HE WANTED TO SCARE YOU AWAY--BECAUSE HE COULDN'T GET AT THIS LOOT WITH THE CLUBHOUSE THERE!
BAH! THERE'S NO BEATING THOSE MARVELS!
The END

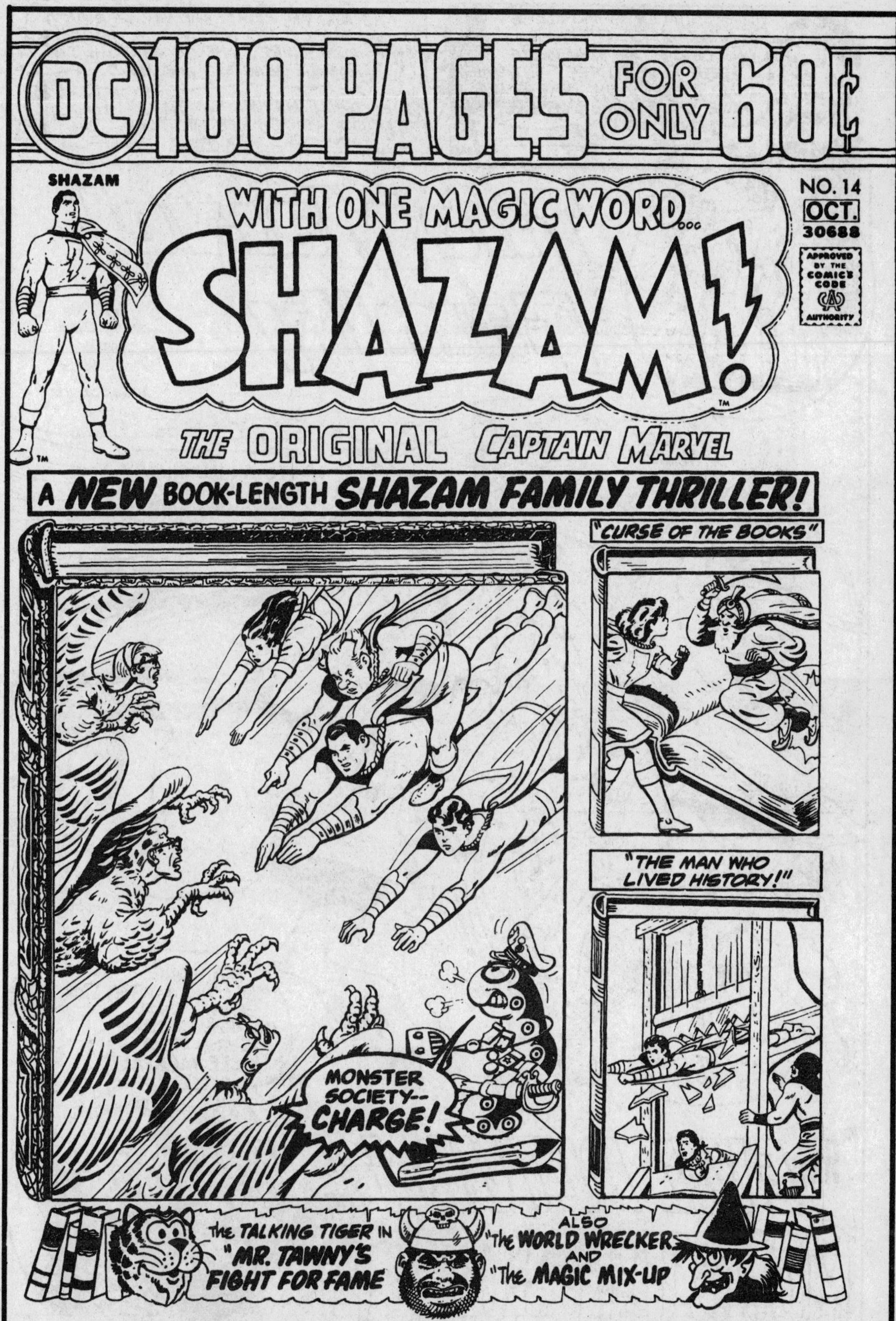
DC
100 PAGES FOR ONLY 60¢
SHAZAM
WITH ONE MAGIC WORD...
SHAZAM!
NO. 14
OCT.
30688
APPROVED BY THE COMICS CODE AUTHORITY
THE ORIGINAL CAPTAIN MARVEL
A NEW BOOK-LENGTH SHAZAM FAMILY THRILLER!
"CURSE OF THE BOOKS"
"THE MAN WHO LIVED HISTORY!"
MONSTER SOCIETY--CHARGE!
The TALKING TIGER IN "MR. TAWNY'S FIGHT FOR FAME
ALSO "The WORLD WRECKER" AND "The MAGIC MIX-UP"

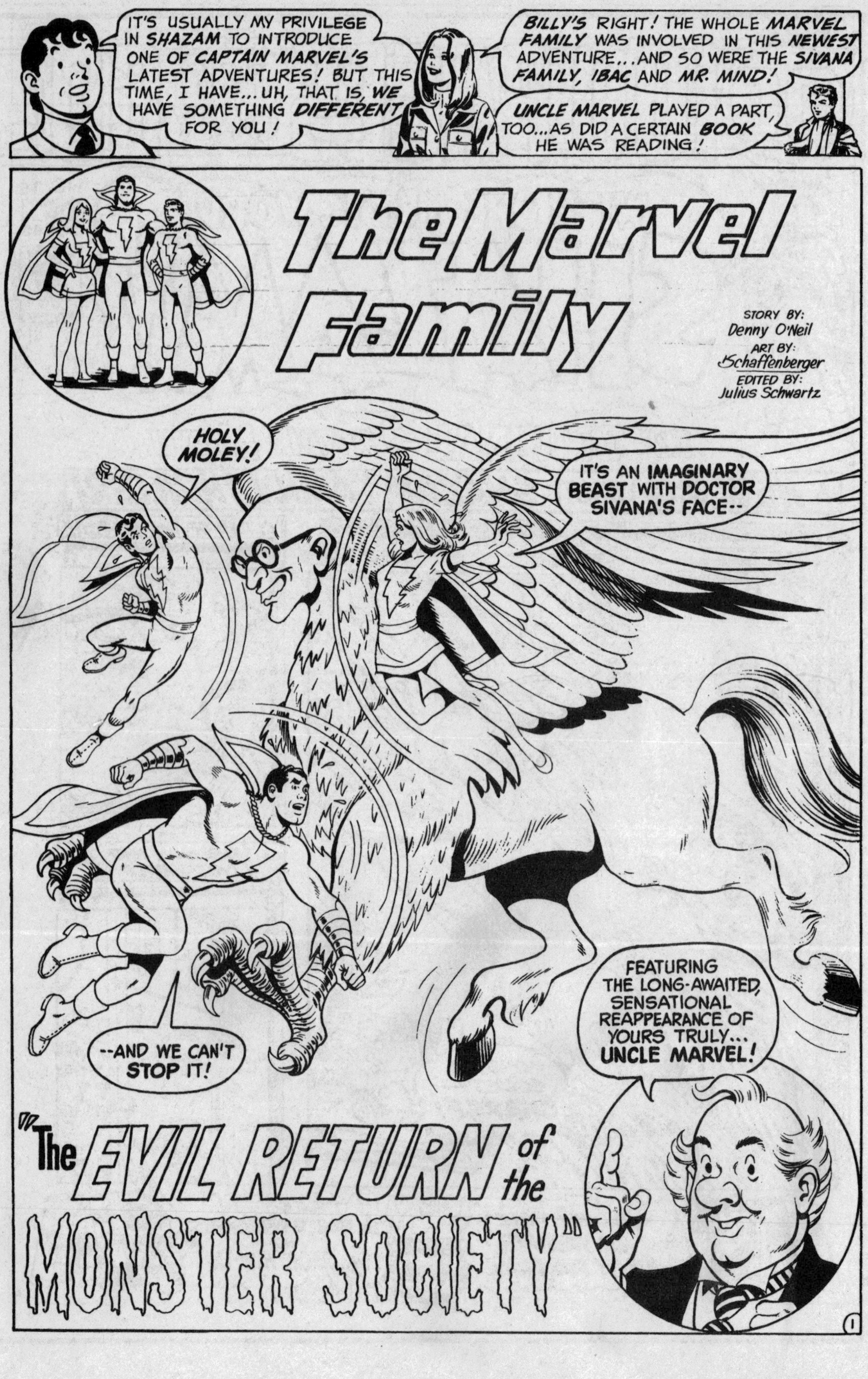
IT'S USUALLY MY PRIVILEGE IN SHAZAM TO INTRODUCE ONE OF CAPTAIN MARVEL'S LATEST ADVENTURES! BUT THIS TIME, I HAVE... UH, THAT IS, WE HAVE SOMETHING DIFFERENT FOR YOU!
BILLY'S RIGHT! THE WHOLE MARVEL FAMILY WAS INVOLVED IN THIS NEWEST ADVENTURE...AND SO WERE THE SIVANA FAMILY, IBAC AND MR. MIND!
UNCLE MARVEL PLAYED A PART, TOO...AS DID A CERTAIN BOOK HE WAS READING!
The Marvel Family
STORY BY: Denny O'Neil
ART BY: Schaffenberger
EDITED BY: Julius Schwartz
HOLY MOLEY!
IT'S AN IMAGINARY BEAST WITH DOCTOR SIVANA'S FACE--
--AND WE CAN'T STOP IT!
FEATURING THE LONG-AWAITED, SENSATIONAL REAPPEARANCE OF YOURS TRULY... UNCLE MARVEL!
"The EVIL RETURN of the MONSTER SOCIETY"
1

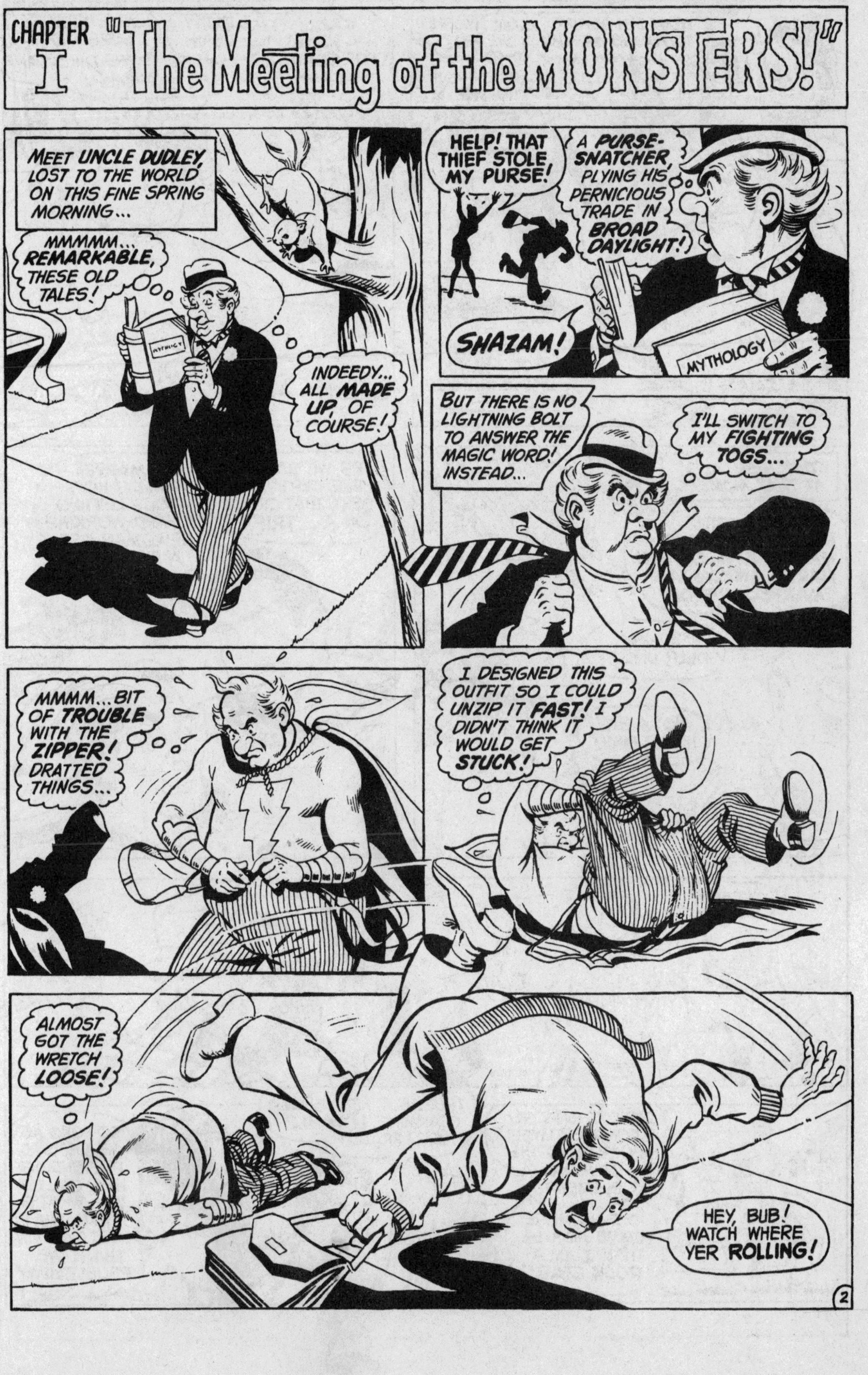
CHAPTER I "The Meeting of the MONSTERS!"
MEET UNCLE DUDLEY, LOST TO THE WORLD ON THIS FINE SPRING MORNING...
MMMMM... REMARKABLE, THESE OLD TALES!
MYTHOLOGY
INDEEDY... ALL MADE UP, OF COURSE!
HELP! THAT THIEF STOLE MY PURSE!
A PURSE-SNATCHER, PLYING HIS PERNICIOUS TRADE IN BROAD DAYLIGHT!
SHAZAM!
MYTHOLOGY
BUT THERE IS NO LIGHTNING BOLT TO ANSWER THE MAGIC WORD! INSTEAD...
I'LL SWITCH TO MY FIGHTING TOGS...
MMMM...BIT OF TROUBLE WITH THE ZIPPER! DRATTED THINGS...
I DESIGNED THIS OUTFIT SO I COULD UNZIP IT FAST! I DIDN'T THINK IT WOULD GET STUCK!
ALMOST GOT THE WRETCH LOOSE!
HEY, BUB! WATCH WHERE YER ROLLING!
2

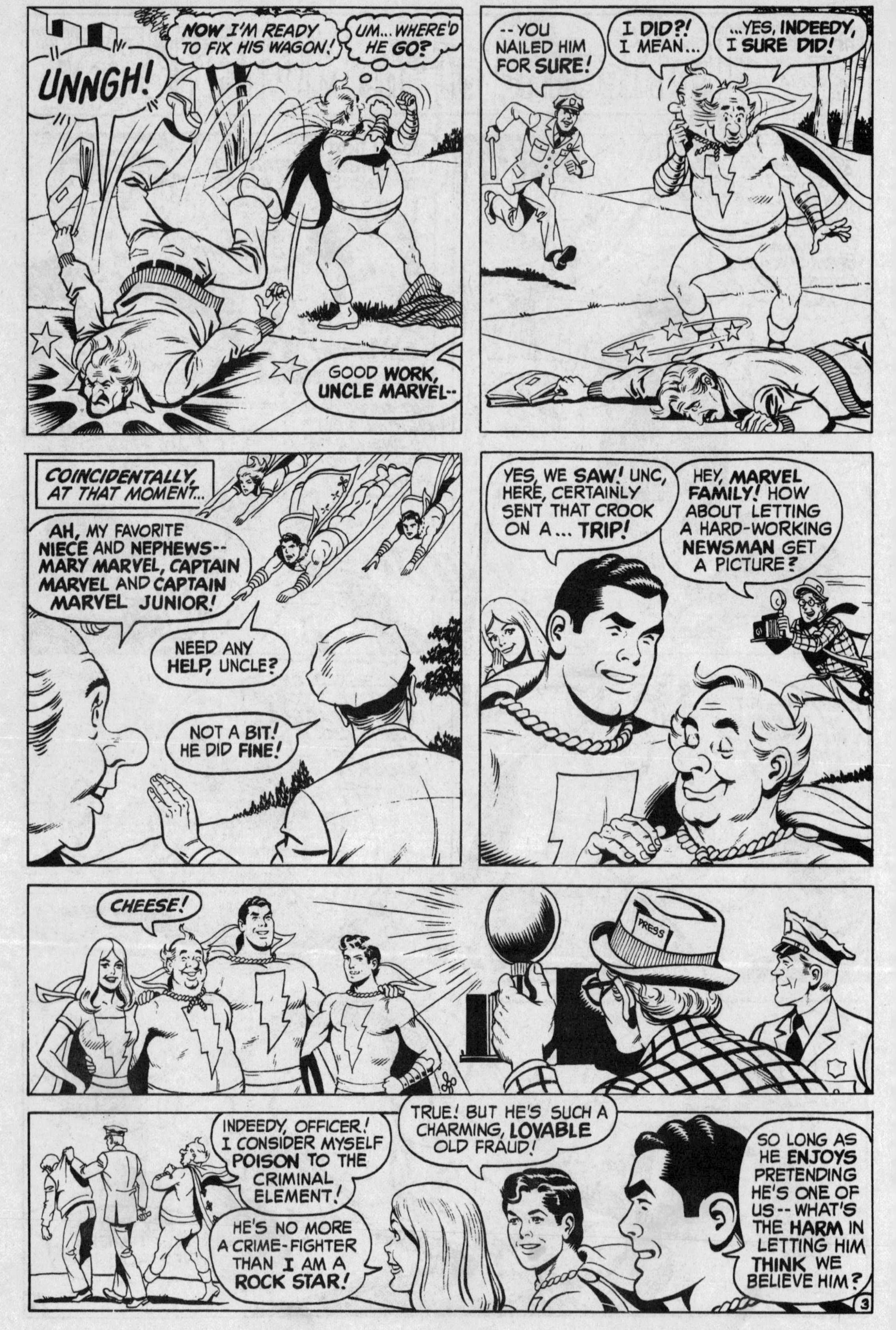
UNNGH!
NOW I'M READY TO FIX HIS WAGON!
UM...WHERE'D HE GO?
GOOD WORK, UNCLE MARVEL--
-- YOU NAILED HIM FOR SURE!
I DID?! I MEAN...
...YES, INDEEDY, I SURE DID!
COINCIDENTALLY, AT THAT MOMENT...
AH, MY FAVORITE NIECE AND NEPHEWS-- MARY MARVEL, CAPTAIN MARVEL AND CAPTAIN MARVEL JUNIOR!
NEED ANY HELP, UNCLE?
NOT A BIT! HE DID FINE!
YES, WE SAW! UNC, HERE, CERTAINLY SENT THAT CROOK ON A... TRIP!
HEY, MARVEL FAMILY! HOW ABOUT LETTING A HARD-WORKING NEWSMAN GET A PICTURE?
CHEESE!
PRESS
INDEEDY, OFFICER! I CONSIDER MYSELF POISON TO THE CRIMINAL ELEMENT!
HE'S NO MORE A CRIME-FIGHTER THAN I AM A ROCK STAR!
TRUE! BUT HE'S SUCH A CHARMING, LOVABLE OLD FRAUD!
SO LONG AS HE ENJOYS PRETENDING HE'S ONE OF US -- WHAT'S THE HARM IN LETTING HIM THINK WE BELIEVE HIM?
3

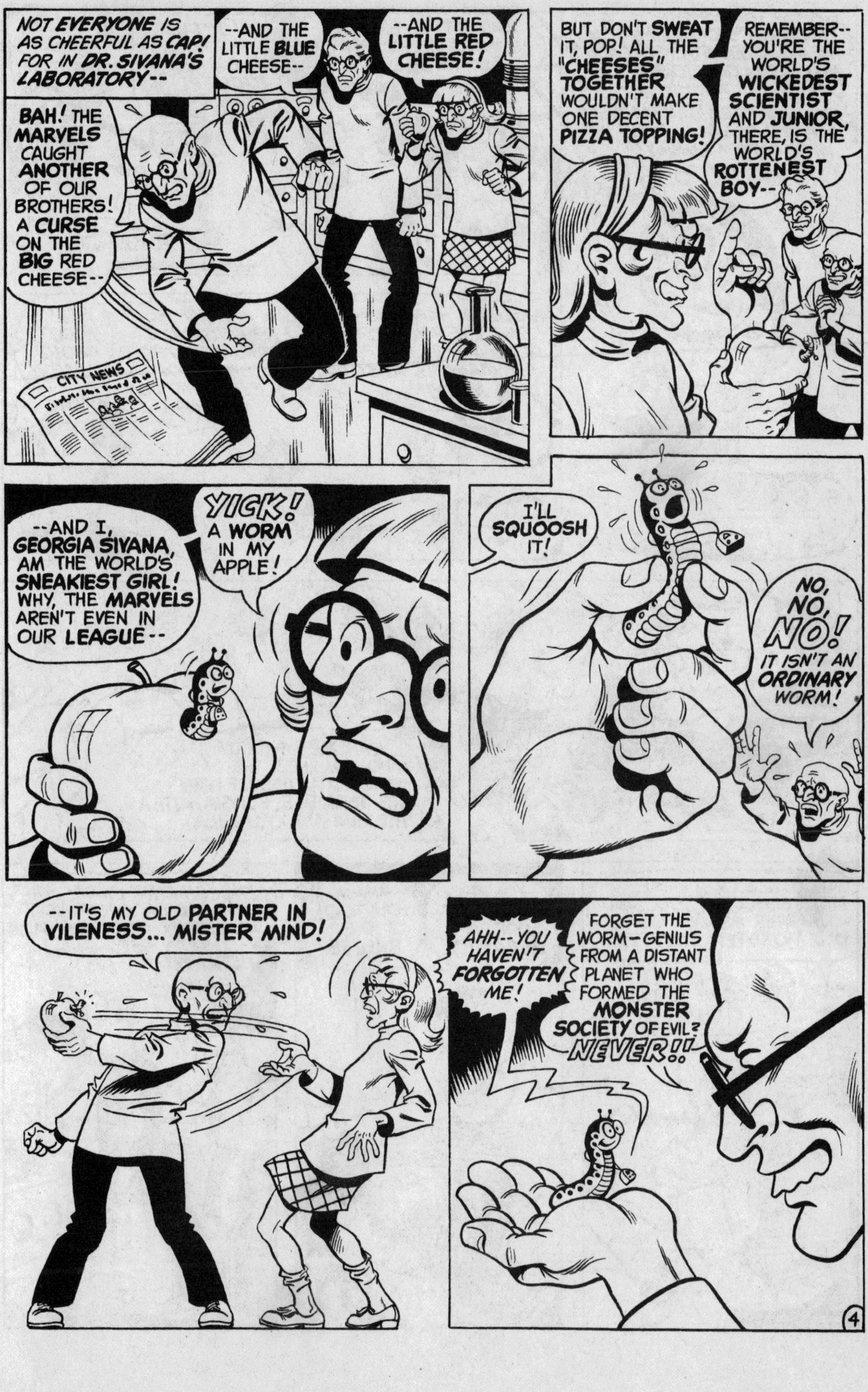
NOT EVERYONE IS AS CHEERFUL AS CAP! FOR IN DR. SIVANA'S LABORATORY--
BAH! THE MARVELS CAUGHT ANOTHER OF OUR BROTHERS! A CURSE ON THE BIG RED CHEESE--
--AND THE LITTLE BLUE CHEESE--
--AND THE LITTLE RED CHEESE!
CITY NEWS
BUT DON'T SWEAT IT, POP! ALL THE "CHEESES" TOGETHER WOULDN'T MAKE ONE DECENT PIZZA TOPPING!
REMEMBER-- YOU'RE THE WORLD'S WICKEDEST SCIENTIST AND JUNIOR, THERE, IS THE WORLD'S ROTTENEST BOY--
--AND I, GEORGIA SIVANA, AM THE WORLD'S SNEAKIEST GIRL! WHY, THE MARVELS AREN'T EVEN IN OUR LEAGUE--
YICK! A WORM IN MY APPLE!
I'LL SQUOOSH IT!
NO, NO, NO! IT ISN'T AN ORDINARY WORM!
--IT'S MY OLD PARTNER IN VILENESS... MISTER MIND!
AHH-- YOU HAVEN'T FORGOTTEN ME!
FORGET THE WORM-GENIUS FROM A DISTANT PLANET WHO FORMED THE MONSTER SOCIETY OF EVIL? NEVER!!
4

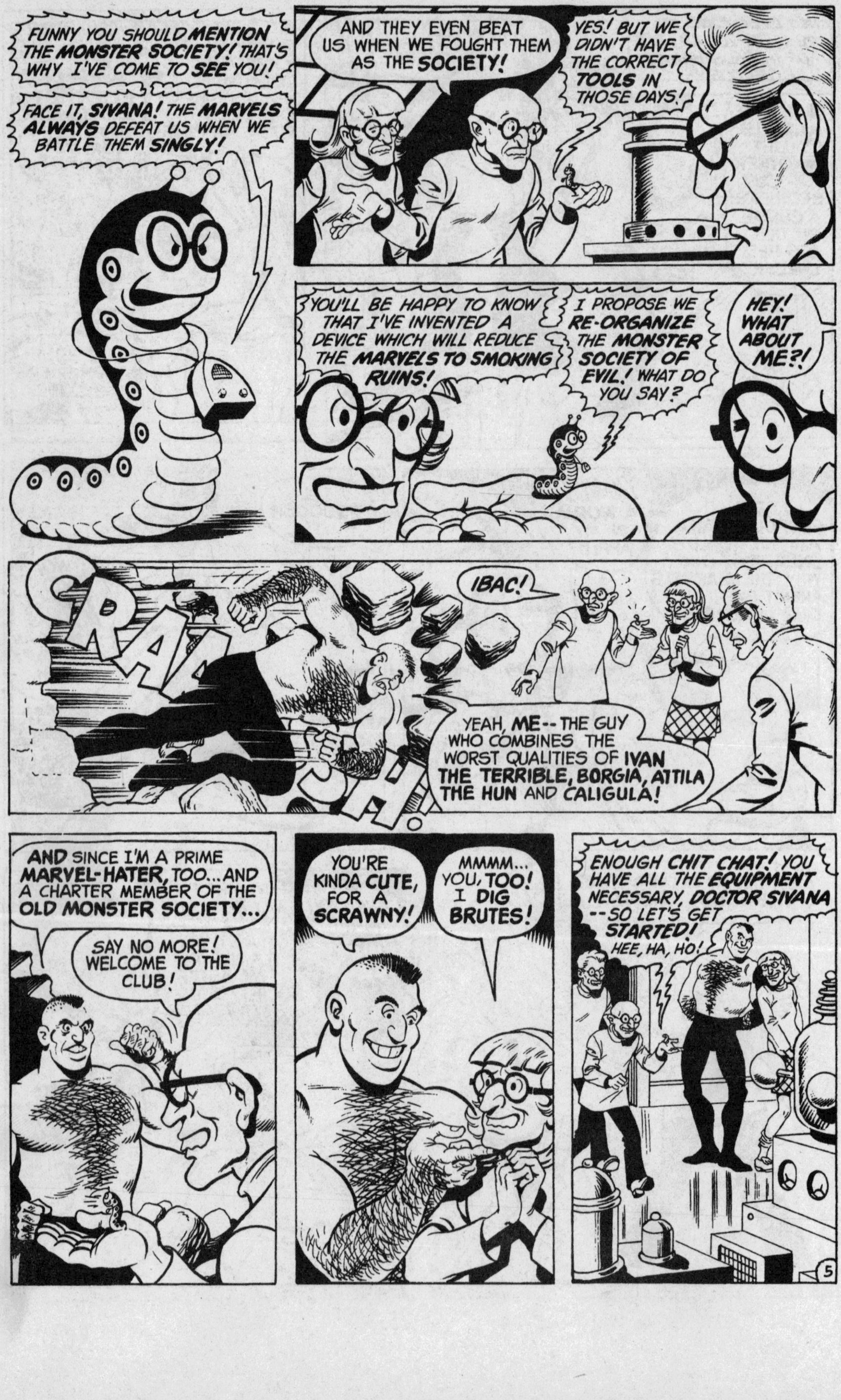
FUNNY YOU SHOULD MENTION THE MONSTER SOCIETY! THAT'S WHY I'VE COME TO SEE YOU!
FACE IT, SIVANA! THE MARVELS ALWAYS DEFEAT US WHEN WE BATTLE THEM SINGLY!
AND THEY EVEN BEAT US WHEN WE FOUGHT THEM AS THE SOCIETY!
YES! BUT WE DIDN'T HAVE THE CORRECT TOOLS IN THOSE DAYS!
YOU'LL BE HAPPY TO KNOW THAT I'VE INVENTED A DEVICE WHICH WILL REDUCE THE MARVELS TO SMOKING RUINS!
I PROPOSE WE RE-ORGANIZE THE MONSTER SOCIETY OF EVIL! WHAT DO YOU SAY?
HEY! WHAT ABOUT ME?!
CRASH!
IBAC!
YEAH, ME-- THE GUY WHO COMBINES THE WORST QUALITIES OF IVAN THE TERRIBLE, BORGIA, ATTILA THE HUN AND CALIGULA!
AND SINCE I'M A PRIME MARVEL-HATER, TOO...AND A CHARTER MEMBER OF THE OLD MONSTER SOCIETY...
SAY NO MORE! WELCOME TO THE CLUB!
YOU'RE KINDA CUTE, FOR A SCRAWNY!
MMMM... YOU, TOO! I DIG BRUTES!
ENOUGH CHIT CHAT! YOU HAVE ALL THE EQUIPMENT NECESSARY, DOCTOR SIVANA --SO LET'S GET STARTED!
HEE, HA, HO!
5

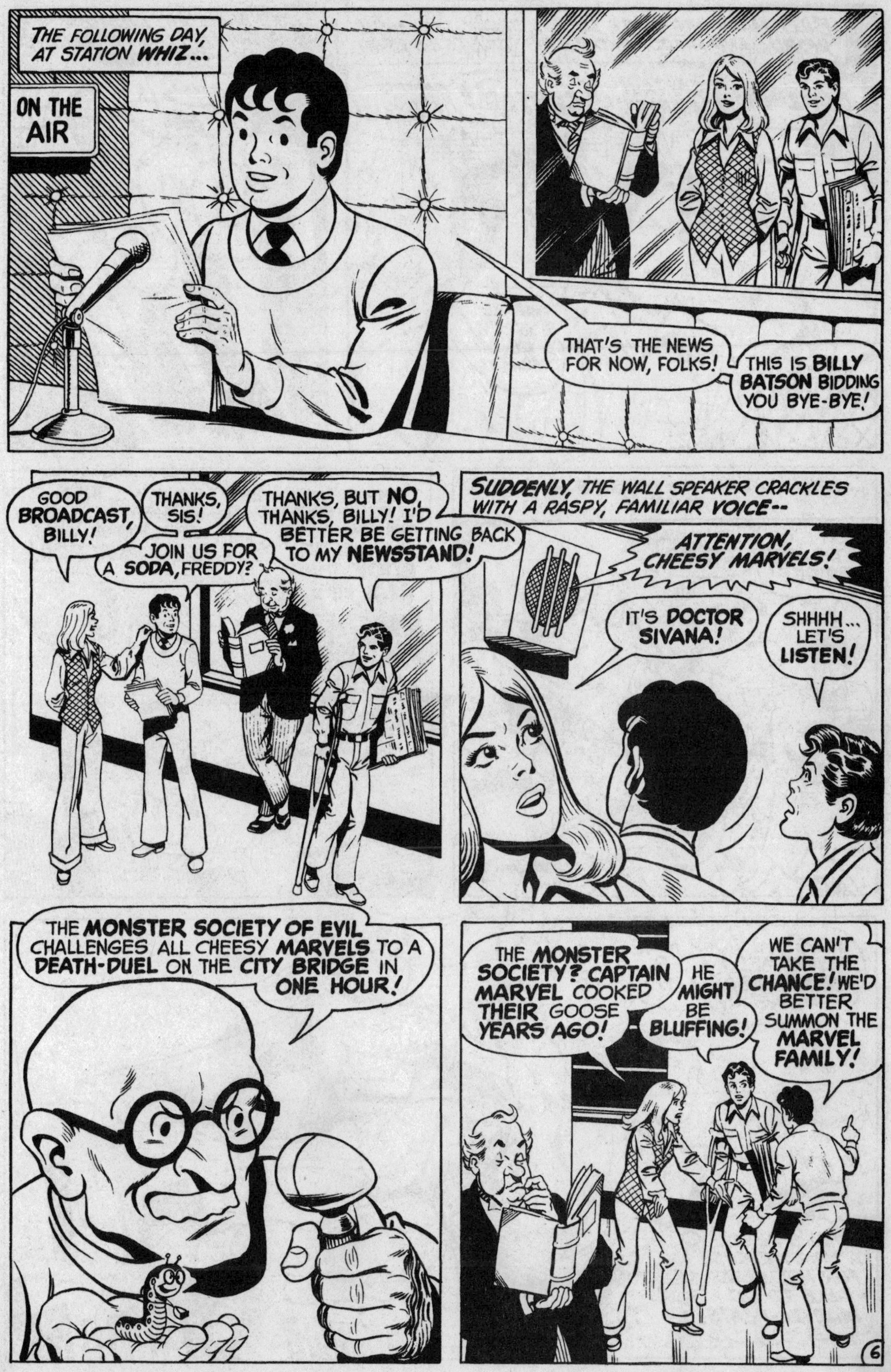
THE FOLLOWING DAY, AT STATION WHIZ...
ON THE AIR
THAT'S THE NEWS FOR NOW, FOLKS!
THIS IS BILLY BATSON BIDDING YOU BYE-BYE!
GOOD BROADCAST, BILLY!
THANKS, SIS!
JOIN US FOR A SODA, FREDDY?
THANKS, BUT NO, THANKS, BILLY! I'D BETTER BE GETTING BACK TO MY NEWSSTAND!
SUDDENLY, THE WALL SPEAKER CRACKLES WITH A RASPY, FAMILIAR VOICE--
ATTENTION, CHEESY MARVELS!
IT'S DOCTOR SIVANA!
SHHHH... LET'S LISTEN!
THE MONSTER SOCIETY OF EVIL CHALLENGES ALL CHEESY MARVELS TO A DEATH-DUEL ON THE CITY BRIDGE IN ONE HOUR!
THE MONSTER SOCIETY? CAPTAIN MARVEL COOKED THEIR GOOSE YEARS AGO!
HE MIGHT BE BLUFFING!
WE CAN'T TAKE THE CHANCE! WE'D BETTER SUMMON THE MARVEL FAMILY!
6

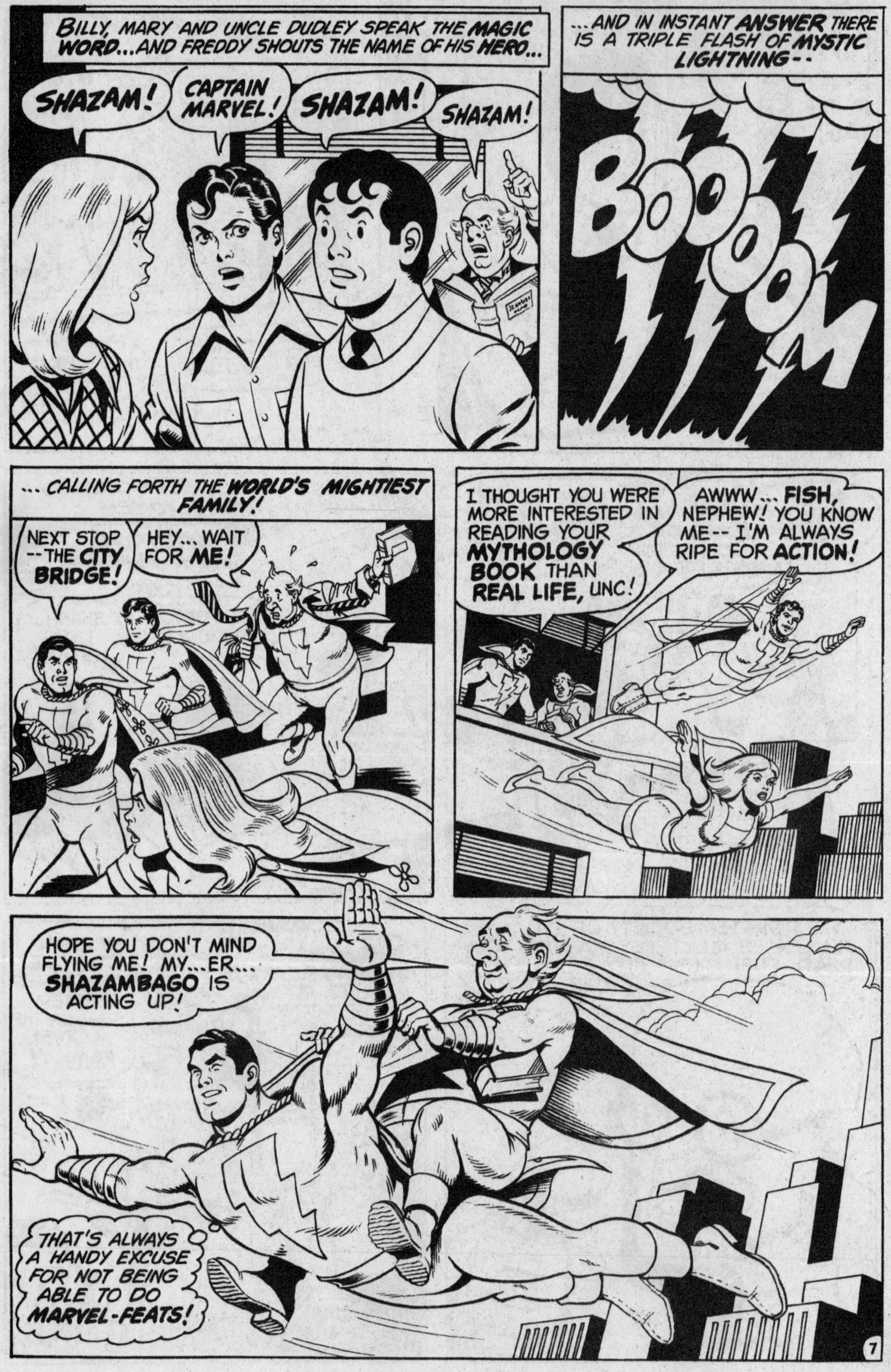

BILLY, MARY AND UNCLE DUDLEY SPEAK THE MAGIC WORD...AND FREDDY SHOUTS THE NAME OF HIS HERO...
SHAZAM!
CAPTAIN MARVEL!
SHAZAM!
SHAZAM!
...AND IN INSTANT ANSWER THERE IS A TRIPLE FLASH OF MYSTIC LIGHTNING--
BOOOOOM
... CALLING FORTH THE WORLD'S MIGHTIEST FAMILY!
NEXT STOP --THE CITY BRIDGE!
HEY... WAIT FOR ME!
I THOUGHT YOU WERE MORE INTERESTED IN READING YOUR MYTHOLOGY BOOK THAN REAL LIFE, UNC!
AWWW... FISH, NEPHEW! YOU KNOW ME-- I'M ALWAYS RIPE FOR ACTION!
HOPE YOU DON'T MIND FLYING ME! MY...ER... SHAZAMBAGO IS ACTING UP!
THAT'S ALWAYS A HANDY EXCUSE FOR NOT BEING ABLE TO DO MARVEL-FEATS!
7

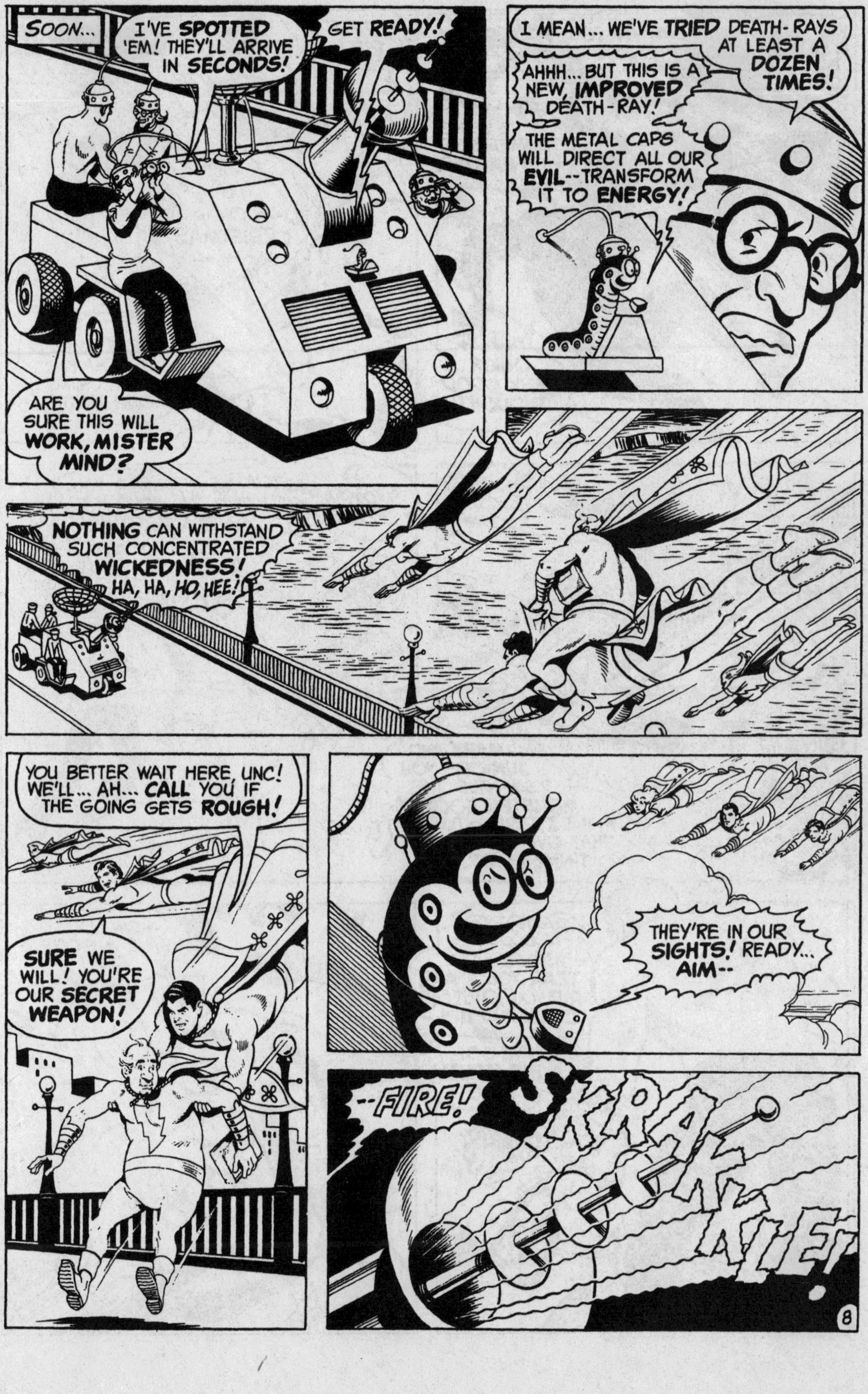
SOON...
I'VE SPOTTED 'EM! THEY'LL ARRIVE IN SECONDS!
GET READY!
ARE YOU SURE THIS WILL WORK, MISTER MIND?
I MEAN... WE'VE TRIED DEATH-RAYS AT LEAST A DOZEN TIMES!
AHHH... BUT THIS IS A NEW, IMPROVED DEATH-RAY!
THE METAL CAPS WILL DIRECT ALL OUR EVIL--TRANSFORM IT TO ENERGY!
NOTHING CAN WITHSTAND SUCH CONCENTRATED WICKEDNESS! HA, HA, HO, HEE!
YOU BETTER WAIT HERE, UNC! WE'LL... AH... CALL YOU IF THE GOING GETS ROUGH!
SURE WE WILL! YOU'RE OUR SECRET WEAPON!
THEY'RE IN OUR SIGHTS! READY... AIM--
--FIRE!
SKRAK KLE!
8

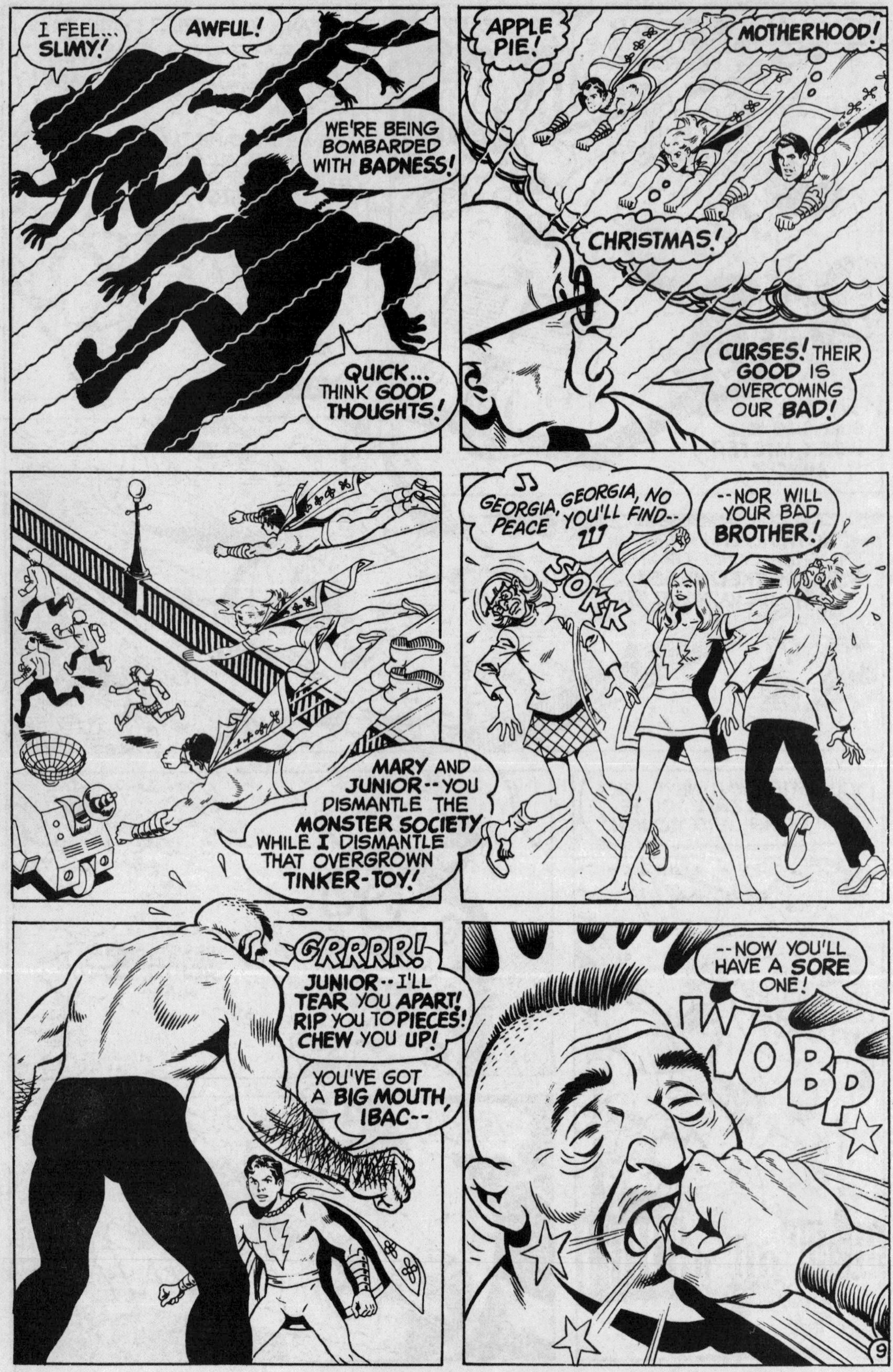
I FEEL... SLIMY!
AWFUL!
WE'RE BEING BOMBARDED WITH BADNESS!
QUICK... THINK GOOD THOUGHTS!
APPLE PIE!
MOTHERHOOD!
CHRISTMAS!
CURSES! THEIR GOOD IS OVERCOMING OUR BAD!
MARY AND JUNIOR-- YOU DISMANTLE THE MONSTER SOCIETY WHILE I DISMANTLE THAT OVERGROWN TINKER-TOY!
GEORGIA, GEORGIA, NO PEACE YOU'LL FIND--
SOKK
--NOR WILL YOUR BAD BROTHER!
GRRRR! JUNIOR-- I'LL TEAR YOU APART! RIP YOU TO PIECES! CHEW YOU UP!
YOU'VE GOT A BIG MOUTH, IBAC--
--NOW YOU'LL HAVE A SORE ONE!
WOBP
9

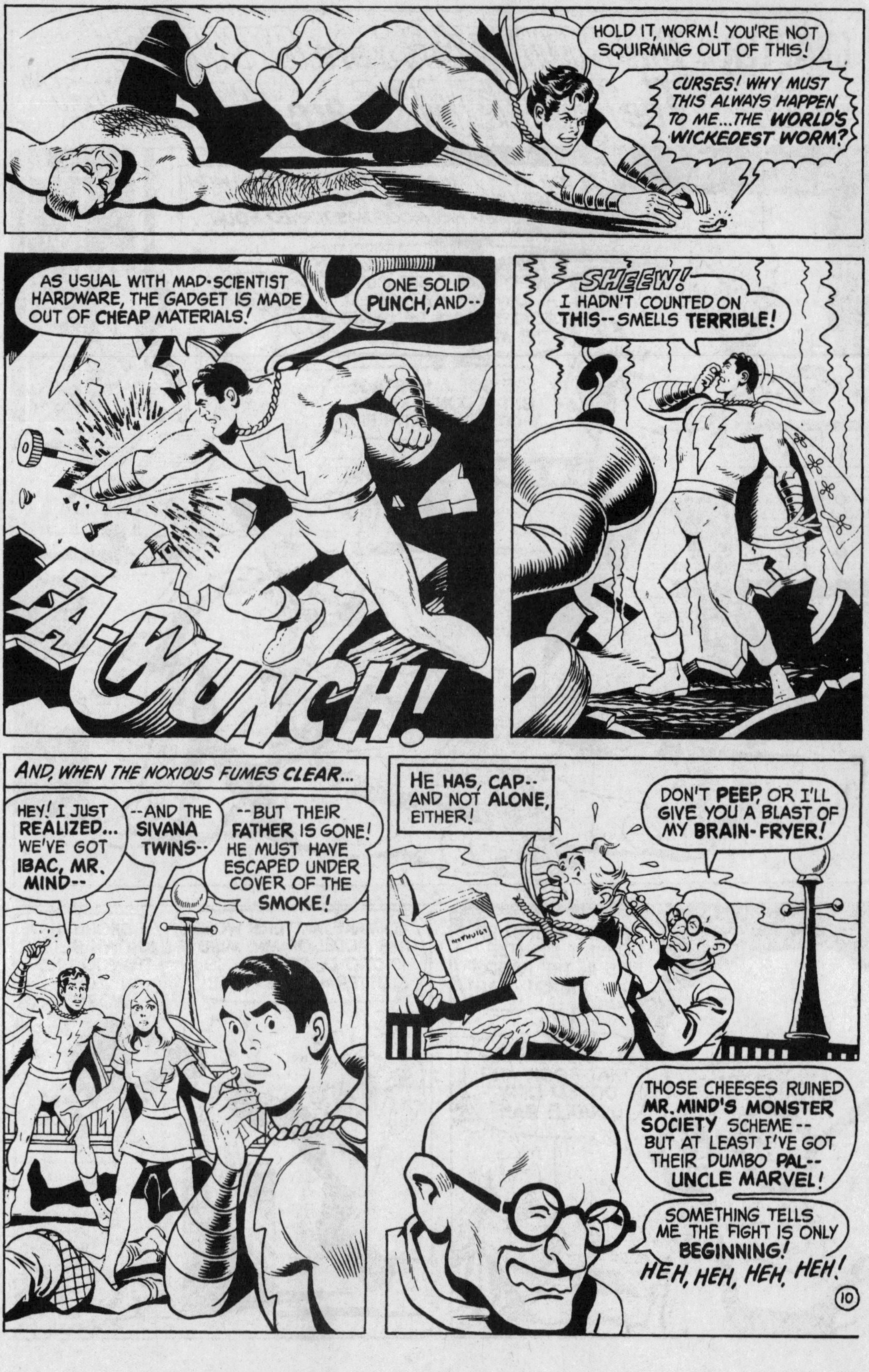

HOLD IT, WORM! YOU'RE NOT SQUIRMING OUT OF THIS!
CURSES! WHY MUST THIS ALWAYS HAPPEN TO ME...THE WORLD'S WICKEDEST WORM?
AS USUAL WITH MAD-SCIENTIST HARDWARE, THE GADGET IS MADE OUT OF CHEAP MATERIALS!
ONE SOLID PUNCH, AND--
FA-WUNCH!
SHEEW! I HADN'T COUNTED ON THIS--SMELLS TERRIBLE!
AND, WHEN THE NOXIOUS FUMES CLEAR...
HEY! I JUST REALIZED... WE'VE GOT IBAC, MR. MIND--
--AND THE SIVANA TWINS--
--BUT THEIR FATHER IS GONE! HE MUST HAVE ESCAPED UNDER COVER OF THE SMOKE!
HE HAS, CAP-- AND NOT ALONE, EITHER!
DON'T PEEP, OR I'LL GIVE YOU A BLAST OF MY BRAIN-FRYER!
THOSE CHEESES RUINED MR. MIND'S MONSTER SOCIETY SCHEME-- BUT AT LEAST I'VE GOT THEIR DUMBO PAL-- UNCLE MARVEL!
SOMETHING TELLS ME THE FIGHT IS ONLY BEGINNING! HEH, HEH, HEH, HEH!
10

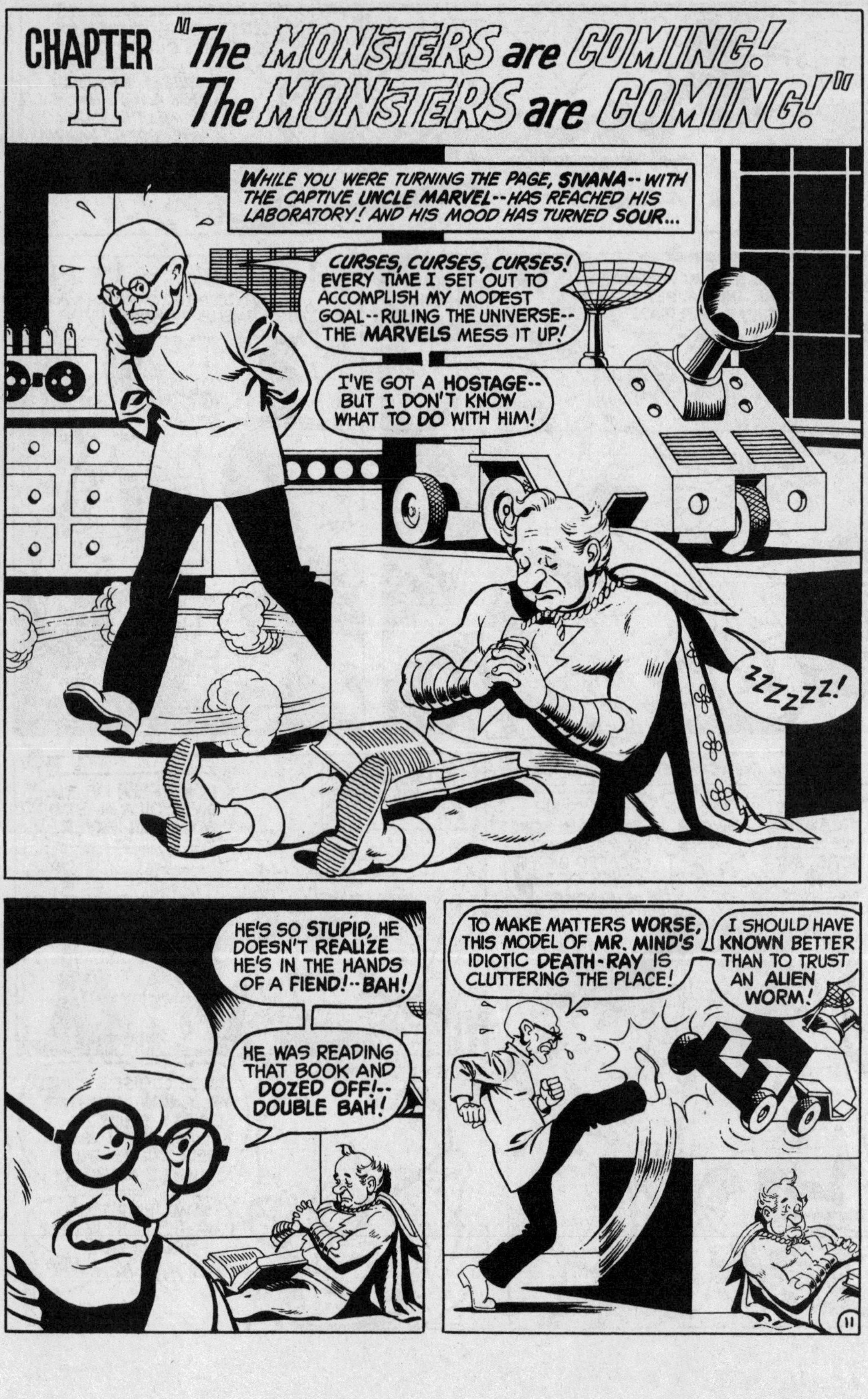
CHAPTER II "The MONSTERS are COMING! The MONSTERS are COMING!"
WHILE YOU WERE TURNING THE PAGE, SIVANA--WITH THE CAPTIVE UNCLE MARVEL--HAS REACHED HIS LABORATORY! AND HIS MOOD HAS TURNED SOUR...
CURSES, CURSES, CURSES! EVERY TIME I SET OUT TO ACCOMPLISH MY MODEST GOAL--RULING THE UNIVERSE--THE MARVELS MESS IT UP!
I'VE GOT A HOSTAGE--BUT I DON'T KNOW WHAT TO DO WITH HIM!
ZZZZZZ!
HE'S SO STUPID, HE DOESN'T REALIZE HE'S IN THE HANDS OF A FIEND!--BAH!
HE WAS READING THAT BOOK AND DOZED OFF!--DOUBLE BAH!
TO MAKE MATTERS WORSE, THIS MODEL OF MR. MIND'S IDIOTIC DEATH-RAY IS CLUTTERING THE PLACE!
I SHOULD HAVE KNOWN BETTER THAN TO TRUST AN ALIEN WORM!
11

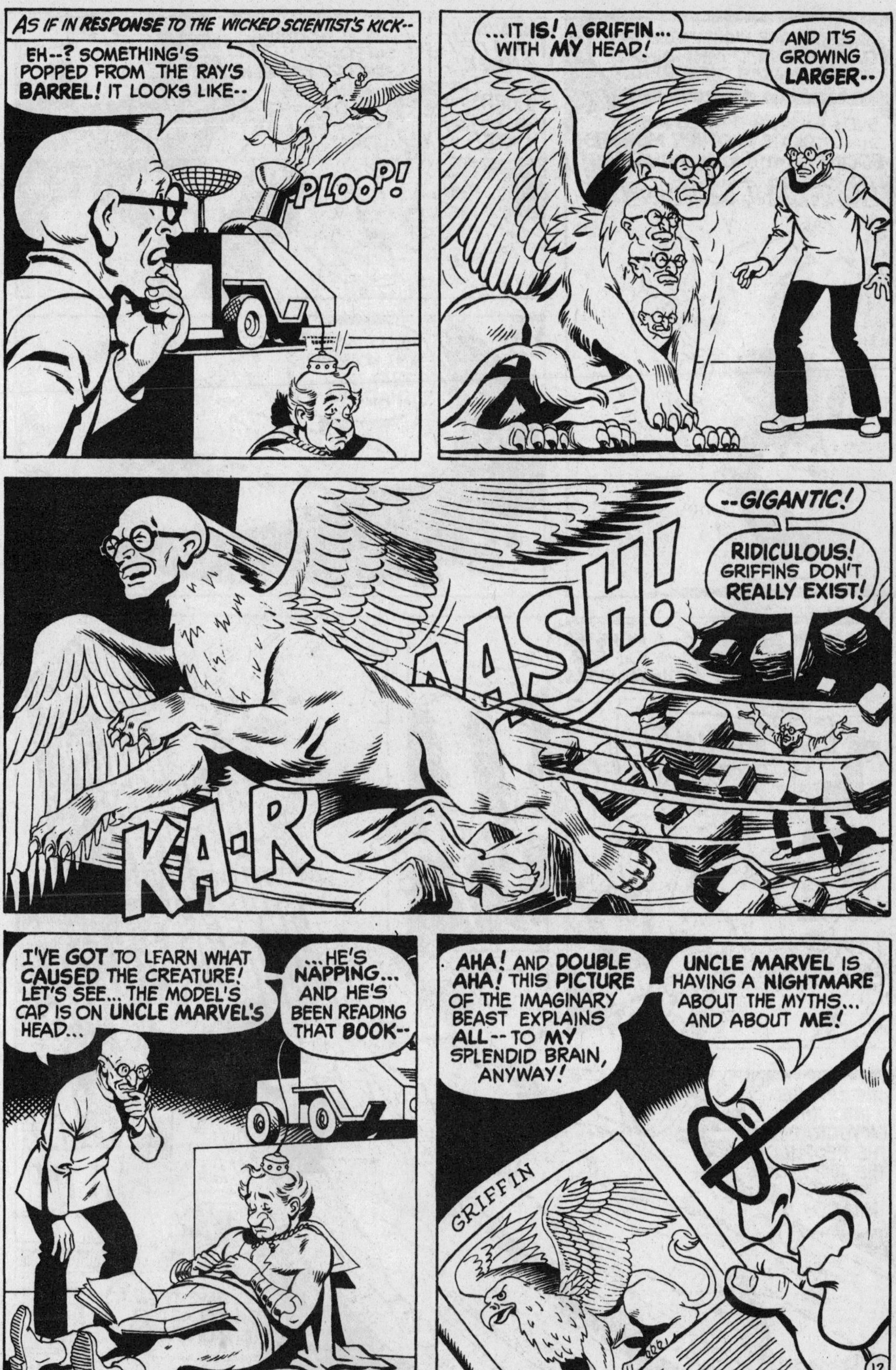
AS IF IN RESPONSE TO THE WICKED SCIENTIST'S KICK--
EH--? SOMETHING'S POPPED FROM THE RAY'S BARREL! IT LOOKS LIKE--
PLOOP!
...IT IS! A GRIFFIN... WITH MY HEAD!
AND IT'S GROWING LARGER--
--GIGANTIC!
RIDICULOUS! GRIFFINS DON'T REALLY EXIST!
KA-RAASH!
I'VE GOT TO LEARN WHAT CAUSED THE CREATURE! LET'S SEE... THE MODEL'S CAP IS ON UNCLE MARVEL'S HEAD...
...HE'S NAPPING... AND HE'S BEEN READING THAT BOOK--
AHA! AND DOUBLE AHA! THIS PICTURE OF THE IMAGINARY BEAST EXPLAINS ALL--TO MY SPLENDID BRAIN, ANYWAY!
UNCLE MARVEL IS HAVING A NIGHTMARE ABOUT THE MYTHS... AND ABOUT ME!
GRIFFIN
12

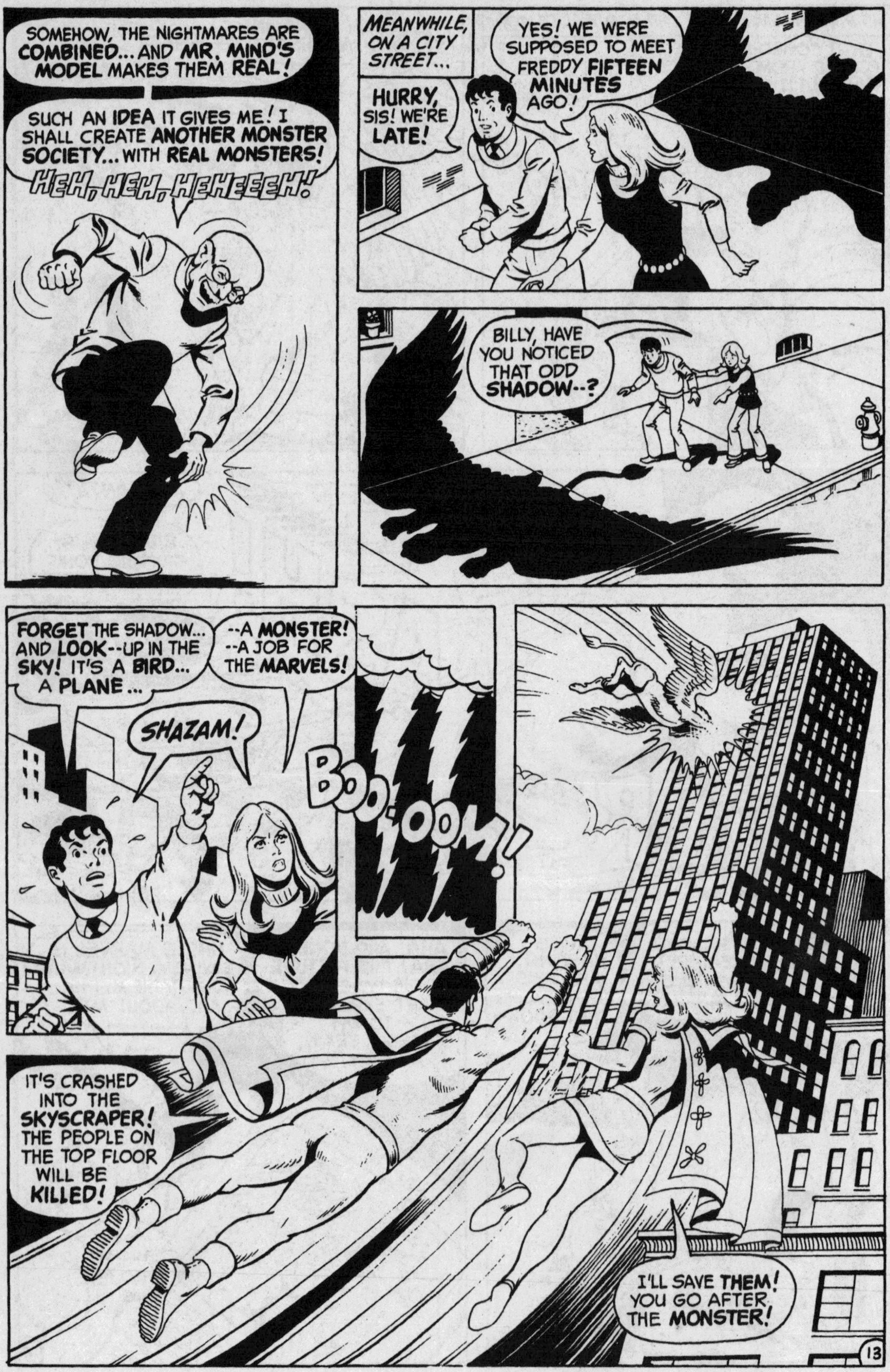
SOMEHOW, THE NIGHTMARES ARE COMBINED... AND MR. MIND'S MODEL MAKES THEM REAL!
SUCH AN IDEA IT GIVES ME! I SHALL CREATE ANOTHER MONSTER SOCIETY... WITH REAL MONSTERS!
HEH, HEH, HEHEEEH!
MEANWHILE, ON A CITY STREET...
HURRY, SIS! WE'RE LATE!
YES! WE WERE SUPPOSED TO MEET FREDDY FIFTEEN MINUTES AGO!
BILLY, HAVE YOU NOTICED THAT ODD SHADOW--?
FORGET THE SHADOW... AND LOOK--UP IN THE SKY! IT'S A BIRD... A PLANE...
--A MONSTER! --A JOB FOR THE MARVELS!
SHAZAM!
BOO-OOM!
IT'S CRASHED INTO THE SKYSCRAPER! THE PEOPLE ON THE TOP FLOOR WILL BE KILLED!
I'LL SAVE THEM! YOU GO AFTER THE MONSTER!
13

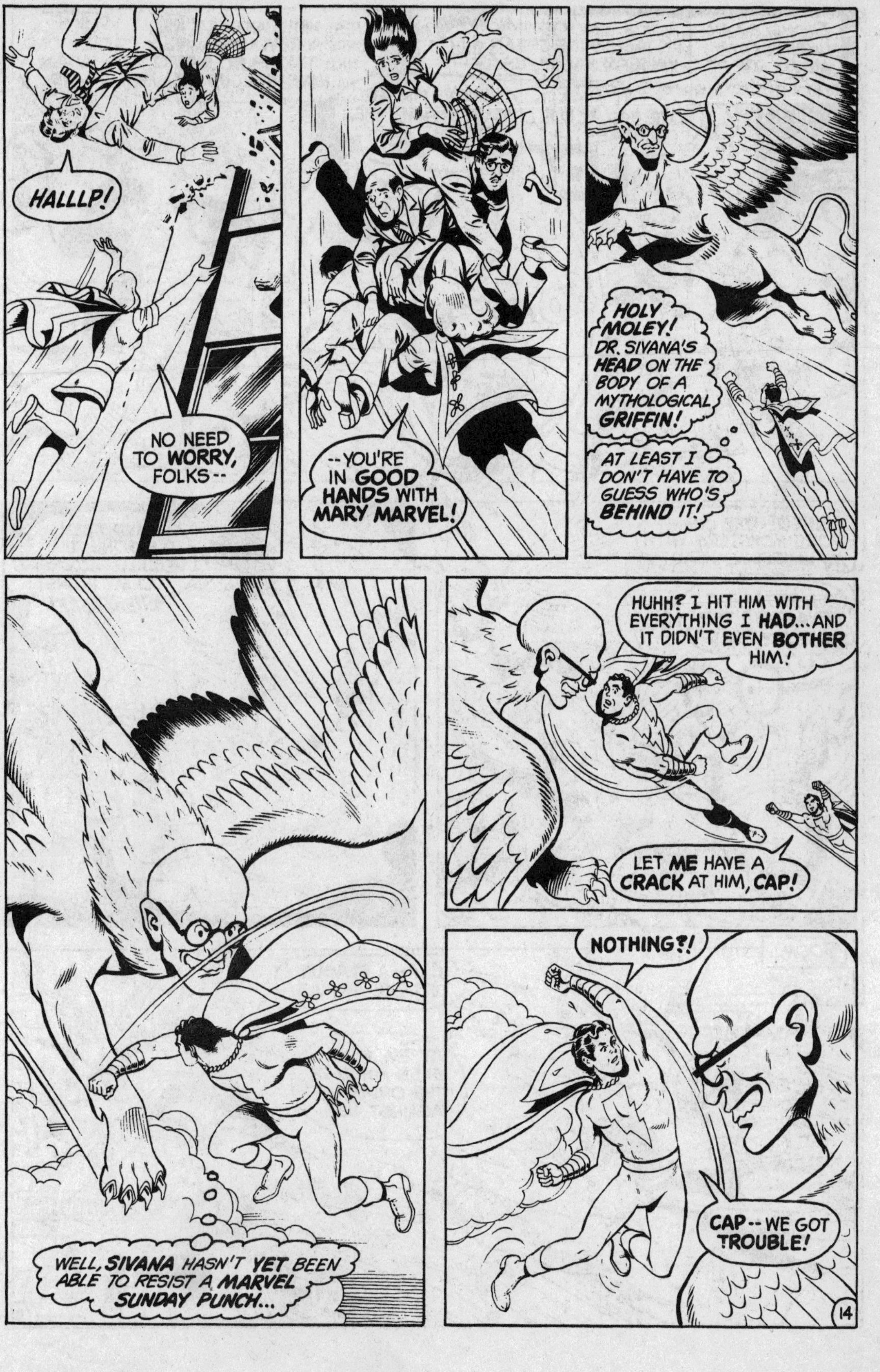
HALLLP!
NO NEED TO WORRY, FOLKS--
--YOU'RE IN GOOD HANDS WITH MARY MARVEL!
HOLY MOLEY! DR. SIVANA'S HEAD ON THE BODY OF A MYTHOLOGICAL GRIFFIN!
AT LEAST I DON'T HAVE TO GUESS WHO'S BEHIND IT!
WELL, SIVANA HASN'T YET BEEN ABLE TO RESIST A MARVEL SUNDAY PUNCH...
HUHH? I HIT HIM WITH EVERYTHING I HAD...AND IT DIDN'T EVEN BOTHER HIM!
LET ME HAVE A CRACK AT HIM, CAP!
NOTHING?!
CAP--WE GOT TROUBLE!
14

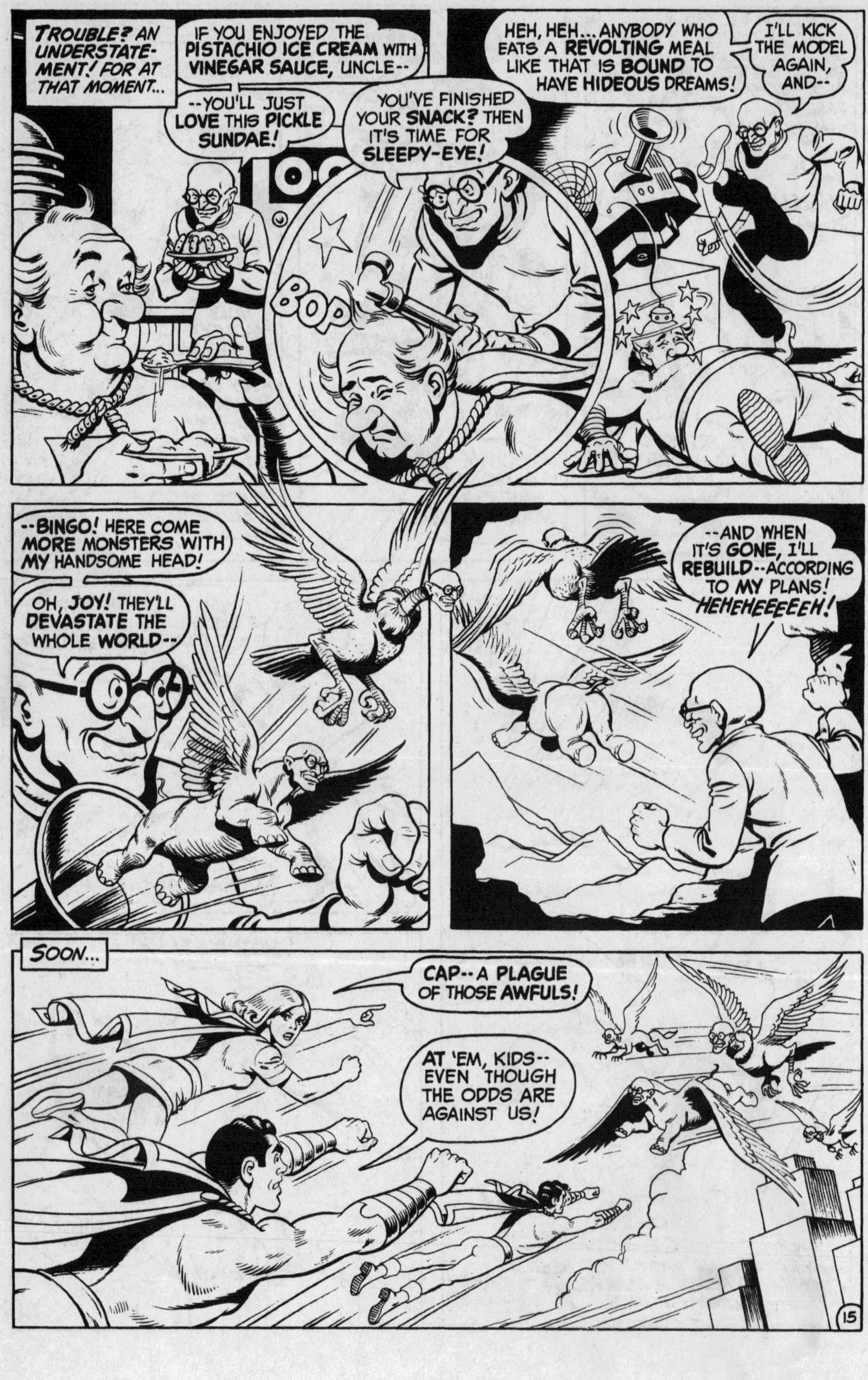
TROUBLE? AN UNDERSTATEMENT! FOR AT THAT MOMENT...
IF YOU ENJOYED THE PISTACHIO ICE CREAM WITH VINEGAR SAUCE, UNCLE--
--YOU'LL JUST LOVE THIS PICKLE SUNDAE!
YOU'VE FINISHED YOUR SNACK? THEN IT'S TIME FOR SLEEPY-EYE!
BOP
HEH, HEH... ANYBODY WHO EATS A REVOLTING MEAL LIKE THAT IS BOUND TO HAVE HIDEOUS DREAMS!
I'LL KICK THE MODEL AGAIN, AND--
--BINGO! HERE COME MORE MONSTERS WITH MY HANDSOME HEAD!
OH, JOY! THEY'LL DEVASTATE THE WHOLE WORLD--
--AND WHEN IT'S GONE, I'LL REBUILD--ACCORDING TO MY PLANS! HEHEHEEEEEEH!
SOON...
CAP--A PLAGUE OF THOSE AWFULS!
AT 'EM, KIDS--EVEN THOUGH THE ODDS ARE AGAINST US!
15

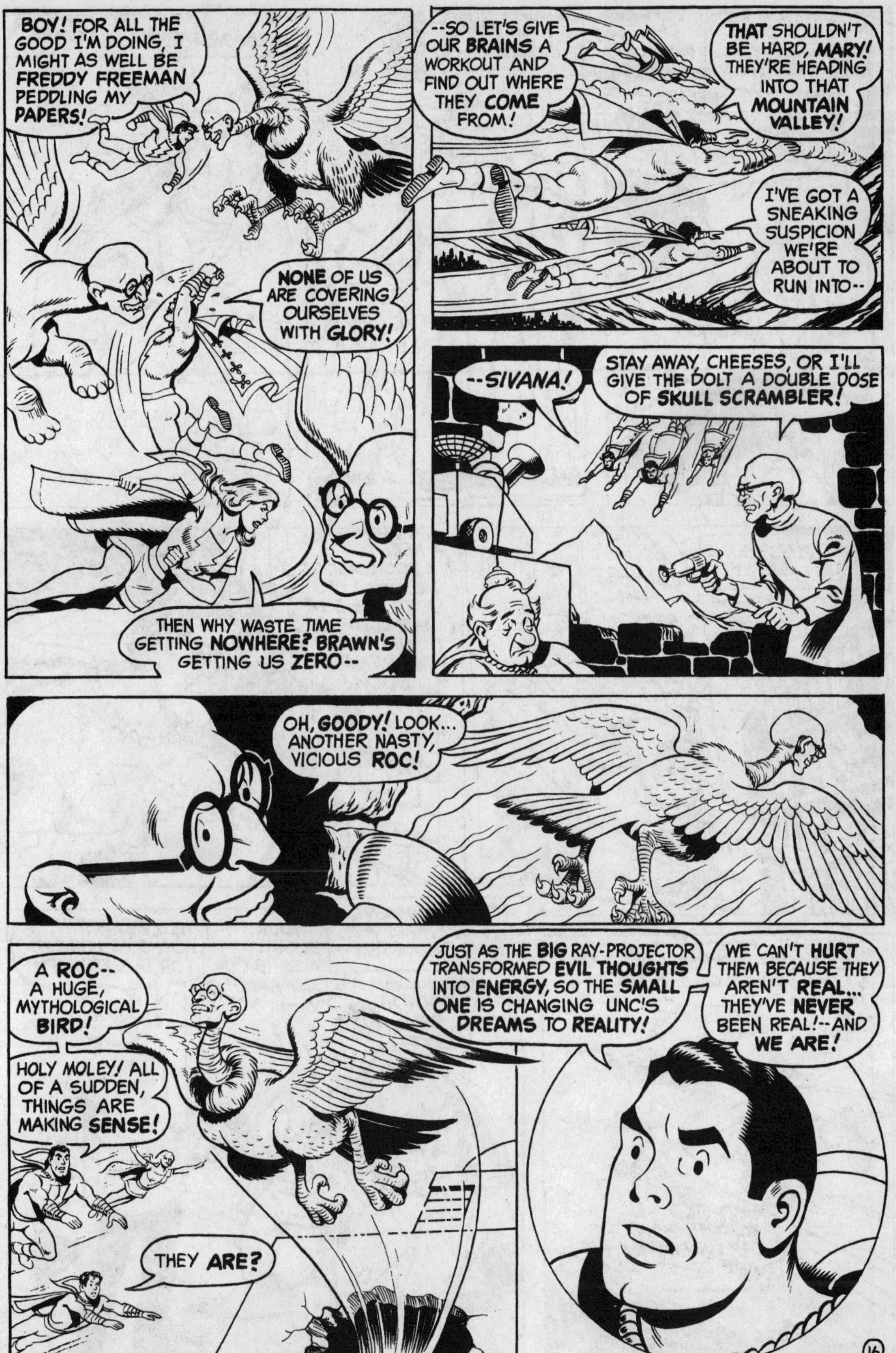
BOY! FOR ALL THE GOOD I'M DOING, I MIGHT AS WELL BE FREDDY FREEMAN PEDDLING MY PAPERS!
NONE OF US ARE COVERING OURSELVES WITH GLORY!
THEN WHY WASTE TIME GETTING NOWHERE? BRAWN'S GETTING US ZERO--
--SO LET'S GIVE OUR BRAINS A WORKOUT AND FIND OUT WHERE THEY COME FROM!
THAT SHOULDN'T BE HARD, MARY! THEY'RE HEADING INTO THAT MOUNTAIN VALLEY!
I'VE GOT A SNEAKING SUSPICION WE'RE ABOUT TO RUN INTO--
--SIVANA!
STAY AWAY, CHEESES, OR I'LL GIVE THE DOLT A DOUBLE DOSE OF SKULL SCRAMBLER!
OH, GOODY! LOOK... ANOTHER NASTY, VICIOUS ROC!
A ROC-- A HUGE, MYTHOLOGICAL BIRD!
HOLY MOLEY! ALL OF A SUDDEN, THINGS ARE MAKING SENSE!
THEY ARE?
JUST AS THE BIG RAY-PROJECTOR TRANSFORMED EVIL THOUGHTS INTO ENERGY, SO THE SMALL ONE IS CHANGING UNC'S DREAMS TO REALITY!
WE CAN'T HURT THEM BECAUSE THEY AREN'T REAL... THEY'VE NEVER BEEN REAL!--AND WE ARE!
16

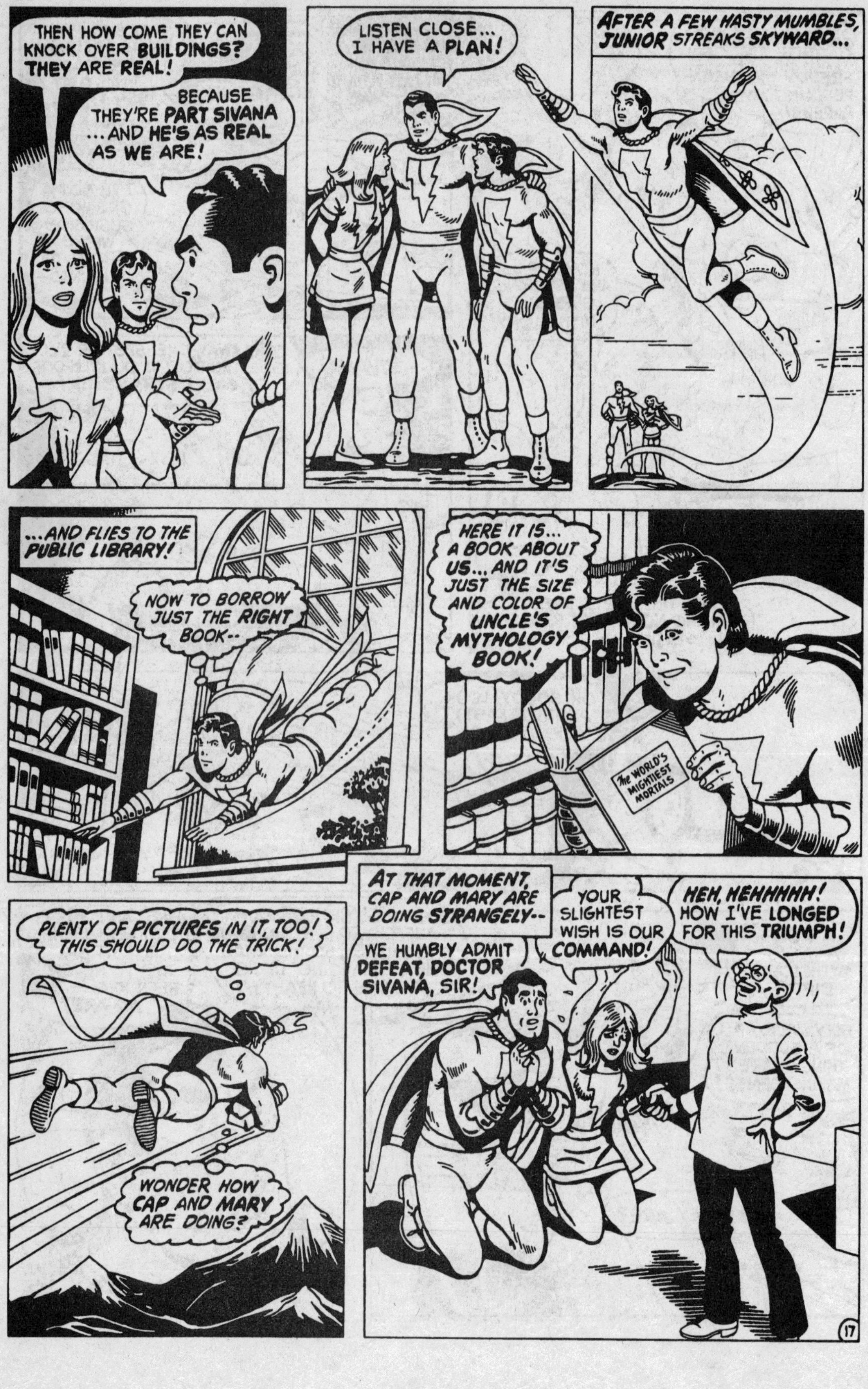
THEN HOW COME THEY CAN KNOCK OVER BUILDINGS? THEY ARE REAL!
BECAUSE THEY'RE PART SIVANA ...AND HE'S AS REAL AS WE ARE!
LISTEN CLOSE... I HAVE A PLAN!
AFTER A FEW HASTY MUMBLES, JUNIOR STREAKS SKYWARD...
...AND FLIES TO THE PUBLIC LIBRARY!
NOW TO BORROW JUST THE RIGHT BOOK--
HERE IT IS... A BOOK ABOUT US... AND IT'S JUST THE SIZE AND COLOR OF UNCLE'S MYTHOLOGY BOOK!
The WORLD'S MIGHTIEST MORTALS
PLENTY OF PICTURES IN IT, TOO! THIS SHOULD DO THE TRICK!
WONDER HOW CAP AND MARY ARE DOING?
AT THAT MOMENT, CAP AND MARY ARE DOING STRANGELY--
WE HUMBLY ADMIT DEFEAT, DOCTOR SIVANA, SIR!
YOUR SLIGHTEST WISH IS OUR COMMAND!
HEH, HEHHHHH! HOW I'VE LONGED FOR THIS TRIUMPH!
17

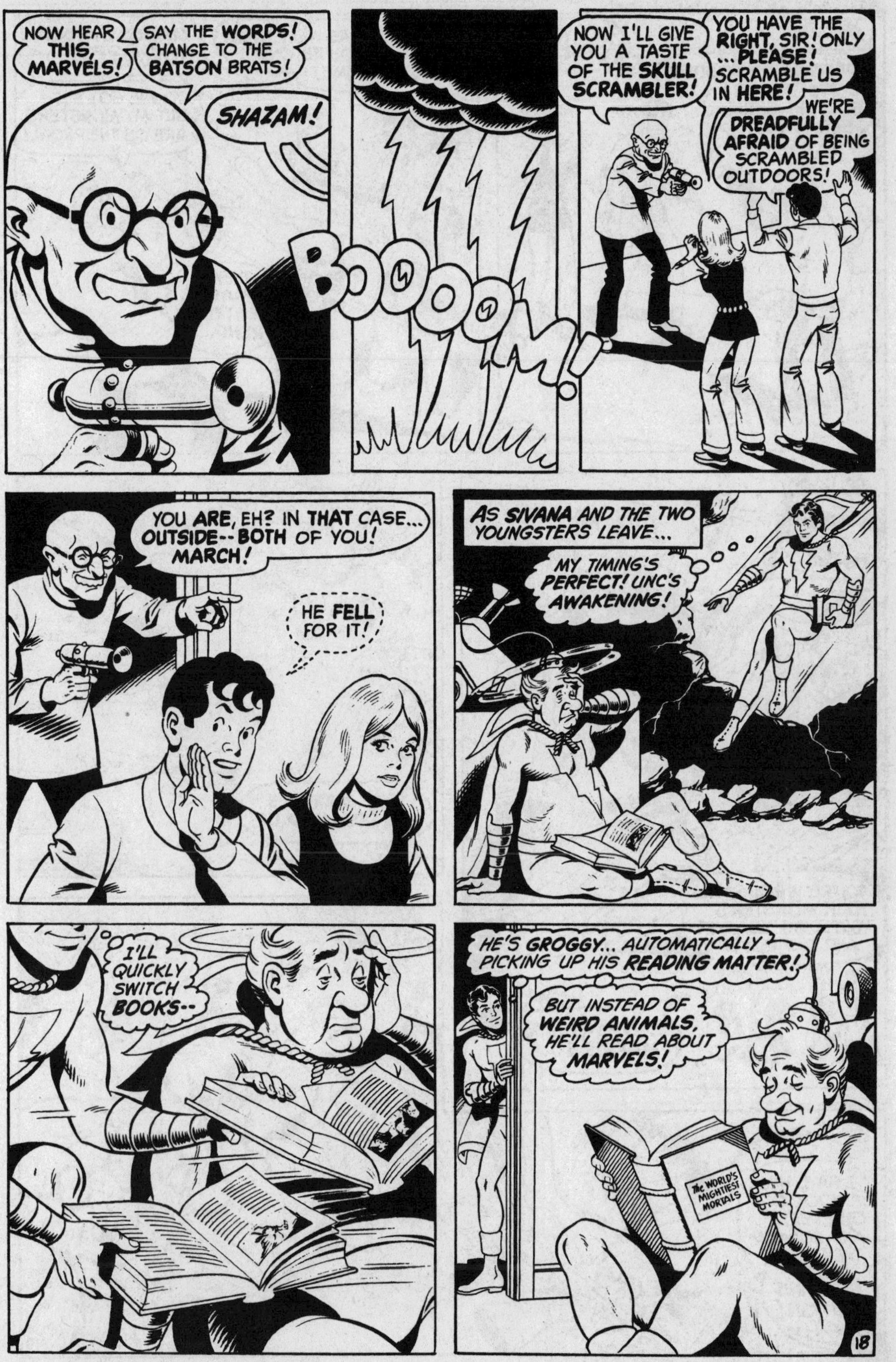
NOW HEAR THIS, MARVELS!
SAY THE WORDS! CHANGE TO THE BATSON BRATS!
SHAZAM!
BOOOOOM!
NOW I'LL GIVE YOU A TASTE OF THE SKULL SCRAMBLER!
YOU HAVE THE RIGHT, SIR! ONLY ...PLEASE! SCRAMBLE US IN HERE!
WE'RE DREADFULLY AFRAID OF BEING SCRAMBLED OUTDOORS!
YOU ARE, EH? IN THAT CASE... OUTSIDE--BOTH OF YOU! MARCH!
HE FELL FOR IT!
AS SIVANA AND THE TWO YOUNGSTERS LEAVE...
MY TIMING'S PERFECT! UNC'S AWAKENING!
I'LL QUICKLY SWITCH BOOKS--
HE'S GROGGY... AUTOMATICALLY PICKING UP HIS READING MATTER!
BUT INSTEAD OF WEIRD ANIMALS, HE'LL READ ABOUT MARVELS!
The WORLD'S MIGHTIEST MORTALS
18

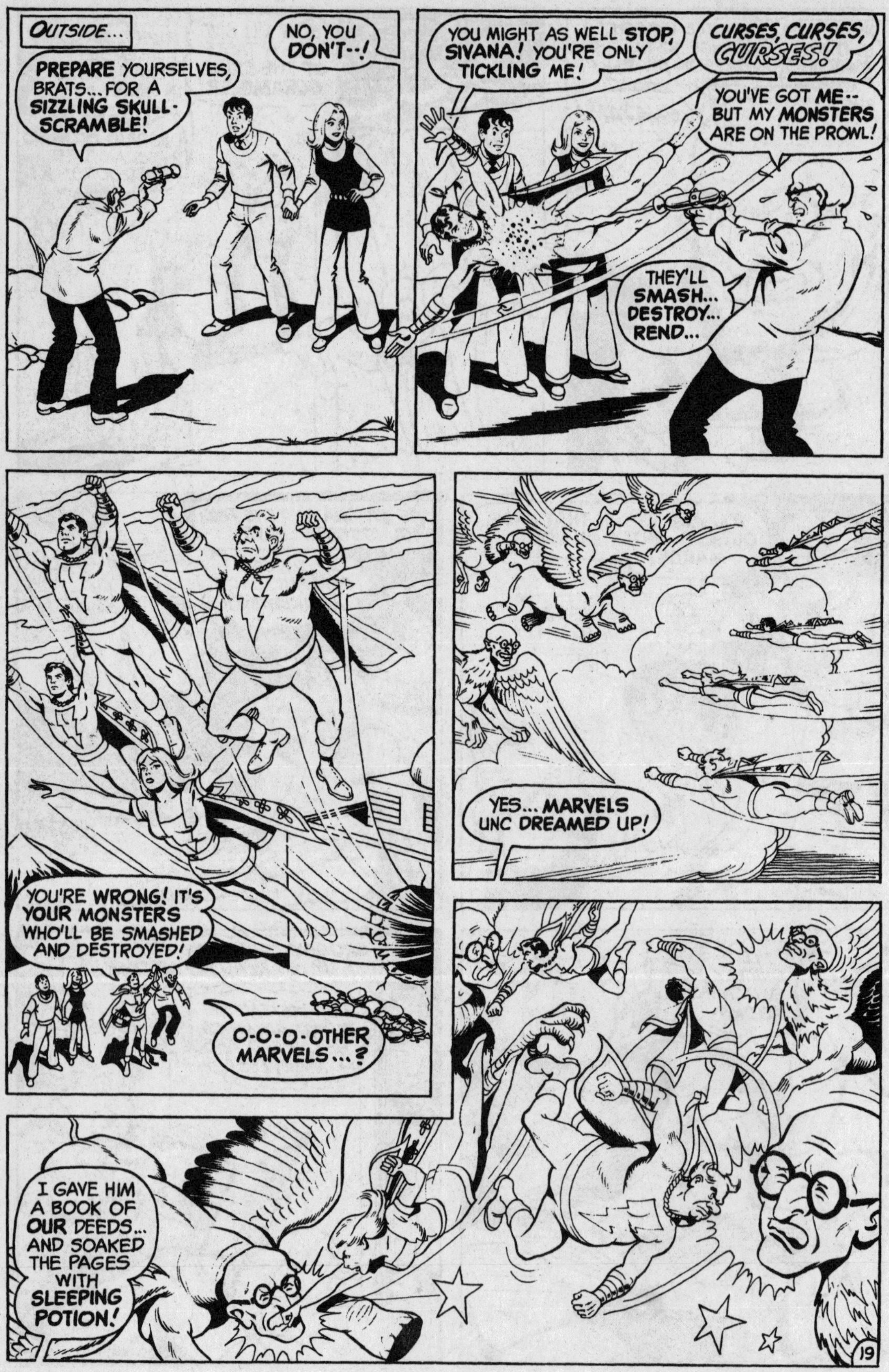
OUTSIDE...
PREPARE YOURSELVES, BRATS... FOR A SIZZLING SKULL-SCRAMBLE!
NO, YOU DON'T--!
YOU MIGHT AS WELL STOP, SIVANA! YOU'RE ONLY TICKLING ME!
CURSES, CURSES, CURSES!
YOU'VE GOT ME-- BUT MY MONSTERS ARE ON THE PROWL!
THEY'LL SMASH... DESTROY... REND...
YOU'RE WRONG! IT'S YOUR MONSTERS WHO'LL BE SMASHED AND DESTROYED!
O-O-O-OTHER MARVELS...?
YES... MARVELS UNC DREAMED UP!
I GAVE HIM A BOOK OF OUR DEEDS... AND SOAKED THE PAGES WITH SLEEPING POTION!
19

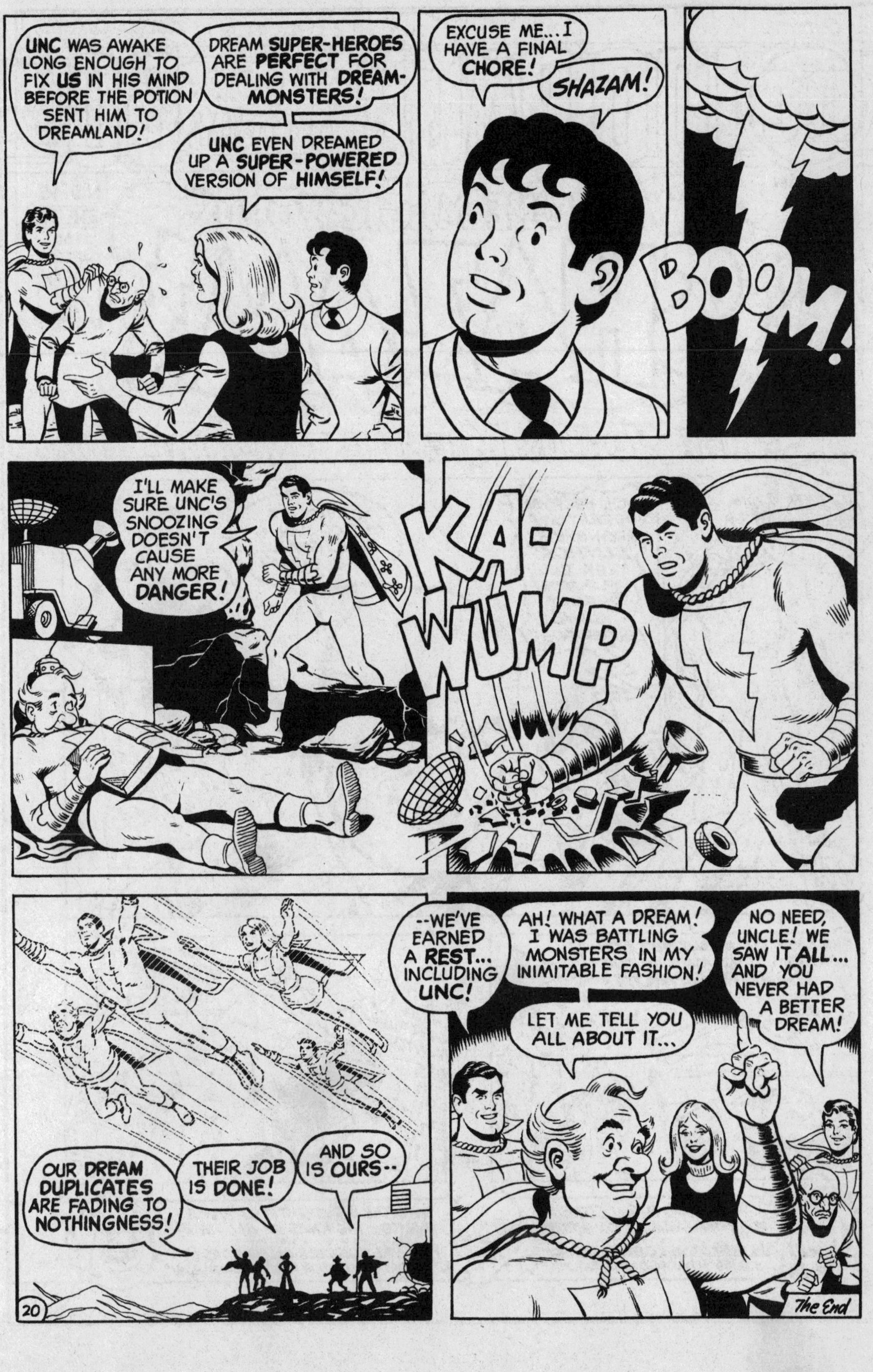
UNC WAS AWAKE LONG ENOUGH TO FIX US IN HIS MIND BEFORE THE POTION SENT HIM TO DREAMLAND!
DREAM SUPER-HEROES ARE PERFECT FOR DEALING WITH DREAM-MONSTERS!
UNC EVEN DREAMED UP A SUPER-POWERED VERSION OF HIMSELF!
EXCUSE ME...I HAVE A FINAL CHORE!
SHAZAM!
BOOM!
I'LL MAKE SURE UNC'S SNOOZING DOESN'T CAUSE ANY MORE DANGER!
KA-WUMP
OUR DREAM DUPLICATES ARE FADING TO NOTHINGNESS!
THEIR JOB IS DONE!
AND SO IS OURS--
20
--WE'VE EARNED A REST... INCLUDING UNC!
AH! WHAT A DREAM! I WAS BATTLING MONSTERS IN MY INIMITABLE FASHION!
LET ME TELL YOU ALL ABOUT IT...
NO NEED, UNCLE! WE SAW IT ALL... AND YOU NEVER HAD A BETTER DREAM!
The End

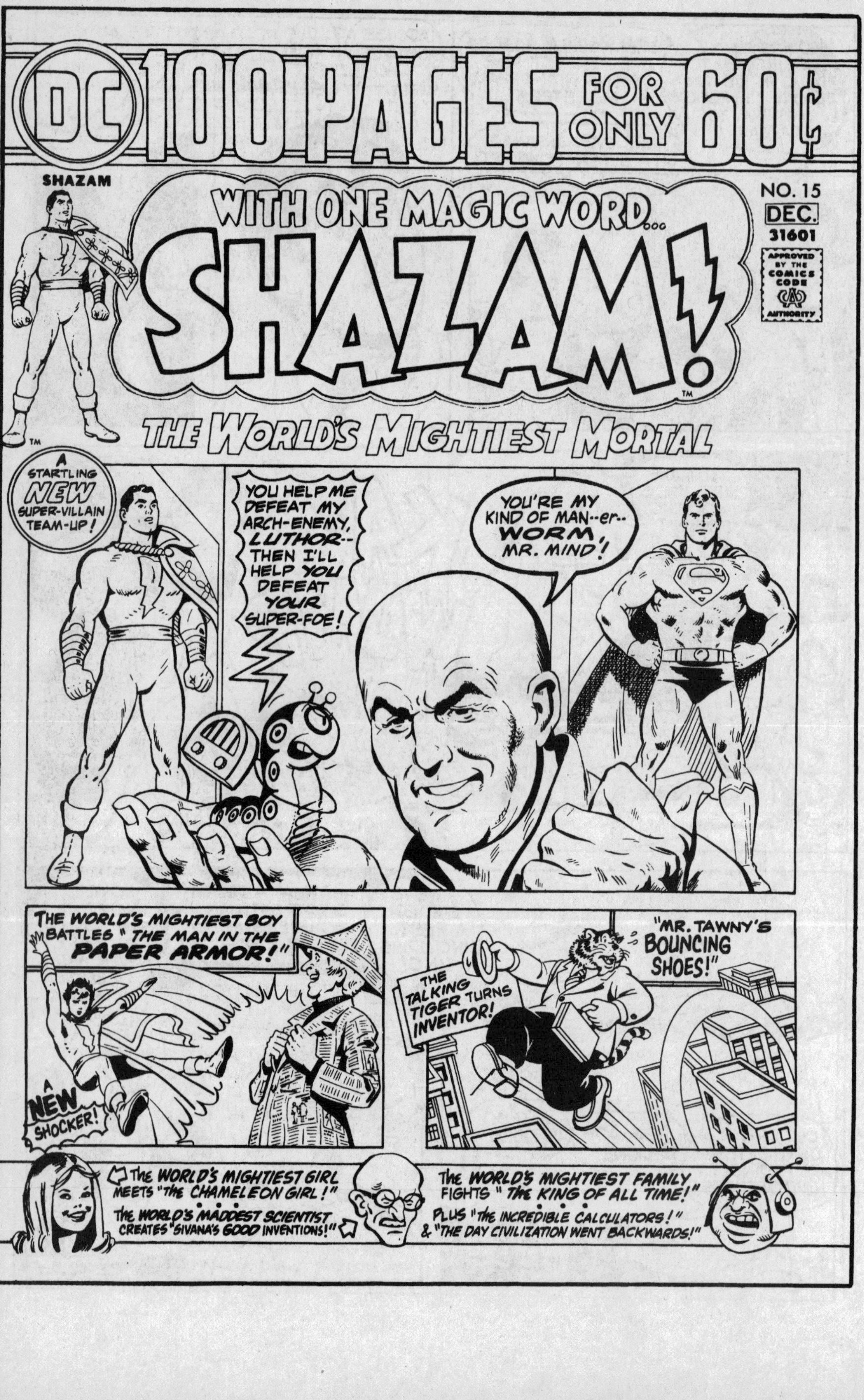

DC
100 PAGES FOR ONLY 60¢
SHAZAM
NO. 15
DEC.
31601
APPROVED BY THE COMICS CODE AUTHORITY
WITH ONE MAGIC WORD...
SHAZAM!
THE WORLD'S MIGHTIEST MORTAL
A STARTLING NEW SUPER-VILLAIN TEAM-UP!
YOU HELP ME DEFEAT MY ARCH-ENEMY, LUTHOR-- THEN I'LL HELP YOU DEFEAT YOUR SUPER-FOE!
YOU'RE MY KIND OF MAN--er-- WORM, MR. MIND!
THE WORLD'S MIGHTIEST BOY BATTLES "THE MAN IN THE PAPER ARMOR!"
A NEW SHOCKER!
"MR. TAWNY'S BOUNCING SHOES!"
THE TALKING TIGER TURNS INVENTOR!
The WORLD'S MIGHTIEST GIRL MEETS "The CHAMELEON GIRL!"
The WORLD'S MADDEST SCIENTIST CREATES "SIVANA'S GOOD INVENTIONS!"
The WORLD'S MIGHTIEST FAMILY FIGHTS "The KING OF ALL TIME!"
PLUS "The INCREDIBLE CALCULATORS!" & "The DAY CIVILIZATION WENT BACKWARDS!"

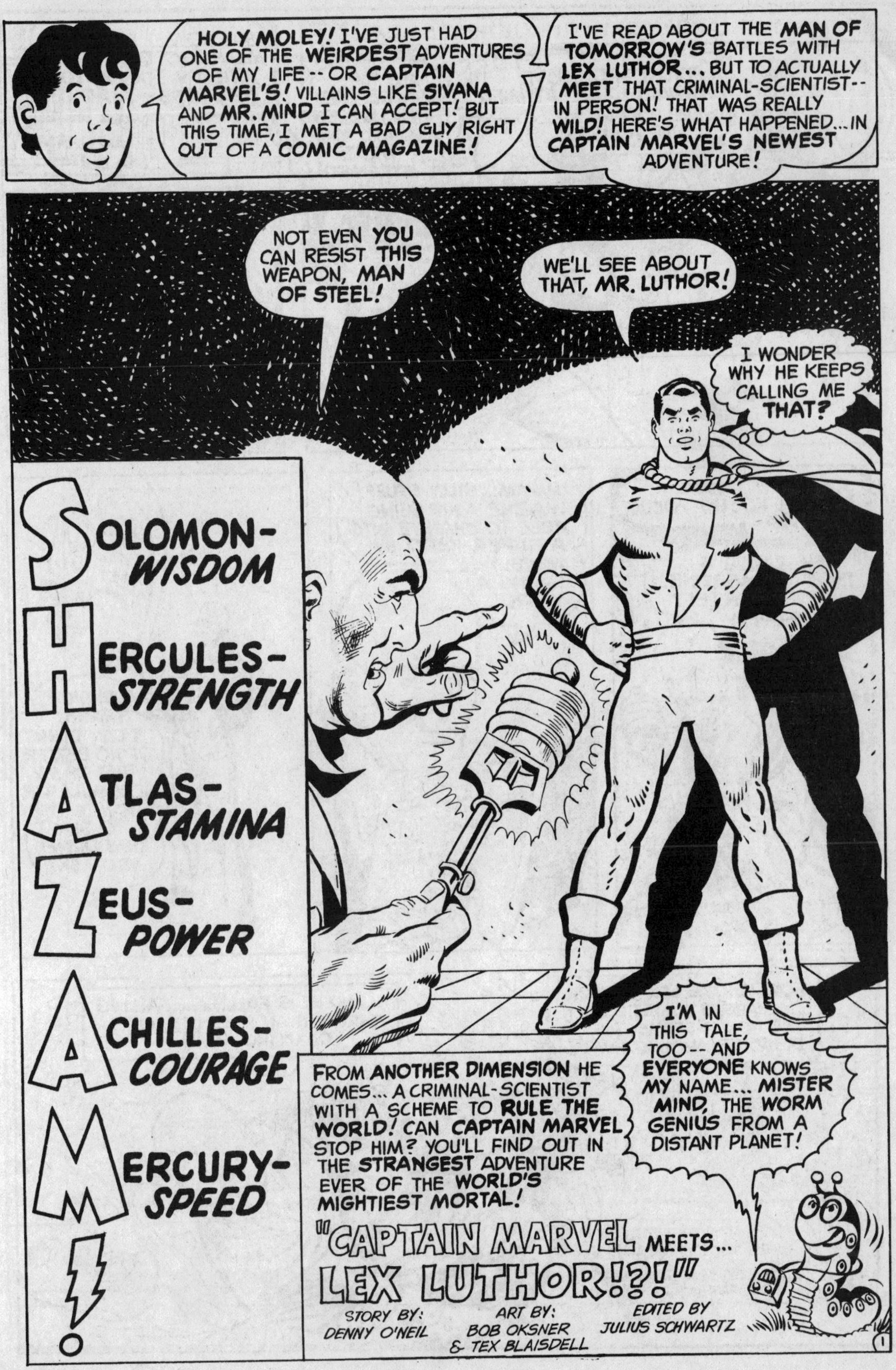
HOLY MOLEY! I'VE JUST HAD ONE OF THE WEIRDEST ADVENTURES OF MY LIFE -- OR CAPTAIN MARVEL'S! VILLAINS LIKE SIVANA AND MR. MIND I CAN ACCEPT! BUT THIS TIME, I MET A BAD GUY RIGHT OUT OF A COMIC MAGAZINE!
I'VE READ ABOUT THE MAN OF TOMORROW'S BATTLES WITH LEX LUTHOR... BUT TO ACTUALLY MEET THAT CRIMINAL-SCIENTIST-- IN PERSON! THAT WAS REALLY WILD! HERE'S WHAT HAPPENED... IN CAPTAIN MARVEL'S NEWEST ADVENTURE!
NOT EVEN YOU CAN RESIST THIS WEAPON, MAN OF STEEL!
WE'LL SEE ABOUT THAT, MR. LUTHOR!
I WONDER WHY HE KEEPS CALLING ME THAT?
SOLOMON- WISDOM
HERCULES- STRENGTH
ATLAS- STAMINA
ZEUS- POWER
ACHILLES- COURAGE
MERCURY- SPEED
!
FROM ANOTHER DIMENSION HE COMES... A CRIMINAL-SCIENTIST WITH A SCHEME TO RULE THE WORLD! CAN CAPTAIN MARVEL STOP HIM? YOU'LL FIND OUT IN THE STRANGEST ADVENTURE EVER OF THE WORLD'S MIGHTIEST MORTAL!
I'M IN THIS TALE, TOO-- AND EVERYONE KNOWS MY NAME... MISTER MIND, THE WORM GENIUS FROM A DISTANT PLANET!
"CAPTAIN MARVEL MEETS... LEX LUTHOR!?!"
STORY BY: DENNY O'NEIL
ART BY: BOB OKSNER & TEX BLAISDELL
EDITED BY JULIUS SCHWARTZ
1

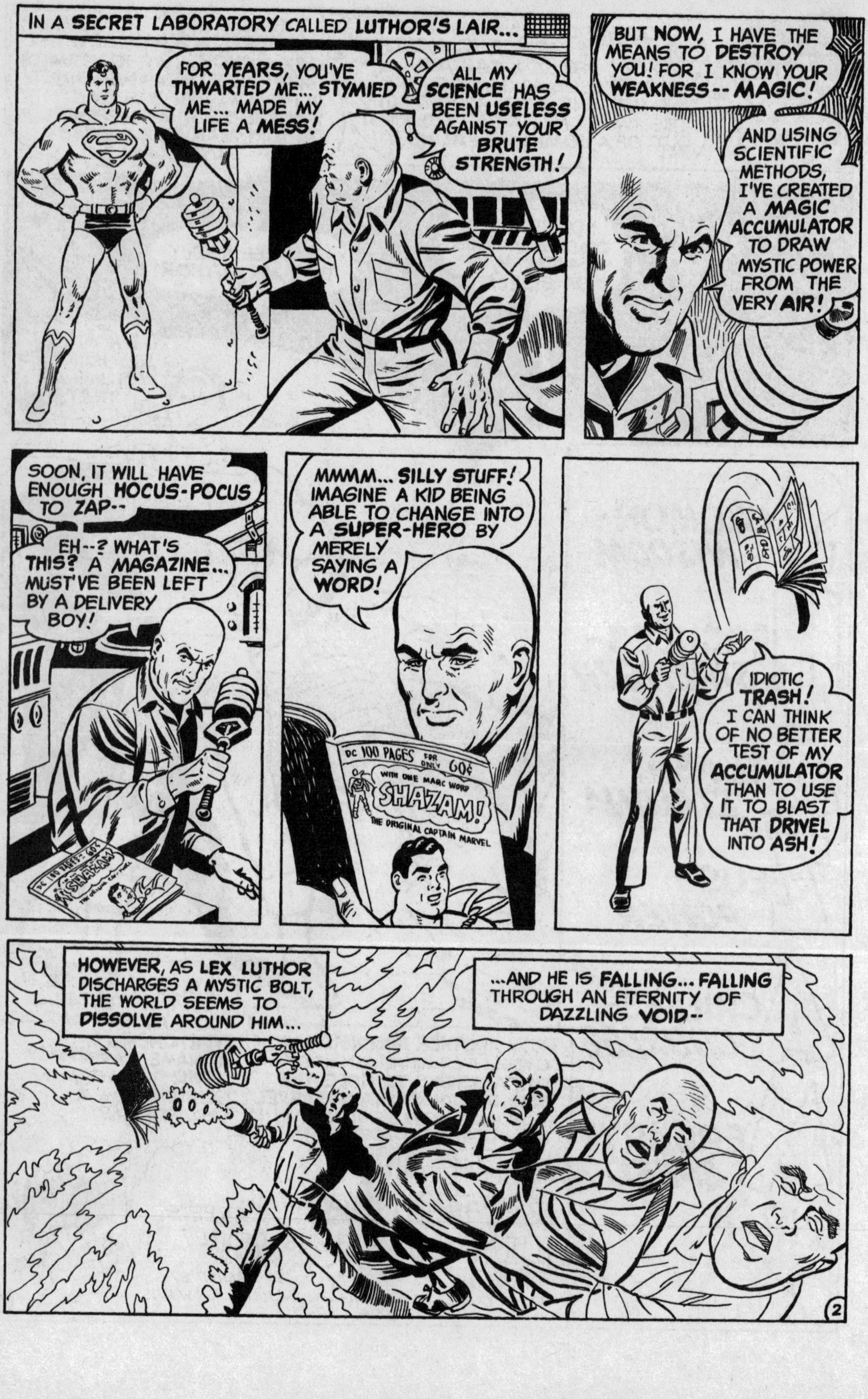
IN A SECRET LABORATORY CALLED LUTHOR'S LAIR...
FOR YEARS, YOU'VE THWARTED ME... STYMIED ME... MADE MY LIFE A MESS!
ALL MY SCIENCE HAS BEEN USELESS AGAINST YOUR BRUTE STRENGTH!
BUT NOW, I HAVE THE MEANS TO DESTROY YOU! FOR I KNOW YOUR WEAKNESS -- MAGIC!
AND USING SCIENTIFIC METHODS, I'VE CREATED A MAGIC ACCUMULATOR TO DRAW MYSTIC POWER FROM THE VERY AIR!
SOON, IT WILL HAVE ENOUGH HOCUS-POCUS TO ZAP--
EH--? WHAT'S THIS? A MAGAZINE... MUST'VE BEEN LEFT BY A DELIVERY BOY!
MMMM... SILLY STUFF! IMAGINE A KID BEING ABLE TO CHANGE INTO A SUPER-HERO BY MERELY SAYING A WORD!
DC 100 PAGES FOR ONLY 60¢
WITH ONE MAGIC WORD
SHAZAM!
THE ORIGINAL CAPTAIN MARVEL
IDIOTIC TRASH! I CAN THINK OF NO BETTER TEST OF MY ACCUMULATOR THAN TO USE IT TO BLAST THAT DRIVEL INTO ASH!
HOWEVER, AS LEX LUTHOR DISCHARGES A MYSTIC BOLT, THE WORLD SEEMS TO DISSOLVE AROUND HIM...
...AND HE IS FALLING... FALLING THROUGH AN ETERNITY OF DAZZLING VOID--
2

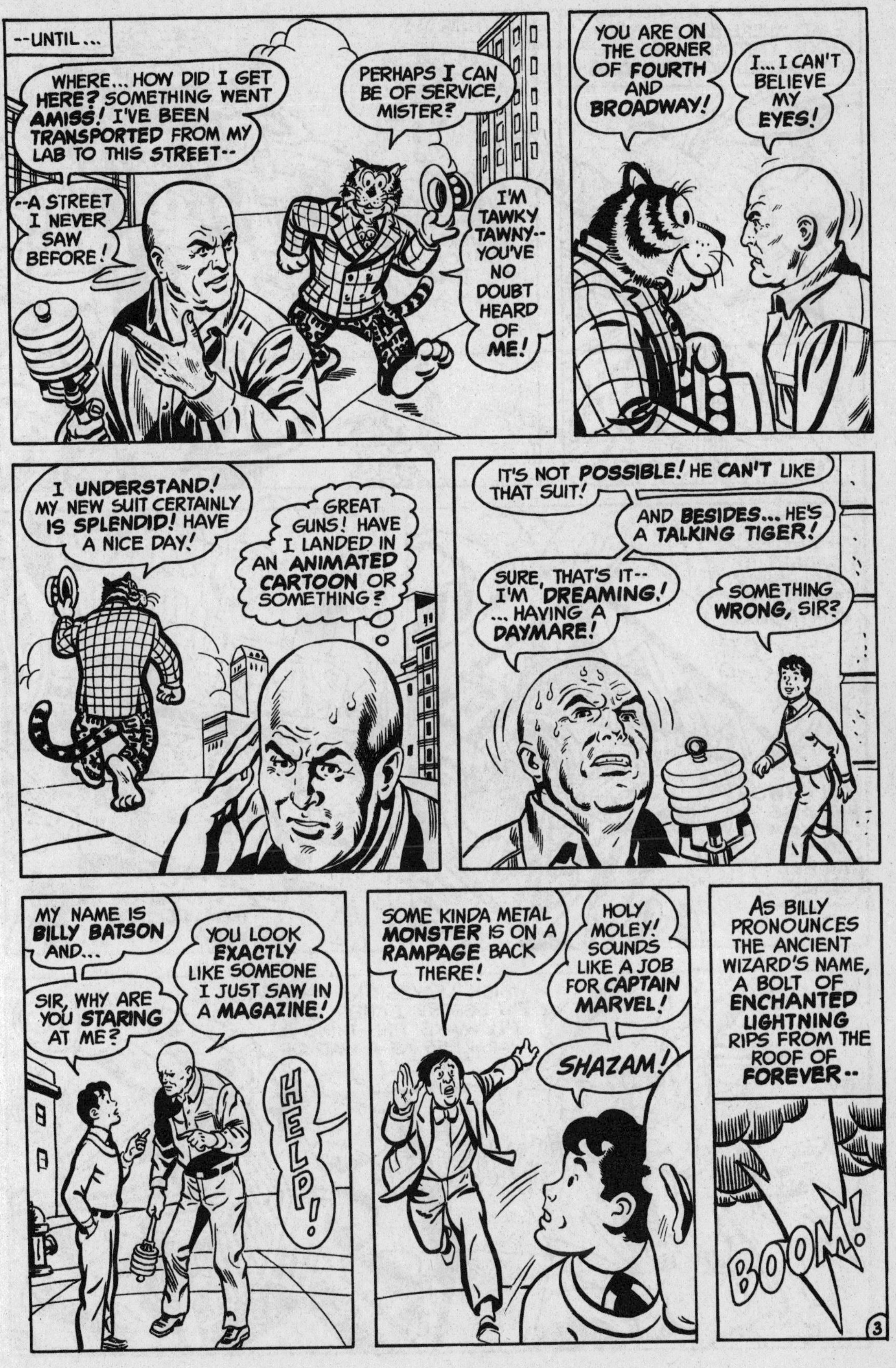
--UNTIL...
WHERE... HOW DID I GET HERE? SOMETHING WENT AMISS! I'VE BEEN TRANSPORTED FROM MY LAB TO THIS STREET--
--A STREET I NEVER SAW BEFORE!
PERHAPS I CAN BE OF SERVICE, MISTER?
I'M TAWKY TAWNY-- YOU'VE NO DOUBT HEARD OF ME!
YOU ARE ON THE CORNER OF FOURTH AND BROADWAY!
I... I CAN'T BELIEVE MY EYES!
I UNDERSTAND! MY NEW SUIT CERTAINLY IS SPLENDID! HAVE A NICE DAY!
GREAT GUNS! HAVE I LANDED IN AN ANIMATED CARTOON OR SOMETHING?
IT'S NOT POSSIBLE! HE CAN'T LIKE THAT SUIT!
AND BESIDES... HE'S A TALKING TIGER!
SURE, THAT'S IT-- I'M DREAMING! ... HAVING A DAYMARE!
SOMETHING WRONG, SIR?
MY NAME IS BILLY BATSON AND...
SIR, WHY ARE YOU STARING AT ME?
YOU LOOK EXACTLY LIKE SOMEONE I JUST SAW IN A MAGAZINE!
HELP!
SOME KINDA METAL MONSTER IS ON A RAMPAGE BACK THERE!
HOLY MOLEY! SOUNDS LIKE A JOB FOR CAPTAIN MARVEL!
SHAZAM!
AS BILLY PRONOUNCES THE ANCIENT WIZARD'S NAME, A BOLT OF ENCHANTED LIGHTNING RIPS FROM THE ROOF OF FOREVER--
BOOM!
3

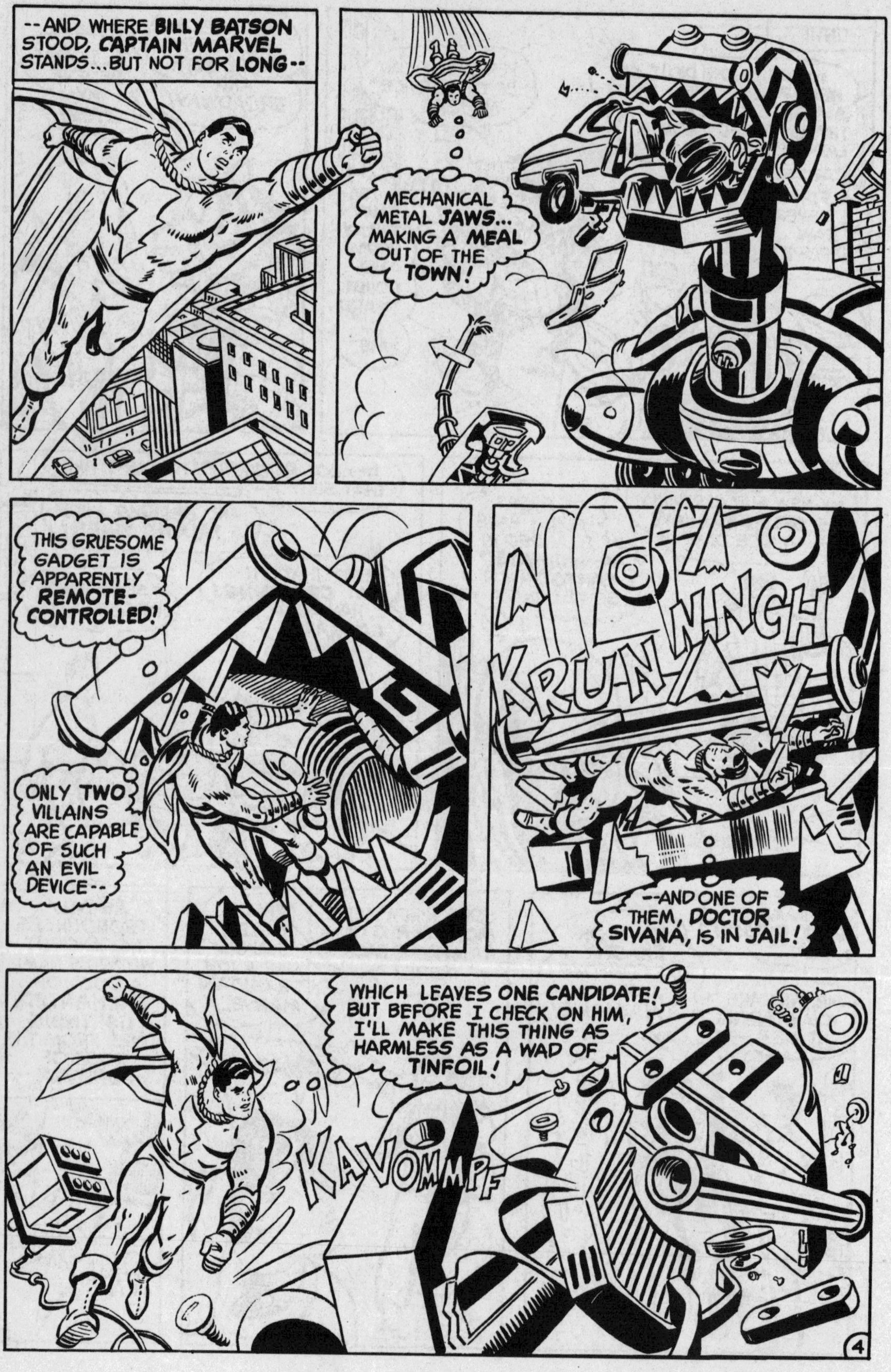
--AND WHERE BILLY BATSON STOOD, CAPTAIN MARVEL STANDS...BUT NOT FOR LONG--
MECHANICAL METAL JAWS... MAKING A MEAL OUT OF THE TOWN!
THIS GRUESOME GADGET IS APPARENTLY REMOTE-CONTROLLED!
ONLY TWO VILLAINS ARE CAPABLE OF SUCH AN EVIL DEVICE--
KRUNNNCH
--AND ONE OF THEM, DOCTOR SIVANA, IS IN JAIL!
WHICH LEAVES ONE CANDIDATE! BUT BEFORE I CHECK ON HIM, I'LL MAKE THIS THING AS HARMLESS AS A WAD OF TINFOIL!
KAVOMMMPF
4

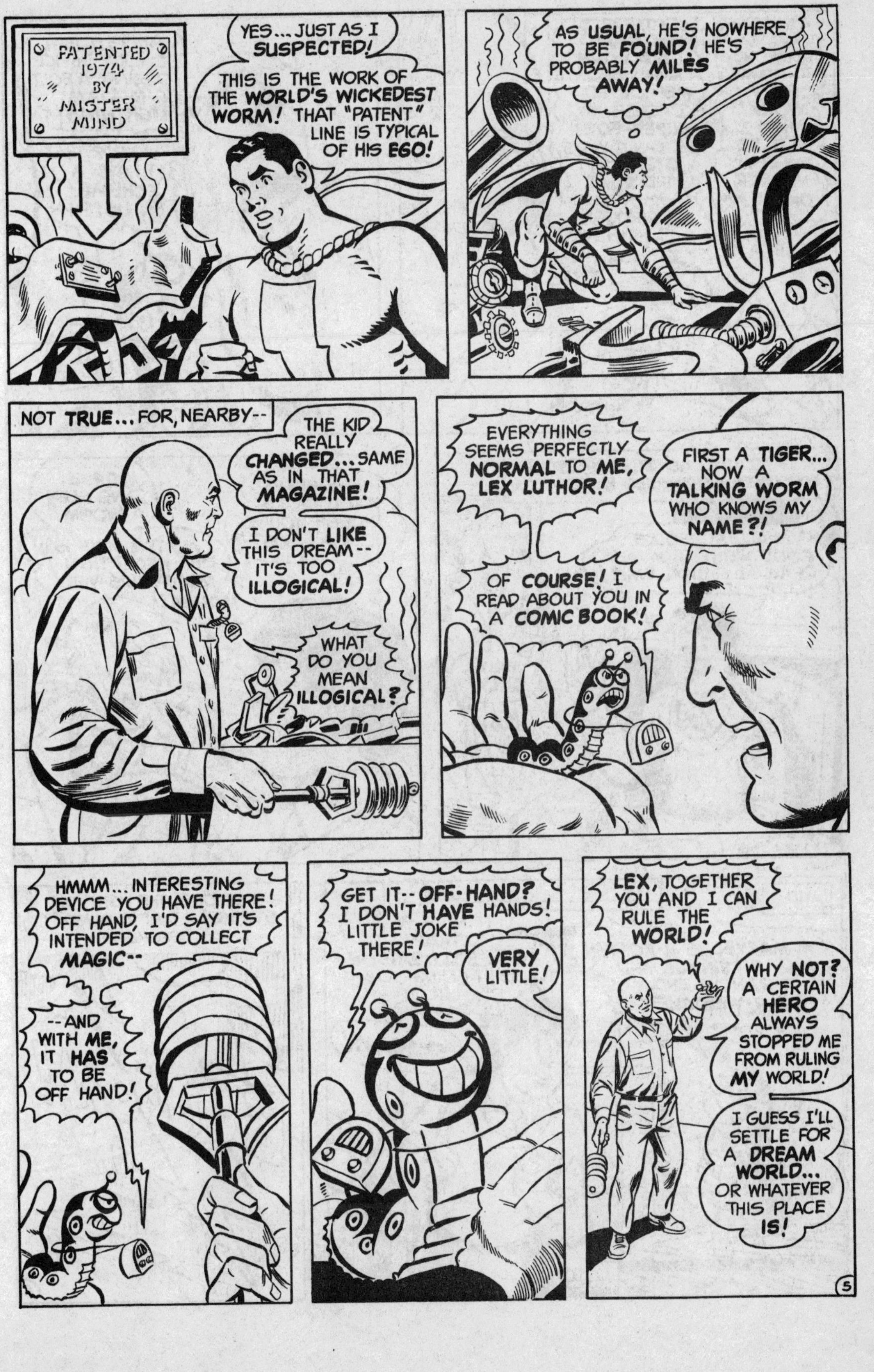
PATENTED 1974 BY MISTER MIND
YES... JUST AS I SUSPECTED!
THIS IS THE WORK OF THE WORLD'S WICKEDEST WORM! THAT "PATENT" LINE IS TYPICAL OF HIS EGO!
AS USUAL, HE'S NOWHERE TO BE FOUND! HE'S PROBABLY MILES AWAY!
NOT TRUE... FOR, NEARBY--
THE KID REALLY CHANGED... SAME AS IN THAT MAGAZINE!
I DON'T LIKE THIS DREAM-- IT'S TOO ILLOGICAL!
WHAT DO YOU MEAN ILLOGICAL?
EVERYTHING SEEMS PERFECTLY NORMAL TO ME, LEX LUTHOR!
FIRST A TIGER... NOW A TALKING WORM WHO KNOWS MY NAME?!
OF COURSE! I READ ABOUT YOU IN A COMIC BOOK!
HMMM... INTERESTING DEVICE YOU HAVE THERE! OFF HAND, I'D SAY IT'S INTENDED TO COLLECT MAGIC--
--AND WITH ME, IT HAS TO BE OFF HAND!
GET IT-- OFF-HAND? I DON'T HAVE HANDS! LITTLE JOKE THERE!
VERY LITTLE!
LEX, TOGETHER YOU AND I CAN RULE THE WORLD!
WHY NOT? A CERTAIN HERO ALWAYS STOPPED ME FROM RULING MY WORLD!
I GUESS I'LL SETTLE FOR A DREAM WORLD... OR WHATEVER THIS PLACE IS!
5

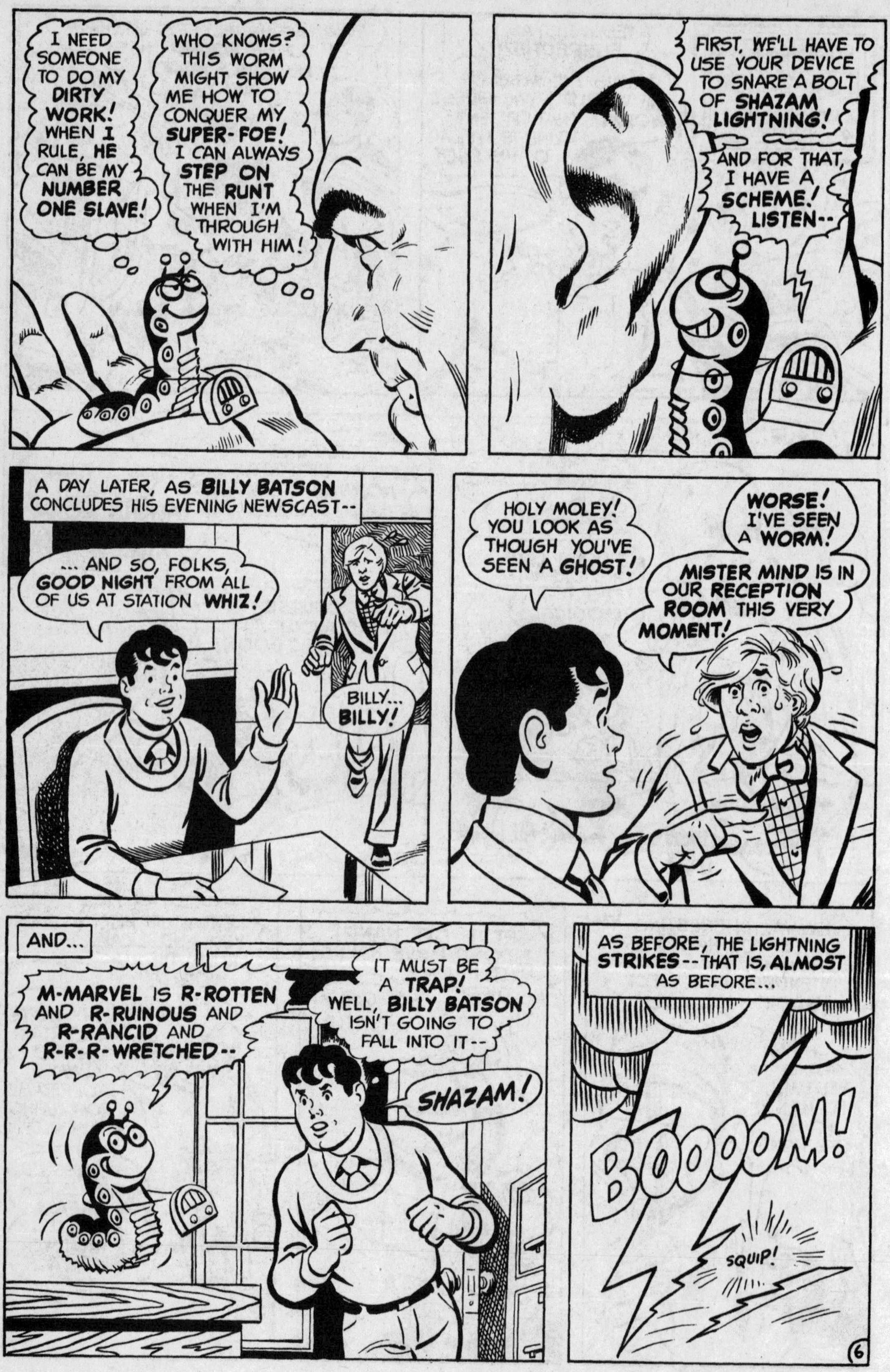
I NEED SOMEONE TO DO MY DIRTY WORK! WHEN I RULE, HE CAN BE MY NUMBER ONE SLAVE!
WHO KNOWS? THIS WORM MIGHT SHOW ME HOW TO CONQUER MY SUPER-FOE! I CAN ALWAYS STEP ON THE RUNT WHEN I'M THROUGH WITH HIM!
FIRST, WE'LL HAVE TO USE YOUR DEVICE TO SNARE A BOLT OF SHAZAM LIGHTNING!
AND FOR THAT, I HAVE A SCHEME! LISTEN--
A DAY LATER, AS BILLY BATSON CONCLUDES HIS EVENING NEWSCAST--
... AND SO, FOLKS, GOOD NIGHT FROM ALL OF US AT STATION WHIZ!
BILLY... BILLY!
HOLY MOLEY! YOU LOOK AS THOUGH YOU'VE SEEN A GHOST!
WORSE! I'VE SEEN A WORM!
MISTER MIND IS IN OUR RECEPTION ROOM THIS VERY MOMENT!
AND...
M-MARVEL IS R-ROTTEN AND R-RUINOUS AND R-RANCID AND R-R-R-WRETCHED--
IT MUST BE A TRAP! WELL, BILLY BATSON ISN'T GOING TO FALL INTO IT--
SHAZAM!
AS BEFORE, THE LIGHTNING STRIKES--THAT IS, ALMOST AS BEFORE...
BOOOOM!
SQUIP!
6

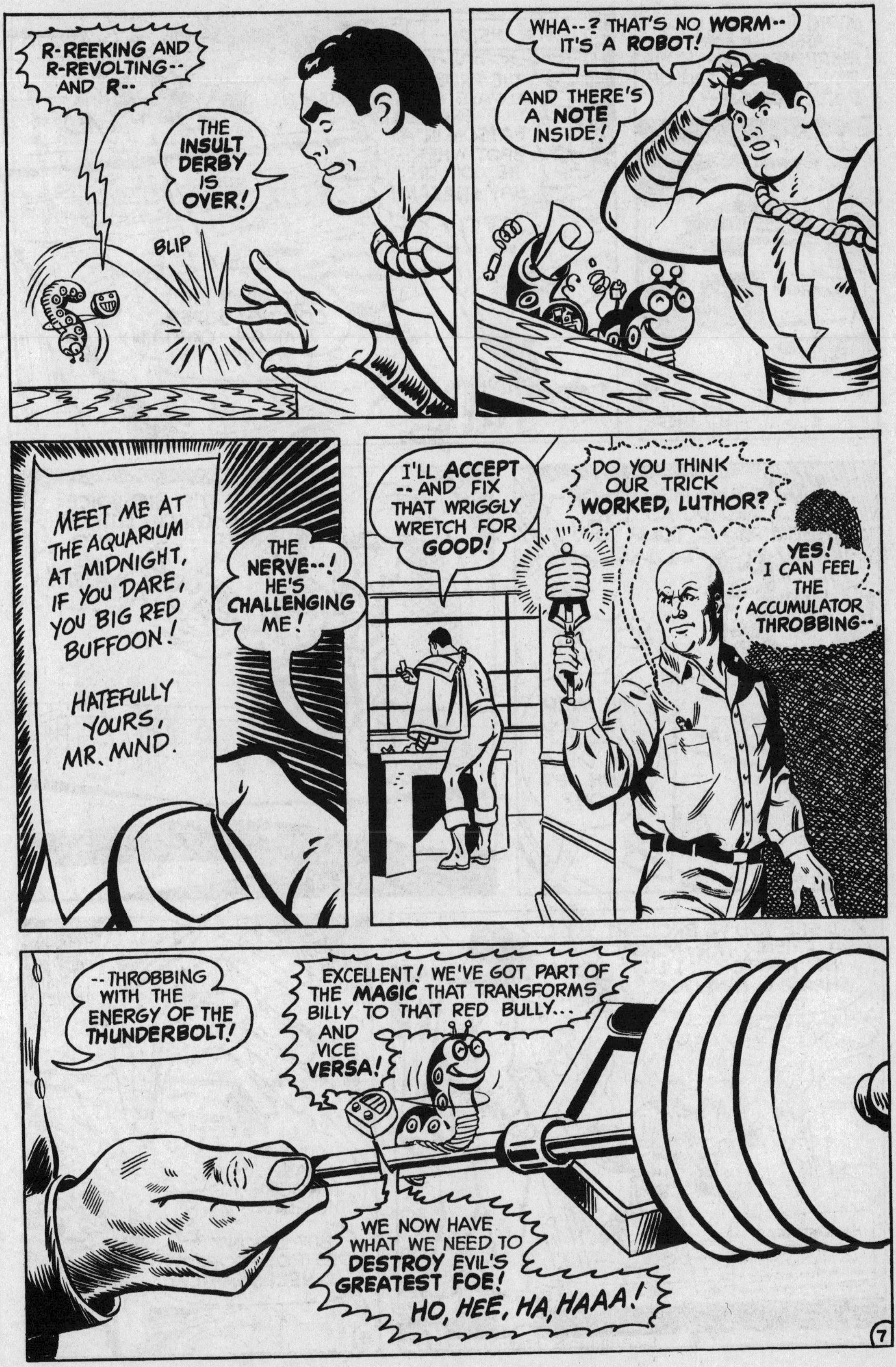
R-REEKING AND R-REVOLTING-- AND R--
THE INSULT DERBY IS OVER!
BLIP
WHA--? THAT'S NO WORM-- IT'S A ROBOT!
AND THERE'S A NOTE INSIDE!
MEET ME AT THE AQUARIUM AT MIDNIGHT, IF YOU DARE, YOU BIG RED BUFFOON!
HATEFULLY YOURS, MR. MIND.
THE NERVE--! HE'S CHALLENGING ME!
I'LL ACCEPT -- AND FIX THAT WRIGGLY WRETCH FOR GOOD!
DO YOU THINK OUR TRICK WORKED, LUTHOR?
YES! I CAN FEEL THE ACCUMULATOR THROBBING--
--THROBBING WITH THE ENERGY OF THE THUNDERBOLT!
EXCELLENT! WE'VE GOT PART OF THE MAGIC THAT TRANSFORMS BILLY TO THAT RED BULLY... AND VICE VERSA!
WE NOW HAVE WHAT WE NEED TO DESTROY EVIL'S GREATEST FOE!
HO, HEE, HA, HAAA!
7

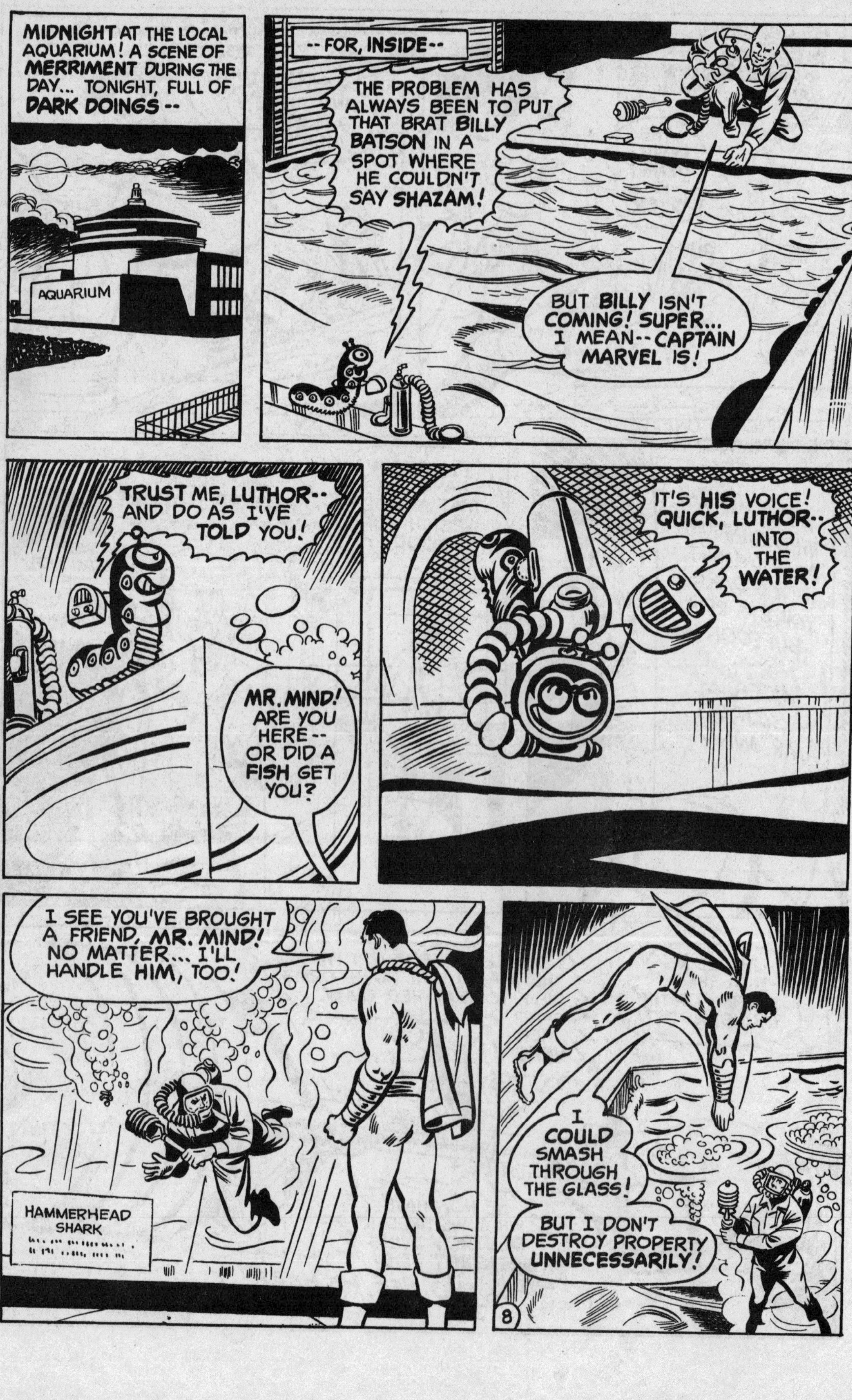
MIDNIGHT AT THE LOCAL AQUARIUM! A SCENE OF MERRIMENT DURING THE DAY... TONIGHT, FULL OF DARK DOINGS --
AQUARIUM
-- FOR, INSIDE --
THE PROBLEM HAS ALWAYS BEEN TO PUT THAT BRAT BILLY BATSON IN A SPOT WHERE HE COULDN'T SAY SHAZAM!
BUT BILLY ISN'T COMING! SUPER... I MEAN-- CAPTAIN MARVEL IS!
TRUST ME, LUTHOR-- AND DO AS I'VE TOLD YOU!
MR. MIND! ARE YOU HERE-- OR DID A FISH GET YOU?
IT'S HIS VOICE! QUICK, LUTHOR-- INTO THE WATER!
I SEE YOU'VE BROUGHT A FRIEND, MR. MIND! NO MATTER... I'LL HANDLE HIM, TOO!
HAMMERHEAD SHARK
I COULD SMASH THROUGH THE GLASS!
BUT I DON'T DESTROY PROPERTY UNNECESSARILY!
8

As CAP DIVES TOWARD HIS FOES--

SPLASH!

--LEX LUTHOR DISCHARGES A MAGIC BOLT AT HIM--

--CAUSING AN UNEXPECTED AND DANGEROUS TRANSFORMATION...

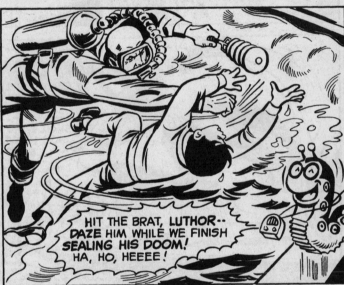

HIT THE BRAT, LUTHOR-- DAZE HIM WHILE WE FINISH SEALING HIS DOOM! HA, HO, HEEEE!

THAT'S IT, LUTHOR! LOCK THE TOP IN PLACE BEFORE HE CAN SURFACE! HA, HEE, HO, HEE, HA!

TOO... THICK! I CAN'T BREAK OUT! CAN'T SAY SHAZAM, EITHER!

HOLY MOLEY! I'M IN THE WORST TROUBLE OF MY LIFE!

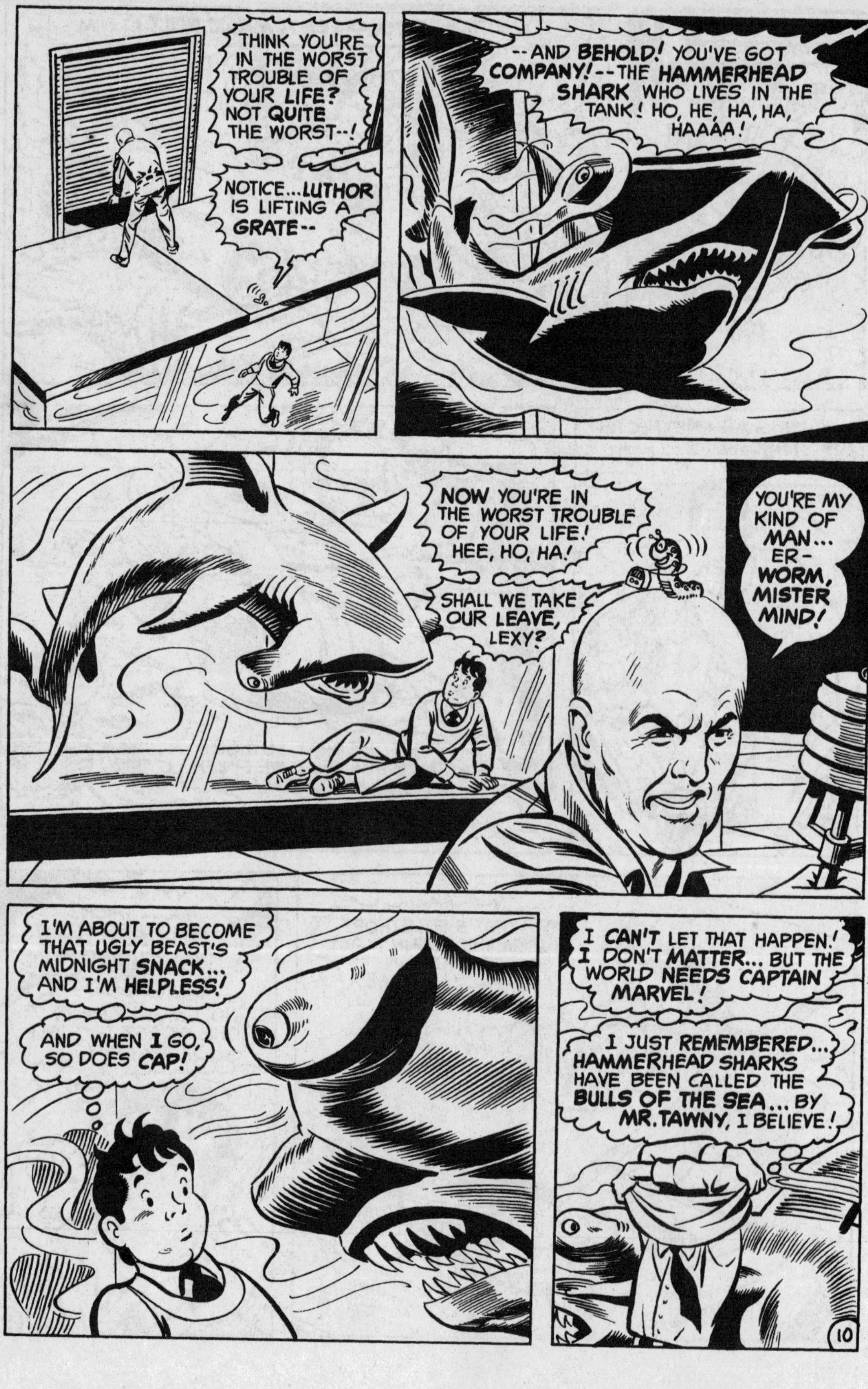
THINK YOU'RE IN THE WORST TROUBLE OF YOUR LIFE? NOT QUITE THE WORST--!
NOTICE...LUTHOR IS LIFTING A GRATE--
--AND BEHOLD! YOU'VE GOT COMPANY!--THE HAMMERHEAD SHARK WHO LIVES IN THE TANK! HO, HE, HA, HA, HAAAA!
NOW YOU'RE IN THE WORST TROUBLE OF YOUR LIFE! HEE, HO, HA!
SHALL WE TAKE OUR LEAVE, LEXY?
YOU'RE MY KIND OF MAN... ER-WORM, MISTER MIND!
I'M ABOUT TO BECOME THAT UGLY BEAST'S MIDNIGHT SNACK... AND I'M HELPLESS!
AND WHEN I GO, SO DOES CAP!
I CAN'T LET THAT HAPPEN! I DON'T MATTER... BUT THE WORLD NEEDS CAPTAIN MARVEL!
I JUST REMEMBERED... HAMMERHEAD SHARKS HAVE BEEN CALLED THE BULLS OF THE SEA... BY MR. TAWNY, I BELIEVE!
10

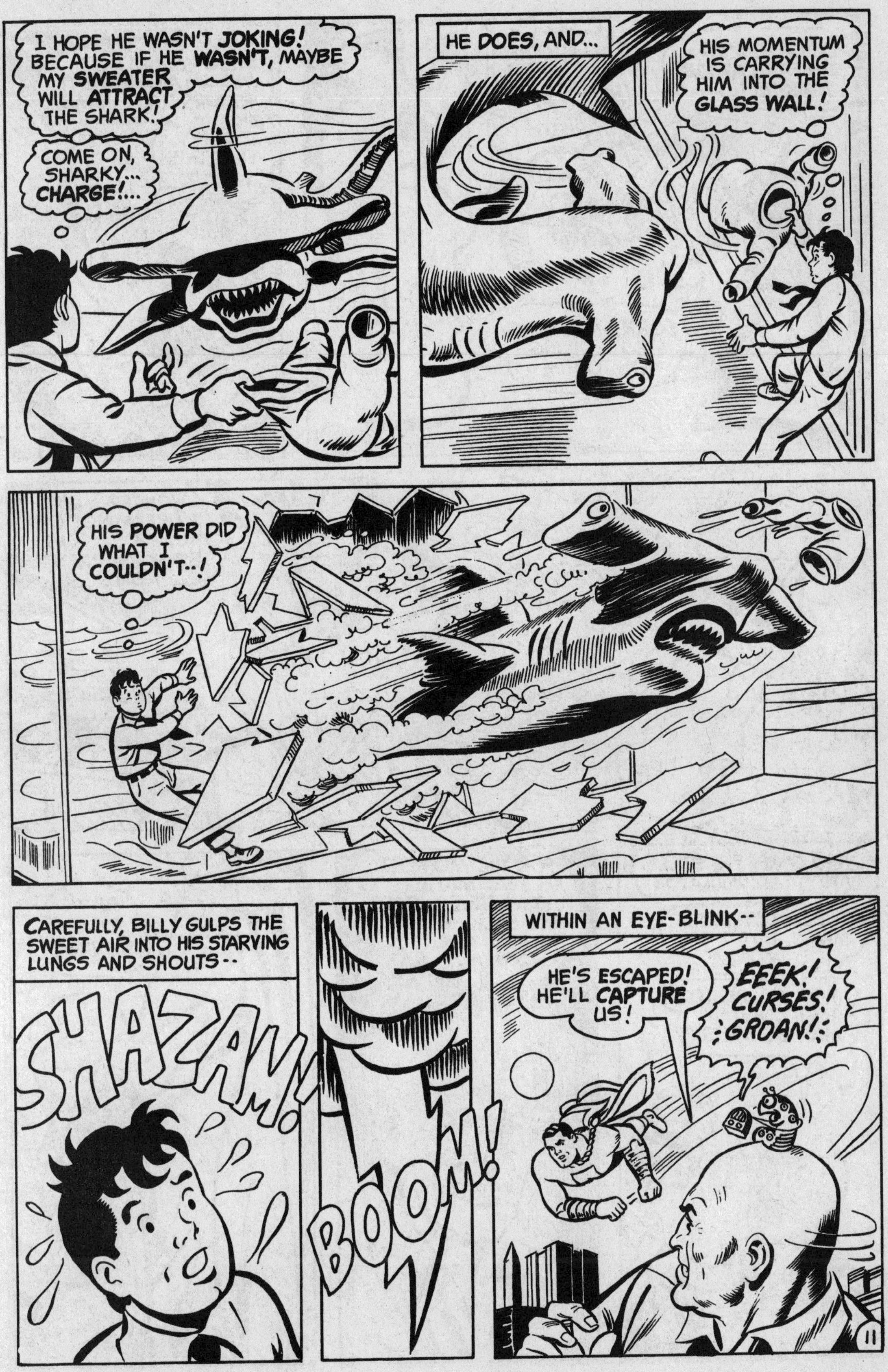
I HOPE HE WASN'T JOKING! BECAUSE IF HE WASN'T, MAYBE MY SWEATER WILL ATTRACT THE SHARK!
COME ON, SHARKY... CHARGE!...
HE DOES, AND...
HIS MOMENTUM IS CARRYING HIM INTO THE GLASS WALL!
HIS POWER DID WHAT I COULDN'T--!
CAREFULLY, BILLY GULPS THE SWEET AIR INTO HIS STARVING LUNGS AND SHOUTS--
SHAZAM!
BOOM!
WITHIN AN EYE-BLINK--
HE'S ESCAPED! HE'LL CAPTURE US!
EEEK! CURSES! GROAN!
11

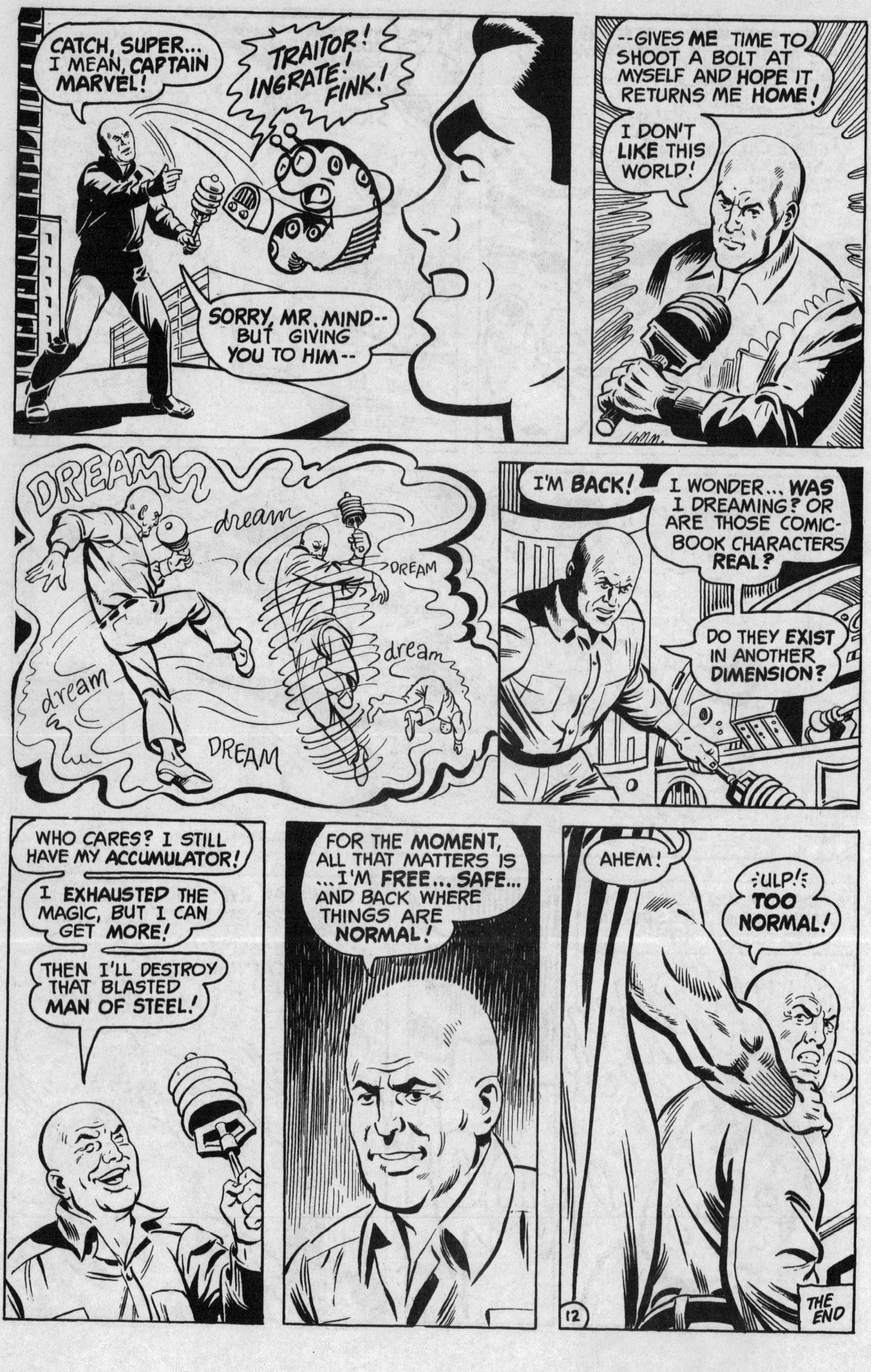
CATCH, SUPER... I MEAN, CAPTAIN MARVEL!
TRAITOR! INGRATE! FINK!
SORRY, MR. MIND-- BUT GIVING YOU TO HIM--
--GIVES ME TIME TO SHOOT A BOLT AT MYSELF AND HOPE IT RETURNS ME HOME!
I DON'T LIKE THIS WORLD!
DREAM
dream
DREAM
dream
dream
DREAM
I'M BACK!
I WONDER... WAS I DREAMING? OR ARE THOSE COMIC-BOOK CHARACTERS REAL?
DO THEY EXIST IN ANOTHER DIMENSION?
WHO CARES? I STILL HAVE MY ACCUMULATOR!
I EXHAUSTED THE MAGIC, BUT I CAN GET MORE!
THEN I'LL DESTROY THAT BLASTED MAN OF STEEL!
FOR THE MOMENT, ALL THAT MATTERS IS ...I'M FREE... SAFE... AND BACK WHERE THINGS ARE NORMAL!
AHEM!
ULP! TOO NORMAL!
12
THE END

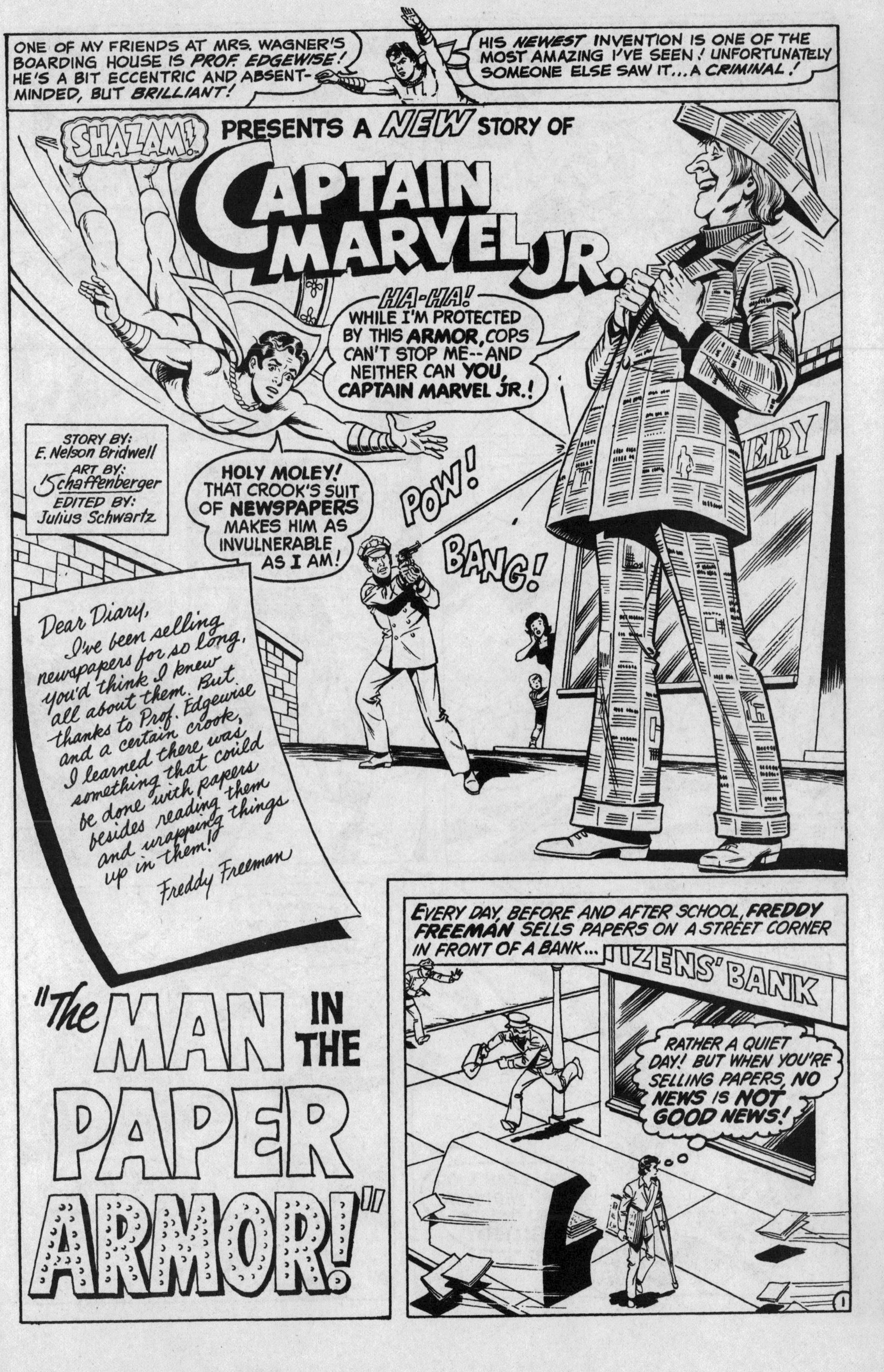
ONE OF MY FRIENDS AT MRS. WAGNER'S BOARDING HOUSE IS PROF. EDGEWISE! HE'S A BIT ECCENTRIC AND ABSENT-MINDED, BUT BRILLIANT!
HIS NEWEST INVENTION IS ONE OF THE MOST AMAZING I'VE SEEN! UNFORTUNATELY SOMEONE ELSE SAW IT... A CRIMINAL!
SHAZAM! PRESENTS A NEW STORY OF
CAPTAIN MARVEL JR.
HA-HA! WHILE I'M PROTECTED BY THIS ARMOR, COPS CAN'T STOP ME--AND NEITHER CAN YOU, CAPTAIN MARVEL JR.!
STORY BY: E. Nelson Bridwell
ART BY: K. Schaffenberger
EDITED BY: Julius Schwartz
HOLY MOLEY! THAT CROOK'S SUIT OF NEWSPAPERS MAKES HIM AS INVULNERABLE AS I AM!
POW!
BANG!
Dear Diary,
I've been selling newspapers for so long, you'd think I knew all about them. But thanks to Prof. Edgewise and a certain crook, I learned there was something that could be done with papers besides reading them and wrapping things up in them!
Freddy Freeman
"The MAN IN THE PAPER ARMOR!"
EVERY DAY, BEFORE AND AFTER SCHOOL, FREDDY FREEMAN SELLS PAPERS ON A STREET CORNER IN FRONT OF A BANK...
...IZENS' BANK
RATHER A QUIET DAY! BUT WHEN YOU'RE SELLING PAPERS, NO NEWS IS NOT GOOD NEWS!
1

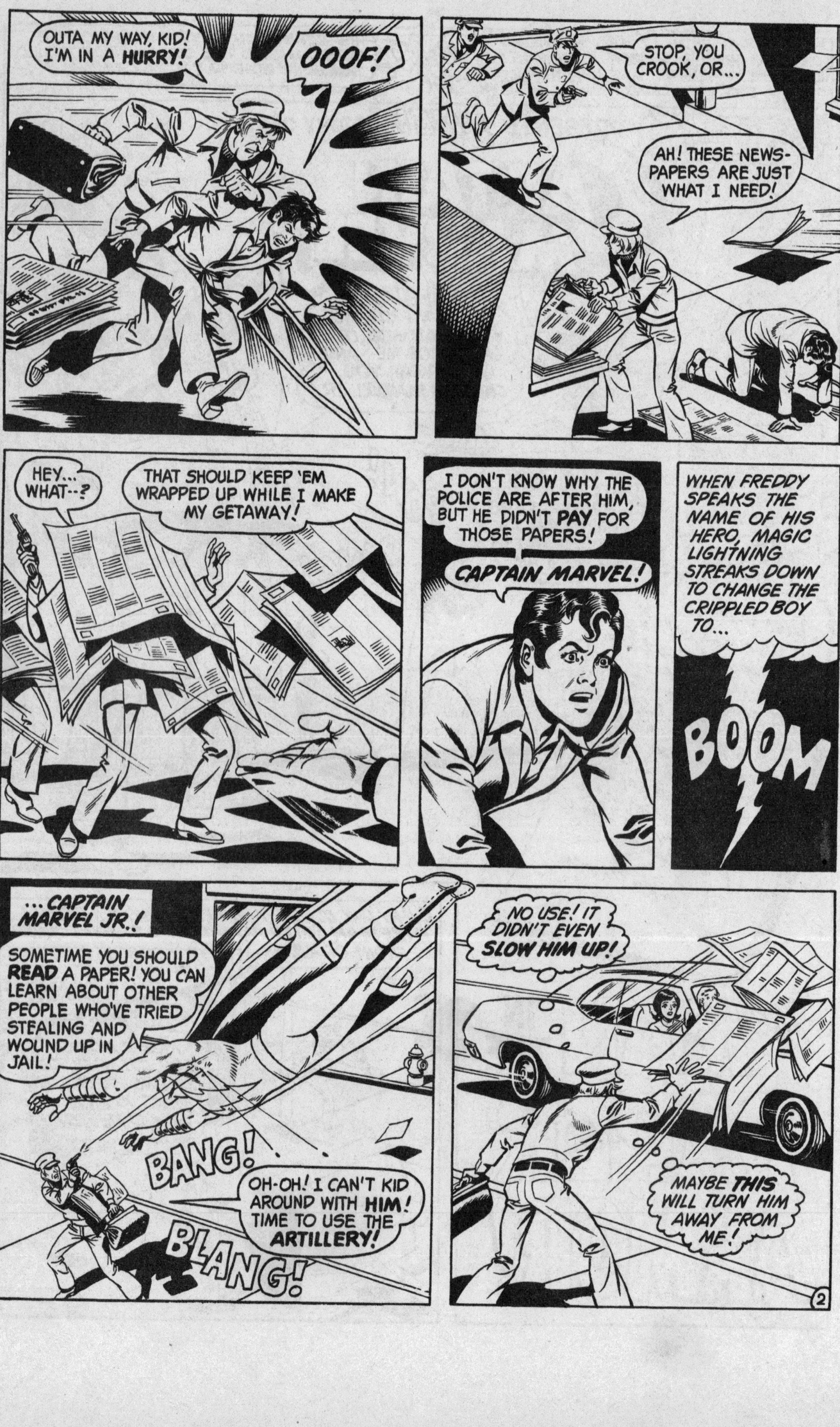
OUTA MY WAY, KID! I'M IN A HURRY!
OOOF!
STOP, YOU CROOK, OR...
AH! THESE NEWS-PAPERS ARE JUST WHAT I NEED!
HEY... WHAT--?
THAT SHOULD KEEP 'EM WRAPPED UP WHILE I MAKE MY GETAWAY!
I DON'T KNOW WHY THE POLICE ARE AFTER HIM, BUT HE DIDN'T PAY FOR THOSE PAPERS!
CAPTAIN MARVEL!
WHEN FREDDY SPEAKS THE NAME OF HIS HERO, MAGIC LIGHTNING STREAKS DOWN TO CHANGE THE CRIPPLED BOY TO...
BOOM
... CAPTAIN MARVEL JR.!
SOMETIME YOU SHOULD READ A PAPER! YOU CAN LEARN ABOUT OTHER PEOPLE WHO'VE TRIED STEALING AND WOUND UP IN JAIL!
BANG!
OH-OH! I CAN'T KID AROUND WITH HIM! TIME TO USE THE ARTILLERY!
BLANG!
NO USE! IT DIDN'T EVEN SLOW HIM UP!
MAYBE THIS WILL TURN HIM AWAY FROM ME!
2

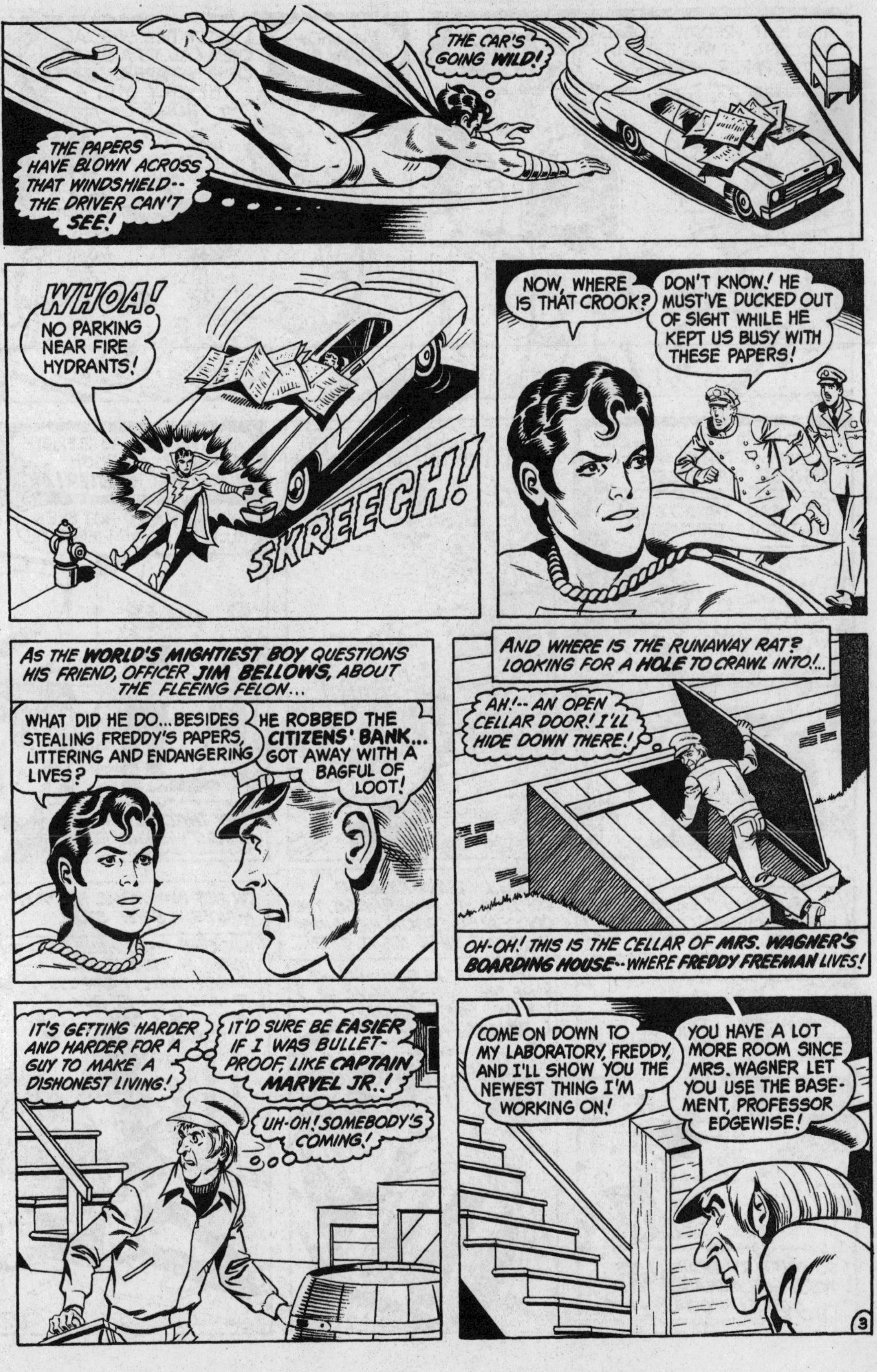
THE CAR'S GOING WILD!
THE PAPERS HAVE BLOWN ACROSS THAT WINDSHIELD-- THE DRIVER CAN'T SEE!
WHOA! NO PARKING NEAR FIRE HYDRANTS!
SKREECH!
NOW, WHERE IS THAT CROOK?
DON'T KNOW! HE MUST'VE DUCKED OUT OF SIGHT WHILE HE KEPT US BUSY WITH THESE PAPERS!
AS THE WORLD'S MIGHTIEST BOY QUESTIONS HIS FRIEND, OFFICER JIM BELLOWS, ABOUT THE FLEEING FELON...
WHAT DID HE DO...BESIDES STEALING FREDDY'S PAPERS, LITTERING AND ENDANGERING LIVES?
HE ROBBED THE CITIZENS' BANK... GOT AWAY WITH A BAGFUL OF LOOT!
AND WHERE IS THE RUNAWAY RAT? LOOKING FOR A HOLE TO CRAWL INTO!...
AH!-- AN OPEN CELLAR DOOR! I'LL HIDE DOWN THERE!
OH-OH! THIS IS THE CELLAR OF MRS. WAGNER'S BOARDING HOUSE-- WHERE FREDDY FREEMAN LIVES!
IT'S GETTING HARDER AND HARDER FOR A GUY TO MAKE A DISHONEST LIVING!
IT'D SURE BE EASIER IF I WAS BULLET-PROOF, LIKE CAPTAIN MARVEL JR.!
UH-OH! SOMEBODY'S COMING!
COME ON DOWN TO MY LABORATORY, FREDDY, AND I'LL SHOW YOU THE NEWEST THING I'M WORKING ON!
YOU HAVE A LOT MORE ROOM SINCE MRS. WAGNER LET YOU USE THE BASEMENT, PROFESSOR EDGEWISE!
3

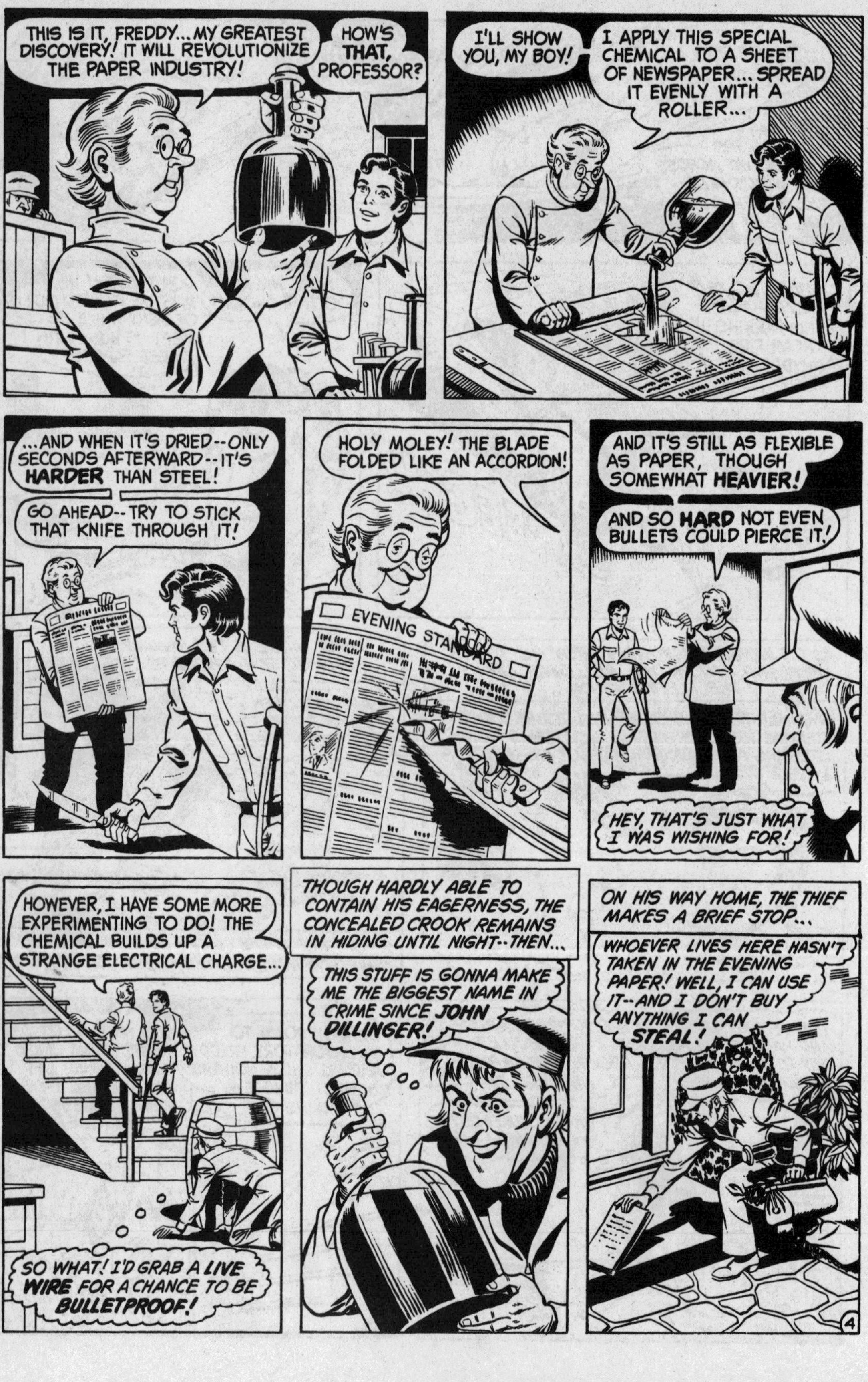
THIS IS IT, FREDDY... MY GREATEST DISCOVERY! IT WILL REVOLUTIONIZE THE PAPER INDUSTRY!
HOW'S THAT, PROFESSOR?
I'LL SHOW YOU, MY BOY!
I APPLY THIS SPECIAL CHEMICAL TO A SHEET OF NEWSPAPER... SPREAD IT EVENLY WITH A ROLLER...
...AND WHEN IT'S DRIED--ONLY SECONDS AFTERWARD--IT'S HARDER THAN STEEL!
GO AHEAD--TRY TO STICK THAT KNIFE THROUGH IT!
HOLY MOLEY! THE BLADE FOLDED LIKE AN ACCORDION!
EVENING STANDARD
AND IT'S STILL AS FLEXIBLE AS PAPER, THOUGH SOMEWHAT HEAVIER!
AND SO HARD NOT EVEN BULLETS COULD PIERCE IT!
HEY, THAT'S JUST WHAT I WAS WISHING FOR!
HOWEVER, I HAVE SOME MORE EXPERIMENTING TO DO! THE CHEMICAL BUILDS UP A STRANGE ELECTRICAL CHARGE...
SO WHAT! I'D GRAB A LIVE WIRE FOR A CHANCE TO BE BULLETPROOF!
THOUGH HARDLY ABLE TO CONTAIN HIS EAGERNESS, THE CONCEALED CROOK REMAINS IN HIDING UNTIL NIGHT--THEN...
THIS STUFF IS GONNA MAKE ME THE BIGGEST NAME IN CRIME SINCE JOHN DILLINGER!
ON HIS WAY HOME, THE THIEF MAKES A BRIEF STOP...
WHOEVER LIVES HERE HASN'T TAKEN IN THE EVENING PAPER! WELL, I CAN USE IT--AND I DON'T BUY ANYTHING I CAN STEAL!
4

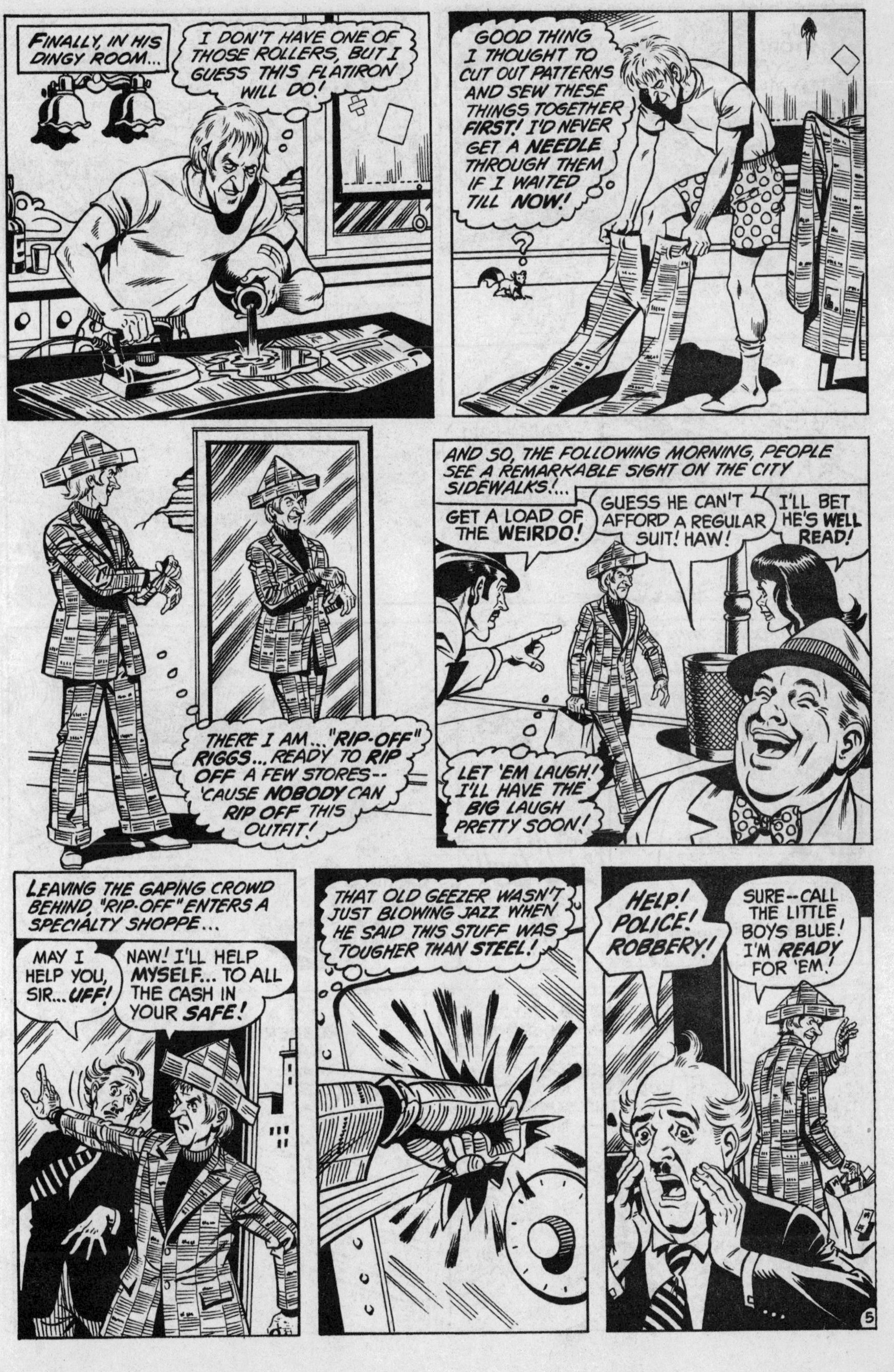
FINALLY, IN HIS DINGY ROOM...
I DON'T HAVE ONE OF THOSE ROLLERS, BUT I GUESS THIS FLATIRON WILL DO!
GOOD THING I THOUGHT TO CUT OUT PATTERNS AND SEW THESE THINGS TOGETHER FIRST! I'D NEVER GET A NEEDLE THROUGH THEM IF I WAITED TILL NOW!
?
THERE I AM..."RIP-OFF" RIGGS... READY TO RIP OFF A FEW STORES-- 'CAUSE NOBODY CAN RIP OFF THIS OUTFIT!
AND SO, THE FOLLOWING MORNING, PEOPLE SEE A REMARKABLE SIGHT ON THE CITY SIDEWALKS!...
GET A LOAD OF THE WEIRDO!
GUESS HE CAN'T AFFORD A REGULAR SUIT! HAW!
I'LL BET HE'S WELL READ!
LET 'EM LAUGH! I'LL HAVE THE BIG LAUGH PRETTY SOON!
LEAVING THE GAPING CROWD BEHIND, "RIP-OFF" ENTERS A SPECIALTY SHOPPE...
MAY I HELP YOU, SIR... UFF!
NAW! I'LL HELP MYSELF... TO ALL THE CASH IN YOUR SAFE!
THAT OLD GEEZER WASN'T JUST BLOWING JAZZ WHEN HE SAID THIS STUFF WAS TOUGHER THAN STEEL!
HELP! POLICE! ROBBERY!
SURE--CALL THE LITTLE BOYS BLUE! I'M READY FOR 'EM!
5

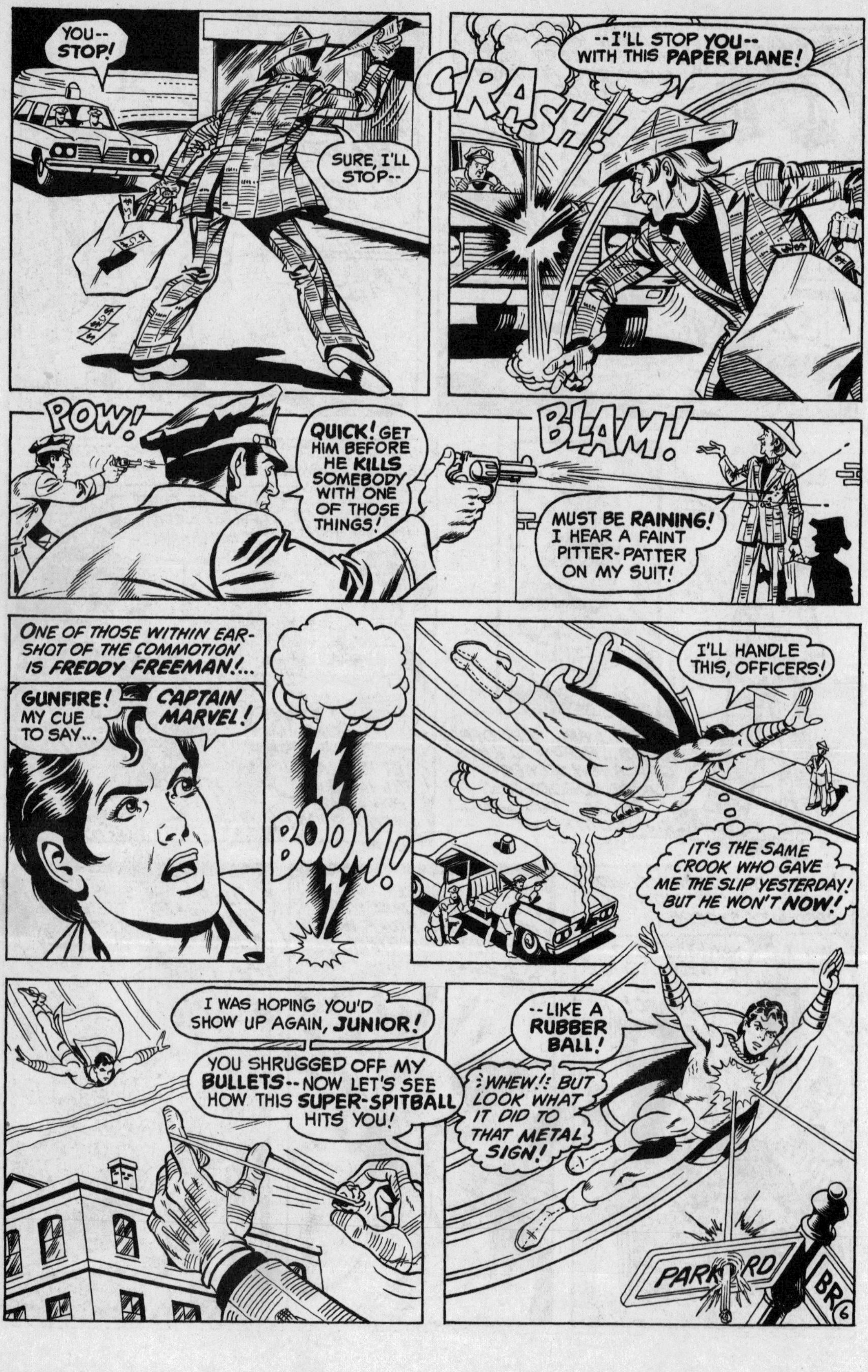

YOU-- STOP!
SURE, I'LL STOP--
CRASH!
--I'LL STOP YOU-- WITH THIS PAPER PLANE!
POW!
QUICK! GET HIM BEFORE HE KILLS SOMEBODY WITH ONE OF THOSE THINGS!
BLAM!
MUST BE RAINING! I HEAR A FAINT PITTER-PATTER ON MY SUIT!
ONE OF THOSE WITHIN EAR-SHOT OF THE COMMOTION IS FREDDY FREEMAN!...
GUNFIRE! MY CUE TO SAY...
CAPTAIN MARVEL!
BOOM!
I'LL HANDLE THIS, OFFICERS!
IT'S THE SAME CROOK WHO GAVE ME THE SLIP YESTERDAY! BUT HE WON'T NOW!
I WAS HOPING YOU'D SHOW UP AGAIN, JUNIOR!
YOU SHRUGGED OFF MY BULLETS--NOW LET'S SEE HOW THIS SUPER-SPITBALL HITS YOU!
--LIKE A RUBBER BALL!
WHEW! BUT LOOK WHAT IT DID TO THAT METAL SIGN!
PARK RD
BR
6

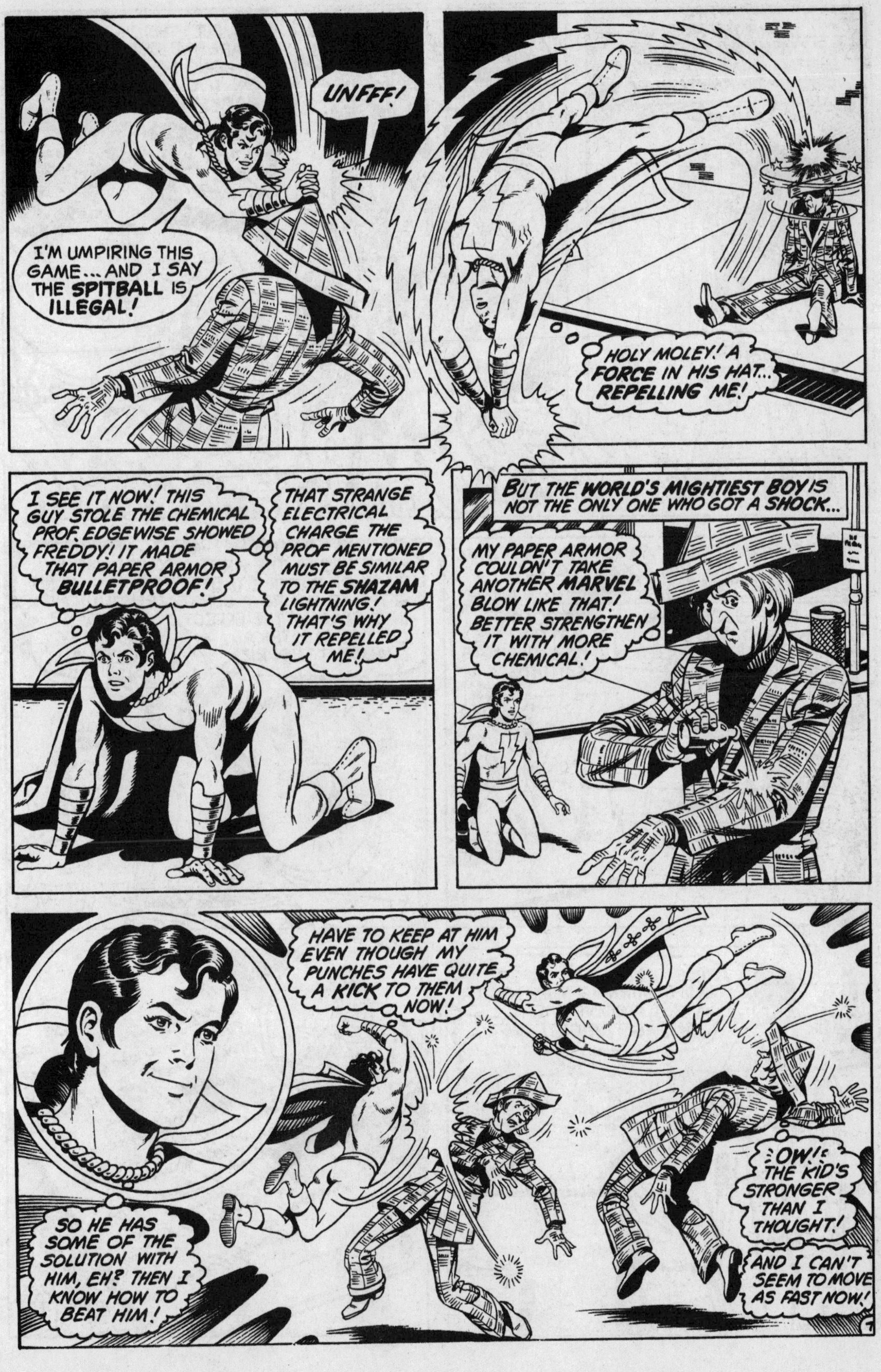
UNFFF!
I'M UMPIRING THIS GAME... AND I SAY THE SPITBALL IS ILLEGAL!
HOLY MOLEY! A FORCE IN HIS HAT... REPELLING ME!
I SEE IT NOW! THIS GUY STOLE THE CHEMICAL PROF. EDGEWISE SHOWED FREDDY! IT MADE THAT PAPER ARMOR BULLETPROOF!
THAT STRANGE ELECTRICAL CHARGE THE PROF MENTIONED MUST BE SIMILAR TO THE SHAZAM LIGHTNING! THAT'S WHY IT REPELLED ME!
BUT THE WORLD'S MIGHTIEST BOY IS NOT THE ONLY ONE WHO GOT A SHOCK...
MY PAPER ARMOR COULDN'T TAKE ANOTHER MARVEL BLOW LIKE THAT! BETTER STRENGTHEN IT WITH MORE CHEMICAL!
HAVE TO KEEP AT HIM EVEN THOUGH MY PUNCHES HAVE QUITE A KICK TO THEM NOW!
SO HE HAS SOME OF THE SOLUTION WITH HIM, EH? THEN I KNOW HOW TO BEAT HIM!
OW!! THE KID'S STRONGER THAN I THOUGHT!
AND I CAN'T SEEM TO MOVE AS FAST NOW!
7

I'LL DUMP THE REST OF THE CHEMICAL OVER ME! THAT'LL MAKE MY ARMOR STAND UP TO ANYTHING!

YIPES! WH- WHAT'S HAPPENING TO ME?

KRUMP!

SIMPLE! THE CHEMICAL MADE THE PAPER HEAVIER! BY USING SO MUCH, YOU PUT ON TOO MUCH... UH... PAPERWEIGHT!

...JUST AS I PLANNED!

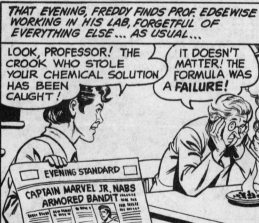

THAT EVENING, FREDDY FINDS PROF. EDGEWISE WORKING IN HIS LAB, FORGETFUL OF EVERYTHING ELSE... AS USUAL...

LOOK, PROFESSOR! THE CROOK WHO STOLE YOUR CHEMICAL SOLUTION HAS BEEN CAUGHT!

IT DOESN'T MATTER! THE FORMULA WAS A FAILURE!

EVENING STANDARD

CAPTAIN MARVEL JR. NABS ARMORED BANDIT

SEE? THIS IS THE FIRST PIECE OF PAPER I TREATED! AFTER 48 HOURS, IT BURST INTO FLAME! THE EFFECT OF THE ELECTRICAL CHARGE, I THEORIZE!

HOLY MOLEY! THEN IT WON'T REVOLUTIONIZE THE PAPER INDUSTRY AFTER ALL!

TRUE-- BUT IF THIS PAPER KEEPS BURNING MUCH LONGER, IT COULD SOLVE THE ENERGY CRISIS!

There's something they call serendipity... where you set out to find one thing and find something else instead! I guess that's what happened this time. Of course, you never can tell how it will turn out... but think of heating this whole boarding house with one piece of burning paper!

Freddy Freeman

THE END

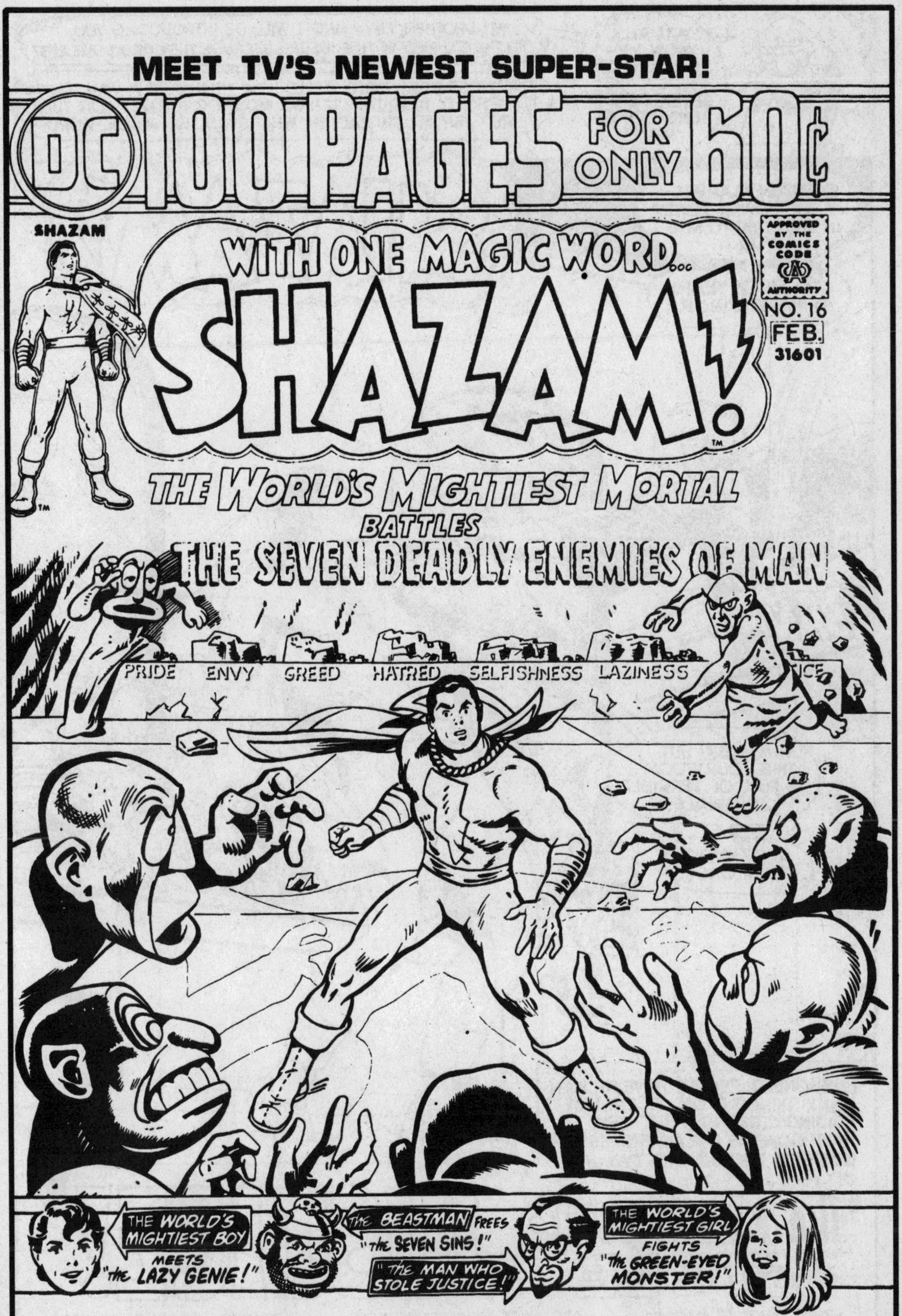
MEET TV'S NEWEST SUPER-STAR!
DC 100 PAGES FOR ONLY 60¢
SHAZAM
APPROVED BY THE COMICS CODE AUTHORITY
NO. 16
FEB.
31601
WITH ONE MAGIC WORD...
SHAZAM!
THE WORLD'S MIGHTIEST MORTAL
BATTLES
THE SEVEN DEADLY ENEMIES OF MAN
PRIDE
ENVY
GREED
HATRED
SELFISHNESS
LAZINESS
THE WORLD'S MIGHTIEST BOY MEETS "THE LAZY GENIE!"
THE BEASTMAN FREES "THE SEVEN SINS!"
"THE MAN WHO STOLE JUSTICE!"
THE WORLD'S MIGHTIEST GIRL FIGHTS "THE GREEN-EYED MONSTER!"

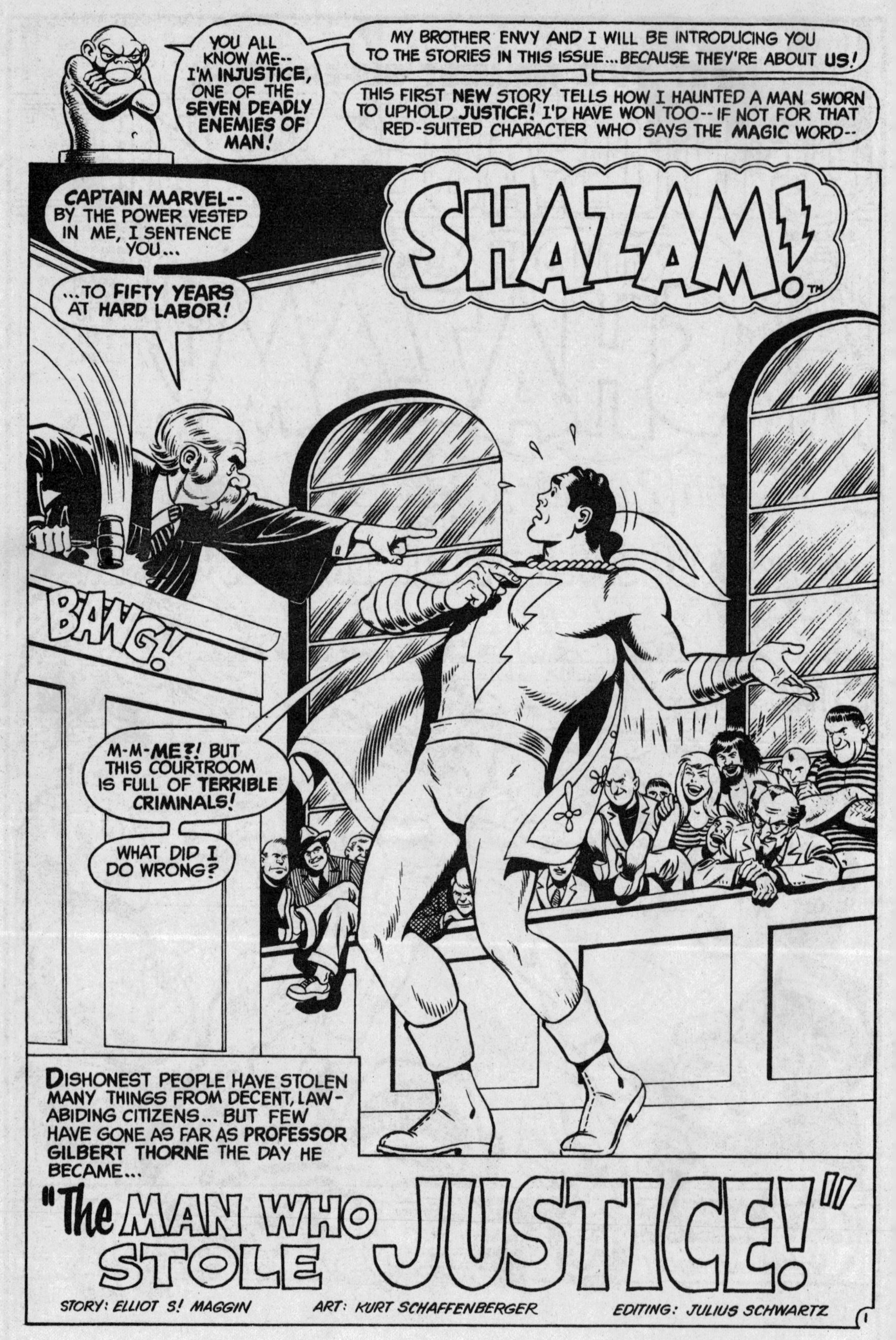
YOU ALL KNOW ME-- I'M INJUSTICE, ONE OF THE SEVEN DEADLY ENEMIES OF MAN!
MY BROTHER ENVY AND I WILL BE INTRODUCING YOU TO THE STORIES IN THIS ISSUE... BECAUSE THEY'RE ABOUT US!
THIS FIRST NEW STORY TELLS HOW I HAUNTED A MAN SWORN TO UPHOLD JUSTICE! I'D HAVE WON TOO-- IF NOT FOR THAT RED-SUITED CHARACTER WHO SAYS THE MAGIC WORD--
SHAZAM!™
CAPTAIN MARVEL-- BY THE POWER VESTED IN ME, I SENTENCE YOU...
...TO FIFTY YEARS AT HARD LABOR!
BANG!
M-M-ME?! BUT THIS COURTROOM IS FULL OF TERRIBLE CRIMINALS!
WHAT DID I DO WRONG?
DISHONEST PEOPLE HAVE STOLEN MANY THINGS FROM DECENT, LAW-ABIDING CITIZENS... BUT FEW HAVE GONE AS FAR AS PROFESSOR GILBERT THORNE THE DAY HE BECAME...
"The MAN WHO STOLE JUSTICE!"
STORY: ELLIOT S! MAGGIN
ART: KURT SCHAFFENBERGER
EDITING: JULIUS SCHWARTZ
1

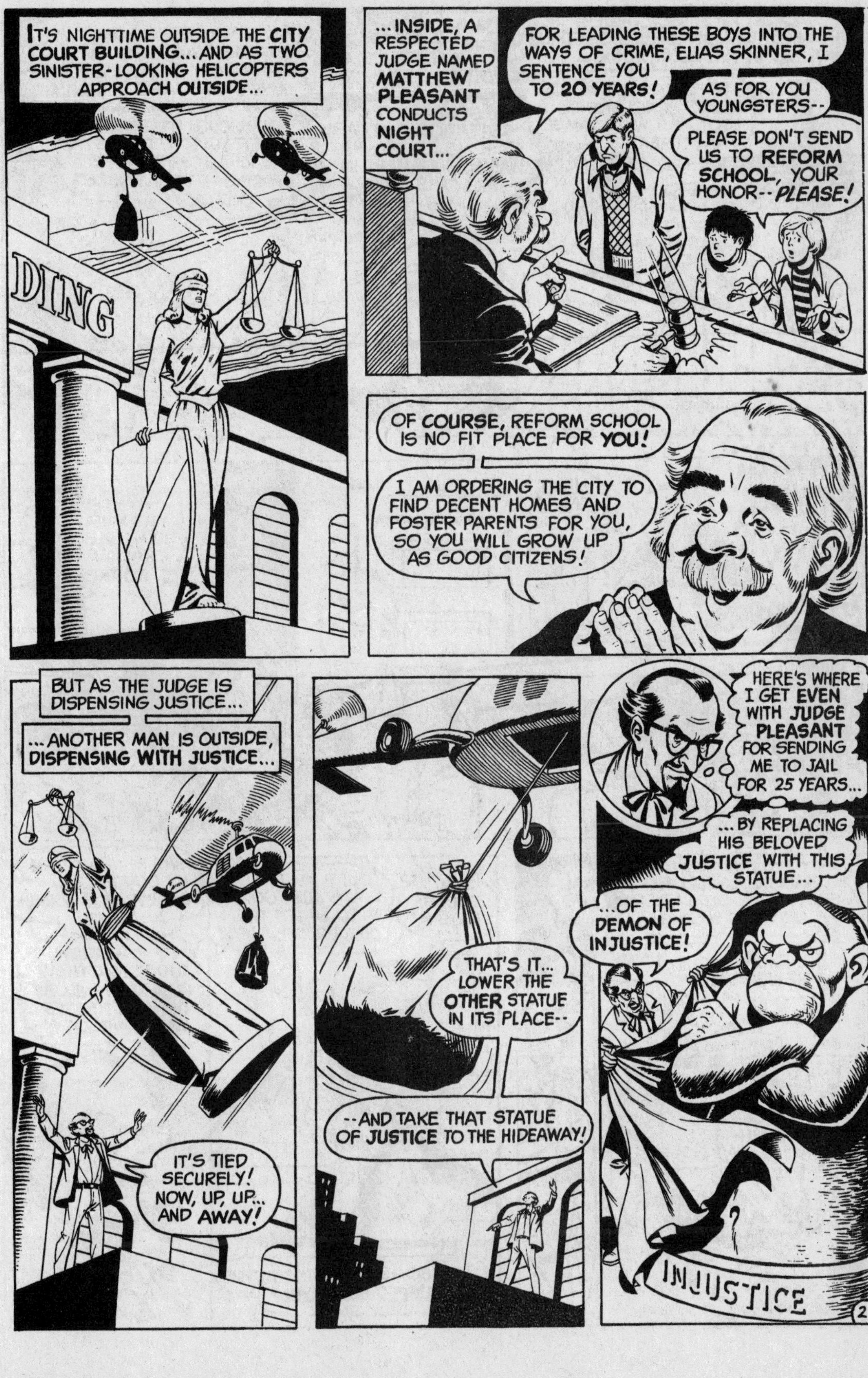

IT'S NIGHTTIME OUTSIDE THE CITY COURT BUILDING... AND AS TWO SINISTER-LOOKING HELICOPTERS APPROACH OUTSIDE...
DING
...INSIDE, A RESPECTED JUDGE NAMED MATTHEW PLEASANT CONDUCTS NIGHT COURT...
FOR LEADING THESE BOYS INTO THE WAYS OF CRIME, ELIAS SKINNER, I SENTENCE YOU TO 20 YEARS!
AS FOR YOU YOUNGSTERS--
PLEASE DON'T SEND US TO REFORM SCHOOL, YOUR HONOR--PLEASE!
OF COURSE, REFORM SCHOOL IS NO FIT PLACE FOR YOU!
I AM ORDERING THE CITY TO FIND DECENT HOMES AND FOSTER PARENTS FOR YOU, SO YOU WILL GROW UP AS GOOD CITIZENS!
BUT AS THE JUDGE IS DISPENSING JUSTICE...
...ANOTHER MAN IS OUTSIDE, DISPENSING WITH JUSTICE...
IT'S TIED SECURELY! NOW, UP, UP... AND AWAY!
THAT'S IT... LOWER THE OTHER STATUE IN ITS PLACE--
--AND TAKE THAT STATUE OF JUSTICE TO THE HIDEAWAY!
HERE'S WHERE I GET EVEN WITH JUDGE PLEASANT FOR SENDING ME TO JAIL FOR 25 YEARS...
...BY REPLACING HIS BELOVED JUSTICE WITH THIS STATUE...
...OF THE DEMON OF INJUSTICE!
INJUSTICE
2

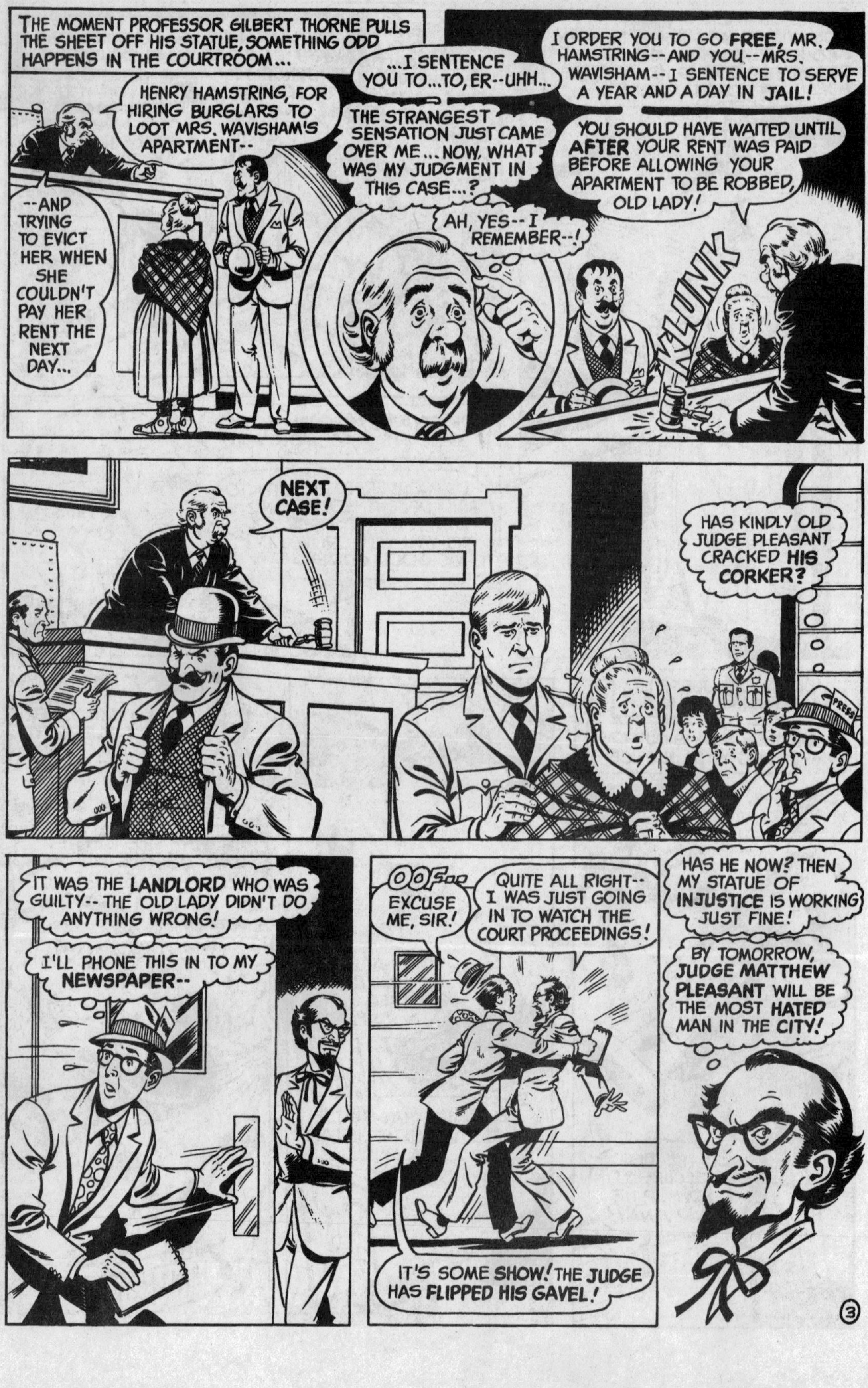
THE MOMENT PROFESSOR GILBERT THORNE PULLS THE SHEET OFF HIS STATUE, SOMETHING ODD HAPPENS IN THE COURTROOM...
HENRY HAMSTRING, FOR HIRING BURGLARS TO LOOT MRS. WAVISHAM'S APARTMENT--
--AND TRYING TO EVICT HER WHEN SHE COULDN'T PAY HER RENT THE NEXT DAY...
...I SENTENCE YOU TO...TO, ER--UHH...
THE STRANGEST SENSATION JUST CAME OVER ME... NOW, WHAT WAS MY JUDGMENT IN THIS CASE...?
AH, YES--I REMEMBER--!
I ORDER YOU TO GO FREE, MR. HAMSTRING--AND YOU--MRS. WAVISHAM--I SENTENCE TO SERVE A YEAR AND A DAY IN JAIL!
YOU SHOULD HAVE WAITED UNTIL AFTER YOUR RENT WAS PAID BEFORE ALLOWING YOUR APARTMENT TO BE ROBBED, OLD LADY!
KLUNK
NEXT CASE!
HAS KINDLY OLD JUDGE PLEASANT CRACKED HIS CORKER?
PRESS
IT WAS THE LANDLORD WHO WAS GUILTY-- THE OLD LADY DIDN'T DO ANYTHING WRONG!
I'LL PHONE THIS IN TO MY NEWSPAPER--
OOF
EXCUSE ME, SIR!
QUITE ALL RIGHT-- I WAS JUST GOING IN TO WATCH THE COURT PROCEEDINGS!
IT'S SOME SHOW! THE JUDGE HAS FLIPPED HIS GAVEL!
HAS HE NOW? THEN MY STATUE OF INJUSTICE IS WORKING JUST FINE!
BY TOMORROW, JUDGE MATTHEW PLEASANT WILL BE THE MOST HATED MAN IN THE CITY!
3

As the night court session goes on, the judge's decisions become more and more topsy-turvy...

FOR PICKING FLOWERS IN THE PARK-- 40 YEARS AT HARD LABOR!

FOR PLAYING YOUR DRUMS AT NIGHT, YOU CAN GO BACK HOME, MR. RUGGLES--

--BUT FOR DISTURBING A BUSY POLICEMAN WITH A COMPLAINT ABOUT IT, YOU GO TO JAIL, MRS. REDGAP!

YOU ARRESTED HIM JUST FOR STEALING A POLICE CAR?!

CASE DISMISSED!

I CAN'T WAIT FOR TOMORROW'S PAPER TO COME OUT!

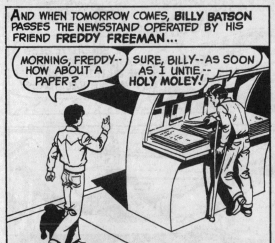

AND WHEN TOMORROW COMES, BILLY BATSON PASSES THE NEWSSTAND OPERATED BY HIS FRIEND FREDDY FREEMAN...

MORNING, FREDDY-- HOW ABOUT A PAPER?

SURE, BILLY--AS SOON AS I UNTIE-- HOLY MOLEY!

LOOK AT THAT HEADLINE!

I DON'T GET IT! JUDGE PLEASANT IS ONE OF THE FINEST MEN IN TOWN!

I'D BETTER LOOK INTO--

DAILY CHRONICLE

JUDGE DISHES OUT INJUSTICE!

MATTHEW PLEASANT DELIVERS UNUSUAL VERDICTS AS STRANGE STATUE APPEARS AT COURT BUILDING

BUT IN THE MIDDLE OF BILLY'S SENTENCE, THE AIR IS DROWNED IN THE SOUND OF...

WHREEEE!

...THE POLICE CHASING A GETAWAY CAR FULL OF CRIMINALS!

LOOK! THE POLICE ARE BLOCKED AT THE RED LIGHT BY THE CEMENT TRUCK!

I'D BETTER GO INTO ACTION!

CAPTAIN MAR--

HOLD IT, FREDDY! DON'T CALL ON CAPTAIN MARVEL JR. WHEN YOU'VE GOT THE NEWSSTAND TO RUN!

I'LL HANDLE IT--

4

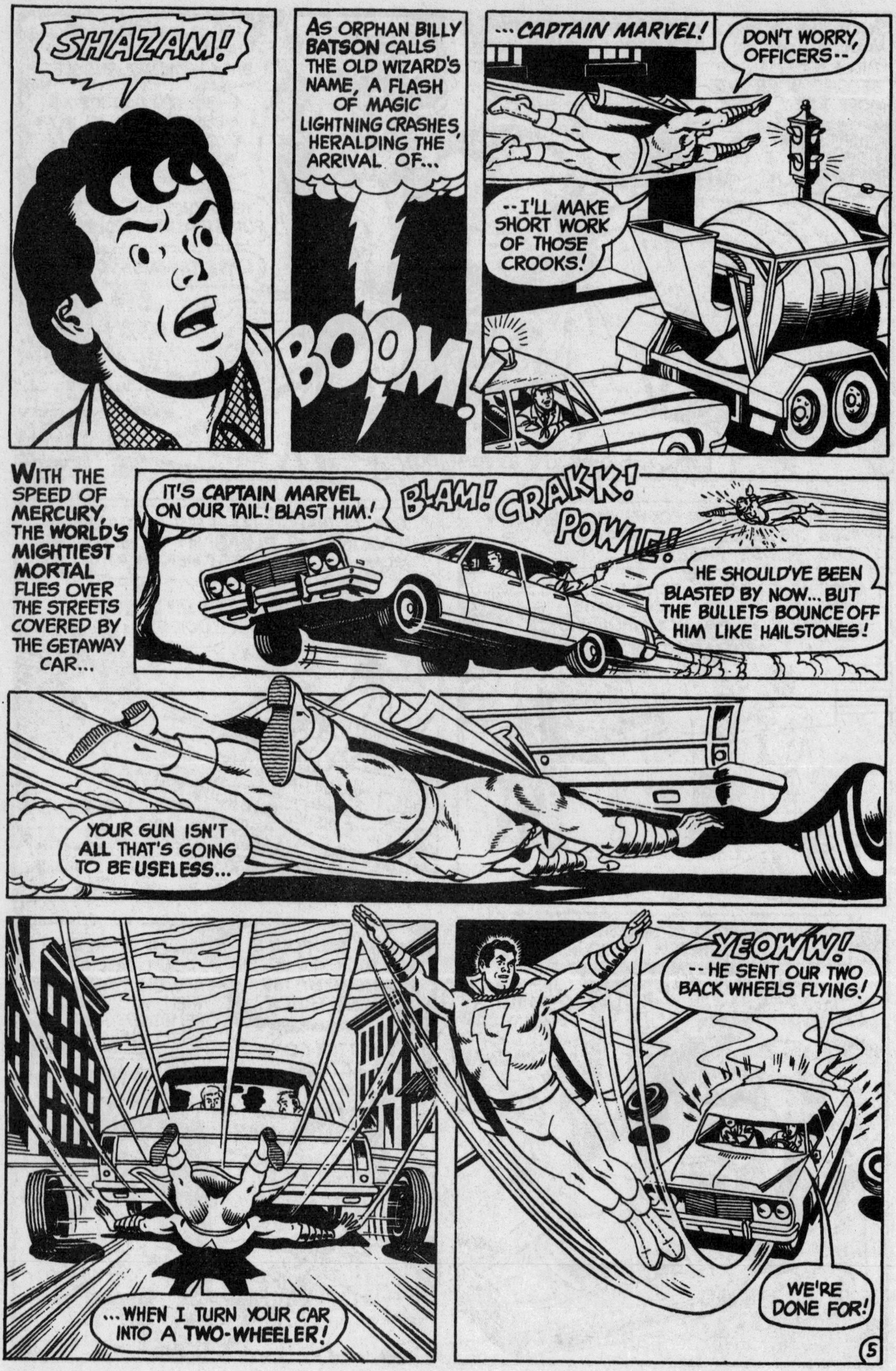
SHAZAM!
AS ORPHAN BILLY BATSON CALLS THE OLD WIZARD'S NAME, A FLASH OF MAGIC LIGHTNING CRASHES, HERALDING THE ARRIVAL OF...
BOOM!
...CAPTAIN MARVEL!
DON'T WORRY, OFFICERS--
--I'LL MAKE SHORT WORK OF THOSE CROOKS!
WITH THE SPEED OF MERCURY, THE WORLD'S MIGHTIEST MORTAL FLIES OVER THE STREETS COVERED BY THE GETAWAY CAR...
IT'S CAPTAIN MARVEL ON OUR TAIL! BLAST HIM!
BLAM! CRAKK!
POW!
HE SHOULD'VE BEEN BLASTED BY NOW... BUT THE BULLETS BOUNCE OFF HIM LIKE HAILSTONES!
YOUR GUN ISN'T ALL THAT'S GOING TO BE USELESS...
...WHEN I TURN YOUR CAR INTO A TWO-WHEELER!
YEOWW! --HE SENT OUR TWO BACK WHEELS FLYING!
WE'RE DONE FOR!
5

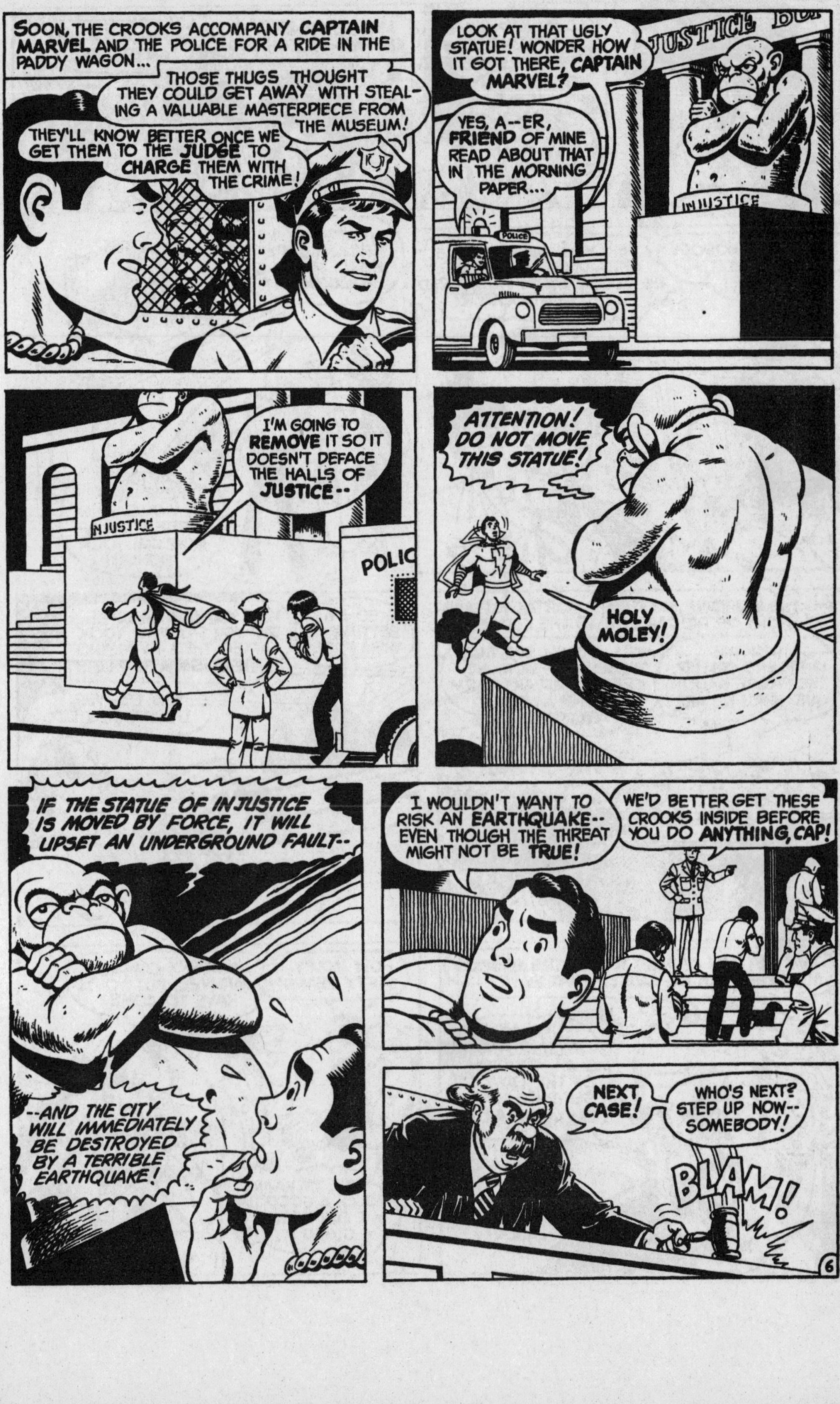
SOON, THE CROOKS ACCOMPANY CAPTAIN MARVEL AND THE POLICE FOR A RIDE IN THE PADDY WAGON...
THOSE THUGS THOUGHT THEY COULD GET AWAY WITH STEALING A VALUABLE MASTERPIECE FROM THE MUSEUM!
THEY'LL KNOW BETTER ONCE WE GET THEM TO THE JUDGE TO CHARGE THEM WITH THE CRIME!
JUSTICE BUI
LOOK AT THAT UGLY STATUE! WONDER HOW IT GOT THERE, CAPTAIN MARVEL?
YES, A--ER, FRIEND OF MINE READ ABOUT THAT IN THE MORNING PAPER...
INJUSTICE
POLICE
I'M GOING TO REMOVE IT SO IT DOESN'T DEFACE THE HALLS OF JUSTICE--
INJUSTICE
POLIC
ATTENTION! DO NOT MOVE THIS STATUE!
HOLY MOLEY!
IF THE STATUE OF INJUSTICE IS MOVED BY FORCE, IT WILL UPSET AN UNDERGROUND FAULT--
--AND THE CITY WILL IMMEDIATELY BE DESTROYED BY A TERRIBLE EARTHQUAKE!
I WOULDN'T WANT TO RISK AN EARTHQUAKE-- EVEN THOUGH THE THREAT MIGHT NOT BE TRUE!
WE'D BETTER GET THESE CROOKS INSIDE BEFORE YOU DO ANYTHING, CAP!
NEXT CASE!
WHO'S NEXT? STEP UP NOW-- SOMEBODY!
BLAM!
6

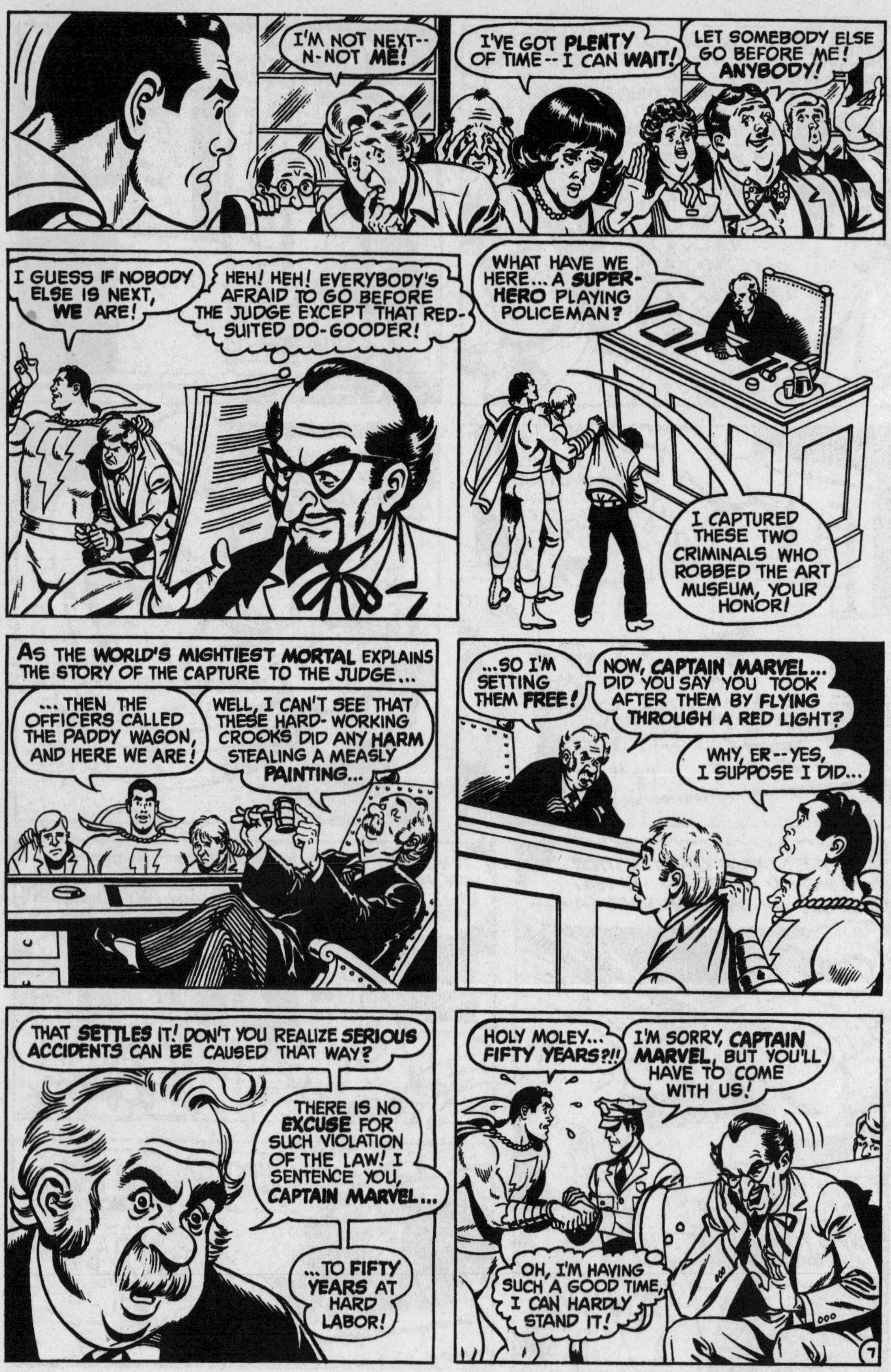
I'M NOT NEXT-- N-NOT ME!
I'VE GOT PLENTY OF TIME -- I CAN WAIT!
LET SOMEBODY ELSE GO BEFORE ME! ANYBODY!
I GUESS IF NOBODY ELSE IS NEXT, WE ARE!
HEH! HEH! EVERYBODY'S AFRAID TO GO BEFORE THE JUDGE EXCEPT THAT RED-SUITED DO-GOODER!
WHAT HAVE WE HERE... A SUPER-HERO PLAYING POLICEMAN?
I CAPTURED THESE TWO CRIMINALS WHO ROBBED THE ART MUSEUM, YOUR HONOR!
AS THE WORLD'S MIGHTIEST MORTAL EXPLAINS THE STORY OF THE CAPTURE TO THE JUDGE...
... THEN THE OFFICERS CALLED THE PADDY WAGON, AND HERE WE ARE!
WELL, I CAN'T SEE THAT THESE HARD-WORKING CROOKS DID ANY HARM STEALING A MEASLY PAINTING...
...SO I'M SETTING THEM FREE!
NOW, CAPTAIN MARVEL... DID YOU SAY YOU TOOK AFTER THEM BY FLYING THROUGH A RED LIGHT?
WHY, ER--YES, I SUPPOSE I DID...
THAT SETTLES IT! DON'T YOU REALIZE SERIOUS ACCIDENTS CAN BE CAUSED THAT WAY?
THERE IS NO EXCUSE FOR SUCH VIOLATION OF THE LAW! I SENTENCE YOU, CAPTAIN MARVEL...
...TO FIFTY YEARS AT HARD LABOR!
HOLY MOLEY... FIFTY YEARS?!!
I'M SORRY, CAPTAIN MARVEL, BUT YOU'LL HAVE TO COME WITH US!
OH, I'M HAVING SUCH A GOOD TIME, I CAN HARDLY STAND IT!
7

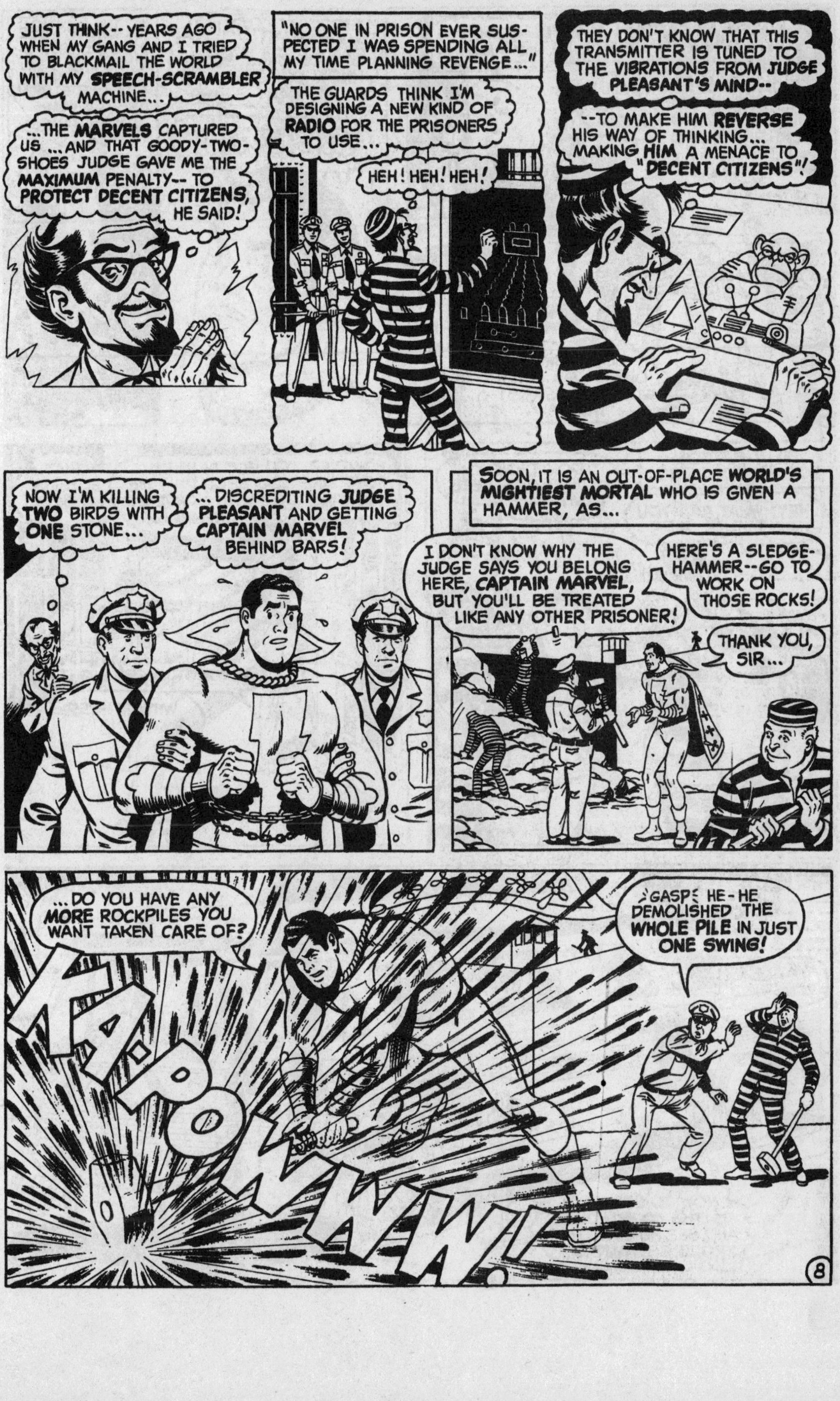
JUST THINK-- YEARS AGO WHEN MY GANG AND I TRIED TO BLACKMAIL THE WORLD WITH MY SPEECH-SCRAMBLER MACHINE...
...THE MARVELS CAPTURED US ... AND THAT GOODY-TWO-SHOES JUDGE GAVE ME THE MAXIMUM PENALTY-- TO PROTECT DECENT CITIZENS, HE SAID!
"NO ONE IN PRISON EVER SUSPECTED I WAS SPENDING ALL MY TIME PLANNING REVENGE..."
THE GUARDS THINK I'M DESIGNING A NEW KIND OF RADIO FOR THE PRISONERS TO USE...
HEH! HEH! HEH!
THEY DON'T KNOW THAT THIS TRANSMITTER IS TUNED TO THE VIBRATIONS FROM JUDGE PLEASANT'S MIND--
--TO MAKE HIM REVERSE HIS WAY OF THINKING... MAKING HIM A MENACE TO "DECENT CITIZENS"!
NOW I'M KILLING TWO BIRDS WITH ONE STONE...
...DISCREDITING JUDGE PLEASANT AND GETTING CAPTAIN MARVEL BEHIND BARS!
SOON, IT IS AN OUT-OF-PLACE WORLD'S MIGHTIEST MORTAL WHO IS GIVEN A HAMMER, AS...
I DON'T KNOW WHY THE JUDGE SAYS YOU BELONG HERE, CAPTAIN MARVEL, BUT YOU'LL BE TREATED LIKE ANY OTHER PRISONER!
HERE'S A SLEDGE-HAMMER--GO TO WORK ON THOSE ROCKS!
THANK YOU, SIR...
...DO YOU HAVE ANY MORE ROCKPILES YOU WANT TAKEN CARE OF?
KA-POWWW!
GASP HE-HE DEMOLISHED THE WHOLE PILE IN JUST ONE SWING!
8

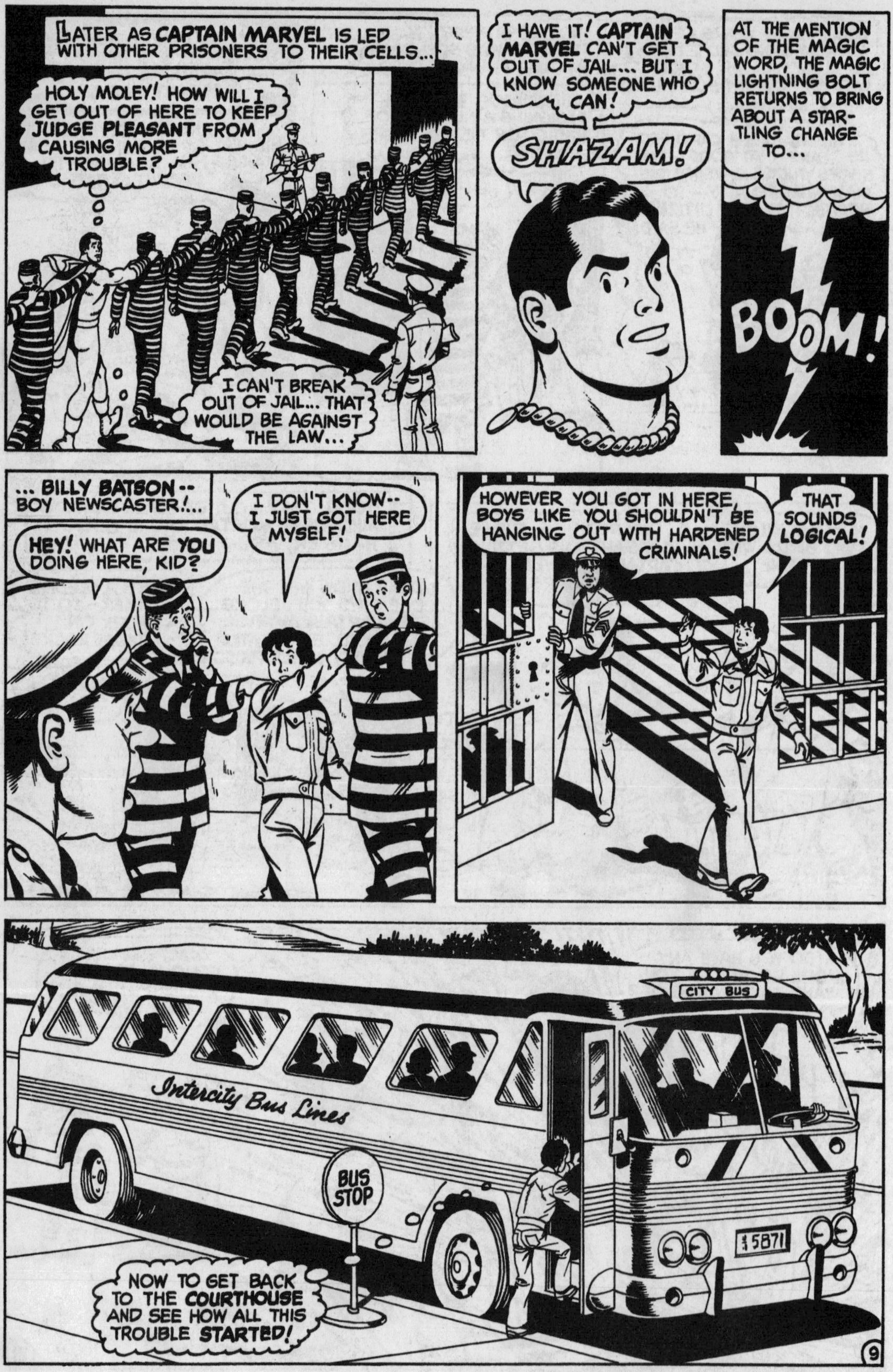
LATER AS CAPTAIN MARVEL IS LED WITH OTHER PRISONERS TO THEIR CELLS...
HOLY MOLEY! HOW WILL I GET OUT OF HERE TO KEEP JUDGE PLEASANT FROM CAUSING MORE TROUBLE?
I CAN'T BREAK OUT OF JAIL... THAT WOULD BE AGAINST THE LAW...
I HAVE IT! CAPTAIN MARVEL CAN'T GET OUT OF JAIL... BUT I KNOW SOMEONE WHO CAN!
SHAZAM!
AT THE MENTION OF THE MAGIC WORD, THE MAGIC LIGHTNING BOLT RETURNS TO BRING ABOUT A STARTLING CHANGE TO...
BOOM!
... BILLY BATSON -- BOY NEWSCASTER!...
HEY! WHAT ARE YOU DOING HERE, KID?
I DON'T KNOW -- I JUST GOT HERE MYSELF!
HOWEVER YOU GOT IN HERE, BOYS LIKE YOU SHOULDN'T BE HANGING OUT WITH HARDENED CRIMINALS!
THAT SOUNDS LOGICAL!
CITY BUS
Intercity Bus Lines
BUS STOP
5871
NOW TO GET BACK TO THE COURTHOUSE AND SEE HOW ALL THIS TROUBLE STARTED!
9

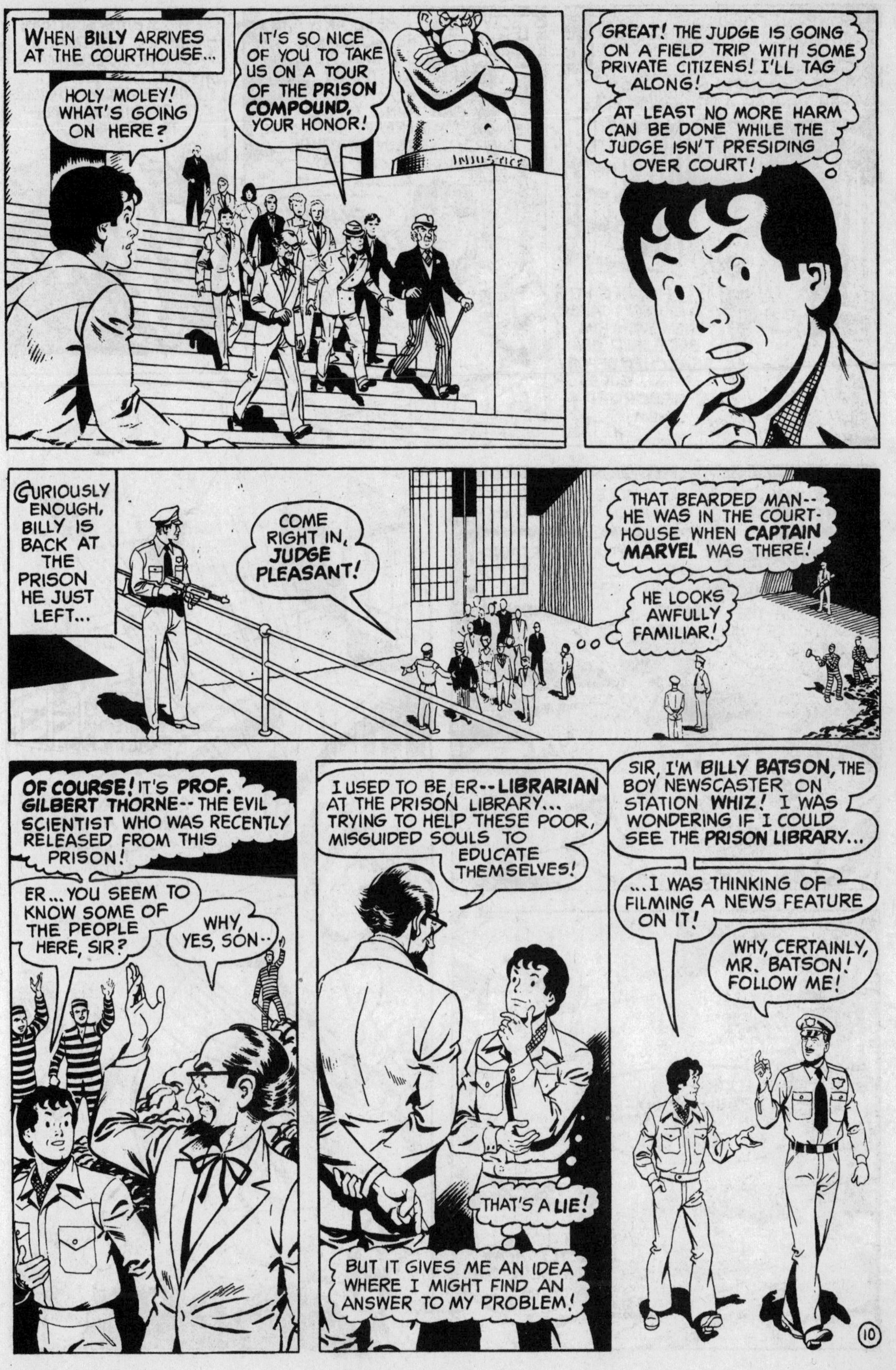
WHEN BILLY ARRIVES AT THE COURTHOUSE...
HOLY MOLEY! WHAT'S GOING ON HERE?
IT'S SO NICE OF YOU TO TAKE US ON A TOUR OF THE PRISON COMPOUND, YOUR HONOR!
INJUSTICE
GREAT! THE JUDGE IS GOING ON A FIELD TRIP WITH SOME PRIVATE CITIZENS! I'LL TAG ALONG!
AT LEAST NO MORE HARM CAN BE DONE WHILE THE JUDGE ISN'T PRESIDING OVER COURT!
CURIOUSLY ENOUGH, BILLY IS BACK AT THE PRISON HE JUST LEFT...
COME RIGHT IN, JUDGE PLEASANT!
THAT BEARDED MAN-- HE WAS IN THE COURTHOUSE WHEN CAPTAIN MARVEL WAS THERE!
HE LOOKS AWFULLY FAMILIAR!
OF COURSE! IT'S PROF. GILBERT THORNE-- THE EVIL SCIENTIST WHO WAS RECENTLY RELEASED FROM THIS PRISON!
ER... YOU SEEM TO KNOW SOME OF THE PEOPLE HERE, SIR?
WHY, YES, SON--
I USED TO BE, ER--LIBRARIAN AT THE PRISON LIBRARY... TRYING TO HELP THESE POOR, MISGUIDED SOULS TO EDUCATE THEMSELVES!
THAT'S A LIE!
BUT IT GIVES ME AN IDEA WHERE I MIGHT FIND AN ANSWER TO MY PROBLEM!
SIR, I'M BILLY BATSON, THE BOY NEWSCASTER ON STATION WHIZ! I WAS WONDERING IF I COULD SEE THE PRISON LIBRARY...
...I WAS THINKING OF FILMING A NEWS FEATURE ON IT!
WHY, CERTAINLY, MR. BATSON! FOLLOW ME!
10

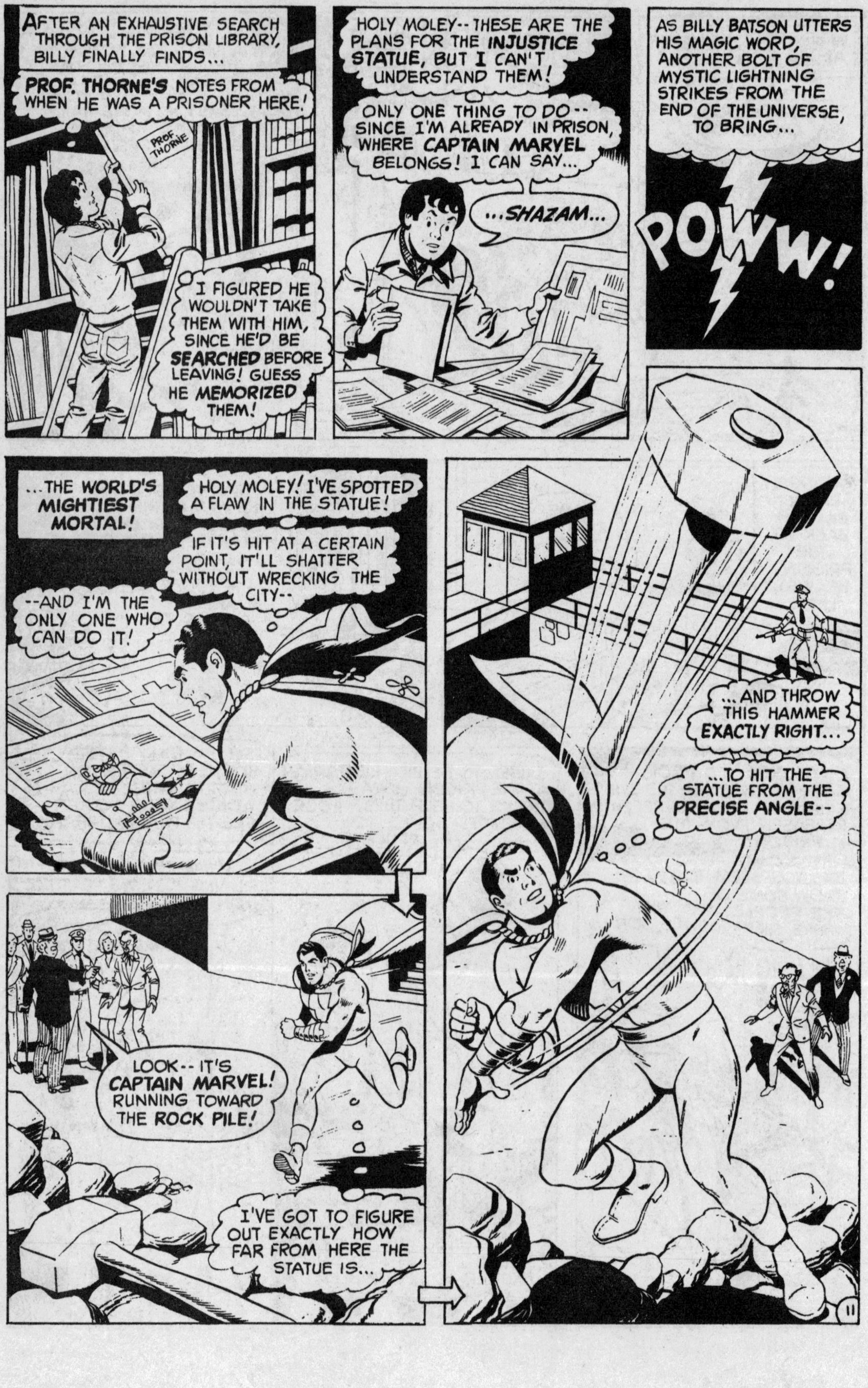
AFTER AN EXHAUSTIVE SEARCH THROUGH THE PRISON LIBRARY, BILLY FINALLY FINDS...
PROF. THORNE'S NOTES FROM WHEN HE WAS A PRISONER HERE!
PROF. THORNE
I FIGURED HE WOULDN'T TAKE THEM WITH HIM, SINCE HE'D BE SEARCHED BEFORE LEAVING! GUESS HE MEMORIZED THEM!
HOLY MOLEY-- THESE ARE THE PLANS FOR THE INJUSTICE STATUE, BUT I CAN'T UNDERSTAND THEM!
ONLY ONE THING TO DO-- SINCE I'M ALREADY IN PRISON, WHERE CAPTAIN MARVEL BELONGS! I CAN SAY...
...SHAZAM...
AS BILLY BATSON UTTERS HIS MAGIC WORD, ANOTHER BOLT OF MYSTIC LIGHTNING STRIKES FROM THE END OF THE UNIVERSE, TO BRING...
POWW!
...THE WORLD'S MIGHTIEST MORTAL!
HOLY MOLEY! I'VE SPOTTED A FLAW IN THE STATUE!
IF IT'S HIT AT A CERTAIN POINT, IT'LL SHATTER WITHOUT WRECKING THE CITY--
--AND I'M THE ONLY ONE WHO CAN DO IT!
LOOK-- IT'S CAPTAIN MARVEL! RUNNING TOWARD THE ROCK PILE!
I'VE GOT TO FIGURE OUT EXACTLY HOW FAR FROM HERE THE STATUE IS...
...AND THROW THIS HAMMER EXACTLY RIGHT...
...TO HIT THE STATUE FROM THE PRECISE ANGLE--
11

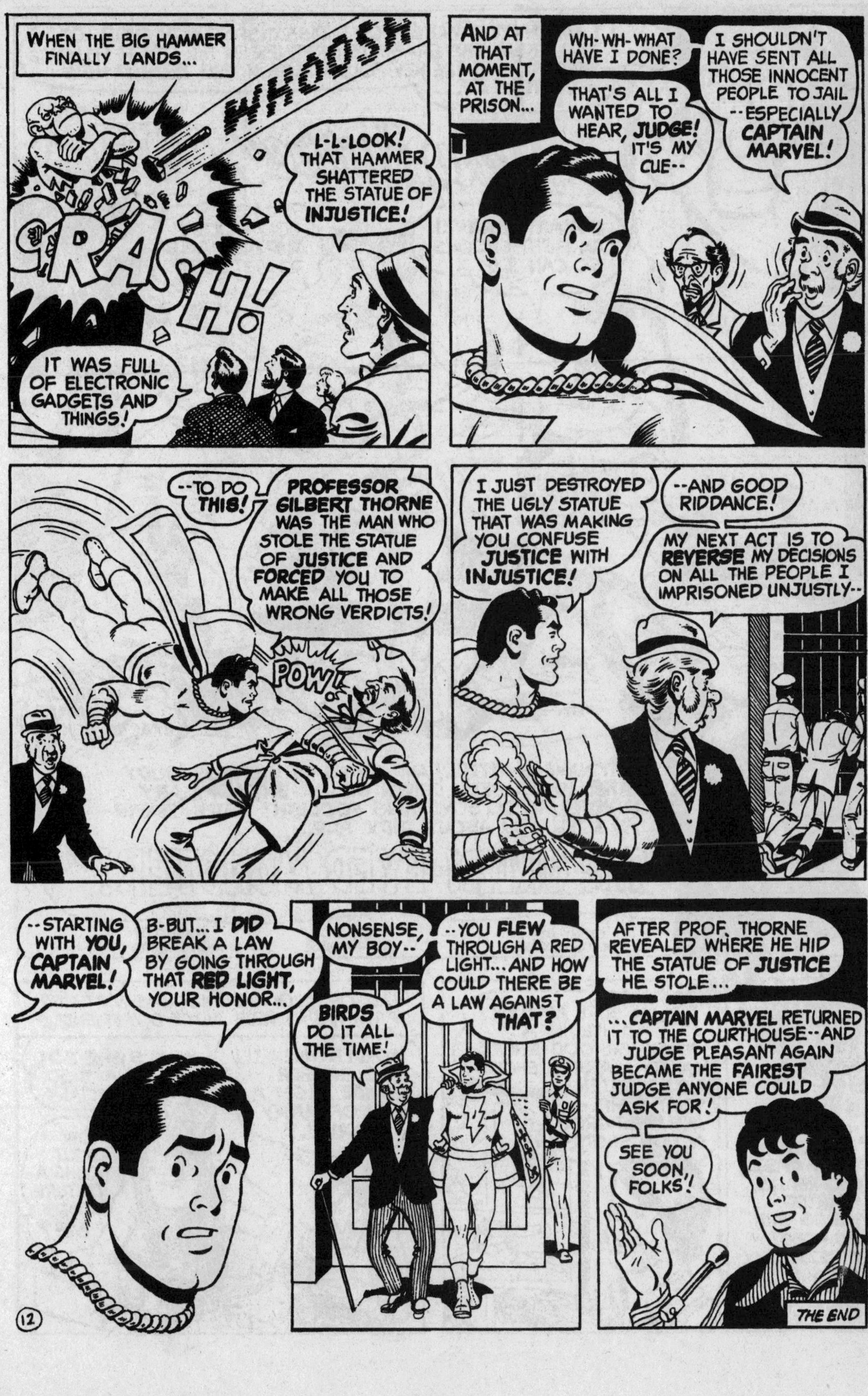
WHEN THE BIG HAMMER FINALLY LANDS...
WHOOSH
CRASH!
L-L-LOOK! THAT HAMMER SHATTERED THE STATUE OF INJUSTICE!
IT WAS FULL OF ELECTRONIC GADGETS AND THINGS!
AND AT THAT MOMENT, AT THE PRISON...
WH-WH-WHAT HAVE I DONE?
I SHOULDN'T HAVE SENT ALL THOSE INNOCENT PEOPLE TO JAIL --ESPECIALLY CAPTAIN MARVEL!
THAT'S ALL I WANTED TO HEAR, JUDGE! IT'S MY CUE--
--TO DO THIS!
PROFESSOR GILBERT THORNE WAS THE MAN WHO STOLE THE STATUE OF JUSTICE AND FORCED YOU TO MAKE ALL THOSE WRONG VERDICTS!
POW!
I JUST DESTROYED THE UGLY STATUE THAT WAS MAKING YOU CONFUSE JUSTICE WITH INJUSTICE!
--AND GOOD RIDDANCE!
MY NEXT ACT IS TO REVERSE MY DECISIONS ON ALL THE PEOPLE I IMPRISONED UNJUSTLY--
--STARTING WITH YOU, CAPTAIN MARVEL!
B-BUT... I DID BREAK A LAW BY GOING THROUGH THAT RED LIGHT, YOUR HONOR...
12
NONSENSE, MY BOY--
--YOU FLEW THROUGH A RED LIGHT... AND HOW COULD THERE BE A LAW AGAINST THAT?
BIRDS DO IT ALL THE TIME!
AFTER PROF. THORNE REVEALED WHERE HE HID THE STATUE OF JUSTICE HE STOLE...
...CAPTAIN MARVEL RETURNED IT TO THE COURTHOUSE--AND JUDGE PLEASANT AGAIN BECAME THE FAIREST JUDGE ANYONE COULD ASK FOR!
SEE YOU SOON, FOLKS!
THE END

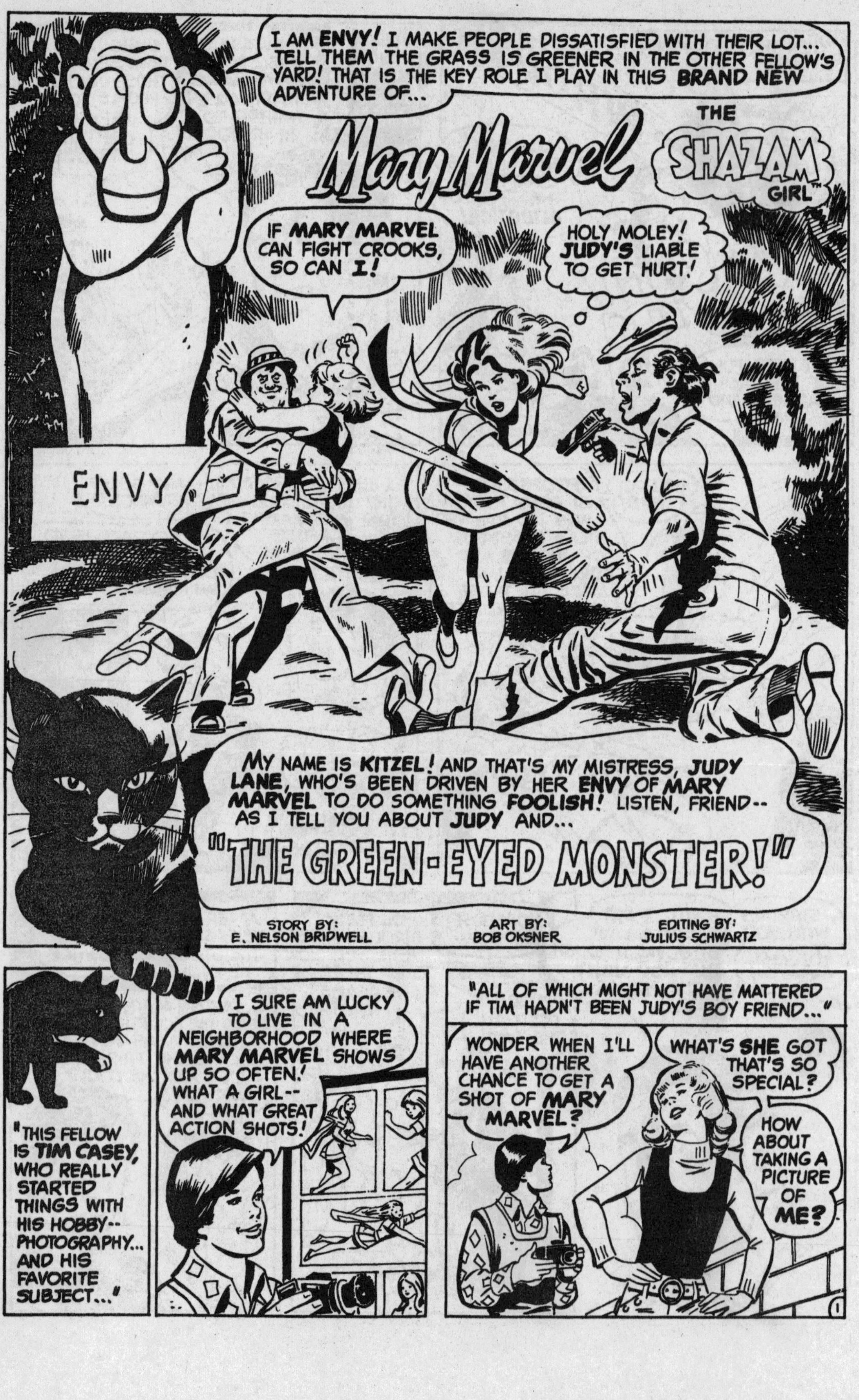
I AM ENVY! I MAKE PEOPLE DISSATISFIED WITH THEIR LOT... TELL THEM THE GRASS IS GREENER IN THE OTHER FELLOW'S YARD! THAT IS THE KEY ROLE I PLAY IN THIS BRAND NEW ADVENTURE OF...
Mary Marvel
THE SHAZAM GIRL™
IF MARY MARVEL CAN FIGHT CROOKS, SO CAN I!
HOLY MOLEY! JUDY'S LIABLE TO GET HURT!
ENVY
MY NAME IS KITZEL! AND THAT'S MY MISTRESS, JUDY LANE, WHO'S BEEN DRIVEN BY HER ENVY OF MARY MARVEL TO DO SOMETHING FOOLISH! LISTEN, FRIEND-- AS I TELL YOU ABOUT JUDY AND...
"THE GREEN-EYED MONSTER!"
STORY BY: E. NELSON BRIDWELL
ART BY: BOB OKSNER
EDITING BY: JULIUS SCHWARTZ
"THIS FELLOW IS TIM CASEY, WHO REALLY STARTED THINGS WITH HIS HOBBY-- PHOTOGRAPHY... AND HIS FAVORITE SUBJECT..."
I SURE AM LUCKY TO LIVE IN A NEIGHBORHOOD WHERE MARY MARVEL SHOWS UP SO OFTEN! WHAT A GIRL-- AND WHAT GREAT ACTION SHOTS!
"ALL OF WHICH MIGHT NOT HAVE MATTERED IF TIM HADN'T BEEN JUDY'S BOY FRIEND..."
WONDER WHEN I'LL HAVE ANOTHER CHANCE TO GET A SHOT OF MARY MARVEL?
WHAT'S SHE GOT THAT'S SO SPECIAL?
HOW ABOUT TAKING A PICTURE OF ME?
1

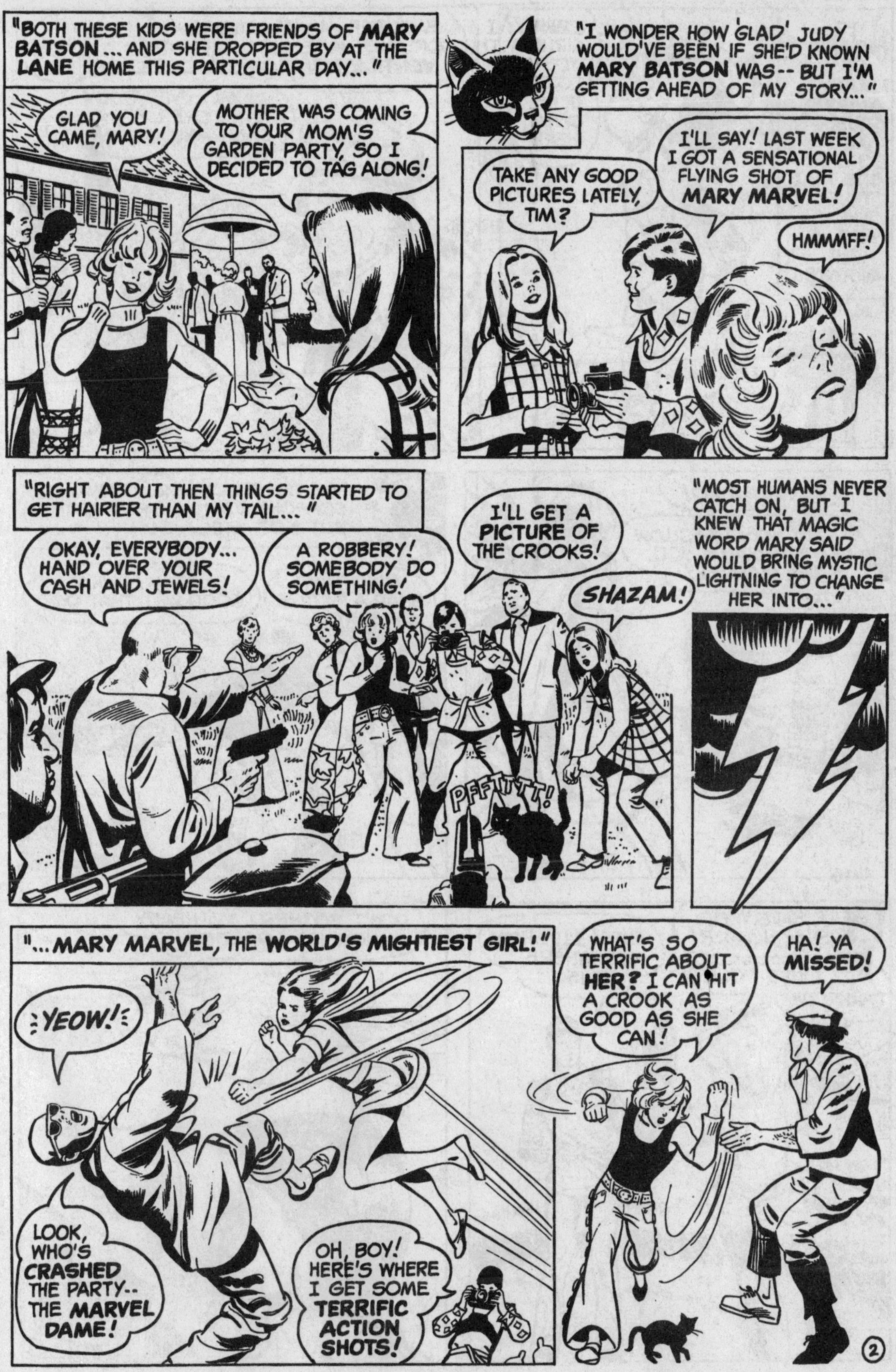
"BOTH THESE KIDS WERE FRIENDS OF MARY BATSON ... AND SHE DROPPED BY AT THE LANE HOME THIS PARTICULAR DAY..."
GLAD YOU CAME, MARY!
MOTHER WAS COMING TO YOUR MOM'S GARDEN PARTY, SO I DECIDED TO TAG ALONG!
"I WONDER HOW 'GLAD' JUDY WOULD'VE BEEN IF SHE'D KNOWN MARY BATSON WAS-- BUT I'M GETTING AHEAD OF MY STORY..."
TAKE ANY GOOD PICTURES LATELY, TIM?
I'LL SAY! LAST WEEK I GOT A SENSATIONAL FLYING SHOT OF MARY MARVEL!
HMMMFF!
"RIGHT ABOUT THEN THINGS STARTED TO GET HAIRIER THAN MY TAIL..."
OKAY, EVERYBODY... HAND OVER YOUR CASH AND JEWELS!
A ROBBERY! SOMEBODY DO SOMETHING!
I'LL GET A PICTURE OF THE CROOKS!
SHAZAM!
PFFTTTT!
"MOST HUMANS NEVER CATCH ON, BUT I KNEW THAT MAGIC WORD MARY SAID WOULD BRING MYSTIC LIGHTNING TO CHANGE HER INTO..."
"...MARY MARVEL, THE WORLD'S MIGHTIEST GIRL!"
YEOW!
LOOK, WHO'S CRASHED THE PARTY.. THE MARVEL DAME!
OH, BOY! HERE'S WHERE I GET SOME TERRIFIC ACTION SHOTS!
WHAT'S SO TERRIFIC ABOUT HER? I CAN HIT A CROOK AS GOOD AS SHE CAN!
HA! YA MISSED!
2

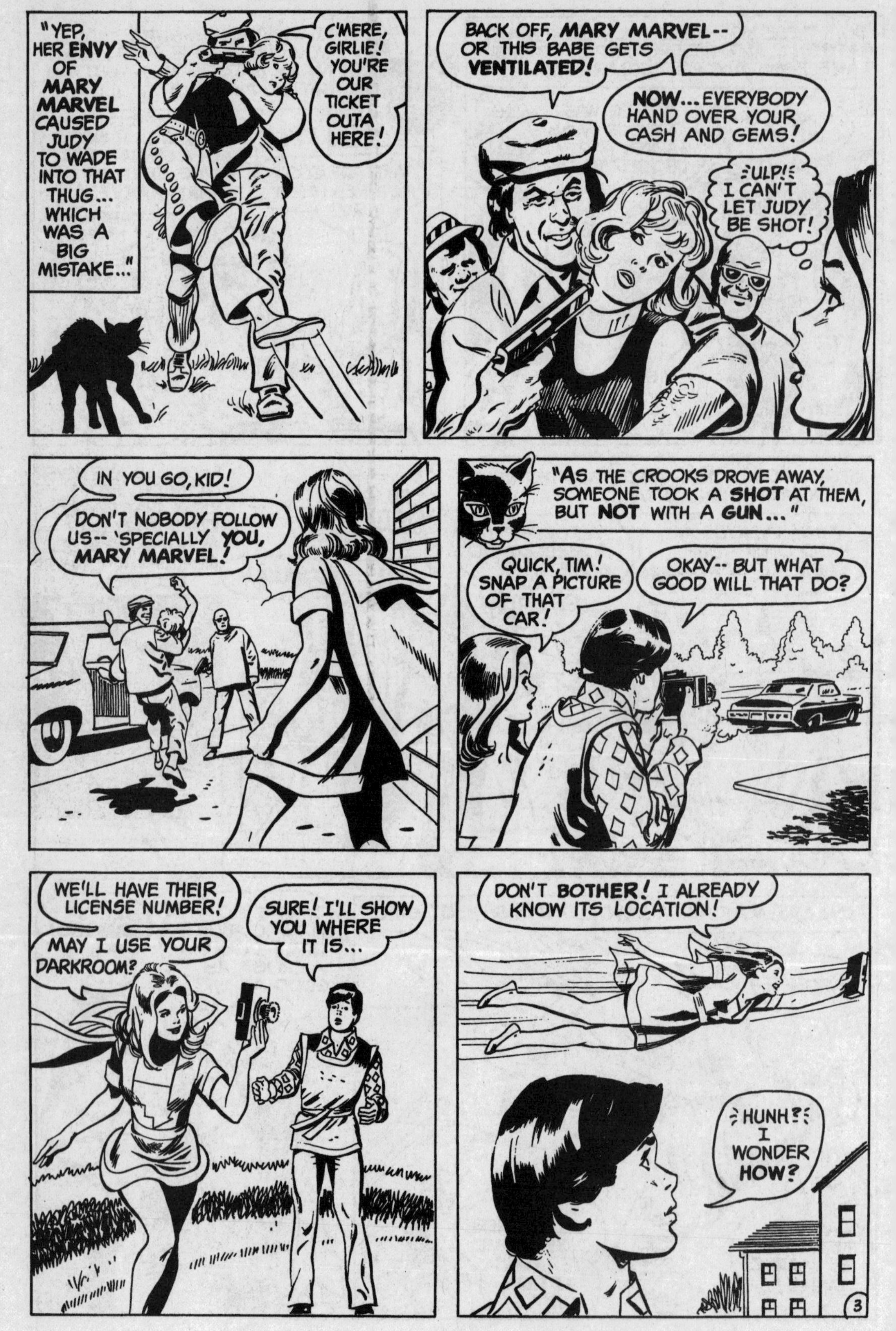
"YEP, HER ENVY OF MARY MARVEL CAUSED JUDY TO WADE INTO THAT THUG... WHICH WAS A BIG MISTAKE..."
C'MERE, GIRLIE! YOU'RE OUR TICKET OUTA HERE!
BACK OFF, MARY MARVEL-- OR THIS BABE GETS VENTILATED!
NOW... EVERYBODY HAND OVER YOUR CASH AND GEMS!
GULP! I CAN'T LET JUDY BE SHOT!
IN YOU GO, KID!
DON'T NOBODY FOLLOW US-- 'SPECIALLY YOU, MARY MARVEL!
"AS THE CROOKS DROVE AWAY, SOMEONE TOOK A SHOT AT THEM, BUT NOT WITH A GUN..."
QUICK, TIM! SNAP A PICTURE OF THAT CAR!
OKAY-- BUT WHAT GOOD WILL THAT DO?
WE'LL HAVE THEIR LICENSE NUMBER!
MAY I USE YOUR DARKROOM?
SURE! I'LL SHOW YOU WHERE IT IS...
DON'T BOTHER! I ALREADY KNOW ITS LOCATION!
HUNH? I WONDER HOW?
3

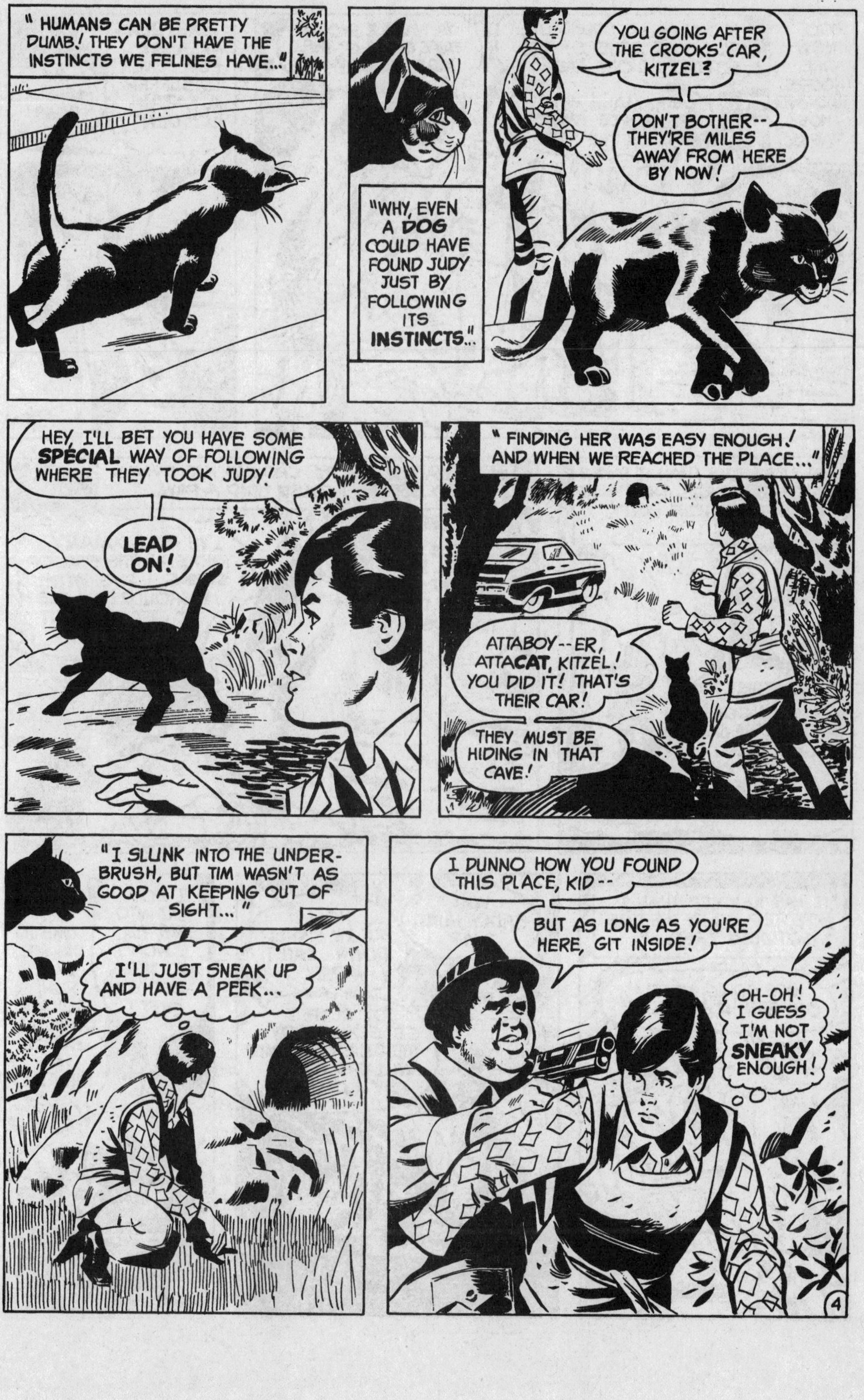
" HUMANS CAN BE PRETTY DUMB! THEY DON'T HAVE THE INSTINCTS WE FELINES HAVE..."
"WHY, EVEN A DOG COULD HAVE FOUND JUDY JUST BY FOLLOWING ITS INSTINCTS."
YOU GOING AFTER THE CROOKS' CAR, KITZEL?
DON'T BOTHER-- THEY'RE MILES AWAY FROM HERE BY NOW!
HEY, I'LL BET YOU HAVE SOME SPECIAL WAY OF FOLLOWING WHERE THEY TOOK JUDY!
LEAD ON!
" FINDING HER WAS EASY ENOUGH! AND WHEN WE REACHED THE PLACE..."
ATTABOY--ER, ATTACAT, KITZEL! YOU DID IT! THAT'S THEIR CAR!
THEY MUST BE HIDING IN THAT CAVE!
" I SLUNK INTO THE UNDER-BRUSH, BUT TIM WASN'T AS GOOD AT KEEPING OUT OF SIGHT... "
I'LL JUST SNEAK UP AND HAVE A PEEK...
I DUNNO HOW YOU FOUND THIS PLACE, KID--
BUT AS LONG AS YOU'RE HERE, GIT INSIDE!
OH-OH! I GUESS I'M NOT SNEAKY ENOUGH!
4

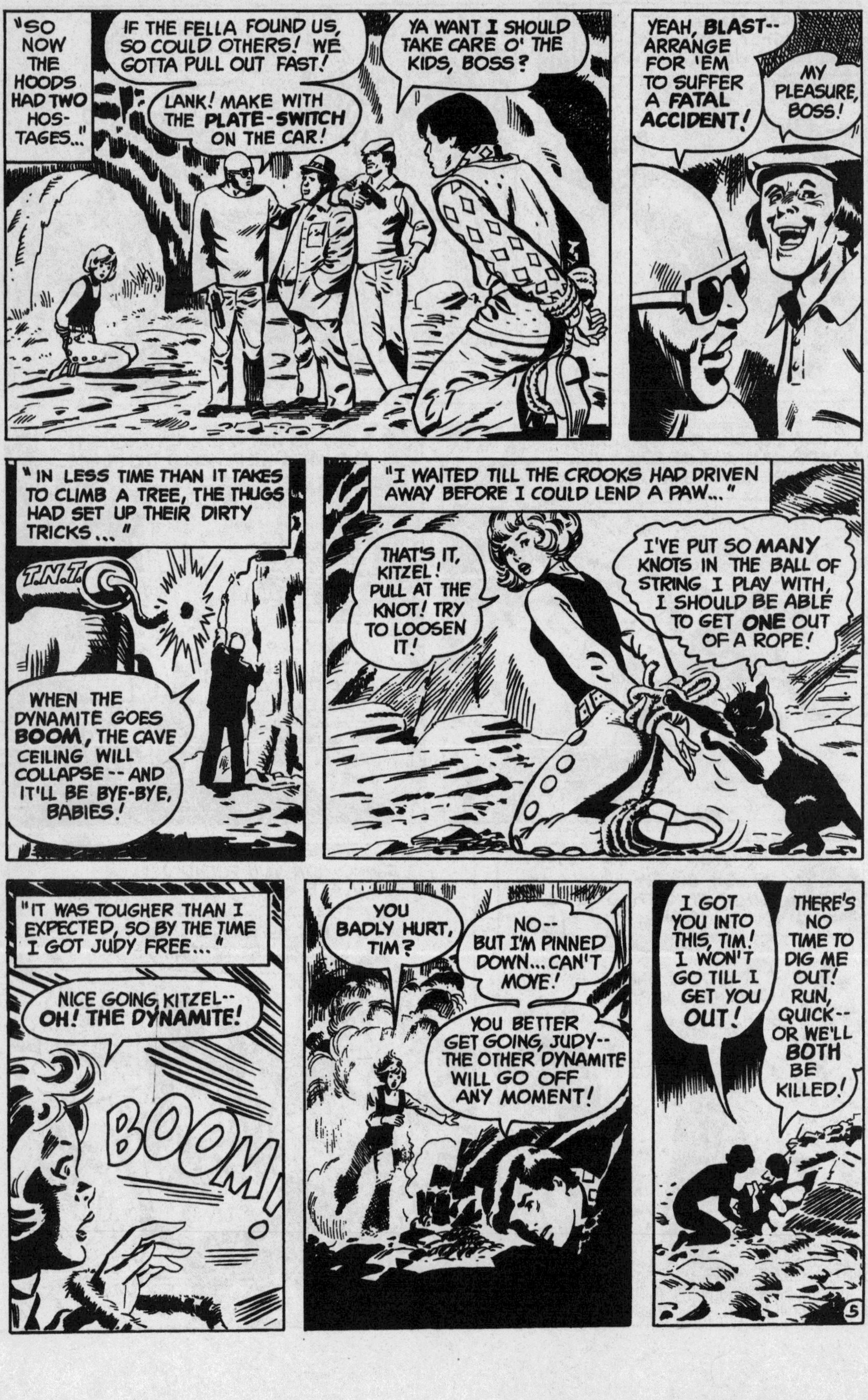
"SO NOW THE HOODS HAD TWO HOS- TAGES..."
IF THE FELLA FOUND US, SO COULD OTHERS! WE GOTTA PULL OUT FAST!
LANK! MAKE WITH THE PLATE-SWITCH ON THE CAR!
YA WANT I SHOULD TAKE CARE O' THE KIDS, BOSS?
YEAH, BLAST-- ARRANGE FOR 'EM TO SUFFER A FATAL ACCIDENT!
MY PLEASURE, BOSS!
"IN LESS TIME THAN IT TAKES TO CLIMB A TREE, THE THUGS HAD SET UP THEIR DIRTY TRICKS..."
T.N.T.
WHEN THE DYNAMITE GOES BOOM, THE CAVE CEILING WILL COLLAPSE-- AND IT'LL BE BYE-BYE, BABIES!
"I WAITED TILL THE CROOKS HAD DRIVEN AWAY BEFORE I COULD LEND A PAW..."
THAT'S IT, KITZEL! PULL AT THE KNOT! TRY TO LOOSEN IT!
I'VE PUT SO MANY KNOTS IN THE BALL OF STRING I PLAY WITH, I SHOULD BE ABLE TO GET ONE OUT OF A ROPE!
"IT WAS TOUGHER THAN I EXPECTED, SO BY THE TIME I GOT JUDY FREE..."
NICE GOING KITZEL-- OH! THE DYNAMITE!
BOOM!
YOU BADLY HURT, TIM?
NO-- BUT I'M PINNED DOWN... CAN'T MOVE!
YOU BETTER GET GOING, JUDY-- THE OTHER DYNAMITE WILL GO OFF ANY MOMENT!
I GOT YOU INTO THIS, TIM! I WON'T GO TILL I GET YOU OUT!
THERE'S NO TIME TO DIG ME OUT! RUN, QUICK-- OR WE'LL BOTH BE KILLED!
5

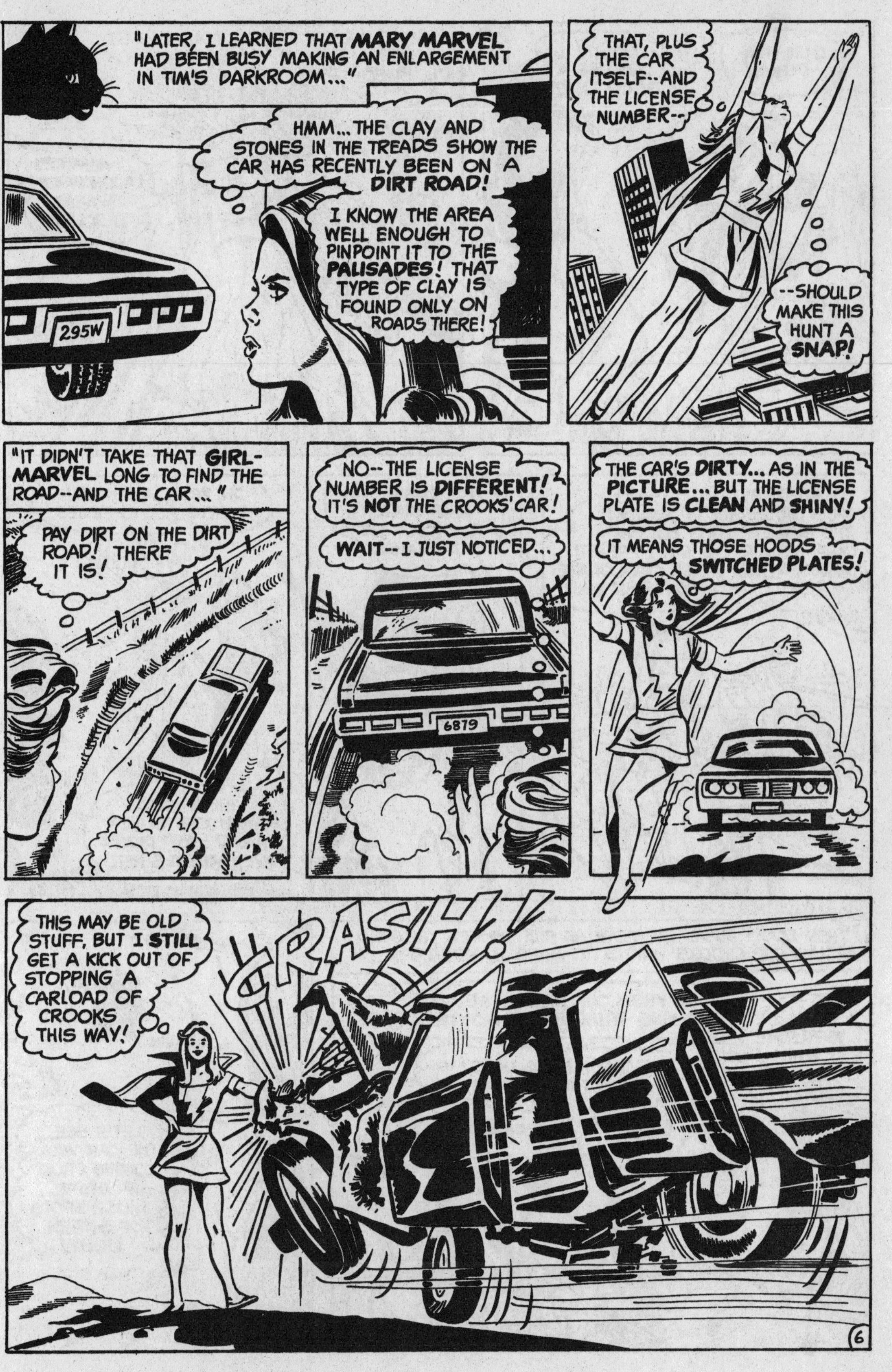
"LATER, I LEARNED THAT MARY MARVEL HAD BEEN BUSY MAKING AN ENLARGEMENT IN TIM'S DARKROOM..."
HMM... THE CLAY AND STONES IN THE TREADS SHOW THE CAR HAS RECENTLY BEEN ON A DIRT ROAD!
I KNOW THE AREA WELL ENOUGH TO PINPOINT IT TO THE PALISADES! THAT TYPE OF CLAY IS FOUND ONLY ON ROADS THERE!
295W
THAT, PLUS THE CAR ITSELF--AND THE LICENSE NUMBER--
--SHOULD MAKE THIS HUNT A SNAP!
"IT DIDN'T TAKE THAT GIRL-MARVEL LONG TO FIND THE ROAD--AND THE CAR..."
PAY DIRT ON THE DIRT ROAD! THERE IT IS!
NO--THE LICENSE NUMBER IS DIFFERENT! IT'S NOT THE CROOKS' CAR!
WAIT--I JUST NOTICED...
6879
THE CAR'S DIRTY... AS IN THE PICTURE... BUT THE LICENSE PLATE IS CLEAN AND SHINY!
IT MEANS THOSE HOODS SWITCHED PLATES!
THIS MAY BE OLD STUFF, BUT I STILL GET A KICK OUT OF STOPPING A CARLOAD OF CROOKS THIS WAY!
CRASH!
6

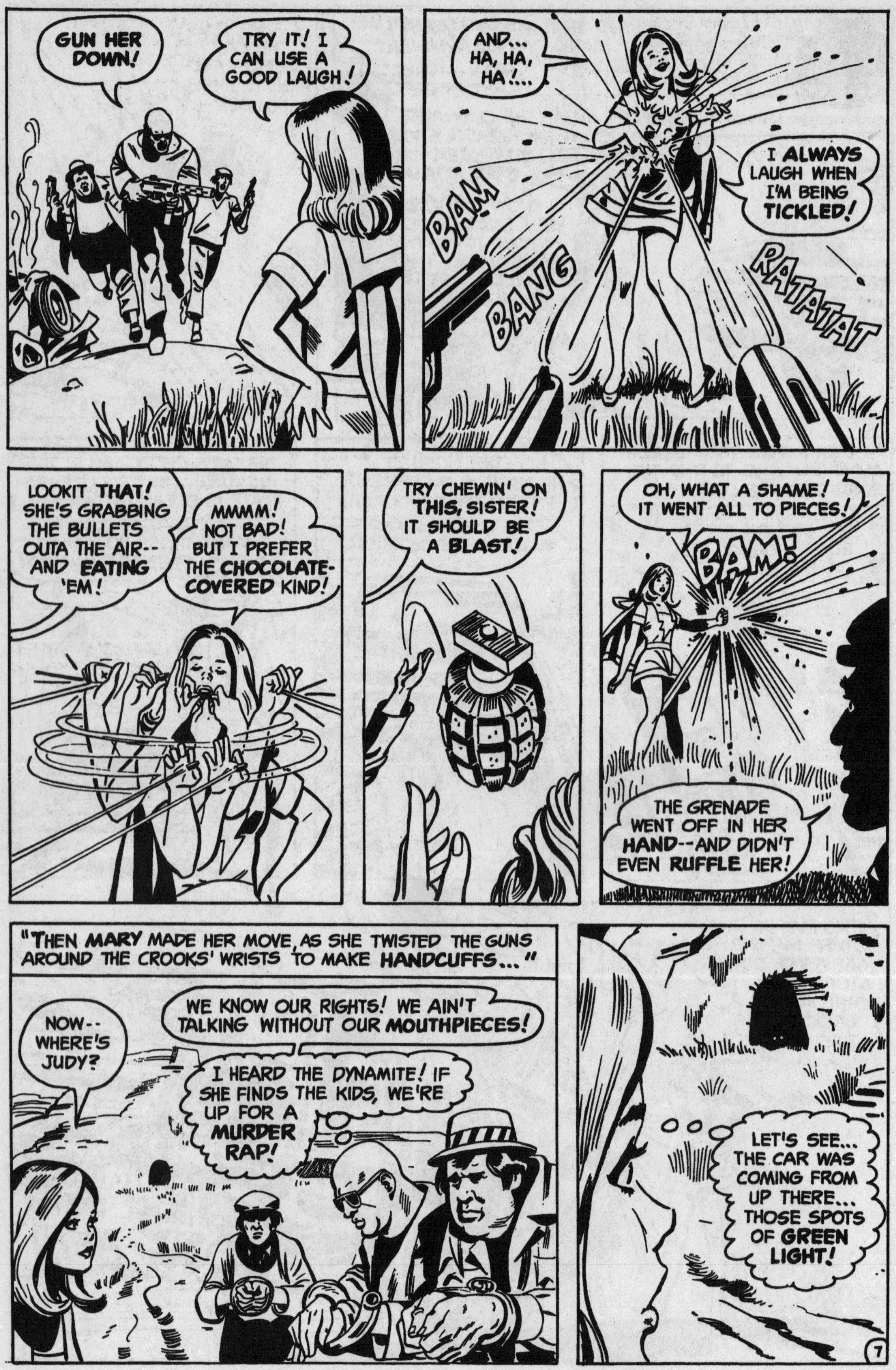
GUN HER DOWN!
TRY IT! I CAN USE A GOOD LAUGH!
AND... HA, HA, HA!...
I ALWAYS LAUGH WHEN I'M BEING TICKLED!
BAM
BANG
RATATAT
LOOKIT THAT! SHE'S GRABBING THE BULLETS OUTA THE AIR-- AND EATING 'EM!
MMMM! NOT BAD! BUT I PREFER THE CHOCOLATE-COVERED KIND!
TRY CHEWIN' ON THIS, SISTER! IT SHOULD BE A BLAST!
OH, WHAT A SHAME! IT WENT ALL TO PIECES!
BAM!
THE GRENADE WENT OFF IN HER HAND--AND DIDN'T EVEN RUFFLE HER!
"THEN MARY MADE HER MOVE, AS SHE TWISTED THE GUNS AROUND THE CROOKS' WRISTS TO MAKE HANDCUFFS..."
NOW-- WHERE'S JUDY?
WE KNOW OUR RIGHTS! WE AIN'T TALKING WITHOUT OUR MOUTHPIECES!
I HEARD THE DYNAMITE! IF SHE FINDS THE KIDS, WE'RE UP FOR A MURDER RAP!
LET'S SEE... THE CAR WAS COMING FROM UP THERE... THOSE SPOTS OF GREEN LIGHT!
7

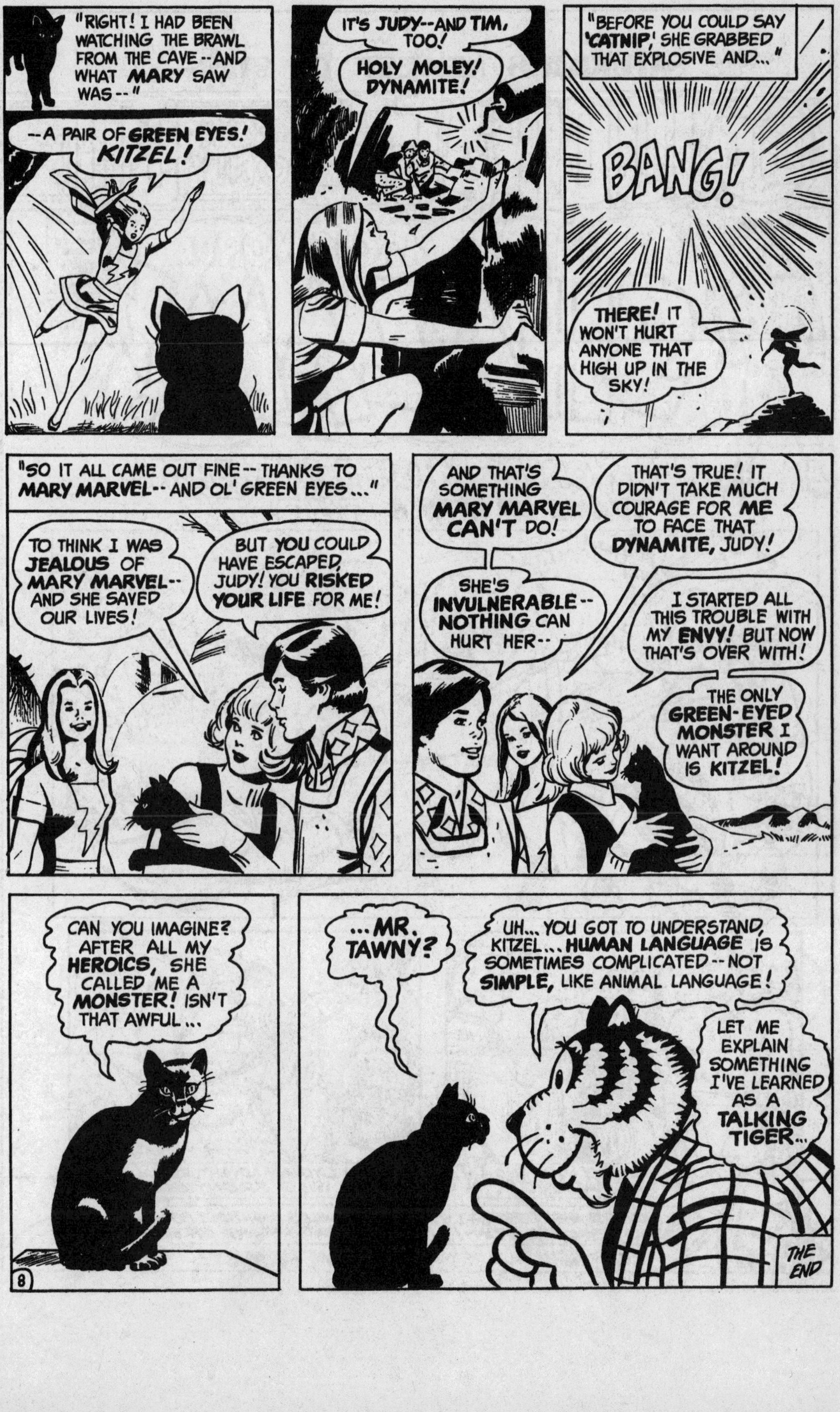
"RIGHT! I HAD BEEN WATCHING THE BRAWL FROM THE CAVE--AND WHAT MARY SAW WAS--"
--A PAIR OF GREEN EYES! KITZEL!
IT'S JUDY--AND TIM, TOO!
HOLY MOLEY! DYNAMITE!
"BEFORE YOU COULD SAY 'CATNIP,' SHE GRABBED THAT EXPLOSIVE AND..."
BANG!
THERE! IT WON'T HURT ANYONE THAT HIGH UP IN THE SKY!
"SO IT ALL CAME OUT FINE--THANKS TO MARY MARVEL--AND OL' GREEN EYES..."
TO THINK I WAS JEALOUS OF MARY MARVEL--AND SHE SAVED OUR LIVES!
BUT YOU COULD HAVE ESCAPED, JUDY! YOU RISKED YOUR LIFE FOR ME!
AND THAT'S SOMETHING MARY MARVEL CAN'T DO!
SHE'S INVULNERABLE--NOTHING CAN HURT HER--
THAT'S TRUE! IT DIDN'T TAKE MUCH COURAGE FOR ME TO FACE THAT DYNAMITE, JUDY!
I STARTED ALL THIS TROUBLE WITH MY ENVY! BUT NOW THAT'S OVER WITH!
THE ONLY GREEN-EYED MONSTER I WANT AROUND IS KITZEL!
CAN YOU IMAGINE? AFTER ALL MY HEROICS, SHE CALLED ME A MONSTER! ISN'T THAT AWFUL...
8
...MR. TAWNY?
UH... YOU GOT TO UNDERSTAND, KITZEL... HUMAN LANGUAGE IS SOMETIMES COMPLICATED--NOT SIMPLE, LIKE ANIMAL LANGUAGE!
LET ME EXPLAIN SOMETHING I'VE LEARNED AS A TALKING TIGER...
THE END

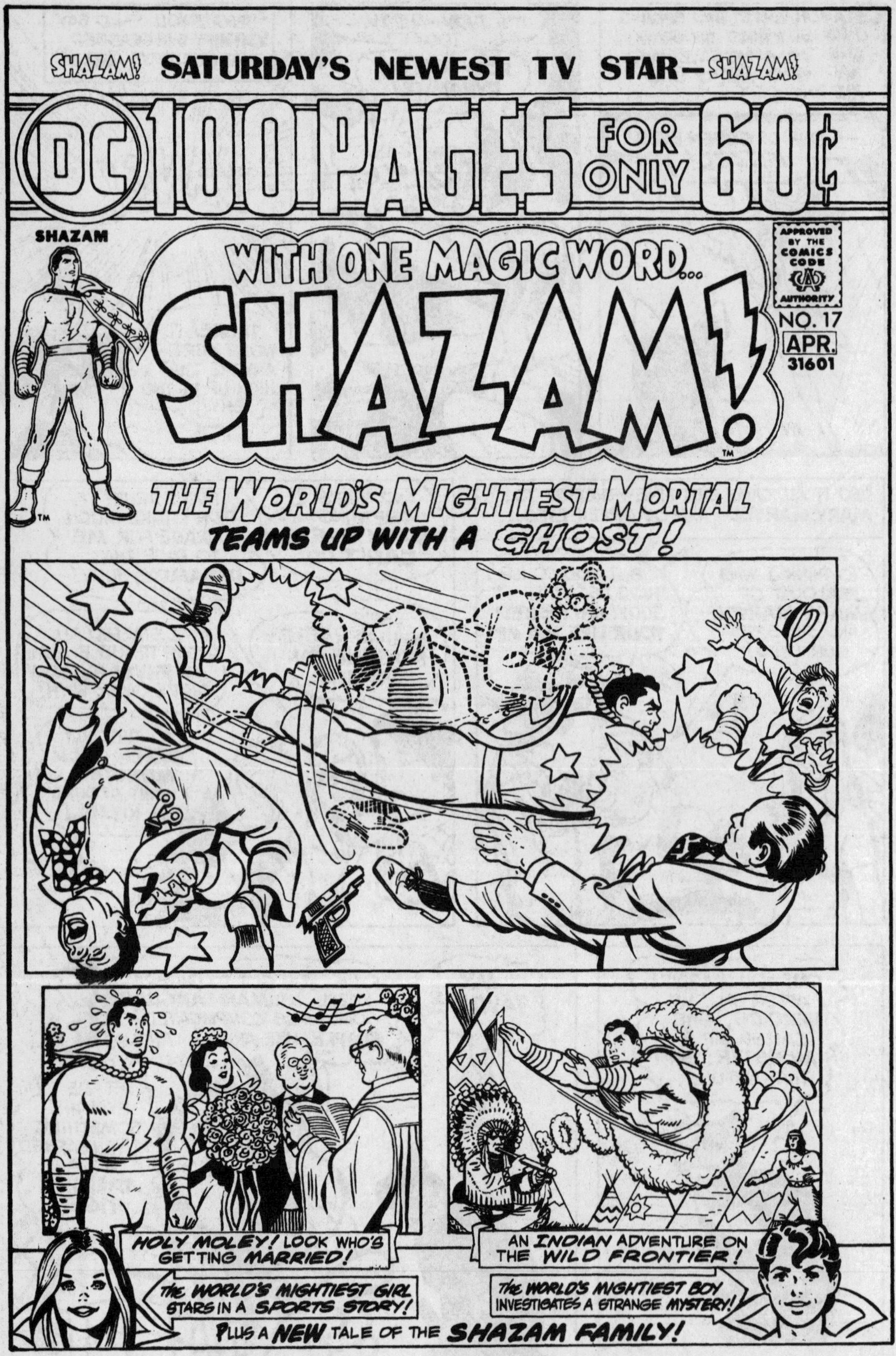
SHAZAM! SATURDAY'S NEWEST TV STAR—SHAZAM!
DC 100 PAGES FOR ONLY 60¢
SHAZAM
APPROVED BY THE COMICS CODE AUTHORITY
NO. 17
APR.
31601
WITH ONE MAGIC WORD...
SHAZAM!
THE WORLD'S MIGHTIEST MORTAL
TEAMS UP WITH A GHOST!
HOLY MOLEY! LOOK WHO'S GETTING MARRIED!
AN INDIAN ADVENTURE ON THE WILD FRONTIER!
THE WORLD'S MIGHTIEST GIRL STARS IN A SPORTS STORY!
THE WORLD'S MIGHTIEST BOY INVESTIGATES A STRANGE MYSTERY!
PLUS A NEW TALE OF THE SHAZAM FAMILY!

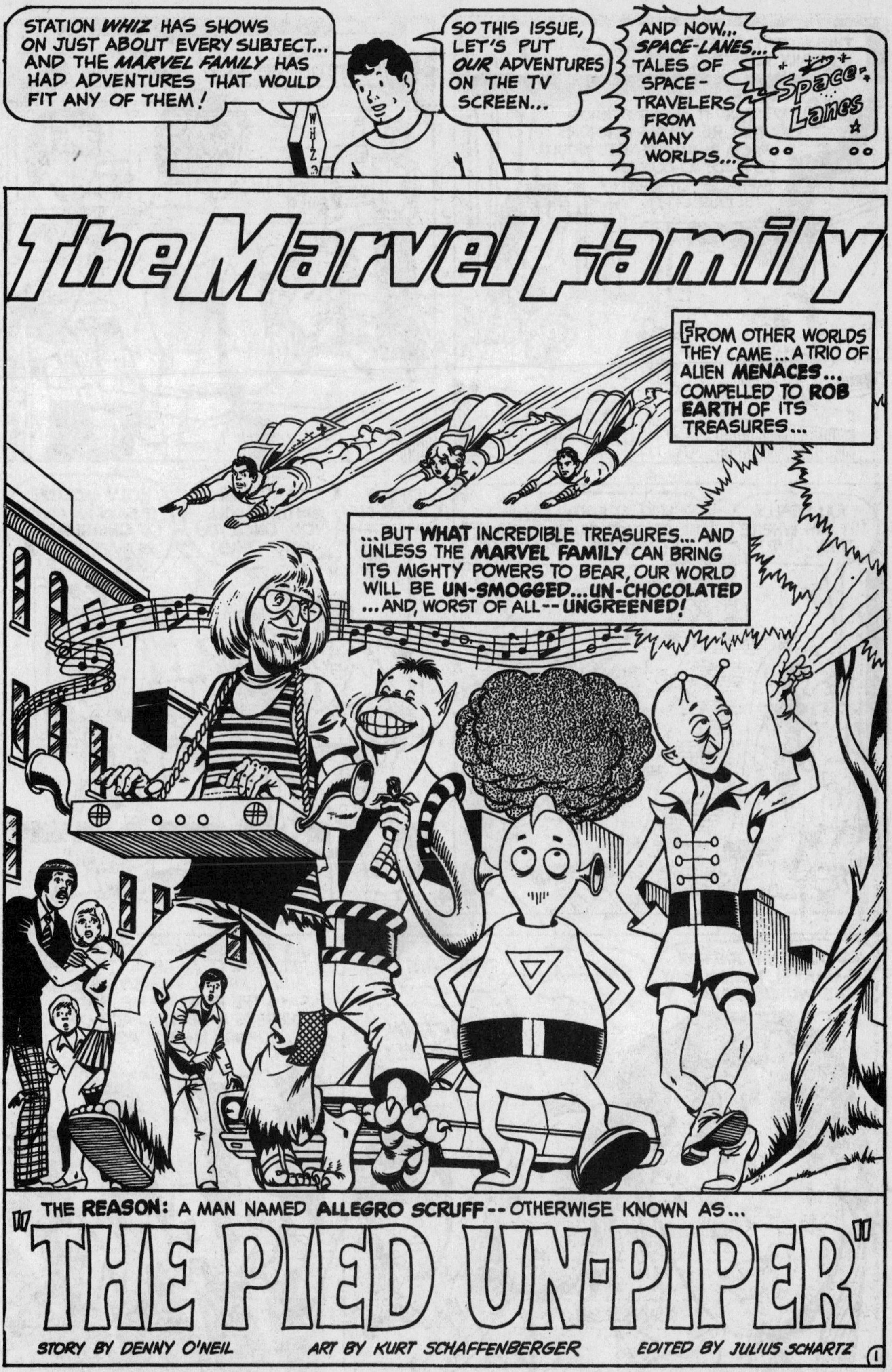
STATION WHIZ HAS SHOWS ON JUST ABOUT EVERY SUBJECT... AND THE MARVEL FAMILY HAS HAD ADVENTURES THAT WOULD FIT ANY OF THEM!
SO THIS ISSUE, LET'S PUT OUR ADVENTURES ON THE TV SCREEN...
AND NOW... SPACE-LANES... TALES OF SPACE-TRAVELERS FROM MANY WORLDS...
Space Lanes
WHIZ
The Marvel Family
FROM OTHER WORLDS THEY CAME... A TRIO OF ALIEN MENACES... COMPELLED TO ROB EARTH OF ITS TREASURES...
...BUT WHAT INCREDIBLE TREASURES... AND UNLESS THE MARVEL FAMILY CAN BRING ITS MIGHTY POWERS TO BEAR, OUR WORLD WILL BE UN-SMOGGED... UN-CHOCOLATED ...AND, WORST OF ALL-- UNGREENED!
THE REASON: A MAN NAMED ALLEGRO SCRUFF -- OTHERWISE KNOWN AS...
"THE PIED UN-PIPER"
STORY BY DENNY O'NEIL
ART BY KURT SCHAFFENBERGER
EDITED BY JULIUS SCHARTZ
1

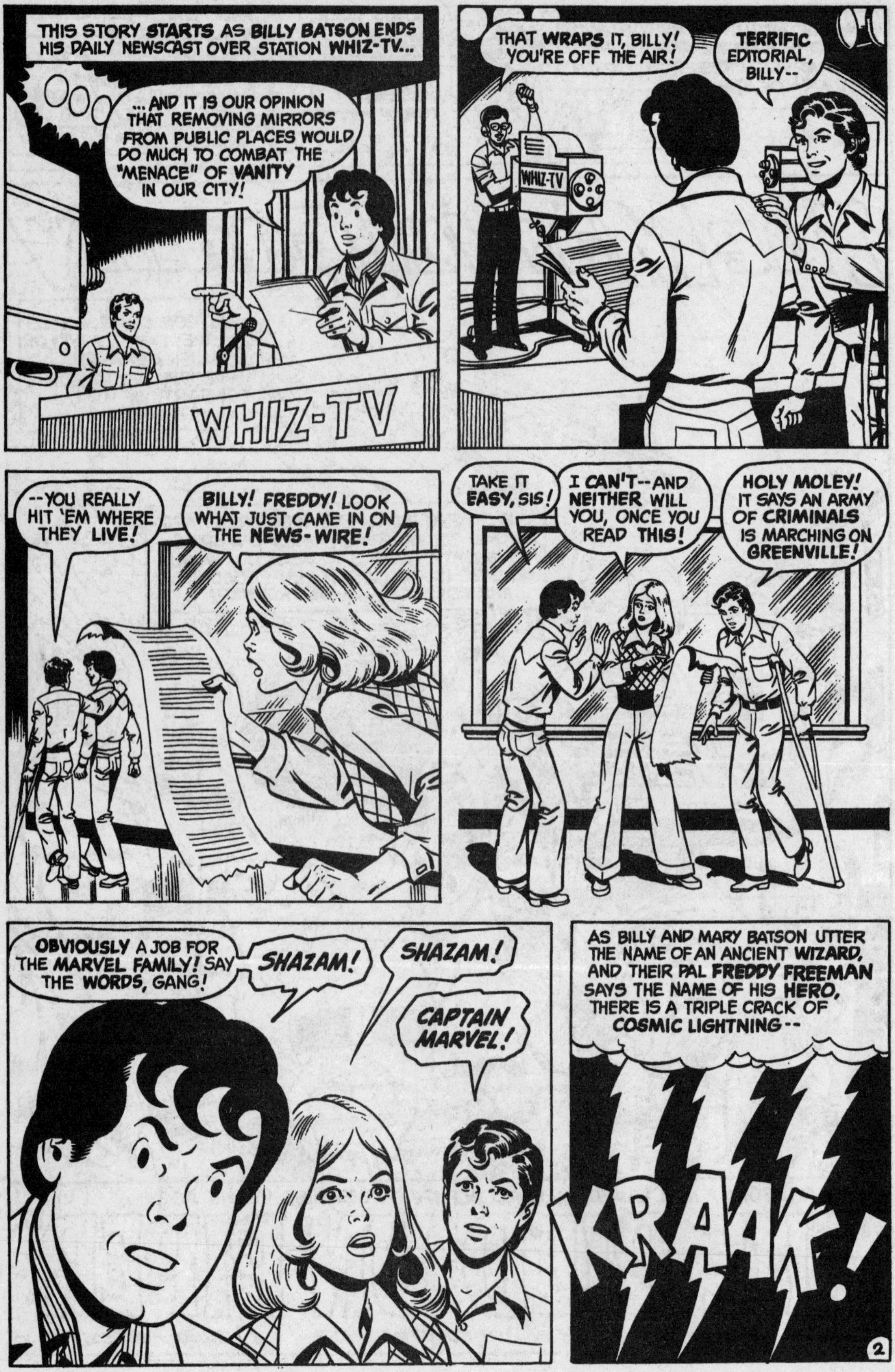

THIS STORY STARTS AS BILLY BATSON ENDS HIS DAILY NEWSCAST OVER STATION WHIZ-TV...
...AND IT IS OUR OPINION THAT REMOVING MIRRORS FROM PUBLIC PLACES WOULD DO MUCH TO COMBAT THE "MENACE" OF VANITY IN OUR CITY!
WHIZ-TV
THAT WRAPS IT, BILLY! YOU'RE OFF THE AIR!
TERRIFIC EDITORIAL, BILLY--
WHIZ-TV
--YOU REALLY HIT 'EM WHERE THEY LIVE!
BILLY! FREDDY! LOOK WHAT JUST CAME IN ON THE NEWS-WIRE!
TAKE IT EASY, SIS!
I CAN'T--AND NEITHER WILL YOU, ONCE YOU READ THIS!
HOLY MOLEY! IT SAYS AN ARMY OF CRIMINALS IS MARCHING ON GREENVILLE!
OBVIOUSLY A JOB FOR THE MARVEL FAMILY! SAY THE WORDS, GANG!
SHAZAM!
SHAZAM!
CAPTAIN MARVEL!
AS BILLY AND MARY BATSON UTTER THE NAME OF AN ANCIENT WIZARD, AND THEIR PAL FREDDY FREEMAN SAYS THE NAME OF HIS HERO, THERE IS A TRIPLE CRACK OF COSMIC LIGHTNING--
KRAAK!
2

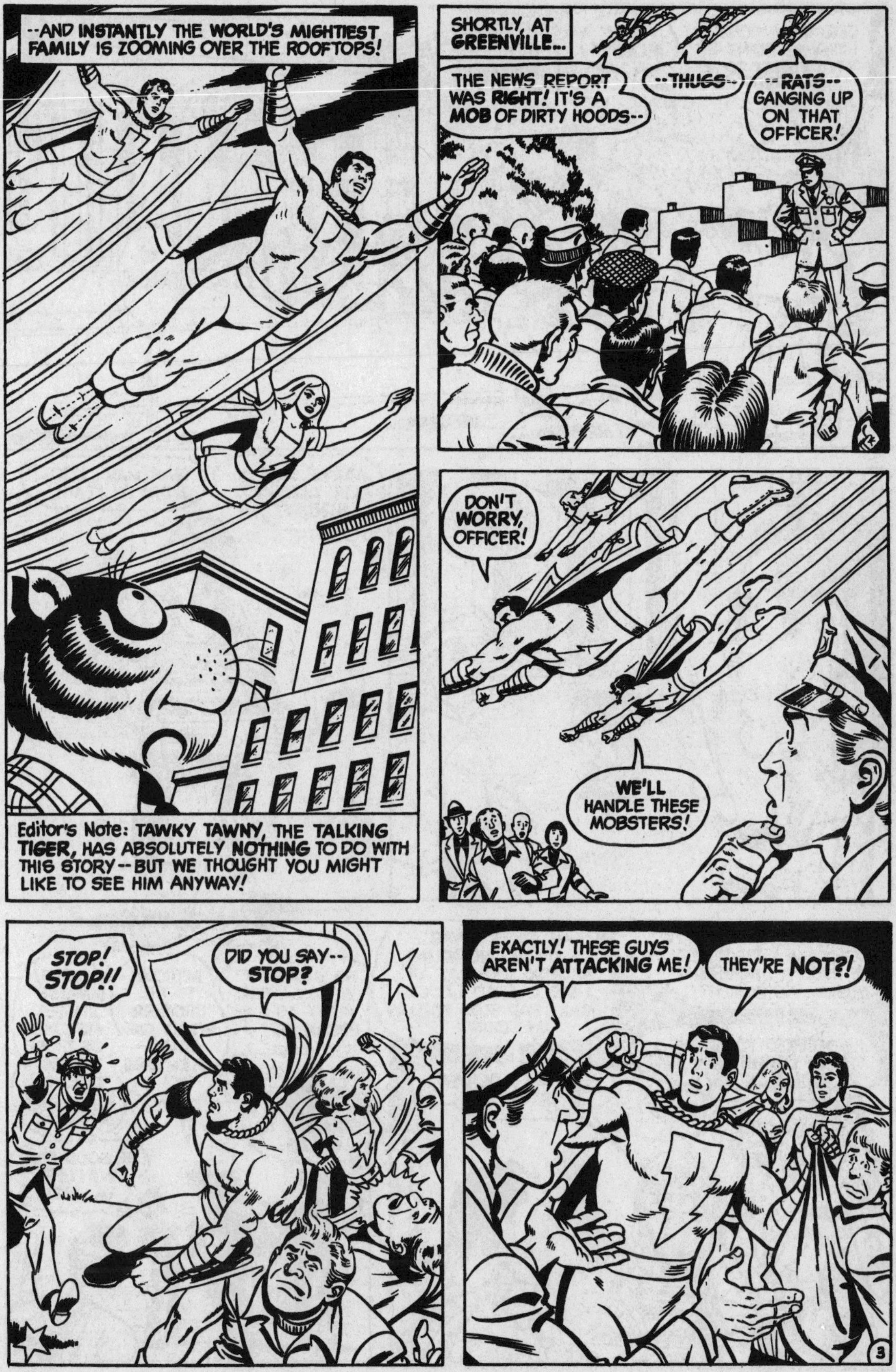
--AND INSTANTLY THE WORLD'S MIGHTIEST FAMILY IS ZOOMING OVER THE ROOFTOPS!
Editor's Note: TAWKY TAWNY, THE TALKING TIGER, HAS ABSOLUTELY NOTHING TO DO WITH THIS STORY--BUT WE THOUGHT YOU MIGHT LIKE TO SEE HIM ANYWAY!
SHORTLY, AT GREENVILLE...
THE NEWS REPORT WAS RIGHT! IT'S A MOB OF DIRTY HOODS--
--THUGS--
--RATS--GANGING UP ON THAT OFFICER!
DON'T WORRY, OFFICER!
WE'LL HANDLE THESE MOBSTERS!
STOP! STOP!!
DID YOU SAY--STOP?
EXACTLY! THESE GUYS AREN'T ATTACKING ME!
THEY'RE NOT?!
3

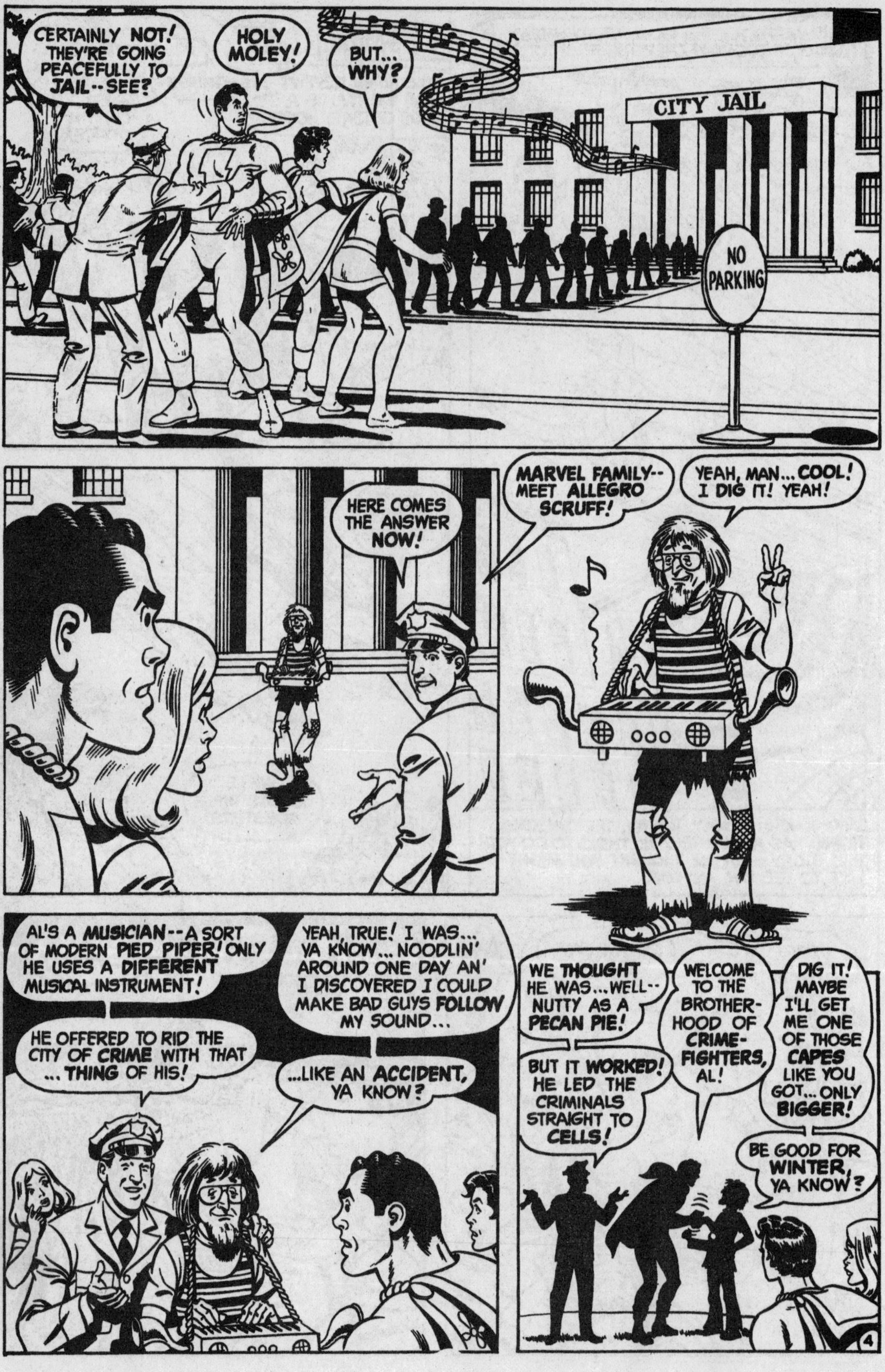
CERTAINLY NOT! THEY'RE GOING PEACEFULLY TO JAIL--SEE?
HOLY MOLEY!
BUT... WHY?
CITY JAIL
NO PARKING
HERE COMES THE ANSWER NOW!
MARVEL FAMILY--MEET ALLEGRO SCRUFF!
YEAH, MAN...COOL! I DIG IT! YEAH!
AL'S A MUSICIAN--A SORT OF MODERN PIED PIPER! ONLY HE USES A DIFFERENT MUSICAL INSTRUMENT!
HE OFFERED TO RID THE CITY OF CRIME WITH THAT ...THING OF HIS!
YEAH, TRUE! I WAS... YA KNOW... NOODLIN' AROUND ONE DAY AN' I DISCOVERED I COULD MAKE BAD GUYS FOLLOW MY SOUND...
...LIKE AN ACCIDENT, YA KNOW?
WE THOUGHT HE WAS...WELL--NUTTY AS A PECAN PIE!
BUT IT WORKED! HE LED THE CRIMINALS STRAIGHT TO CELLS!
WELCOME TO THE BROTHERHOOD OF CRIME-FIGHTERS, AL!
DIG IT! MAYBE I'LL GET ME ONE OF THOSE CAPES LIKE YOU GOT...ONLY BIGGER!
BE GOOD FOR WINTER, YA KNOW?
4

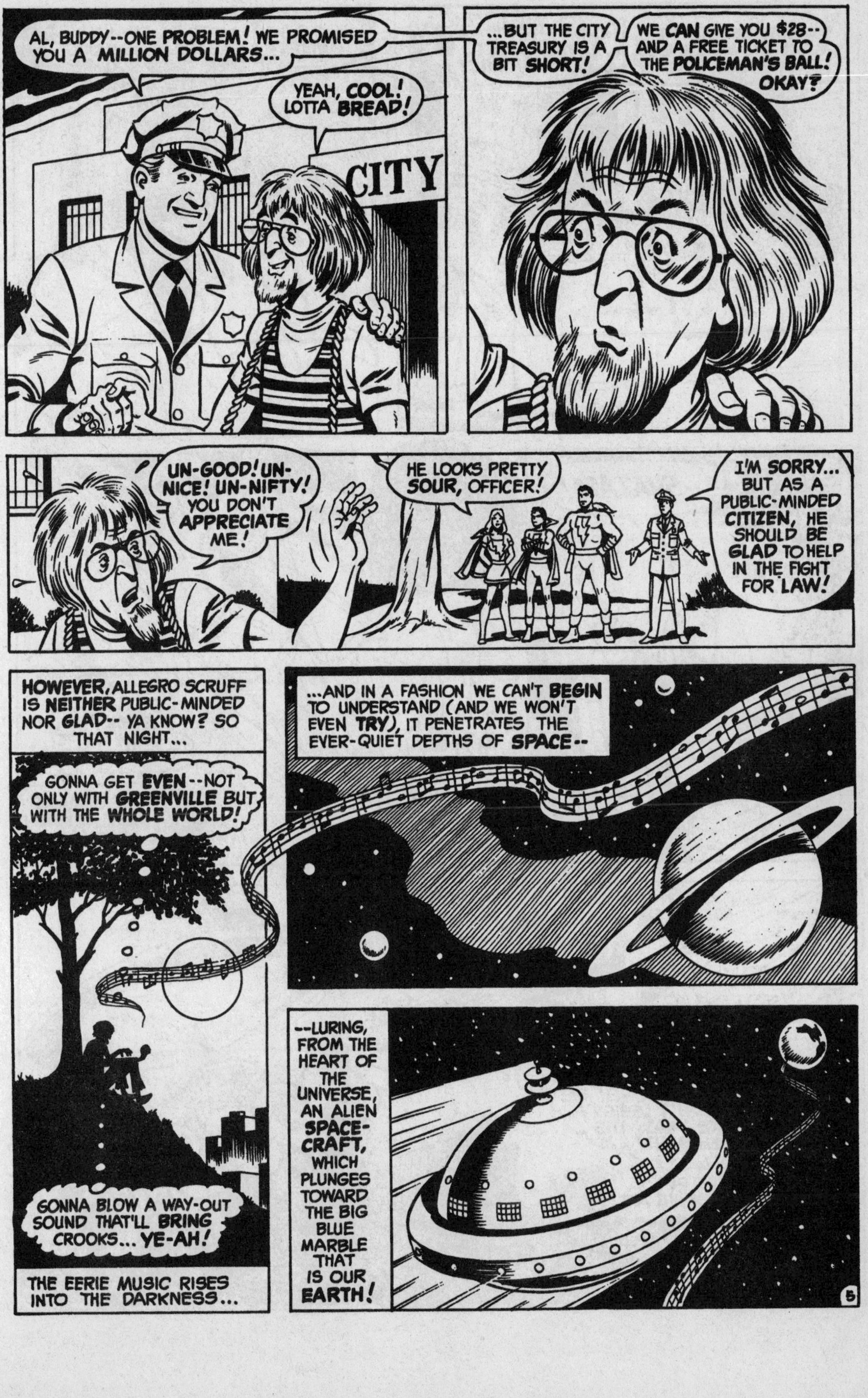
AL, BUDDY--ONE PROBLEM! WE PROMISED YOU A MILLION DOLLARS...
YEAH, COOL! LOTTA BREAD!
CITY
...BUT THE CITY TREASURY IS A BIT SHORT!
WE CAN GIVE YOU $28--AND A FREE TICKET TO THE POLICEMAN'S BALL! OKAY?
UN-GOOD! UN-NICE! UN-NIFTY! YOU DON'T APPRECIATE ME!
HE LOOKS PRETTY SOUR, OFFICER!
I'M SORRY... BUT AS A PUBLIC-MINDED CITIZEN, HE SHOULD BE GLAD TO HELP IN THE FIGHT FOR LAW!
HOWEVER, ALLEGRO SCRUFF IS NEITHER PUBLIC-MINDED NOR GLAD-- YA KNOW? SO THAT NIGHT...
GONNA GET EVEN--NOT ONLY WITH GREENVILLE BUT WITH THE WHOLE WORLD!
GONNA BLOW A WAY-OUT SOUND THAT'LL BRING CROOKS... YE-AH!
THE EERIE MUSIC RISES INTO THE DARKNESS...
...AND IN A FASHION WE CAN'T BEGIN TO UNDERSTAND (AND WE WON'T EVEN TRY), IT PENETRATES THE EVER-QUIET DEPTHS OF SPACE--
--LURING, FROM THE HEART OF THE UNIVERSE, AN ALIEN SPACE-CRAFT, WHICH PLUNGES TOWARD THE BIG BLUE MARBLE THAT IS OUR EARTH!
5

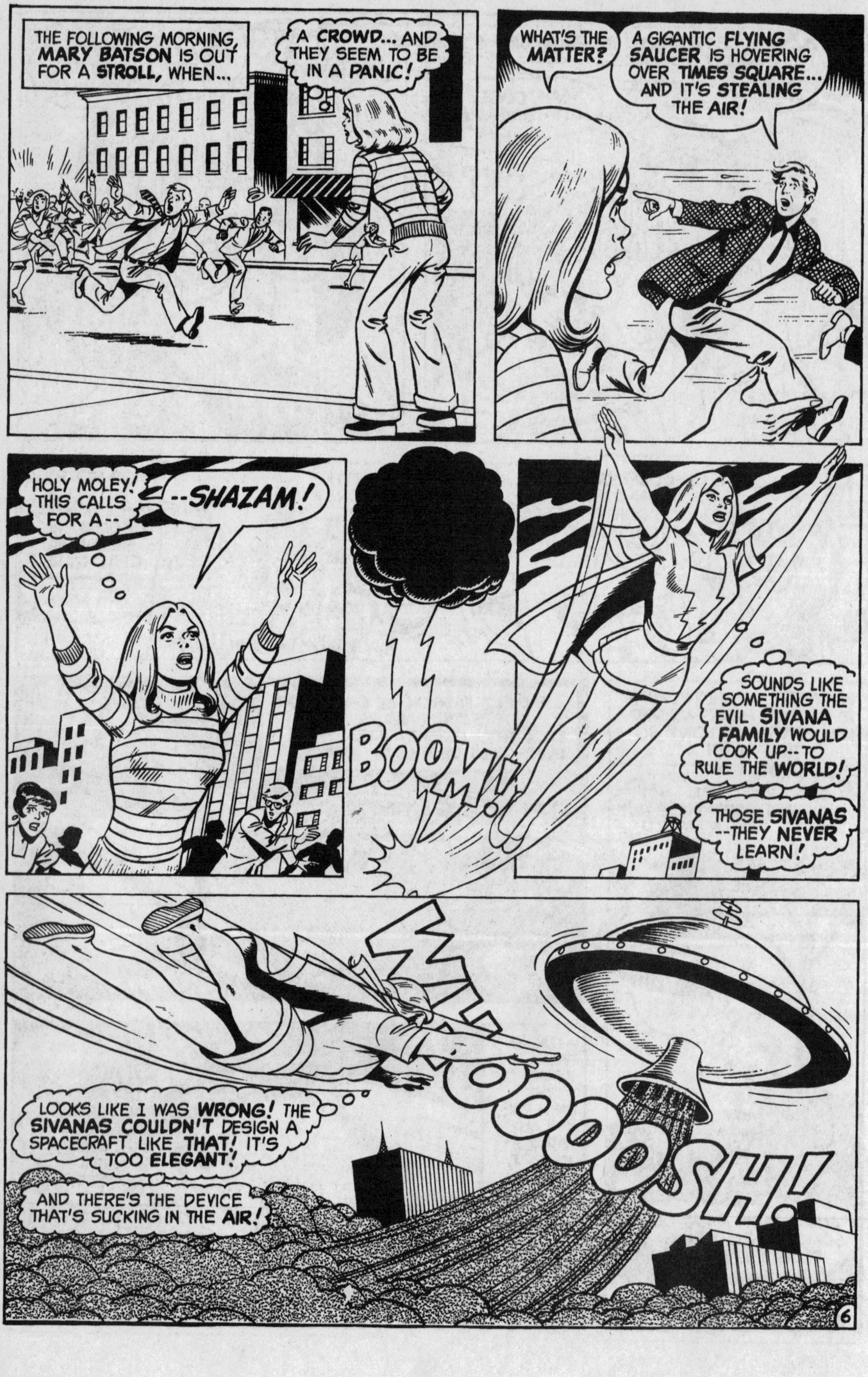
THE FOLLOWING MORNING, MARY BATSON IS OUT FOR A STROLL, WHEN...
A CROWD... AND THEY SEEM TO BE IN A PANIC!
WHAT'S THE MATTER?
A GIGANTIC FLYING SAUCER IS HOVERING OVER TIMES SQUARE... AND IT'S STEALING THE AIR!
HOLY MOLEY! THIS CALLS FOR A--
--SHAZAM!
BOOM!
SOUNDS LIKE SOMETHING THE EVIL SIVANA FAMILY WOULD COOK UP--TO RULE THE WORLD!
THOSE SIVANAS --THEY NEVER LEARN!
WHOOOOOOSH!
LOOKS LIKE I WAS WRONG! THE SIVANAS COULDN'T DESIGN A SPACECRAFT LIKE THAT! IT'S TOO ELEGANT!
AND THERE'S THE DEVICE THAT'S SUCKING IN THE AIR!
6

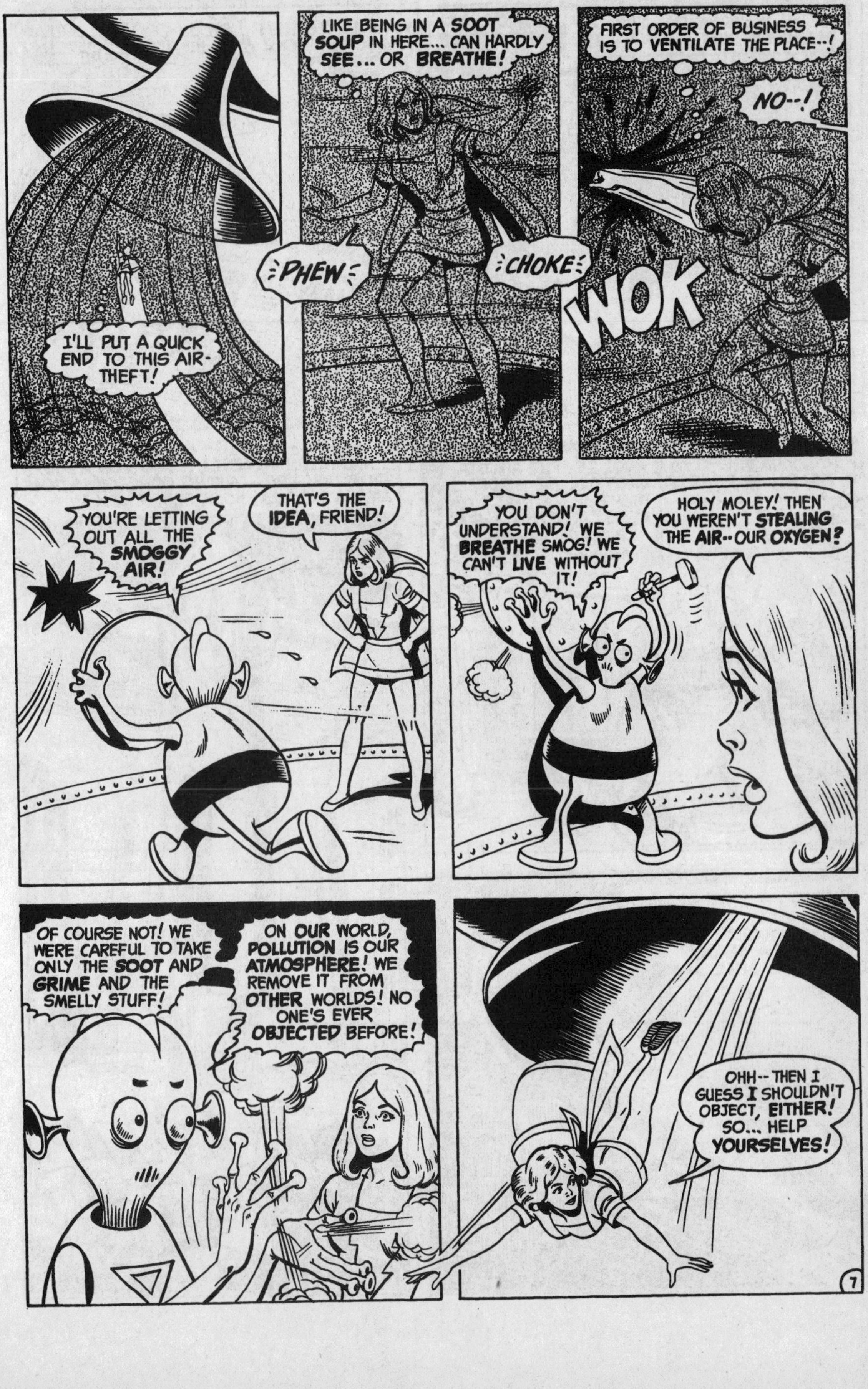
I'LL PUT A QUICK END TO THIS AIR-THEFT!
LIKE BEING IN A SOOT SOUP IN HERE... CAN HARDLY SEE... OR BREATHE!
PHEW
CHOKE
FIRST ORDER OF BUSINESS IS TO VENTILATE THE PLACE--!
NO--!
WOK
YOU'RE LETTING OUT ALL THE SMOGGY AIR!
THAT'S THE IDEA, FRIEND!
YOU DON'T UNDERSTAND! WE BREATHE SMOG! WE CAN'T LIVE WITHOUT IT!
HOLY MOLEY! THEN YOU WEREN'T STEALING THE AIR-- OUR OXYGEN?
OF COURSE NOT! WE WERE CAREFUL TO TAKE ONLY THE SOOT AND GRIME AND THE SMELLY STUFF!
ON OUR WORLD, POLLUTION IS OUR ATMOSPHERE! WE REMOVE IT FROM OTHER WORLDS! NO ONE'S EVER OBJECTED BEFORE!
OHH-- THEN I GUESS I SHOULDN'T OBJECT, EITHER! SO... HELP YOURSELVES!
7

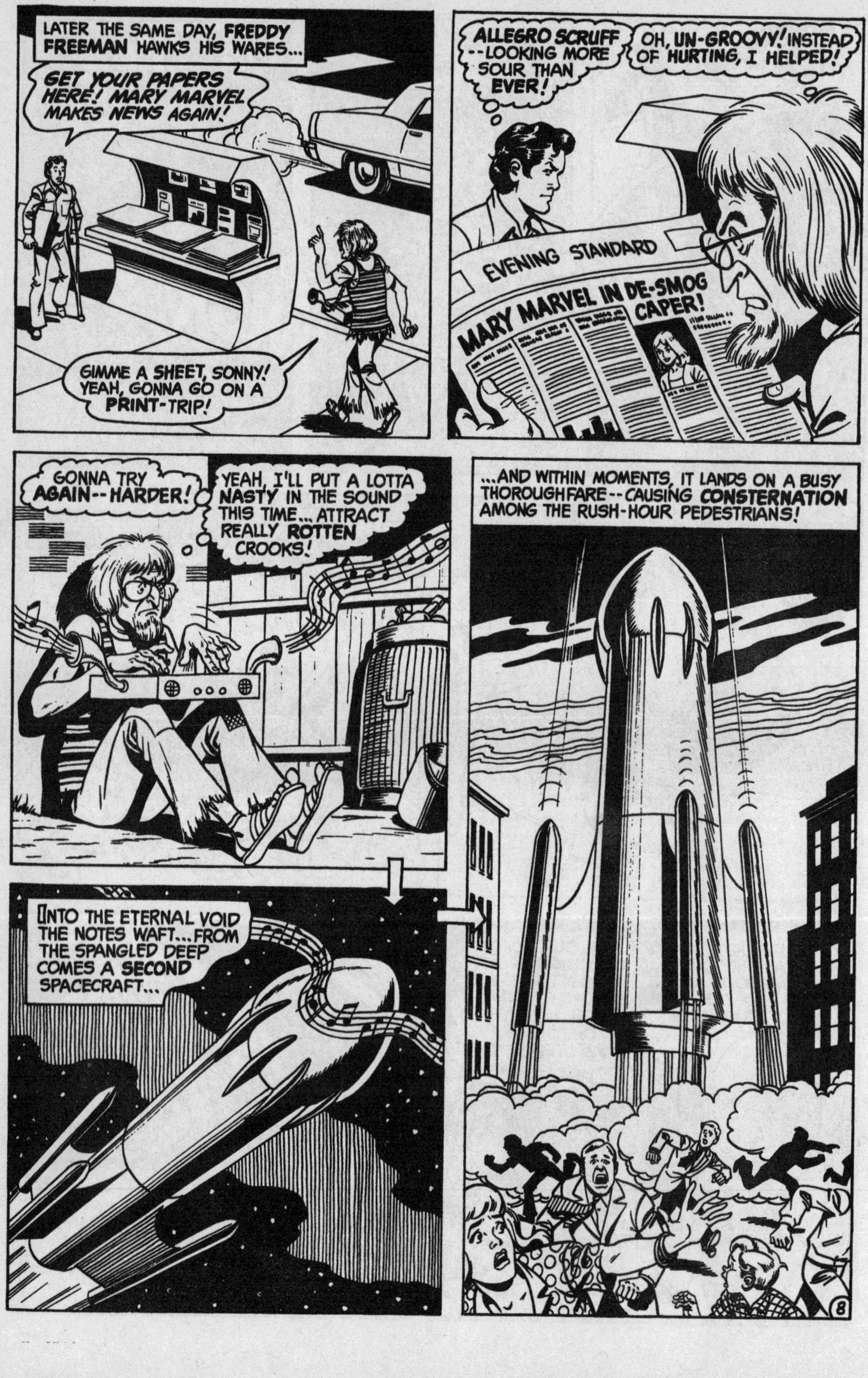
LATER THE SAME DAY, FREDDY FREEMAN HAWKS HIS WARES...
GET YOUR PAPERS HERE! MARY MARVEL MAKES NEWS AGAIN!
GIMME A SHEET, SONNY! YEAH, GONNA GO ON A PRINT-TRIP!
ALLEGRO SCRUFF --LOOKING MORE SOUR THAN EVER!
OH, UN-GROOVY! INSTEAD OF HURTING, I HELPED!
EVENING STANDARD
MARY MARVEL IN DE-SMOG CAPER!
GONNA TRY AGAIN--HARDER!
YEAH, I'LL PUT A LOTTA NASTY IN THE SOUND THIS TIME... ATTRACT REALLY ROTTEN CROOKS!
INTO THE ETERNAL VOID THE NOTES WAFT...FROM THE SPANGLED DEEP COMES A SECOND SPACECRAFT...
...AND WITHIN MOMENTS, IT LANDS ON A BUSY THOROUGHFARE--CAUSING CONSTERNATION AMONG THE RUSH-HOUR PEDESTRIANS!
8

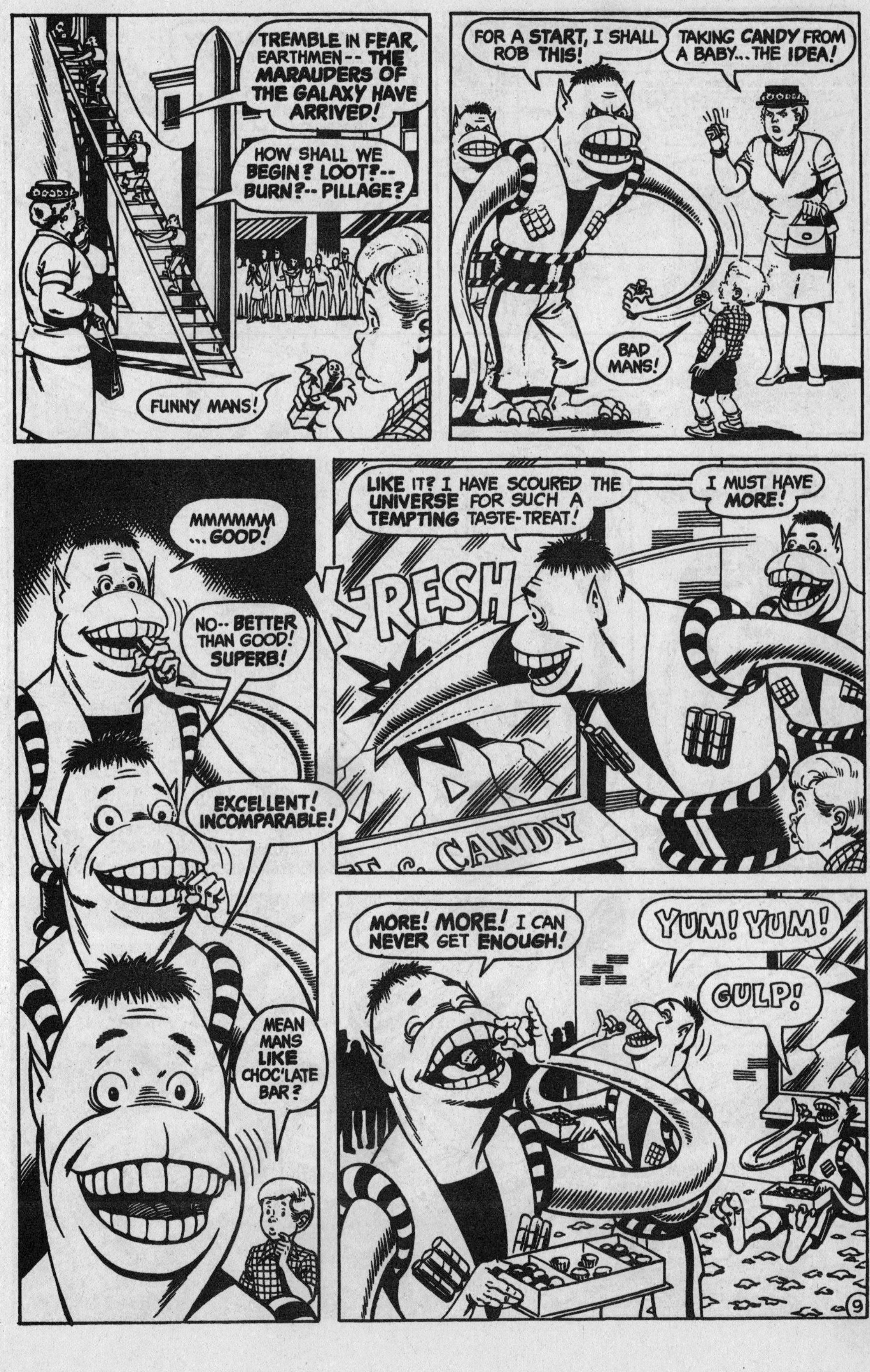
TREMBLE IN FEAR, EARTHMEN-- THE MARAUDERS OF THE GALAXY HAVE ARRIVED!
HOW SHALL WE BEGIN? LOOT?-- BURN?-- PILLAGE?
FUNNY MANS!
FOR A START, I SHALL ROB THIS!
TAKING CANDY FROM A BABY...THE IDEA!
BAD MANS!
MMMMMM ...GOOD!
NO-- BETTER THAN GOOD! SUPERB!
EXCELLENT! INCOMPARABLE!
MEAN MANS LIKE CHOC'LATE BAR?
LIKE IT? I HAVE SCOURED THE UNIVERSE FOR SUCH A TEMPTING TASTE-TREAT!
I MUST HAVE MORE!
K-RESH
CANDY
MORE! MORE! I CAN NEVER GET ENOUGH!
YUM! YUM!
GULP!
9

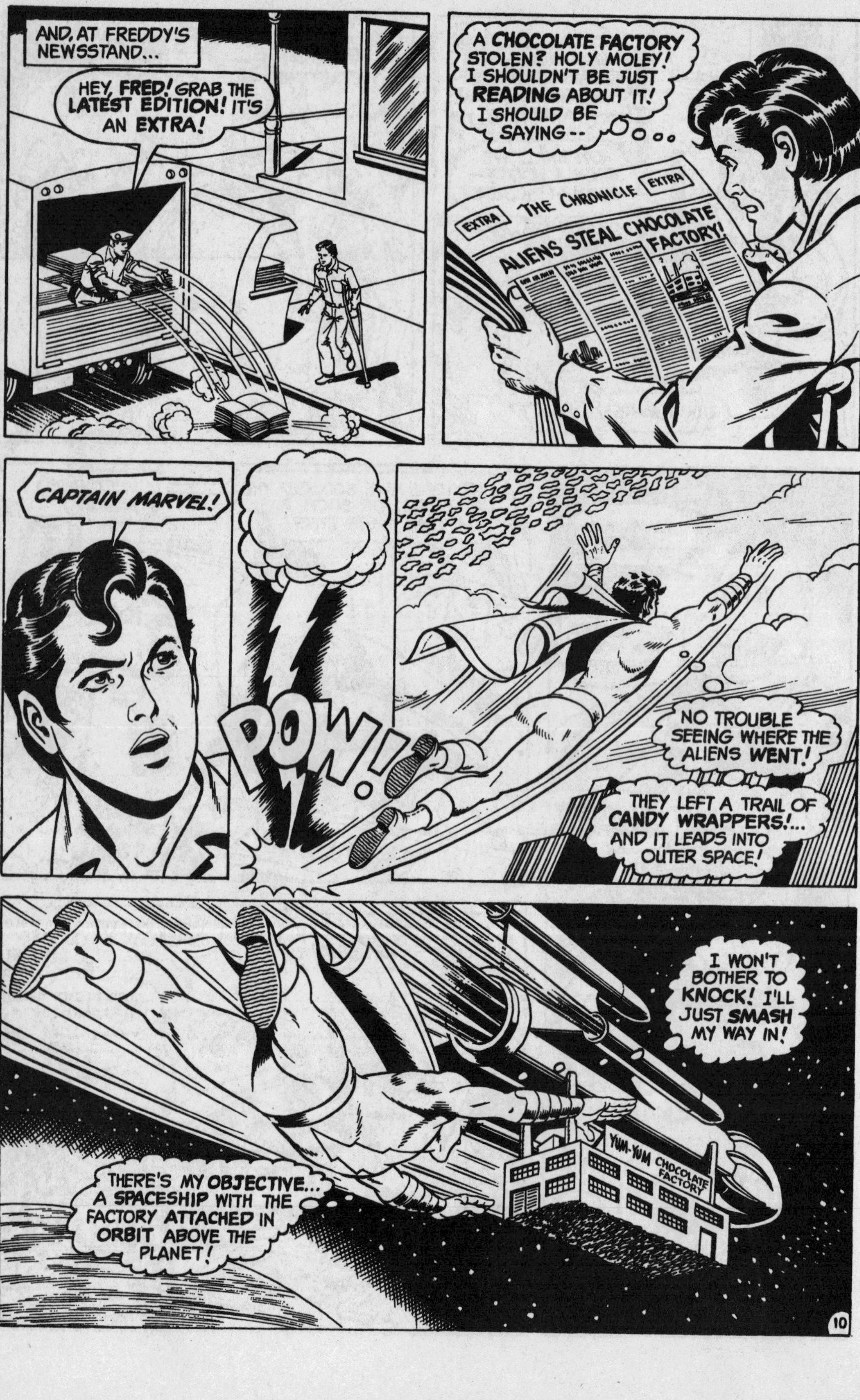
AND, AT FREDDY'S NEWSSTAND...
HEY, FRED! GRAB THE LATEST EDITION! IT'S AN EXTRA!
A CHOCOLATE FACTORY STOLEN? HOLY MOLEY! I SHOULDN'T BE JUST READING ABOUT IT! I SHOULD BE SAYING--
EXTRA THE CHRONICLE EXTRA
ALIENS STEAL CHOCOLATE FACTORY!
CAPTAIN MARVEL!
POW!!
NO TROUBLE SEEING WHERE THE ALIENS WENT!
THEY LEFT A TRAIL OF CANDY WRAPPERS!... AND IT LEADS INTO OUTER SPACE!
I WON'T BOTHER TO KNOCK! I'LL JUST SMASH MY WAY IN!
THERE'S MY OBJECTIVE... A SPACESHIP WITH THE FACTORY ATTACHED IN ORBIT ABOVE THE PLANET!
YUM-YUM CHOCOLATE FACTORY
10

BUT THEN...

PLASMIC ENERGY-BOLTS! AND DO THEY STING!

IF I WERE A NORMAL BOY, I'D BE FRIED TO A CRISP!

LIKE FIGHTING MY WAY INTO A HORNETS' NEST!

CAN'T FIGHT THROUGH THE ENERGY-BOLTS!

I'LL HAVE TO REAR BACK AND REALLY GIVE THEM MY BEST!

SUDDENLY...

HUH? THEY'VE STOPPED FIRING!

WONDER WHY?

YUM-YUM!

I'LL SEE FOR MYSELF!

RIPP!

AS THOUGH HE WERE TEARING TISSUE, THE WORLD'S MIGHTIEST BOY RIPS OPEN THE HULL!

OOOEEEE!

OWWOOOOO!

HOLY MOLEY! IT LOOKS LIKE--SOUNDS LIKE THE ALIEN MENACES HAVE--

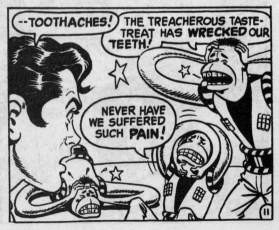

--TOOTHACHES! THE TREACHEROUS TASTE-TREAT HAS WRECKED OUR TEETH!

NEVER HAVE WE SUFFERED SUCH PAIN!

11

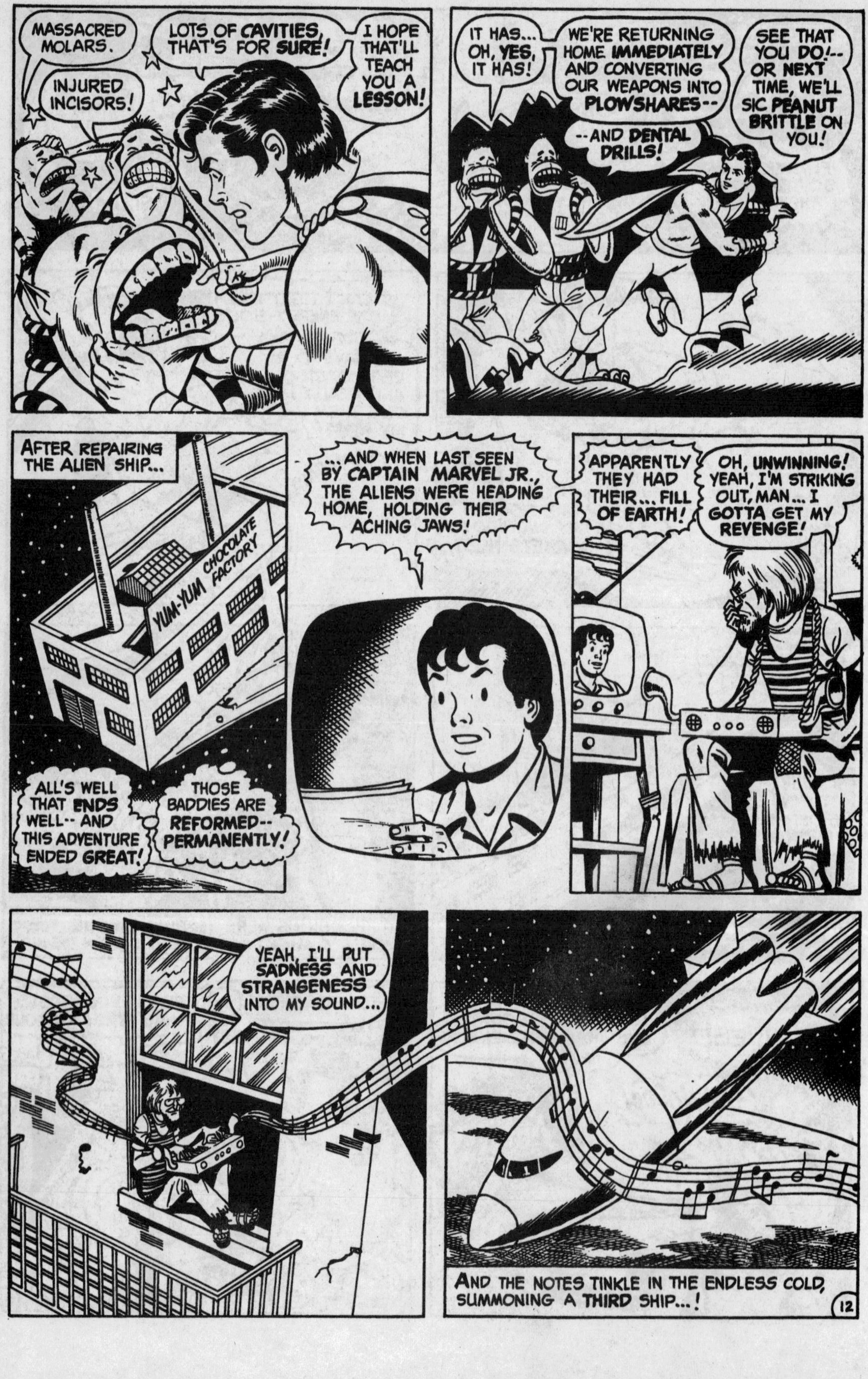
MASSACRED MOLARS.
INJURED INCISORS!
LOTS OF CAVITIES, THAT'S FOR SURE!
I HOPE THAT'LL TEACH YOU A LESSON!
IT HAS... OH, YES, IT HAS!
WE'RE RETURNING HOME IMMEDIATELY AND CONVERTING OUR WEAPONS INTO PLOWSHARES--
--AND DENTAL DRILLS!
SEE THAT YOU DO!-- OR NEXT TIME, WE'LL SIC PEANUT BRITTLE ON YOU!
AFTER REPAIRING THE ALIEN SHIP...
YUM-YUM CHOCOLATE FACTORY
ALL'S WELL THAT ENDS WELL-- AND THIS ADVENTURE ENDED GREAT!
THOSE BADDIES ARE REFORMED-- PERMANENTLY!
...AND WHEN LAST SEEN BY CAPTAIN MARVEL JR., THE ALIENS WERE HEADING HOME, HOLDING THEIR ACHING JAWS!
APPARENTLY THEY HAD THEIR... FILL OF EARTH!
OH, UNWINNING! YEAH, I'M STRIKING OUT, MAN... I GOTTA GET MY REVENGE!
YEAH, I'LL PUT SADNESS AND STRANGENESS INTO MY SOUND...
AND THE NOTES TINKLE IN THE ENDLESS COLD, SUMMONING A THIRD SHIP...!
12

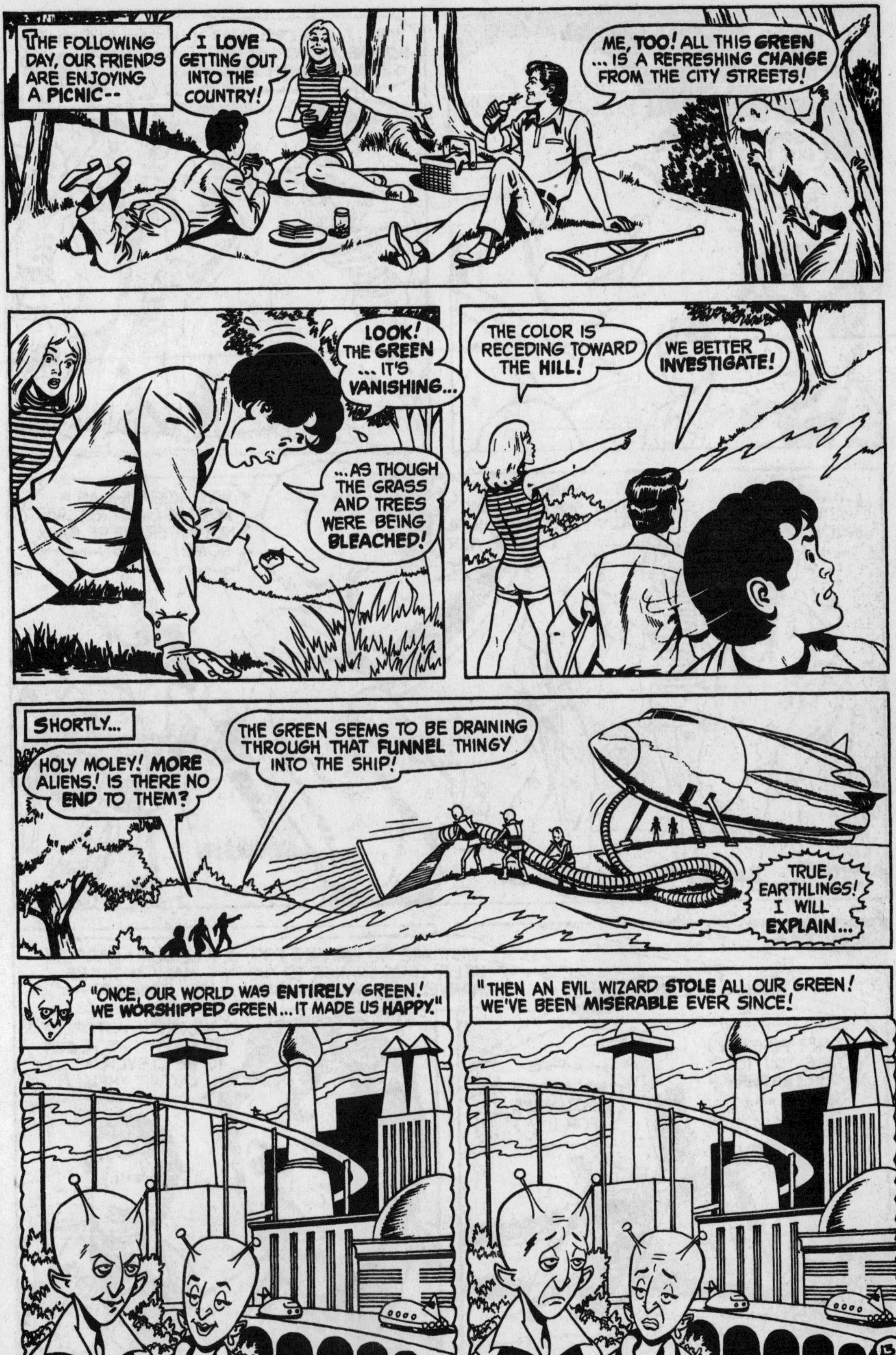
THE FOLLOWING DAY, OUR FRIENDS ARE ENJOYING A PICNIC--
I LOVE GETTING OUT INTO THE COUNTRY!
ME, TOO! ALL THIS GREEN ... IS A REFRESHING CHANGE FROM THE CITY STREETS!
LOOK! THE GREEN ... IT'S VANISHING...
...AS THOUGH THE GRASS AND TREES WERE BEING BLEACHED!
THE COLOR IS RECEDING TOWARD THE HILL!
WE BETTER INVESTIGATE!
SHORTLY...
HOLY MOLEY! MORE ALIENS! IS THERE NO END TO THEM?
THE GREEN SEEMS TO BE DRAINING THROUGH THAT FUNNEL THINGY INTO THE SHIP!
TRUE, EARTHLINGS! I WILL EXPLAIN...
"ONCE, OUR WORLD WAS ENTIRELY GREEN! WE WORSHIPPED GREEN... IT MADE US HAPPY."
"THEN AN EVIL WIZARD STOLE ALL OUR GREEN! WE'VE BEEN MISERABLE EVER SINCE!
13

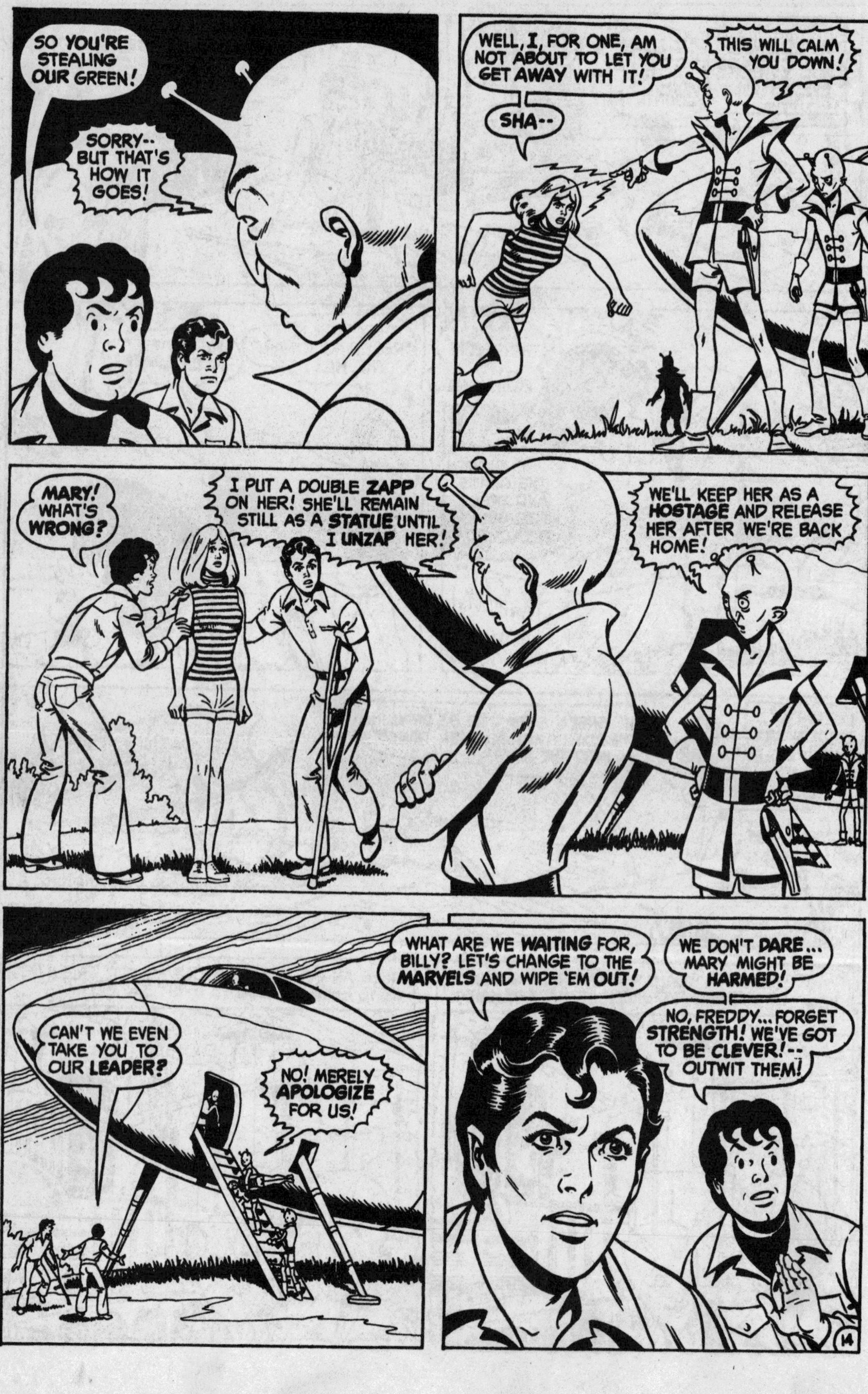

SO YOU'RE STEALING OUR GREEN!
SORRY-- BUT THAT'S HOW IT GOES!
WELL, I, FOR ONE, AM NOT ABOUT TO LET YOU GET AWAY WITH IT!
SHA--
THIS WILL CALM YOU DOWN!
MARY! WHAT'S WRONG?
I PUT A DOUBLE ZAPP ON HER! SHE'LL REMAIN STILL AS A STATUE UNTIL I UNZAP HER!
WE'LL KEEP HER AS A HOSTAGE AND RELEASE HER AFTER WE'RE BACK HOME!
CAN'T WE EVEN TAKE YOU TO OUR LEADER?
NO! MERELY APOLOGIZE FOR US!
WHAT ARE WE WAITING FOR, BILLY? LET'S CHANGE TO THE MARVELS AND WIPE 'EM OUT!
WE DON'T DARE... MARY MIGHT BE HARMED!
NO, FREDDY... FORGET STRENGTH! WE'VE GOT TO BE CLEVER!-- OUTWIT THEM!
14

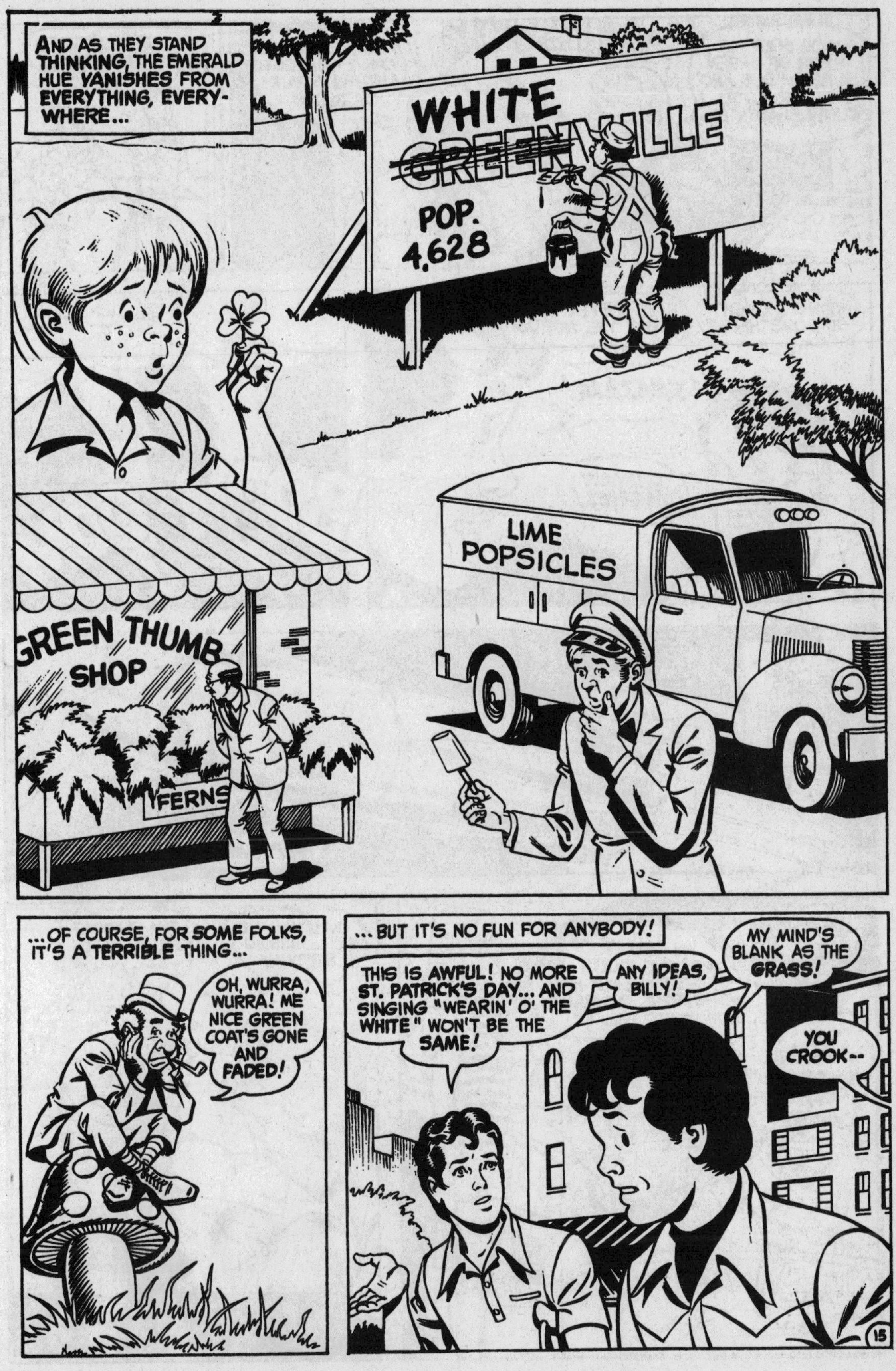
AND AS THEY STAND THINKING, THE EMERALD HUE VANISHES FROM EVERYTHING, EVERYWHERE...
WHITE
GREENVILLE
POP. 4,628
LIME POPSICLES
GREEN THUMB SHOP
FERNS
...OF COURSE, FOR SOME FOLKS, IT'S A TERRIBLE THING...
OH, WURRA, WURRA! ME NICE GREEN COAT'S GONE AND FADED!
... BUT IT'S NO FUN FOR ANYBODY!
THIS IS AWFUL! NO MORE ST. PATRICK'S DAY... AND SINGING "WEARIN' O' THE WHITE" WON'T BE THE SAME!
ANY IDEAS, BILLY!
MY MIND'S BLANK AS THE GRASS!
YOU CROOK--
15

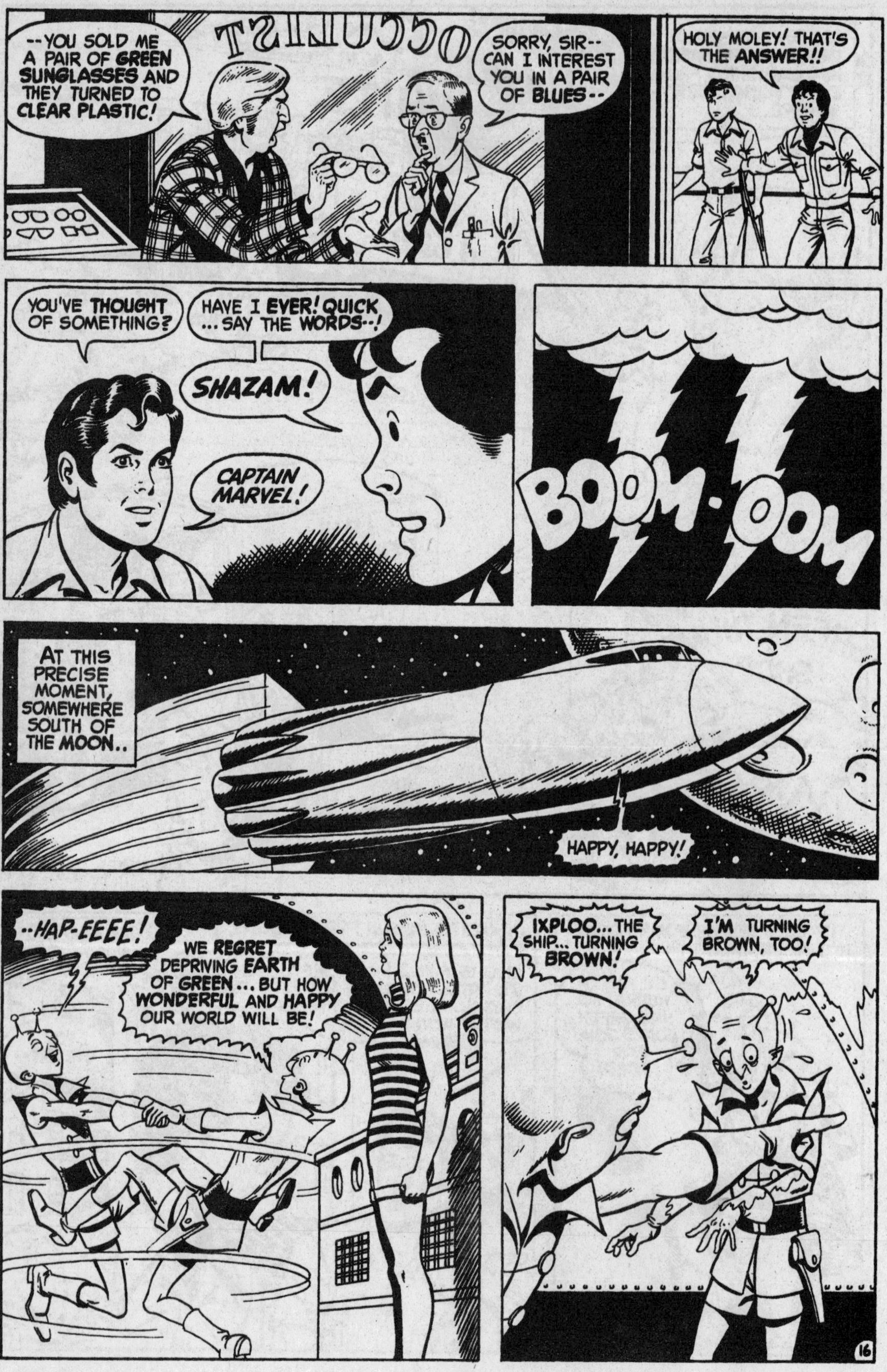
OCCULIST
--YOU SOLD ME A PAIR OF GREEN SUNGLASSES AND THEY TURNED TO CLEAR PLASTIC!
SORRY, SIR-- CAN I INTEREST YOU IN A PAIR OF BLUES--
HOLY MOLEY! THAT'S THE ANSWER!!
YOU'VE THOUGHT OF SOMETHING?
HAVE I EVER! QUICK ... SAY THE WORDS--!
SHAZAM!
CAPTAIN MARVEL!
BOOM-OOM
AT THIS PRECISE MOMENT, SOMEWHERE SOUTH OF THE MOON..
HAPPY, HAPPY!
..HAP-EEEE!
WE REGRET DEPRIVING EARTH OF GREEN ... BUT HOW WONDERFUL AND HAPPY OUR WORLD WILL BE!
IXPLOO... THE SHIP... TURNING BROWN!
I'M TURNING BROWN, TOO!
16

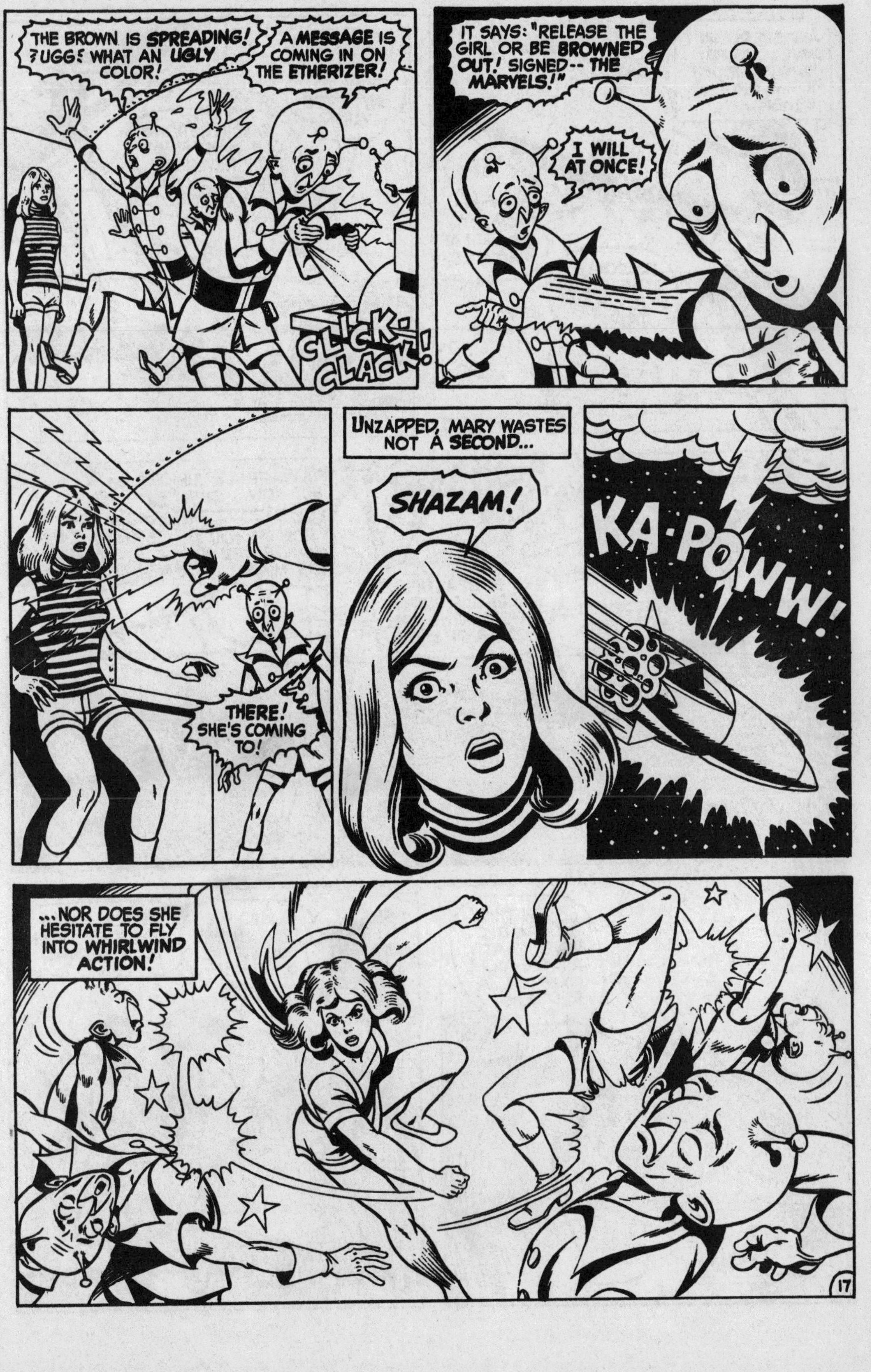
THE BROWN IS SPREADING! ?UGG! WHAT AN UGLY COLOR!
A MESSAGE IS COMING IN ON THE ETHERIZER!
CLICK-CLACK!
IT SAYS: "RELEASE THE GIRL OR BE BROWNED OUT! SIGNED-- THE MARVELS!"
I WILL AT ONCE!
THERE! SHE'S COMING TO!
UNZAPPED, MARY WASTES NOT A SECOND...
SHAZAM!
KA-POWW!
...NOR DOES SHE HESITATE TO FLY INTO WHIRLWIND ACTION!
17

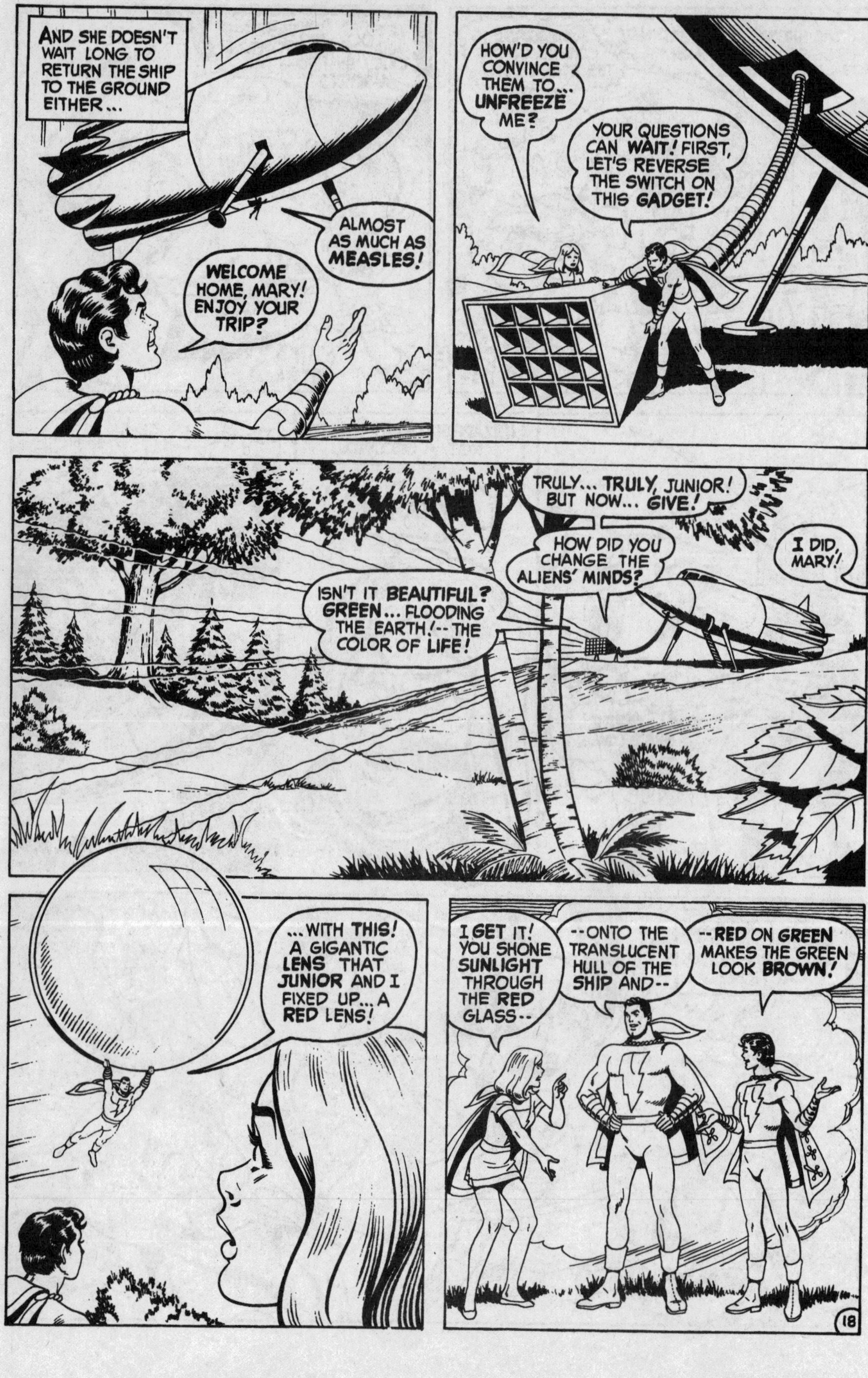
AND SHE DOESN'T WAIT LONG TO RETURN THE SHIP TO THE GROUND EITHER...
WELCOME HOME, MARY! ENJOY YOUR TRIP?
ALMOST AS MUCH AS MEASLES!
HOW'D YOU CONVINCE THEM TO... UNFREEZE ME?
YOUR QUESTIONS CAN WAIT! FIRST, LET'S REVERSE THE SWITCH ON THIS GADGET!
ISN'T IT BEAUTIFUL? GREEN... FLOODING THE EARTH!-- THE COLOR OF LIFE!
TRULY... TRULY, JUNIOR! BUT NOW... GIVE!
HOW DID YOU CHANGE THE ALIENS' MINDS?
I DID, MARY!
...WITH THIS! A GIGANTIC LENS THAT JUNIOR AND I FIXED UP... A RED LENS!
I GET IT! YOU SHONE SUNLIGHT THROUGH THE RED GLASS--
--ONTO THE TRANSLUCENT HULL OF THE SHIP AND--
--RED ON GREEN MAKES THE GREEN LOOK BROWN!
18

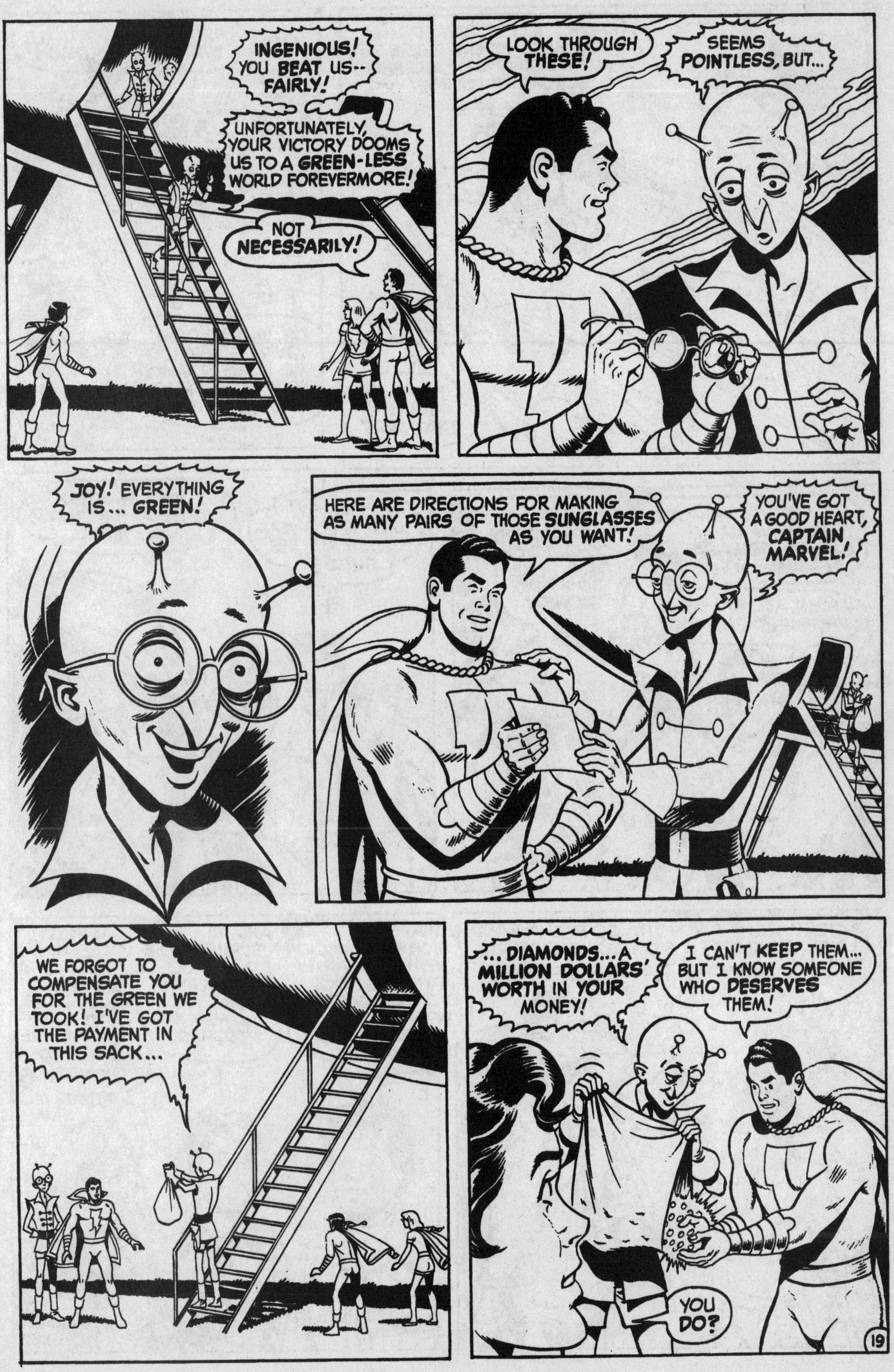
INGENIOUS! YOU BEAT US-- FAIRLY!
UNFORTUNATELY, YOUR VICTORY DOOMS US TO A GREEN-LESS WORLD FOREVERMORE!
NOT NECESSARILY!
LOOK THROUGH THESE!
SEEMS POINTLESS, BUT...
JOY! EVERYTHING IS ... GREEN!
HERE ARE DIRECTIONS FOR MAKING AS MANY PAIRS OF THOSE SUNGLASSES AS YOU WANT!
YOU'VE GOT A GOOD HEART, CAPTAIN MARVEL!
WE FORGOT TO COMPENSATE YOU FOR THE GREEN WE TOOK! I'VE GOT THE PAYMENT IN THIS SACK...
... DIAMONDS... A MILLION DOLLARS' WORTH IN YOUR MONEY!
I CAN'T KEEP THEM... BUT I KNOW SOMEONE WHO DESERVES THEM!
YOU DO?
19

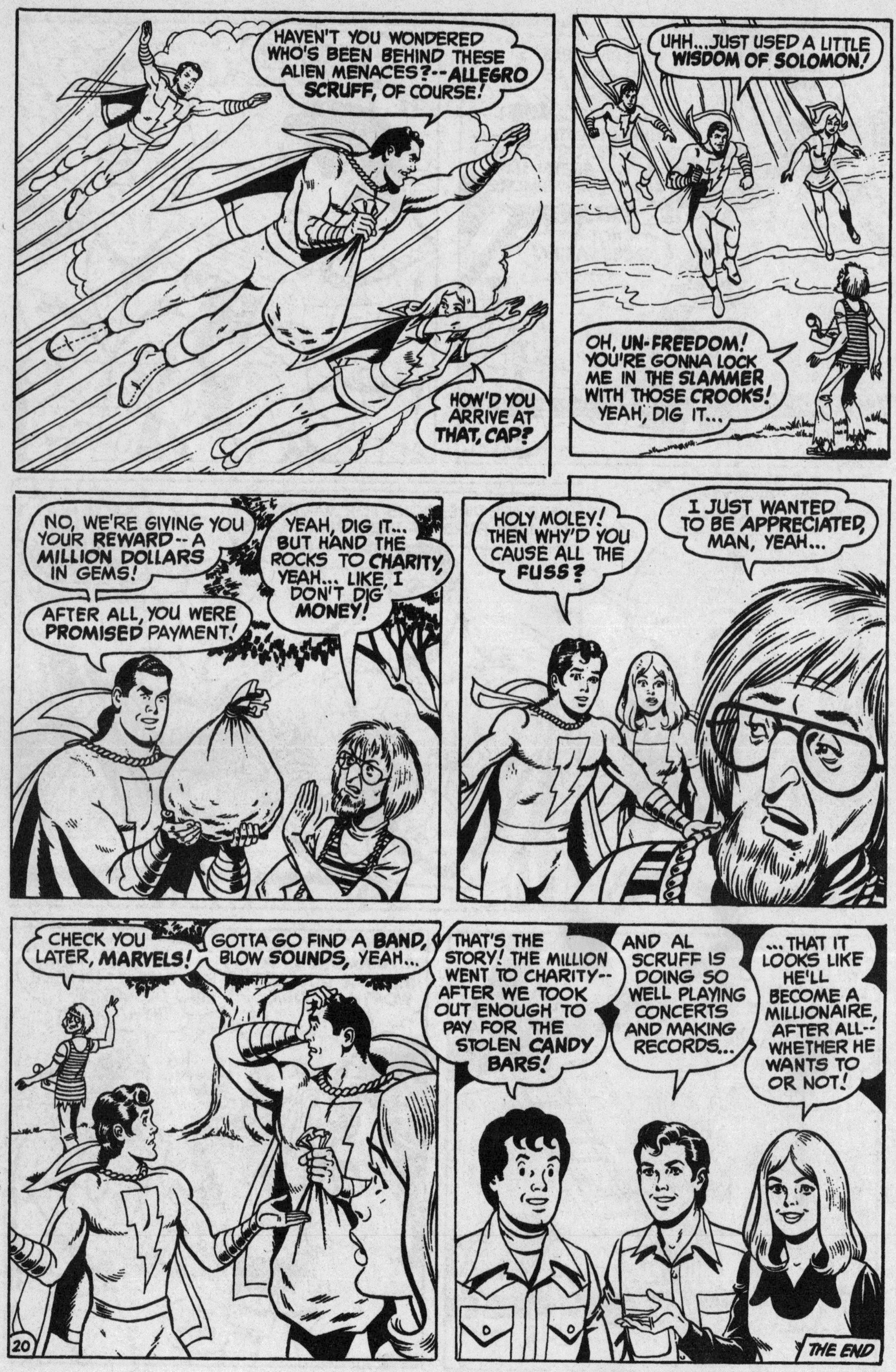
HAVEN'T YOU WONDERED WHO'S BEEN BEHIND THESE ALIEN MENACES?--ALLEGRO SCRUFF, OF COURSE!
HOW'D YOU ARRIVE AT THAT, CAP?
UHH...JUST USED A LITTLE WISDOM OF SOLOMON!
OH, UN-FREEDOM! YOU'RE GONNA LOCK ME IN THE SLAMMER WITH THOSE CROOKS! YEAH, DIG IT...
NO, WE'RE GIVING YOU YOUR REWARD--A MILLION DOLLARS IN GEMS!
AFTER ALL, YOU WERE PROMISED PAYMENT!
YEAH, DIG IT... BUT HAND THE ROCKS TO CHARITY, YEAH... LIKE, I DON'T DIG MONEY!
HOLY MOLEY! THEN WHY'D YOU CAUSE ALL THE FUSS?
I JUST WANTED TO BE APPRECIATED, MAN, YEAH...
CHECK YOU LATER, MARVELS!
GOTTA GO FIND A BAND, BLOW SOUNDS, YEAH...
20
THAT'S THE STORY! THE MILLION WENT TO CHARITY--AFTER WE TOOK OUT ENOUGH TO PAY FOR THE STOLEN CANDY BARS!
AND AL SCRUFF IS DOING SO WELL PLAYING CONCERTS AND MAKING RECORDS...
...THAT IT LOOKS LIKE HE'LL BECOME A MILLIONAIRE, AFTER ALL--WHETHER HE WANTS TO OR NOT!
THE END

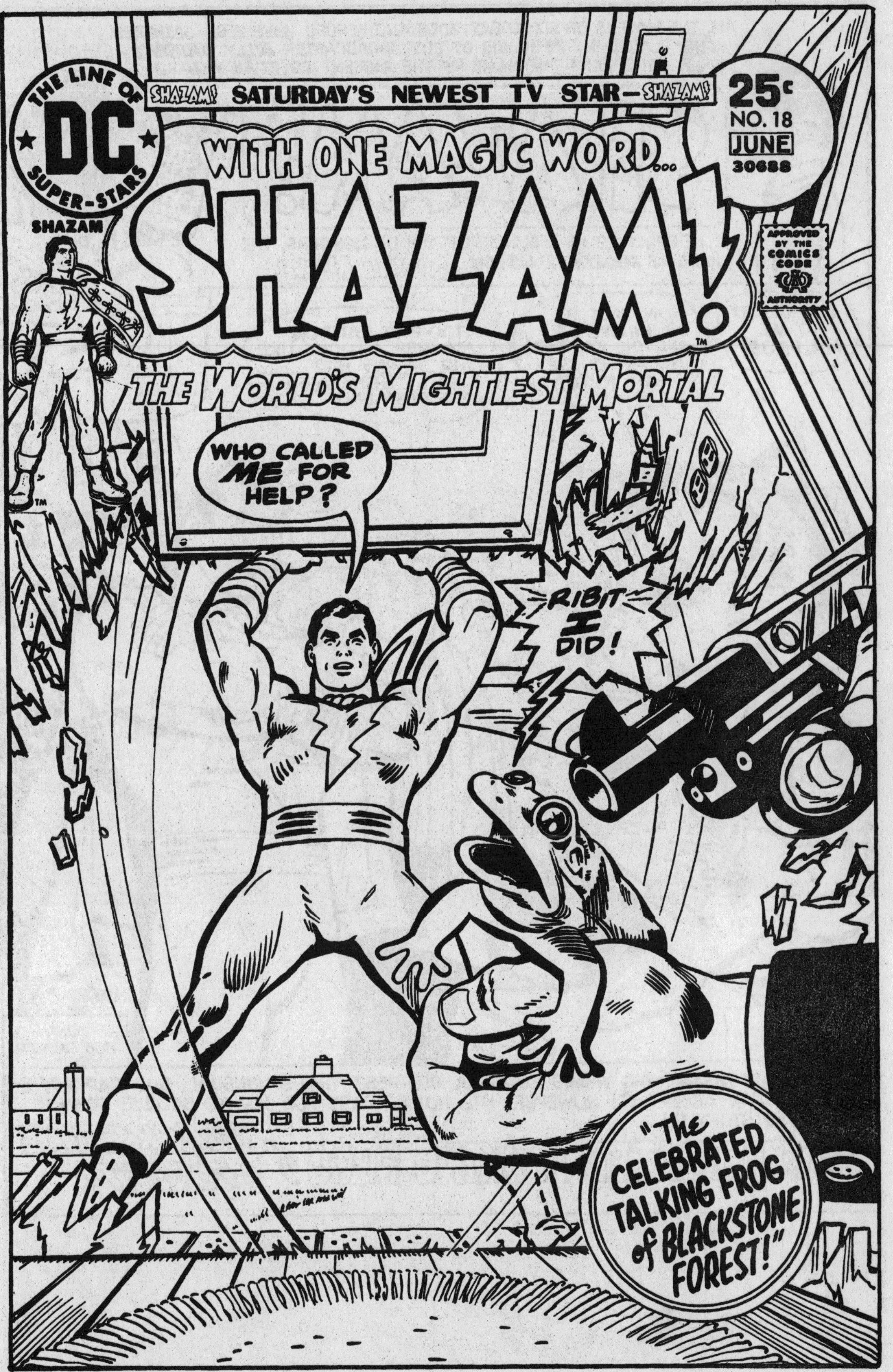
THE LINE OF DC SUPER-STARS
SHAZAM
SHAZAM! SATURDAY'S NEWEST TV STAR—SHAZAM!
25¢
NO. 18
JUNE
30688
WITH ONE MAGIC WORD...
SHAZAM!
THE WORLD'S MIGHTIEST MORTAL
APPROVED BY THE COMICS CODE AUTHORITY
WHO CALLED ME FOR HELP?
RIBIT I DID!
"The CELEBRATED TALKING FROG of BLACKSTONE FOREST!"

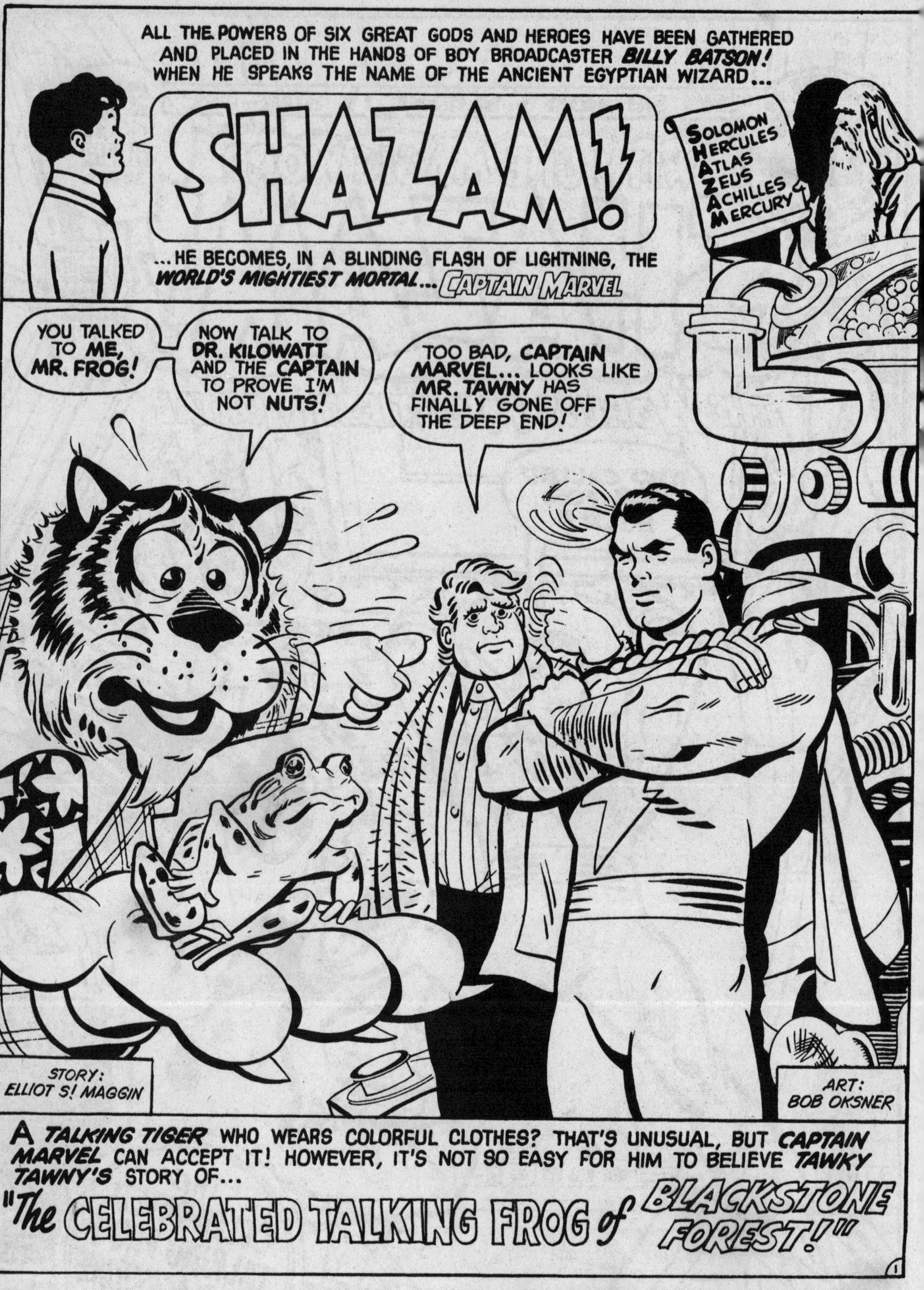
ALL THE POWERS OF SIX GREAT GODS AND HEROES HAVE BEEN GATHERED AND PLACED IN THE HANDS OF BOY BROADCASTER BILLY BATSON! WHEN HE SPEAKS THE NAME OF THE ANCIENT EGYPTIAN WIZARD...
SHAZAM!
SOLOMON
HERCULES
ATLAS
ZEUS
ACHILLES
MERCURY
...HE BECOMES, IN A BLINDING FLASH OF LIGHTNING, THE WORLD'S MIGHTIEST MORTAL... CAPTAIN MARVEL
YOU TALKED TO ME, MR. FROG!
NOW TALK TO DR. KILOWATT AND THE CAPTAIN TO PROVE I'M NOT NUTS!
TOO BAD, CAPTAIN MARVEL... LOOKS LIKE MR. TAWNY HAS FINALLY GONE OFF THE DEEP END!
STORY: ELLIOT S! MAGGIN
ART: BOB OKSNER
A TALKING TIGER WHO WEARS COLORFUL CLOTHES? THAT'S UNUSUAL, BUT CAPTAIN MARVEL CAN ACCEPT IT! HOWEVER, IT'S NOT SO EASY FOR HIM TO BELIEVE TAWKY TAWNY'S STORY OF...
"The CELEBRATED TALKING FROG of BLACKSTONE FOREST!"
1

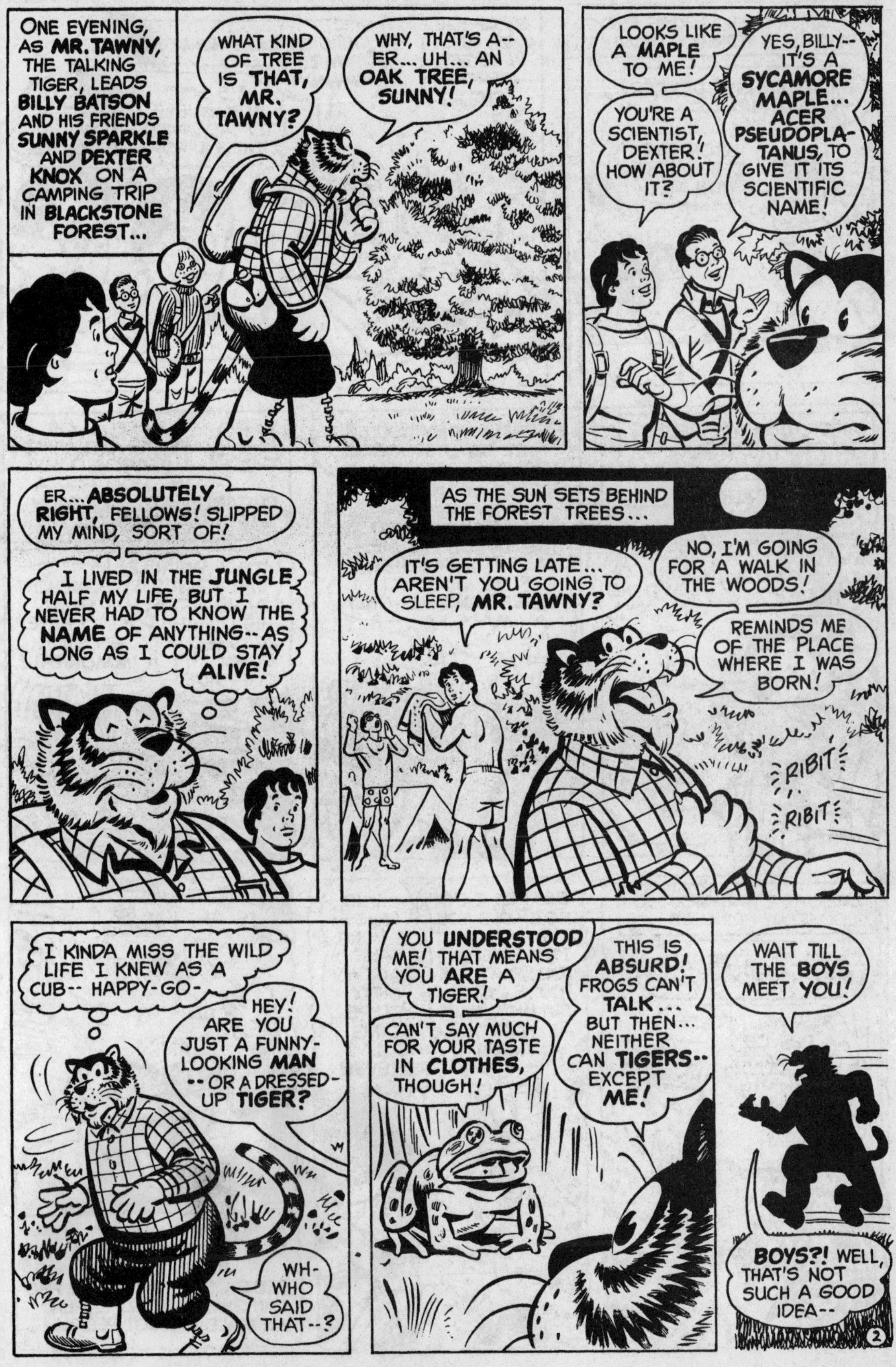
ONE EVENING, AS MR. TAWNY, THE TALKING TIGER, LEADS BILLY BATSON AND HIS FRIENDS SUNNY SPARKLE AND DEXTER KNOX ON A CAMPING TRIP IN BLACKSTONE FOREST...
WHAT KIND OF TREE IS THAT, MR. TAWNY?
WHY, THAT'S A-- ER... UH... AN OAK TREE, SUNNY!
LOOKS LIKE A MAPLE TO ME!
YOU'RE A SCIENTIST, DEXTER! HOW ABOUT IT?
YES, BILLY-- IT'S A SYCAMORE MAPLE... ACER PSEUDOPLATANUS, TO GIVE IT ITS SCIENTIFIC NAME!
ER... ABSOLUTELY RIGHT, FELLOWS! SLIPPED MY MIND, SORT OF!
I LIVED IN THE JUNGLE HALF MY LIFE, BUT I NEVER HAD TO KNOW THE NAME OF ANYTHING--AS LONG AS I COULD STAY ALIVE!
AS THE SUN SETS BEHIND THE FOREST TREES...
IT'S GETTING LATE... AREN'T YOU GOING TO SLEEP, MR. TAWNY?
NO, I'M GOING FOR A WALK IN THE WOODS!
REMINDS ME OF THE PLACE WHERE I WAS BORN!
RIBIT
RIBIT
I KINDA MISS THE WILD LIFE I KNEW AS A CUB-- HAPPY-GO-
HEY! ARE YOU JUST A FUNNY-LOOKING MAN --OR A DRESSED-UP TIGER?
WH-WHO SAID THAT--?
YOU UNDERSTOOD ME! THAT MEANS YOU ARE A TIGER!
CAN'T SAY MUCH FOR YOUR TASTE IN CLOTHES, THOUGH!
THIS IS ABSURD! FROGS CAN'T TALK... BUT THEN... NEITHER CAN TIGERS-- EXCEPT ME!
WAIT TILL THE BOYS MEET YOU!
BOYS?! WELL, THAT'S NOT SUCH A GOOD IDEA--
2

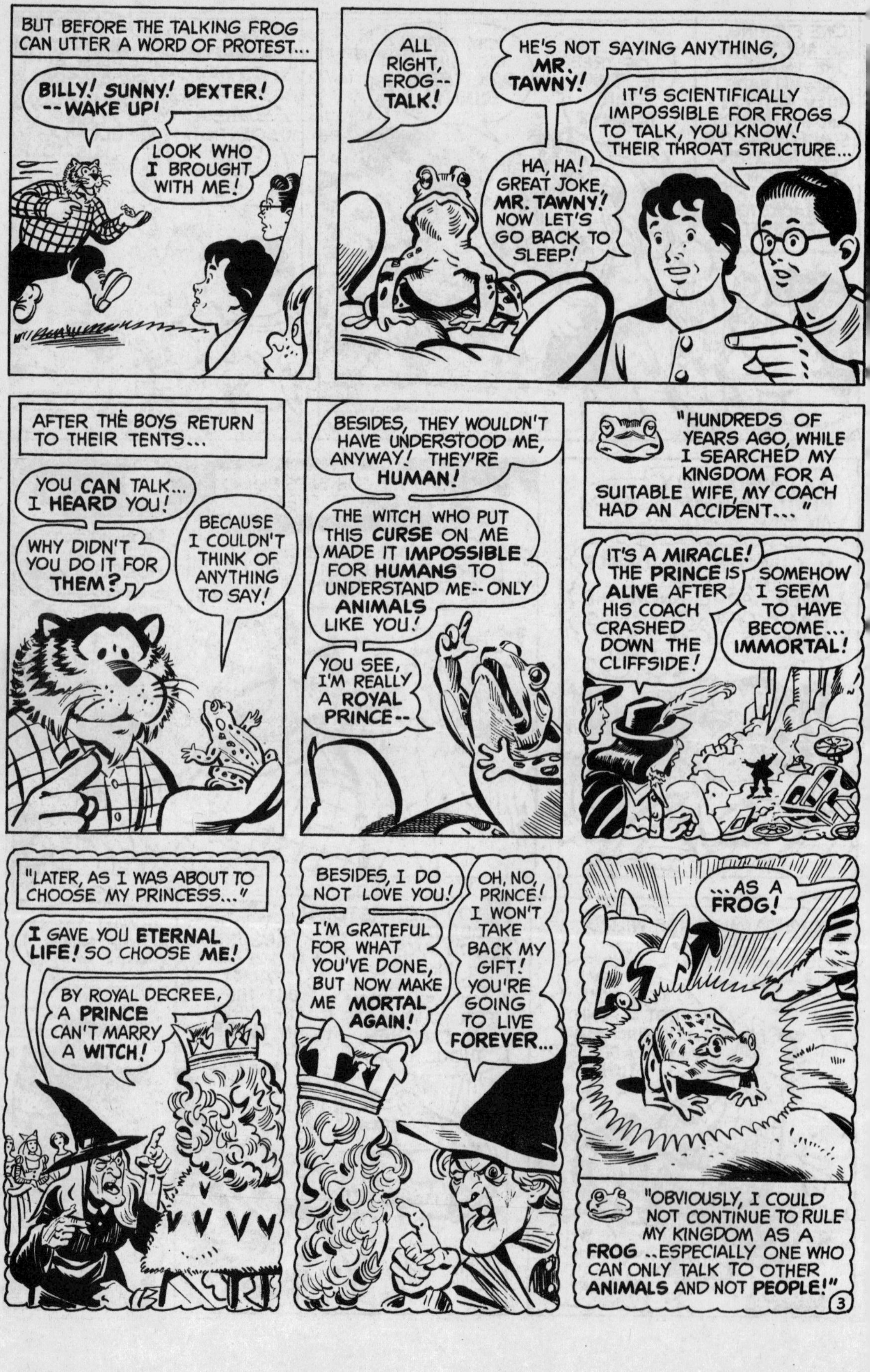
BUT BEFORE THE TALKING FROG CAN UTTER A WORD OF PROTEST...
BILLY! SUNNY! DEXTER! --WAKE UP!
LOOK WHO I BROUGHT WITH ME!
ALL RIGHT, FROG-- TALK!
HE'S NOT SAYING ANYTHING, MR. TAWNY!
IT'S SCIENTIFICALLY IMPOSSIBLE FOR FROGS TO TALK, YOU KNOW! THEIR THROAT STRUCTURE...
HA, HA! GREAT JOKE, MR. TAWNY! NOW LET'S GO BACK TO SLEEP!
AFTER THE BOYS RETURN TO THEIR TENTS...
YOU CAN TALK... I HEARD YOU!
WHY DIDN'T YOU DO IT FOR THEM?
BECAUSE I COULDN'T THINK OF ANYTHING TO SAY!
BESIDES, THEY WOULDN'T HAVE UNDERSTOOD ME, ANYWAY! THEY'RE HUMAN!
THE WITCH WHO PUT THIS CURSE ON ME MADE IT IMPOSSIBLE FOR HUMANS TO UNDERSTAND ME--ONLY ANIMALS LIKE YOU!
YOU SEE, I'M REALLY A ROYAL PRINCE--
"HUNDREDS OF YEARS AGO, WHILE I SEARCHED MY KINGDOM FOR A SUITABLE WIFE, MY COACH HAD AN ACCIDENT..."
IT'S A MIRACLE! THE PRINCE IS ALIVE AFTER HIS COACH CRASHED DOWN THE CLIFFSIDE!
SOMEHOW I SEEM TO HAVE BECOME... IMMORTAL!
"LATER, AS I WAS ABOUT TO CHOOSE MY PRINCESS..."
I GAVE YOU ETERNAL LIFE! SO CHOOSE ME!
BY ROYAL DECREE, A PRINCE CAN'T MARRY A WITCH!
BESIDES, I DO NOT LOVE YOU!
I'M GRATEFUL FOR WHAT YOU'VE DONE, BUT NOW MAKE ME MORTAL AGAIN!
OH, NO, PRINCE! I WON'T TAKE BACK MY GIFT! YOU'RE GOING TO LIVE FOREVER...
...AS A FROG!
"OBVIOUSLY, I COULD NOT CONTINUE TO RULE MY KINGDOM AS A FROG ..ESPECIALLY ONE WHO CAN ONLY TALK TO OTHER ANIMALS AND NOT PEOPLE!"
3

THE NEXT DAY...

I **STILL** DON'T SEE WHY YOU THINK THAT'S A SUPER-SMART FROG!

I HAVE MY REASONS-- AND HOW BETTER TO PROVE IT THAN WITH **DR. KILOWATT?**

DR. THOMAS A. KILOWATT

PHONOGRAPH HILL

IN THE GREAT INVENTOR'S HOME...

BILLY--TAWKY TAWNY--SO **THAT** IS THE FABULOUS FROG!

RIGHT THIS WAY--TO MY **BRAIN·O·METER!**

INTELLIGENCE METER

CHIMPANZEE
GORILLA
LION
DOG
MOUSE
FROG
FISH
CLAM
AMOEBA

EXTRAORDINARY! THE **MERCURY** IS PASSING THE NORMAL INTELLIGENCE LEVEL FOR A FROG... AND I HAVEN'T EVEN CLOSED HIM IN YET!

INTELLIG METE

CHIMPAN
GORILLA
LION
DOG
MOUSE
FROG
FISH
CLAM
AMOEBA

DR. KILOWATT! THE MACHINE IS STARTING TO **BREAK** APART!

THE FROG'S **HIGH INTELLIGENCE** IS OVERLOADING IT--

--IT'LL **EXPLODE** AND THE WHOLE **HOUSE** WITH IT...

HOLY MOLEY! I CAN'T SAVE MR. TAWNY AND DR. KILOWATT-- BUT I KNOW **WHO** CAN!

SHAZAM!

INTELLIGENCE METER

CHIMPANZEE
GORILLA
LION
DOG
MOUSE
FROG
FISH
CLAM
AMOEBA

AND WITH A FLASH OF LIGHT AS SUDDEN AND BRILLIANT AS A TRILLION **FOURTH OF JULYS,** THE BOY NEWSCASTER IS REPLACED BY THE **WORLD'S MIGHTIEST MORTAL** ...

BOOM!

4

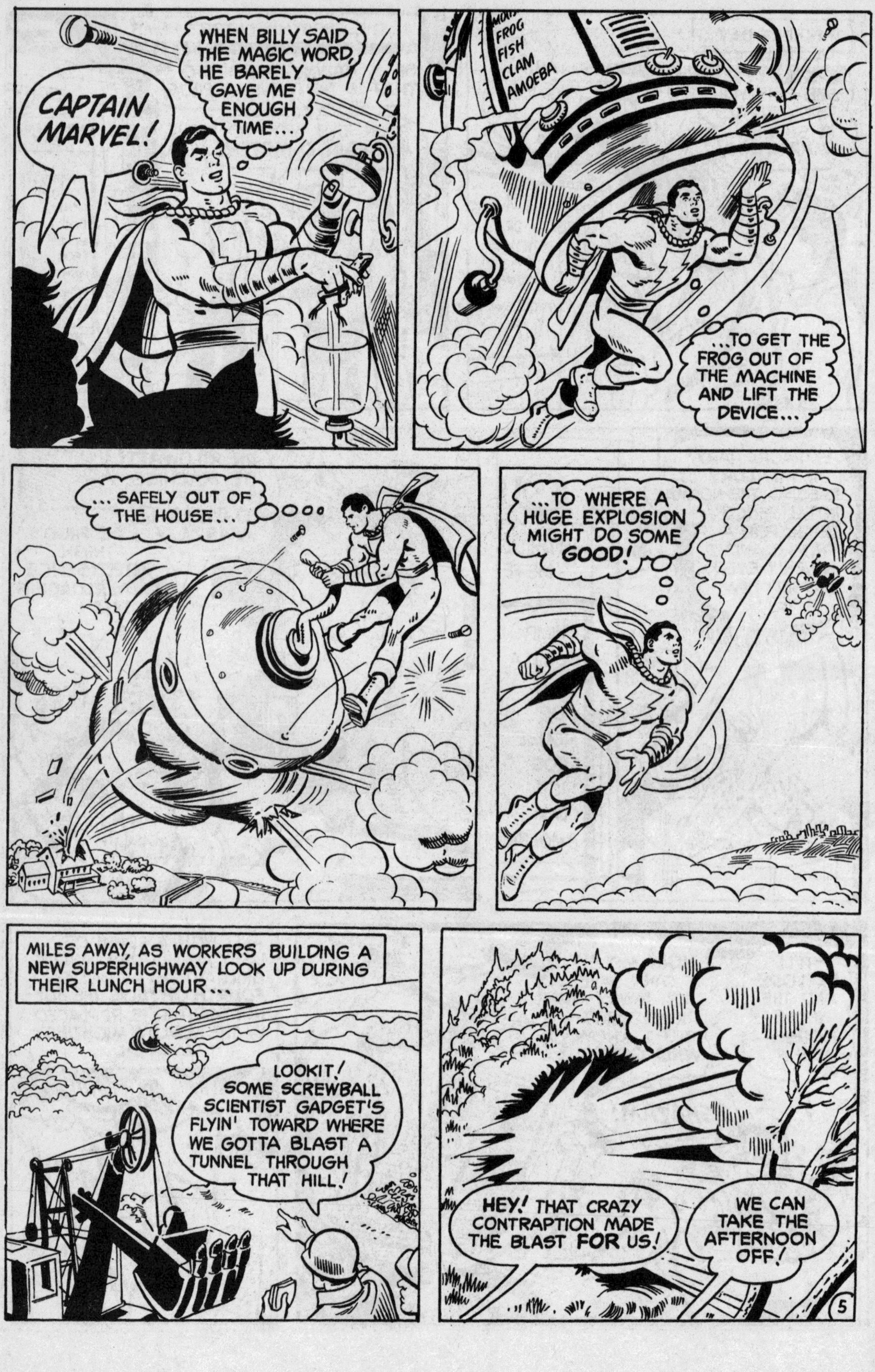
WHEN BILLY SAID THE MAGIC WORD, HE BARELY GAVE ME ENOUGH TIME...
CAPTAIN MARVEL!
FROG
FISH
CLAM
AMOEBA
...TO GET THE FROG OUT OF THE MACHINE AND LIFT THE DEVICE...
... SAFELY OUT OF THE HOUSE...
...TO WHERE A HUGE EXPLOSION MIGHT DO SOME GOOD!
MILES AWAY, AS WORKERS BUILDING A NEW SUPERHIGHWAY LOOK UP DURING THEIR LUNCH HOUR...
LOOKIT! SOME SCREWBALL SCIENTIST GADGET'S FLYIN' TOWARD WHERE WE GOTTA BLAST A TUNNEL THROUGH THAT HILL!
HEY! THAT CRAZY CONTRAPTION MADE THE BLAST FOR US!
WE CAN TAKE THE AFTERNOON OFF!
5

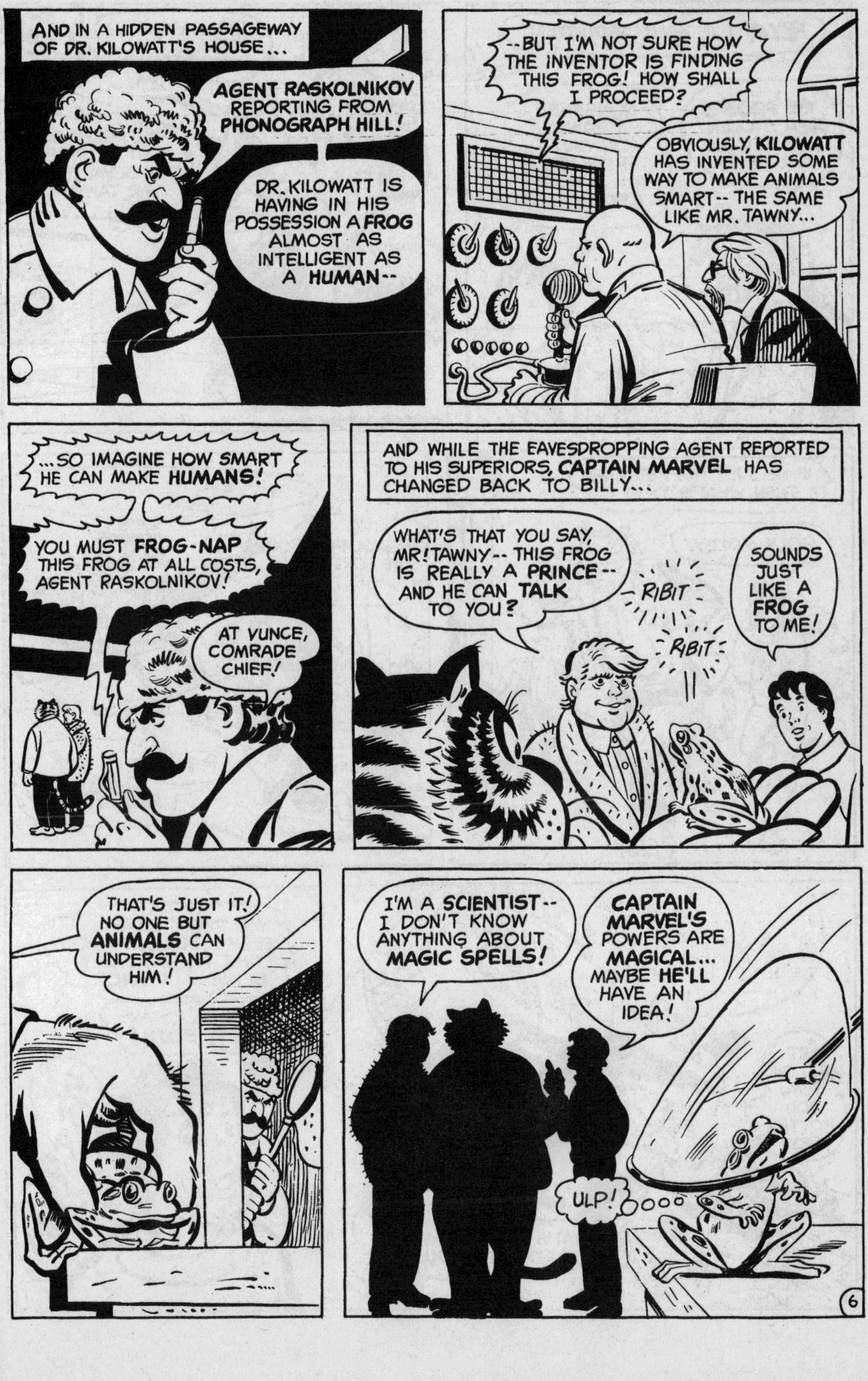
AND IN A HIDDEN PASSAGEWAY OF DR. KILOWATT'S HOUSE...
AGENT RASKOLNIKOV REPORTING FROM PHONOGRAPH HILL!
DR. KILOWATT IS HAVING IN HIS POSSESSION A FROG ALMOST AS INTELLIGENT AS A HUMAN--
--BUT I'M NOT SURE HOW THE INVENTOR IS FINDING THIS FROG! HOW SHALL I PROCEED?
OBVIOUSLY, KILOWATT HAS INVENTED SOME WAY TO MAKE ANIMALS SMART-- THE SAME LIKE MR. TAWNY...
...SO IMAGINE HOW SMART HE CAN MAKE HUMANS!
YOU MUST FROG-NAP THIS FROG AT ALL COSTS, AGENT RASKOLNIKOV!
AT VUNCE, COMRADE CHIEF!
AND WHILE THE EAVESDROPPING AGENT REPORTED TO HIS SUPERIORS, CAPTAIN MARVEL HAS CHANGED BACK TO BILLY...
WHAT'S THAT YOU SAY, MR. TAWNY-- THIS FROG IS REALLY A PRINCE-- AND HE CAN TALK TO YOU?
RIBIT
RIBIT
SOUNDS JUST LIKE A FROG TO ME!
THAT'S JUST IT! NO ONE BUT ANIMALS CAN UNDERSTAND HIM!
I'M A SCIENTIST-- I DON'T KNOW ANYTHING ABOUT MAGIC SPELLS!
CAPTAIN MARVEL'S POWERS ARE MAGICAL... MAYBE HE'LL HAVE AN IDEA!
ULP!
6

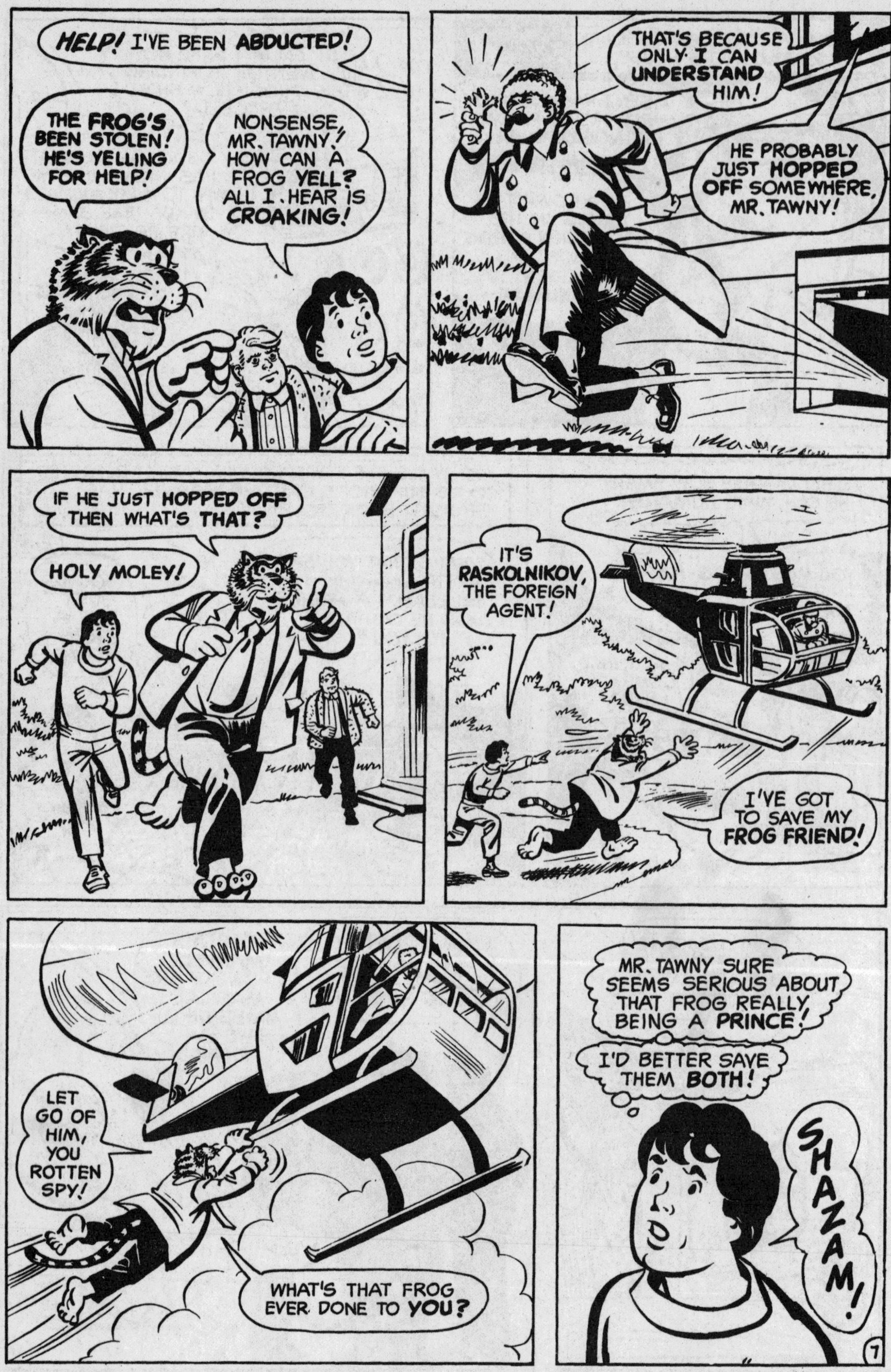
HELP! I'VE BEEN ABDUCTED!
THE FROG'S BEEN STOLEN! HE'S YELLING FOR HELP!
NONSENSE, MR. TAWNY! HOW CAN A FROG YELL? ALL I. HEAR IS CROAKING!
THAT'S BECAUSE ONLY I CAN UNDERSTAND HIM!
HE PROBABLY JUST HOPPED OFF SOMEWHERE, MR. TAWNY!
IF HE JUST HOPPED OFF THEN WHAT'S THAT?
HOLY MOLEY!
IT'S RASKOLNIKOV, THE FOREIGN AGENT!
I'VE GOT TO SAVE MY FROG FRIEND!
LET GO OF HIM, YOU ROTTEN SPY!
WHAT'S THAT FROG EVER DONE TO YOU?
MR. TAWNY SURE SEEMS SERIOUS ABOUT THAT FROG REALLY BEING A PRINCE!
I'D BETTER SAVE THEM BOTH!
SHAZAM!
7

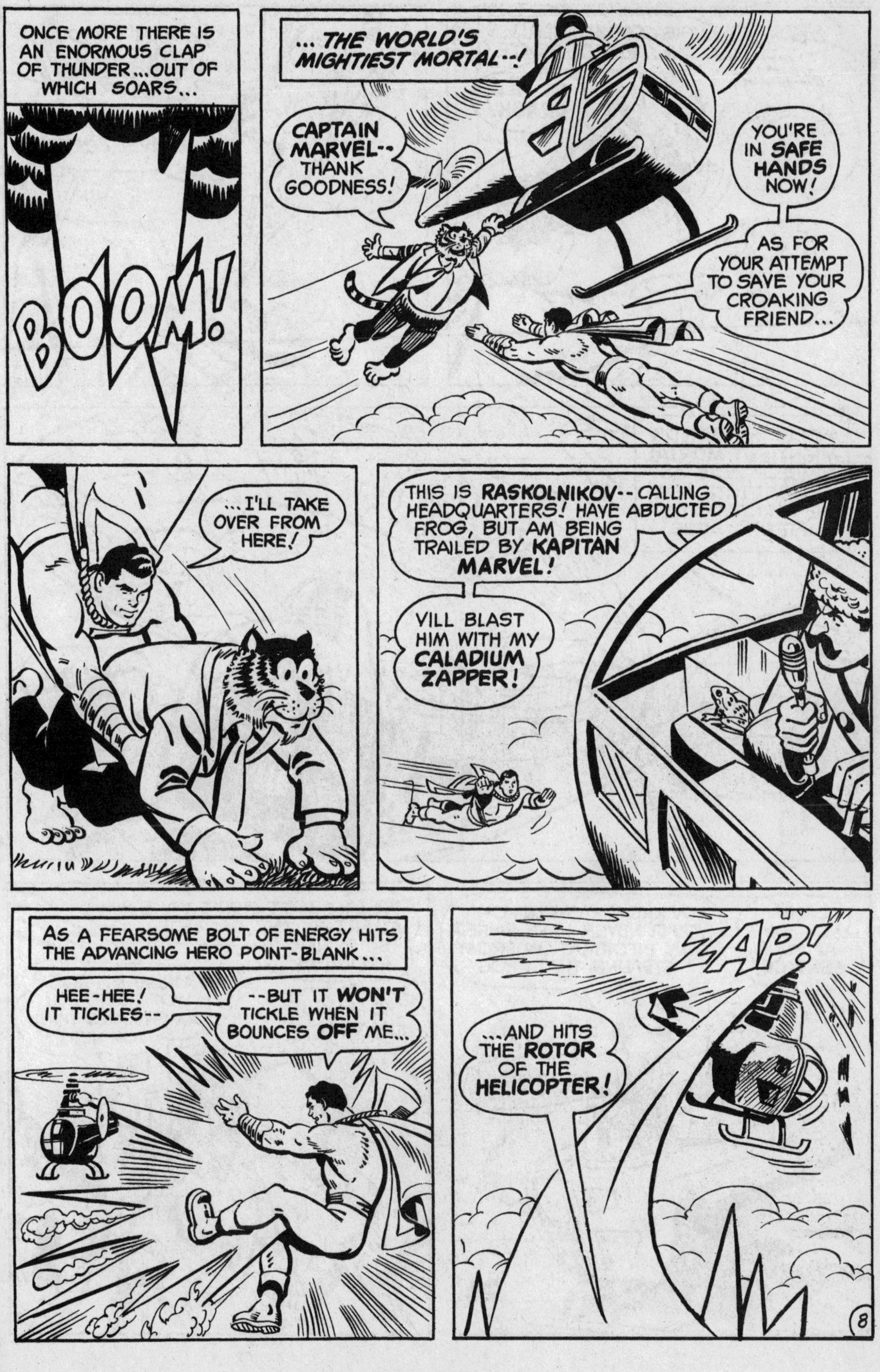
ONCE MORE THERE IS AN ENORMOUS CLAP OF THUNDER...OUT OF WHICH SOARS...
BOOM!
...THE WORLD'S MIGHTIEST MORTAL--!
CAPTAIN MARVEL-- THANK GOODNESS!
YOU'RE IN SAFE HANDS NOW!
AS FOR YOUR ATTEMPT TO SAVE YOUR CROAKING FRIEND...
...I'LL TAKE OVER FROM HERE!
THIS IS RASKOLNIKOV--CALLING HEADQUARTERS! HAVE ABDUCTED FROG, BUT AM BEING TRAILED BY KAPITAN MARVEL!
VILL BLAST HIM WITH MY CALADIUM ZAPPER!
AS A FEARSOME BOLT OF ENERGY HITS THE ADVANCING HERO POINT-BLANK...
HEE-HEE! IT TICKLES--
--BUT IT WON'T TICKLE WHEN IT BOUNCES OFF ME...
ZAP!
...AND HITS THE ROTOR OF THE HELICOPTER!
8

RIBIT

THE **COPTER BLADES** -- THEY **DISINTEGRATE!**

VE VILL **CRASH!**

WHAT DO YOU WANT WITH THAT **METAL ROTOR**... WHEN YOU CAN HAVE A **MARVEL-COPTER?**

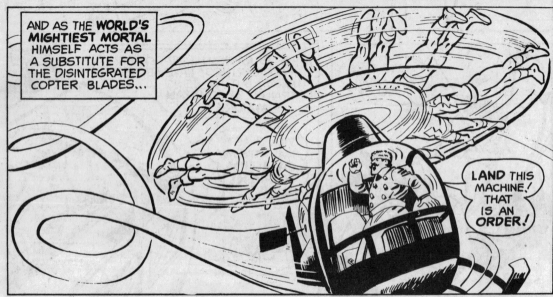

AND AS THE **WORLD'S MIGHTIEST MORTAL** HIMSELF ACTS AS A SUBSTITUTE FOR THE DISINTEGRATED COPTER BLADES...

LAND THIS MACHINE! THAT IS AN **ORDER!**

LAND, YOU SAY? AT YOUR **SERVICE!**

YOU KNOW, RASKOLNIKOV -- YOU'D NEVER HAVE GAINED ANY INFORMATION FROM STEALING THAT FROG!

DR. KILOWATT DIDN'T MAKE HIM SMART BY ANY SECRET SCIENTIFIC PROCESS!

THE FROG IS **HUMAN!**

A HUMAN FROG? VOT VON'T YOU **AMERICANS** THINK OF NEXT!

9

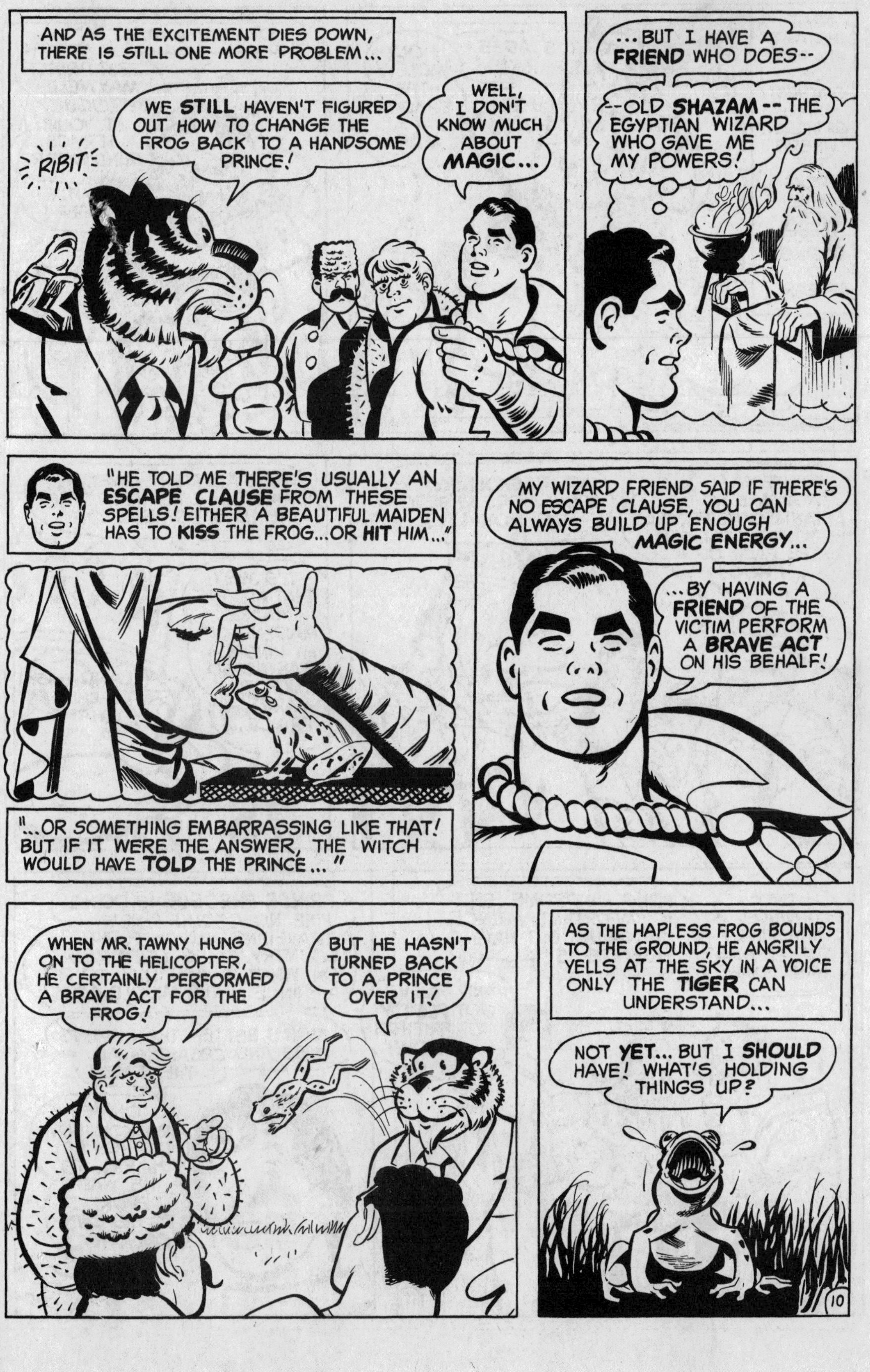
AND AS THE EXCITEMENT DIES DOWN, THERE IS STILL ONE MORE PROBLEM...
RIBIT
WE STILL HAVEN'T FIGURED OUT HOW TO CHANGE THE FROG BACK TO A HANDSOME PRINCE!
WELL, I DON'T KNOW MUCH ABOUT MAGIC...
...BUT I HAVE A FRIEND WHO DOES--
--OLD SHAZAM -- THE EGYPTIAN WIZARD WHO GAVE ME MY POWERS!
"HE TOLD ME THERE'S USUALLY AN ESCAPE CLAUSE FROM THESE SPELLS! EITHER A BEAUTIFUL MAIDEN HAS TO KISS THE FROG...OR HIT HIM..."
"...OR SOMETHING EMBARRASSING LIKE THAT! BUT IF IT WERE THE ANSWER, THE WITCH WOULD HAVE TOLD THE PRINCE..."
MY WIZARD FRIEND SAID IF THERE'S NO ESCAPE CLAUSE, YOU CAN ALWAYS BUILD UP ENOUGH MAGIC ENERGY...
...BY HAVING A FRIEND OF THE VICTIM PERFORM A BRAVE ACT ON HIS BEHALF!
WHEN MR. TAWNY HUNG ON TO THE HELICOPTER, HE CERTAINLY PERFORMED A BRAVE ACT FOR THE FROG!
BUT HE HASN'T TURNED BACK TO A PRINCE OVER IT!
AS THE HAPLESS FROG BOUNDS TO THE GROUND, HE ANGRILY YELLS AT THE SKY IN A VOICE ONLY THE TIGER CAN UNDERSTAND...
NOT YET... BUT I SHOULD HAVE! WHAT'S HOLDING THINGS UP?
10

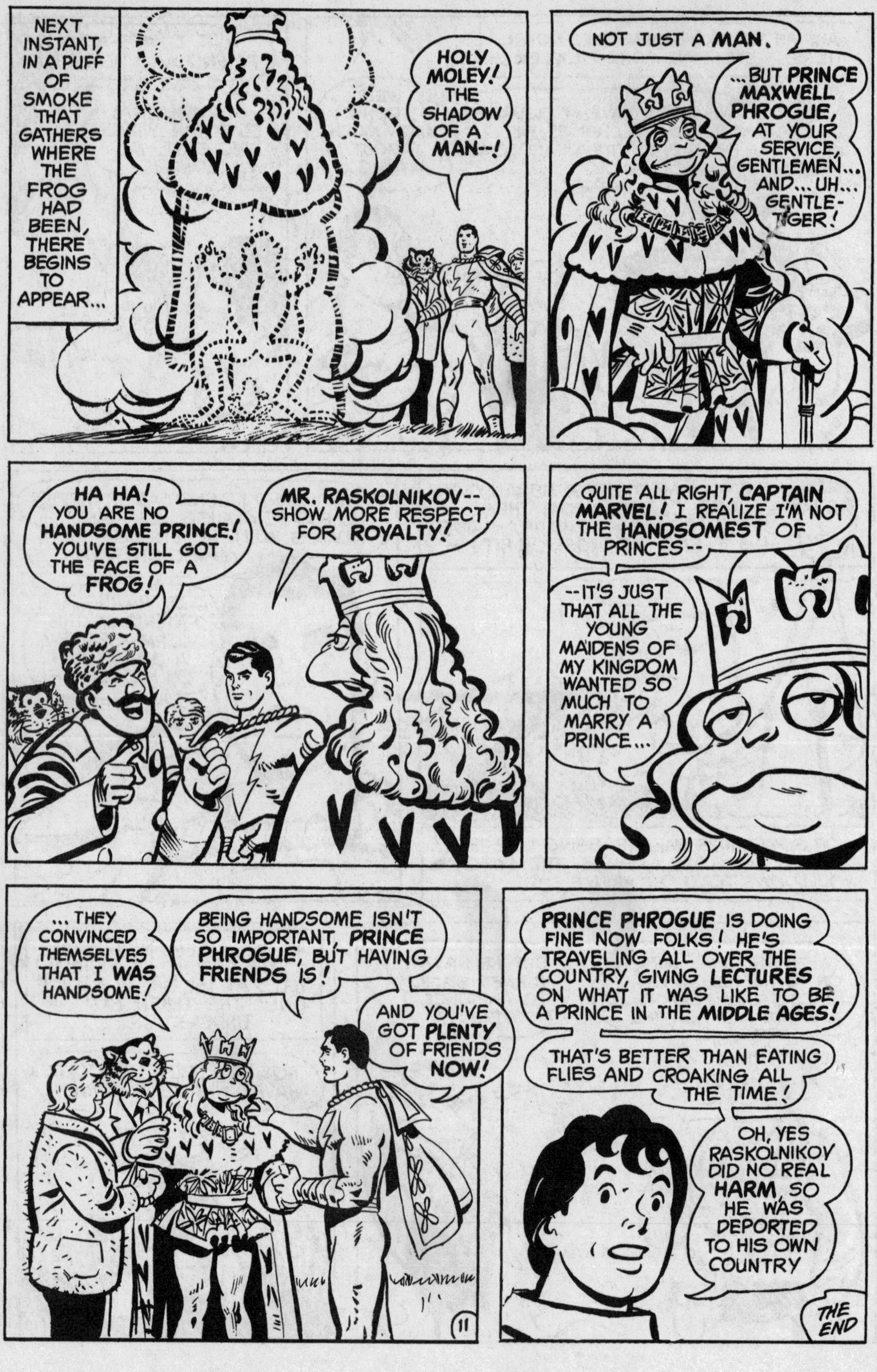
NEXT INSTANT, IN A PUFF OF SMOKE THAT GATHERS WHERE THE FROG HAD BEEN, THERE BEGINS TO APPEAR...
HOLY MOLEY! THE SHADOW OF A MAN--!
NOT JUST A MAN.
...BUT PRINCE MAXWELL PHROGUE, AT YOUR SERVICE, GENTLEMEN... AND... UH... GENTLE-TIGER!
HA HA! YOU ARE NO HANDSOME PRINCE! YOU'VE STILL GOT THE FACE OF A FROG!
MR. RASKOLNIKOV-- SHOW MORE RESPECT FOR ROYALTY!
QUITE ALL RIGHT, CAPTAIN MARVEL! I REALIZE I'M NOT THE HANDSOMEST OF PRINCES--
--IT'S JUST THAT ALL THE YOUNG MAIDENS OF MY KINGDOM WANTED SO MUCH TO MARRY A PRINCE...
...THEY CONVINCED THEMSELVES THAT I WAS HANDSOME!
BEING HANDSOME ISN'T SO IMPORTANT, PRINCE PHROGUE, BUT HAVING FRIENDS IS!
AND YOU'VE GOT PLENTY OF FRIENDS NOW!
11
PRINCE PHROGUE IS DOING FINE NOW FOLKS! HE'S TRAVELING ALL OVER THE COUNTRY, GIVING LECTURES ON WHAT IT WAS LIKE TO BE A PRINCE IN THE MIDDLE AGES!
THAT'S BETTER THAN EATING FLIES AND CROAKING ALL THE TIME!
OH, YES RASKOLNIKOV DID NO REAL HARM, SO HE WAS DEPORTED TO HIS OWN COUNTRY
THE END

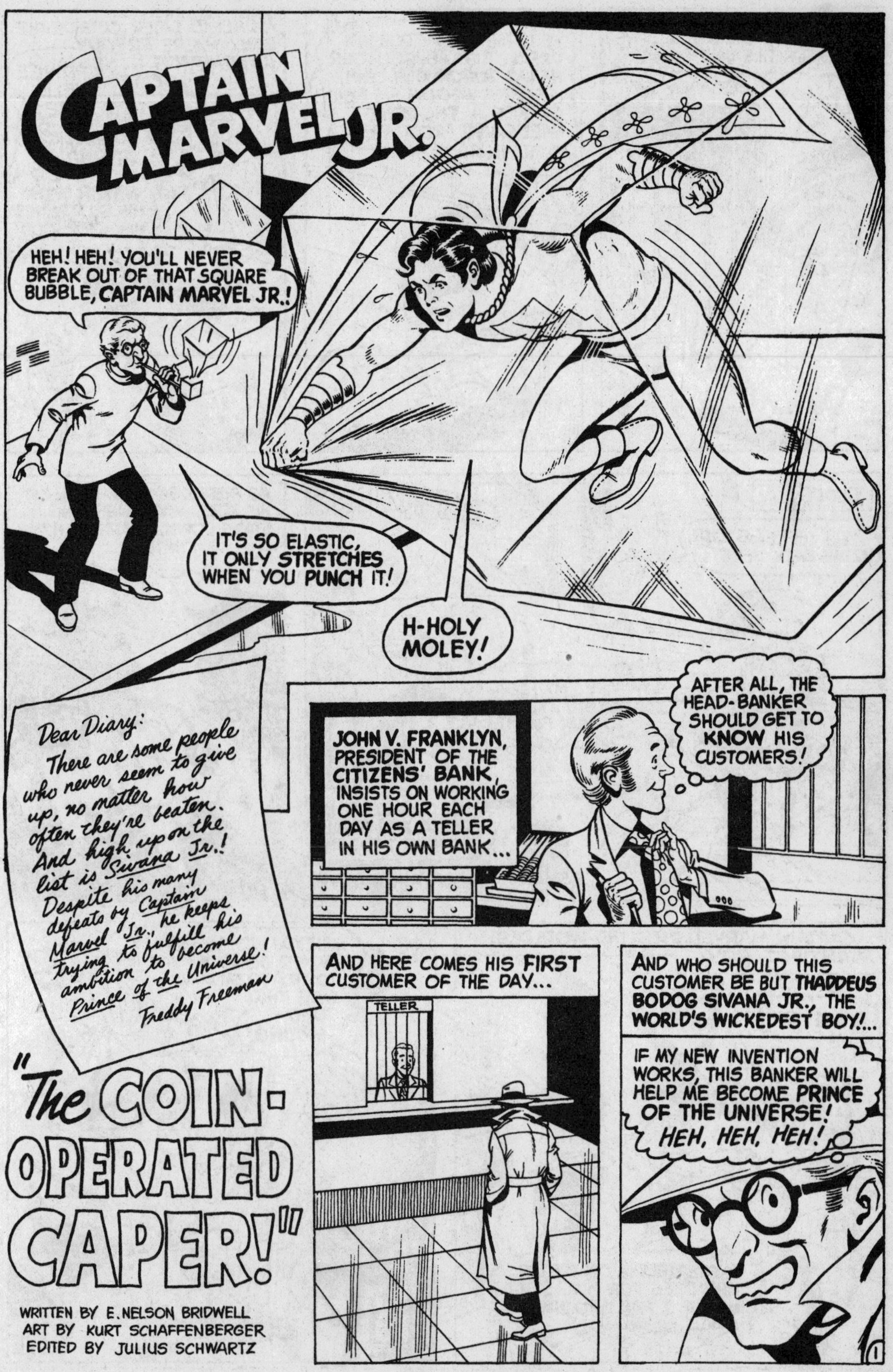
CAPTAIN MARVEL JR.
HEH! HEH! YOU'LL NEVER BREAK OUT OF THAT SQUARE BUBBLE, CAPTAIN MARVEL JR.!
IT'S SO ELASTIC, IT ONLY STRETCHES WHEN YOU PUNCH IT!
H-HOLY MOLEY!
Dear Diary: There are some people who never seem to give up, no matter how often they're beaten. And high up on the list is Sivana Jr.! Despite his many defeats by Captain Marvel Jr., he keeps trying to fulfill his ambition to become Prince of the Universe! Freddy Freeman
"The COIN-OPERATED CAPER!"
WRITTEN BY E. NELSON BRIDWELL
ART BY KURT SCHAFFENBERGER
EDITED BY JULIUS SCHWARTZ
JOHN V. FRANKLYN, PRESIDENT OF THE CITIZENS' BANK, INSISTS ON WORKING ONE HOUR EACH DAY AS A TELLER IN HIS OWN BANK...
AFTER ALL, THE HEAD-BANKER SHOULD GET TO KNOW HIS CUSTOMERS!
AND HERE COMES HIS FIRST CUSTOMER OF THE DAY...
TELLER
AND WHO SHOULD THIS CUSTOMER BE BUT THADDEUS BODOG SIVANA JR., THE WORLD'S WICKEDEST BOY!...
IF MY NEW INVENTION WORKS, THIS BANKER WILL HELP ME BECOME PRINCE OF THE UNIVERSE! HEH, HEH, HEH!
1

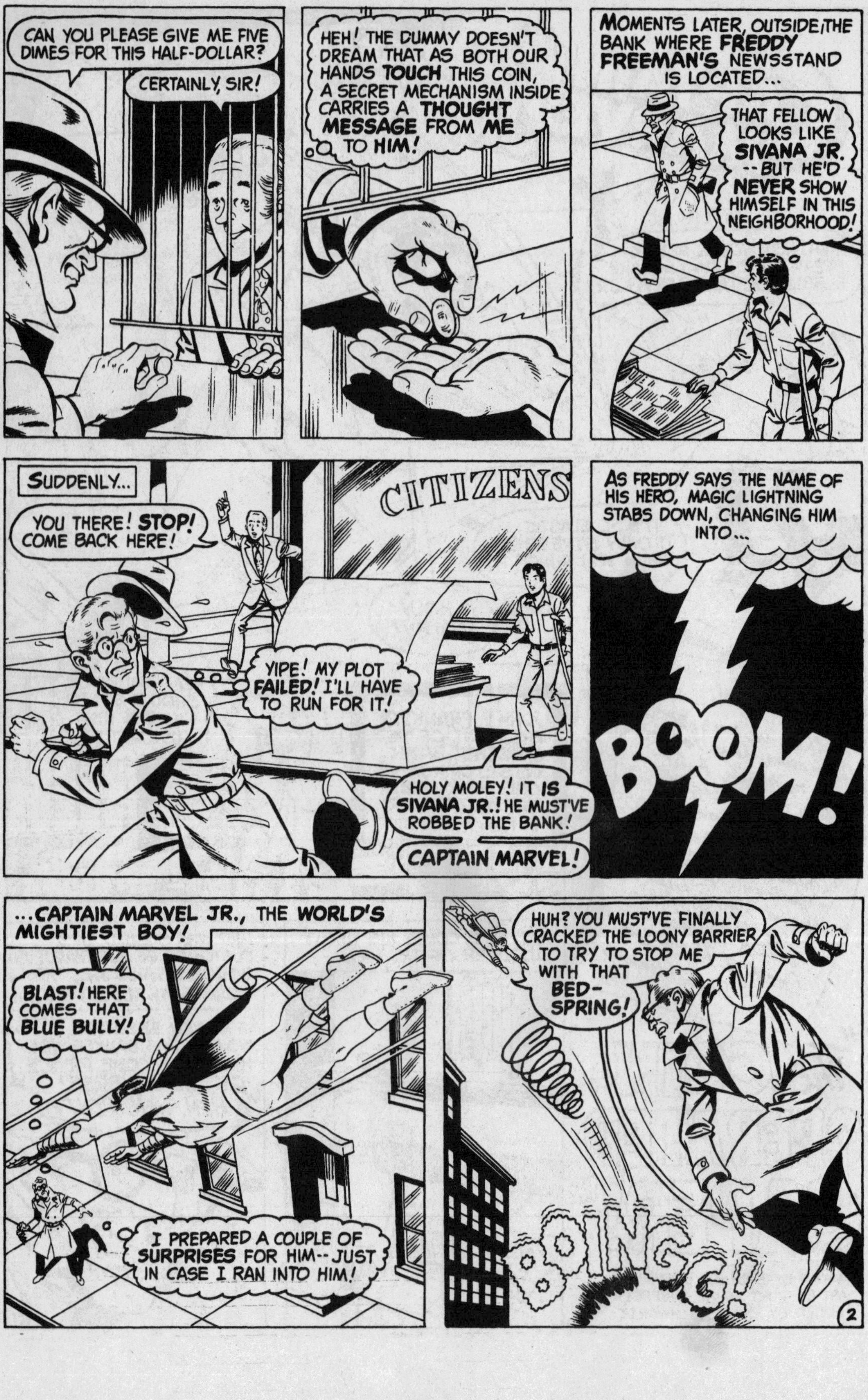

CAN YOU PLEASE GIVE ME FIVE DIMES FOR THIS HALF-DOLLAR?
CERTAINLY, SIR!
HEH! THE DUMMY DOESN'T DREAM THAT AS BOTH OUR HANDS TOUCH THIS COIN, A SECRET MECHANISM INSIDE CARRIES A THOUGHT MESSAGE FROM ME TO HIM!
MOMENTS LATER, OUTSIDE THE BANK WHERE FREDDY FREEMAN'S NEWSSTAND IS LOCATED...
THAT FELLOW LOOKS LIKE SIVANA JR. --BUT HE'D NEVER SHOW HIMSELF IN THIS NEIGHBORHOOD!
SUDDENLY...
CITIZENS
YOU THERE! STOP! COME BACK HERE!
YIPE! MY PLOT FAILED! I'LL HAVE TO RUN FOR IT!
HOLY MOLEY! IT IS SIVANA JR.! HE MUST'VE ROBBED THE BANK!
CAPTAIN MARVEL!
AS FREDDY SAYS THE NAME OF HIS HERO, MAGIC LIGHTNING STABS DOWN, CHANGING HIM INTO...
BOOM!
...CAPTAIN MARVEL JR., THE WORLD'S MIGHTIEST BOY!
BLAST! HERE COMES THAT BLUE BULLY!
I PREPARED A COUPLE OF SURPRISES FOR HIM--JUST IN CASE I RAN INTO HIM!
HUH? YOU MUST'VE FINALLY CRACKED THE LOONY BARRIER TO TRY TO STOP ME WITH THAT BED-SPRING!
BOINGG!
2

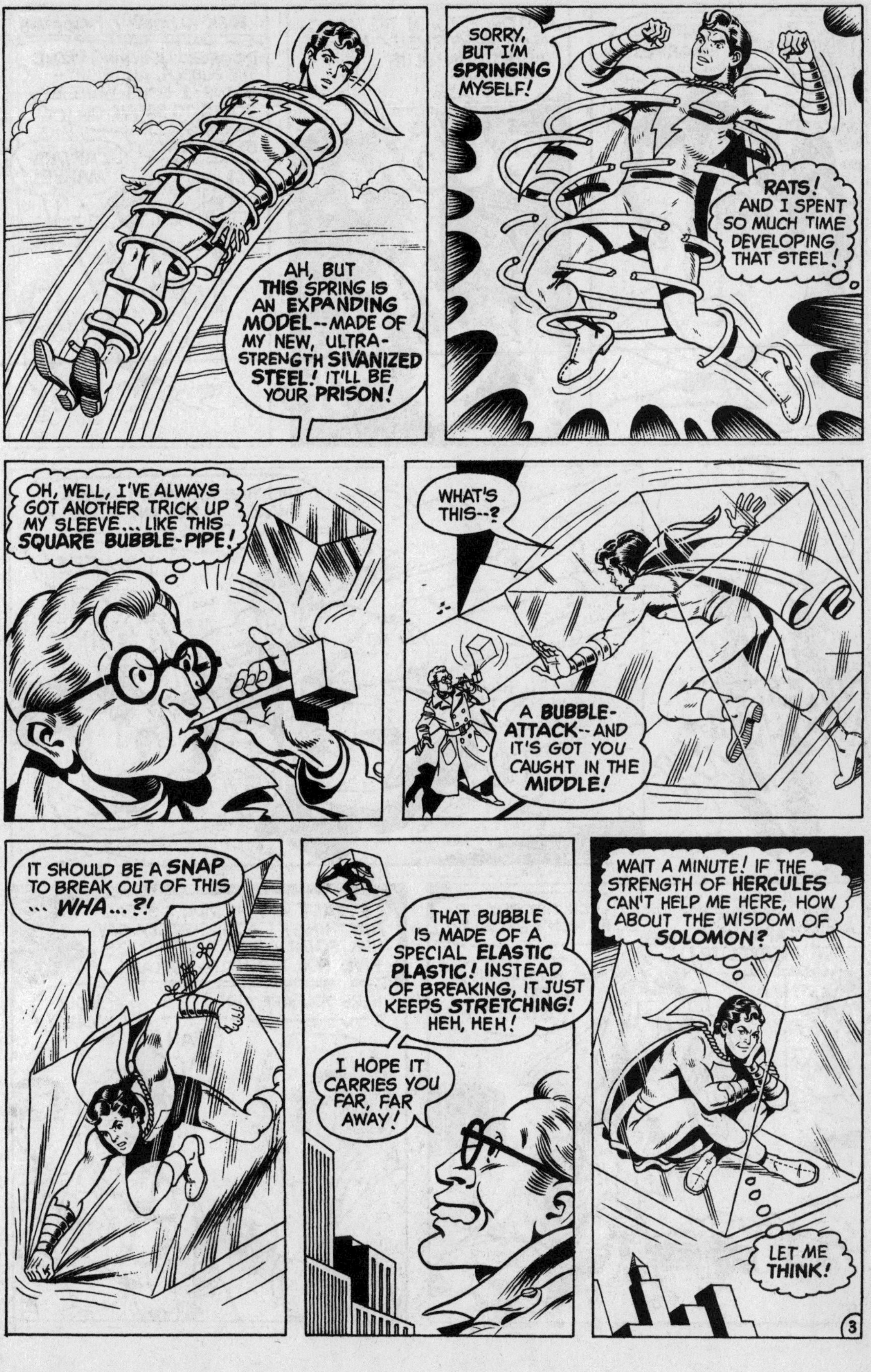
AH, BUT THIS SPRING IS AN EXPANDING MODEL--MADE OF MY NEW, ULTRA-STRENGTH SIVANIZED STEEL! IT'LL BE YOUR PRISON!
SORRY, BUT I'M SPRINGING MYSELF!
RATS! AND I SPENT SO MUCH TIME DEVELOPING THAT STEEL!
OH, WELL, I'VE ALWAYS GOT ANOTHER TRICK UP MY SLEEVE... LIKE THIS SQUARE BUBBLE-PIPE!
WHAT'S THIS--?
A BUBBLE-ATTACK--AND IT'S GOT YOU CAUGHT IN THE MIDDLE!
IT SHOULD BE A SNAP TO BREAK OUT OF THIS ... WHA...?!
THAT BUBBLE IS MADE OF A SPECIAL ELASTIC PLASTIC! INSTEAD OF BREAKING, IT JUST KEEPS STRETCHING! HEH, HEH!
I HOPE IT CARRIES YOU FAR, FAR AWAY!
WAIT A MINUTE! IF THE STRENGTH OF HERCULES CAN'T HELP ME HERE, HOW ABOUT THE WISDOM OF SOLOMON?
LET ME THINK!
3

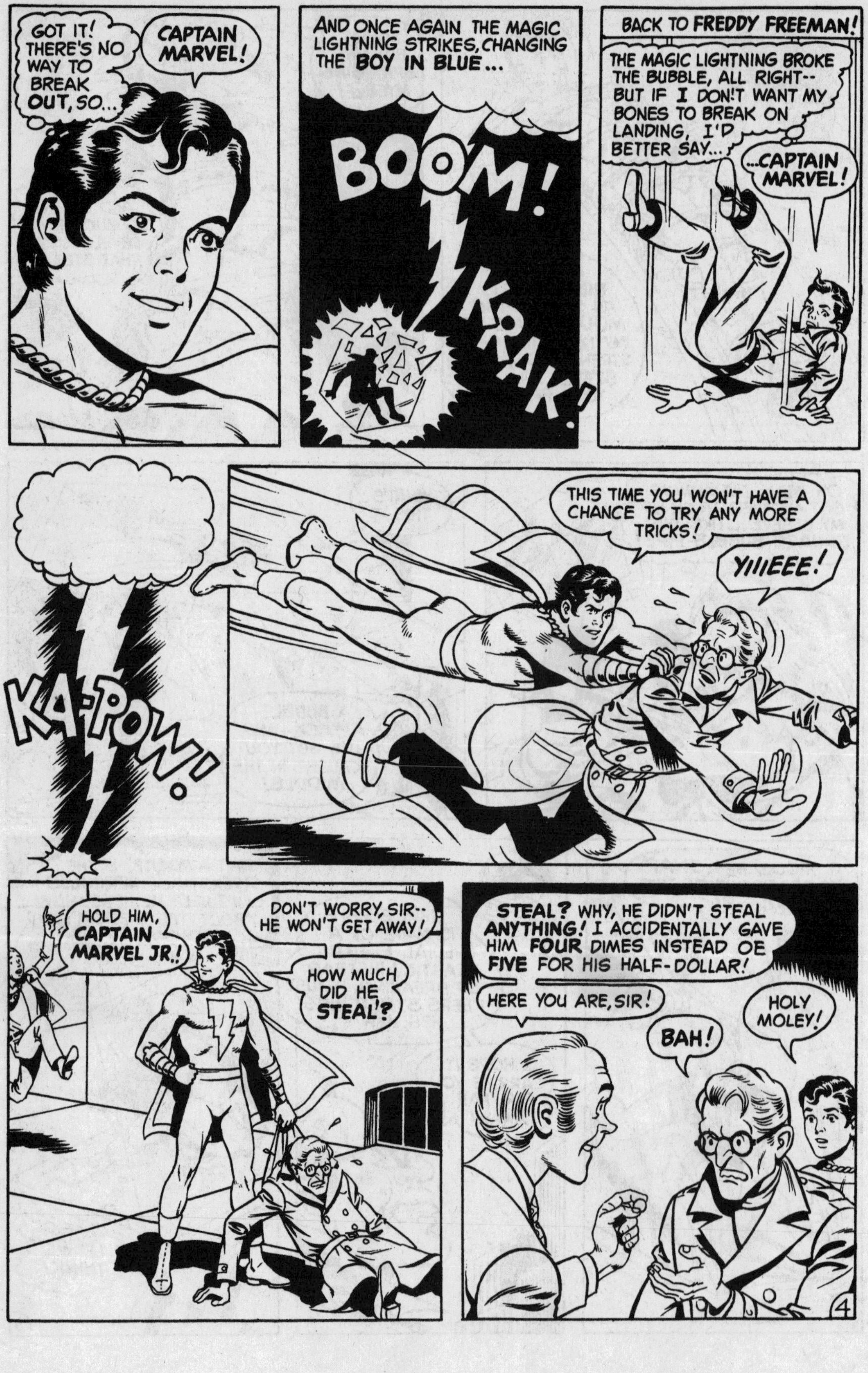
GOT IT! THERE'S NO WAY TO BREAK OUT, SO...
CAPTAIN MARVEL!
AND ONCE AGAIN THE MAGIC LIGHTNING STRIKES, CHANGING THE BOY IN BLUE...
BOOM!
KRAK!
BACK TO FREDDY FREEMAN!
THE MAGIC LIGHTNING BROKE THE BUBBLE, ALL RIGHT-- BUT IF I DON'T WANT MY BONES TO BREAK ON LANDING, I'D BETTER SAY...
...CAPTAIN MARVEL!
KA-POW!
THIS TIME YOU WON'T HAVE A CHANCE TO TRY ANY MORE TRICKS!
YIIIEEE!
HOLD HIM, CAPTAIN MARVEL JR.!
DON'T WORRY, SIR-- HE WON'T GET AWAY!
HOW MUCH DID HE STEAL?
STEAL? WHY, HE DIDN'T STEAL ANYTHING! I ACCIDENTALLY GAVE HIM FOUR DIMES INSTEAD OF FIVE FOR HIS HALF-DOLLAR!
HERE YOU ARE, SIR!
BAH!
HOLY MOLEY!
4

HOW ABOUT THAT? I HAVE TO CHASE **SIVANA JR.** TO LET SOMEONE **GIVE** HIM MONEY! AND HE LOOKS **ANGRY** ABOUT IT!

HMMPFF! IF THE **MIND-CONTROL DEVICE** IN MY HALF-DOLLAR HAD WORKED PROPERLY, THAT BANKER WOULD NEVER HAVE BEEN ABLE TO CORRECT HIS ERROR!

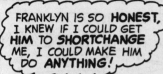

FRANKLYN IS SO **HONEST,** I KNEW IF I COULD GET **HIM** TO **SHORTCHANGE** ME, I COULD MAKE HIM DO **ANYTHING!**

BUT THE EFFECT WORE OFF ALMOST IMMEDIATELY! I MUST IMPROVE THE MECHANISM!

AND WHEN I DO, I'LL SEE TO IT THAT **CAPTAIN MARVEL JR.** NEVER INTERFERES WITH MY SCHEMES AGAIN!

NEXT DAY, AT FREDDY'S NEWSSTAND...

GIVE ME A PAPER, PLEASE!

YES, SIR! I....

HOLY MOLEY! SIVANA JR. AGAIN!

CAP... CAP...

HEH, HEH! YOU TRYING TO SAY **SOMETHING?**

CA... CAP... C-C-CAP...

TRY ALL YOU LIKE -- BUT YOU'LL **NEVER SAY YOUR MAGIC WORDS AGAIN!**

5

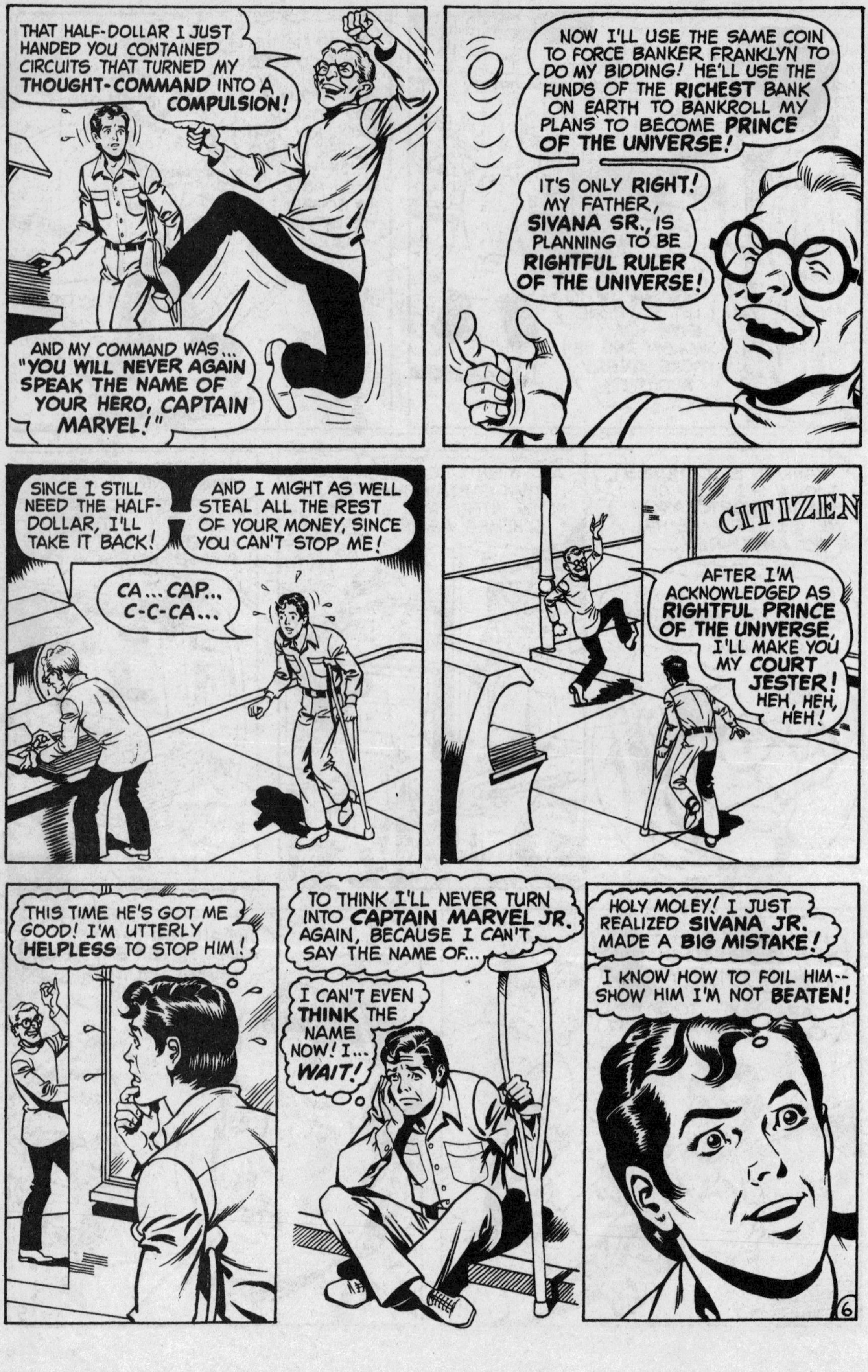
THAT HALF-DOLLAR I JUST HANDED YOU CONTAINED CIRCUITS THAT TURNED MY THOUGHT-COMMAND INTO A COMPULSION!
AND MY COMMAND WAS... "YOU WILL NEVER AGAIN SPEAK THE NAME OF YOUR HERO, CAPTAIN MARVEL!"
NOW I'LL USE THE SAME COIN TO FORCE BANKER FRANKLYN TO DO MY BIDDING! HE'LL USE THE FUNDS OF THE RICHEST BANK ON EARTH TO BANKROLL MY PLANS TO BECOME PRINCE OF THE UNIVERSE!
IT'S ONLY RIGHT! MY FATHER, SIVANA SR., IS PLANNING TO BE RIGHTFUL RULER OF THE UNIVERSE!
SINCE I STILL NEED THE HALF-DOLLAR, I'LL TAKE IT BACK!
AND I MIGHT AS WELL STEAL ALL THE REST OF YOUR MONEY, SINCE YOU CAN'T STOP ME!
CA... CAP... C-C-CA...
CITIZEN
AFTER I'M ACKNOWLEDGED AS RIGHTFUL PRINCE OF THE UNIVERSE, I'LL MAKE YOU MY COURT JESTER! HEH, HEH, HEH!
THIS TIME HE'S GOT ME GOOD! I'M UTTERLY HELPLESS TO STOP HIM!
TO THINK I'LL NEVER TURN INTO CAPTAIN MARVEL JR. AGAIN, BECAUSE I CAN'T SAY THE NAME OF...
I CAN'T EVEN THINK THE NAME NOW! I... WAIT!
HOLY MOLEY! I JUST REALIZED SIVANA JR. MADE A BIG MISTAKE!
I KNOW HOW TO FOIL HIM--SHOW HIM I'M NOT BEATEN!
6

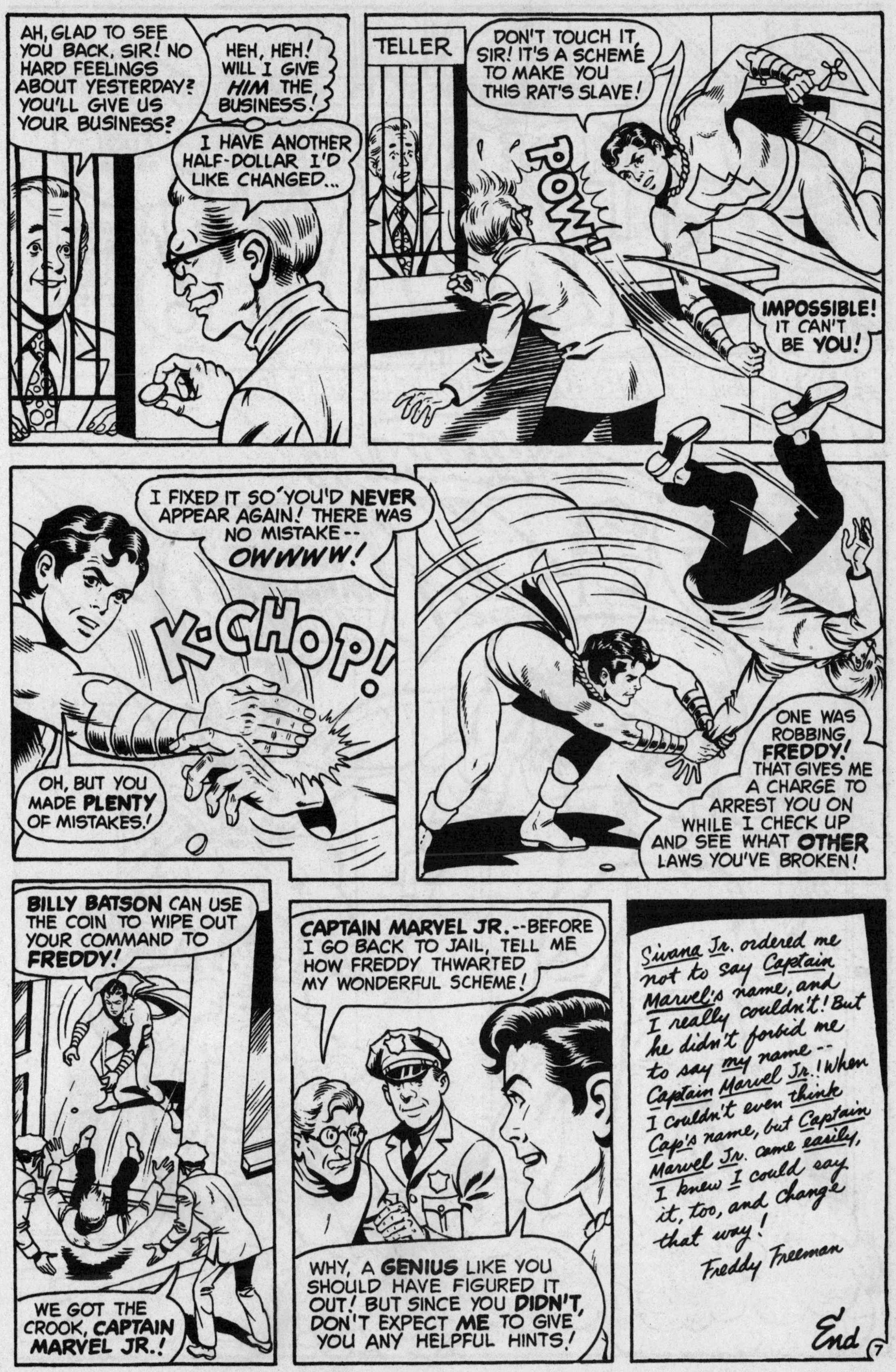
AH, GLAD TO SEE YOU BACK, SIR! NO HARD FEELINGS ABOUT YESTERDAY? YOU'LL GIVE US YOUR BUSINESS?
HEH, HEH! WILL I GIVE HIM THE BUSINESS!
I HAVE ANOTHER HALF-DOLLAR I'D LIKE CHANGED...
TELLER
DON'T TOUCH IT, SIR! IT'S A SCHEME TO MAKE YOU THIS RAT'S SLAVE!
POW!
IMPOSSIBLE! IT CAN'T BE YOU!
I FIXED IT SO YOU'D NEVER APPEAR AGAIN! THERE WAS NO MISTAKE-- OWWWW!
K-CHOP!
OH, BUT YOU MADE PLENTY OF MISTAKES!
ONE WAS ROBBING FREDDY! THAT GIVES ME A CHARGE TO ARREST YOU ON WHILE I CHECK UP AND SEE WHAT OTHER LAWS YOU'VE BROKEN!
BILLY BATSON CAN USE THE COIN TO WIPE OUT YOUR COMMAND TO FREDDY!
WE GOT THE CROOK, CAPTAIN MARVEL JR.!
CAPTAIN MARVEL JR.--BEFORE I GO BACK TO JAIL, TELL ME HOW FREDDY THWARTED MY WONDERFUL SCHEME!
WHY, A GENIUS LIKE YOU SHOULD HAVE FIGURED IT OUT! BUT SINCE YOU DIDN'T, DON'T EXPECT ME TO GIVE YOU ANY HELPFUL HINTS!
Sivana Jr. ordered me not to say Captain Marvel's name, and I really couldn't! But he didn't forbid me to say my name -- Captain Marvel Jr.! When I couldn't even think Cap's name, but Captain Marvel Jr. came easily, I knew I could say it, too, and change that way!
Freddy Freeman
End
7

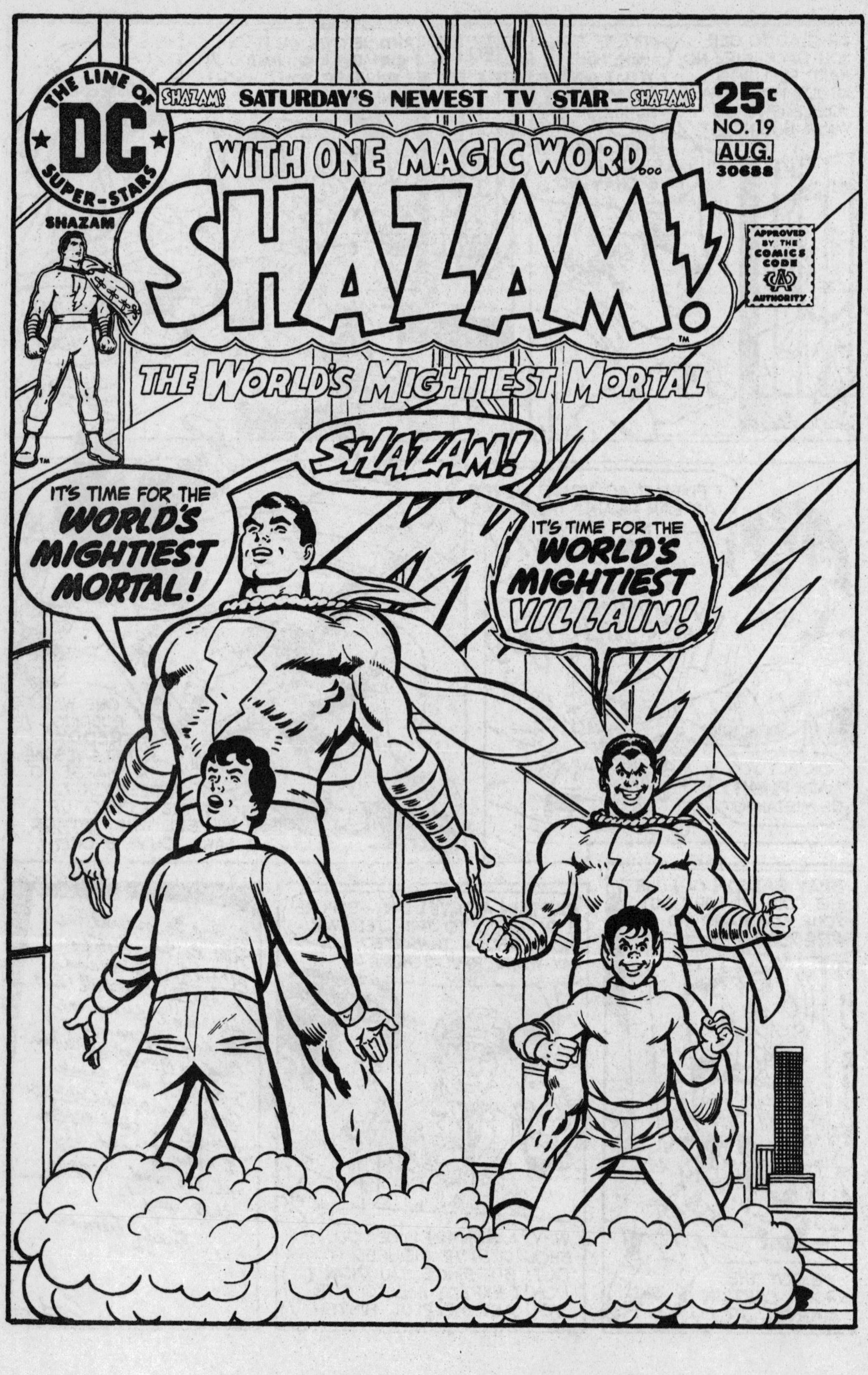
THE LINE OF DC SUPER-STARS
SHAZAM
SHAZAM! SATURDAY'S NEWEST TV STAR—SHAZAM!
25¢
NO. 19
AUG.
30688
WITH ONE MAGIC WORD...
SHAZAM!
APPROVED BY THE COMICS CODE AUTHORITY
THE WORLD'S MIGHTIEST MORTAL
SHAZAM!
IT'S TIME FOR THE WORLD'S MIGHTIEST MORTAL!
IT'S TIME FOR THE WORLD'S MIGHTIEST VILLAIN!

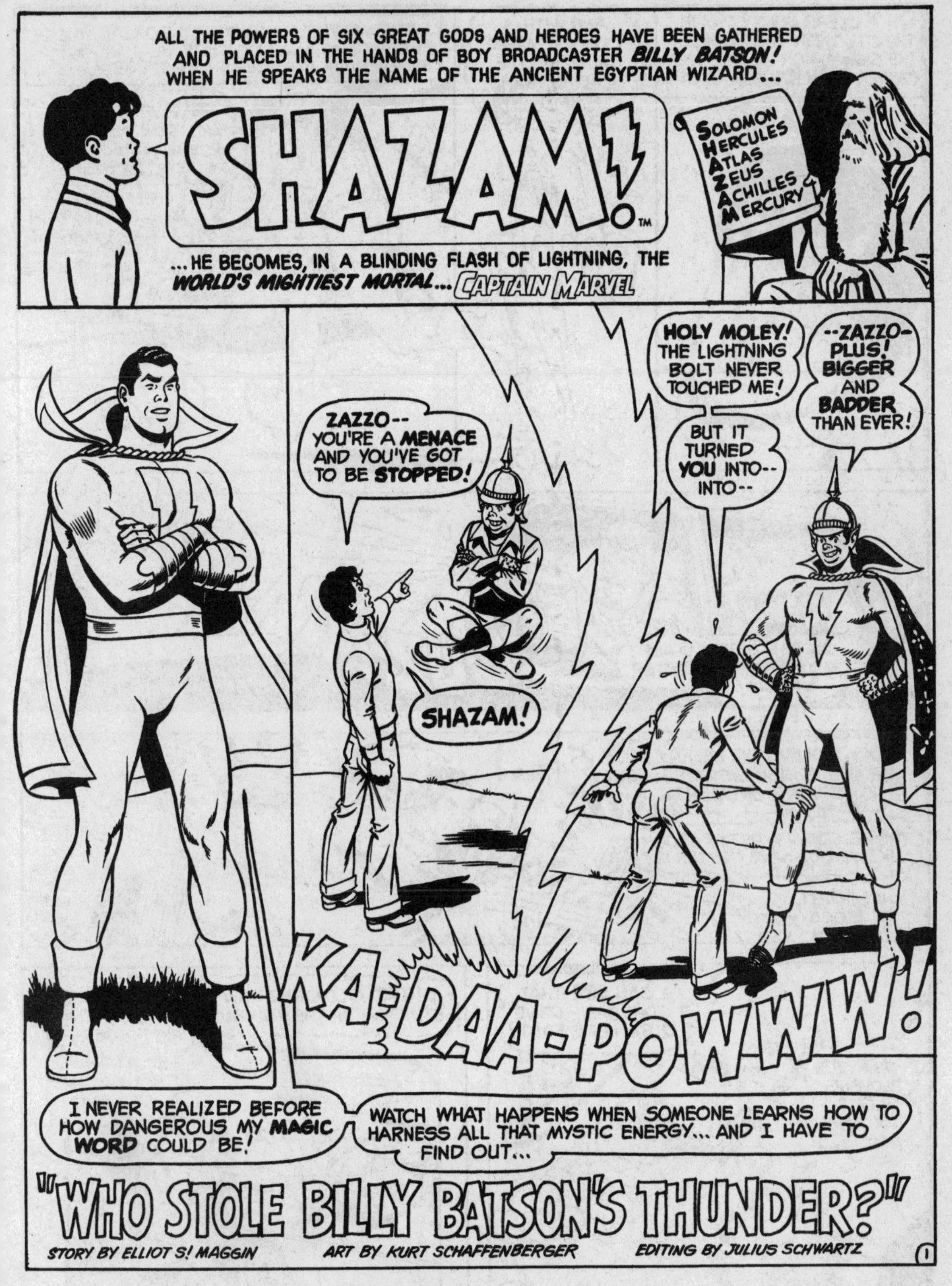
ALL THE POWERS OF SIX GREAT GODS AND HEROES HAVE BEEN GATHERED AND PLACED IN THE HANDS OF BOY BROADCASTER BILLY BATSON! WHEN HE SPEAKS THE NAME OF THE ANCIENT EGYPTIAN WIZARD...
SHAZAM!™
SOLOMON
HERCULES
ATLAS
ZEUS
ACHILLES
MERCURY
...HE BECOMES, IN A BLINDING FLASH OF LIGHTNING, THE WORLD'S MIGHTIEST MORTAL... CAPTAIN MARVEL
ZAZZO-- YOU'RE A MENACE AND YOU'VE GOT TO BE STOPPED!
SHAZAM!
HOLY MOLEY! THE LIGHTNING BOLT NEVER TOUCHED ME!
BUT IT TURNED YOU INTO-- INTO--
--ZAZZO-PLUS! BIGGER AND BADDER THAN EVER!
KA-DAA-POWWW!
I NEVER REALIZED BEFORE HOW DANGEROUS MY MAGIC WORD COULD BE!
WATCH WHAT HAPPENS WHEN SOMEONE LEARNS HOW TO HARNESS ALL THAT MYSTIC ENERGY... AND I HAVE TO FIND OUT...
"WHO STOLE BILLY BATSON'S THUNDER?"
STORY BY ELLIOT S! MAGGIN
ART BY KURT SCHAFFENBERGER
EDITING BY JULIUS SCHWARTZ
1

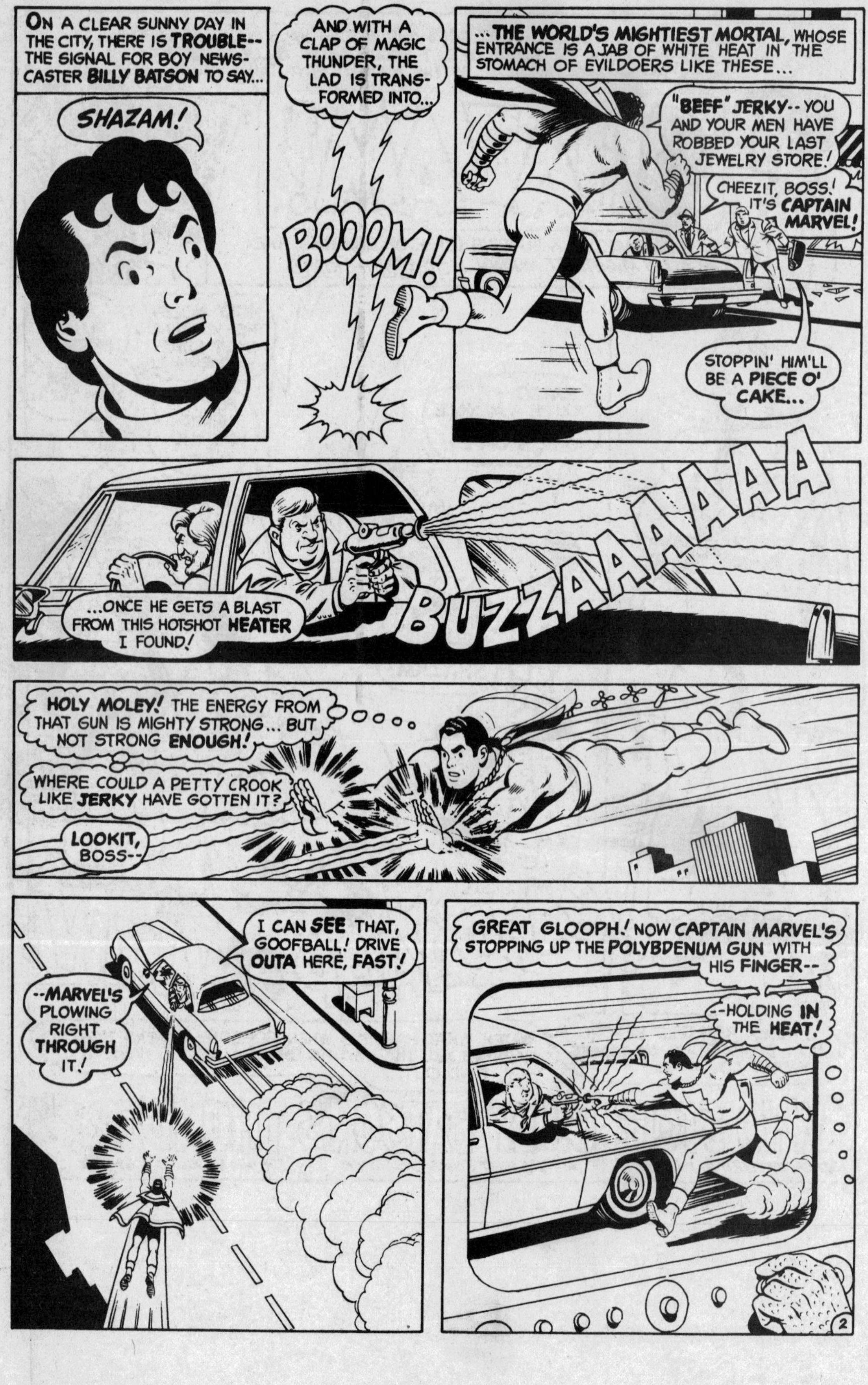
ON A CLEAR SUNNY DAY IN THE CITY, THERE IS TROUBLE-- THE SIGNAL FOR BOY NEWSCASTER BILLY BATSON TO SAY...
SHAZAM!
AND WITH A CLAP OF MAGIC THUNDER, THE LAD IS TRANSFORMED INTO...
BOOOM!
...THE WORLD'S MIGHTIEST MORTAL, WHOSE ENTRANCE IS A JAB OF WHITE HEAT IN THE STOMACH OF EVILDOERS LIKE THESE...
"BEEF" JERKY-- YOU AND YOUR MEN HAVE ROBBED YOUR LAST JEWELRY STORE!
CHEEZIT, BOSS! IT'S CAPTAIN MARVEL!
STOPPIN' HIM'LL BE A PIECE O' CAKE...
...ONCE HE GETS A BLAST FROM THIS HOTSHOT HEATER I FOUND!
BUZZAAAAAAA
HOLY MOLEY! THE ENERGY FROM THAT GUN IS MIGHTY STRONG... BUT NOT STRONG ENOUGH!
WHERE COULD A PETTY CROOK LIKE JERKY HAVE GOTTEN IT?
LOOKIT, BOSS--
--MARVEL'S PLOWING RIGHT THROUGH IT!
I CAN SEE THAT, GOOFBALL! DRIVE OUTA HERE, FAST!
GREAT GLOOPH! NOW CAPTAIN MARVEL'S STOPPING UP THE POLYBDENUM GUN WITH HIS FINGER--
--HOLDING IN THE HEAT!
2

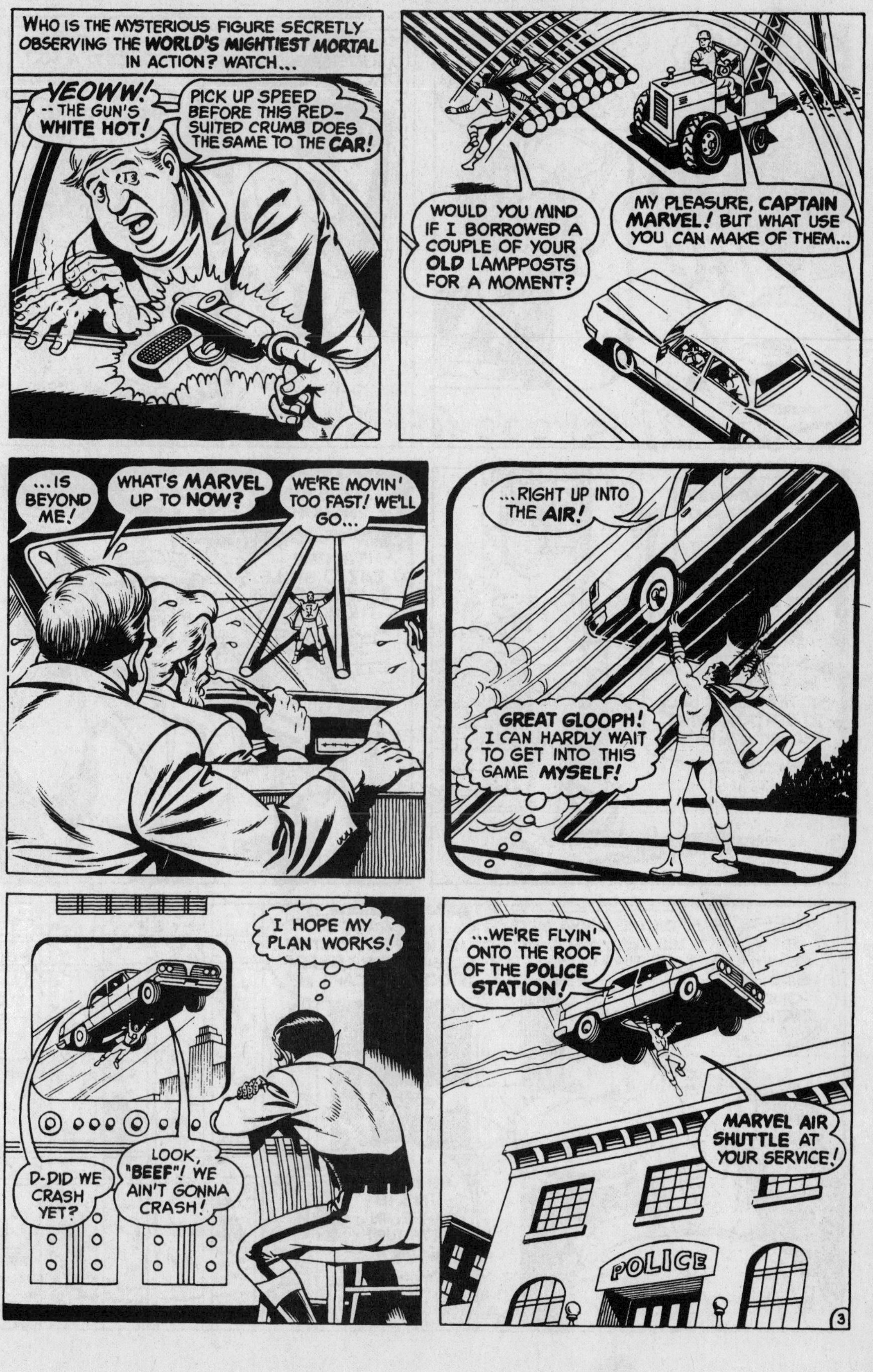
WHO IS THE MYSTERIOUS FIGURE SECRETLY OBSERVING THE WORLD'S MIGHTIEST MORTAL IN ACTION? WATCH...
YEOWW! -- THE GUN'S WHITE HOT!
PICK UP SPEED BEFORE THIS RED-SUITED CRUMB DOES THE SAME TO THE CAR!
WOULD YOU MIND IF I BORROWED A COUPLE OF YOUR OLD LAMPPOSTS FOR A MOMENT?
MY PLEASURE, CAPTAIN MARVEL! BUT WHAT USE YOU CAN MAKE OF THEM...
...IS BEYOND ME!
WHAT'S MARVEL UP TO NOW?
WE'RE MOVIN' TOO FAST! WE'LL GO...
...RIGHT UP INTO THE AIR!
GREAT GLOOPH! I CAN HARDLY WAIT TO GET INTO THIS GAME MYSELF!
I HOPE MY PLAN WORKS!
D-DID WE CRASH YET?
LOOK, "BEEF"! WE AIN'T GONNA CRASH!
...WE'RE FLYIN' ONTO THE ROOF OF THE POLICE STATION!
MARVEL AIR SHUTTLE AT YOUR SERVICE!
POLICE
3

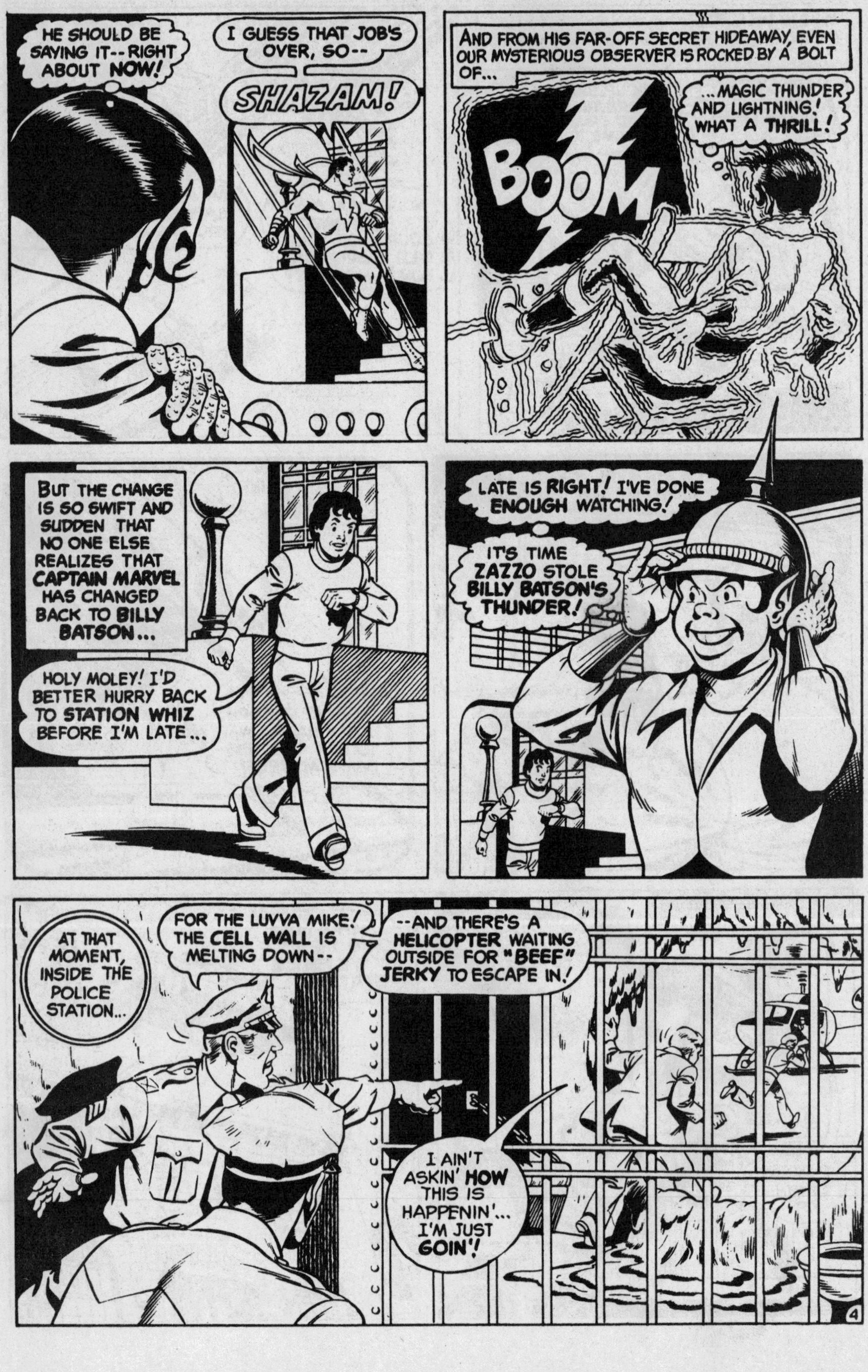
HE SHOULD BE SAYING IT--RIGHT ABOUT NOW!
I GUESS THAT JOB'S OVER, SO--
SHAZAM!
AND FROM HIS FAR-OFF SECRET HIDEAWAY, EVEN OUR MYSTERIOUS OBSERVER IS ROCKED BY A BOLT OF...
BOOM
...MAGIC THUNDER AND LIGHTNING! WHAT A THRILL!
BUT THE CHANGE IS SO SWIFT AND SUDDEN THAT NO ONE ELSE REALIZES THAT CAPTAIN MARVEL HAS CHANGED BACK TO BILLY BATSON...
HOLY MOLEY! I'D BETTER HURRY BACK TO STATION WHIZ BEFORE I'M LATE...
LATE IS RIGHT! I'VE DONE ENOUGH WATCHING!
IT'S TIME ZAZZO STOLE BILLY BATSON'S THUNDER!
AT THAT MOMENT, INSIDE THE POLICE STATION...
FOR THE LUVVA MIKE! THE CELL WALL IS MELTING DOWN--
--AND THERE'S A HELICOPTER WAITING OUTSIDE FOR "BEEF" JERKY TO ESCAPE IN!
I AIN'T ASKIN' HOW THIS IS HAPPENIN'... I'M JUST GOIN'!
4

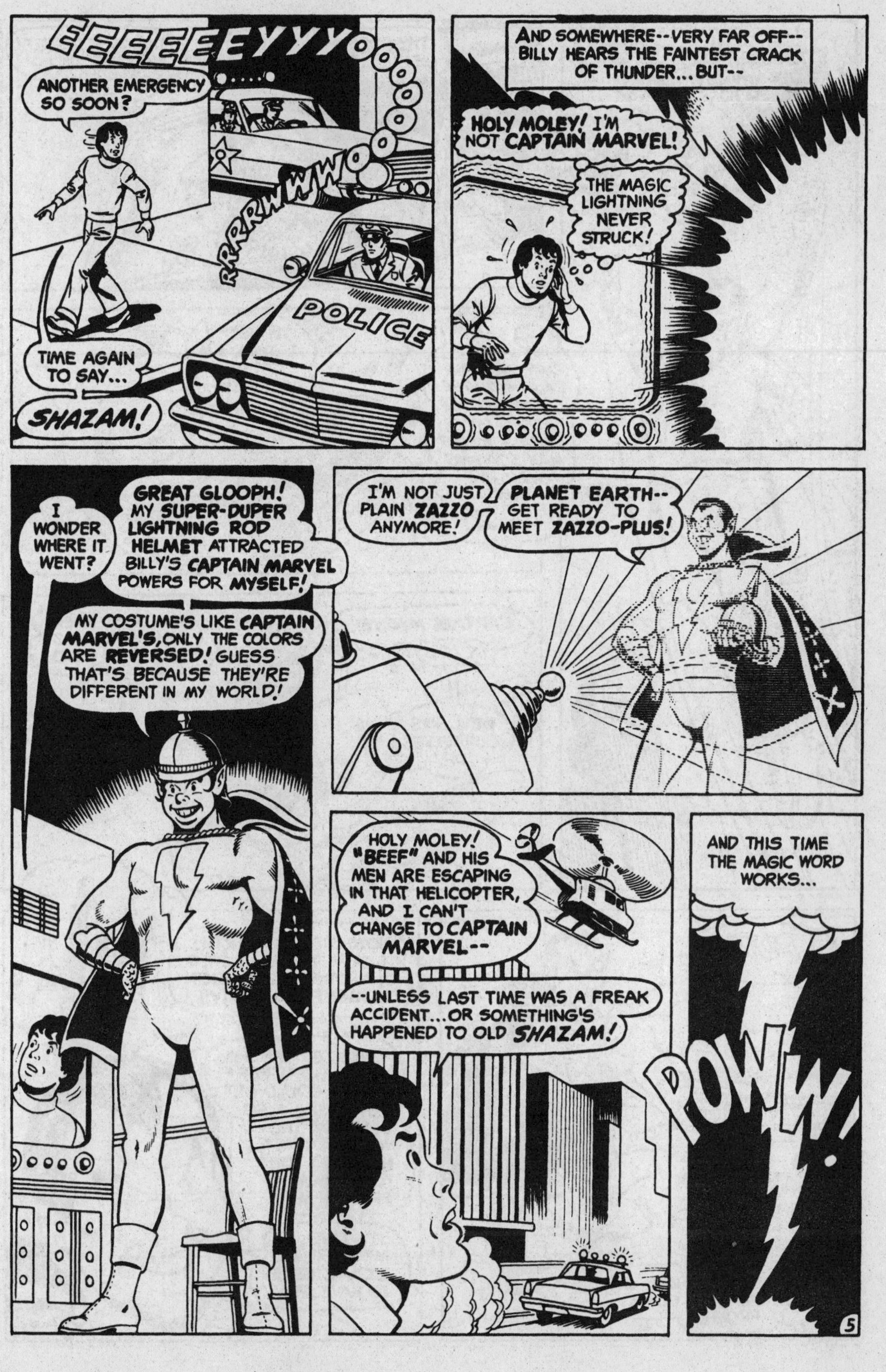
EEEEEEYYYYOOOOOOOOO
ANOTHER EMERGENCY SO SOON?
RRRRWWWWOOO
POLICE
TIME AGAIN TO SAY...
SHAZAM!
AND SOMEWHERE--VERY FAR OFF--BILLY HEARS THE FAINTEST CRACK OF THUNDER...BUT--
HOLY MOLEY! I'M NOT CAPTAIN MARVEL!
THE MAGIC LIGHTNING NEVER STRUCK!
I WONDER WHERE IT WENT?
GREAT GLOOPH! MY SUPER-DUPER LIGHTNING ROD HELMET ATTRACTED BILLY'S CAPTAIN MARVEL POWERS FOR MYSELF!
MY COSTUME'S LIKE CAPTAIN MARVEL'S, ONLY THE COLORS ARE REVERSED! GUESS THAT'S BECAUSE THEY'RE DIFFERENT IN MY WORLD!
I'M NOT JUST PLAIN ZAZZO ANYMORE!
PLANET EARTH--GET READY TO MEET ZAZZO-PLUS!
HOLY MOLEY! "BEEF" AND HIS MEN ARE ESCAPING IN THAT HELICOPTER, AND I CAN'T CHANGE TO CAPTAIN MARVEL--
--UNLESS LAST TIME WAS A FREAK ACCIDENT...OR SOMETHING'S HAPPENED TO OLD SHAZAM!
AND THIS TIME THE MAGIC WORD WORKS...
POWW!
5

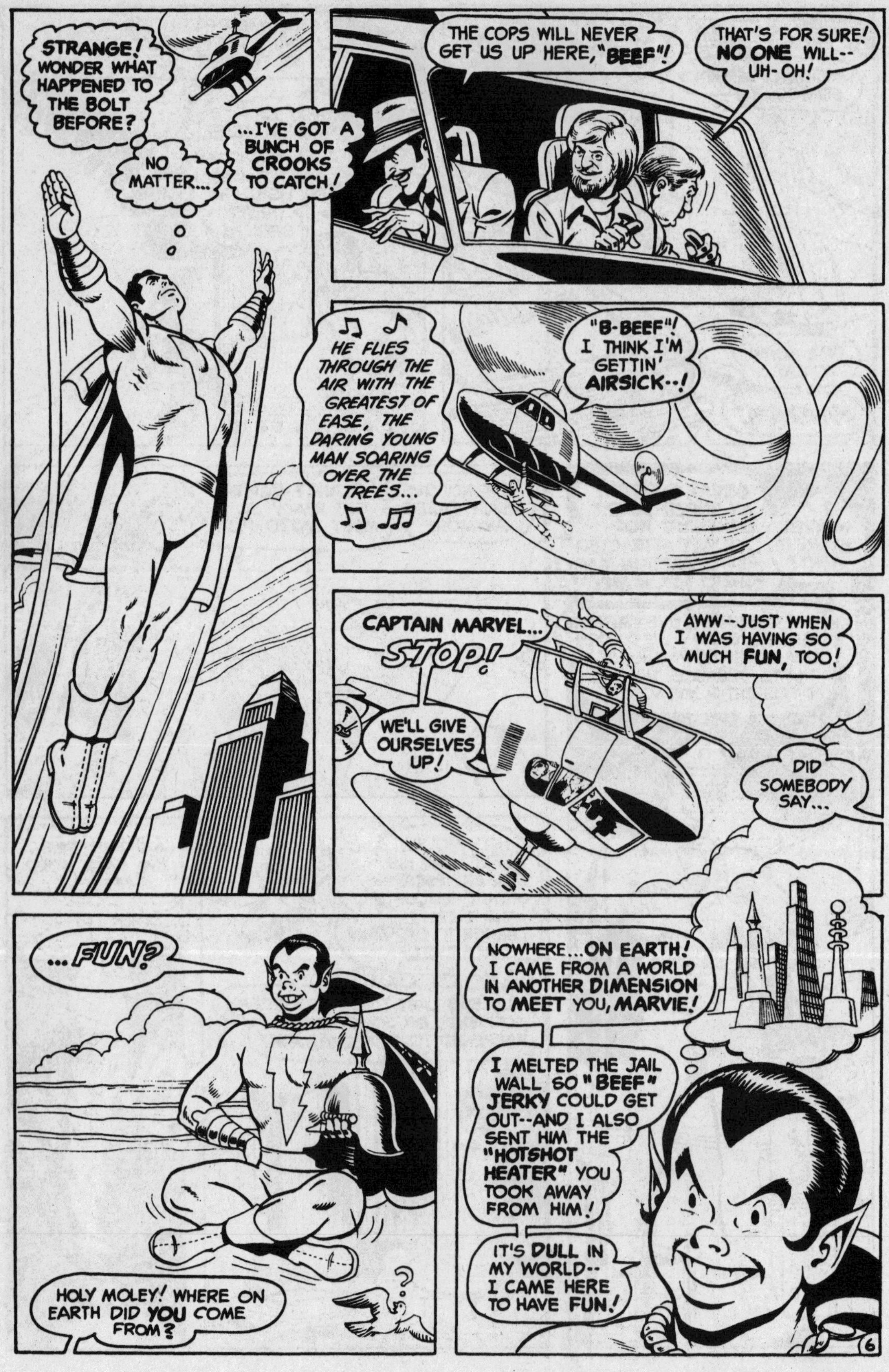
STRANGE! WONDER WHAT HAPPENED TO THE BOLT BEFORE?
NO MATTER...
...I'VE GOT A BUNCH OF CROOKS TO CATCH!
THE COPS WILL NEVER GET US UP HERE, "BEEF"!
THAT'S FOR SURE! NO ONE WILL-- UH-OH!
♫ ♪ HE FLIES THROUGH THE AIR WITH THE GREATEST OF EASE, THE DARING YOUNG MAN SOARING OVER THE TREES... ♫ ♫
"B-BEEF"! I THINK I'M GETTIN' AIRSICK--!
CAPTAIN MARVEL... STOP!
WE'LL GIVE OURSELVES UP!
AWW--JUST WHEN I WAS HAVING SO MUCH FUN, TOO!
DID SOMEBODY SAY...
...FUN?
HOLY MOLEY! WHERE ON EARTH DID YOU COME FROM?
NOWHERE...ON EARTH! I CAME FROM A WORLD IN ANOTHER DIMENSION TO MEET YOU, MARVIE!
I MELTED THE JAIL WALL SO "BEEF" JERKY COULD GET OUT--AND I ALSO SENT HIM THE "HOTSHOT HEATER" YOU TOOK AWAY FROM HIM!
IT'S DULL IN MY WORLD-- I CAME HERE TO HAVE FUN!
6

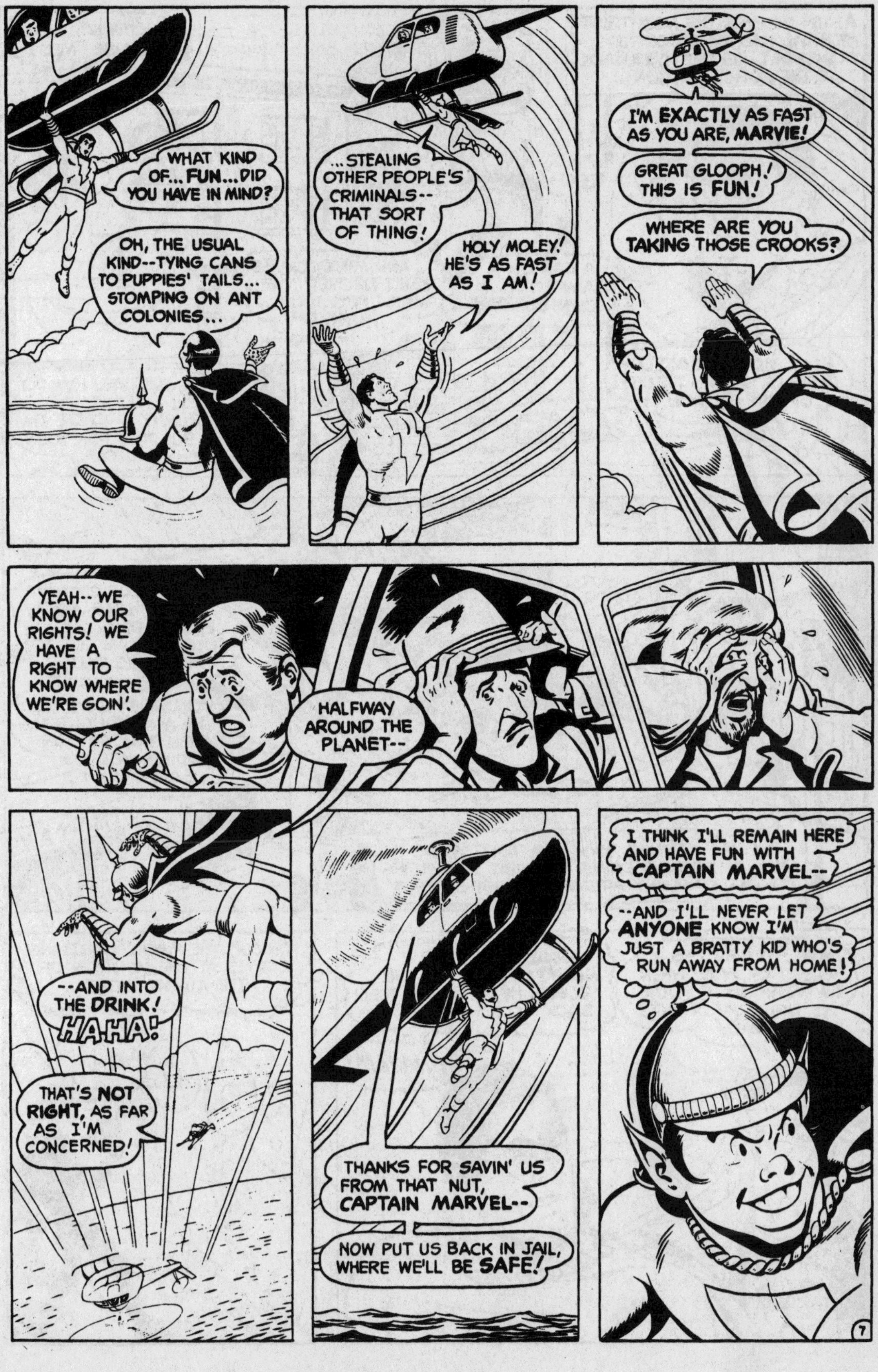
WHAT KIND OF... FUN... DID YOU HAVE IN MIND?
OH, THE USUAL KIND--TYING CANS TO PUPPIES' TAILS... STOMPING ON ANT COLONIES...
...STEALING OTHER PEOPLE'S CRIMINALS--THAT SORT OF THING!
HOLY MOLEY! HE'S AS FAST AS I AM!
I'M EXACTLY AS FAST AS YOU ARE, MARVIE!
GREAT GLOOPH! THIS IS FUN!
WHERE ARE YOU TAKING THOSE CROOKS?
YEAH-- WE KNOW OUR RIGHTS! WE HAVE A RIGHT TO KNOW WHERE WE'RE GOIN'.
HALFWAY AROUND THE PLANET--
--AND INTO THE DRINK! HAHA!
THAT'S NOT RIGHT, AS FAR AS I'M CONCERNED!
THANKS FOR SAVIN' US FROM THAT NUT, CAPTAIN MARVEL--
NOW PUT US BACK IN JAIL, WHERE WE'LL BE SAFE!
I THINK I'LL REMAIN HERE AND HAVE FUN WITH CAPTAIN MARVEL--
--AND I'LL NEVER LET ANYONE KNOW I'M JUST A BRATTY KID WHO'S RUN AWAY FROM HOME!
7

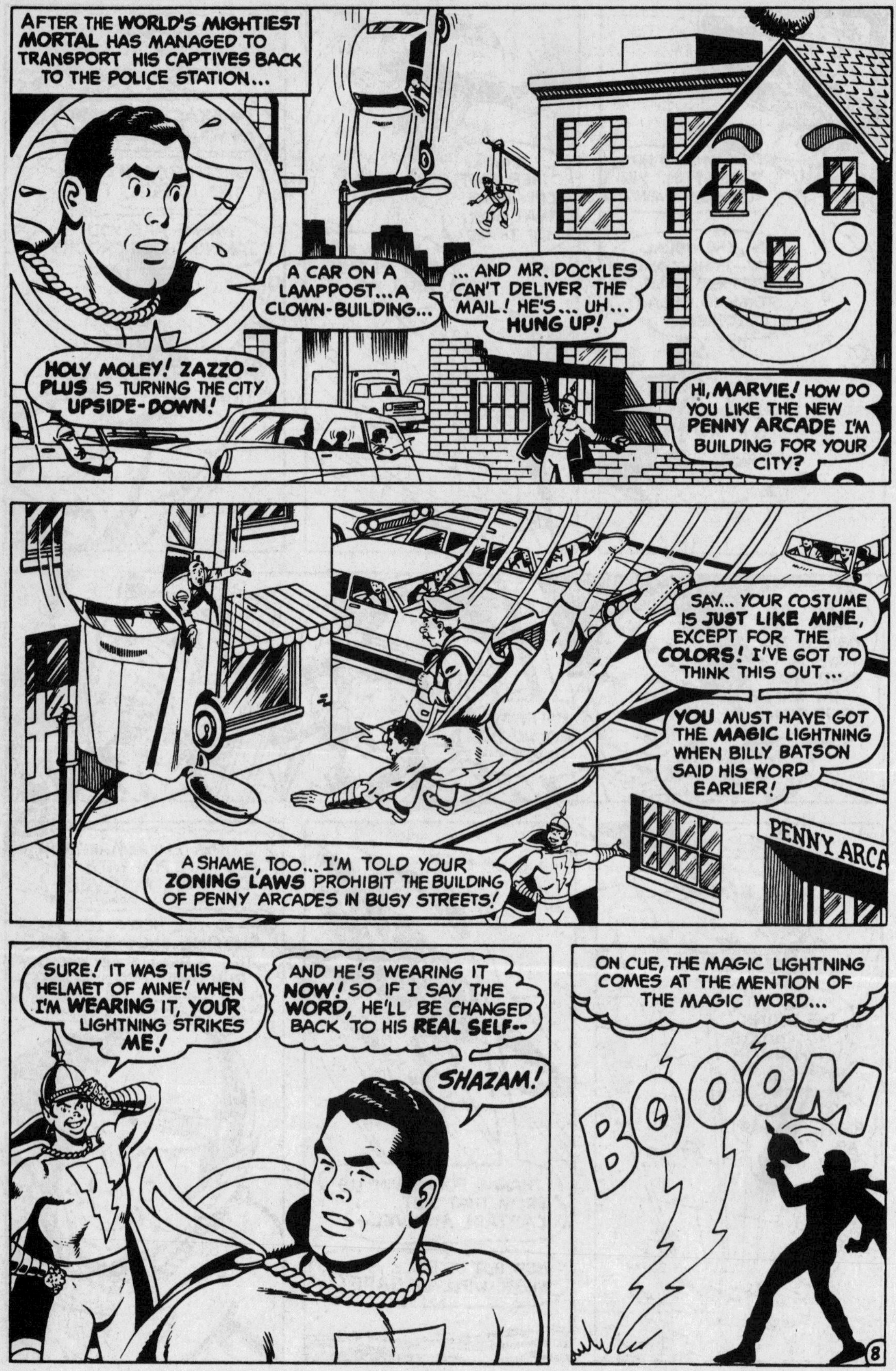
AFTER THE WORLD'S MIGHTIEST MORTAL HAS MANAGED TO TRANSPORT HIS CAPTIVES BACK TO THE POLICE STATION...
A CAR ON A LAMPPOST...A CLOWN-BUILDING...
... AND MR. DOCKLES CAN'T DELIVER THE MAIL! HE'S... UH... HUNG UP!
HOLY MOLEY! ZAZZO-PLUS IS TURNING THE CITY UPSIDE-DOWN!
HI, MARVIE! HOW DO YOU LIKE THE NEW PENNY ARCADE I'M BUILDING FOR YOUR CITY?
SAY... YOUR COSTUME IS JUST LIKE MINE, EXCEPT FOR THE COLORS! I'VE GOT TO THINK THIS OUT...
YOU MUST HAVE GOT THE MAGIC LIGHTNING WHEN BILLY BATSON SAID HIS WORD EARLIER!
A SHAME, TOO... I'M TOLD YOUR ZONING LAWS PROHIBIT THE BUILDING OF PENNY ARCADES IN BUSY STREETS!
PENNY ARCA
SURE! IT WAS THIS HELMET OF MINE! WHEN I'M WEARING IT, YOUR LIGHTNING STRIKES ME!
AND HE'S WEARING IT NOW! SO IF I SAY THE WORD, HE'LL BE CHANGED BACK TO HIS REAL SELF--
SHAZAM!
ON CUE, THE MAGIC LIGHTNING COMES AT THE MENTION OF THE MAGIC WORD...
BOOOM
8

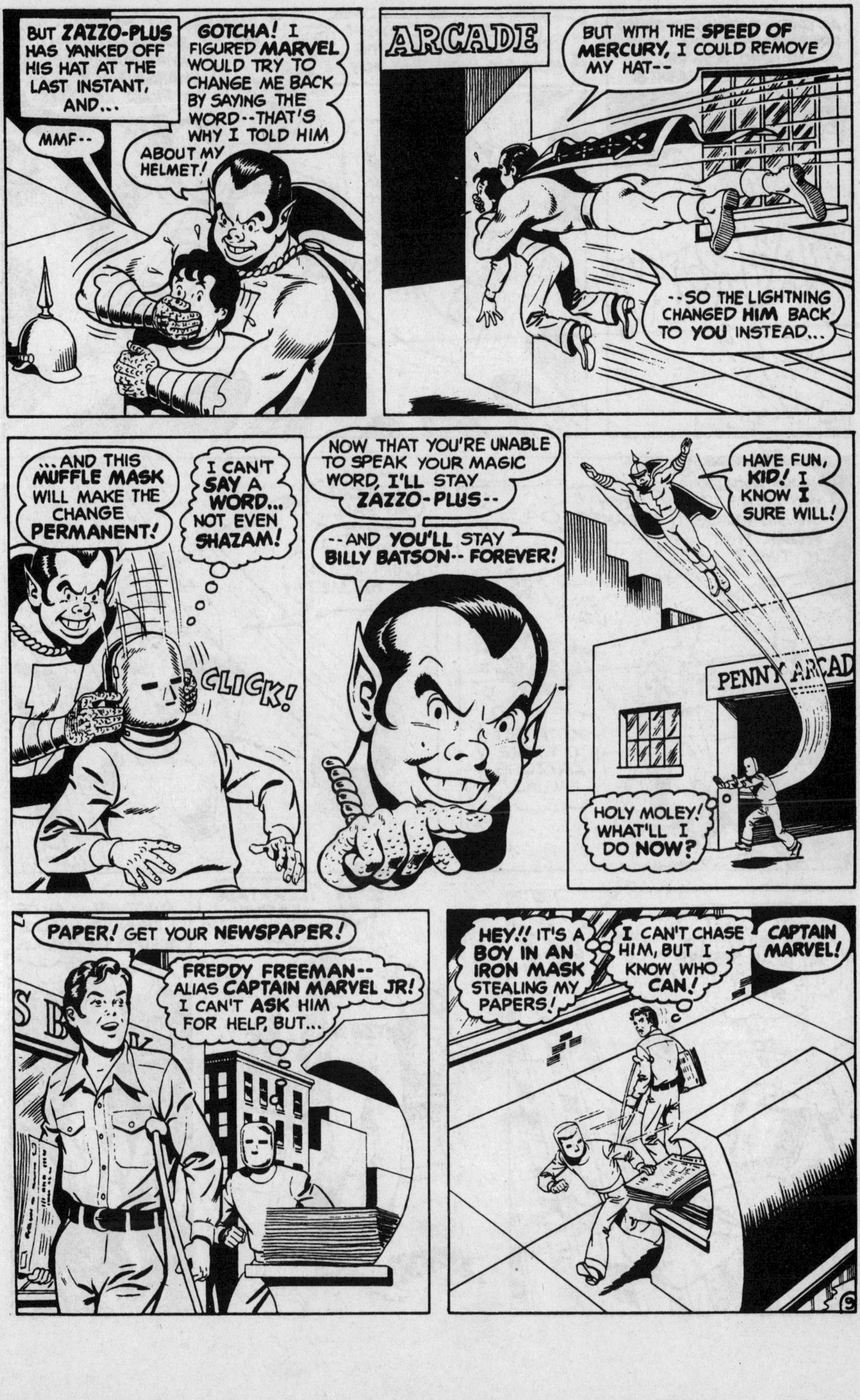
BUT ZAZZO-PLUS HAS YANKED OFF HIS HAT AT THE LAST INSTANT, AND...
MMF--
GOTCHA! I FIGURED MARVEL WOULD TRY TO CHANGE ME BACK BY SAYING THE WORD--THAT'S WHY I TOLD HIM ABOUT MY HELMET!
ARCADE
BUT WITH THE SPEED OF MERCURY, I COULD REMOVE MY HAT--
--SO THE LIGHTNING CHANGED HIM BACK TO YOU INSTEAD...
...AND THIS MUFFLE MASK WILL MAKE THE CHANGE PERMANENT!
I CAN'T SAY A WORD... NOT EVEN SHAZAM!
CLICK!
NOW THAT YOU'RE UNABLE TO SPEAK YOUR MAGIC WORD, I'LL STAY ZAZZO-PLUS--
--AND YOU'LL STAY BILLY BATSON-- FOREVER!
HAVE FUN, KID! I KNOW I SURE WILL!
PENNY ARCAD
HOLY MOLEY! WHAT'LL I DO NOW?
PAPER! GET YOUR NEWSPAPER!
FREDDY FREEMAN-- ALIAS CAPTAIN MARVEL JR! I CAN'T ASK HIM FOR HELP, BUT...
HEY!! IT'S A BOY IN AN IRON MASK STEALING MY PAPERS!
I CAN'T CHASE HIM, BUT I KNOW WHO CAN!
CAPTAIN MARVEL!
9

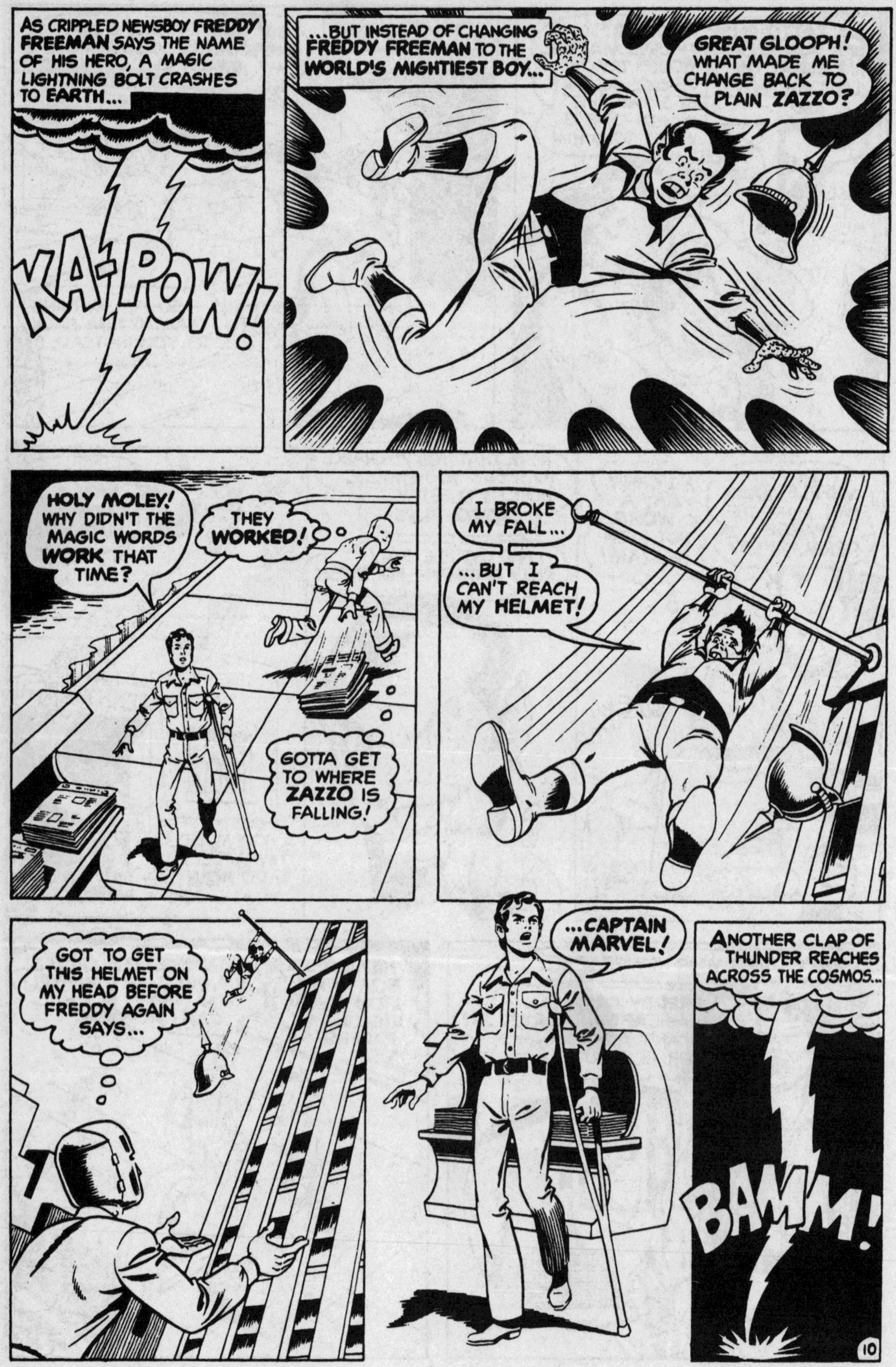
AS CRIPPLED NEWSBOY FREDDY FREEMAN SAYS THE NAME OF HIS HERO, A MAGIC LIGHTNING BOLT CRASHES TO EARTH...
KA-POW!
...BUT INSTEAD OF CHANGING FREDDY FREEMAN TO THE WORLD'S MIGHTIEST BOY...
GREAT GLOOPH! WHAT MADE ME CHANGE BACK TO PLAIN ZAZZO?
HOLY MOLEY! WHY DIDN'T THE MAGIC WORDS WORK THAT TIME?
THEY WORKED!
GOTTA GET TO WHERE ZAZZO IS FALLING!
I BROKE MY FALL...
...BUT I CAN'T REACH MY HELMET!
GOT TO GET THIS HELMET ON MY HEAD BEFORE FREDDY AGAIN SAYS...
...CAPTAIN MARVEL!
ANOTHER CLAP OF THUNDER REACHES ACROSS THE COSMOS...
BAMM!
10

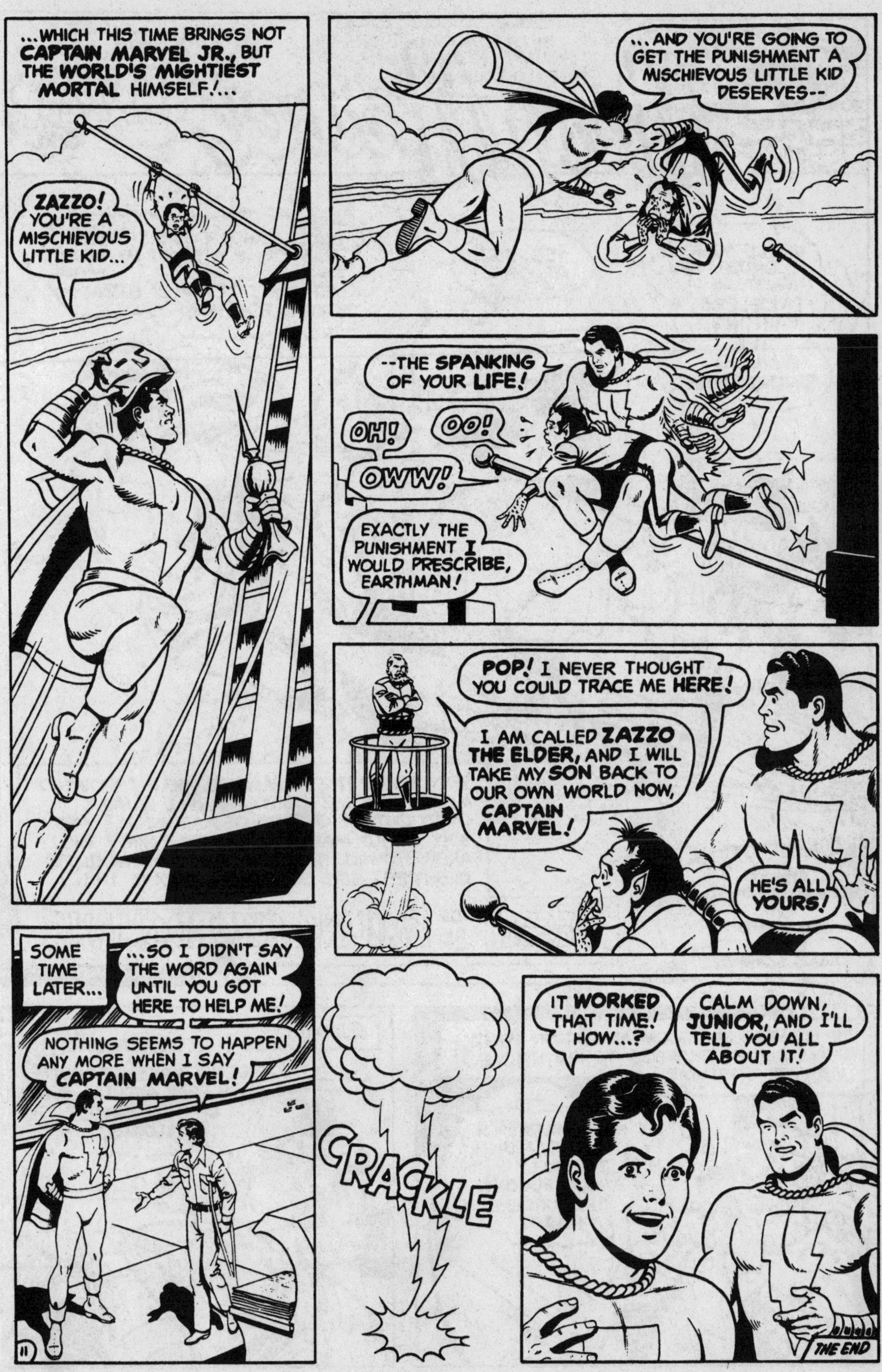
...WHICH THIS TIME BRINGS NOT CAPTAIN MARVEL JR., BUT THE WORLD'S MIGHTIEST MORTAL HIMSELF!...
ZAZZO! YOU'RE A MISCHIEVOUS LITTLE KID...
...AND YOU'RE GOING TO GET THE PUNISHMENT A MISCHIEVOUS LITTLE KID DESERVES--
--THE SPANKING OF YOUR LIFE!
OH!
OO!
OWW!
EXACTLY THE PUNISHMENT I WOULD PRESCRIBE, EARTHMAN!
POP! I NEVER THOUGHT YOU COULD TRACE ME HERE!
I AM CALLED ZAZZO THE ELDER, AND I WILL TAKE MY SON BACK TO OUR OWN WORLD NOW, CAPTAIN MARVEL!
HE'S ALL YOURS!
SOME TIME LATER...
...SO I DIDN'T SAY THE WORD AGAIN UNTIL YOU GOT HERE TO HELP ME!
NOTHING SEEMS TO HAPPEN ANY MORE WHEN I SAY CAPTAIN MARVEL!
11
CRACKLE
IT WORKED THAT TIME! HOW...?
CALM DOWN, JUNIOR, AND I'LL TELL YOU ALL ABOUT IT!
THE END

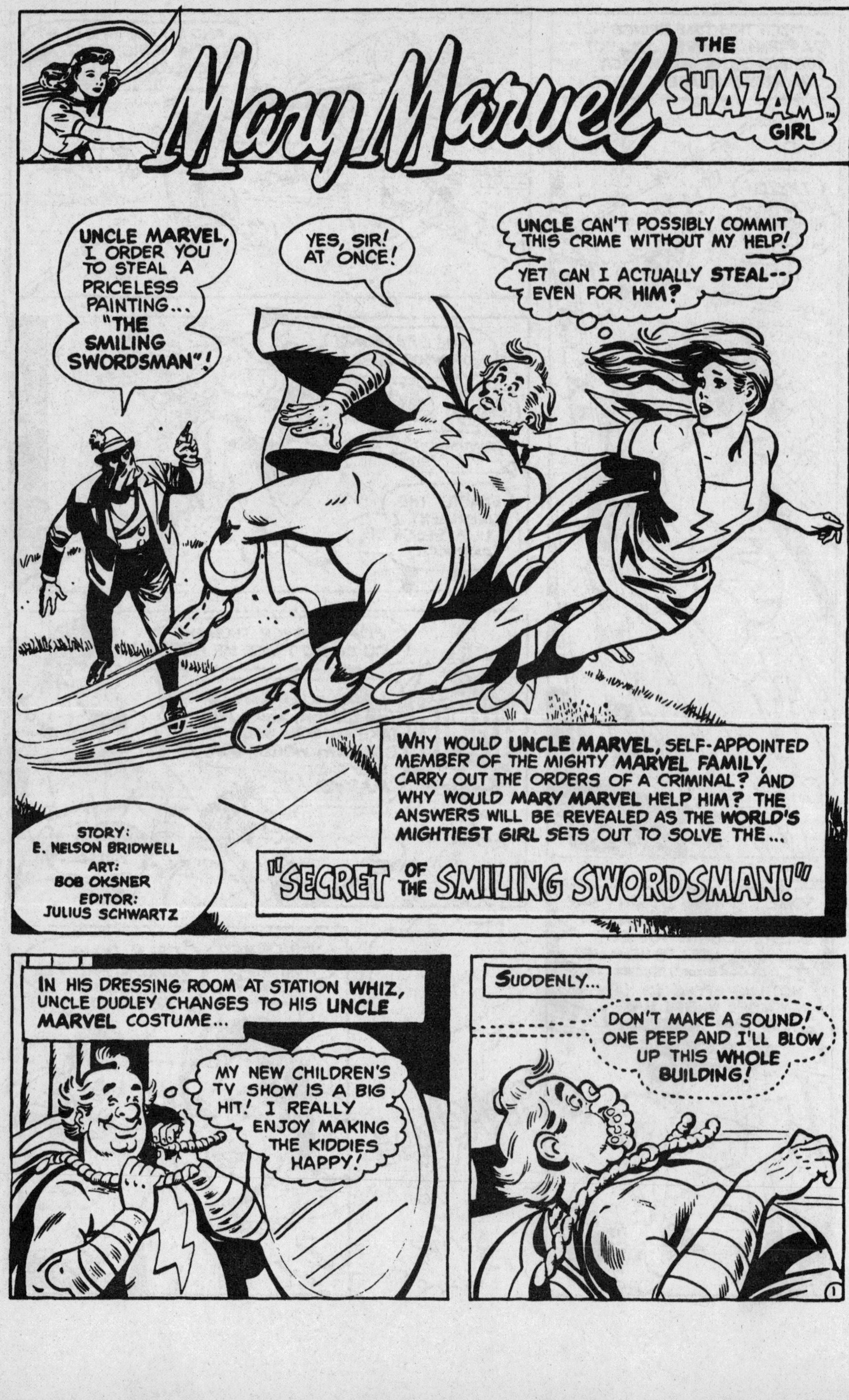

Mary Marvel
THE SHAZAM GIRL
UNCLE MARVEL, I ORDER YOU TO STEAL A PRICELESS PAINTING... "THE SMILING SWORDSMAN"!
YES, SIR! AT ONCE!
UNCLE CAN'T POSSIBLY COMMIT THIS CRIME WITHOUT MY HELP!
YET CAN I ACTUALLY STEAL-- EVEN FOR HIM?
WHY WOULD UNCLE MARVEL, SELF-APPOINTED MEMBER OF THE MIGHTY MARVEL FAMILY, CARRY OUT THE ORDERS OF A CRIMINAL? AND WHY WOULD MARY MARVEL HELP HIM? THE ANSWERS WILL BE REVEALED AS THE WORLD'S MIGHTIEST GIRL SETS OUT TO SOLVE THE...
STORY: E. NELSON BRIDWELL
ART: BOB OKSNER
EDITOR: JULIUS SCHWARTZ
"SECRET OF THE SMILING SWORDSMAN!"
IN HIS DRESSING ROOM AT STATION WHIZ, UNCLE DUDLEY CHANGES TO HIS UNCLE MARVEL COSTUME...
MY NEW CHILDREN'S TV SHOW IS A BIG HIT! I REALLY ENJOY MAKING THE KIDDIES HAPPY!
SUDDENLY...
DON'T MAKE A SOUND! ONE PEEP AND I'LL BLOW UP THIS WHOLE BUILDING!
1

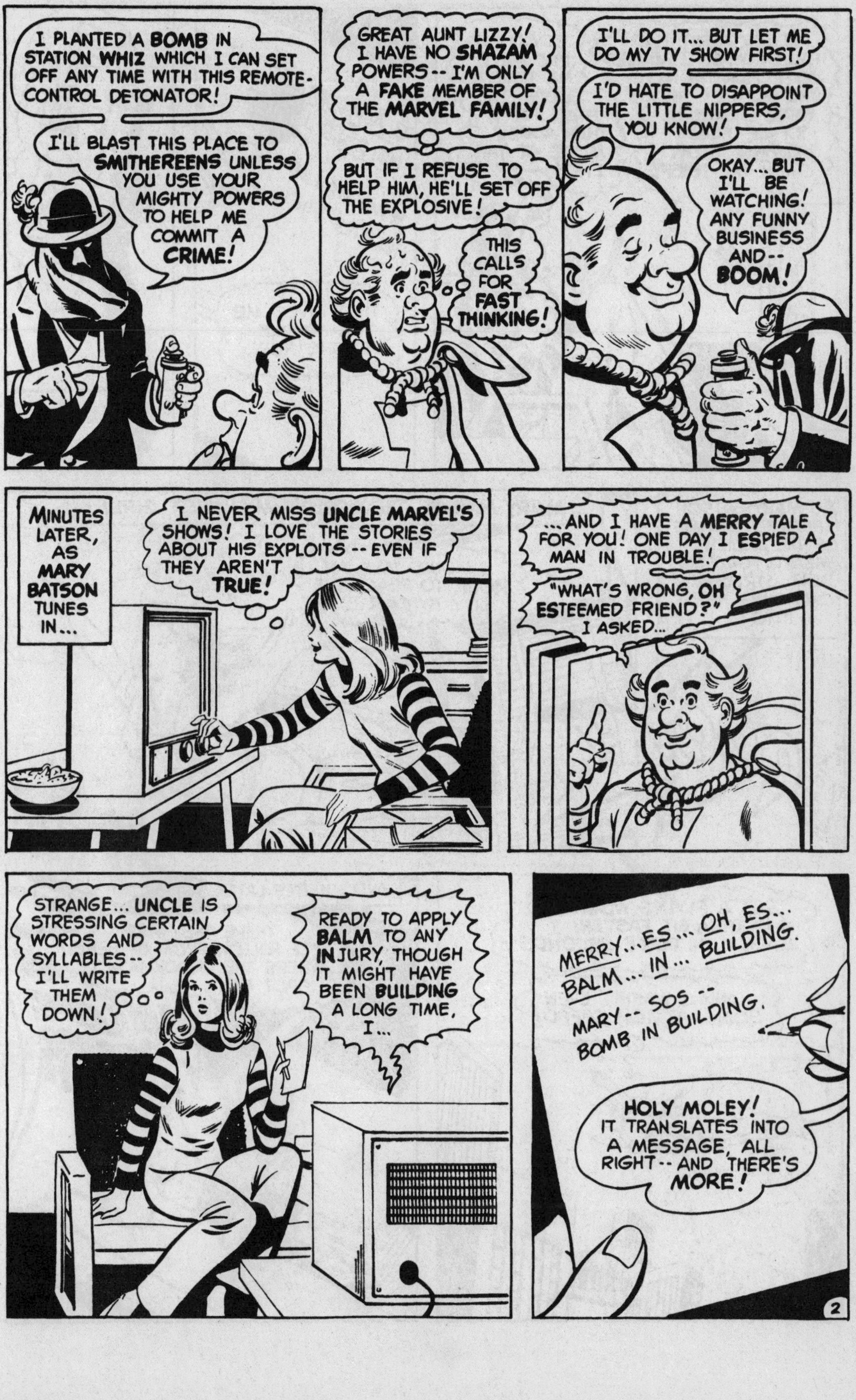
I PLANTED A BOMB IN STATION WHIZ WHICH I CAN SET OFF ANY TIME WITH THIS REMOTE-CONTROL DETONATOR!
I'LL BLAST THIS PLACE TO SMITHEREENS UNLESS YOU USE YOUR MIGHTY POWERS TO HELP ME COMMIT A CRIME!
GREAT AUNT LIZZY! I HAVE NO SHAZAM POWERS -- I'M ONLY A FAKE MEMBER OF THE MARVEL FAMILY!
BUT IF I REFUSE TO HELP HIM, HE'LL SET OFF THE EXPLOSIVE!
THIS CALLS FOR FAST THINKING!
I'LL DO IT... BUT LET ME DO MY TV SHOW FIRST!
I'D HATE TO DISAPPOINT THE LITTLE NIPPERS, YOU KNOW!
OKAY... BUT I'LL BE WATCHING! ANY FUNNY BUSINESS AND -- BOOM!
MINUTES LATER, AS MARY BATSON TUNES IN...
I NEVER MISS UNCLE MARVEL'S SHOWS! I LOVE THE STORIES ABOUT HIS EXPLOITS -- EVEN IF THEY AREN'T TRUE!
...AND I HAVE A MERRY TALE FOR YOU! ONE DAY I ESPIED A MAN IN TROUBLE!
"WHAT'S WRONG, OH ESTEEMED FRIEND?" I ASKED...
STRANGE... UNCLE IS STRESSING CERTAIN WORDS AND SYLLABLES -- I'LL WRITE THEM DOWN!
READY TO APPLY BALM TO ANY INJURY, THOUGH IT MIGHT HAVE BEEN BUILDING A LONG TIME, I...
MERRY... ES... OH, ES...
BALM... IN... BUILDING.
MARY -- SOS --
BOMB IN BUILDING.
HOLY MOLEY! IT TRANSLATES INTO A MESSAGE, ALL RIGHT -- AND THERE'S MORE!
2

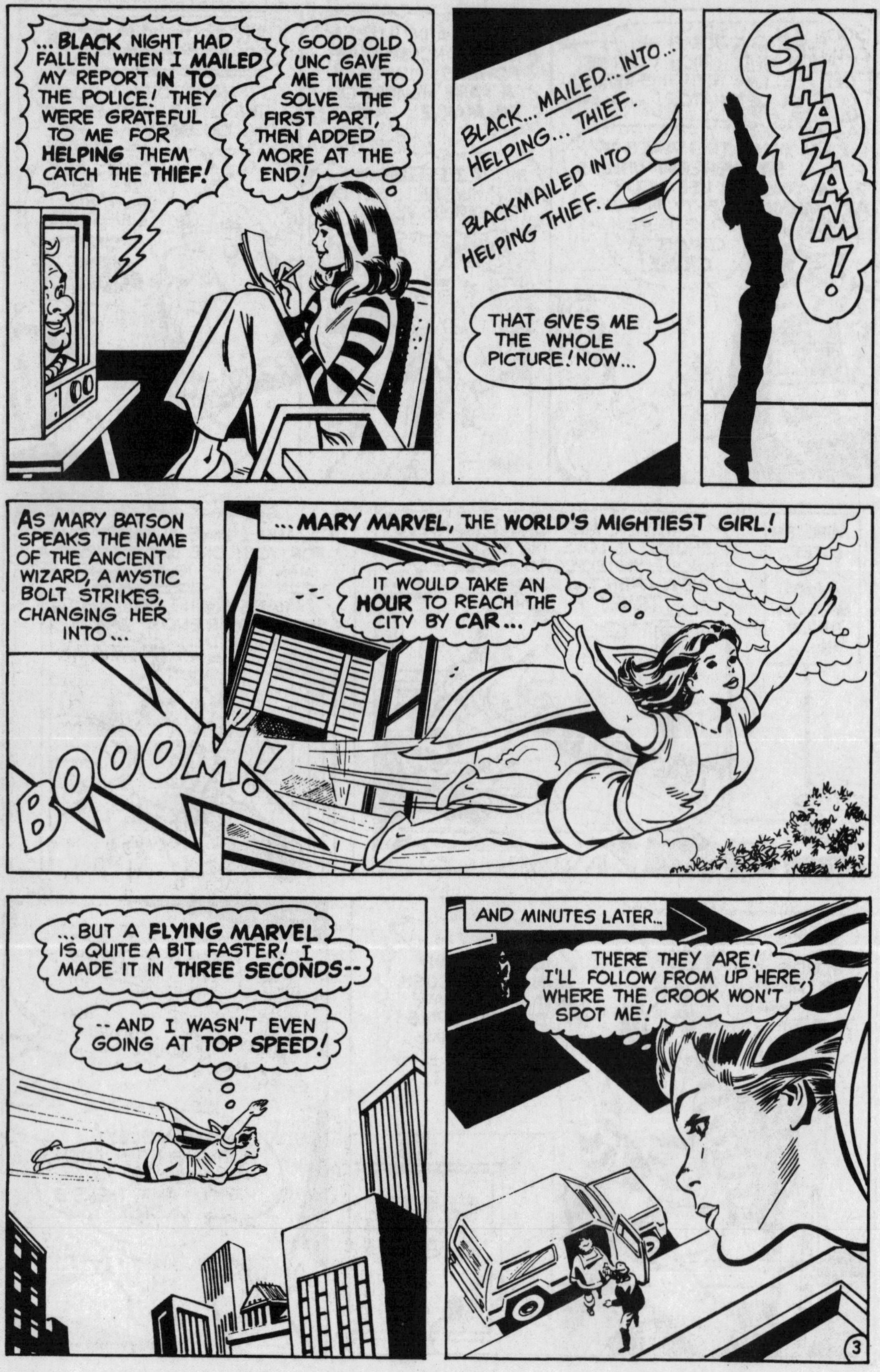
...BLACK NIGHT HAD FALLEN WHEN I MAILED MY REPORT IN TO THE POLICE! THEY WERE GRATEFUL TO ME FOR HELPING THEM CATCH THE THIEF!
GOOD OLD UNC GAVE ME TIME TO SOLVE THE FIRST PART, THEN ADDED MORE AT THE END!
BLACK... MAILED... INTO... HELPING... THIEF.
BLACKMAILED INTO HELPING THIEF.
THAT GIVES ME THE WHOLE PICTURE! NOW...
SHAZAM!
AS MARY BATSON SPEAKS THE NAME OF THE ANCIENT WIZARD, A MYSTIC BOLT STRIKES, CHANGING HER INTO...
...MARY MARVEL, THE WORLD'S MIGHTIEST GIRL!
IT WOULD TAKE AN HOUR TO REACH THE CITY BY CAR...
BOOOM!
...BUT A FLYING MARVEL IS QUITE A BIT FASTER! I MADE IT IN THREE SECONDS--
--AND I WASN'T EVEN GOING AT TOP SPEED!
AND MINUTES LATER...
THERE THEY ARE! I'LL FOLLOW FROM UP HERE, WHERE THE CROOK WON'T SPOT ME!
3

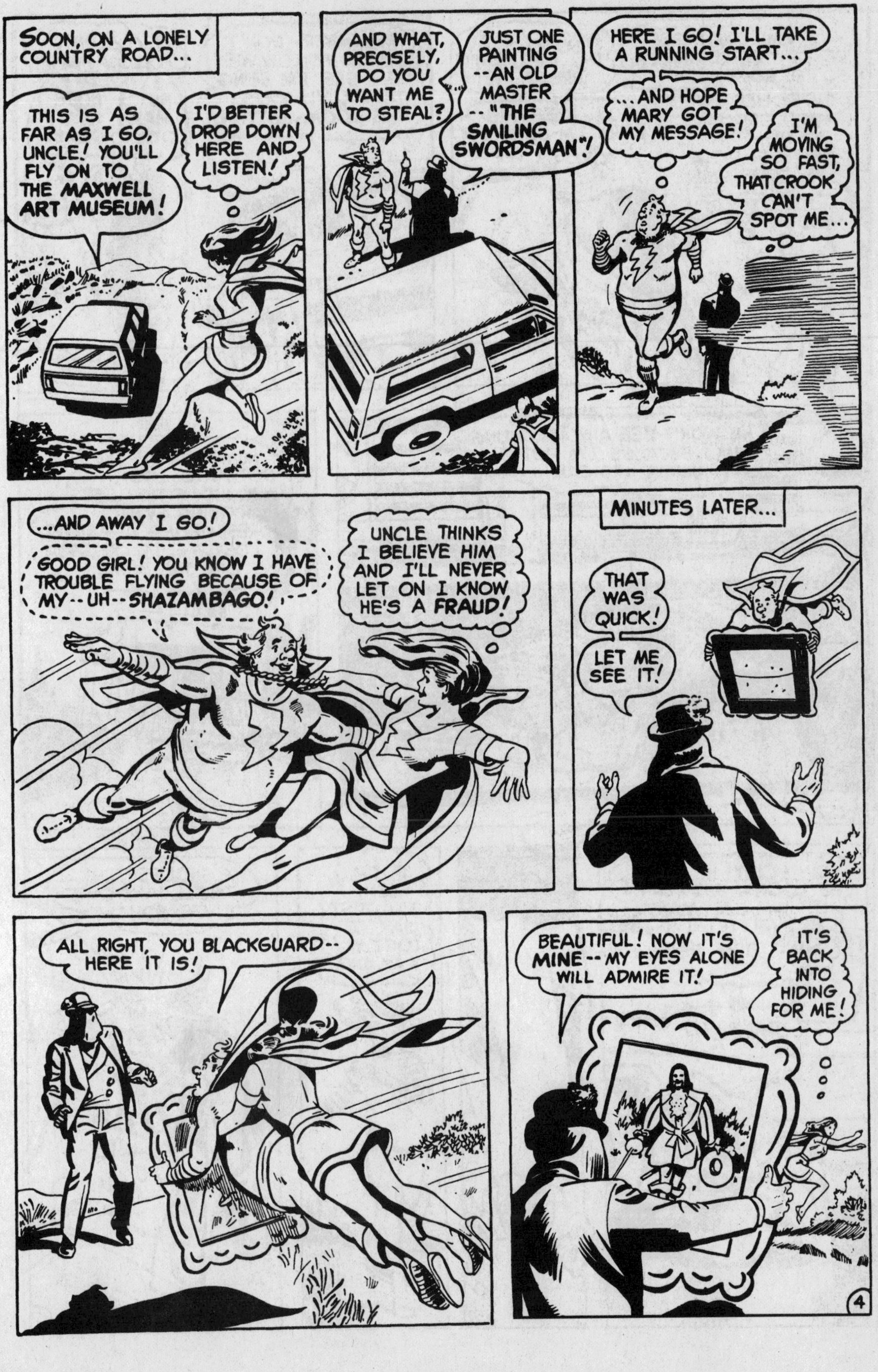
SOON, ON A LONELY COUNTRY ROAD...
THIS IS AS FAR AS I GO, UNCLE! YOU'LL FLY ON TO THE MAXWELL ART MUSEUM!
I'D BETTER DROP DOWN HERE AND LISTEN!
AND WHAT, PRECISELY, DO YOU WANT ME TO STEAL?
JUST ONE PAINTING --AN OLD MASTER -- "THE SMILING SWORDSMAN"!
HERE I GO! I'LL TAKE A RUNNING START...
...AND HOPE MARY GOT MY MESSAGE!
I'M MOVING SO FAST, THAT CROOK CAN'T SPOT ME...
...AND AWAY I GO!
GOOD GIRL! YOU KNOW I HAVE TROUBLE FLYING BECAUSE OF MY--UH--SHAZAMBAGO!
UNCLE THINKS I BELIEVE HIM AND I'LL NEVER LET ON I KNOW HE'S A FRAUD!
MINUTES LATER...
THAT WAS QUICK!
LET ME SEE IT!
ALL RIGHT, YOU BLACKGUARD-- HERE IT IS!
BEAUTIFUL! NOW IT'S MINE--MY EYES ALONE WILL ADMIRE IT!
IT'S BACK INTO HIDING FOR ME!
4

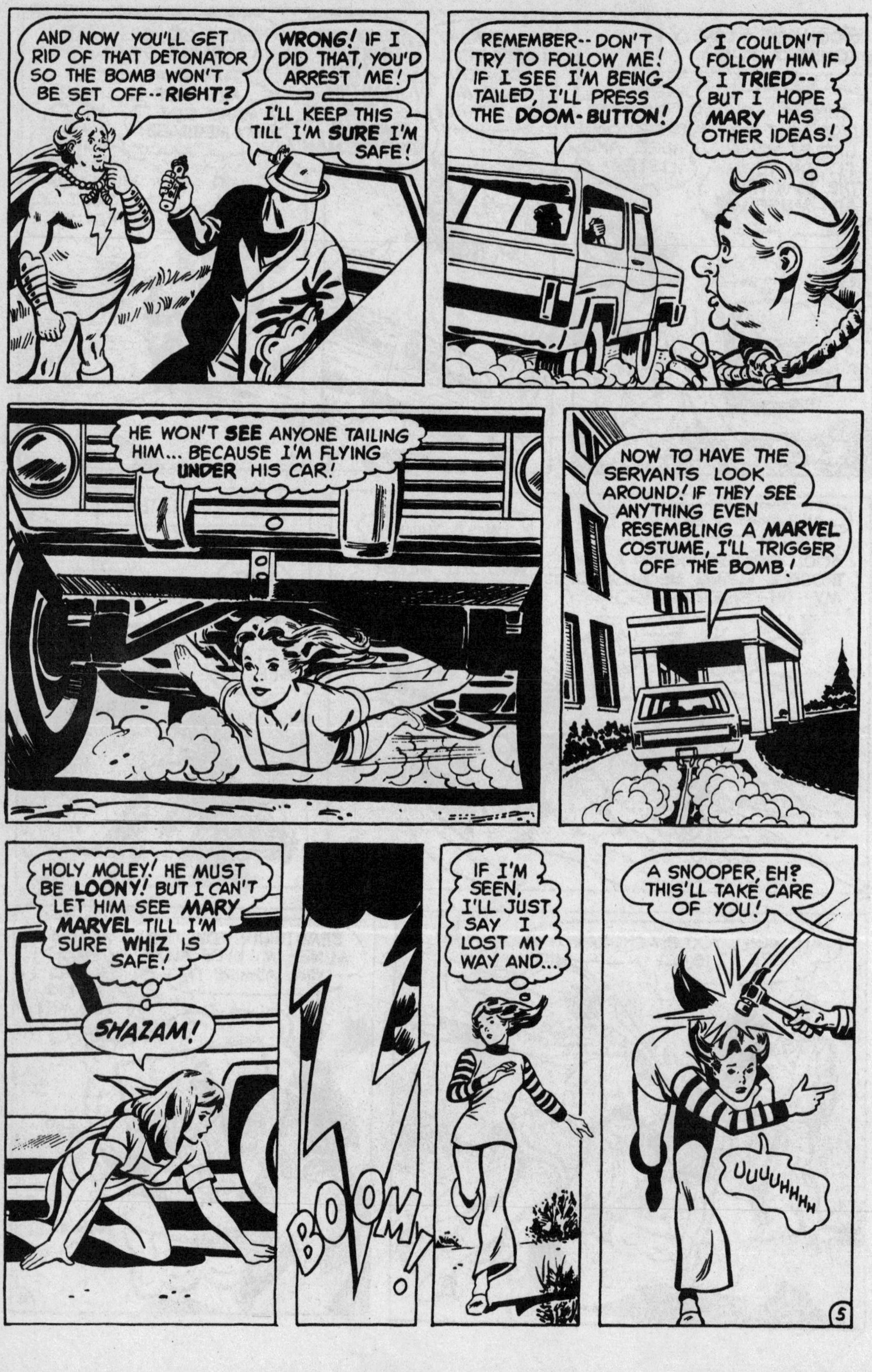
AND NOW YOU'LL GET RID OF THAT DETONATOR SO THE BOMB WON'T BE SET OFF--RIGHT?
WRONG! IF I DID THAT, YOU'D ARREST ME!
I'LL KEEP THIS TILL I'M SURE I'M SAFE!
REMEMBER--DON'T TRY TO FOLLOW ME! IF I SEE I'M BEING TAILED, I'LL PRESS THE DOOM-BUTTON!
I COULDN'T FOLLOW HIM IF I TRIED--BUT I HOPE MARY HAS OTHER IDEAS!
HE WON'T SEE ANYONE TAILING HIM... BECAUSE I'M FLYING UNDER HIS CAR!
NOW TO HAVE THE SERVANTS LOOK AROUND! IF THEY SEE ANYTHING EVEN RESEMBLING A MARVEL COSTUME, I'LL TRIGGER OFF THE BOMB!
HOLY MOLEY! HE MUST BE LOONY! BUT I CAN'T LET HIM SEE MARY MARVEL TILL I'M SURE WHIZ IS SAFE!
SHAZAM!
BOOOM!
IF I'M SEEN, I'LL JUST SAY I LOST MY WAY AND...
A SNOOPER, EH? THIS'LL TAKE CARE OF YOU!
UUUUHHHH
5

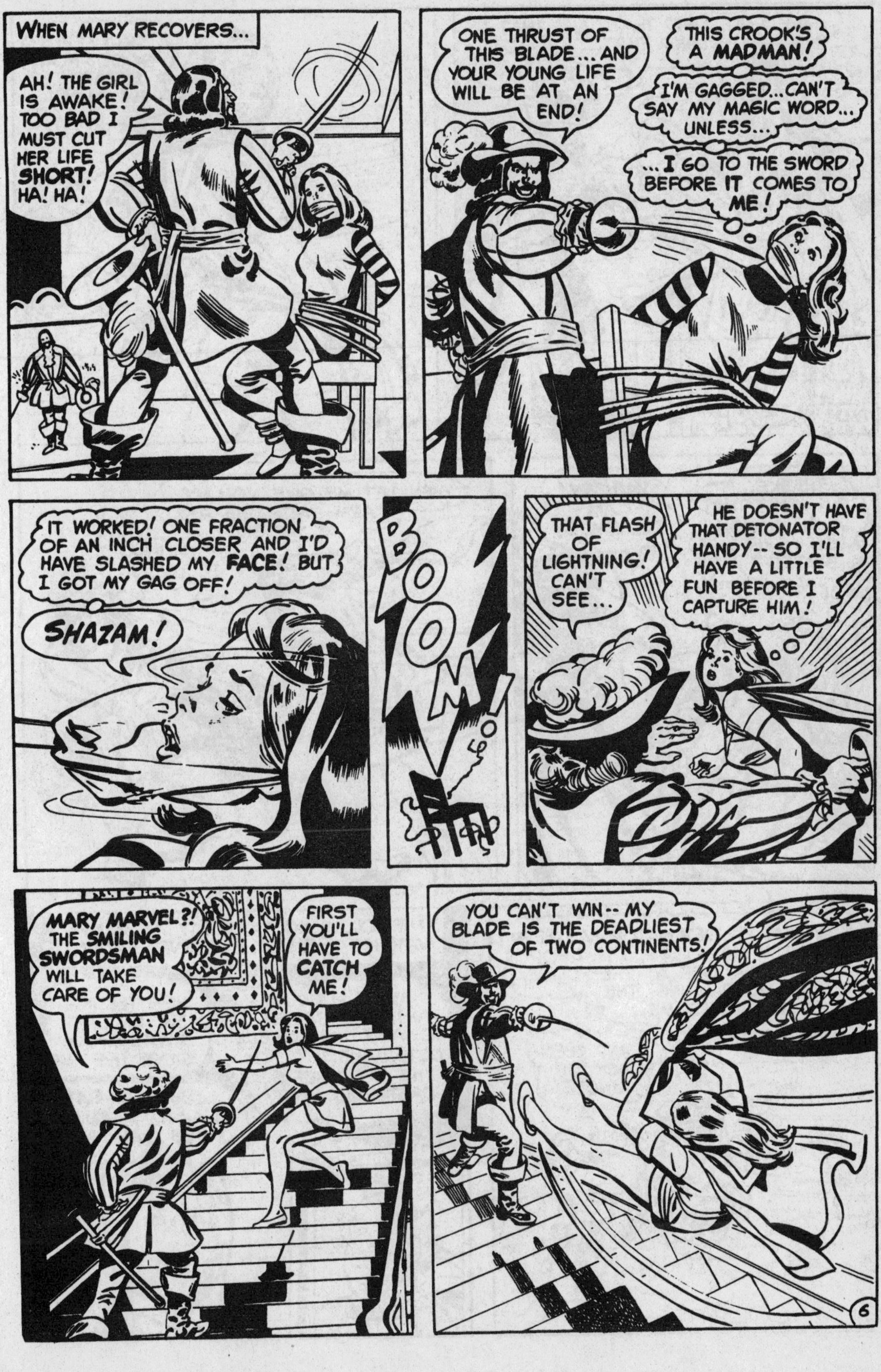
WHEN MARY RECOVERS...
AH! THE GIRL IS AWAKE! TOO BAD I MUST CUT HER LIFE SHORT! HA! HA!
ONE THRUST OF THIS BLADE... AND YOUR YOUNG LIFE WILL BE AT AN END!
THIS CROOK'S A MADMAN!
I'M GAGGED... CAN'T SAY MY MAGIC WORD... UNLESS...
...I GO TO THE SWORD BEFORE IT COMES TO ME!
IT WORKED! ONE FRACTION OF AN INCH CLOSER AND I'D HAVE SLASHED MY FACE! BUT I GOT MY GAG OFF!
SHAZAM!
BOOM!
THAT FLASH OF LIGHTNING! CAN'T SEE...
HE DOESN'T HAVE THAT DETONATOR HANDY -- SO I'LL HAVE A LITTLE FUN BEFORE I CAPTURE HIM!
MARY MARVEL?! THE SMILING SWORDSMAN WILL TAKE CARE OF YOU!
FIRST YOU'LL HAVE TO CATCH ME!
YOU CAN'T WIN -- MY BLADE IS THE DEADLIEST OF TWO CONTINENTS!
6

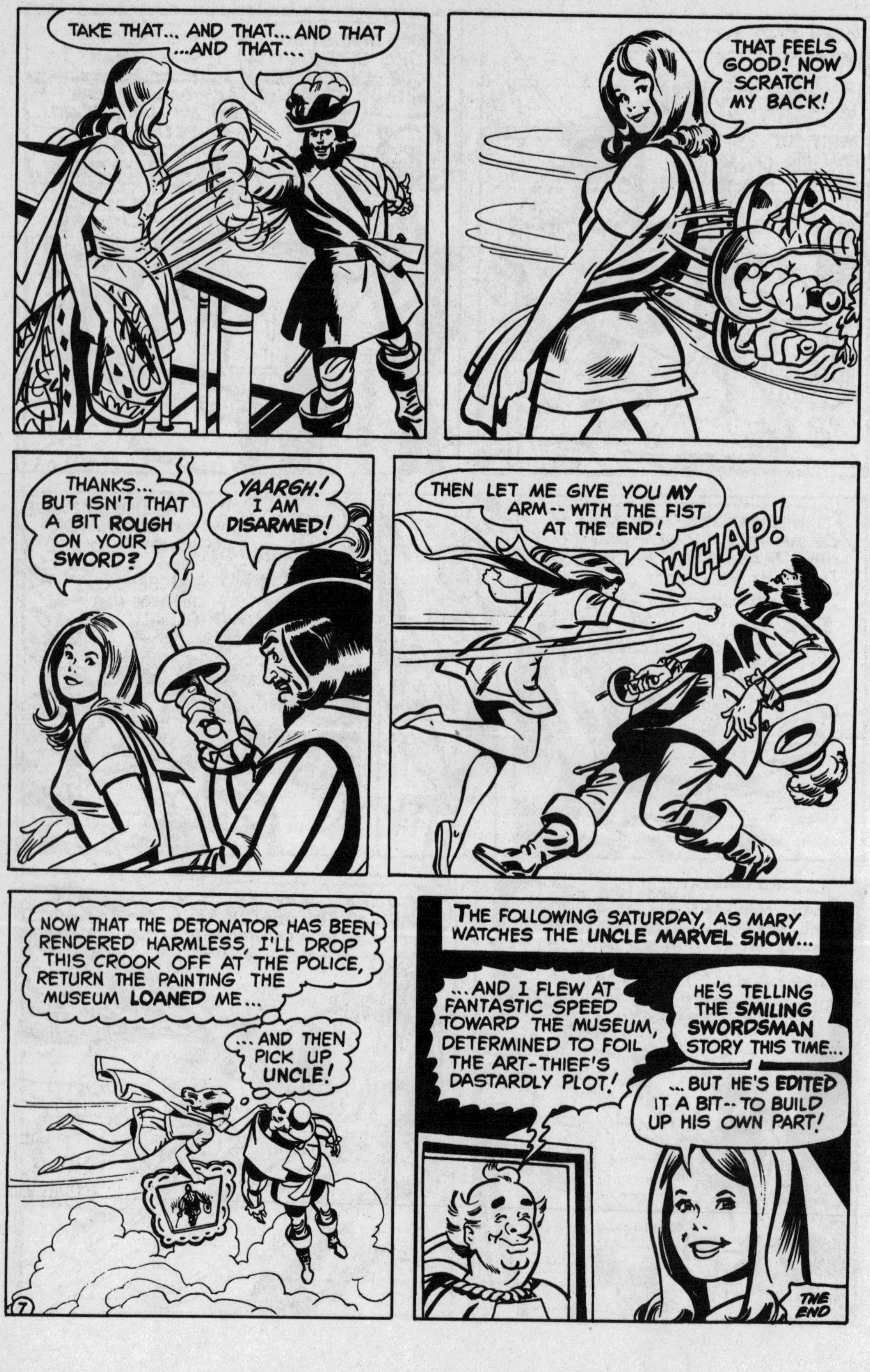
TAKE THAT... AND THAT... AND THAT ...AND THAT...
THAT FEELS GOOD! NOW SCRATCH MY BACK!
THANKS... BUT ISN'T THAT A BIT ROUGH ON YOUR SWORD?
YAARGH! I AM DISARMED!
THEN LET ME GIVE YOU MY ARM-- WITH THE FIST AT THE END!
WHAP!
NOW THAT THE DETONATOR HAS BEEN RENDERED HARMLESS, I'LL DROP THIS CROOK OFF AT THE POLICE, RETURN THE PAINTING THE MUSEUM LOANED ME...
...AND THEN PICK UP UNCLE!
7
THE FOLLOWING SATURDAY, AS MARY WATCHES THE UNCLE MARVEL SHOW...
...AND I FLEW AT FANTASTIC SPEED TOWARD THE MUSEUM, DETERMINED TO FOIL THE ART-THIEF'S DASTARDLY PLOT!
HE'S TELLING THE SMILING SWORDSMAN STORY THIS TIME...
...BUT HE'S EDITED IT A BIT-- TO BUILD UP HIS OWN PART!
THE END

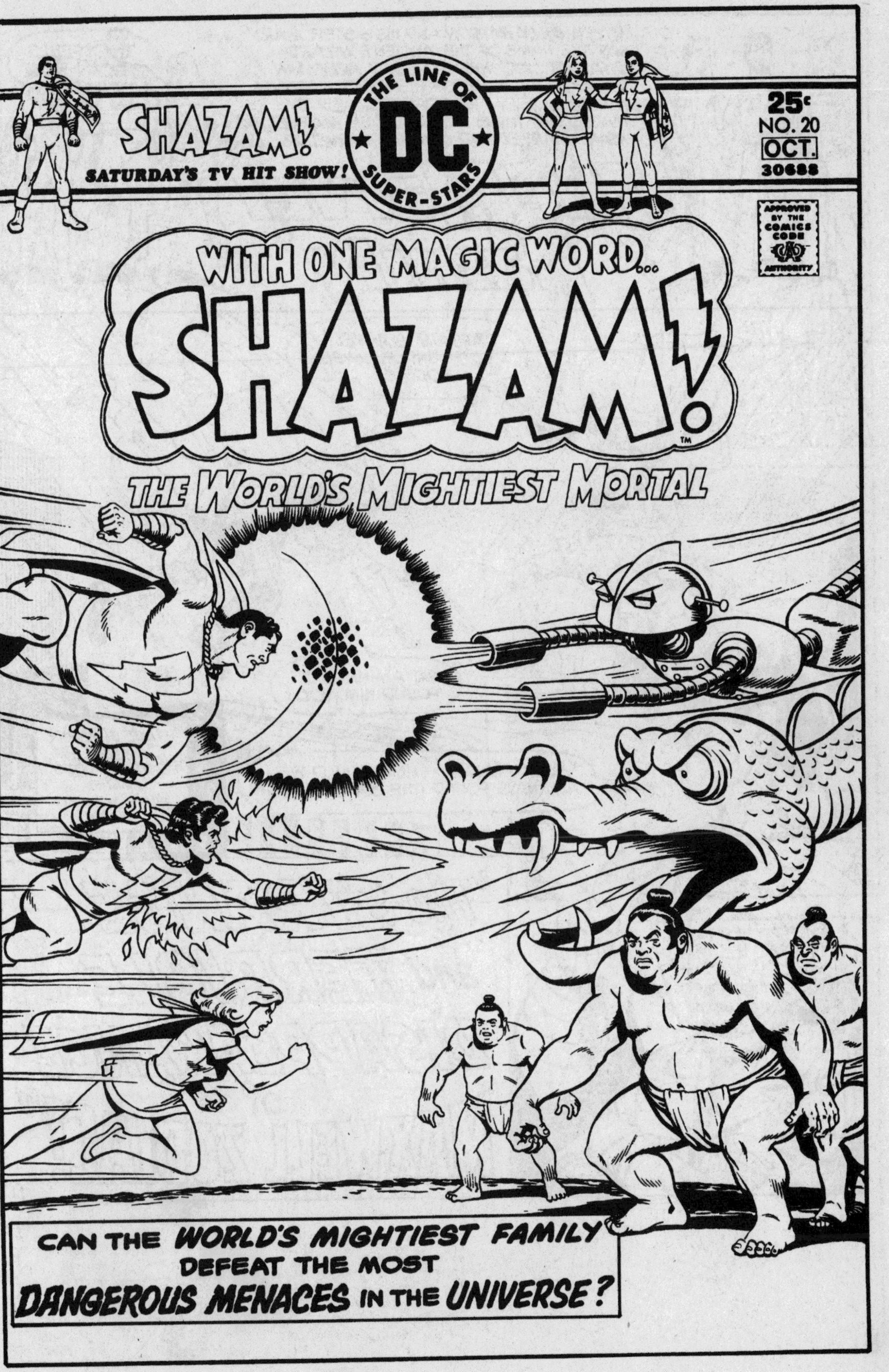
SHAZAM!
SATURDAY'S TV HIT SHOW!
THE LINE OF DC SUPER-STARS
25¢
NO. 20
OCT.
30688
APPROVED BY THE COMICS CODE AUTHORITY
WITH ONE MAGIC WORD...
SHAZAM!
THE WORLD'S MIGHTIEST MORTAL
CAN THE WORLD'S MIGHTIEST FAMILY
DEFEAT THE MOST
DANGEROUS MENACES IN THE UNIVERSE?

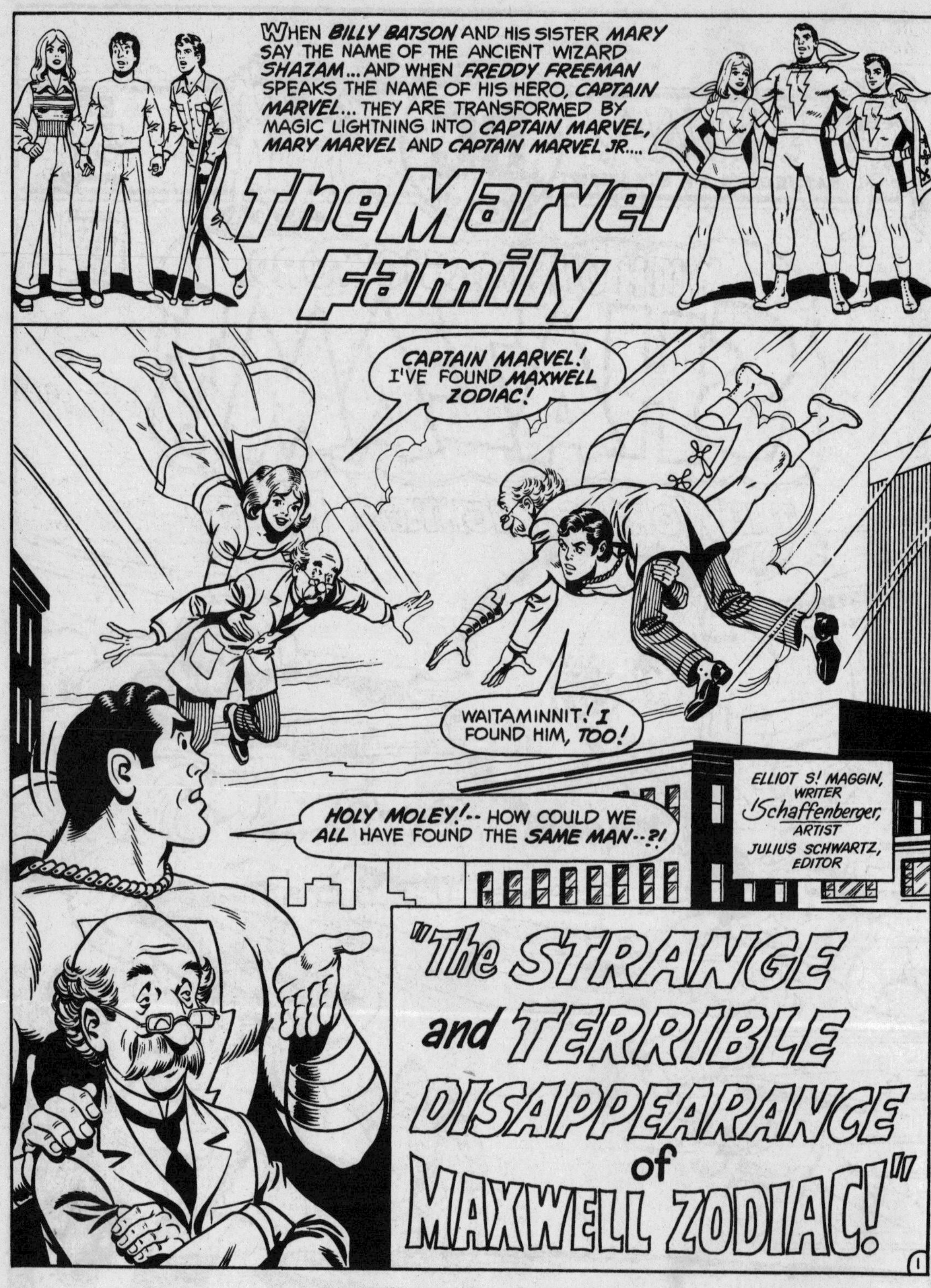
WHEN BILLY BATSON AND HIS SISTER MARY SAY THE NAME OF THE ANCIENT WIZARD SHAZAM... AND WHEN FREDDY FREEMAN SPEAKS THE NAME OF HIS HERO, CAPTAIN MARVEL... THEY ARE TRANSFORMED BY MAGIC LIGHTNING INTO CAPTAIN MARVEL, MARY MARVEL AND CAPTAIN MARVEL JR....
The Marvel Family
CAPTAIN MARVEL! I'VE FOUND MAXWELL ZODIAC!
WAITAMINNIT! I FOUND HIM, TOO!
HOLY MOLEY!-- HOW COULD WE ALL HAVE FOUND THE SAME MAN--?!
ELLIOT S! MAGGIN, WRITER
Schaffenberger, ARTIST
JULIUS SCHWARTZ, EDITOR
"The STRANGE and TERRIBLE DISAPPEARANCE of MAXWELL ZODIAC!"
1

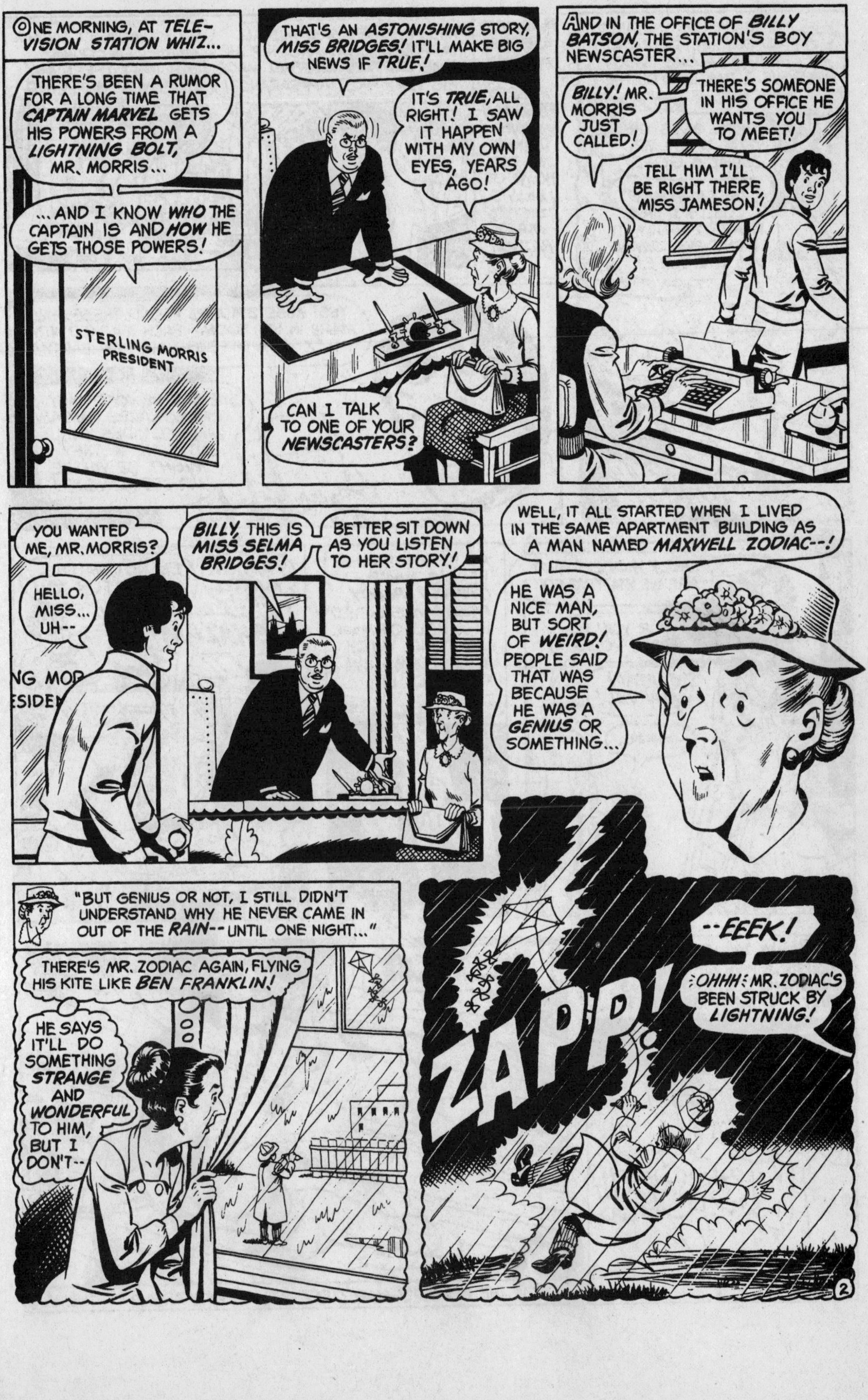
ONE MORNING, AT TELE-VISION STATION WHIZ...
THERE'S BEEN A RUMOR FOR A LONG TIME THAT CAPTAIN MARVEL GETS HIS POWERS FROM A LIGHTNING BOLT, MR. MORRIS...
...AND I KNOW WHO THE CAPTAIN IS AND HOW HE GETS THOSE POWERS!
STERLING MORRIS PRESIDENT
THAT'S AN ASTONISHING STORY, MISS BRIDGES! IT'LL MAKE BIG NEWS IF TRUE!
IT'S TRUE, ALL RIGHT! I SAW IT HAPPEN WITH MY OWN EYES, YEARS AGO!
CAN I TALK TO ONE OF YOUR NEWSCASTERS?
AND IN THE OFFICE OF BILLY BATSON, THE STATION'S BOY NEWSCASTER...
BILLY! MR. MORRIS JUST CALLED!
THERE'S SOMEONE IN HIS OFFICE HE WANTS YOU TO MEET!
TELL HIM I'LL BE RIGHT THERE, MISS JAMESON!
YOU WANTED ME, MR. MORRIS?
HELLO, MISS... UH--
BILLY, THIS IS MISS SELMA BRIDGES!
BETTER SIT DOWN AS YOU LISTEN TO HER STORY!
WELL, IT ALL STARTED WHEN I LIVED IN THE SAME APARTMENT BUILDING AS A MAN NAMED MAXWELL ZODIAC--!
HE WAS A NICE MAN, BUT SORT OF WEIRD! PEOPLE SAID THAT WAS BECAUSE HE WAS A GENIUS OR SOMETHING...
"BUT GENIUS OR NOT, I STILL DIDN'T UNDERSTAND WHY HE NEVER CAME IN OUT OF THE RAIN--UNTIL ONE NIGHT..."
THERE'S MR. ZODIAC AGAIN, FLYING HIS KITE LIKE BEN FRANKLIN!
HE SAYS IT'LL DO SOMETHING STRANGE AND WONDERFUL TO HIM, BUT I DON'T--
--EEEK!
OHHH! MR. ZODIAC'S BEEN STRUCK BY LIGHTNING!
ZAPP!
2

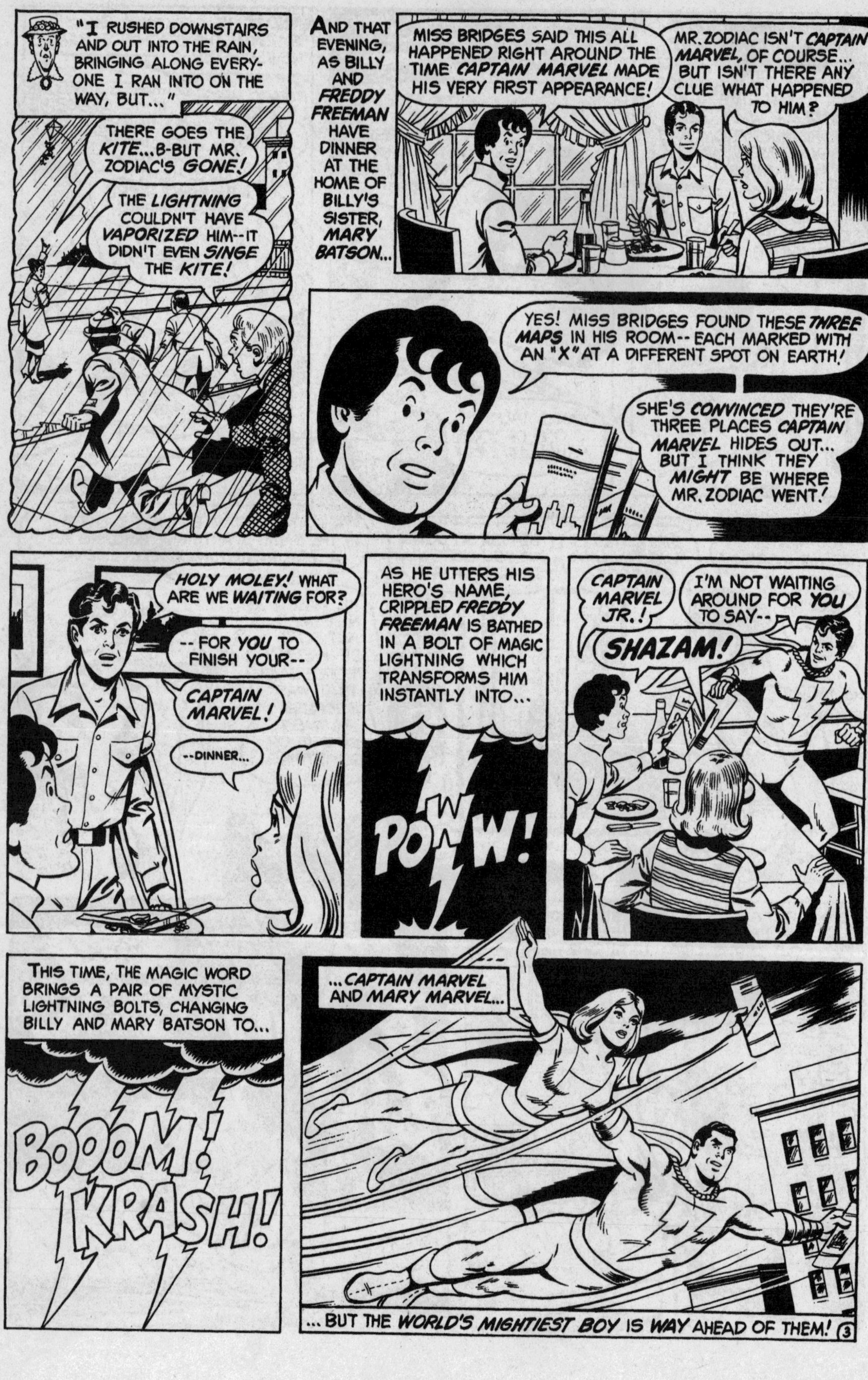
"I RUSHED DOWNSTAIRS AND OUT INTO THE RAIN, BRINGING ALONG EVERYONE I RAN INTO ON THE WAY, BUT..."
THERE GOES THE KITE...B-BUT MR. ZODIAC'S GONE!
THE LIGHTNING COULDN'T HAVE VAPORIZED HIM--IT DIDN'T EVEN SINGE THE KITE!
AND THAT EVENING, AS BILLY AND FREDDY FREEMAN HAVE DINNER AT THE HOME OF BILLY'S SISTER, MARY BATSON...
MISS BRIDGES SAID THIS ALL HAPPENED RIGHT AROUND THE TIME CAPTAIN MARVEL MADE HIS VERY FIRST APPEARANCE!
MR. ZODIAC ISN'T CAPTAIN MARVEL, OF COURSE... BUT ISN'T THERE ANY CLUE WHAT HAPPENED TO HIM?
YES! MISS BRIDGES FOUND THESE THREE MAPS IN HIS ROOM-- EACH MARKED WITH AN "X" AT A DIFFERENT SPOT ON EARTH!
SHE'S CONVINCED THEY'RE THREE PLACES CAPTAIN MARVEL HIDES OUT... BUT I THINK THEY MIGHT BE WHERE MR. ZODIAC WENT!
HOLY MOLEY! WHAT ARE WE WAITING FOR?
-- FOR YOU TO FINISH YOUR--
CAPTAIN MARVEL!
--DINNER...
AS HE UTTERS HIS HERO'S NAME, CRIPPLED FREDDY FREEMAN IS BATHED IN A BOLT OF MAGIC LIGHTNING WHICH TRANSFORMS HIM INSTANTLY INTO...
POWW!
CAPTAIN MARVEL JR.!
I'M NOT WAITING AROUND FOR YOU TO SAY--
SHAZAM!
THIS TIME, THE MAGIC WORD BRINGS A PAIR OF MYSTIC LIGHTNING BOLTS, CHANGING BILLY AND MARY BATSON TO...
BOOOM! KRASH!
...CAPTAIN MARVEL AND MARY MARVEL...
... BUT THE WORLD'S MIGHTIEST BOY IS WAY AHEAD OF THEM!
3

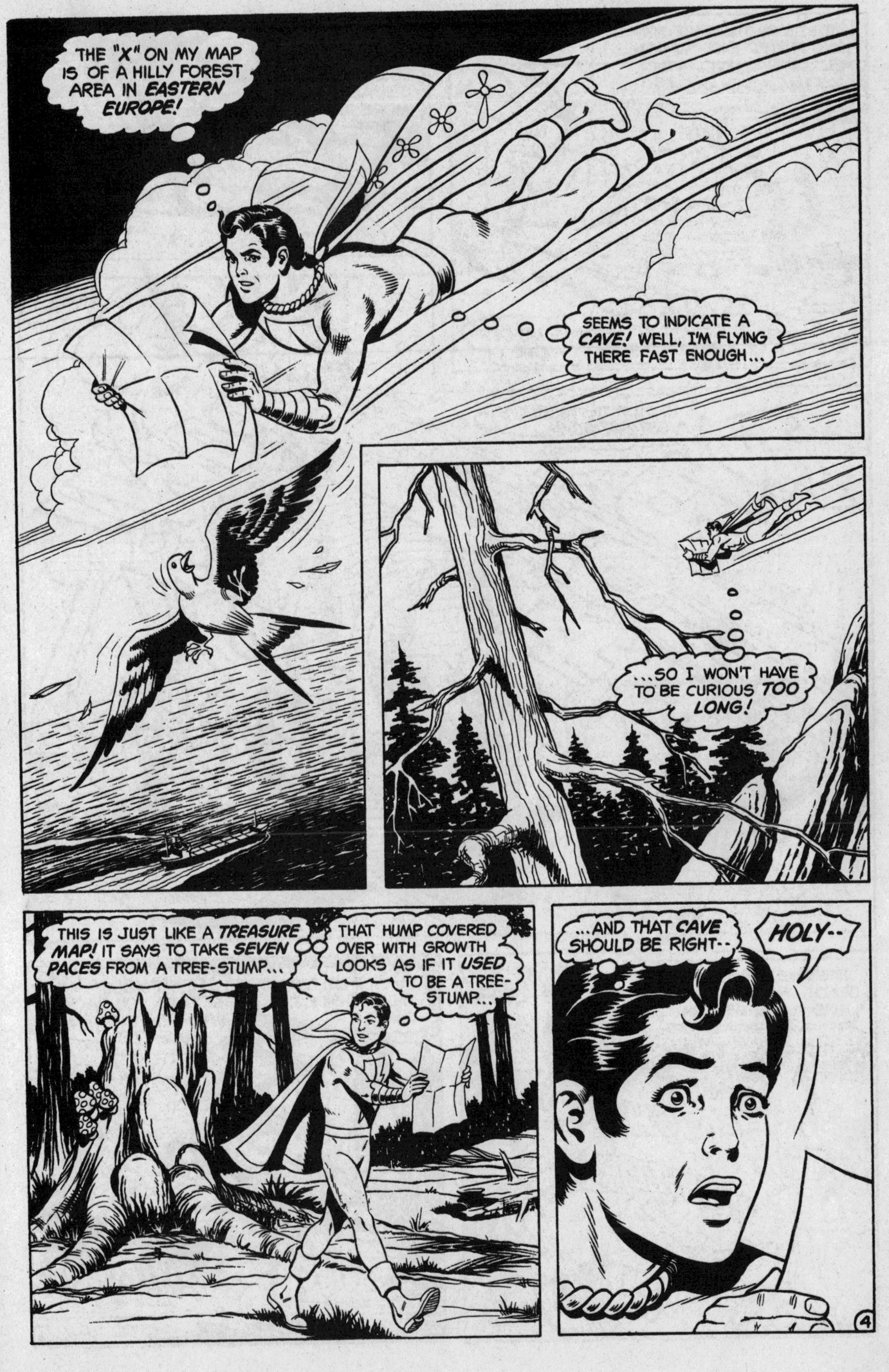
THE "X" ON MY MAP IS OF A HILLY FOREST AREA IN EASTERN EUROPE!
SEEMS TO INDICATE A CAVE! WELL, I'M FLYING THERE FAST ENOUGH...
...SO I WON'T HAVE TO BE CURIOUS TOO LONG!
THIS IS JUST LIKE A TREASURE MAP! IT SAYS TO TAKE SEVEN PACES FROM A TREE-STUMP...
THAT HUMP COVERED OVER WITH GROWTH LOOKS AS IF IT USED TO BE A TREE-STUMP...
...AND THAT CAVE SHOULD BE RIGHT--
HOLY--
4

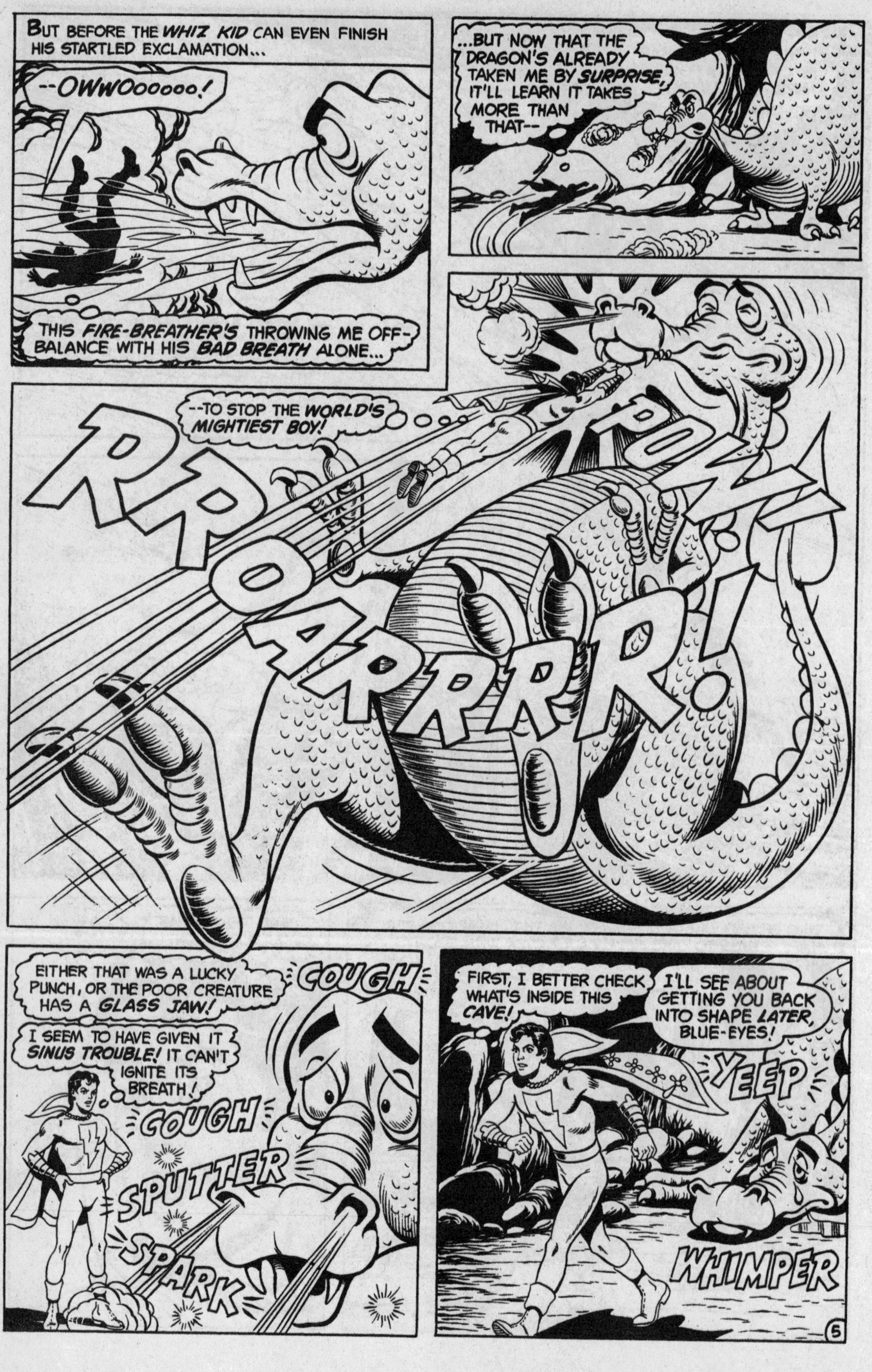
BUT BEFORE THE WHIZ KID CAN EVEN FINISH HIS STARTLED EXCLAMATION...
--OWWOoooooo!
THIS FIRE-BREATHER'S THROWING ME OFF-BALANCE WITH HIS BAD BREATH ALONE...
...BUT NOW THAT THE DRAGON'S ALREADY TAKEN ME BY SURPRISE, IT'LL LEARN IT TAKES MORE THAN THAT--
--TO STOP THE WORLD'S MIGHTIEST BOY!
POW!
RROARRRR!
EITHER THAT WAS A LUCKY PUNCH, OR THE POOR CREATURE HAS A GLASS JAW!
I SEEM TO HAVE GIVEN IT SINUS TROUBLE! IT CAN'T IGNITE ITS BREATH!
COUGH
COUGH
SPUTTER
SPARK
FIRST, I BETTER CHECK WHAT'S INSIDE THIS CAVE!
I'LL SEE ABOUT GETTING YOU BACK INTO SHAPE LATER, BLUE-EYES!
YEEP
WHIMPER
5

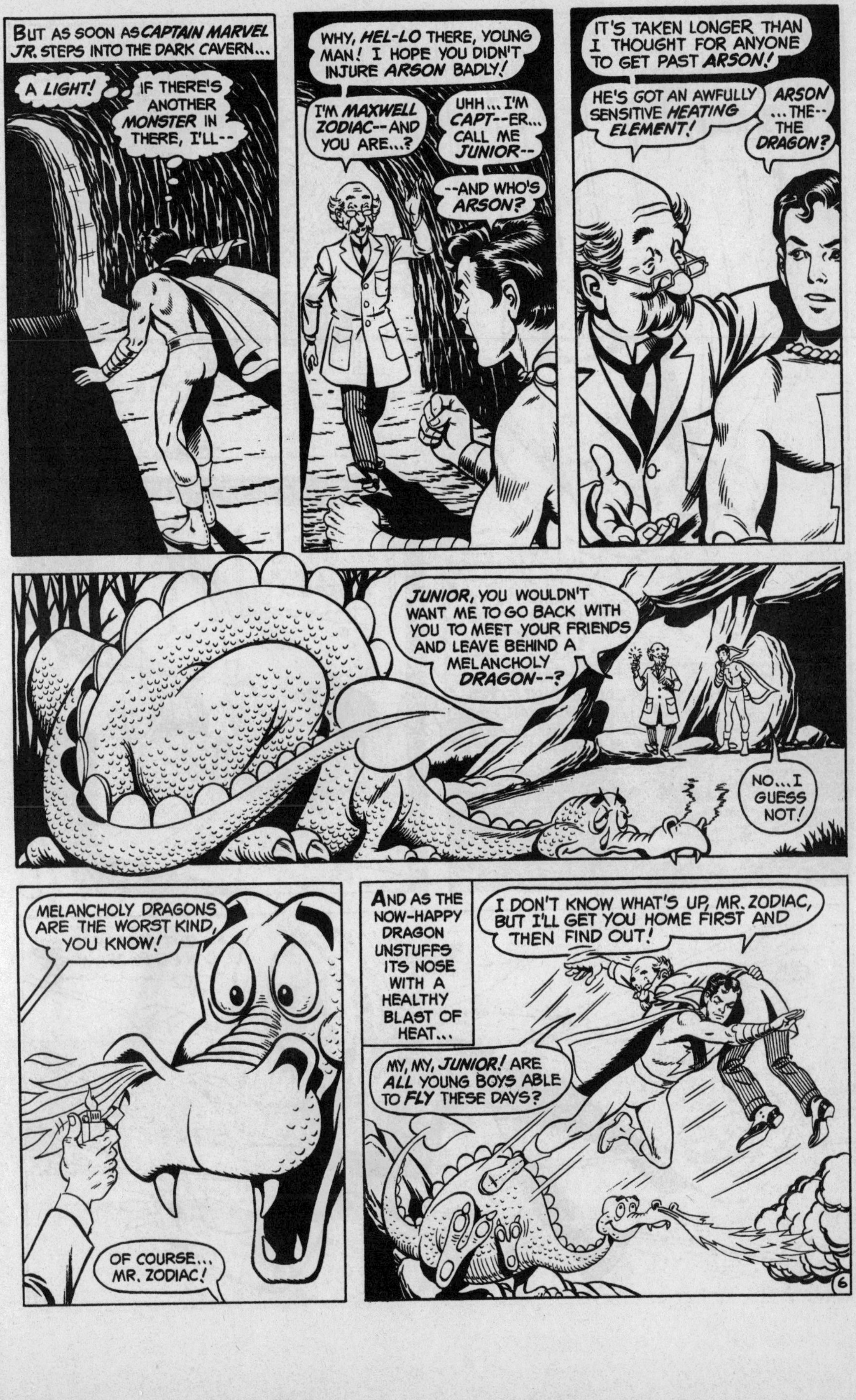

BUT AS SOON AS CAPTAIN MARVEL JR. STEPS INTO THE DARK CAVERN...
A LIGHT!
IF THERE'S ANOTHER MONSTER IN THERE, I'LL--
WHY, HEL-LO THERE, YOUNG MAN! I HOPE YOU DIDN'T INJURE ARSON BADLY!
I'M MAXWELL ZODIAC--AND YOU ARE...?
UHH... I'M CAPT--ER... CALL ME JUNIOR--
--AND WHO'S ARSON?
IT'S TAKEN LONGER THAN I THOUGHT FOR ANYONE TO GET PAST ARSON!
HE'S GOT AN AWFULLY SENSITIVE HEATING ELEMENT!
ARSON ...THE-- THE DRAGON?
JUNIOR, YOU WOULDN'T WANT ME TO GO BACK WITH YOU TO MEET YOUR FRIENDS AND LEAVE BEHIND A MELANCHOLY DRAGON--?
NO...I GUESS NOT!
MELANCHOLY DRAGONS ARE THE WORST KIND, YOU KNOW!
OF COURSE... MR. ZODIAC!
AND AS THE NOW-HAPPY DRAGON UNSTUFFS ITS NOSE WITH A HEALTHY BLAST OF HEAT...
I DON'T KNOW WHAT'S UP, MR. ZODIAC, BUT I'LL GET YOU HOME FIRST AND THEN FIND OUT!
MY, MY, JUNIOR! ARE ALL YOUNG BOYS ABLE TO FLY THESE DAYS?
6

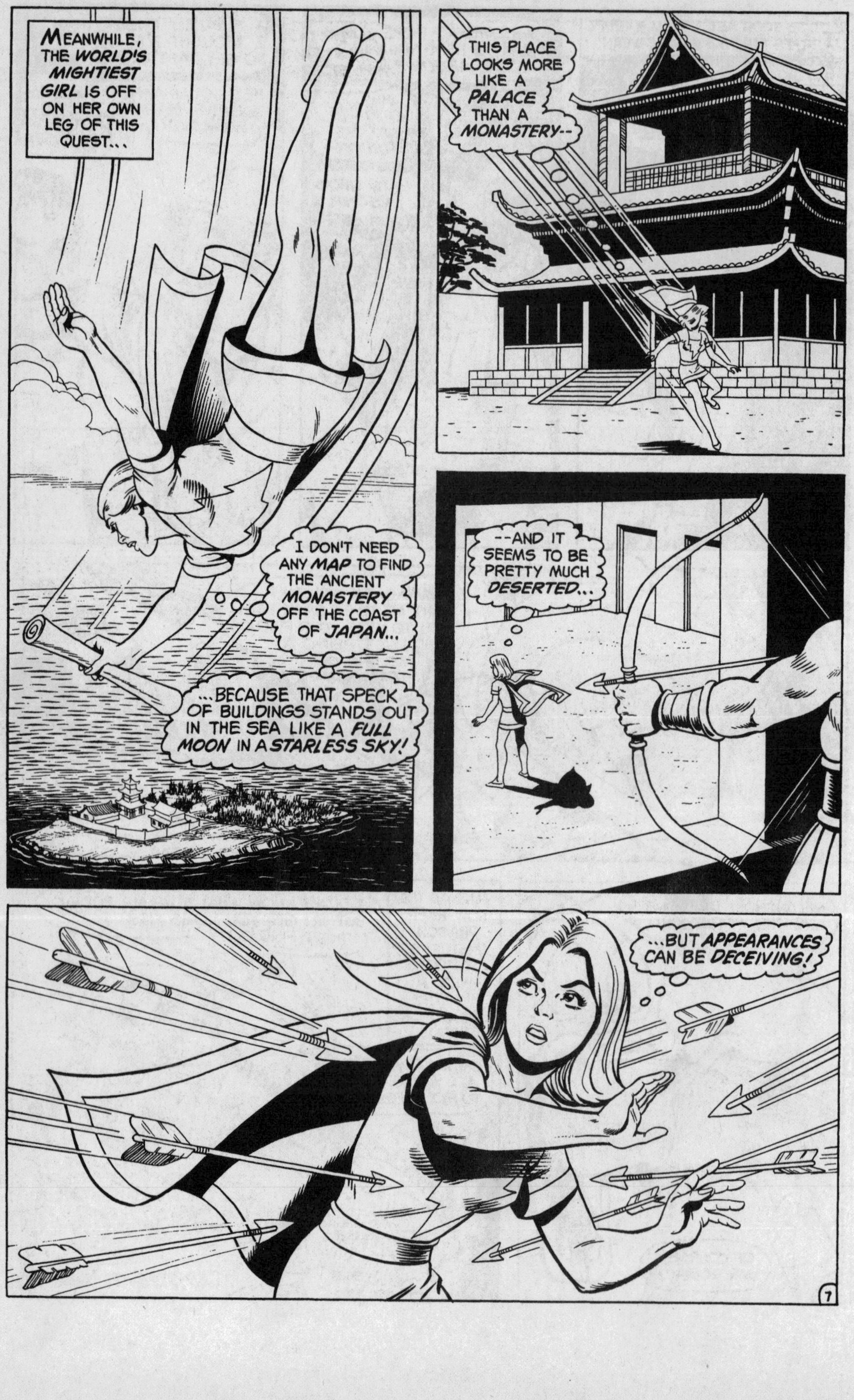
MEANWHILE, THE WORLD'S MIGHTIEST GIRL IS OFF ON HER OWN LEG OF THIS QUEST...
I DON'T NEED ANY MAP TO FIND THE ANCIENT MONASTERY OFF THE COAST OF JAPAN...
...BECAUSE THAT SPECK OF BUILDINGS STANDS OUT IN THE SEA LIKE A FULL MOON IN A STARLESS SKY!
THIS PLACE LOOKS MORE LIKE A PALACE THAN A MONASTERY--
--AND IT SEEMS TO BE PRETTY MUCH DESERTED...
...BUT APPEARANCES CAN BE DECEIVING!
7

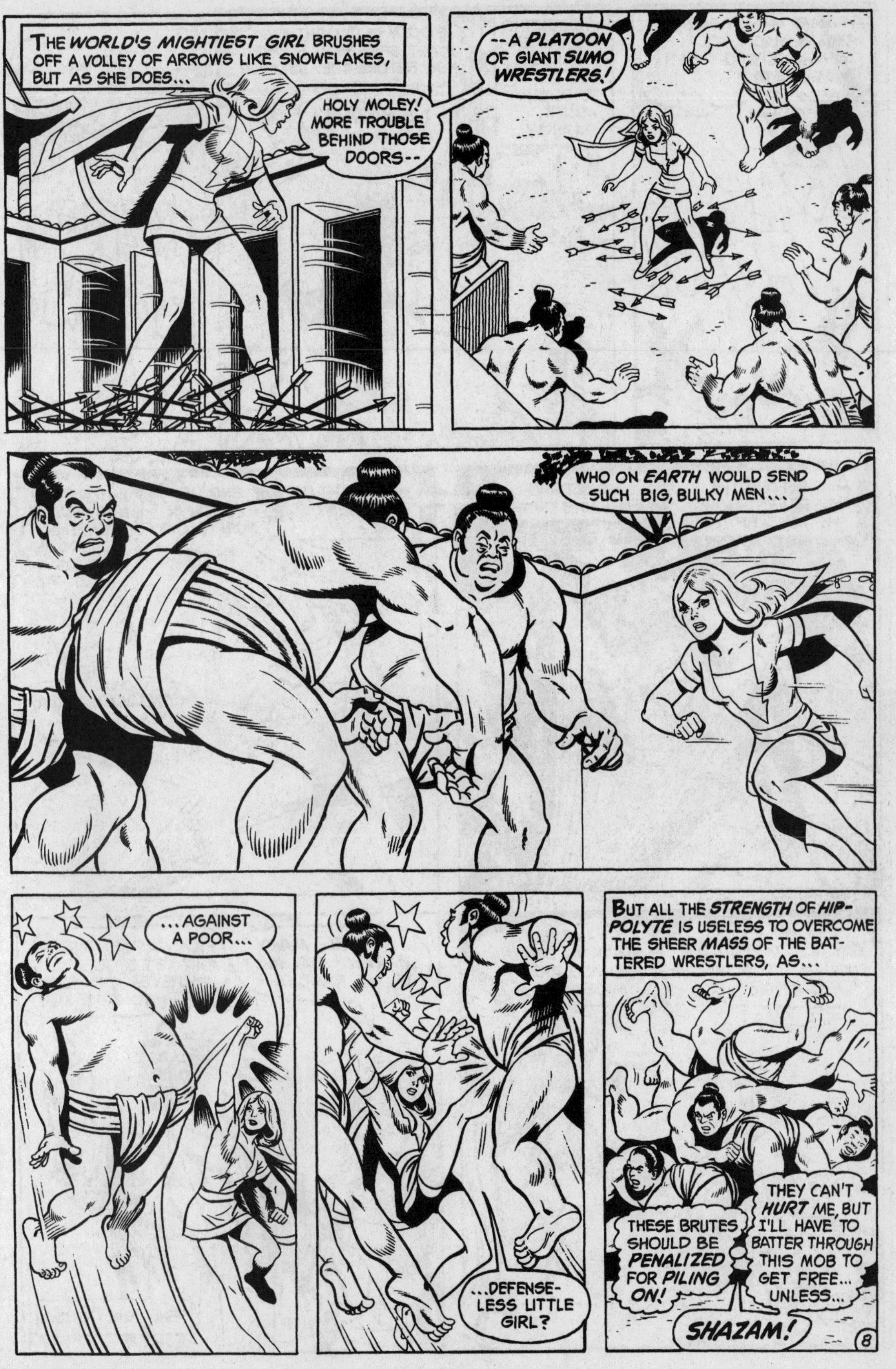
THE WORLD'S MIGHTIEST GIRL BRUSHES OFF A VOLLEY OF ARROWS LIKE SNOWFLAKES, BUT AS SHE DOES...
HOLY MOLEY! MORE TROUBLE BEHIND THOSE DOORS--
--A PLATOON OF GIANT SUMO WRESTLERS!
WHO ON EARTH WOULD SEND SUCH BIG, BULKY MEN...
...AGAINST A POOR...
...DEFENSE-LESS LITTLE GIRL?
BUT ALL THE STRENGTH OF HIP-POLYTE IS USELESS TO OVERCOME THE SHEER MASS OF THE BAT-TERED WRESTLERS, AS...
THESE BRUTES SHOULD BE PENALIZED FOR PILING ON!
THEY CAN'T HURT ME, BUT I'LL HAVE TO BATTER THROUGH THIS MOB TO GET FREE... UNLESS...
SHAZAM!
8

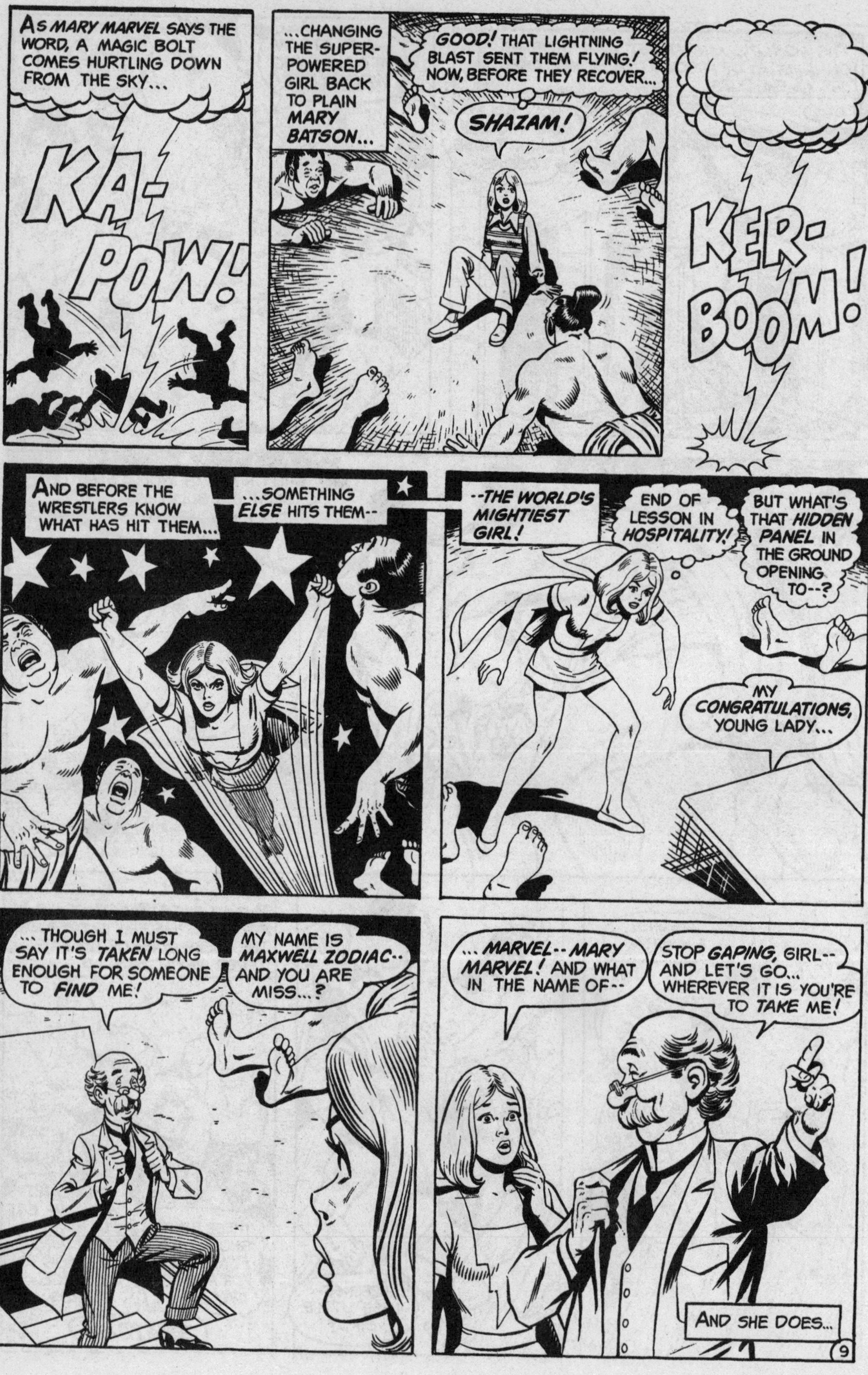
AS MARY MARVEL SAYS THE WORD, A MAGIC BOLT COMES HURTLING DOWN FROM THE SKY...
KA-POW!
...CHANGING THE SUPER-POWERED GIRL BACK TO PLAIN MARY BATSON...
GOOD! THAT LIGHTNING BLAST SENT THEM FLYING! NOW, BEFORE THEY RECOVER...
SHAZAM!
KER-BOOM!
AND BEFORE THE WRESTLERS KNOW WHAT HAS HIT THEM...
...SOMETHING ELSE HITS THEM--
--THE WORLD'S MIGHTIEST GIRL!
END OF LESSON IN HOSPITALITY!
BUT WHAT'S THAT HIDDEN PANEL IN THE GROUND OPENING TO--?
MY CONGRATULATIONS, YOUNG LADY...
... THOUGH I MUST SAY IT'S TAKEN LONG ENOUGH FOR SOMEONE TO FIND ME!
MY NAME IS MAXWELL ZODIAC-- AND YOU ARE MISS...?
... MARVEL-- MARY MARVEL! AND WHAT IN THE NAME OF--
STOP GAPING, GIRL-- AND LET'S GO... WHEREVER IT IS YOU'RE TO TAKE ME!
AND SHE DOES...
9

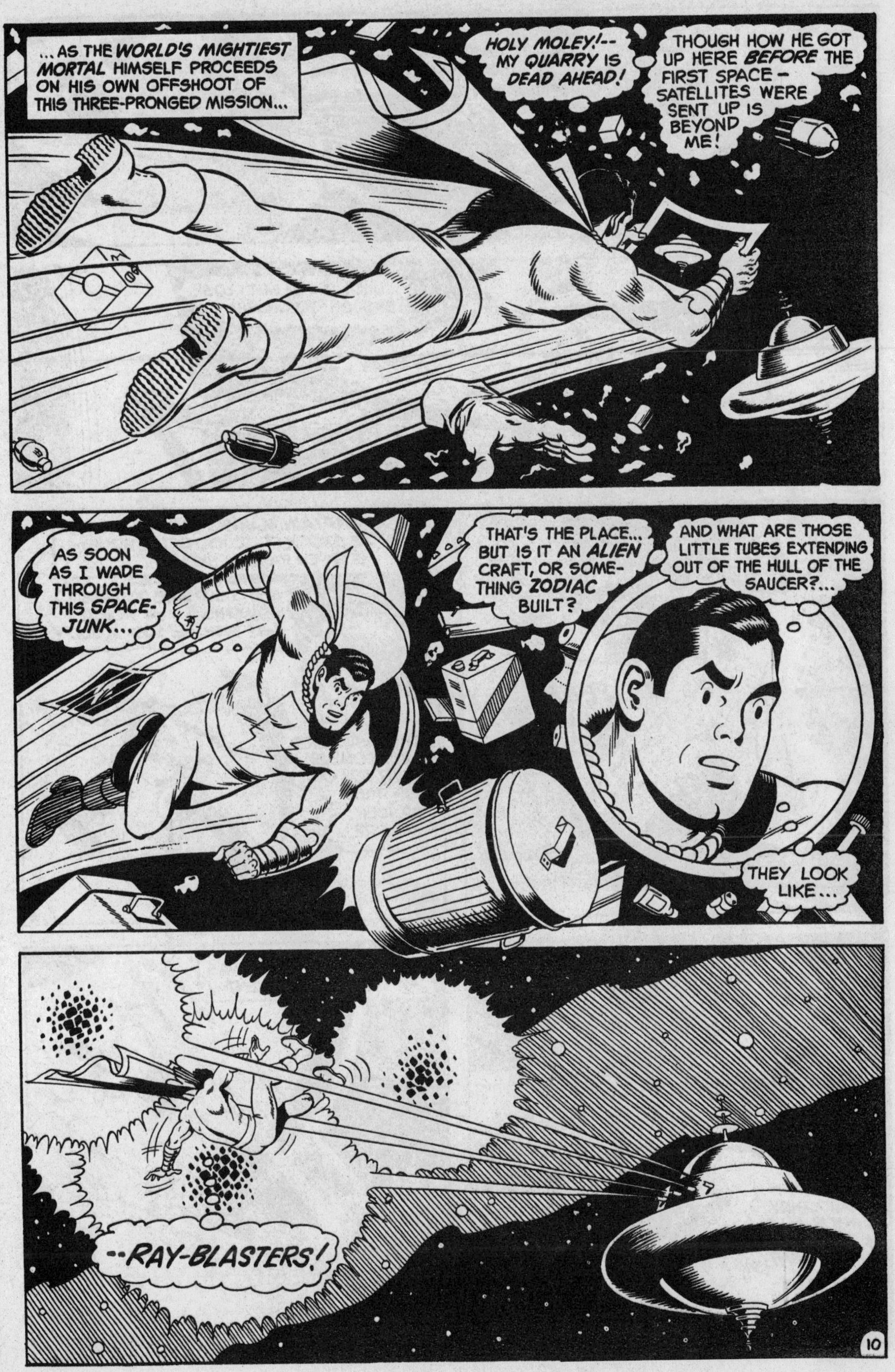
...AS THE WORLD'S MIGHTIEST MORTAL HIMSELF PROCEEDS ON HIS OWN OFFSHOOT OF THIS THREE-PRONGED MISSION...
HOLY MOLEY!-- MY QUARRY IS DEAD AHEAD!
THOUGH HOW HE GOT UP HERE BEFORE THE FIRST SPACE-SATELLITES WERE SENT UP IS BEYOND ME!
AS SOON AS I WADE THROUGH THIS SPACE-JUNK...
THAT'S THE PLACE... BUT IS IT AN ALIEN CRAFT, OR SOMETHING ZODIAC BUILT?
AND WHAT ARE THOSE LITTLE TUBES EXTENDING OUT OF THE HULL OF THE SAUCER?...
THEY LOOK LIKE...
--RAY-BLASTERS!
10

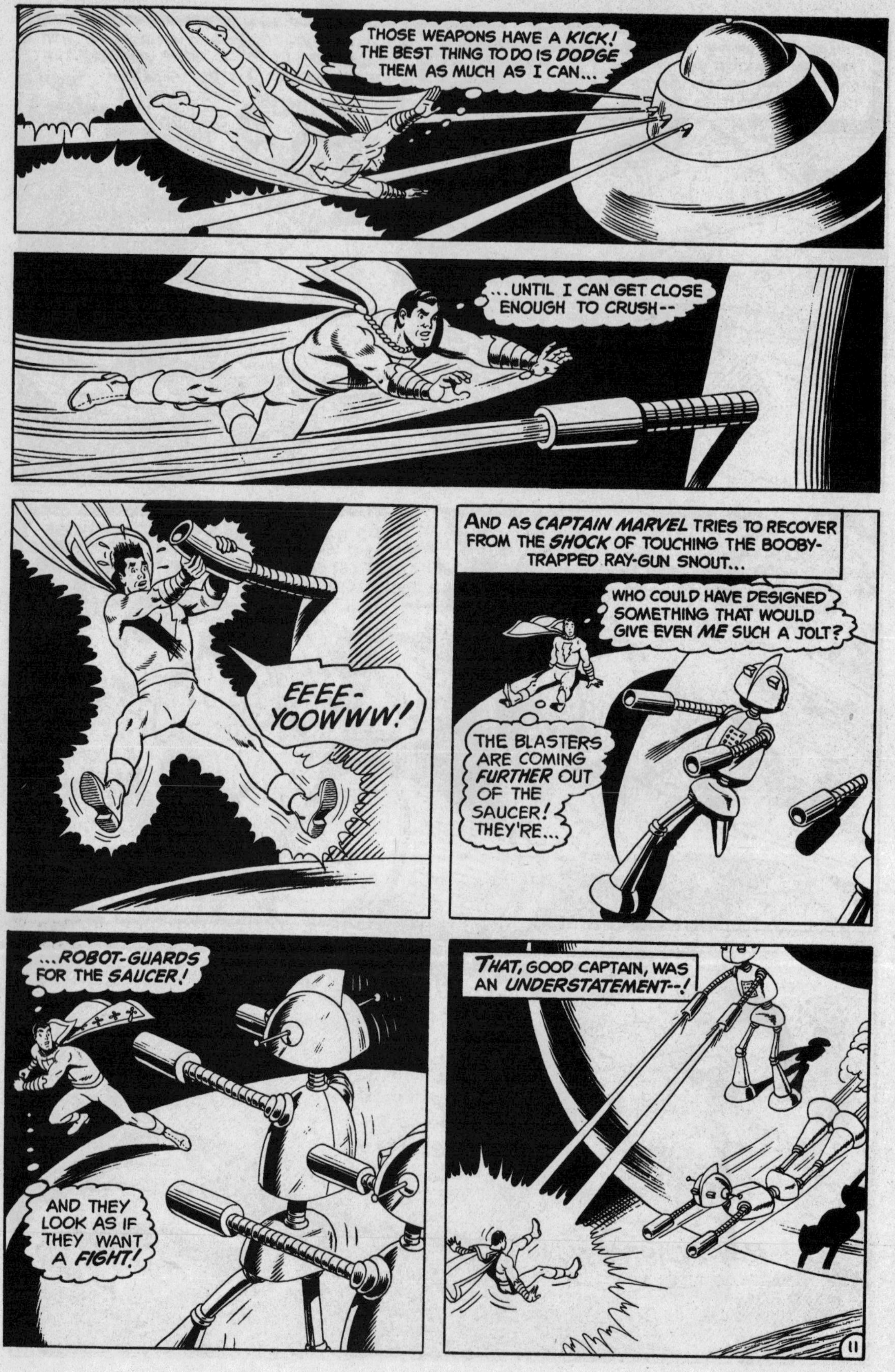
THOSE WEAPONS HAVE A *KICK*! THE BEST THING TO DO IS *DODGE* THEM AS MUCH AS I CAN...
...UNTIL I CAN GET CLOSE ENOUGH TO CRUSH--
EEEE-YOOWWW!
AND AS *CAPTAIN MARVEL* TRIES TO RECOVER FROM THE *SHOCK* OF TOUCHING THE BOOBY-TRAPPED RAY-GUN SNOUT...
WHO COULD HAVE DESIGNED SOMETHING THAT WOULD GIVE EVEN *ME* SUCH A JOLT?
THE BLASTERS ARE COMING *FURTHER* OUT OF THE SAUCER! THEY'RE...
...*ROBOT-GUARDS* FOR THE *SAUCER*!
AND THEY LOOK AS IF THEY WANT A *FIGHT*!
THAT, GOOD CAPTAIN, WAS AN *UNDERSTATEMENT*--!
11

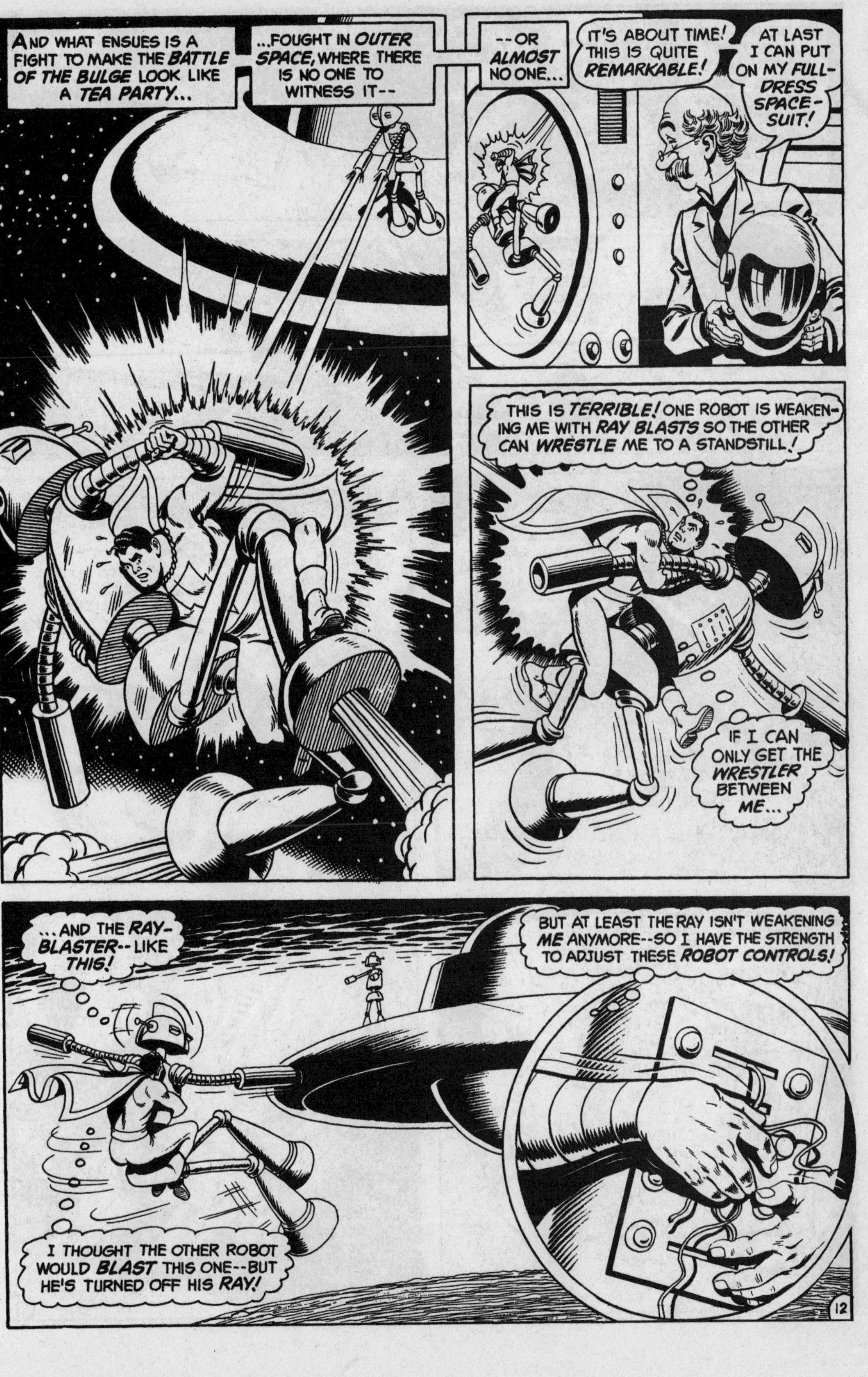
AND WHAT ENSUES IS A FIGHT TO MAKE THE BATTLE OF THE BULGE LOOK LIKE A TEA PARTY...
...FOUGHT IN OUTER SPACE, WHERE THERE IS NO ONE TO WITNESS IT--
--OR ALMOST NO ONE...
IT'S ABOUT TIME! THIS IS QUITE REMARKABLE!
AT LAST I CAN PUT ON MY FULL-DRESS SPACE-SUIT!
THIS IS TERRIBLE! ONE ROBOT IS WEAKENING ME WITH RAY BLASTS SO THE OTHER CAN WRESTLE ME TO A STANDSTILL!
IF I CAN ONLY GET THE WRESTLER BETWEEN ME...
...AND THE RAY-BLASTER--LIKE THIS!
BUT AT LEAST THE RAY ISN'T WEAKENING ME ANYMORE--SO I HAVE THE STRENGTH TO ADJUST THESE ROBOT CONTROLS!
I THOUGHT THE OTHER ROBOT WOULD BLAST THIS ONE--BUT HE'S TURNED OFF HIS RAY!
12

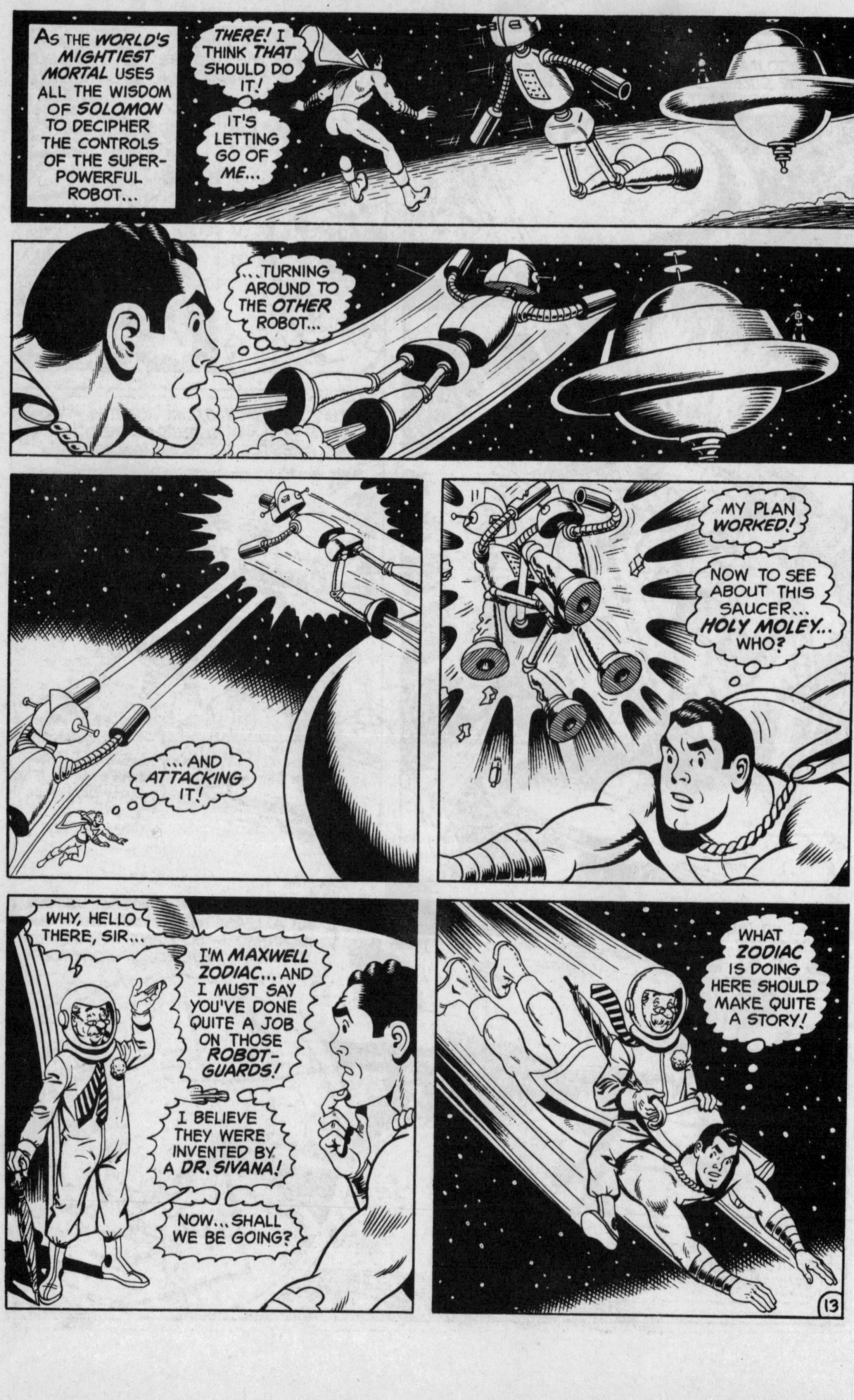

AS THE WORLD'S MIGHTIEST MORTAL USES ALL THE WISDOM OF SOLOMON TO DECIPHER THE CONTROLS OF THE SUPER-POWERFUL ROBOT...
THERE! I THINK THAT SHOULD DO IT!
IT'S LETTING GO OF ME...
...TURNING AROUND TO THE OTHER ROBOT...
...AND ATTACKING IT!
MY PLAN WORKED!
NOW TO SEE ABOUT THIS SAUCER... HOLY MOLEY... WHO?
WHY, HELLO THERE, SIR...
I'M MAXWELL ZODIAC... AND I MUST SAY YOU'VE DONE QUITE A JOB ON THOSE ROBOT-GUARDS!
I BELIEVE THEY WERE INVENTED BY A DR. SIVANA!
NOW... SHALL WE BE GOING?
WHAT ZODIAC IS DOING HERE SHOULD MAKE QUITE A STORY!
13

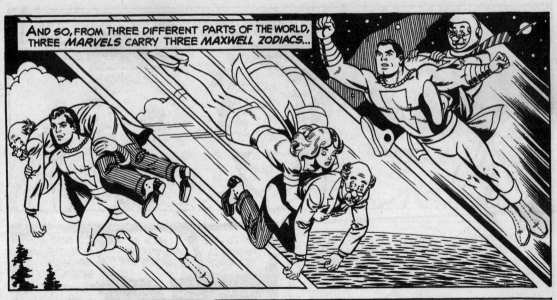

AND SO, FROM THREE DIFFERENT PARTS OF THE WORLD, THREE *MARVELS* CARRY THREE *MAXWELL ZODIACS*...

...UNTIL ALL SIX PEOPLE *ZOOM* DOWN *TOWARD* THE *WHIZ* BUILDING, TO AN OVERPOWERING...

HOLY MOLEY!?!

GOOD TO SEE YOU AGAIN, FELLOW ZODIACS!

IT'S BEEN LONGER THAN I FIGURED--

OH, THIS WILL BE A MOST PLEASANT EXPERIENCE!

BY NOW WE'RE ALMOST READY TO -- YES, *CAPTAIN?*

WE'VE GOT A *MYSTERY* TO SOLVE... AND *YOU'RE* INVOLVED!

MISS SELMA BRIDGES WANTS TO KNOW WHAT HAPPENED TO YOU!

BRIDGES?! THAT SNOOPY *BLABBER-MOUTH* WILL RUIN *EVERYTHING!*

AND MOMENTARILY, BEFORE STATION *WHIZ* CAMERAS...

MR. ZODIAC?

MR. ZODIAC?

MR. ZODIAC?!?

MR. ZODIAC?

GOODNESS! THERE ARE *THREE* OF YOU! WHAT DID THAT HORRIBLE LIGHTNING BOLT *DO* TO YOU--?

CALM DOWN AND WE'LL *EXPLAIN*--

14

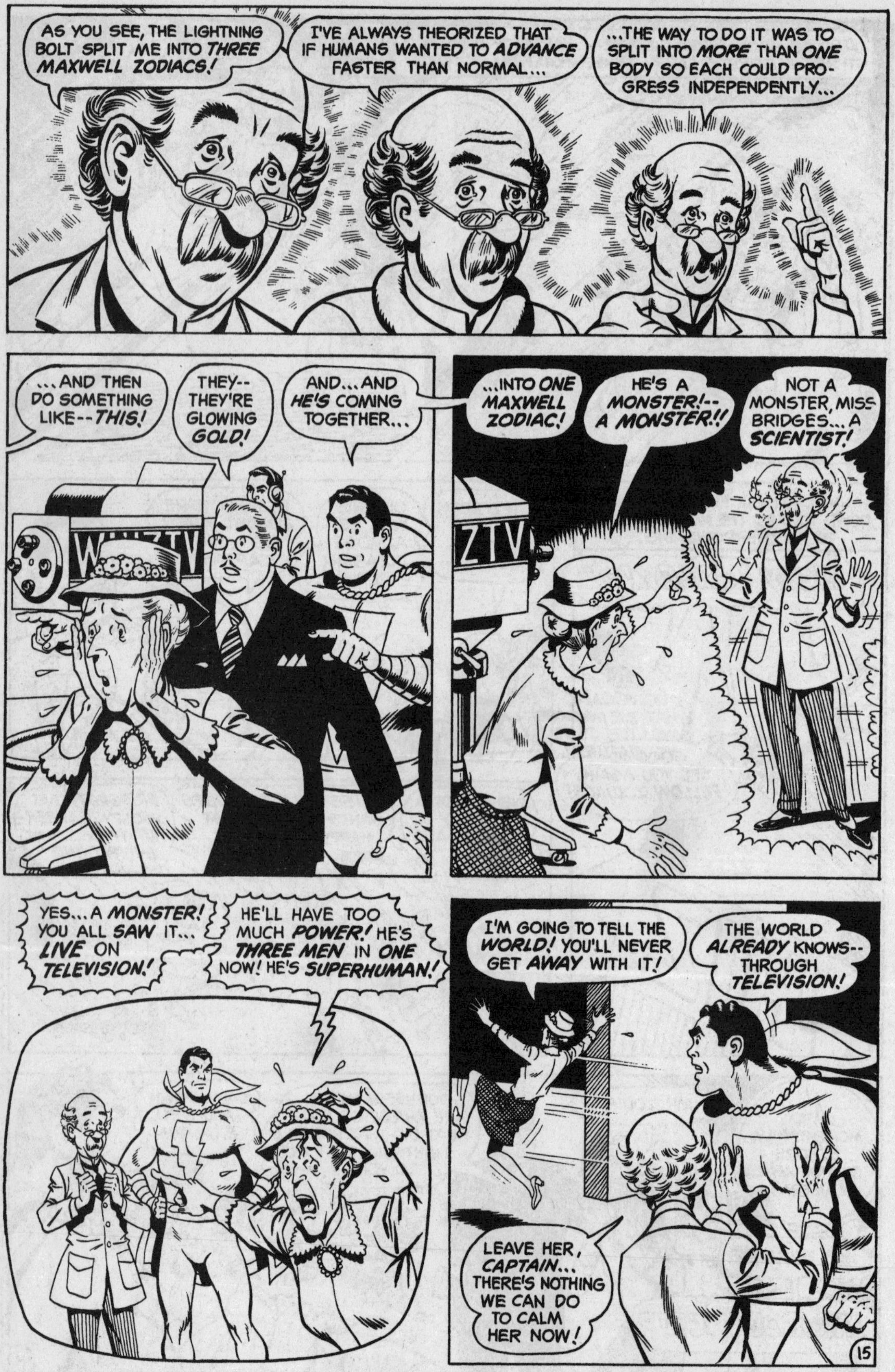
AS YOU SEE, THE LIGHTNING BOLT SPLIT ME INTO THREE MAXWELL ZODIACS!
I'VE ALWAYS THEORIZED THAT IF HUMANS WANTED TO ADVANCE FASTER THAN NORMAL...
...THE WAY TO DO IT WAS TO SPLIT INTO MORE THAN ONE BODY SO EACH COULD PROGRESS INDEPENDENTLY...
...AND THEN DO SOMETHING LIKE--THIS!
THEY--THEY'RE GLOWING GOLD!
AND...AND HE'S COMING TOGETHER...
...INTO ONE MAXWELL ZODIAC!
HE'S A MONSTER!--A MONSTER!!
NOT A MONSTER, MISS BRIDGES... A SCIENTIST!
YES... A MONSTER! YOU ALL SAW IT... LIVE ON TELEVISION!
HE'LL HAVE TOO MUCH POWER! HE'S THREE MEN IN ONE NOW! HE'S SUPERHUMAN!
I'M GOING TO TELL THE WORLD! YOU'LL NEVER GET AWAY WITH IT!
THE WORLD ALREADY KNOWS--THROUGH TELEVISION!
LEAVE HER, CAPTAIN... THERE'S NOTHING WE CAN DO TO CALM HER NOW!
15

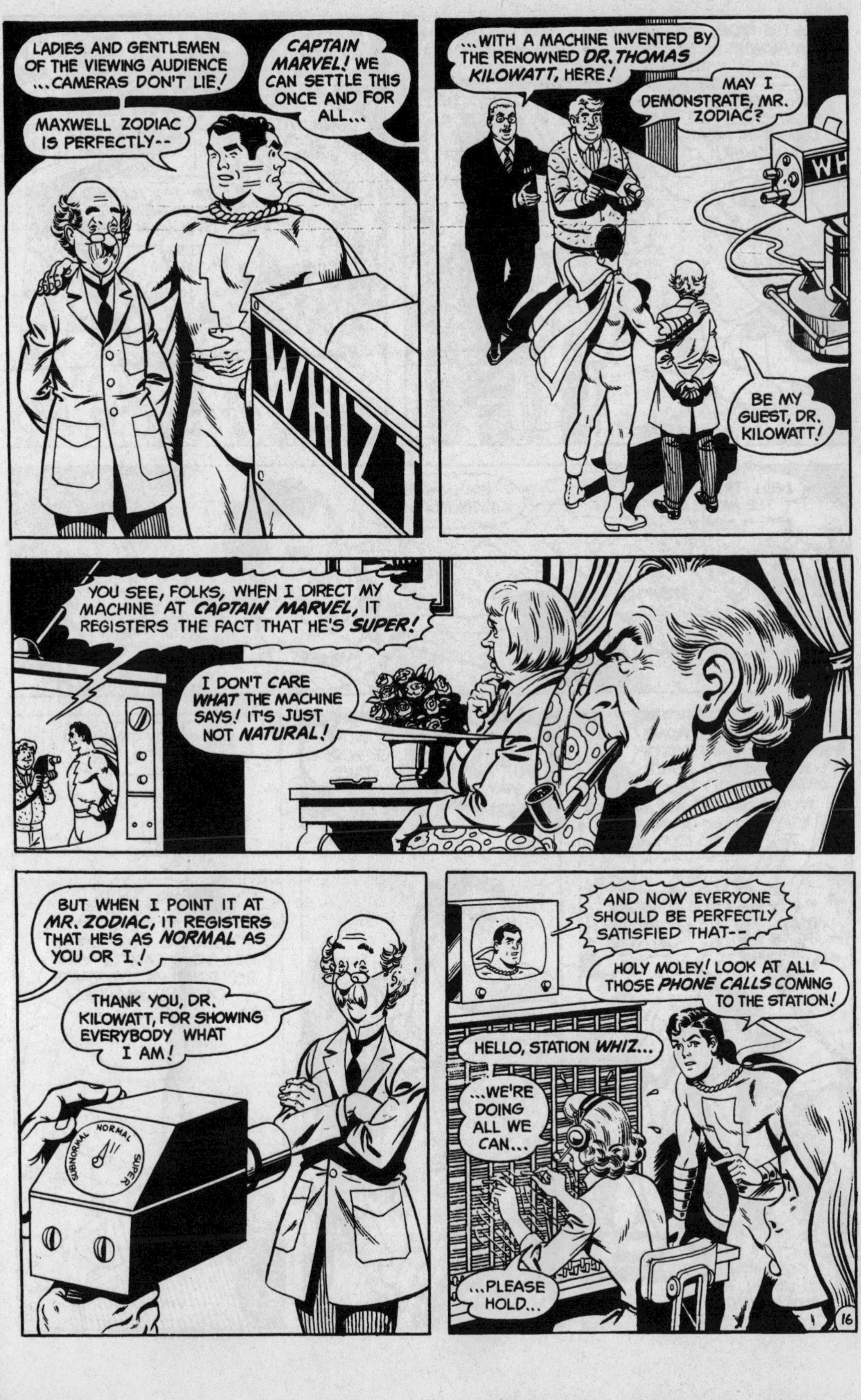
LADIES AND GENTLEMEN OF THE VIEWING AUDIENCE ...CAMERAS DON'T LIE!
MAXWELL ZODIAC IS PERFECTLY--
CAPTAIN MARVEL! WE CAN SETTLE THIS ONCE AND FOR ALL...
WHIZ T
...WITH A MACHINE INVENTED BY THE RENOWNED DR. THOMAS KILOWATT, HERE!
MAY I DEMONSTRATE, MR. ZODIAC?
WH
BE MY GUEST, DR. KILOWATT!
YOU SEE, FOLKS, WHEN I DIRECT MY MACHINE AT CAPTAIN MARVEL, IT REGISTERS THE FACT THAT HE'S SUPER!
I DON'T CARE WHAT THE MACHINE SAYS! IT'S JUST NOT NATURAL!
BUT WHEN I POINT IT AT MR. ZODIAC, IT REGISTERS THAT HE'S AS NORMAL AS YOU OR I!
THANK YOU, DR. KILOWATT, FOR SHOWING EVERYBODY WHAT I AM!
SUBNORMAL NORMAL SUPER
AND NOW EVERYONE SHOULD BE PERFECTLY SATISFIED THAT--
HOLY MOLEY! LOOK AT ALL THOSE PHONE CALLS COMING TO THE STATION!
HELLO, STATION WHIZ...
...WE'RE DOING ALL WE CAN...
...PLEASE HOLD...
16

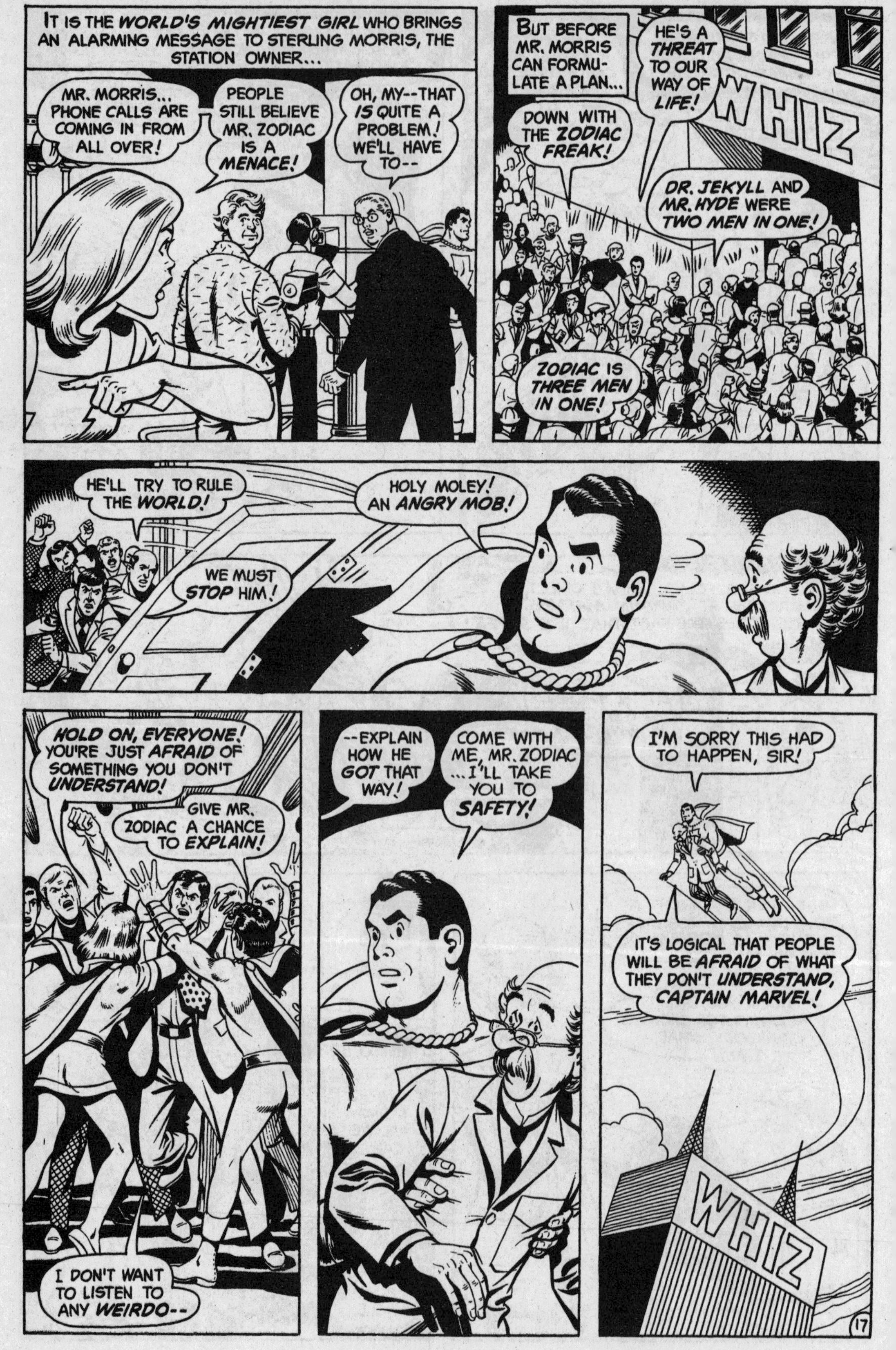
IT IS THE WORLD'S MIGHTIEST GIRL WHO BRINGS AN ALARMING MESSAGE TO STERLING MORRIS, THE STATION OWNER...
MR. MORRIS... PHONE CALLS ARE COMING IN FROM ALL OVER!
PEOPLE STILL BELIEVE MR. ZODIAC IS A MENACE!
OH, MY--THAT IS QUITE A PROBLEM! WE'LL HAVE TO--
BUT BEFORE MR. MORRIS CAN FORMULATE A PLAN...
HE'S A THREAT TO OUR WAY OF LIFE!
WHIZ
DOWN WITH THE ZODIAC FREAK!
DR. JEKYLL AND MR. HYDE WERE TWO MEN IN ONE!
ZODIAC IS THREE MEN IN ONE!
HE'LL TRY TO RULE THE WORLD!
HOLY MOLEY! AN ANGRY MOB!
WE MUST STOP HIM!
HOLD ON, EVERYONE! YOU'RE JUST AFRAID OF SOMETHING YOU DON'T UNDERSTAND!
GIVE MR. ZODIAC A CHANCE TO EXPLAIN!
I DON'T WANT TO LISTEN TO ANY WEIRDO--
--EXPLAIN HOW HE GOT THAT WAY!
COME WITH ME, MR. ZODIAC ...I'LL TAKE YOU TO SAFETY!
I'M SORRY THIS HAD TO HAPPEN, SIR!
IT'S LOGICAL THAT PEOPLE WILL BE AFRAID OF WHAT THEY DON'T UNDERSTAND, CAPTAIN MARVEL!
WHIZ
17

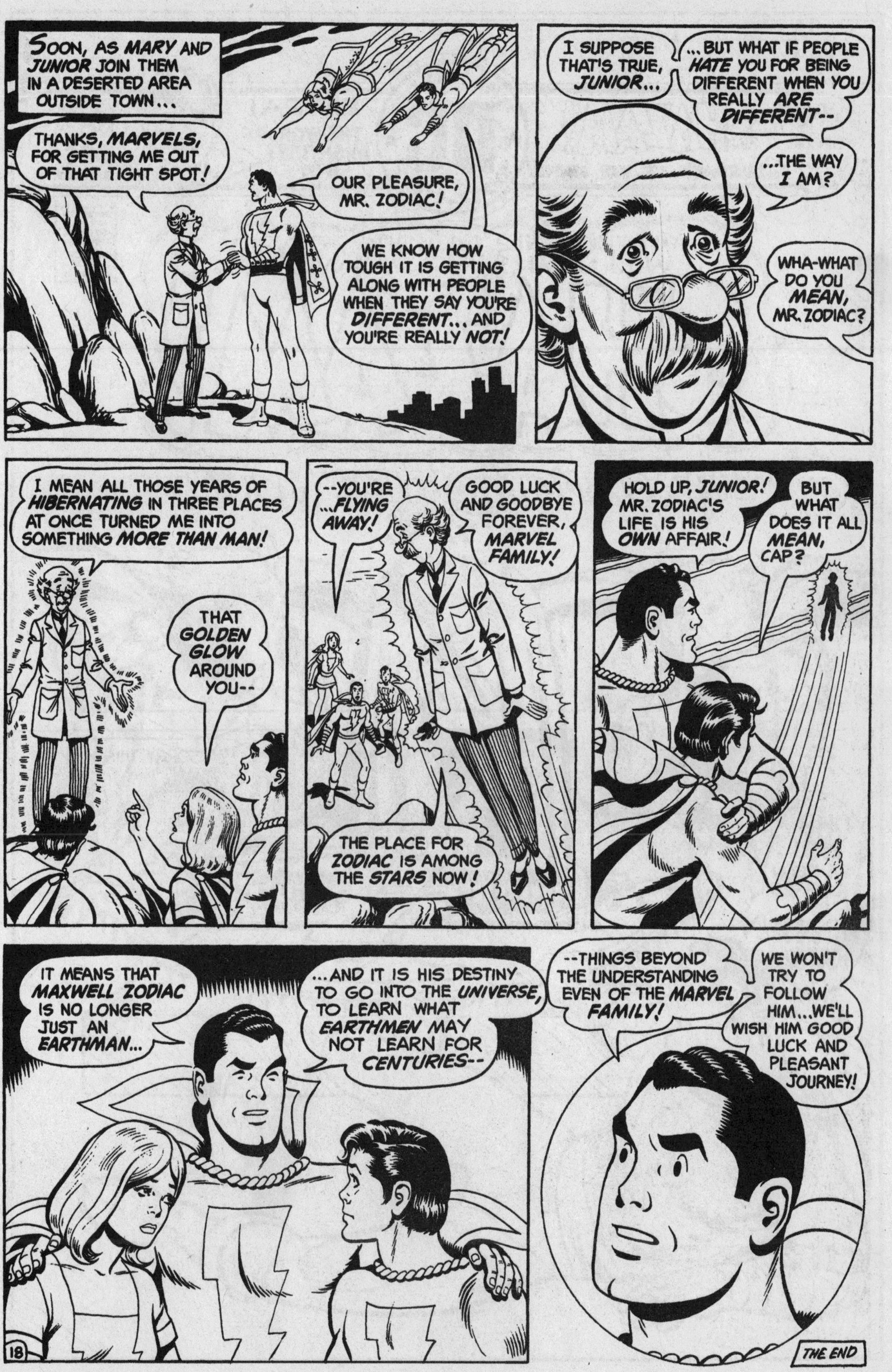
SOON, AS MARY AND JUNIOR JOIN THEM IN A DESERTED AREA OUTSIDE TOWN...
THANKS, MARVELS, FOR GETTING ME OUT OF THAT TIGHT SPOT!
OUR PLEASURE, MR. ZODIAC!
WE KNOW HOW TOUGH IT IS GETTING ALONG WITH PEOPLE WHEN THEY SAY YOU'RE DIFFERENT... AND YOU'RE REALLY NOT!
I SUPPOSE THAT'S TRUE, JUNIOR...
...BUT WHAT IF PEOPLE HATE YOU FOR BEING DIFFERENT WHEN YOU REALLY ARE DIFFERENT--
...THE WAY I AM?
WHA-WHAT DO YOU MEAN, MR. ZODIAC?
I MEAN ALL THOSE YEARS OF HIBERNATING IN THREE PLACES AT ONCE TURNED ME INTO SOMETHING MORE THAN MAN!
THAT GOLDEN GLOW AROUND YOU--
--YOU'RE ...FLYING AWAY!
GOOD LUCK AND GOODBYE FOREVER, MARVEL FAMILY!
THE PLACE FOR ZODIAC IS AMONG THE STARS NOW!
HOLD UP, JUNIOR! MR. ZODIAC'S LIFE IS HIS OWN AFFAIR!
BUT WHAT DOES IT ALL MEAN, CAP?
IT MEANS THAT MAXWELL ZODIAC IS NO LONGER JUST AN EARTHMAN...
...AND IT IS HIS DESTINY TO GO INTO THE UNIVERSE, TO LEARN WHAT EARTHMEN MAY NOT LEARN FOR CENTURIES--
--THINGS BEYOND THE UNDERSTANDING EVEN OF THE MARVEL FAMILY!
WE WON'T TRY TO FOLLOW HIM...WE'LL WISH HIM GOOD LUCK AND PLEASANT JOURNEY!
18
THE END

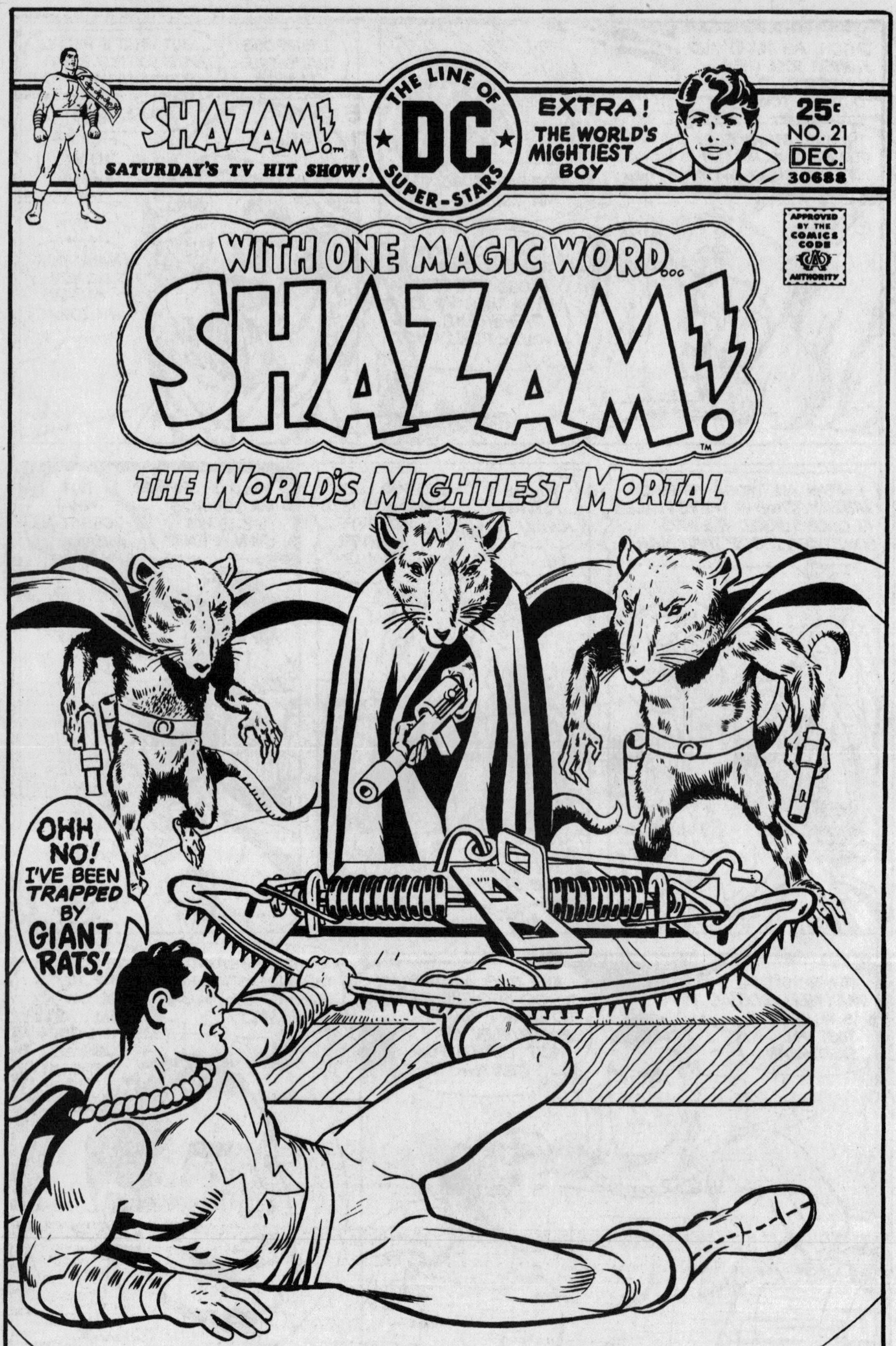
SHAZAM!
SATURDAY'S TV HIT SHOW!
THE LINE OF DC SUPER-STARS
EXTRA! THE WORLD'S MIGHTIEST BOY
25¢
NO. 21
DEC.
30688
APPROVED BY THE COMICS CODE AUTHORITY
WITH ONE MAGIC WORD...
SHAZAM!
THE WORLD'S MIGHTIEST MORTAL
OHH NO! I'VE BEEN TRAPPED BY GIANT RATS!

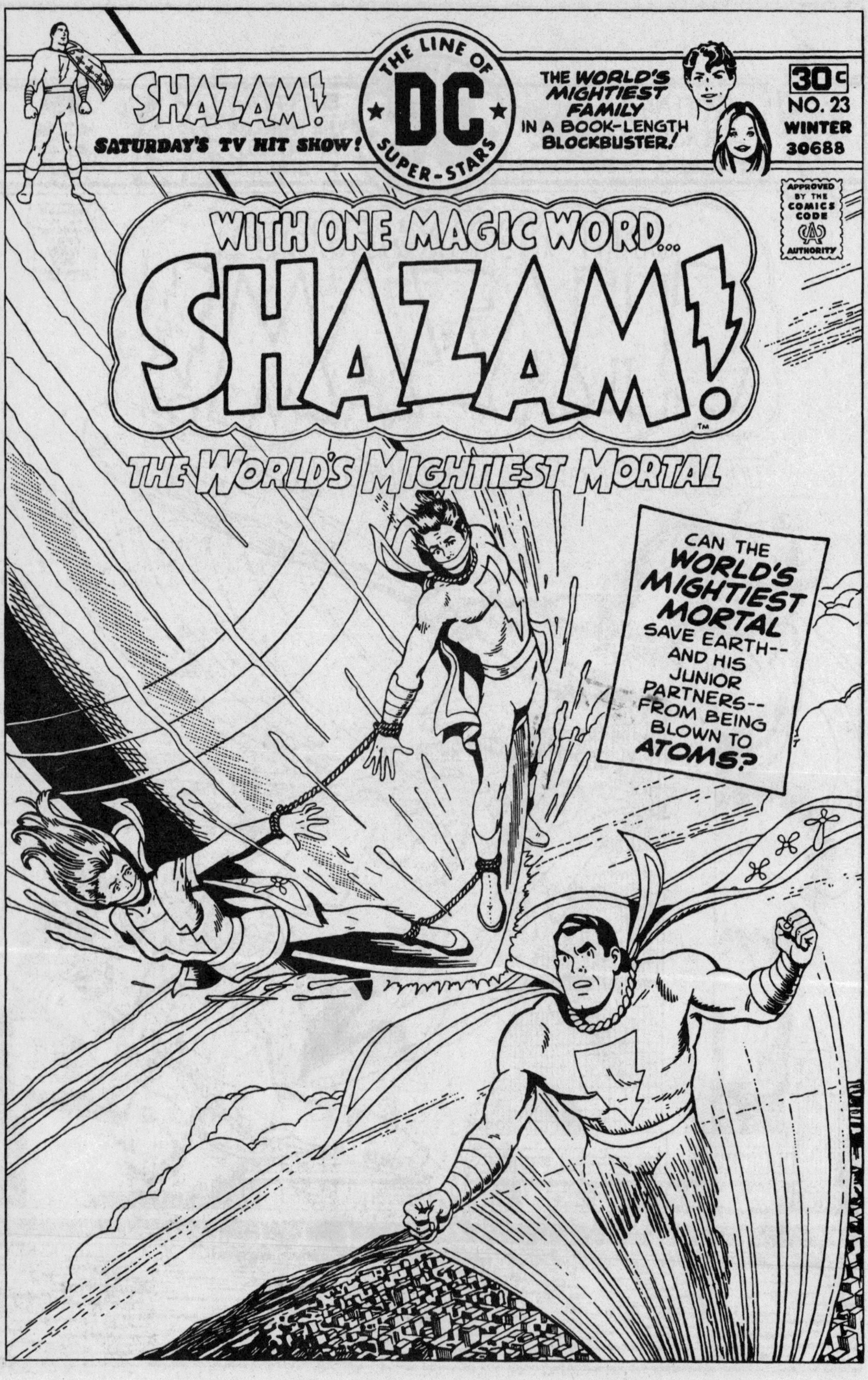
SHAZAM!
SATURDAY'S TV HIT SHOW!
THE LINE OF DC SUPER-STARS
THE WORLD'S MIGHTIEST FAMILY IN A BOOK-LENGTH BLOCKBUSTER!
30¢
NO. 23
WINTER
30688
APPROVED BY THE COMICS CODE AUTHORITY
WITH ONE MAGIC WORD...
SHAZAM!
THE WORLD'S MIGHTIEST MORTAL
CAN THE WORLD'S MIGHTIEST MORTAL SAVE EARTH-- AND HIS JUNIOR PARTNERS-- FROM BEING BLOWN TO ATOMS?

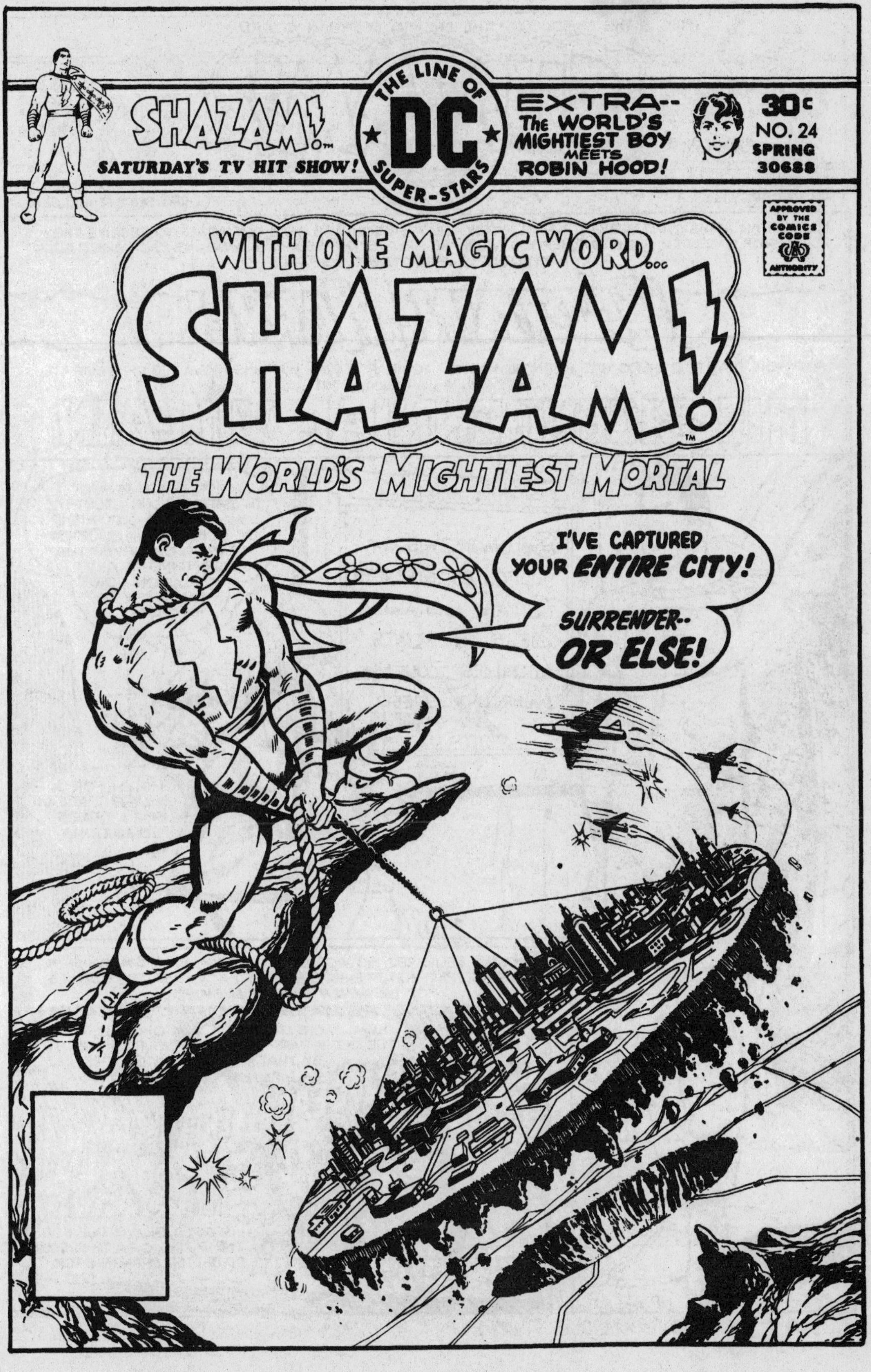
SHAZAM!
SATURDAY'S TV HIT SHOW!
THE LINE OF DC SUPER-STARS
EXTRA-- The WORLD'S MIGHTIEST BOY MEETS ROBIN HOOD!
30¢
NO. 24
SPRING
30688
APPROVED BY THE COMICS CODE AUTHORITY
WITH ONE MAGIC WORD...
SHAZAM!
THE WORLD'S MIGHTIEST MORTAL
I'VE CAPTURED YOUR ENTIRE CITY!
SURRENDER-- OR ELSE!

This is the throne of the ancient Egyptian wizard...

SHAZAM!

STORY:
E. NELSON BRIDWELL

EDITOR:
JOE ORLANDO

ART:
KURT SCHAFFENBERGER

Here, in an abandoned subway tunnel, young Billy Batson was once summoned to receive the powers of six elder gods and heroes. When he speaks the wizard's name, he is changed into the *WORLD'S MIGHTIEST MORTAL*...

CAPTAIN MARVEL

And here that very hero has been summoned to hear a dire warning from the spirit of *SHAZAM*, a warning about...

THE BICENTENNIAL VILLAIN

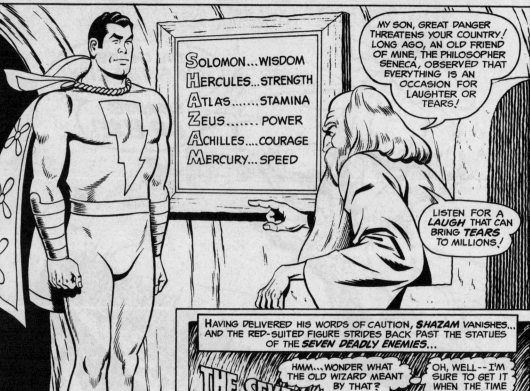

Solomon...Wisdom
Hercules...Strength
Atlas.......Stamina
Zeus.......Power
Achilles....Courage
Mercury...Speed

My son, great danger threatens your country! Long ago, an old friend of mine, the philosopher Seneca, observed that everything is an occasion for laughter or tears!

Listen for a *LAUGH* that can bring *TEARS* to millions!

Having delivered his words of caution, *SHAZAM* vanishes... and the red-suited figure strides back past the statues of the *SEVEN DEADLY ENEMIES*...

THE SEVEN DEADLY ENEMIES OF MAN

HMM...WONDER WHAT THE OLD WIZARD MEANT BY THAT?

OH, WELL-- I'M SURE TO GET IT WHEN THE TIME COMES!

BESIDES, BILLY'S DUE FOR THE TAPING OF A TV SPECIAL! I'D BETTER CHANGE BACK!

PRIDE   ENVY   GREED

SOON, IN *CENTRAL PARK*, BILLY AND HIS ASSISTANT, WHITEY MURPHY, PREPARE FOR A MOST UNUSUAL DOCUMENTARY...

THEN THIS SPECIAL WILL BE ALL ABOUT *YOUNG PEOPLE* IN AMERICAN HISTORY, BILLY?

RIGHT, WHITEY! AND THE ACTORS WILL ALL BE STUDENTS FROM THE LOCAL SCHOOLS!

SEEMS LIKE MOST OF THE HISTORY BOOKS CONCENTRATE ON OLD GUYS-- LIKE *BENJAMIN FRANKLIN!*

BUT BEN WAS APPRENTICED AS A PRINTER WHEN HE WAS *TEN*...

...TO HIS OLDER BROTHER! AND AT 16, BEN SECRETLY WROTE A SERIES OF BRILLIANT LETTERS...

WHAT A WRITER THIS *SILENCE DOGOOD* IS! SHE HAS WIT AND INSIGHT!

WOULD HE BE SURPRISED TO LEARN *I* AM "SILENCE DOGOOD"!

AND HOW ABOUT *POCAHONTAS?* SHE WAS ONLY 12 OR 13 WHEN SHE SAVED CAPTAIN JOHN SMITH!

OUR FIRST SCENE WILL SHOW YOUNG *KIT CARSON*, AT 17, WHEN HE FIRST WENT WEST. HE BECAME A GREAT SCOUT, TRAPPER, MOUNTAIN MAN, TRANSLATOR ...

YIPES! THIS ISN'T IN THE SCRIPT!

RRAAAARRR

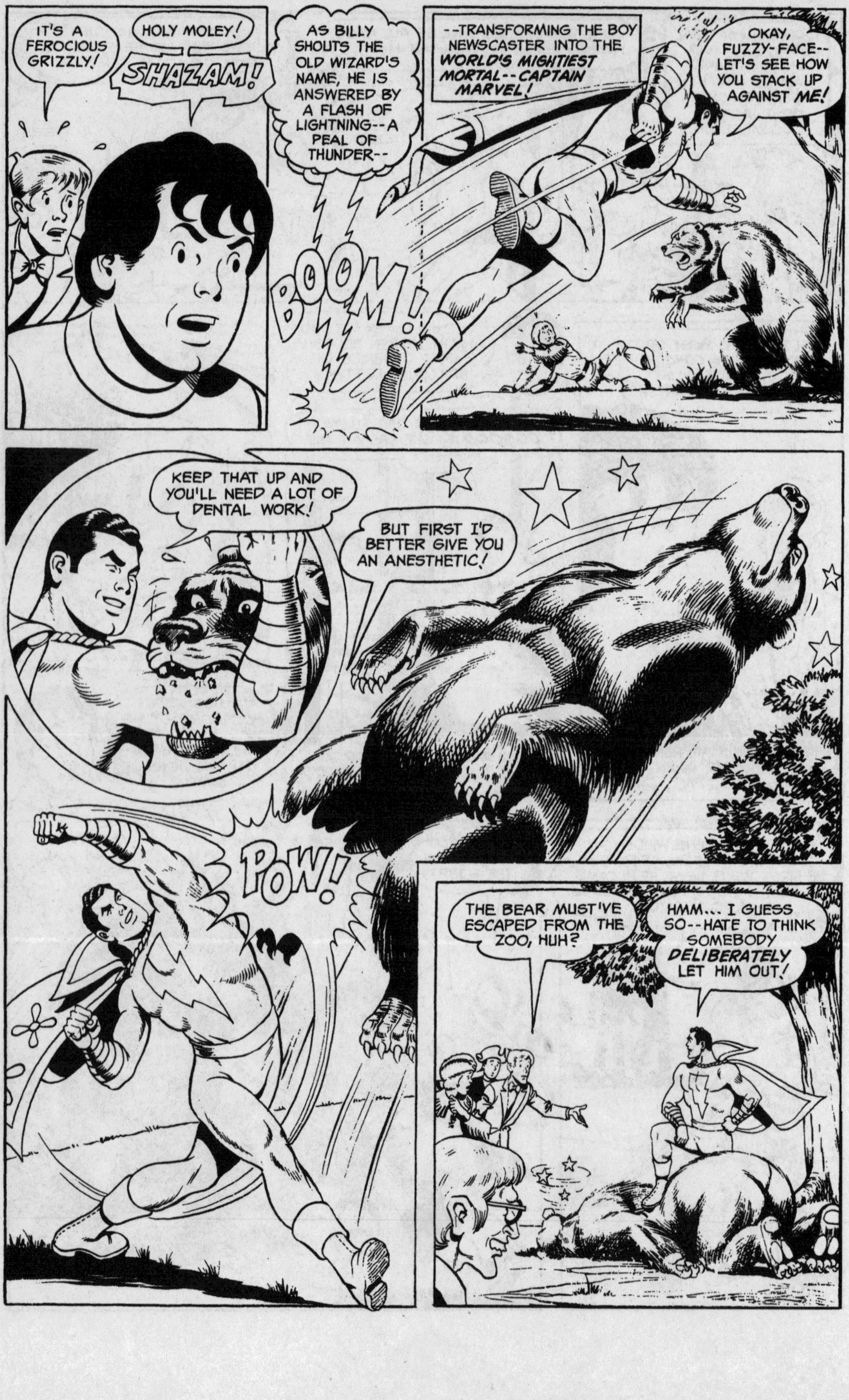
IT'S A FEROCIOUS GRIZZLY!
HOLY MOLEY!
SHAZAM!
AS BILLY SHOUTS THE OLD WIZARD'S NAME, HE IS ANSWERED BY A FLASH OF LIGHTNING--A PEAL OF THUNDER--
BOOM!
--TRANSFORMING THE BOY NEWSCASTER INTO THE WORLD'S MIGHTIEST MORTAL--CAPTAIN MARVEL!
OKAY, FUZZY-FACE-- LET'S SEE HOW YOU STACK UP AGAINST ME!
KEEP THAT UP AND YOU'LL NEED A LOT OF DENTAL WORK!
BUT FIRST I'D BETTER GIVE YOU AN ANESTHETIC!
POW!
THE BEAR MUST'VE ESCAPED FROM THE ZOO, HUH?
HMM... I GUESS SO--HATE TO THINK SOMEBODY DELIBERATELY LET HIM OUT!

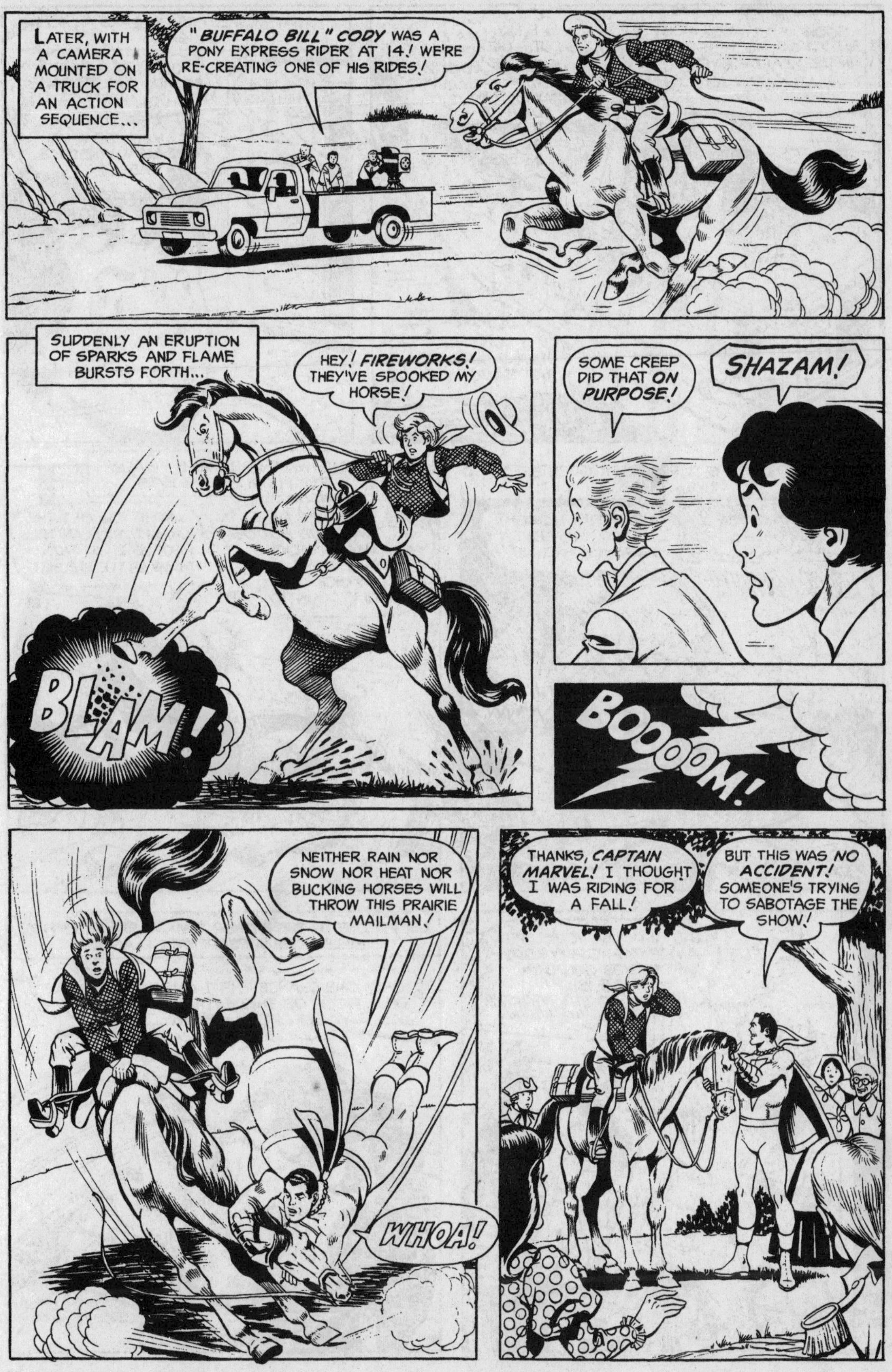
LATER, WITH A CAMERA MOUNTED ON A TRUCK FOR AN ACTION SEQUENCE...
"BUFFALO BILL" CODY WAS A PONY EXPRESS RIDER AT 14! WE'RE RE-CREATING ONE OF HIS RIDES!
SUDDENLY AN ERUPTION OF SPARKS AND FLAME BURSTS FORTH...
HEY! FIREWORKS! THEY'VE SPOOKED MY HORSE!
BLAM!
SOME CREEP DID THAT ON PURPOSE!
SHAZAM!
BOOOOM!
NEITHER RAIN NOR SNOW NOR HEAT NOR BUCKING HORSES WILL THROW THIS PRAIRIE MAILMAN!
WHOA!
THANKS, CAPTAIN MARVEL! I THOUGHT I WAS RIDING FOR A FALL!
BUT THIS WAS NO ACCIDENT! SOMEONE'S TRYING TO SABOTAGE THE SHOW!

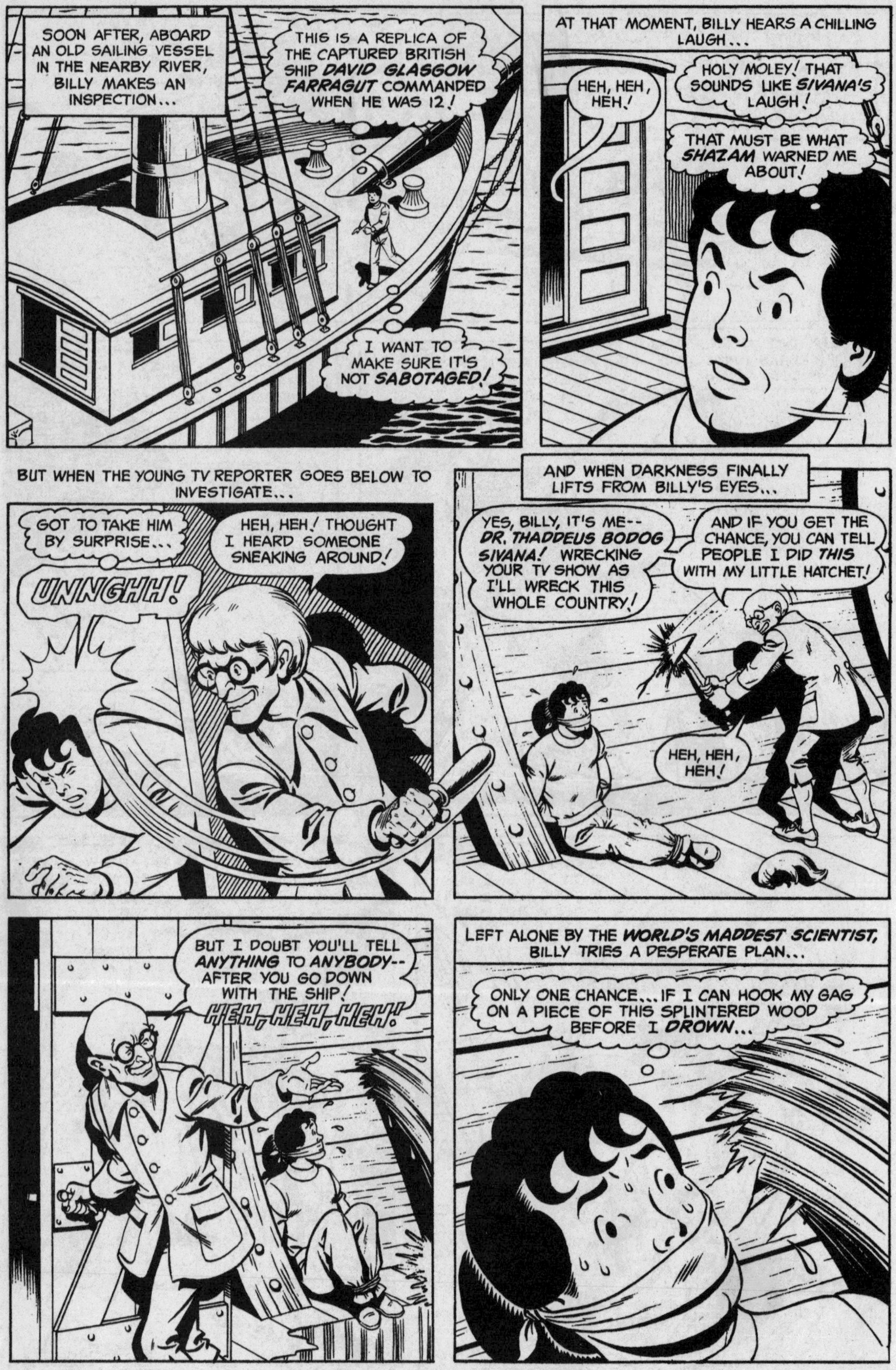
SOON AFTER, ABOARD AN OLD SAILING VESSEL IN THE NEARBY RIVER, BILLY MAKES AN INSPECTION...
THIS IS A REPLICA OF THE CAPTURED BRITISH SHIP *DAVID GLASGOW FARRAGUT* COMMANDED WHEN HE WAS 12!
I WANT TO MAKE SURE IT'S NOT *SABOTAGED!*
AT THAT MOMENT, BILLY HEARS A CHILLING LAUGH...
HEH, HEH, HEH!
HOLY MOLEY! THAT SOUNDS LIKE *SIVANA'S* LAUGH!
THAT MUST BE WHAT *SHAZAM* WARNED ME ABOUT!
BUT WHEN THE YOUNG TV REPORTER GOES BELOW TO INVESTIGATE...
GOT TO TAKE HIM BY SURPRISE...
HEH, HEH! THOUGHT I HEARD SOMEONE SNEAKING AROUND!
UNNGHH!
AND WHEN DARKNESS FINALLY LIFTS FROM BILLY'S EYES...
YES, BILLY, IT'S ME-- *DR. THADDEUS BODOG SIVANA!* WRECKING YOUR TV SHOW AS I'LL WRECK THIS WHOLE COUNTRY!
AND IF YOU GET THE CHANCE, YOU CAN TELL PEOPLE I DID *THIS* WITH MY LITTLE HATCHET!
HEH, HEH, HEH!
BUT I DOUBT YOU'LL TELL *ANYTHING* TO *ANYBODY*-- AFTER YOU GO DOWN WITH THE SHIP!
HEH, HEH, HEH!
LEFT ALONE BY THE *WORLD'S MADDEST SCIENTIST,* BILLY TRIES A DESPERATE PLAN...
ONLY ONE CHANCE... IF I CAN HOOK MY GAG ON A PIECE OF THIS SPLINTERED WOOD BEFORE I *DROWN*...

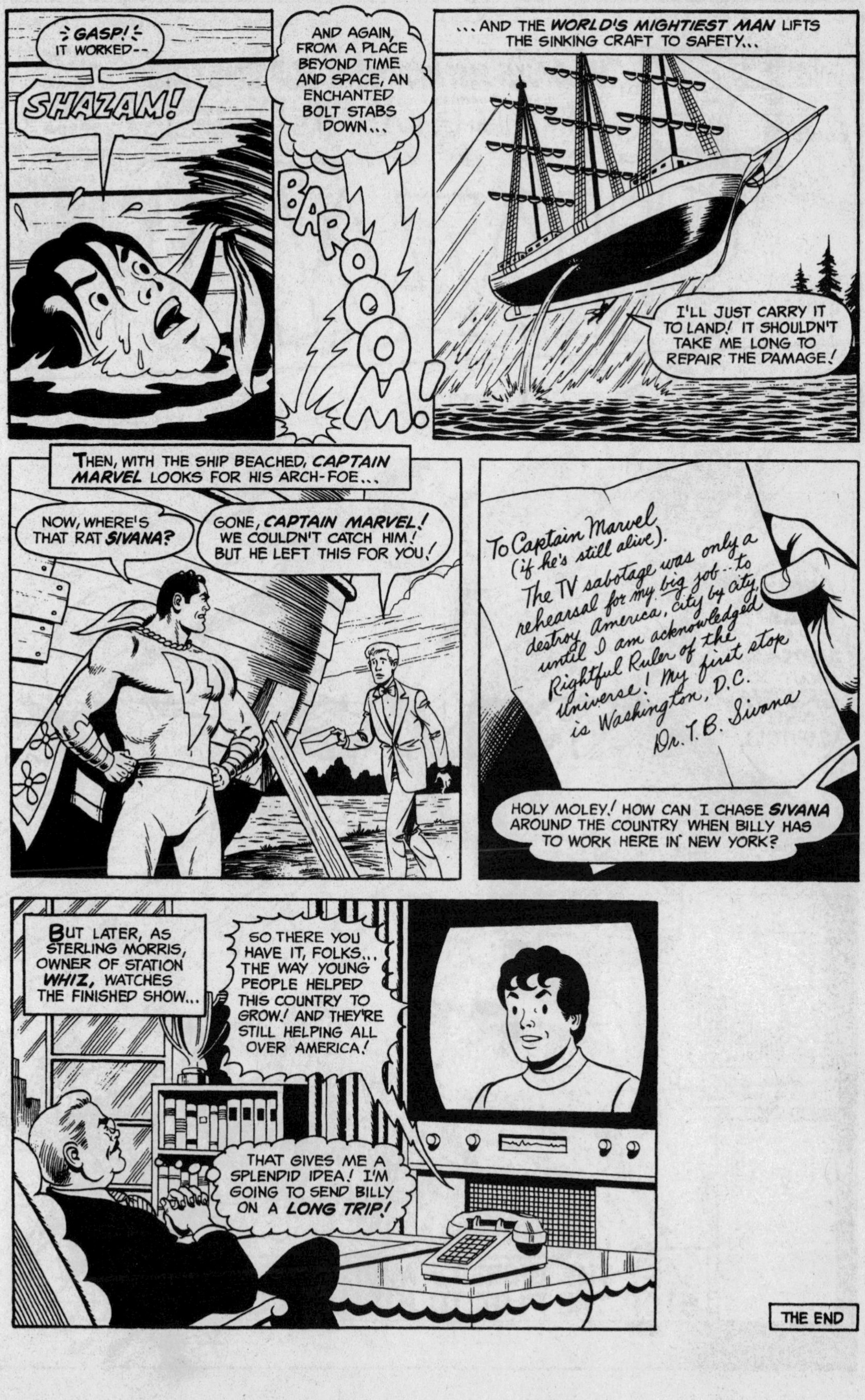
GASP! IT WORKED--
SHAZAM!
AND AGAIN, FROM A PLACE BEYOND TIME AND SPACE, AN ENCHANTED BOLT STABS DOWN...
BAROOOOM!
...AND THE WORLD'S MIGHTIEST MAN LIFTS THE SINKING CRAFT TO SAFETY...
I'LL JUST CARRY IT TO LAND! IT SHOULDN'T TAKE ME LONG TO REPAIR THE DAMAGE!
THEN, WITH THE SHIP BEACHED, CAPTAIN MARVEL LOOKS FOR HIS ARCH-FOE...
NOW, WHERE'S THAT RAT SIVANA?
GONE, CAPTAIN MARVEL! WE COULDN'T CATCH HIM! BUT HE LEFT THIS FOR YOU!
To Captain Marvel (if he's still alive). The TV sabotage was only a rehearsal for my big job...to destroy America, city by city until I am acknowledged Rightful Ruler of the Universe! My first stop is Washington, D.C. Dr. T.B. Sivana
HOLY MOLEY! HOW CAN I CHASE SIVANA AROUND THE COUNTRY WHEN BILLY HAS TO WORK HERE IN NEW YORK?
BUT LATER, AS STERLING MORRIS, OWNER OF STATION WHIZ, WATCHES THE FINISHED SHOW...
SO THERE YOU HAVE IT, FOLKS... THE WAY YOUNG PEOPLE HELPED THIS COUNTRY TO GROW! AND THEY'RE STILL HELPING ALL OVER AMERICA!
THAT GIVES ME A SPLENDID IDEA! I'M GOING TO SEND BILLY ON A LONG TRIP!
THE END

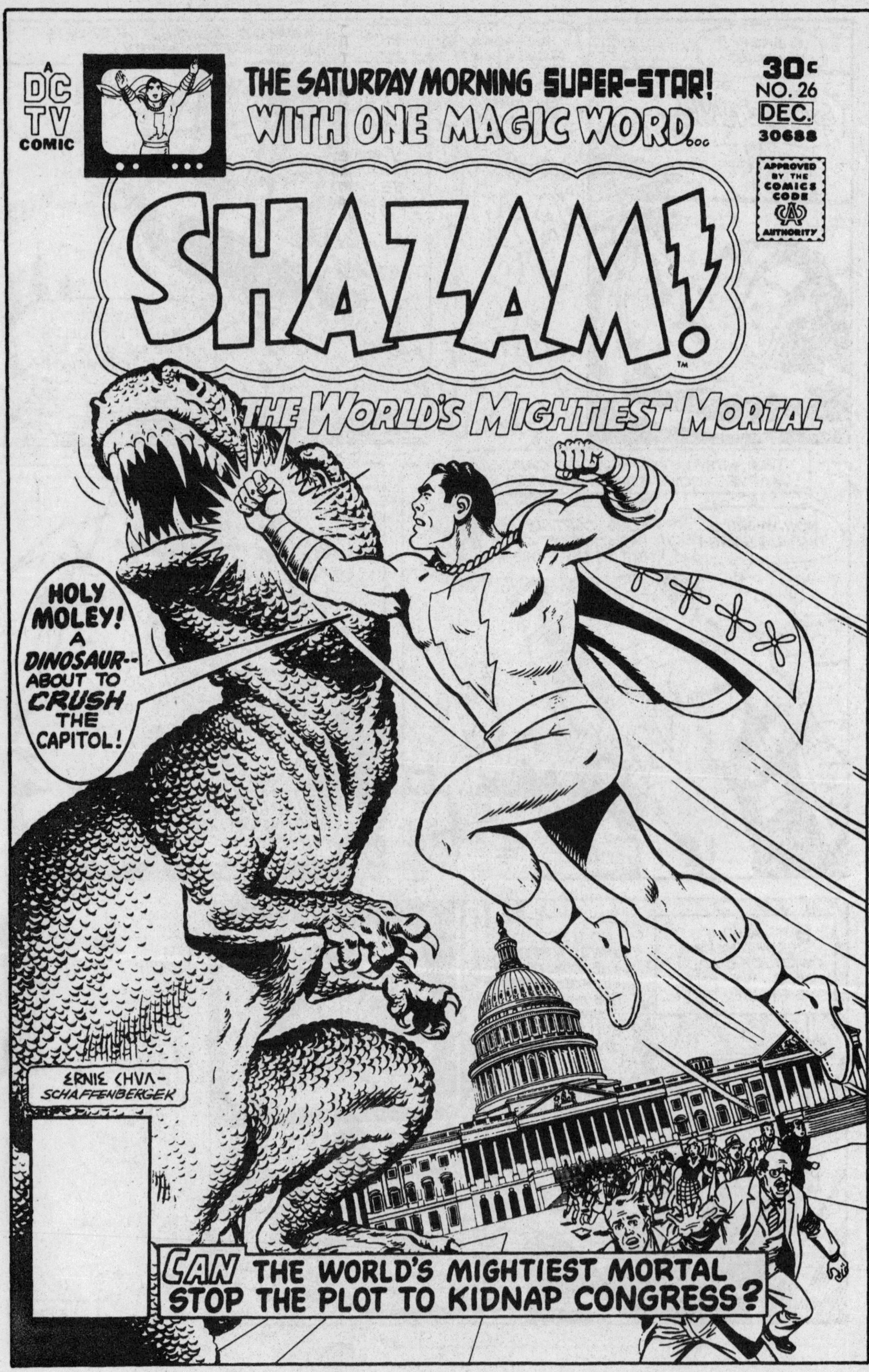
A DC TV COMIC
THE SATURDAY MORNING SUPER-STAR!
WITH ONE MAGIC WORD...
30¢
NO. 26
DEC.
30688
APPROVED BY THE COMICS CODE AUTHORITY
SHAZAM!
THE WORLD'S MIGHTIEST MORTAL
HOLY MOLEY! A DINOSAUR-- ABOUT TO CRUSH THE CAPITOL!
ERNIE CHUA-SCHAFFENBERGER
CAN THE WORLD'S MIGHTIEST MORTAL STOP THE PLOT TO KIDNAP CONGRESS?

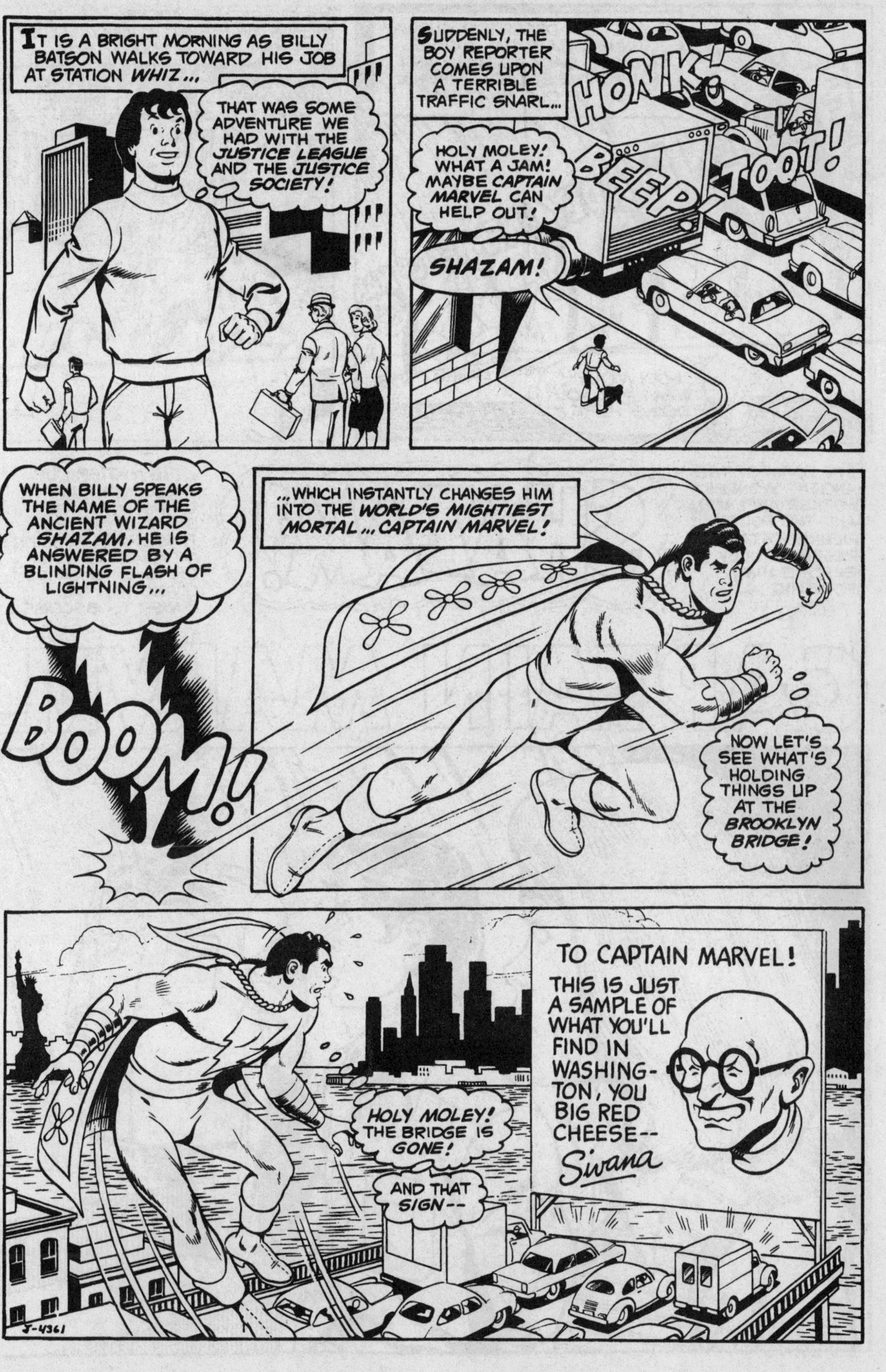
IT IS A BRIGHT MORNING AS BILLY BATSON WALKS TOWARD HIS JOB AT STATION WHIZ...
THAT WAS SOME ADVENTURE WE HAD WITH THE JUSTICE LEAGUE AND THE JUSTICE SOCIETY!
SUDDENLY, THE BOY REPORTER COMES UPON A TERRIBLE TRAFFIC SNARL...
HONK!
BEEP!
TOOT!
HOLY MOLEY! WHAT A JAM! MAYBE CAPTAIN MARVEL CAN HELP OUT!
SHAZAM!
WHEN BILLY SPEAKS THE NAME OF THE ANCIENT WIZARD SHAZAM, HE IS ANSWERED BY A BLINDING FLASH OF LIGHTNING...
BOOM!
...WHICH INSTANTLY CHANGES HIM INTO THE WORLD'S MIGHTIEST MORTAL...CAPTAIN MARVEL!
NOW LET'S SEE WHAT'S HOLDING THINGS UP AT THE BROOKLYN BRIDGE!
TO CAPTAIN MARVEL!
THIS IS JUST A SAMPLE OF WHAT YOU'LL FIND IN WASHING-TON, YOU BIG RED CHEESE--
Sivana
HOLY MOLEY! THE BRIDGE IS GONE!
AND THAT SIGN--
J-4361

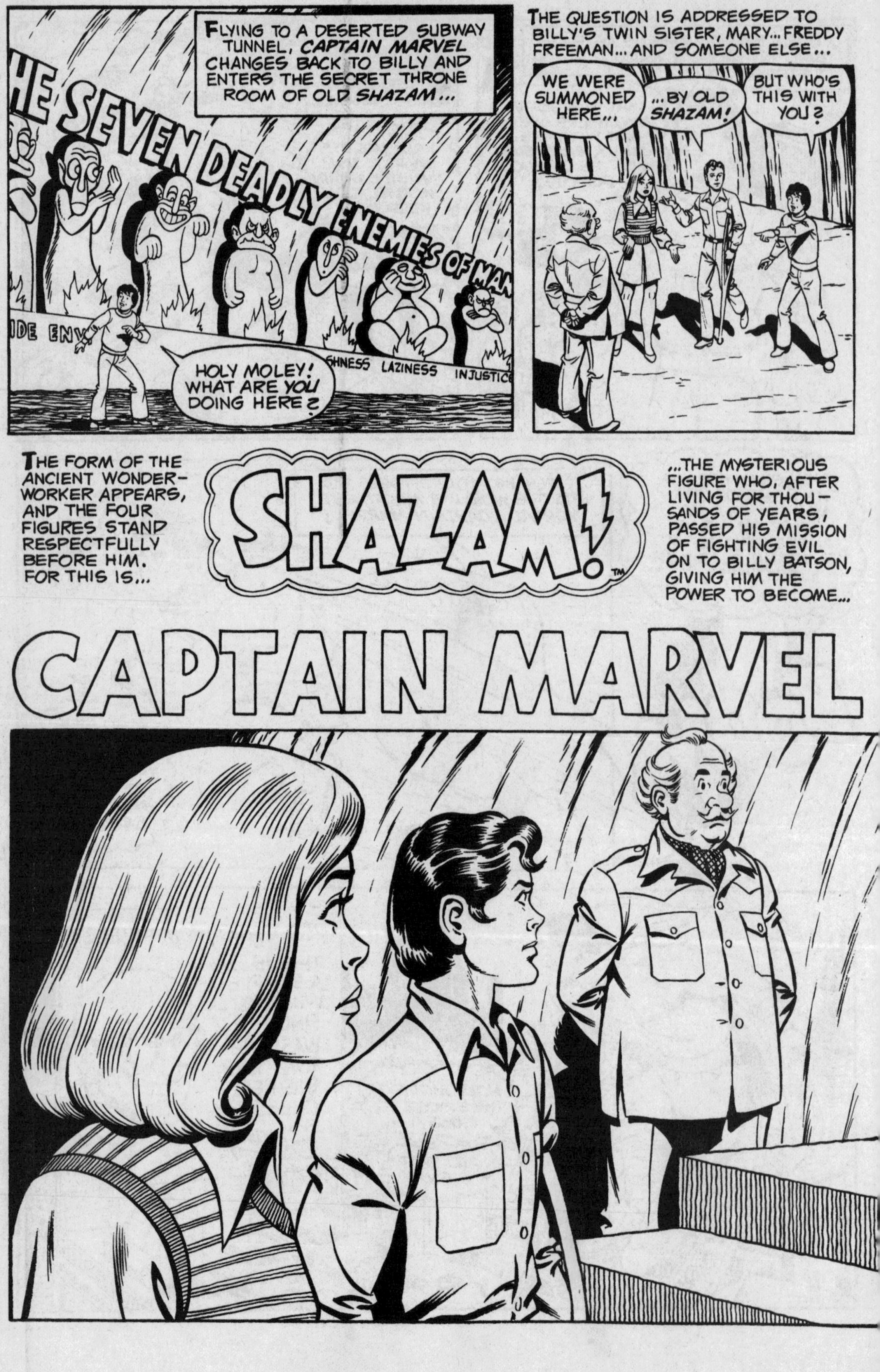
FLYING TO A DESERTED SUBWAY TUNNEL, CAPTAIN MARVEL CHANGES BACK TO BILLY AND ENTERS THE SECRET THRONE ROOM OF OLD SHAZAM...
HE SEVEN DEADLY ENEMIES OF MAN
IDE ENV
SHNESS LAZINESS INJUSTICE
HOLY MOLEY! WHAT ARE YOU DOING HERE?
THE QUESTION IS ADDRESSED TO BILLY'S TWIN SISTER, MARY... FREDDY FREEMAN... AND SOMEONE ELSE...
WE WERE SUMMONED HERE...
...BY OLD SHAZAM!
BUT WHO'S THIS WITH YOU?
THE FORM OF THE ANCIENT WONDER-WORKER APPEARS, AND THE FOUR FIGURES STAND RESPECTFULLY BEFORE HIM. FOR THIS IS...
SHAZAM!™
...THE MYSTERIOUS FIGURE WHO, AFTER LIVING FOR THOUSANDS OF YEARS, PASSED HIS MISSION OF FIGHTING EVIL ON TO BILLY BATSON, GIVING HIM THE POWER TO BECOME...
CAPTAIN MARVEL

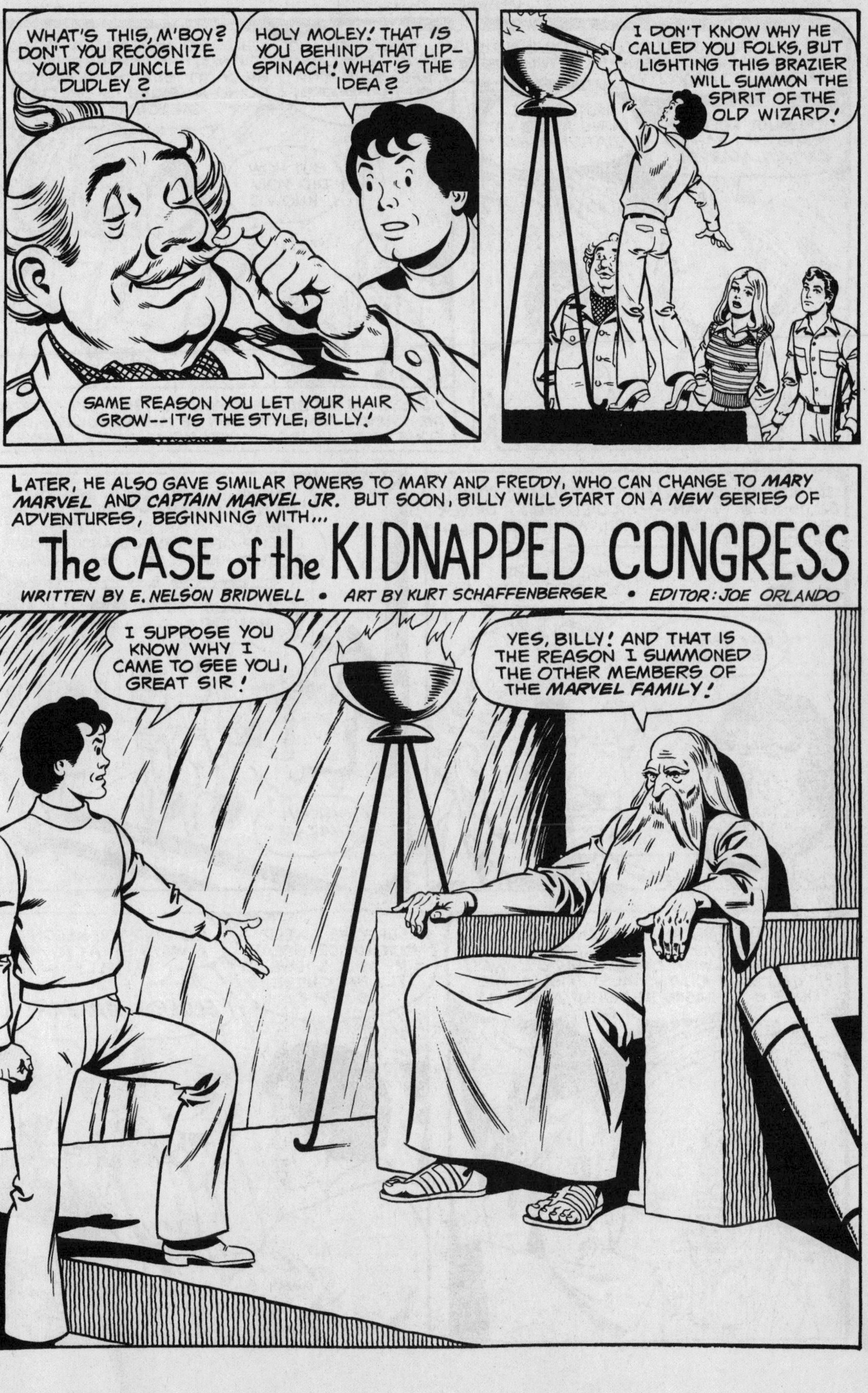
WHAT'S THIS, M'BOY? DON'T YOU RECOGNIZE YOUR OLD UNCLE DUDLEY?
HOLY MOLEY! THAT IS YOU BEHIND THAT LIP-SPINACH! WHAT'S THE IDEA?
SAME REASON YOU LET YOUR HAIR GROW--IT'S THE STYLE, BILLY!
I DON'T KNOW WHY HE CALLED YOU FOLKS, BUT LIGHTING THIS BRAZIER WILL SUMMON THE SPIRIT OF THE OLD WIZARD!
LATER, HE ALSO GAVE SIMILAR POWERS TO MARY AND FREDDY, WHO CAN CHANGE TO MARY MARVEL AND CAPTAIN MARVEL JR. BUT SOON, BILLY WILL START ON A NEW SERIES OF ADVENTURES, BEGINNING WITH...
The CASE of the KIDNAPPED CONGRESS
WRITTEN BY E. NELSON BRIDWELL • ART BY KURT SCHAFFENBERGER • EDITOR: JOE ORLANDO
I SUPPOSE YOU KNOW WHY I CAME TO SEE YOU, GREAT SIR!
YES, BILLY! AND THAT IS THE REASON I SUMMONED THE OTHER MEMBERS OF THE MARVEL FAMILY!

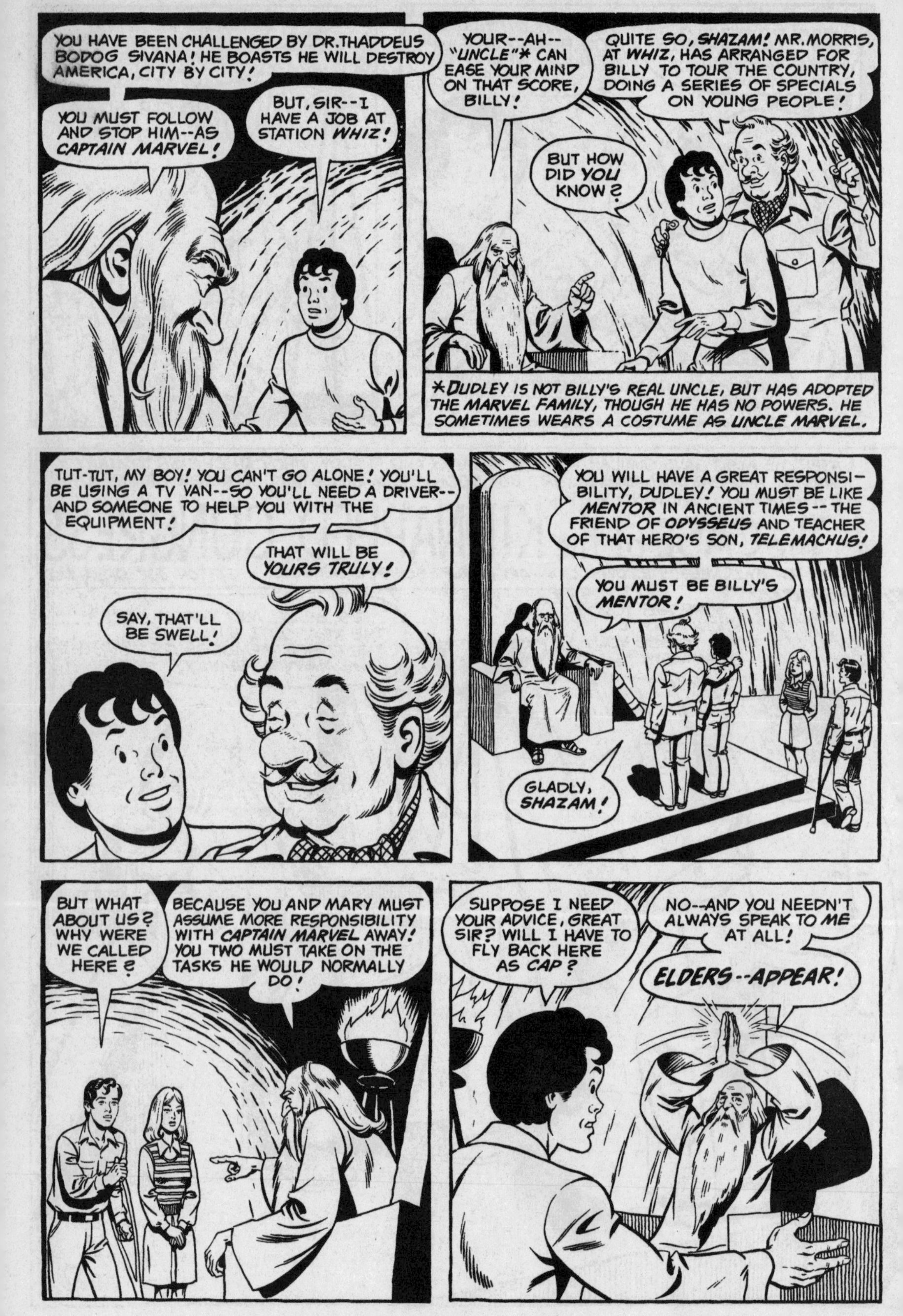
YOU HAVE BEEN CHALLENGED BY DR. THADDEUS BODOG SIVANA! HE BOASTS HE WILL DESTROY AMERICA, CITY BY CITY!
YOU MUST FOLLOW AND STOP HIM--AS CAPTAIN MARVEL!
BUT, SIR--I HAVE A JOB AT STATION WHIZ!
YOUR--AH--"UNCLE"* CAN EASE YOUR MIND ON THAT SCORE, BILLY!
QUITE SO, SHAZAM! MR. MORRIS, AT WHIZ, HAS ARRANGED FOR BILLY TO TOUR THE COUNTRY, DOING A SERIES OF SPECIALS ON YOUNG PEOPLE!
BUT HOW DID YOU KNOW?
*DUDLEY IS NOT BILLY'S REAL UNCLE, BUT HAS ADOPTED THE MARVEL FAMILY, THOUGH HE HAS NO POWERS. HE SOMETIMES WEARS A COSTUME AS UNCLE MARVEL.
TUT-TUT, MY BOY! YOU CAN'T GO ALONE! YOU'LL BE USING A TV VAN--SO YOU'LL NEED A DRIVER--AND SOMEONE TO HELP YOU WITH THE EQUIPMENT!
THAT WILL BE YOURS TRULY!
SAY, THAT'LL BE SWELL!
YOU WILL HAVE A GREAT RESPONSIBILITY, DUDLEY! YOU MUST BE LIKE MENTOR IN ANCIENT TIMES--THE FRIEND OF ODYSSEUS AND TEACHER OF THAT HERO'S SON, TELEMACHUS!
YOU MUST BE BILLY'S MENTOR!
GLADLY, SHAZAM!
BUT WHAT ABOUT US? WHY WERE WE CALLED HERE?
BECAUSE YOU AND MARY MUST ASSUME MORE RESPONSIBILITY WITH CAPTAIN MARVEL AWAY! YOU TWO MUST TAKE ON THE TASKS HE WOULD NORMALLY DO!
SUPPOSE I NEED YOUR ADVICE, GREAT SIR? WILL I HAVE TO FLY BACK HERE AS CAP?
NO--AND YOU NEEDN'T ALWAYS SPEAK TO ME AT ALL!
ELDERS--APPEAR!

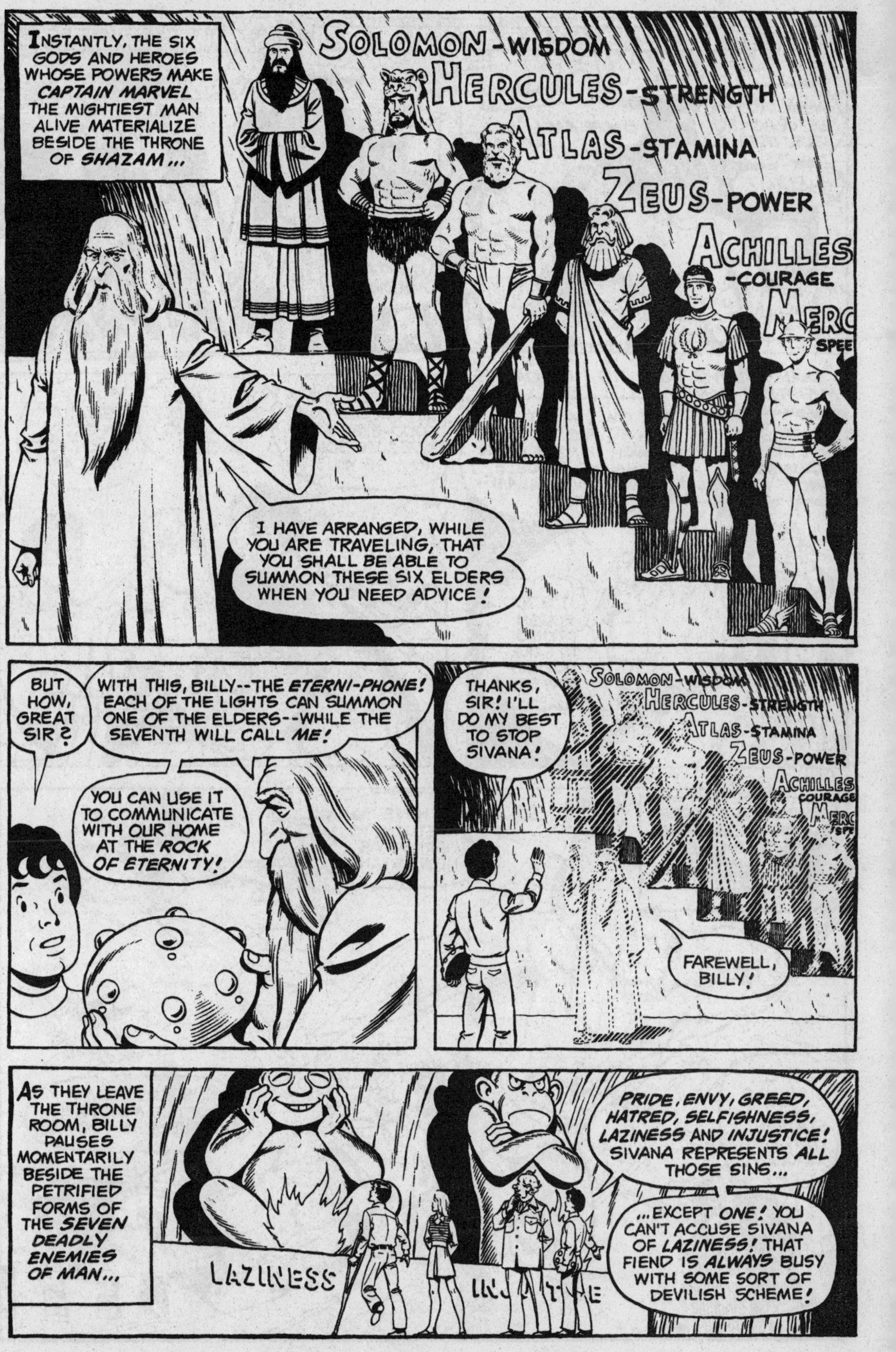
INSTANTLY, THE SIX GODS AND HEROES WHOSE POWERS MAKE CAPTAIN MARVEL THE MIGHTIEST MAN ALIVE MATERIALIZE BESIDE THE THRONE OF SHAZAM...
SOLOMON-WISDOM
HERCULES-STRENGTH
ATLAS-STAMINA
ZEUS-POWER
ACHILLES -COURAGE
I HAVE ARRANGED, WHILE YOU ARE TRAVELING, THAT YOU SHALL BE ABLE TO SUMMON THESE SIX ELDERS WHEN YOU NEED ADVICE!
BUT HOW, GREAT SIR?
WITH THIS, BILLY--THE ETERNI-PHONE! EACH OF THE LIGHTS CAN SUMMON ONE OF THE ELDERS--WHILE THE SEVENTH WILL CALL ME!
YOU CAN USE IT TO COMMUNICATE WITH OUR HOME AT THE ROCK OF ETERNITY!
THANKS, SIR! I'LL DO MY BEST TO STOP SIVANA!
SOLOMON-WISDOM
HERCULES-STRENGTH
ATLAS-STAMINA
ZEUS-POWER
ACHILLES COURAGE
FAREWELL, BILLY!
AS THEY LEAVE THE THRONE ROOM, BILLY PAUSES MOMENTARILY BESIDE THE PETRIFIED FORMS OF THE SEVEN DEADLY ENEMIES OF MAN...
LAZINESS
PRIDE, ENVY, GREED, HATRED, SELFISHNESS, LAZINESS AND INJUSTICE! SIVANA REPRESENTS ALL THOSE SINS...
...EXCEPT ONE! YOU CAN'T ACCUSE SIVANA OF LAZINESS! THAT FIEND IS ALWAYS BUSY WITH SOME SORT OF DEVILISH SCHEME!

OUTSIDE, THE THREE YOUNG PEOPLE SPEAK THEIR MAGIC WORDS...

WE'D BETTER GET BACK TO OUR WORK!

SHAZAM!

SHAZAM!

CAPTAIN MARVEL!

AND THIS TIME, *THREE* BOLTS OF MYSTICAL LIGHTNING STRIKE...

BA-MA-MA-M

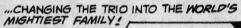

...CHANGING THE TRIO INTO THE *WORLD'S MIGHTIEST FAMILY!*

WHY, UNCLE! WHY DIDN'T YOU CHANGE TO *UNCLE MARVEL?*

OH, I'M GETTING A BIT TOO OLD FOR SUCH THINGS! BEEN HAVING TROUBLE WITH MY *SHAZAM-BAGO!*

IT'S TOO ROUGH TRYING TO FAKE SUPER-POWERS!

I--I GUESS WE'D BETTER GET OUR GOOD-BYES SAID, KIDS! I'M GOING TO MISS YOU!

WE'LL MISS YOU TERRIBLY, TOO--AND UNCLE!

GIVE SIVANA AN EXTRA PUNCH FOR ME, *CAP!*

AND SO THE THREE COLORFUL FIGURES TAKE TO THE SKY, EACH FLYING IN A DIFFERENT DIRECTION...

I HAVE TO RETURN TO FREDDY'S NEWSSTAND.

I WILL, *JUNIOR!* ON TO STATION *WHIZ*, EH, UNCLE?

IT'S BACK TO MY ADOPTIVE MOTHER IN THE SUBURBS FOR ME!

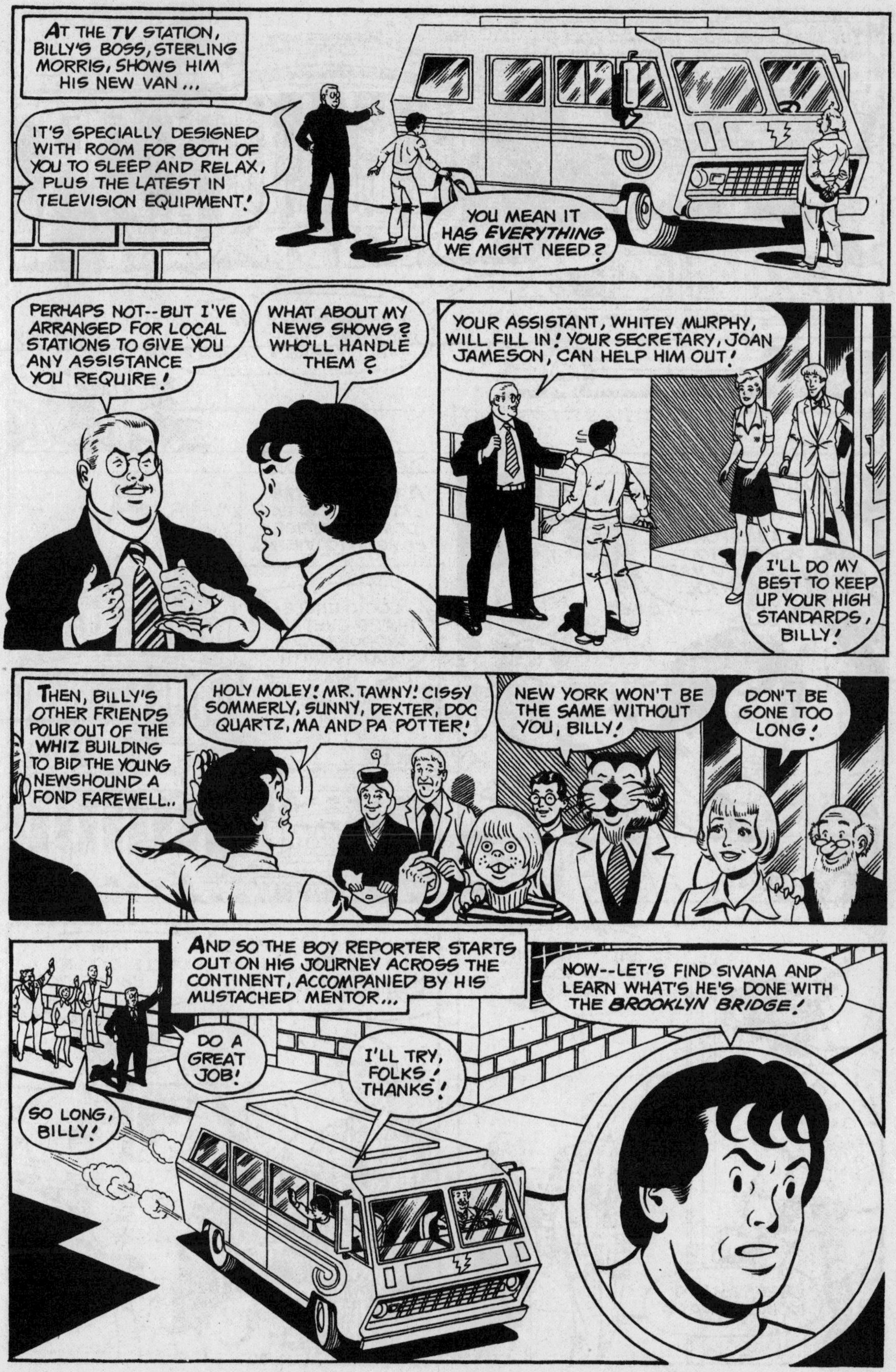
AT THE TV STATION, BILLY'S BOSS, STERLING MORRIS, SHOWS HIM HIS NEW VAN...
IT'S SPECIALLY DESIGNED WITH ROOM FOR BOTH OF YOU TO SLEEP AND RELAX, PLUS THE LATEST IN TELEVISION EQUIPMENT!
YOU MEAN IT HAS EVERYTHING WE MIGHT NEED?
PERHAPS NOT--BUT I'VE ARRANGED FOR LOCAL STATIONS TO GIVE YOU ANY ASSISTANCE YOU REQUIRE!
WHAT ABOUT MY NEWS SHOWS? WHO'LL HANDLE THEM?
YOUR ASSISTANT, WHITEY MURPHY, WILL FILL IN! YOUR SECRETARY, JOAN JAMESON, CAN HELP HIM OUT!
I'LL DO MY BEST TO KEEP UP YOUR HIGH STANDARDS, BILLY!
THEN, BILLY'S OTHER FRIENDS POUR OUT OF THE WHIZ BUILDING TO BID THE YOUNG NEWSHOUND A FOND FAREWELL..
HOLY MOLEY! MR. TAWNY! CISSY SOMMERLY, SUNNY, DEXTER, DOC QUARTZ, MA AND PA POTTER!
NEW YORK WON'T BE THE SAME WITHOUT YOU, BILLY!
DON'T BE GONE TOO LONG!
AND SO THE BOY REPORTER STARTS OUT ON HIS JOURNEY ACROSS THE CONTINENT, ACCOMPANIED BY HIS MUSTACHED MENTOR...
NOW--LET'S FIND SIVANA AND LEARN WHAT'S HE'S DONE WITH THE BROOKLYN BRIDGE!
DO A GREAT JOB!
I'LL TRY, FOLKS! THANKS!
SO LONG, BILLY!

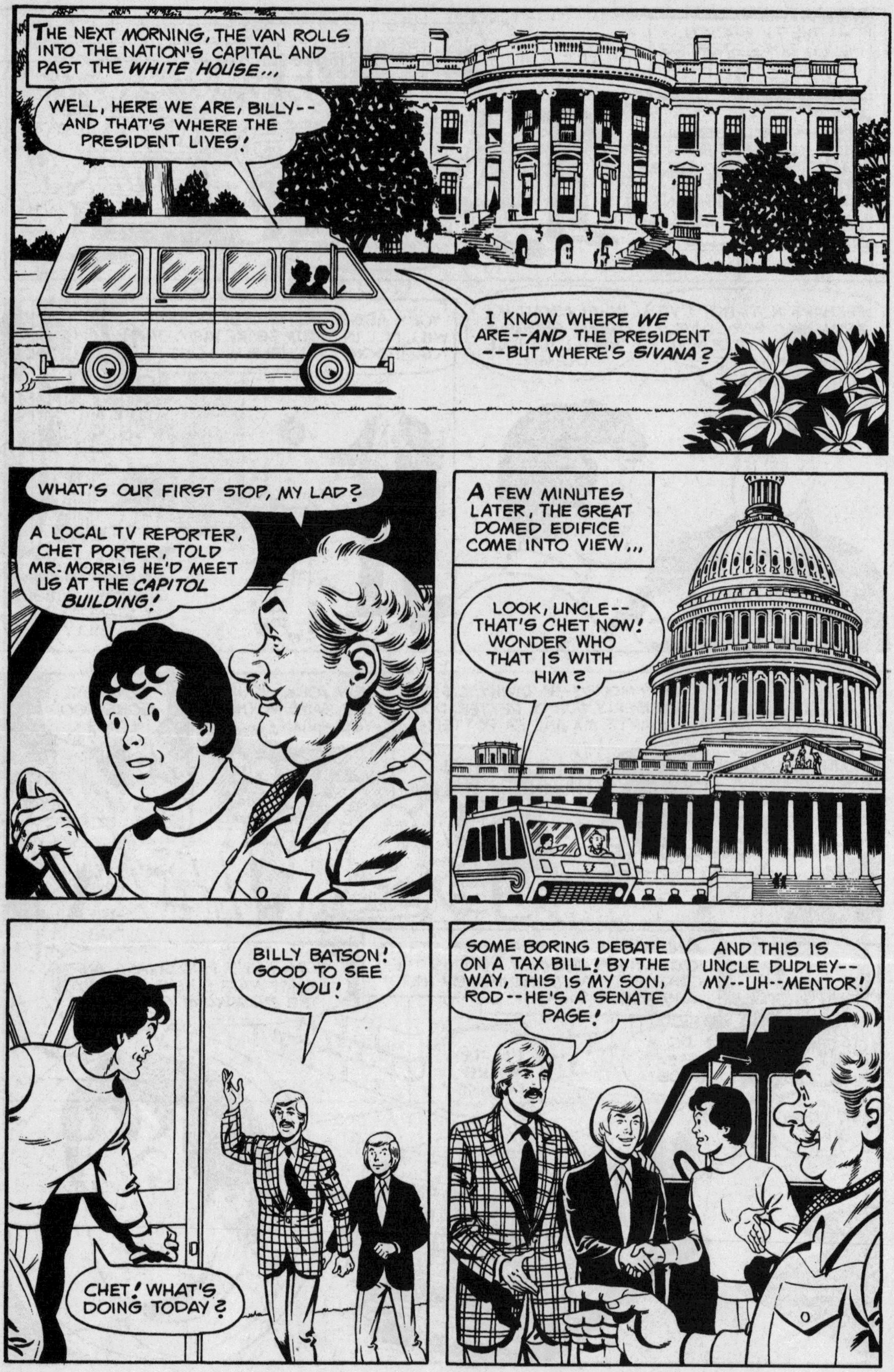
THE NEXT MORNING, THE VAN ROLLS INTO THE NATION'S CAPITAL AND PAST THE WHITE HOUSE...,
WELL, HERE WE ARE, BILLY-- AND THAT'S WHERE THE PRESIDENT LIVES!
I KNOW WHERE WE ARE--AND THE PRESIDENT --BUT WHERE'S SIVANA?
WHAT'S OUR FIRST STOP, MY LAD?
A LOCAL TV REPORTER, CHET PORTER, TOLD MR. MORRIS HE'D MEET US AT THE CAPITOL BUILDING!
A FEW MINUTES LATER, THE GREAT DOMED EDIFICE COME INTO VIEW...
LOOK, UNCLE-- THAT'S CHET NOW! WONDER WHO THAT IS WITH HIM?
BILLY BATSON! GOOD TO SEE YOU!
CHET! WHAT'S DOING TODAY?
SOME BORING DEBATE ON A TAX BILL! BY THE WAY, THIS IS MY SON, ROD--HE'S A SENATE PAGE!
AND THIS IS UNCLE DUDLEY-- MY--UH--MENTOR!

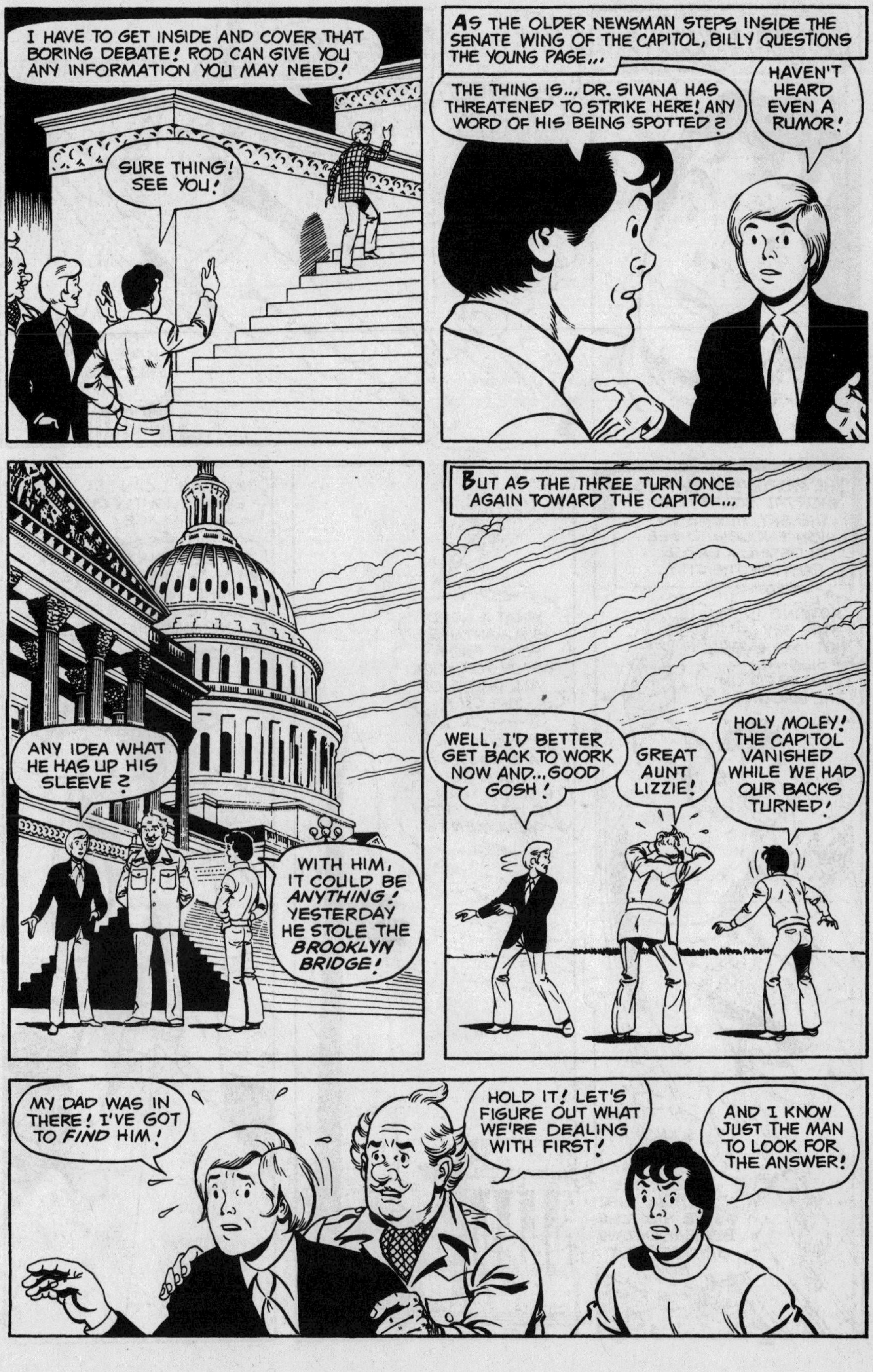
I HAVE TO GET INSIDE AND COVER THAT BORING DEBATE! ROD CAN GIVE YOU ANY INFORMATION YOU MAY NEED!
SURE THING! SEE YOU!
AS THE OLDER NEWSMAN STEPS INSIDE THE SENATE WING OF THE CAPITOL, BILLY QUESTIONS THE YOUNG PAGE...
THE THING IS... DR. SIVANA HAS THREATENED TO STRIKE HERE! ANY WORD OF HIS BEING SPOTTED?
HAVEN'T HEARD EVEN A RUMOR!
ANY IDEA WHAT HE HAS UP HIS SLEEVE?
WITH HIM, IT COULD BE *ANYTHING!* YESTERDAY HE STOLE THE *BROOKLYN BRIDGE!*
BUT AS THE THREE TURN ONCE AGAIN TOWARD THE CAPITOL...
WELL, I'D BETTER GET BACK TO WORK NOW AND...GOOD GOSH!
GREAT AUNT LIZZIE!
HOLY MOLEY! THE CAPITOL VANISHED WHILE WE HAD OUR BACKS TURNED!
MY DAD WAS IN THERE! I'VE GOT TO *FIND* HIM!
HOLD IT! LET'S FIGURE OUT WHAT WE'RE DEALING WITH FIRST!
AND I KNOW JUST THE MAN TO LOOK FOR THE ANSWER!

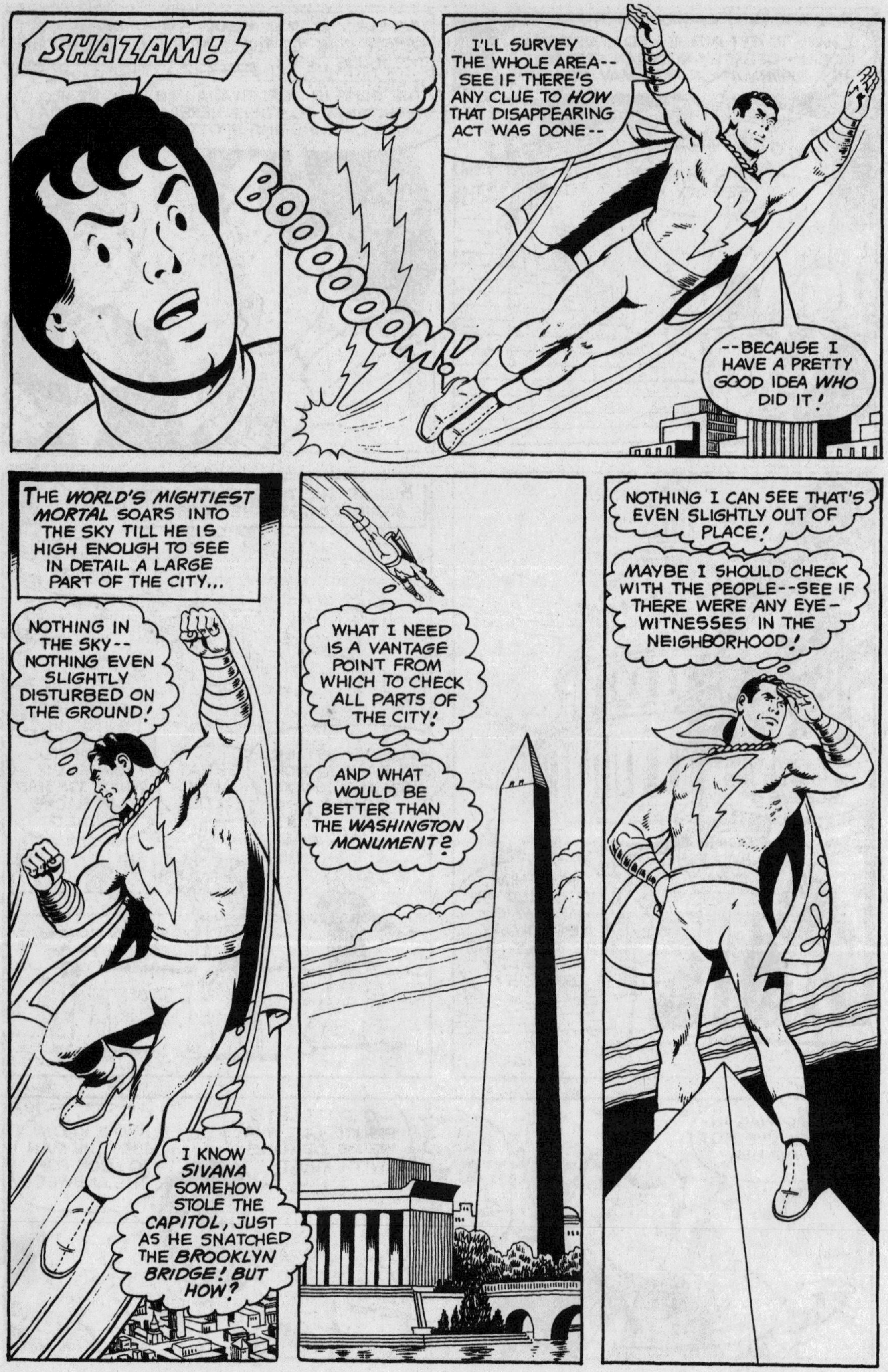
SHAZAM!
BOOOOOOM!
I'LL SURVEY THE WHOLE AREA-- SEE IF THERE'S ANY CLUE TO HOW THAT DISAPPEARING ACT WAS DONE--
--BECAUSE I HAVE A PRETTY GOOD IDEA WHO DID IT!
THE WORLD'S MIGHTIEST MORTAL SOARS INTO THE SKY TILL HE IS HIGH ENOUGH TO SEE IN DETAIL A LARGE PART OF THE CITY...
NOTHING IN THE SKY-- NOTHING EVEN SLIGHTLY DISTURBED ON THE GROUND!
I KNOW SIVANA SOMEHOW STOLE THE CAPITOL, JUST AS HE SNATCHED THE BROOKLYN BRIDGE! BUT HOW?
WHAT I NEED IS A VANTAGE POINT FROM WHICH TO CHECK ALL PARTS OF THE CITY!
AND WHAT WOULD BE BETTER THAN THE WASHINGTON MONUMENT?
NOTHING I CAN SEE THAT'S EVEN SLIGHTLY OUT OF PLACE!
MAYBE I SHOULD CHECK WITH THE PEOPLE--SEE IF THERE WERE ANY EYE-WITNESSES IN THE NEIGHBORHOOD!

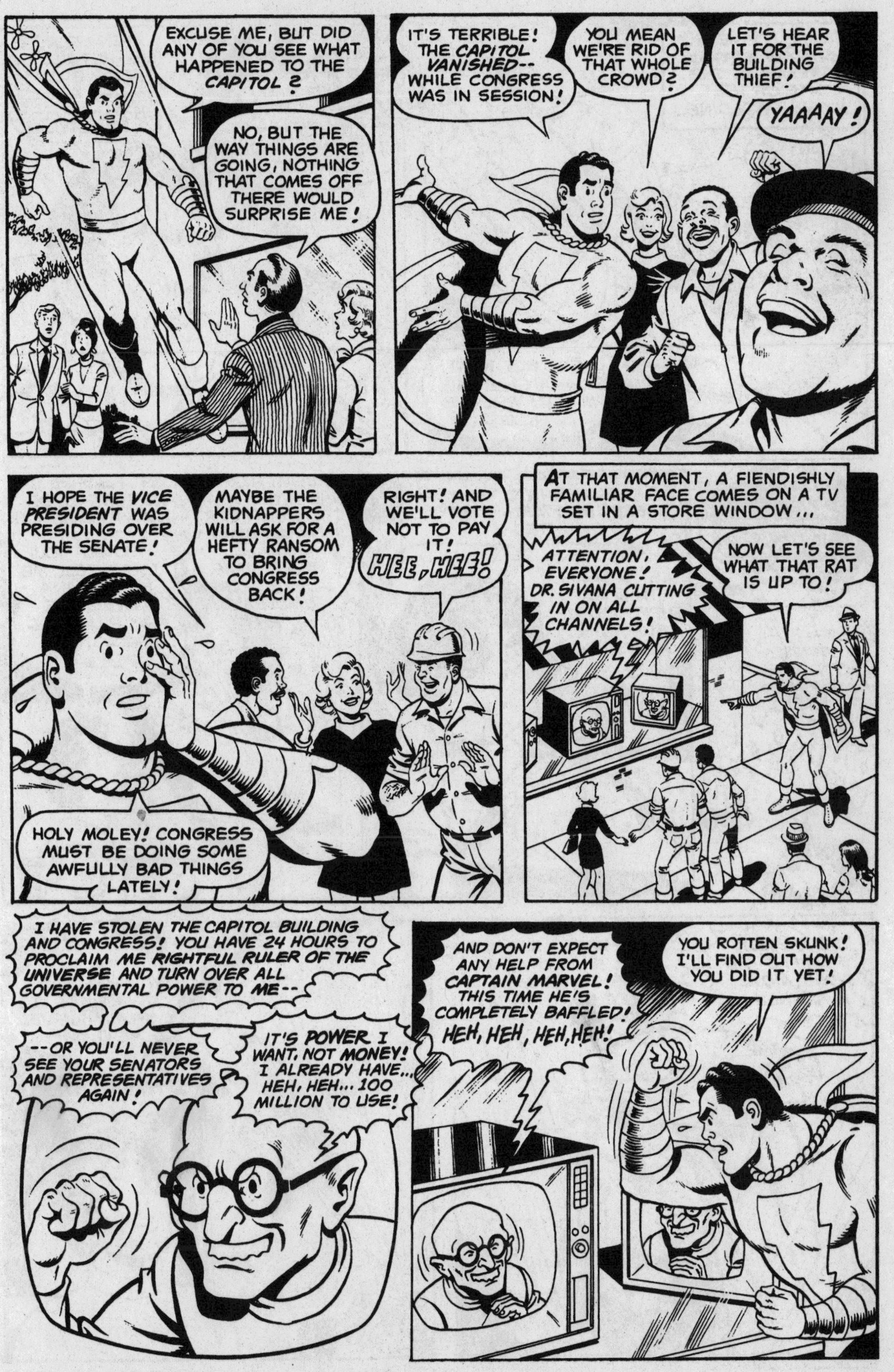
EXCUSE ME, BUT DID ANY OF YOU SEE WHAT HAPPENED TO THE CAPITOL ?
NO, BUT THE WAY THINGS ARE GOING, NOTHING THAT COMES OFF THERE WOULD SURPRISE ME!
IT'S TERRIBLE! THE CAPITOL VANISHED-- WHILE CONGRESS WAS IN SESSION!
YOU MEAN WE'RE RID OF THAT WHOLE CROWD?
LET'S HEAR IT FOR THE BUILDING THIEF!
YAAAAY!
I HOPE THE VICE PRESIDENT WAS PRESIDING OVER THE SENATE!
MAYBE THE KIDNAPPERS WILL ASK FOR A HEFTY RANSOM TO BRING CONGRESS BACK!
RIGHT! AND WE'LL VOTE NOT TO PAY IT! HEE, HEE!
HOLY MOLEY! CONGRESS MUST BE DOING SOME AWFULLY BAD THINGS LATELY!
AT THAT MOMENT, A FIENDISHLY FAMILIAR FACE COMES ON A TV SET IN A STORE WINDOW...
ATTENTION, EVERYONE! DR. SIVANA CUTTING IN ON ALL CHANNELS!
NOW LET'S SEE WHAT THAT RAT IS UP TO!
I HAVE STOLEN THE CAPITOL BUILDING AND CONGRESS! YOU HAVE 24 HOURS TO PROCLAIM ME RIGHTFUL RULER OF THE UNIVERSE AND TURN OVER ALL GOVERNMENTAL POWER TO ME--
--OR YOU'LL NEVER SEE YOUR SENATORS AND REPRESENTATIVES AGAIN!
IT'S POWER I WANT, NOT MONEY! I ALREADY HAVE... HEH, HEH... 100 MILLION TO USE!
AND DON'T EXPECT ANY HELP FROM CAPTAIN MARVEL! THIS TIME HE'S COMPLETELY BAFFLED! HEH, HEH, HEH, HEH!
YOU ROTTEN SKUNK! I'LL FIND OUT HOW YOU DID IT YET!

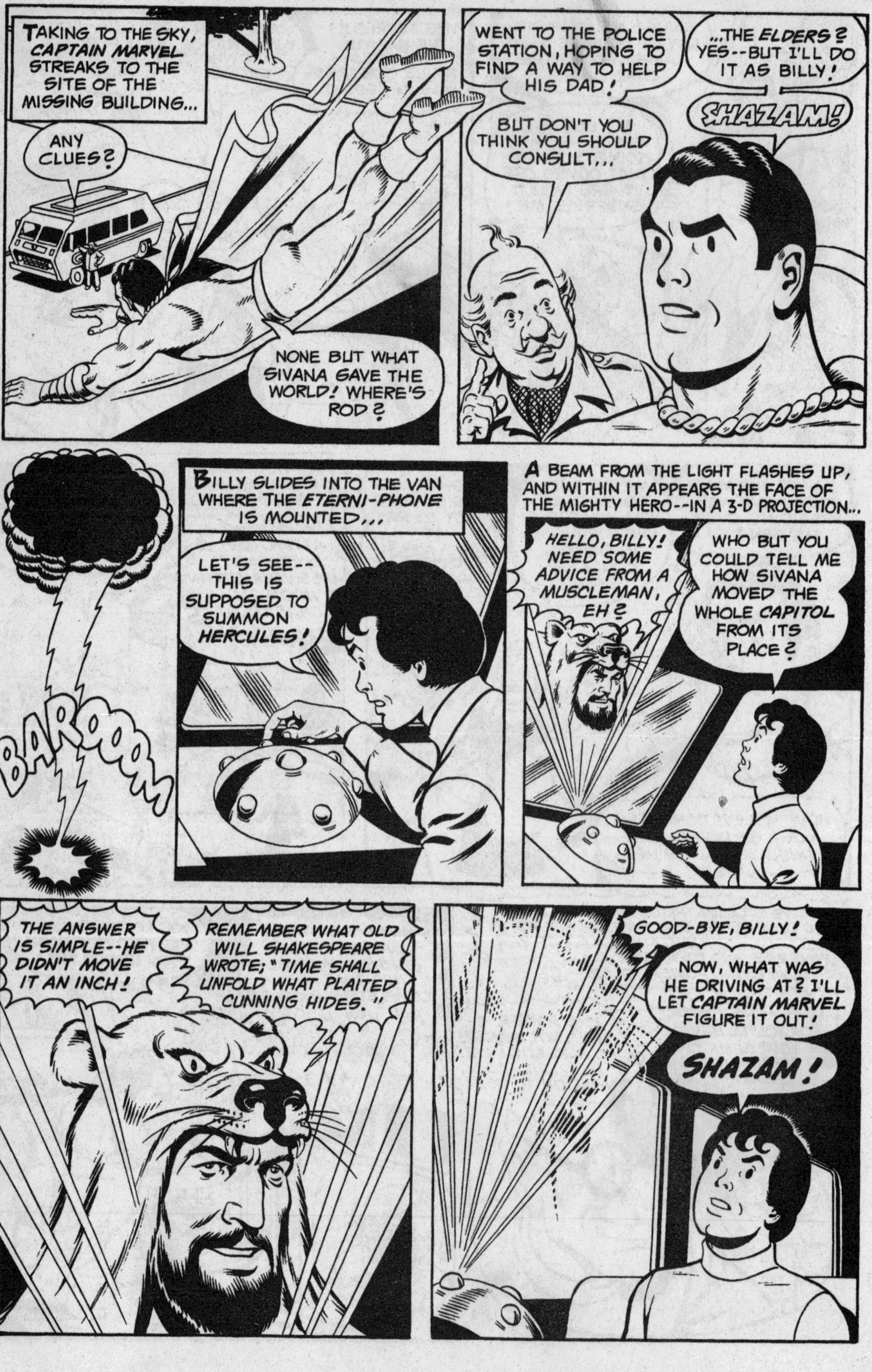
TAKING TO THE SKY, CAPTAIN MARVEL STREAKS TO THE SITE OF THE MISSING BUILDING...
ANY CLUES?
NONE BUT WHAT SIVANA GAVE THE WORLD! WHERE'S ROD?
WENT TO THE POLICE STATION, HOPING TO FIND A WAY TO HELP HIS DAD!
BUT DON'T YOU THINK YOU SHOULD CONSULT...
...THE ELDERS? YES--BUT I'LL DO IT AS BILLY!
SHAZAM!
BAROOOM
BILLY SLIDES INTO THE VAN WHERE THE ETERNI-PHONE IS MOUNTED...
LET'S SEE-- THIS IS SUPPOSED TO SUMMON HERCULES!
A BEAM FROM THE LIGHT FLASHES UP, AND WITHIN IT APPEARS THE FACE OF THE MIGHTY HERO--IN A 3-D PROJECTION...
HELLO, BILLY! NEED SOME ADVICE FROM A MUSCLEMAN, EH?
WHO BUT YOU COULD TELL ME HOW SIVANA MOVED THE WHOLE CAPITOL FROM ITS PLACE?
THE ANSWER IS SIMPLE--HE DIDN'T MOVE IT AN INCH!
REMEMBER WHAT OLD WILL SHAKESPEARE WROTE; "TIME SHALL UNFOLD WHAT PLAITED CUNNING HIDES."
GOOD-BYE, BILLY!
NOW, WHAT WAS HE DRIVING AT? I'LL LET CAPTAIN MARVEL FIGURE IT OUT!
SHAZAM!

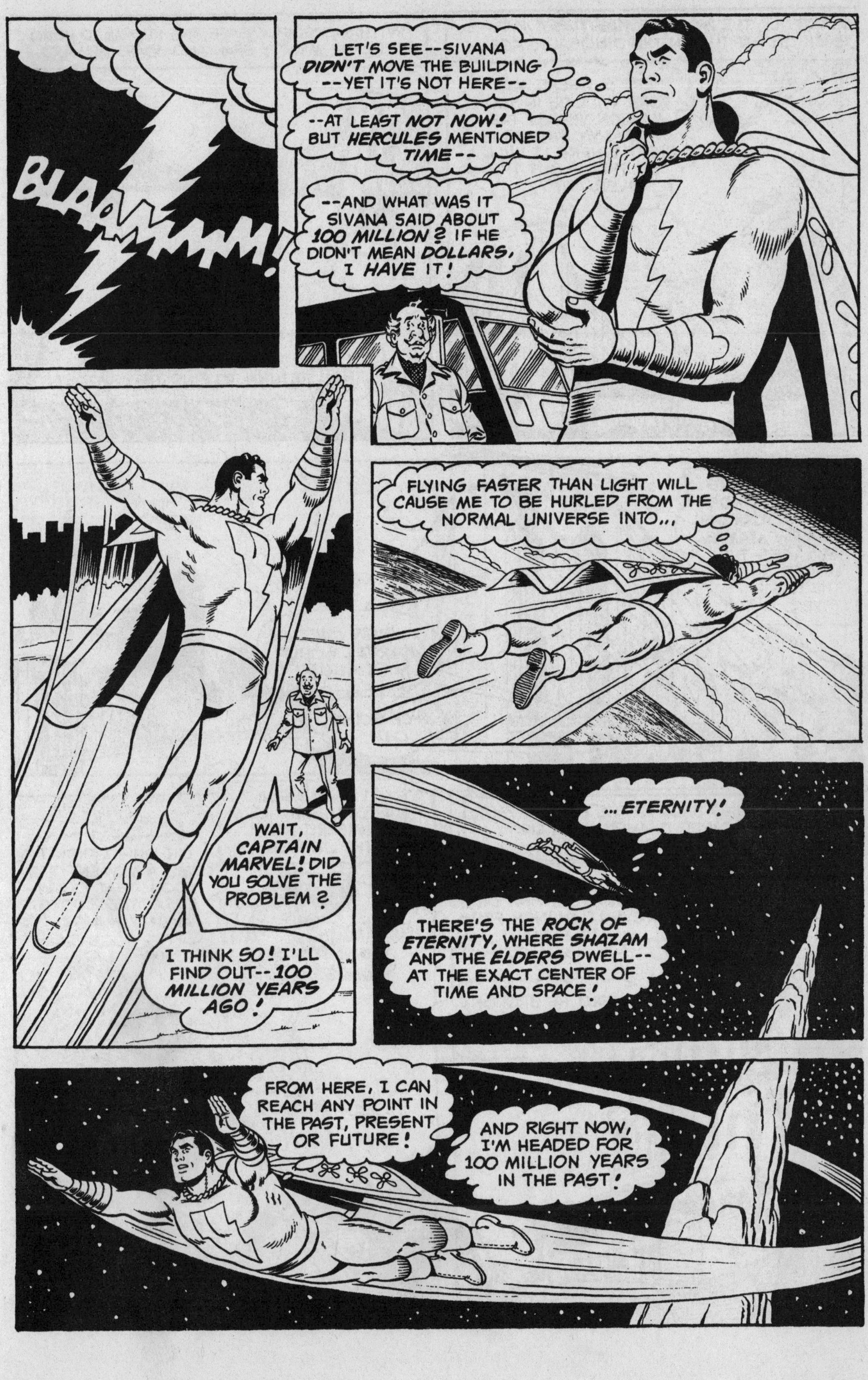
BLAAAMMM!
LET'S SEE--SIVANA DIDN'T MOVE THE BUILDING --YET IT'S NOT HERE--
--AT LEAST NOT NOW! BUT HERCULES MENTIONED TIME--
--AND WHAT WAS IT SIVANA SAID ABOUT 100 MILLION? IF HE DIDN'T MEAN DOLLARS, I HAVE IT!
WAIT, CAPTAIN MARVEL! DID YOU SOLVE THE PROBLEM?
I THINK SO! I'LL FIND OUT--100 MILLION YEARS AGO!
FLYING FASTER THAN LIGHT WILL CAUSE ME TO BE HURLED FROM THE NORMAL UNIVERSE INTO...
...ETERNITY!
THERE'S THE ROCK OF ETERNITY, WHERE SHAZAM AND THE ELDERS DWELL-- AT THE EXACT CENTER OF TIME AND SPACE!
FROM HERE, I CAN REACH ANY POINT IN THE PAST, PRESENT OR FUTURE!
AND RIGHT NOW, I'M HEADED FOR 100 MILLION YEARS IN THE PAST!

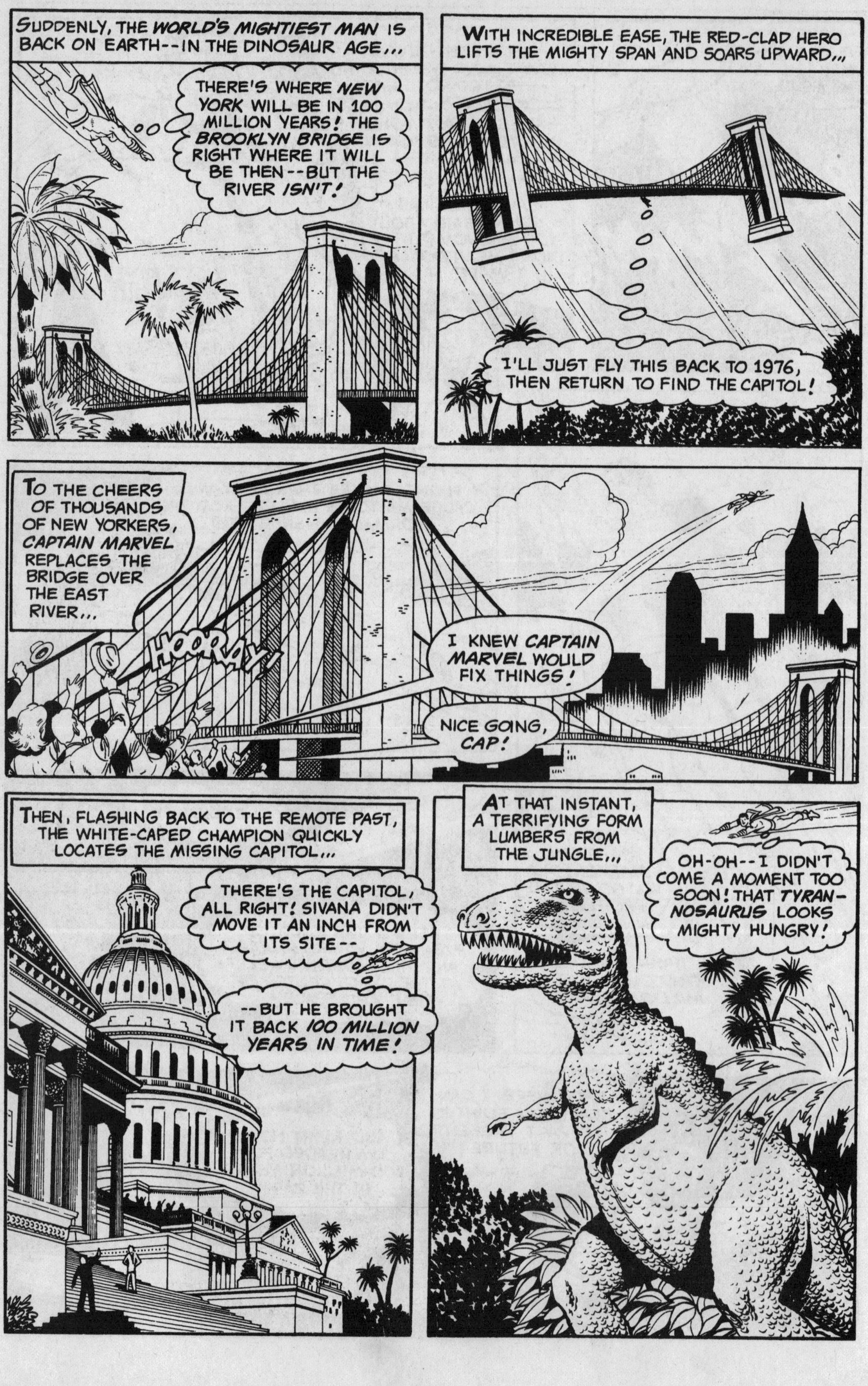
SUDDENLY, THE WORLD'S MIGHTIEST MAN IS BACK ON EARTH--IN THE DINOSAUR AGE...
THERE'S WHERE NEW YORK WILL BE IN 100 MILLION YEARS! THE BROOKLYN BRIDGE IS RIGHT WHERE IT WILL BE THEN--BUT THE RIVER ISN'T!
WITH INCREDIBLE EASE, THE RED-CLAD HERO LIFTS THE MIGHTY SPAN AND SOARS UPWARD...
I'LL JUST FLY THIS BACK TO 1976, THEN RETURN TO FIND THE CAPITOL!
TO THE CHEERS OF THOUSANDS OF NEW YORKERS, CAPTAIN MARVEL REPLACES THE BRIDGE OVER THE EAST RIVER...
HOORAY!
I KNEW CAPTAIN MARVEL WOULD FIX THINGS!
NICE GOING, CAP!
THEN, FLASHING BACK TO THE REMOTE PAST, THE WHITE-CAPED CHAMPION QUICKLY LOCATES THE MISSING CAPITOL...
THERE'S THE CAPITOL, ALL RIGHT! SIVANA DIDN'T MOVE IT AN INCH FROM ITS SITE--
--BUT HE BROUGHT IT BACK 100 MILLION YEARS IN TIME!
AT THAT INSTANT, A TERRIFYING FORM LUMBERS FROM THE JUNGLE...
OH-OH--I DIDN'T COME A MOMENT TOO SOON! THAT TYRANNOSAURUS LOOKS MIGHTY HUNGRY!

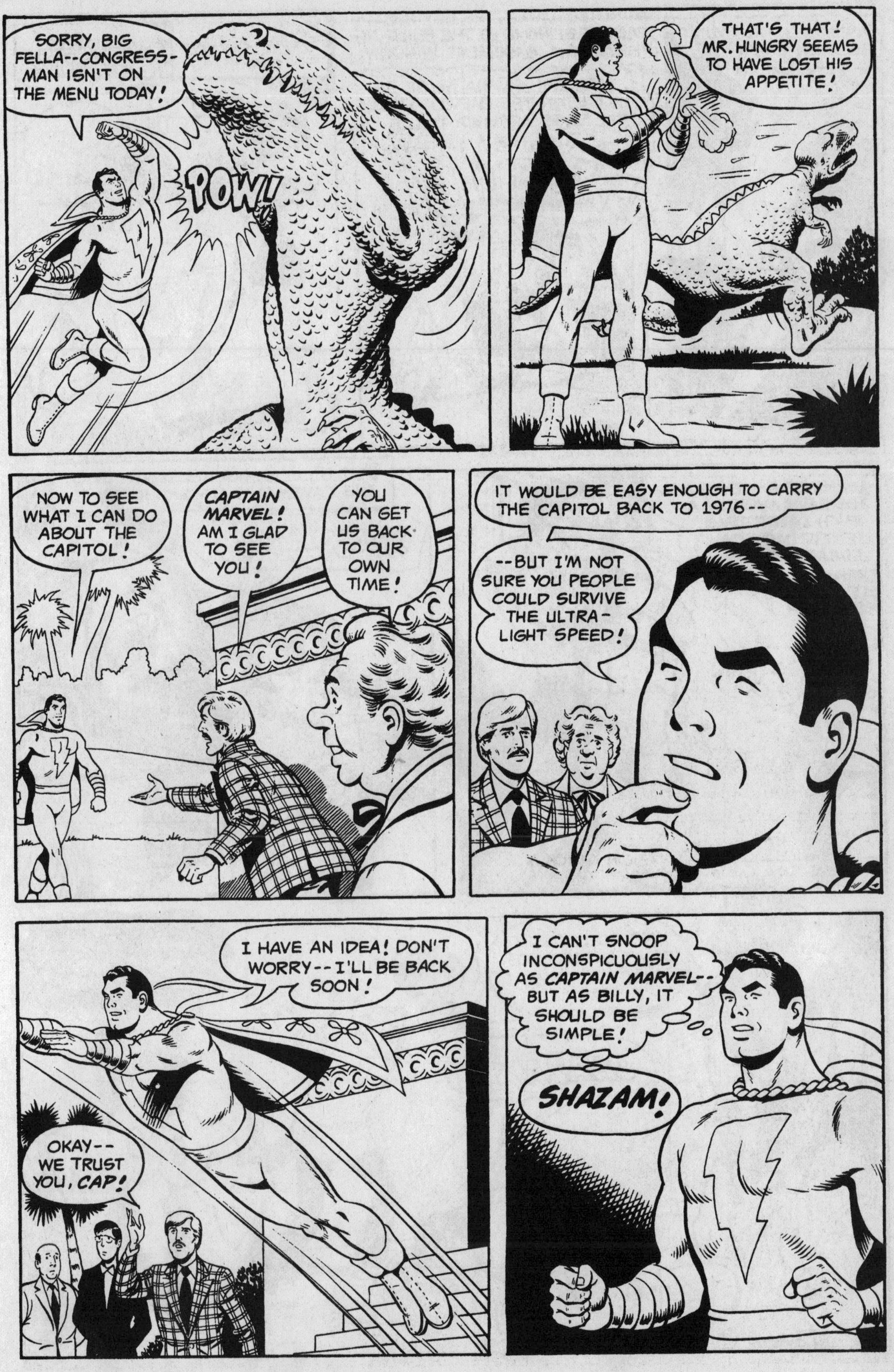
SORRY, BIG FELLA--CONGRESSMAN ISN'T ON THE MENU TODAY!
POW!
THAT'S THAT! MR. HUNGRY SEEMS TO HAVE LOST HIS APPETITE!
NOW TO SEE WHAT I CAN DO ABOUT THE CAPITOL!
CAPTAIN MARVEL! AM I GLAD TO SEE YOU!
YOU CAN GET US BACK TO OUR OWN TIME!
IT WOULD BE EASY ENOUGH TO CARRY THE CAPITOL BACK TO 1976--
--BUT I'M NOT SURE YOU PEOPLE COULD SURVIVE THE ULTRA-LIGHT SPEED!
I HAVE AN IDEA! DON'T WORRY--I'LL BE BACK SOON!
OKAY--WE TRUST YOU, CAP!
I CAN'T SNOOP INCONSPICUOUSLY AS CAPTAIN MARVEL--BUT AS BILLY, IT SHOULD BE SIMPLE!
SHAZAM!

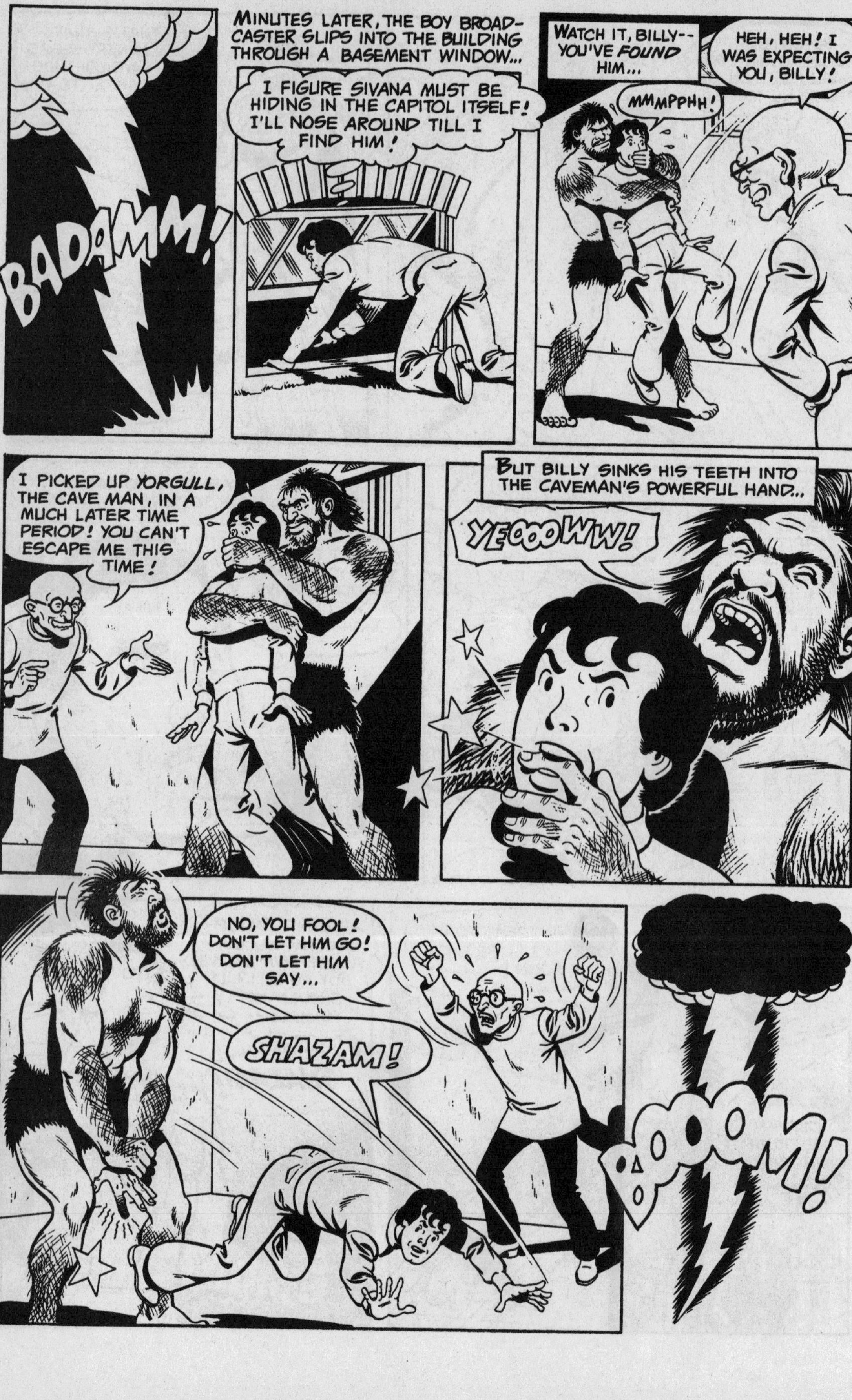
BADAMM!
MINUTES LATER, THE BOY BROADCASTER SLIPS INTO THE BUILDING THROUGH A BASEMENT WINDOW...
I FIGURE SIVANA MUST BE HIDING IN THE CAPITOL ITSELF! I'LL NOSE AROUND TILL I FIND HIM!
WATCH IT, BILLY--YOU'VE FOUND HIM...
HEH, HEH! I WAS EXPECTING YOU, BILLY!
MMMPPHH!
I PICKED UP YORGULL, THE CAVE MAN, IN A MUCH LATER TIME PERIOD! YOU CAN'T ESCAPE ME THIS TIME!
BUT BILLY SINKS HIS TEETH INTO THE CAVEMAN'S POWERFUL HAND...
YEOOOWW!
NO, YOU FOOL! DON'T LET HIM GO! DON'T LET HIM SAY...
SHAZAM!
BOOOOM!

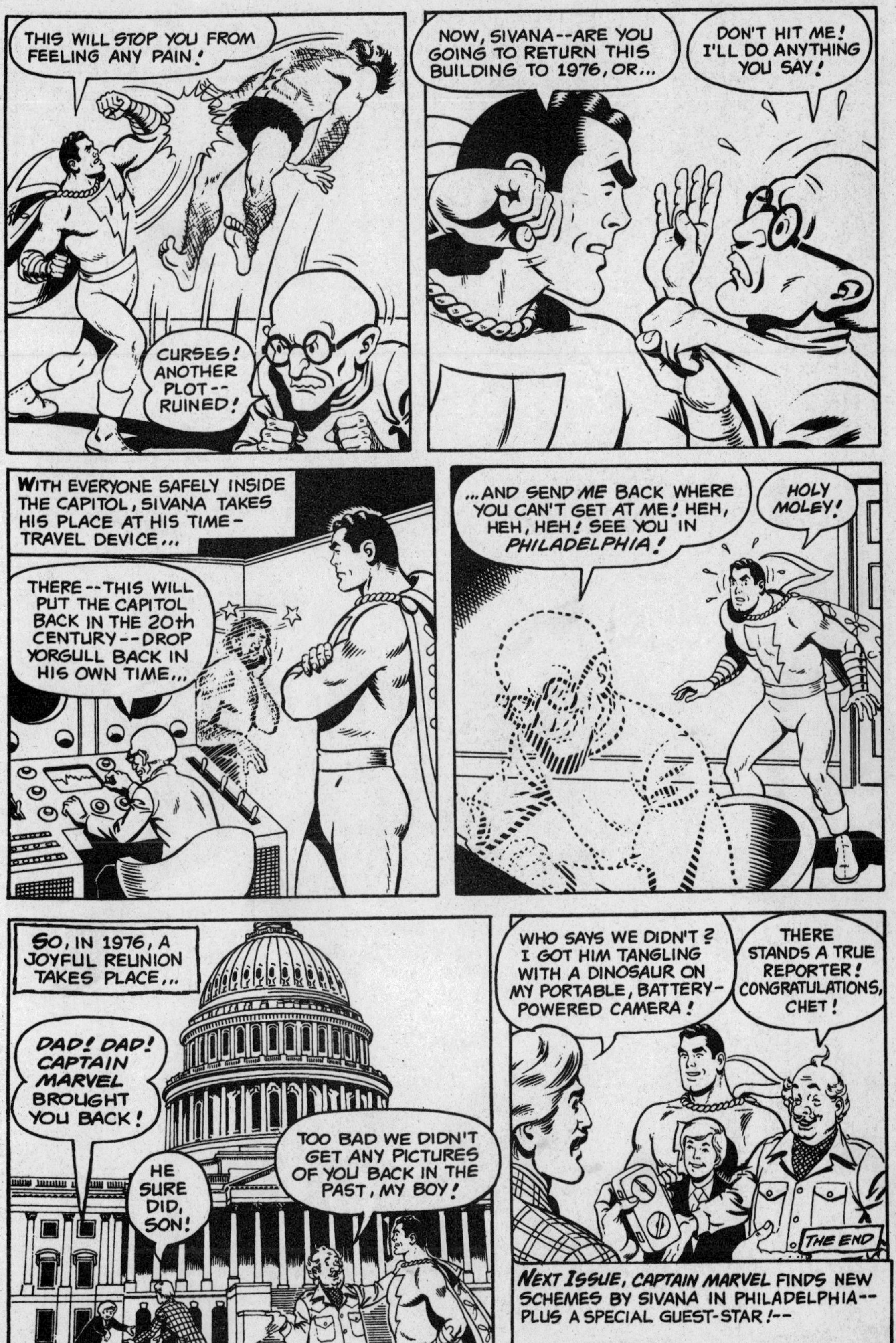
THIS WILL STOP YOU FROM FEELING ANY PAIN!
CURSES! ANOTHER PLOT--RUINED!
NOW, SIVANA--ARE YOU GOING TO RETURN THIS BUILDING TO 1976, OR...
DON'T HIT ME! I'LL DO ANYTHING YOU SAY!
WITH EVERYONE SAFELY INSIDE THE CAPITOL, SIVANA TAKES HIS PLACE AT HIS TIME-TRAVEL DEVICE...
THERE--THIS WILL PUT THE CAPITOL BACK IN THE 20th CENTURY--DROP YORGULL BACK IN HIS OWN TIME...
...AND SEND ME BACK WHERE YOU CAN'T GET AT ME! HEH, HEH, HEH! SEE YOU IN PHILADELPHIA!
HOLY MOLEY!
SO, IN 1976, A JOYFUL REUNION TAKES PLACE...
DAD! DAD! CAPTAIN MARVEL BROUGHT YOU BACK!
HE SURE DID, SON!
TOO BAD WE DIDN'T GET ANY PICTURES OF YOU BACK IN THE PAST, MY BOY!
WHO SAYS WE DIDN'T? I GOT HIM TANGLING WITH A DINOSAUR ON MY PORTABLE, BATTERY-POWERED CAMERA!
THERE STANDS A TRUE REPORTER! CONGRATULATIONS, CHET!
THE END
NEXT ISSUE, CAPTAIN MARVEL FINDS NEW SCHEMES BY SIVANA IN PHILADELPHIA--PLUS A SPECIAL GUEST-STAR!--

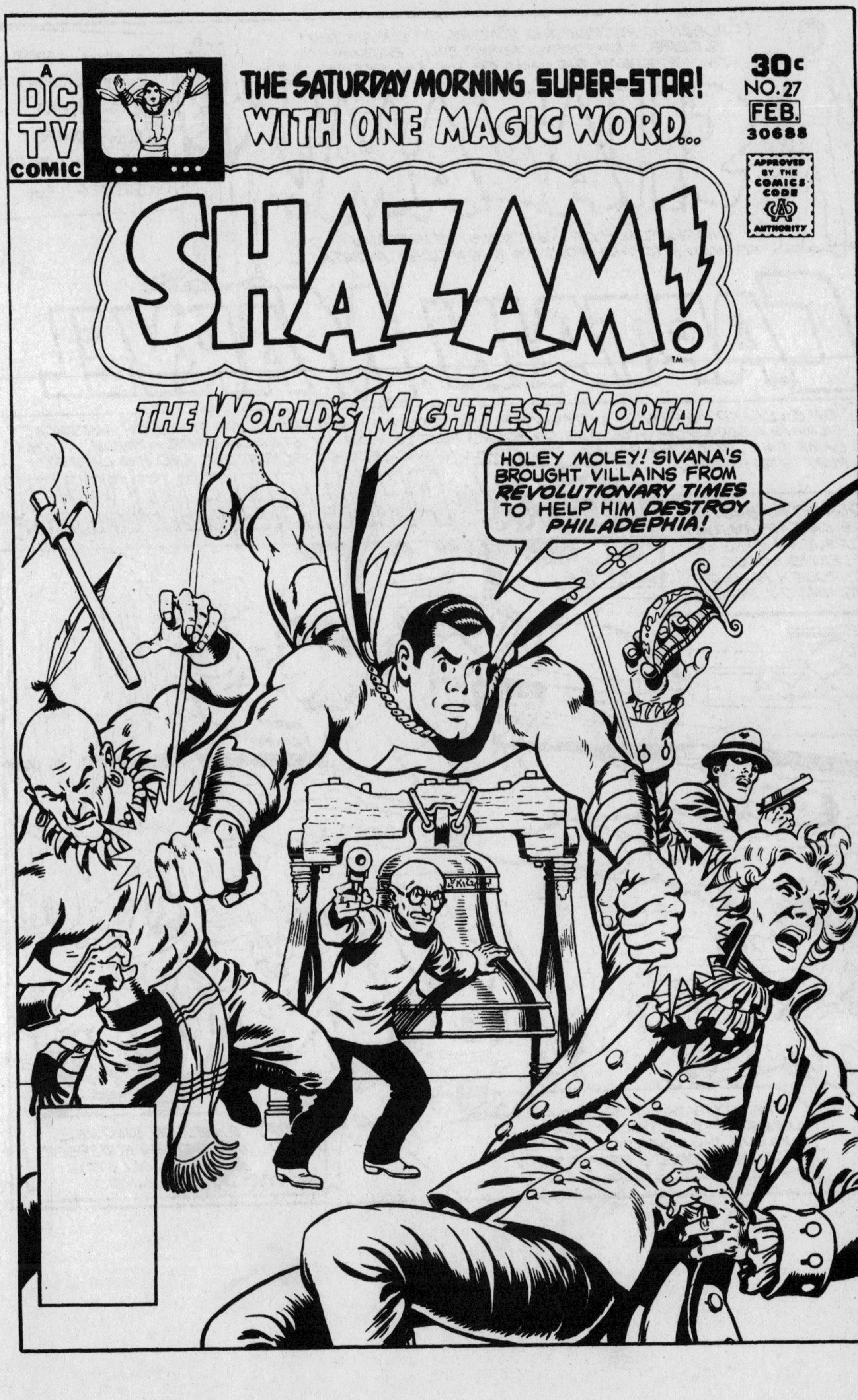
A DC TV COMIC
THE SATURDAY MORNING SUPER-STAR!
WITH ONE MAGIC WORD...
30¢
NO. 27
FEB.
30688
APPROVED BY THE COMICS CODE AUTHORITY
SHAZAM!
THE WORLD'S MIGHTIEST MORTAL
HOLEY MOLEY! SIVANA'S BROUGHT VILLAINS FROM REVOLUTIONARY TIMES TO HELP HIM DESTROY PHILADEPHIA!

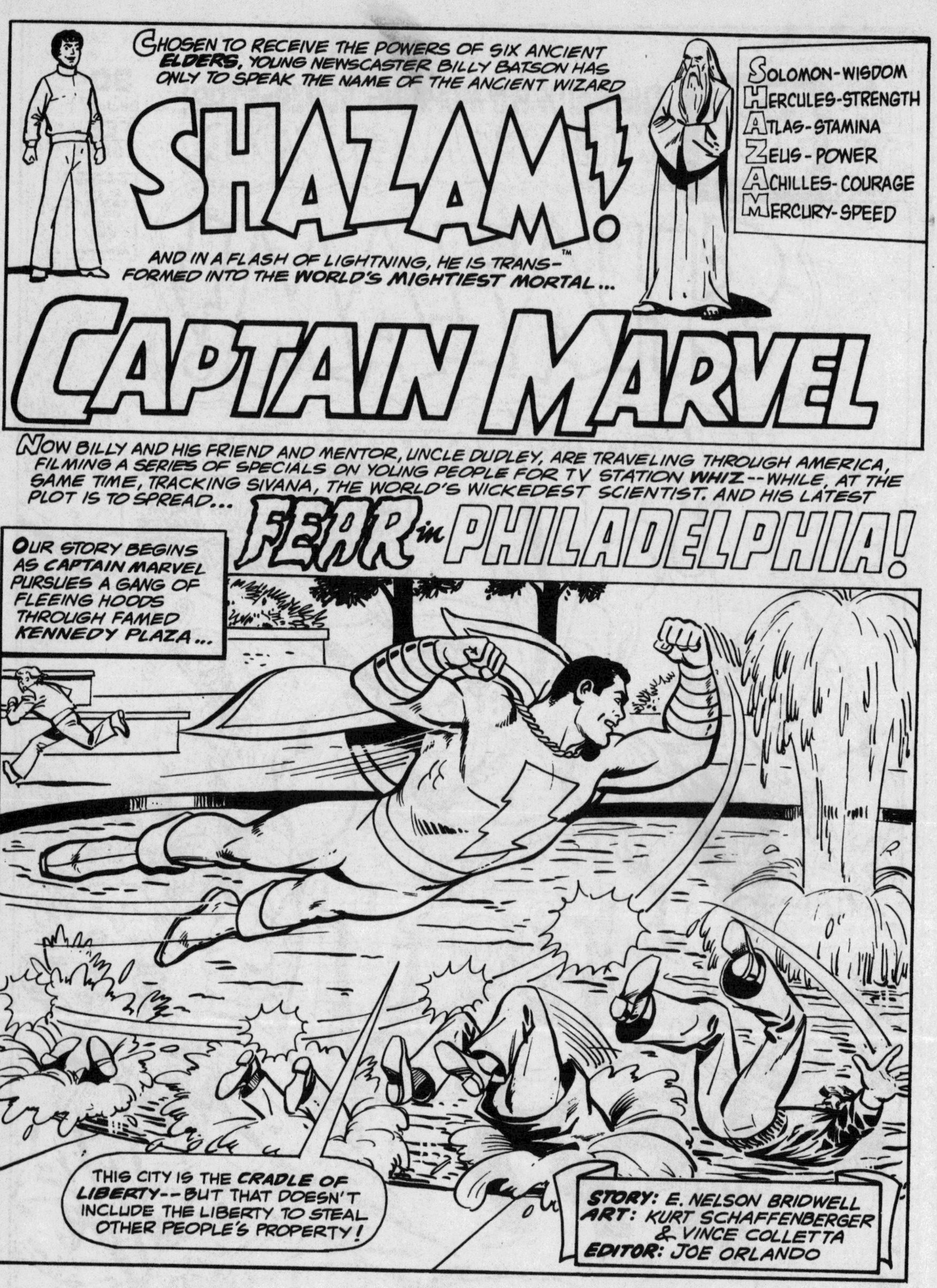
CHOSEN TO RECEIVE THE POWERS OF SIX ANCIENT ELDERS, YOUNG NEWSCASTER BILLY BATSON HAS ONLY TO SPEAK THE NAME OF THE ANCIENT WIZARD
SHAZAM!
SOLOMON-WISDOM
HERCULES-STRENGTH
ATLAS-STAMINA
ZEUS-POWER
ACHILLES-COURAGE
MERCURY-SPEED
AND IN A FLASH OF LIGHTNING, HE IS TRANSFORMED INTO THE WORLD'S MIGHTIEST MORTAL...
CAPTAIN MARVEL
NOW BILLY AND HIS FRIEND AND MENTOR, UNCLE DUDLEY, ARE TRAVELING THROUGH AMERICA, FILMING A SERIES OF SPECIALS ON YOUNG PEOPLE FOR TV STATION WHIZ--WHILE, AT THE SAME TIME, TRACKING SIVANA, THE WORLD'S WICKEDEST SCIENTIST. AND HIS LATEST PLOT IS TO SPREAD...
FEAR in PHILADELPHIA!
OUR STORY BEGINS AS CAPTAIN MARVEL PURSUES A GANG OF FLEEING HOODS THROUGH FAMED KENNEDY PLAZA...
THIS CITY IS THE CRADLE OF LIBERTY--BUT THAT DOESN'T INCLUDE THE LIBERTY TO STEAL OTHER PEOPLE'S PROPERTY!
STORY: E. NELSON BRIDWELL
ART: KURT SCHAFFENBERGER & VINCE COLLETTA
EDITOR: JOE ORLANDO

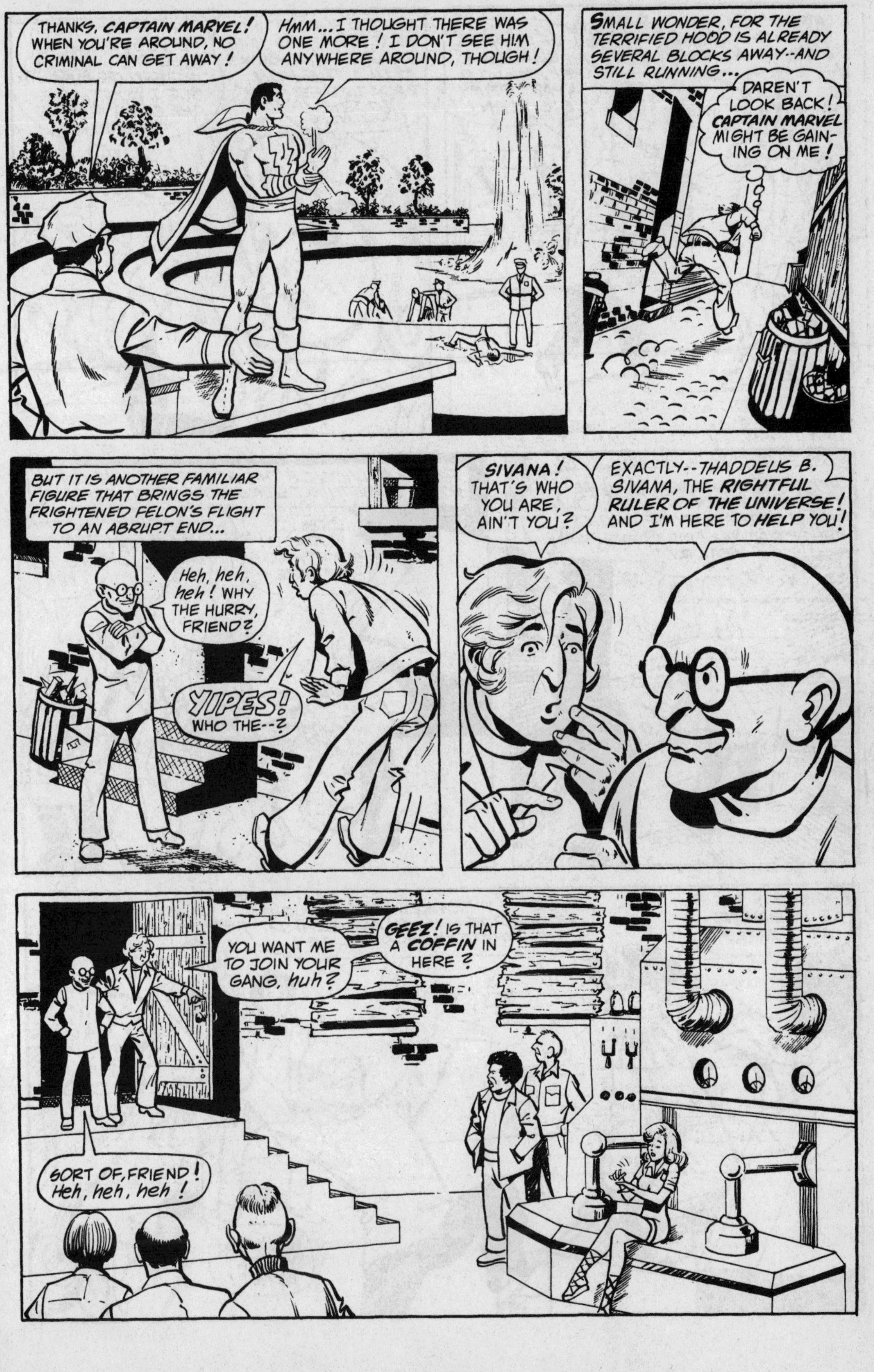
THANKS, CAPTAIN MARVEL! WHEN YOU'RE AROUND, NO CRIMINAL CAN GET AWAY!
HMM... I THOUGHT THERE WAS ONE MORE! I DON'T SEE HIM ANYWHERE AROUND, THOUGH!
SMALL WONDER, FOR THE TERRIFIED HOOD IS ALREADY SEVERAL BLOCKS AWAY--AND STILL RUNNING...
DAREN'T LOOK BACK! CAPTAIN MARVEL MIGHT BE GAINING ON ME!
BUT IT IS ANOTHER FAMILIAR FIGURE THAT BRINGS THE FRIGHTENED FELON'S FLIGHT TO AN ABRUPT END...
Heh, heh, heh! WHY THE HURRY, FRIEND?
YIPES! WHO THE--?
SIVANA! THAT'S WHO YOU ARE, AIN'T YOU?
EXACTLY--THADDEUS B. SIVANA, THE RIGHTFUL RULER OF THE UNIVERSE! AND I'M HERE TO HELP YOU!
YOU WANT ME TO JOIN YOUR GANG, huh?
SORT OF, FRIEND! Heh, heh, heh!
GEEZ! IS THAT A COFFIN IN HERE?

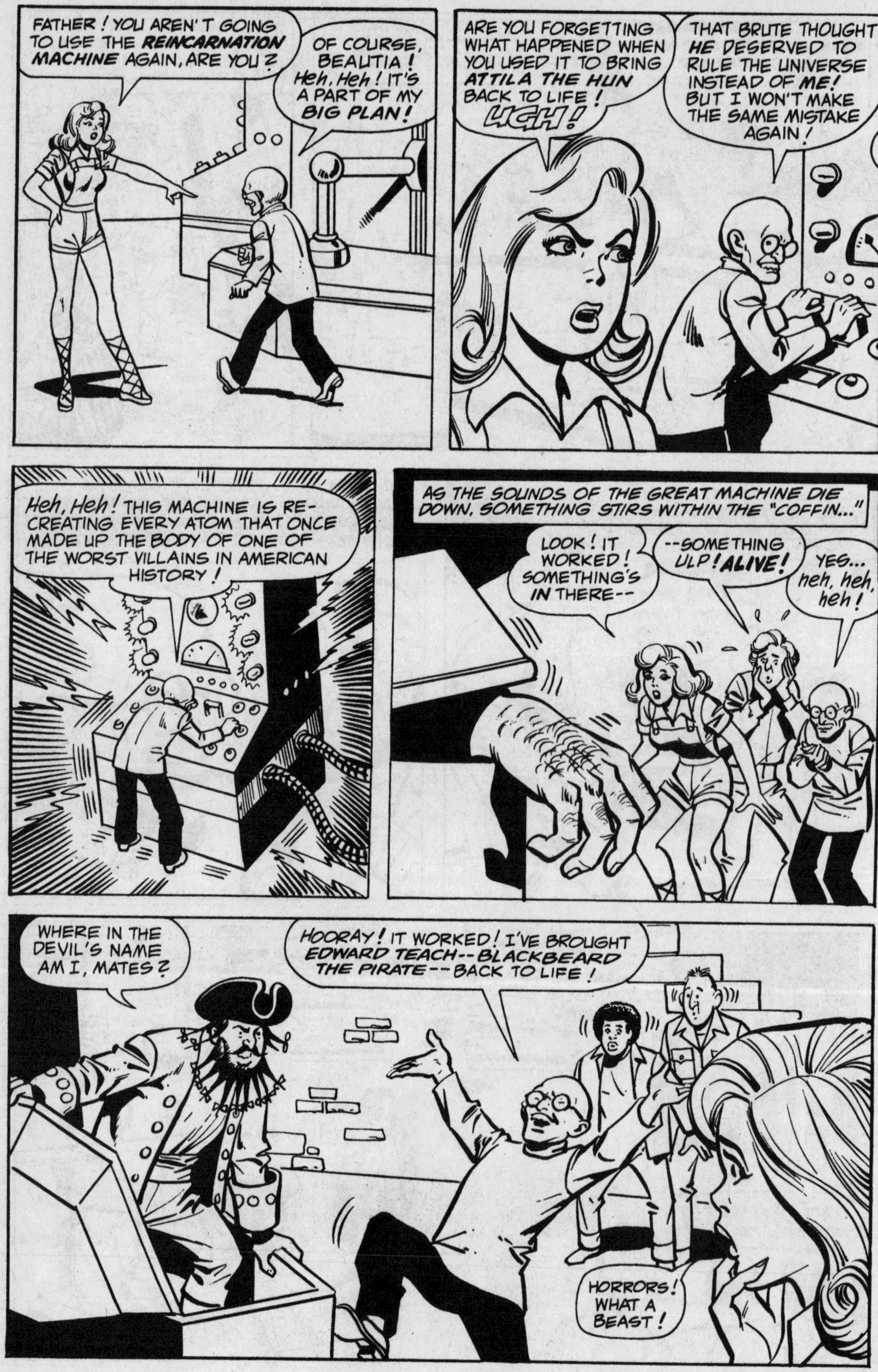

FATHER! YOU AREN'T GOING TO USE THE REINCARNATION MACHINE AGAIN, ARE YOU?
OF COURSE, BEAUTIA! Heh, Heh! IT'S A PART OF MY BIG PLAN!
ARE YOU FORGETTING WHAT HAPPENED WHEN YOU USED IT TO BRING ATTILA THE HUN BACK TO LIFE! UGH!
THAT BRUTE THOUGHT HE DESERVED TO RULE THE UNIVERSE INSTEAD OF ME! BUT I WON'T MAKE THE SAME MISTAKE AGAIN!
Heh, Heh! THIS MACHINE IS RE-CREATING EVERY ATOM THAT ONCE MADE UP THE BODY OF ONE OF THE WORST VILLAINS IN AMERICAN HISTORY!
AS THE SOUNDS OF THE GREAT MACHINE DIE DOWN, SOMETHING STIRS WITHIN THE "COFFIN..."
LOOK! IT WORKED! SOMETHING'S IN THERE--
--SOMETHING ULP! ALIVE!
YES... heh, heh, heh!
WHERE IN THE DEVIL'S NAME AM I, MATES?
HOORAY! IT WORKED! I'VE BROUGHT EDWARD TEACH--BLACKBEARD THE PIRATE--BACK TO LIFE!
HORRORS! WHAT A BEAST!

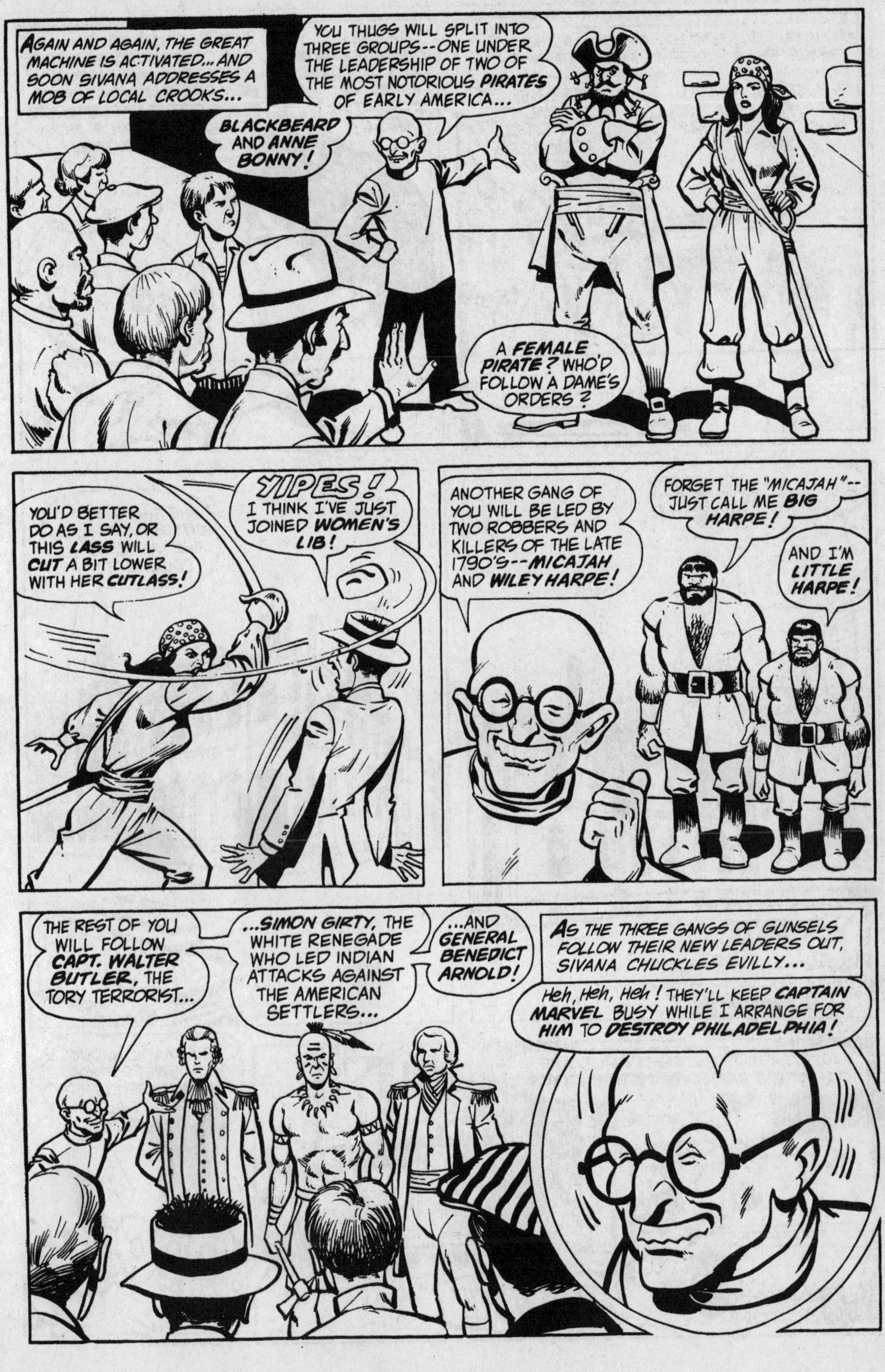
AGAIN AND AGAIN, THE GREAT MACHINE IS ACTIVATED... AND SOON SIVANA ADDRESSES A MOB OF LOCAL CROOKS...
YOU THUGS WILL SPLIT INTO THREE GROUPS--ONE UNDER THE LEADERSHIP OF TWO OF THE MOST NOTORIOUS PIRATES OF EARLY AMERICA...
BLACKBEARD AND ANNE BONNY!
A FEMALE PIRATE? WHO'D FOLLOW A DAME'S ORDERS?
YOU'D BETTER DO AS I SAY, OR THIS LASS WILL CUT A BIT LOWER WITH HER CUTLASS!
YIPES! I THINK I'VE JUST JOINED WOMEN'S LIB!
ANOTHER GANG OF YOU WILL BE LED BY TWO ROBBERS AND KILLERS OF THE LATE 1790'S--MICAJAH AND WILEY HARPE!
FORGET THE "MICAJAH"-- JUST CALL ME BIG HARPE!
AND I'M LITTLE HARPE!
THE REST OF YOU WILL FOLLOW CAPT. WALTER BUTLER, THE TORY TERRORIST...
...SIMON GIRTY, THE WHITE RENEGADE WHO LED INDIAN ATTACKS AGAINST THE AMERICAN SETTLERS...
...AND GENERAL BENEDICT ARNOLD!
AS THE THREE GANGS OF GUNSELS FOLLOW THEIR NEW LEADERS OUT, SIVANA CHUCKLES EVILLY...
Heh, Heh, Heh! THEY'LL KEEP CAPTAIN MARVEL BUSY WHILE I ARRANGE FOR HIM TO DESTROY PHILADELPHIA!

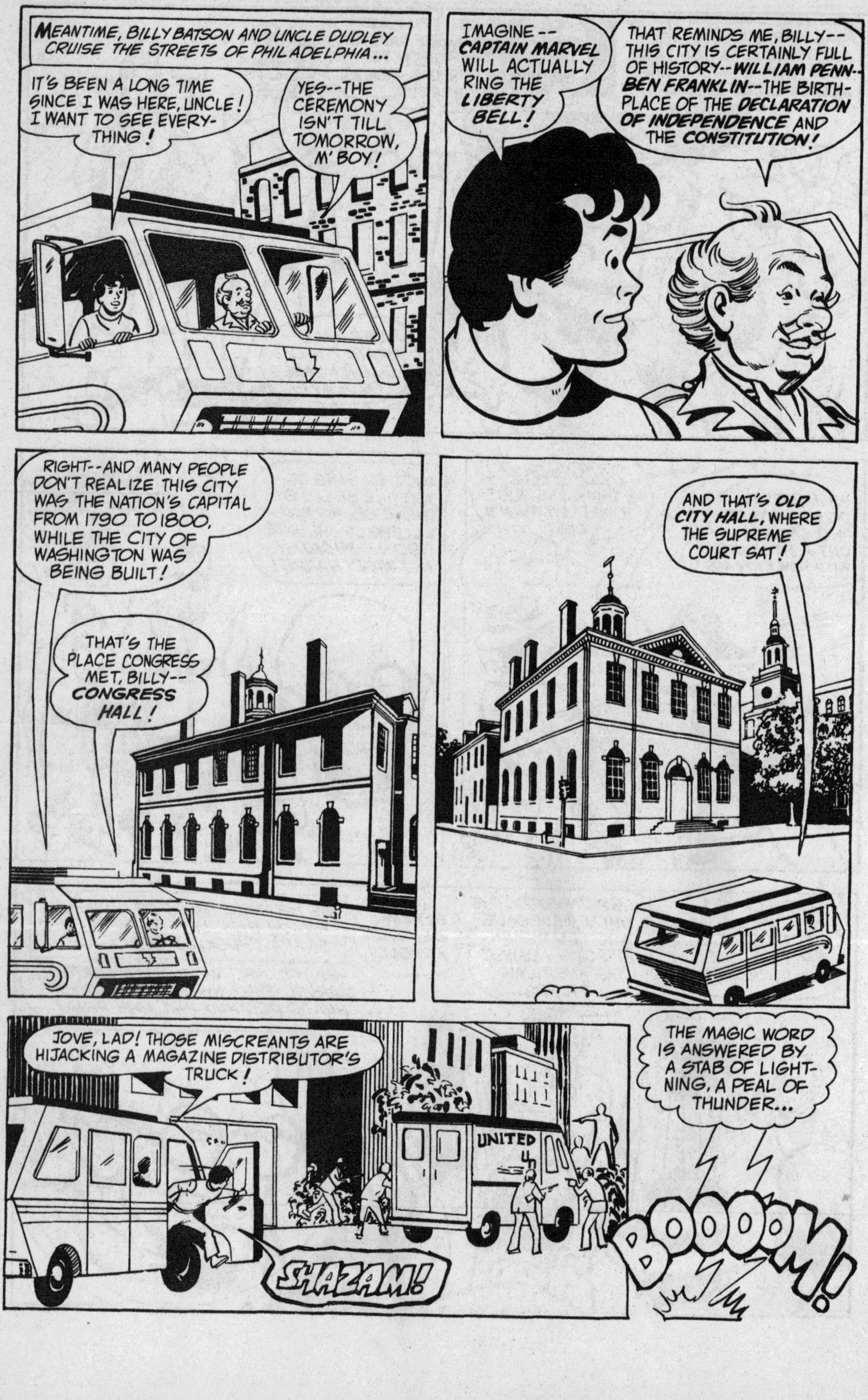
MEANTIME, BILLY BATSON AND UNCLE DUDLEY CRUISE THE STREETS OF PHILADELPHIA...
IT'S BEEN A LONG TIME SINCE I WAS HERE, UNCLE! I WANT TO SEE EVERYTHING!
YES--THE CEREMONY ISN'T TILL TOMORROW, M' BOY!
IMAGINE -- CAPTAIN MARVEL WILL ACTUALLY RING THE LIBERTY BELL!
THAT REMINDS ME, BILLY-- THIS CITY IS CERTAINLY FULL OF HISTORY--WILLIAM PENN-- BEN FRANKLIN--THE BIRTHPLACE OF THE DECLARATION OF INDEPENDENCE AND THE CONSTITUTION!
RIGHT--AND MANY PEOPLE DON'T REALIZE THIS CITY WAS THE NATION'S CAPITAL FROM 1790 TO 1800, WHILE THE CITY OF WASHINGTON WAS BEING BUILT!
THAT'S THE PLACE CONGRESS MET, BILLY-- CONGRESS HALL!
AND THAT'S OLD CITY HALL, WHERE THE SUPREME COURT SAT!
JOVE, LAD! THOSE MISCREANTS ARE HIJACKING A MAGAZINE DISTRIBUTOR'S TRUCK!
UNITED
SHAZAM!
THE MAGIC WORD IS ANSWERED BY A STAB OF LIGHTNING, A PEAL OF THUNDER...
BOOOOM!

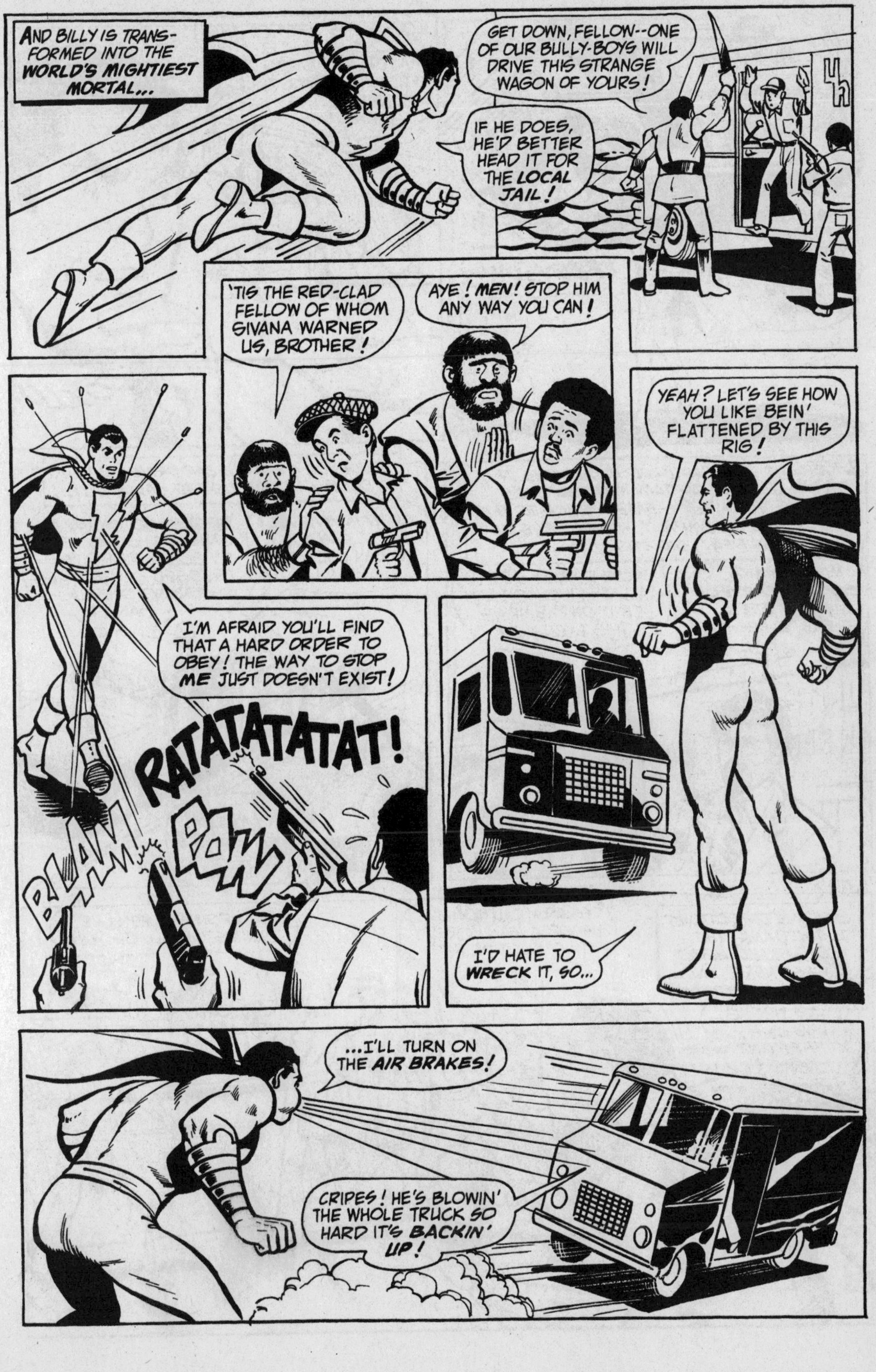
AND BILLY IS TRANS-FORMED INTO THE WORLD'S MIGHTIEST MORTAL...
GET DOWN, FELLOW--ONE OF OUR BULLY-BOYS WILL DRIVE THIS STRANGE WAGON OF YOURS!
IF HE DOES, HE'D BETTER HEAD IT FOR THE LOCAL JAIL!
'TIS THE RED-CLAD FELLOW OF WHOM SIVANA WARNED US, BROTHER!
AYE! MEN! STOP HIM ANY WAY YOU CAN!
I'M AFRAID YOU'LL FIND THAT A HARD ORDER TO OBEY! THE WAY TO STOP ME JUST DOESN'T EXIST!
RATATATATAT!
BLAM
POW
YEAH? LET'S SEE HOW YOU LIKE BEIN' FLATTENED BY THIS RIG!
I'D HATE TO WRECK IT, SO...
...I'LL TURN ON THE AIR BRAKES!
CRIPES! HE'S BLOWIN' THE WHOLE TRUCK SO HARD IT'S BACKIN' UP!

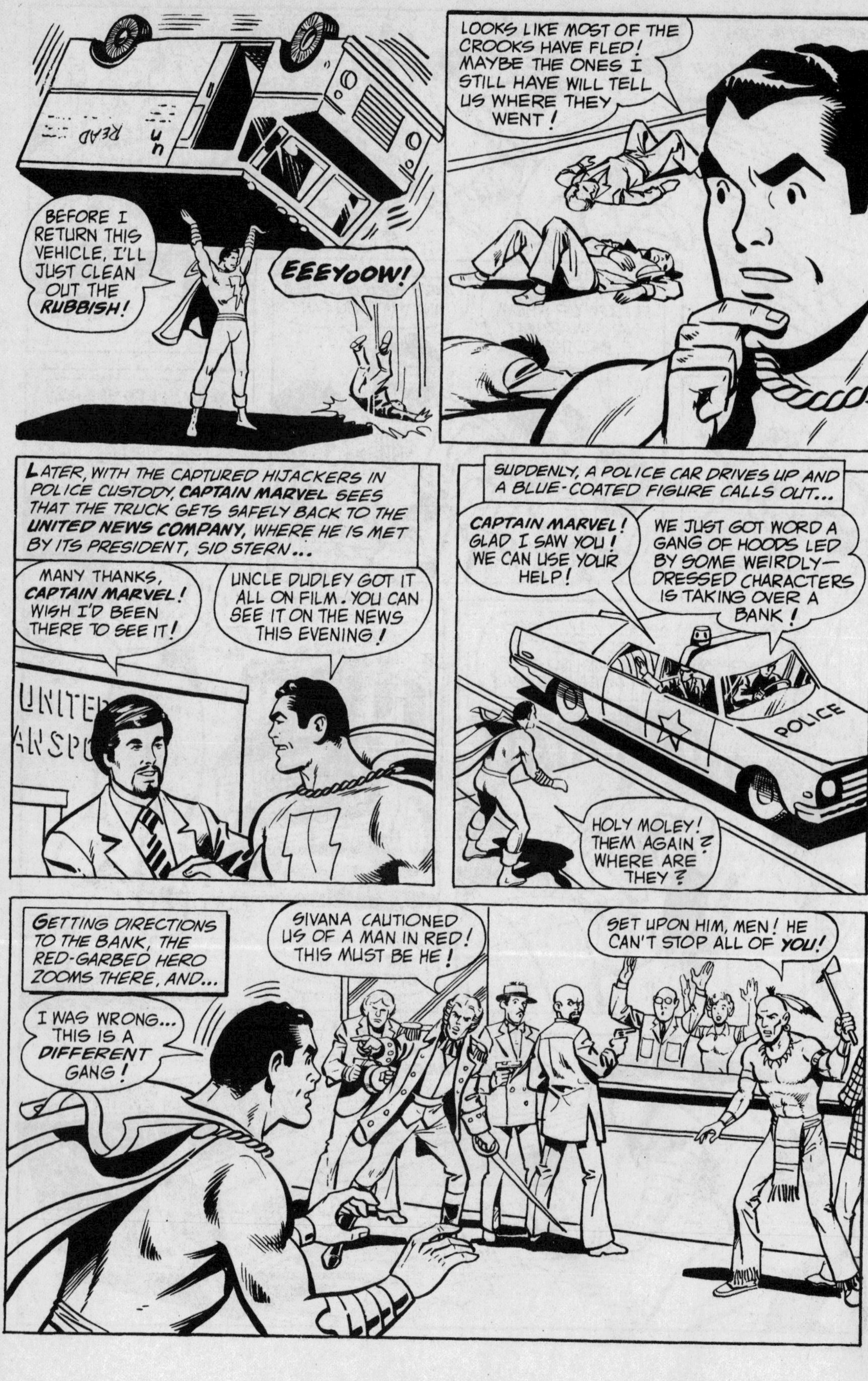
BEFORE I RETURN THIS VEHICLE, I'LL JUST CLEAN OUT THE RUBBISH!
EEEYOOW!
LOOKS LIKE MOST OF THE CROOKS HAVE FLED! MAYBE THE ONES I STILL HAVE WILL TELL US WHERE THEY WENT!
LATER, WITH THE CAPTURED HIJACKERS IN POLICE CUSTODY, CAPTAIN MARVEL SEES THAT THE TRUCK GETS SAFELY BACK TO THE UNITED NEWS COMPANY, WHERE HE IS MET BY ITS PRESIDENT, SID STERN...
MANY THANKS, CAPTAIN MARVEL! WISH I'D BEEN THERE TO SEE IT!
UNCLE DUDLEY GOT IT ALL ON FILM. YOU CAN SEE IT ON THE NEWS THIS EVENING!
SUDDENLY, A POLICE CAR DRIVES UP AND A BLUE-COATED FIGURE CALLS OUT...
CAPTAIN MARVEL! GLAD I SAW YOU! WE CAN USE YOUR HELP!
WE JUST GOT WORD A GANG OF HOODS LED BY SOME WEIRDLY-DRESSED CHARACTERS IS TAKING OVER A BANK!
POLICE
HOLY MOLEY! THEM AGAIN? WHERE ARE THEY?
GETTING DIRECTIONS TO THE BANK, THE RED-GARBED HERO ZOOMS THERE, AND...
I WAS WRONG... THIS IS A DIFFERENT GANG!
SIVANA CAUTIONED US OF A MAN IN RED! THIS MUST BE HE!
SET UPON HIM, MEN! HE CAN'T STOP ALL OF YOU!

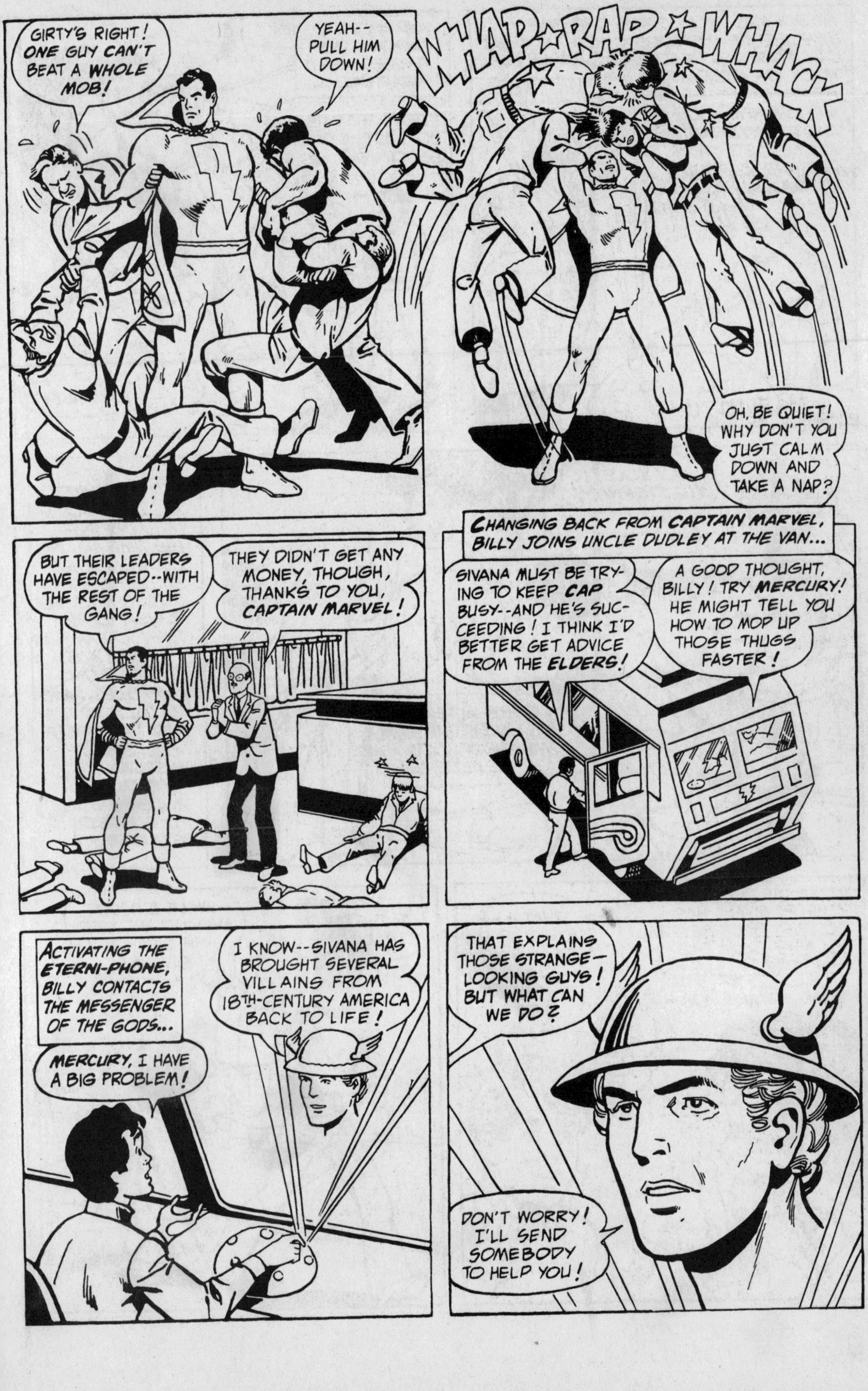
GIRTY'S RIGHT! ONE GUY CAN'T BEAT A WHOLE MOB!
YEAH-- PULL HIM DOWN!
WHAP☆RAP☆WHACK
OH, BE QUIET! WHY DON'T YOU JUST CALM DOWN AND TAKE A NAP?
BUT THEIR LEADERS HAVE ESCAPED--WITH THE REST OF THE GANG!
THEY DIDN'T GET ANY MONEY, THOUGH, THANKS TO YOU, CAPTAIN MARVEL!
CHANGING BACK FROM CAPTAIN MARVEL, BILLY JOINS UNCLE DUDLEY AT THE VAN...
SIVANA MUST BE TRYING TO KEEP CAP BUSY--AND HE'S SUCCEEDING! I THINK I'D BETTER GET ADVICE FROM THE ELDERS!
A GOOD THOUGHT, BILLY! TRY MERCURY! HE MIGHT TELL YOU HOW TO MOP UP THOSE THUGS FASTER!
ACTIVATING THE ETERNI-PHONE, BILLY CONTACTS THE MESSENGER OF THE GODS...
MERCURY, I HAVE A BIG PROBLEM!
I KNOW--SIVANA HAS BROUGHT SEVERAL VILLAINS FROM 18TH-CENTURY AMERICA BACK TO LIFE!
THAT EXPLAINS THOSE STRANGE-LOOKING GUYS! BUT WHAT CAN WE DO?
DON'T WORRY! I'LL SEND SOMEBODY TO HELP YOU!

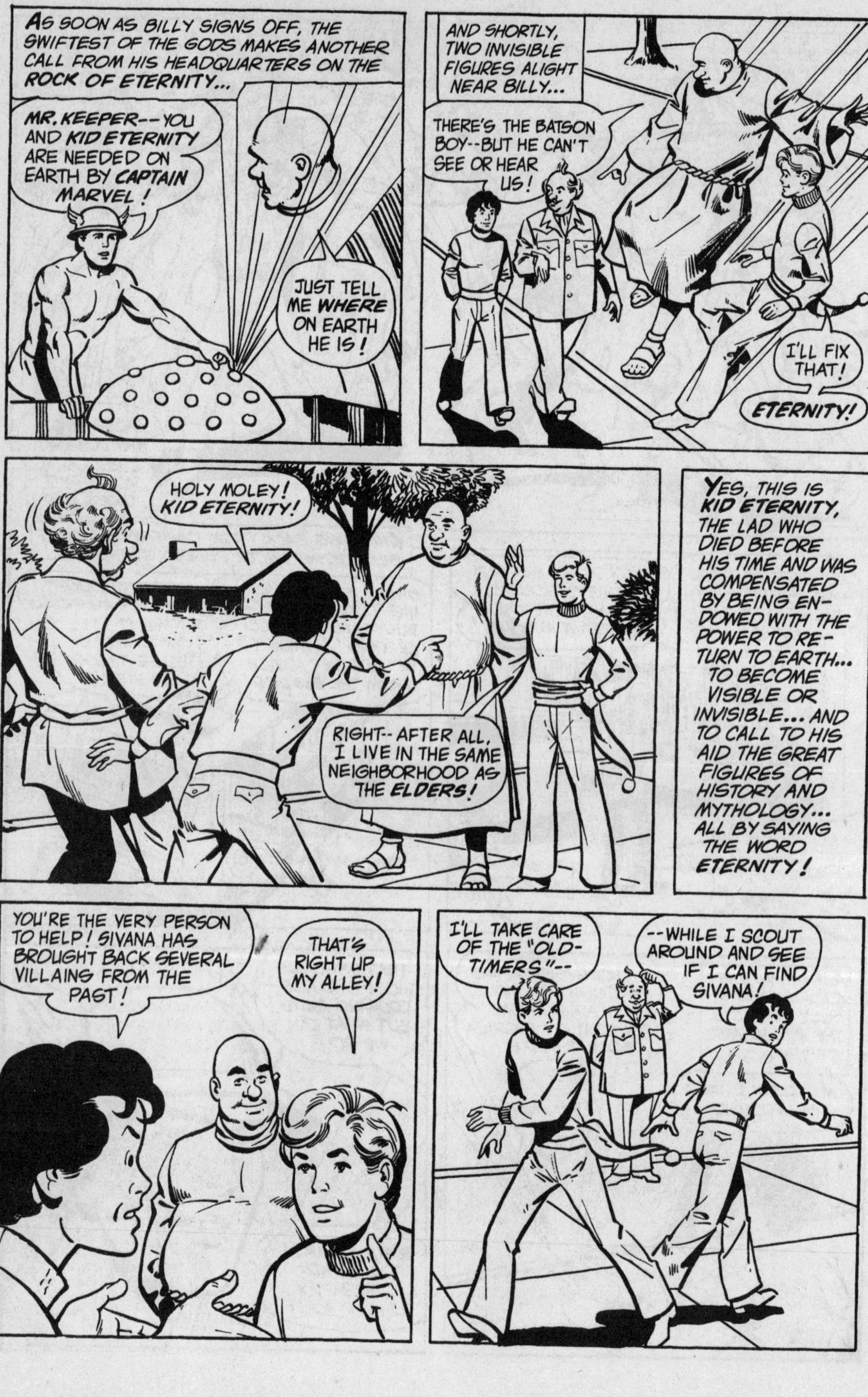
AS SOON AS BILLY SIGNS OFF, THE SWIFTEST OF THE GODS MAKES ANOTHER CALL FROM HIS HEADQUARTERS ON THE ROCK OF ETERNITY...
MR. KEEPER--YOU AND KID ETERNITY ARE NEEDED ON EARTH BY CAPTAIN MARVEL!
JUST TELL ME WHERE ON EARTH HE IS!
AND SHORTLY, TWO INVISIBLE FIGURES ALIGHT NEAR BILLY...
THERE'S THE BATSON BOY--BUT HE CAN'T SEE OR HEAR US!
I'LL FIX THAT!
ETERNITY!
HOLY MOLEY! KID ETERNITY!
RIGHT--AFTER ALL, I LIVE IN THE SAME NEIGHBORHOOD AS THE ELDERS!
YES, THIS IS KID ETERNITY, THE LAD WHO DIED BEFORE HIS TIME AND WAS COMPENSATED BY BEING ENDOWED WITH THE POWER TO RETURN TO EARTH... TO BECOME VISIBLE OR INVISIBLE... AND TO CALL TO HIS AID THE GREAT FIGURES OF HISTORY AND MYTHOLOGY... ALL BY SAYING THE WORD ETERNITY!
YOU'RE THE VERY PERSON TO HELP! SIVANA HAS BROUGHT BACK SEVERAL VILLAINS FROM THE PAST!
THAT'S RIGHT UP MY ALLEY!
I'LL TAKE CARE OF THE "OLD-TIMERS"--
--WHILE I SCOUT AROUND AND SEE IF I CAN FIND SIVANA!

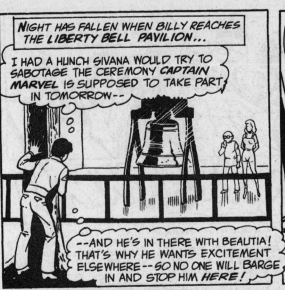

NIGHT HAS FALLEN WHEN BILLY REACHES THE *LIBERTY BELL* PAVILION...

I HAD A HUNCH SIVANA WOULD TRY TO SABOTAGE THE CEREMONY *CAPTAIN MARVEL* IS SUPPOSED TO TAKE PART IN TOMORROW--

--AND HE'S IN THERE WITH BEAUTIA! THAT'S WHY HE WANTS EXCITEMENT ELSEWHERE -- SO NO ONE WILL BARGE IN AND STOP HIM *HERE*!

HMM...IT SAYS HERE THE MAYOR IS HAVING TROUBLE WITH HIS POLITICAL OPPONENTS!

WELL, SOON HIS WORRIES WILL BE *OVER*!

I'VE CHANGED THE ATOMS OF THE *BELL* TO MAKE IT A HUGE *ATOMIC BOMB*! WHEN *CAPTAIN MARVEL* RINGS IT--

--*BOOM*! NO MORE TROUBLES FOR THE MAYOR--BECAUSE THERE'LL BE NO MORE *CITY*! Heh, Heh!

BUT THE LISTENING BILLY HAS HEARD THE PLOT...

SO THAT'S WHAT HE'S UP TO! *CAPTAIN MARVEL* WILL FIX HIM--

SHA...

GOTCHA, SNOOPER!

MMMPPHHH!

I CAUGHT THIS KID LISTENIN' OUTSIDE, BOSS!

THIS MEANS I'LL HAVE TO CHANGE MY PLANS--BUT PERHAPS FOR THE BETTER!

WHEN PHILADELPHIA GOES, SO WILL BILLY--AND THERE'LL BE NO MORE *CAPTAIN MARVEL*!

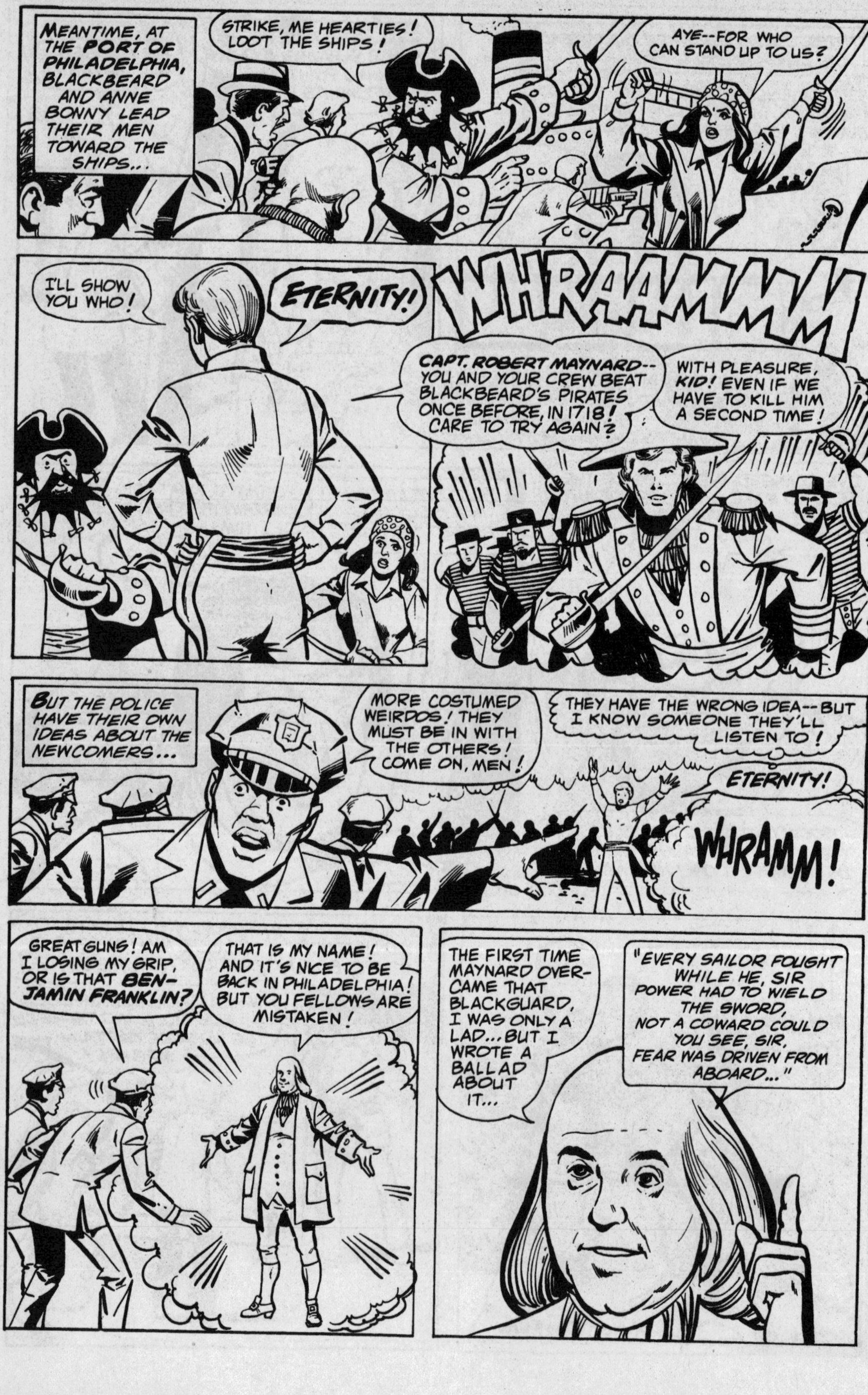
MEANTIME, AT THE PORT OF PHILADELPHIA, BLACKBEARD AND ANNE BONNY LEAD THEIR MEN TOWARD THE SHIPS...
STRIKE, ME HEARTIES! LOOT THE SHIPS!
AYE--FOR WHO CAN STAND UP TO US?
I'LL SHOW YOU WHO!
ETERNITY!
WHRAAMMM
CAPT. ROBERT MAYNARD-- YOU AND YOUR CREW BEAT BLACKBEARD'S PIRATES ONCE BEFORE, IN 1718! CARE TO TRY AGAIN?
WITH PLEASURE, KID! EVEN IF WE HAVE TO KILL HIM A SECOND TIME!
BUT THE POLICE HAVE THEIR OWN IDEAS ABOUT THE NEWCOMERS...
MORE COSTUMED WEIRDOS! THEY MUST BE IN WITH THE OTHERS! COME ON, MEN!
THEY HAVE THE WRONG IDEA--BUT I KNOW SOMEONE THEY'LL LISTEN TO!
ETERNITY!
WHRAMM!
GREAT GUNS! AM I LOSING MY GRIP, OR IS THAT BENJAMIN FRANKLIN?
THAT IS MY NAME! AND IT'S NICE TO BE BACK IN PHILADELPHIA! BUT YOU FELLOWS ARE MISTAKEN!
THE FIRST TIME MAYNARD OVERCAME THAT BLACKGUARD, I WAS ONLY A LAD... BUT I WROTE A BALLAD ABOUT IT...
"EVERY SAILOR FOUGHT WHILE HE, SIR POWER HAD TO WIELD THE SWORD, NOT A COWARD COULD YOU SEE, SIR, FEAR WAS DRIVEN FROM ABOARD..."

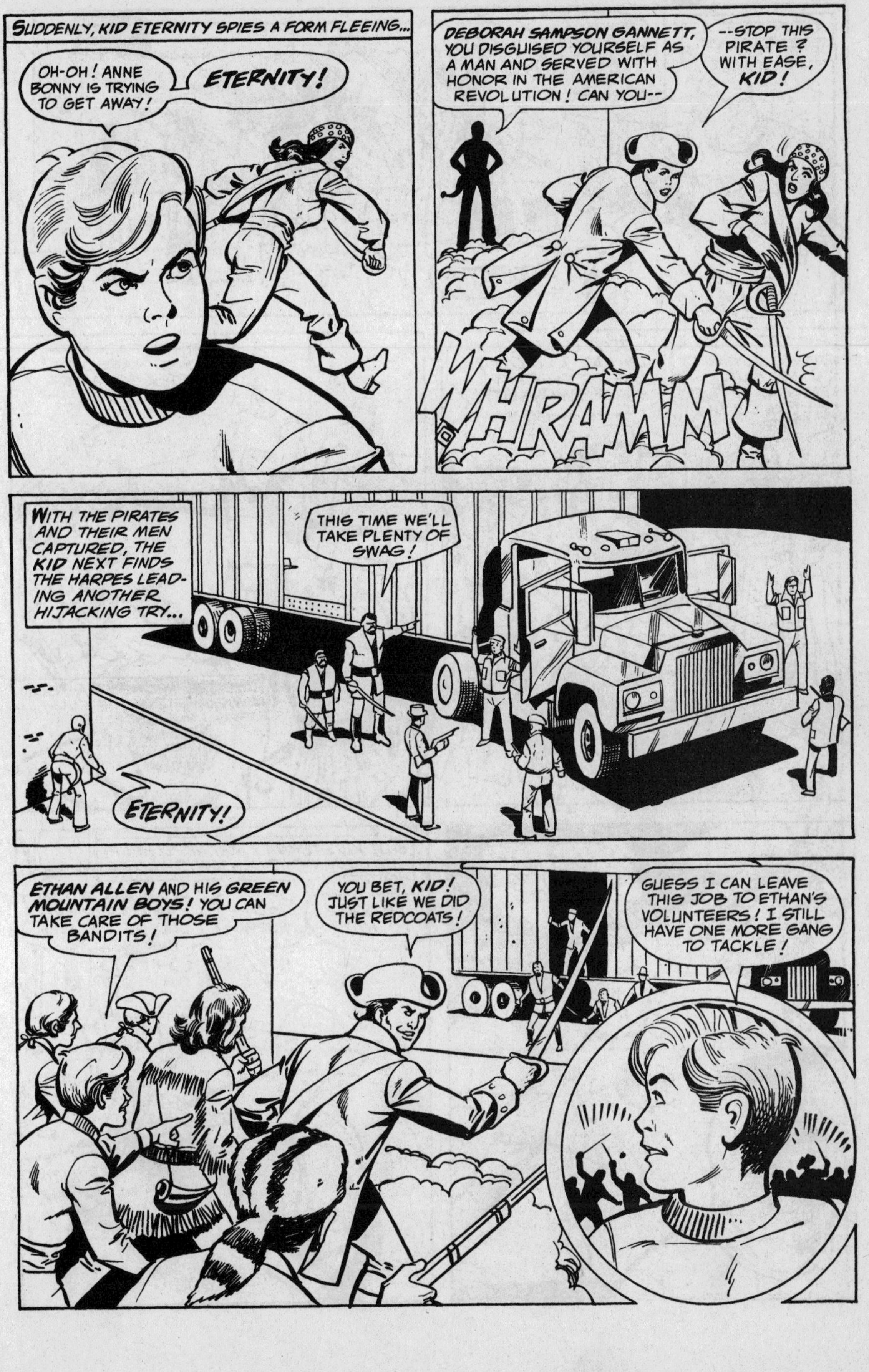
SUDDENLY, KID ETERNITY SPIES A FORM FLEEING...
OH-OH! ANNE BONNY IS TRYING TO GET AWAY!
ETERNITY!
DEBORAH SAMPSON GANNETT, YOU DISGUISED YOURSELF AS A MAN AND SERVED WITH HONOR IN THE AMERICAN REVOLUTION! CAN YOU--
--STOP THIS PIRATE? WITH EASE, KID!
WHRAMM
WITH THE PIRATES AND THEIR MEN CAPTURED, THE KID NEXT FINDS THE HARPES LEADING ANOTHER HIJACKING TRY...
THIS TIME WE'LL TAKE PLENTY OF SWAG!
ETERNITY!
ETHAN ALLEN AND HIS GREEN MOUNTAIN BOYS! YOU CAN TAKE CARE OF THOSE BANDITS!
YOU BET, KID! JUST LIKE WE DID THE REDCOATS!
GUESS I CAN LEAVE THIS JOB TO ETHAN'S VOLUNTEERS! I STILL HAVE ONE MORE GANG TO TACKLE!

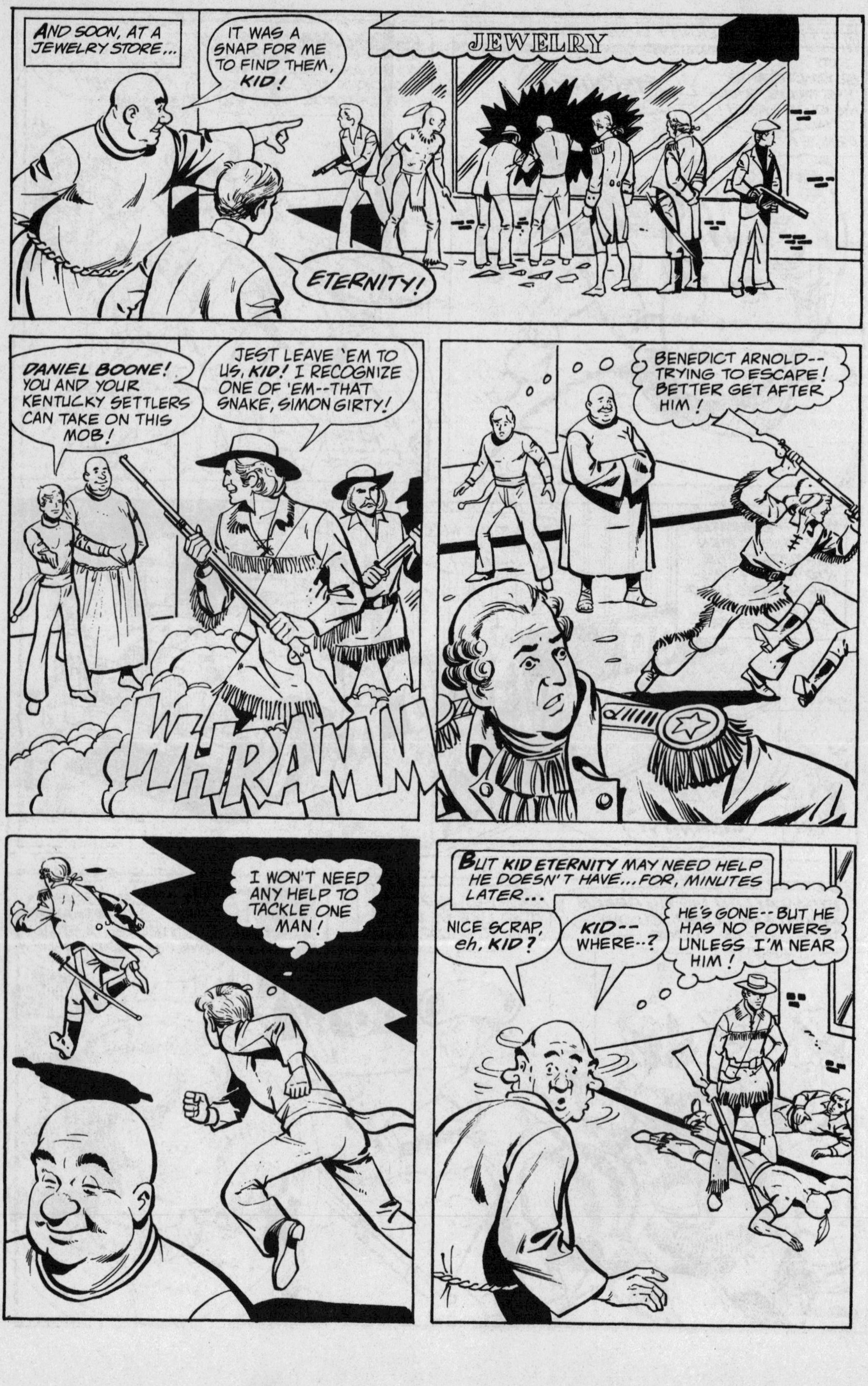
AND SOON, AT A JEWELRY STORE...
IT WAS A SNAP FOR ME TO FIND THEM, KID!
JEWELRY
ETERNITY!
DANIEL BOONE! YOU AND YOUR KENTUCKY SETTLERS CAN TAKE ON THIS MOB!
JEST LEAVE 'EM TO US, KID! I RECOGNIZE ONE OF 'EM--THAT SNAKE, SIMON GIRTY!
WHRAMM
BENEDICT ARNOLD-- TRYING TO ESCAPE! BETTER GET AFTER HIM!
I WON'T NEED ANY HELP TO TACKLE ONE MAN!
BUT KID ETERNITY MAY NEED HELP HE DOESN'T HAVE... FOR, MINUTES LATER...
NICE SCRAP, eh, KID?
KID-- WHERE--?
HE'S GONE--BUT HE HAS NO POWERS UNLESS I'M NEAR HIM!

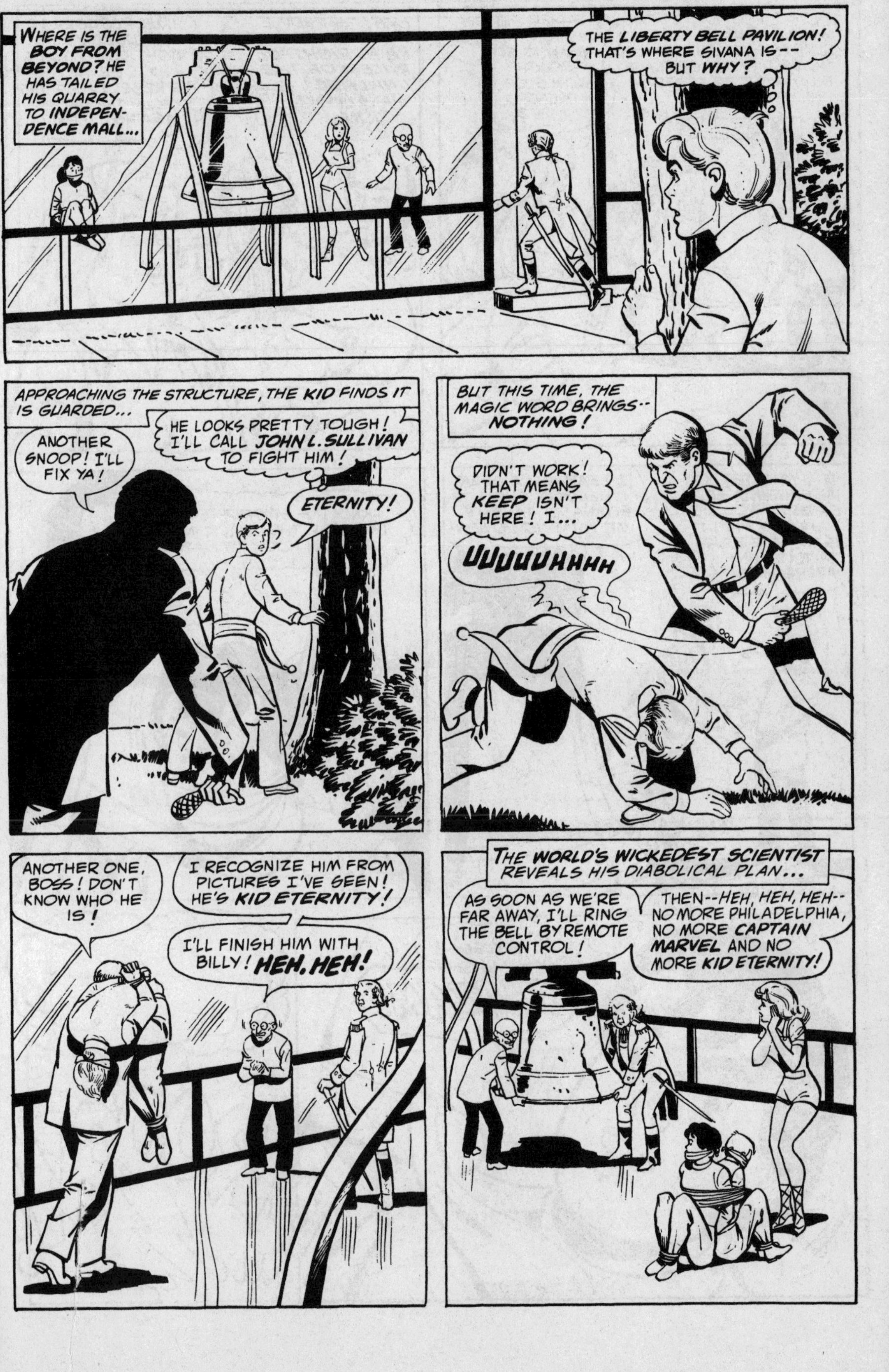
WHERE IS THE BOY FROM BEYOND? HE HAS TAILED HIS QUARRY TO INDEPENDENCE MALL...
THE LIBERTY BELL PAVILION! THAT'S WHERE SIVANA IS-- BUT WHY?
APPROACHING THE STRUCTURE, THE KID FINDS IT IS GUARDED...
ANOTHER SNOOP! I'LL FIX YA!
HE LOOKS PRETTY TOUGH! I'LL CALL JOHN L. SULLIVAN TO FIGHT HIM!
ETERNITY!
BUT THIS TIME, THE MAGIC WORD BRINGS-- NOTHING!
DIDN'T WORK! THAT MEANS KEEP ISN'T HERE! I...
UUUUUHHHH
ANOTHER ONE, BOSS! DON'T KNOW WHO HE IS!
I RECOGNIZE HIM FROM PICTURES I'VE SEEN! HE'S KID ETERNITY!
I'LL FINISH HIM WITH BILLY! HEH, HEH!
THE WORLD'S WICKEDEST SCIENTIST REVEALS HIS DIABOLICAL PLAN...
AS SOON AS WE'RE FAR AWAY, I'LL RING THE BELL BY REMOTE CONTROL!
THEN--HEH, HEH, HEH-- NO MORE PHILADELPHIA, NO MORE CAPTAIN MARVEL AND NO MORE KID ETERNITY!

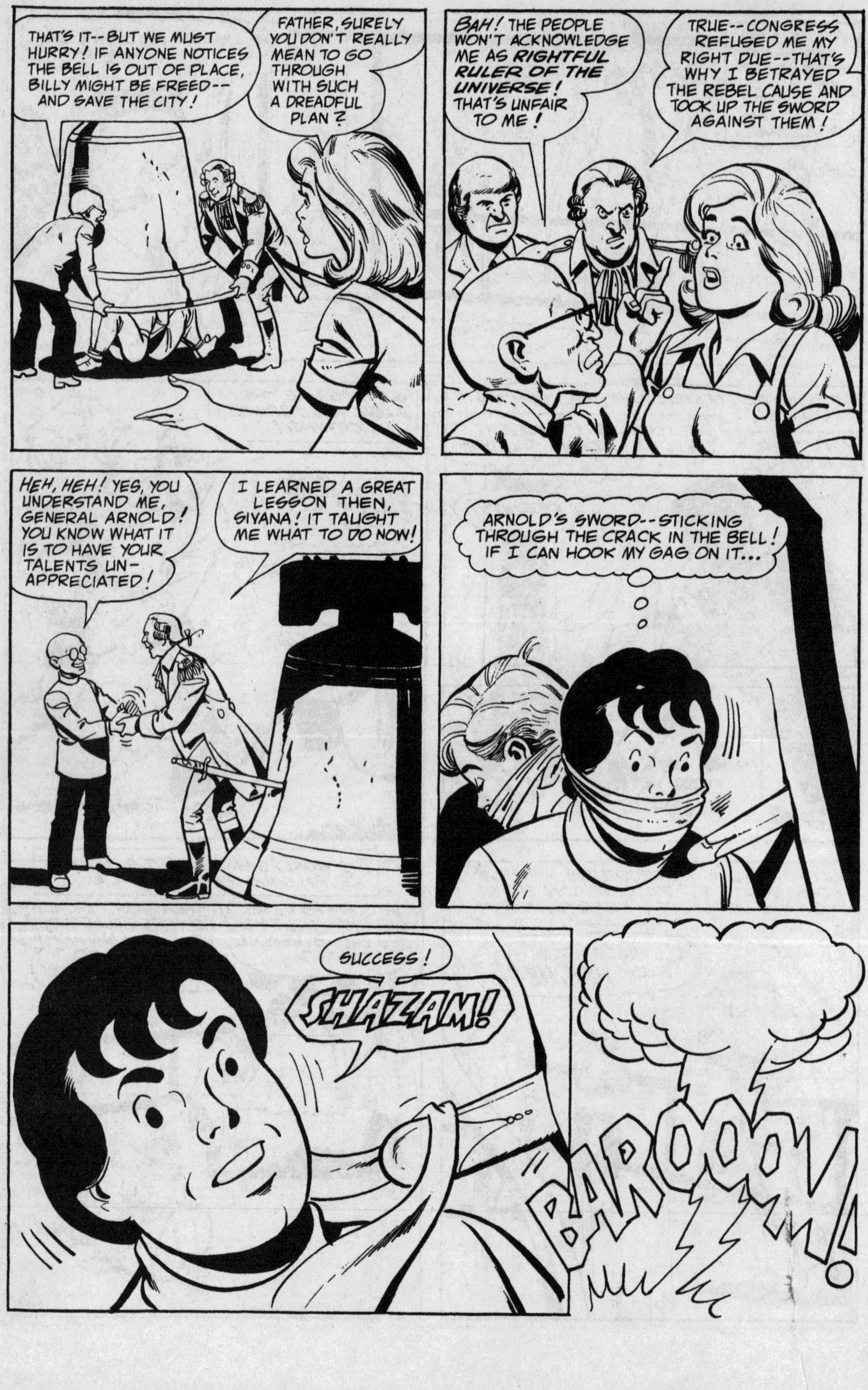
THAT'S IT--BUT WE MUST HURRY! IF ANYONE NOTICES THE BELL IS OUT OF PLACE, BILLY MIGHT BE FREED--AND SAVE THE CITY!
FATHER, SURELY YOU DON'T REALLY MEAN TO GO THROUGH WITH SUCH A DREADFUL PLAN?
BAH! THE PEOPLE WON'T ACKNOWLEDGE ME AS RIGHTFUL RULER OF THE UNIVERSE! THAT'S UNFAIR TO ME!
TRUE--CONGRESS REFUSED ME MY RIGHT DUE--THAT'S WHY I BETRAYED THE REBEL CAUSE AND TOOK UP THE SWORD AGAINST THEM!
HEH, HEH! YES, YOU UNDERSTAND ME, GENERAL ARNOLD! YOU KNOW WHAT IT IS TO HAVE YOUR TALENTS UN-APPRECIATED!
I LEARNED A GREAT LESSON THEN, SIVANA! IT TAUGHT ME WHAT TO DO NOW!
ARNOLD'S SWORD--STICKING THROUGH THE CRACK IN THE BELL! IF I CAN HOOK MY GAG ON IT...
SUCCESS!
SHAZAM!
BAROOOM!

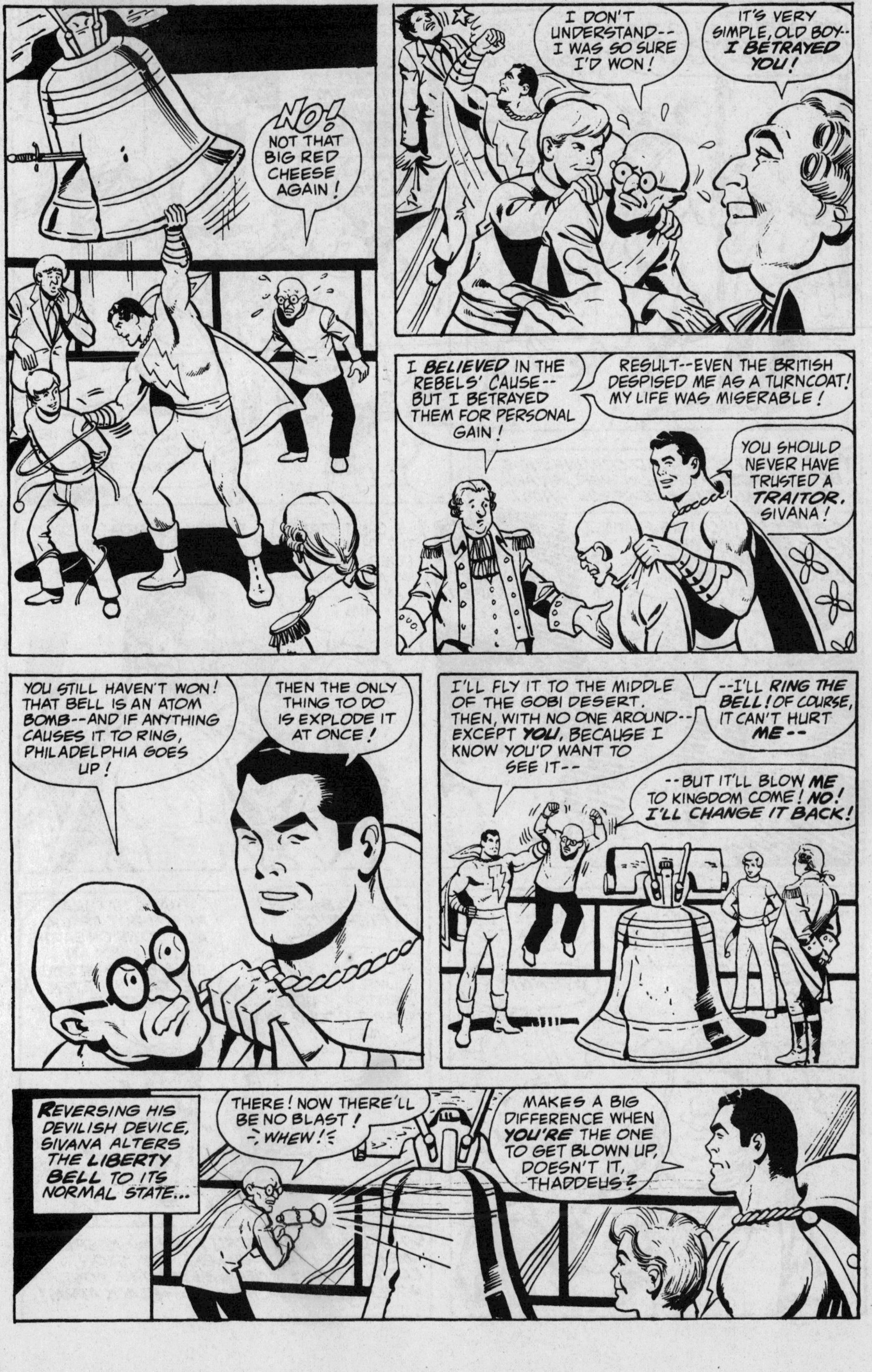
NO! NOT THAT BIG RED CHEESE AGAIN!
I DON'T UNDERSTAND-- I WAS SO SURE I'D WON!
IT'S VERY SIMPLE, OLD BOY-- I BETRAYED YOU!
I BELIEVED IN THE REBELS' CAUSE-- BUT I BETRAYED THEM FOR PERSONAL GAIN!
RESULT--EVEN THE BRITISH DESPISED ME AS A TURNCOAT! MY LIFE WAS MISERABLE!
YOU SHOULD NEVER HAVE TRUSTED A TRAITOR, SIVANA!
YOU STILL HAVEN'T WON! THAT BELL IS AN ATOM BOMB--AND IF ANYTHING CAUSES IT TO RING, PHILADELPHIA GOES UP!
THEN THE ONLY THING TO DO IS EXPLODE IT AT ONCE!
I'LL FLY IT TO THE MIDDLE OF THE GOBI DESERT. THEN, WITH NO ONE AROUND-- EXCEPT YOU, BECAUSE I KNOW YOU'D WANT TO SEE IT--
--I'LL RING THE BELL! OF COURSE, IT CAN'T HURT ME--
--BUT IT'LL BLOW ME TO KINGDOM COME! NO! I'LL CHANGE IT BACK!
REVERSING HIS DEVILISH DEVICE, SIVANA ALTERS THE LIBERTY BELL TO ITS NORMAL STATE...
THERE! NOW THERE'LL BE NO BLAST! WHEW!
MAKES A BIG DIFFERENCE WHEN YOU'RE THE ONE TO GET BLOWN UP, DOESN'T IT, THADDEUS?

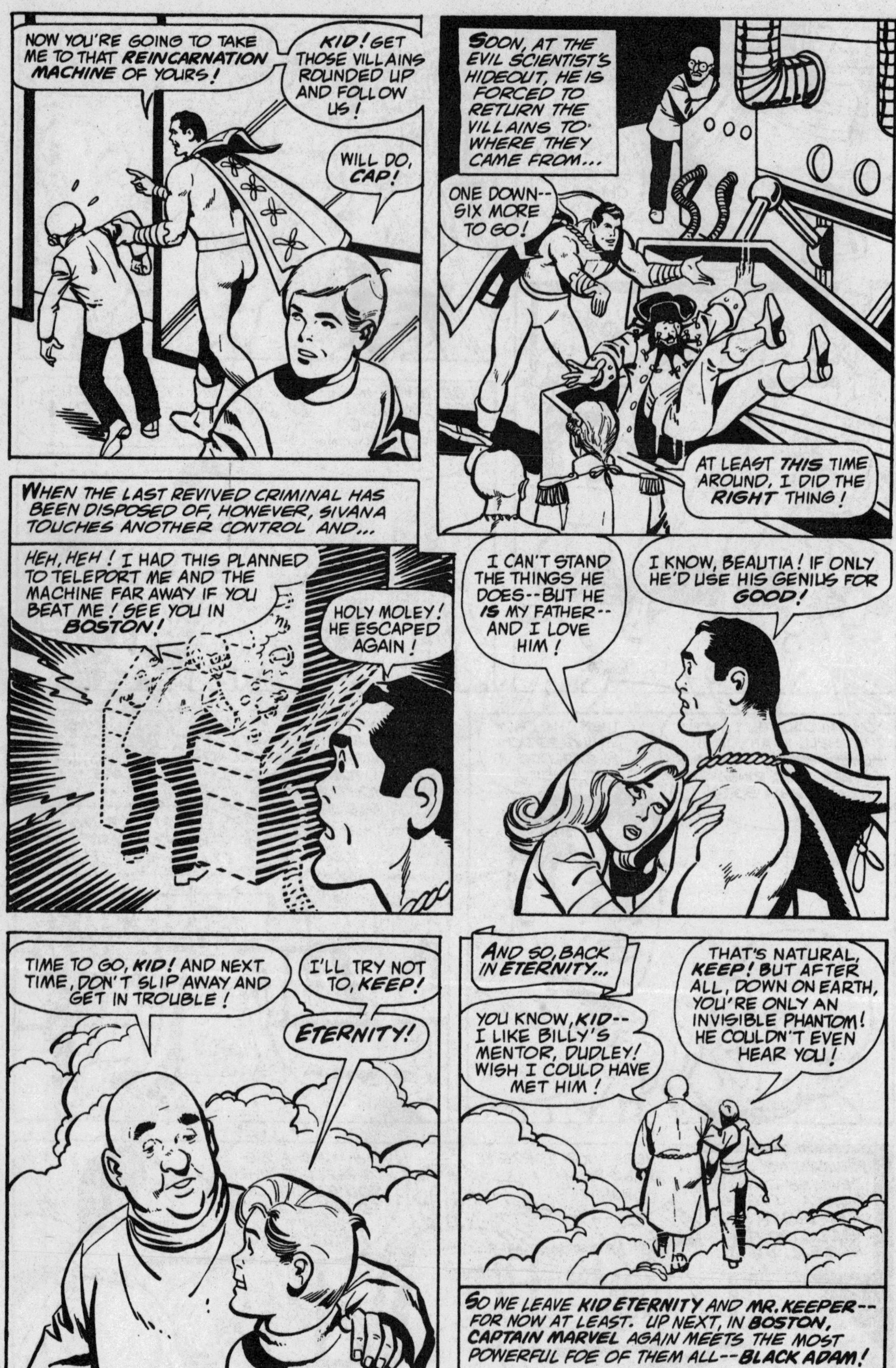
NOW YOU'RE GOING TO TAKE ME TO THAT REINCARNATION MACHINE OF YOURS!
KID! GET THOSE VILLAINS ROUNDED UP AND FOLLOW US!
WILL DO, CAP!
SOON, AT THE EVIL SCIENTIST'S HIDEOUT, HE IS FORCED TO RETURN THE VILLAINS TO WHERE THEY CAME FROM...
ONE DOWN--SIX MORE TO GO!
AT LEAST THIS TIME AROUND, I DID THE RIGHT THING!
WHEN THE LAST REVIVED CRIMINAL HAS BEEN DISPOSED OF, HOWEVER, SIVANA TOUCHES ANOTHER CONTROL AND...
HEH, HEH! I HAD THIS PLANNED TO TELEPORT ME AND THE MACHINE FAR AWAY IF YOU BEAT ME! SEE YOU IN BOSTON!
HOLY MOLEY! HE ESCAPED AGAIN!
I CAN'T STAND THE THINGS HE DOES--BUT HE IS MY FATHER--AND I LOVE HIM!
I KNOW, BEAUTIA! IF ONLY HE'D USE HIS GENIUS FOR GOOD!
TIME TO GO, KID! AND NEXT TIME, DON'T SLIP AWAY AND GET IN TROUBLE!
I'LL TRY NOT TO, KEEP!
ETERNITY!
AND SO, BACK IN ETERNITY...
YOU KNOW, KID--I LIKE BILLY'S MENTOR, DUDLEY! WISH I COULD HAVE MET HIM!
THAT'S NATURAL, KEEP! BUT AFTER ALL, DOWN ON EARTH, YOU'RE ONLY AN INVISIBLE PHANTOM! HE COULDN'T EVEN HEAR YOU!
SO WE LEAVE KID ETERNITY AND MR. KEEPER--FOR NOW AT LEAST. UP NEXT, IN BOSTON, CAPTAIN MARVEL AGAIN MEETS THE MOST POWERFUL FOE OF THEM ALL--BLACK ADAM!

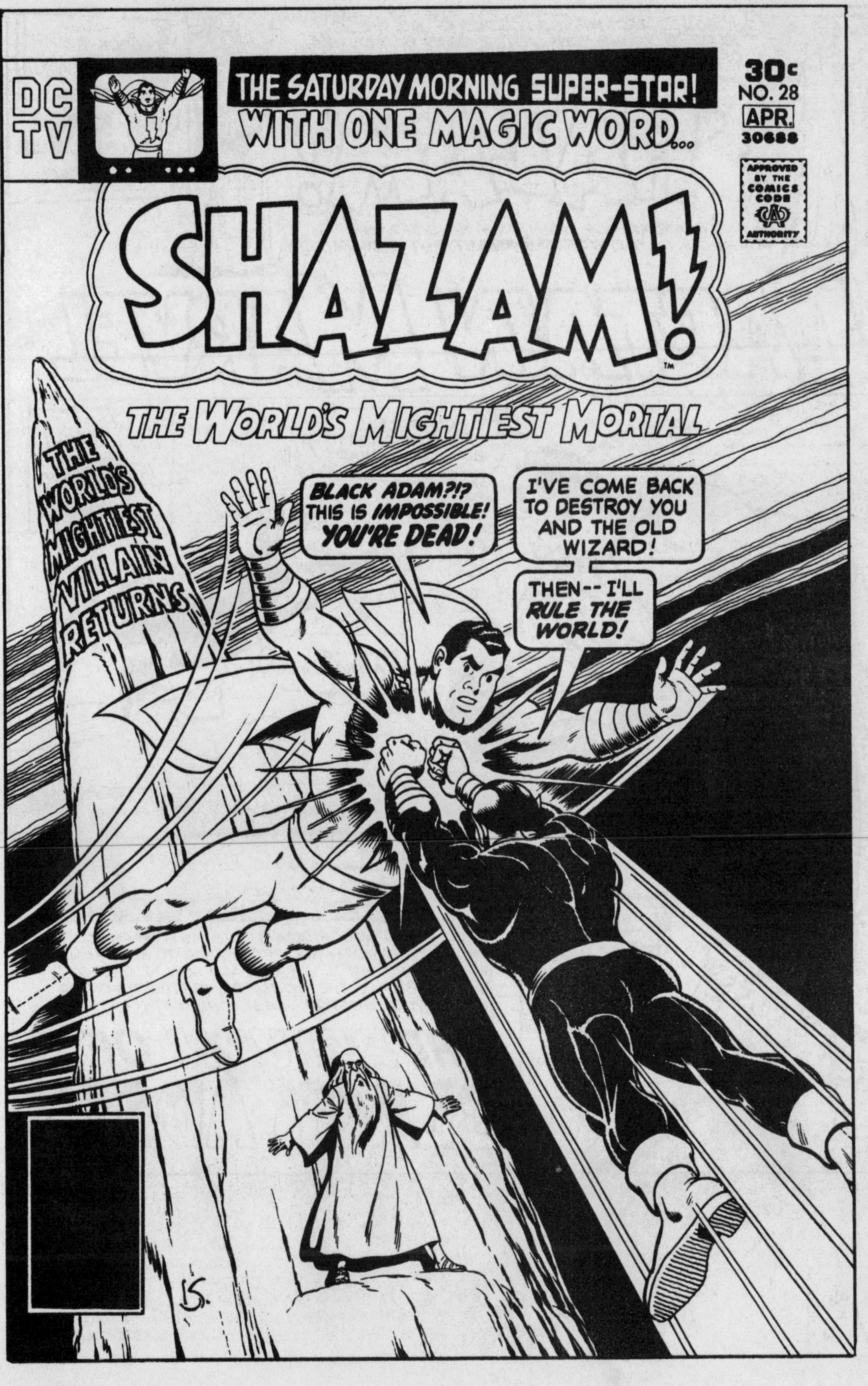
DC TV
THE SATURDAY MORNING SUPER-STAR!
WITH ONE MAGIC WORD...
30¢
NO. 28
APR.
30688
APPROVED BY THE COMICS CODE AUTHORITY
SHAZAM!
THE WORLD'S MIGHTIEST MORTAL
THE WORLD'S MIGHTIEST VILLAIN RETURNS
BLACK ADAM?!? THIS IS IMPOSSIBLE! YOU'RE DEAD!
I'VE COME BACK TO DESTROY YOU AND THE OLD WIZARD!
THEN-- I'LL RULE THE WORLD!

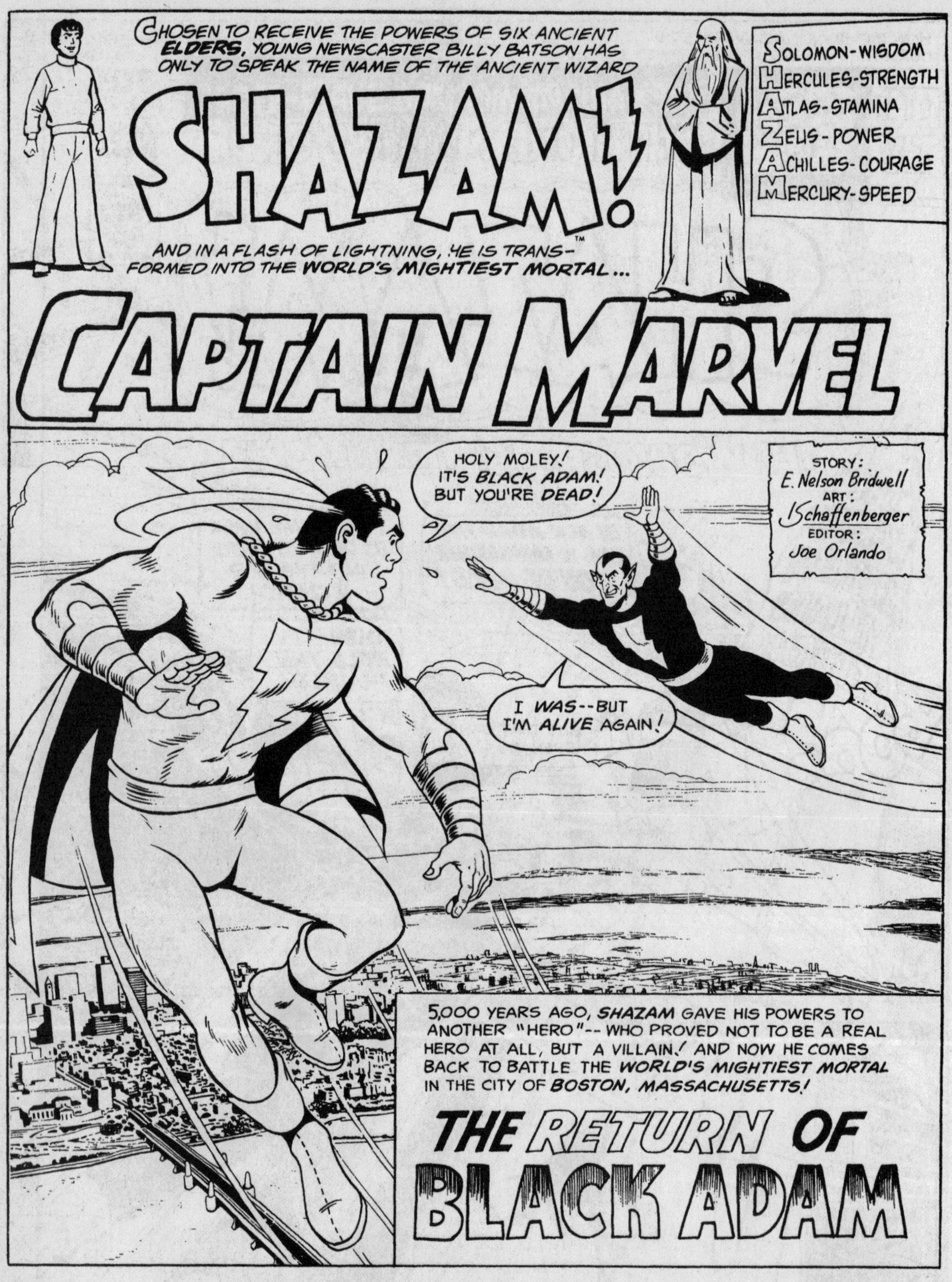
CHOSEN TO RECEIVE THE POWERS OF SIX ANCIENT ELDERS, YOUNG NEWSCASTER BILLY BATSON HAS ONLY TO SPEAK THE NAME OF THE ANCIENT WIZARD
SHAZAM!
SOLOMON-WISDOM
HERCULES-STRENGTH
ATLAS-STAMINA
ZEUS-POWER
ACHILLES-COURAGE
MERCURY-SPEED
AND IN A FLASH OF LIGHTNING, HE IS TRANS-FORMED INTO THE WORLD'S MIGHTIEST MORTAL...
CAPTAIN MARVEL
STORY: E. Nelson Bridwell
ART: I Schaffenberger
EDITOR: Joe Orlando
HOLY MOLEY! IT'S BLACK ADAM! BUT YOU'RE DEAD!
I WAS--BUT I'M ALIVE AGAIN!
5,000 YEARS AGO, SHAZAM GAVE HIS POWERS TO ANOTHER "HERO"-- WHO PROVED NOT TO BE A REAL HERO AT ALL, BUT A VILLAIN! AND NOW HE COMES BACK TO BATTLE THE WORLD'S MIGHTIEST MORTAL IN THE CITY OF BOSTON, MASSACHUSETTS!
THE RETURN OF BLACK ADAM

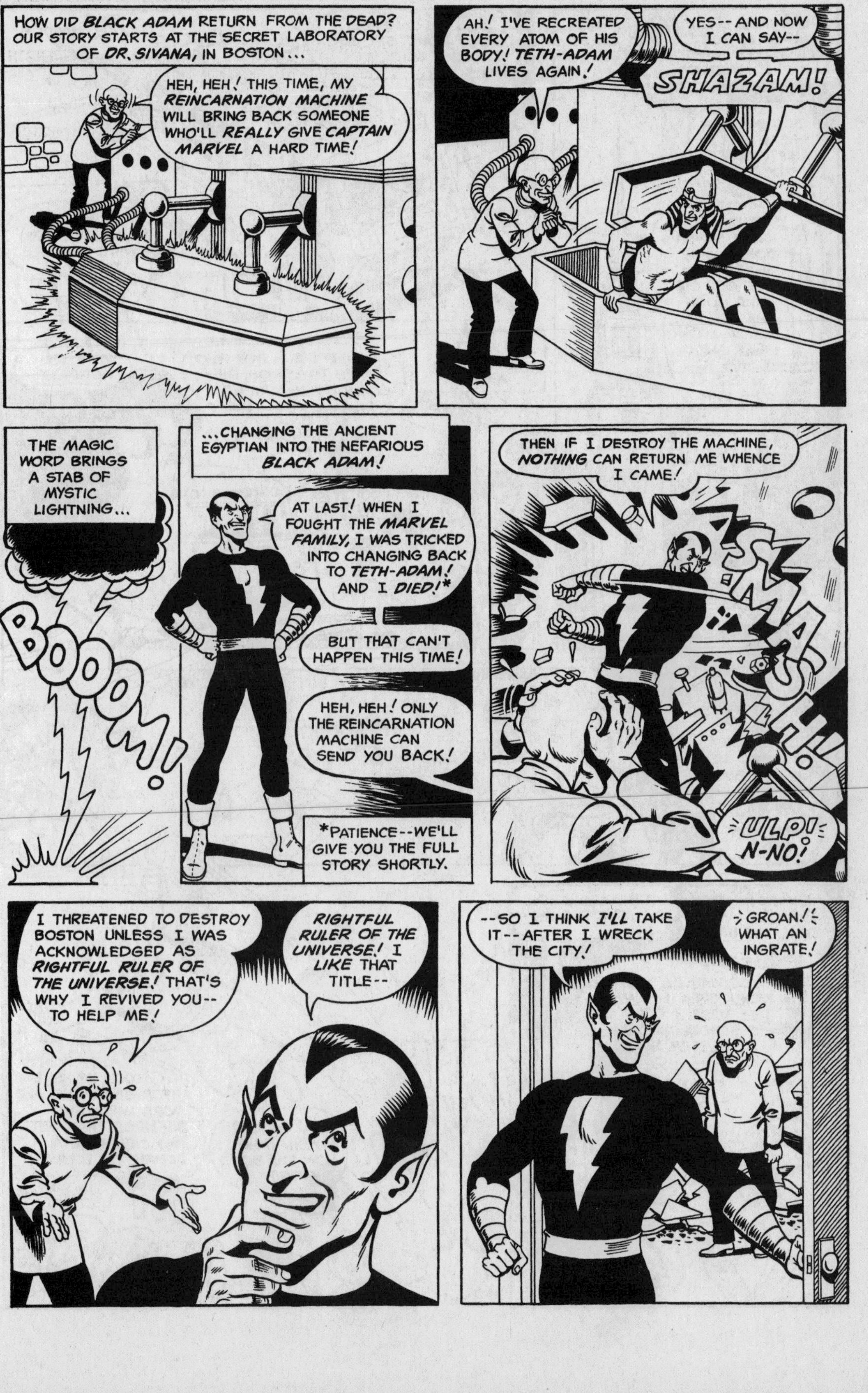
HOW DID BLACK ADAM RETURN FROM THE DEAD? OUR STORY STARTS AT THE SECRET LABORATORY OF DR. SIVANA, IN BOSTON...
HEH, HEH! THIS TIME, MY REINCARNATION MACHINE WILL BRING BACK SOMEONE WHO'LL REALLY GIVE CAPTAIN MARVEL A HARD TIME!
AH! I'VE RECREATED EVERY ATOM OF HIS BODY! TETH-ADAM LIVES AGAIN!
YES--AND NOW I CAN SAY--
SHAZAM!
THE MAGIC WORD BRINGS A STAB OF MYSTIC LIGHTNING...
BOOOM!
...CHANGING THE ANCIENT EGYPTIAN INTO THE NEFARIOUS BLACK ADAM!
AT LAST! WHEN I FOUGHT THE MARVEL FAMILY, I WAS TRICKED INTO CHANGING BACK TO TETH-ADAM! AND I DIED!*
BUT THAT CAN'T HAPPEN THIS TIME!
HEH, HEH! ONLY THE REINCARNATION MACHINE CAN SEND YOU BACK!
*PATIENCE--WE'LL GIVE YOU THE FULL STORY SHORTLY.
THEN IF I DESTROY THE MACHINE, NOTHING CAN RETURN ME WHENCE I CAME!
SMASH!
ULP! N-NO!
I THREATENED TO DESTROY BOSTON UNLESS I WAS ACKNOWLEDGED AS RIGHTFUL RULER OF THE UNIVERSE! THAT'S WHY I REVIVED YOU--TO HELP ME!
RIGHTFUL RULER OF THE UNIVERSE! I LIKE THAT TITLE--
--SO I THINK I'LL TAKE IT--AFTER I WRECK THE CITY!
GROAN! WHAT AN INGRATE!

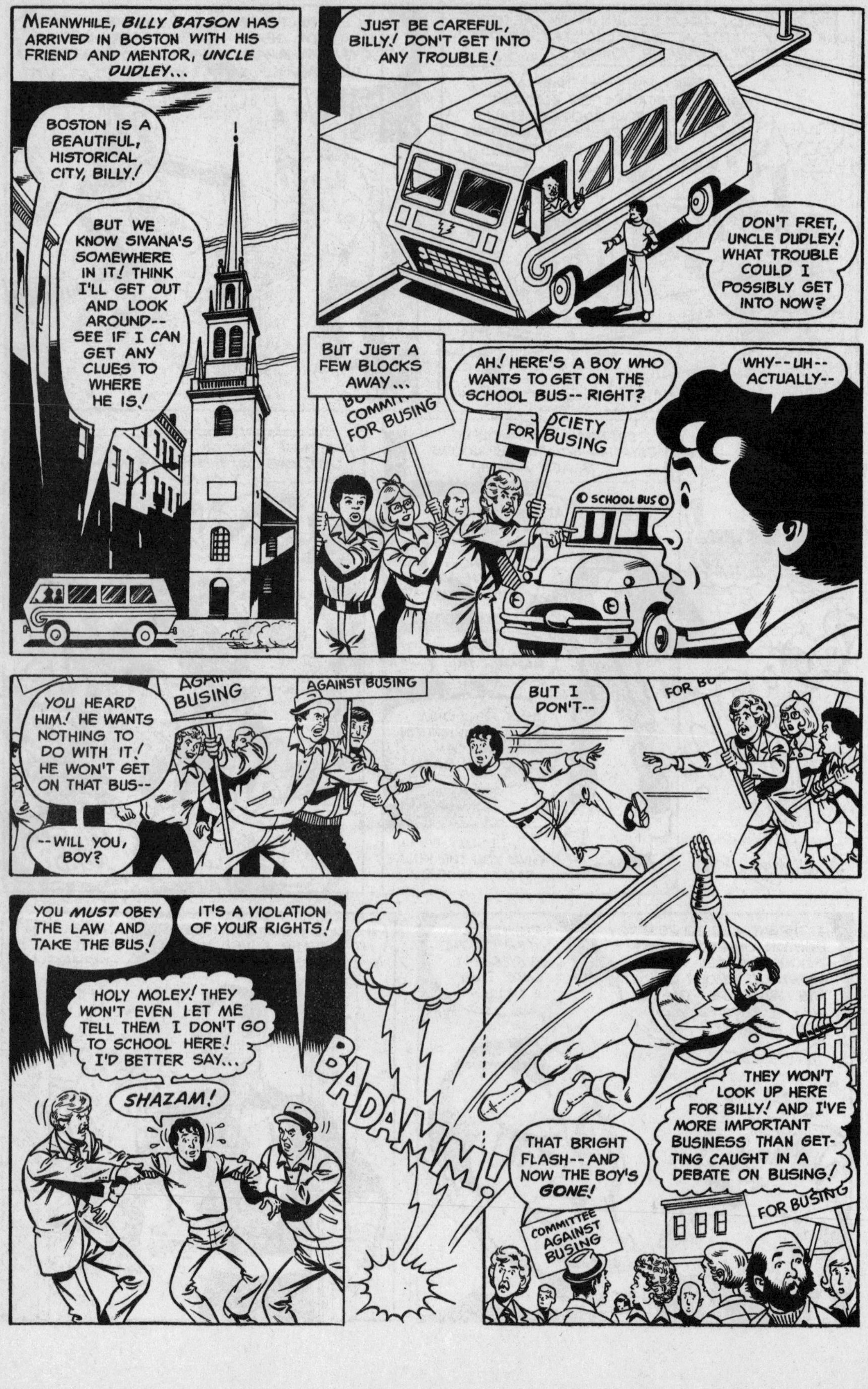
MEANWHILE, BILLY BATSON HAS ARRIVED IN BOSTON WITH HIS FRIEND AND MENTOR, UNCLE DUDLEY...
BOSTON IS A BEAUTIFUL, HISTORICAL CITY, BILLY!
BUT WE KNOW SIVANA'S SOMEWHERE IN IT! THINK I'LL GET OUT AND LOOK AROUND-- SEE IF I CAN GET ANY CLUES TO WHERE HE IS!
JUST BE CAREFUL, BILLY! DON'T GET INTO ANY TROUBLE!
DON'T FRET, UNCLE DUDLEY! WHAT TROUBLE COULD I POSSIBLY GET INTO NOW?
BUT JUST A FEW BLOCKS AWAY...
COMMI FOR BUSING
FOR BUSING
SCHOOL BUS
AH! HERE'S A BOY WHO WANTS TO GET ON THE SCHOOL BUS-- RIGHT?
WHY-- UH-- ACTUALLY--
BUSING
AGAINST BUSING
FOR BU
YOU HEARD HIM! HE WANTS NOTHING TO DO WITH IT! HE WON'T GET ON THAT BUS--
--WILL YOU, BOY?
BUT I DON'T--
YOU MUST OBEY THE LAW AND TAKE THE BUS!
IT'S A VIOLATION OF YOUR RIGHTS!
HOLY MOLEY! THEY WON'T EVEN LET ME TELL THEM I DON'T GO TO SCHOOL HERE! I'D BETTER SAY...
SHAZAM!
BADAMM!
THEY WON'T LOOK UP HERE FOR BILLY! AND I'VE MORE IMPORTANT BUSINESS THAN GETTING CAUGHT IN A DEBATE ON BUSING!
THAT BRIGHT FLASH-- AND NOW THE BOY'S GONE!
COMMITTEE AGAINST BUSING
FOR BUSING

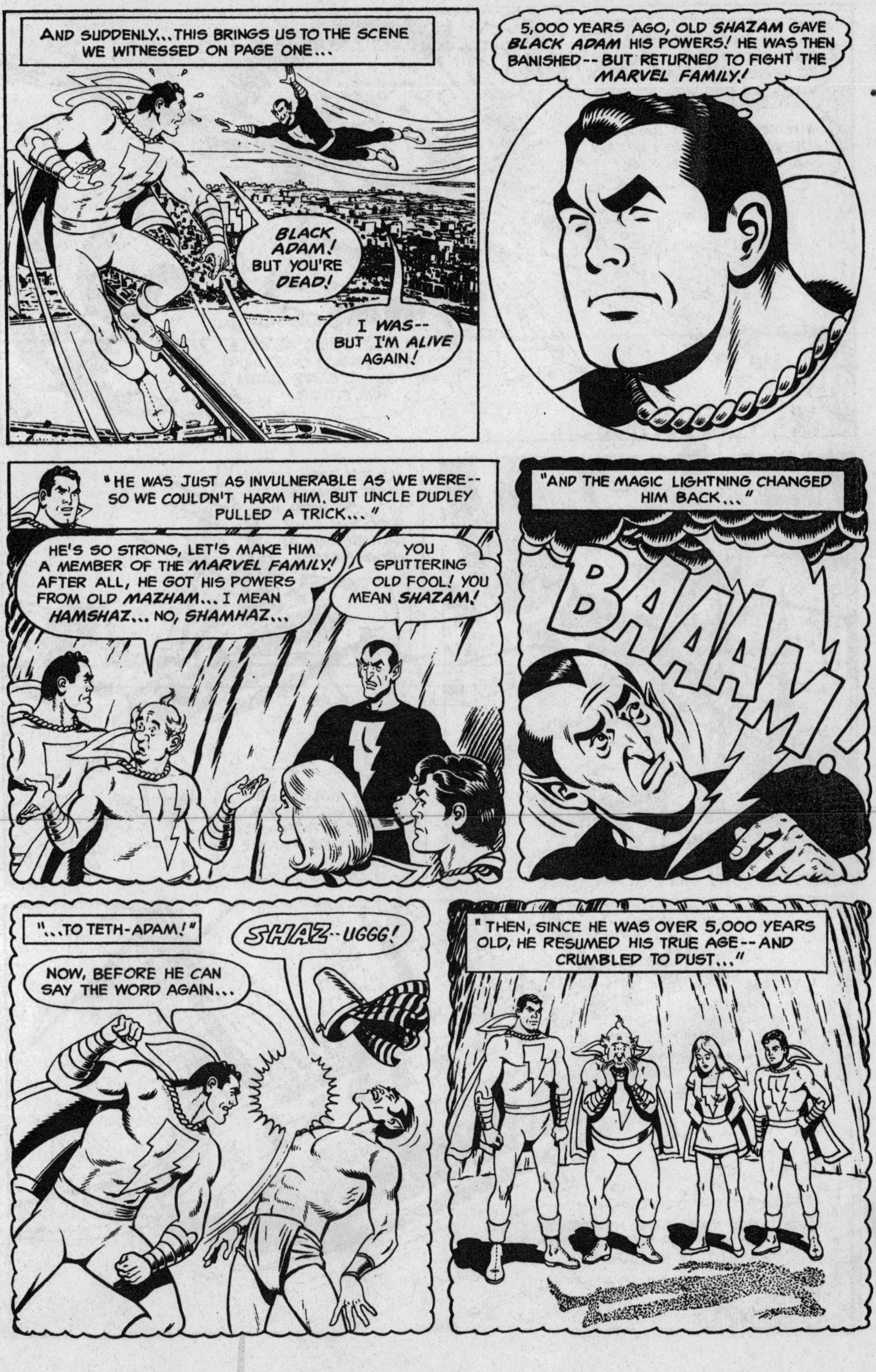
AND SUDDENLY... THIS BRINGS US TO THE SCENE WE WITNESSED ON PAGE ONE...
BLACK ADAM! BUT YOU'RE DEAD!
I WAS-- BUT I'M ALIVE AGAIN!
5,000 YEARS AGO, OLD SHAZAM GAVE BLACK ADAM HIS POWERS! HE WAS THEN BANISHED-- BUT RETURNED TO FIGHT THE MARVEL FAMILY!
"HE WAS JUST AS INVULNERABLE AS WE WERE-- SO WE COULDN'T HARM HIM. BUT UNCLE DUDLEY PULLED A TRICK..."
HE'S SO STRONG, LET'S MAKE HIM A MEMBER OF THE MARVEL FAMILY! AFTER ALL, HE GOT HIS POWERS FROM OLD MAZHAM... I MEAN HAMSHAZ... NO, SHAMHAZ...
YOU SPUTTERING OLD FOOL! YOU MEAN SHAZAM!
"AND THE MAGIC LIGHTNING CHANGED HIM BACK..."
BAAAM!
"...TO TETH-ADAM!"
SHAZ--UGGG!
NOW, BEFORE HE CAN SAY THE WORD AGAIN...
"THEN, SINCE HE WAS OVER 5,000 YEARS OLD, HE RESUMED HIS TRUE AGE--AND CRUMBLED TO DUST..."

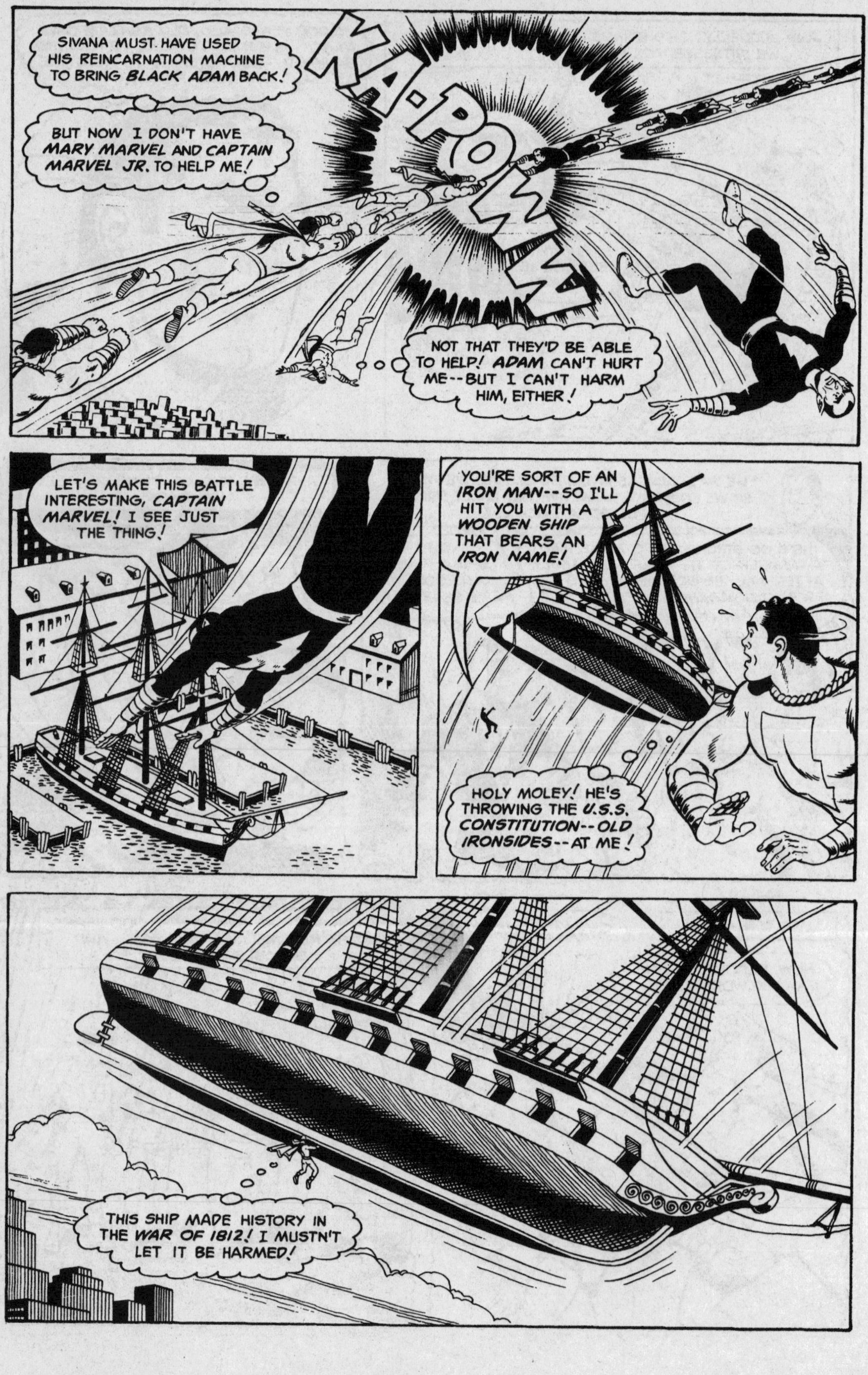
SIVANA MUST HAVE USED HIS REINCARNATION MACHINE TO BRING BLACK ADAM BACK!
BUT NOW I DON'T HAVE MARY MARVEL AND CAPTAIN MARVEL JR. TO HELP ME!
KA-POWW
NOT THAT THEY'D BE ABLE TO HELP! ADAM CAN'T HURT ME--BUT I CAN'T HARM HIM, EITHER!
LET'S MAKE THIS BATTLE INTERESTING, CAPTAIN MARVEL! I SEE JUST THE THING!
YOU'RE SORT OF AN IRON MAN--SO I'LL HIT YOU WITH A WOODEN SHIP THAT BEARS AN IRON NAME!
HOLY MOLEY! HE'S THROWING THE U.S.S. CONSTITUTION--OLD IRONSIDES--AT ME!
THIS SHIP MADE HISTORY IN THE WAR OF 1812! I MUSTN'T LET IT BE HARMED!

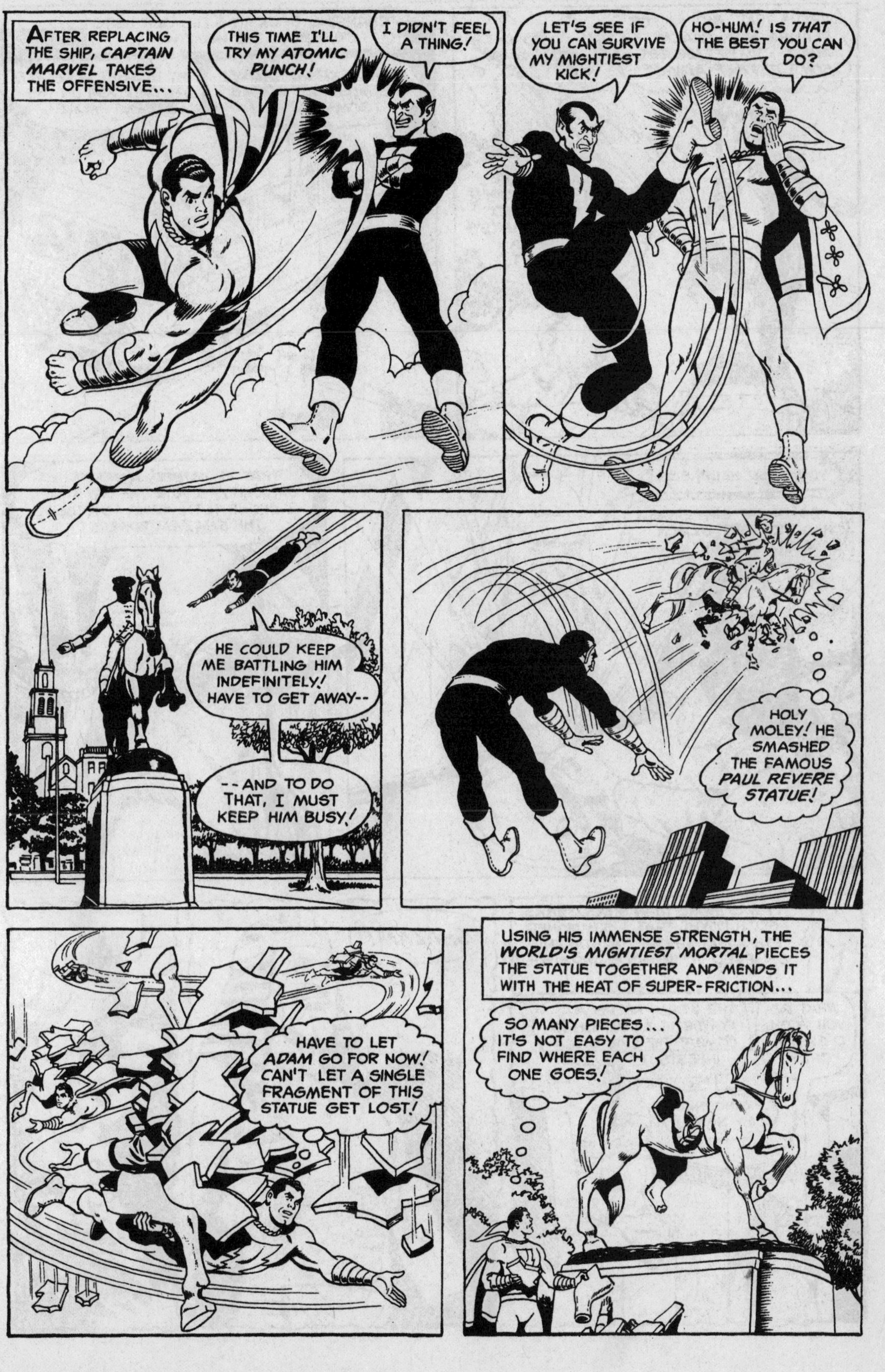
AFTER REPLACING THE SHIP, CAPTAIN MARVEL TAKES THE OFFENSIVE...
THIS TIME I'LL TRY MY ATOMIC PUNCH!
I DIDN'T FEEL A THING!
LET'S SEE IF YOU CAN SURVIVE MY MIGHTIEST KICK!
HO-HUM! IS THAT THE BEST YOU CAN DO?
HE COULD KEEP ME BATTLING HIM INDEFINITELY! HAVE TO GET AWAY--
--AND TO DO THAT, I MUST KEEP HIM BUSY!
HOLY MOLEY! HE SMASHED THE FAMOUS PAUL REVERE STATUE!
HAVE TO LET ADAM GO FOR NOW! CAN'T LET A SINGLE FRAGMENT OF THIS STATUE GET LOST!
USING HIS IMMENSE STRENGTH, THE WORLD'S MIGHTIEST MORTAL PIECES THE STATUE TOGETHER AND MENDS IT WITH THE HEAT OF SUPER-FRICTION...
SO MANY PIECES... IT'S NOT EASY TO FIND WHERE EACH ONE GOES!

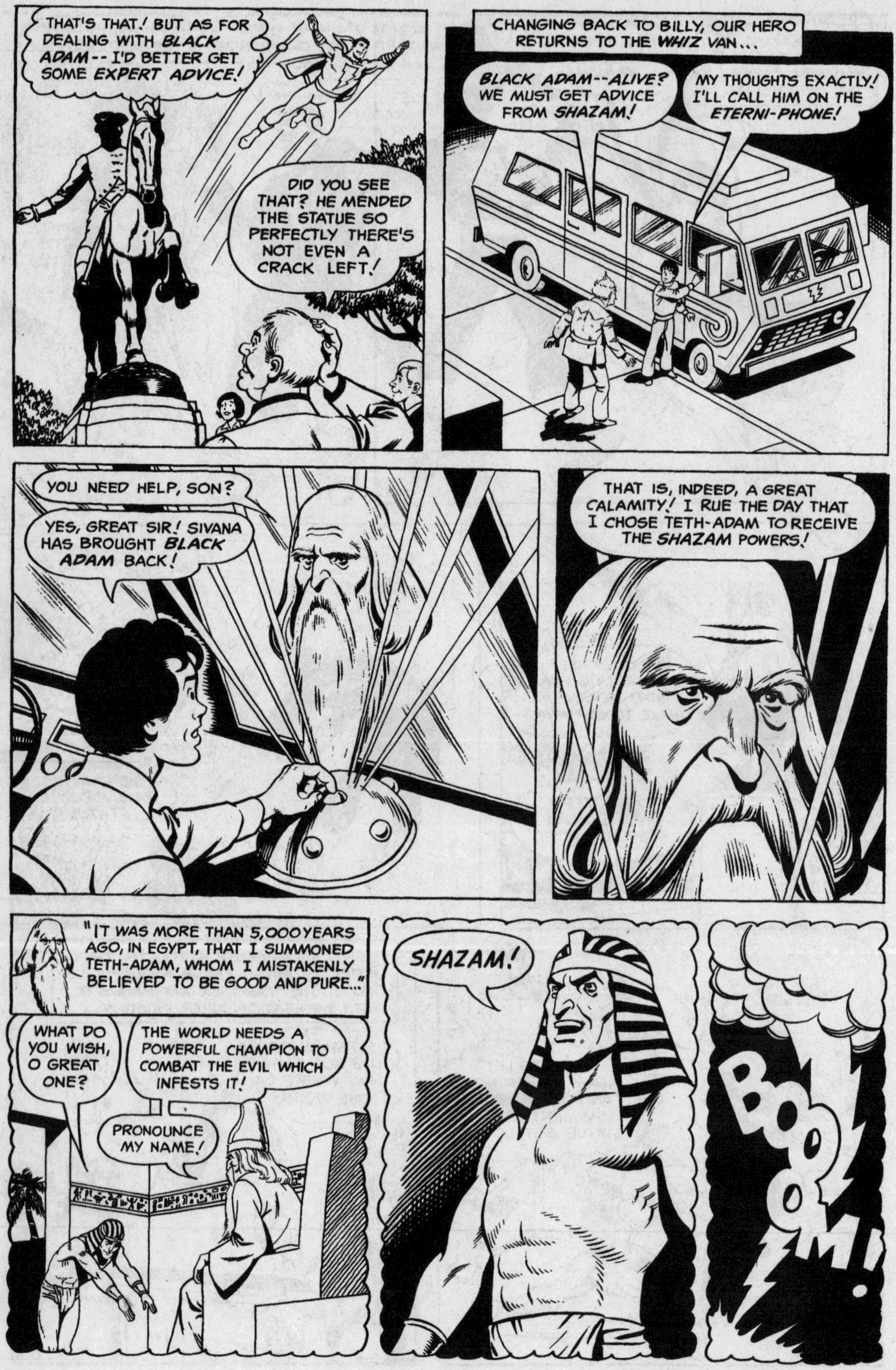
THAT'S THAT! BUT AS FOR DEALING WITH BLACK ADAM-- I'D BETTER GET SOME EXPERT ADVICE!
DID YOU SEE THAT? HE MENDED THE STATUE SO PERFECTLY THERE'S NOT EVEN A CRACK LEFT!
CHANGING BACK TO BILLY, OUR HERO RETURNS TO THE WHIZ VAN...
BLACK ADAM--ALIVE? WE MUST GET ADVICE FROM SHAZAM!
MY THOUGHTS EXACTLY! I'LL CALL HIM ON THE ETERNI-PHONE!
YOU NEED HELP, SON?
YES, GREAT SIR! SIVANA HAS BROUGHT BLACK ADAM BACK!
THAT IS, INDEED, A GREAT CALAMITY! I RUE THE DAY THAT I CHOSE TETH-ADAM TO RECEIVE THE SHAZAM POWERS!
"IT WAS MORE THAN 5,000 YEARS AGO, IN EGYPT, THAT I SUMMONED TETH-ADAM, WHOM I MISTAKENLY BELIEVED TO BE GOOD AND PURE..."
WHAT DO YOU WISH, O GREAT ONE?
THE WORLD NEEDS A POWERFUL CHAMPION TO COMBAT THE EVIL WHICH INFESTS IT!
PRONOUNCE MY NAME!
SHAZAM!
BOOOM!

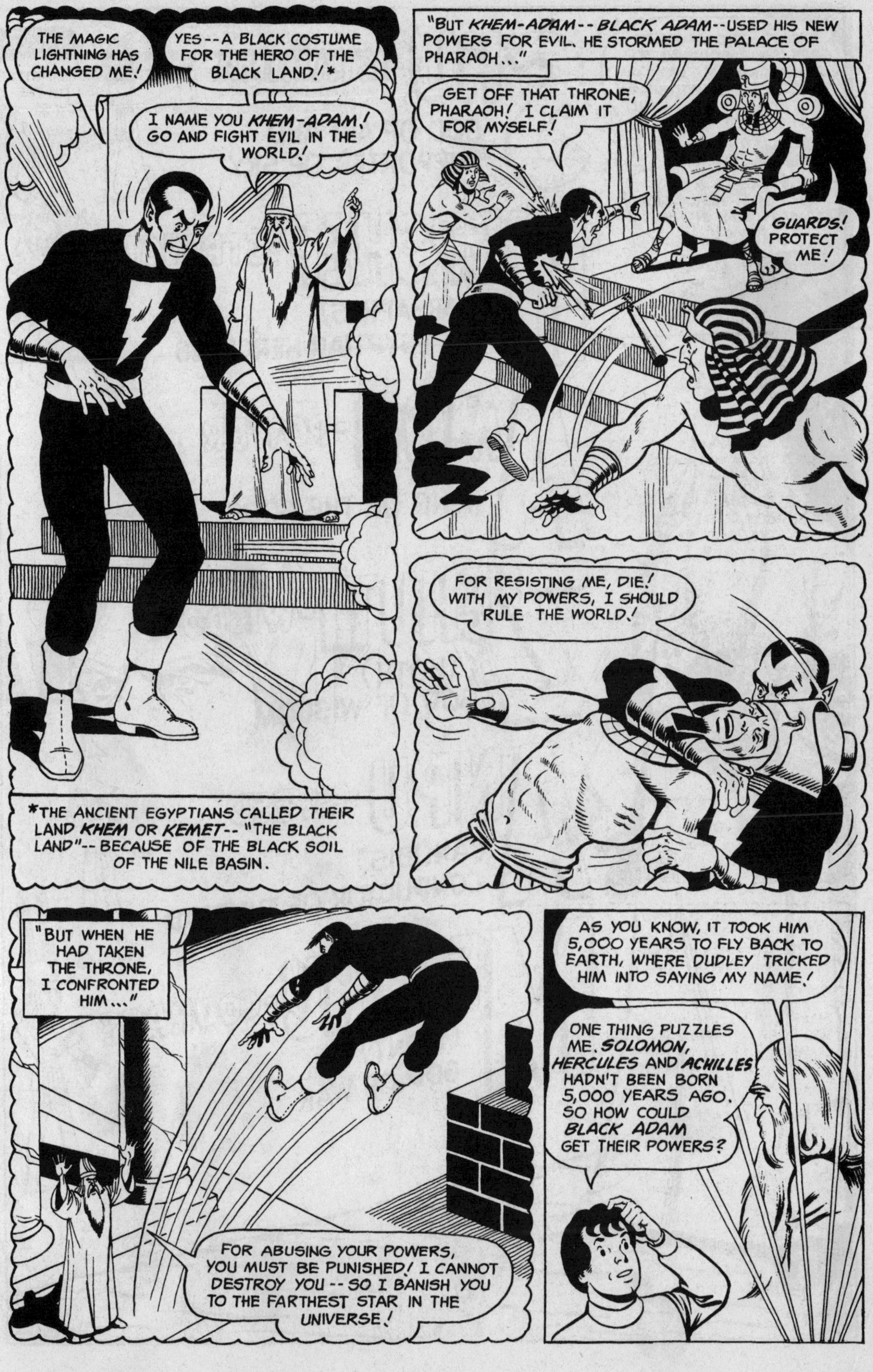
THE MAGIC LIGHTNING HAS CHANGED ME!
YES--A BLACK COSTUME FOR THE HERO OF THE BLACK LAND!*
I NAME YOU KHEM-ADAM! GO AND FIGHT EVIL IN THE WORLD!
*THE ANCIENT EGYPTIANS CALLED THEIR LAND KHEM OR KEMET-- "THE BLACK LAND"-- BECAUSE OF THE BLACK SOIL OF THE NILE BASIN.
"BUT KHEM-ADAM--BLACK ADAM--USED HIS NEW POWERS FOR EVIL. HE STORMED THE PALACE OF PHARAOH..."
GET OFF THAT THRONE, PHARAOH! I CLAIM IT FOR MYSELF!
GUARDS! PROTECT ME!
FOR RESISTING ME, DIE! WITH MY POWERS, I SHOULD RULE THE WORLD!
"BUT WHEN HE HAD TAKEN THE THRONE, I CONFRONTED HIM..."
FOR ABUSING YOUR POWERS, YOU MUST BE PUNISHED! I CANNOT DESTROY YOU--SO I BANISH YOU TO THE FARTHEST STAR IN THE UNIVERSE!
AS YOU KNOW, IT TOOK HIM 5,000 YEARS TO FLY BACK TO EARTH, WHERE DUDLEY TRICKED HIM INTO SAYING MY NAME!
ONE THING PUZZLES ME. SOLOMON, HERCULES AND ACHILLES HADN'T BEEN BORN 5,000 YEARS AGO. SO HOW COULD BLACK ADAM GET THEIR POWERS?

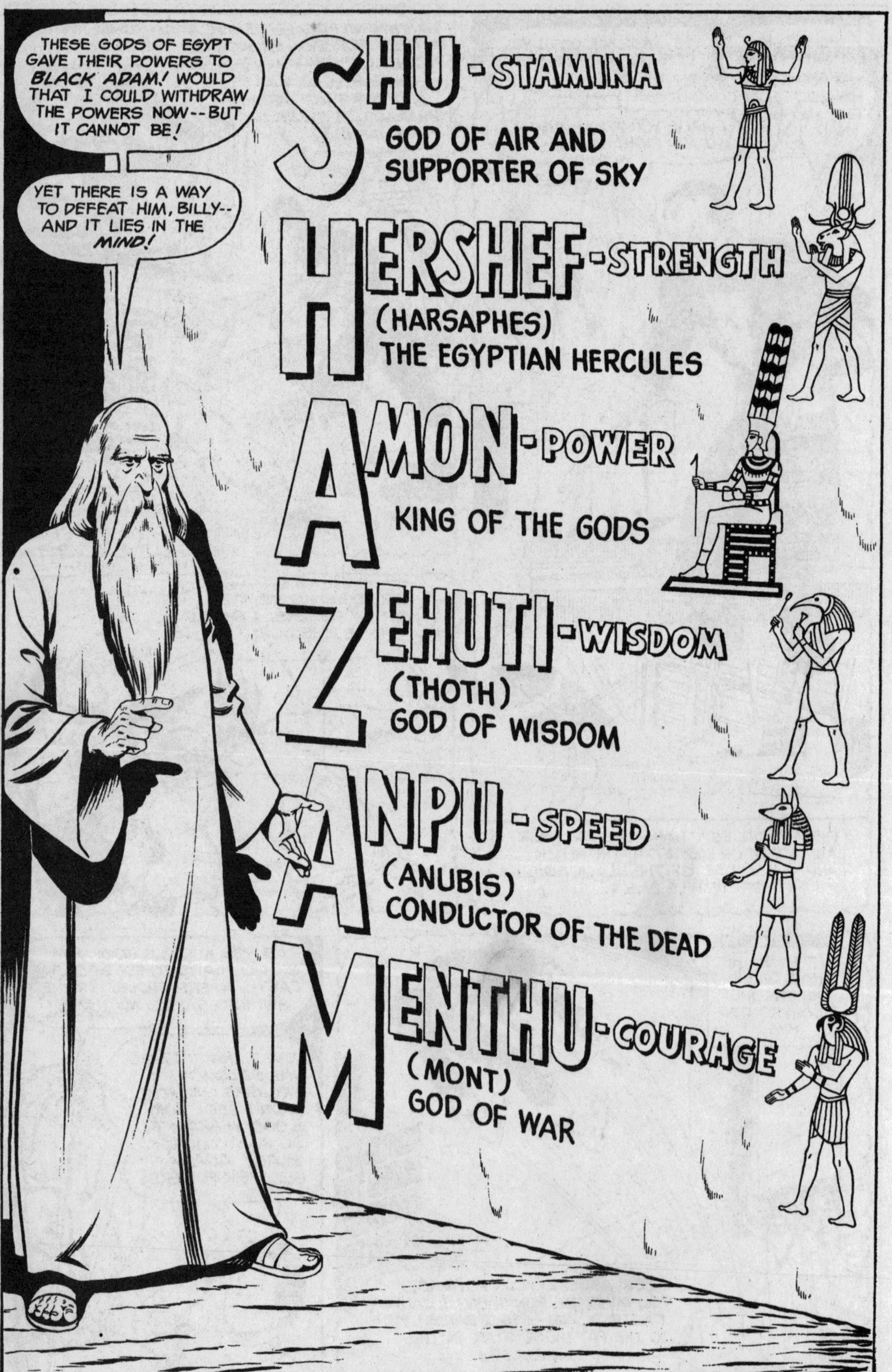
THESE GODS OF EGYPT GAVE THEIR POWERS TO BLACK ADAM! WOULD THAT I COULD WITHDRAW THE POWERS NOW--BUT IT CANNOT BE!
YET THERE IS A WAY TO DEFEAT HIM, BILLY-- AND IT LIES IN THE MIND!
SHU - STAMINA
GOD OF AIR AND SUPPORTER OF SKY
HERSHEF - STRENGTH
(HARSAPHES)
THE EGYPTIAN HERCULES
AMON - POWER
KING OF THE GODS
ZEHUTI - WISDOM
(THOTH)
GOD OF WISDOM
ANPU - SPEED
(ANUBIS)
CONDUCTOR OF THE DEAD
MENTHU - COURAGE
(MONT)
GOD OF WAR

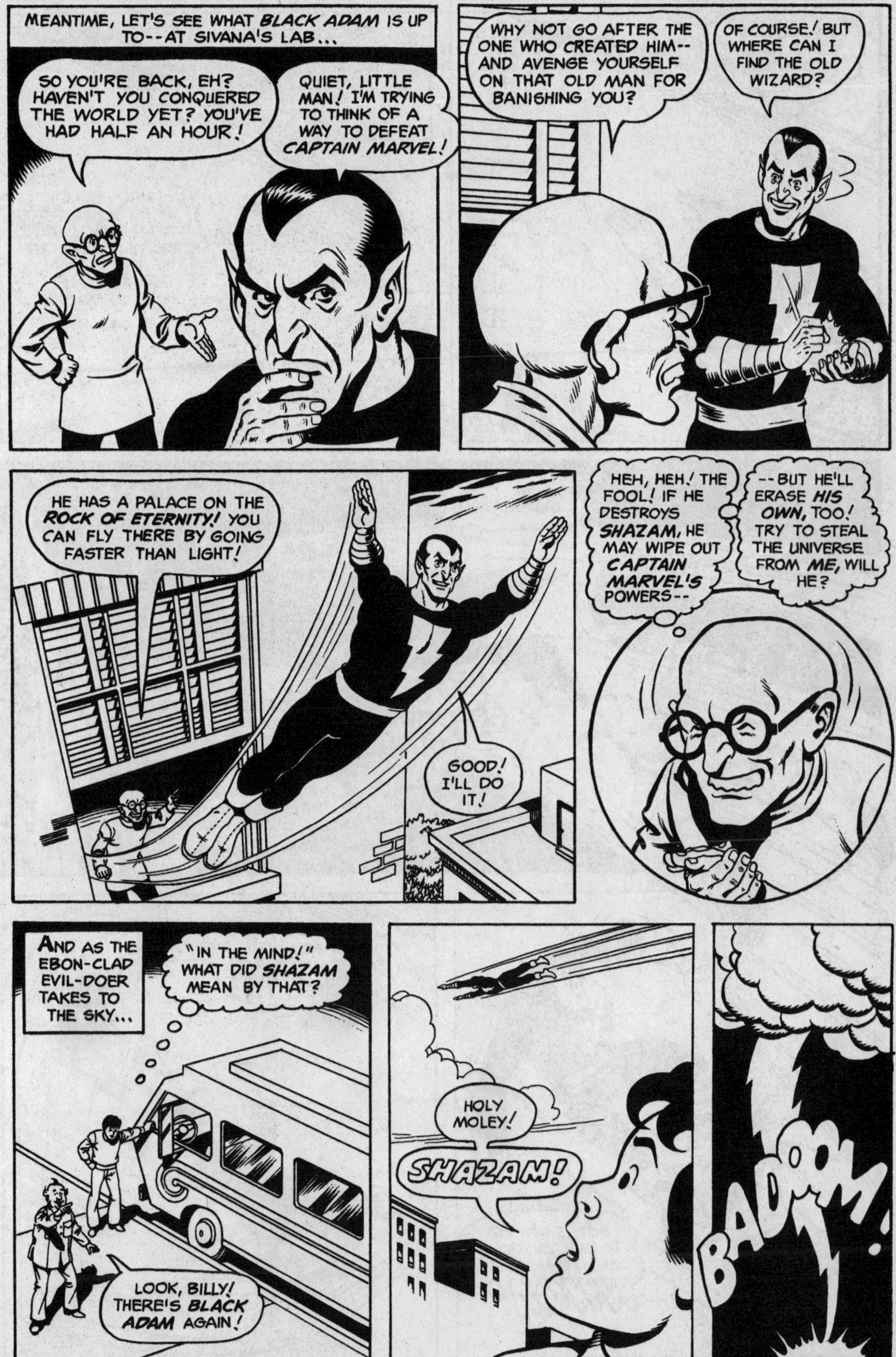
MEANTIME, LET'S SEE WHAT BLACK ADAM IS UP TO--AT SIVANA'S LAB...
SO YOU'RE BACK, EH? HAVEN'T YOU CONQUERED THE WORLD YET? YOU'VE HAD HALF AN HOUR!
QUIET, LITTLE MAN! I'M TRYING TO THINK OF A WAY TO DEFEAT CAPTAIN MARVEL!
WHY NOT GO AFTER THE ONE WHO CREATED HIM-- AND AVENGE YOURSELF ON THAT OLD MAN FOR BANISHING YOU?
OF COURSE! BUT WHERE CAN I FIND THE OLD WIZARD?
HE HAS A PALACE ON THE ROCK OF ETERNITY! YOU CAN FLY THERE BY GOING FASTER THAN LIGHT!
GOOD! I'LL DO IT!
HEH, HEH! THE FOOL! IF HE DESTROYS SHAZAM, HE MAY WIPE OUT CAPTAIN MARVEL'S POWERS--
--BUT HE'LL ERASE HIS OWN, TOO! TRY TO STEAL THE UNIVERSE FROM ME, WILL HE?
AND AS THE EBON-CLAD EVIL-DOER TAKES TO THE SKY...
"IN THE MIND!" WHAT DID SHAZAM MEAN BY THAT?
LOOK, BILLY! THERE'S BLACK ADAM AGAIN!
HOLY MOLEY!
SHAZAM!
BADOOM!

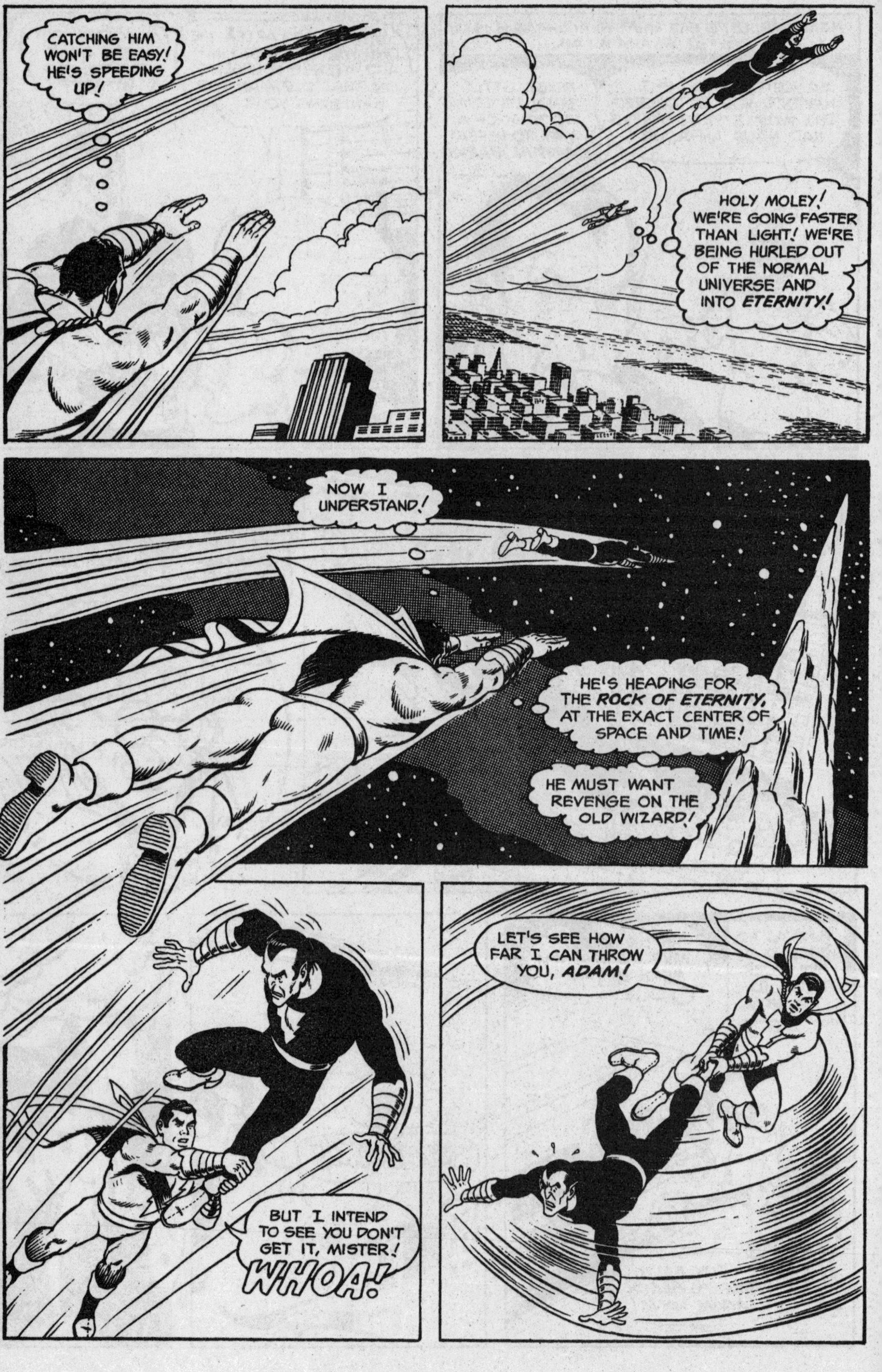
CATCHING HIM WON'T BE EASY! HE'S SPEEDING UP!
HOLY MOLEY! WE'RE GOING FASTER THAN LIGHT! WE'RE BEING HURLED OUT OF THE NORMAL UNIVERSE AND INTO ETERNITY!
NOW I UNDERSTAND!
HE'S HEADING FOR THE ROCK OF ETERNITY, AT THE EXACT CENTER OF SPACE AND TIME!
HE MUST WANT REVENGE ON THE OLD WIZARD!
BUT I INTEND TO SEE YOU DON'T GET IT, MISTER!
WHOA!
LET'S SEE HOW FAR I CAN THROW YOU, ADAM!

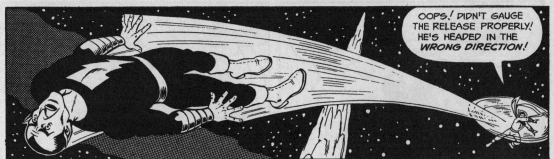

OOPS! DIDN'T GAUGE THE RELEASE PROPERLY! HE'S HEADED IN THE *WRONG DIRECTION!*

As *CAPTAIN MARVEL* FOLLOWS THE HURTLING FIGURE...

HOLY MOLEY! HE LANDED IN *BOSTON HARBOR*-- OVER *200 YEARS* IN THE PAST!

THOSE BOATS FILLED WITH FAKE "INDIANS"--THIS IS THE NIGHT OF DECEMBER 16, 1773-- THE *BOSTON TEA PARTY!*

BUT MY CONCERN IS *BLACK ADAM!* HE'S FLYING TO ONE OF THE TEA SHIPS!

CURSE YOU, *CAPTAIN MARVEL!* I'LL GET YOU YET!

THE JAILS ARE FULL OF CHARACTERS WHO SAID *THAT!*

KEEP IT UP, *ADAM!* YOU'RE ONLY *HELPING* THE COLONISTS BY DESTROYING THE CHESTS OF TEA BEFORE *THEY* GET A CHANCE TO DO IT!

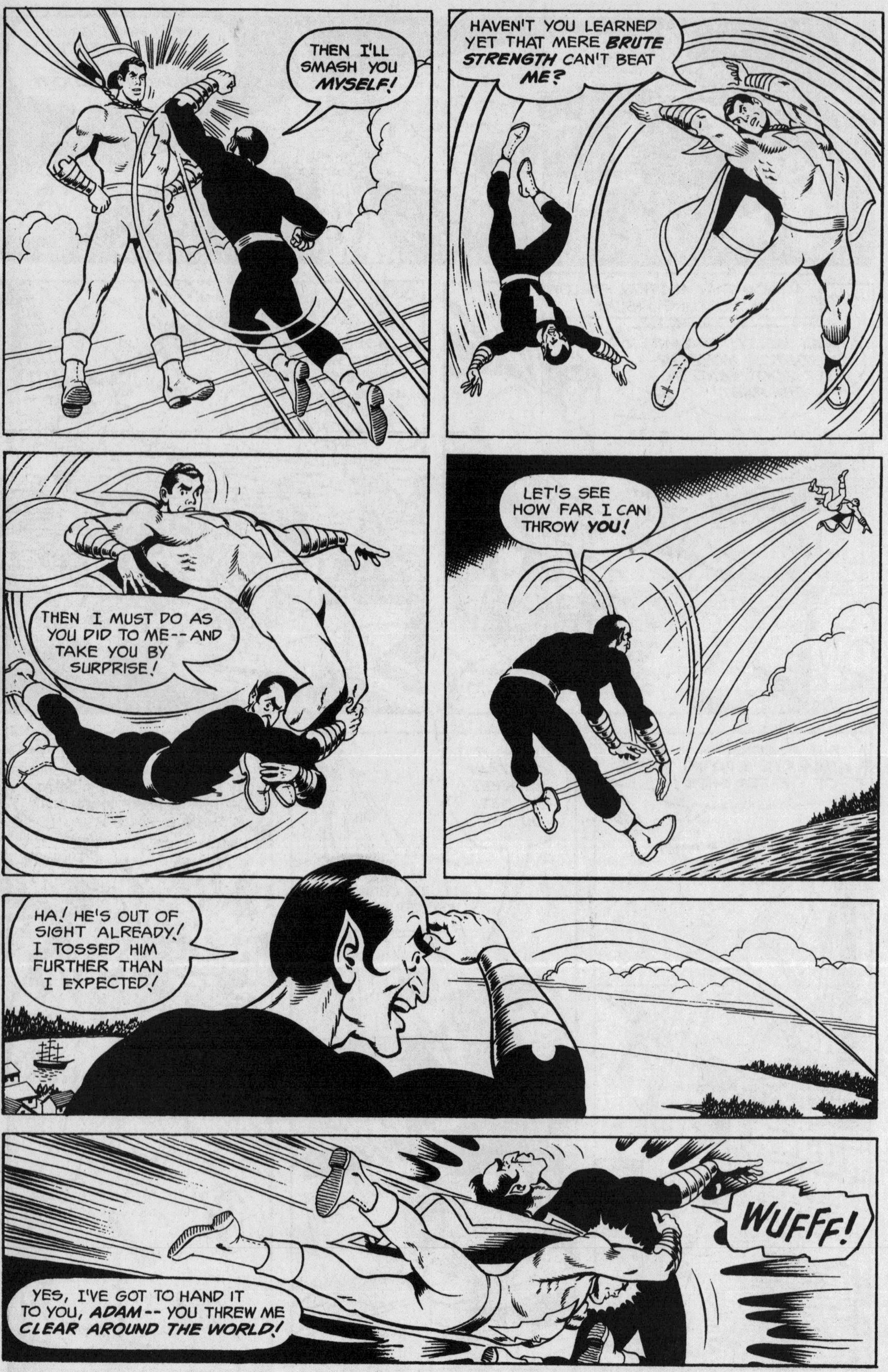
THEN I'LL SMASH YOU MYSELF!
HAVEN'T YOU LEARNED YET THAT MERE BRUTE STRENGTH CAN'T BEAT ME?
THEN I MUST DO AS YOU DID TO ME--AND TAKE YOU BY SURPRISE!
LET'S SEE HOW FAR I CAN THROW YOU!
HA! HE'S OUT OF SIGHT ALREADY! I TOSSED HIM FURTHER THAN I EXPECTED!
WUFFF!
YES, I'VE GOT TO HAND IT TO YOU, ADAM-- YOU THREW ME CLEAR AROUND THE WORLD!

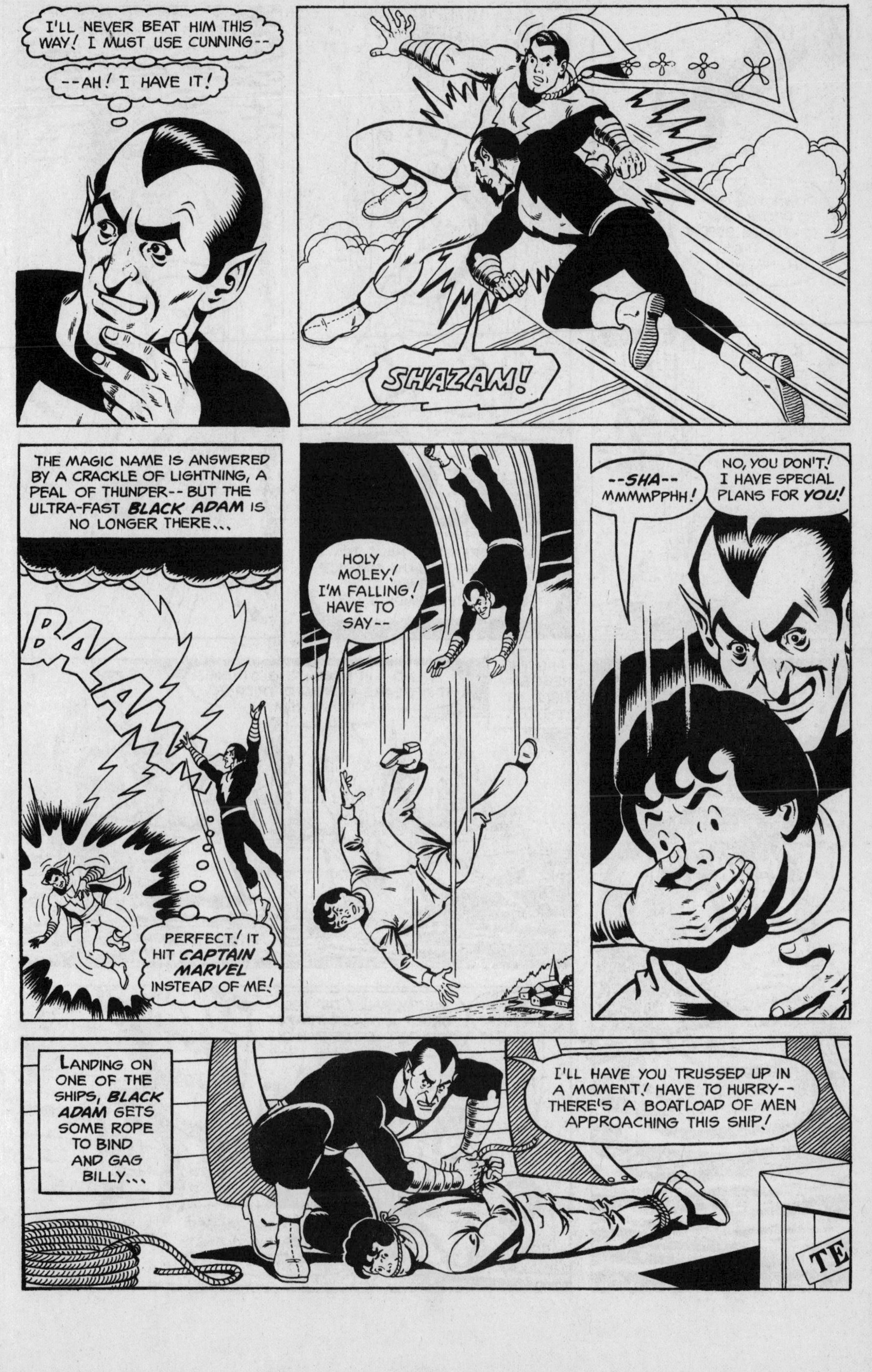
I'LL NEVER BEAT HIM THIS WAY! I MUST USE CUNNING--
--AH! I HAVE IT!
SHAZAM!
THE MAGIC NAME IS ANSWERED BY A CRACKLE OF LIGHTNING, A PEAL OF THUNDER-- BUT THE ULTRA-FAST BLACK ADAM IS NO LONGER THERE...
BALAM
PERFECT! IT HIT CAPTAIN MARVEL INSTEAD OF ME!
HOLY MOLEY! I'M FALLING! HAVE TO SAY--
--SHA-- MMMMPPHH!
NO, YOU DON'T! I HAVE SPECIAL PLANS FOR YOU!
LANDING ON ONE OF THE SHIPS, BLACK ADAM GETS SOME ROPE TO BIND AND GAG BILLY...
I'LL HAVE YOU TRUSSED UP IN A MOMENT! HAVE TO HURRY-- THERE'S A BOATLOAD OF MEN APPROACHING THIS SHIP!
TE

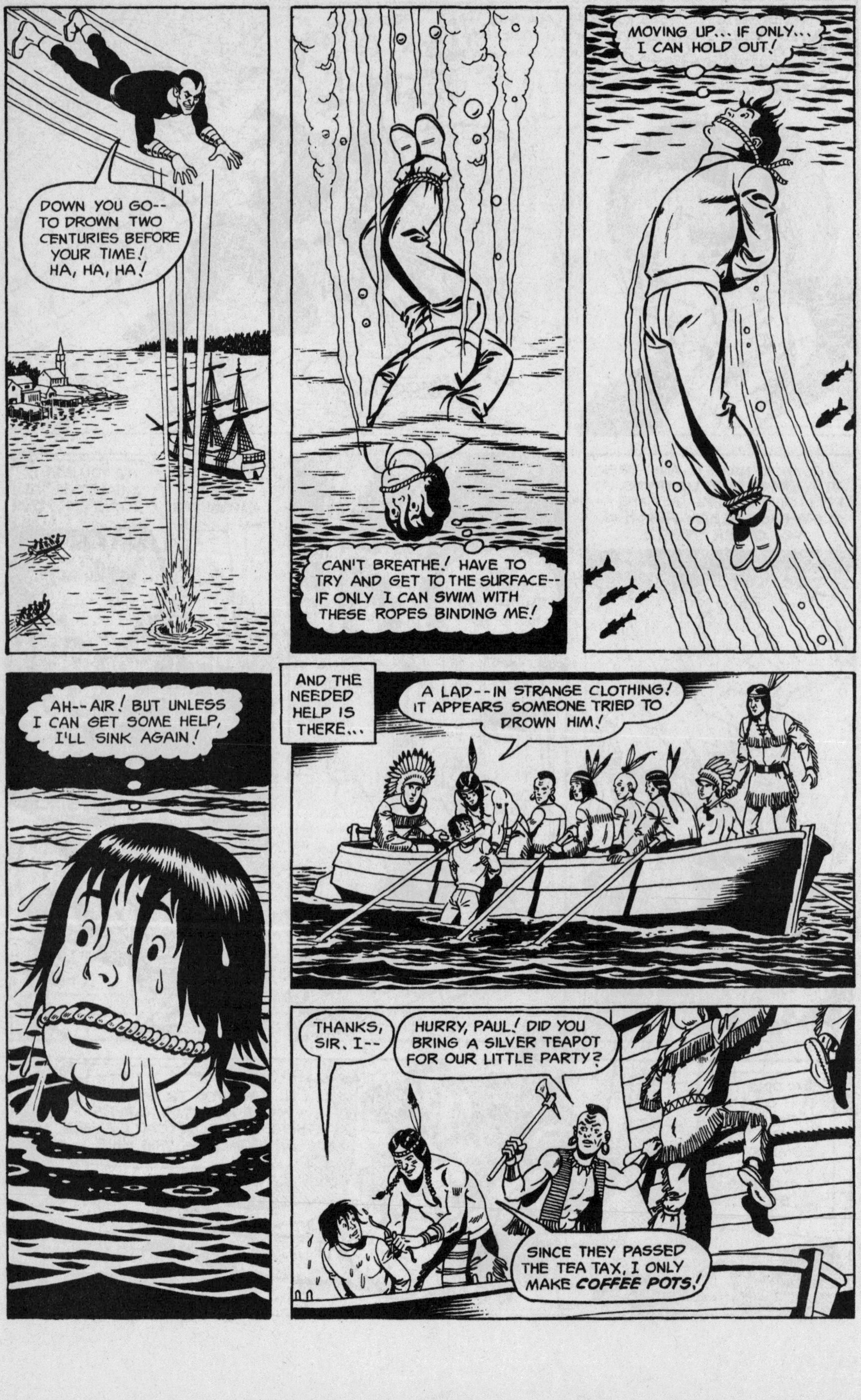
DOWN YOU GO-- TO DROWN TWO CENTURIES BEFORE YOUR TIME! HA, HA, HA!
CAN'T BREATHE! HAVE TO TRY AND GET TO THE SURFACE-- IF ONLY I CAN SWIM WITH THESE ROPES BINDING ME!
MOVING UP... IF ONLY... I CAN HOLD OUT!
AH--AIR! BUT UNLESS I CAN GET SOME HELP, I'LL SINK AGAIN!
AND THE NEEDED HELP IS THERE...
A LAD--IN STRANGE CLOTHING! IT APPEARS SOMEONE TRIED TO DROWN HIM!
THANKS, SIR. I--
HURRY, PAUL! DID YOU BRING A SILVER TEAPOT FOR OUR LITTLE PARTY?
SINCE THEY PASSED THE TEA TAX, I ONLY MAKE COFFEE POTS!

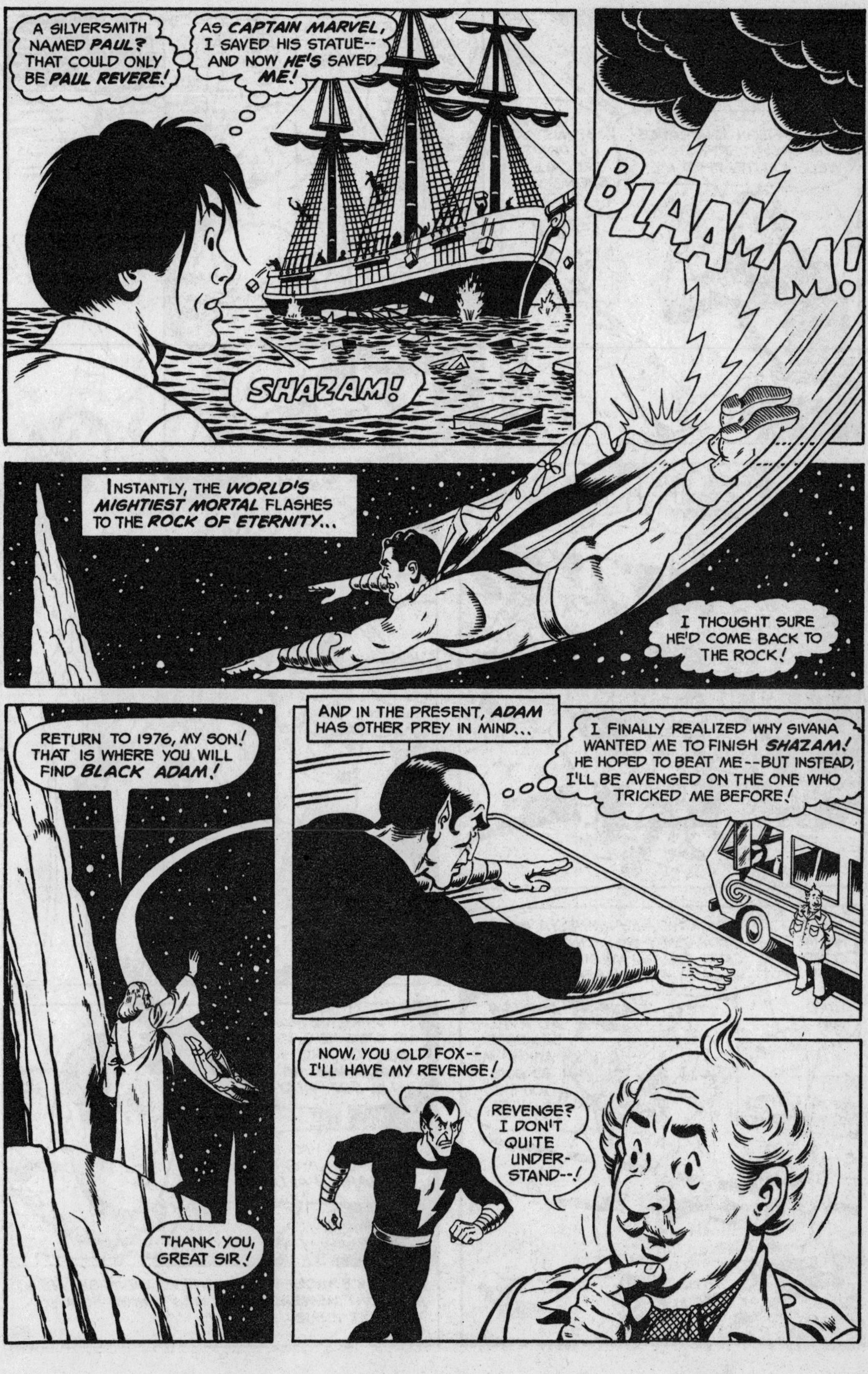
A SILVERSMITH NAMED PAUL? THAT COULD ONLY BE PAUL REVERE!
AS CAPTAIN MARVEL, I SAVED HIS STATUE-- AND NOW HE'S SAVED ME!
SHAZAM!
BLAAMMM!
INSTANTLY, THE WORLD'S MIGHTIEST MORTAL FLASHES TO THE ROCK OF ETERNITY...
I THOUGHT SURE HE'D COME BACK TO THE ROCK!
RETURN TO 1976, MY SON! THAT IS WHERE YOU WILL FIND BLACK ADAM!
THANK YOU, GREAT SIR!
AND IN THE PRESENT, ADAM HAS OTHER PREY IN MIND...
I FINALLY REALIZED WHY SIVANA WANTED ME TO FINISH SHAZAM! HE HOPED TO BEAT ME--BUT INSTEAD, I'LL BE AVENGED ON THE ONE WHO TRICKED ME BEFORE!
NOW, YOU OLD FOX-- I'LL HAVE MY REVENGE!
REVENGE? I DON'T QUITE UNDER-STAND--!

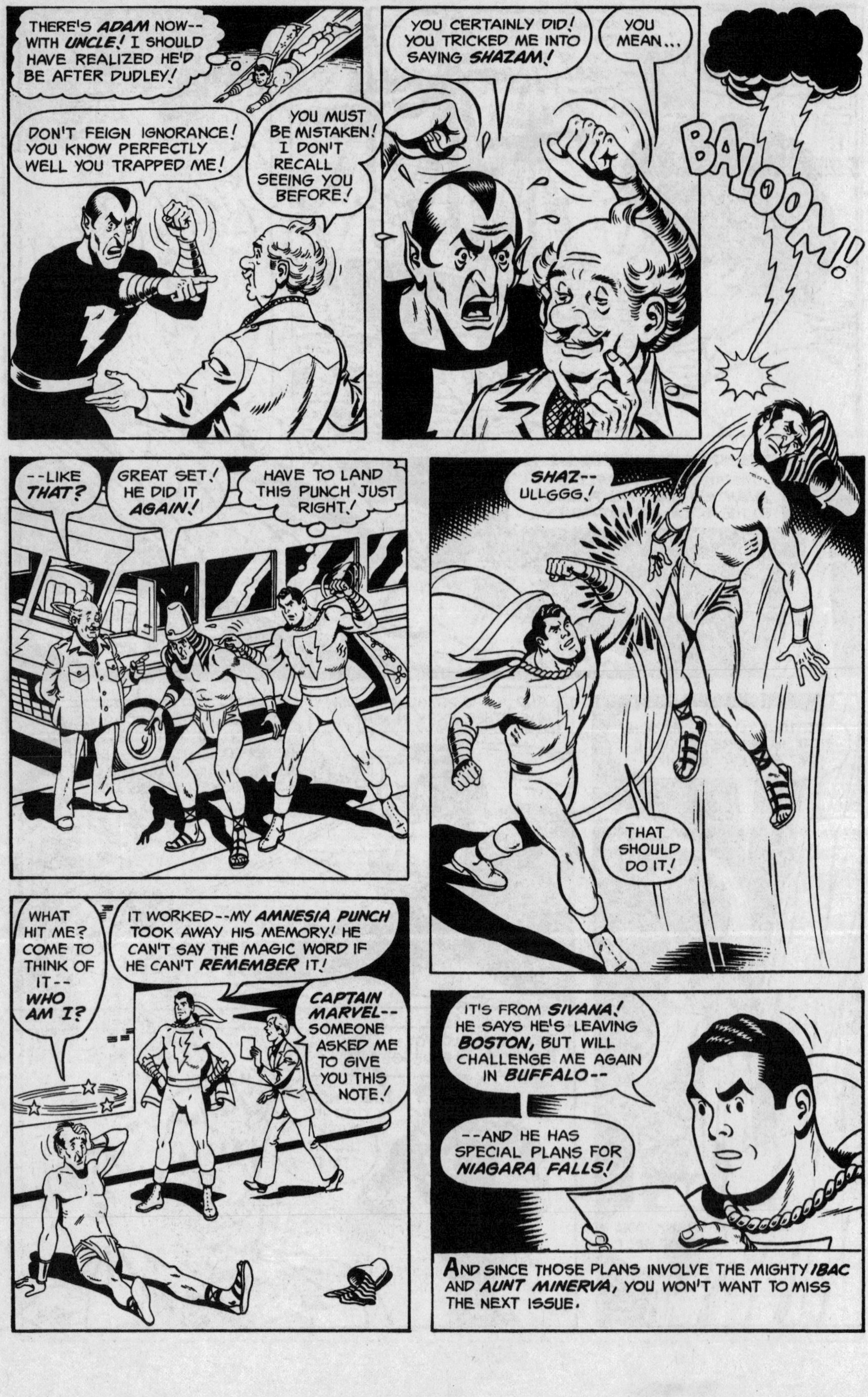
THERE'S ADAM NOW-- WITH UNCLE! I SHOULD HAVE REALIZED HE'D BE AFTER DUDLEY!
DON'T FEIGN IGNORANCE! YOU KNOW PERFECTLY WELL YOU TRAPPED ME!
YOU MUST BE MISTAKEN! I DON'T RECALL SEEING YOU BEFORE!
YOU CERTAINLY DID! YOU TRICKED ME INTO SAYING SHAZAM!
YOU MEAN...
BALOOM!
--LIKE THAT?
GREAT SET! HE DID IT AGAIN!
HAVE TO LAND THIS PUNCH JUST RIGHT!
SHAZ-- ULLGGG!
THAT SHOULD DO IT!
WHAT HIT ME? COME TO THINK OF IT-- WHO AM I?
IT WORKED--MY AMNESIA PUNCH TOOK AWAY HIS MEMORY! HE CAN'T SAY THE MAGIC WORD IF HE CAN'T REMEMBER IT!
CAPTAIN MARVEL-- SOMEONE ASKED ME TO GIVE YOU THIS NOTE!
IT'S FROM SIVANA! HE SAYS HE'S LEAVING BOSTON, BUT WILL CHALLENGE ME AGAIN IN BUFFALO--
--AND HE HAS SPECIAL PLANS FOR NIAGARA FALLS!
AND SINCE THOSE PLANS INVOLVE THE MIGHTY IBAC AND AUNT MINERVA, YOU WON'T WANT TO MISS THE NEXT ISSUE.

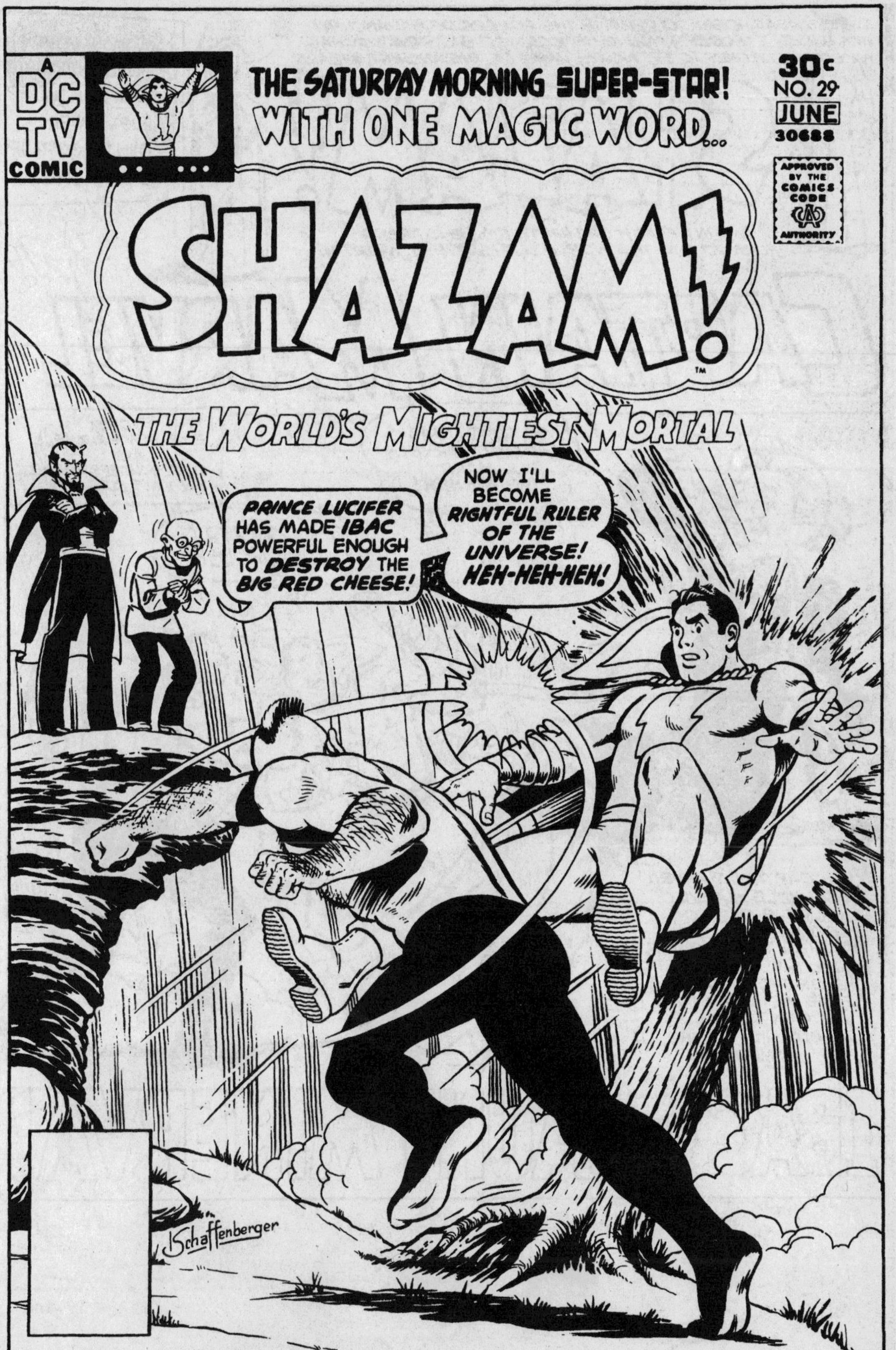
A DC TV COMIC
THE SATURDAY MORNING SUPER-STAR!
WITH ONE MAGIC WORD...
30¢
NO. 29
JUNE
30688
APPROVED BY THE COMICS CODE AUTHORITY
SHAZAM!
THE WORLD'S MIGHTIEST MORTAL
PRINCE LUCIFER HAS MADE IBAC POWERFUL ENOUGH TO DESTROY THE BIG RED CHEESE!
NOW I'LL BECOME RIGHTFUL RULER OF THE UNIVERSE! HEH-HEH-HEH!
Schaffenberger

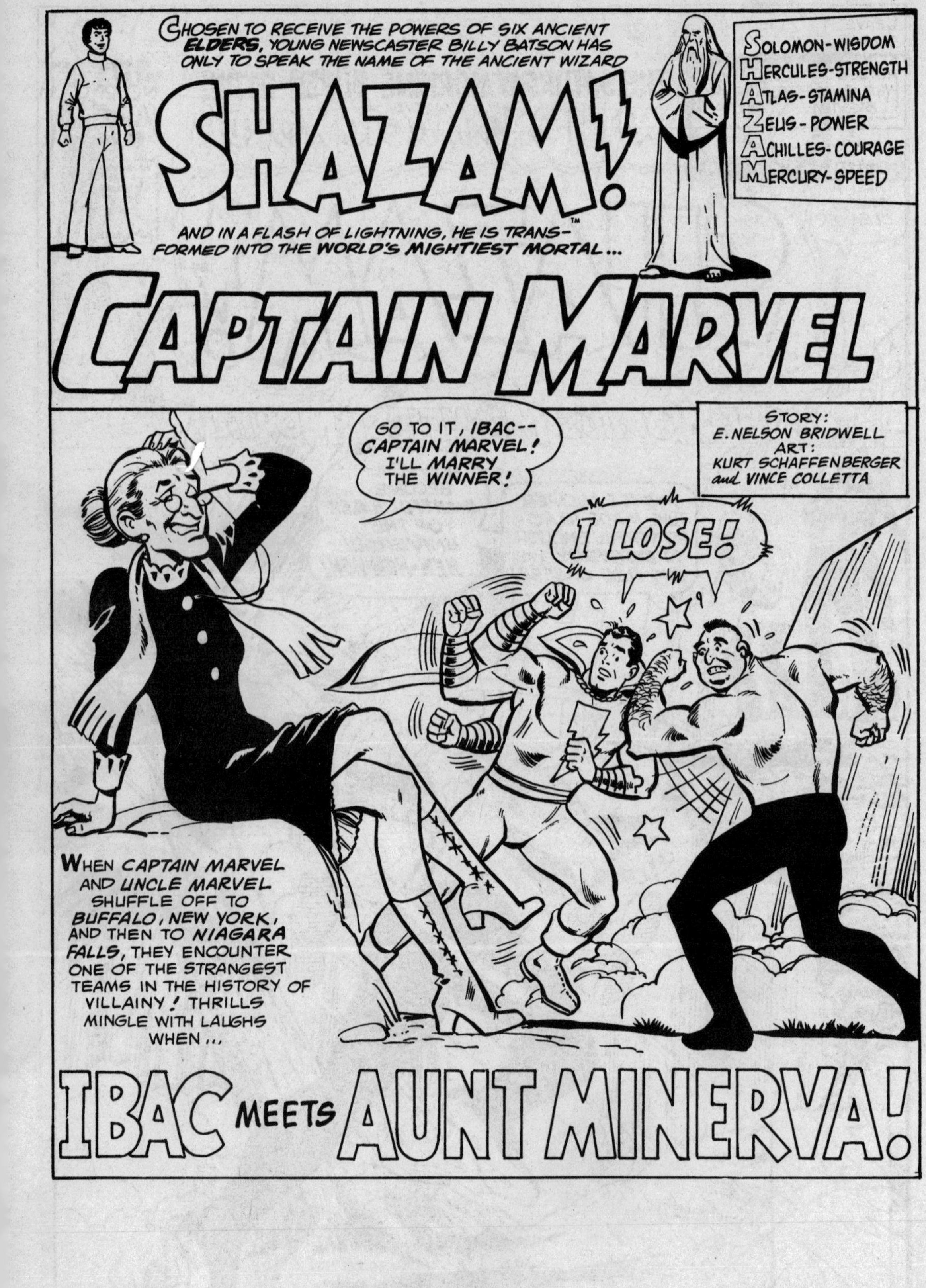
CHOSEN TO RECEIVE THE POWERS OF SIX ANCIENT ELDERS, YOUNG NEWSCASTER BILLY BATSON HAS ONLY TO SPEAK THE NAME OF THE ANCIENT WIZARD
SHAZAM!™
AND IN A FLASH OF LIGHTNING, HE IS TRANSFORMED INTO THE WORLD'S MIGHTIEST MORTAL...
SOLOMON-WISDOM
HERCULES-STRENGTH
ATLAS-STAMINA
ZEUS-POWER
ACHILLES-COURAGE
MERCURY-SPEED
CAPTAIN MARVEL
GO TO IT, IBAC-- CAPTAIN MARVEL! I'LL MARRY THE WINNER!
STORY: E. NELSON BRIDWELL ART: KURT SCHAFFENBERGER and VINCE COLLETTA
I LOSE!
WHEN CAPTAIN MARVEL AND UNCLE MARVEL SHUFFLE OFF TO BUFFALO, NEW YORK, AND THEN TO NIAGARA FALLS, THEY ENCOUNTER ONE OF THE STRANGEST TEAMS IN THE HISTORY OF VILLAINY! THRILLS MINGLE WITH LAUGHS WHEN...
IBAC MEETS AUNT MINERVA!

LEAVE IT TO DR. THADDEUS B. SIVANA... NOW HE'S BROUGHT A KIDNAP VICTIM TO HIS LABORATORY HIDEOUT IN UPSTATE NEW YORK. WHO IS HE? A MILLIONAIRE? A BIG-TIME POLITICIAN?

B-BUT I'M ONLY A *STREET-CLEANER!*

ONLY A STREET-CLEANER? WHEN YOU SAY YOUR MAGIC WORD, YOU'RE SOMETHING ELSE, STANLEY PRINTWHISTLE!

YES-- AND WHAT'S HAPPENED EVERY TIME I SAID THE WORD? I BECAME A SUPER-POWERED VILLAIN WHO GOT BEAT UP BY *CAPTAIN MARVEL*--

SO YOU MUST *HATE* THAT BIG RED CHEESE AS *I* DO! YOU *MUST* BECOME *IBAC* AGAIN!

YES, YOU MUST!

YIPES! YOU MUST BE...,

PRINCE LUCIFER-- THE ONE WHO GAVE STANLEY HIS *IBAC* POWERS -- BACK WHEN HE WAS A TWO-BIT CROOK CALLED *"STINKY" PRINTWHISTLE!*

BUT I DID NOT MAKE YOU POWERFUL ENOUGH! THIS TIME YOU WILL BE *MORE* POWERFUL!

SAY YOUR WORD, STANLEY!

IBAC!

THE WORD IS ANSWERED BY A BURST OF GREEN FIRE... CONTAINING THE WORST QUALITIES OF FOUR VILLAINS OF HISTORY...

IVAN THE TERRIBLE -- TERROR
BORGIA -- CUNNING
ATTILA -- FIERCENESS
CALIGULA -- CRUELTY

ZZEEESEE!

AND PRINTWHISTLE BECOMES *IBAC THE CURSED!*

AT LAST I'VE CHANGED FROM THAT WEAKLING! I FEEL *MIGHTIER* THAN EVER!

HEH, HEH! WAIT TILL *CAPTAIN MARVEL* SEES YOU NOW!

2

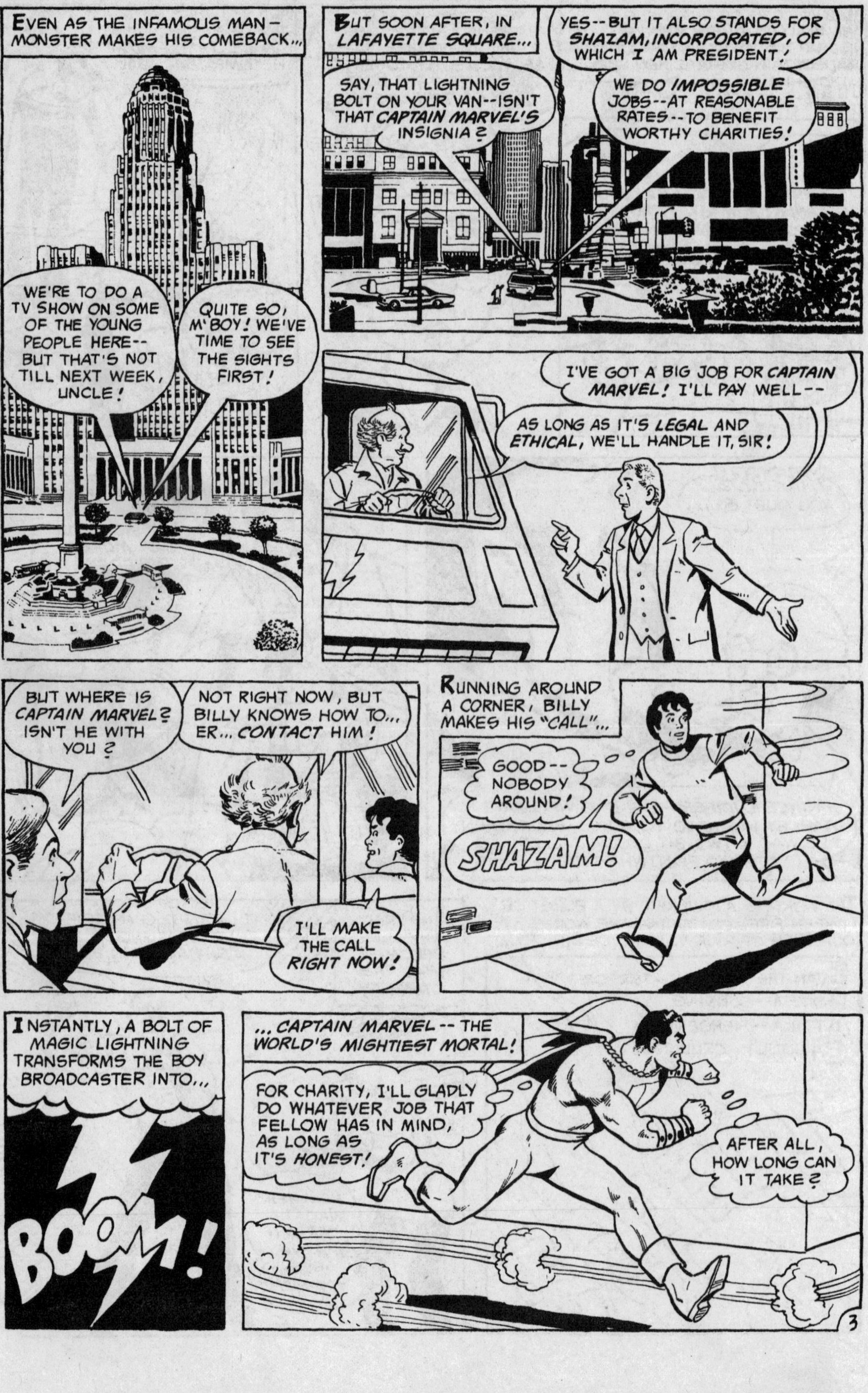
EVEN AS THE INFAMOUS MAN-MONSTER MAKES HIS COMEBACK...
WE'RE TO DO A TV SHOW ON SOME OF THE YOUNG PEOPLE HERE-- BUT THAT'S NOT TILL NEXT WEEK, UNCLE!
QUITE SO, M'BOY! WE'VE TIME TO SEE THE SIGHTS FIRST!
BUT SOON AFTER, IN LAFAYETTE SQUARE...
SAY, THAT LIGHTNING BOLT ON YOUR VAN--ISN'T THAT CAPTAIN MARVEL'S INSIGNIA?
YES--BUT IT ALSO STANDS FOR SHAZAM, INCORPORATED, OF WHICH I AM PRESIDENT!
WE DO IMPOSSIBLE JOBS--AT REASONABLE RATES--TO BENEFIT WORTHY CHARITIES!
I'VE GOT A BIG JOB FOR CAPTAIN MARVEL! I'LL PAY WELL--
AS LONG AS IT'S LEGAL AND ETHICAL, WE'LL HANDLE IT, SIR!
BUT WHERE IS CAPTAIN MARVEL? ISN'T HE WITH YOU?
NOT RIGHT NOW, BUT BILLY KNOWS HOW TO... ER... CONTACT HIM!
I'LL MAKE THE CALL RIGHT NOW!
RUNNING AROUND A CORNER, BILLY MAKES HIS "CALL"...
GOOD--NOBODY AROUND!
SHAZAM!
INSTANTLY, A BOLT OF MAGIC LIGHTNING TRANSFORMS THE BOY BROADCASTER INTO...
BOOM!
...CAPTAIN MARVEL--THE WORLD'S MIGHTIEST MORTAL!
FOR CHARITY, I'LL GLADLY DO WHATEVER JOB THAT FELLOW HAS IN MIND, AS LONG AS IT'S HONEST!
AFTER ALL, HOW LONG CAN IT TAKE?
3

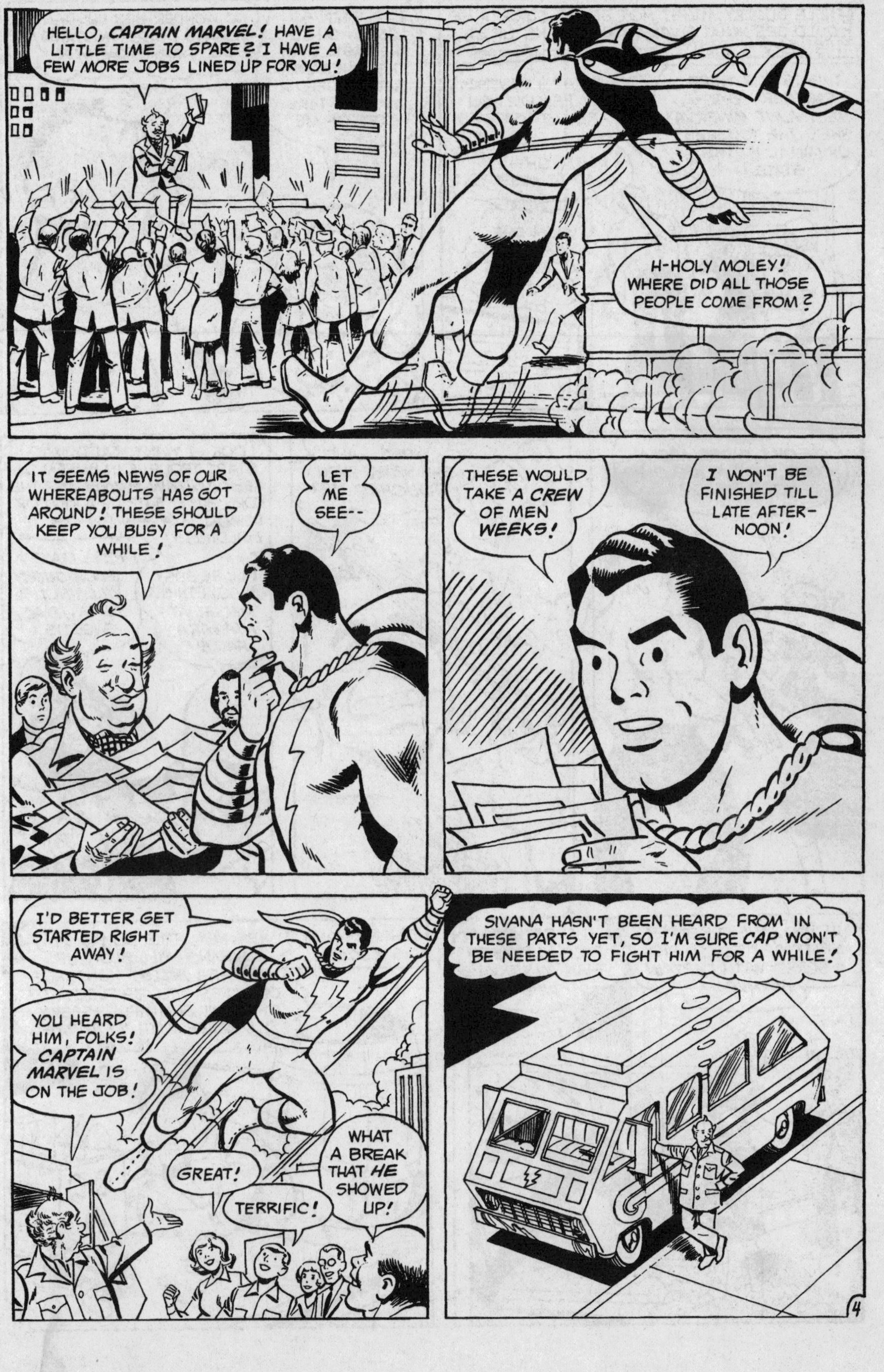
HELLO, CAPTAIN MARVEL! HAVE A LITTLE TIME TO SPARE? I HAVE A FEW MORE JOBS LINED UP FOR YOU!
H-HOLY MOLEY! WHERE DID ALL THOSE PEOPLE COME FROM?
IT SEEMS NEWS OF OUR WHEREABOUTS HAS GOT AROUND! THESE SHOULD KEEP YOU BUSY FOR A WHILE!
LET ME SEE--
THESE WOULD TAKE A CREW OF MEN WEEKS!
I WON'T BE FINISHED TILL LATE AFTER-NOON!
I'D BETTER GET STARTED RIGHT AWAY!
YOU HEARD HIM, FOLKS! CAPTAIN MARVEL IS ON THE JOB!
GREAT!
TERRIFIC!
WHAT A BREAK THAT HE SHOWED UP!
SIVANA HASN'T BEEN HEARD FROM IN THESE PARTS YET, SO I'M SURE CAP WON'T BE NEEDED TO FIGHT HIM FOR A WHILE!
4

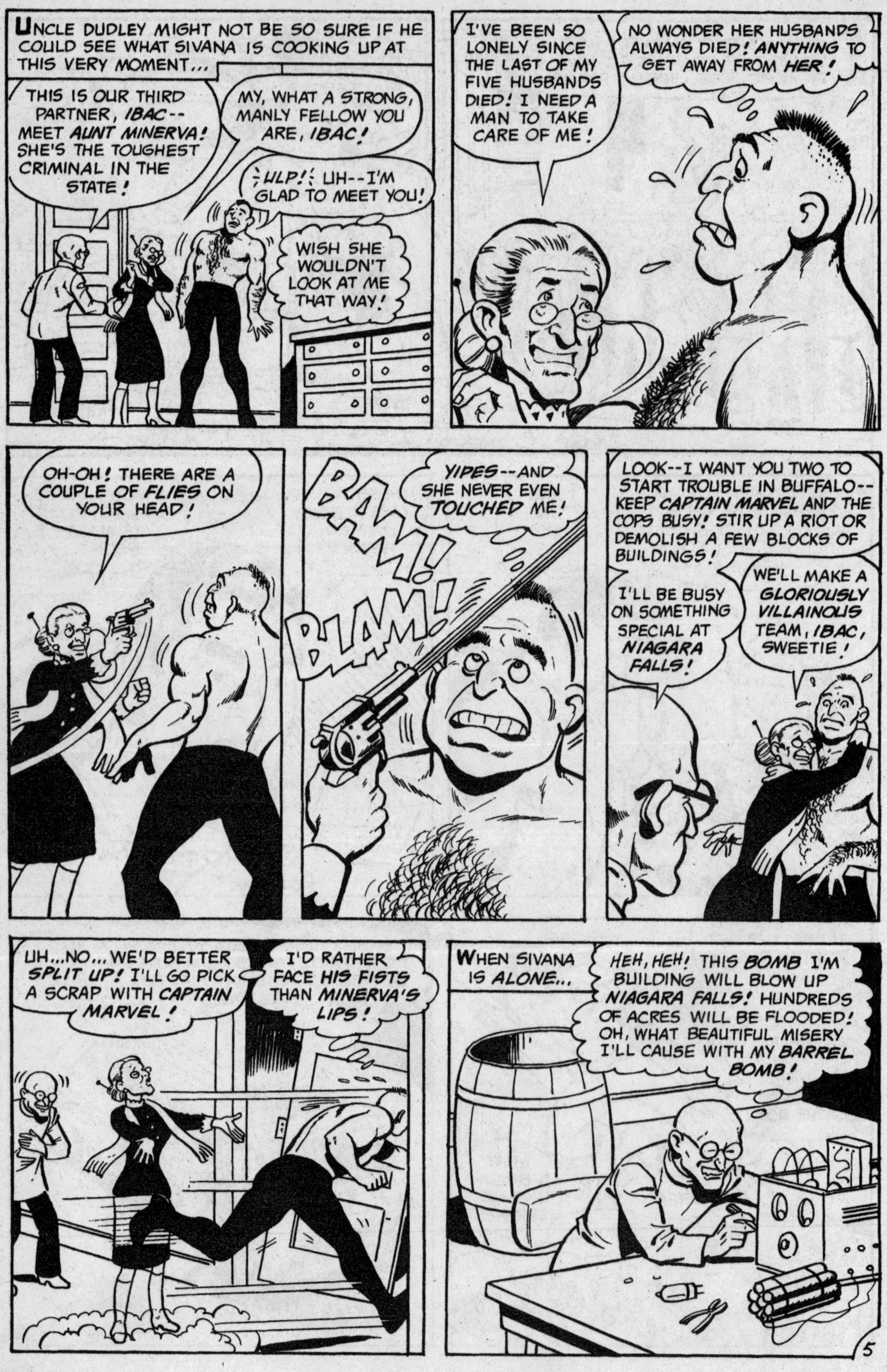
UNCLE DUDLEY MIGHT NOT BE SO SURE IF HE COULD SEE WHAT SIVANA IS COOKING UP AT THIS VERY MOMENT...
THIS IS OUR THIRD PARTNER, IBAC-- MEET AUNT MINERVA! SHE'S THE TOUGHEST CRIMINAL IN THE STATE!
MY, WHAT A STRONG, MANLY FELLOW YOU ARE, IBAC!
ULP! UH--I'M GLAD TO MEET YOU!
WISH SHE WOULDN'T LOOK AT ME THAT WAY!
I'VE BEEN SO LONELY SINCE THE LAST OF MY FIVE HUSBANDS DIED! I NEED A MAN TO TAKE CARE OF ME!
NO WONDER HER HUSBANDS ALWAYS DIED! ANYTHING TO GET AWAY FROM HER!
OH-OH! THERE ARE A COUPLE OF FLIES ON YOUR HEAD!
BAM! BLAM!
YIPES--AND SHE NEVER EVEN TOUCHED ME!
LOOK--I WANT YOU TWO TO START TROUBLE IN BUFFALO--KEEP CAPTAIN MARVEL AND THE COPS BUSY! STIR UP A RIOT OR DEMOLISH A FEW BLOCKS OF BUILDINGS!
I'LL BE BUSY ON SOMETHING SPECIAL AT NIAGARA FALLS!
WE'LL MAKE A GLORIOUSLY VILLAINOUS TEAM, IBAC, SWEETIE!
UH...NO...WE'D BETTER SPLIT UP! I'LL GO PICK A SCRAP WITH CAPTAIN MARVEL!
I'D RATHER FACE HIS FISTS THAN MINERVA'S LIPS!
WHEN SIVANA IS ALONE...
HEH, HEH! THIS BOMB I'M BUILDING WILL BLOW UP NIAGARA FALLS! HUNDREDS OF ACRES WILL BE FLOODED! OH, WHAT BEAUTIFUL MISERY I'LL CAUSE WITH MY BARREL BOMB!
5

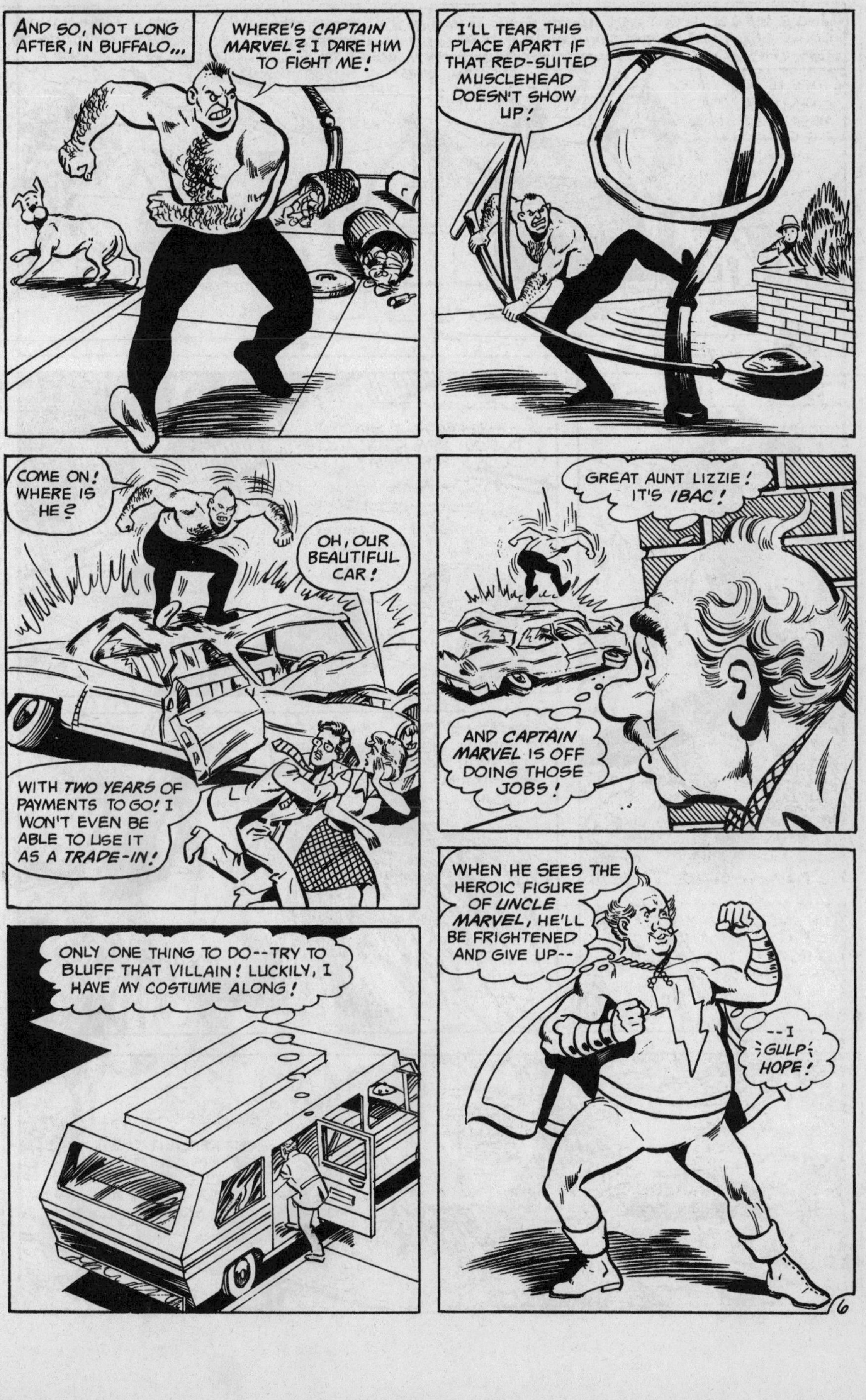
AND SO, NOT LONG AFTER, IN BUFFALO...
WHERE'S CAPTAIN MARVEL? I DARE HIM TO FIGHT ME!
I'LL TEAR THIS PLACE APART IF THAT RED-SUITED MUSCLEHEAD DOESN'T SHOW UP!
COME ON! WHERE IS HE?
OH, OUR BEAUTIFUL CAR!
WITH TWO YEARS OF PAYMENTS TO GO! I WON'T EVEN BE ABLE TO USE IT AS A TRADE-IN!
GREAT AUNT LIZZIE! IT'S IBAC!
AND CAPTAIN MARVEL IS OFF DOING THOSE JOBS!
ONLY ONE THING TO DO--TRY TO BLUFF THAT VILLAIN! LUCKILY, I HAVE MY COSTUME ALONG!
WHEN HE SEES THE HEROIC FIGURE OF UNCLE MARVEL, HE'LL BE FRIGHTENED AND GIVE UP--
--I GULP HOPE!
6

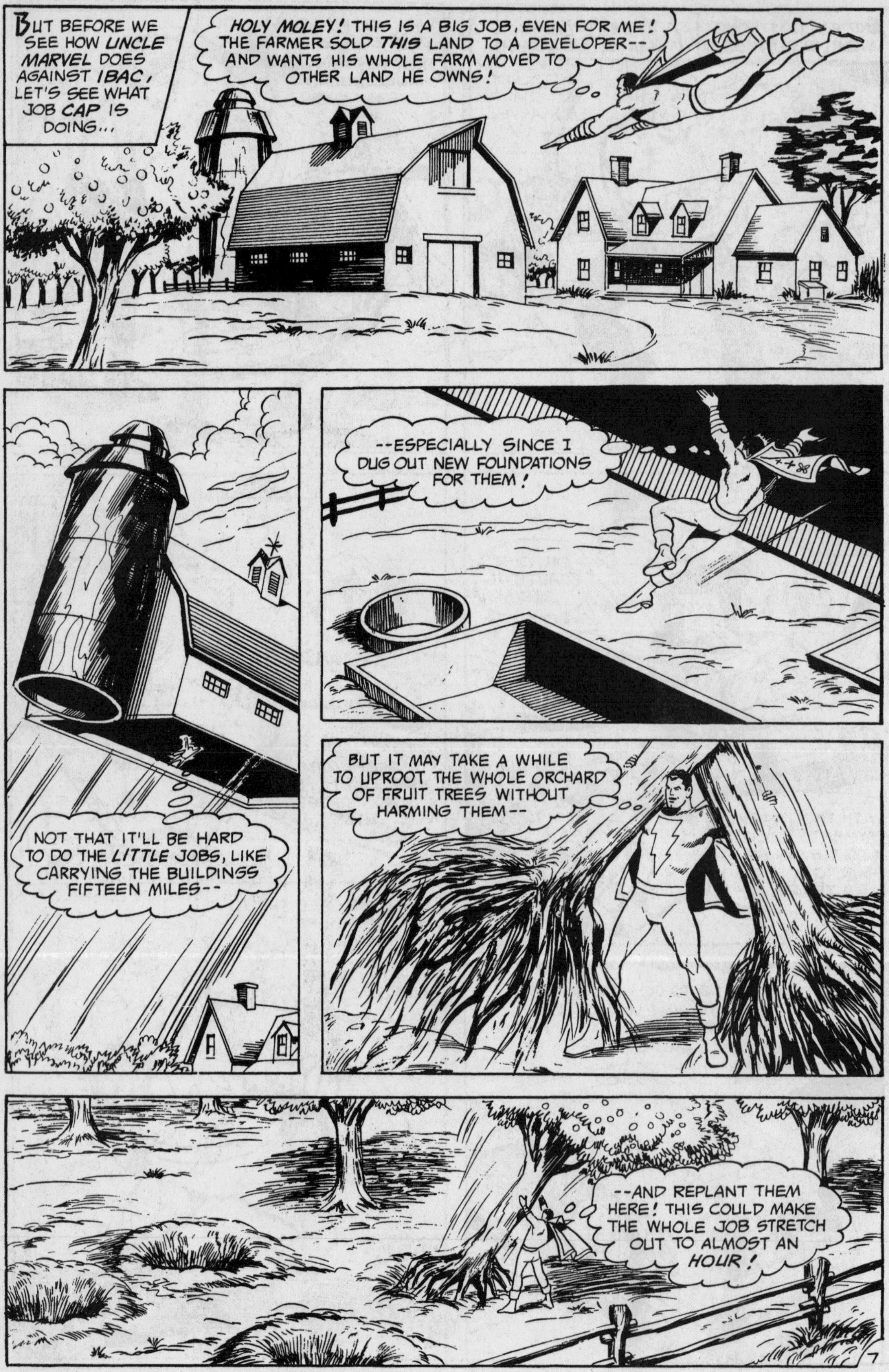
BUT BEFORE WE SEE HOW UNCLE MARVEL DOES AGAINST IBAC, LET'S SEE WHAT JOB CAP IS DOING...
HOLY MOLEY! THIS IS A BIG JOB, EVEN FOR ME! THE FARMER SOLD THIS LAND TO A DEVELOPER-- AND WANTS HIS WHOLE FARM MOVED TO OTHER LAND HE OWNS!
NOT THAT IT'LL BE HARD TO DO THE LITTLE JOBS, LIKE CARRYING THE BUILDINGS FIFTEEN MILES--
--ESPECIALLY SINCE I DUG OUT NEW FOUNDATIONS FOR THEM!
BUT IT MAY TAKE A WHILE TO UPROOT THE WHOLE ORCHARD OF FRUIT TREES WITHOUT HARMING THEM--
--AND REPLANT THEM HERE! THIS COULD MAKE THE WHOLE JOB STRETCH OUT TO ALMOST AN HOUR!
7

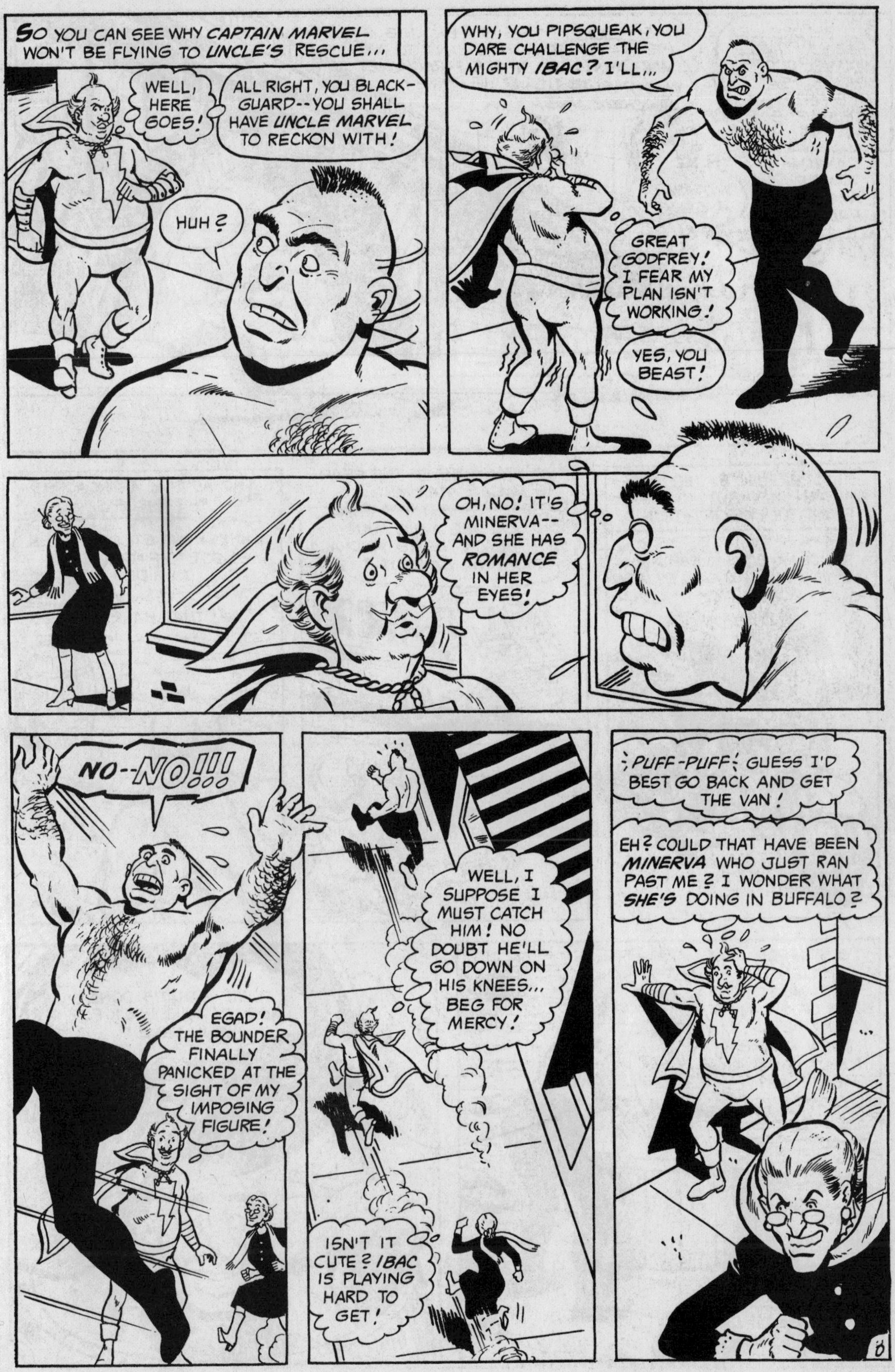
SO YOU CAN SEE WHY CAPTAIN MARVEL WON'T BE FLYING TO UNCLE'S RESCUE...
WELL, HERE GOES!
ALL RIGHT, YOU BLACK-GUARD--YOU SHALL HAVE UNCLE MARVEL TO RECKON WITH!
HUH?
WHY, YOU PIPSQUEAK, YOU DARE CHALLENGE THE MIGHTY IBAC? I'LL...
GREAT GODFREY! I FEAR MY PLAN ISN'T WORKING!
YES, YOU BEAST!
OH, NO! IT'S MINERVA--AND SHE HAS ROMANCE IN HER EYES!
NO--NO!!!
EGAD! THE BOUNDER FINALLY PANICKED AT THE SIGHT OF MY IMPOSING FIGURE!
WELL, I SUPPOSE I MUST CATCH HIM! NO DOUBT HE'LL GO DOWN ON HIS KNEES... BEG FOR MERCY!
ISN'T IT CUTE? IBAC IS PLAYING HARD TO GET!
PUFF-PUFF GUESS I'D BEST GO BACK AND GET THE VAN!
EH? COULD THAT HAVE BEEN MINERVA WHO JUST RAN PAST ME? I WONDER WHAT SHE'S DOING IN BUFFALO?

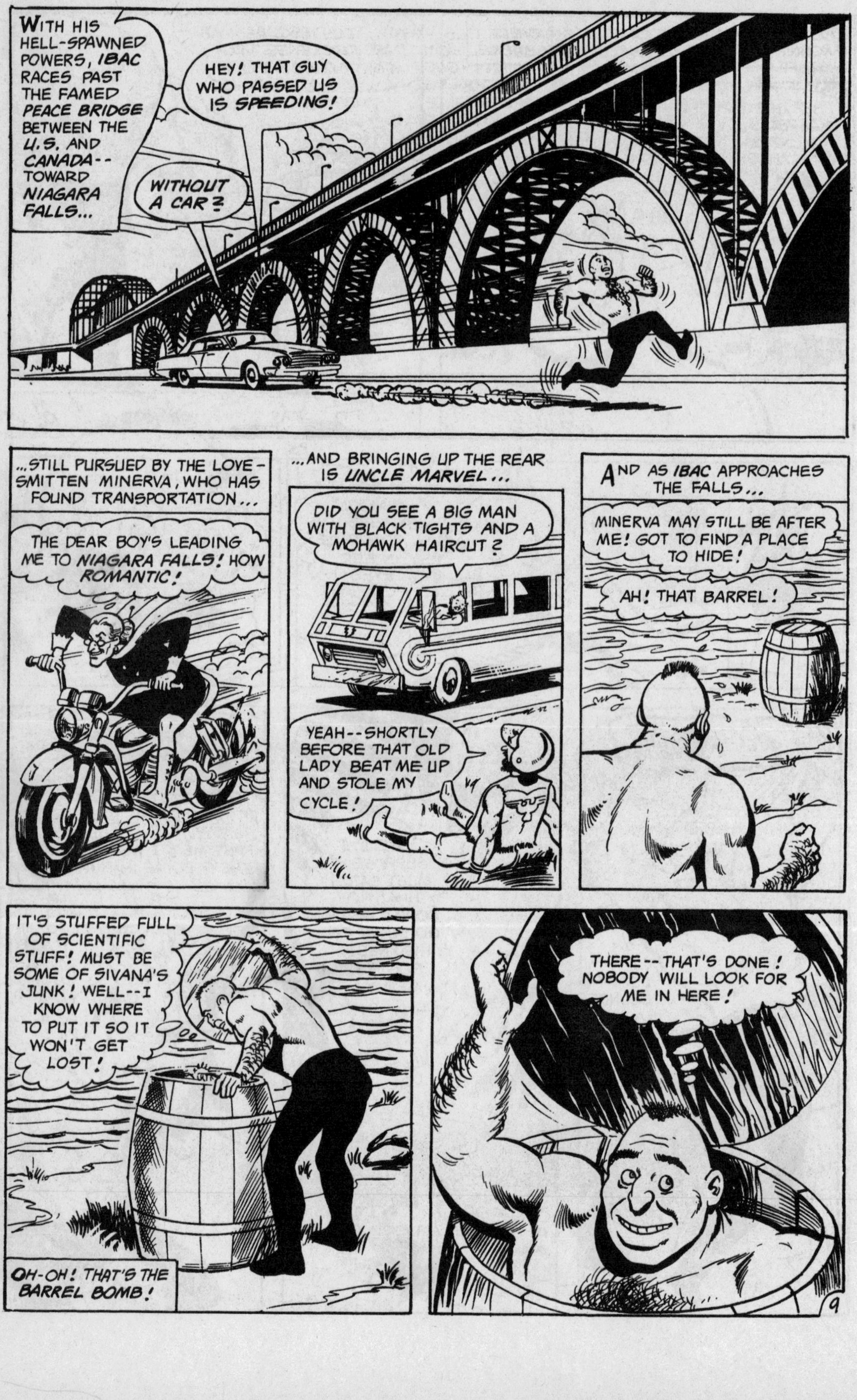
WITH HIS HELL-SPAWNED POWERS, IBAC RACES PAST THE FAMED PEACE BRIDGE BETWEEN THE U.S. AND CANADA-- TOWARD NIAGARA FALLS...
HEY! THAT GUY WHO PASSED US IS SPEEDING!
WITHOUT A CAR?
...STILL PURSUED BY THE LOVE-SMITTEN MINERVA, WHO HAS FOUND TRANSPORTATION...
THE DEAR BOY'S LEADING ME TO NIAGARA FALLS! HOW ROMANTIC!
...AND BRINGING UP THE REAR IS UNCLE MARVEL...
DID YOU SEE A BIG MAN WITH BLACK TIGHTS AND A MOHAWK HAIRCUT?
YEAH--SHORTLY BEFORE THAT OLD LADY BEAT ME UP AND STOLE MY CYCLE!
AND AS IBAC APPROACHES THE FALLS...
MINERVA MAY STILL BE AFTER ME! GOT TO FIND A PLACE TO HIDE!
AH! THAT BARREL!
IT'S STUFFED FULL OF SCIENTIFIC STUFF! MUST BE SOME OF SIVANA'S JUNK! WELL--I KNOW WHERE TO PUT IT SO IT WON'T GET LOST!
OH-OH! THAT'S THE BARREL BOMB!
THERE--THAT'S DONE! NOBODY WILL LOOK FOR ME IN HERE!
9

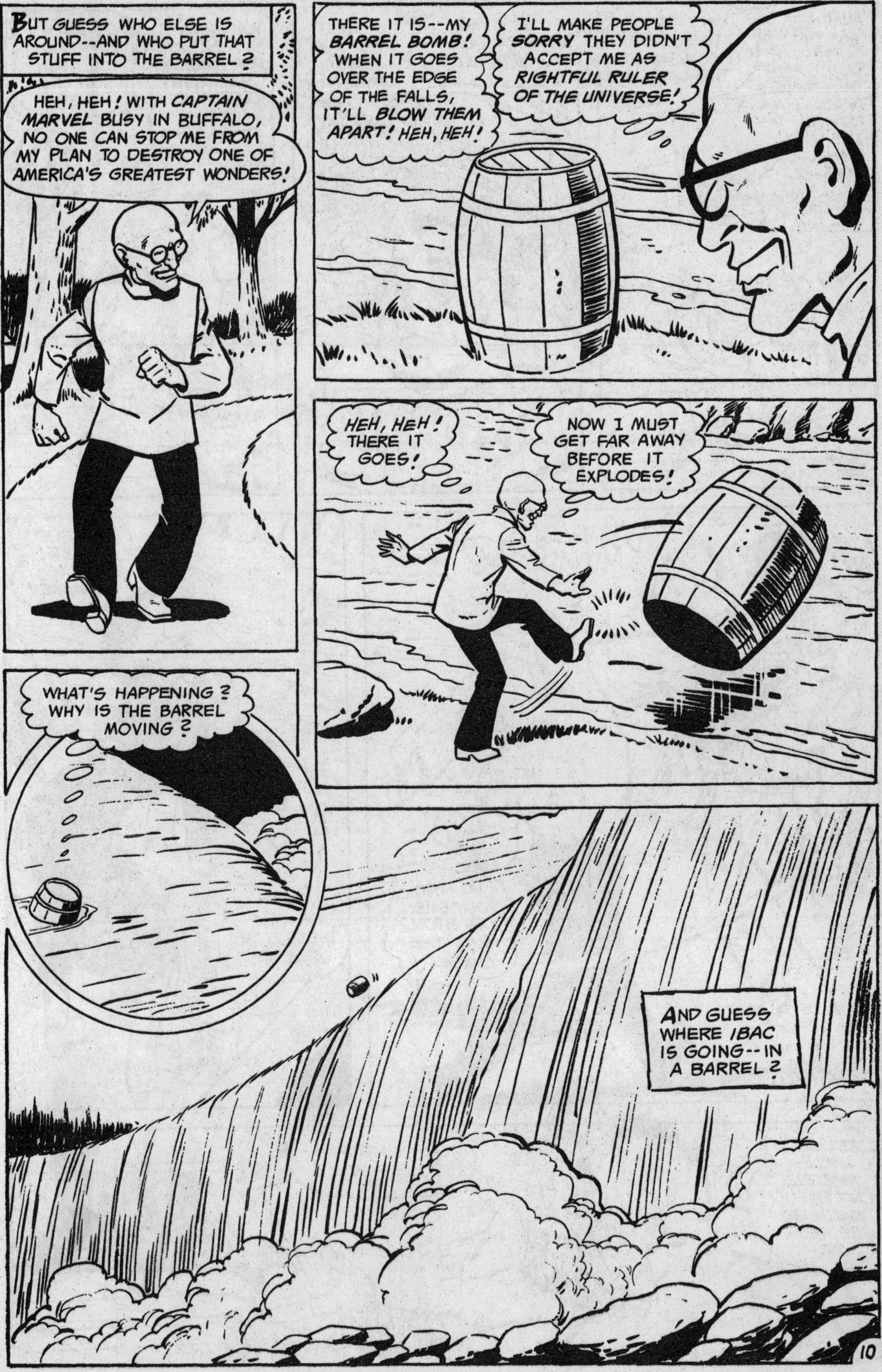
BUT GUESS WHO ELSE IS AROUND--AND WHO PUT THAT STUFF INTO THE BARREL?
HEH, HEH! WITH CAPTAIN MARVEL BUSY IN BUFFALO, NO ONE CAN STOP ME FROM MY PLAN TO DESTROY ONE OF AMERICA'S GREATEST WONDERS!
THERE IT IS--MY BARREL BOMB! WHEN IT GOES OVER THE EDGE OF THE FALLS, IT'LL BLOW THEM APART! HEH, HEH!
I'LL MAKE PEOPLE SORRY THEY DIDN'T ACCEPT ME AS RIGHTFUL RULER OF THE UNIVERSE!
HEH, HEH! THERE IT GOES!
NOW I MUST GET FAR AWAY BEFORE IT EXPLODES!
WHAT'S HAPPENING? WHY IS THE BARREL MOVING?
AND GUESS WHERE IBAC IS GOING--IN A BARREL?
10

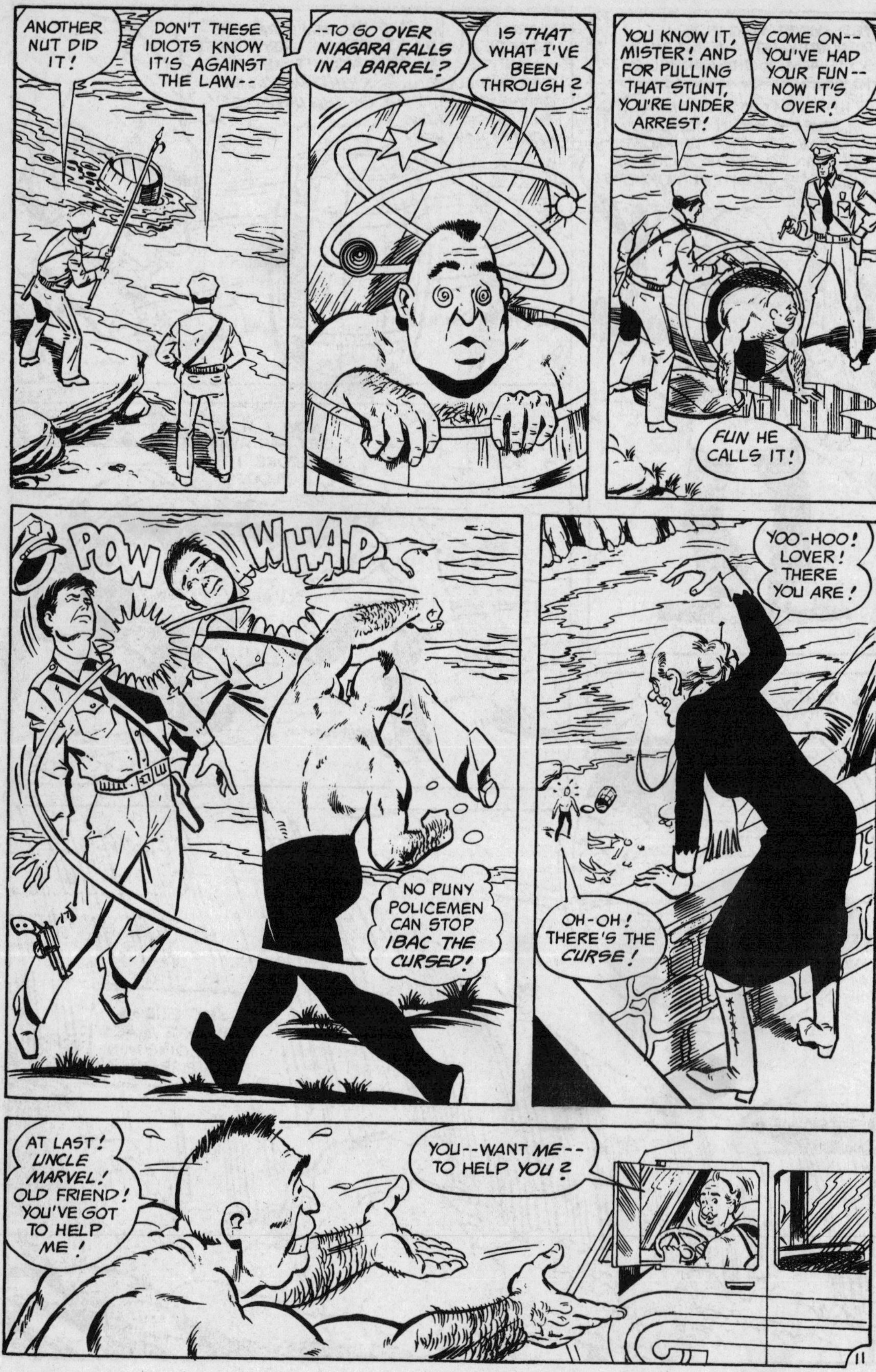
ANOTHER NUT DID IT!
DON'T THESE IDIOTS KNOW IT'S AGAINST THE LAW--
--TO GO OVER NIAGARA FALLS IN A BARREL?
IS THAT WHAT I'VE BEEN THROUGH?
YOU KNOW IT, MISTER! AND FOR PULLING THAT STUNT, YOU'RE UNDER ARREST!
COME ON--YOU'VE HAD YOUR FUN--NOW IT'S OVER!
FUN HE CALLS IT!
POW
WHAP
NO PUNY POLICEMEN CAN STOP IBAC THE CURSED!
YOO-HOO! LOVER! THERE YOU ARE!
OH-OH! THERE'S THE CURSE!
AT LAST! UNCLE MARVEL! OLD FRIEND! YOU'VE GOT TO HELP ME!
YOU--WANT ME--TO HELP YOU?
11

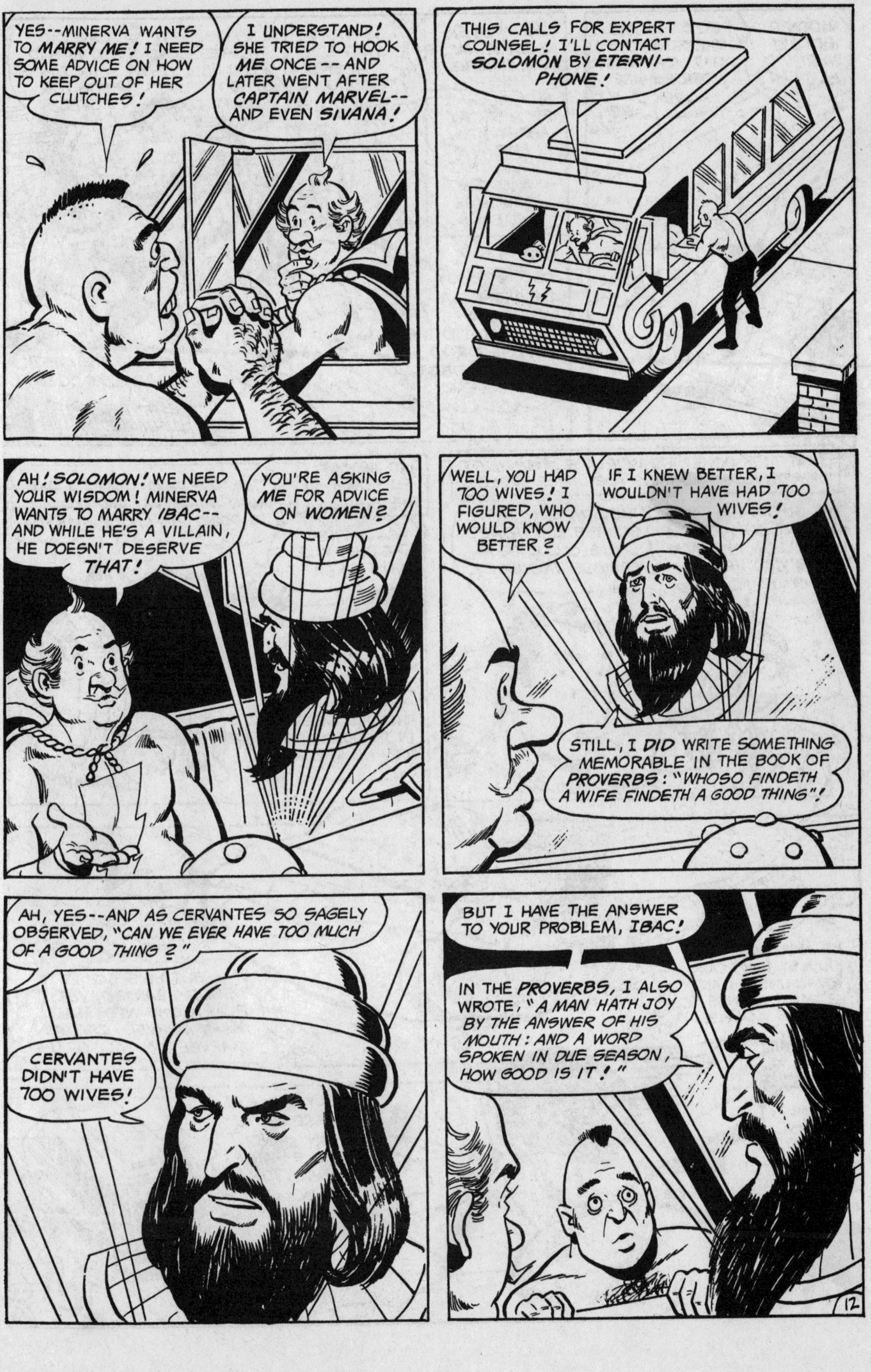
YES--MINERVA WANTS TO MARRY ME! I NEED SOME ADVICE ON HOW TO KEEP OUT OF HER CLUTCHES!
I UNDERSTAND! SHE TRIED TO HOOK ME ONCE--AND LATER WENT AFTER CAPTAIN MARVEL--AND EVEN SIVANA!
THIS CALLS FOR EXPERT COUNSEL! I'LL CONTACT SOLOMON BY ETERNI-PHONE!
AH! SOLOMON! WE NEED YOUR WISDOM! MINERVA WANTS TO MARRY IBAC--AND WHILE HE'S A VILLAIN, HE DOESN'T DESERVE THAT!
YOU'RE ASKING ME FOR ADVICE ON WOMEN?
WELL, YOU HAD 700 WIVES! I FIGURED, WHO WOULD KNOW BETTER?
IF I KNEW BETTER, I WOULDN'T HAVE HAD 700 WIVES!
STILL, I DID WRITE SOMETHING MEMORABLE IN THE BOOK OF PROVERBS: "WHOSO FINDETH A WIFE FINDETH A GOOD THING"!
AH, YES--AND AS CERVANTES SO SAGELY OBSERVED, "CAN WE EVER HAVE TOO MUCH OF A GOOD THING?"
CERVANTES DIDN'T HAVE 700 WIVES!
BUT I HAVE THE ANSWER TO YOUR PROBLEM, IBAC!
IN THE PROVERBS, I ALSO WROTE, "A MAN HATH JOY BY THE ANSWER OF HIS MOUTH: AND A WORD SPOKEN IN DUE SEASON, HOW GOOD IS IT!"
12

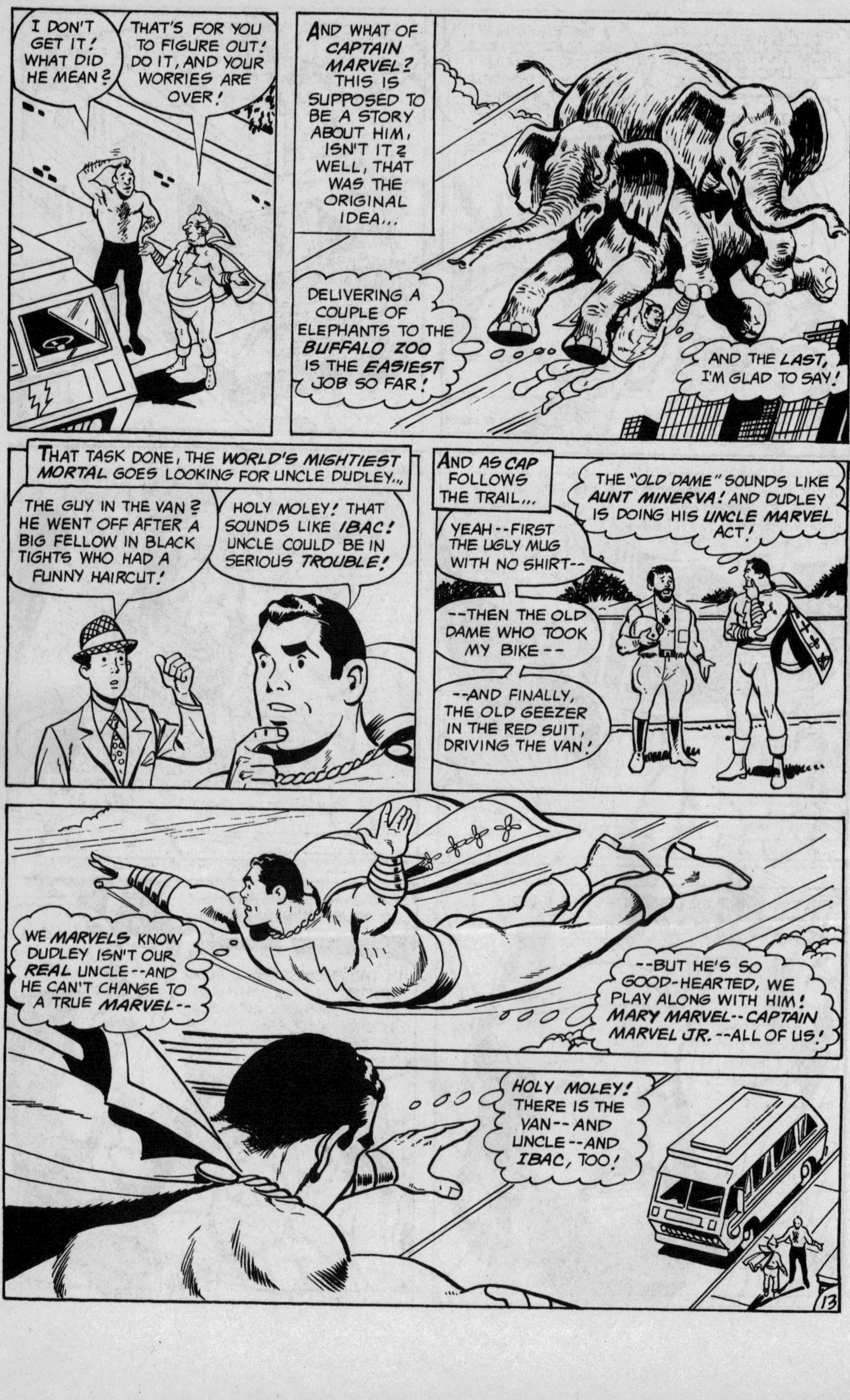
I DON'T GET IT! WHAT DID HE MEAN?
THAT'S FOR YOU TO FIGURE OUT! DO IT, AND YOUR WORRIES ARE OVER!
AND WHAT OF CAPTAIN MARVEL? THIS IS SUPPOSED TO BE A STORY ABOUT HIM, ISN'T IT? WELL, THAT WAS THE ORIGINAL IDEA...
DELIVERING A COUPLE OF ELEPHANTS TO THE BUFFALO ZOO IS THE EASIEST JOB SO FAR!
AND THE LAST, I'M GLAD TO SAY!
THAT TASK DONE, THE WORLD'S MIGHTIEST MORTAL GOES LOOKING FOR UNCLE DUDLEY...
THE GUY IN THE VAN? HE WENT OFF AFTER A BIG FELLOW IN BLACK TIGHTS WHO HAD A FUNNY HAIRCUT!
HOLY MOLEY! THAT SOUNDS LIKE IBAC! UNCLE COULD BE IN SERIOUS TROUBLE!
AND AS CAP FOLLOWS THE TRAIL...
YEAH--FIRST THE UGLY MUG WITH NO SHIRT--
--THEN THE OLD DAME WHO TOOK MY BIKE--
--AND FINALLY, THE OLD GEEZER IN THE RED SUIT, DRIVING THE VAN!
THE "OLD DAME" SOUNDS LIKE AUNT MINERVA! AND DUDLEY IS DOING HIS UNCLE MARVEL ACT!
WE MARVELS KNOW DUDLEY ISN'T OUR REAL UNCLE--AND HE CAN'T CHANGE TO A TRUE MARVEL--
--BUT HE'S SO GOOD-HEARTED, WE PLAY ALONG WITH HIM! MARY MARVEL--CAPTAIN MARVEL JR.--ALL OF US!
HOLY MOLEY! THERE IS THE VAN--AND UNCLE--AND IBAC, TOO!
13

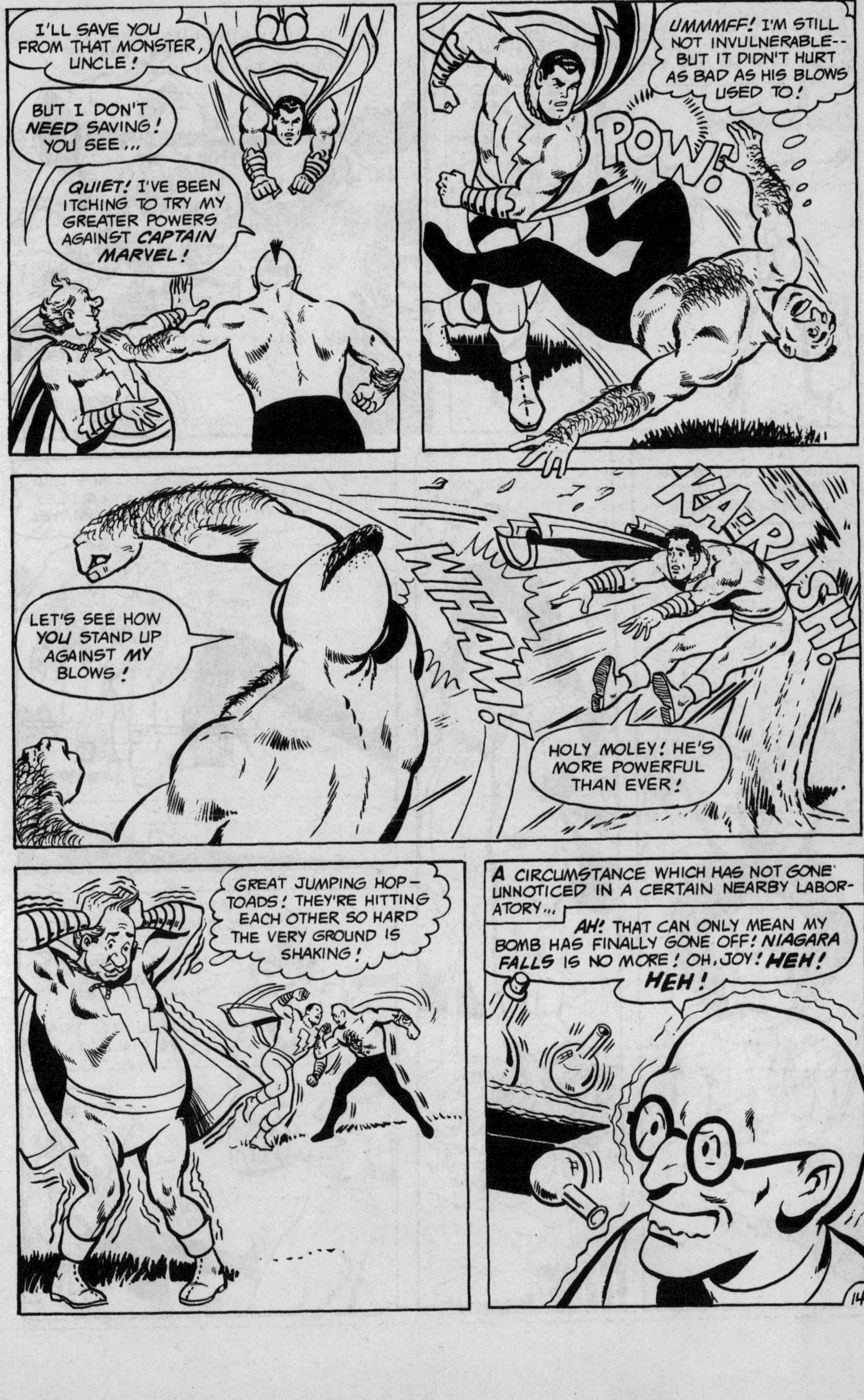
I'LL SAVE YOU FROM THAT MONSTER, UNCLE!
BUT I DON'T NEED SAVING! YOU SEE...
QUIET! I'VE BEEN ITCHING TO TRY MY GREATER POWERS AGAINST CAPTAIN MARVEL!
UMMMFF! I'M STILL NOT INVULNERABLE-- BUT IT DIDN'T HURT AS BAD AS HIS BLOWS USED TO!
POW!
LET'S SEE HOW YOU STAND UP AGAINST MY BLOWS!
WHAM!
KA-RASH!
HOLY MOLEY! HE'S MORE POWERFUL THAN EVER!
GREAT JUMPING HOP-TOADS! THEY'RE HITTING EACH OTHER SO HARD THE VERY GROUND IS SHAKING!
A CIRCUMSTANCE WHICH HAS NOT GONE UNNOTICED IN A CERTAIN NEARBY LABORATORY...
AH! THAT CAN ONLY MEAN MY BOMB HAS FINALLY GONE OFF! NIAGARA FALLS IS NO MORE! OH, JOY! HEH! HEH!
14

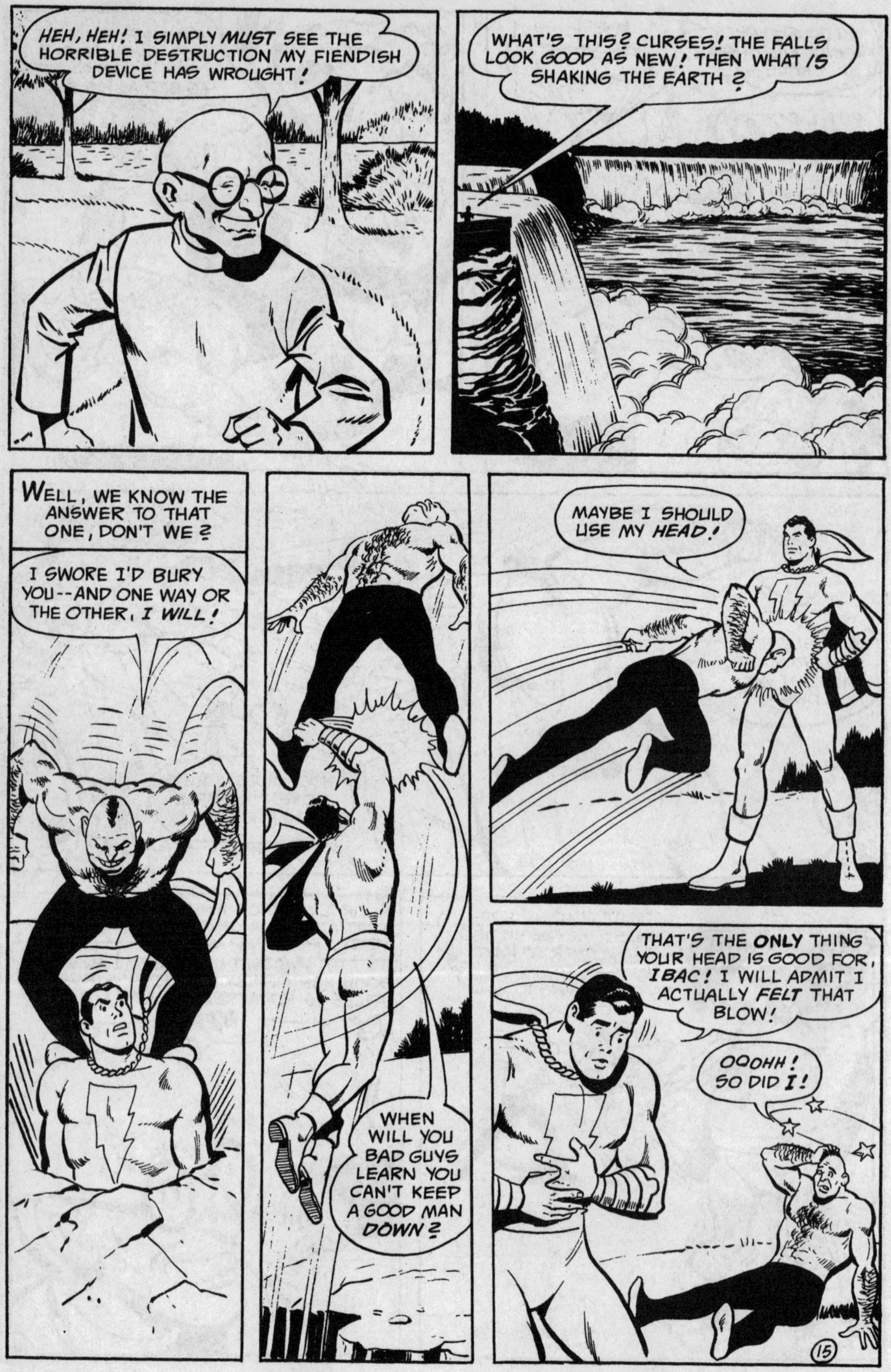
HEH, HEH! I SIMPLY MUST SEE THE HORRIBLE DESTRUCTION MY FIENDISH DEVICE HAS WROUGHT!
WHAT'S THIS? CURSES! THE FALLS LOOK GOOD AS NEW! THEN WHAT IS SHAKING THE EARTH?
WELL, WE KNOW THE ANSWER TO THAT ONE, DON'T WE?
I SWORE I'D BURY YOU--AND ONE WAY OR THE OTHER, I WILL!
WHEN WILL YOU BAD GUYS LEARN YOU CAN'T KEEP A GOOD MAN DOWN?
MAYBE I SHOULD USE MY HEAD!
THAT'S THE ONLY THING YOUR HEAD IS GOOD FOR, IBAC! I WILL ADMIT I ACTUALLY FELT THAT BLOW!
OOOHH! SO DID I!
15

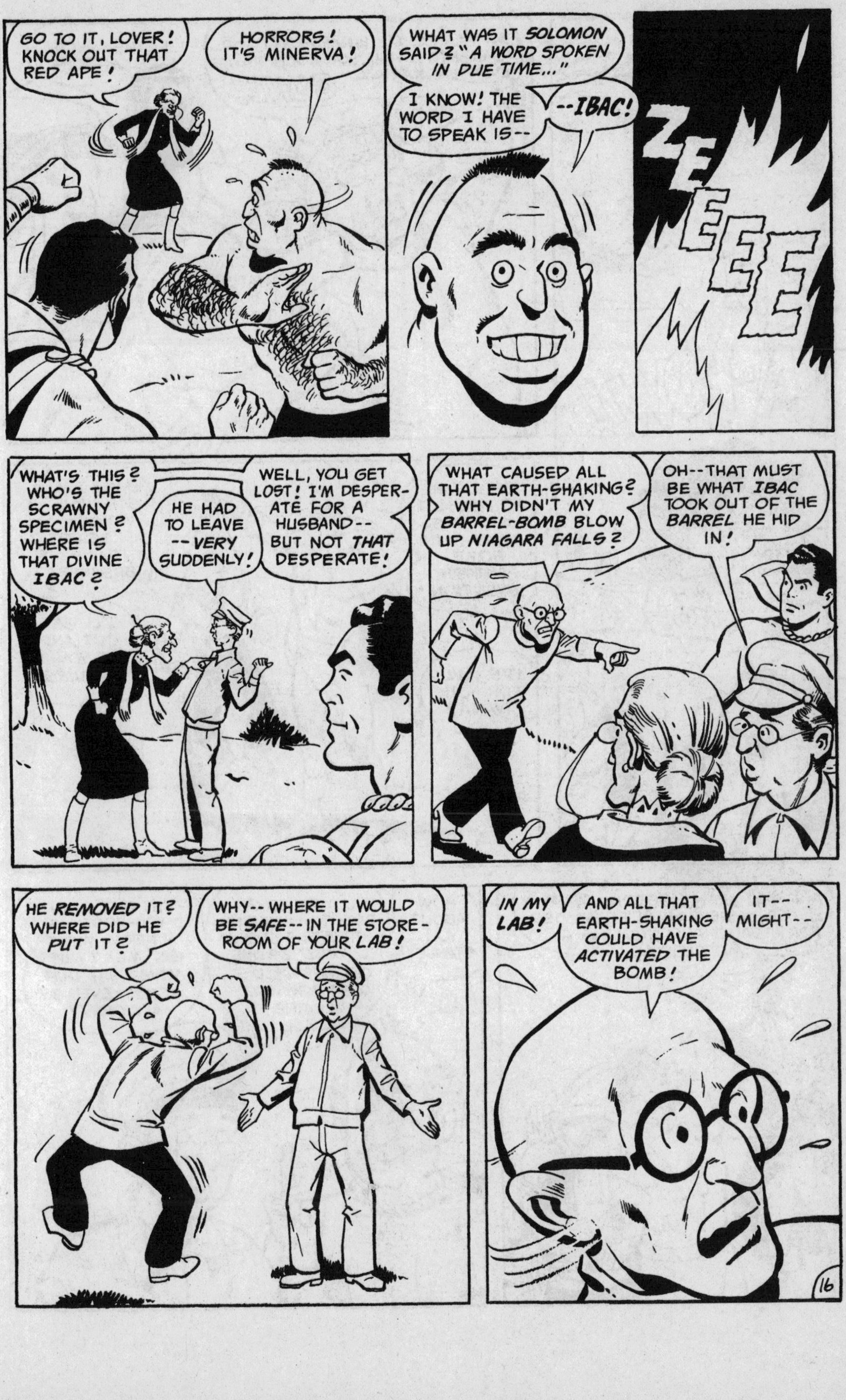
GO TO IT, LOVER! KNOCK OUT THAT RED APE!
HORRORS! IT'S MINERVA!
WHAT WAS IT SOLOMON SAID? "A WORD SPOKEN IN DUE TIME..."
I KNOW! THE WORD I HAVE TO SPEAK IS--
--IBAC!
ZEEEE
WHAT'S THIS? WHO'S THE SCRAWNY SPECIMEN? WHERE IS THAT DIVINE IBAC?
HE HAD TO LEAVE --VERY SUDDENLY!
WELL, YOU GET LOST! I'M DESPERATE FOR A HUSBAND-- BUT NOT THAT DESPERATE!
WHAT CAUSED ALL THAT EARTH-SHAKING? WHY DIDN'T MY BARREL-BOMB BLOW UP NIAGARA FALLS?
OH--THAT MUST BE WHAT IBAC TOOK OUT OF THE BARREL HE HID IN!
HE REMOVED IT? WHERE DID HE PUT IT?
WHY-- WHERE IT WOULD BE SAFE--IN THE STOREROOM OF YOUR LAB!
IN MY LAB!
AND ALL THAT EARTH-SHAKING COULD HAVE ACTIVATED THE BOMB!
IT-- MIGHT--
16

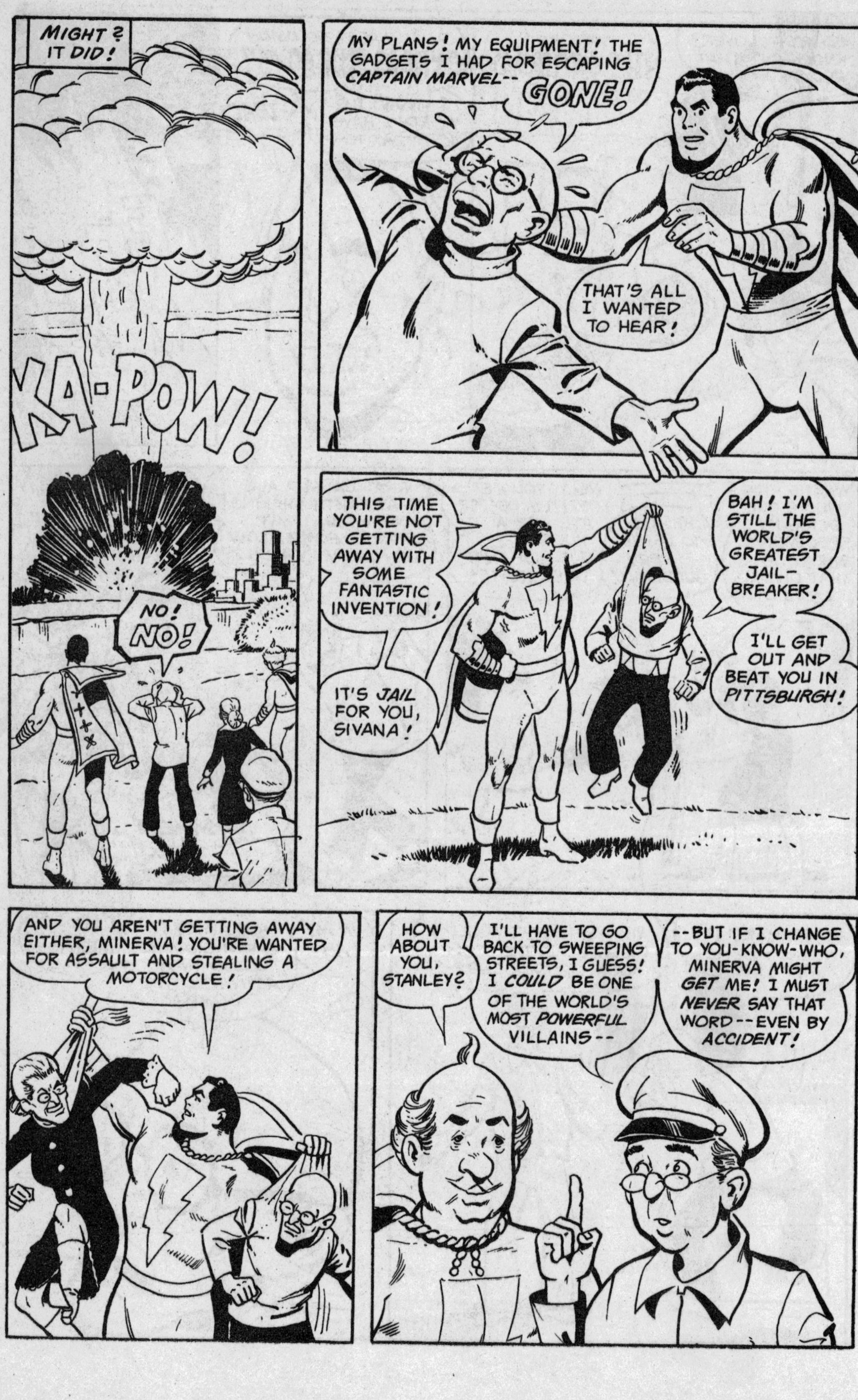
MIGHT? IT DID!
KA-POW!
NO! NO!
MY PLANS! MY EQUIPMENT! THE GADGETS I HAD FOR ESCAPING CAPTAIN MARVEL-- GONE!
THAT'S ALL I WANTED TO HEAR!
THIS TIME YOU'RE NOT GETTING AWAY WITH SOME FANTASTIC INVENTION!
IT'S JAIL FOR YOU, SIVANA!
BAH! I'M STILL THE WORLD'S GREATEST JAIL-BREAKER!
I'LL GET OUT AND BEAT YOU IN PITTSBURGH!
AND YOU AREN'T GETTING AWAY EITHER, MINERVA! YOU'RE WANTED FOR ASSAULT AND STEALING A MOTORCYCLE!
HOW ABOUT YOU, STANLEY?
I'LL HAVE TO GO BACK TO SWEEPING STREETS, I GUESS! I COULD BE ONE OF THE WORLD'S MOST POWERFUL VILLAINS--
--BUT IF I CHANGE TO YOU-KNOW-WHO, MINERVA MIGHT GET ME! I MUST NEVER SAY THAT WORD--EVEN BY ACCIDENT!

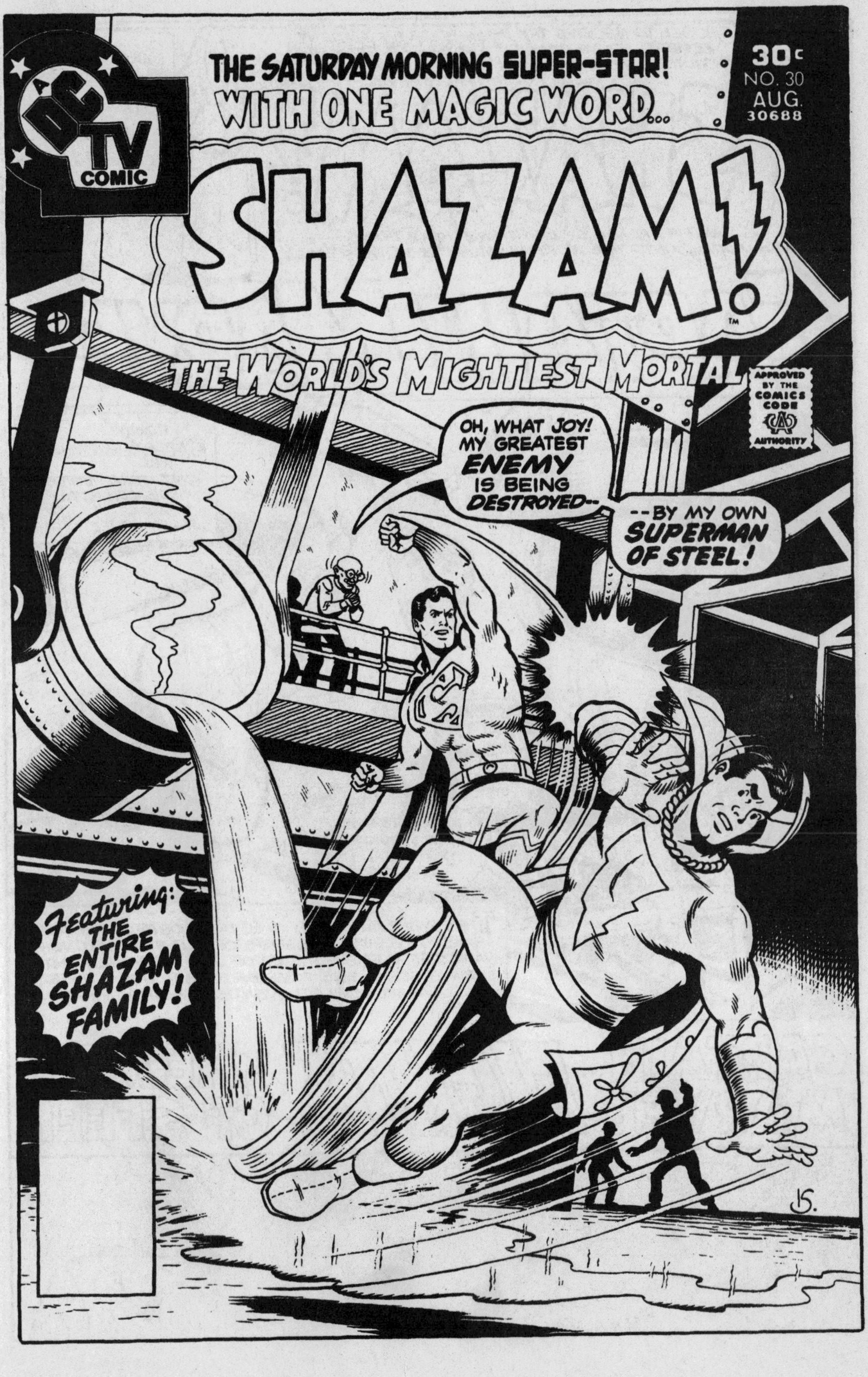
THE SATURDAY MORNING SUPER-STAR!
WITH ONE MAGIC WORD...
30¢
NO. 30
AUG.
30688
DC TV COMIC
SHAZAM!
THE WORLD'S MIGHTIEST MORTAL
APPROVED BY THE COMICS CODE AUTHORITY
OH, WHAT JOY! MY GREATEST ENEMY IS BEING DESTROYED--
--BY MY OWN SUPERMAN OF STEEL!
Featuring: THE ENTIRE SHAZAM FAMILY!

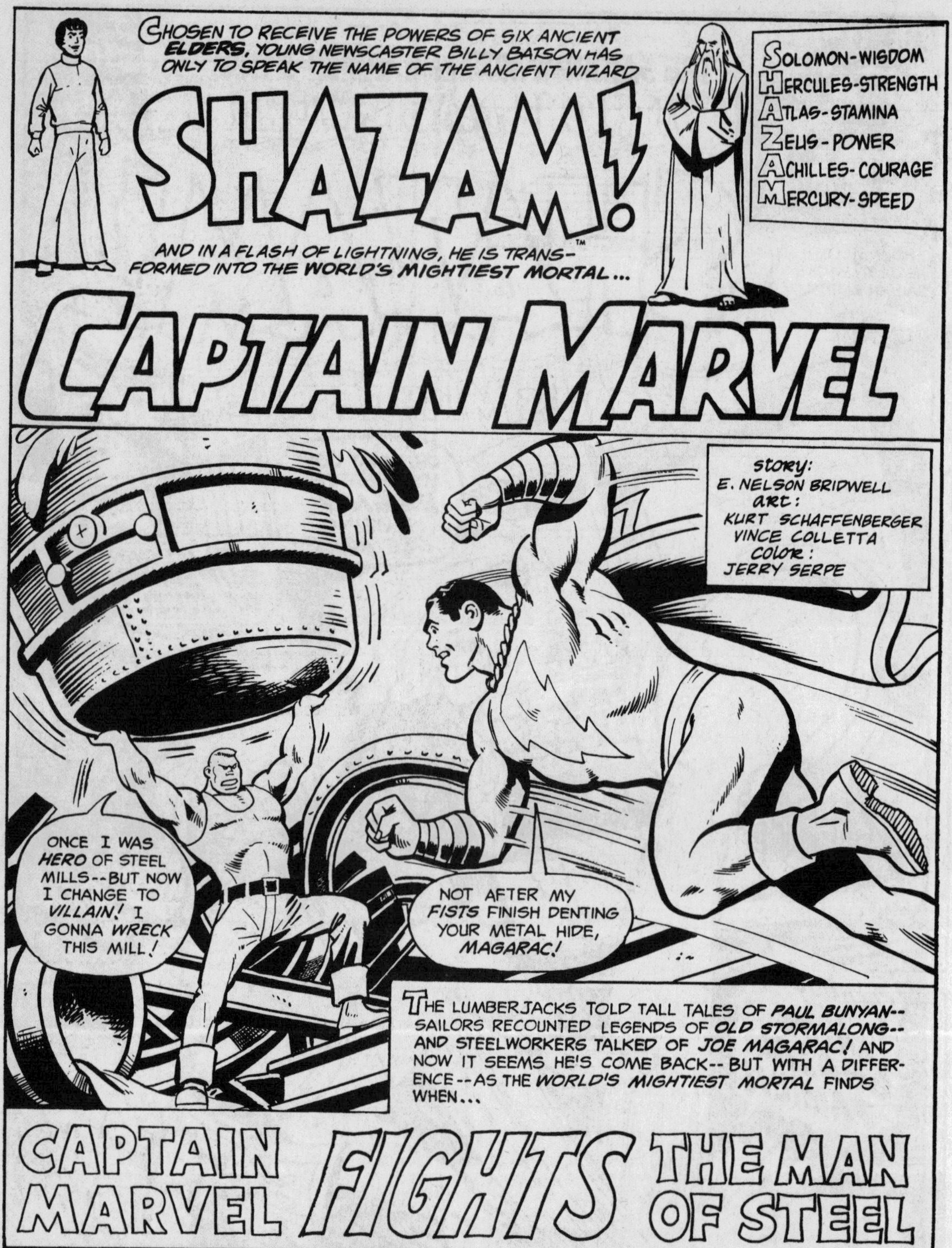
CHOSEN TO RECEIVE THE POWERS OF SIX ANCIENT ELDERS, YOUNG NEWSCASTER BILLY BATSON HAS ONLY TO SPEAK THE NAME OF THE ANCIENT WIZARD
SHAZAM!™
SOLOMON-WISDOM
HERCULES-STRENGTH
ATLAS-STAMINA
ZEUS-POWER
ACHILLES-COURAGE
MERCURY-SPEED
AND IN A FLASH OF LIGHTNING, HE IS TRANSFORMED INTO THE WORLD'S MIGHTIEST MORTAL...
CAPTAIN MARVEL
STORY: E. NELSON BRIDWELL ART: KURT SCHAFFENBERGER VINCE COLLETTA COLOR: JERRY SERPE
ONCE I WAS HERO OF STEEL MILLS--BUT NOW I CHANGE TO VILLAIN! I GONNA WRECK THIS MILL!
NOT AFTER MY FISTS FINISH DENTING YOUR METAL HIDE, MAGARAC!
THE LUMBERJACKS TOLD TALL TALES OF PAUL BUNYAN--SAILORS RECOUNTED LEGENDS OF OLD STORMALONG--AND STEELWORKERS TALKED OF JOE MAGARAC! AND NOW IT SEEMS HE'S COME BACK--BUT WITH A DIFFERENCE--AS THE WORLD'S MIGHTIEST MORTAL FINDS WHEN...
CAPTAIN MARVEL FIGHTS THE MAN OF STEEL

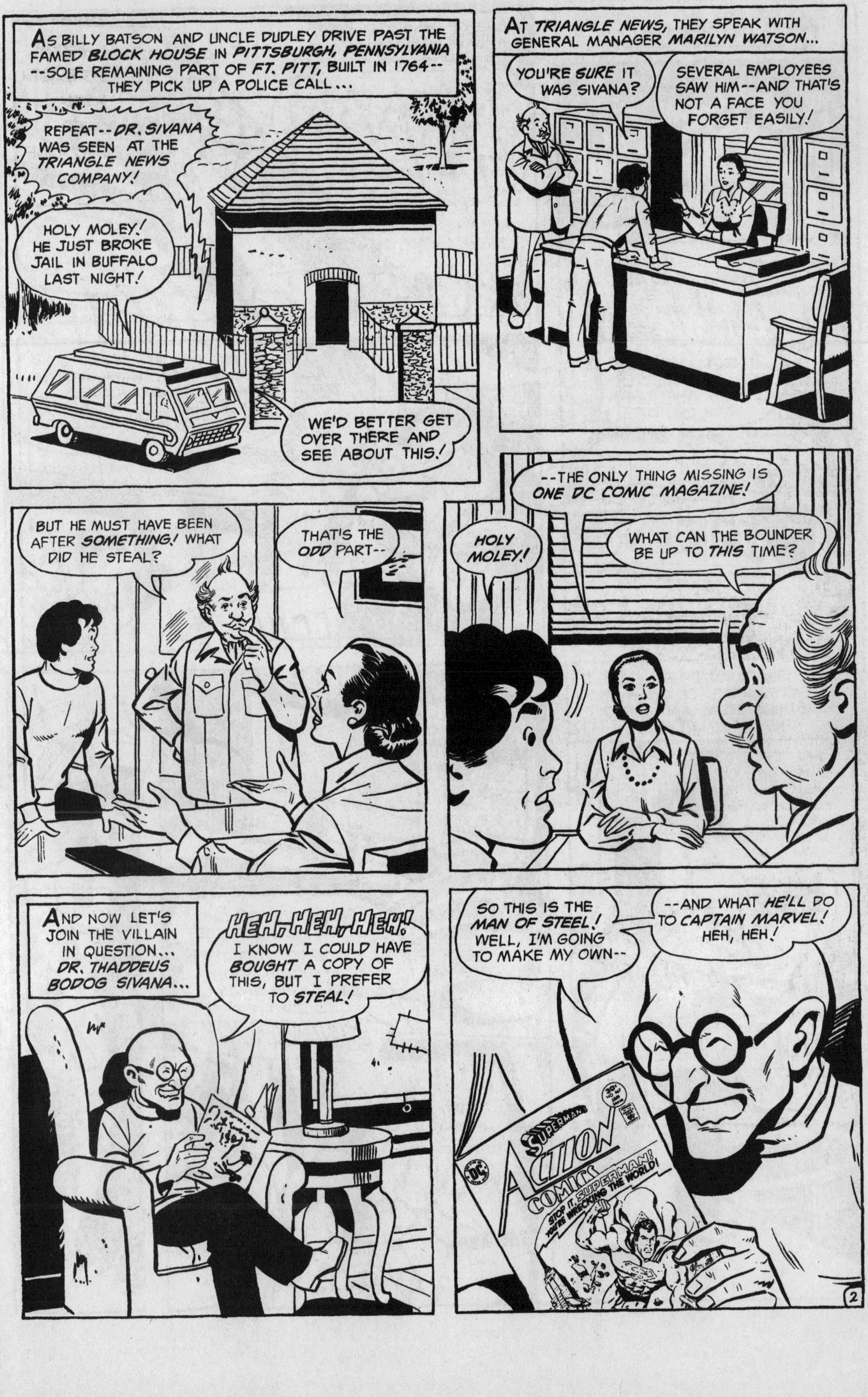
AS BILLY BATSON AND UNCLE DUDLEY DRIVE PAST THE FAMED BLOCK HOUSE IN PITTSBURGH, PENNSYLVANIA --SOLE REMAINING PART OF FT. PITT, BUILT IN 1764-- THEY PICK UP A POLICE CALL...
REPEAT--DR. SIVANA WAS SEEN AT THE TRIANGLE NEWS COMPANY!
HOLY MOLEY! HE JUST BROKE JAIL IN BUFFALO LAST NIGHT!
WE'D BETTER GET OVER THERE AND SEE ABOUT THIS!
AT TRIANGLE NEWS, THEY SPEAK WITH GENERAL MANAGER MARILYN WATSON...
YOU'RE SURE IT WAS SIVANA?
SEVERAL EMPLOYEES SAW HIM--AND THAT'S NOT A FACE YOU FORGET EASILY!
BUT HE MUST HAVE BEEN AFTER SOMETHING! WHAT DID HE STEAL?
THAT'S THE ODD PART--
--THE ONLY THING MISSING IS ONE DC COMIC MAGAZINE!
HOLY MOLEY!
WHAT CAN THE BOUNDER BE UP TO THIS TIME?
AND NOW LET'S JOIN THE VILLAIN IN QUESTION... DR. THADDEUS BODOG SIVANA...
HEH, HEH, HEH! I KNOW I COULD HAVE BOUGHT A COPY OF THIS, BUT I PREFER TO STEAL!
SO THIS IS THE MAN OF STEEL! WELL, I'M GOING TO MAKE MY OWN--
--AND WHAT HE'LL DO TO CAPTAIN MARVEL! HEH, HEH!
SUPERMAN
ACTION COMICS
STOP IT, SUPERMAN! YOU'RE WRECKING THE WORLD!
2

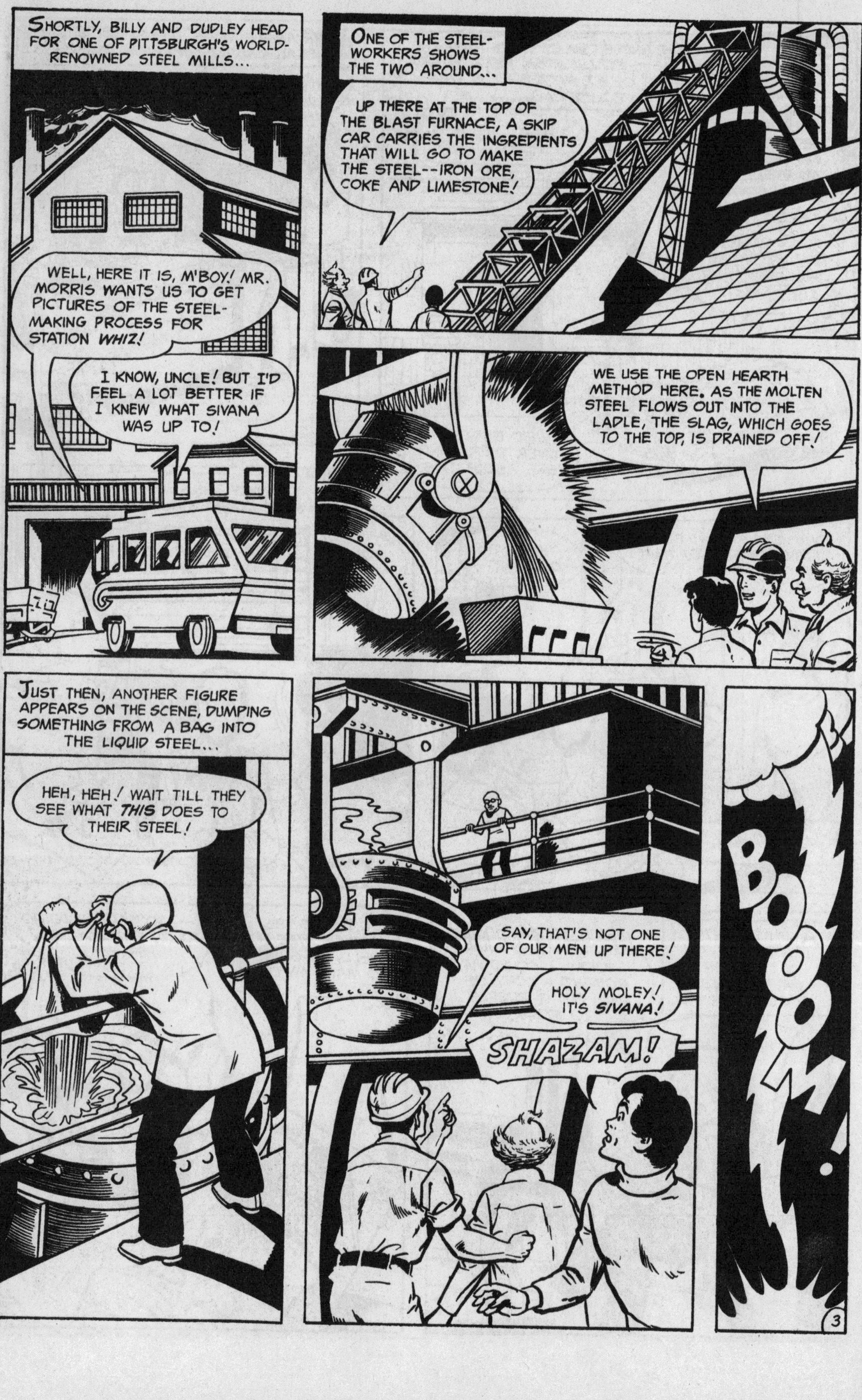
SHORTLY, BILLY AND DUDLEY HEAD FOR ONE OF PITTSBURGH'S WORLD-RENOWNED STEEL MILLS...
WELL, HERE IT IS, M'BOY! MR. MORRIS WANTS US TO GET PICTURES OF THE STEEL-MAKING PROCESS FOR STATION WHIZ!
I KNOW, UNCLE! BUT I'D FEEL A LOT BETTER IF I KNEW WHAT SIVANA WAS UP TO!
ONE OF THE STEEL-WORKERS SHOWS THE TWO AROUND...
UP THERE AT THE TOP OF THE BLAST FURNACE, A SKIP CAR CARRIES THE INGREDIENTS THAT WILL GO TO MAKE THE STEEL--IRON ORE, COKE AND LIMESTONE!
WE USE THE OPEN HEARTH METHOD HERE. AS THE MOLTEN STEEL FLOWS OUT INTO THE LADLE, THE SLAG, WHICH GOES TO THE TOP, IS DRAINED OFF!
JUST THEN, ANOTHER FIGURE APPEARS ON THE SCENE, DUMPING SOMETHING FROM A BAG INTO THE LIQUID STEEL...
HEH, HEH! WAIT TILL THEY SEE WHAT THIS DOES TO THEIR STEEL!
SAY, THAT'S NOT ONE OF OUR MEN UP THERE!
HOLY MOLEY! IT'S SIVANA!
SHAZAM!
BOOOM!
3

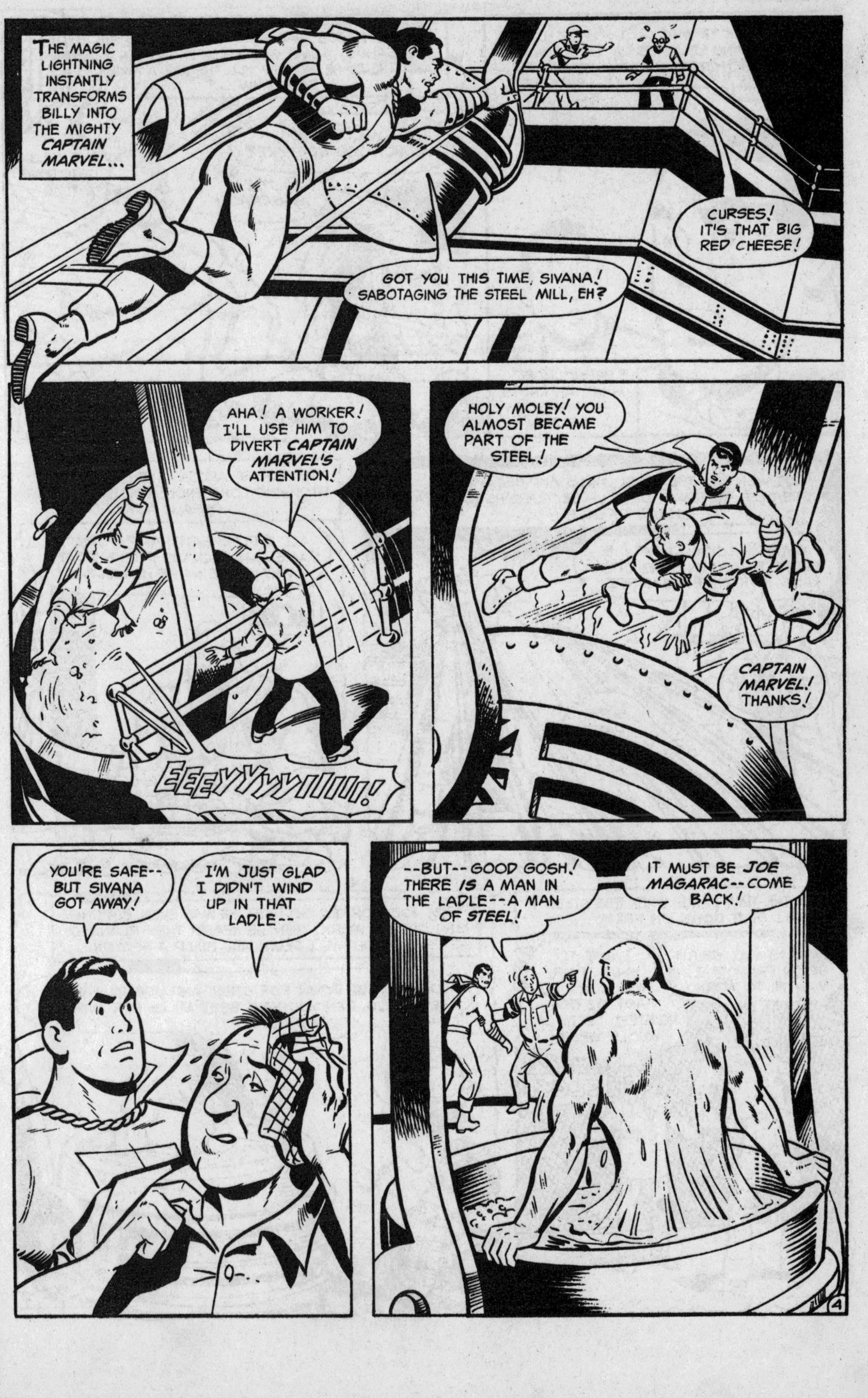
THE MAGIC LIGHTNING INSTANTLY TRANSFORMS BILLY INTO THE MIGHTY CAPTAIN MARVEL...
GOT YOU THIS TIME, SIVANA! SABOTAGING THE STEEL MILL, EH?
CURSES! IT'S THAT BIG RED CHEESE!
AHA! A WORKER! I'LL USE HIM TO DIVERT CAPTAIN MARVEL'S ATTENTION!
EEEYYYYYIIIII!
HOLY MOLEY! YOU ALMOST BECAME PART OF THE STEEL!
CAPTAIN MARVEL! THANKS!
YOU'RE SAFE--BUT SIVANA GOT AWAY!
I'M JUST GLAD I DIDN'T WIND UP IN THAT LADLE--
--BUT--GOOD GOSH! THERE IS A MAN IN THE LADLE--A MAN OF STEEL!
IT MUST BE JOE MAGARAC--COME BACK!
4

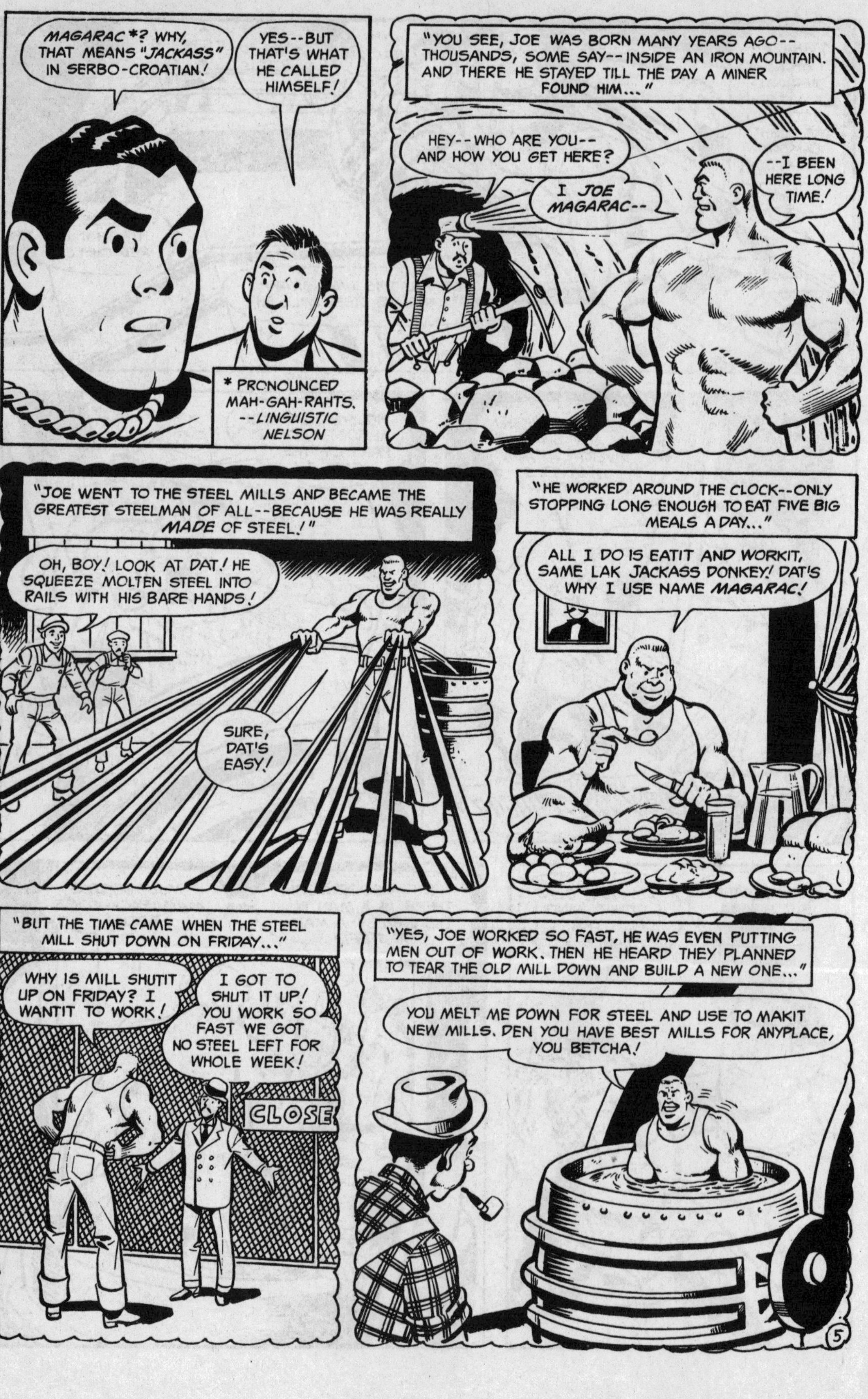
MAGARAC*? WHY, THAT MEANS "JACKASS" IN SERBO-CROATIAN!
YES--BUT THAT'S WHAT HE CALLED HIMSELF!
* PRONOUNCED MAH-GAH-RAHTS. --LINGUISTIC NELSON
"YOU SEE, JOE WAS BORN MANY YEARS AGO--THOUSANDS, SOME SAY--INSIDE AN IRON MOUNTAIN. AND THERE HE STAYED TILL THE DAY A MINER FOUND HIM..."
HEY--WHO ARE YOU--AND HOW YOU GET HERE?
I JOE MAGARAC--
--I BEEN HERE LONG TIME!
"JOE WENT TO THE STEEL MILLS AND BECAME THE GREATEST STEELMAN OF ALL--BECAUSE HE WAS REALLY MADE OF STEEL!"
OH, BOY! LOOK AT DAT! HE SQUEEZE MOLTEN STEEL INTO RAILS WITH HIS BARE HANDS!
SURE, DAT'S EASY!
"HE WORKED AROUND THE CLOCK--ONLY STOPPING LONG ENOUGH TO EAT FIVE BIG MEALS A DAY..."
ALL I DO IS EATIT AND WORKIT, SAME LAK JACKASS DONKEY! DAT'S WHY I USE NAME MAGARAC!
"BUT THE TIME CAME WHEN THE STEEL MILL SHUT DOWN ON FRIDAY..."
WHY IS MILL SHUTIT UP ON FRIDAY? I WANTIT TO WORK!
I GOT TO SHUT IT UP! YOU WORK SO FAST WE GOT NO STEEL LEFT FOR WHOLE WEEK!
CLOSE
"YES, JOE WORKED SO FAST, HE WAS EVEN PUTTING MEN OUT OF WORK. THEN HE HEARD THEY PLANNED TO TEAR THE OLD MILL DOWN AND BUILD A NEW ONE..."
YOU MELT ME DOWN FOR STEEL AND USE TO MAKIT NEW MILLS. DEN YOU HAVE BEST MILLS FOR ANYPLACE, YOU BETCHA!
5

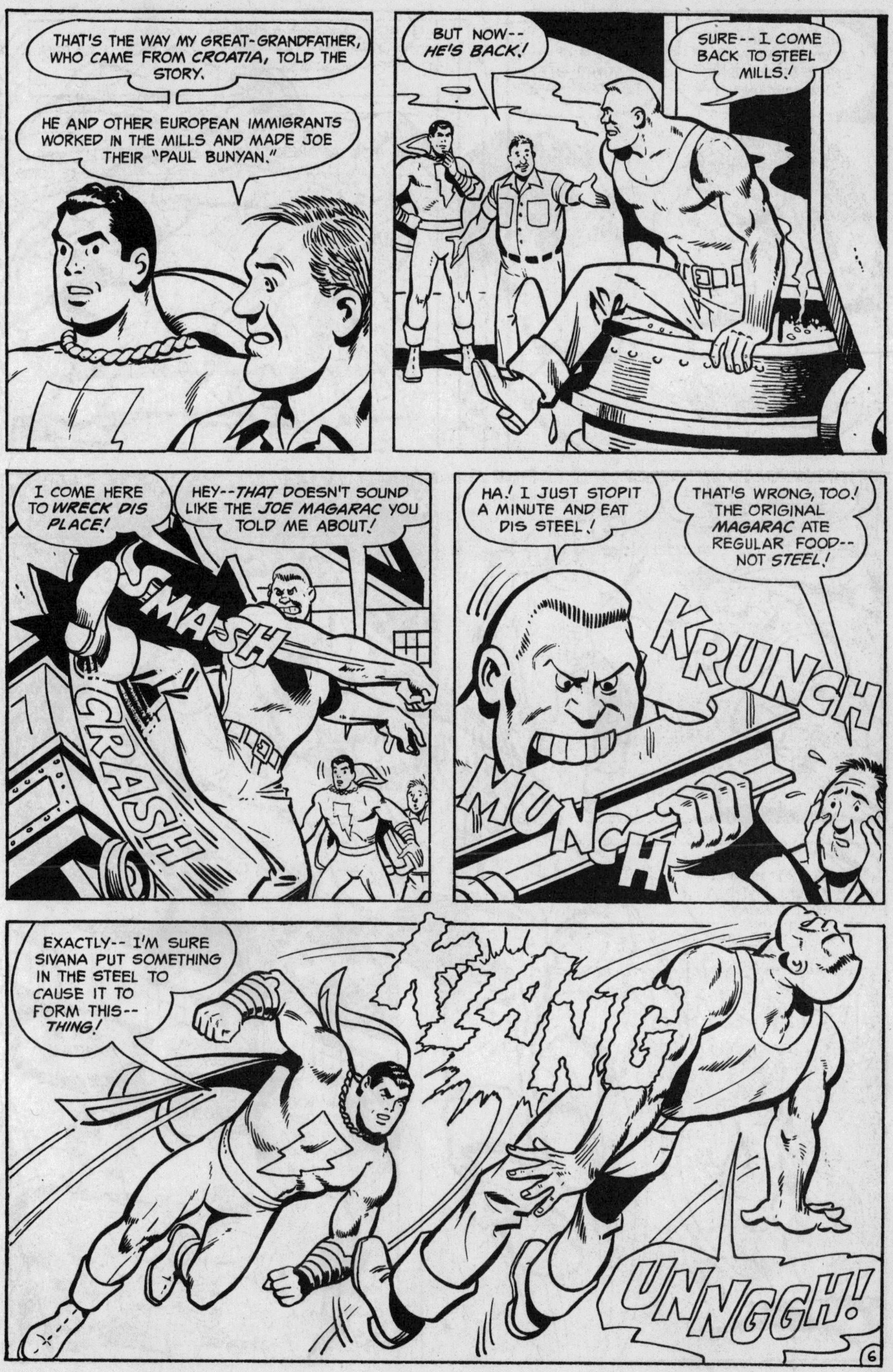
THAT'S THE WAY MY GREAT-GRANDFATHER, WHO CAME FROM CROATIA, TOLD THE STORY.
HE AND OTHER EUROPEAN IMMIGRANTS WORKED IN THE MILLS AND MADE JOE THEIR "PAUL BUNYAN."
BUT NOW-- HE'S BACK!
SURE-- I COME BACK TO STEEL MILLS!
I COME HERE TO WRECK DIS PLACE!
HEY--THAT DOESN'T SOUND LIKE THE JOE MAGARAC YOU TOLD ME ABOUT!
SMASH
CRASH
HA! I JUST STOPIT A MINUTE AND EAT DIS STEEL!
THAT'S WRONG, TOO! THE ORIGINAL MAGARAC ATE REGULAR FOOD-- NOT STEEL!
KRUNCH
MUNCH
EXACTLY-- I'M SURE SIVANA PUT SOMETHING IN THE STEEL TO CAUSE IT TO FORM THIS-- THING!
KLANG
UNNGGH!
6

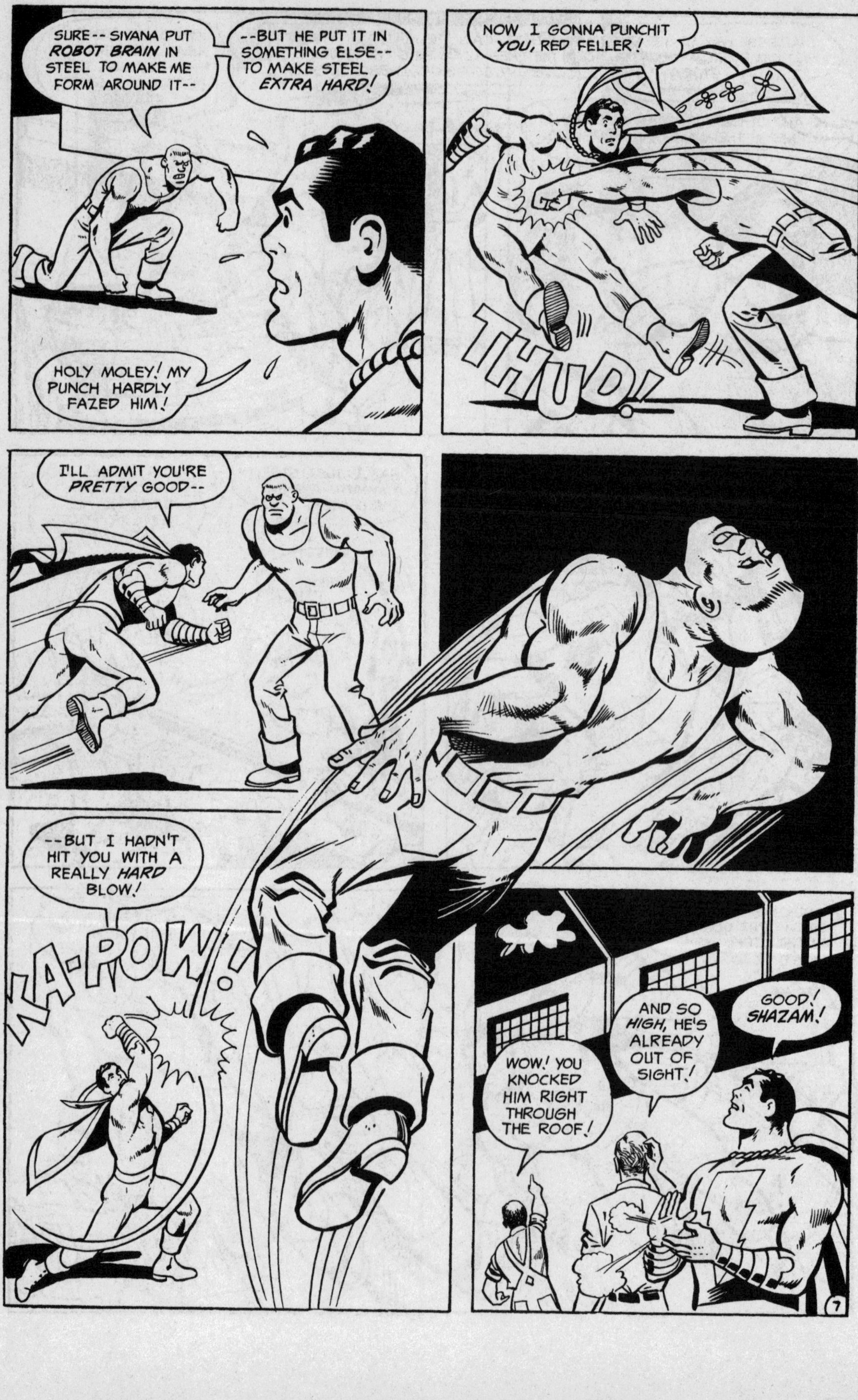
SURE-- SIVANA PUT ROBOT BRAIN IN STEEL TO MAKE ME FORM AROUND IT--
--BUT HE PUT IT IN SOMETHING ELSE-- TO MAKE STEEL EXTRA HARD!
HOLY MOLEY! MY PUNCH HARDLY FAZED HIM!
NOW I GONNA PUNCHIT YOU, RED FELLER!
THUD!
I'LL ADMIT YOU'RE PRETTY GOOD--
--BUT I HADN'T HIT YOU WITH A REALLY HARD BLOW!
KA-POW!
WOW! YOU KNOCKED HIM RIGHT THROUGH THE ROOF!
AND SO HIGH, HE'S ALREADY OUT OF SIGHT!
GOOD! SHAZAM!
7

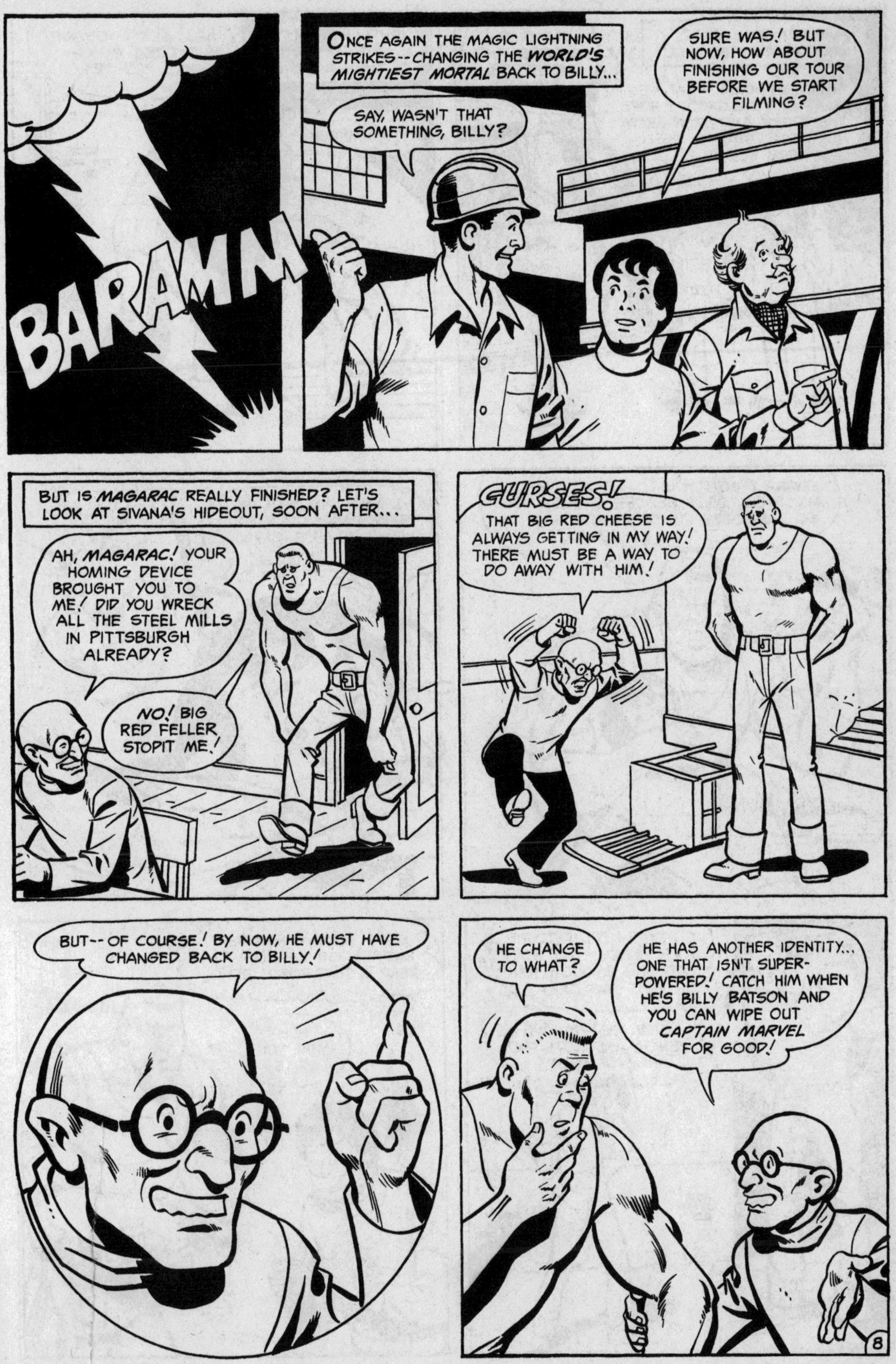
BARAMM
ONCE AGAIN THE MAGIC LIGHTNING STRIKES--CHANGING THE WORLD'S MIGHTIEST MORTAL BACK TO BILLY...
SAY, WASN'T THAT SOMETHING, BILLY?
SURE WAS! BUT NOW, HOW ABOUT FINISHING OUR TOUR BEFORE WE START FILMING?
BUT IS MAGARAC REALLY FINISHED? LET'S LOOK AT SIVANA'S HIDEOUT, SOON AFTER...
AH, MAGARAC! YOUR HOMING DEVICE BROUGHT YOU TO ME! DID YOU WRECK ALL THE STEEL MILLS IN PITTSBURGH ALREADY?
NO! BIG RED FELLER STOPIT ME!
CURSES!
THAT BIG RED CHEESE IS ALWAYS GETTING IN MY WAY! THERE MUST BE A WAY TO DO AWAY WITH HIM!
BUT--OF COURSE! BY NOW, HE MUST HAVE CHANGED BACK TO BILLY!
HE CHANGE TO WHAT?
HE HAS ANOTHER IDENTITY... ONE THAT ISN'T SUPER-POWERED! CATCH HIM WHEN HE'S BILLY BATSON AND YOU CAN WIPE OUT CAPTAIN MARVEL FOR GOOD!
8

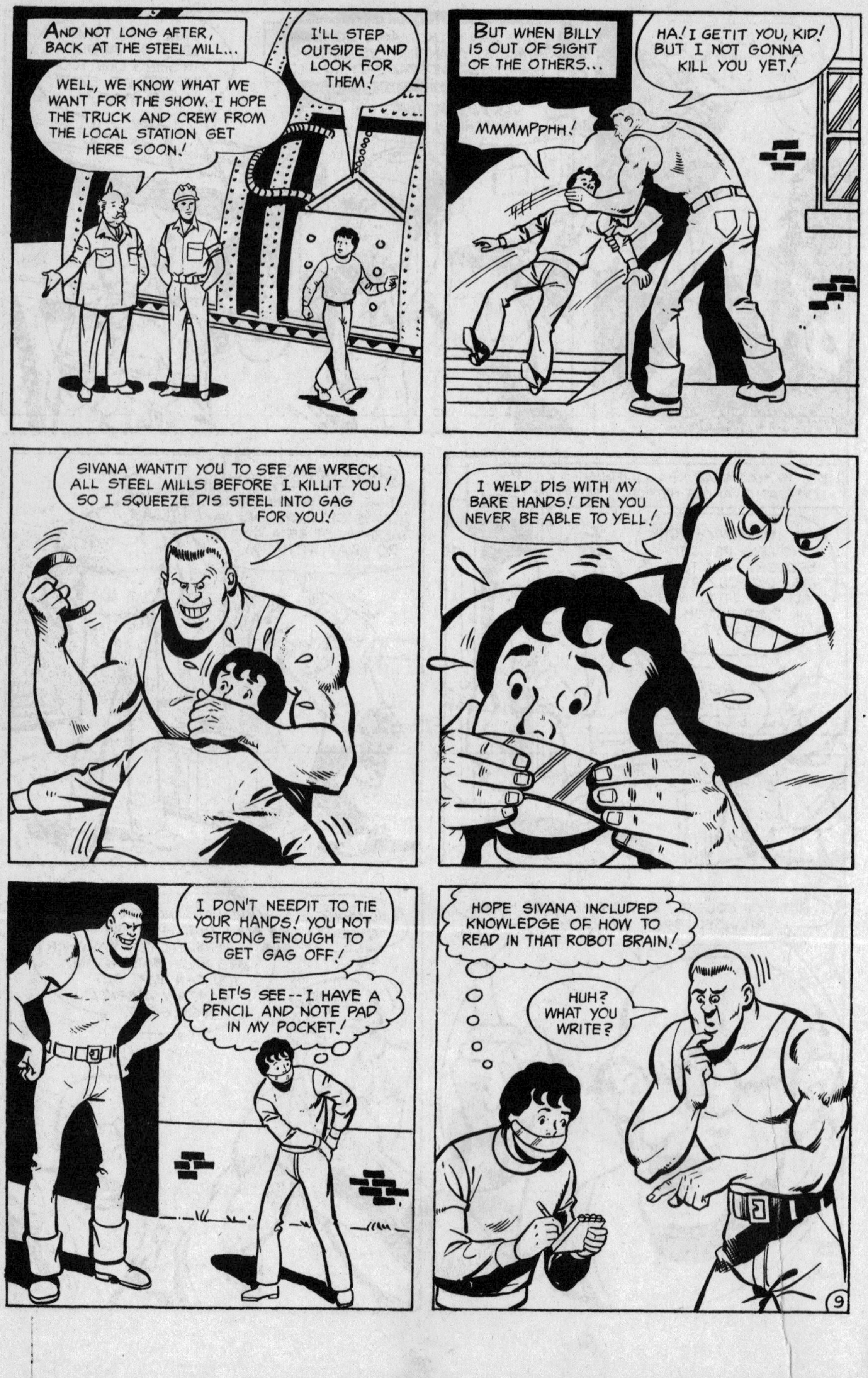
AND NOT LONG AFTER, BACK AT THE STEEL MILL...
WELL, WE KNOW WHAT WE WANT FOR THE SHOW. I HOPE THE TRUCK AND CREW FROM THE LOCAL STATION GET HERE SOON!
I'LL STEP OUTSIDE AND LOOK FOR THEM!
BUT WHEN BILLY IS OUT OF SIGHT OF THE OTHERS...
HA! I GETIT YOU, KID! BUT I NOT GONNA KILL YOU YET!
MMMMPPHH!
SIVANA WANTIT YOU TO SEE ME WRECK ALL STEEL MILLS BEFORE I KILLIT YOU! SO I SQUEEZE DIS STEEL INTO GAG FOR YOU!
I WELD DIS WITH MY BARE HANDS! DEN YOU NEVER BE ABLE TO YELL!
I DON'T NEEDIT TO TIE YOUR HANDS! YOU NOT STRONG ENOUGH TO GET GAG OFF!
LET'S SEE--I HAVE A PENCIL AND NOTE PAD IN MY POCKET!
HOPE SIVANA INCLUDED KNOWLEDGE OF HOW TO READ IN THAT ROBOT BRAIN!
HUH? WHAT YOU WRITE?
9

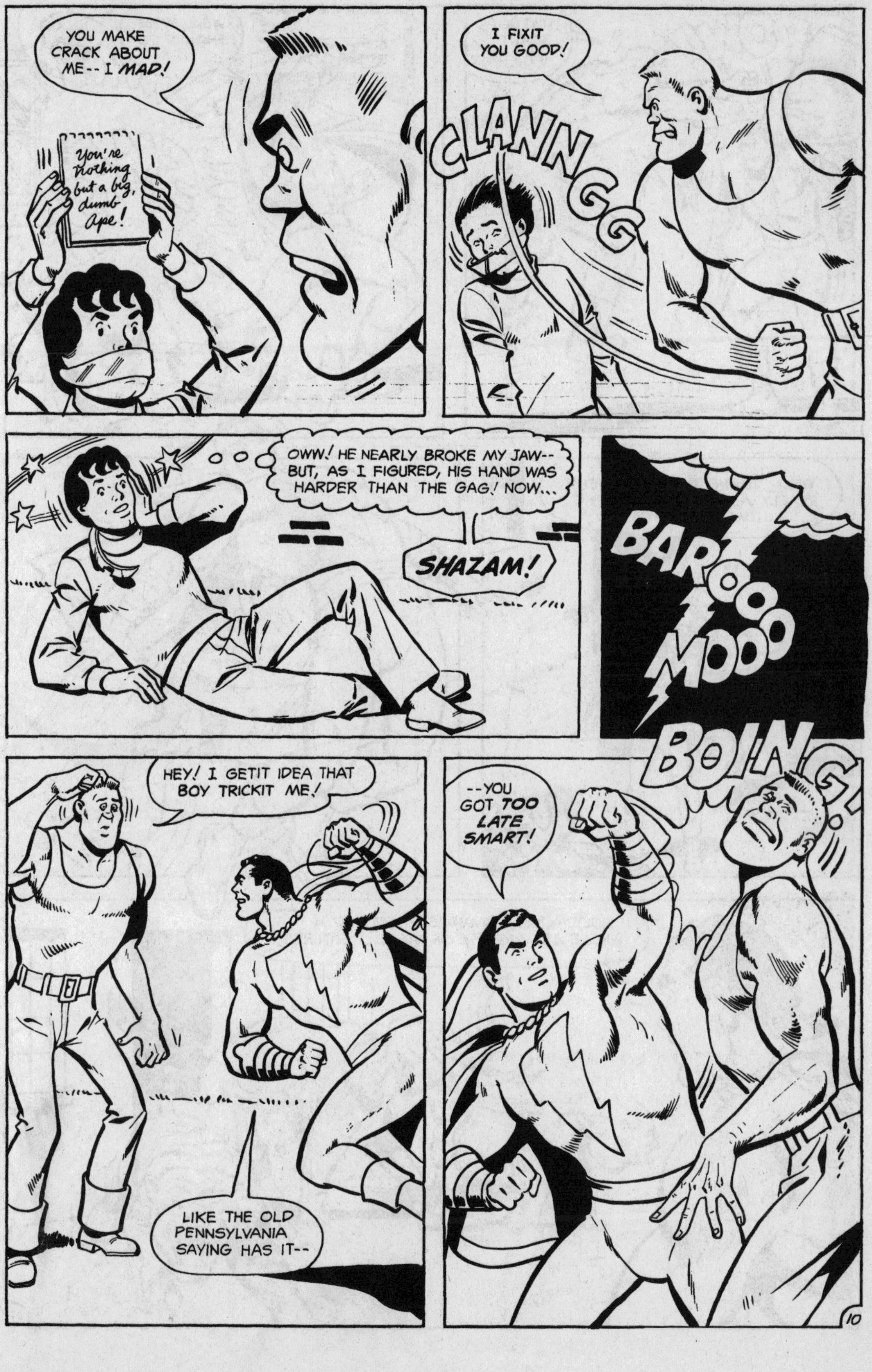
YOU MAKE CRACK ABOUT ME-- I MAD!
You're nothing but a big, dumb Ape!
I FIXIT YOU GOOD!
CLANNGG
OWW! HE NEARLY BROKE MY JAW-- BUT, AS I FIGURED, HIS HAND WAS HARDER THAN THE GAG! NOW...
SHAZAM!
BAROOO MOOO
BOING!
HEY! I GETIT IDEA THAT BOY TRICKIT ME!
LIKE THE OLD PENNSYLVANIA SAYING HAS IT--
--YOU GOT TOO LATE SMART!
10

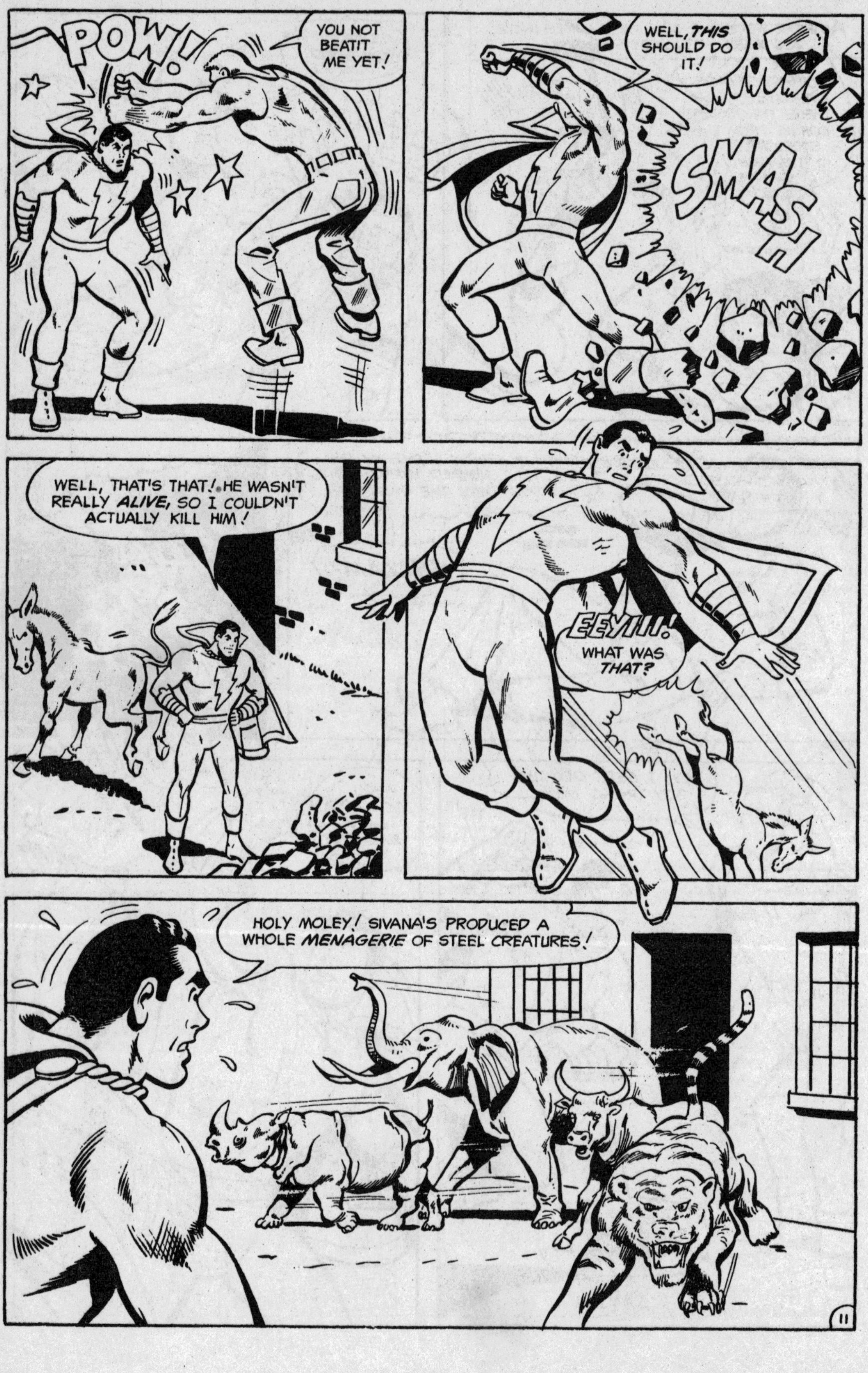
POW!
YOU NOT BEATIT ME YET!
WELL, THIS SHOULD DO IT!
SMASH
WELL, THAT'S THAT! HE WASN'T REALLY ALIVE, SO I COULDN'T ACTUALLY KILL HIM!
EEYIII! WHAT WAS THAT?
HOLY MOLEY! SIVANA'S PRODUCED A WHOLE MENAGERIE OF STEEL CREATURES!
11

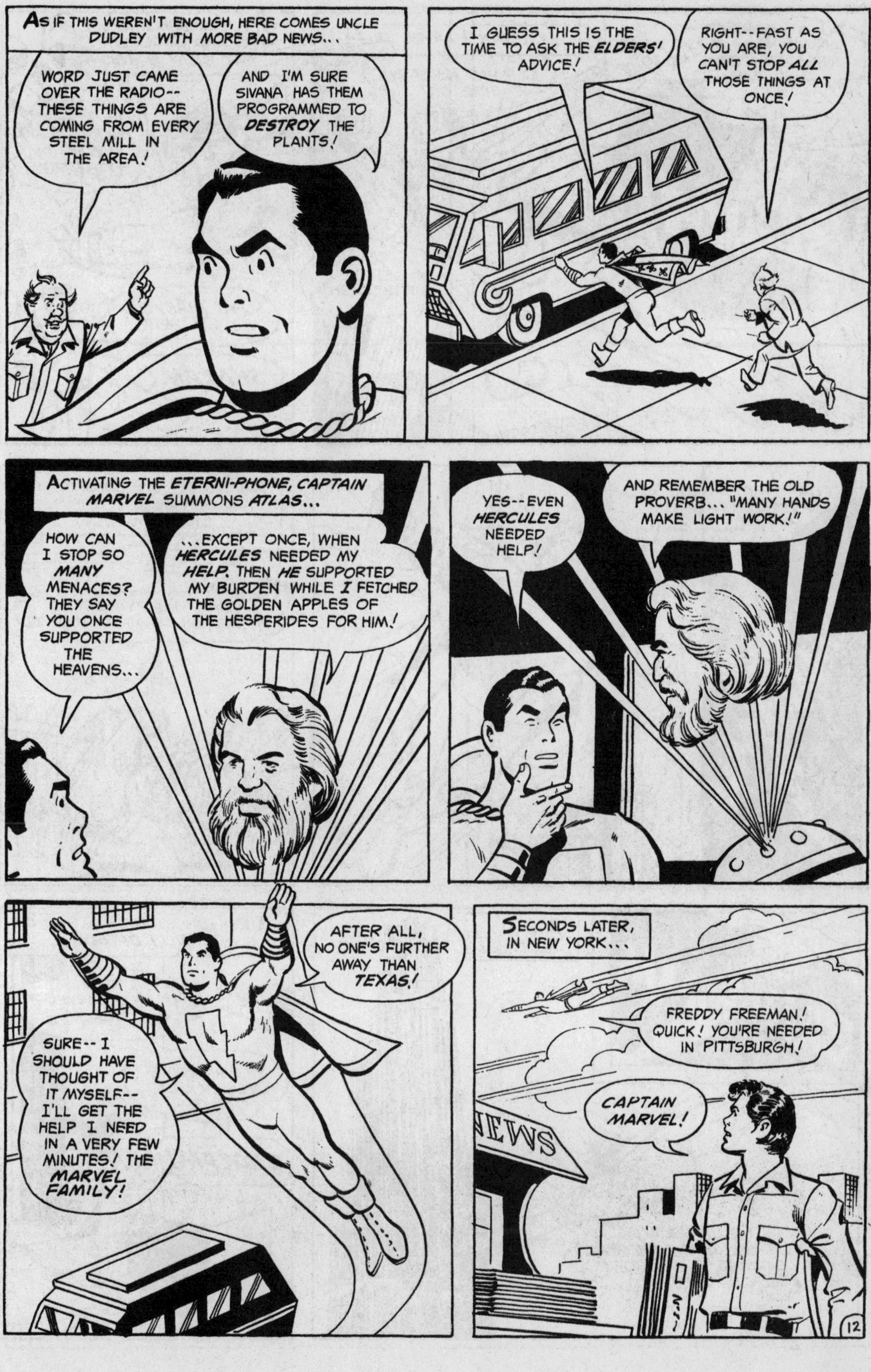
AS IF THIS WEREN'T ENOUGH, HERE COMES UNCLE DUDLEY WITH MORE BAD NEWS...
WORD JUST CAME OVER THE RADIO-- THESE THINGS ARE COMING FROM EVERY STEEL MILL IN THE AREA!
AND I'M SURE SIVANA HAS THEM PROGRAMMED TO DESTROY THE PLANTS!
I GUESS THIS IS THE TIME TO ASK THE ELDERS' ADVICE!
RIGHT--FAST AS YOU ARE, YOU CAN'T STOP ALL THOSE THINGS AT ONCE!
ACTIVATING THE ETERNI-PHONE, CAPTAIN MARVEL SUMMONS ATLAS...
HOW CAN I STOP SO MANY MENACES? THEY SAY YOU ONCE SUPPORTED THE HEAVENS...
...EXCEPT ONCE, WHEN HERCULES NEEDED MY HELP. THEN HE SUPPORTED MY BURDEN WHILE I FETCHED THE GOLDEN APPLES OF THE HESPERIDES FOR HIM!
YES--EVEN HERCULES NEEDED HELP!
AND REMEMBER THE OLD PROVERB... "MANY HANDS MAKE LIGHT WORK!"
AFTER ALL, NO ONE'S FURTHER AWAY THAN TEXAS!
SURE-- I SHOULD HAVE THOUGHT OF IT MYSELF-- I'LL GET THE HELP I NEED IN A VERY FEW MINUTES! THE MARVEL FAMILY!
SECONDS LATER, IN NEW YORK...
FREDDY FREEMAN! QUICK! YOU'RE NEEDED IN PITTSBURGH!
CAPTAIN MARVEL!
NEWS
12

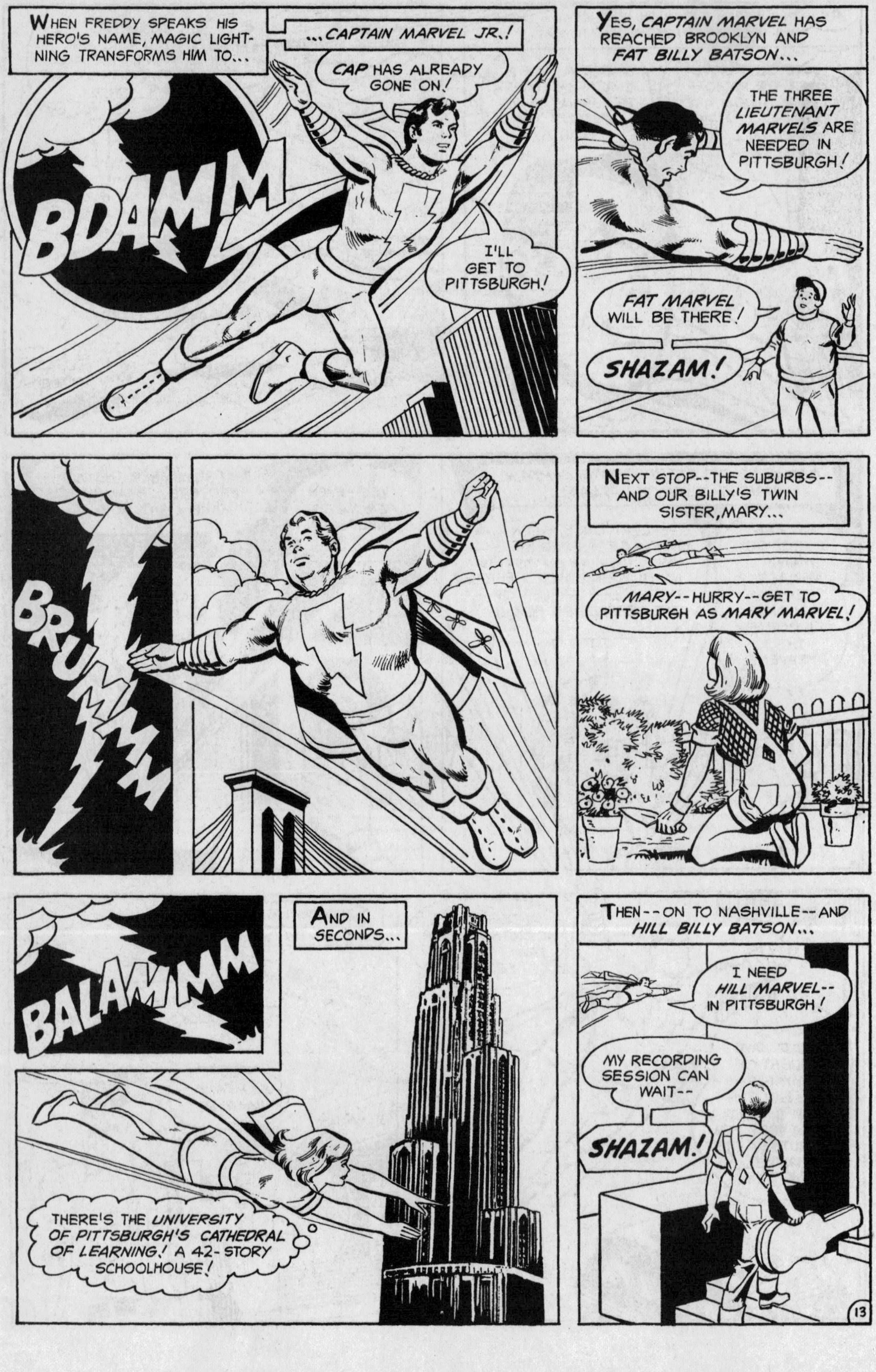
WHEN FREDDY SPEAKS HIS HERO'S NAME, MAGIC LIGHTNING TRANSFORMS HIM TO...
BDAMM
...CAPTAIN MARVEL JR.!
CAP HAS ALREADY GONE ON!
I'LL GET TO PITTSBURGH!
YES, CAPTAIN MARVEL HAS REACHED BROOKLYN AND FAT BILLY BATSON...
THE THREE LIEUTENANT MARVELS ARE NEEDED IN PITTSBURGH!
FAT MARVEL WILL BE THERE!
SHAZAM!
BRUMMMM
NEXT STOP--THE SUBURBS--AND OUR BILLY'S TWIN SISTER, MARY...
MARY--HURRY--GET TO PITTSBURGH AS MARY MARVEL!
BALAMMM
AND IN SECONDS...
THERE'S THE UNIVERSITY OF PITTSBURGH'S CATHEDRAL OF LEARNING! A 42-STORY SCHOOLHOUSE!
THEN--ON TO NASHVILLE--AND HILL BILLY BATSON...
I NEED HILL MARVEL--IN PITTSBURGH!
MY RECORDING SESSION CAN WAIT--
SHAZAM!
13

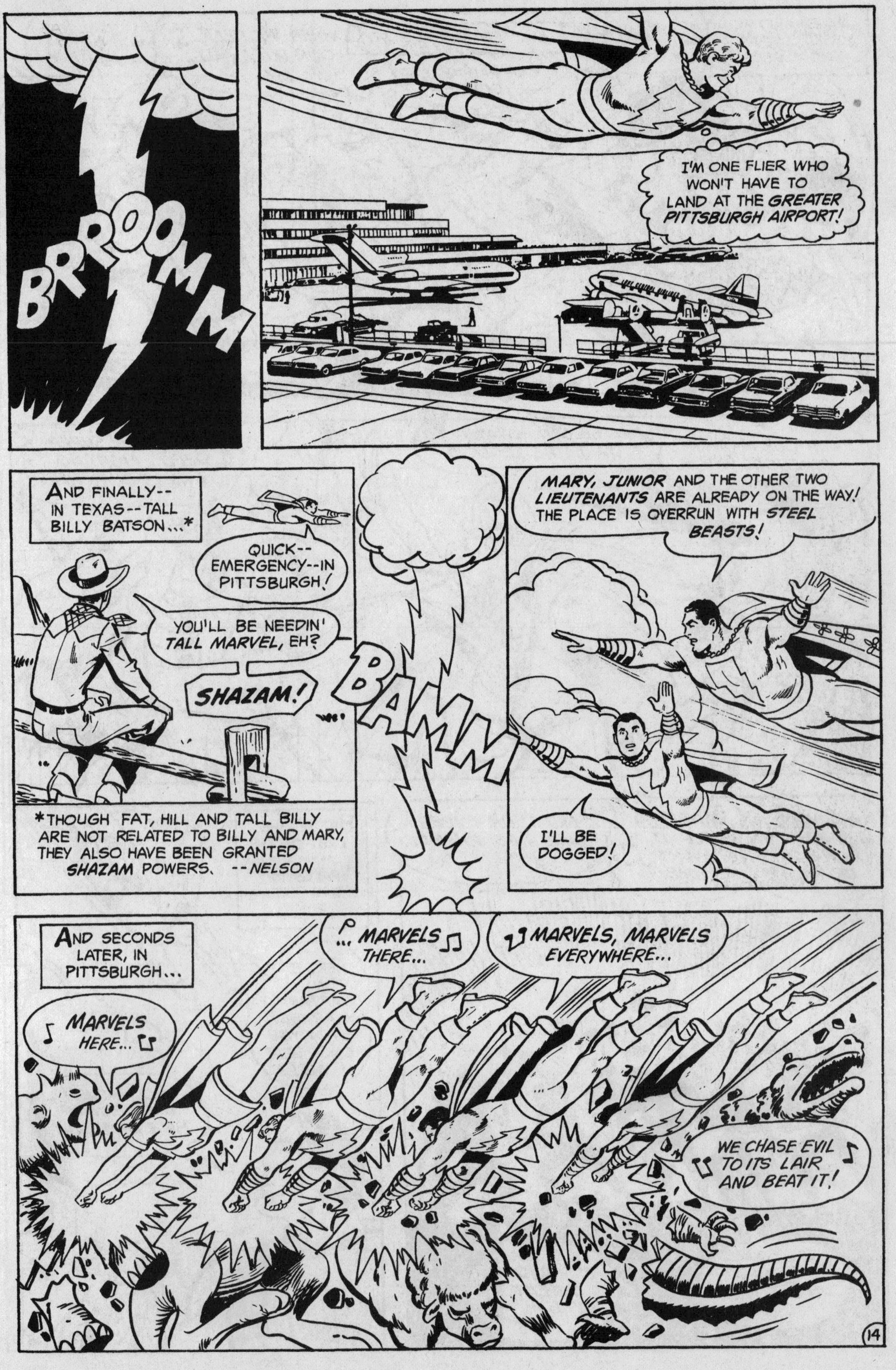
BRROOMMM
I'M ONE FLIER WHO WON'T HAVE TO LAND AT THE GREATER PITTSBURGH AIRPORT!
AND FINALLY-- IN TEXAS--TALL BILLY BATSON...*
QUICK--EMERGENCY--IN PITTSBURGH!
YOU'LL BE NEEDIN' TALL MARVEL, EH?
SHAZAM!
BAMM
MARY, JUNIOR AND THE OTHER TWO LIEUTENANTS ARE ALREADY ON THE WAY! THE PLACE IS OVERRUN WITH STEEL BEASTS!
I'LL BE DOGGED!
*THOUGH FAT, HILL AND TALL BILLY ARE NOT RELATED TO BILLY AND MARY, THEY ALSO HAVE BEEN GRANTED SHAZAM POWERS. --NELSON
AND SECONDS LATER, IN PITTSBURGH...
MARVELS HERE...
...MARVELS THERE...
MARVELS, MARVELS EVERYWHERE...
WE CHASE EVIL TO ITS LAIR AND BEAT IT!
14

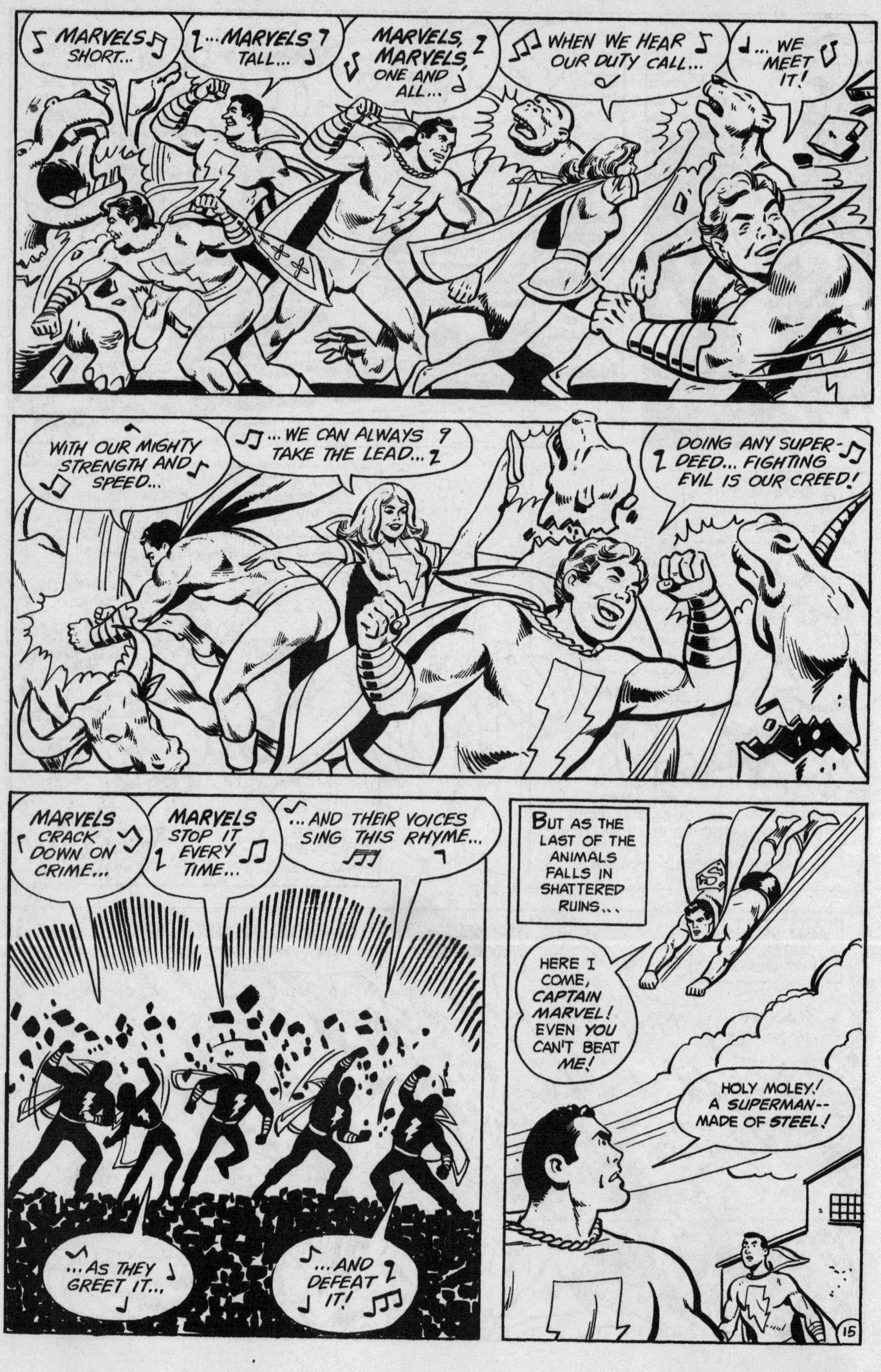
MARVELS SHORT...
...MARVELS TALL...
MARVELS, MARVELS, ONE AND ALL...
WHEN WE HEAR OUR DUTY CALL...
...WE MEET IT!
WITH OUR MIGHTY STRENGTH AND SPEED...
...WE CAN ALWAYS TAKE THE LEAD...
DOING ANY SUPER-DEED... FIGHTING EVIL IS OUR CREED!
MARVELS CRACK DOWN ON CRIME...
MARVELS STOP IT EVERY TIME...
...AND THEIR VOICES SING THIS RHYME...
...AS THEY GREET IT...
...AND DEFEAT IT!
BUT AS THE LAST OF THE ANIMALS FALLS IN SHATTERED RUINS...
HERE I COME, CAPTAIN MARVEL! EVEN YOU CAN'T BEAT ME!
HOLY MOLEY! A SUPERMAN--MADE OF STEEL!
15

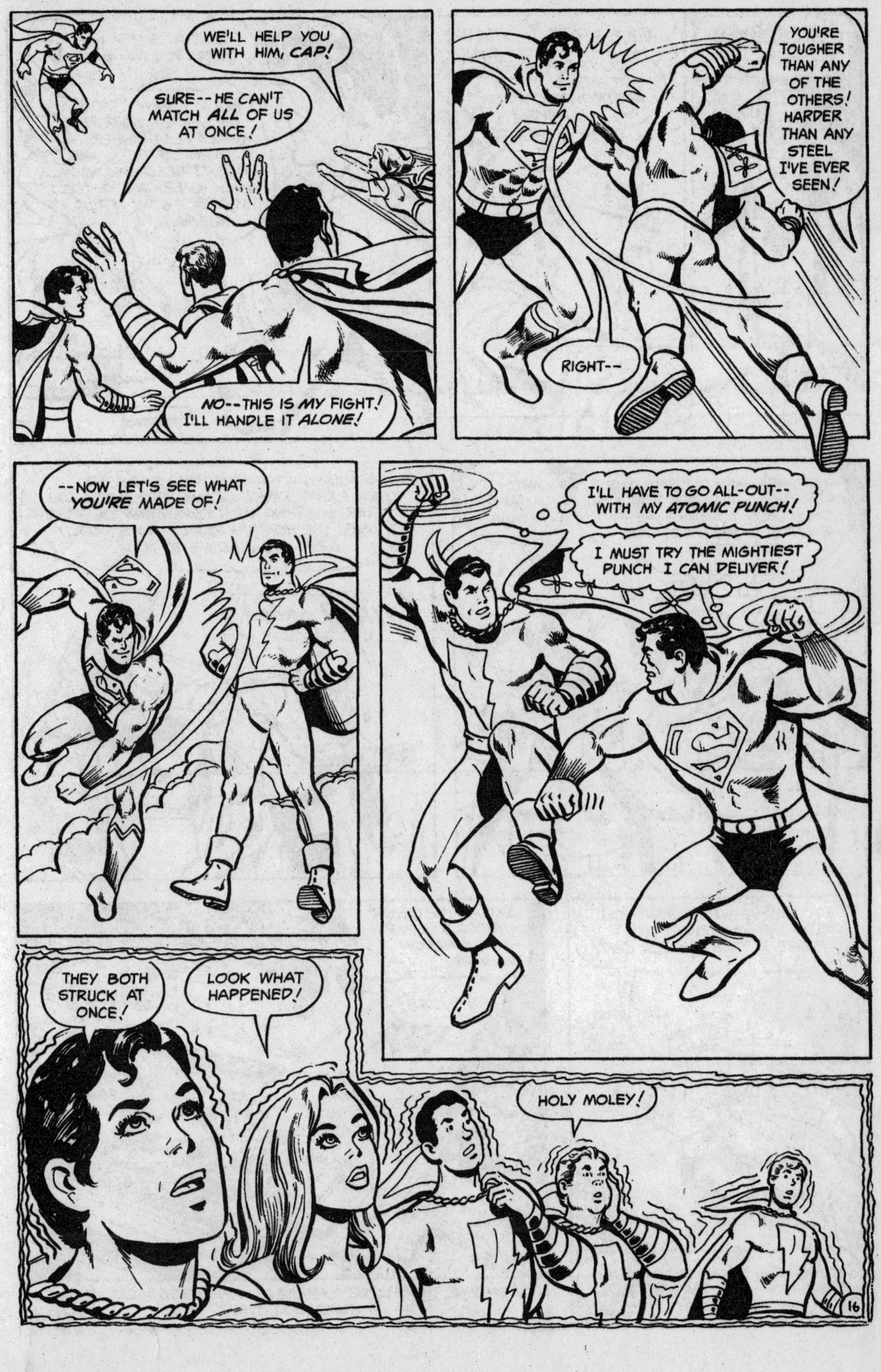
WE'LL HELP YOU WITH HIM, CAP!
SURE--HE CAN'T MATCH ALL OF US AT ONCE!
NO--THIS IS MY FIGHT! I'LL HANDLE IT ALONE!
RIGHT--
YOU'RE TOUGHER THAN ANY OF THE OTHERS! HARDER THAN ANY STEEL I'VE EVER SEEN!
--NOW LET'S SEE WHAT YOU'RE MADE OF!
I'LL HAVE TO GO ALL-OUT-- WITH MY ATOMIC PUNCH!
I MUST TRY THE MIGHTIEST PUNCH I CAN DELIVER!
THEY BOTH STRUCK AT ONCE!
LOOK WHAT HAPPENED!
HOLY MOLEY!
16

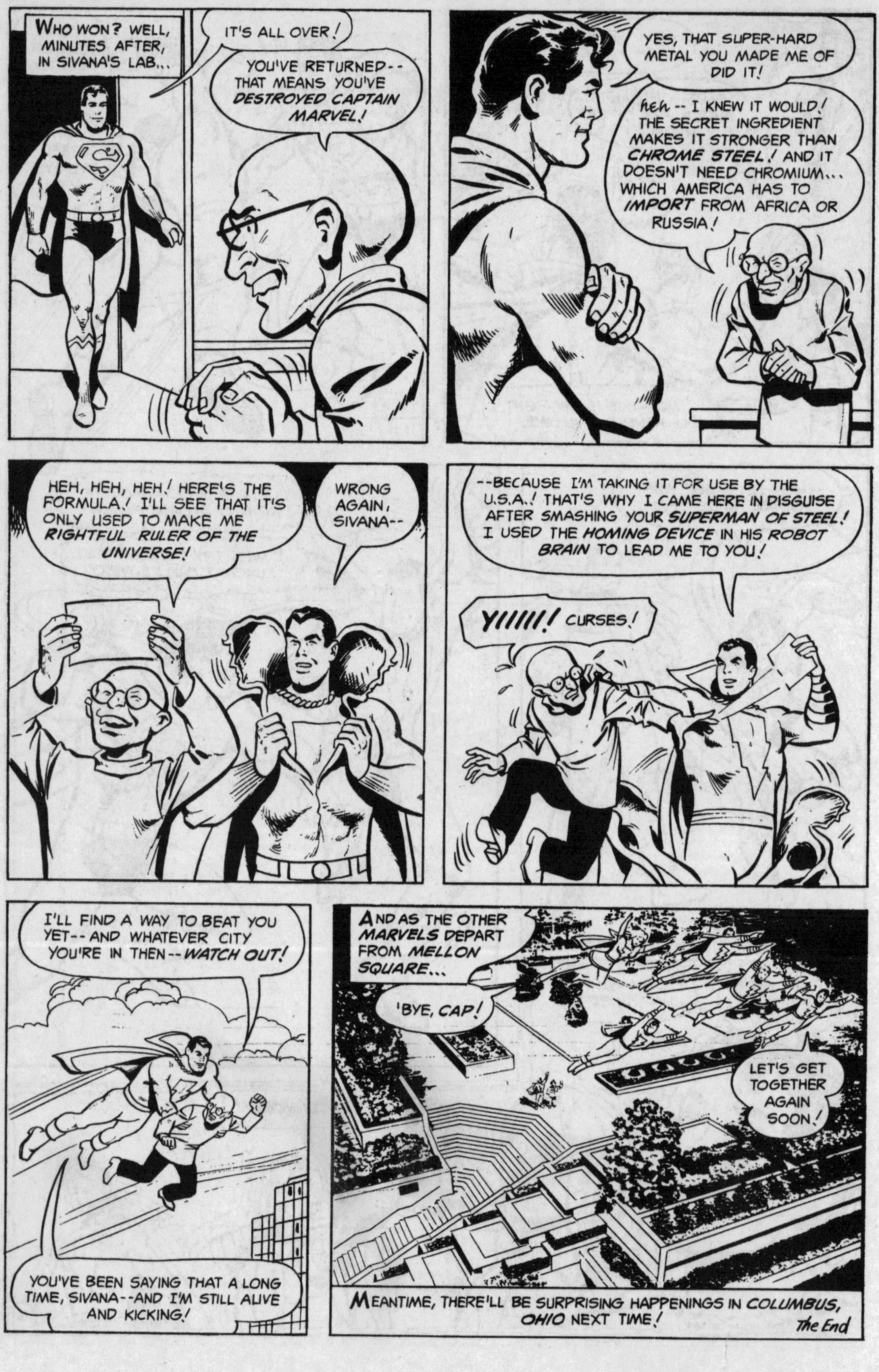
WHO WON? WELL, MINUTES AFTER, IN SIVANA'S LAB...
IT'S ALL OVER!
YOU'VE RETURNED-- THAT MEANS YOU'VE DESTROYED CAPTAIN MARVEL!
YES, THAT SUPER-HARD METAL YOU MADE ME OF DID IT!
heh -- I KNEW IT WOULD! THE SECRET INGREDIENT MAKES IT STRONGER THAN CHROME STEEL! AND IT DOESN'T NEED CHROMIUM... WHICH AMERICA HAS TO IMPORT FROM AFRICA OR RUSSIA!
HEH, HEH, HEH! HERE'S THE FORMULA! I'LL SEE THAT IT'S ONLY USED TO MAKE ME RIGHTFUL RULER OF THE UNIVERSE!
WRONG AGAIN, SIVANA--
--BECAUSE I'M TAKING IT FOR USE BY THE U.S.A.! THAT'S WHY I CAME HERE IN DISGUISE AFTER SMASHING YOUR SUPERMAN OF STEEL! I USED THE HOMING DEVICE IN HIS ROBOT BRAIN TO LEAD ME TO YOU!
YIIII! CURSES!
I'LL FIND A WAY TO BEAT YOU YET-- AND WHATEVER CITY YOU'RE IN THEN--WATCH OUT!
YOU'VE BEEN SAYING THAT A LONG TIME, SIVANA--AND I'M STILL ALIVE AND KICKING!
AND AS THE OTHER MARVELS DEPART FROM MELLON SQUARE...
'BYE, CAP!
LET'S GET TOGETHER AGAIN SOON!
MEANTIME, THERE'LL BE SURPRISING HAPPENINGS IN COLUMBUS, OHIO NEXT TIME!
The End

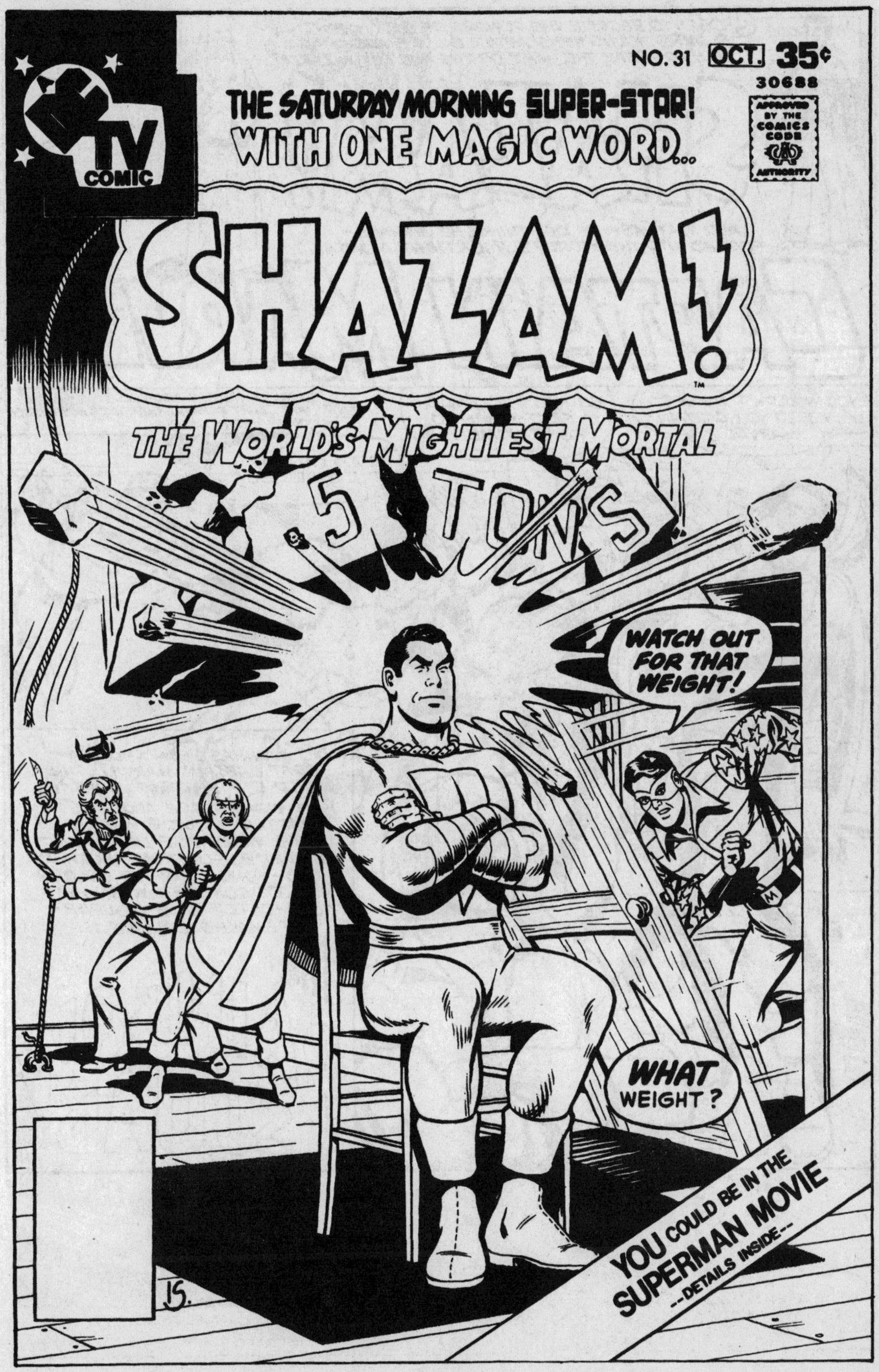
TV COMIC
NO. 31 OCT. 35¢
30688
APPROVED BY THE COMICS CODE AUTHORITY
THE SATURDAY MORNING SUPER-STAR!
WITH ONE MAGIC WORD...
SHAZAM!
THE WORLD'S MIGHTIEST MORTAL
5 TONS
WATCH OUT FOR THAT WEIGHT!
WHAT WEIGHT?
YOU COULD BE IN THE SUPERMAN MOVIE
--DETAILS INSIDE--

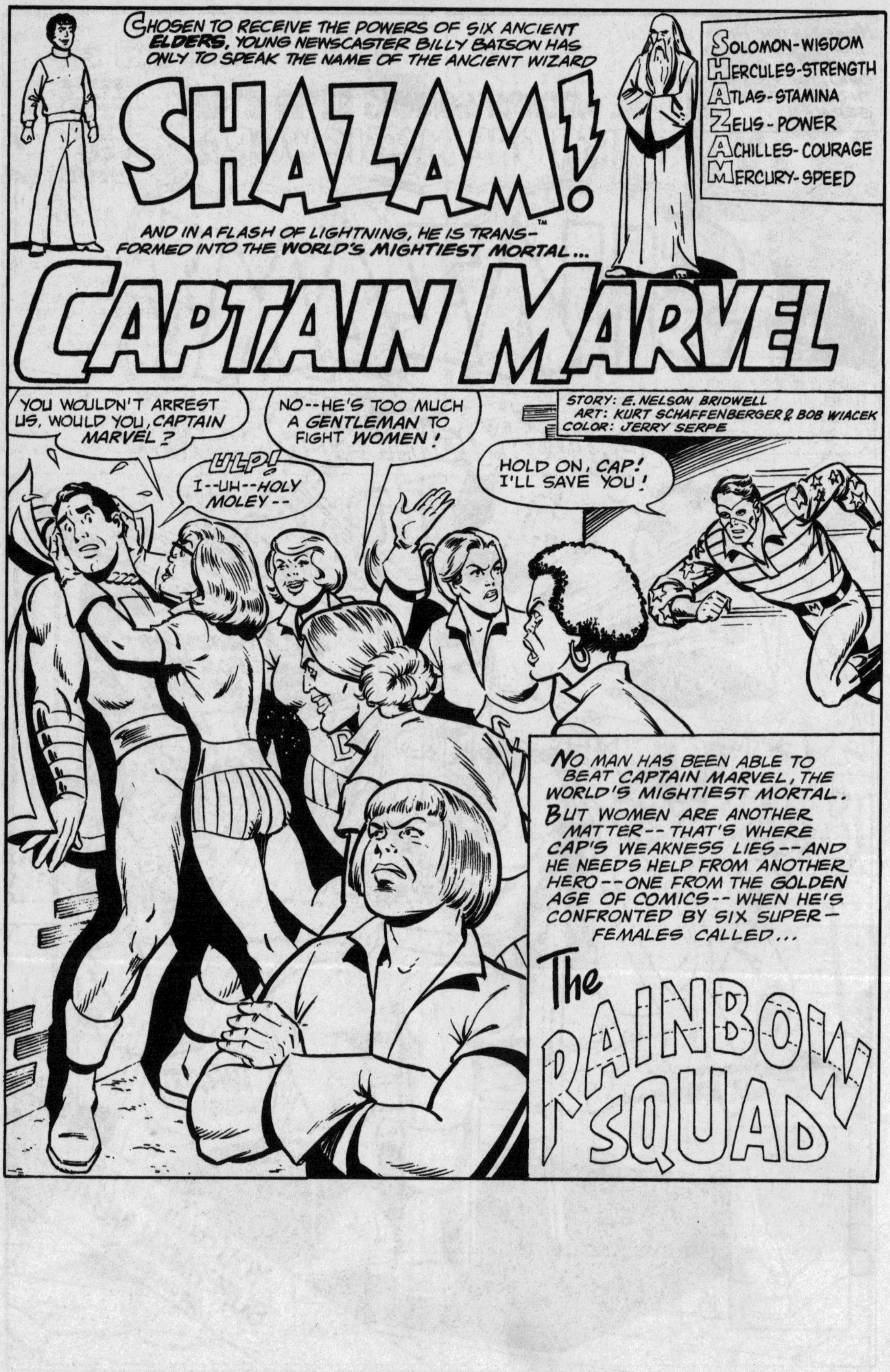

CHOSEN TO RECEIVE THE POWERS OF SIX ANCIENT ELDERS, YOUNG NEWSCASTER BILLY BATSON HAS ONLY TO SPEAK THE NAME OF THE ANCIENT WIZARD
SHAZAM!
SOLOMON-WISDOM
HERCULES-STRENGTH
ATLAS-STAMINA
ZEUS-POWER
ACHILLES-COURAGE
MERCURY-SPEED
AND IN A FLASH OF LIGHTNING, HE IS TRANSFORMED INTO THE WORLD'S MIGHTIEST MORTAL...
CAPTAIN MARVEL
YOU WOULDN'T ARREST US, WOULD YOU, CAPTAIN MARVEL?
NO--HE'S TOO MUCH A GENTLEMAN TO FIGHT WOMEN!
STORY: E. NELSON BRIDWELL
ART: KURT SCHAFFENBERGER & BOB WIACEK
COLOR: JERRY SERPE
ULP! I--UH--HOLY MOLEY--
HOLD ON, CAP! I'LL SAVE YOU!
NO MAN HAS BEEN ABLE TO BEAT CAPTAIN MARVEL, THE WORLD'S MIGHTIEST MORTAL. BUT WOMEN ARE ANOTHER MATTER--THAT'S WHERE CAP'S WEAKNESS LIES--AND HE NEEDS HELP FROM ANOTHER HERO--ONE FROM THE GOLDEN AGE OF COMICS--WHEN HE'S CONFRONTED BY SIX SUPER-FEMALES CALLED...
The RAINBOW SQUAD

NEWSCASTER BILLY BATSON AND UNCLE DUDLEY HAVE ARRIVED IN *COLUMBUS*, *OHIO*, WHERE THEY PASS THROUGH THE FAMOUS *GERMAN VILLAGE*...

ABOUT TIME WE STOPPED FOR LUNCH, ISN'T IT, BILLY?

SURE, UNCLE! AND WE HAVE AN INVITATION TO *JACK WESTON'S* RESTAURANT!

AND WHO IS JACK WESTON? YOU'RE ABOUT TO FIND OUT...

BILLY--AND DUDLEY! GOOD TO SEE YOU AGAIN!

IT'S BEEN A LONG TIME, JACK! I NEVER EXPECTED YOU'D WIND UP AS A RESTAURATEUR!

WELL, WHY NOT? WHEN I WAS PRIVATE JACK WESTON, U.S. ARMY, I SPENT ENOUGH TIME ON *K.P.*!

ONLY BECAUSE THE SERGEANT DIDN'T KNOW YOU WERE REALLY *MINUTE MAN*, THE *ONE-MAN ARMY!* *

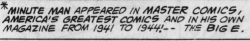

*MINUTE MAN APPEARED IN MASTER COMICS, AMERICA'S GREATEST COMICS AND IN HIS OWN MAGAZINE FROM 1941 TO 1944!-- THE BIG E.

YES--AND GENERAL MILTON DIDN'T ALWAYS HAVE A CHANCE TO GET ME A LEAVE WHEN *MINUTE MAN* WAS NEEDED! NO ONE ELSE IN THE MILITARY KNEW ABOUT MY DOUBLE LIFE!

I'VE ALREADY ORDERED FOR YOU--THE FOOD WILL BE HERE IN A FEW MOMENTS!

AND SO, SHORTLY...

GODFREY! I SEE AN OLD FRIEND ENTERING--*RON SCHEER*--VICE PRESIDENT OF THE SCOTT KRAUSS NEWS AGENCY!

RON--COME OVER AND JOIN US!

YES--THE FOOD IS GREAT!

I HADN'T EVEN HEARD YOU WERE IN TOWN! IS *CAPTAIN MARVEL* HERE, TOO?

WHY--UH--HE'S NEVER FAR AWAY!

QUITE SO! THOUGH WE'VE HAD NO--UH--CONTACT WITH HIM SINCE HE ARRESTED *SIVANA* IN PITTSBURGH!

2

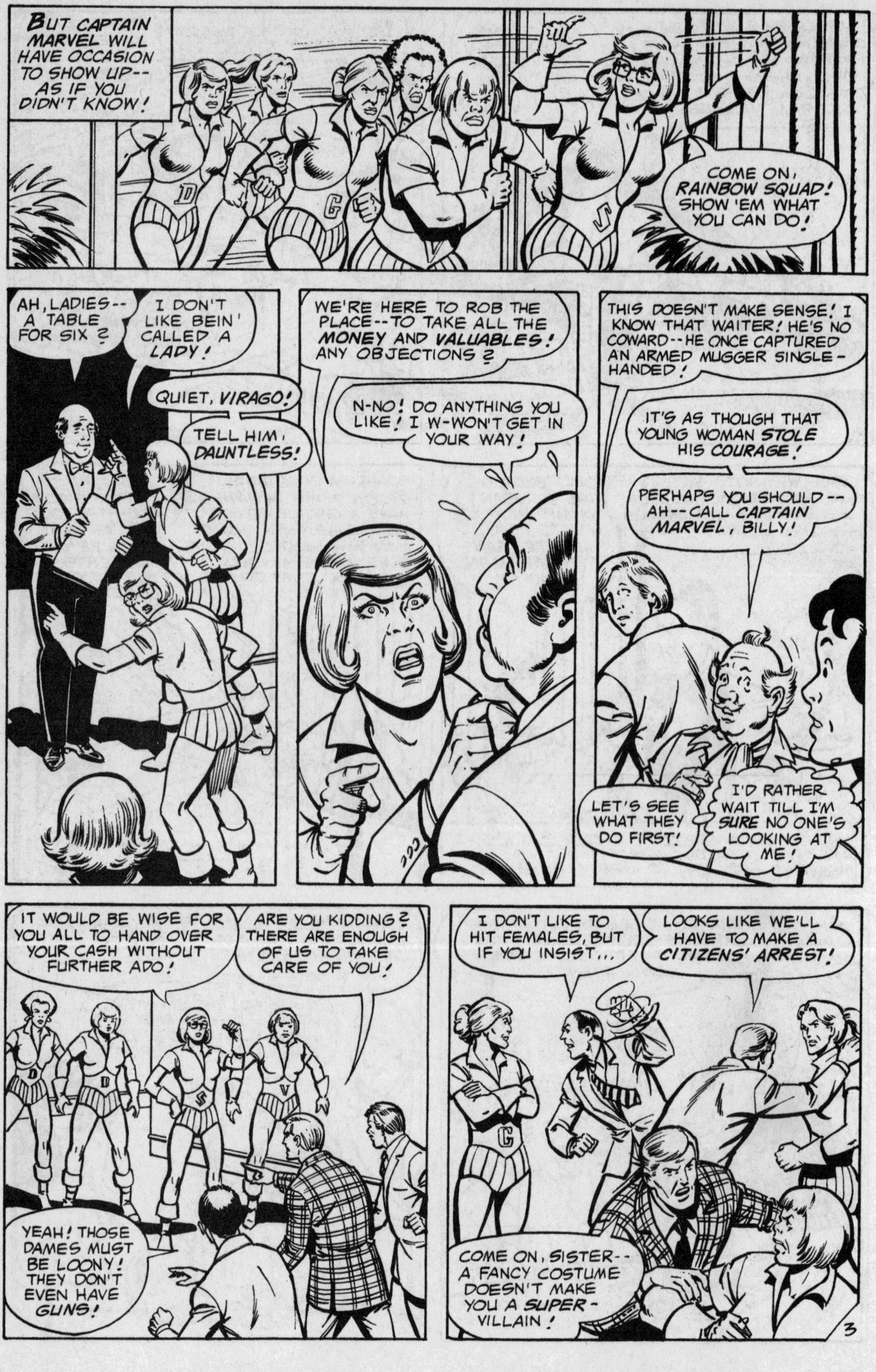
BUT CAPTAIN MARVEL WILL HAVE OCCASION TO SHOW UP-- AS IF YOU DIDN'T KNOW!
COME ON, RAINBOW SQUAD! SHOW 'EM WHAT YOU CAN DO!
AH, LADIES-- A TABLE FOR SIX ?
I DON'T LIKE BEIN' CALLED A LADY!
QUIET, VIRAGO!
TELL HIM, DAUNTLESS!
WE'RE HERE TO ROB THE PLACE--TO TAKE ALL THE MONEY AND VALUABLES! ANY OBJECTIONS ?
N-NO! DO ANYTHING YOU LIKE! I W-WON'T GET IN YOUR WAY!
THIS DOESN'T MAKE SENSE! I KNOW THAT WAITER! HE'S NO COWARD--HE ONCE CAPTURED AN ARMED MUGGER SINGLE-HANDED!
IT'S AS THOUGH THAT YOUNG WOMAN STOLE HIS COURAGE!
PERHAPS YOU SHOULD--AH--CALL CAPTAIN MARVEL, BILLY!
LET'S SEE WHAT THEY DO FIRST!
I'D RATHER WAIT TILL I'M SURE NO ONE'S LOOKING AT ME!
IT WOULD BE WISE FOR YOU ALL TO HAND OVER YOUR CASH WITHOUT FURTHER ADO!
ARE YOU KIDDING ? THERE ARE ENOUGH OF US TO TAKE CARE OF YOU!
YEAH! THOSE DAMES MUST BE LOONY! THEY DON'T EVEN HAVE GUNS!
I DON'T LIKE TO HIT FEMALES, BUT IF YOU INSIST...
LOOKS LIKE WE'LL HAVE TO MAKE A CITIZENS' ARREST!
COME ON, SISTER-- A FANCY COSTUME DOESN'T MAKE YOU A SUPER-VILLAIN!
3

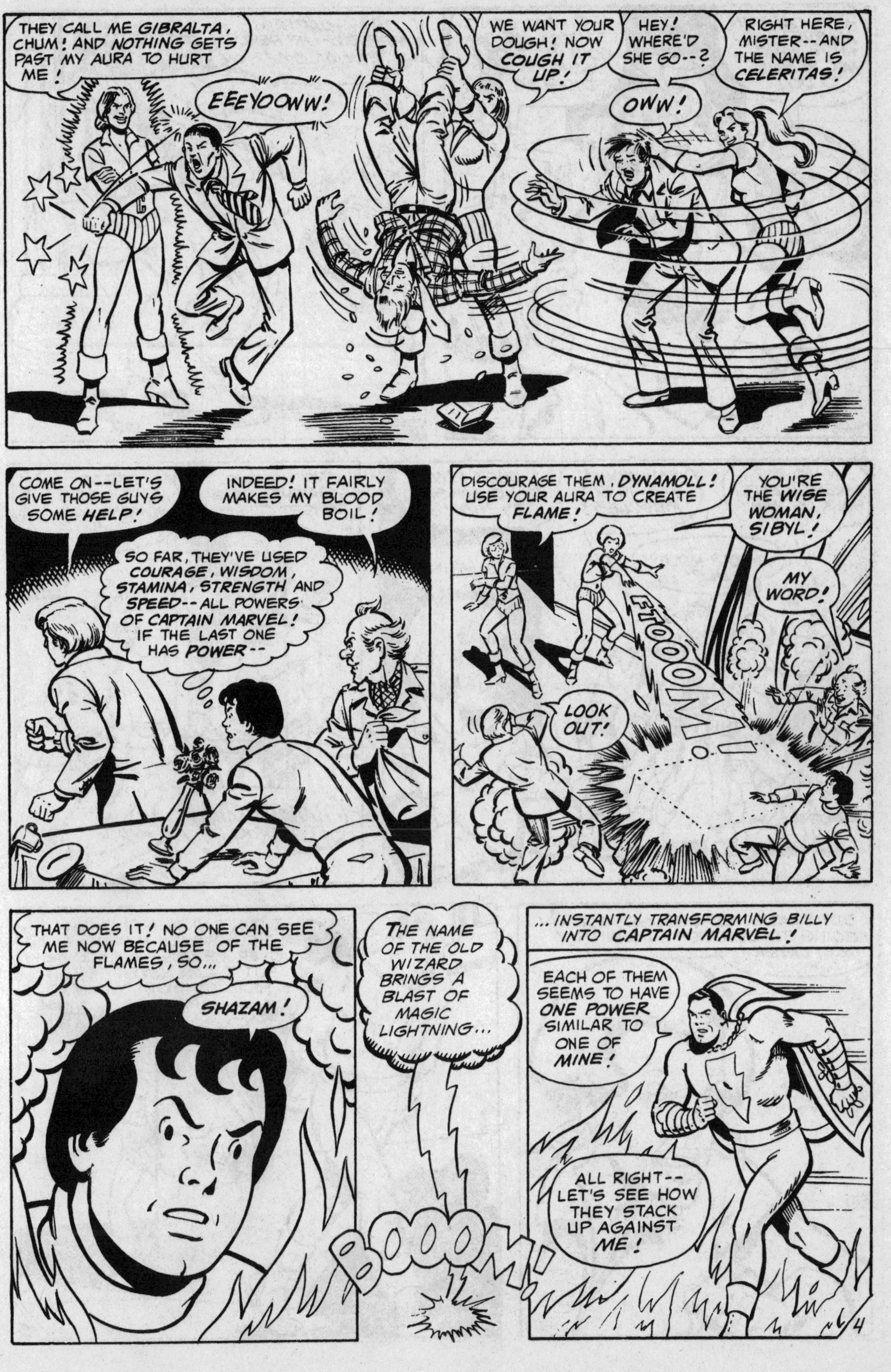
THEY CALL ME GIBRALTA, CHUM! AND NOTHING GETS PAST MY AURA TO HURT ME!
EEEYOOWW!
WE WANT YOUR DOUGH! NOW COUGH IT UP!
HEY! WHERE'D SHE GO--?
OWW!
RIGHT HERE, MISTER--AND THE NAME IS CELERITAS!
COME ON--LET'S GIVE THOSE GUYS SOME HELP!
INDEED! IT FAIRLY MAKES MY BLOOD BOIL!
SO FAR, THEY'VE USED COURAGE, WISDOM, STAMINA, STRENGTH AND SPEED--ALL POWERS OF CAPTAIN MARVEL! IF THE LAST ONE HAS POWER--
DISCOURAGE THEM, DYNAMOLL! USE YOUR AURA TO CREATE FLAME!
YOU'RE THE WISE WOMAN, SIBYL!
MY WORD!
FTOOOOM!
LOOK OUT!
THAT DOES IT! NO ONE CAN SEE ME NOW BECAUSE OF THE FLAMES, SO...
SHAZAM!
THE NAME OF THE OLD WIZARD BRINGS A BLAST OF MAGIC LIGHTNING...
BOOOOM!
...INSTANTLY TRANSFORMING BILLY INTO CAPTAIN MARVEL!
EACH OF THEM SEEMS TO HAVE ONE POWER SIMILAR TO ONE OF MINE!
ALL RIGHT--LET'S SEE HOW THEY STACK UP AGAINST ME!
4

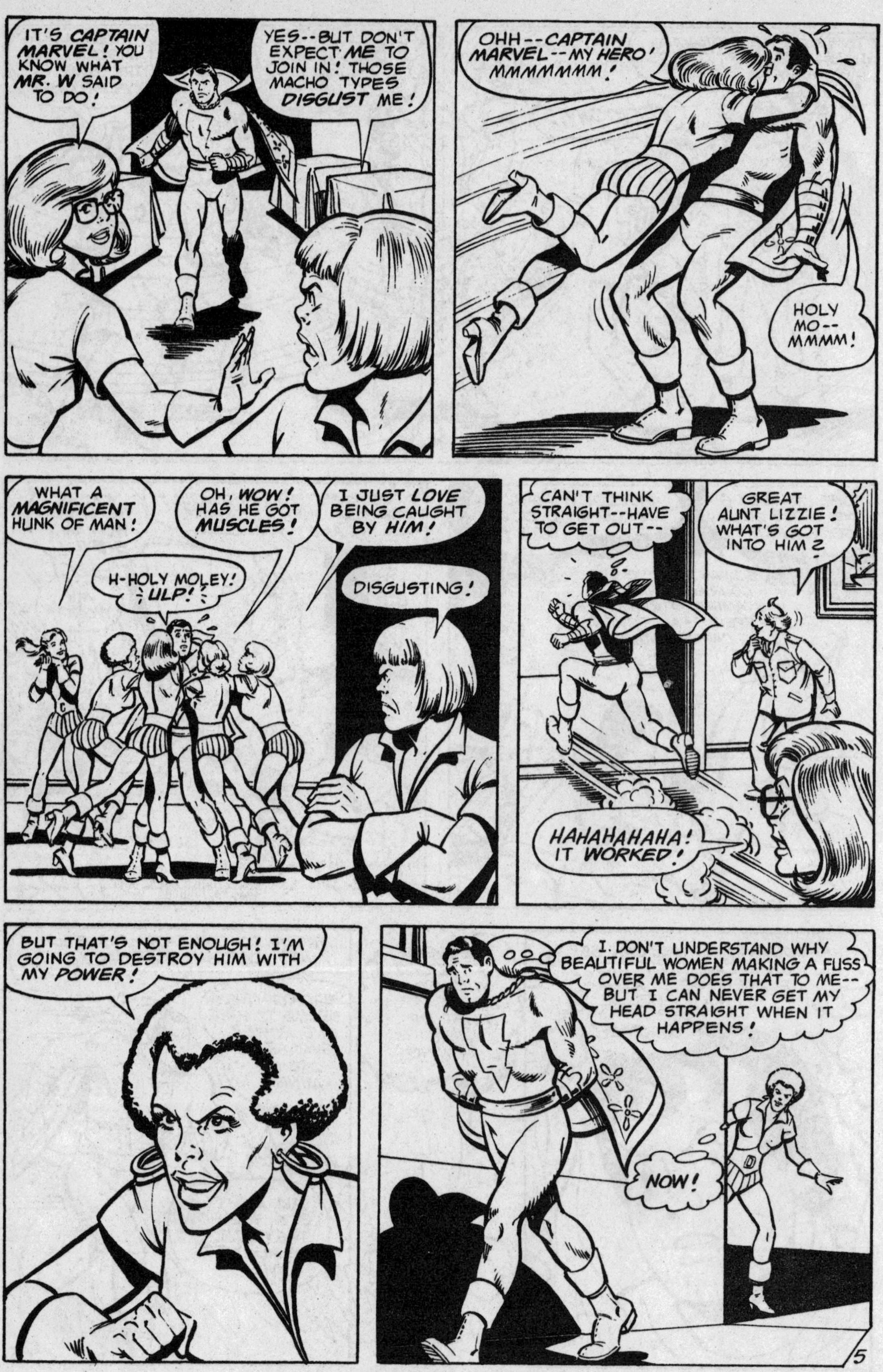
IT'S CAPTAIN MARVEL! YOU KNOW WHAT MR. W SAID TO DO!
YES--BUT DON'T EXPECT ME TO JOIN IN! THOSE MACHO TYPES DISGUST ME!
OHH--CAPTAIN MARVEL--MY HERO! MMMMMMM!
HOLY MO--MMMM!
WHAT A MAGNIFICENT HUNK OF MAN!
OH, WOW! HAS HE GOT MUSCLES!
I JUST LOVE BEING CAUGHT BY HIM!
H-HOLY MOLEY! ULP!
DISGUSTING!
CAN'T THINK STRAIGHT--HAVE TO GET OUT--
GREAT AUNT LIZZIE! WHAT'S GOT INTO HIM?
HAHAHAHAHA! IT WORKED!
BUT THAT'S NOT ENOUGH! I'M GOING TO DESTROY HIM WITH MY POWER!
I DON'T UNDERSTAND WHY BEAUTIFUL WOMEN MAKING A FUSS OVER ME DOES THAT TO ME--BUT I CAN NEVER GET MY HEAD STRAIGHT WHEN IT HAPPENS!
NOW!
5

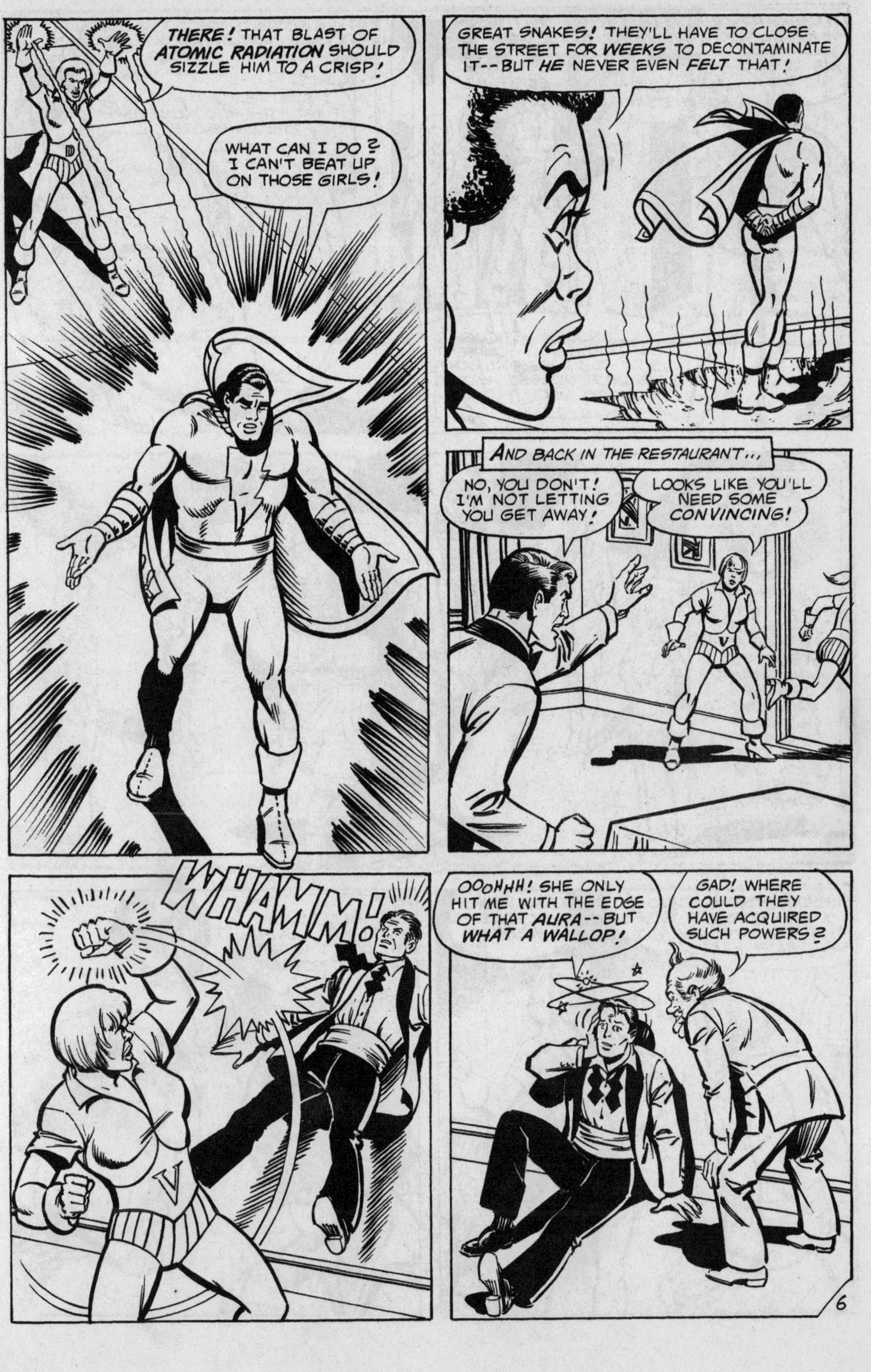
THERE! THAT BLAST OF ATOMIC RADIATION SHOULD SIZZLE HIM TO A CRISP!
WHAT CAN I DO? I CAN'T BEAT UP ON THOSE GIRLS!
GREAT SNAKES! THEY'LL HAVE TO CLOSE THE STREET FOR WEEKS TO DECONTAMINATE IT--BUT HE NEVER EVEN FELT THAT!
AND BACK IN THE RESTAURANT...
NO, YOU DON'T! I'M NOT LETTING YOU GET AWAY!
LOOKS LIKE YOU'LL NEED SOME CONVINCING!
WHAMM!
OOOHHH! SHE ONLY HIT ME WITH THE EDGE OF THAT AURA--BUT WHAT A WALLOP!
GAD! WHERE COULD THEY HAVE ACQUIRED SUCH POWERS?
6

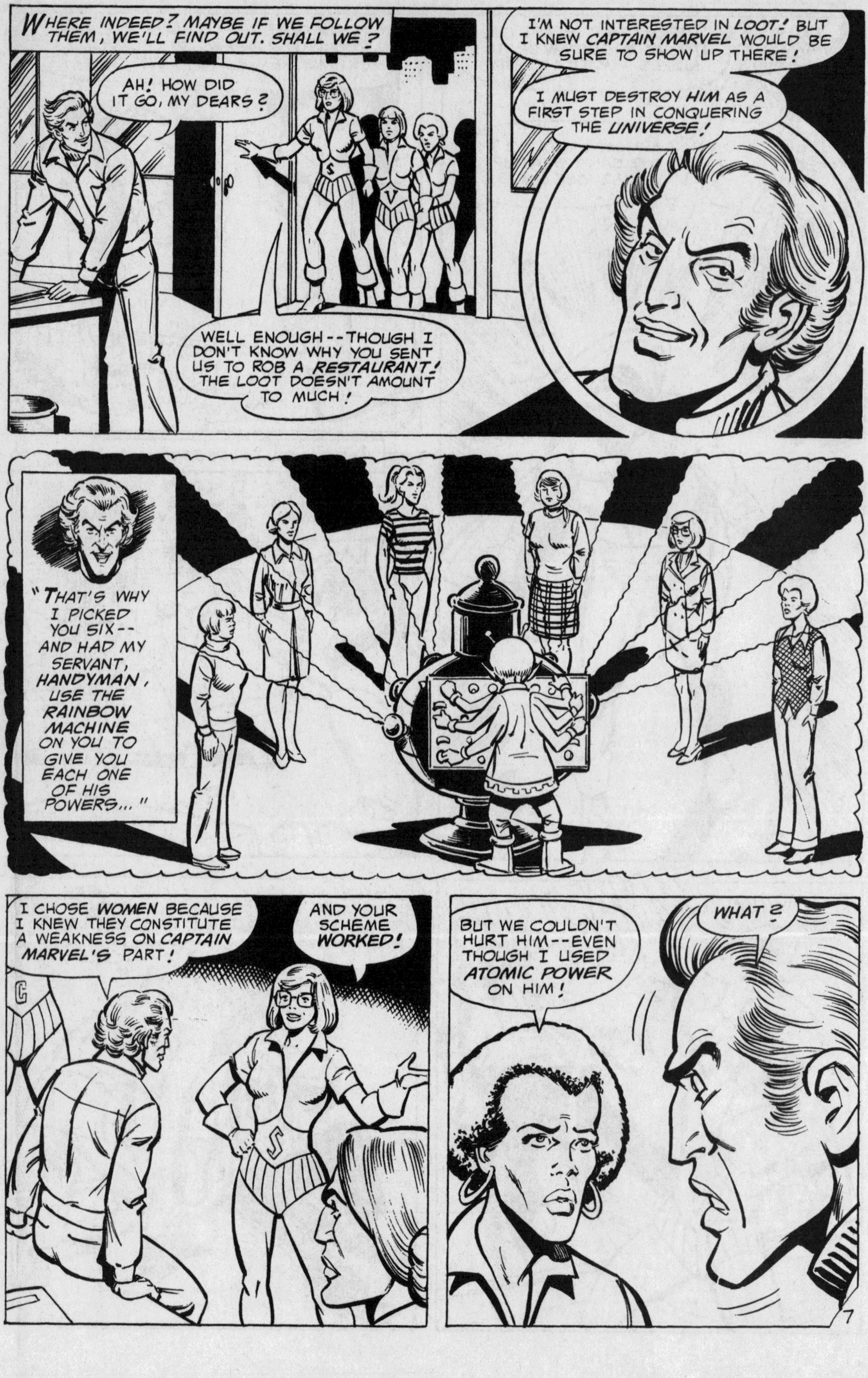
WHERE INDEED? MAYBE IF WE FOLLOW THEM, WE'LL FIND OUT. SHALL WE?
AH! HOW DID IT GO, MY DEARS?
WELL ENOUGH--THOUGH I DON'T KNOW WHY YOU SENT US TO ROB A RESTAURANT! THE LOOT DOESN'T AMOUNT TO MUCH!
I'M NOT INTERESTED IN LOOT! BUT I KNEW CAPTAIN MARVEL WOULD BE SURE TO SHOW UP THERE!
I MUST DESTROY HIM AS A FIRST STEP IN CONQUERING THE UNIVERSE!
"THAT'S WHY I PICKED YOU SIX--AND HAD MY SERVANT, HANDYMAN, USE THE RAINBOW MACHINE ON YOU TO GIVE YOU EACH ONE OF HIS POWERS..."
I CHOSE WOMEN BECAUSE I KNEW THEY CONSTITUTE A WEAKNESS ON CAPTAIN MARVEL'S PART!
AND YOUR SCHEME WORKED!
BUT WE COULDN'T HURT HIM--EVEN THOUGH I USED ATOMIC POWER ON HIM!
WHAT?
7

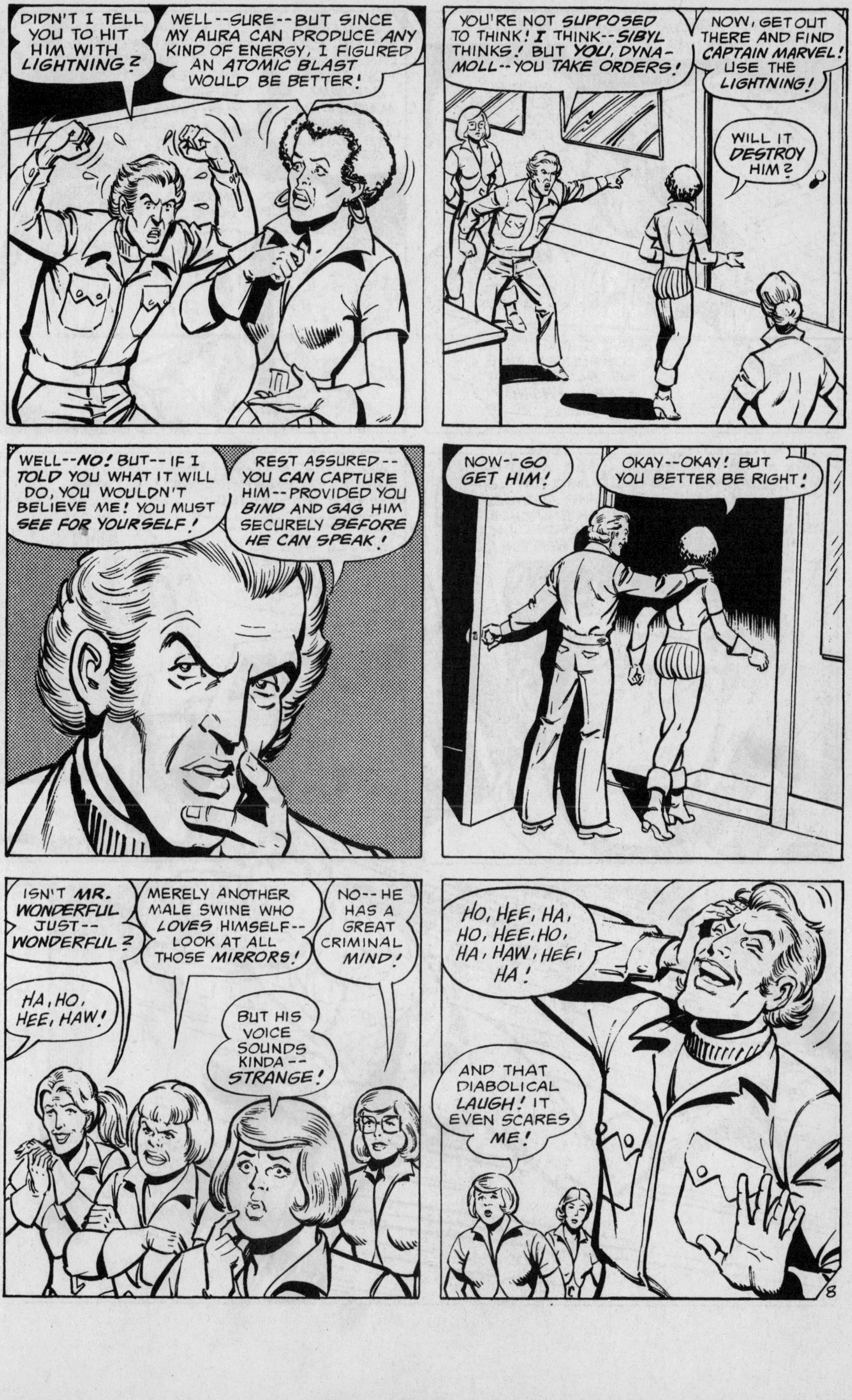
DIDN'T I TELL YOU TO HIT HIM WITH LIGHTNING?
WELL--SURE--BUT SINCE MY AURA CAN PRODUCE ANY KIND OF ENERGY, I FIGURED AN ATOMIC BLAST WOULD BE BETTER!
YOU'RE NOT SUPPOSED TO THINK! I THINK--SIBYL THINKS! BUT YOU, DYNA-MOLL--YOU TAKE ORDERS!
NOW, GET OUT THERE AND FIND CAPTAIN MARVEL! USE THE LIGHTNING!
WILL IT DESTROY HIM?
WELL--NO! BUT--IF I TOLD YOU WHAT IT WILL DO, YOU WOULDN'T BELIEVE ME! YOU MUST SEE FOR YOURSELF!
REST ASSURED--YOU CAN CAPTURE HIM--PROVIDED YOU BIND AND GAG HIM SECURELY BEFORE HE CAN SPEAK!
NOW--GO GET HIM!
OKAY--OKAY! BUT YOU BETTER BE RIGHT!
ISN'T MR. WONDERFUL JUST--WONDERFUL?
MERELY ANOTHER MALE SWINE WHO LOVES HIMSELF--LOOK AT ALL THOSE MIRRORS!
NO--HE HAS A GREAT CRIMINAL MIND!
HA, HO, HEE, HAW!
BUT HIS VOICE SOUNDS KINDA--STRANGE!
HO, HEE, HA, HO, HEE, HO, HA, HAW, HEE, HA!
AND THAT DIABOLICAL LAUGH! IT EVEN SCARES ME!
8

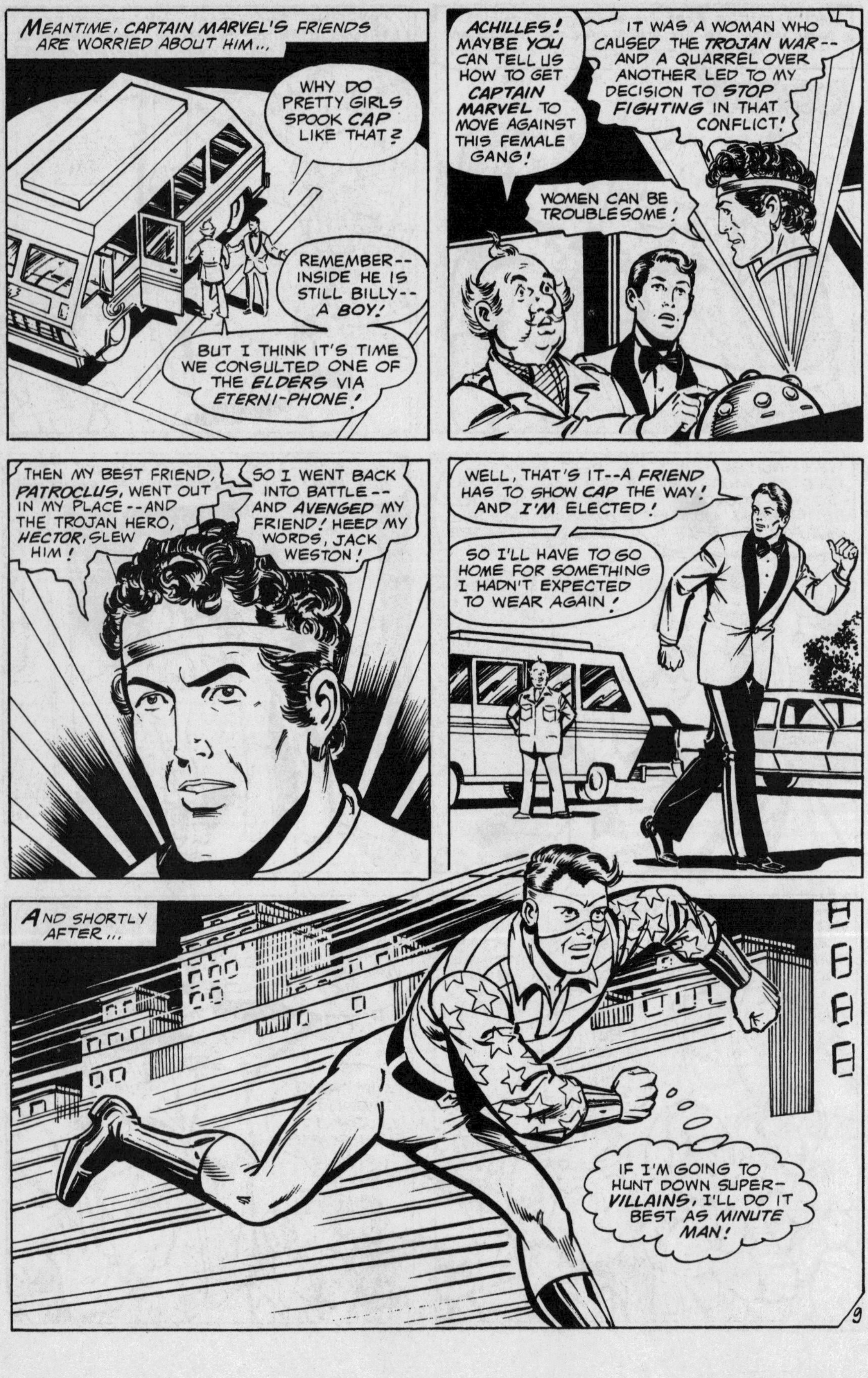
MEANTIME, CAPTAIN MARVEL'S FRIENDS ARE WORRIED ABOUT HIM...
WHY DO PRETTY GIRLS SPOOK CAP LIKE THAT?
REMEMBER-- INSIDE HE IS STILL BILLY-- A BOY!
BUT I THINK IT'S TIME WE CONSULTED ONE OF THE ELDERS VIA ETERNI-PHONE!
ACHILLES! MAYBE YOU CAN TELL US HOW TO GET CAPTAIN MARVEL TO MOVE AGAINST THIS FEMALE GANG!
IT WAS A WOMAN WHO CAUSED THE TROJAN WAR-- AND A QUARREL OVER ANOTHER LED TO MY DECISION TO STOP FIGHTING IN THAT CONFLICT!
WOMEN CAN BE TROUBLESOME!
THEN MY BEST FRIEND, PATROCLUS, WENT OUT IN MY PLACE--AND THE TROJAN HERO, HECTOR, SLEW HIM!
SO I WENT BACK INTO BATTLE-- AND AVENGED MY FRIEND! HEED MY WORDS, JACK WESTON!
WELL, THAT'S IT--A FRIEND HAS TO SHOW CAP THE WAY! AND I'M ELECTED!
SO I'LL HAVE TO GO HOME FOR SOMETHING I HADN'T EXPECTED TO WEAR AGAIN!
AND SHORTLY AFTER...
IF I'M GOING TO HUNT DOWN SUPER-VILLAINS, I'LL DO IT BEST AS MINUTE MAN!
9

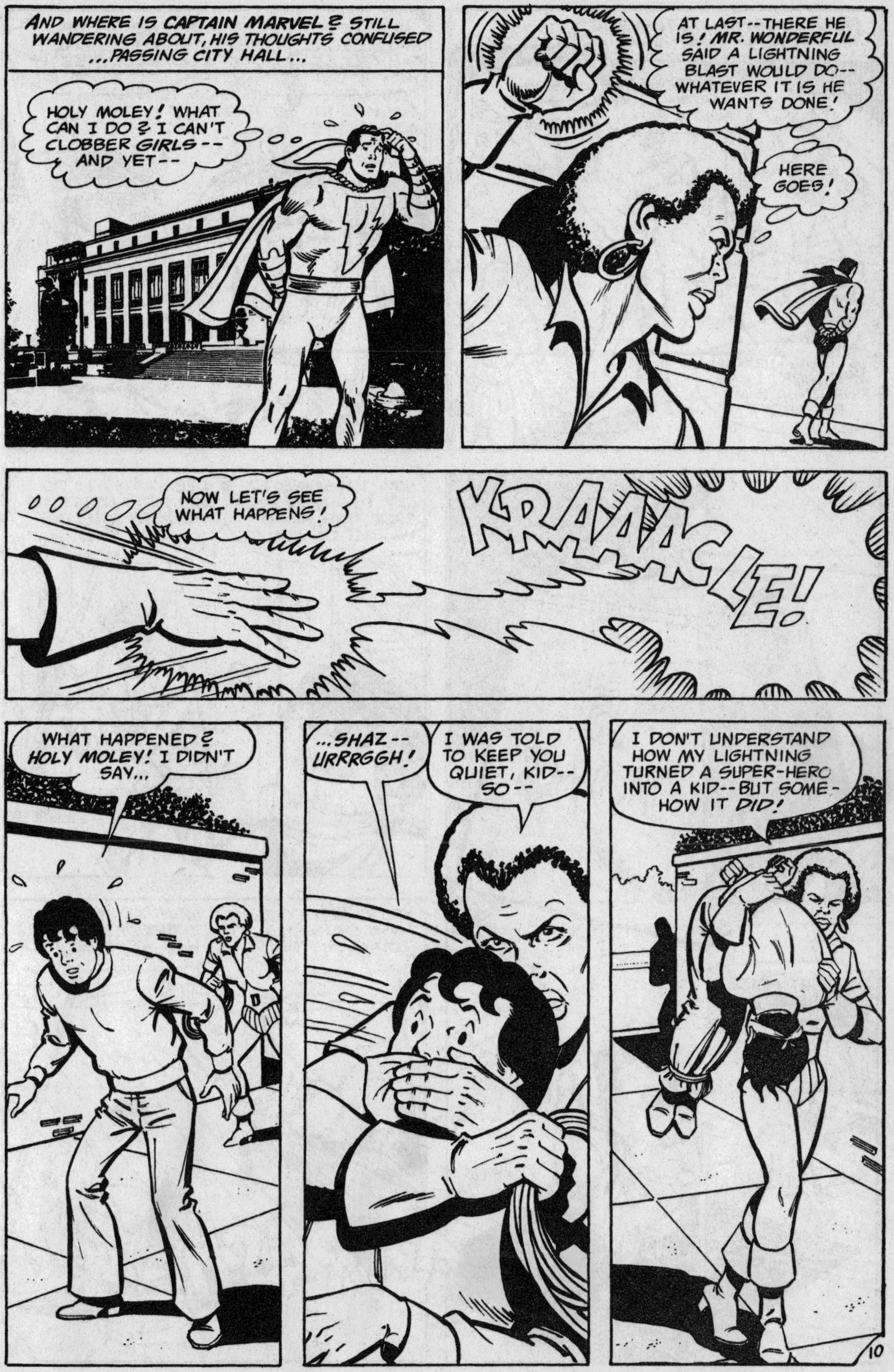
AND WHERE IS CAPTAIN MARVEL? STILL WANDERING ABOUT, HIS THOUGHTS CONFUSED ...PASSING CITY HALL...
HOLY MOLEY! WHAT CAN I DO? I CAN'T CLOBBER GIRLS -- AND YET --
AT LAST--THERE HE IS! MR. WONDERFUL SAID A LIGHTNING BLAST WOULD DO-- WHATEVER IT IS HE WANTS DONE!
HERE GOES!
NOW LET'S SEE WHAT HAPPENS!
KRAAACLE!
WHAT HAPPENED? HOLY MOLEY! I DIDN'T SAY...
...SHAZ-- URRRGGH!
I WAS TOLD TO KEEP YOU QUIET, KID-- SO--
I DON'T UNDERSTAND HOW MY LIGHTNING TURNED A SUPER-HERO INTO A KID--BUT SOME-HOW IT DID!
10

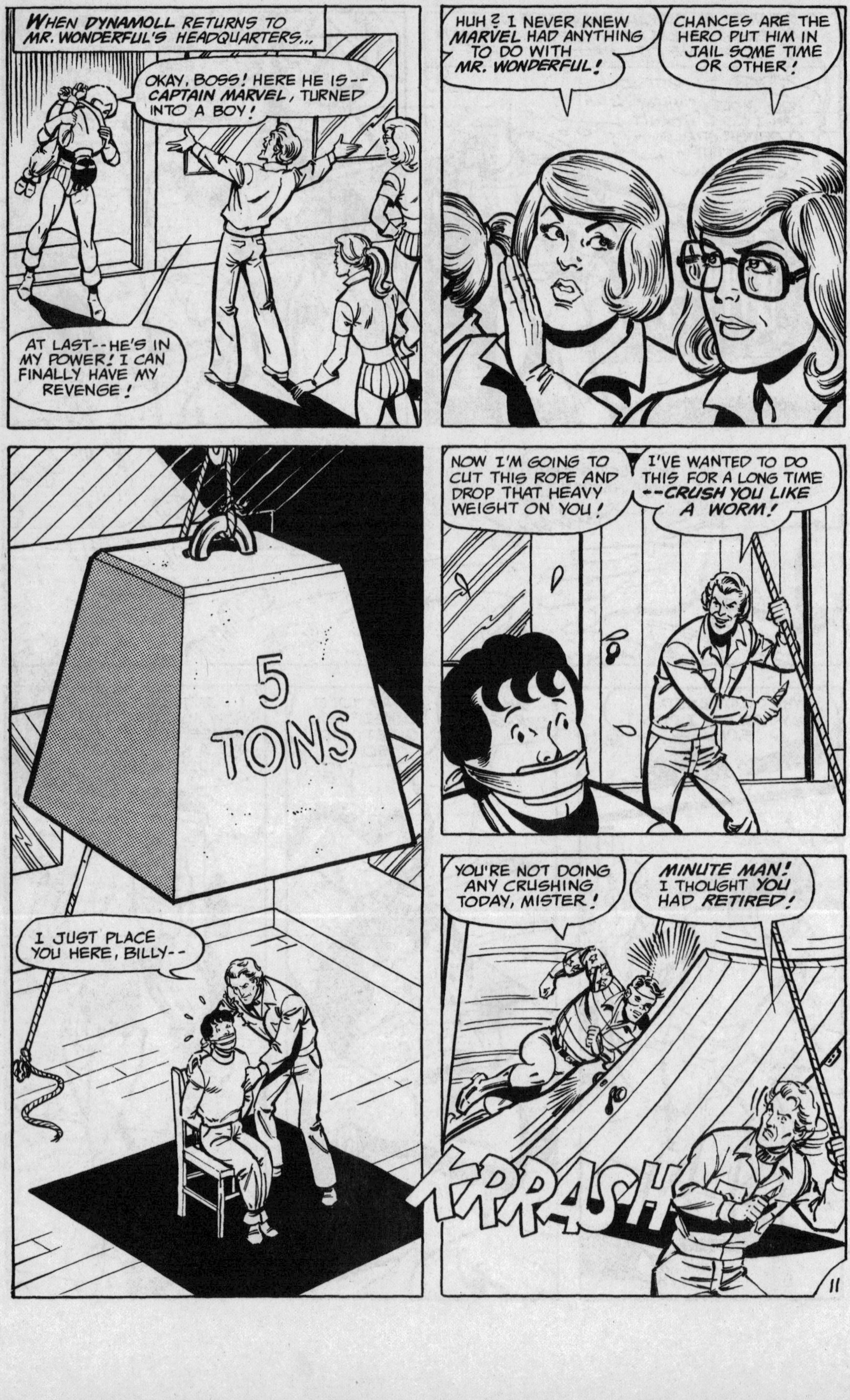
WHEN DYNAMOLL RETURNS TO MR. WONDERFUL'S HEADQUARTERS...
OKAY, BOSS! HERE HE IS-- CAPTAIN MARVEL, TURNED INTO A BOY!
AT LAST--HE'S IN MY POWER! I CAN FINALLY HAVE MY REVENGE!
HUH? I NEVER KNEW MARVEL HAD ANYTHING TO DO WITH MR. WONDERFUL!
CHANCES ARE THE HERO PUT HIM IN JAIL SOME TIME OR OTHER!
5 TONS
I JUST PLACE YOU HERE, BILLY--
NOW I'M GOING TO CUT THIS ROPE AND DROP THAT HEAVY WEIGHT ON YOU!
I'VE WANTED TO DO THIS FOR A LONG TIME --CRUSH YOU LIKE A WORM!
YOU'RE NOT DOING ANY CRUSHING TODAY, MISTER!
MINUTE MAN! I THOUGHT YOU HAD RETIRED!
KRRASH
11

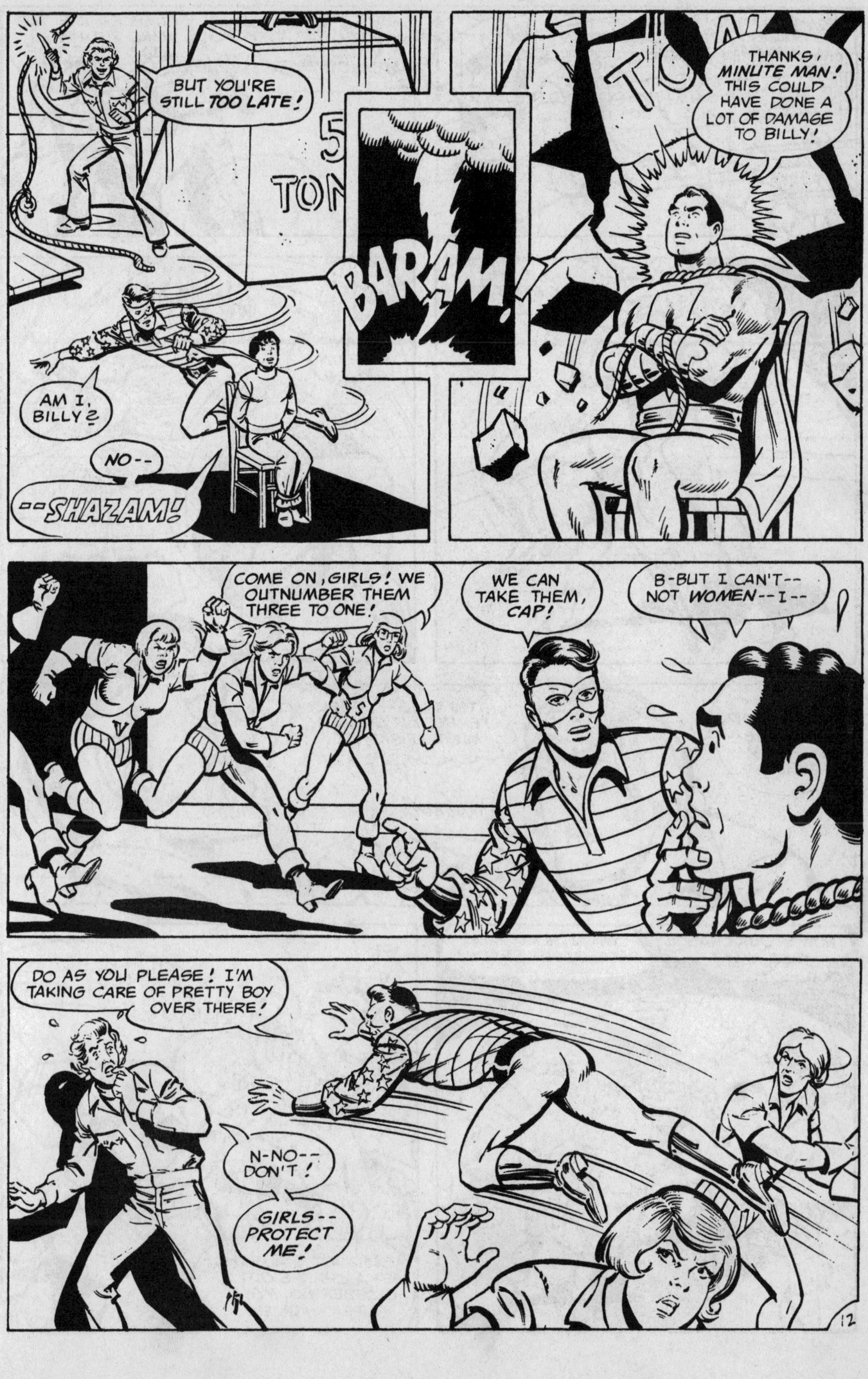
BUT YOU'RE STILL TOO LATE!
5 TON
AM I, BILLY?
NO--
--SHAZAM!
BARAM!
TON
THANKS, MINUTE MAN! THIS COULD HAVE DONE A LOT OF DAMAGE TO BILLY!
COME ON, GIRLS! WE OUTNUMBER THEM THREE TO ONE!
WE CAN TAKE THEM, CAP!
B-BUT I CAN'T-- NOT WOMEN--I--
DO AS YOU PLEASE! I'M TAKING CARE OF PRETTY BOY OVER THERE!
N-NO-- DON'T!
GIRLS-- PROTECT ME!
12

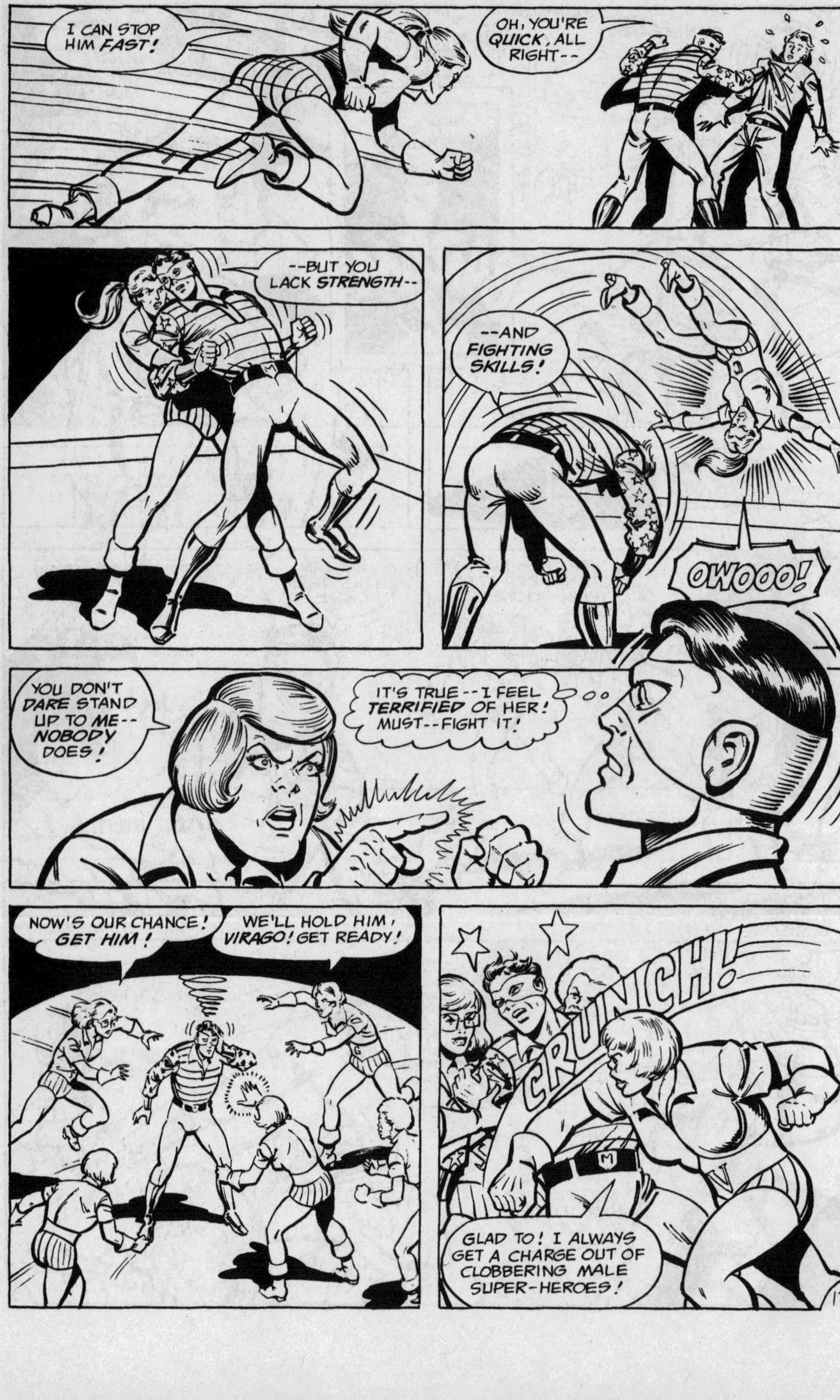
I CAN STOP HIM FAST!
OH, YOU'RE QUICK, ALL RIGHT--
--BUT YOU LACK STRENGTH--
--AND FIGHTING SKILLS!
OWOOO!
YOU DON'T DARE STAND UP TO ME--NOBODY DOES!
IT'S TRUE--I FEEL TERRIFIED OF HER! MUST--FIGHT IT!
NOW'S OUR CHANCE! GET HIM!
WE'LL HOLD HIM, VIRAGO! GET READY!
CRUNCH!
GLAD TO! I ALWAYS GET A CHARGE OUT OF CLOBBERING MALE SUPER-HEROES!
13

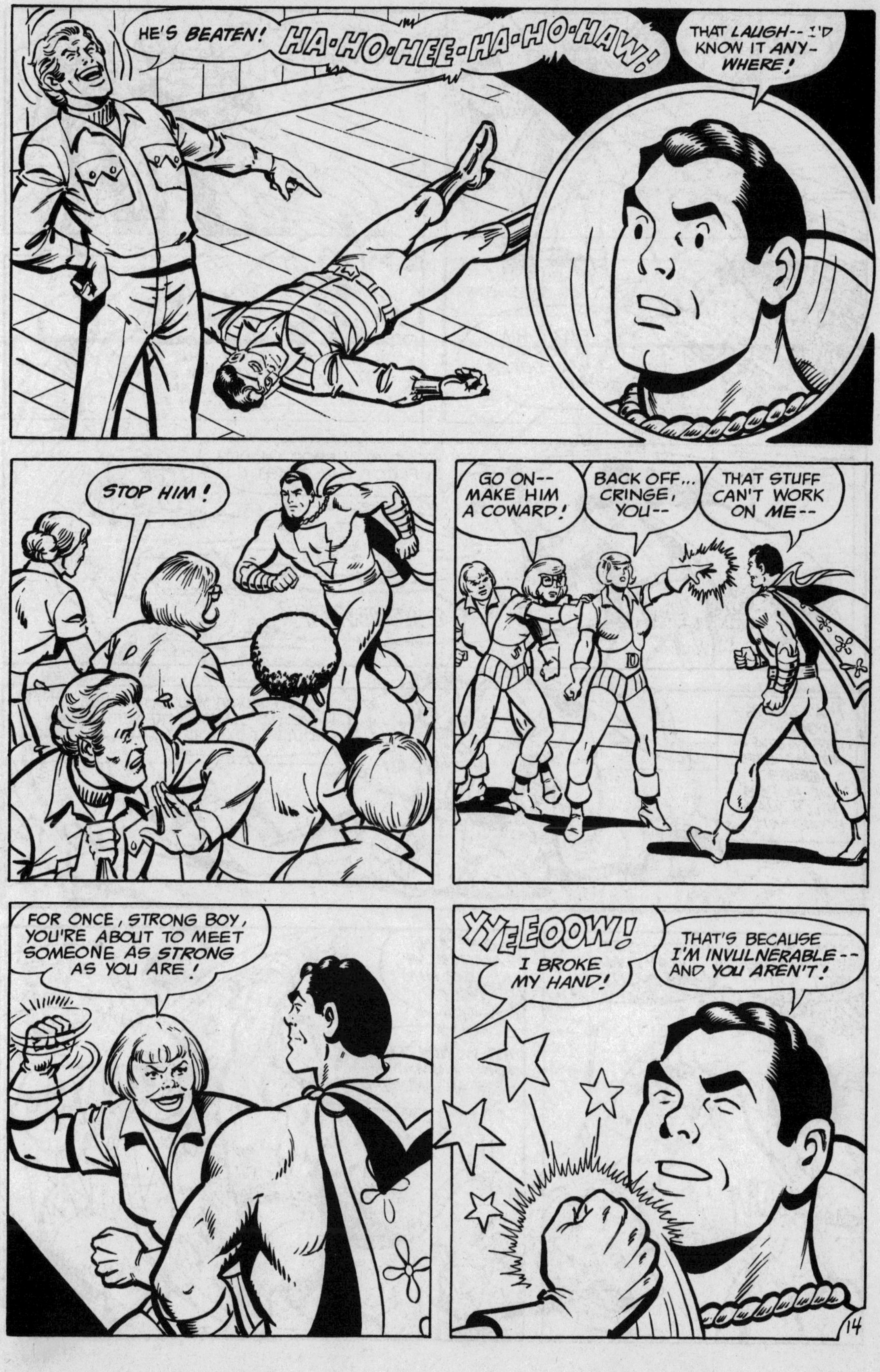
HE'S BEATEN!
HA-HO-HEE-HA-HO-HAW!
THAT LAUGH-- I'D KNOW IT ANYWHERE!
STOP HIM!
GO ON-- MAKE HIM A COWARD!
BACK OFF... CRINGE, YOU--
THAT STUFF CAN'T WORK ON ME--
FOR ONCE, STRONG BOY, YOU'RE ABOUT TO MEET SOMEONE AS STRONG AS YOU ARE!
YYEEOOW!
I BROKE MY HAND!
THAT'S BECAUSE I'M INVULNERABLE-- AND YOU AREN'T!
14

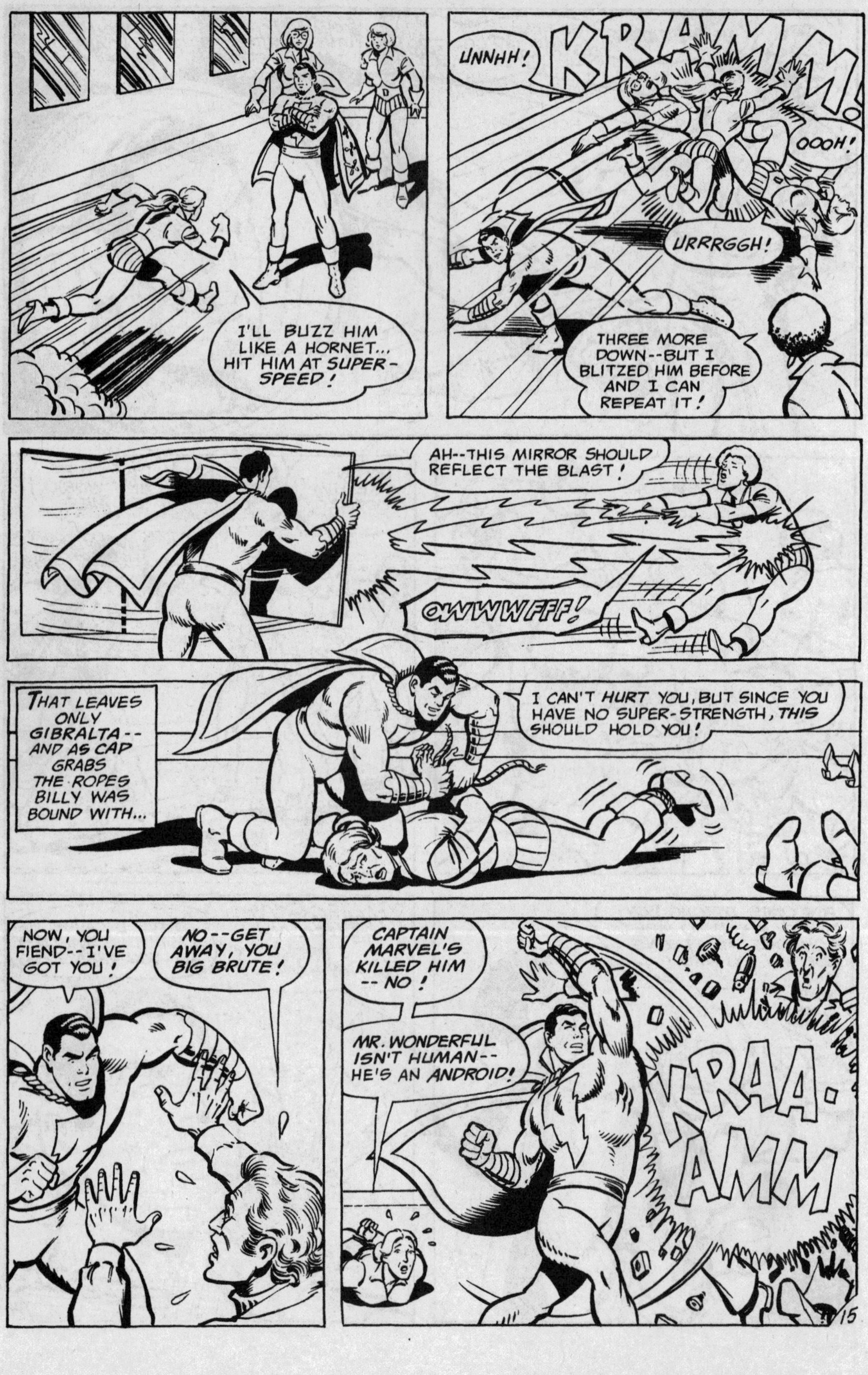
I'LL BUZZ HIM LIKE A HORNET... HIT HIM AT SUPER-SPEED!
UNNHH!
KRAMM!
OOOH!
URRRGGH!
THREE MORE DOWN--BUT I BLITZED HIM BEFORE AND I CAN REPEAT IT!
AH--THIS MIRROR SHOULD REFLECT THE BLAST!
OWWWFFF!
THAT LEAVES ONLY GIBRALTA--AND AS CAP GRABS THE ROPES BILLY WAS BOUND WITH...
I CAN'T HURT YOU, BUT SINCE YOU HAVE NO SUPER-STRENGTH, THIS SHOULD HOLD YOU!
NOW, YOU FIEND--I'VE GOT YOU!
NO--GET AWAY, YOU BIG BRUTE!
CAPTAIN MARVEL'S KILLED HIM --NO!
MR. WONDERFUL ISN'T HUMAN--HE'S AN ANDROID!
KRAA-AMM
15

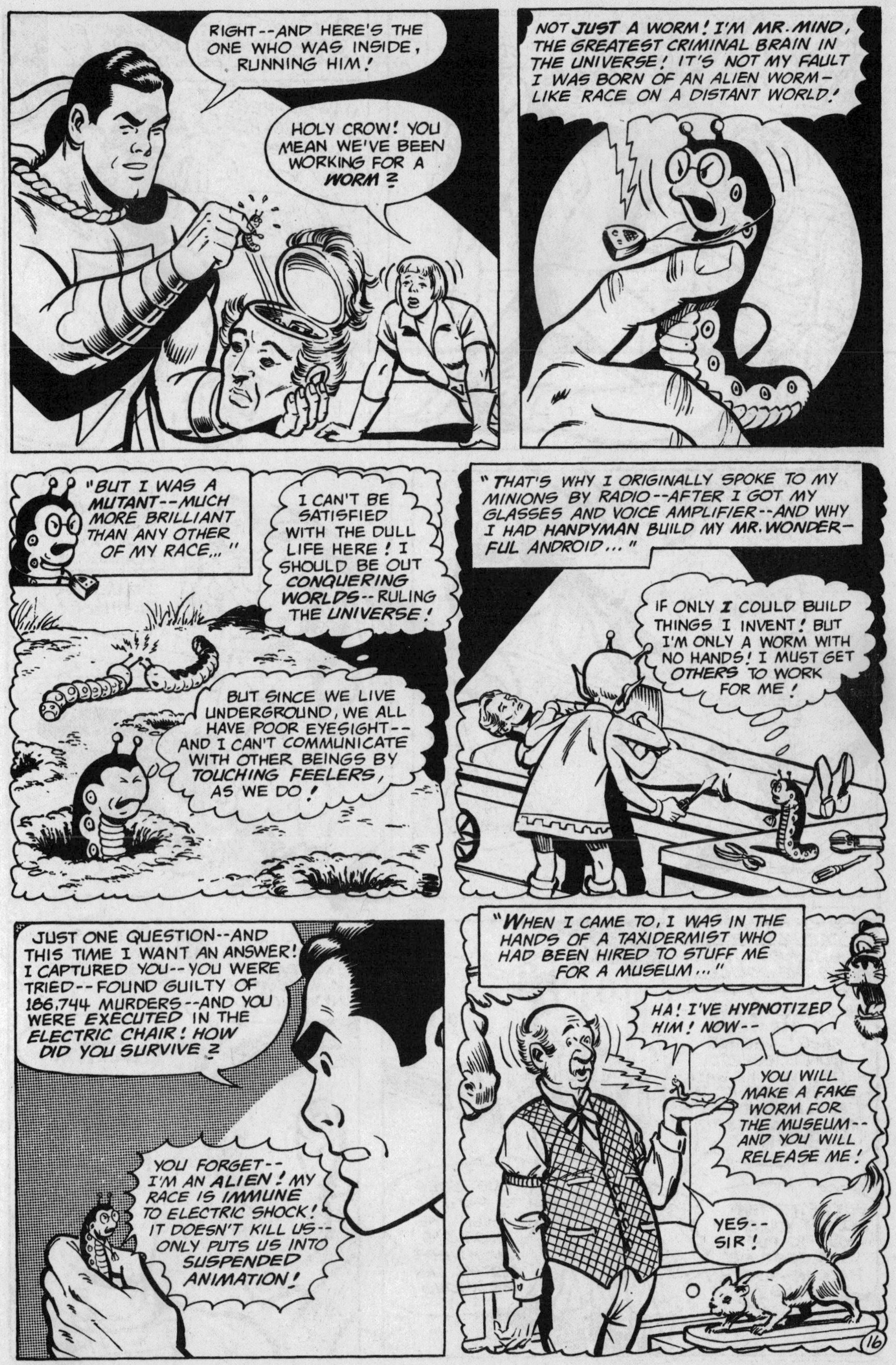
RIGHT--AND HERE'S THE ONE WHO WAS INSIDE, RUNNING HIM!
HOLY CROW! YOU MEAN WE'VE BEEN WORKING FOR A WORM?
NOT JUST A WORM! I'M MR. MIND, THE GREATEST CRIMINAL BRAIN IN THE UNIVERSE! IT'S NOT MY FAULT I WAS BORN OF AN ALIEN WORM-LIKE RACE ON A DISTANT WORLD!
"BUT I WAS A MUTANT--MUCH MORE BRILLIANT THAN ANY OTHER OF MY RACE..."
I CAN'T BE SATISFIED WITH THE DULL LIFE HERE! I SHOULD BE OUT CONQUERING WORLDS--RULING THE UNIVERSE!
BUT SINCE WE LIVE UNDERGROUND, WE ALL HAVE POOR EYESIGHT--AND I CAN'T COMMUNICATE WITH OTHER BEINGS BY TOUCHING FEELERS, AS WE DO!
"THAT'S WHY I ORIGINALLY SPOKE TO MY MINIONS BY RADIO--AFTER I GOT MY GLASSES AND VOICE AMPLIFIER--AND WHY I HAD HANDYMAN BUILD MY MR. WONDERFUL ANDROID..."
IF ONLY I COULD BUILD THINGS I INVENT! BUT I'M ONLY A WORM WITH NO HANDS! I MUST GET OTHERS TO WORK FOR ME!
JUST ONE QUESTION--AND THIS TIME I WANT AN ANSWER! I CAPTURED YOU--YOU WERE TRIED--FOUND GUILTY OF 186,744 MURDERS--AND YOU WERE EXECUTED IN THE ELECTRIC CHAIR! HOW DID YOU SURVIVE?
YOU FORGET--I'M AN ALIEN! MY RACE IS IMMUNE TO ELECTRIC SHOCK! IT DOESN'T KILL US--ONLY PUTS US INTO SUSPENDED ANIMATION!
"WHEN I CAME TO, I WAS IN THE HANDS OF A TAXIDERMIST WHO HAD BEEN HIRED TO STUFF ME FOR A MUSEUM..."
HA! I'VE HYPNOTIZED HIM! NOW--
YOU WILL MAKE A FAKE WORM FOR THE MUSEUM--AND YOU WILL RELEASE ME!
YES--SIR!
16

OOOOH! MAN, DOES THAT BABE PACK A WALLOP!

MINUTE MAN! THANK HEAVENS YOU'RE NOT BADLY HURT!

BUT, HIS ATTENTION DISTRACTED, CAPTAIN MARVEL LOOSENS HIS GRIP EVER SO SLIGHTLY--AND...

HAW-HA-HEE-HO-HOO-HEE! I'M FREE!

HEY!

DOWN THIS CRACK AND I'M SAFE! I HAVE BUSINESS IN DETROIT!

JUST MISSED HIM!

HMMM--IF MR. MIND HAS SOME DEVILTRY PLANNED FOR DETROIT, I'D BETTER BE THERE!

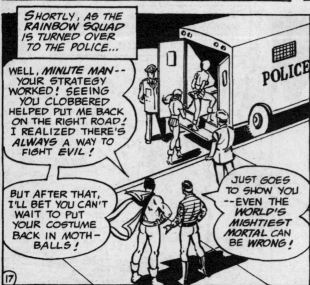

SHORTLY, AS THE RAINBOW SQUAD IS TURNED OVER TO THE POLICE...

WELL, MINUTE MAN-- YOUR STRATEGY WORKED! SEEING YOU CLOBBERED HELPED PUT ME BACK ON THE RIGHT ROAD! I REALIZED THERE'S ALWAYS A WAY TO FIGHT EVIL!

BUT AFTER THAT, I'LL BET YOU CAN'T WAIT TO PUT YOUR COSTUME BACK IN MOTH-BALLS!

JUST GOES TO SHOW YOU --EVEN THE WORLD'S MIGHTIEST MORTAL CAN BE WRONG!

POLICE

⑰

I REALIZE NOW WHAT MY LIFE'S BEEN LACKING THESE LAST FEW YEARS-- EXCITEMENT! YOU MAY BE SEEING MINUTE MAN IN HARNESS A LOT FROM NOW ON!

WELCOME BACK, PAL!

THE END

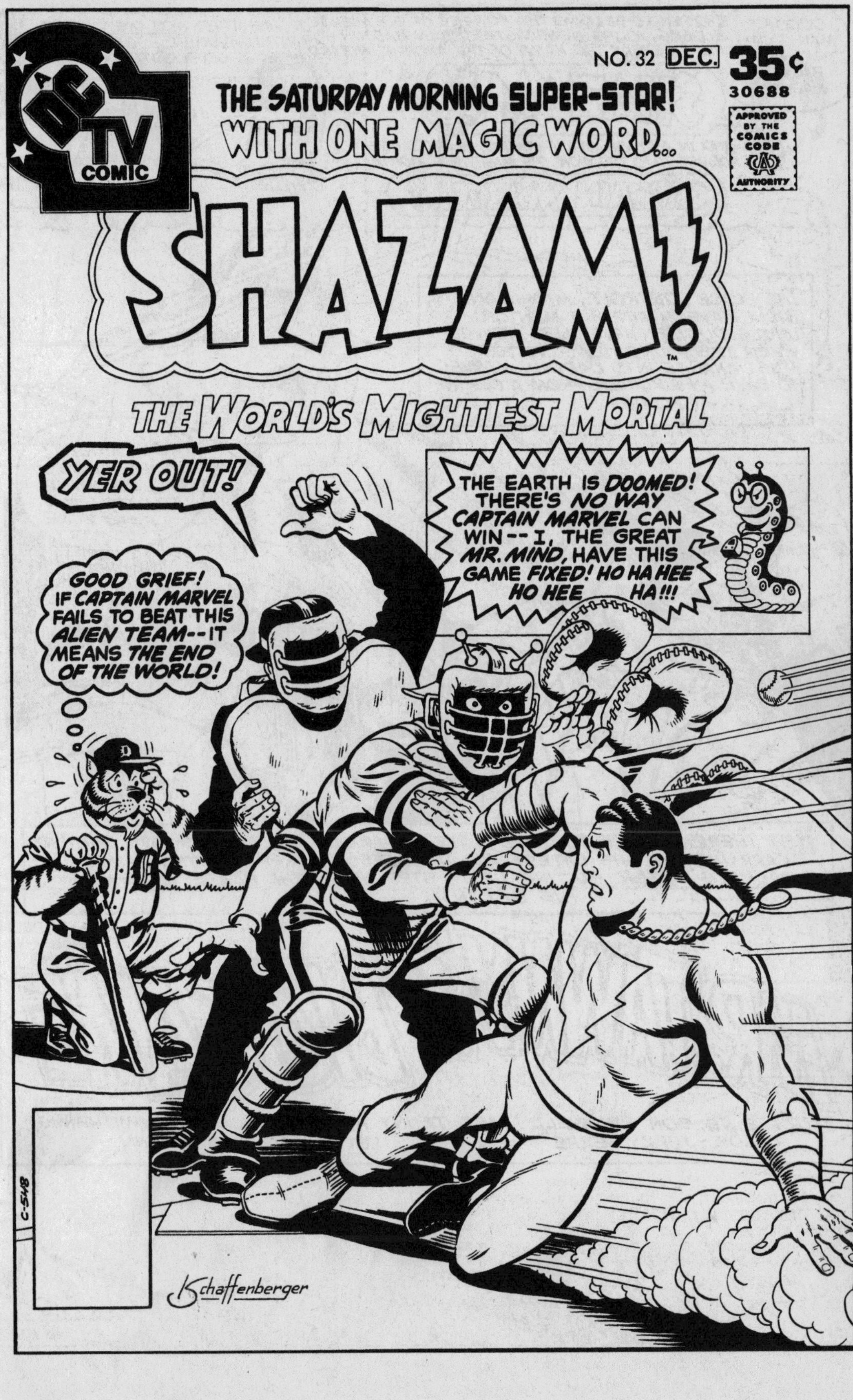
A DC TV COMIC
NO. 32 DEC.
35¢
30688
APPROVED BY THE COMICS CODE AUTHORITY
THE SATURDAY MORNING SUPER-STAR!
WITH ONE MAGIC WORD...
SHAZAM!
THE WORLD'S MIGHTIEST MORTAL
YER OUT!
THE EARTH IS DOOMED! THERE'S NO WAY CAPTAIN MARVEL CAN WIN -- I, THE GREAT MR. MIND, HAVE THIS GAME FIXED! HO HA HEE HO HEE HA!!!
GOOD GRIEF! IF CAPTAIN MARVEL FAILS TO BEAT THIS ALIEN TEAM--IT MEANS THE END OF THE WORLD!
C-548
KSchaffenberger

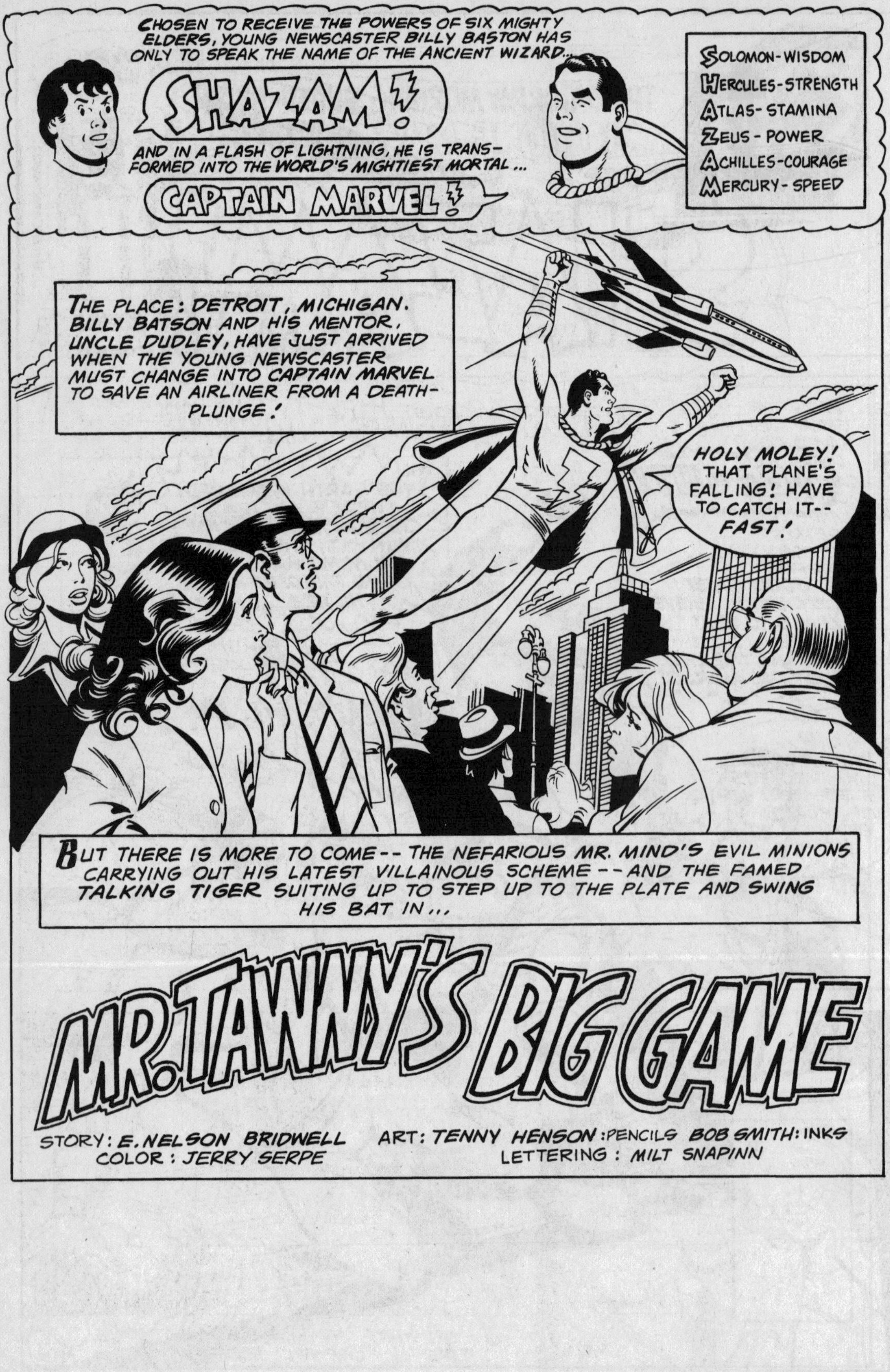
CHOSEN TO RECEIVE THE POWERS OF SIX MIGHTY ELDERS, YOUNG NEWSCASTER BILLY BASTON HAS ONLY TO SPEAK THE NAME OF THE ANCIENT WIZARD...
SHAZAM!
AND IN A FLASH OF LIGHTNING, HE IS TRANS-FORMED INTO THE WORLD'S MIGHTIEST MORTAL ...
CAPTAIN MARVEL!
SOLOMON-WISDOM
HERCULES-STRENGTH
ATLAS-STAMINA
ZEUS-POWER
ACHILLES-COURAGE
MERCURY-SPEED
THE PLACE: DETROIT, MICHIGAN. BILLY BATSON AND HIS MENTOR, UNCLE DUDLEY, HAVE JUST ARRIVED WHEN THE YOUNG NEWSCASTER MUST CHANGE INTO CAPTAIN MARVEL TO SAVE AN AIRLINER FROM A DEATH-PLUNGE!
HOLY MOLEY! THAT PLANE'S FALLING! HAVE TO CATCH IT-- FAST!
BUT THERE IS MORE TO COME-- THE NEFARIOUS MR. MIND'S EVIL MINIONS CARRYING OUT HIS LATEST VILLAINOUS SCHEME--AND THE FAMED TALKING TIGER SUITING UP TO STEP UP TO THE PLATE AND SWING HIS BAT IN...
MR. TAWNY'S BIG GAME
STORY: E. NELSON BRIDWELL ART: TENNY HENSON: PENCILS BOB SMITH: INKS
COLOR: JERRY SERPE LETTERING: MILT SNAPINN

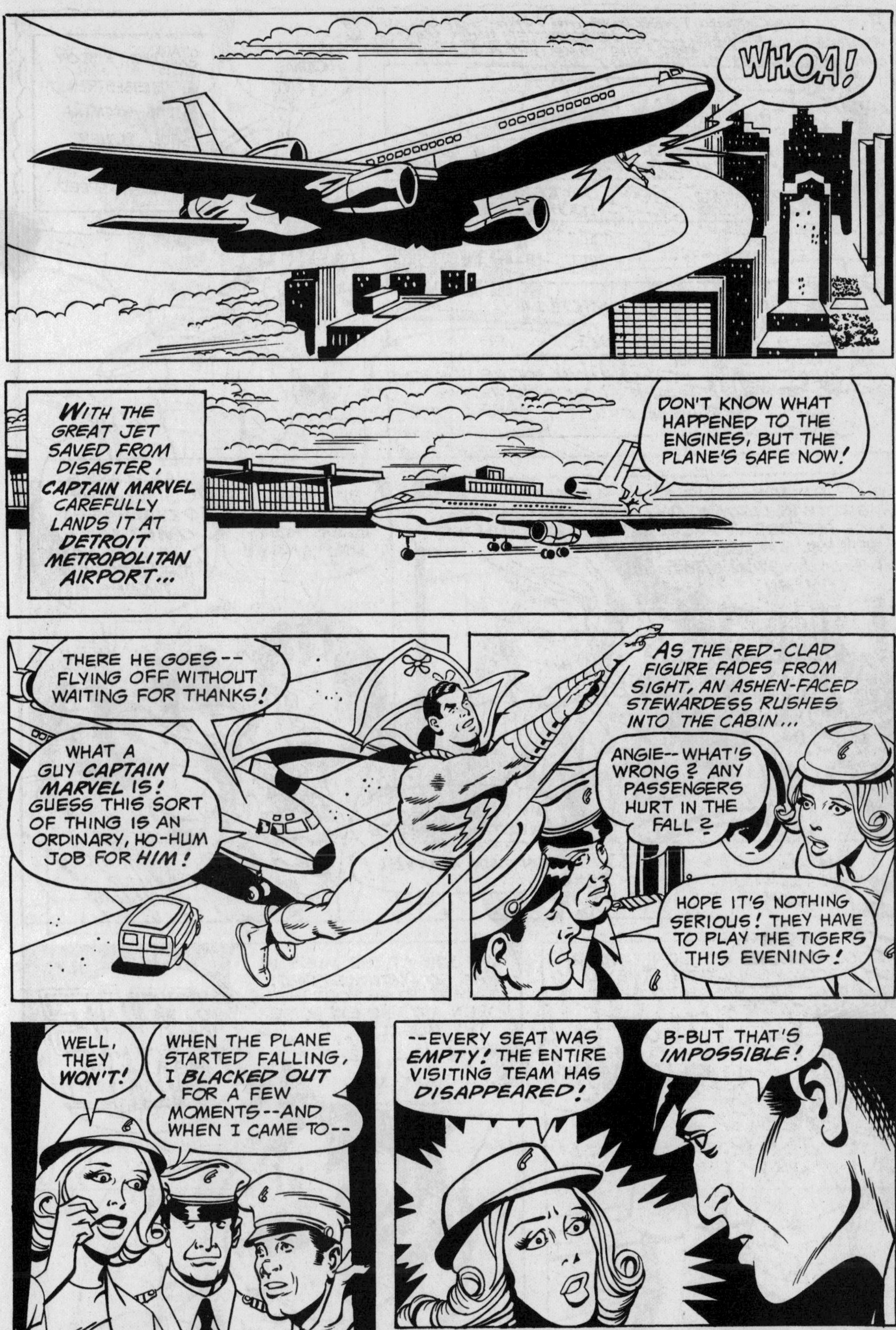
WHOA!
WITH THE GREAT JET SAVED FROM DISASTER, CAPTAIN MARVEL CAREFULLY LANDS IT AT DETROIT METROPOLITAN AIRPORT...
DON'T KNOW WHAT HAPPENED TO THE ENGINES, BUT THE PLANE'S SAFE NOW!
THERE HE GOES-- FLYING OFF WITHOUT WAITING FOR THANKS!
WHAT A GUY CAPTAIN MARVEL IS! GUESS THIS SORT OF THING IS AN ORDINARY, HO-HUM JOB FOR HIM!
AS THE RED-CLAD FIGURE FADES FROM SIGHT, AN ASHEN-FACED STEWARDESS RUSHES INTO THE CABIN...
ANGIE-- WHAT'S WRONG? ANY PASSENGERS HURT IN THE FALL?
HOPE IT'S NOTHING SERIOUS! THEY HAVE TO PLAY THE TIGERS THIS EVENING!
WELL, THEY WON'T!
WHEN THE PLANE STARTED FALLING, I BLACKED OUT FOR A FEW MOMENTS--AND WHEN I CAME TO--
--EVERY SEAT WAS EMPTY! THE ENTIRE VISITING TEAM HAS DISAPPEARED!
B-BUT THAT'S IMPOSSIBLE!
AN ORDINARY "HO-HUM JOB"? NOT THIS TIME--AS CAP WILL SOON FIND OUT!
2

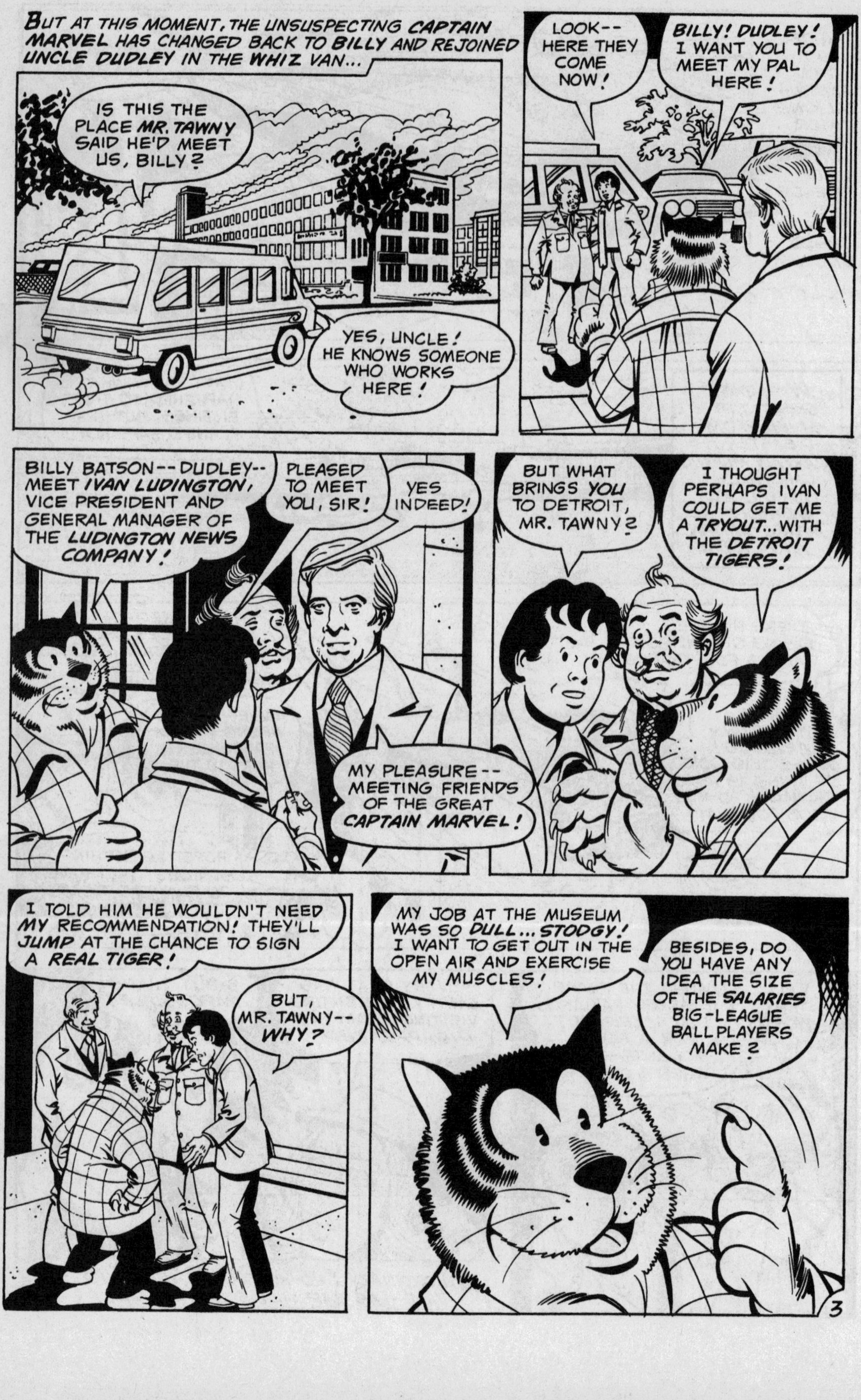
BUT AT THIS MOMENT, THE UNSUSPECTING CAPTAIN MARVEL HAS CHANGED BACK TO BILLY AND REJOINED UNCLE DUDLEY IN THE WHIZ VAN...
IS THIS THE PLACE MR. TAWNY SAID HE'D MEET US, BILLY?
YES, UNCLE! HE KNOWS SOMEONE WHO WORKS HERE!
LOOK-- HERE THEY COME NOW!
BILLY! DUDLEY! I WANT YOU TO MEET MY PAL HERE!
BILLY BATSON--DUDLEY-- MEET IVAN LUDINGTON, VICE PRESIDENT AND GENERAL MANAGER OF THE LUDINGTON NEWS COMPANY!
PLEASED TO MEET YOU, SIR!
YES INDEED!
MY PLEASURE-- MEETING FRIENDS OF THE GREAT CAPTAIN MARVEL!
BUT WHAT BRINGS YOU TO DETROIT, MR. TAWNY?
I THOUGHT PERHAPS IVAN COULD GET ME A TRYOUT...WITH THE DETROIT TIGERS!
I TOLD HIM HE WOULDN'T NEED MY RECOMMENDATION! THEY'LL JUMP AT THE CHANCE TO SIGN A REAL TIGER!
BUT, MR. TAWNY-- WHY?
MY JOB AT THE MUSEUM WAS SO DULL... STODGY! I WANT TO GET OUT IN THE OPEN AIR AND EXERCISE MY MUSCLES!
BESIDES, DO YOU HAVE ANY IDEA THE SIZE OF THE SALARIES BIG-LEAGUE BALLPLAYERS MAKE?
3

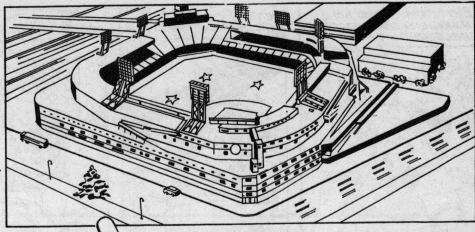

AND SO THE FAMOUS TALKING TIGER GOES WITH HIS FRIENDS TO FAMED TIGER STADIUM...

...AND AFTER HASTY NEGOTIATIONS, TAWKY TAWNY IS SUITED UP AND READY TO TRY OUT...

ALL RIGHT--LET'S HAVE A PITCH--AND DON'T HOLD BACK!

STRIKE ONE!

WHIFF

LET'S TRY IT AGAIN-- UMPH!

WHOOF

STRIKE TWO!

CRACK!

AH! GOT IT THAT TIME!

NOT BAD--A LITTLE MORE WOOD AND YOU MIGHT'VE HAD A HOMER!

THAT'S GOOD FOR EXTRA BASES AS IT IS!

4

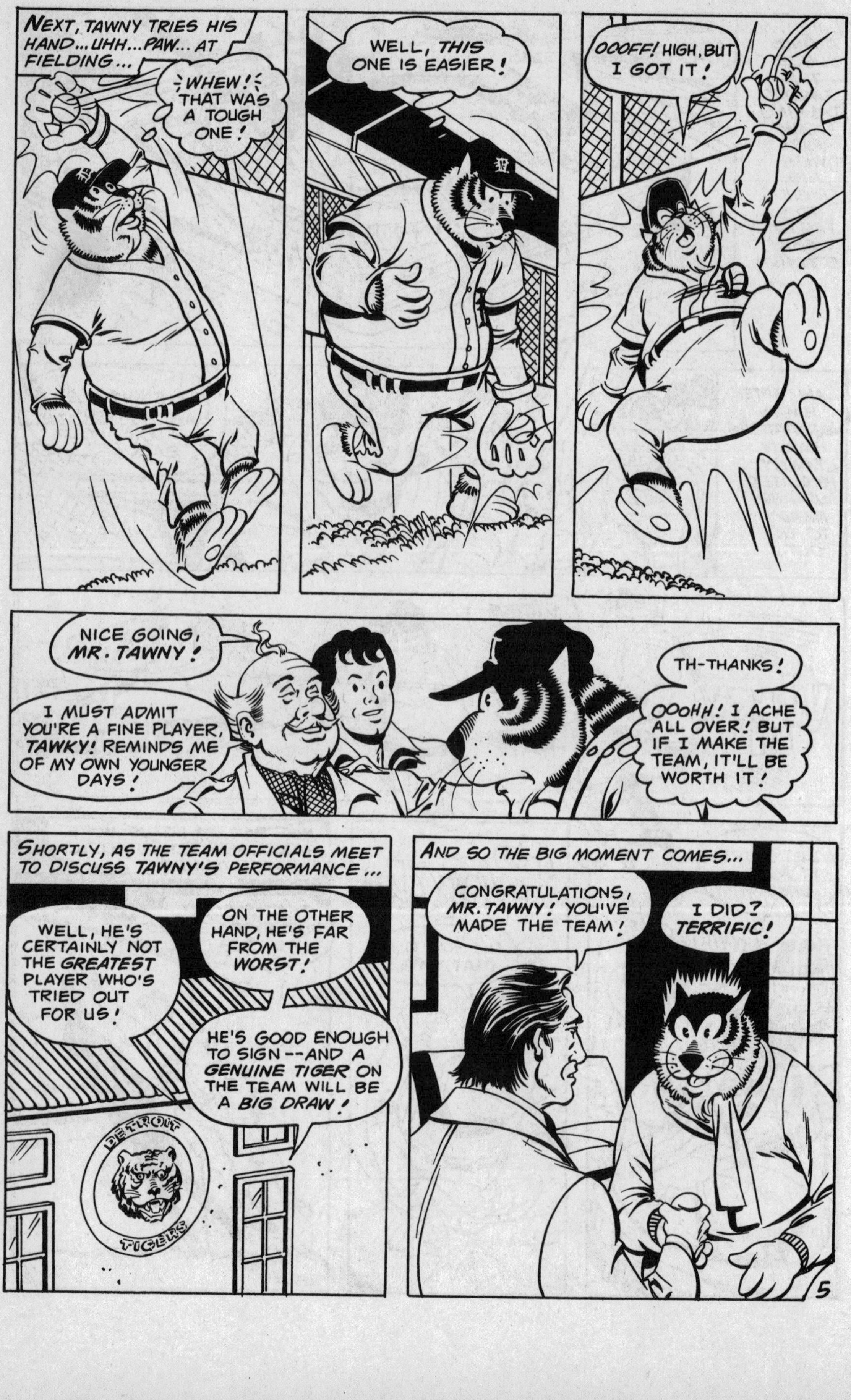
NEXT, TAWNY TRIES HIS HAND... UHH... PAW... AT FIELDING...
WHEW! THAT WAS A TOUGH ONE!
WELL, THIS ONE IS EASIER!
OOOFF! HIGH, BUT I GOT IT!
NICE GOING, MR. TAWNY!
I MUST ADMIT YOU'RE A FINE PLAYER, TAWKY! REMINDS ME OF MY OWN YOUNGER DAYS!
TH-THANKS!
OOOHH! I ACHE ALL OVER! BUT IF I MAKE THE TEAM, IT'LL BE WORTH IT!
SHORTLY, AS THE TEAM OFFICIALS MEET TO DISCUSS TAWNY'S PERFORMANCE...
WELL, HE'S CERTAINLY NOT THE GREATEST PLAYER WHO'S TRIED OUT FOR US!
ON THE OTHER HAND, HE'S FAR FROM THE WORST!
HE'S GOOD ENOUGH TO SIGN--AND A GENUINE TIGER ON THE TEAM WILL BE A BIG DRAW!
DETROIT
TIGERS
AND SO THE BIG MOMENT COMES...
CONGRATULATIONS, MR. TAWNY! YOU'VE MADE THE TEAM!
I DID? TERRIFIC!
5

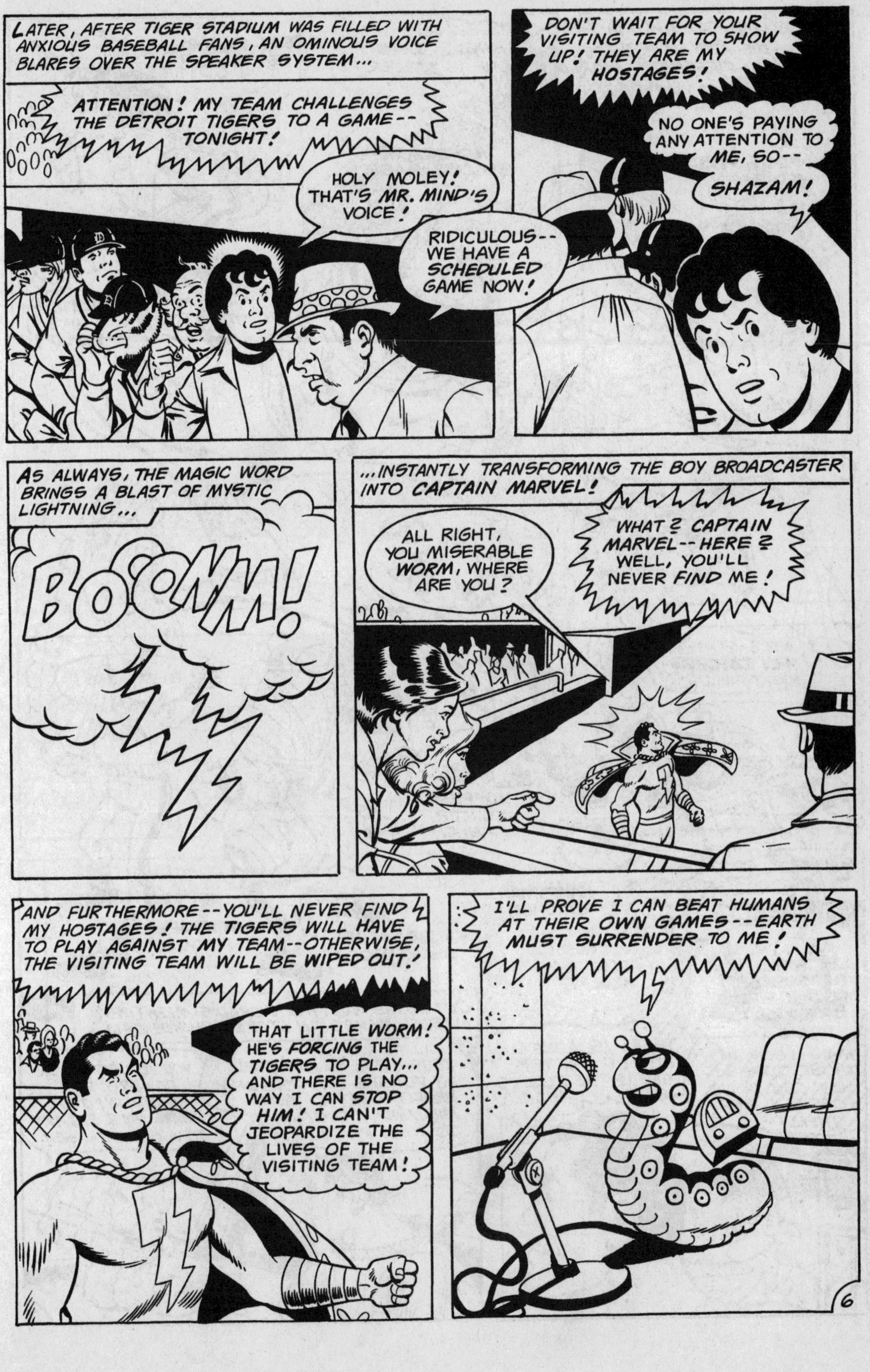
LATER, AFTER TIGER STADIUM WAS FILLED WITH ANXIOUS BASEBALL FANS, AN OMINOUS VOICE BLARES OVER THE SPEAKER SYSTEM...
ATTENTION! MY TEAM CHALLENGES THE DETROIT TIGERS TO A GAME-- TONIGHT!
HOLY MOLEY! THAT'S MR. MIND'S VOICE!
RIDICULOUS-- WE HAVE A SCHEDULED GAME NOW!
DON'T WAIT FOR YOUR VISITING TEAM TO SHOW UP! THEY ARE MY HOSTAGES!
NO ONE'S PAYING ANY ATTENTION TO ME, SO--
SHAZAM!
AS ALWAYS, THE MAGIC WORD BRINGS A BLAST OF MYSTIC LIGHTNING...
BOOOMM!
...INSTANTLY TRANSFORMING THE BOY BROADCASTER INTO CAPTAIN MARVEL!
ALL RIGHT, YOU MISERABLE WORM, WHERE ARE YOU?
WHAT? CAPTAIN MARVEL--HERE? WELL, YOU'LL NEVER FIND ME!
AND FURTHERMORE--YOU'LL NEVER FIND MY HOSTAGES! THE TIGERS WILL HAVE TO PLAY AGAINST MY TEAM--OTHERWISE, THE VISITING TEAM WILL BE WIPED OUT!
THAT LITTLE WORM! HE'S FORCING THE TIGERS TO PLAY... AND THERE IS NO WAY I CAN STOP HIM! I CAN'T JEOPARDIZE THE LIVES OF THE VISITING TEAM!
I'LL PROVE I CAN BEAT HUMANS AT THEIR OWN GAMES--EARTH MUST SURRENDER TO ME!
6

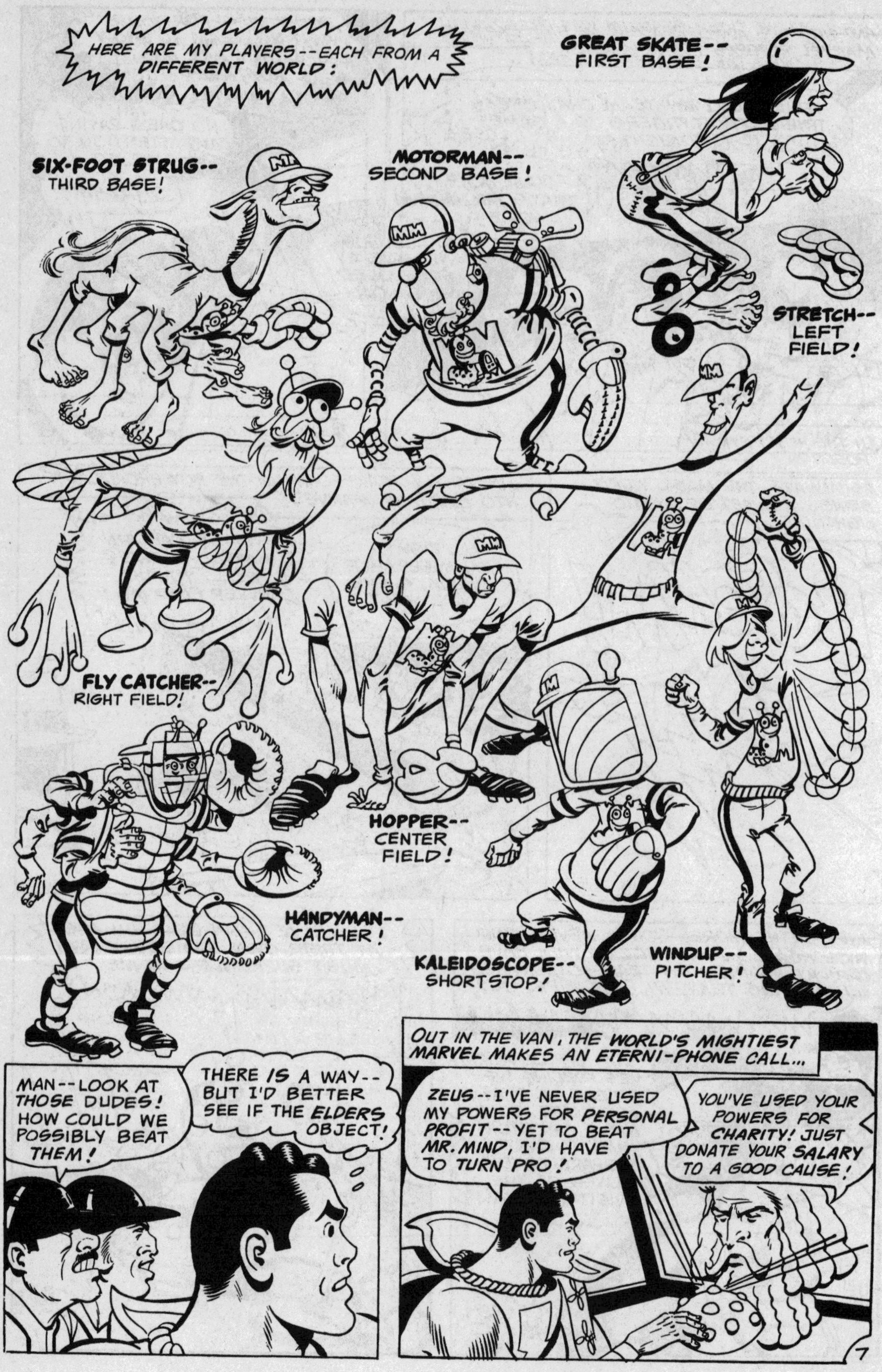
HERE ARE MY PLAYERS--EACH FROM A DIFFERENT WORLD:
GREAT SKATE-- FIRST BASE!
SIX-FOOT STRUG-- THIRD BASE!
MOTORMAN-- SECOND BASE!
STRETCH-- LEFT FIELD!
FLY CATCHER-- RIGHT FIELD!
HOPPER-- CENTER FIELD!
HANDYMAN-- CATCHER!
KALEIDOSCOPE-- SHORTSTOP!
WINDUP-- PITCHER!
MAN--LOOK AT THOSE DUDES! HOW COULD WE POSSIBLY BEAT THEM!
THERE IS A WAY-- BUT I'D BETTER SEE IF THE ELDERS OBJECT!
OUT IN THE VAN, THE WORLD'S MIGHTIEST MARVEL MAKES AN ETERNI-PHONE CALL...
ZEUS--I'VE NEVER USED MY POWERS FOR PERSONAL PROFIT--YET TO BEAT MR. MIND, I'D HAVE TO TURN PRO!
YOU'VE USED YOUR POWERS FOR CHARITY! JUST DONATE YOUR SALARY TO A GOOD CAUSE!
7

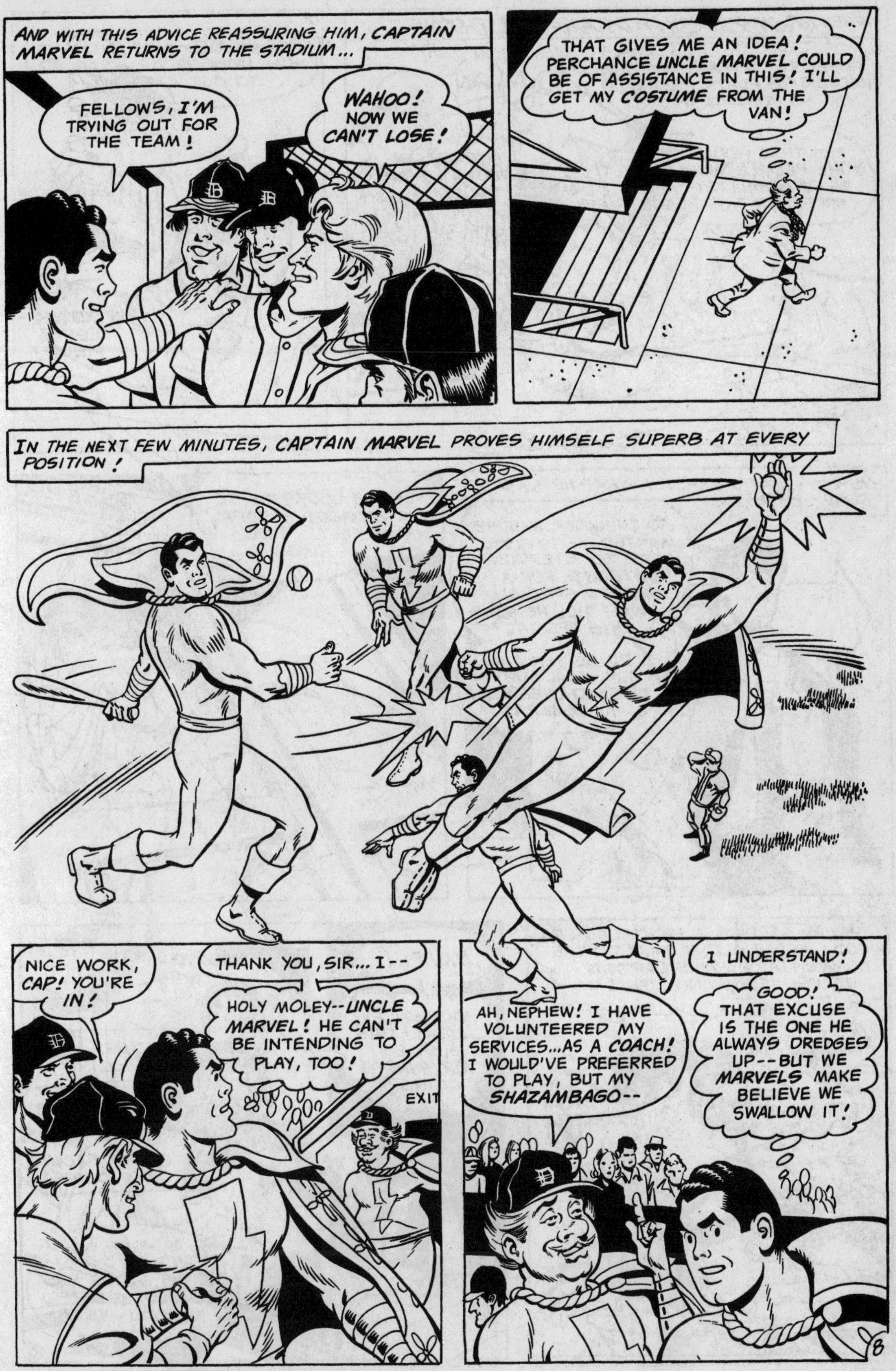
AND WITH THIS ADVICE REASSURING HIM, CAPTAIN MARVEL RETURNS TO THE STADIUM...
FELLOWS, I'M TRYING OUT FOR THE TEAM!
WAHOO! NOW WE CAN'T LOSE!
THAT GIVES ME AN IDEA! PERCHANCE UNCLE MARVEL COULD BE OF ASSISTANCE IN THIS! I'LL GET MY COSTUME FROM THE VAN!
IN THE NEXT FEW MINUTES, CAPTAIN MARVEL PROVES HIMSELF SUPERB AT EVERY POSITION!
NICE WORK, CAP! YOU'RE IN!
THANK YOU, SIR... I--
HOLY MOLEY--UNCLE MARVEL! HE CAN'T BE INTENDING TO PLAY, TOO!
EXIT
AH, NEPHEW! I HAVE VOLUNTEERED MY SERVICES...AS A COACH! I WOULD'VE PREFERRED TO PLAY, BUT MY SHAZAMBAGO--
I UNDERSTAND!
GOOD! THAT EXCUSE IS THE ONE HE ALWAYS DREDGES UP--BUT WE MARVELS MAKE BELIEVE WE SWALLOW IT!
8

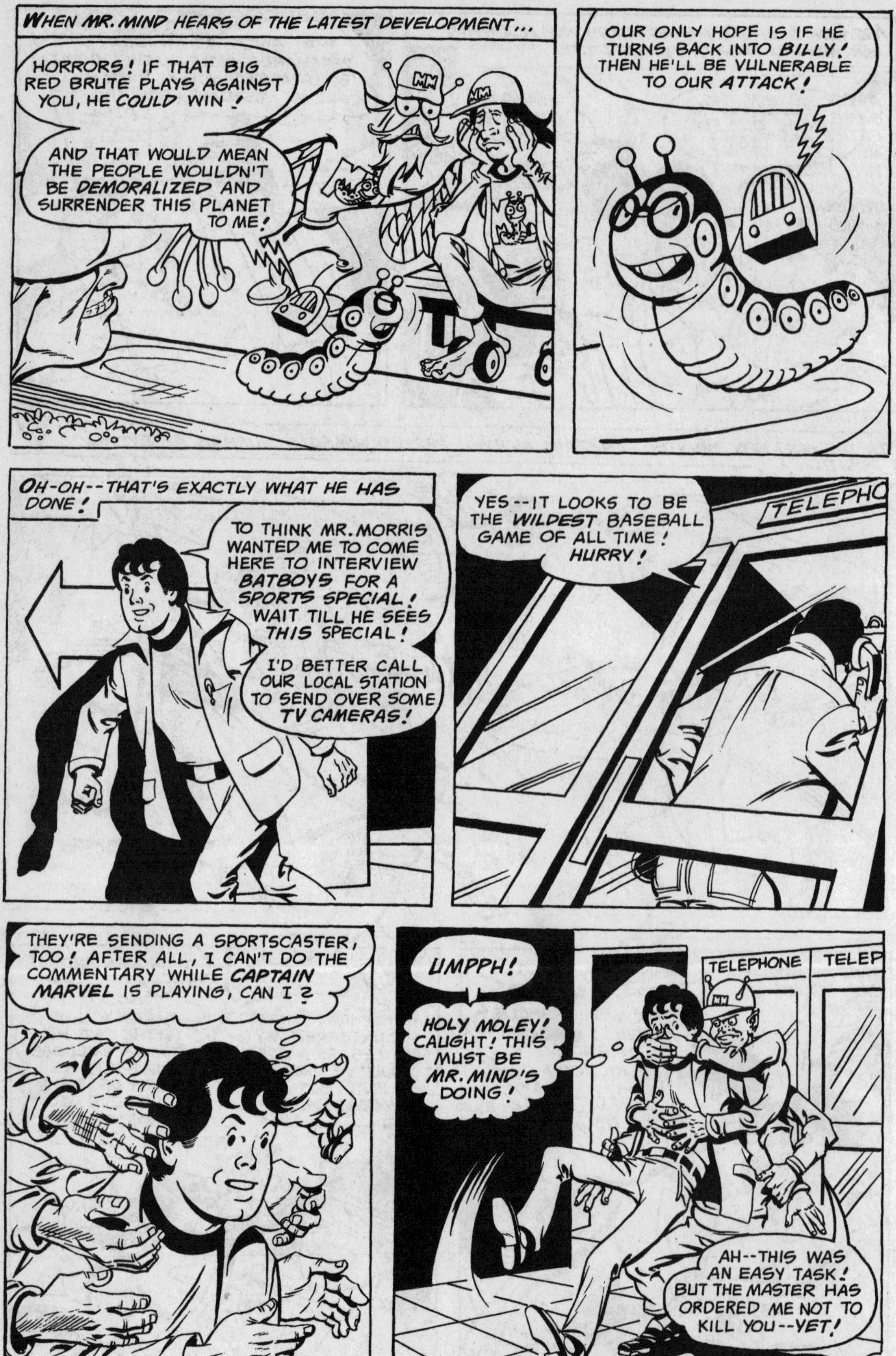
WHEN MR. MIND HEARS OF THE LATEST DEVELOPMENT...
HORRORS! IF THAT BIG RED BRUTE PLAYS AGAINST YOU, HE COULD WIN!
AND THAT WOULD MEAN THE PEOPLE WOULDN'T BE DEMORALIZED AND SURRENDER THIS PLANET TO ME!
MM
OUR ONLY HOPE IS IF HE TURNS BACK INTO BILLY! THEN HE'LL BE VULNERABLE TO OUR ATTACK!
OH-OH--THAT'S EXACTLY WHAT HE HAS DONE!
TO THINK MR. MORRIS WANTED ME TO COME HERE TO INTERVIEW BATBOYS FOR A SPORTS SPECIAL! WAIT TILL HE SEES THIS SPECIAL!
I'D BETTER CALL OUR LOCAL STATION TO SEND OVER SOME TV CAMERAS!
YES--IT LOOKS TO BE THE WILDEST BASEBALL GAME OF ALL TIME! HURRY!
TELEPHO
THEY'RE SENDING A SPORTSCASTER, TOO! AFTER ALL, I CAN'T DO THE COMMENTARY WHILE CAPTAIN MARVEL IS PLAYING, CAN I?
UMPPH!
HOLY MOLEY! CAUGHT! THIS MUST BE MR. MIND'S DOING!
TELEPHONE TELEP
AH--THIS WAS AN EASY TASK! BUT THE MASTER HAS ORDERED ME NOT TO KILL YOU--YET!
9

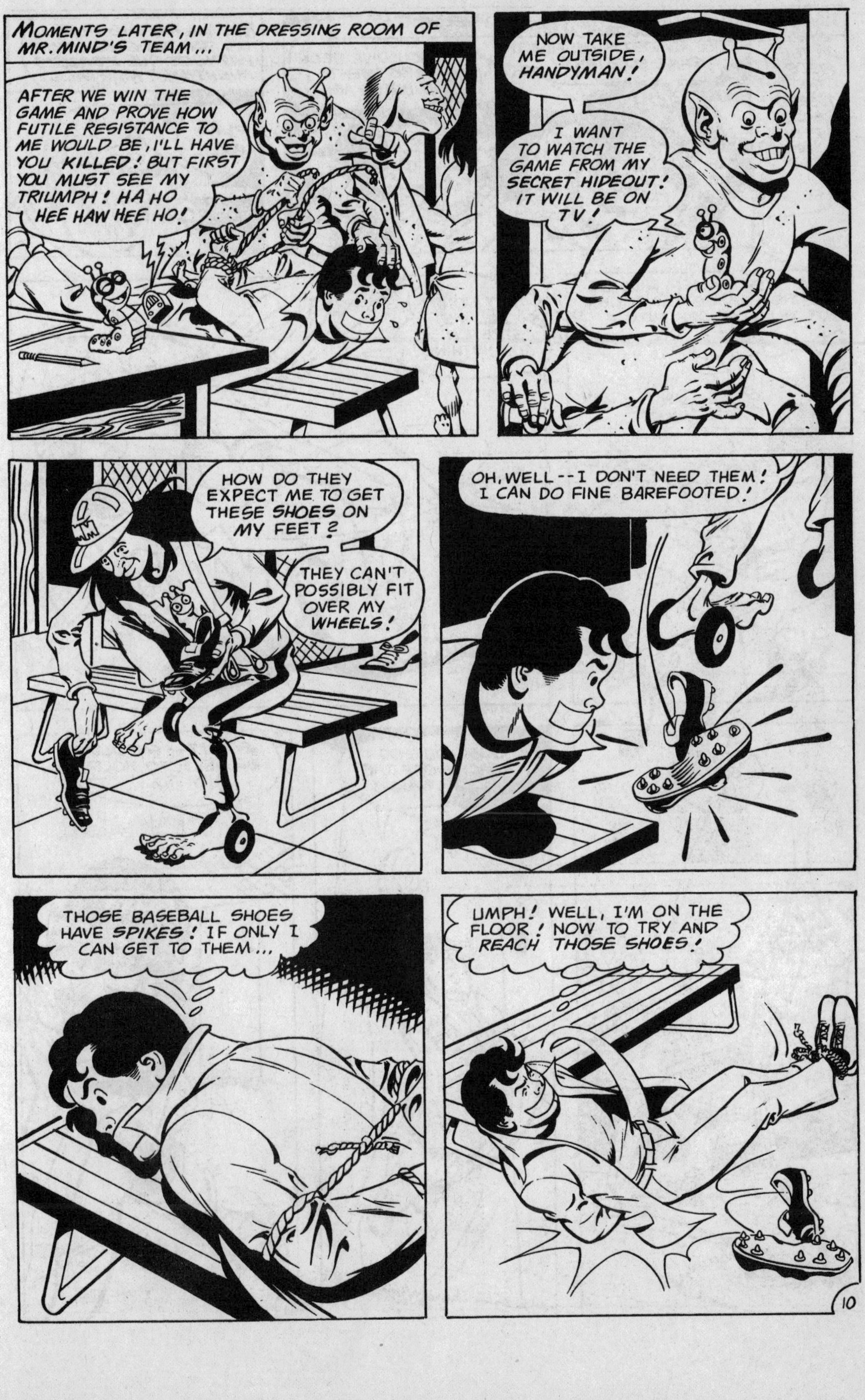
MOMENTS LATER, IN THE DRESSING ROOM OF MR. MIND'S TEAM...
AFTER WE WIN THE GAME AND PROVE HOW FUTILE RESISTANCE TO ME WOULD BE, I'LL HAVE YOU KILLED! BUT FIRST YOU MUST SEE MY TRIUMPH! HA HO HEE HAW HEE HO!
NOW TAKE ME OUTSIDE, HANDYMAN!
I WANT TO WATCH THE GAME FROM MY SECRET HIDEOUT! IT WILL BE ON TV!
HOW DO THEY EXPECT ME TO GET THESE SHOES ON MY FEET?
THEY CAN'T POSSIBLY FIT OVER MY WHEELS!
OH, WELL--I DON'T NEED THEM! I CAN DO FINE BAREFOOTED!
THOSE BASEBALL SHOES HAVE SPIKES! IF ONLY I CAN GET TO THEM...
UMPH! WELL, I'M ON THE FLOOR! NOW TO TRY AND REACH THOSE SHOES!
10

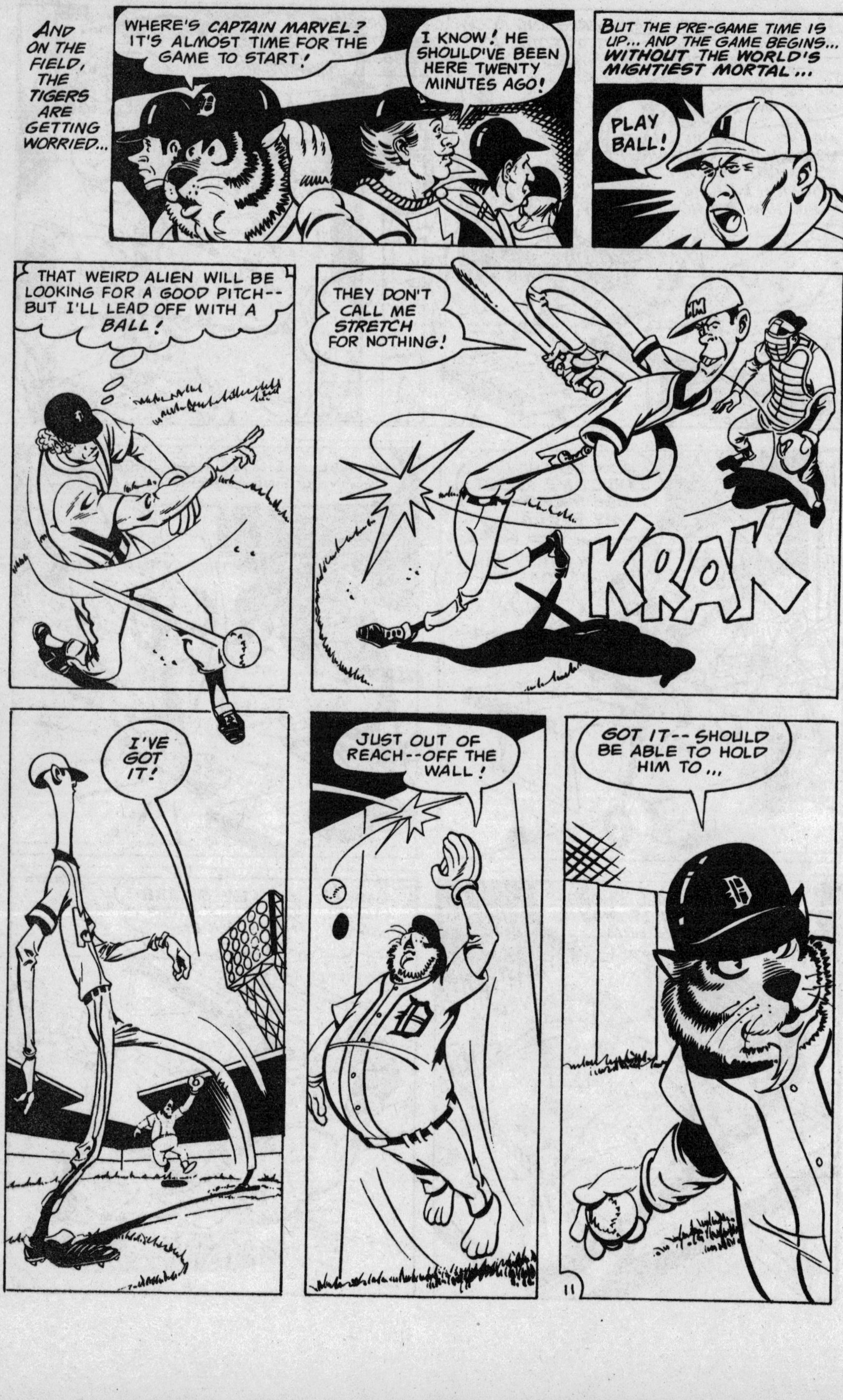
AND ON THE FIELD, THE TIGERS ARE GETTING WORRIED...
WHERE'S CAPTAIN MARVEL? IT'S ALMOST TIME FOR THE GAME TO START!
I KNOW! HE SHOULD'VE BEEN HERE TWENTY MINUTES AGO!
BUT THE PRE-GAME TIME IS UP... AND THE GAME BEGINS... WITHOUT THE WORLD'S MIGHTIEST MORTAL...
PLAY BALL!
THAT WEIRD ALIEN WILL BE LOOKING FOR A GOOD PITCH-- BUT I'LL LEAD OFF WITH A BALL!
THEY DON'T CALL ME STRETCH FOR NOTHING!
KRAK
I'VE GOT IT!
JUST OUT OF REACH--OFF THE WALL!
GOT IT-- SHOULD BE ABLE TO HOLD HIM TO...
11

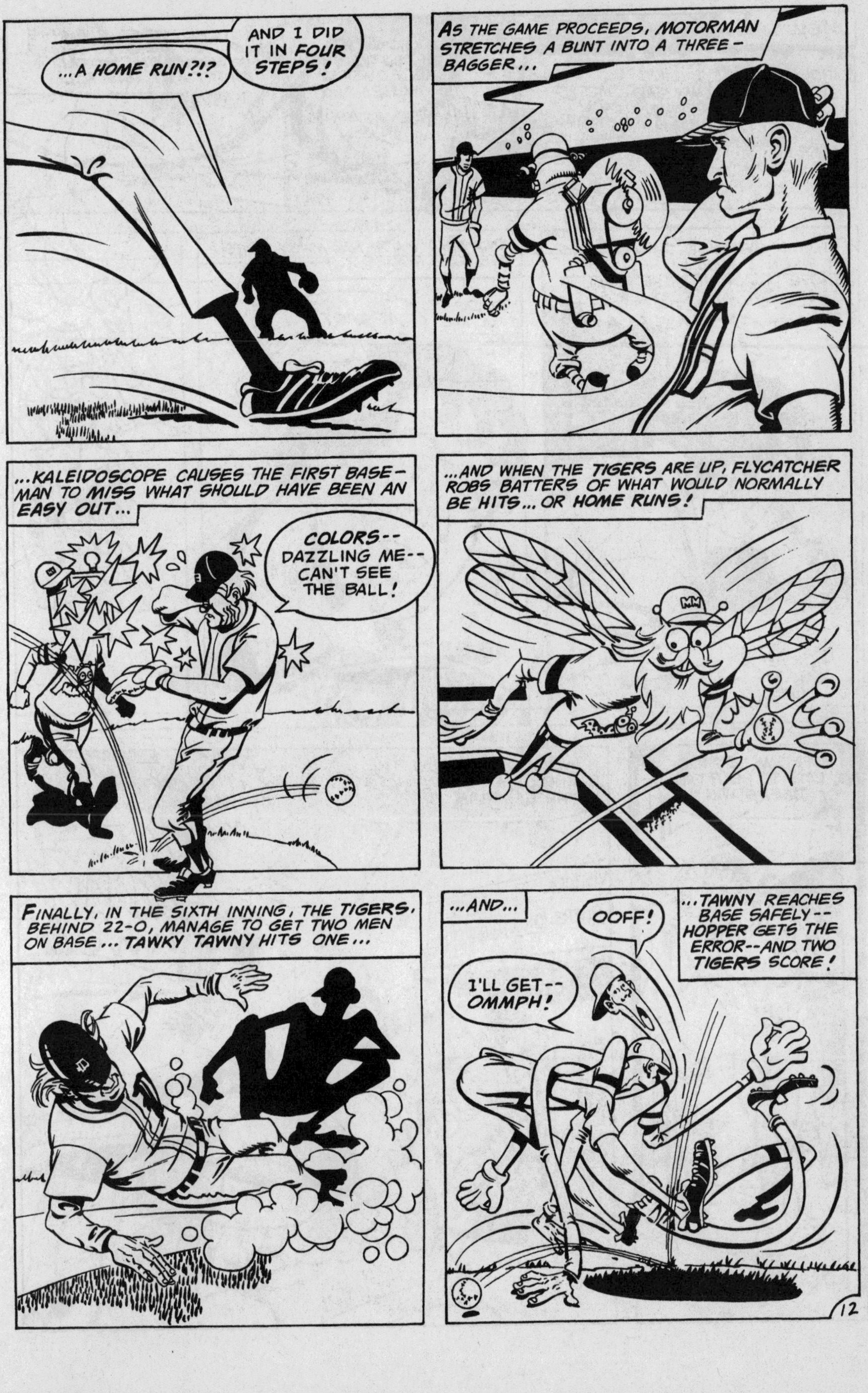
...A HOME RUN?!?
AND I DID IT IN FOUR STEPS!
AS THE GAME PROCEEDS, MOTORMAN STRETCHES A BUNT INTO A THREE-BAGGER...
...KALEIDOSCOPE CAUSES THE FIRST BASE-MAN TO MISS WHAT SHOULD HAVE BEEN AN EASY OUT...
COLORS-- DAZZLING ME-- CAN'T SEE THE BALL!
...AND WHEN THE TIGERS ARE UP, FLYCATCHER ROBS BATTERS OF WHAT WOULD NORMALLY BE HITS... OR HOME RUNS!
FINALLY, IN THE SIXTH INNING, THE TIGERS, BEHIND 22-0, MANAGE TO GET TWO MEN ON BASE... TAWKY TAWNY HITS ONE...
...AND...
OOFF!
...TAWNY REACHES BASE SAFELY-- HOPPER GETS THE ERROR--AND TWO TIGERS SCORE!
I'LL GET-- OMMPH!
12

MEANTIME...

HOLY MOLEY! I CAN'T SEEM TO HOOK MY GAG ON THE SPIKES! WHEN I TRY, THE SHOES *MOVE*!

THAT'S BECAUSE I'M *PUSHING* IT WHEN I TOUCH IT--BUT IF I SHOVE IT AGAINST THE *WALL*, IT CAN'T MOVE ANY FURTHER!

AND FINALLY, AFTER MANY TRIES, THE GAG HOOKS...

AT LAST!

SHAZAM!

BARAMMM

HOPE I'M NOT TOO LATE TO HELP THE *TIGERS* WIN!

HOLY MOLEY! AT THE END OF *EIGHT INNINGS*, THE SCORE IS *28 TO 2*!

IT'S CAPTAIN MARVEL!

YAAAY!

VISITORS:	3	2	6	4	3	4	5	1
TIGERS:	0	0	0	0	0	2	0	0

13

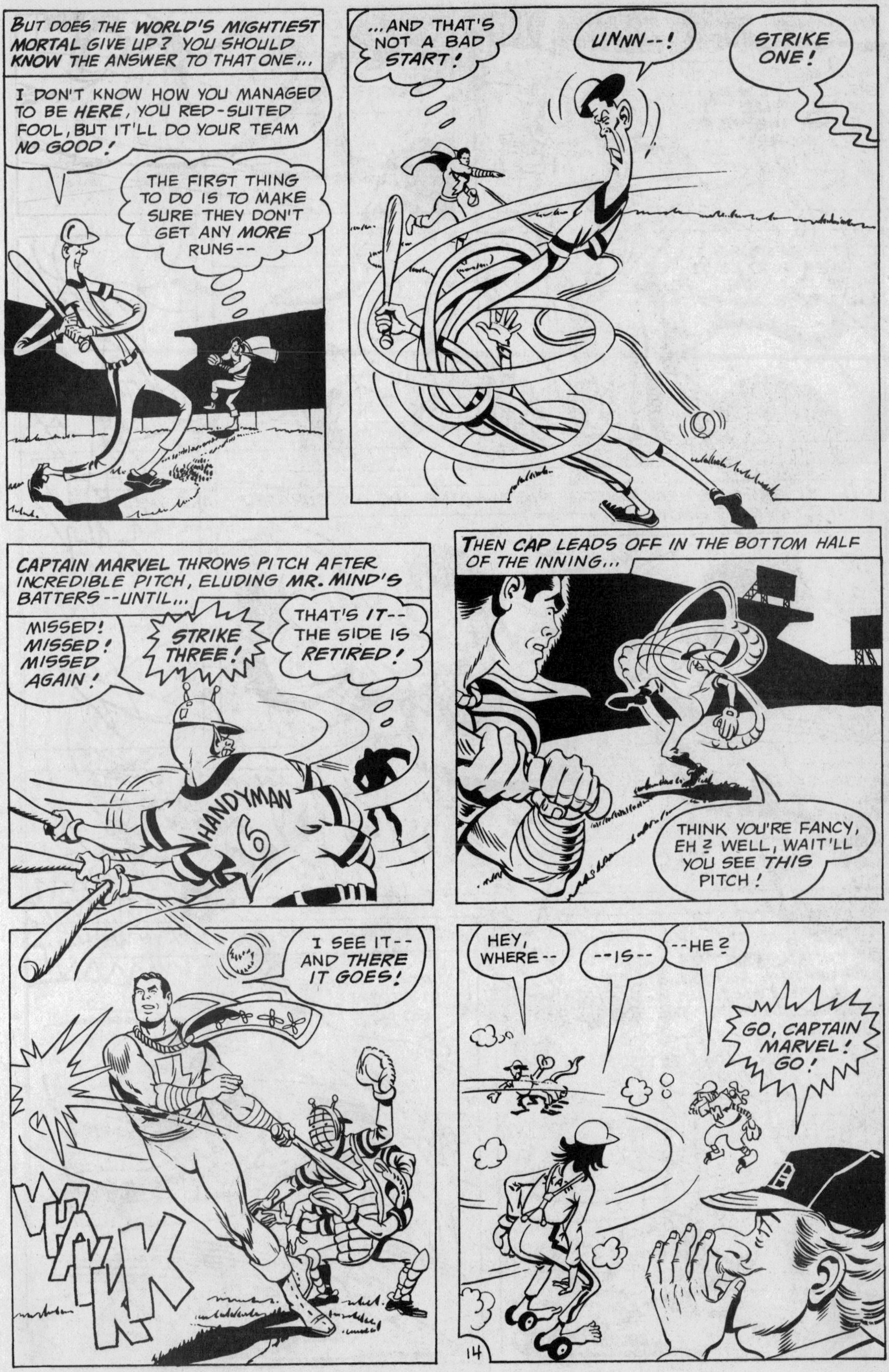
BUT DOES THE WORLD'S MIGHTIEST MORTAL GIVE UP? YOU SHOULD KNOW THE ANSWER TO THAT ONE...
I DON'T KNOW HOW YOU MANAGED TO BE HERE, YOU RED-SUITED FOOL, BUT IT'LL DO YOUR TEAM NO GOOD!
THE FIRST THING TO DO IS TO MAKE SURE THEY DON'T GET ANY MORE RUNS--
...AND THAT'S NOT A BAD START!
UNNN--!
STRIKE ONE!
CAPTAIN MARVEL THROWS PITCH AFTER INCREDIBLE PITCH, ELUDING MR. MIND'S BATTERS--UNTIL...
MISSED! MISSED! MISSED AGAIN!
STRIKE THREE!
THAT'S IT-- THE SIDE IS RETIRED!
HANDYMAN
6
THEN CAP LEADS OFF IN THE BOTTOM HALF OF THE INNING...
THINK YOU'RE FANCY, EH? WELL, WAIT'LL YOU SEE THIS PITCH!
I SEE IT-- AND THERE IT GOES!
HEY, WHERE--
--IS--
--HE?
GO, CAPTAIN MARVEL! GO!
14

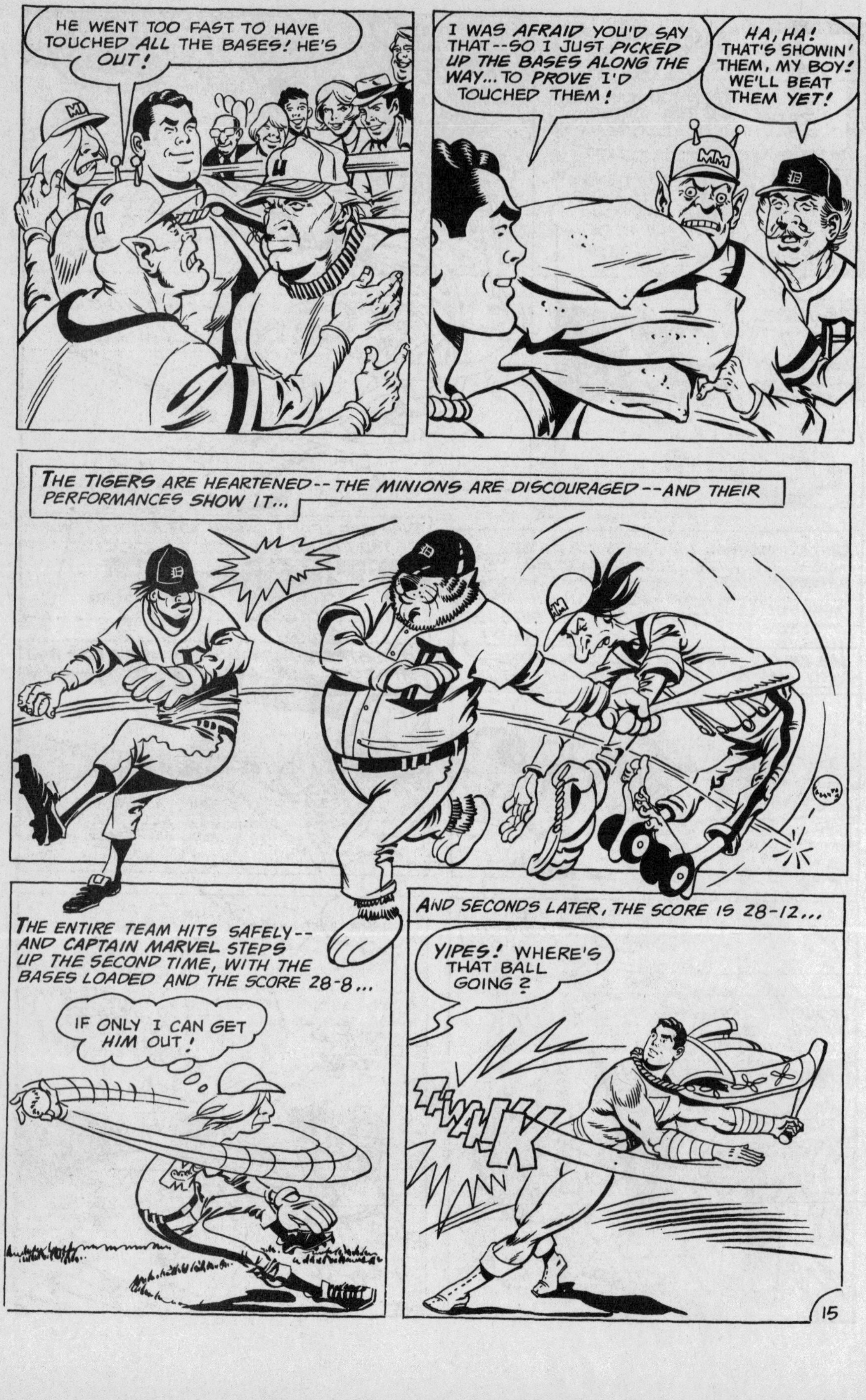
HE WENT TOO FAST TO HAVE TOUCHED ALL THE BASES! HE'S OUT!
I WAS AFRAID YOU'D SAY THAT--SO I JUST PICKED UP THE BASES ALONG THE WAY... TO PROVE I'D TOUCHED THEM!
HA, HA! THAT'S SHOWIN' THEM, MY BOY! WE'LL BEAT THEM YET!
THE TIGERS ARE HEARTENED--THE MINIONS ARE DISCOURAGED--AND THEIR PERFORMANCES SHOW IT...
THE ENTIRE TEAM HITS SAFELY--AND CAPTAIN MARVEL STEPS UP THE SECOND TIME, WITH THE BASES LOADED AND THE SCORE 28-8...
IF ONLY I CAN GET HIM OUT!
AND SECONDS LATER, THE SCORE IS 28-12...
YIPES! WHERE'S THAT BALL GOING?
TWAK
15

WHERE DID THE BALL GO? ALL THE WAY TO THE MOON!

THE TIGERS ARE ROLLING... SEVEN MORE RUNS -- A MAN ON -- AND NOBODY OUT -- AS CAP COMES TO BAT FOR THE THIRD TIME IN THE INNING!

LET'S SEE YOU HIT THIS FASTBALL!

AND THE WORLD'S MIGHTIEST MORTAL DOES -- WITH SUCH FORCE HE DRILLS IT RIGHT THROUGH THE STADIUM WALL!

KWHAM!

MR. TAWNY DRAWS A WALK... THEN THE NEXT MAN UP HITS A GOOD, HIGH ONE...

BUT STRETCH FINALLY MAKES UP FOR THAT STRIKEOUT WITH AN UNASSISTED DOUBLE-PLAY!

HOWEVER, THE REST OF THE TIGERS BAT SAFELY... AND THE SCORE IS 28-24 AS CAP COMES TO BAT AGAIN...

HOLY MOLEY! THAT SHORTSTOP IS PRACTICALLY BLINDING ME -- I CAN'T SEE THE BALL!

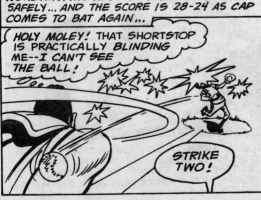

STRIKE TWO!

I'LL SWING THE BAT MANY TIMES SO FAST NO ONE WILL SEE I'M COVERING THE WHOLE STRIKE ZONE --

16

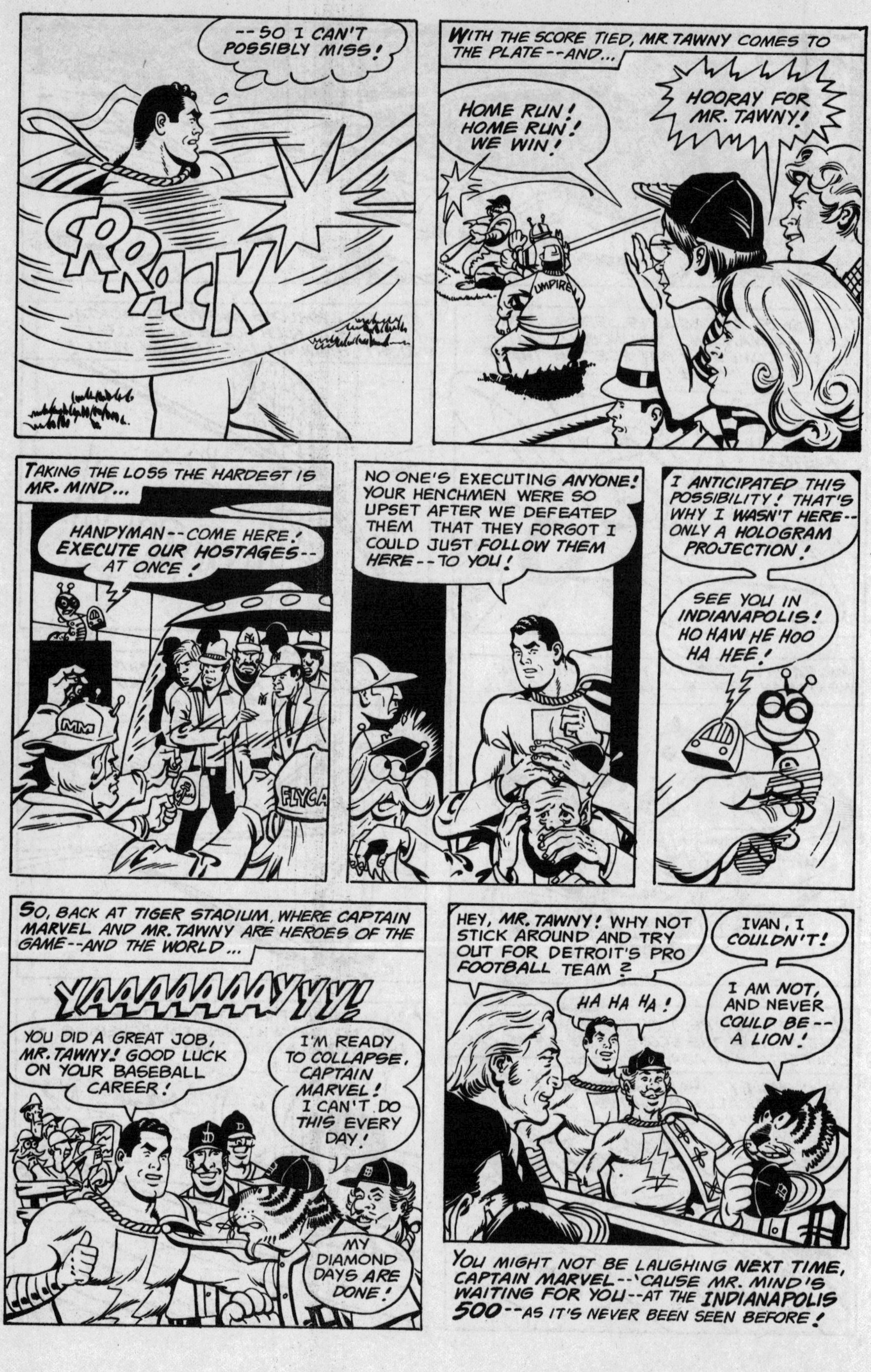
--SO I CAN'T POSSIBLY MISS!
CRRACK
WITH THE SCORE TIED, MR. TAWNY COMES TO THE PLATE--AND...
HOME RUN! HOME RUN! WE WIN!
HOORAY FOR MR. TAWNY!
UMPIRE
TAKING THE LOSS THE HARDEST IS MR. MIND...
HANDYMAN--COME HERE! EXECUTE OUR HOSTAGES--AT ONCE!
MM
FLYCA
NO ONE'S EXECUTING ANYONE! YOUR HENCHMEN WERE SO UPSET AFTER WE DEFEATED THEM THAT THEY FORGOT I COULD JUST FOLLOW THEM HERE--TO YOU!
I ANTICIPATED THIS POSSIBILITY! THAT'S WHY I WASN'T HERE--ONLY A HOLOGRAM PROJECTION!
SEE YOU IN INDIANAPOLIS! HO HAW HE HOO HA HEE!
SO, BACK AT TIGER STADIUM, WHERE CAPTAIN MARVEL AND MR. TAWNY ARE HEROES OF THE GAME--AND THE WORLD...
YAAAAAAAYYY!
YOU DID A GREAT JOB, MR. TAWNY! GOOD LUCK ON YOUR BASEBALL CAREER!
I'M READY TO COLLAPSE, CAPTAIN MARVEL! I CAN'T DO THIS EVERY DAY!
MY DIAMOND DAYS ARE DONE!
HEY, MR. TAWNY! WHY NOT STICK AROUND AND TRY OUT FOR DETROIT'S PRO FOOTBALL TEAM?
HA HA HA!
IVAN, I COULDN'T!
I AM NOT, AND NEVER COULD BE--A LION!
YOU MIGHT NOT BE LAUGHING NEXT TIME, CAPTAIN MARVEL--'CAUSE MR. MIND'S WAITING FOR YOU--AT THE INDIANAPOLIS 500--AS IT'S NEVER BEEN SEEN BEFORE!

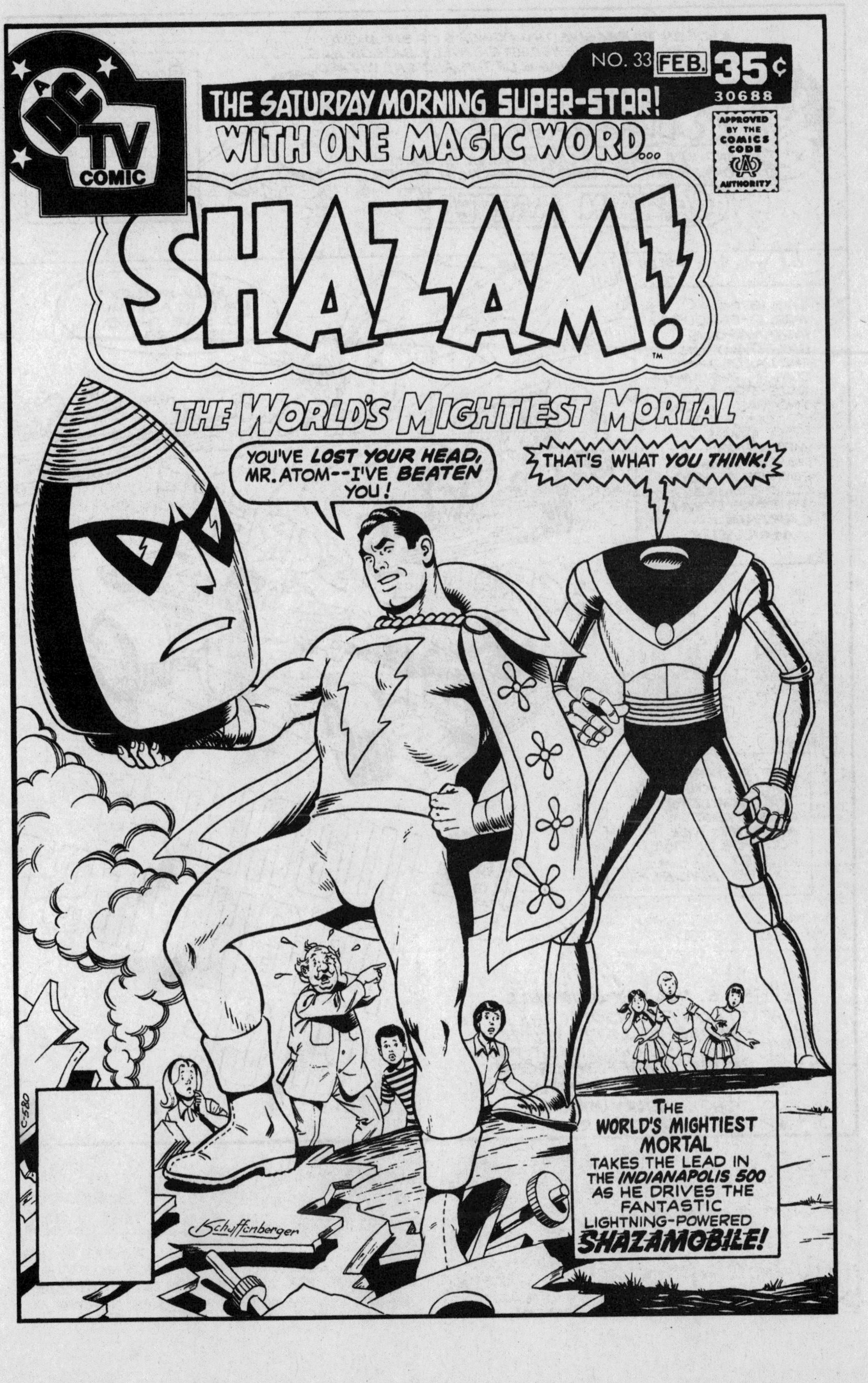
A DC TV COMIC
NO. 33 FEB. 35¢
30688
APPROVED BY THE COMICS CODE AUTHORITY
THE SATURDAY MORNING SUPER-STAR!
WITH ONE MAGIC WORD...
SHAZAM!
THE WORLD'S MIGHTIEST MORTAL
YOU'VE LOST YOUR HEAD, MR. ATOM--I'VE BEATEN YOU!
THAT'S WHAT YOU THINK!
THE WORLD'S MIGHTIEST MORTAL TAKES THE LEAD IN THE INDIANAPOLIS 500 AS HE DRIVES THE FANTASTIC LIGHTNING-POWERED SHAZAMOBILE!
Schaffenberger
C-580

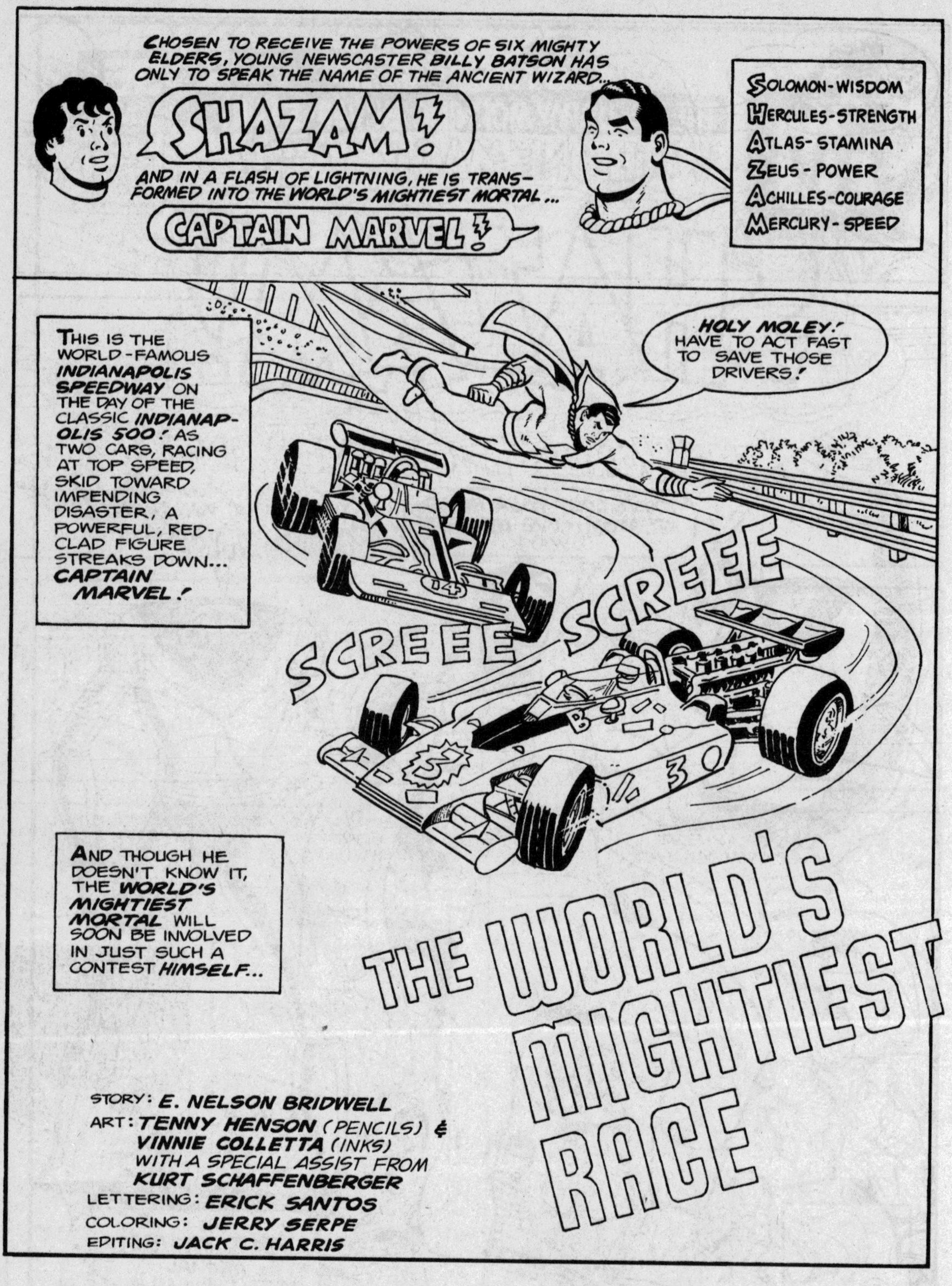
CHOSEN TO RECEIVE THE POWERS OF SIX MIGHTY ELDERS, YOUNG NEWSCASTER BILLY BATSON HAS ONLY TO SPEAK THE NAME OF THE ANCIENT WIZARD...
SHAZAM!
AND IN A FLASH OF LIGHTNING, HE IS TRANS-FORMED INTO THE WORLD'S MIGHTIEST MORTAL ...
CAPTAIN MARVEL!
SOLOMON-WISDOM
HERCULES-STRENGTH
ATLAS-STAMINA
ZEUS-POWER
ACHILLES-COURAGE
MERCURY-SPEED
THIS IS THE WORLD-FAMOUS INDIANAPOLIS SPEEDWAY ON THE DAY OF THE CLASSIC INDIANAPOLIS 500! AS TWO CARS, RACING AT TOP SPEED, SKID TOWARD IMPENDING DISASTER, A POWERFUL, RED-CLAD FIGURE STREAKS DOWN... CAPTAIN MARVEL!
HOLY MOLEY! HAVE TO ACT FAST TO SAVE THOSE DRIVERS!
SCREEE
SCREEE
AND THOUGH HE DOESN'T KNOW IT, THE WORLD'S MIGHTIEST MORTAL WILL SOON BE INVOLVED IN JUST SUCH A CONTEST HIMSELF...
THE WORLD'S MIGHTIEST RACE
STORY: E. NELSON BRIDWELL
ART: TENNY HENSON (PENCILS) & VINNIE COLLETTA (INKS) WITH A SPECIAL ASSIST FROM KURT SCHAFFENBERGER
LETTERING: ERICK SANTOS
COLORING: JERRY SERPE
EDITING: JACK C. HARRIS

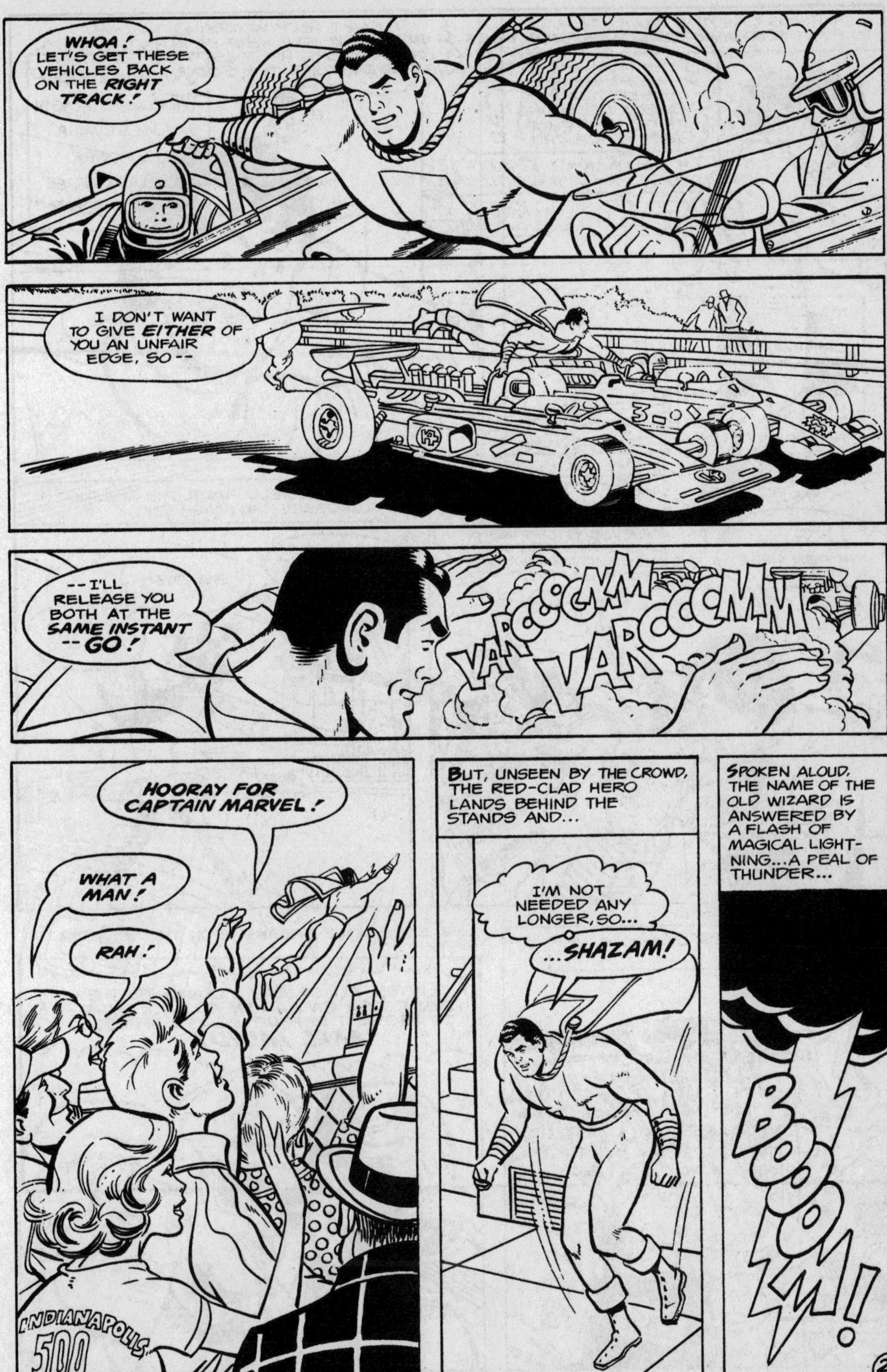
WHOA! LET'S GET THESE VEHICLES BACK ON THE RIGHT TRACK!
I DON'T WANT TO GIVE EITHER OF YOU AN UNFAIR EDGE, SO--
--I'LL RELEASE YOU BOTH AT THE SAME INSTANT --GO!
VARCCCCMM
VARCCCCNM
HOORAY FOR CAPTAIN MARVEL!
WHAT A MAN!
RAH!
INDIANAPOLIS 500
BUT, UNSEEN BY THE CROWD, THE RED-CLAD HERO LANDS BEHIND THE STANDS AND...
I'M NOT NEEDED ANY LONGER, SO...
...SHAZAM!
SPOKEN ALOUD, THE NAME OF THE OLD WIZARD IS ANSWERED BY A FLASH OF MAGICAL LIGHTNING...A PEAL OF THUNDER...
BOOOOM!
2

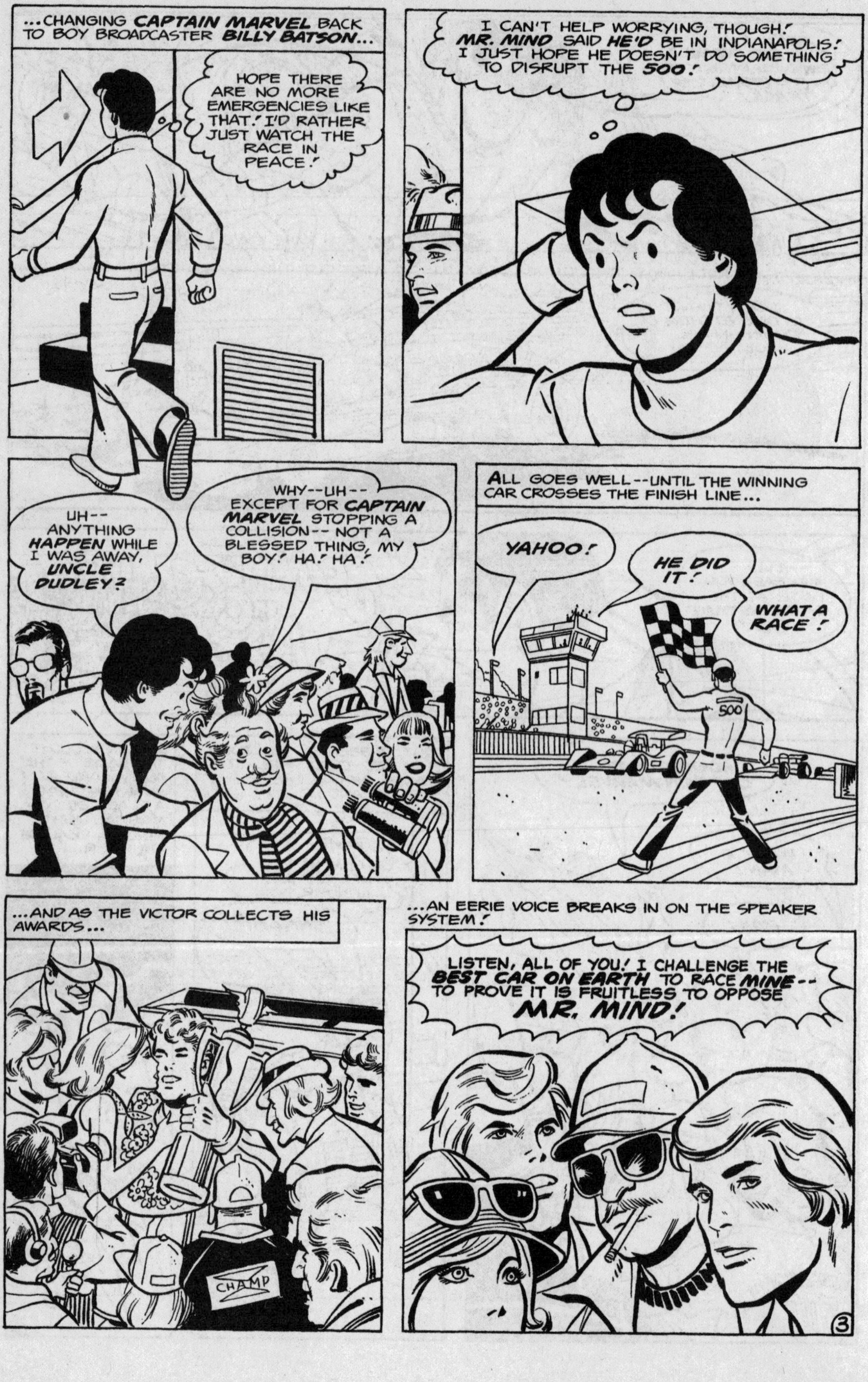
...CHANGING CAPTAIN MARVEL BACK TO BOY BROADCASTER BILLY BATSON...
HOPE THERE ARE NO MORE EMERGENCIES LIKE THAT! I'D RATHER JUST WATCH THE RACE IN PEACE!
I CAN'T HELP WORRYING, THOUGH! MR. MIND SAID HE'D BE IN INDIANAPOLIS! I JUST HOPE HE DOESN'T DO SOMETHING TO DISRUPT THE 500!
UH-- ANYTHING HAPPEN WHILE I WAS AWAY, UNCLE DUDLEY?
WHY--UH-- EXCEPT FOR CAPTAIN MARVEL STOPPING A COLLISION-- NOT A BLESSED THING, MY BOY! HA! HA!
ALL GOES WELL--UNTIL THE WINNING CAR CROSSES THE FINISH LINE...
YAHOO!
HE DID IT!
WHAT A RACE!
500
...AND AS THE VICTOR COLLECTS HIS AWARDS...
CHAMP
...AN EERIE VOICE BREAKS IN ON THE SPEAKER SYSTEM!
LISTEN, ALL OF YOU! I CHALLENGE THE BEST CAR ON EARTH TO RACE MINE-- TO PROVE IT IS FRUITLESS TO OPPOSE MR. MIND!
3

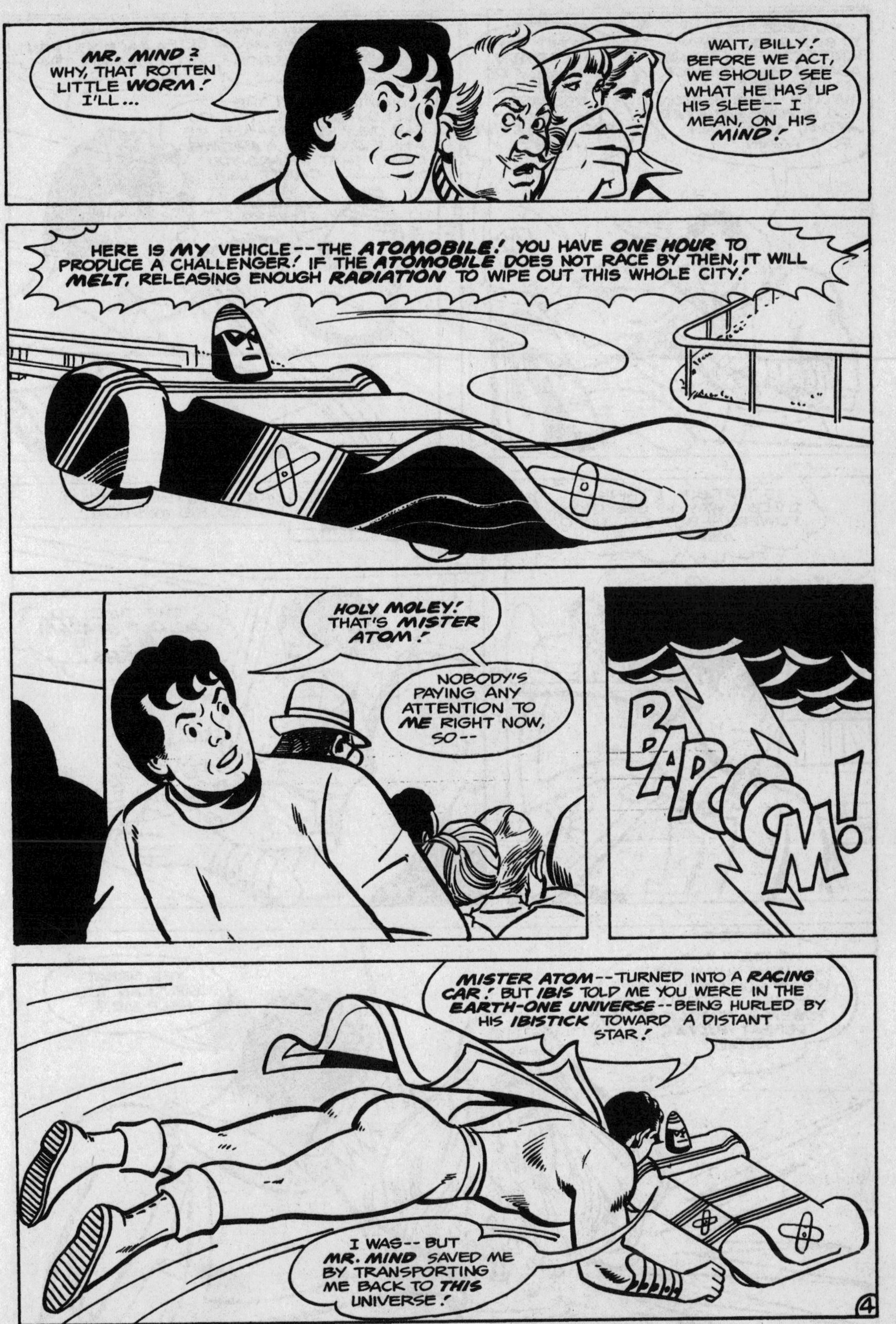
MR. MIND? WHY, THAT ROTTEN LITTLE WORM! I'LL...
WAIT, BILLY! BEFORE WE ACT, WE SHOULD SEE WHAT HE HAS UP HIS SLEE-- I MEAN, ON HIS MIND!
HERE IS MY VEHICLE--THE ATOMOBILE! YOU HAVE ONE HOUR TO PRODUCE A CHALLENGER! IF THE ATOMOBILE DOES NOT RACE BY THEN, IT WILL MELT, RELEASING ENOUGH RADIATION TO WIPE OUT THIS WHOLE CITY!
HOLY MOLEY! THAT'S MISTER ATOM!
NOBODY'S PAYING ANY ATTENTION TO ME RIGHT NOW, SO--
BAPOOOM!
MISTER ATOM--TURNED INTO A RACING CAR! BUT IBIS TOLD ME YOU WERE IN THE EARTH-ONE UNIVERSE--BEING HURLED BY HIS IBISTICK TOWARD A DISTANT STAR!
I WAS-- BUT MR. MIND SAVED ME BY TRANSPORTING ME BACK TO THIS UNIVERSE!
4

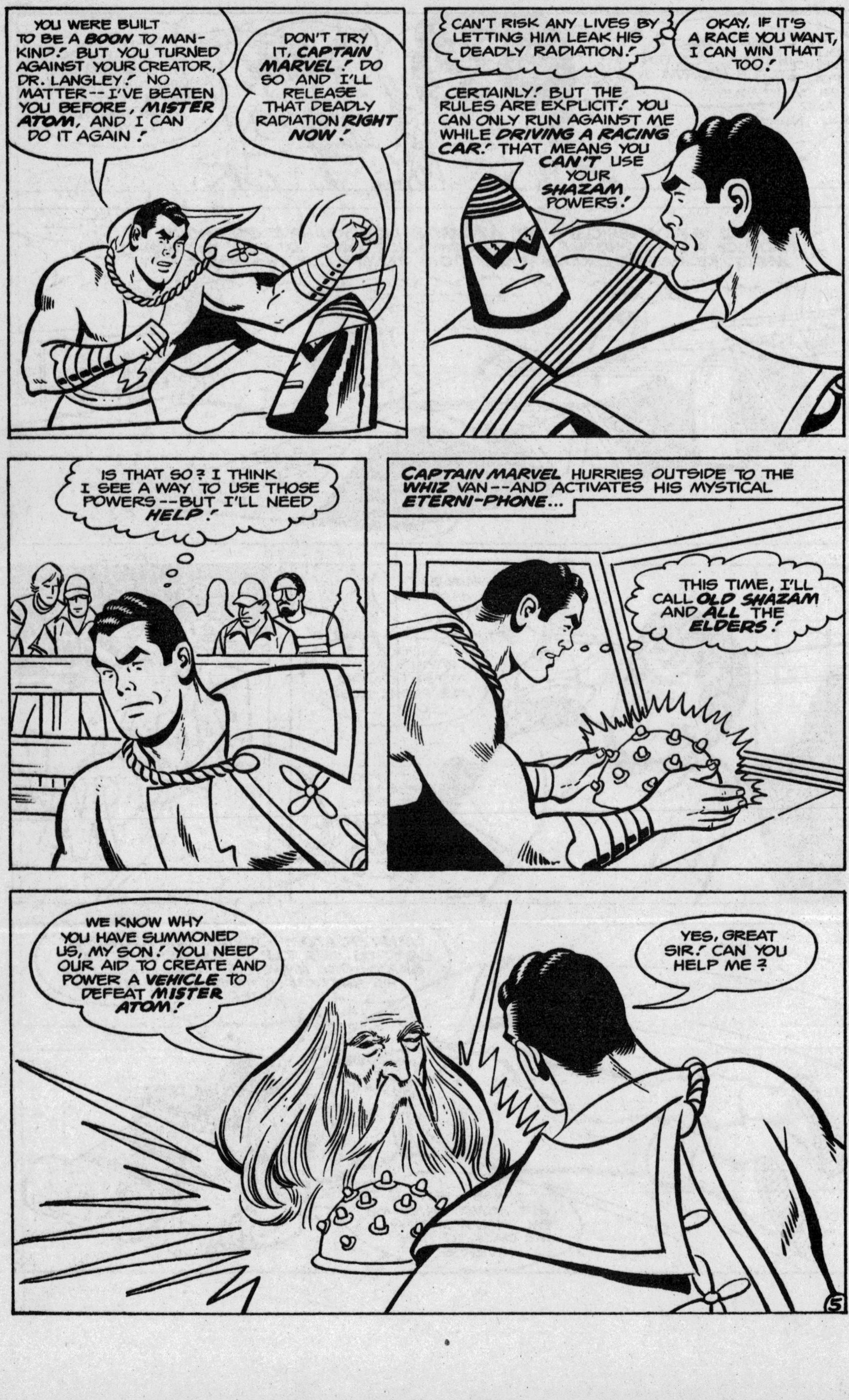
YOU WERE BUILT TO BE A BOON TO MAN-KIND! BUT YOU TURNED AGAINST YOUR CREATOR, DR. LANGLEY! NO MATTER -- I'VE BEATEN YOU BEFORE, MISTER ATOM, AND I CAN DO IT AGAIN!
DON'T TRY IT, CAPTAIN MARVEL! DO SO AND I'LL RELEASE THAT DEADLY RADIATION RIGHT NOW!
CAN'T RISK ANY LIVES BY LETTING HIM LEAK HIS DEADLY RADIATION!
OKAY. IF IT'S A RACE YOU WANT, I CAN WIN THAT TOO!
CERTAINLY! BUT THE RULES ARE EXPLICIT! YOU CAN ONLY RUN AGAINST ME WHILE DRIVING A RACING CAR! THAT MEANS YOU CAN'T USE YOUR SHAZAM POWERS!
IS THAT SO? I THINK I SEE A WAY TO USE THOSE POWERS--BUT I'LL NEED HELP!
CAPTAIN MARVEL HURRIES OUTSIDE TO THE WHIZ VAN--AND ACTIVATES HIS MYSTICAL ETERNI-PHONE...
THIS TIME, I'LL CALL OLD SHAZAM AND ALL THE ELDERS!
WE KNOW WHY YOU HAVE SUMMONED US, MY SON! YOU NEED OUR AID TO CREATE AND POWER A VEHICLE TO DEFEAT MISTER ATOM!
YES, GREAT SIR! CAN YOU HELP ME?
5

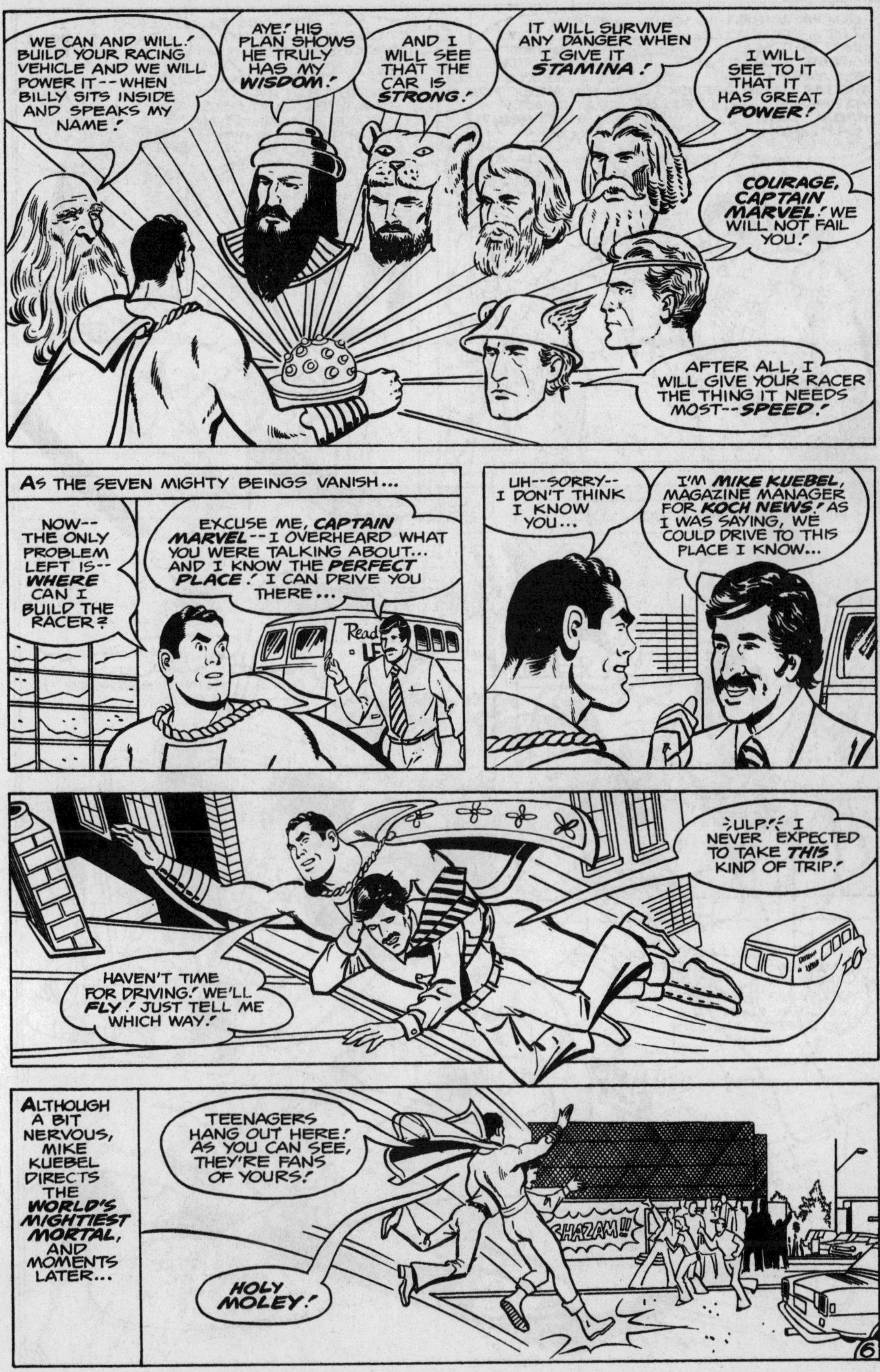
WE CAN AND WILL! BUILD YOUR RACING VEHICLE AND WE WILL POWER IT--WHEN BILLY SITS INSIDE AND SPEAKS MY NAME!
AYE! HIS PLAN SHOWS HE TRULY HAS MY WISDOM!
AND I WILL SEE THAT THE CAR IS STRONG!
IT WILL SURVIVE ANY DANGER WHEN I GIVE IT STAMINA!
I WILL SEE TO IT THAT IT HAS GREAT POWER!
COURAGE, CAPTAIN MARVEL! WE WILL NOT FAIL YOU!
AFTER ALL, I WILL GIVE YOUR RACER THE THING IT NEEDS MOST--SPEED!
AS THE SEVEN MIGHTY BEINGS VANISH...
NOW--THE ONLY PROBLEM LEFT IS--WHERE CAN I BUILD THE RACER?
EXCUSE ME, CAPTAIN MARVEL--I OVERHEARD WHAT YOU WERE TALKING ABOUT... AND I KNOW THE PERFECT PLACE! I CAN DRIVE YOU THERE...
UH--SORRY--I DON'T THINK I KNOW YOU...
I'M MIKE KUEBEL, MAGAZINE MANAGER FOR KOCH NEWS! AS I WAS SAYING, WE COULD DRIVE TO THIS PLACE I KNOW...
HAVEN'T TIME FOR DRIVING! WE'LL FLY! JUST TELL ME WHICH WAY!
ULP! I NEVER EXPECTED TO TAKE THIS KIND OF TRIP!
ALTHOUGH A BIT NERVOUS, MIKE KUEBEL DIRECTS THE WORLD'S MIGHTIEST MORTAL, AND MOMENTS LATER...
TEENAGERS HANG OUT HERE! AS YOU CAN SEE, THEY'RE FANS OF YOURS!
SHAZAM!!
HOLY MOLEY!
6

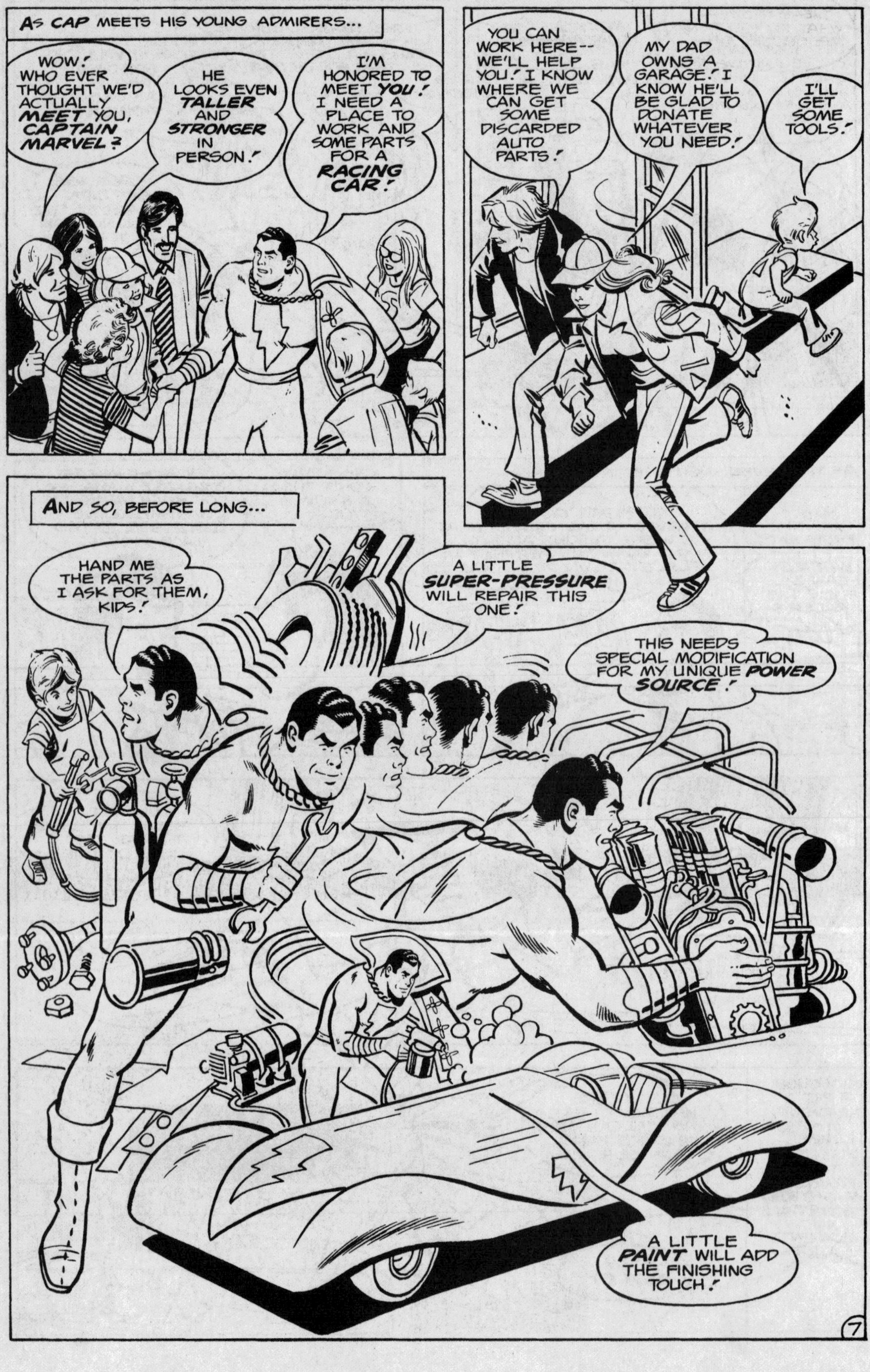
AS CAP MEETS HIS YOUNG ADMIRERS...
WOW! WHO EVER THOUGHT WE'D ACTUALLY MEET YOU, CAPTAIN MARVEL?
HE LOOKS EVEN TALLER AND STRONGER IN PERSON!
I'M HONORED TO MEET YOU! I NEED A PLACE TO WORK AND SOME PARTS FOR A RACING CAR!
YOU CAN WORK HERE-- WE'LL HELP YOU! I KNOW WHERE WE CAN GET SOME DISCARDED AUTO PARTS!
MY DAD OWNS A GARAGE! I KNOW HE'LL BE GLAD TO DONATE WHATEVER YOU NEED!
I'LL GET SOME TOOLS!
AND SO, BEFORE LONG...
HAND ME THE PARTS AS I ASK FOR THEM, KIDS!
A LITTLE SUPER-PRESSURE WILL REPAIR THIS ONE!
THIS NEEDS SPECIAL MODIFICATION FOR MY UNIQUE POWER SOURCE!
A LITTLE PAINT WILL ADD THE FINISHING TOUCH!
7

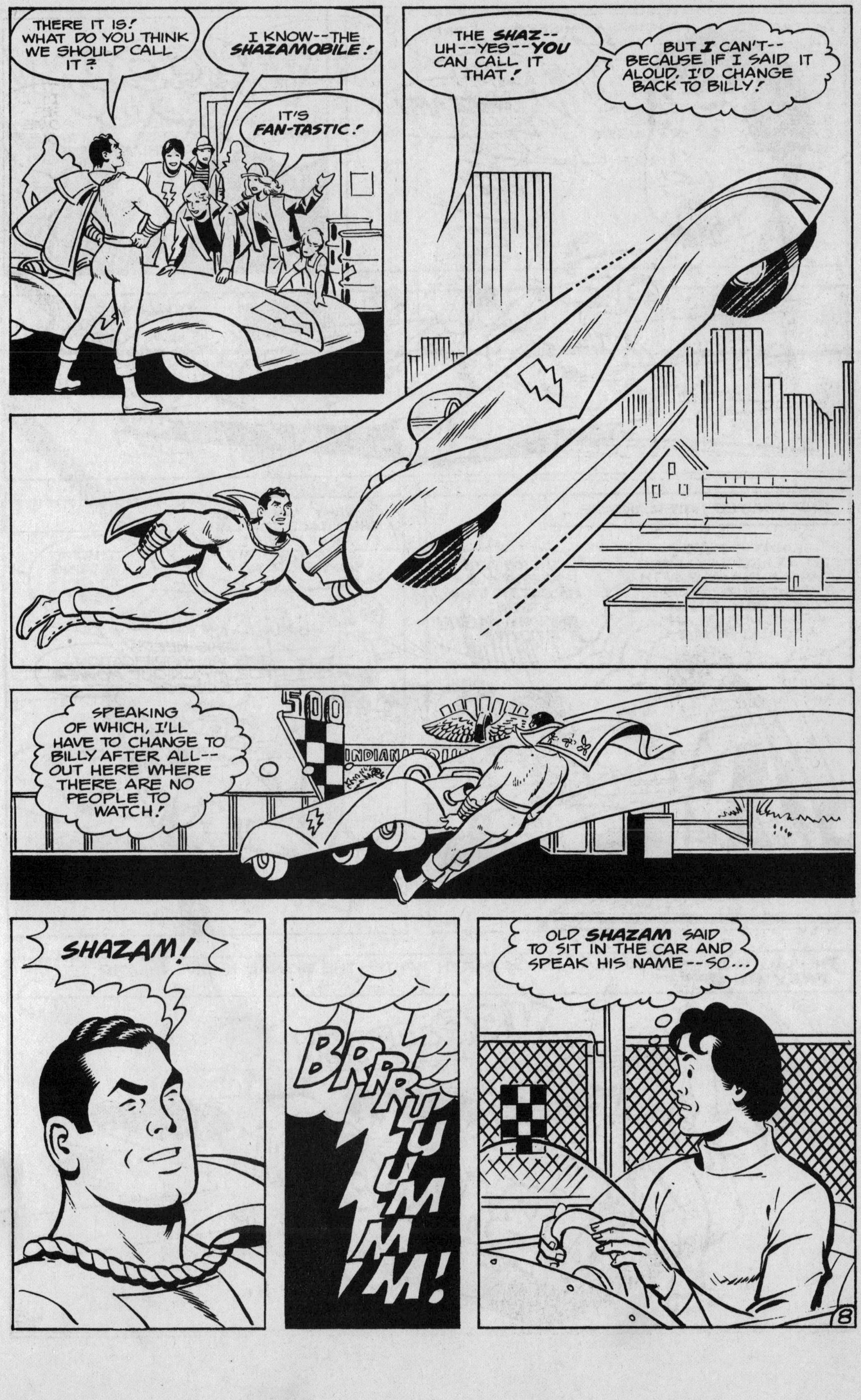
THERE IT IS! WHAT DO YOU THINK WE SHOULD CALL IT?
I KNOW--THE SHAZAMOBILE!
IT'S FAN-TASTIC!
THE SHAZ-- UH--YES--YOU CAN CALL IT THAT!
BUT I CAN'T--BECAUSE IF I SAID IT ALOUD, I'D CHANGE BACK TO BILLY!
SPEAKING OF WHICH, I'LL HAVE TO CHANGE TO BILLY AFTER ALL--OUT HERE WHERE THERE ARE NO PEOPLE TO WATCH!
500
INDIANAPOLIS
SHAZAM!
BRRRRUUUMMM!
OLD SHAZAM SAID TO SIT IN THE CAR AND SPEAK HIS NAME--SO...
8

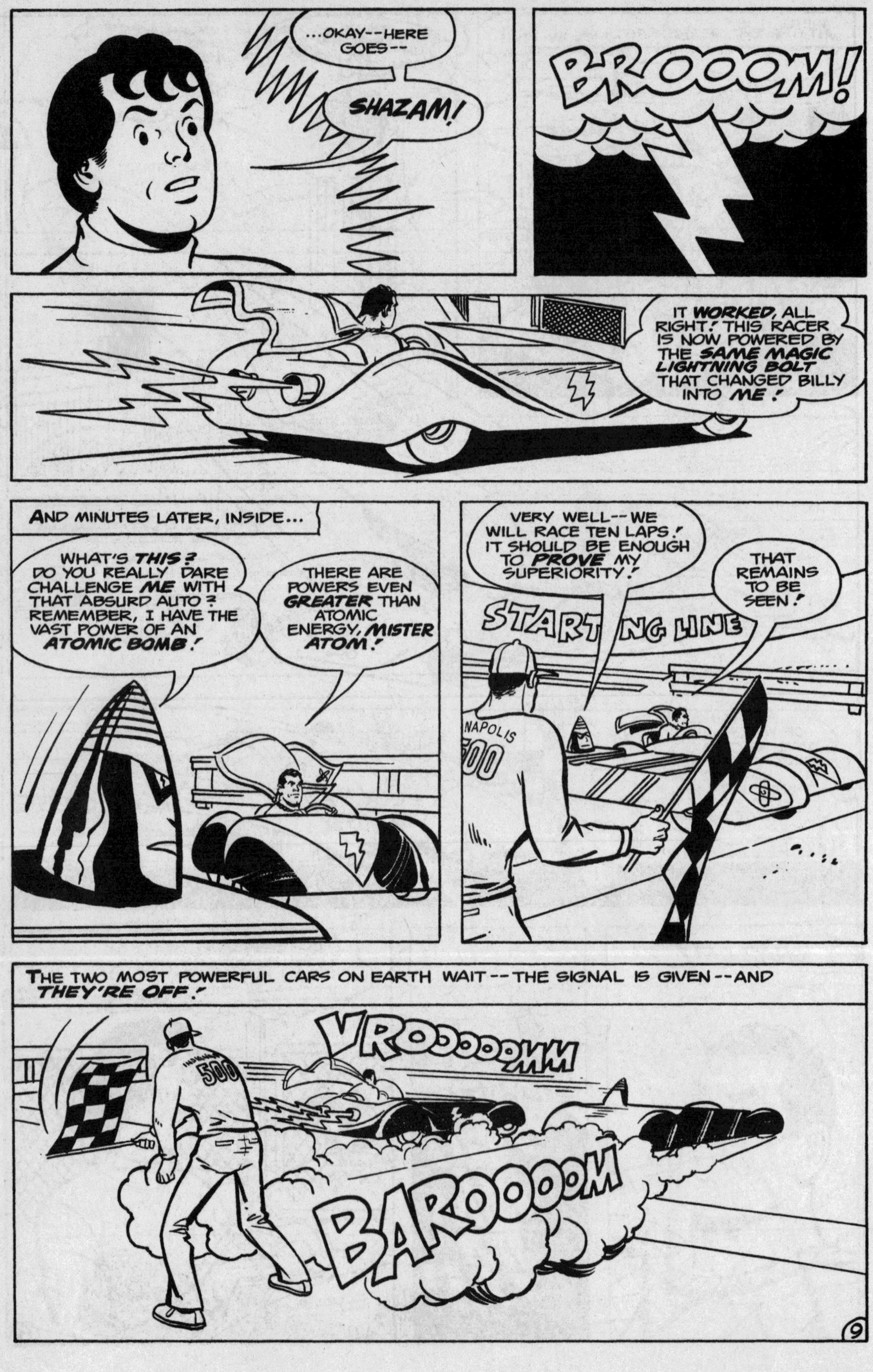
...OKAY--HERE GOES--
SHAZAM!
BROOOM!
IT WORKED, ALL RIGHT! THIS RACER IS NOW POWERED BY THE SAME MAGIC LIGHTNING BOLT THAT CHANGED BILLY INTO ME!
AND MINUTES LATER, INSIDE...
WHAT'S THIS? DO YOU REALLY DARE CHALLENGE ME WITH THAT ABSURD AUTO? REMEMBER, I HAVE THE VAST POWER OF AN ATOMIC BOMB!
THERE ARE POWERS EVEN GREATER THAN ATOMIC ENERGY, MISTER ATOM!
VERY WELL--WE WILL RACE TEN LAPS! IT SHOULD BE ENOUGH TO PROVE MY SUPERIORITY!
THAT REMAINS TO BE SEEN!
START NG LINE
NAPOLIS
500
THE TWO MOST POWERFUL CARS ON EARTH WAIT--THE SIGNAL IS GIVEN--AND THEY'RE OFF!
VROOOOOMM
500
BAROOOOM
9

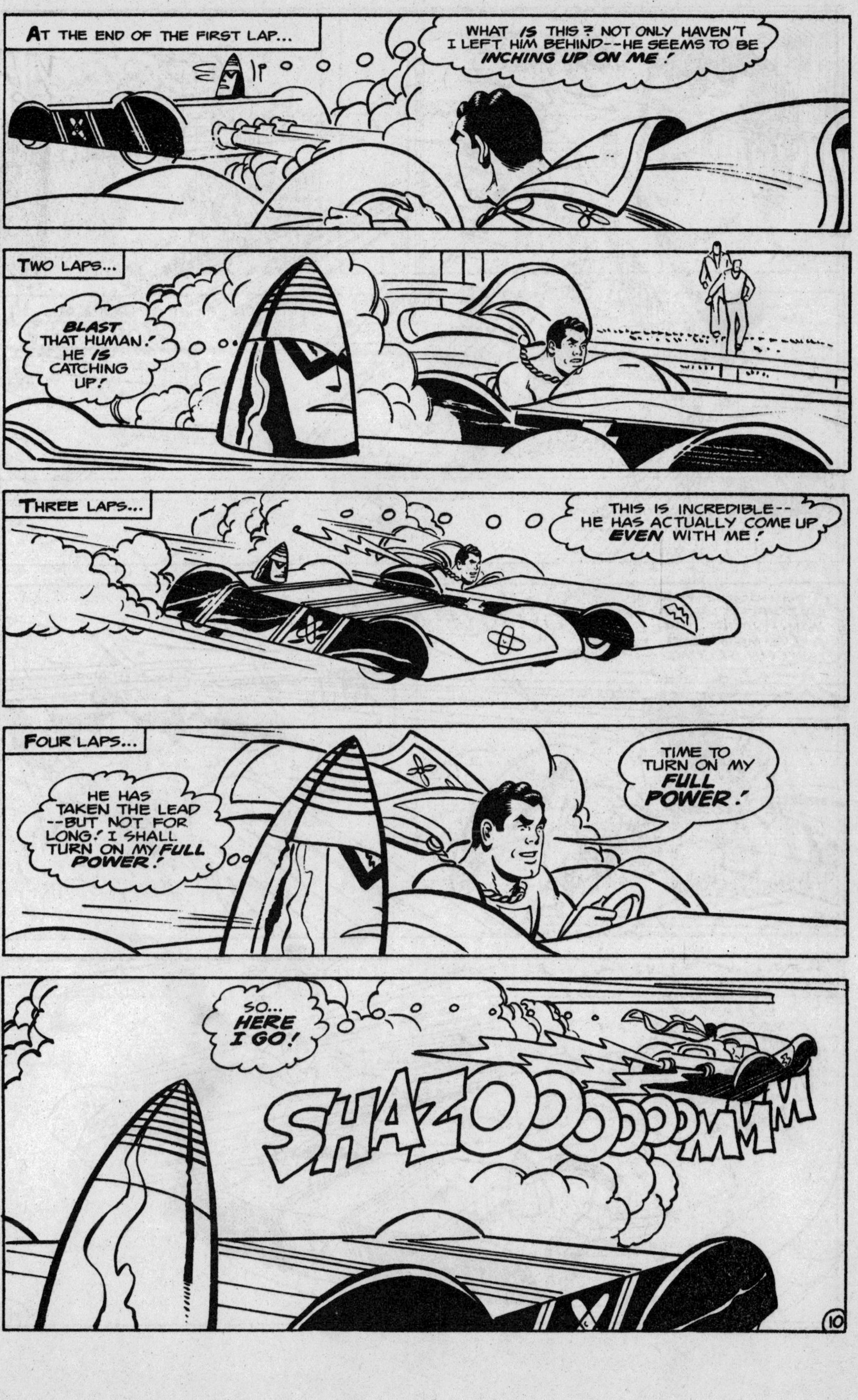
AT THE END OF THE FIRST LAP...
WHAT IS THIS? NOT ONLY HAVEN'T I LEFT HIM BEHIND--HE SEEMS TO BE INCHING UP ON ME!
TWO LAPS...
BLAST THAT HUMAN! HE IS CATCHING UP!
THREE LAPS...
THIS IS INCREDIBLE--HE HAS ACTUALLY COME UP EVEN WITH ME!
FOUR LAPS...
HE HAS TAKEN THE LEAD --BUT NOT FOR LONG! I SHALL TURN ON MY FULL POWER!
TIME TO TURN ON MY FULL POWER!
SO... HERE I GO!
SHAZOOOOOOMMMM
10

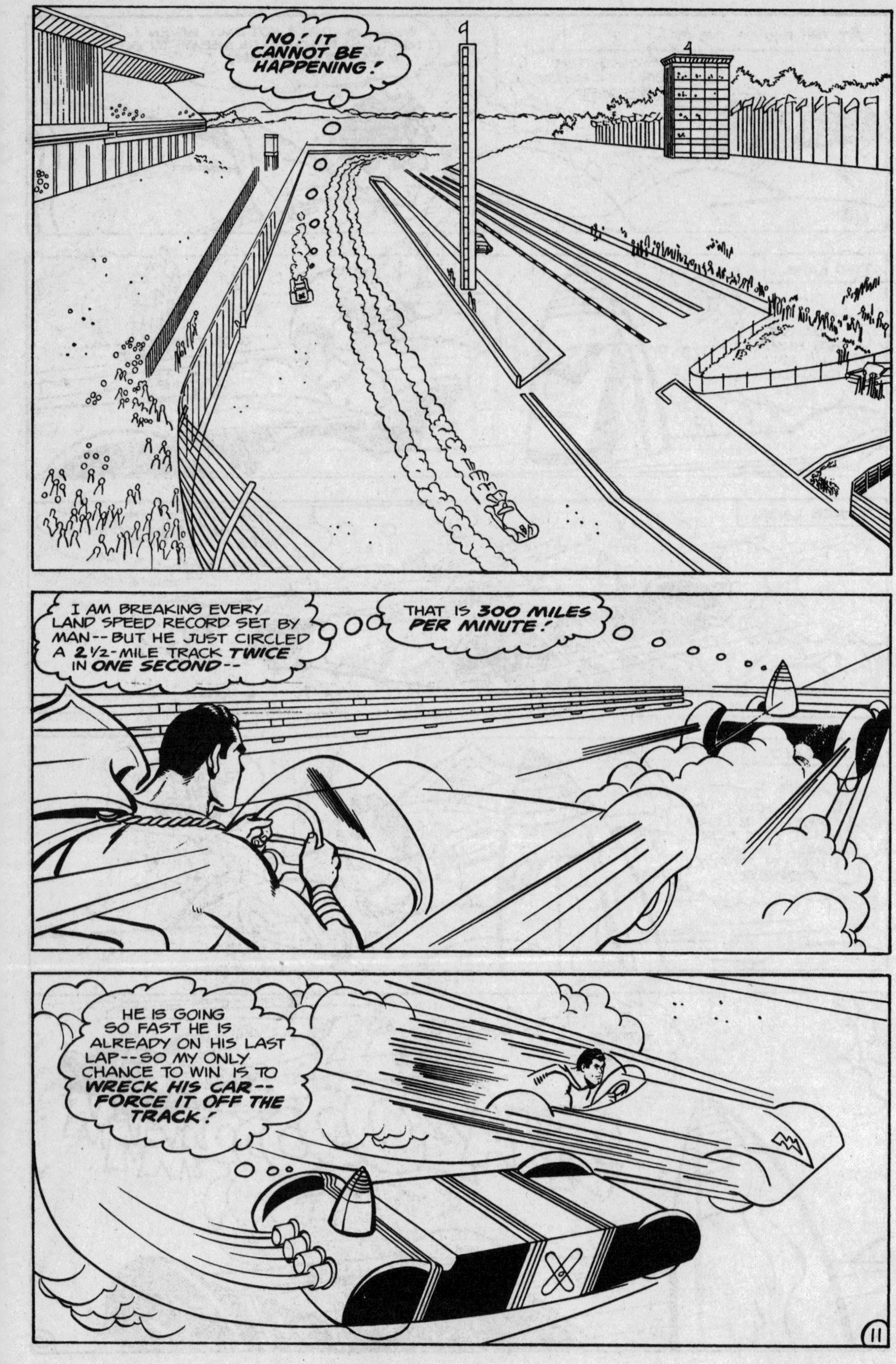
NO! IT CANNOT BE HAPPENING!
I AM BREAKING EVERY LAND SPEED RECORD SET BY MAN--BUT HE JUST CIRCLED A 2 1/2-MILE TRACK TWICE IN ONE SECOND--
THAT IS 300 MILES PER MINUTE!
HE IS GOING SO FAST HE IS ALREADY ON HIS LAST LAP--SO MY ONLY CHANCE TO WIN IS TO WRECK HIS CAR--FORCE IT OFF THE TRACK!
11

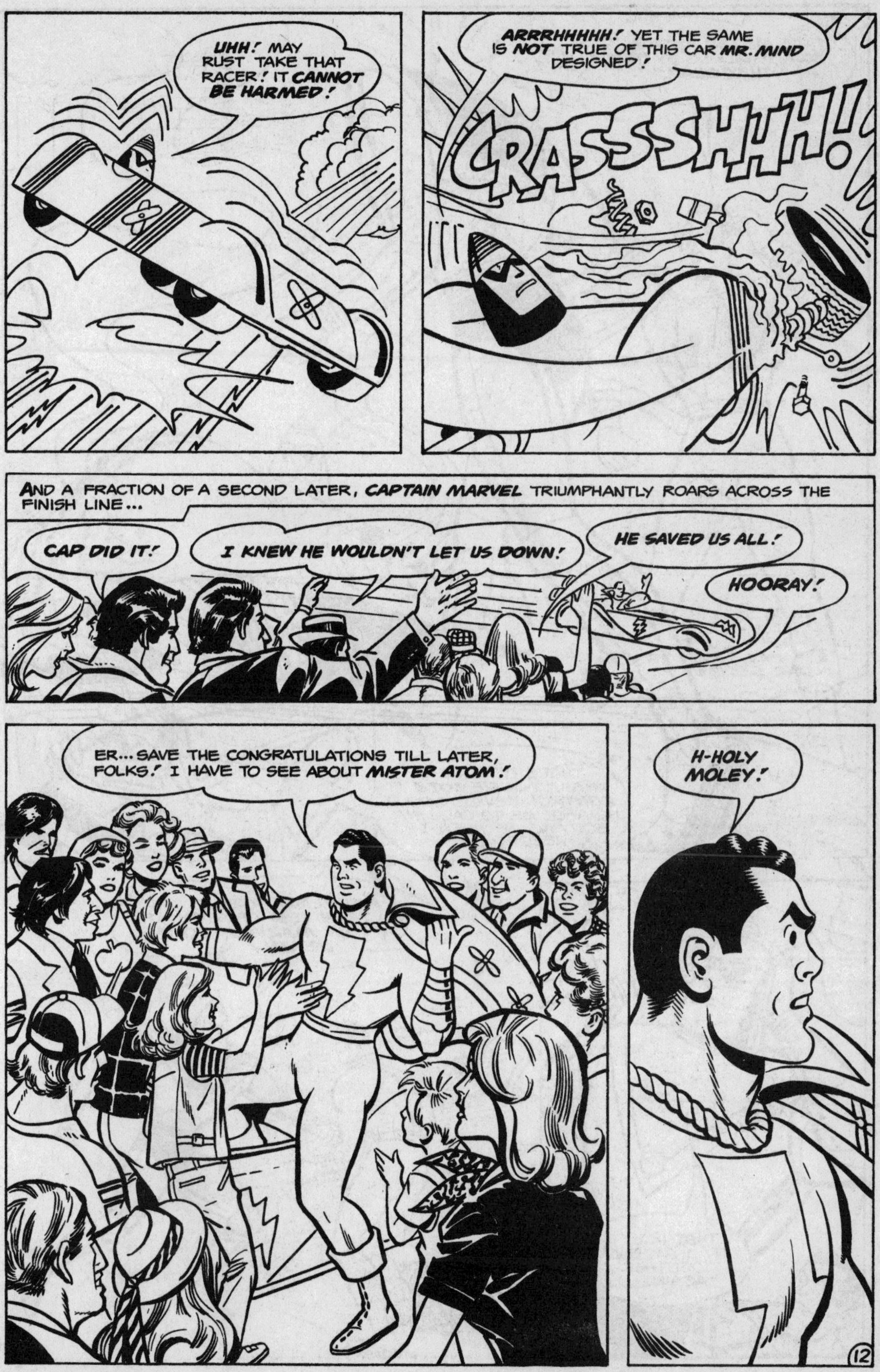
UHH! MAY RUST TAKE THAT RACER! IT CANNOT BE HARMED!
ARRRHHHHH! YET THE SAME IS NOT TRUE OF THIS CAR MR. MIND DESIGNED!
CRASSSHHH!
AND A FRACTION OF A SECOND LATER, CAPTAIN MARVEL TRIUMPHANTLY ROARS ACROSS THE FINISH LINE...
CAP DID IT!
I KNEW HE WOULDN'T LET US DOWN!
HE SAVED US ALL!
HOORAY!
ER... SAVE THE CONGRATULATIONS TILL LATER, FOLKS! I HAVE TO SEE ABOUT MISTER ATOM!
H-HOLY MOLEY!
12

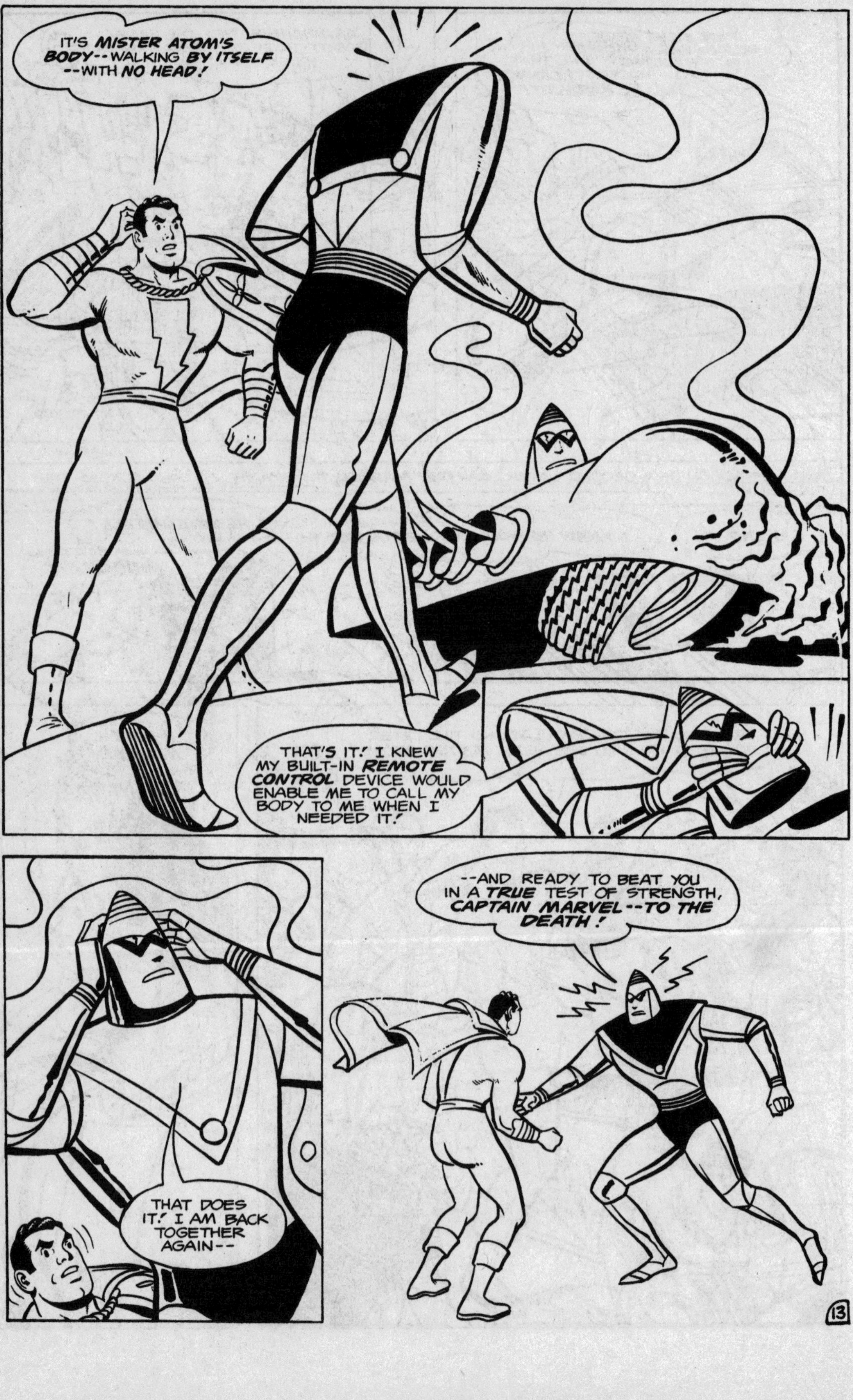
IT'S MISTER ATOM'S BODY--WALKING BY ITSELF --WITH NO HEAD!
THAT'S IT! I KNEW MY BUILT-IN REMOTE CONTROL DEVICE WOULD ENABLE ME TO CALL MY BODY TO ME WHEN I NEEDED IT!
THAT DOES IT! I AM BACK TOGETHER AGAIN--
--AND READY TO BEAT YOU IN A TRUE TEST OF STRENGTH, CAPTAIN MARVEL--TO THE DEATH!
13

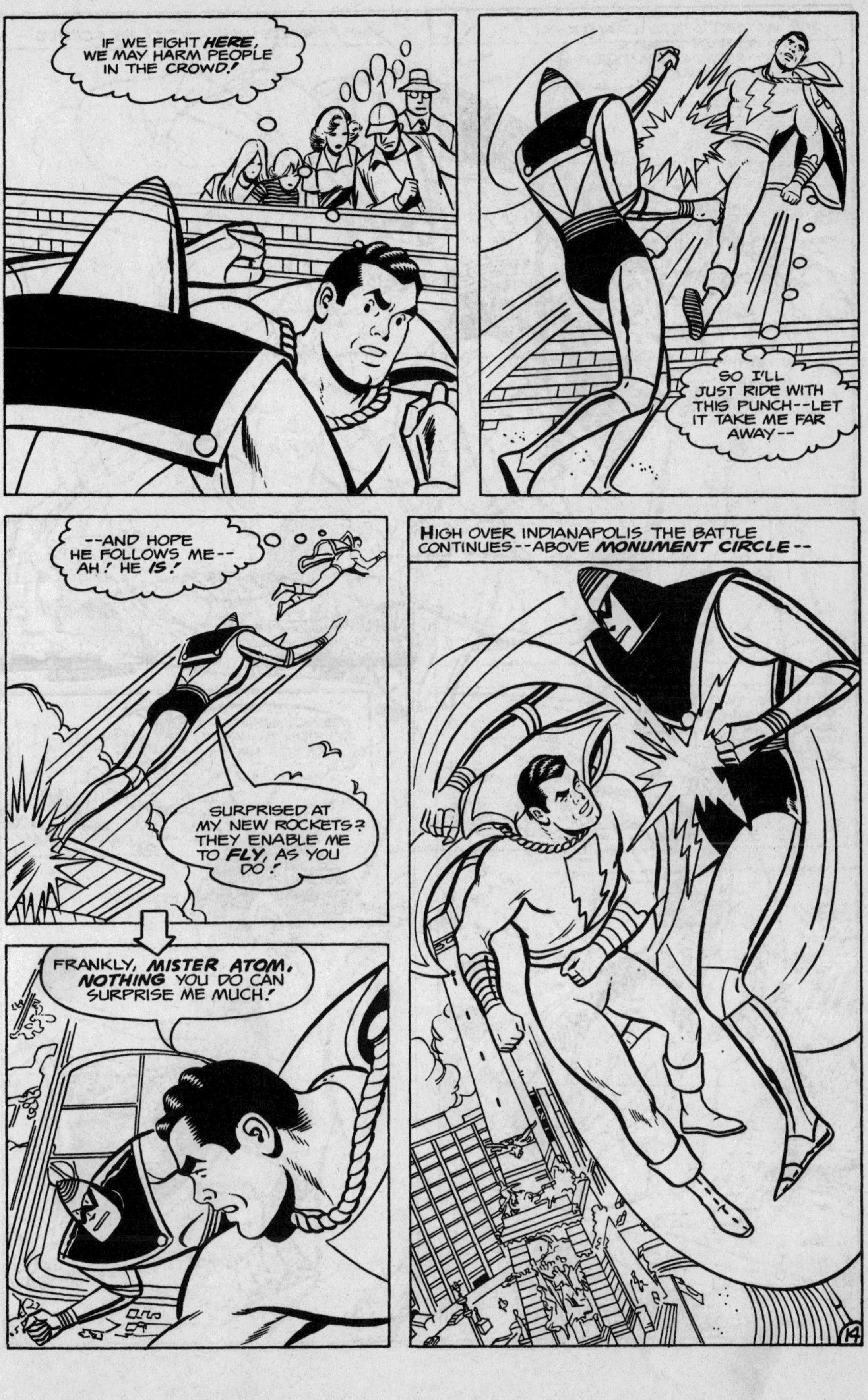
IF WE FIGHT HERE, WE MAY HARM PEOPLE IN THE CROWD!
SO I'LL JUST RIDE WITH THIS PUNCH--LET IT TAKE ME FAR AWAY--
--AND HOPE HE FOLLOWS ME-- AH! HE IS!
SURPRISED AT MY NEW ROCKETS? THEY ENABLE ME TO FLY, AS YOU DO!
FRANKLY, MISTER ATOM, NOTHING YOU DO CAN SURPRISE ME MUCH!
HIGH OVER INDIANAPOLIS THE BATTLE CONTINUES--ABOVE MONUMENT CIRCLE--
14

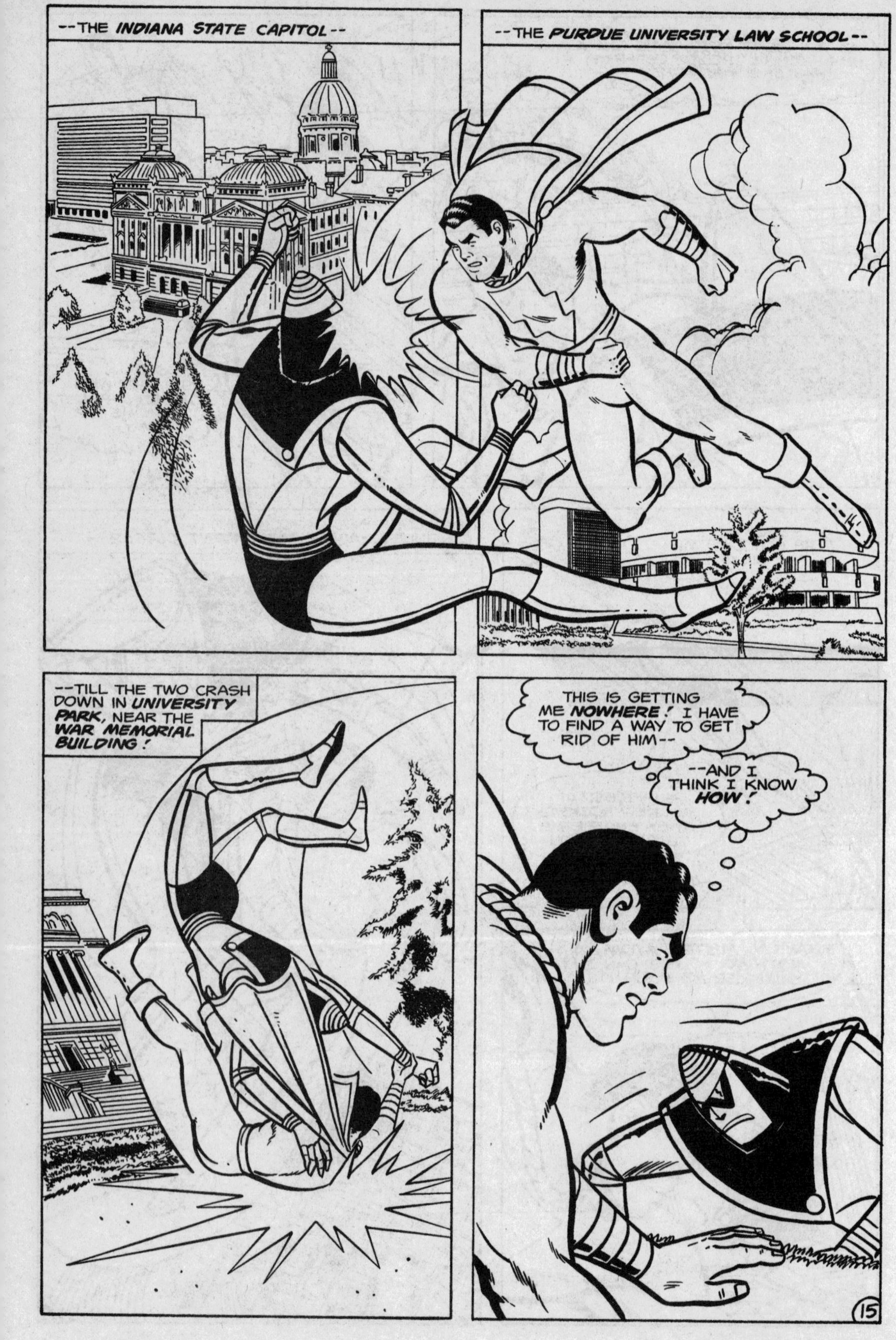
--THE INDIANA STATE CAPITOL--
--THE PURDUE UNIVERSITY LAW SCHOOL--
--TILL THE TWO CRASH DOWN IN UNIVERSITY PARK, NEAR THE WAR MEMORIAL BUILDING!
THIS IS GETTING ME NOWHERE! I HAVE TO FIND A WAY TO GET RID OF HIM--
--AND I THINK I KNOW HOW!
15

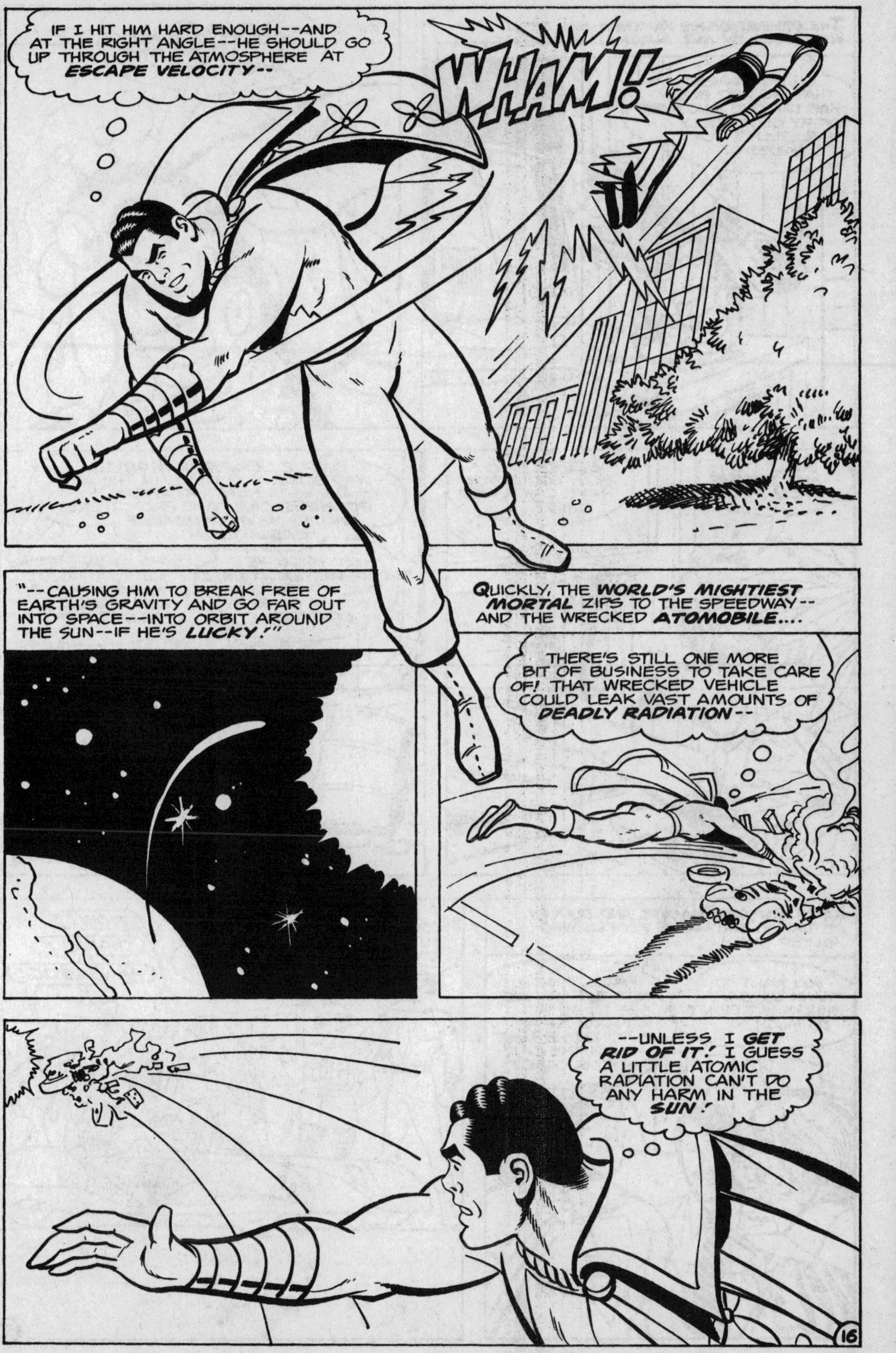
IF I HIT HIM HARD ENOUGH--AND AT THE RIGHT ANGLE--HE SHOULD GO UP THROUGH THE ATMOSPHERE AT ESCAPE VELOCITY--
WHAM!
"--CAUSING HIM TO BREAK FREE OF EARTH'S GRAVITY AND GO FAR OUT INTO SPACE--INTO ORBIT AROUND THE SUN--IF HE'S LUCKY!"
QUICKLY, THE WORLD'S MIGHTIEST MORTAL ZIPS TO THE SPEEDWAY--AND THE WRECKED ATOMOBILE....
THERE'S STILL ONE MORE BIT OF BUSINESS TO TAKE CARE OF! THAT WRECKED VEHICLE COULD LEAK VAST AMOUNTS OF DEADLY RADIATION--
--UNLESS I GET RID OF IT! I GUESS A LITTLE ATOMIC RADIATION CAN'T DO ANY HARM IN THE SUN!
16

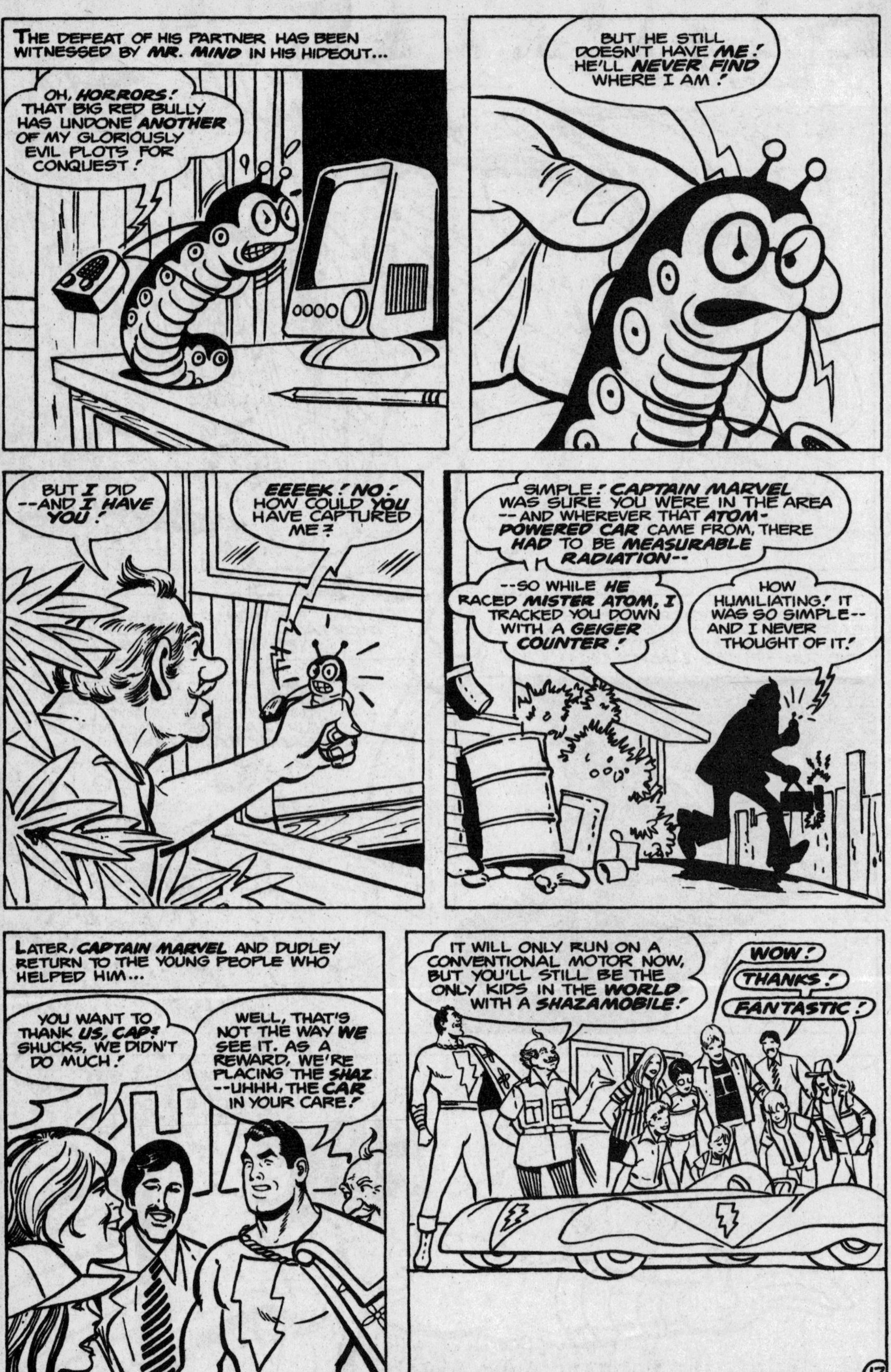
THE DEFEAT OF HIS PARTNER HAS BEEN WITNESSED BY MR. MIND IN HIS HIDEOUT...
OH, HORRORS! THAT BIG RED BULLY HAS UNDONE ANOTHER OF MY GLORIOUSLY EVIL PLOTS FOR CONQUEST!
BUT HE STILL DOESN'T HAVE ME! HE'LL NEVER FIND WHERE I AM!
BUT I DID --AND I HAVE YOU!
EEEEK! NO! HOW COULD YOU HAVE CAPTURED ME?
SIMPLE! CAPTAIN MARVEL WAS SURE YOU WERE IN THE AREA --AND WHEREVER THAT ATOM-POWERED CAR CAME FROM, THERE HAD TO BE MEASURABLE RADIATION--
--SO WHILE HE RACED MISTER ATOM, I TRACKED YOU DOWN WITH A GEIGER COUNTER!
HOW HUMILIATING! IT WAS SO SIMPLE-- AND I NEVER THOUGHT OF IT!
LATER, CAPTAIN MARVEL AND DUDLEY RETURN TO THE YOUNG PEOPLE WHO HELPED HIM...
YOU WANT TO THANK US, CAP? SHUCKS, WE DIDN'T DO MUCH!
WELL, THAT'S NOT THE WAY WE SEE IT. AS A REWARD, WE'RE PLACING THE SHAZ --UHHH, THE CAR IN YOUR CARE!
IT WILL ONLY RUN ON A CONVENTIONAL MOTOR NOW, BUT YOU'LL STILL BE THE ONLY KIDS IN THE WORLD WITH A SHAZAMOBILE!
WOW!
THANKS!
FANTASTIC!
17

SHOWCASE
PRESENTS

OVER 500 PAGES OF DC'S CLASSIC HEROES AND STORIES PRESENTED IN EACH VOLUME!

**GREEN LANTERN
VOL. 1**

**SUPERMAN
VOL. 1**

**SUPERMAN
VOL. 2**

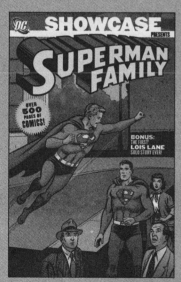

**SUPERMAN FAMILY
VOL. 1**

**JONAH HEX
VOL. 1**

**METAMORPHO
VOL. 1**

SHOWCASE

PRESENTS

OVER 500 PAGES OF DC'S CLASSIC HEROES AND STORIES PRESENTED IN EACH VOLUME!

**BATMAN
VOL. 1**

**JUSTICE LEAGUE OF
AMERICA
VOL. 1**

**THE ELONGATED MAN
VOL. 1**

**THE CHALLENGERS OF THE
UNKNOWN
VOL. 1**

**THE HAUNTED TANK
VOL. 1**

**THE PHANTOM STRANGER
VOL. 1**

SEARCH THE GRAPHIC NOVELS S   3 1901 04836 9799

www.DCCOMICS.com

FOR ART AND INFORMATION ON ALL OF OUR BOOKS!